k_{RF} Rate of return on a risk-free security

k_s (1) Cost of retained earnings

     (2) Required return on a stock

LP   Liquidity premium

M   Maturity value of a bond

M/B   Market-to-book ratio

MCC   Marginal cost of capital

MIRR   Modified internal rate of return

MRP   Maturity risk premium

MVA   Market value added

N   Calculator key denoting number of periods

n   (1) Life of a project or investment

     (2) Number of shares outstanding

NPV   Net present value

NWC   Net working capital

P   (1) Price of a share of stock; P_0 = price today

     (2) Sales price per unit of product sold

PPP   Purchase power parity

P_f Price of good in foreign country

P_h Price of good in home country

P/E   Price/earnings ratio

PMT   Payment of an annuity

PV   Present value

PVA_n Present value of an annuity for n years

PVIF   Present value interest factor for a lump sum

PVIFA   Present value interest factor for an annuity

Q   Quantity produced or sold

r   Correlation coefficient

ROA   Return on assets

ROE   Return on equity

RP   Risk premium

RP_M Market risk premium

S   Sales

SML   Security Market Line

Σ Summation sign (capital sigma)

σ Standard deviation (lowercase sigma)

σ^2 Variance

t   Time period

T   Marginal income tax rate

TIE   Times interest earned

V   Variable cost per unit

V_B Bond value

VC   Total variable costs

WACC   Weighted average cost of capital

YTC   Yield to call

YTM   Yield to maturity

FUNDAMENTALS
OF
FINANCIAL
MANAGEMENT

EIGHTH EDITION

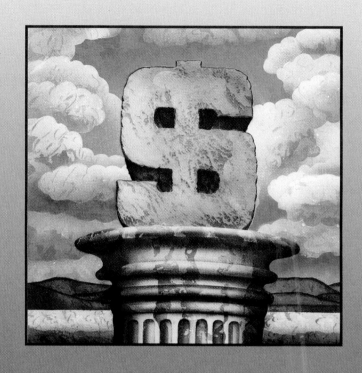

FUNDAMENTALS
OF
FINANCIAL
MANAGEMENT

EIGHTH EDITION

EUGENE F. BRIGHAM
University of Florida

JOEL F. HOUSTON
University of Florida

The Dryden Press
Harcourt Brace College Publishers

Fort Worth   Philadelphia   San Diego   New York   Orlando   Austin   San Antonio

Toronto   Montreal   London   Sydney   Tokyo

Publisher	George Provol
Executive Editor	Mike Reynolds
Product Manager	Craig Johnson
Senior Developmental Editor	Anita Fallon
Project Editor	Dee Salisbury
Production Manager	Carlyn Hauser
Art Director	Jeanette Barber
Project Management	Elm Street Publishing Services, Inc.
Cover Image	Conrad Represents/Pierre Fortin

Requests for permission to make copies of any part of the work should be mailed to: Permissions Department, Harcourt Brace & Company, 6277 Sea Harbor Drive, Orlando, FL 32887-6777.

Some material in this work previously appeared in *Fundamentals of Financial Management: The Concise Edition* by Eugene F. Brigham and Joel F. Houston

Address for Orders
The Dryden Press, 6277 Sea Harbor Drive, Orlando, FL 32887-6777; 1-800-782-4479

Address for Editorial Correspondence
The Dryden Press, The Public Ledger Building, 150 South Independence Mall West, Suite 1250, Philadelphia, PA 19106-3412

Web site address:
http://www.hbcollege.com

THE DRYDEN PRESS, DRYDEN, and the DP Logo are trademarks of Harcourt Brace & Company.

ISBN: 0-03-024418-8

Annotated Instructor's Edition ISBN: 0-03-024436-6

Library of Congress Catalog Card Number: 96-80089

Printed in the United States of America

8 9 0 1 2 3 4 5 6   0 4 8   9 8 7 6 5 4 3

The Dryden Press
Harcourt Brace College Publishers

The Dryden Press Series in Finance

Sandburg
Discovering Your Finance Career
CD-ROM

Sears and Trennepohl
Investment Management

Seitz and Ellison
Capital Budgeting and Long-Term Financing Decisions
Second Edition

Siegel and Siegel
Futures Markets

Smith and Spudeck
Interest Rates: Principles and Applications

Stickney
*Financial Reporting and Statement Analysis:
A Strategic Perspective*
Third Edition

Weston, Besley, and Brigham
Essentials of Managerial Finance
Eleventh Edition

PREFACE

When *Fundamentals of Financial Management* was first published more than 20 years ago, our intent was to write an introductory finance text that students could truly understand. Today, 20 years later, *Fundamentals* has become the leading undergraduate finance text. Our goal with the eighth edition has been to produce a book and ancillary package that holds its position and sets yet another new standard for finance textbooks.

The eighth edition continues to offer the most complete and integrated teaching system available.

As teachers and authors, we have always tried to incorporate current innovations in the fields of finance, education, and publishing into *Fundamentals* and its related ancillaries. The eighth edition's new look and new ancillary items provide the most complete and integrated teaching system available. Of course, our commitment to quality, accuracy, and student accessibility remains as strong as ever.

Finance is an exciting, challenging, and ever-changing discipline. In developing and improving *Fundamentals,* we strive to convey the excitement and ever-changing nature of finance, and most students do quickly realize its importance and relevance. More often than not, students are pleased and surprised to discover that finance is more interesting and exciting than they had anticipated. Nevertheless, finance remains a difficult subject for many students, and we kept this in mind as we developed the text and supporting materials. Without sacrificing rigor, we try to explain each topic clearly and completely. However, an introductory finance course should be more than just a series of topics — to fully understand the basic financial concepts, students must understand how the various topics fit together.

With this in mind, we begin *Fundamentals* with a discussion of financial objectives, and we show how both managers and investors use accounting statements to assess how well firms are meeting those objectives. We also describe early on the financial environment, the fundamental trade-off between risk and return, and the time value of money. We build on these basic concepts to develop the principles of security valuation and to explain how prices and rates are established in the stock and bond markets. Subsequent chapters explain how financial tools and techniques can be used to help firms maximize value by improving decisions relating to capital budgeting, capital structure, and working capital management. The final part of the book deals with a number of related topics, including multinational financial management, derivatives and risk management, hybrid financing, and mergers. Our organization has four important advantages:

Four of the many advantages of the eighth edition's organization.

1. Explaining early how accounting data are used, how financial markets operate, and how security prices are determined helps students see how financial management affects stock prices. Also, early coverage of risk analysis, the time value of money, and valuation techniques permits us to use and reinforce those concepts throughout the remainder of the book.

2. Structuring the book around markets and valuation enhances continuity and helps students see how the various topics are related to one another.

3. Most students — even those who do not plan to major in finance — are interested in stock and bond valuation, rates of return, and the like. Because the ability to learn a topic is a function of interest and motivation, and because *Fundamentals* covers security markets and stock and bond values early, our organization is pedagogically sound.

4. Once the basic concepts have been established, it is much easier for students to understand how corporations make important investment and financing decisions, and how they establish working capital policies. Also, the later chapters make sense only after the basics have been covered.

RELATIONSHIP TO OTHER DRYDEN PRESS BOOKS AND OUR OTHER BOOKS

The growing body of knowledge makes it difficult, it not impossible, to include all that one might want in the text. This led Gene Brigham to coauthor (with Lou Gapenski) two other texts which deal with materials that go beyond what can be covered in an introductory course — an upper level undergraduate text (*Intermediate Financial Management,* fifth edition) and a comprehensive book aimed primarily at MBAs (*Financial Management: Theory and Practice,* eighth edition).

Although we have limited the scope of *Fundamentals,* some professors indicated a preference for a smaller, more streamlined textbook. With this in mind, we created another text, *Fundamentals of Financial Management: The Concise Edition.* The development of *Concise* forced us to systematically rethink all aspects of the book with the goal of removing nonessential and/or redundant materials. This led to improvements which we carried over to *Fundamentals* and which helped make this eighth edition a better book.

Although *Concise* was well received, there are still two significant advantages to a more complete book such as *Fundamentals:*

1. *Fundamentals* affords professors more flexibility in designing their courses.

2. *Fundamentals* provides a more complete reference book for students after they complete the course. This is especially important for nonfinance majors, who will not otherwise have access to the materials contained in *Fundamentals* but omitted from *Concise.* In this regard, it should be noted that the *Fundamentals* chapters are written in a modular, self-contained format, designed to make it easy for students to read them on their own.

INTENDED MARKET

Fundamentals is intended for use in the introductory finance course. The key chapters can be covered in a one-term course or, supplemented with cases and some outside readings, used in a two-term course. If it is used in a one-term course, most instructors generally cover only selected chapters, leaving the others for students to examine on their own or to use as references in conjunction with work in later courses and after graduation. Note that we made every effort to write the chapters in a flexible, modular format, which will help instructors cover the material in whatever sequence they choose.

All chapters are written in a flexible, modular format.

INNOVATIONS FOR THE EIGHTH EDITION

Both financial issues and teaching technology are dynamic, so textbooks must be continually updated to reflect important new developments. Consequently, we are always on the lookout for ways to improve the book, and we work with a team of reviewers to systematically seek potential improvements. As a result, several important changes were made in this edition, the most important of which are discussed here.

INCREASED COVERAGE OF INTERNATIONAL FINANCE

Increased global perspective.

It has become a cliché to argue that world capital markets have become increasingly integrated and that investors and corporations should think globally when they make important financial decisions. Like most clichés, this one is true, but even so, most introductory finance textbooks have not paid much attention to international issues. However, as international issues become increasingly important, this omission becomes increasingly serious. With this in mind, we have taken several steps to improve our coverage of international finance.

Strengthened and repositioned multinational chapter.

As a starting point, we reworked the multinational financial management chapter (now Chapter 18) to incorporate such important topics as interest rate and purchasing power parity. We also expanded the sections on capital structure and capital budgeting across countries, and the implications of cross-country differences for financial managers. In addition, we discuss the implications of recent developments in the global marketplace, including the creation of the European Monetary System. Finally, we moved the international chapter forward in the text, which is consistent with its increasing importance.

It is not enough to just have a chapter on international finance — international topics should be integrated and discussed throughout the text. With this in mind, we added a new series of boxes, entitled "Global Perspectives," which look at the issues covered in the chapters from a global viewpoint.

New Global Perspectives boxes expand on issues covered in chapters.

A number of people helped us with the international materials. Chapter 18 was coauthored with two international specialists, Roy Crum and Subu Venkataraman. Roy teaches international finance at the University of Florida, and Subu teaches international finance at Northwestern University and also deals with international issues as a senior economist at the Federal Reserve Bank of Chicago. Andy Naranjo, another international expert at Florida, gave us many suggestions for the Global Perspectives boxes and also helped us integrate international topics throughout the text.

SEPARATE CHAPTERS FOR STOCKS AND BONDS

Previous editions of *Fundamentals* contained a single chapter early in the book on stock and bond valuation, and later chapters then described the institutional characteristics of common stock, investment banking, and long-term debt. A number of instructors suggested that this organization was less than ideal, primarily because students found it hard to fully understand the stock and bond valuation material without the background provided by the institutional materials covered later in the book. While developing *Concise,* we decided to divide the material covered in the three previous chapters into two new chapters, one on bonds and one on stocks. The bond chapter covers types of bonds, bond ratings, and the bond market, and it then discusses bond valuation. The stock chapter provides background information on the stock market, the rights of stockholders, and investment banking, then covers stock valuation and rates of return.

The new arrangement worked wonderfully well with *Concise,* so we carried it over to *Fundamentals.*

REORGANIZATION OF THE WORKING CAPITAL CHAPTERS

Again taking a cue from the lessons we learned while developing *Concise,* we also reorganized the material on working capital into two chapters, one entitled "Managing Current Assets" and the other "Financing Current Assets." The chapter on current assets describes the general trade-offs firms face when establishing policy related to cash management, inventory management, and accounts receivable. In the seventh edition, these topics were covered in three separate chapters.

The new approach enables us to tie things together better, which makes it easier for students to see the "big picture." When we reduced the number of chapters, we also eliminated some details that did little to help students understand the basic issues. In effect, students had difficulty seeing the forest for the trees, and it helped to remove a few trees. Finally, covering the key working capital materials in two rather than three chapters makes it easier to fit this important topic into a crowded syllabus.

A NEW CHAPTER ON DERIVATIVES AND RISK MANAGEMENT

Derivatives and their use in risk management are a rapidly growing and important part of the financial landscape, so we included a new chapter entitled "Derivatives and Risk Management." Here we explain what derivatives are and how they can be used to help manage risk. Although we highlight some of the high-profile real-world cases where mismanagement of derivatives had led to large losses, the primary thrust of the chapter is to describe situations in which derivatives can reduce risk and enhance shareholder value, which is really why this market has seen such explosive growth.

STARTER PROBLEMS

All instructors recognize that answering questions and working through problems is an integral part of the learning process. Consequently, *Fundamentals* has always included a large and diverse set of problems in each chapter, including Questions, Self-Test Problems, Problems, Exam-Type Problems, an Integrated Case, and Computer-Related Problems. In the eighth edition we added a new component, entitled Starter Problems, which are easy problems designed to let students work some basic exercises before moving on to more challenging problems. The Starter Problems help students get going, and they also provide a useful check as to whether students need to reread the chapter before going on.

IMPROVEMENTS TO THE ANCILLARY PACKAGE

We also made a number of improvements to the ancillary materials:

Lecture presentation now in *PowerPoint*.

♦ The computerized slide show which illustrates the key concepts of each chapter has been thoroughly overhauled. First, based on our own usage and suggestions from others, we did a lot of fine-tuning which improved the slides. Second, a number of professors indicated that they would like to be able to modify the slide show by adding some slides of their own and/or deleting some of ours. Since most were familiar with *Microsoft Office,* including its *PowerPoint* software, we decided to switch from *Aldus Persuasion* to *Microsoft PowerPoint.* Since *PowerPoint* is more familiar and easier to learn, the switch gives instructors greater flexibility to modify our slides or add slides of their own, thereby tailoring the slide show to meet their needs.

By popular demand! A unique student note-taking manual based on the *PowerPoint* slides.

♦ The format of *Blueprints* was completely revamped. *Blueprints* is now based on a hard copy of the *PowerPoint* slides, plus exam-type problems which can be worked by students or discussed in class. We made this change in *Concise,* and 100 percent of our reviewers and students felt that the new format represents a huge improvement. We are convinced that this change will be well received by those who currently use the slides, and we strongly recommend that nonusers look over the new slides and seriously consider using them. Of course, not all schools have the necessary projection equipment, but the new version of the slide show does represent a real breakthrough, and its use, along with *Blueprints* to facilitate student note-taking, can help students get the most out of lectures and save instructors preparation time in the process.

New footage!

♦ The finance video series has been significantly updated. New footage has been filmed to coincide with changes in the text and to provide more current examples of how many of the concepts discussed in the book are applied in the real world.

New! World Wide Web links in every chapter.

♦ One new feature that many students and professors will like is a set of marginal note references entitled, "On the WWW." These notes direct readers to interesting sites on the World Wide Web that are relevant to the subject being covered at that point in the text. These references are found throughout the book.

Additional instructional support for lectures.

♦ The Annotated Instructor's Edition, which was first included in the seventh edition, has been significantly enhanced and updated. The points made in the annotations can be quite useful for getting discussions started.

We describe other aspects of the ancillary package next, when we discuss other features of the book.

ADDITIONAL IMPROVEMENTS

As always, we updated and clarified the text and end-of-chapter problems, and we made numerous improvements in the pedagogy. In particular, we updated the real-world examples and pointed out key recent developments in the financial environment. We also expanded the coverage of certain topics as they became more important, and, in other instances, we deleted redundant material to streamline the discussion and make the text flow better. Here is a sampling of the changes:

♦ In Chapter 1, we describe in more detail the importance of globalization.

♦ In Chapter 2, we expanded our discussion of Economic Value Added (EVA), and we also expanded and improved the section which describes the relationship between accounting income and cash flow.

♦ In Chapter 4, we clarified our discussion of the term structure of interest rates, and we also described some of the risks that arise when one invests overseas.

♦ In Chapter 5, we now explain the nature of rates of return before discussing their riskiness, we bring in more real-world data on the risks of and returns on various investments over time, and we discuss the benefits and limitations of diversifying internationally.

♦ As noted earlier, we now have separate chapters for bonds and stocks (Chapters 7 and 8), and we provide background material on these securities before going into the analytics of their valuation.

♦ We reworked and simplified Chapter 9 on the cost of capital. For example, we streamlined the discussion of break points in the cost of capital schedule. Our earlier discussion was unnecessarily complicated, and we spent too much time on something that is only marginally relevant for real-world decision makers. We also point out the connection between EVA and the cost of capital, and we bring in some recent evidence regarding the magnitude of flotation costs.

♦ We moved the material on bond refunding to Chapter 11 (as an appendix) to reflect the fact that the decision to call a bond is in essence a capital budgeting replacement decision.

♦ We also streamlined the chapter on capital structure (Chapter 13). Our reviewers convinced us that while the algebraic material on degree of leverage is interesting, it made the chapter too long and complicated. So, we moved it to an appendix. We also updated and expanded the discussion of capital structure in various industries and capital structures across countries.

♦ In Chapter 14, we expanded our discussion of stock repurchases to reflect their increased use as an alternative to cash dividends, and we discuss more completely the issues that arise when companies contemplate changing their dividend policies.

♦ In Chapter 15, we simplified the use of projected financial statements for financial forecasting. This material was not conceptually difficult, but as it was set up, students had to wade through more time-consuming number crunching than the effort was worth. This change makes it much easier for instructors and students to get through the material in a reasonable amount of time.

♦ Options are now covered in the new chapter on derivatives and risk management (Chapter 19) rather than as part of the chapter on hybrid securities. We introduce students to the Black-Scholes model, but in an intuitive, nontechnical manner.

♦ Given the increased importance of mergers, and the shift toward strategic mergers as opposed to ones based primarily on "financial engineering," we significantly updated the chapter on mergers and divestitures (Chapter 21).

FEATURES OF THE BOOK

A large number of pedagogical elements and supporting materials have helped make *Fundamentals* successful. Included are the following:

♦ Each chapter opens with a vignette describing how an actual corporation has contended with the issues discussed in the chapter. These vignettes heighten students' interest by pointing out the real-world relevance and applicability of what might otherwise seem to be dry, technical material.

♦ Throughout the book, there are "Industry Practice" and "Global Perspectives" boxes which provide real-world illustrations of how finance concepts are applied in practice.

♦ An Integrated Case, which is generally related to the vignette, appears at the end of each chapter. These "mini-cases" both illustrate and tie together the key topics covered in the chapter, thus providing an ideal platform for lectures which systematically cover the key materials in the chapter.

♦ The end-of-chapter materials contain a large number of Questions, Problems, Exam-Type Problems, and Starter Problems, which vary in level of difficulty and cover all the topics discussed in the chapter.

♦ Most chapters contain a Computer-Related Problem, which enables students to use a computer spreadsheet program such as *Lotus 1-2-3* or *Microsoft Excel* to answer a set of questions. These problems reinforce the concepts covered in the chapter and provide students with an opportunity to become more proficient with computers. Models for the problems are available to instructors, who can, if they choose, make them available to students.

♦ Throughout the textbook, key terms are highlighted in the text and defined in the margins. These "marginal glossaries" enable students to quickly find and review key topics within the chapter. International references are also defined in the margins.

♦ Self-Test Questions, which serve as checkpoints for students to test their understanding, follow each major section in the chapters.

THE INSTRUCTIONAL PACKAGE: AN INTEGRATED SYSTEM

Fundamentals includes a broad range of ancillary materials designed both to enhance students' learning and to make it easier for instructors to prepare for and conduct classes. The ancillaries are described here:

The most comprehensive manual available.

1. **Instructor's Manual.** This comprehensive manual contains answers to all text questions and problems, plus detailed solutions to the integrated cases. If a computerized version of the IM would help in class preparation, instructors can contact The Dryden Press for a copy.

Now in *PowerPoint*.

2. **Lecture Presentation Software, or Computerized Lecture Slide Show.** This ancillary, written in *Microsoft PowerPoint*, is a computer graphics slide show covering all the essential issues presented in the chapter. Graphs, tables, lists, and calculations are developed sequentially, much as one might develop them on a blackboard. However, the slides are more crisp, clear, and colorful, and color coding is used to tie elements of a given slide together. The new slide

show is far more polished than anything previously available. Based on our end-of-course evaluations, students overwhelmingly like the slides and recommend that we continue using them as an integral part of our lectures. The slides were initially developed with the assistance of Dr. Larry Wolken of Texas A&M University.

When we first began using the slide show, we were concerned about the lack of flexibility in the classroom, thinking that although one can navigate easily from slide to slide, one cannot change the slides themselves in the classroom. Our fears were unfounded. First, because we had spent a great deal of time designing the slides, our examples and materials turned out to be appropriate in most lecture situations. Second, when we used the slides in class, we found that we could easily depart from them by going to the blackboard, which also provided variety and spontaneity. Now, the slides provide the backbone of our lectures, but we spice them up by going to the blackboard to address current events, to present alternative examples, and to help answer questions.

Now follows PowerPoint slide show.

3. **Blueprints.** This supplement, which is based on the Integrated Cases, was developed several years ago to help guide students through the chapter in a systematic manner. Since the Integrated Cases cover the key points in the chapters, including definitions, logical relationships, and calculations, and since they show how finance is actually used in practice, they were ideal for this purpose.

As technology advanced and our lectures moved away from the blackboard, it became increasingly important to provide students with a hard copy of the lecture materials. Students must have hard copies if they are to focus on the lecture yet still develop a complete and useful set of notes. With this in mind, we concluded that *Blueprints* would be most useful if it actually consisted of copies of the slides. So, each chapter of the new *Blueprints* begins with the case itself and is followed by copies of each slide, along with space for notes and comments. Moreover, at the end of each *Blueprints* chapter we include several exam-type problems which can be covered in class if time permits or left up to the students to solve on their own. Now students can watch and listen to the lecture, yet still end up with a good set of notes.

The new *Blueprints* has several other advantages. First, it offers more flexibility for presenting alternative examples and discussing current events. As noted earlier, *Blueprints* provides students with an almost complete set of notes, so it is less necessary for instructors to lecture on everything in class. Second, because our discussion in class is tied directly to the slides, students can place their notes in the spaces provided right next to (or on) the relevant slide. This enables students to develop a better set of notes.

Each term, we use a course pack consisting of our syllabus, a calculator tutorial, some old exams, and *Blueprints*. This package can be provided by The Dryden Press through bookstores or else made available to students through an off-campus copy center. We have 10- to 12-page write-ups on several popular calculators (see the section on the *Technology Supplement*), and we include one (or more) of these in the course pack or else provide them to students separately.

Many new class-tested questions.

4. **Test Bank.** Although some instructors do not like multiple-choice questions, they do provide a useful means for testing students in many situations. It is critically important, however, that the questions be both unambiguous and

consistent with the lectures and assigned readings. To meet this need, we developed a large *Test Bank* containing more than 1,200 class-tested questions and problems. It is available both in book form and on diskettes. A number of new and thoroughly class-tested conceptual questions and problems, which range in level of difficulty, have been added to the eighth edition's *Test Bank*. Information regarding the topics, degree of difficulty, and the correct answers, along with complete solutions for all numerical problems, is provided with each question. Questions which require the use of a financial calculator are grouped together in a separate section at the end of each *Test Bank* chapter.

The *Test Bank* is available in book form and in Dryden's computerized test bank form (EXAMaster+). This software has many features that make test preparation, scoring, and grade recording easy. For example, EXAMaster+ allows automatic conversion of multiple-choice questions and problems into free response questions. The sequence of test questions can be altered to make different versions of a given test, and the software makes it easy to add to or edit the existing test items, or to compile a test which covers specific topics.

The *Test Bank* is also available in word-processing format for instructors who are more comfortable with that format. Answer keys are automatically generated for each version of an exam, and the solutions always follow the problems. One can, of course, utilize all the features of word processors to customize tests.

Now available via the Internet at *http://www.dryden.com/ finance/fincase/*

5. **Cases in Financial Management: Dryden Request.** More than 64 cases written by Eugene F. Brigham, Louis C. Gapenski, and Linda Klein are now available via the World Wide Web, with new cases added every year. The *Cases in Financial Management: Dryden Request* series is a customized case database which allows instructors to select cases and create their own customized casebooks. These cases can be used as supplements to illustrate the various topics covered in the textbook. The cases come in directed and non-directed versions (that is, with and without guidance questions), and most of the cases have accompanying spreadsheet models. The models are not essential for working the cases, but they do reduce number crunching and thus leave more time for students to consider conceptual issues. They also show students quite clearly the usefulness of computers for helping to make better financial decisions.

More testing questions!

6. **Supplemental Test Bank.** A *Supplemental Test Bank* will be provided in the future. Instructors obviously can use the *Test Bank* for exams, but some also like to provide students with sample questions for study purposes or pre-exam reviews. This multiple usage can exhaust even the largest of *Test Banks,* but since we develop new problems in our own classes each term, we plan to provide new problems on a timely basis through the use of an annual *Supplemental Test Bank.*

Additional problems for tests, quizzes, or practice.

7. **Supplemental Problems.** An additional set of problems similar to the end-of-chapter problems, organized according to topic and level of difficulty, is also available. The Dryden Press will provide this problem set to instructors upon request.

Now in *Excel.*

8. **Problem Diskette.** A diskette containing spreadsheet models for the computer-related end-of-chapter problems is also available. To obtain the diskette, instructors should contact their Dryden Press representative.

9. **Data Disk.** In the textbook itself we incorporate many real-company examples to show how the concepts apply to actual companies. However, several professors involved in a focus group suggested that we should take this one step further and provide instructors with real company data on a floppy disk. Although most introductory students do not have time to do much computer work, this may change in the not-so-distant future. Thus, we have put together a set of financial data from several companies along with a set of key economic statistics, including interest rates and stock market indexes and made it available on the Web.

10. **Technology Supplement.** The *Technology Supplement* contains tutorials for five commonly used financial calculators and for both *Microsoft Excel* and *Lotus 1-2-3*. The calculator tutorials cover everything a student needs to know about the calculator to work the problems in the text, and we provide them as a part of our course pack. These tutorials are generally about 12 typewritten pages. Some students are intimidated by the rather large manuals that accompany the calculators, and they find our brief, course-specific tutorials far easier to use.

Professionally developed videos linked to chapters with concept introductions and interesting news footage.

11. **Video Package: Integrating Print and Video Technologies.** Brand-new videos feature financial concepts explained in terms of how companies do business today. Companies featured include Southwest Airlines, Pier 1 Imports, Paradigm Simulations, Cadillac, and Marriott International.

These videos are based on chapter opening vignettes and serve to capture students' attention for further discussion. For instance, how has K-Mart managed its dividend policy while losing market value (Chapter 14)? Another case looks at how Southwest airlines grew from one plane to its current fleet (Chapter 16).

Those professors preferring more traditional lecture videos with animated graphs and more detailed discussions of financial concepts can access the seventh edition videos. These were prepared with the help of Department Chair Sarah Bryant and Scott Weiss of the University of Columbia's Department of Finance and International Business, and they fit nearly perfectly into the pedagogy of this eighth edition.

Although the videos, vignettes, and integrated cases are related to one another, instructors do not have to assign one in order to use another. Each stands on its own. There are many different classroom settings and course objectives, and our video format will not meet all needs. However, many instructors will find these videos extremely useful, and The Dryden Press will provide them to adopting instructors upon request.

Now available through the Internet at *http://www.dryden.com/finance*

12. **Finance NewsWire.** One of the problems inherent in textbooks is keeping them current in a constantly changing world. When Orange County goes bankrupt or Baring Bank collapses or Procter & Gamble loses $200 million, it would be useful to relate these events to the textbook. Fortunately, the advent of the World Wide Web can help us keep up to date. Adopters of this text will have access to a portion of the Dryden Press Web site, where they will be provided with summaries of one or two recent articles in *The Wall Street Journal, Business Week,* or some other major business publication, along with discussion questions and references to the text. This will facilitate incorporating late-breaking news into classroom discussions. One can also use the accompanying questions for quizzes and/or exams.

A number of additional items are offered specifically for students, as described here:

1. **Study Guide.** This supplement lists the key learning objectives for each chapter, outlines the key sections, provides students with self-test questions, and provides a set of problems similar to those in the text and in the *Test Bank* but with fully worked-out solutions.

2. **Spreadsheet Books.** The Dryden Press has published several books on spreadsheets, including both *Microsoft Excel* and *Lotus 1-2-3*. Included are *Financial Analysis with Microsoft Excel* and *Financial Analysis with Lotus 1-2-3*, both by Timothy R. Mayes and Todd M. Shank. These books are based on Windows 95. A DOS-based book, *Finance with Lotus 1-2-3*, by Eugene F. Brigham, Dana A. Aberwald, and Louis C. Gapenski, is also available from The Dryden Press. All of these books enable students to learn, on their own, how to use spreadsheets and apply them to financial decisions.

The Dryden Press will provide complimentary supplements or supplement packages to those adopters qualified under Dryden's adoption policy. Please contact your sales representative to learn how you may qualify. If, as an adopter or potential user, you receive supplements you do not need, please return them to your sales representative or send them to the following address: Attn: Returns Department, Troy Warehouse, 465 South Lincoln Drive, Troy, MO 63379.

ACKNOWLEDGMENTS

This textbook reflects the efforts of a great many people who have worked on *Fundamentals* and our related books over a number of years, as well as those who have worked specifically on this eighth edition. First, we would like to thank Dana Aberwald Clark, who worked closely with us at every stage of the revision — her assistance was absolutely invaluable. Also, our colleagues Lou Gapenski, Andy Naranjo, M. Nimalendran, Jay Ritter, Mike Ryngaert, and Carolyn Takeda gave us many useful suggestions regarding the ancillaries and many parts of the book, including the integrated cases. Next, we would like to thank the following professors, who reviewed this edition in detail and provided many useful comments and suggestions: Sharif Ahkam, Rhode Island College; John Andrews, Emory University; Gilbert W. Bickum, Eastern Kentucky University; Rick Boulware, University of South Carolina; Larry Brown, University of Mary; Paul Bursik, St. Norbert College; James D'Mello, Western Michigan University; Frank Draper, University of Maryland; U. Elike, Alabama A&M University; L. Franklin Fant, University of New Hampshire; Robert Fiore, Springfield College; Armand Gilinsky, Jr., Sonoma State University; Zhenhn Jin, Illinois Wesleyan University; Sally Joyner, Texas A&M University; John Kaminarides, Arkansas State University; Robert Kleiman, Oakland University; Erich Knehans, Allentown College; David Lange, Auburn University; Surendra Mansinghka, San Francisco State University; Timothy Manuel, University of Montana; William Nelson, Indiana University Northwest; Bruce Niendorf, University of Montana; Dean Olson, Evergreen State College; Dianna Preece, University of Louisville; David Schirm, John Carroll University; Robert Schwebach, University of Wyoming; Patricia Matisz Smith, North Carolina Wesleyan; Eugene Swinnerton, University of Detroit; Madeline Thimmes, Utah State University; Arlene Thurman, North Georgia College; Janet Todd, University of

Delaware; Richard Whiston, Hudson Valley Community College; and John Zietlow, Indiana State University.

We would also like to thank the following professors, whose reviews and comments on companion books have contributed to this edition: Robert Adams, Mike Adler, Syed Ahmad, Ed Altman, Bruce Anderson, Ron Anderson, Bob Angell, Vince Apilado, Harvey Arbalaez, Henry Arnold, Bob Aubey, Gil Babcock, Peter Bacon, Kent Baker, Robert Balik, Tom Bankston, Babu Baradwai, Les Barenbaum, Charles Barngrover, Bill Beedles, Moshe Ben-Horim, Bill Beranek, Tom Berry, Will Bertin, Scott Besley, Dan Best, Roger Bey, Dalton Bigbee, John Bildersee, Laurence E. Blose, Russ Boisjoly, Bob Boldin, Keith Boles, Michael Bond, Geof Booth, Waldo Born, Kenneth Boudreaux, Helen Bowers, Oswald Bowlin, Don Boyd, G. Michael Boyd, Pat Boyer, Joe Brandt, Elizabeth Brannigan, Greg Bauer, Mary Broske, David T. Brown, Kate Brown, Bill Brueggeman, Paul Bursik, Bill Campsey, Bob Carlson, Severin Carlson, David Cary, Steve Celec, Mary Chaffin, Don Chance, Antony Chang, Susan Chaplinsky, K. C. Chen, Jay Choi, S. K. Choudhary, Lal Chugh, Maclyn Clouse, Bruce Collins, Margaret Considine, Phil Cooley, Joe Copeland, David Cordell, Marsha Cornett, M. P. Corrigan, John Cotner, Charles Cox, David Crary, John Crockett, Jr., Roy Crum, Brent Dalrymple, Bill Damon, Joel Dauten, Steve Dawson, Sankar De, Fred Dellva, Chad Denson, James Desreumaux, Bodie Dickerson, Bernard Dill, Gregg Dimkoff, Les Dlabay, Mark Dorfman, Gene Drzycimski, Dean Dudley, David Durst, Ed Dyl, Richard Edelman, Charles Edwards, John Ellis, Suzanne Erickson, Dave Ewert, John Ezzell, Michael Ferri, Jim Filkins, John Finnerty, Susan Fischer, Steven Flint, Russ Fogler, Jennifer Fraizer, Dan French, Michael Garlington, David Garraty, Sharon Garrison, Jim Garven, Adam Gehr, Jr., Jim Gentry, Philip Glasgo, Rudyard Goode, Walt Goulet, Bernie Grablowsky, Theoharry Grammatikos, Owen Gregory, Ed Grossnickle, John Groth, Alan Grunewald, Manak Gupta, Darryl Gurley, Sam Hadaway, Don Hakala, Gerald Hamsmith, William Hardin, John Harris, Paul Hastings, Bob Haugen, Steve Hawke, Del Hawley, Robert Hehre, David Heskel, George Hettenhouse, Hans Heymann, Kendall Hill, Roger Hill, Tom Hindelang, Linda Hittle, Ralph Hocking, J. Ronald Hoffmeister, Robert Hollinger, Jim Horrigan, John Houston, John Howe, Keith Howe, Steve Isberg, Jim Jackson, Vahan Janjigian, Kose John, Craig Johnson, Keith Johnson, Ramon Johnson, Steven Johnson, Ray Jones, Frank Jordan, Manuel Jose, Alfred Kahl, Gus Kalogeras, Rajiv Kalra, Ravi Kamath, Michael Keenan, Bill Kennedy, James Keys, Carol Kiefer, Joe Kiernan, Richard Kish, Don Knight, Ladd Kochman, Dorothy Koehl, Jaroslaw Komarynsky, Duncan Kretovich, Harold Krogh, Charles Kroncke, Don Kummer, Reinhold Lamb, Joan Lamm, Larry Lang, P. Lange, Howard Lanser, Edward Lawrence, Martin Lawrence, Wayne Lee, Jim LePage, David E. LeTourneau, Jules Levine, John Lewis, Jason Lin, Chuck Linke, Bill Lloyd, Susan Long, Judy Maese, Bob Magee, Ileen Malitz, Bob Malko, Phil Malone, Abbas Mamoozadeh, Terry Maness, Chris Manning, S. K. Mansinghka, Terry Martell, David Martin, D. J. Masson, John Mathys, Ralph May, John McAlhany, Andy McCollough, Ambrose McCoy, Thomas McCue, Bill McDaniel, John McDowell, Charles McKinney, Robyn McLaughlin, James McNulty, Jeanette Medewitz-Diamond, Jamshid Mehran, Larry Merville, Rick Meyer, Jim Millar, Ed Miller, John Miller, John Mitchell, Carol Moerdyk, Bob Moore, Scott Moore, Barry Morris, Gene Morris, Fred Morrissey, Chris Muscarella, David Nachman, Tim Nantell, Don Nast, Bill Nelson, Bob Nelson, Bob Niendorf, Tom O'Brien, William O'Connell, Dennis O'Connor, John O'Donnell, Jim Olsen, Robert Olsen, Jim Pappas, Stephen Parrish, Helen Pawlowski, Michael Pescow, Glenn Petry, Jim Pettijohn, Rich Pettit, Dick Pettway, Aaron Phillips, Hugo Phillips, H. R. Pickett, John Pinkerton, Gerald Pogue, Eugene Poindexter, R. Potter, Franklin Potts, R. Powell, Chris Prestopino, Jerry Prock, Howard Puckett, Herbert Quigley, George Racette, Bob Radcliffe, Bill Rentz, Ken Riener, Charles Rini, John Ritchie, Pietra Rivoli, Antonio Rodriguez, James Rosenfeld, Stuart Rosenstein, E. N. Roussakis, Dexter Rowell, Marjorie Rubash, Bob Ryan, Jim Sachlis, Abdul Sadik, Thomas Scampini, Kevin Scanlon, Frederick Schadeler, Mary Jane Scheuer, Carl Schweser, John Settle, Alan Severn, James Sfiridis, Sol Shalit, Frederic Shipley, Dilip Shome, Ron Shrieves, Neil Sicherman, J. B. Silvers, Clay Singleton, Joe Sinkey, Stacy Sirmans, Jaye Smith, Patricia Smith, Steve Smith, Don Sorensen, David Speairs, Ken Stanley, Ed Stendardi, Alan Stephens, Don Stevens, Jerry Stevens, Glen Strasburg, David Suk, Katherine Sullivan, Philip Swensen, Bruce Swenson, Ernest Swift, Paul Swink, Gary Tallman, Dular Talukdar, Dennis Tanner, Craig Tapley, Russ Taussig, Richard Teweles, Ted Teweles, Francis C. Thomas, Andrew Thompson, John Thompson, Dogan Tirtirogu, Holland J. Toles, George Tsetsekos, William Tozer, Emery Trahan, George Trivoli, David Upton, Howard Van Auken, Pretorious Van den Dool, Pieter Vandenberg, Paul Vanderheiden, JoAnn Vaughan, Jim Verbrugge, Patrick Vincent, Steve Vinson, Susan Visscher, John Wachowicz, Mike Walker, Sam Weaver, Al Webster, Kuo-Chiang Wei, Bill Welch, Fred Weston, Norm Williams, Tony Wingler, Ed Wolfe, Criss Woodruff, Don Woods, Michael Yonan, Dennis Zocco, and Kent Zumwalt.

Special thanks are due to Chris Barry, Texas Christian University, and Shirley Love, Idaho State University, who wrote many of the boxes relating to small-business issues; to Dilip Shome, Virginia Polytechnic Institute, who helped greatly with the capital structure chapter; to Dave Brown and Mike Ryngaert, University of Florida, who helped us with the bankruptcy and merger material; to Roy Crum, Andy Naranjo, and Subu Venkataraman, who worked with us on the international materials; to Scott Below of East Carolina University, who developed the Web site information and references; to Laurie and Stan Eakins of East Carolina, who developed the materials on *Microsoft Excel* for the *Technology Supplement;* and to Larry Wolken, Texas A&M University, who offered his hard work and advice for the development of the *Lecture Presentation Software*. Susan Purcell and Bryan Jecko typed and helped proof the various manuscripts. Finally, the Dryden Press and Elm Street Publishing Services staffs, especially Anita Fallon, Karen Hill, Craig Johnson, Shana Lum, Sue Nodine, and Mike Reynolds, helped greatly with all phases of the textbook's development and production.

ERRORS IN THE TEXTBOOK

At this point, most authors make a statement like this: "We appreciate all the help we received from the people listed here, but any remaining errors are, of course, our own responsibility." And generally there are more than enough remaining errors! Having experienced difficulties with errors ourselves, both as students and as instructors, we resolved to avoid this problem in *Fundamentals*. As a result of our detection procedures, we are convinced that this book is relatively free of significant errors, meaning those that either confuse or distract readers.

Partly because of our confidence that few such errors remain, but primarily because we want very much to detect any errors that may have slipped by to correct them in subsequent printings, we decided to offer a reward of $10 per error to the first person who reports it to us. For purposes of this reward, errors are defined as misspelled words, nonrounding numerical errors, incorrect statements, and any other error that inhibits comprehension. Typesetting problems such as irregular spacing and differences in opinion regarding grammatical or punctuation conventions do not qualify for this reward. Given the ever-changing nature of the World Wide Web, changes in Web addresses also do not qualify as errors. Finally, any qualifying error that has follow-through effects is counted as two errors only. Please report any errors to us at the address below.

CONCLUSION

Finance is, in a real sense, the cornerstone of the enterprise system — good financial management is vitally important to the economic health of business firms, hence to the nation and the world. Because of its importance, finance should be widely and thoroughly understood, but this is easier said than done. The field is relatively complex, and it is undergoing constant change in response to shifts in economic conditions. All of this makes finance stimulating and exciting, but also challenging and sometimes perplexing. We sincerely hope that this eighth edition of *Fundamentals* will meet its own challenge by contributing to a better understanding of our financial system.

EUGENE F. BRIGHAM
JOEL F. HOUSTON
College of Business Administration
University of Florida
Gainesville, Florida 32611-7160

August 1997

BRIEF CONTENTS

Contents

FUNDAMENTALS OF FINANCIAL MANAGEMENT

EIGHTH EDITION

P A R T

INTRODUCTION TO FINANCIAL MANAGEMENT

CHAPTER 1
AN OVERVIEW OF FINANCIAL
MANAGEMENT

CHAPTER 2
FINANCIAL STATEMENTS, CASH
FLOW, AND TAXES

CHAPTER 3
ANALYSIS OF FINANCIAL
STATEMENTS

CHAPTER 4
THE FINANCIAL ENVIRONMENT:
MARKETS, INSTITUTIONS, AND
INTEREST RATES

CHAPTER 1

AN OVERVIEW OF FINANCIAL MANAGEMENT

ON THE WWW

See *http://www.benjerry.com/ mission.html* for *Ben and Jerry's interesting mission statement. It might be a good idea to print it out and take it to class for discussion.*

STRIKING THE RIGHT BALANCE

For many companies, the decision would have been both easy and positive. However, Ben and Jerry's Homemade Inc. has always taken pride in doing things differently. Faced with declining profits, the company was offered an opportunity to sell its premium ice cream in the lucrative Japanese market. However, Ben and Jerry's turned down the business because the Japanese firm that would have distributed their product had failed to develop a reputation for promoting social causes. Robert Holland Jr., Ben and Jerry's CEO at the time, commented that, "The only reason to take the opportunity was to make money." Clearly, Holland, who resigned from the company in late 1996, thought there was more to running a business than just making money.

The company's cofounders, Ben Cohen and Jerry Greenfield, opened the first Ben and Jerry's ice cream shop in 1978 in a vacant Vermont gas station with just $12,000 of capital plus a commitment to run the business in a manner consistent with their underlying values. Even though it is more expensive, the company only buys milk and cream from small local farms in Vermont. In addition, 7.5 percent of the company's before-tax income is donated to charity, and each of the company's 700 employees receives three free pints of ice cream each day. Moreover, the company had a policy of restricting the CEO's compensation to just seven times the salary of the company's lowest paid worker.

Until recently, Ben and Jerry's philosophy and commitment to social causes had not hindered its ability to make a lot of money. The company's stock grew by leaps and bounds up through the early 1990s, and its 1995 sales exceeded $150 million. However, in recent years the stock price fell from $33 to a 1995 low of $10 a share. Part of the problem has been increased competition in the premium ice cream market, along with a leveling off of sales in that market. Other problems include production inefficiencies and a slow, haphazard product development strategy.

The company lost money for the first time in 1994, and as a result, Cohen stepped down as CEO. Then Holland, a former consultant for McKinsey & Co. with a reputation as a turnaround specialist, was tapped as Cohen's replacement. To get Holland, though, the company had to abandon its old pay policy, for he was paid $326,000 in 1995, more than 14 times what an ice cream scooper made. Holland immediately took steps to improve the company's bottom line. As a result, sales increased, the company began making money, and its stock price climbed 70 percent, to $17, by mid-1996. Nevertheless, the recent decision not to enter the Japanese market demonstrates that the company has not abandoned its social consciousness.

All of this suggests that, in the future, Holland's successor will have to continue balancing the need for stronger financial performance against the desire to maintain the company's founding values. As you will see throughout the book, many of today's companies face challenges similar to those of Ben and Jerry's. Every day, corporations struggle with decisions such as these: Does it make sense to shift production overseas? What is the appropriate level of compensation for senior management? In general, how do we balance social concerns against the need to create value for our shareholders?

The purpose of this chapter is to give you an idea of what financial management is all about. After you finish the chapter, you should have a reasonably good idea of what finance majors might do after graduation. You should also have a better understanding of (1) some of the forces that will affect financial management in the future; (2) the place of finance in a firm's organization; (3) the relationships between financial managers and their counterparts in the accounting, marketing, production, and personnel departments; (4) the goals of a firm; and (5) the way financial managers can contribute to the attainment of these goals.

CAREER OPPORTUNITIES IN FINANCE

Finance consists of three interrelated areas: (1) *money and capital markets,* which deals with securities markets and financial institutions; (2) *investments,* which focuses on the decisions made by both individual and institutional investors as they choose securities for their investment portfolios; and (3) *financial management,* or "business finance," which involves decisions within firms. The career opportunities within each field are many and varied, but financial managers must have a knowledge of all three areas if they are to do their jobs well.

MONEY AND CAPITAL MARKETS

Many finance majors go to work for financial institutions, including banks, insurance companies, mutual funds, and investment banking firms. For success here, one needs a knowledge of valuation techniques, the factors that cause interest rates to rise and fall, the regulations to which financial institutions are subject, and the various types of financial instruments (mortgages, auto loans, certificates of deposit, and so on). One also needs a general knowledge of all aspects of business administration, because the management of a financial institution involves accounting, marketing, personnel, and computer systems, as well as financial management. An ability to communicate, both orally and in writing, is important, and "people skills," or the ability to get others to do their jobs well, are critical.

One common entry-level job in this area is a bank officer trainee, where one goes into bank operations and learns about the business, from tellers' work, to cash management, to making loans. One could expect to spend a year or so being rotated among these different areas, after which he or she would settle into a department, often as an assistant manager in a branch. Alternatively, one might become a specialist in some area such as real estate, and be authorized to make loans going into millions of dollars, or in the management of trusts, estates, and pension funds. Similar career paths are available with insurance companies, investment companies, credit unions, and consumer loan companies.

ON THE WWW

Consult http://www.cob.ohio-state.edu/dept/fin/osujobs.htm for an excellent site containing information on a variety of business career areas, listings of current jobs, and a variety of other reference materials.

INVESTMENTS

Finance graduates who go into investments often work for a brokerage house such as Merrill Lynch, either in sales or as a security analyst. Others work for banks, mutual funds, or insurance companies in the management of their investment portfolios; for financial consulting firms advising individual investors or pension funds on how to invest their capital; or for an investment banker, whose primary function is to help businesses raise new capital. The three main functions in the investments area are sales, the analysis of individual securities, and determining the optimal mix of securities for a given investor.

FINANCIAL MANAGEMENT

Financial management is the broadest of the three areas, and the one with the greatest number of job opportunities. Financial management is important in all types of businesses, including banks and other financial institutions, as well as industrial and retail firms. Financial management is also important in governmental operations, from schools to hospitals to highway departments. The job opportunities in financial management range from making decisions regarding plant expansions to choosing what types of securities to issue when financing expansion. Financial managers also have the responsibility for deciding the credit terms under which customers may buy, how much inventory the firm should carry, how much cash to keep on hand, whether to acquire other firms (merger analysis), and how much of the firm's earnings to plow back into the business versus pay out as dividends.

Regardless of which area a finance major goes into, he or she will need a knowledge of all three areas. For example, a bank lending officer cannot do his or her job well without a good understanding of financial management, because he or she must be able to judge how well a business is being operated. The same thing holds true for Merrill Lynch's security analysts and stockbrokers, who must have an understanding of general financial principles if they are to give their customers intelligent advice. Similarly, corporate financial managers need to know what their bankers are thinking about, and they also need to know how investors judge a firm's performance and thus determine its stock price. So, if you decide to make finance your career, you will need to know something about all three areas.

But suppose you do not plan to major in finance. Is the subject still important to you? Absolutely, for two reasons: (1) You need a knowledge of finance to make many personal decisions, ranging from investing for your retirement to deciding whether to lease versus buy a car. (2) Virtually all important business decisions have financial implications, so important decisions are generally made by teams from the accounting, finance, legal, marketing, personnel, and production departments. Therefore, if you want to succeed in the business arena, you must be highly competent in your own area, say, marketing, but you must also have a familiarity with the other business disciplines, including finance.

Thus, there are financial implications in virtually all business decisions, and nonfinancial executives simply must know enough finance to work these implications into their own specialized analyses.[1] Because of this, every student of

---

[1]It is an interesting fact that the course "Financial Management for Nonfinancial Executives" has the highest enrollment in most executive development programs.

business, regardless of his or her major, should be concerned with financial management.

SELF-TEST QUESTIONS   ??????

What are the three main areas of finance?

If you have definite plans to go into one area, why is it necessary that you know something about the other areas?

Why is it necessary for business students who do not plan to major in finance to understand the basics of finance?

FINANCIAL MANAGEMENT IN THE 1990s

When financial management emerged as a separate field of study in the early 1900s, the emphasis was on the legal aspects of mergers, the formation of new firms, and the various types of securities firms could issue to raise capital. During the Depression of the 1930s, the emphasis shifted to bankruptcy and reorganization, to corporate liquidity, and to the regulation of security markets. During the 1940s and early 1950s, finance continued to be taught as a descriptive, institutional subject, viewed more from the standpoint of an outsider rather than from that of a manager. However, a movement toward theoretical analysis began during the late 1950s, and the focus shifted to managerial decisions regarding the choice of assets and liabilities with the goal of maximizing the value of the firm. The focus on value maximization has continued on into the 1990s. However, two other trends have become increasingly important in recent years: (1) the globalization of business and (2) the increased use of information technology. These trends will undoubtedly continue in the years ahead.

GLOBALIZATION OF BUSINESS

Many companies today rely to a large and increasing extent on overseas operations. Table 1-1 summarizes the percentage of overseas revenues and profits for 10 well-known corporations. Very clearly, these 10 "American" companies are really international concerns.

Four factors have led to increased globalization of businesses: (1) Improvements in transportation and communications, which lowered shipping costs and made international trade more feasible. (2) The increasing political clout of consumers, who desire low-cost, high-quality products, has helped lower trade barriers designed to protect inefficient, high-cost domestic manufacturers. (3) As technology has become more advanced, the cost of developing new products has increased. These rising costs have led to joint ventures between such companies as General Motors and Toyota, and to global operations for many firms as they seek to expand markets and thus spread development costs over higher unit sales. (4) In a world populated with multinational firms able to shift production to wherever costs are lowest, a firm whose manufacturing operations are restricted to one country cannot compete unless costs in its home country happen to be low, a condition that does not necessarily exist for many U.S. corporations. As a result of these four factors, survival requires that most manufacturers produce and sell globally.

GLOBAL PERSPECTIVES

MCDONALD'S LOOKS OVERSEAS

As Table 1-1 demonstrates, many large corporations are truly global enterprises. For example, consider McDonald's Corp. As of mid-1996, the company owned, operated, or licensed more than 17,000 eateries, and nearly 7,000 of them were located in 84 overseas nations. Moreover, McDonald's has been growing much faster overseas than at home in the United States.

This trend will undoubtedly continue, as demonstrated by the firm's plans for operations in China. It currently has two restaurants in China, but it plans to have 500 by the year 2000.

Not suprisingly, McDonald's overall financial performance is heavily influenced by its overseas business. Because markets are less saturated and competition is less keen, its international profit margins are higher than they are in the United States. As a result, McDonald's disclosed in a recent report that even though its domestic revenues were only up a lackluster 4 percent, it had a healthy overall increase in earnings because revenues generated outside the United States rose by 15 percent.

Service companies, including banks, advertising agencies, and accounting firms, are also being forced to "go global," because such firms can better serve their multinational clients if they have worldwide operations. There will, of course, always be some purely domestic companies, but the most dynamic growth, and the best employment opportunities, are often with companies that operate worldwide.

Even businesses that operate exclusively in the United States are not immune to the effects of globalization. For example, the costs to a homebuilder in rural Nebraska are affected by interest rates and lumber prices—both of which are determined by worldwide supply and demand conditions. Furthermore, demand for the homebuilder's houses are influenced by interest rates and by conditions in the local farm economy, which depend to a large extent on foreign demand for

TABLE 1-1	Percentage of Revenue and Net Income from Overseas Operations for 10 Well-Known Corporations, 1995

COMPANY	PERCENTAGE OF REVENUE ORIGINATED OVERSEAS	PERCENTAGE OF NET INCOME GENERATED OVERSEAS
Citicorp	59.3	57.9
Coca-Cola	70.5	68.7
Exxon	77.8	76.5
Ford Motor	30.5	14.0
General Electric	25.5	13.4
General Motors	29.0	53.9
IBM	62.8	85.4
McDonald's	54.3	56.3
Merck	32.1	26.3
Walt Disney	20.9	1.8

NOTE: Disney's 1995 income from overseas operations was depressed by EuroDisney.

SOURCE: *Forbes* Magazine's 1995 Ranking of the Top 100 U.S. Multinationals.

wheat. To operate efficiently, the Nebraska builder must be able to forecast the demand for houses, and that demand depends on worldwide events. So, at least some knowledge of global economic conditions is important to virtually everyone, not just to those involved with businesses that operate internationally.

INFORMATION TECHNOLOGY

The remainder of the 1990s will see continued advances in computer and communications technology, and this will continue to revolutionize the way financial decisions are made. Companies are linking networks of personal computers to one another, to the firms' own mainframe computers, to the Internet and the World Wide Web, and to their customers' and suppliers' computers. Thus, financial managers are increasingly able to share information and to have "face-to-face" meetings with distant colleagues through video teleconferencing. The ability to access and analyze data on a real-time basis also means that quantitative analysis is becoming more important, and "gut feel" less sufficient, in business decisions. As a result, the next generation of financial managers will need stronger computer and quantitative skills than were required in the past.

SELF-TEST QUESTIONS ??????

What are two key trends to look for in the 1990s and beyond?

How has financial management changed from the early 1900s to the 1990s?

How might a person become better prepared for a career in financial management?

THE FINANCIAL STAFF'S RESPONSIBILITIES

The financial staff's task is to acquire and then help employ resources so as to maximize the value of the firm. Here are some specific activities:

1. **Forecasting and planning.** The financial staff must coordinate the planning process. This means they must interact with people from other departments as they look ahead and lay the plans which will shape the firm's future.

2. **Major investment and financing decisions.** A successful firm usually has rapid growth in sales, which requires investments in plant, equipment, and inventory. The financial staff must help determine the optimal sales growth rate, and finance people must help decide what specific assets to acquire and the best way to finance those assets. For example, should the firm finance with debt, equity, or some combination of the two, and if debt is used, how much should be long term and how much should be short term?

3. **Coordination and control.** The financial staff must interact with other personnel to ensure that the firm is operated as efficiently as possible. All business decisions have financial implications, and all managers — financial and otherwise — need to take this into account. For example, marketing decisions affect sales growth, which in turn influences investment requirements. Thus, marketing decision makers must take account of how their actions affect and are affected by such factors as the availability of funds, inventory policies, and plant capacity utilization.

4. **Dealing with the financial markets.** The financial staff must deal with the money and capital markets. As we shall see in Chapter 4, each firm affects and is affected by the general financial markets where funds are raised, where the firm's securities are traded, and where investors either make or lose money.

5. **Risk management.** All businesses face risks, including natural disasters such as fires and floods, uncertainties in commodity and security prices, volatile interest rates, and fluctuating foreign exchange rates. However, many of these risks can be reduced by purchasing insurance or by hedging in the derivatives markets. The financial staff is responsible for the firm's overall risk management program, including identifying the risks that should be hedged and then hedging them in the most efficient manner.

In summary, people working in financial management make decisions regarding which assets their firms should acquire, how those assets should be financed, and how the firm should manage its existing resources. If these responsibilities are performed optimally, financial managers will help to maximize the values of their firms, and this will also contribute to the welfare of consumers and employees.

SELF-TEST QUESTION ??????

What are five specific activities with which finance people are involved?

ALTERNATIVE FORMS OF BUSINESS ORGANIZATION

There are three main forms of business organization: (1) sole proprietorships, (2) partnerships, and (3) corporations, plus several hybrid forms. In terms of numbers, about 80 percent of businesses are operated as sole proprietorships, while most of the remainder are divided equally between partnerships and corporations. Based on dollar value of sales, however, about 80 percent of all business is conducted by corporations, about 13 percent by sole proprietorships, and about 7 percent by partnerships and hybrids. Because most business is conducted by corporations, we will concentrate on them in this book. However, it is important to understand the differences among the various forms.

SOLE PROPRIETORSHIP

Sole Proprietorship
An unincorporated business owned by one individual.

A **sole proprietorship** is an unincorporated business owned by one individual. Going into business as a sole proprietor is easy — one merely begins business operations. However, even the smallest businesses normally must be licensed by a governmental unit.

The proprietorship has three important advantages: (1) It is easily and inexpensively formed, (2) it is subject to few government regulations, and (3) the business avoids corporate income taxes.

The proprietorship also has three important limitations: (1) It is difficult for a proprietorship to obtain large sums of capital; (2) the proprietor has unlimited personal liability for the business's debts, which can result in losses that exceed the money he or she invested in the company; and (3) the life of a business organized as a proprietorship is limited to the life of the individual who created it.

For these three reasons, sole proprietorships are used primarily for small-business operations. However, businesses are frequently started as proprietorships and then converted to corporations when their growth causes the disadvantages of being a proprietorship to outweigh the advantages.

PARTNERSHIP

Partnership
An unincorporated business owned by two or more persons.

A **partnership** exists whenever two or more persons associate to conduct a non-corporate business. Partnerships may operate under different degrees of formality, ranging from informal, oral understandings to formal agreements filed with the secretary of the state in which the partnership was formed. The major advantage of a partnership is its low cost and ease of formation. The disadvantages are similar to those associated with proprietorships: (1) unlimited liability, (2) limited life of the organization, (3) difficulty of transferring ownership, and (4) difficulty of raising large amounts of capital. The tax treatment of a partnership is similar to that for proprietorships, which is often an advantage, as we demonstrate in Chapter 2.

Regarding liability, the partners can potentially lose all of their personal assets, even assets not invested in the business, because under partnership law, each partner is liable for the business's debts. Therefore, if any partner is unable to meet his or her pro rata liability in the event the partnership goes bankrupt, the remaining partners must make good on the unsatisfied claims, drawing on their personal assets to the extent necessary. The partners of the national accounting firm Laventhol and Horwath, a huge partnership which went bankrupt as a result of suits filed by investors who relied on faulty audit statements, learned all about the perils of doing business as a partnership. Thus, a Texas partner who audits a business which goes under can bring ruin to a millionaire New York partner who never went near the client company.

The first three disadvantages — unlimited liability, impermanence of the organization, and difficulty of transferring ownership — lead to the fourth, the difficulty partnerships have in attracting substantial amounts of capital. This is generally not a problem for a slow-growing business, but if a business's products or services really catch on, and if it needs to raise large amounts of capital to capitalize on its opportunities, the difficulty in attracting capital becomes a real drawback. Thus, growth companies such as Hewlett-Packard and Microsoft generally begin life as a proprietorship or partnership, but at some point their founders find it necessary to convert to a corporation.

CORPORATION

Corporation
A legal entity created by a state, separate and distinct from its owners and managers, having unlimited life, easy transferability of ownership, and limited liability.

A **corporation** is a legal entity created by a state, and it is separate and distinct from its owners and managers. This separateness gives the corporation three major advantages: (1) *Unlimited life.* A corporation can continue after its original owners and managers are deceased. (2) *Easy transferability of ownership interest.* Ownership interests can be divided into shares of stock, which, in turn, can be transferred far more easily than can proprietorship or partnership interests. (3) *Limited liability.* Losses are limited to the actual funds invested. To illustrate limited liability, suppose you invested $10,000 in a partnership which then went bankrupt owing $1 million. Because the owners are liable for the debts of a partnership, you could be assessed for a share of the company's debt, and you could be held liable for the entire $1 million if your partners could not pay their shares. Thus, an investor in a partnership is exposed to unlimited liability. On the other hand, if you invested $10,000 in the stock of a corporation which then went bankrupt, your potential loss on the investment would be limited to your $10,000 investment.[2] These three factors — unlimited life, easy transferability of ownership interest, and limited liability — make it much easier for corporations than for proprietorships or partnerships to raise money in the capital markets.

The corporate form offers significant advantages over proprietorships and partnerships, but it also has two disadvantages: (1) Corporate earnings may be subject to double taxation — the earnings of the corporation are taxed at the corporate level, and then any earnings paid out as dividends are taxed again as income to the stockholders. (2) Setting up a corporation, and filing the many required state and federal reports, is more complex and time-consuming than for a proprietorship or a partnership.

A proprietorship or a partnership can commence operations without much paperwork, but setting up a corporation requires that the incorporators prepare a charter and a set of bylaws. Although personal computer software that creates charters and bylaws is now available, a lawyer is required if the fledgling corporation has any nonstandard features. The *charter* includes the following information: (1) name of the proposed corporation, (2) types of activities it will pursue, (3) amount of capital stock, (4) number of directors, and (5) names and addresses of directors. The charter is filed with the secretary of the state in which the firm will be incorporated, and when it is approved, the corporation is officially in existence.[3] Then, after the corporation is in operation, quarterly and annual employment, financial, and tax reports must be filed with state and federal authorities.

The *bylaws* are a set of rules drawn up by the founders of the corporation. Included are such points as (1) how directors are to be elected (all elected each year, or perhaps one-third each year for three-year terms); (2) whether the existing stockholders will have the first right to buy any new shares the firm issues; and (3) procedures for changing the bylaws themselves, should conditions require it.

The value of any business other than a very small one will probably be maximized if it is organized as a corporation for the following three reasons:

1. Limited liability reduces the risks borne by investors, and, other things held constant, *the lower the firm's risk, the higher its value.*

2. A firm's value is dependent on its *growth opportunities*, which in turn are dependent on the firm's ability to attract capital. Since corporations can attract capital more easily than can unincorporated businesses, they are better able to take advantage of growth opportunities.

3. The value of an asset also depends on its *liquidity,* which means the ease of selling the asset and converting it to cash at a "fair market value." Since an investment in the stock of a corporation is much more liquid than a similar investment in a proprietorship or partnership, this too enhances the value of a corporation.

As we will see later in the chapter, most firms are managed with value maximization in mind, and this, in turn, has caused most large businesses to be organized as corporations.

---

[2]In the case of small corporations, the limited liability feature is often a fiction, because bankers and other lenders frequently require personal guarantees from the stockholders of small, weak businesses.

[3]Note that more than 60 percent of major U.S. corporations are chartered in Delaware, which has, over the years, provided a favorable legal environment for corporations. It is not necessary for a firm to be headquartered, or even to conduct operations, in its state of incorporation.

HYBRID FORMS OF ORGANIZATION

Although the three basic types of organization — proprietorships, partnerships, and corporations — dominate the business scene, several hybrid forms are gaining popularity. For example, there are some specialized types of partnerships that have somewhat different characteristics than the "plain vanilla" kind. First, it is possible to limit the liabilities of some of the partners by establishing a **limited partnership**, wherein certain partners are designated *general partners* and others *limited partners*. In a limited partnership, the limited partners are liable only for the amount of their investment in the partnership, while the general partners have unlimited liability. However, the limited partners typically have no control, which rests solely with the general partners, and their returns are likewise limited. Limited partnerships are common in real estate, oil, and equipment leasing ventures, but they are not widely used in general business situations because no one partner is usually willing to be the general partner and thus accept the majority of the business's risk, while would-be limited partners are unwilling to give up all control.

The **limited liability partnership (LLP)**, sometimes called a **limited liability company (LLC)**, is a relatively new type of partnership that is now permitted in many states. In both regular and limited partnerships, at least one partner is liable for the debts of the partnership. However, in an LLP, all partners enjoy limited liability with regard to the business's liabilities, and, in that regard, they are similar to shareholders in a corporation. In effect, the LLP form of organization combines the limited liability advantage of a corporation with the tax advantages of a partnership. Of course, those who do business with an LLP as opposed to a regular partnership are aware of the situation, which increases the risk faced by lenders, customers, and others who deal with the LLP.

There are also several different types of corporations. One type that is common among professionals such as doctors, lawyers, and accountants is the **professional corporation (PC)**, or in some states, the **professional association (PA)**. All 50 states have statutes that prescribe the requirements for such corporations, which provide most of the benefits of incorporation but do not relieve the participants of professional (malpractice) liability. Indeed, the primary motivation behind the professional corporation was to provide a way for groups of professionals to incorporate and thus avoid certain types of unlimited liability, yet still be held responsible for professional liability.

Finally, note that if certain requirements are met, particularly with regard to size and number of stockholders, one (or more) individuals can establish a corporation but elect to be taxed as if the business were a proprietorship or partnership. Such firms, which differ not in organizational form but only in how their owners are taxed, are called *S corporations*. Although S corporations are similar in many ways to limited liability partnerships, LLPs frequently offer more flexibility and benefits to their owners — so many that large numbers of S corporation businesses are converting to this relatively new organizational form.

Limited Partnership
A hybrid form of organization consisting of general partners, who have unlimited liability for the partnership's debts, and limited partners, whose liability is limited to the amount of their investment.

Limited Liability Partnership (Limited Liability Company)
A hybrid form of organization in which all partners enjoy limited liability for the business's debts. It combines the limited liability advantage of a corporation with the tax advantages of a partnership.

Professional Corporation (Professional Association)
A type of corporation common among professionals that provides most of the benefits of incorporation but does not relieve the participants of malpractice liability.

SELF-TEST QUESTIONS

What are the key differences between sole proprietorships, partnerships, and corporations?

Explain why the value of any business other than a very small one will probably be maximized if it is organized as a corporation.

Identify the hybrid forms of organization discussed in the text, and explain the differences among them.

FINANCE IN THE ORGANIZATIONAL STRUCTURE OF THE FIRM

Organizational structures vary from firm to firm, but Figure 1-1 presents a fairly typical picture of the role of finance within a corporation. The chief financial officer (CFO) generally has the title of vice-president: finance, and he or she reports to the president. The financial vice-president's key subordinates are the treasurer and the controller. In most firms the treasurer has direct responsibility for managing the firm's cash and marketable securities, for planning its capital structure, for selling stocks and bonds to raise capital, for overseeing the corporate pension plan, and for managing risk. The treasurer also supervises the credit manager, the inventory manager, and the director of capital budgeting (who analyzes decisions related to investments in fixed assets). The controller is typically responsible for the activities of the accounting and tax departments.

SELF-TEST QUESTION   ??????

Identify the two primary subordinates who report to the firm's chief financial officer, and indicate the primary responsibilities of each.

FIGURE   1 - 1   Role of Finance in a Typical Business Organization

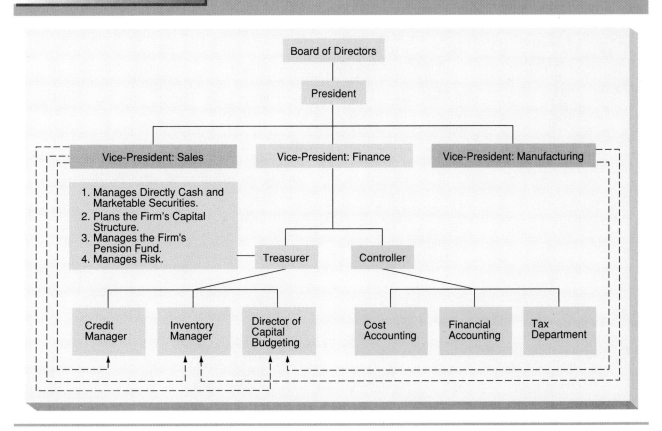

THE GOALS OF THE CORPORATION

Stockholder Wealth Maximization
The primary goal for management decisions; considers the risk and timing associated with expected earnings per share in order to maximize the price of the firm's common stock.

Shareholders are the owners of a corporation, and they purchase stocks because they are looking for a financial return. In most cases, shareholders elect directors, who then hire managers to run the corporation on a day-to-day basis. Since managers are working on behalf of shareholders, it follows that they should pursue policies which enhance shareholder value. Consequently, throughout this book we operate on the assumption that management's primary goal is **stockholder wealth maximization,** which translates into *maximizing the price of the firm's common stock*. Firms do, of course, have other objectives — in particular, the managers who make the actual decisions are interested in their own personal satisfaction, in their employees' welfare, and in the good of the community and of society at large. Still, for the reasons set forth in the following sections, *stock price maximization is the most important goal in most corporations*.

MANAGERIAL INCENTIVES TO MAXIMIZE SHAREHOLDER WEALTH

Stockholders own the firm and elect the board of directors, which then elects the management team. Management, in turn, is supposed to operate in the best interests of the stockholders. We know, however, that because the stock of most large firms is widely held, managers of large corporations have a great deal of autonomy. This being the case, might not managers pursue goals other than stock price maximization? For example, some have argued that the managers of a large, well-entrenched corporation could work just hard enough to keep stockholder returns at a "reasonable" level and then devote the remainder of their effort and resources to public service activities, to employee benefits, to higher executive salaries, or to golf.

It is almost impossible to determine whether a particular management team is trying to maximize shareholder wealth or is merely attempting to keep stockholders satisfied while pursuing other goals. For example, how can we tell whether employee or community benefit programs are in the long-run best interests of the stockholders? Similarly, are huge executive salaries really necessary to attract and retain excellent managers, or are they just another example of managers taking advantage of stockholders?

It is impossible to give definitive answers to these questions. However, we do know that the managers of a firm operating in a competitive market will be forced to undertake actions that are reasonably consistent with shareholder wealth maximization. If they depart from this goal, they run the risk of being removed from their jobs, either by the firm's board of directors or by outside forces. We will have more to say about this in a later section.

SOCIAL RESPONSIBILITY

Social Responsibility
The concept that businesses should be actively concerned with the welfare of society at large.

Another issue that deserves consideration is **social responsibility:** Should businesses operate strictly in their stockholders' best interests, or are firms also responsible for the welfare of their employees, customers, and the communities in which they operate? Certainly firms have an ethical responsibility to provide a safe working environment, to avoid polluting the air or water, and to produce safe products. However, socially responsible actions have costs, and not all businesses would voluntarily incur all such costs. If some firms act in a socially

Normal Profits/Rates of Return
Those profits and rates of return that are close to the average for all firms and are just sufficient to attract capital.

responsible manner while others do not, then the socially responsible firms will be at a disadvantage in attracting capital. To illustrate, suppose all firms in a given industry have close to **"normal" profits** and **rates of return on investment,** that is, close to the average for all firms and just sufficient to attract capital. If one company attempts to exercise social responsibility, it will have to raise prices to cover the added costs. If other firms in its industry do not follow suit, their costs and prices will be lower. The socially responsible firm will not be able to compete, and it will be forced to abandon its efforts. Thus, any voluntary socially responsible acts that raise costs will be difficult, if not impossible, in industries that are subject to keen competition.

What about oligopolistic firms with profits above normal levels — cannot such firms devote resources to social projects? Undoubtedly they can, and many large, successful firms do engage in community projects, employee benefit programs, and the like to a greater degree than would appear to be called for by pure profit or wealth maximization goals.[4] Furthermore, many such firms contribute large sums to charities. Still, publicly owned firms are constrained by capital market forces. To illustrate, suppose a saver who has funds to invest is considering two alternative firms. One devotes a substantial part of its resources to social actions, while the other concentrates on profits and stock prices. Many investors would shun the socially oriented firm, thus putting it at a disadvantage in the capital market. After all, why should the stockholders of one corporation subsidize society to a greater extent than those of other businesses? For this reason, even highly profitable firms (unless they are closely held rather than publicly owned) are generally constrained against taking unilateral cost-increasing social actions.

Does all this mean that firms should not exercise social responsibility? Not at all. But it does mean that most significant cost-increasing actions will have to be put on a *mandatory* rather than a voluntary basis to ensure that the burden falls uniformly on all businesses. Thus, such social benefit programs as fair hiring practices, minority training, product safety, pollution abatement, and antitrust actions are most likely to be effective if realistic rules are established initially and then enforced by government agencies. Of course, it is critical that industry and government cooperate in establishing the rules of corporate behavior, and that the costs as well as the benefits of such actions be estimated accurately and then taken into account.

In spite of the fact that many socially responsible actions must be mandated by government, in recent years numerous firms have voluntarily taken such actions, especially in the area of environmental protection, because they helped sales. For example, many detergent manufacturers now use recycled paper for their containers, and food companies are packaging more and more products in materials that consumers can recycle or that are biodegradable. To illustrate, McDonald's replaced its styrofoam boxes, which take years to break down in landfills, with paper wrappers that are less bulky and decompose more rapidly. Some companies, such as the Body Shop and Ben & Jerry's Ice Cream, go to great lengths to be socially responsible. According to the president of the Body Shop, the role of business is to promote the public good, not just the good of the firm's shareholders. Furthermore, she argues that it is impossible to separate business from social responsibility. For some firms, socially responsible actions may not de facto be costly — the companies heavily advertise their actions, and many

ON THE WWW
Go to http://www.the-body-shop.com/values/index.html to see the corporate values The Body Shop embraces.

[4]Even firms like these often find it necessary to justify such projects at stockholder meetings by stating that these programs will contribute to long-run profit maximization.

INDUSTRY PRACTICE

ARE CEOS OVERPAID?

At first glance the number is hard to believe: $203 million. That's what Disney's chief, Michael Eisner, received as compensation in 1993. This happened in a year when Disney's net income fell 63 percent, partly in response to losses at EuroDisney. In fact, Eisner's compensation was not that much less than Disney's 1993 net income, which totaled $229.8 million. A cynic might think, "If someone reduced net income by 63 percent and still earned $203 million, how much would the company pay if earnings actually rose?"

What is interesting is that Eisner's compensation received little or no resistance from the company's shareholders. Why? During his tenure as Disney's CEO, Eisner has made shareholders rich. Disney's market value has skyrocketed from $2.2 billion in 1984, when he took over as CEO, to more than $40 billion by mid-1996. If you had invested $1,000 in Disney stock in 1984, and reinvested all of your dividends, your investment would be worth nearly $30,000 today.

Eisner's record haul came largely in the form of stock options. His salary and bonus in 1993 totaled only $750,000, but he exercised long-term stock options worth more than $202 million. Clearly, those stock options provided Eisner with a significant incentive to raise the company's stock price, and he delivered.

Concerns about "excessive compensation" are most likely to arise when CEOs receive exorbitant levels of pay at the same time the firm's stock price is underperforming the market. Even in these instances, the issues may not be all that straightforward. The stock price may fall for reasons having nothing to do with the CEO — indeed, you could argue that CEOs probably work especially hard when the company's fortunes are declining. Also, you need to look at the long-run track record of the CEO and the firm. In Disney's case, the company's performance over time has been outstanding, even though during the year in which Eisner exercised his options and had a reported income of $203 million, the company's performance was lackluster.

Some critics argue that although performance incentives are entirely appropriate as a method of compensation, the overall level of CEO compensation is still too high. Would Eisner have been unwilling to take the job if he had been offered only half as many stock options? Would he have put forth less effort, and would the stock price not have gone up as much? It is hard to say.

Eisner's compensation was extraordinary, but it was largely a one-time payment. The typical CEO of a large corporation generally receives annual compensation of less than $1 million. Although this certainly is respectable, it pales compared with the salaries sports stars and other entertainers receive. For example, it has been estimated that director Steven Spielberg earned more than $165 million in 1994, while the preschool icon Barney the Dinosaur earned $59 million for his creators in 1993 and another $25 million in 1994. More recently, Michael Jordan just signed a $25 million one-year contract to play basketball, a 20-year-old Tiger Woods quit school to play golf for about $50 million, and actors Jim Carrey and Sylvester Stallone have signed deals which earn them $20 million per picture.

consumers prefer to buy from socially responsible companies rather than from those that shun social responsibility.

STOCK PRICE MAXIMIZATION AND SOCIAL WELFARE

If a firm attempts to maximize its stock price, is this good or bad for society? In general, it is good. Aside from such illegal actions as attempting to form monopolies, violating safety codes, and failing to meet pollution control requirements, *the same actions that maximize stock prices also benefit society*. First, note that stock price maximization requires efficient, low-cost businesses that produce high-quality goods and services at the lowest possible cost. Second, stock price maximization requires the development of products and services that consumers want and need, so the profit motive leads to new technology, to new products, and to new jobs. Finally, stock price maximization necessitates efficient and courteous service, adequate stocks of merchandise, and well-located business establishments — these are the factors which lead to sales, which in turn are necessary for profits. Therefore, most actions which help a firm increase the price of its stock also benefit society at large. This is why profit-motivated, free-enterprise economies have been so much more successful than socialistic and communistic economic systems. Since financial management plays a crucial role in the operations of successful firms, and since successful firms are absolutely necessary for a healthy, productive economy, it is easy to see why finance is important from a social standpoint.[5]

SELF-TEST QUESTIONS

What is management's primary goal?

What actions could be taken to remove a management team if it departs from the goal of maximizing shareholder wealth?

What would happen if one firm attempted to exercise costly socially responsible programs but its competitors did *not* follow suit?

How does the goal of stock price maximization benefit society at large?

BUSINESS ETHICS

Business Ethics
A company's attitude and conduct toward its employees, customers, community, and stockholders.

The word *ethics* is defined in Webster's dictionary as "standards of conduct or moral behavior." **Business ethics** can be thought of as a company's attitude and conduct toward its employees, customers, community, and stockholders. High standards of ethical behavior demand that a firm treat each party that it deals with in a fair and honest manner. A firm's commitment to business ethics can be measured by the tendency of the firm and its employees to adhere to laws and regulations relating to such factors as product safety and quality, fair employment practices, fair marketing and selling practices, the use of confidential information for personal gain, community involvement, bribery, and illegal payments to obtain business.

There are many instances of firms engaging in unethical behavior. For example, in recent years the employees of several prominent Wall Street investment banking houses have been sentenced to prison for illegally using insider information on proposed mergers for their own personal gain, and E. F. Hutton, a large brokerage firm, lost its independence through a forced merger after it was convicted of cheating its banks out of millions of dollars in a check kiting scheme. Drexel Burnham Lambert, one of the largest investment banking firms, went bankrupt, and its "junk bond king," Michael Milken, who had earned $550 million in just one year, was sentenced to 10 years in prison plus charged a huge fine for securities-law violations. Another investment bank, Salomon Brothers, was implicated in a Treasury bond scandal which resulted in the firing of its chairman and other top officers.

---

[5]People sometimes argue that firms, in their efforts to raise profits and stock prices, increase product prices and gouge the public. In a reasonably competitive economy, which we have, prices are constrained by competition and consumer resistance. If a firm raises its prices beyond reasonable levels, it will simply lose its market share. Even giant firms like General Motors lose business to the Japanese and Germans, as well as to Ford and Chrysler, if they set prices above levels necessary to cover production costs plus a "normal" profit. Of course, firms *want* to earn more, and they constantly try to cut costs, to develop new products, and so on, and thereby to earn above-normal profits. Note, though, that if they are indeed successful and do earn above-normal profits, those very profits will attract competition which will eventually drive prices down, so again the main long-term beneficiary is the consumer.

These cases received a lot of notoriety, but the results of a recent study indicate that the executives of most major firms in the United States believe that firms do try to maintain high ethical standards in all of their business dealings. Furthermore, most executives believe that there is a positive correlation between ethics and long-run profitability. For example, Chase Bank suggested that ethical behavior has increased its profitability because such behavior helped it (1) avoid fines and legal expenses, (2) build public trust, (3) attract business from customers who appreciate and support its policies, (4) attract and keep employees of the highest caliber, and (5) support the economic viability of the communities in which it operates.

Most firms today have in place strong codes of ethical behavior, and they also conduct training programs designed to ensure that employees understand the correct behavior in different business situations. However, it is imperative that top management — the chairman, president, and vice-presidents — be openly committed to ethical behavior, and that they communicate this commitment through their own personal actions as well as through company policies, directives, and punishment/reward systems.

When conflicts arise between profits and ethics, sometimes the ethical considerations are so strong that they clearly dominate. However, in many cases the choice between ethics and profits is not clear cut. For example, suppose Norfolk Southern's managers know that its coal trains are polluting the air along its routes, but the amount of pollution is within legal limits and preventive actions would be costly. Are the managers ethically bound to reduce pollution? Similarly, suppose a medical products company's own research indicates that one of its new products may cause problems. However, the evidence is relatively weak, other evidence regarding benefits to patients is strong, and independent government tests show no adverse effects. Should the company make the potential problem known to the public? If it does release the negative (but questionable) information, this will hurt sales and profits, and possibly keep some patients who would benefit from the new product from using it. There are no obvious answers to questions such as these, but companies must deal with them on a regular basis, and a failure to handle the situation properly can lead to huge product liability suits and even to bankruptcy. Just ask Dow-Corning's executives.

SELF-TEST QUESTIONS

How would you define "business ethics"?

Is "being ethical" good for profits in the long run? In the short run?

AGENCY RELATIONSHIPS

It has long been recognized that managers may have personal goals that compete with shareholder wealth maximization. Managers are empowered by the owners of the firm — the shareholders — to make decisions, and that creates a potential conflict of interest known as *agency theory*.

An *agency relationship* arises whenever one or more individuals, called *principals,* hires another individual or organization, called an *agent*, to perform some service and then delegates decision-making authority to that agent. Within the financial management context, the primary agency relationships are those (1) between stockholders and managers and (2) between managers and debt-holders.[6]

STOCKHOLDERS VERSUS MANAGERS

Agency Problem
A potential conflict of interest between the agent (manager) and (1) the outside stockholders or (2) the creditors (debtholders).

A potential **agency problem** arises whenever the manager of a firm owns less than 100 percent of the firm's common stock. If the firm is a proprietorship managed by its owner, the owner-manager will presumably operate so as to maximize his or her own welfare, with welfare measured in the form of increased personal wealth, more leisure, or perquisites.[7] However, if the owner-manager incorporates and then sells some of the stock to outsiders, a potential conflict of interests immediately arises. Now the owner-manager may decide to lead a more relaxed lifestyle and not work as strenuously to maximize shareholder wealth, because less of this wealth will accrue to him or her. Also, the owner-manager may decide to consume more perquisites, because some of these costs will be borne by the outside shareholders. In essence, the fact that the owner-manager will neither gain all the benefits of the wealth created by his or her efforts nor bear all of the costs of perquisites will increase the incentive to take actions that are not in the best interests of other shareholders.

In most large corporations, potential agency conflicts are important, because large firms' managers generally own only a small percentage of the stock. In this situation, shareholder wealth maximization could take a back seat to any number of conflicting managerial goals. For example, people have argued that some managers' primary goal seems to be to maximize the size of their firms.[8] By creating a large, rapidly growing firm, managers (1) increase their job security, because a hostile takeover is less likely; (2) increase their own power, status, and salaries; and (3) create more opportunities for their lower- and middle-level managers. Furthermore, since the managers of most large firms own only a small percentage of the stock, it has been argued that they have a voracious appetite for salaries and perquisites, and that they generously contribute corporate dollars to their favorite charities because they get the glory but outside stockholders bear the cost.

Managers can be encouraged to act in stockholders' best interests through incentives which reward them for good performance but punish them for poor performance. Some specific mechanisms used to motivate managers to act in shareholders' best interests include (1) managerial compensation, (2) direct intervention by shareholders, (3) the threat of firing, and (4) the threat of takeover.

1. **Managerial compensation.** Managers obviously must be compensated, and the structure of the compensation package can and should be designed to meet two primary objectives: (a) to attract and retain able managers and (b) to align manager's actions as closely as possible with the interests of stockholders, who are primarily interested in stock price maximization. Different companies follow different compensation practices, but a typical senior executive's compensation is structured in three parts: (a) a specified annual salary, which is

---

[6]The classic work on the application of agency theory to financial management is Michael C. Jensen and William H. Meckling, "Theory of the Firm, Managerial Behavior, Agency Costs, and Ownership Structure," *Journal of Financial Economics,* October 1976, 305–360.

[7]*Perquisites* are executive fringe benefits such as luxurious offices, executive assistants, expense accounts, limousines, corporate jets, generous retirement plans, and the like.

[8]See J.R. Wildsmith, *Managerial Theories of the Firm* (New York: Dunellen, 1974).

necessary to meet living expenses; (b) a bonus paid at the end of the year, which depends on the company's profitability during the year; and (c) options to buy stock, or actual shares of stock, which reward the executive for long-term performance.

Performance Shares
Stock which is awarded to executives on the basis of the company's performance.

Managers are more likely to focus on maximizing stock prices if they are themselves large shareholders. Often, companies grant senior managers **performance shares,** where the executive receives a number of shares dependent upon the company's actual performance and the executive's continued service. For example, in 1991 Coca-Cola granted one million shares of stock worth $81 million to its CEO, Roberto Goizueta. The award was based on Coke's performance under Goizueta's leadership, but it also stipulated that Goizueta would receive the shares only if he stayed with the company for the remainder of his career.

Executive Stock Option
An option to buy stock at a stated price within a specified time period that is granted to an executive as part of his or her compensation package.

Most large corporations also provide **executive stock options,** which allow managers to purchase stock at some future time at a given price. Obviously, a manager who has an option to buy, say, 10,000 shares of stock at a price of $10 during the next 5 years will have an incentive to help raise the stock's value to an amount greater than $10.

The number of performance shares or options awarded is generally based on objective criteria. Years ago, the primary criteria were accounting measures such as earnings per share (EPS) and return on equity (ROE). Today, though, the focus is more on the market value of the firm's shares or, better yet, on the performance of its shares relative to other stocks in its industry. Various procedures are used to structure compensation programs, and good programs are relatively complicated. Still, it has been thoroughly established that a well-designed compensation program can do wonders to improve a company's financial performance.

2. **Direct intervention by shareholders.** Years ago most stock was owned by individuals, but today the majority is owned by institutional investors such as insurance companies, pension funds, and mutual funds. Therefore, the institutional money managers have the clout, if they choose to use it, to exercise considerable influence over most firms' operations. First, they can talk with a firm's management and make suggestions regarding how the business should be run. In effect, institutional investors act as lobbyists for the body of stockholders. Second, any shareholder who has owned at least $1,000 of a company's stock for one year can sponsor a proposal which must be voted on at the annual stockholders' meeting, even if the proposal is opposed by management. Although shareholder-sponsored proposals are nonbinding and are limited to issues outside of day-to-day operations, the results of such votes are clearly heard by top management.

3. **The threat of firing.** Until recently, the probability of a large firm's management being ousted by its stockholders was so remote that it posed little threat. This situation existed because the shares of most firms were so widely distributed, and management's control over the voting mechanism was so strong, that it was almost impossible for dissident stockholders to get the votes needed to overthrow a management team. However, as noted above, that situation is changing.

Consider the case of Baltimore Bancorp. Recently its chairman, Harry L. Robinson, spurned a friendly $17-per-share takeover offer from rival First Maryland Bancorp. Dismayed stockholders saw the stock price drop to $5 a share, and, led by a Baltimore businessman, they revolted. A slate of dissident directors was nominated, and they lined up the support of T. Rowe Price, a Baltimore mutual fund management company that held about 9 percent of the stock. At Baltimore Bancorp's next annual meeting, shareholders elected the dissident directors, who won all six of the board seats that were up for election. Then the board ousted Robinson, and a new management team was put in place.

For every obvious case of shareholders' directly ousting current management, there have been dozens of indirect ousters. For example, the CEOs or other top executives at American Express, Goodyear, General Motors, Kodak, and IBM all resigned recently amid speculation that their departures were due to their companies' poor performance. More and more, the reasons for executive departures are shifting from "poor health" and "personal reasons" to "at the request of the board."

Hostile Takeover
The acquisition of a company over the opposition of its management.

4. **The threat of takeovers. Hostile takeovers** (when management does not want the firm to be taken over) are most likely to occur when a firm's stock is undervalued relative to its potential because of poor management. In a hostile takeover, the managers of the acquired firm are generally fired, and any who manage to stay on lose status and authority. Thus, managers have a strong incentive to take actions designed to maximize stock prices. In the words of one company president, "If you want to keep your job, don't let your stock sell at a bargain price."

STOCKHOLDERS (THROUGH MANAGERS) VERSUS CREDITORS

In addition to conflicts between stockholders and managers, there can also be conflicts between creditors and stockholders. Creditors have a claim on part of the firm's earnings stream for payment of interest and principal on the debt, and they have a claim on the firm's assets in the event of bankruptcy. However, stockholders have control (through the managers) of decisions that affect the profitability and risk of the firm. Creditors lend funds at rates that are based on (1) the riskiness of the firm's existing assets, (2) expectations concerning the riskiness of future asset additions, (3) the firm's existing capital structure (that is, the amount of debt financing used), and (4) expectations concerning future capital structure decisions. These are the primary determinants of the riskiness of a firm's cash flows, hence the safety of its debt issues.

Now suppose stockholders, acting through management, cause a firm to take on a large new project that is far riskier than was anticipated by the creditors. This increased risk will cause the required rate of return on the firm's debt to increase, and that will cause the value of the outstanding debt to fall. If the risky project is successful, all the benefits go to the stockholders, because creditors' returns are fixed at the old, low-risk rate. However, if the project is unsuccessful, the bondholders may have to share in the losses. From the stockholders' point of view, this amounts to a game of "heads I win, tails you lose," which is obviously not good for the creditors. Similarly, suppose its managers borrow additional funds and use the proceeds to repurchase some of the firm's outstanding stock in an effort to "leverage up" stockholders' return on equity. The value of the debt will probably decrease, because more debt will have a claim against the firm's cash flows and assets. In both the riskier asset and the increased leverage situations, stockholders tend to gain at the expense of creditors.

Can and should stockholders, through their managers/agents, try to expropriate wealth from creditors? In general, the answer is no, for there is no room for unethical behavior in the business world. Indeed, creditors attempt to protect themselves against stockholders by placing restrictive covenants in debt agreements. Moreover, if creditors perceive that a firm's managers are trying to take advantage of them, they will either refuse to deal further with the firm or else will charge a higher than normal interest rate to compensate for the risk of possible exploitation. Thus, firms which deal unfairly with creditors either lose access to the debt markets or are saddled with high interest rates and restrictive covenants, all of which are detrimental to shareholders.

In view of these constraints, it follows that to best serve their shareholders in the long run, managers must play fairly with creditors. Managers, as agents of both shareholders and creditors, must act in a manner that is fairly balanced between the interests of the two classes of security holders. Similarly, because of other constraints and sanctions, management actions which would expropriate wealth from any of the firm's other *stakeholders,* including its employees, customers, suppliers, and community, will ultimately be to the detriment of its shareholders. In our society, stock price maximization requires fair treatment for all parties whose economic positions are affected by managerial decisions.

SELF-TEST QUESTIONS   ??????

What are agency costs, and who bears them?

What are some mechanisms that encourage managers to act in the best interests of stockholders? To not take advantage of bondholders?

Why should managers not take actions that are unfair to any of the firm's stakeholders?

MANAGERIAL ACTIONS TO MAXIMIZE SHAREHOLDER WEALTH

What types of actions can management take to maximize the price of a firm's stock? To answer this question, we first need to ask, "What factors determine the price of a company's stock?" While we will address this issue in detail in Chapter 8, we can lay out three basic facts here. (1) Any financial asset, including a company's stock, is valuable only to the extent that the asset generates cash flows. (2) The timing of the cash flows matter — cash received sooner is better, because it can be reinvested to produce additional income. (3) Investors are generally averse to risk, so all else equal, they will pay more for a stock whose cash flows are relatively certain than for one with relatively risky cash flows. Because of these three factors, managers can enhance their firms' value (and the stock price) by increasing their firms' expected cash flows, by speeding them up, and by reducing their riskiness.

Within the firm, managers make investment decisions regarding the types of products or services produced, as well as the way goods and services are produced and delivered. Also, managers must decide *how to finance the firm* — what mix of debt and equity should be used, and what specific types of debt and equity securities should be issued? In addition, the financial manager must decide what percentage of current earnings to pay out as dividends rather than to

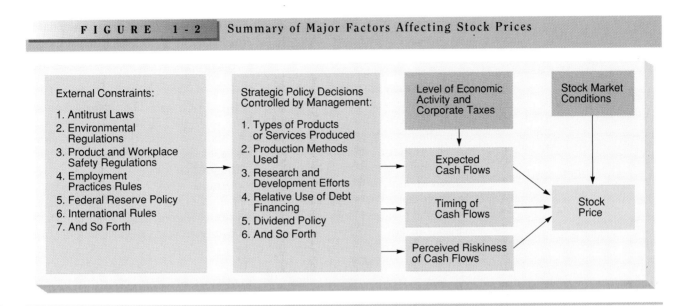

FIGURE 1-2   Summary of Major Factors Affecting Stock Prices

Dividend Policy Decision
The decision as to how much of current earnings to pay out as dividends rather than to retain for reinvestment in the firm.

retain and reinvest; this is called the **dividend policy decision**. Each of these investment and financing decisions is likely to affect the level, timing, and riskiness of the firm's cash flows, and, therefore, the price of its stock. Naturally, managers should make investment and financing decisions designed to maximize the firm's stock price.

Although managerial actions affect the value of a firm's stock, stock prices are also affected by such external factors as legal constraints, the general level of economic activity, tax laws, interest rates, and conditions in the stock market. Figure 1-2 diagrams these general relationships. Working within the set of external constraints shown in the box at the extreme left, management makes a set of long-run strategic policy decisions which chart a future course for the firm. These policy decisions, along with the general level of economic activity and the level of corporate income taxes, influence the firm's expected cash flows, their timing, their eventual payment to stockholders as dividends, and their perceived riskiness. These factors all affect the price of the stock, but so does another factor, conditions in the stock market as a whole.

SELF-TEST QUESTION   ??????

Identify some factors beyond a firm's control which influence its stock price.

DOES IT MAKE SENSE TO TRY TO MAXIMIZE EARNINGS PER SHARE?

Profit Maximization
The maximization of the firm's net income.

Earnings Per Share (EPS)
Net income divided by the number of shares of common stock outstanding.

In arguing that managers should take steps to maximize the firm's stock price, we have said nothing about the traditional objective, **profit maximization**, or the maximization of **earnings per share (EPS)**. Indeed, while a growing number of analysts rely on cash flow projections to assess performance, at least as much attention is still paid to accounting measures, especially EPS. The traditional accounting performance measures are appealing because (1) they are easy to use and understand; (2) they are calculated on the basis of (more or less) standardized accounting practices, which reflect the accounting profession's best efforts to measure financial performance on a consistent basis both across firms and over time; and (3) net income is supposed to be reflective of the firm's potential to produce cash flows over time.

Generally, there is a high correlation between EPS, cash flow, and stock price, and all of them will probably rise if a firm's sales rise. Nevertheless, as we will see in the next chapter, (1) there are also important distinctions between earnings and cash flow, and (2) a firm's stock price is affected by both its performance this year and its expected performance in the future.

Even though cash flows ultimately determine stockholder value, financial managers cannot ignore the effects of their decisions on reported EPS, because earnings announcements send messages to investors. Say, for example, a manager makes a decision which will ultimately enhance cash flows and stock price, yet the short-run effect is a decline in this year's profitability and EPS. Such a decision might be a change in inventory accounting policy which increases reported expenses but also increases cash flow because it reduces current taxes. In this case, it makes sense for the manager to adopt the policy because it generates additional cash, even though it reduces reported profits. Note, though, that management must communicate the reason for the earnings decline, for otherwise the company's stock price would probably decline after the earnings announcement.

SELF-TEST QUESTIONS

Is profit maximization an appropriate goal for financial managers?

Should financial managers concentrate strictly on cash flow and ignore the impact of their decisions on EPS?

ORGANIZATION OF THE BOOK

The primary goal of all managers is to help maximize the value of the firm. To achieve this goal, all managers must have a general understanding of how businesses are organized, how financial markets operate, how interest rates are determined, how the tax system operates, and how accounting data are used to evaluate a business's performance. In addition, managers must have a good understanding of such fundamental concepts as time value of money, risk measurement, asset valuation, and evaluation of specific investment opportunities. This background information is essential for *anyone* involved with the kinds of decisions that affect the value of a firm's securities.

The organization of this book reflects these considerations, so Part I presents some background material in four chapters. Chapter 1 discusses the goals of the firm and the "philosophy" of financial management. Chapter 2 describes the key financial statements, discusses what they are designed to do, and then explains how our tax system affects earnings, cash flows, stock prices, and managerial decisions. Chapter 3 shows how financial statements are analyzed, and Chapter 4 discusses how financial markets operate and how interest rates are determined.

Part II considers two of the most fundamental concepts in financial management — risk and the time value of money. First, Chapter 5 explains how risk is measured and how it affects security prices and rates of return. Next, Chapter 6 discusses the time value of money and its effects on asset values and rates of return.

Part III covers issues related to financial assets, primarily stocks and bonds. Chapter 7 focuses on bonds, and Chapter 8 considers stocks. Both chapters describe the relevant institutional details, then explain how risk and time value jointly determine stock and bond prices.

Part IV, "Investing in Long-Term Assets: Capital Budgeting," applies the concepts covered in earlier chapters to decisions related to long-term, fixed asset investments. First, Chapter 9 explains how to measure the cost of the funds used to acquire fixed assets, or the cost of capital. Next, Chapter 10 shows how this information is used to evaluate potential capital investments by answering this question: Can we expect a project to provide a higher rate of return than the cost of the funds used to finance it? Only if the expected return exceeds the cost of capital will accepting a project increase stockholders' wealth. Chapter 11 goes into more detail on capital budgeting decisions, looking at replacement projects versus expansion projects, the effects of inflation, and the like. Finally, Chapter 12 shows how projects' riskiness is taken into account, and how the total capital budget should be determined.

Part V discusses how firms should finance their long-term assets. First, Chapter 13 examines capital structure theory, or the issue of how much debt versus equity the firm should use. Then, Chapter 14 considers dividend policy, or the decision to retain earnings versus paying them out as dividends.

In Part VI, our focus shifts from long-term, strategic decisions to short-term, day-to-day operating decisions. Operating decisions are made within the context of a financial plan, or forecast, so we begin, in Chapter 15, with a discussion of financial planning and forecasting. Then, in Chapters 16 and 17, we see how cash, inventories, and accounts receivable are managed, and the best way of financing these current assets.

Finally, in Part VII, we address several special topics, including multinational financial management, risk management, derivatives, hybrid financing, and mergers. Proper treatment of these topics requires a knowledge of the basics presented in the earlier chapters, so they were deferred to the end.

It is worth noting that some instructors may choose to cover the chapters in a different sequence from their order in the book. The chapters are written to a large extent in a modular, self-contained manner, so such reordering should present no major difficulties.

SUMMARY

This chapter has provided an overview of financial management. The key concepts covered are listed below.

♦ Finance consists of three interrelated areas: (1) **money and capital markets,** (2) **investments,** and (3) **financial management.**

♦ In recent years the two most important trends in finance have been the **increased globalization of business** and the growing use of **computers and information technology.** These trends are likely to continue in the future.

♦ The **financial staff's** task is to **obtain** and **use funds** so as to **maximize the value of the firm.**

♦ The three main forms of business organization are the **sole proprietorship,** the **partnership,** and the **corporation.**

♦ Although each form of organization offers advantages and disadvantages, **most business is conducted by corporations because this organizational form maximizes larger firms' values.**

♦ The primary goal of management should be to **maximize stockholders' wealth,** and this means **maximizing the firm's stock price.** However, actions which maximize stock prices also increase social welfare.

♦ An **agency problem** is a potential conflict of interests that can arise between a principal and an agent. Two important agency relationships are (1) those between the owners of the firm and its management and (2) those between the managers, acting for stockholders, and the debtholders.

♦ There are a number of ways to **motivate managers to act in the best interests of stockholders,** including (1) properly structured **managerial compensation,** (2) **direct intervention by stockholders,** (3) the **threat of firing,** and (4) the **threat of takeovers.**

♦ The **price of a firm's stock** depends on the **cash flows paid to shareholders,** the **timing of the cash flows,** and their **riskiness.** The level and riskiness of cash flows are affected by the **financial environment** as well as by **investment, financing,** and **dividend policy decisions** made by financial managers.

QUESTIONS

1-1 What are the three principal forms of business organization? What are the advantages and disadvantages of each?

1-2 Would the "normal" rate of return on investment be the same in all industries? Would "normal" rates of return change over time? Explain.

1-3 Would the role of a financial manager be likely to increase or decrease in importance relative to other executives if the rate of inflation increased? Explain.

1-4 Should stockholder wealth maximization be thought of as a long-term or a short-term goal — for example, if one action would probably increase the firm's stock price from a current level of $20 to $25 in 6 months and then to $30 in 5 years but another action would probably keep the stock at $20 for several years but then increase it to $40 in 5 years, which action would be better? Can you think of some specific corporate actions which might have these general tendencies?

1-5 Drawing on your background in accounting, can you think of any accounting differences that might make it difficult to compare the relative performance of different firms?

1-6 Would the management of a firm in an oligopolistic or in a competitive industry be more likely to engage in what might be called "socially conscious" practices? Explain your reasoning.

1-7 What's the difference between stock price maximization and profit maximization? Under what conditions might profit maximization *not* lead to stock price maximization?

1-8 If you were the president of a large, publicly owned corporation, would you make decisions to maximize stockholders' welfare or your own personal interests? What are some actions stockholders could take to ensure that management's interests and those of stockholders coincided? What are some other factors that might influence management's actions?

1-9 The president of Southern Semiconductor Corporation (SSC) made this statement in the company's annual report: "SSC's primary goal is to increase the value of the common stockholders' equity over time." Later on in the report, the following announcements were made:

a. The company contributed $1.5 million to the symphony orchestra in Birmingham, Alabama, its headquarters city.

b. The company is spending $500 million to open a new plant in Mexico. No revenues will be produced by the plant for 4 years, so earnings will be depressed during this period versus what they would have been had the decision not been made to open the new plant.

c. The company is increasing its relative use of debt. Whereas assets were formerly financed with 35 percent debt and 65 percent equity, henceforth the financing mix will be 50-50.

d. The company uses a great deal of electricity in its manufacturing operations, and it generates most of this power itself. Plans are to utilize nuclear fuel rather than coal to produce electricity in the future.

e. The company has been paying out half of its earnings as dividends and retaining the other half. Henceforth, it will pay out only 30 percent as dividends.

Discuss how each of these actions would be reacted to by SSC's stockholders and customers, and then how each action might affect SSC's stock price.

1-10 Assume that you are serving on the board of directors of a medium-sized corporation and that you are responsible for establishing the compensation policies of senior management. You believe that the company's CEO is very talented, but your concern is that she is always looking for a better job and may want to boost the company's short-run performance (perhaps at the expense of long-run profitability) to make herself more marketable to other corporations. What effect would these concerns have on the compensation policy you put in place?

1-11 If the overall stock market is extremely volatile, and if many analysts foresee the possibility of a stock market crash, how might these factors influence the way corporations choose to compensate their senior executives?

1-12 Teacher's Insurance and Annuity Association–College Retirement Equity Fund (TIAA–CREF) is the largest institutional shareholder in the United States, controlling $125 billion in pension funds. Traditionally, TIAA–CREF has acted as a passive investor. However, TIAA–CREF announced a tough new corporate governance policy beginning October 5, 1993.

In a statement mailed to all 1,500 companies in which it invests, TIAA–CREF outlined a policy designed to improve corporate performance, including a goal of higher stock prices for the $52 billion in stock assets it holds, and to encourage corporate boards to have a majority of independent (outside) directors. TIAA–CREF wants to see management more accountable to shareholder interests, as evidenced by its statement that the fund will vote against any director "where companies don't have an effective, independent board which can challenge the CEO."

Historically, TIAA–CREF did not quickly sell poor-performing stocks. In addition, the fund invested a large part of its assets to match performance of the major market indexes, locking TIAA–CREF into ownership of certain companies. Further complicating the problem, TIAA–CREF owns stakes of from 1 percent to 10 percent in several companies, and selling such large blocks of stock would depress their prices.

Common stock ownership confers a right to sponsor initiatives to shareholders regarding the corporation. A corresponding voting right exists for shareholders.

a. Is TIAA–CREF an ordinary shareholder?

b. Due to its asset size, TIAA–CREF assumes large positions with which it plans to actively vote. However, who owns TIAA–CREF?

c. Should the investment managers of a fund like TIAA–CREF determine the voting practices of the fund's shares, or should the voting rights be passed on to TIAA–CREF's stakeholders?

SELF-TEST PROBLEM (Solution Appears in Appendix B)

ST-1
Key terms

Define each of the following terms:

a. Sole proprietorship; partnership; corporation

b. Limited partnership; limited liability partnership; professional corporation

c. Stockholder wealth maximization

d. Social responsibility; business ethics

e. Normal profits; normal rate of return
f. Agency problem
g. Performance shares; executive stock options
h. Hostile takeover
i. Profit maximization
j. Earnings per share
k. Dividend policy decision

INTEGRATED CASE

THE JOHNSONS

1-1 Financial Management Overview   Jennifer Johnson went home for a quick visit early in the term, and, over the course of the weekend, her brother, who received his finance degree three years ago, asked her to tell him about the courses she is taking. After she told him that financial management was one of the courses, he asked her the following questions:

a. What kinds of career opportunities are open to finance majors?

b. What are the most important financial management issues of the 1990s?

c. What are the primary responsibilities of a corporate financial staff?

d. (1) What are the alternative forms of business organization?

(2) What are their advantages and disadvantages?

e. What is the primary goal of the corporation?

(1) Do firms have any responsibilities to society at large?

(2) Is stock price maximization good or bad for society?

(3) Should firms behave ethically?

f. What is an agency relationship?

(1) What agency relationships exist within a corporation?

(2) What mechanisms exist to influence managers to act in shareholders' best interests?

(3) Should shareholders (through managers) take actions that are detrimental to bondholders?

g. What factors affect stock prices?

h. What factors affect the level and riskiness of cash flows?

CHAPTER 2

FINANCIAL STATEMENTS, CASH FLOW, AND TAXES

DOING YOUR HOMEWORK WITH FINANCIAL STATEMENTS

Suppose you are a small investor who knows a little about finance and accounting. Could you compete successfully against large institutional investors with armies of analysts, high-powered computers, and state-of-the-art trading strategies?

The answer, according to one Wall Street legend, is a resounding yes! Peter Lynch, who had an outstanding track record as manager of the $10 billion Fidelity Magellan fund and who went on to become the best-selling author of *One Up on Wall Street* and *Beating the Street,* has long argued that small investors can beat the market by using common sense and information available to all of us as we go about our day-to-day lives.

For example, a college student may be more adept at scouting out the new and interesting products which will become tomorrow's success stories than is an investment banker who works 75 hours a week in a New York office. Parents of young children are likely to know which baby foods will succeed, or which diapers are best. Couch potatoes may have the best feel for which tortilla chips have the brightest future, or whether a new remote control is worth its price.

The trick is to find a product which will boom, yet whose manufacturer's stock is undervalued. If this sounds too easy, you are right. Lynch argues that once you have discovered a good product, there is still much homework to be done. This involves combing through the vast amount of financial information that is regularly provided by companies. It also requires taking a closer and more critical look at how the company conducts its business — Lynch refers to this as "kicking the tires."

To illustrate his point, Lynch relates his experience with Dunkin' Donuts. As a consumer, Lynch was impressed with the quality of the product. This impression led him to take a closer look at the company's financial statements and operations. He liked what he saw, and Dunkin' Donuts became one of the best investments in his portfolio.

The next two chapters discuss what financial statements are and how they are analyzed. Once you have identified a good product as a possible investment, the principles discussed in these chapters will help you "do your homework."

A manager's primary goal is to maximize the value of his or her firm's stock. Value is based on the stream of earnings and cash flows the firm will generate in the future. But how does an investor go about estimating future earnings and cash flows, and how does a manager decide which actions are most likely to increase future earnings and cash flows? The answers to both questions lie in a study of the financial statements which publicly traded firms must provide to investors. Here "investors" include both institutions (banks, insurance companies, pension funds, and the like) and individuals. Thus, this chapter begins with a discussion of what the basic financial statements are, how they are used, and what kinds of financial information users need.

The value of any business asset — whether it is a *financial asset* such as a stock or a bond, or a *real (physical) asset* such as land, buildings, and equipment — depends on the usable, after-tax cash flows the asset is expected to produce. Therefore, the chapter also explains the difference between accounting income and cash flow. Finally, since it is *after-tax* cash flow that is important, the chapter provides an overview of the federal income tax system.

Much of the material in this chapter reviews concepts covered in basic accounting courses. However, the information is important enough to go over again — accounting is used to "keep score," and if a firm's managers do not know the score, they cannot tell if their actions are appropriate. If you took midterm exams but were not told how you were doing, you would have a difficult time improving your grades. The same thing holds in business. If a firm's managers — whether they are in marketing, personnel, production, or finance — do not understand financial statements, they will not be able to judge the effects of their actions, and the firm will not be successful. Although only accountants need to know how to *make* financial statements, everyone involved with business needs to know how to *interpret* them.

A BRIEF HISTORY OF ACCOUNTING AND FINANCIAL STATEMENTS

Financial statements are pieces of paper with numbers written on them, but it is important to also think about the real assets that underlie the numbers. If you understand how and why accounting began, and how financial statements are used, you can better visualize what is going on, and why accounting information is so important.

Thousands of years ago, individuals (or families) were self-contained in the sense that they gathered their own food, made their own clothes, and built their own shelters. Then specialization began — some people became good at making pots, others at making arrowheads, others at making clothing, and so on.

As specialization began, so did trading, initially in the form of barter. At first, each artisan worked alone, and trade was strictly local. Eventually, though, master craftsmen set up small factories and employed workers, money (in the form of clamshells) began to be used, and trade expanded beyond the local area. As these developments occurred, a primitive form of banking began, with wealthy merchants lending profits from past dealings to enterprising factory owners who needed capital to expand or to young traders who needed money to buy wagons, ships, and merchandise.

When the first loans were made, lenders could physically inspect borrowers' assets and judge the likelihood of the loan's being repaid. Eventually, though, lending became more complex — borrowers were developing larger factories, traders were acquiring fleets of ships and wagons, and loans were being made to develop distant mines and trading posts. At that point, lenders could no longer personally inspect the assets that backed their loans, and they needed some way of summarizing borrowers' assets. Also, some investments were made on a share-of-the-profits basis, and this meant that profits (or income) had to be determined. At the same time, factory owners and large merchants needed reports to see how effectively their own enterprises were being run, and governments needed information for use in assessing taxes. For all these reasons, a need arose for financial statements, for accountants to prepare those statements, and for auditors to verify the accuracy of the accountants' work.

The economic system has grown enormously since its beginning, and accounting has become more complex. However, the original reasons for financial statements still apply: Bankers and other investors need accounting information to make intelligent decisions, managers need it to operate their businesses efficiently, and taxing authorities need it to assess taxes in a reasonable way.

It should be intuitively clear that it is not easy to translate physical assets into numbers, which is what accountants do when they construct financial statements. The numbers shown on balance sheets generally represent the historical costs of assets. However, inventories may be spoiled, obsolete, or even missing; fixed assets such as machinery and buildings may have higher or lower values than their historical costs; and accounts receivable may be uncollectable. Also, some liabilities such as obligations to pay retirees' medical costs may not even show up on the balance sheet. Similarly, some costs reported on the income statement may be understated, as would be true if a plant with a useful life of 10 years were being depreciated over 40 years. When you examine a set of financial statements, you should keep in mind that a physical reality lies behind the numbers, and you should also realize that the translation from physical assets to "correct" numbers is far from precise.

FINANCIAL STATEMENTS AND REPORTS

Annual Report
A report issued annually by a corporation to its stockholders. It contains basic financial statements, as well as management's opinion of the past year's operations and the firm's future prospects.

ON THE WWW

For an excellent example of a complete 1995 annual report on the Web, see J.P. Morgan's at http://www.jpmorgan.com/ CorpInfo/FinancialInformation/ AnnualReport/1995/contents.html. The complete report is also available in Adobe Acrobat format from this site.

Of the various reports corporations issue to their stockholders, the **annual report** is probably the most important. Two types of information are given in this report. First, there is a verbal section, often presented as a letter from the chairman, that describes the firm's operating results during the past year and discusses new developments that will affect future operations. Second, the annual report presents four basic financial statements — the *balance sheet,* the *income statement,* the *statement of retained earnings,* and the *statement of cash flows.* Taken together, these statements give an accounting picture of the firm's operations and financial position. Detailed data are provided for the two or three most recent years, along with historical summaries of key operating statistics for the past five or ten years.[1]

---

[1]Firms also provide quarterly reports, but these are much less comprehensive. In addition, larger firms file even more detailed statements, giving breakdowns for each major division or subsidiary, with the Securities and Exchange Commission (SEC). These reports, called *10-K reports,* are made available to stockholders upon request to a company's corporate secretary. Finally, many larger firms also publish *statistical supplements,* which give financial statement data and key ratios going back 10 to 20 years, and their reports are available on the World Wide Web.

The quantitative and verbal information are equally important. The financial statements report *what has actually happened* to assets, earnings, and dividends over the past few years, whereas the verbal statements attempt to explain why things turned out the way they did.

For illustrative purposes, we shall use data taken from Allied Food Products, a processor and distributor of a wide variety of staple foods, to discuss the basic financial statements. Formed in 1977 when several regional firms merged, Allied has grown steadily, and it has earned a reputation for being one of the best firms in its industry. Allied's earnings dropped a bit in 1997, to $113.5 million versus $118 million in 1996. Management reported that the drop resulted from losses associated with a drought and from increased costs due to a three-month strike. However, management then went on to paint a more optimistic picture for the future, stating that full operations had been resumed, that several unprofitable businesses had been eliminated, and that 1998 profits were expected to rise sharply. Of course, an increase in profitability may not occur, and analysts should compare management's past statements with subsequent results. In any event, *the information contained in an annual report is used by investors to help form expectations about future earnings and dividends.* Therefore, the annual report is obviously of great interest to investors.

SELF-TEST QUESTIONS

What is the annual report, and what two types of information are given in it?

Why is the annual report of great interest to investors?

What four types of financial statements are typically included in the annual report?

THE BALANCE SHEET

Balance Sheet
A statement of the firm's financial position at a specific point in time.

The left-hand side of Allied's year-end 1997 and 1996 **balance sheets,** which are given in Table 2-1, shows the firm's assets, while the right-hand side shows the liabilities and equity, or the claims against these assets. The assets are listed in order of their "liquidity," or the length of time it typically takes to convert them to cash. The claims are listed in the order in which they must be paid: Accounts payable must generally be paid within 30 days, notes payable within 90 days, and so on, down to the stockholders' equity accounts, which represent ownership and need never be "paid off."

Some additional points about the balance sheet are worth noting:

1. **Cash versus other assets.** Although the assets are all stated in terms of dollars, only cash represents actual money. (Marketable securities can be converted to cash in a day or two, so they are about like cash and are reported with cash on the balance sheet.) Receivables are bills others owe Allied. Inventories show the dollars the company has invested in raw materials, work-in-process, and finished goods available for sale. And net plant and equipment reflect the amount of money Allied paid for its fixed assets when it acquired those assets in the past, less accumulated depreciation. Allied can write checks for a total of $10 million (versus current liabilities of $310 million due within a year). The noncash assets should produce cash over time, but they do not represent cash in hand, and the amount of cash they would bring if they were sold today could be higher or lower than the values at which they are carried on the books.

| TABLE 2-1 | Allied Food Products: December 31 Balance Sheets (Millions of Dollars) | | | | |

ASSETS	1997	1996	LIABILITIES AND EQUITY	1997	1996
Cash and marketable securities	$ 10	$ 80	Accounts payable	$ 60	$ 30
Accounts receivable	375	315	Notes payable	110	60
Inventories	615	415	Accruals	140	130
Total current assets	$1,000	$ 810	Total current liabilities	$ 310	$ 220
Net plant and equipment	1,000	870	Long-term bonds	754	580
			Total debt	$1,064	$ 800
			Preferred stock (400,000 shares)	40	40
			Common stock (50,000,000 shares)	130	130
			Retained earnings	766	710
			Total common equity	$ 896	$ 840
Total assets	$2,000	$1,680	Total liabilities and equity	$2,000	$1,680

NOTE: The bonds have a sinking fund requirement of $20 million a year. Sinking funds are discussed in Chapter 7, but in brief, a sinking fund simply involves the repayment of long-term debt. Thus, Allied was required to pay off $20 million of its mortgage bonds during 1997. The current portion of the long-term debt is included in notes payable here, although in a more detailed balance sheet it would be shown as a separate item under current liabilities.

Common Stockholders' Equity (Net Worth)
The capital supplied by common stockholders — capital stock, paid-in capital, retained earnings, and, occasionally, certain reserves. *Total equity* is common equity plus preferred stock.

2. **Liabilities versus stockholders' equity.** The claims against assets are of two types — liabilities (or money the company owes) and the stockholders' ownership position.[2] The **common stockholders' equity,** or **net worth,** is a residual. For example, at the end of 1997,

$$\text{Assets} - \text{Liabilities} - \text{Preferred stock} = \text{Common stockholders' equity.}$$

$$\$2,000,000,000 - \$1,064,000,000 - \$40,000,000 = \$896,000,000.$$

Suppose assets decline in value — for example, suppose some of the accounts receivable are written off as bad debts. Liabilities and preferred stock remain constant, so the value of the common stockholders' equity must decline. Therefore, the risk of asset value fluctuations is borne by the common stockholders. Note, however, that if asset values rise (perhaps because of inflation), these benefits will accrue exclusively to the common stockholders.

3. **Preferred versus common stock.** As we will see in Chapter 20, preferred stock is a hybrid, or a cross between common stock and debt. In the event of bankruptcy, preferred stock ranks below debt but above common stock. Also, the preferred dividend is fixed, so preferred stockholders do not benefit if the company's earnings grow. Finally, many firms do not use any preferred stock, and those that do generally do not use much of it. Therefore, when the term

---

[2]One could divide liabilities into (1) debts owed to someone and (2) other items, such as deferred taxes, reserves, and so on. Because we do not make this distinction, the terms *debt* and *liabilities* are used synonymously. It should be noted that firms occasionally set up reserves for certain contingencies, such as the potential costs involved in a lawsuit currently in the courts. These reserves represent an accounting transfer from retained earnings to the reserve account. If the company wins the suit, retained earnings will be credited, and the reserve will be eliminated. If it loses, a loss will be recorded, cash will be reduced, and the reserve will be eliminated.

"equity" is used in finance, we generally mean "common equity" unless the word "total" is included.

4. **Breakdown of the common equity accounts.** The common equity section is divided into two accounts — "common stock" and "retained earnings." The **retained earnings** account is built up over time as the firm "saves" a part of its earnings rather than paying all earnings out as dividends. The common stock account arises from the issuance of stock to raise capital, as discussed in Chapter 8.

Retained Earnings
That portion of the firm's earnings that has been saved rather than paid out as dividends.

The breakdown of the common equity accounts is important for some purposes but not for others. For example, a potential stockholder would want to know whether the company actually earned the funds reported in its equity accounts or whether the funds came mainly from selling stock. A potential creditor, on the other hand, would be more interested in the total equity the owners have in the firm and would be less concerned with the source of the equity. In the remainder of this chapter, we generally aggregate the two common equity accounts and call this sum *common equity* or *net worth*.

5. **Inventory accounting.** Allied uses the FIFO (first-in, first-out) method to determine the inventory value shown on its balance sheet ($615 million). It could have used the LIFO (last-in, first-out) method. During a period of rising prices, by taking out old, low-cost inventory and leaving in new, high-cost items, FIFO will produce a higher balance sheet inventory value but a lower cost of goods sold on the income statement. (This is strictly accounting; companies actually use older items first.) Since Allied uses FIFO, and since inflation has been occurring, (a) its balance sheet inventories are higher than they would have been had it used LIFO, (b) its cost of goods sold is lower than it would have been under LIFO, and (c) its reported profits are therefore higher. In Allied's case, if the company had elected to switch to LIFO in 1997, its balance sheet figure for inventories would have been $585,000,000 rather than $615,000,000, and its earnings (which will be discussed in the next section) would have been reduced by $18,000,000. Thus, the inventory valuation method can have a significant effect on financial statements. This is important when an analyst is comparing different companies.

6. **Depreciation methods.** Most companies prepare two sets of financial statements — one for tax purposes and one for reporting to stockholders. Generally, they use the most accelerated method permitted under the law to calculate depreciation for tax purposes, but they use straight line, which results in a lower depreciation charge, for stockholder reporting. However, Allied has elected to use rapid depreciation for both stockholder reporting and tax purposes. Had Allied elected to use straight line depreciation for stockholder reporting, its 1997 depreciation expense would have been $25,000,000 less, so the $1 billion shown for "net plant" on its balance sheet, hence its retained earnings, would have been $25,000,000 higher. Its net income would also have been higher.

7. **The time dimension.** The balance sheet may be thought of as a snapshot of the firm's financial position *at a point in time* — for example, on December 31, 1996. Thus, on December 31, 1996, Allied had $80 million of cash and marketable securities, but this account had been reduced to $10 million by the end of 1997. The balance sheet changes every day as inventories are increased or decreased, as fixed assets are added or retired, as bank loans are increased or decreased, and so on. Companies whose businesses are seasonal have especially large changes in their balance sheets. Allied's inventories are low just before the harvest season, but they are high just after the fall crops

have been brought in and processed. Similarly, most retailers have large inventories just before Christmas but low inventories and high accounts receivable just after Christmas. Therefore, firms' balance sheets change over the year, depending on when the statement is constructed.

SELF-TEST QUESTIONS

What is the balance sheet, and what information does it provide?

How is the order of the information shown on the balance sheet determined?

Why might a company's December 31 balance sheet differ from its June 30 balance sheet?

THE INCOME STATEMENT

Income Statement
A statement summarizing the firm's revenues and expenses over an accounting period, generally a quarter or a year.

Table 2-2 gives the 1997 and 1996 **income statements** for Allied Food Products. Net sales are shown at the top of each statement, after which various costs, including income taxes, are subtracted to obtain the net income available to common stockholders. A report on earnings and dividends per share is given at the bottom of the statement. Earnings per share (EPS) is called "the bottom line," denoting that of all the items on the income statement, EPS is the most important. Allied earned $2.27 per share in 1997, down from $2.36 in 1996, but it still raised the dividend from $1.06 to $1.15.

While the balance sheet can be thought of as a snapshot in time, the income statement reports on operations *over a period of time,* for example, during the calendar year 1997. During 1997 Allied had sales of $3 billion, and its net income available to common stockholders was $113.5 million. Income statements can cover any period of time, but they are usually prepared monthly, quarterly, or annually. Of course, sales, costs, and profits will be larger the longer the reporting period, and the sum of the last 12 monthly (or 4 quarterly) income statements should equal the values shown on the annual income statement.

For planning and control purposes, management generally forecasts monthly (or perhaps quarterly) income statements, and it then compares actual results to the budgeted statements. If revenues are below and costs above the forecasted levels, then management should take corrective steps before the problem becomes too serious.

SELF-TEST QUESTIONS

What is an income statement, and what information does it provide?

Why is earnings per share called "the bottom line"?

Regarding the time period reported, how does the income statement differ from the balance sheet?

STATEMENT OF RETAINED EARNINGS

Statement of Retained Earnings
A statement reporting how much of the firm's earnings were retained in the business rather than paid out in dividends. The figure for retained earnings that appears here is the sum of the annual retained earnings for each year of the firm's history.

Changes in retained earnings between balance sheet dates are reported in the **statement of retained earnings.** Table 2-3 shows that Allied earned $113.5 million during 1997, paid out $57.5 million in common dividends, and plowed $56

TABLE 2-2	Allied Food Products: Income Statements for Years Ending December 31 (Millions of Dollars, Except for Per-Share Data)

	1997	1996
Net sales	$3,000.0	$2,850.0
Costs excluding depreciation	2,616.2	2,497.0
Depreciation	100.0	90.0
Total operating costs	$2,716.2	$2,587.0
Earnings before interest and taxes (EBIT)	$ 283.8	$ 263.0
Less interest	88.0	60.0
Earnings before taxes (EBT)	$ 195.8	$ 203.0
Taxes (40%)	78.3	81.0
Net income before preferred dividends	$ 117.5	$ 122.0
Preferred dividends	4.0	4.0
Net income available to common stockholders	$ 113.5	$ 118.0
Common dividends	$ 57.5	$ 53.0
Addition to retained earnings	$ 56.0	$ 65.0
Per-share data:		
Common stock price	$23.00	$24.00
Earnings per share (EPS)[a]	$ 2.27	$ 2.36
Dividends per share (DPS)[a]	$ 1.15	$ 1.06
Book value per share (BVPS)[a]	$17.92	$16.80

[a]There are 50,000,000 shares of common stock outstanding. Note that EPS is based on earnings after preferred dividends — that is, on net income available to common stockholders. Calculations of EPS, DPS, and BVPS for 1997 are as follows:

$$EPS = \frac{\text{Net income}}{\text{Common shares outstanding}} = \frac{\$113,500,000}{50,000,000} = \$2.27.$$

$$DPS = \frac{\text{Dividends paid to common stockholders}}{\text{Common shares outstanding}} = \frac{\$57,500,000}{50,000,000} = \$1.15.$$

$$BVPS = \frac{\text{Total common equity}}{\text{Common shares outstanding}} = \frac{\$896,000,000}{50,000,000} = \$17.92.$$

million back into the business. Thus, the balance sheet item "Retained earnings" increased from $710 million at the end of 1996 to $766 million at the end of 1997.

Note that "Retained earnings" represents a *claim against assets,* not assets per se. Moreover, firms retain earnings primarily to expand the business, and this means investing in plant and equipment, in inventories, and so on, *not* piling up cash in a bank account. Changes in retained earnings occur because common stockholders allow the firm to reinvest funds that otherwise could be distributed as dividends. *Thus, retained earnings as reported on the balance sheet do not represent cash and are not "available" for the payment of dividends or anything else.*[3]

---

[3]The amount reported in the retained earnings account is *not* an indication of the amount of cash the firm has. Cash (as of the balance sheet date) is found in the cash account — an asset account. A

| TABLE 2-3 | Allied Food Products: Statement of Retained Earnings for Year Ending December 31, 1997 (Millions of Dollars) |

Balance of retained earnings, December 31, 1996	$710.0
Add: Net income, 1997	113.5
Less: Dividends to common stockholders	(57.5)[a]
Balance of retained earnings, December 31, 1997	$766.0

[a]Here, and throughout the book, parentheses are used to denote negative numbers.

SELF-TEST QUESTIONS

What is the statement of retained earnings, and what information does it provide?

Why do changes in retained earnings occur?

Explain why the following statement is true: "Retained earnings as reported on the balance sheet do not represent cash and are not 'available' for the payment of dividends or anything else."

ACCOUNTING INCOME VERSUS CASH FLOW

Net Cash Flow
The actual net cash, as opposed to accounting net income, that a firm generates during some specified period.

When you studied income statements in accounting, the emphasis was probably on the firm's net income. In finance, however, we focus on **net cash flow.** The value of an asset (or a whole firm) is determined by the cash flow it generates. The firm's net income is important, but cash flow is even more important because dividends must be paid in cash and because cash is necessary to purchase the assets required to continue operations.

As we discussed in Chapter 1, the firm's goal should be to maximize its stock price. Since the value of any asset, including a share of stock, depends on the cash flow produced by the asset, managers should strive to maximize the cash flow available to investors over the long run. A business's *net cash flow* generally differs from its **accounting profit** because some of the revenues and expenses listed on the income statement were not paid in cash during the year. The relationship between net cash flow and net income can be expressed as follows:

Accounting Profit
A firm's net income as reported on its income statement.

$$\text{Net cash flow} = \text{Net income} - \text{Noncash revenues} + \text{Noncash charges.} \quad (2\text{-}1)$$

The primary example of a noncash charge is depreciation. This item reduces net income but is not paid out in cash, so we add it back to net income when calculating net cash flow. Likewise, some taxes may be deferred and some revenues may not be collected in cash during the year, and these items must be subtracted from net income when calculating net cash flow. Typically, though, depreciation

positive number in the retained earnings account indicates only that in the past the firm has earned some income, but its dividends have been less than its earnings. Even though a company reports record earnings and shows an increase in the retained earnings account, it still may be short of cash.

The same situation holds for individuals. You might own a new BMW (no loan), lots of clothes, and an expensive stereo, hence have a high net worth, but if you had only 23 cents in your pocket plus $5 in your checking account, you would still be short of cash.

is by far the largest noncash item, and the other items often roughly net out to zero. Therefore, unless otherwise indicated, we will assume that noncash items other than depreciation sum to zero. Given this assumption, net cash flow equals net income plus depreciation:

$$\text{Net cash flow} = \text{Net income} + \text{Depreciation}. \qquad (2\text{-}2)$$

We can illustrate Equation 2-2 with 1997 data for Allied taken from Table 2-2:

$$\text{Net cash flow} = \$117.5 + \$100.0 = \$217.5 \text{ million}.$$

Depreciation
The charge for assets used in production. Depreciation is not a cash outlay.

To see this more clearly, recall from accounting that **depreciation** is an annual charge against income which reflects the estimated dollar cost of the capital equipment used up in the production process. For example, suppose a machine with a life of five years and a zero expected salvage value was purchased in 1996 for $100,000 and placed into service in 1997. This $100,000 cost is not expensed in the purchase year; rather, it is charged against production over the machine's five-year depreciable life. If the depreciation expense were not taken, profits would be overstated, and taxes would be too high. So, the annual depreciation charge is deducted from sales revenues, along with such other costs as labor and raw materials, to determine income. However, because the $100,000 was actually expended back in 1996, the depreciation charged against income in 1997 and subsequent years is not a cash outlay, as are labor or raw materials charges. *Depreciation is a noncash charge, so it must be added back to net income to obtain the net cash flow.* Once again, assuming all other noncash items sum to zero, we see that net cash flow is equal to net income plus depreciation.

Investors and managers often find it useful to distinguish between *operating cash flow* and *net cash flow*. The essential difference is that operating cash flow reflects only the results of normal, ongoing operations, whereas net cash flow reflects both operating and financing decisions. Thus, **operating cash flow** is defined as the difference between sales revenues and cash operating expenses, after taxes on operating income, and it can be calculated as follows:[4]

Operating Cash Flow
That cash flow which arises from normal operations; the difference between sales revenues and cash operating expenses, after taxes on operating income.

$$\text{Operating cash flow} = (\text{Operating income})(1 - \text{Tax rate}) + \text{Depreciation}. \quad (2\text{-}3)$$

In 1997 Allied Food Products had operating income, or EBIT, of $283.8 million, depreciation of $100 million, and a 40 percent tax rate. Thus, its operating cash flow was

$$\text{Operating cash flow} = (283.8)(0.6) + \$100 = \$170.3 + \$100 = \$270.3 \text{ million}.$$

Note that Allied's operating cash flow, $270.3 million, is greater than its net cash flow, $217.5 million. Why is this? The answer is that after-tax interest expenses must be deducted from operating cash flow to obtain net cash flow. As we will see later in the chapter, interest is a deductible expense. Allied has operating

---

[4]Operating cash flow = Operating income (or EBIT) − Taxes − Depreciation

$$= \text{Operating income} - (\text{Operating income})(\text{Tax rate}) + \text{Depreciation}$$

$$= \text{Operating income}\,(1 - \text{Tax rate}) + \text{Depreciation}. \qquad \textbf{(2\text{-}3)}$$

Note that if the firm uses debt, its *taxable* income will be less than its operating income by the amount of interest paid. Therefore, actual taxes will be less than the tax that would otherwise be due on operating income. This means that debt provides a tax shelter, or shield, which reduces the taxes the firm would otherwise have to pay. The definition of operating cash flow given in Equation 2-3 includes the taxes attributable to operating income, not the actual taxes paid. Therefore, the equation attributes the tax shield from debt to the financing decision to use debt, not to operations. This distinction is important, for it permits one to measure the effects of operating versus financing decisions.

INDUSTRY PRACTICE

SHERLOCK HOLMES, OR CORPORATE ENEMY NUMBER 1?

Is there more than meets the eye when it comes to looking at financial statements? One American University accounting professor certainly thinks so. His name is Howard Schilit, and he is recognized as a leading "forensic" accountant. As an independent consultant, Schilit works as a detective to search for the truth among the financial statements that companies make available to the public. *Business Week* has labeled Schilit the "Sherlock Holmes of Accounting." It is safe to say that many of the companies that have been targeted by Schilit would characterize his work less charitably.

Schilit pores over financial statements and looks for cases where companies adopt accounting practices which overstate their true positions. These practices, which are generally legal and even consistent with generally accepted accounting principles (GAAP), are frequently referred to as "window dressing." In many instances, companies have considerable latitude in deciding how to account for various activities in their financial statements. Schilit objects, however, when he believes these statements result in an inaccurate picture of a company's financial health.

Business Week also reported that in a recent one-year period, Schilit investigated 39 companies and wrote negative reports on 24 of them. During this time, the average price of these 24 companies' stocks fell by 31 percent. Schilit has particularly targeted firms which recently went public (issued shares of stock to the public for the first time). These firms are often under pressure to quickly demonstrate strong performance, so they are tempted to use accounting gimmicks to boost profits.

Consider Kendall Square Research Corporation, which went public in 1992 at a price of $10 per share. Within the first year, its stock price more than doubled, to $22 a share, and its revenues increased from less than $1 million to nearly $21 million. Fidelity Investments, a large institutional investor, hired Schilit to see if this was too good to be true. Schilit concluded that it was. His report, along with a later report by the company's independent auditor, led to a dramatic restatement of the company's financial statements. The company ended up reporting a large loss for 1993, and in early 1994, its stock price fell to just over $2 per share. In an additional blow to investors, the company was delisted by the National Association of Securities Dealers (NASDAQ).

SOURCE: Adapted from "The Sherlock Holmes of Accounting," *Business Week*, September 5, 1994, 48–52.

---

cash flow of $270.3 million, interest charges of $88 million, and a tax rate of 40 percent. Thus, its net cash flow can be calculated as follows:

$$\text{Net cash flow} = \text{Operating cash flow} - (\text{Interest charges})(1 - \text{Tax rate}) \quad \textbf{(2-4)}$$
$$= \$270.3 + \$88(0.6) = \$270.3 - \$52.8 = \$217.5 \text{ million.}$$

This answer agrees with the one based on Equation 2-2.

SELF-TEST QUESTIONS

?????

Differentiate between net cash flow and accounting profit.

Differentiate between operating cash flow and net cash flow.

In accounting, the emphasis is on the determination of net income. What is emphasized in finance, and why is that emphasis important?

Assuming that depreciation is the only noncash cost, how can someone calculate a business's cash flow?

STATEMENT OF CASH FLOWS

Net cash flow is the actual cash produced by a business in a given year. The fact that a company generates high cash flow does not necessarily mean, however, that the *amount of cash* reported on its balance sheet will also be high. The cash flow may be used in a variety of ways. For example, the firm may use its cash flow to pay dividends, to increase inventories, to finance accounts receivable, to invest in fixed assets, to reduce debt, or to buy back common stock. Indeed, the company's cash position as reported on the balance sheet is affected by a great many factors, including the following:

1. **Cash flow.** Other things held constant, a positive net cash flow will lead to more cash in the bank. However, as we discuss below, other things are generally not held constant.

2. **Changes in working capital.** Net working capital, which is discussed in detail in Chapter 16, is defined as current assets minus current liabilities. Increases in current assets other than cash, such as inventories and accounts receivable, decrease cash, whereas decreases in these accounts increase cash. For example, if inventories are to increase, the firm must use some of its cash to buy the additional inventory, whereas if inventories decrease, this generally means the firm is selling off inventories and not replacing them, hence generating cash. On the other hand, increases in current liabilities such as accounts payable increase cash, whereas decreases in current liabilities decrease it. For example, if payables increase, the firm has received additional credit from its suppliers, which saves cash, but if payables decrease, this means the firm has used cash to pay off its suppliers.

3. **Fixed assets.** If a company invests in fixed assets, this will reduce its cash position. On the other hand, the sale of fixed assets will increase cash.

4. **Security transactions.** If a company issues stock or bonds during the year, the funds raised will enhance its cash position. On the other hand, if the company uses cash to buy back outstanding debt or equity, or pays dividends to its shareholders, this will reduce its cash.

Statement of Cash Flows
A statement reporting the impact of a firm's operating, investing, and financing activities on cash flows over an accounting period.

Each of the above factors is reflected in the **statement of cash flows,** which summarizes the changes in a company's cash position. The statement separates activities into three categories:

1. *Operating activities,* which includes net income, depreciation, and changes in current assets and current liabilities other than cash and short-term debt.

2. *Investing activities,* which includes investments in or sales of fixed assets.

3. *Financing activities,* which includes cash raised during the year by issuing short-term debt, long-term debt, or stock. Also, since dividends paid or cash used to buy back outstanding stock or bonds reduce the company's cash, such transactions are included here.

Accounting texts explain how to prepare the statement of cash flows, but the statement is used to help answer questions such as these: Is the firm generating enough cash to purchase the additional assets required for growth? Is the firm generating any extra cash that can be used to repay debt or to invest in new products? Such information is useful both for managers and investors, so the statement of cash flows is an important part of the annual report. Financial managers generally use this statement, along with the cash budget, when forecasting their companies' cash positions. This issue is considered in more detail in Chapter 16.

Table 2-4 is Allied's statement of cash flows as it would appear in the company's annual report. The top part of the table shows cash flows generated by and used in operations — for Allied, operations provided net cash flows of *minus* $2.5

TABLE 2 - 4 Allied Food Products: Statement of Cash Flows for 1997 (Millions of Dollars)

OPERATING ACTIVITIES	
Net income	$117.5
Additions (Sources of Cash)	
Depreciation[a]	100.0
Increase in accounts payable	30.0
Increase in accruals	10.0
Subtractions (Uses of Cash)	
Increase in accounts receivable	(60.0)
Increase in inventories	(200.0)
Net cash provided by operating activities	($ 2.5)
LONG-TERM INVESTING ACTIVITIES	
Cash used to acquire fixed assets[b]	($230.0)
FINANCING ACTIVITIES	
Increase in notes payable	$ 50.0
Increase in bonds	174.0
Payment of common and preferred dividends	(61.5)
Net cash provided by financing activities	$162.5
Net decrease in cash and marketable securities	($ 70.0)
Cash and securities at beginning of year	80.0
Cash and securities at end of year	$ 10.0

[a]Depreciation is a noncash expense that was deducted when calculating net income. It must be added back to show the correct cash flow from operations.
[b]The net increase in fixed assets is $130 million; however, this net amount is after a deduction for the year's depreciation expense. Depreciation expense should be added back to show the increase in gross fixed assets. From the company's income statement, we see that the 1997 depreciation expense is $100 million; thus, expenditures on fixed assets were actually $230 million.

million. The operating cash flows are generated in the normal course of business, and this amount is determined by adjusting the net income figure to account for depreciation plus other cash flows related to operations. Allied's day-to-day operations in 1997 provided $257.5 million; however, the increase in receivables and inventories more than offset this amount, resulting in a *negative* $2.5 million cash flow from operations.

The second section shows long-term fixed-asset investing activities. Allied purchased fixed assets totaling $230 million; this was the only long-term investment it made during 1997.

Allied's financing activities, shown in the third section, include borrowing from banks (notes payable), selling new bonds, and paying dividends on its common and preferred stock. Allied raised $224 million by borrowing, but it paid $61.5 million in preferred and common dividends, so its net inflow of funds from financing activities was $162.5 million.

When all of these sources and uses of cash are totaled, we see that Allied's cash outflows exceeded its cash inflows by $70 million during 1997. It met that shortfall by drawing down its cash and marketable securities holdings by $70 million, as shown in Table 2-1, the firm's balance sheet.

Allied's statement of cash flows should be worrisome to its managers and to outside analysts. The company had a $2.5 million cash shortfall from operations, it spent an additional $230 million on new fixed assets, and it paid out another $61.5 million in dividends. It covered these cash outlays by borrowing heavily and by selling off most of its marketable securities. Obviously, this situation cannot continue year after year, so something will have to be done. In Chapter 3, we will consider some of the actions Allied's financial staff might recommend to ease the cash flow problem.[5]

SELF-TEST QUESTION

What is the statement of cash flows, and what types of questions does it answer?

MVA AND EVA

While accounting data provide us with much useful information, accounting does have limitations. In response to these limitations, analysts have come up with adjustments which provide alternative measures of performance. In this section, we consider some measures of profitability which have been used to evaluate managerial performance in recent years.

MARKET VALUE ADDED (MVA)

The primary goal of most firms is to maximize shareholders' wealth. This goal obviously benefits shareholders, but it also ensures that scarce resources are allocated efficiently, which benefits the economy. Shareholder wealth is maximized by maximizing the *difference* between the market value of the firm's equity and the amount of equity capital that was supplied by investors. This difference is called the **Market Value Added (MVA):**[6]

Market Value Added (MVA)
The difference between the market value of equity and the amount of equity capital that investors supplied.

$$\text{MVA} = \text{Market value of equity} - \text{Equity capital supplied by investors}$$
$$= (\text{Shares outstanding})(\text{Stock price}) - \text{Total common equity}. \quad (2\text{-}5)$$

To illustrate, consider Coca-Cola. In 1995, its total equity value was $69 billion, while its balance sheet showed that stockholders had put up only $8 billion. Thus, Coca-Cola's MVA was $69 − $8 = $61 billion. This $61 billion represents the difference between the money that Coca-Cola's stockholders have invested in the corporation since its founding — including retained earnings — and the cash they could get if they sold the business. By maximizing this spread, management maximizes the wealth of its shareholders.

[5]We should also mention the term *free cash flow*, which is defined as the difference between operating cash inflows and the required expenditures necessary to maintain operating cash flows in the future. Management has discretion in the use of free cash flow, so the larger the free cash flow, the greater the firm's potential for financing growth, increasing dividends, paying off debt, and so forth. Consequently, financial analysts give much attention to free cash flow. Allied had negative free cash flow during 1997.

[6]MVA can also be defined in terms of total capital supplied, including both debt and equity. However, the definition presented here, which focuses solely on equity capital, is easier to use and is generally consistent with the broader definition.

While Coca-Cola's managers have done a spectacular job of maximizing shareholder wealth, General Motors' managers have done poorly. In 1995, GM's total market value was $69 billion, which, on the surface, makes it look as though its managers have done as good a job as those of Coca-Cola. However, investors have supplied GM with $87 billion of capital, so GM's MVA was a *negative* $18 billion. In effect, GM has only $0.79 of wealth remaining for every dollar investors put up, whereas Coca-Cola has turned $1 of investment into $8.63. Therefore, Coca-Cola's managers have created $61 billion of wealth for its stockholders, while GM's managers have vaporized $18 billion.

ECONOMIC VALUE ADDED (EVA)

Economic Value Added
Value added to shareholders by management during a given year.

Whereas MVA measures the effects of managerial actions since the very inception of a company, **Economic Value Added (EVA)** focuses on managerial effectiveness in a given year. The basic formula for EVA is as follows:

$$\text{EVA} = \text{After-tax operating profit} - \text{After-tax cost of capital} \qquad (2\text{-}6)$$

$$= \text{EBIT} (1 - \text{Corporate tax rate}) - (\text{Total capital})(\text{After-tax cost of capital}).$$

Total capital includes long-term debt, preferred stock, and common equity. Thus, EVA is an estimate of a business's true economic profit for the year, and it differs sharply from accounting profit.[7] EVA represents the residual income that remains after the cost of *all* capital, including equity capital, has been deducted, whereas accounting profit is determined without imposing a charge for equity capital. As we will discuss more completely in Chapter 9, equity capital has a cost, because funds provided by shareholders could have been invested elsewhere where they would have earned a return. In other words, shareholders give up the opportunity to invest funds elsewhere when they provide capital to the firm. The return they could earn elsewhere in investments of equal risk represents the cost of equity capital. This cost is an *opportunity cost* rather than an *accounting cost*, but it is quite real nevertheless.

Notice that when calculating EVA we do not add back depreciation. Although not a cash expense, depreciation is a cost, and is therefore deducted when determining both net income and EVA. Our calculation of EVA assumes that the true economic depreciation of the company's fixed assets exactly equals the depreciation level used for accounting and tax purposes. If this were not the case, adjustments would have to be made to obtain a more accurate measure of EVA.

EVA provides a good measure of whether the firm has added to shareholder value. Therefore, if managers focus on EVA, this will help to ensure that they operate in a manner that is consistent with maximizing shareholder value. Note too that EVA can be determined for divisions as well as for the company as a whole, so it provides a useful basis for determining managerial compensation at all levels. As a result of all this, EVA is being used by an increasing number of firms as the primary basis for determining managerial compensation.

 ON THE WWW

An excellent site for students to access is http://www.mediapool.com/offtherecord/eva.html. The site contains a description of EVA and numerous audio clips from interviews with executives about EVA. The audio clips are accessible with the "Real Audio Player," which is available free of charge at http://www.realaudio.com.

---

[7]The most important reason EVA differs from accounting profit is that the cost of equity capital is deducted when EVA is calculated. Other factors that could lead to differences include adjustments that might be made to depreciation, to research and development costs, to inventory valuations, and so on. See G. Bennett Stewart III, *The Quest for Value* (New York: HarperCollins Publishers Inc., 1991).

ECONOMIC VALUE ADDED (EVA)—TODAY'S HOTTEST FINANCIAL IDEA

According to *Fortune* magazine, "Economic Value Added (EVA)" is today's hottest financial idea. Developed and popularized by the consulting firm Stern Stewart & Co., EVA helps managers ensure that a given business unit is adding to stockholder value, while investors can use it to spot stocks that are likely to increase in value. Right now, relatively few managers and investors are using EVA, so those who do use it have a competitive advantage. However, *Fortune* thinks this situation won't last long, as more managers and investors are catching the EVA fever every day.

What exactly is EVA? EVA is a way to measure an operation's true profitability. The cost of debt capital (interest expense) is deducted when calculating net income, but no cost is deducted to account for the cost of common equity. Therefore, in an economic sense, net income overstates "true" income. EVA overcomes this flaw in conventional accounting.

EVA is found by taking the after-tax operating profit and subtracting the annual cost of *all* the capital a firm uses. Such highly successful giants as Coca-Cola, AT&T, Quaker Oats, Briggs & Stratton, and CSX have jumped on the EVA bandwagon and attribute much of their success to its use. According to AT&T financial executive William H. Kurtz, EVA played a major role in AT&T's decision to acquire McCaw Cellular. In addition, AT&T made EVA the primary measure of its business unit managers' performance. Quaker Oats's CEO William Smithburg said, "EVA makes managers act like shareholders. It's the true corporate faith for the 1990s."

Surprisingly, many corporate executives have no idea how much capital they are using or what that capital costs. The cost of debt capital is easy to determine because it shows up in financial statements as interest expense; however, the cost of equity capital, which is actually much larger than the cost of debt capital, does not appear in financial statements. As a result, managers often regard equity as free capital, even though it actually has a high cost. So, until a management team determines its cost of capital, it cannot know whether it is covering all costs and thereby adding value to the firm.

Although EVA is perhaps the most widely discussed concept in finance today, it is not completely new; the need to earn more than the cost of capital is actually one of the oldest ideas in business. However, the idea is often lost because of a misguided focus on conventional accounting.

John Snow, the chief executive officer who introduced the EVA concept to CSX Corporation in 1988, notes that CSX has lots of capital tied up in its fleets of locomotives, containers, trailers, and railcars, and in its tracks and rights-of-way, and that CSX's effectiveness in using that capital determines its market value. Snow's stiffest challenge has been in the fast-growing, but low-margin, intermodal business, where trains rush freight to waiting trucks or ships. In 1988, CSX Intermodal lost $70 million after all capital costs were considered — thus, its EVA was a negative $70 million. The division was told that it must break even by 1993 or be sold. Intermodal's employees realized what would happen to their jobs if the division were sold, so they worked hard and were able to increase freight volume by 25 percent even as they reduced capital by selling off containers, trailers, and loco-

motives. Wall Street has also noticed the improvement. CSX's stock price was $28 when Snow introduced the EVA concept in 1988, but it had climbed to $82.50 by 1993.

Briggs & Stratton, a maker of gasoline engines, tells a similar success story. When EVA was introduced in 1990, management was earning a return of only 7.7 percent on capital versus a cost of 12 percent. Drastic changes were made, the return on capital was pushed up over its cost, and, as a result, the stock price quadrupled in four years.

Coca-Cola formally introduced the EVA concept to its managers after Roberto Goizueta took over as CEO in 1981. Since then, Coke has restructured its business, sharply lowered its average cost of capital, and increased its EVA even more sharply. As a result, its stock price increased from $3 to $57.

One of EVA's greatest virtues is its direct link to stock prices. AT&T found an almost perfect correlation between its EVA and its stock price. Moreover, security analysts have found that stock prices track EVA far more closely than other factors such as earnings per share, operating margin, or return on equity. This correlation occurs because EVA is what investors really care about, namely, the net cash return on their capital. Therefore, more and more security analysts are calculating companies' EVAs and using them to help identify good buys in the stock market.

SOURCES: "The Real Key to Creating Wealth," *Fortune,* September 20, 1993, 38–44; "America's Best Wealth Creators," *Fortune*, November 28, 1994, 143–162.

Define the terms "Market Value Added (MVA)" and "Economic Value Added (EVA)."

How does EVA differ from accounting profit?

THE FEDERAL INCOME TAX SYSTEM

The value of any financial asset (including stocks, bonds, and mortgages) as well as most real assets such as plants or even entire firms depends on the stream of cash flows produced by the asset. Cash flows from an asset consist of *usable* income plus depreciation, and usable income means income *after taxes*.

Our tax laws can be changed by Congress, and in recent years changes have occurred frequently. Indeed, a major change has occurred, on average, every three to four years since 1913, when our federal income tax system began. Further, certain parts of our tax system are tied to the rate of inflation, so changes occur automatically each year, depending on the rate of inflation during the previous year. Therefore, although this section will give you a good background on the basic nature of our tax system, you should consult current rate schedules and other data published by the Internal Revenue Service (available in U.S. post offices) before you file your personal or business tax returns.

Currently (1997), federal income tax rates for individuals go up to 39.6 percent, and, when Social Security, Medicare, and state and city income taxes are included, the marginal tax rate on an individual's income can easily exceed 50 percent. Business income is also taxed heavily. The income from partnerships and proprietorships is reported by the individual owners as personal income and, consequently, is taxed at federal-plus-state rates going up to 50 percent or more. Corporate profits are subject to federal income tax rates of up to 39 percent, plus state income taxes. Furthermore, corporations pay taxes and then distribute after-tax income to their stockholders as dividends, which are also taxed. So, corporate income is really subject to double taxation. *Because of the magnitude of the tax bite, taxes play a critical role in many financial decisions.*

As this text is being written, a Republican Congress and a Democratic administration are debating the merits of different changes in the tax laws. To stimulate investment, depreciation schedules may be liberalized, and capital gains may be taxed at a lower rate. Even in the unlikely event that no explicit changes are made in the tax laws, changes will still occur because certain aspects of the tax calculation are tied to the inflation rate. Thus, by the time you read this chapter, tax rates and other factors will almost certainly be different from those we provide. Still, if you understand this section, you will understand the basics of our tax system, and you will know how to operate under the revised tax code.

Taxes are so complicated that university law schools offer master's degrees in taxation to lawyers, many of whom are also CPAs. In a field complicated enough to warrant such detailed study, only the highlights can be covered in a book such as this. This is really enough, though, because business managers and investors should and do rely on tax specialists rather than trusting their own limited knowledge. Still, it is important to know the basic elements of the tax system as a starting point for discussions with tax experts.

INDIVIDUAL INCOME TAXES

Progressive Tax
A tax system where the tax rate is higher on higher incomes. The personal income tax in the United States, which goes from 0 percent on the lowest increments of income to 39.6 percent, is progressive.

Taxable Income
Gross income minus exemptions and allowable deductions as set forth in the Tax Code.

Marginal Tax Rate
The tax rate applicable to the last unit of a person's income.

Average Tax Rate
Taxes paid divided by taxable income.

Bracket Creep
A situation that occurs when progressive tax rates combine with inflation to cause a greater portion of each taxpayer's real income to be paid as taxes.

Individuals pay taxes on wages and salaries, on investment income (dividends, interest, and profits from the sale of securities), and on the profits of proprietorships and partnerships. Our tax rates are **progressive** — that is, the higher one's income, the larger the percentage paid in taxes. Table 2-5 gives the tax rates for single individuals and married couples filing joint returns under the rate schedules that were in effect in April 1997.

1. **Taxable income** is defined as gross income less a set of exemptions and deductions which are spelled out in the instructions to the tax forms individuals must file. When filing a tax return in 1997 for the tax year 1996, each taxpayer received an exemption of $2,550 for each dependent, including the taxpayer, which reduces taxable income. However, this exemption is indexed to rise with inflation, and the exemption is phased out (taken away) for high-income taxpayers. Also, certain expenses including mortgage interest paid, state and local income taxes paid, and charitable contributions, can be deducted and thus be used to reduce taxable income, but again, high-income taxpayers lose most of these deductions.

2. The **marginal tax rate** is defined as the tax rate on the last unit of income. Marginal rates begin at 15 percent and rise to 39.6 percent. Note, though, that when consideration is given to the phase-out of exemptions and deductions, to Social Security and Medicare taxes, and to state taxes, the marginal tax rate can actually exceed 50 percent.

3. One can calculate **average tax rates** from the data in Table 2-5. For example, if Jill Smith, a single individual, had taxable income of $35,000, her tax bill would be $3,600 + ($35,000 − $24,000)(0.28) = $3,600 + $3,080 = $6,680. Her *average tax rate* would be $6,680/$35,000 = 19.1% versus a *marginal rate* of 28 percent. If Jill received a raise of $1,000, bringing her income to $36,000, she would have to pay $280 of it as taxes, so her after-tax raise would be $720. In addition, her Social Security and Medicare taxes would increase by $76.50, which would cut her net raise to $643.50.

4. As indicated in the notes to the table, the tax code indexes tax brackets to inflation to avoid the **bracket creep** that occurred several years ago and that in reality raised tax rates substantially.[8]

TAXES ON DIVIDEND AND INTEREST INCOME. Dividend and interest income received by individuals from corporate securities is added to other income and thus is taxed at rates going up to about 50 percent.[9] Since corporations pay dividends

---

[8]For example, if you were single and had a taxable income of $24,000, your tax bill would be $3,600. Now suppose inflation caused prices to double and your income, being tied to a cost-of-living index, rose to $48,000. Because our tax rates are progressive, if tax brackets were not indexed, your taxes would jump to $10,320. Your after-tax income would thus increase from $20,400 to $37,680, but, because prices have doubled, your real income would *decline* from $20,400 to $18,840 (calculated as one-half of $37,680). You would be in a higher tax bracket, so you would be paying a higher percentage of your real income in taxes. If this happened to everyone, and if Congress failed to change tax rates sufficiently, real disposable incomes would decline because the federal government would be taking a larger share of the national product. This is called the federal government's "inflation dividend." However, since tax brackets are now indexed, if your income doubled due to inflation, your tax bill would double, but your after-tax real income would remain constant at $20,400. Bracket creep was a real problem until the 1980s, but indexing put an end to it. A change in the way the Consumer Price Index is calculated would affect real income tax rates.

[9]You do not pay Social Security and Medicare taxes on interest, dividends, and capital gains, only on earned income, but state taxes are generally imposed on dividends, interest, and capital gains.

TABLE 2-5   Individual Tax Rates in April 1997

SINGLE INDIVIDUALS

If Your Taxable Income Is	You Pay This Amount on the Base of the Bracket	Plus This Percentage on the Excess over the Base	Average Tax Rate at Top of Bracket
Up to $24,000	$ 0	15.0%	15.0%
$24,000–$58,150	3,600.00	28.0	22.6
$58,150–$121,300	13,162.00	31.0	27.0
$121,300–$263,750	32,738.50	36.0	31.9
Over $263,750	84,020.50	39.6	39.6

MARRIED COUPLES FILING JOINT RETURNS

If Your Taxable Income Is	You Pay This Amount on the Base of the Bracket	Plus This Percentage on the Excess over the Base	Average Tax Rate at Top of Bracket
Up to $40,100	$ 0	15.0%	15.0%
$40,100–$96,900	6,015.00	28.0	22.6
$96,900–$147,700	21,919.00	31.0	25.5
$147,700–$263,750	37,667.00	36.0	30.1
Over $263,750	79,445.00	39.6	39.6

Notes:

a. These are the tax rates in April 1997. The income ranges at which each tax rate takes effect, as well as the ranges for the additional taxes discussed below, are indexed with inflation each year, so they will change from those shown in the table.

b. The average tax rate approaches 39.6 percent as taxable income rises without limit. At $1 million of taxable income, the average tax rates for single individuals and married couples filing joint returns are 37.6 percent and 37.1 percent, respectively, while at $10 million it is 39.4 percent.

c. In 1996, a *personal exemption* of $2,550 per person or dependent could be deducted from gross income to determine taxable income. Thus, a husband and wife with two children would have a 1996 exemption of 4 × $2,550 = $10,200. The amount of the exemption is scheduled to increase with inflation. However, if the gross income exceeds certain limits ($176,950 for joint returns and $117,950 for single individuals in 1996), the exemption is phased out, and this has the effect of raising the effective tax rate on incomes over the specified limit by about 0.5 percent per family member, or 2.0 percent for a family of four. In addition, taxpayers can claim *itemized deductions* for charitable contributions and certain other items, but these deductions are reduced if the gross income exceeds $117,950 (for both single individuals and joint returns), and this raises the effective tax rate for high-income taxpayers by another 1 percent or so. The combined effect of the loss of exemptions and the reduction of itemized deductions is about 3 percent, so the marginal federal tax rate for high-income individuals goes up to about 42.6 percent.

In addition, there is the Social Security tax, which amounts to 6.2 percent (12.4 percent for a self-employed person) on up to $62,700 of earned income, plus a 1.45 percent Medicare payroll tax (2.9 percent for self-employed individuals) on *all* earned income. Finally, older high-income taxpayers who receive Social Security payments must pay taxes on 85 percent of their Social Security receipts, up from 50 percent in 1994. All of this pushes the effective tax rate up even further.

out of earnings that have already been taxed, there is *double taxation* of corporate income — income is first taxed at the corporate rate, and when what is left is paid out as dividends, it is taxed again at the personal rate.

It should be noted that under U.S. tax laws, interest on most state and local government bonds, called *municipals* or *"munis,"* is not subject to federal income taxes. Thus, investors get to keep all of the interest received from most municipal bonds but only a fraction of the interest received from bonds issued by corporations or by the U.S. government. This means that a lower-yielding muni can provide the same after-tax return as a higher-yielding corporate bond. For example, a taxpayer in the 39.6 percent marginal tax bracket who could buy a muni that yielded 5.5 percent would have to receive a before-tax yield of 9.11 percent on a corporate or U.S. Treasury bond to have the same after-tax income:

$$\frac{\text{Equivalent pre-tax yield}}{\text{on taxable bond}} = \frac{\text{Yield on muni}}{1 - \text{Marginal tax rate}}$$

$$= \frac{5.5\%}{1 - 0.396} = 9.11\%.$$

If we know the yield on the taxable bond, we can use the following equation to find the equivalent yield on a muni:

$$\text{Equivalent yield on muni} = \left(\begin{array}{c} \text{Pre-tax yield} \\ \text{on taxable} \\ \text{bond} \end{array} \right) (1 - \text{Marginal tax rate})$$

$$= 9.11\% \ (1 - 0.396) = 9.11\%(0.604) = 5.5\%.$$

The exemption from federal taxes stems from the separation of federal and state powers, and its primary effect is to help state and local governments borrow at lower rates than they otherwise could.

Munis always yield less than corporate bonds with similar risk, maturity, and liquidity. Because of this, it would make no sense for someone in a zero or very low tax bracket to buy munis. Therefore, most munis are owned by high-bracket investors.

Capital Gain or Loss
The profit (loss) from the sale of a capital asset for more (less) than its purchase price.

CAPITAL GAINS VERSUS ORDINARY INCOME. Assets such as stocks, bonds, and real estate are defined as *capital assets*. If you buy a capital asset and later sell it for more than your purchase price, the profit is called a **capital gain;** if you suffer a loss, it is called a **capital loss.** An asset sold within one year of the time it was purchased produces a *short-term gain or loss,* whereas one held for more than one year produces a *long-term gain or loss.* Thus, if you buy 100 shares of Disney stock for $42 per share and sell it for $52 per share, you make a capital gain of $100 \times \$10$, or $1,000. However, if you sell the stock for $32 per share, you will have a $1,000 capital loss. If you hold the stock for more than one year, the gain or loss is long-term; otherwise, it is short-term. If you sell the stock for exactly $42 per share, you make neither a gain nor a loss; you simply get your $4,200 back, and no tax is due.

Short-term capital gains are added to such ordinary income as wages, dividends, and interest and then are taxed at the same rate as ordinary income. However, long-term capital gains are taxed differently in that the rate on long-term capital gains is capped at 28 percent. Thus, if in 1996 you were in a tax bracket of 28 percent or less, any capital gains you earned would be taxed just like ordinary income, but if you were in the 31, 36, or 39.6 percent bracket, your long-term capital gains would only be taxed at a 28 percent rate. Thus, long-term capital gains are better than ordinary income for many people because more of it is left after taxes.

Capital gains tax rates have varied over time, but they have generally been lower than rates on ordinary income. The reason is simple — Congress wants the economy to grow, for growth we need investment in productive assets, and low

T A B L E 2 - 6	Corporate Tax Rates as of January 1997

IF A CORPORATION'S TAXABLE INCOME IS	IT PAYS THIS AMOUNT ON THE BASE OF THE BRACKET	PLUS THIS PERCENTAGE ON THE EXCESS OVER THE BASE	AVERAGE TAX RATE AT TOP OF BRACKET
Up to $50,000	$ 0	15%	15.0%
$50,000–$75,000	7,500	25	18.3
$75,000–$100,000	13,750	34	22.3
$100,000–$335,000	22,250	39	34.0
$335,000–$10,000,000	113,900	34	34.0
$10,000,000–$15,000,000	3,400,000	35	34.3
$15,000,000–$18,333,333	5,150,000	38	35.0
Over $18,333,333	6,416,667	35	35.0

capital gains tax rates encourage investment. To see why, suppose you owned a company that earned $1 million after corporate taxes. Because it is your company, you could have it pay out the entire $1 million profit as dividends, or you could have it retain and reinvest all or part of the income to expand the business. If it paid dividends, they would be taxable to you at a rate of 39.6 percent. However, if the company reinvests its income, that reinvestment should cause the company's earnings and stock price to increase. Then, if you wait for a year and then sell some of your stock at a now-higher price, you will have earned capital gains, but they will be taxed at only 28 percent. Further, you can postpone the capital gains tax indefinitely by simply not selling the stock.

It should be clear that a lower tax rate on capital gains will encourage investment. The owners of small businesses will want to reinvest income to get capital gains, as will stockholders in large corporations. Individuals with money to invest will understand the tax advantages associated with investing in newly formed companies versus buying bonds, so new ventures will have an easier time attracting equity capital. All in all, lower capital gains tax rates stimulate capital formation and investment.[10]

CORPORATE INCOME TAXES

The corporate tax structure, shown in Table 2-6, is relatively simple. To illustrate, if a firm had $65,000 of taxable income, its tax bill would be

$$\text{Taxes} = \$7,500 + 0.25(\$15,000)$$
$$= \$7,500 + \$3,750 = \$11,250,$$

---

[10]Capital gains on the newly issued stock of certain small companies are taxed at one-half the regular capital gains tax rate, provided the small-company stock is held for five years or longer. Thus, if one bought newly issued stock from a qualifying small company and held it for at least five years, any capital gains would be taxed at a maximum rate of 14 percent. This provision was designed to help small businesses obtain equity capital.

and its average tax rate would be $11,250/$65,000 = 17.3\%$. Note that corporate income above $18,333,333 has an average and marginal tax rate of 35 percent.[11]

INTEREST AND DIVIDEND INCOME RECEIVED BY A CORPORATION. Interest income received by a corporation is taxed as ordinary income at regular corporate tax rates. *However, 70 percent of the dividends received by one corporation from another is excluded from taxable income, while the remaining 30 percent is taxed at the ordinary tax rate.*[12] Thus, a corporation earning more than $18,333,333 and paying a 35 percent marginal tax rate would pay only $(0.30)(0.35) = 0.105 = 10.5\%$ of its dividend income as taxes, so its effective tax rate on dividends received would be 10.5 percent. If this firm had $10,000 in pre-tax dividend income, its after-tax dividend income would be $8,950:

$$
\begin{aligned}
\frac{\text{After-tax}}{\text{income}} &= \text{Before-tax income} - \text{Taxes} \\
&= \text{Before-tax income} - (\text{Before-tax income})(\text{Effective tax rate}) \\
&= \text{Before-tax income}(1 - \text{Effective tax rate}) \\
&= \$10,000\,[1 - (0.30)(0.35)] \\
&= \$10,000(1 - 0.105) = \$10,000(0.895) = \$8,950.
\end{aligned}
$$

If the corporation pays its own after-tax income out to its stockholders as dividends, the income is ultimately subjected to *triple taxation:* (1) the original corporation is first taxed, (2) the second corporation is then taxed on the dividends it received, and (3) the individuals who receive the final dividends are taxed again. This is the reason for the 70 percent exclusion on intercorporate dividends.

If a corporation has surplus funds that can be invested in marketable securities, the tax factor favors investment in stocks, which pay dividends, rather than in bonds, which pay interest. For example, suppose GE had $100,000 to invest, and it could buy either bonds that paid interest of $8,000 per year or preferred stock that paid dividends of $7,000. GE is in the 35 percent tax bracket; therefore, its tax on the interest, if it bought bonds, would be $0.35(\$8,000) = \$2,800$, and its after-tax income would be $5,200. If it bought preferred (or common) stock, its tax would be $0.35[(0.30)(\$7,000)] = \$735$, and its after-tax income would

---

[11]Prior to 1987, many large, profitable corporations such as General Electric and Boeing paid no income taxes. The reasons for this were as follows: (1) expenses, especially depreciation, were defined differently for calculating taxable income than for reporting earnings to stockholders, so some companies reported positive profits to stockholders but losses — hence no taxes — to the Internal Revenue Service; and (2) some companies which did have tax liabilities used various tax credits to offset taxes that would otherwise have been payable. This situation was effectively eliminated in 1987.

The principal method used to eliminate this situation is the Alternative Minimum Tax (AMT). Under the AMT, both corporate and individual taxpayers must figure their taxes in two ways, the "regular" way and the AMT way, and then pay the higher of the two. The AMT is calculated as follows: (1) Figure your regular taxes. (2) Take your taxable income under the regular method and then add back certain items, especially income on certain municipal bonds, depreciation in excess of straight line depreciation, certain research and drilling costs, itemized or standard deductions (for individuals), and a number of other items. (3) The income determined in (2) is defined as AMT income, and it must then be multiplied by the AMT tax rate to determine the tax due under the AMT system. An individual or corporation must then pay the higher of the regular tax or the AMT tax. In 1996, there were two AMT tax rates for individuals (26 percent and 28 percent, depending on the level of AMT income and filing status); the corporate AMT remained unchanged at 20 percent.

[12]The size of the dividend exclusion actually depends on the degree of ownership. Corporations that own less than 20 percent of the stock of the dividend-paying company can exclude 70 percent of the dividends received; firms that own more than 20 percent but less than 80 percent can exclude 80 percent of the dividends; and firms that own more than 80 percent can exclude the entire dividend payment. We will, in general, assume a 70 percent dividend exclusion.

be $6,265. Other factors might lead GE to invest in bonds, but the tax factor certainly favors stock investments when the investor is a corporation.[13]

INTEREST AND DIVIDENDS PAID BY A CORPORATION. A firm's operations can be financed with either debt or equity capital. If it uses debt, it must pay interest on this debt, whereas if it uses equity, it is expected to pay dividends to the equity investors (stockholders). The interest *paid* by a corporation is deducted from its operating income to obtain its taxable income, but dividends paid are not deductible. Therefore, a firm needs $1 of pre-tax income to pay $1 of interest, but if it is in the 40 percent federal-plus-state tax bracket, it needs $1.67 of pre-tax income to pay $1 of dividends:

$$\frac{\text{Pre-tax income needed}}{\text{to pay \$1 of dividends}} = \frac{\$1}{1 - \text{Tax rate}} = \frac{\$1}{0.60} = \$1.67.$$

$$\text{Proof: After-tax income} = \$1.67 - \text{Tax} = \$1.67 - \$1.67(0.4)$$
$$= \$1.67(1 - 0.4) = \$1.00.$$

Table 2-7 shows the situation for a firm with $10 million of assets, sales of $5 million, and $1.5 million of earnings before interest and taxes (EBIT). As shown in Column 1, if the firm were financed entirely by bonds, and if it made interest payments of $1.5 million, its taxable income would be zero, taxes would be zero, and its investors would receive the entire $1.5 million. (The term *investors* includes both stockholders and bondholders.) However, as shown in Column 2, if the firm had no debt and was therefore financed only by stock, all of the $1.5 million of EBIT would be taxable income to the corporation, the tax would be

---

[13]This illustration demonstrates why corporations favor investing in lower-yielding preferred stocks over higher-yielding bonds. When tax consequences are considered, the yield on the preferred stock, $[1 - 0.35(0.30)](7.0\%) = 6.265\%$, is higher than the yield on the bond, $(1 - 0.35)(8.0\%) = 5.200\%$. Also, note that corporations are restricted in their use of borrowed funds to purchase other firms' preferred or common stocks. Without such restrictions, firms could engage in *tax arbitrage,* whereby the interest on borrowed funds reduces taxable income on a dollar-for-dollar basis, but taxable income is increased by only $0.30 per dollar of dividend income. Thus, current tax laws reduce the 70 percent dividend exclusion in proportion to the amount of borrowed funds used to purchase the stock.

TABLE 2-7 Cash Flows to Investors under Bond and Stock Financing

	USE BONDS (1)	USE STOCK (2)
Sales	$5,000,000	$5,000,000
Operating costs	3,500,000	3,500,000
Earnings before interest and taxes (EBIT)	$1,500,000	$1,500,000
Interest	1,500,000	0
Taxable income	$ 0	$1,500,000
Federal-plus-state taxes (40%)	0	600,000
After-tax income	$ 0	$ 900,000
Income to investors	$1,500,000	$ 900,000
Rate of return on $10 million of assets	15.0%	9.0%

$1,500,000(0.40) = $600,000, and investors would receive only $0.9 million versus $1.5 million under debt financing. The rate of return to investors on their $10 million investment is therefore much higher if debt is used.

Of course, it is generally not possible to finance exclusively with debt capital, and the risk of doing so would offset the benefits of the higher expected income. *Still, the fact that interest is a deductible expense has a profound effect on the way businesses are financed—our corporate tax system favors debt financing over equity financing.* This point is discussed in more detail in Chapters 9 and 13.

CORPORATE CAPITAL GAINS. Before 1987, corporate long-term capital gains were taxed at lower rates than corporate ordinary income, so the situation was similar for corporations and individuals. Under current law, however, corporations' capital gains are taxed at the same rates as their operating income.

CORPORATE LOSS CARRY-BACK AND CARRY-FORWARD. Ordinary corporate operating losses can be carried back **(carry-back)** to each of the preceding 3 years and forward **(carry-forward)** for the next 15 years and used to offset taxable income in those years. For example, an operating loss in 1998 could be carried back and used to reduce taxable income in 1995, 1996, and 1997, and forward, if necessary, and used in 1999, 2000, and so on, to the year 2013. The loss is typically applied first to the earliest year, then to the next earliest year, and so on, until losses have been used up or the 15-year carry-forward limit has been reached.

To illustrate, suppose Apex Corporation had $2 million of *pre-tax* profits (taxable income) in 1995, 1996, and 1997, and then, in 1998, Apex lost $12 million. Also, assume that Apex's federal-plus-state tax rate is 40 percent. As shown in Table 2-8, the company would use the carry-back feature to recompute its taxes for 1995, using $2 million of the 1998 operating losses to reduce the 1995 pre-tax profit to zero. This would permit it to recover the taxes paid in 1995. Therefore, in 1998 Apex would receive a refund of its 1995 taxes because of the loss

Tax Loss Carry-Back and Carry-Forward
Ordinary corporate operating losses can be carried backward for 3 years or forward for 15 years to offset taxable income in a given year.

| TABLE 2-8 | Apex Corporation: Calculation of Loss Carry-Back and Carry-Forward for 1995–1997 Using a $12 Million 1998 Loss |

	1995	**1996**	**1997**
Original taxable income	$2,000,000	$2,000,000	$2,000,000
Carry-back credit	− 2,000,000	− 2,000,000	− 2,000,000
Adjusted profit	$ 0	$ 0	$ 0
Taxes previously paid (40%)	800,000	800,000	800,000
Difference = Tax refund	$ 800,000	$ 800,000	$ 800,000

Total refund check received in 1999: $800,000 + $800,000 + $800,000 = $2,400,000.

Amount of loss carry-forward available for use in 1999–2013:

1998 loss	$12,000,000
Carry-back losses used	$ 6,000,000
Carry-forward losses still available	$ 6,000,000

experienced in 1998. Because $10 million of the unrecovered losses would still be available, Apex would repeat this procedure for 1996 and 1997. Thus, in 1998 the company would pay zero taxes for 1998 and also would receive a refund for taxes paid from 1995 through 1997. Apex would still have $6 million of unrecovered losses to carry forward, subject to the 15-year limit. This $6 million could be used until the entire $12 million loss had been used to offset taxable income. The purpose of permitting this loss treatment is to avoid penalizing corporations whose incomes fluctuate substantially from year to year.

Improper Accumulation
Retention of earnings by a business for the purpose of enabling stockholders to avoid personal income taxes.

IMPROPER ACCUMULATION TO AVOID PAYMENT OF DIVIDENDS. Corporations could refrain from paying dividends and thus permit their stockholders to avoid personal income taxes on dividends. To prevent this, the Tax Code contains an **improper accumulation** provision which states that earnings accumulated by a corporation are subject to penalty rates *if the purpose of the accumulation is to enable stockholders to avoid personal income taxes.* A cumulative total of $250,000 (the balance sheet item "retained earnings") is by law exempted from the improper accumulation tax for most corporations. This is a benefit primarily to small corporations.

The improper accumulation penalty applies only if the retained earnings in excess of $250,000 are *shown by the IRS to be unnecessary to meet the reasonable needs of the business.* A great many companies do indeed have legitimate reasons for retaining more than $250,000 of earnings. For example, earnings may be retained and used to pay off debt, to finance growth, or to provide the corporation with a cushion against possible cash drains caused by losses. How much a firm should properly accumulate for uncertain contingencies is a matter of judgment. We shall consider this matter again in Chapter 14, which deals with corporate dividend policy.

CONSOLIDATED CORPORATE TAX RETURNS. If a corporation owns 80 percent or more of another corporation's stock, it can aggregate income and file one consolidated tax return; thus, the losses of one company can be used to offset the profits of another. (Similarly, one division's losses can be used to offset another division's profits.) No business ever wants to incur losses (you can go broke losing $1 to save 35¢ in taxes), but tax offsets do help make it more feasible for large, multidivisional corporations to undertake risky new ventures or ventures that will suffer losses during a developmental period.

TAXATION OF SMALL BUSINESSES: S CORPORATIONS

S Corporation
A small corporation which, under Subchapter S of the Internal Revenue Code, elects to be taxed as a proprietorship or a partnership yet retains limited liability and other benefits of the corporate form of organization.

The Tax Code provides that small businesses which meet certain restrictions as spelled out in the code may be set up as corporations and thus receive the benefits of the corporate form of organization—especially limited liability—yet still be taxed as proprietorships or partnerships rather than as corporations. These corporations are called **S corporations.** ("Regular" corporations are called C corporations.) If a corporation elects S corporation status for tax purposes, all of the business's income is reported as personal income by its stockholders, on a pro rata basis, and thus is taxed at the rates that apply to individuals. This is an important benefit to the owners of small corporations in which all or most of the income earned each year will be distributed as dividends, because then the income is taxed only once, at the individual level.

GLOBAL PERSPECTIVES

TAX HAVENS

Many multinational corporations have found an interesting but controversial way to reduce their tax burdens: By shifting some of their operations to countries with low or nonexistent taxes, they can significantly reduce their total tax bills. Over the years, several countries have passed tax laws which make the countries *tax havens* designed to attract foreign investment. Notable examples include the Bahamas, the Grand Caymans, and the Netherlands Antilles.

Rupert Murdoch, chairman of global media giant News Corporation, has in some years paid virtually no taxes on his U.S. businesses, despite the fact that these businesses represent roughly 70 percent of his total operating profit. How has Murdoch been able to reduce his tax burden? By shifting profits to a News Corp. subsidiary which is incorporated in the Netherlands Antilles. As Murdoch puts it, "Moving assets around like that is one of the advantages of being global."

While activities such as Murdoch's are legal, some have questioned their ethics. Clearly, shareholders want corporations to take legal steps to reduce taxes. Indeed, many argue that managers have a fiduciary responsibility to take such actions whenever they are cost effective. Moreover, citizens of the various tax havens benefit from foreign investment. Who loses? Obviously, the United States loses tax revenue whenever a domestic corporation establishes a subsidiary in a tax haven. Ultimately, this loss of tax revenue either reduces services or raises the tax burden on other corporations and individuals. Nevertheless, even the U.S. government is itself somewhat ambivalent about the establishment of off-shore subsidiaries — it does not like to lose tax revenues, but it does like to encourage foreign investment.

SELF-TEST QUESTIONS

??????

Explain what is meant by the statement: "Our tax rates are progressive."

Are tax rates progressive for all income ranges?

Explain the difference between marginal tax rates and average tax rates.

What are capital gains and losses, and how are they differentiated from ordinary income?

How does the federal income tax system treat corporate dividends received by a corporation versus those received by an individual? Why is this distinction made?

What is the difference in the tax treatment of interest and dividends paid by a corporation? Does this difference favor debt or equity financing?

Briefly explain how tax loss carry-back and carry-forward procedures work.

What is a "municipal bond," and how are these bonds taxed?

DEPRECIATION

Depreciation plays an important role in income tax calculations — the larger the depreciation, the lower the taxable income, the lower the tax bill, hence the higher the cash flow from operations. Congress specifies, in the Tax Code, both the life over which assets can be depreciated for tax purposes and the methods of depreciation which can be used. We will discuss in detail how depreciation is calculated, and how it affects income and cash flows, when we take up capital budgeting in Chapters 10, 11, and 12.

SUMMARY

The primary purposes of this chapter were (1) to describe the basic financial statements, (2) to present some background information on cash flows, and (3) to provide an overview of the federal income tax system. The key concepts covered are listed below.

- The four basic statements contained in the **annual report** are the balance sheet, the income statement, the statement of retained earnings, and the statement of cash flows. Investors use the information provided in these statements to form expectations about the future levels of earnings and dividends, and about the firm's riskiness.

- A firm's **balance sheet** shows its assets on the left-hand side and its liabilities and equity, or claims against assets, on the right-hand side. The balance sheet may be thought of as a snapshot of the firm's financial position at a particular point in time.

- A firm's **income statement** reports the results of operations over a period of time, and it shows earnings per share as its "bottom line."

- A firm's **statement of retained earnings** shows the change in retained earnings between the balance sheet dates. Retained earnings represent a claim against assets, not assets per se.

- A firm's **statement of cash flows** reports the impact of operating, investing, and financing activities on cash flows over an accounting period.

- **Net cash flow** differs from **accounting profit** because some of the revenues and expenses reflected in accounting profits may not have been received or paid out in cash during the year. Depreciation is typically the largest noncash item, so net cash flow is often expressed as net income plus depreciation. Investors are at least as interested in a firm's projected net cash flow as in reported earnings because it is cash, not paper profit, that is paid out as dividends and plowed back into the business to produce growth.

- **Operating cash flow** arises from normal operations, and it is the difference between cash revenues and cash costs, including taxes on operating income. Operating cash flow differs from net cash flow because operating cash flow does not include interest expense.

- **Market Value Added (MVA)** represents the difference between the market value of a firm's stock and the amount of equity its investors have supplied.

- **Economic Value Added (EVA)** is found as the difference between after-tax operating profit and the total cost of capital, including the cost of equity capital. EVA is an estimate of the value created by management during the year, and it differs substantially from accounting profit because no charge for the use of equity capital is reflected in accounting profit.

- The value of any asset depends on the stream of **after-tax cash flows** it produces. Tax rates and other aspects of our tax system are changed by Congress every year or so.

- In the United States, tax rates are **progressive** — the higher one's income, the larger the percentage paid in taxes, up to a point.

- Assets such as stocks, bonds, and real estate are defined as **capital assets.** If a capital asset is sold for more than its cost, the profit is called a **capital gain.** If the asset is sold for a loss, it is called a **capital loss.** Assets held for over a year provide **long-term** gains or losses.

♦ Operating income paid out as dividends is subject to **double taxation:** the income is first taxed at the corporate level, and then shareholders must pay personal taxes on their dividends.

♦ Interest income received by a corporation is taxed as **ordinary income;** however, 70 percent of the dividends received by one corporation from another are excluded from **taxable income.** The reason for this exclusion is that corporate dividend income is ultimately subjected to **triple taxation**.

♦ Because interest paid by a corporation is a **deductible** expense while dividends are not, our tax system favors debt over equity financing.

♦ Ordinary corporate operating losses can be **carried back** to each of the preceding 3 years and **forward** for the next 15 years and used to offset taxable income in those years.

♦ **S corporations** are small businesses which have the limited-liability benefits of the corporate form of organization yet are taxed as a partnership or a proprietorship.

QUESTIONS

2-1 What four statements are contained in most annual reports?

2-2 If a "typical" firm reports $20 million of retained earnings on its balance sheet, could its directors declare a $20 million cash dividend without any qualms whatsoever?

2-3 Explain the following statement: "While the balance sheet can be thought of as a snapshot of the firm's financial position *at a point in time,* the income statement reports on operations *over a period of time.*"

2-4 Differentiate between accounting income and net cash flow. Why might these two numbers differ?

2-5 Differentiate between operating cash flow and net cash flow. Why might these two numbers differ?

2-6 What do the numbers on financial statements actually represent?

2-7 Who are some of the basic users of financial statements, and how do they use them?

2-8 In what way does the Tax Code discourage corporations from paying high dividends to their shareholders?

2-9 What does *double taxation of corporate income* mean?

2-10 If you were starting a business, what tax considerations might cause you to prefer to set it up as a proprietorship or a partnership rather than as a corporation?

2-11 Explain how the federal income tax structure affects the choice of financing (use of debt versus equity) of U.S. business firms.

2-12 For someone planning to start a new business, is the average or the marginal tax rate more relevant?

SELF-TEST PROBLEMS   (Solutions Appear in Appendix B)

ST-1
Key terms

Define each of the following terms:
a. Annual report; balance sheet; income statement
b. Common stockholders' equity, or net worth; paid-in capital; retained earnings
c. Statement of retained earnings; statement of cash flows
d. Depreciation; inventory valuation methods
e. Accounting profit; net cash flow; operating cash flow
f. Market value added; Economic value added
g. Progressive tax; taxable income

h. Marginal and average tax rates
i. Bracket creep
j. Capital gain or loss
k. Tax loss carry-back and carry-forward
l. Improper accumulation
m. S corporation

ST-2
Net income, cash flow, and EVA

Last year Rattner Robotics had $5,000,000 in operating income (EBIT). The company had a depreciation expense of $1,000,000 and an interest expense of $1,000,000; its corporate tax rate was 40 percent. The company has a total of $25,000,000 of capital, and it estimates that its after-tax cost of capital is 10 percent. Assume that Rattner's only noncash item was depreciation.
a. What was the company's net income for the year?
b. What was the company's net cash flow?
c. What was the company's operating cash flow?
d. What was the company's economic value added (EVA)?

ST-3
Effect of form of organization on taxes

Mary Henderson is planning to start a new business, MH Enterprises, and she must decide whether to incorporate or to do business as a sole proprietorship. Under either form, Henderson will initially own 100 percent of the firm, and tax considerations are important to her. She plans to finance the firm's expected growth by drawing a salary just sufficient for her family living expenses, which she estimates will be about $40,000, and by retaining all other income in the business. Assume that as a married woman with one child, she files a joint return. She has income tax exemptions of $3 \times \$2,550 = \$7,650$, and she estimates that her itemized deductions for each of the 3 years will be $9,700. She expects MH Enterprises to grow and to earn income of $52,700 in 1998, $90,000 in 1999, and $150,000 in 2000. Which form of business organization will allow Henderson to pay the lowest taxes (and retain the most income) during the period from 1998 to 2000? Assume that the tax rates given in the chapter are applicable for all future years. (Social Security taxes would also have to be paid, but ignore them.)

STARTER PROBLEMS

2-1
Income statement

Little Books Inc. recently reported net income of $3 million. Its operating income (EBIT) was $6 million, and the company pays a 40 percent tax rate. What was the company's interest expense for the year? [Hint: Divide $3 million by $(1 - T) = 0.6$ to find taxable income.]

2-2
Net cash flow

Kendall Corners Inc. recently reported net income of $3.1 million. The company's depreciation expense was $500,000. What is the company's approximate net cash flow?

2-3
After-tax yield

An investor recently purchased a corporate bond which yields 9 percent. The investor is in the 36 percent tax bracket. What is the bond's after-tax yield?

2-4
Personal taxes

Joe and Jane Keller are a married couple who file a joint income tax return. The couple's taxable income was $97,000. How much federal taxes did they owe? Use the tax tables given in the chapter.

2-5
After-tax-yield

Corporate bonds issued by Johnson Corporation currently yield 8 percent. Municipal bonds of equal risk currently yield 6 percent. At what tax rate would an investor be indifferent between these two bonds?

EXAM-TYPE PROBLEMS

The problems included in this section are set up in such a way that they could be used as multiple-choice exam problems.

2-6
Corporate tax liability

The Talley Corporation had a 1997 taxable income of $365,000 from operations after all operating costs but before (1) interest charges of $50,000, (2) dividends received of $15,000, (3) dividends paid of $25,000, and (4) income taxes. What is the firm's income tax liability and its after-tax income? What are the company's marginal and average tax rates on taxable income?

2-7
Corporate tax liability
The Wendt Corporation had $10.5 million of taxable income from operations in 1997.
a. What is the company's federal income tax bill for the year?
b. Assume the firm receives an additional $1 million of interest income from some bonds it owns. What is the tax on this interest income?
c. Now assume that Wendt does not receive the interest income but does receive an additional $1 million as dividends on some stock it owns. What is the tax on this dividend income?

2-8
After-tax yield
The Shrieves Corporation has $10,000 which it plans to invest in marketable securities. It is choosing between AT&T bonds, which yield 7.5 percent, state of Florida muni bonds, which yield 5 percent, and AT&T preferred stock, with a dividend yield of 6 percent. Shrieves' corporate tax rate is 35 percent, and 70 percent of the dividends received are tax exempt. Assuming that the investments are equally risky and that Shrieves chooses strictly on the basis of after-tax returns, which security should be selected? What is the after-tax rate of return on the highest-yielding security?

2-9
After-tax yield
Your personal tax rate is 36 percent. You can invest in either corporate bonds which yield 9 percent or municipal bonds (of equal risk) which yield 7 percent. Which investment should you choose? (Ignore state income taxes.)

2-10
Cash flow
The Klaven Corporation has operating income (EBIT) of $750,000. The company's depreciation expense is $200,000. Klaven is 100 percent equity financed, and it faces a 40 percent tax rate. What is the company's net income? What is its net cash flow? What is its operating cash flow?

2-11
Balance sheet
Which of the following actions will, all else equal, increase the amount of cash on a company's balance sheet?
a. The company issues $2 million in new common stock.
b. The company invests $3 million in new plant and equipment.
c. The company generates negative net income and negative net cash flow during the year.
d. The company increases the dividend paid on its common stock.

PROBLEMS

Note: By the time this book is published, Congress might have changed rates and/or other provisions of current tax law — as noted in the chapter, such changes occur fairly often. Work all problems on the assumption that the information in the chapter is applicable.

2-12
Financial statements
The Smythe-Davidson Corporation just issued its annual report. The current year's balance sheet and income statement as they appeared in the annual report are given below. Answer the questions that follow based on information given in the financial statements.

SMYTHE-DAVIDSON CORPORATION: BALANCE SHEET AS OF DECEMBER 31, 1997 (MILLIONS OF DOLLARS)

ASSETS		LIABILITIES AND EQUITY	
Cash and marketable securities	$ 15	Accounts payable	$ 120
Accounts receivable	515	Notes payable	220
Inventories	880	Accruals	280
Total current assets	$1,410	Total current liabilities	$ 620
Net plant and equipment	2,590	Long-term bonds	1,520
		Total debt	$2,140
		Preferred stock (800,000 shares)	80
		Common stock (100 million shares)	260
		Retained earnings	1,520
		Common equity	$1,780
Total assets	$4,000	Total liabilities and equity	$4,000

SMYTHE-DAVIDSON CORPORATION: INCOME STATEMENT FOR YEAR ENDING DECEMBER 31, 1997 (MILLIONS OF DOLLARS)

Sales	$6,250
Operating costs excluding depreciation	5,230
Depreciation	220
EBIT	$ 800
Less: Interest	180
EBT	$ 620
Taxes (40%)	248
Net income before preferred dividends	372
Preferred dividends	8
Net income available to common stockholders	$ 364
Common dividends paid	$ 146
Earnings per share	$3.64

a. Assume that all of the firm's revenues were received in cash during the year and that all costs except depreciation were paid in cash during the year. What is the firm's net cash flow available to common stockholders for the year? How is this number different from the accounting profit reported by the firm?

b. Construct the firm's Statement of Retained Earnings for December 31, 1997.

c. How much money has the firm reinvested in itself over the years instead of paying out dividends?

d. At the present time, how large a check could the firm write without it bouncing?

e. How much money must the firm pay its current creditors within the next year?

2-13
Income and cash flow analysis

The Menendez Corporation expects to have sales of $12 million in 1998. Costs other than depreciation are expected to be 75 percent of sales, and depreciation is expected to be $1.5 million. All sales revenues will be collected in cash, and costs other than depreciation must be paid for during the year. Menendez's federal-plus-state tax rate is 40 percent.

a. Set up an income statement. What is Menendez's expected net cash flow?

b. Suppose Congress changed the tax laws so that Menendez's depreciation expenses doubled. No changes in operations occurred. What would happen to reported profit and to net cash flow?

c. Now suppose that Congress, instead of doubling Menendez's depreciation, reduced it by 50 percent. How would profit and net cash flow be affected?

d. If this were your company, would you prefer Congress to cause your depreciation expense to be doubled or halved? Why?

e. In the situation in which depreciation doubled, would this possibly have an adverse effect on the company's stock price and on its ability to borrow money?

2-14
Income statement

Last year Martin Motors reported the following income statement:

Sales	$2,000,000
Cost of goods sold	1,200,000
Depreciation	500,000
Total operating costs	$1,700,000
Operating income (EBIT)	$ 300,000
Interest expense	100,000
Taxable income (EBT)	$ 200,000
Taxes (40%)	80,000
Net income	$ 120,000

The company's CEO, Joe Lawrence, was unhappy with the firm's performance. This year, he would like to see net income doubled to $240,000. Depreciation, interest expense, and tax rate will all remain constant, and the cost of goods sold will also remain at 60 percent of sales. How much sales revenue must the company generate to achieve the CEO's net income target?

2-15
Loss carry-back, carry-forward

The Herrmann Company has made $150,000 before taxes during each of the last 15 years, and it expects to make $150,000 a year before taxes in the future. However, in 1997 the firm incurred a loss of $650,000. The firm will claim a tax credit at the time it files its 1997 income tax return, and it will receive a check from the U.S. Treasury. Show how it calculates this credit, and then indicate the firm's tax liability for each of the next 5 years. Assume a 40 percent tax rate on *all* income to ease the calculations.

2-16
Loss carry-back, carry-forward

The projected taxable income of the McAlhany Corporation, formed in 1998, is indicated in the table below. (Losses are shown in parentheses.) What is the corporate tax liability for each year? Assume a constant federal-plus-state tax rate of 40 percent.

YEAR	TAXABLE INCOME
1998	($ 95,000,000)
1999	70,000,000
2000	55,000,000
2001	80,000,000
2002	(150,000,000)

2-17
Form of organization

Susan Visscher has operated her small restaurant as a sole proprietorship for several years, but projected changes in her business's income have led her to consider incorporating. Visscher is married and has two children. Her family's only income, an annual salary of $52,000, is from operating the business. (The business actually earns more than $52,000, but Susan reinvests the additional earnings in the business.) She itemizes deductions, and she is able to deduct $8,600. These deductions, combined with her four personal exemptions for $4 \times \$2,550 = \$10,200$, give her a taxable income of $52,000 - $8,600 - $10,200. (Assume the personal exemption remains at $2,550.) Of course, her actual taxable income, if she does not incorporate, would be higher by the amount of reinvested income. Visscher estimates that her business earnings before salary and taxes for the period 1998 to 2000 will be:

YEAR	EARNINGS BEFORE SALARY AND TAXES
1998	$ 70,000
1999	$ 95,000
2000	$110,000

a. What would her total taxes (corporate plus personal) be in each year under
   (1) A non-S corporate form of organization? (1998 tax = $7,680.)
   (2) A proprietorship? (1998 tax = $9,123.)
b. Should Visscher incorporate? Discuss.

2-18
Personal taxes

Mary Jarvis, a single individual, has this situation for the year 1997: salary of $82,000; dividend income of $12,000; interest on Disney bonds of $5,000; interest on state of Florida municipal bonds of $10,000; proceeds of $22,000 from the sale of Disney stock purchased in 1984 at a cost of $9,000; and proceeds of $22,000 from the November 1997 sale of Disney stock purchased in October 1997 at a cost of $21,000. Jarvis gets one exemption ($2,550), and she has allowable itemized deductions of $4,900; these amounts will be deducted from her gross income to determine her taxable income.
a. What is Jarvis's federal tax liability for 1997?
b. What are her marginal and average tax rates?
c. If she had $5,000 to invest and was offered a choice of either state of Florida bonds with a yield of 6 percent or more Disney bonds with a yield of 8 percent, which should she choose, and why?
d. At what marginal tax rate would Jarvis be indifferent in her choice between the Florida and Disney bonds?

I N T E G R A T E D   C A S E

D'LEON INC., PART I

2-19 SECTION I: Financial Statements Donna Jamison, a 1993 graduate of the University of Florida with four years of banking experience, was recently brought in as assistant to the chairman of the board of D'Leon Inc., a small food producer which operates in north Florida and whose specialty is high-quality pecan and other nut products sold in the snack-foods market. D'Leon's president, Al Watkins, decided in 1996 to undertake a major expansion and to "go national" in competition with Frito-Lay, Eagle, and other major snack-food companies. Watkins felt that D'Leon's products were of a higher quality than the competition's, that this quality differential would enable it to charge a premium price, and that the end result would be greatly increased sales, profits, and stock price.

The company doubled its plant capacity, opened new sales offices outside its home territory, and launched an expensive advertising campaign. D'Leon's results were not satisfactory, to put it mildly. Its board of directors, which consisted of its president and vice-president plus its major stockholders (who were all local business people) was most upset when directors learned how the expansion was going. Suppliers were being paid late and were unhappy, and the bank was complaining about the deteriorating situation and threatening to cut off credit. As a result, President Watkins was informed that changes would have to be made, and quickly, or he would be fired. Also, at the board's insistence Donna Jamison was brought in and given the job of assistant to Fred Campo, a retired banker who was D'Leon's chairman and largest stockholder. Campo agreed to give up a few of his golfing days and to help nurse the company back to health, with Jamison's help.

Jamison began by gathering the financial statements and other data given in Tables IC2-1, IC2-2, IC2-3, and IC2-4. Assume that you are Jamison's assistant, and you must help her answer the following questions for Campo. (Note: We will continue with this case in Chapter 3, and you will feel more comfortable with the analysis there, but answering these questions will help prepare you for Chapter 3. Provide clear explanations, not just yes or no answers!)

a. What effect did the company's expansion have on its net cash flow and operating cash flow?
b. Jamison also has asked you to estimate D'Leon's EVA. She estimates that the after-tax total cost of capital was $125,000 in 1996 and $275,000 in 1997.

TABLE IC2-1 Balance Sheets

	1997	1996
Assets		
Cash	$ 7,282	$ 57,600
Accounts receivable	632,160	351,200
Inventories	1,287,360	715,200
Total current assets	$1,926,802	$1,124,000
Gross fixed assets	1,202,950	491,000
Less accumulated depreciation	263,160	146,200
Net fixed assets	$ 939,790	$ 344,800
Total assets	$2,866,592	$1,468,800
Liabilities and Equity		
Accounts payable	$ 524,160	$ 145,600
Notes payable	720,000	200,000
Accruals	489,600	136,000
Total current liabilities	$1,733,760	$ 481,600
Long-term debt	1,000,000	323,432
Common stock (100,000 shares)	460,000	460,000
Retained earnings	(327,168)	203,768
Total equity	$ 132,832	$ 663,768
Total liabilities and equity	$2,866,592	$1,468,800

TABLE IC 2-2 Income Statements

	1997	1996
Sales	$5,834,400	$3,432,000
Cost of goods sold	5,728,000	2,864,000
Other expenses	680,000	340,000
Depreciation	116,960	18,900
Total operating costs	$6,524,960	$3,222,900
EBIT	($ 690,560)	$ 209,100
Interest expense	176,000	62,500
EBT	($ 866,560)	$ 146,600
Taxes (40%)	(346,624)	58,640
Net income	($ 519,936)	$ 87,960
EPS	($ 5.199)	$ 0.880
DPS	$ 0.110	$ 0.220
Book value per share	$ 1.328	$ 6.638
Stock price	$ 2.25	$ 8.50
Shares outstanding	100,000	100,000
Tax rate	40.00%	40.00%
Lease payments	40,000	40,000
Sinking fund payments	0	0

TABLE IC 2-3 Statement of Retained Earnings, 1997

Balance of retained earnings, 12/31/96	$203,768
Add: Net income, 1997	(519,936)
Less: Dividends paid	(11,000)
Balance of retained earnings, 12/31/97	($327,168)

c. Looking at D'Leon's stock price today, would you conclude that the expansion increased or decreased MVA?

d. D'Leon purchases materials on 30-day terms, meaning that it is supposed to pay for purchases within 30 days of receipt. Judging from its 1997 balance sheet, do you think D'Leon pays suppliers on time? Explain. If not, what problems might this lead to?

e. D'Leon spends money for labor, materials, and fixed assets (depreciation) to make products, and still more money to sell those products. Then, it makes sales which result in receivables, which eventually result in cash inflows. Does it appear that D'Leon's sales price exceeds its costs per unit sold? How does this affect the cash balance?

f. Suppose D'Leon's sales manager told the sales staff to start offering 60-day credit terms rather than the 30-day terms now being offered. D'Leon's competitors react by offering similar terms, so sales remain constant. What effect would this have on the cash account? How would the cash account be affected if sales doubled as a result of the credit policy change?

g. Can you imagine a situation in which the sales price exceeds the cost of producing and selling a unit of output, yet a dramatic increase in sales volume causes the cash balance to decline?

h. In general, could a company like D'Leon increase sales without a corresponding increase in inventory and other assets? Would the asset increase occur before the increase in sales, and, if so, how would that affect the cash account and the statement of cash flows?

i. Did D'Leon finance its expansion program with internally generated funds (additions to retained earnings plus depreciation) or with external capital? How does the choice of financing affect the company's financial strength?

| TABLE IC 2-4 | Statement of Cash Flows, 1997 |

OPERATING ACTIVITIES	
Net income	($ 519,936)
Additions (Sources of Cash)	
Depreciation	116,960
Increase in accounts payable	378,560
Increase in accruals	353,600
Subtractions (Uses of Cash)	
Increase in accounts receivable	(280,960)
Increase in inventories	(572,160)
Net cash provided by operating activities	($ 523,936)
LONG-TERM INVESTING ACTIVITIES	
Cash used to acquire fixed assets	($ 711,950)
FINANCING ACTIVITIES	
Increase in notes payable	$ 520,000
Increase in long-term debt	676,568
Payment of cash dividends	(11,000)
Net cash provided by financing activities	$1,185,568
Sum: net decrease in cash	($ 50,318)
Plus: cash at beginning of year	57,600
Cash at end of year	$ 7,282

j. Refer to Tables IC2-2 and IC2-4. Suppose D'Leon broke even in 1997 in the sense that sales revenues equaled total operating costs plus interest charges. Would the asset expansion have caused the company to experience a cash shortage which required it to raise external capital?

k. If D'Leon started depreciating fixed assets over 7 years rather than 10 years, would that affect (1) the physical stock of assets, (2) the balance sheet account for fixed assets, (3) the company's reported net income, and (4) its cash position? Assume the same depreciation method is used for stockholder reporting and for tax calculations, and the accounting change has no effect on assets' physical lives.

l. Explain how (1) inventory valuation methods, (2) the accounting policy regarding expensing versus capitalizing research and development, and (3) the policy with regard to funding future retirement plan costs (retirement pay and retirees' health benefits) could affect the financial statements.

m. D'Leon's stock sells for $2.25 per share even though the company had large losses. Does the positive stock price indicate that some investors are irrational?

n. D'Leon followed the standard practice of paying dividends on a quarterly basis. It paid a dividend during the first two quarters of 1997, then eliminated the dividend when management realized that a loss would be incurred for the year. The dividend was cut before the losses were announced,

and at that point the stock price fell from $8.50 to $3.50. Why would an $0.11, or even a $0.22, dividend reduction lead to a $5.00 stock price reduction?

o. Explain how earnings per share, dividends per share, and book value per share are calculated, and what they mean. Why does the market price per share *not* equal the book value per share?

p. How much new money did D'Leon borrow from its bank during 1997? How much additional credit did its suppliers extend? Its employees and the taxing authorities?

q. If you were D'Leon's banker, or the credit manager of one of its suppliers, would you be worried about your job? If you were a current D'Leon employee, a retiree, or a stockholder, should you be concerned?

r. The 1997 income statement shows negative taxes, that is, a tax credit. How much taxes would the company have had to pay in the past to actually get this credit? If taxes paid within the last 3 years had been less than $346,624, what would have happened? Would this have affected the statement of cash flows and the ending cash balance?

SECTION II: Taxes

s. Working with Jamison has required you to put in a lot of overtime, so you have had very little time to spend on your private finances. It's now April 1, and you have only two weeks left to file your income tax return. You have managed to get all the information together that you will need to complete your return. D'Leon paid you a salary of $45,000, and you received $3,000 in dividends from common stock that you own. You are single, so your personal exemption is $2,550, and your itemized deductions are $4,550.

(1) On the basis of the information above and the April 1997 individual tax rate schedule, what is your tax liability?

(2) What are your marginal and average tax rates?

t. Assume that a corporation has $100,000 of taxable income from operations plus $5,000 of interest income and $10,000 of dividend income. What is the company's tax liability?

u. Assume that after paying your personal income tax as calculated in Part s, you have $5,000 to invest. You have narrowed your investment choices down to California bonds with a yield of 7 percent or equally risky Exxon bonds with a yield of 10 percent. Which one should you choose and why? At what marginal tax rate would you be indifferent to the choice between California and Exxon bonds?

COMPUTER-RELATED PROBLEM

Work the problem in this section only if you are using the computer problem diskette.

2-20

Effect of form of organization on taxes

The problem requires you to rework Problem 2-17, using the data given below. Use File C2 on the computer problem diskette.

a. Suppose Visscher decides to pay out (1) 50 percent or (2) 100 percent of the after-salary corporate income in each year as dividends. Would such dividend policy changes affect her decision about whether or not to incorporate?

b. Suppose business improves, and actual earnings before salary and taxes in each year are twice the original estimate. Assume that if Visscher chooses to incorporate she will continue to receive a salary of $52,000, and to reinvest additional earnings in the business. (No dividends would be paid.) What would be the effect of this increase in business income on Visscher's decision to incorporate or not incorporate?

CHAPTER 3

ANALYSIS OF FINANCIAL STATEMENTS

© Geoff Brightling/Masterfile

Note: We have covered this chapter both early in the course and toward the end. Early coverage gives students an overview of how financial decisions affect financial statements and results, and thus of what financial management is all about. Later coverage, after students have an understanding of stock valuation, risk analysis, capital budgeting, capital structure, and working capital management, helps students appreciate why ratios are the way they are and how they are used for different purposes. Depending on students' backgrounds, instructors may want to cover the chapter early or late.

TAKING A CHAIN SAW TO SUNBEAM

Sunbeam Corporation, the well-known manufacturer of toasters, blenders, bread makers, outdoor grills, and other consumer products, took on too much debt in the 1980s, and that debt forced it into bankruptcy. These problems were cleared up in 1990, and from 1990 to 1994 the company experienced strong growth in earnings. However, its business took a surprising downturn in 1995, and then things went from bad to worse. The 1995 profit margin shrunk to just over 4 percent from nearly 9 percent in 1994. At the same time, sales stagnated, and the return on equity dropped to a paltry 5.4 percent. Not surprisingly, Sunbeam's stock, which sold for $26 a share in 1994, fell to $12 in 1996.

Superstar money managers Michael Price and Michael Steinhardt had taken control of the company while Sunbeam was in bankruptcy, and in 1996 they still held 42 percent of its shares. Needless to say, Price and Steinhardt have been disappointed with the company's recent performance. As a result, they fired Sunbeam's chief executive officer and brought in a turnaround specialist, "Chain Saw" Al Dunlap, to straighten things out.

Dunlap earned his nickname as a result of his actions at other troubled companies, most recently Scott Paper. During his 18-month tenure at Scott, Dunlap dramatically cut costs, and he eliminated more than 11,000 jobs. As a result of these actions, Scott's stock price rose sharply, and Dunlap was able to sell the company to Kimberly Clark at a price which increased Scott's stockholders' value by $6.5 billion. For his efforts, Dunlap received incentive compensation to the tune of $100 million.

The day Dunlap's appointment at Sunbeam was announced, its stock jumped 49 percent, from $12½ to $18⅝, thereby raising the company's market value by nearly $500 million. Obviously, Sunbeam's stockholders thought Dunlap could do with it what he had done with Scott Paper. Quickly, he fired a number of top managers and announced plans to cut the work force in half. In addition, he announced plans to reduce corporate overhead by 60 percent, and that he intends to sell off any part of the company that cannot be made profitable.

While the market's response to Dunlap's appointment was enthusiastic, some skeptics doubt that he will be able to turn Sunbeam around quickly. To restore profitability, Dunlap will have to boost sales by improving products, developing innovative new products, and expanding into new markets.

As you study this chapter, think about Sunbeam. An analysis of any firm's financial statements can highlight its shortcomings, and that information then can be used to improve performance. In addition, financial analysis can be used to forecast how such strategic decisions as the sale of a division, a major marketing program, or expanding

a plant are likely to affect future financial performance. Chain Saw Al will undoubtedly use financial analysis as he attempts in the months ahead to improve Sunbeam's performance — his next $100 million depends on it.

The primary goal of financial management is to maximize the stock price, not to maximize accounting measures such as net income or EPS. However, accounting data do influence stock prices, and to understand why a company is performing the way it is and to forecast where it is heading, one needs to evaluate the accounting information reported in the financial statements. Chapter 2 described the primary financial statements and showed how they change as a firm's operations undergo change. Now, in Chapter 3, we show how financial statements are used by managers to improve performance, by lenders to evaluate the likelihood of collecting on loans, and by stockholders to forecast earnings, dividends, and stock prices.

If management is to maximize a firm's value, it must take advantage of the firm's strengths and, simultaneously, correct its weaknesses. Financial statement analysis involves (1) comparing the firm's performance with that of other firms in the same industry and (2) evaluating trends in the firm's financial position over time. These studies help management identify deficiencies and then take actions to improve performance. In this chapter, we focus on how financial managers (and investors) evaluate a firm's current financial position. Then, in the remaining chapters, we examine the types of actions managements can take to improve performance and thus increase their stock prices.

This chapter should, for the most part, be a review of concepts you learned in accounting. However, accounting focuses on how financial statements are *made,* whereas our focus is on how they are *used* by management to improve the firm's performance and by investors when they set values on the firm's stock and bonds.

RATIO ANALYSIS

Financial statements report both on a firm's position at a point in time and on its operations over some past period. However, the real value of financial statements lies in the fact that they can be used to help predict future earnings and dividends. From an investor's standpoint, *predicting the future is what financial statement analysis is all about*, while from management's standpoint, *financial statement analysis is useful both to help anticipate future conditions and, more important, as a starting point for planning actions that will affect the future course of events.*

Financial ratios are designed to help one evaluate a financial statement. For example, Firm A might have debt of $5,248,760 and interest charges of $419,900, while Firm B might have debt of $52,647,980 and interest charges of $3,948,600. Which company is stronger? The burden of these debts, and the companies' ability to repay them, can best be evaluated (1) by comparing each firm's debt to its assets and (2) by comparing the interest it must pay to the income it has available for payment of interest. Such comparisons are made by *ratio analysis*.

In the paragraphs which follow, we will calculate the 1997 financial ratios for Allied Food Products, using data from the balance sheets and income statements given in Tables 2-1 and 2-2 back in Chapter 2. We will also evaluate the ratios in relation to the industry averages.[1] Note that all dollar amounts in the ratio calculations are in millions.

LIQUIDITY RATIOS

Liquid Asset
An asset that can be converted to cash quickly without having to reduce the asset's price very much.

A **liquid asset** is one that trades in an active market and hence can be quickly converted to cash at the going market price, and a firm's "liquidity position" deals with this question: Will the firm be able to pay off its debts as they come due over the next year or so? As shown in Table 2-1 in Chapter 2, Allied has debts totaling $310 million that must be paid off within the coming year. Will it have trouble satisfying those obligations? A full liquidity analysis requires the use of cash budgets, but by relating the amount of cash and other current assets to current obligations, ratio analysis provides a quick, easy-to-use measure of liquidity. Two commonly used **liquidity ratios** are discussed in this section.

Liquidity Ratios
Ratios that show the relationship of a firm's cash and other current assets to its current liabilities.

ABILITY TO MEET SHORT-TERM OBLIGATIONS: THE CURRENT RATIO

Current Ratio
This ratio is calculated by dividing current assets by current liabilities. It indicates the extent to which current liabilities are covered by those assets expected to be converted to cash in the near future.

The **current ratio** is calculated by dividing current assets by current liabilities:

$$\text{Current ratio} = \frac{\text{Current assets}}{\text{Current liabilities}}$$

$$= \frac{\$1,000}{\$310} = 3.2 \text{ times.}$$

Industry average = 4.2 times.

Current assets normally include cash, marketable securities, accounts receivable, and inventories. Current liabilities consist of accounts payable, short-term notes payable, current maturities of long-term debt, accrued taxes, and other accrued expenses (principally wages).

If a company is getting into financial difficulty, it begins paying its bills (accounts payable) more slowly, borrowing from its bank, and so on. If current liabilities are rising faster than current assets, the current ratio will fall, and this could spell trouble. Because the current ratio provides the best single indicator of the extent to which the claims of short-term creditors are covered by assets that are expected to be converted to cash fairly quickly, it is the most commonly used measure of short-term solvency.

Allied's current ratio is well below the average for its industry, 4.2, so its liquidity position is relatively weak. Still, since current assets are scheduled to be converted to cash in the near future, it is highly probable that they could be liquidated at close to their stated value. With a current ratio of 3.2, Allied could liquidate current assets at only 31 percent of book value and still pay off current creditors in full.[2]

---

[1]In addition to the ratios discussed in this section, financial analysts also employ a tool known as *common size* balance sheets and income statements. To form a common size balance sheet, one simply divides each asset and liability item by total assets and then expresses the result as a percentage. The resultant percentage statement can be compared with statements of larger or smaller firms, or with those of the same firm over time. To form a common size income statement, one simply divides each income statement item by sales.

[2]1/3.2 = 0.31, or 31 percent. Note that 0.31($1,000) = $310, the amount of current liabilities.

Although industry average figures are discussed later in some detail, it should be noted at this point that an industry average is not a magic number that all firms should strive to maintain — in fact, some very well-managed firms will be above the average while other good firms will be below it. However, if a firm's ratios are far removed from the averages for its industry, an analyst should be concerned about why this variance occurs. Thus, a deviation from the industry average should signal the analyst (or management) to check further.

QUICK, OR ACID TEST, RATIO

Quick (Acid Test) Ratio
This ratio is calculated by deducting inventories from current assets and dividing the remainder by current liabilities.

The **quick,** or **acid test, ratio** is calculated by deducting inventories from current assets and then dividing the remainder by current liabilities:

$$\text{Quick, or acid test, ratio} = \frac{\text{Current assets} - \text{Inventories}}{\text{Current liabilities}}$$

$$= \frac{\$385}{\$310} = 1.2 \text{ times.}$$

$$\text{Industry average} = 2.1 \text{ times.}$$

Inventories are typically the least liquid of a firm's current assets, hence they are the assets on which losses are most likely to occur in the event of liquidation. Therefore, a measure of the firm's ability to pay off short-term obligations without relying on the sale of inventories is important.

The industry average quick ratio is 2.1, so Allied's 1.2 ratio is low in comparison with other firms in its industry. Still, if the accounts receivable can be collected, the company can pay off its current liabilities without having to liquidate its inventory.

SELF-TEST QUESTIONS   ?????

Identify two ratios that are used to analyze a firm's liquidity position, and write out their equations.

What are the characteristics of a liquid asset? Give some examples.

Which current asset is typically the least liquid?

ASSET MANAGEMENT RATIOS

Asset Management Ratios
A set of ratios which measure how effectively a firm is managing its assets.

The second group of ratios, the **asset management ratios,** measures how effectively the firm is managing its assets. These ratios are designed to answer this question: Does the total amount of each type of asset as reported on the balance sheet seem reasonable, too high, or too low in view of current and projected sales levels? When they acquire assets, Allied and other companies must borrow or obtain capital from other sources. If a firm has too many assets, its cost of capital will be too high, hence its profits will be depressed. On the other hand, if assets are too low, profitable sales will be lost. Ratios which analyze the different types of assets are described in this section.

EVALUATING INVENTORIES: THE INVENTORY TURNOVER RATIO

Inventory Turnover Ratio
The ratio calculated by dividing sales by inventories.

The **inventory turnover ratio** is defined as sales divided by inventories:

$$\text{Inventory turnover ratio} = \frac{\text{Sales}}{\text{Inventories}}$$

$$= \frac{\$3,000}{\$615} = 4.9 \text{ times.}$$

Industry average = 9.0 times.

As a rough approximation, each item of Allied's inventory is sold out and restocked, or "turned over," 4.9 times per year. "Turnover" is a term that originated many years ago with the old Yankee peddler, who would load up his wagon with goods, then go off on his route to peddle his wares. The merchandise was called "working capital" because it was what he actually sold, or "turned over," to produce his profits, whereas his "turnover" was the number of trips he took each year. Annual sales divided by inventory equaled turnover, or trips per year. If he made 10 trips per year, stocked 100 pans, and made a gross profit of $5 per pan, his annual gross profit would be (100)($5)(10) = $5,000. If he went faster and made 20 trips per year, his gross profit would double, other things held constant. So, his turnover directly affected his profits.

Allied's turnover of 4.9 times is much lower than the industry average of 9 times. This suggests that Allied is holding excessive stocks of inventory. Excess stocks are, of course, unproductive, and they represent an investment with a low or zero rate of return. Allied's low inventory turnover ratio also makes us question the current ratio. With such a low turnover, we must wonder whether the firm is actually holding damaged or obsolete goods not worth their stated value.[3]

Note that sales occur over the entire year, whereas the inventory figure is for one point in time. For this reason, it is better to use an average inventory measure.[4] If the firm's business is highly seasonal, or if there has been a strong upward or downward sales trend during the year, it is essential to make some such adjustment. To maintain comparability with industry averages, however, we did not use the average inventory figure.

EVALUATING RECEIVABLES: THE DAYS SALES OUTSTANDING

Days Sales Outstanding (DSO)
The ratio calculated by dividing accounts receivable by average sales per day; indicates the average length of time the firm must wait after making a sale before receiving cash.

Days sales outstanding (DSO), also called the "average collection period" (ACP), is used to appraise accounts receivable, and it is calculated by dividing accounts receivable by average daily sales to find the number of days' sales that are tied up in receivables. Thus, the DSO represents the average length of time that the firm must wait after making a sale before receiving cash, which is the average

---

[3] A problem arises calculating and analyzing the inventory turnover ratio. Sales are stated at market prices, so if inventories are carried at cost, as they generally are, the calculated turnover overstates the true turnover ratio. Therefore, it would be more appropriate to use cost of goods sold in place of sales in the formula's numerator. However, established compilers of financial ratio statistics such as Dun & Bradstreet use the ratio of sales to inventories carried at cost. To develop a figure that can be compared with those published by Dun & Bradstreet and similar organizations, it is necessary to measure inventory turnover with sales in the numerator, as we do here.

[4] Preferably, the average inventory value should be calculated by summing the monthly figures during the year and dividing by 12. If monthly data are not available, one can add the beginning and ending figures and divide by 2. Both methods adjust for growth but not for seasonal effects.

collection period. Allied has 45 days sales outstanding, well above the 36-day industry average.[5]

$$DSO = \begin{array}{c} \text{Days} \\ \text{sales} \\ \text{outstanding} \end{array} = \frac{\text{Receivables}}{\text{Average sales per day}} = \frac{\text{Receivables}}{\text{Annual sales}/360}$$

$$= \frac{\$375}{\$3,000/360} = \frac{\$375}{\$8.333} = 45 \text{ days.}$$

Industry average = 36 days.

The DSO can also be evaluated by comparison with the terms on which the firm sells its goods. For example, Allied's sales terms call for payment within 30 days, so the fact that 45 days' sales, not 30 days', are outstanding indicates that customers, on the average, are not paying their bills on time. This deprives Allied of funds which it could use to invest in productive assets. Moreover, in some instances the fact that a customer is paying its bills late may signal that the customer is in financial trouble, in which case Allied may have a hard time ever collecting what is owed. Therefore, if the trend in DSO over the past few years has been rising, but the credit policy has not been changed, this would be strong evidence that steps should be taken to expedite the collection of accounts receivable.

EVALUATING FIXED ASSETS: THE FIXED ASSETS TURNOVER RATIO

Fixed Assets Turnover Ratio
The ratio of sales to net fixed assets.

The **fixed assets turnover ratio** measures how effectively the firm uses its plant and equipment. It is the ratio of sales to net fixed assets:

$$\text{Fixed assets turnover ratio} = \frac{\text{Sales}}{\text{Net fixed assets}}$$

$$= \frac{\$3,000}{\$1,000} = 3.0 \text{ times.}$$

Industry average = 3.0 times.

Allied's ratio of 3.0 times is equal to the industry average, indicating that the firm is using its fixed assets about as intensively as are other firms in its industry. Therefore, Allied seems to have about the right amount of fixed assets in relation to other firms.

A potential problem can exist when interpreting the fixed assets turnover ratio. Recall from accounting that fixed assets reflect the historical costs of the assets. Inflation has caused the value of many assets that were purchased in the past to be seriously understated. Therefore, if we were comparing an old firm which had acquired many of its fixed assets years ago at low prices with a new company which had acquired its fixed assets only recently, we probably would find that the old firm had the higher fixed assets turnover ratio. However, this

---

[5]Note that by convention the financial community generally uses 360 rather than 365 as the number of days in the year. Also, it would be better to use *average* receivables, either an average of the monthly figures or (beginning receivables + ending receivables)/2 = ($315 + $375)/2 = $345 in the formula. Had the annual average receivables been used, Allied's DSO would have been $345.00/$8.333 = 41 days. The 41-day figure is the more accurate one, but because the industry average was based on year-end receivables, we used 45 days for our comparison. The DSO is discussed further in Chapter 16.

would be more reflective of the difficulty accountants have in dealing with inflation than of any inefficiency on the part of the new firm. The accounting profession is trying to devise ways of making financial statements reflect current values rather than historical values. If balance sheets were actually stated on a current value basis, this would help us make better comparisons, but at the moment the problem still exists. Since financial analysts typically do not have the data necessary to make adjustments, they simply recognize that a problem exists and deal with it judgmentally. In Allied's case, the issue is not a serious one because all firms in the industry have been expanding at about the same rate, hence the balance sheets of the comparison firms are reasonably comparable.[6]

EVALUATING TOTAL ASSETS: THE TOTAL ASSETS TURNOVER RATIO

Total Assets Turnover Ratio
The ratio calculated by dividing sales by total assets.

The final asset management ratio, the **total assets turnover ratio**, measures the turnover of all the firm's assets; it is calculated by dividing sales by total assets:

$$\text{Total assets turnover ratio} = \frac{\text{Sales}}{\text{Total assets}}$$

$$= \frac{\$3,000}{\$2,000} = 1.5 \text{ times.}$$

$$\text{Industry average} = 1.8 \text{ times.}$$

Allied's ratio is somewhat below the industry average, indicating that the company is not generating a sufficient volume of business given its total asset investment. Sales should be increased, some assets should be disposed of, or a combination of these steps should be taken.

SELF-TEST QUESTIONS   ??????

Identify four ratios that are used to measure how effectively a firm is managing its assets, and write out their equations.

What potential problem might arise with the inventory turnover ratio?

What potential problem might arise when comparing different firms' fixed assets turnover ratios?

DEBT MANAGEMENT RATIOS

Financial Leverage
The use of debt financing.

The extent to which a firm uses debt financing, or **financial leverage**, has three important implications: (1) By raising funds through debt, stockholders can maintain control of a firm while limiting their investment. (2) Creditors look to the equity, or owner-supplied funds, to provide a margin of safety, so if the stockholders have provided only a small proportion of the total financing, the risks of the enterprise are borne mainly by its creditors. (3) If the firm earns more on investments financed with borrowed funds than it pays in interest, the return on the owners' capital is magnified, or "leveraged."

---

[6]See FASB #33, *Financial Reporting and Changing Prices* (September 1979), for a discussion of the effects of inflation on financial statements.

To understand better how financial leverage affects risk and return, consider Table 3-1. Here we analyze two companies that are identical except for the way they are financed. Firm U (for "unleveraged") has no debt, whereas Firm L (for "leveraged") is financed half with equity and half with debt that costs 15 percent. Both companies have $100 of assets and $100 of sales, and their expected operating income (also called earnings before interest and taxes, or EBIT) is $30. Thus, both firms *expect* to earn $30, before taxes, on their assets. Of course, things could turn out badly, in which case EBIT would be lower; in the second column of the table, we show EBIT declining from $30 to $2.50 under bad conditions.

T A B L E   3 - 1   Effects of Financial Leverage on Stockholders' Returns

FIRM U (UNLEVERAGED)

Current assets	$ 50	Debt	$ 0
Fixed assets	50	Common equity	100
Total assets	$100	Total liabilities and equity	$100

	EXPECTED CONDITIONS (1)	BAD CONDITIONS (2)
Sales	$100.00	$82.50
Operating costs	70.00	80.00
Operating income (EBIT)	$ 30.00	$ 2.50
Interest	0.00	0.00
Earnings before taxes (EBT)	$ 30.00	$ 2.50
Taxes (40%)	12.00	1.00
Net income (NI)	$ 18.00	$ 1.50
ROE_U = NI/Common equity = NI/$100 =	18.00%	1.50%

FIRM L (LEVERAGED)

Current assets	$ 50	Debt (interest = 15%)	$ 50
Fixed assets	50	Common equity	50
Total assets	$100	Total liabilities and equity	$100

	EXPECTED CONDITIONS (1)	BAD CONDITIONS (2)
Sales	$100.00	$82.50
Operating costs	70.00	80.00
Operating income (EBIT)	$ 30.00	$ 2.50
Interest (15%)	7.50	7.50
Earnings before taxes (EBT)	$ 22.50	($ 5.00)
Taxes (40%)	9.00	(2.00)
Net income (NI)	$ 13.50	($ 3.00)
ROE_L = NI/Common equity = NI/$50 =	27.00%	(6.00%)

Even though both companies' assets produce the same expected EBIT, under-normal conditions Firm L should provide its stockholders with a return on equity of 27 percent versus only 18 percent for Firm U. This difference is caused by Firm L's use of debt, which raises the expected rate of return to stockholders for two reasons: (1) Since interest is deductible, the use of debt lowers the tax bill and leaves more of the firm's operating income available to its investors. (2) If the expected rate of return on assets (EBIT/Total assets) exceeds the interest rate on debt, as it generally does, then a company can use debt to acquire assets, pay the interest on the debt, and have something left over as a "bonus" for its stockholders. For our hypothetical firms, these two effects combine to push Firm L's ex-pected rate of return on equity up far above that of Firm U. Thus, debt can be used to "leverage up" the rate of return on equity.

However, financial leverage can cut both ways. As we show in Column 2, if sales are lower and costs are higher than were expected, the return on assets will also be lower than was expected. Under these conditions, the leveraged firm's return on equity falls especially sharply, and losses occur. For example, under the "bad conditions" in Table 3-1, the debt-free firm still shows a profit, but Firm L shows a loss and thus has a negative return on equity. This occurs because Firm L needs cash to service its debt, while Firm U does not. Firm U, because of its strong balance sheet, could ride out the recession and be ready for the next boom. Firm L, on the other hand, must pay interest of $7.50 regardless of its level of sales. Since in the recession its operations do not generate enough income to meet the interest payments, cash would be depleted, and the firm probably would need to raise additional funds. Because it would be running a loss, Firm L would have a hard time selling stock to raise capital, and its losses would cause lenders to raise the interest rate, increasing L's problems still further. As a result, Firm L just might not survive to enjoy the next boom.

We see, then, that firms with relatively high debt ratios have higher expected returns when the economy is normal, but they are exposed to risk of loss when the economy goes into a recession. Thus, firms with low debt ratios are less risky, but they also forgo the opportunity to leverage up their return on equity. The prospects of high returns are desirable, but investors are averse to risk. Therefore, decisions about the use of debt require firms to balance higher expected returns against increased risk. Determining the optimal amount of debt for a given firm is a complicated process, and we defer a discussion of this topic until Chapter 13. For now, we will simply look at two procedures analysts use to examine the firm's debt: (1) They check the balance sheet to determine the extent to which borrowed funds have been used to finance assets, and (2) they review the income statement to see the extent to which fixed charges are covered by operating profits.

HOW THE FIRM IS FINANCED: TOTAL DEBT TO TOTAL ASSETS

Debt Ratio
The ratio of total debt to total assets.

The ratio of total debt to total assets, generally called the **debt ratio**, measures the percentage of funds provided by creditors:

$$\text{Debt ratio} = \frac{\text{Total debt}}{\text{Total assets}}$$

$$= \frac{\$310 + \$754}{\$2,000} = \frac{\$1,064}{\$2,000} = 53.2\%.$$

$$\text{Industry average} = 40.0\%.$$

Total debt includes both current liabilities and long-term debt. Creditors prefer low debt ratios because the lower the ratio, the greater the cushion against creditors' losses in the event of liquidation. Stockholders, on the other hand, may want more leverage because it magnifies expected earnings.

Allied's debt ratio is 53.2 percent, which means that its creditors have supplied more than half the firm's total financing. As we will discuss in Chapter 13, there are a variety of factors which determine a company's optimal debt ratio. Even within the same industry, optimal debt ratios may differ considerably. Nevertheless, the fact that Allied's debt ratio exceeds the industry average of 40 percent raises a red flag and may make it costly for Allied to borrow additional funds without first raising more equity capital. Creditors may be reluctant to lend the firm more money, and management would probably be subjecting the firm to the risk of bankruptcy if it sought to increase the debt ratio any further by borrowing additional funds.[7]

ABILITY TO PAY INTEREST: TIMES INTEREST EARNED

Times-Interest-Earned (TIE) Ratio
The ratio of earnings before interest and taxes (EBIT) to interest charges; measures the ability of the firm to meet its annual interest payments.

The **times-interest-earned (TIE) ratio** is determined by dividing earnings before interest and taxes (EBIT in Table 2-2) by the interest charges:

$$\text{Times-interest-earned (TIE) ratio} = \frac{\text{EBIT}}{\text{Interest charges}}$$

$$= \frac{\$283.8}{\$88} = 3.2 \text{ times.}$$

$$\text{Industry average} = 6.0 \text{ times.}$$

The TIE ratio measures the extent to which operating income can decline before the firm is unable to meet its annual interest costs. Failure to meet this obligation can bring legal action by the firm's creditors, possibly resulting in bankruptcy. Note that earnings before interest and taxes, rather than net income, is used in the numerator. Because interest is paid with pre-tax dollars, the firm's ability to pay current interest is not affected by taxes.

Allied's interest is covered 3.2 times. Since the industry average is 6 times, Allied is covering its interest charges by a relatively low margin of safety. Thus, the TIE ratio reinforces our conclusion based on the debt ratio that Allied would face difficulties if it attempted to borrow additional funds.

ABILITY TO SERVICE DEBT: THE FIXED CHARGE COVERAGE RATIO

Fixed Charge Coverage Ratio
This ratio extends the TIE ratio to include the firm's annual long-term lease and sinking fund obligations.

The **fixed charge coverage ratio** is similar to the times-interest-earned ratio, but it is more inclusive because it recognizes that many firms lease assets and also must make sinking fund payments.[8] Leasing has become widespread in certain

---

[7]The ratio of debt to equity is also used in financial analysis. The debt-to-assets (D/A) and debt-to-equity (D/E) ratios are simply transformations of each other:

$$D/E = \frac{D/A}{1 - D/A}, \text{ and } D/A = \frac{D/E}{1 + D/E}.$$

[8]A sinking fund is a required annual payment designed to reduce the balance of a bond or preferred stock issue. Sinking funds are discussed in Chapter 7.

industries in recent years, making this ratio preferable to the times-interest-earned ratio for many purposes. Allied's annual lease payments are $28 million, and it must make an annual $20 million sinking fund payment to help retire its debt. Because sinking fund payments must be paid with after-tax dollars, whereas interest and lease payments are paid with pre-tax dollars, the sinking fund payment must be "grossed up" by dividing by (1 − Tax rate) to find the before-tax income required to pay taxes and still have enough left to make the sinking fund payment.[9]

Fixed charges include interest, annual long-term lease obligations, and sinking fund payments, and the fixed charge coverage ratio is defined as follows:

$$\text{Fixed charge coverage ratio} = \frac{\text{EBIT} + \text{Lease payments}}{\text{Interest charges} + \text{Lease payments} + \frac{\text{Sinking fund payments}}{(1 - \text{Tax rate})}}$$

$$= \frac{\$283.8 + \$28}{\$88 + \$28 + \frac{\$20}{0.6}} = 2.1 \text{ times.}$$

$$\text{Industry average} = 5.5 \text{ times.}$$

Allied's fixed charges are covered only 2.1 times, versus an industry average of 5.5 times. Again, this indicates that the firm is weaker than average, and this reinforces the argument that Allied would probably encounter difficulties if it attempted to increase its debt.

SELF-TEST QUESTIONS

How does the use of financial leverage affect stockholders' control position?

In what way do taxes influence a firm's willingness to finance with debt?

In what way does the decision to use debt involve a risk-versus-return trade-off?

Explain the following statement: "Analysts look at both balance sheet and income statement ratios when appraising a firm's financial condition."

Name three ratios that are used to measure the extent to which a firm uses financial leverage, and write out their equations.

PROFITABILITY RATIOS

Profitability Ratios
A group of ratios which show the combined effects of liquidity, asset management, and debt on operating results.

Profitability is the net result of a number of policies and decisions. The ratios examined thus far provide useful clues as to the effectiveness of a firm's operations, but the **profitability ratios** show the combined effects of liquidity, asset management, and debt on operating results.

---

[9]Note that $20/0.6 = $33.33. Therefore, if the company had pre-tax income of $33.33, it could pay taxes at a 40 percent rate and have exactly $20 left with which to make the sinking fund payment. Thus, a $20 sinking fund requirement requires $20/0.6 = $33.33 of pre-tax income. Dividing by (1 − T) is called "grossing up" an after-tax value to find the corresponding pre-tax value.

PROFIT MARGIN ON SALES

Profit Margin on Sales
This ratio measures income per dollar of sales; it is calculated by dividing net income by sales.

The **profit margin on sales,** calculated by dividing net income by sales, gives the profit per dollar of sales:

$$\text{Profit margin on sales} = \frac{\text{Net income available to common stockholders}}{\text{Sales}}$$

$$= \frac{\$113.5}{\$3,000} = 3.8\%.$$

Industry average = 5.0%.

Allied's profit margin is below the industry average of 5 percent. This sub-par result occurs because costs are too high. High costs, in turn, generally occur because of inefficient operations. However, Allied's low profit margin is also a result of its heavy use of debt. Recall that net income is income *after interest.* Therefore, if two firms have identical operations in the sense that their sales, operating costs, and EBIT are the same, but if one firm uses more debt than the other, it will have higher interest charges. Those interest charges will pull net income down, and since sales are constant, the result will be a relatively low profit margin. In such a case, the low profit margin would not indicate an operating problem, just a difference in financing strategies, and the firm with the low margin might well end up with a higher rate of return on its stockholders' investment due to its use of financial leverage. We will see exactly how profit margins and the use of debt interact to affect stockholder returns shortly.

GLOBAL PERSPECTIVES

INTERNATIONAL ACCOUNTING DIFFERENCES CREATE HEADACHES FOR INVESTORS

You must be a good financial detective to analyze financial statements, especially if the company operates overseas. Despite attempts to standardize accounting practices, there are many differences in the way financial information is reported in different countries, and these differences create headaches for investors trying to make cross-border company comparisons.

A study by three Rider College accounting professors demonstrated that huge differences can exist. The professors constructed a computer model to evaluate the net income of a hypothetical but typical company operating in different countries. Applying the standard accounting practices of each country, the hypothetical company would have reported net income of $34,600 in the United States, $250,000 in the United Kingdom, $240,000 in Australia, and $10,402 in Germany.

Such variances occur for a number of reasons. In most countries, including the United States, an asset's balance sheet value is reported at original cost less any accumulated depreciation. However, in some countries, asset values are adjusted to more accurately reflect current market values. Also, inventory valuation methods vary from country to country, as does the treatment of goodwill. Other differences arise from the treatment of leases, research and development costs, and pension plans.

Differences in accounting practices arise from a variety of legal, historical, cultural, and economic factors. For example, in Germany and Japan large banks are the key source of both debt and equity capital, whereas in the United States public capital markets are most important. As a result, U.S. corporations disclose a great deal of information to the public, while German and Japanese corporations use very conservative accounting practices which appeal to the banks.

BASIC EARNING POWER (BEP)

Basic Earning Power (BEP) Ratio
This ratio indicates the ability of the firm's assets to generate operating income; calculated by dividing EBIT by total assets.

The **basic earning power (BEP) ratio** is calculated by dividing earnings before interest and taxes (EBIT) by total assets:

$$\text{Basic earning power ratio (BEP)} = \frac{\text{EBIT}}{\text{Total assets}}$$

$$= \frac{\$283.8}{\$2,000} = 14.2\%.$$

Industry average = 17.2%.

This ratio shows the raw earning power of the firm's assets, before the influence of taxes and leverage, and it is useful for comparing firms with different tax situations and different degrees of financial leverage. Because of its low turnover ratios and low profit margin on sales, Allied is not getting as high a return on its assets as is the average food-processing company.[10]

RETURN ON TOTAL ASSETS

Return on Total Assets (ROA)
The ratio of net income to total assets.

The ratio of net income to total assets measures the **return on total assets (ROA)** after interest and taxes:

$$\frac{\text{Return on}}{\text{total assets}} = \text{ROA} = \frac{\text{Net income available to common stockholders}}{\text{Total assets}}$$

$$= \frac{\$113.5}{\$2,000} = 5.7\%.$$

Industry average = 9.0%.

Allied's 5.7 percent return is well below the 9 percent average for the industry. This low return results from (1) the company's low basic earning power plus (2) its high interest costs which results from its above-average use of debt, both of which cause its net income to be relatively low.

RETURN ON COMMON EQUITY

Return on Common Equity (ROE)
The ratio of net income to common equity; measures the rate of return on common stockholders' investment.

The ratio of net income to common equity measures the **return on common equity (ROE),** or the *rate of return on stockholders' investment*:

$$\frac{\text{Return on}}{\text{common equity}} = \text{ROE} = \frac{\text{Net income available to common stockholders}}{\text{Common equity}}$$

$$= \frac{\$113.5}{\$896} = 12.7\%.$$

Industry average = 15.0%.

---

[10]Notice that EBIT is earned throughout the year, whereas the total assets figure is an end-of-the-year number. Therefore, it would be conceptually better to calculate this ratio as EBIT/Average assets = EBIT/[(Beginning assets + Ending assets)/2]. We have not made this adjustment because the published ratios used for comparative purposes do not include it. However, when we construct our own comparative ratios, we do make the adjustment. Incidentally, the same adjustment would also be appropriate for the next two ratios, ROA and ROE.

Allied's 12.7 percent return is below the 15 percent industry average, but not as far below as the return on total assets. This somewhat better result is due to the company's greater use of debt, a point that is analyzed in detail later in the chapter.

SELF-TEST QUESTIONS   ??????

Identify and write out the equations for four ratios that show the combined effects of liquidity, asset management, and debt management on profitability.

Why is the basic earning power ratio useful?

What does ROE measure? Does using debt lower ROE?

Why does the use of debt lower the ROA?

MARKET VALUE RATIOS

Market Value Ratios
A set of ratios that relate the firm's stock price to its earnings and book value per share.

A final group of ratios, the **market value ratios,** relates the firm's stock price to its earnings and book value per share. These ratios give management an indication of what investors think of the company's past performance and future prospects. If the liquidity, asset management, debt management, and profitability ratios are all good, then the market value ratios will be high, and the stock price will probably be as high as can be expected.

PRICE/EARNINGS RATIO

Price/Earnings (P/E) Ratio
The ratio of the price per share to earnings per share; shows the dollar amount investors will pay for $1 of current earnings.

The **price/earnings (P/E) ratio** shows how much investors are willing to pay per dollar of reported profits. Allied's stock sells for $23, so with an EPS of $2.27 its P/E ratio is 10.1:

$$\text{Price/earnings (P/E) ratio} = \frac{\text{Price per share}}{\text{Earnings per share}}$$

$$= \frac{\$23.00}{\$2.27} = 10.1 \text{ times.}$$

$$\text{Industry average} = 12.5 \text{ times.}$$

As we will see in Chapter 8, P/E ratios are higher for firms with strong growth prospects, other things held constant, but they are lower for riskier firms. Since Allied's P/E ratio is below the average for other food processors, this suggests that the company is regarded as being somewhat riskier than most, as having poorer growth prospects, or both.

MARKET/BOOK RATIO

The ratio of a stock's market price to its book value gives another indication of how investors regard the company. Companies with relatively high rates of return on equity generally sell at higher multiples of book value than those with low returns. First, we find Allied's book value per share:

$$\text{Book value per share} = \frac{\text{Common equity}}{\text{Shares outstanding}}$$

$$= \frac{\$896}{50} = \$17.92.$$

Market/Book (M/B) Ratio
The ratio of a stock's market price to its book value.

Now we divide the market price per share by the book value to get a **market/book (M/B) ratio** of 1.3 times:

$$\text{Market/book ratio} = M/B = \frac{\text{Market price per share}}{\text{Book value per share}}$$

$$= \frac{\$23.00}{\$17.92} = 1.3 \text{ times.}$$

$$\text{Industry average} = 1.7 \text{ times.}$$

Investors are willing to pay less for a dollar of Allied's book value than for one of an average food-processing company.

The average company followed by the *Value Line Investment Survey* had a market/book ratio of about 2.35 during 1996. Since M/B ratios typically exceed 1.0, this means that investors are willing to pay more for stocks than their accounting book values. This situation occurs primarily because asset values, as reported by accountants on corporate balance sheets, do not reflect either inflation or "goodwill." Thus, assets purchased years ago at preinflation prices are carried at their original costs, even though inflation might have caused their actual values to rise substantially, and going concerns have a value greater than their historical costs.

If a company earns a low rate of return on its assets, then its M/B ratio will be relatively low versus an average company. Thus, many airlines, which have not fared well in recent years, sell at M/B ratios below 1.0, while very successful firms such as Microsoft (which makes the operating systems for virtually all PCs) achieve high rates of return on their assets, and their market values are well in excess of their book values. In early 1997, Microsoft's book value per share was $7 versus a market price of $82, so its market/book ratio was $82/$7 = 11.7 times.

SELF-TEST QUESTIONS ??????

Describe two ratios that relate a firm's stock price to its earnings and book value per share, and write out their equations.

How do market value ratios reflect what investors think about a stock's risk and expected rate of return?

What does the price/earnings (P/E) ratio show? If one firm's P/E ratio is lower than that of another firm, name some factors that might explain the difference.

How is book value per share calculated? Explain how inflation and "goodwill" cause book values to deviate from market values.

TREND ANALYSIS

Trend Analysis
An analysis of a firm's financial ratios over time; used to estimate the likelihood of improvement or deterioration in its financial situation.

It is important to analyze trends in ratios as well as their absolute levels, for trends give clues as to whether the financial situation is likely to improve or to deteriorate. To do a **trend analysis**, one simply plots a ratio over time, as shown in Figure 3-1. This graph shows that Allied's rate of return on common equity has been declining since 1994, even though the industry average has been relatively stable. All the other ratios could be analyzed similarly.

FIGURE 3-1 | Rate of Return on Common Equity, 1993–1997

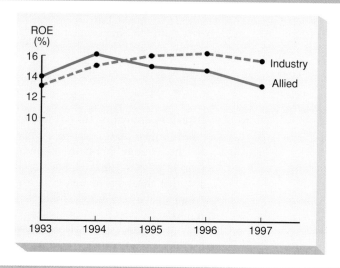

SELF-TEST QUESTIONS ??????

How does one do a trend analysis?

What important information does a trend analysis provide?

TYING THE RATIOS TOGETHER: THE DU PONT CHART AND EQUATION

Du Pont Chart
A chart designed to show the relationships among return on investment, asset turnover, the profit margin, and leverage.

Table 3-2 summarizes Allied's ratios, and Figure 3-2, which is called a modified **Du Pont chart** because that company's managers developed the general approach, shows how the return on equity is affected by asset turnover, the profit margin, and leverage. The left-hand side of the chart develops the *profit margin on sales*. The various expense items are listed and then summed to obtain Allied's total cost, which is subtracted from sales to obtain the company's net income. When we divide net income by sales, we find that 3.8 percent of each sales dollar is left over for stockholders. If the profit margin is low or trending down, one can examine the individual expense items to identify and then correct problems.

The right-hand side of Figure 3-2 lists the various categories of assets, totals them, and then divides sales by total assets to find the number of times Allied "turns its assets over" each year. The company's total assets turnover ratio is 1.5 times.

Du Pont Equation
A formula which shows that the rate of return on assets can be found as the product of the profit margin times the total assets turnover.

The profit margin times the total assets turnover is called the **Du Pont equation,** and it gives the rate of return on assets (ROA):

$$ROA = \text{Profit margin} \times \text{Total assets turnover}$$

$$= \frac{\text{Net income}}{\text{Sales}} \times \frac{\text{Sales}}{\text{Total assets}} \tag{3-1}$$

$$= 3.8\% \times 1.5 = 5.7\%.$$

TABLE 3-2	Allied Food Products: Summary of Financial Ratios (Millions of Dollars)

RATIO	FORMULA FOR CALCULATION	CALCULATION	RATIO	INDUSTRY AVERAGE	COMMENT
Liquidity					
Current	$\dfrac{\text{Current assets}}{\text{Current liabilities}}$	$\dfrac{\$1,000}{\$310}$	= 3.2×	4.2×	Poor
Quick, or acid, test	$\dfrac{\text{Current assets} - \text{Inventories}}{\text{Current liabilities}}$	$\dfrac{\$385}{\$310}$	= 1.2×	2.1×	Poor
Asset Management					
Inventory turnover	$\dfrac{\text{Sales}}{\text{Inventories}}$	$\dfrac{\$3,000}{\$615}$	= 4.9×	9.0×	Poor
Days sales outstanding (DSO)	$\dfrac{\text{Receivables}}{\text{Annual sales}/360}$	$\dfrac{\$375}{\$8.333}$	= 45 days	36 days	Poor
Fixed assets turnover	$\dfrac{\text{Sales}}{\text{Net fixed assets}}$	$\dfrac{\$3,000}{\$1,000}$	= 3.0×	3.0×	OK
Total assets turnover	$\dfrac{\text{Sales}}{\text{Total assets}}$	$\dfrac{\$3,000}{\$2,000}$	= 1.5×	1.8×	Somewhat low
Debt Management					
Total debt to total assets	$\dfrac{\text{Total debt}}{\text{Total assets}}$	$\dfrac{\$1,064}{\$2,000}$	= 53.2%	40.0%	High (risky)
Times-interest-earned (TIE)	$\dfrac{\text{Earnings before interest and taxes (EBIT)}}{\text{Interest charges}}$	$\dfrac{\$283.8}{\$88}$	= 3.2×	6.0×	Low (risky)
Fixed charge coverage	$\dfrac{\text{Earnings before interest and taxes} + \text{Lease payments}}{\text{Interest charges} + \text{Lease payments} + \dfrac{\text{SF payments}}{(1 - T)}}$	$\dfrac{\$311.8}{\$149.3}$	= 2.1×	5.5×	Low (risky)
Profitability					
Profit margin on sales	$\dfrac{\text{Net income available to common stockholders}}{\text{Sales}}$	$\dfrac{\$113.5}{\$3,000}$	= 3.8%	5.0%	Poor
Basic earning power (BEP)	$\dfrac{\text{Earnings before interest and taxes (EBIT)}}{\text{Total assets}}$	$\dfrac{\$283.8}{\$2,000}$	= 14.2%	17.2%	Poor
Return on total assets (ROA)	$\dfrac{\text{Net income available to common stockholders}}{\text{Total assets}}$	$\dfrac{\$113.5}{\$2,000}$	= 5.7%	9.0%	Poor
Return on common equity (ROE)	$\dfrac{\text{Net income available to common stockholders}}{\text{Common equity}}$	$\dfrac{\$113.5}{\$896}$	= 12.7%	15.0%	Poor
Market Value					
Price/earnings (P/E)	$\dfrac{\text{Price per share}}{\text{Earnings per share}}$	$\dfrac{\$23.00}{\$2.27}$	= 10.1×	12.5×	Low
Market/book (M/B)	$\dfrac{\text{Market price per share}}{\text{Book value per share}}$	$\dfrac{\$23.00}{\$17.92}$	= 1.3×	1.7×	Low

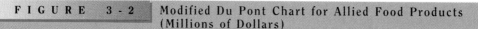

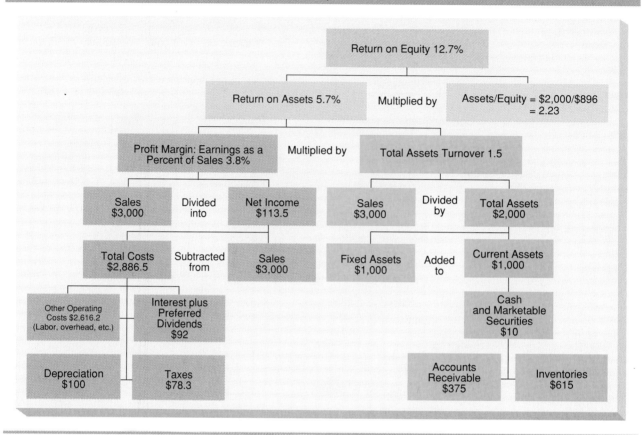

Allied made 3.8 percent, or 3.8 cents, on each dollar of sales, and assets were "turned over" 1.5 times during the year. Therefore, the company earned a return of 5.7 percent on its assets.

If the company were financed only with common equity, the rate of return on assets (ROA) and the return on equity (ROE) would be the same because the total assets would equal the common equity:

$$\text{ROA} = \frac{\text{Net income}}{\text{Total assets}} = \frac{\text{Net income}}{\text{Common equity}} = \text{ROE}.$$

This equality holds if and only if Total assets = Common equity, that is, if the company uses no debt. Allied does use debt, so its common equity is less than total assets. Therefore, the return to the common stockholders (ROE) must be greater than the ROA of 5.7 percent. Specifically, the rate of return on assets (ROA) can be multiplied by the *equity multiplier*, which is the ratio of assets to common equity.

Note that firms which use a large amount of debt financing (more leverage) will necessarily have a high equity multiplier — the more the debt, the less the equity, hence the higher the equity multiplier, Assets/Equity. For example, if a firm has $1,000 of assets and is financed with $800, or 80 percent debt, then its equity will be $200, and its equity multiplier will be $1,000/$200 = 5. Had it used only $200 of debt, then its equity would have been $800, and its equity multiplier would have been only $1,000/$800 = 1.25.[11]

The firm's return on equity (ROE) depends on its ROA and its use of leverage:[12]

$$\text{ROE} = \text{ROA} \times \text{Equity multiplier}$$
$$= \frac{\text{Net income}}{\text{Total assets}} \times \frac{\text{Total assets}}{\text{Common equity}} \qquad (3\text{-}2)$$
$$= 5.7\% \times \$2,000/\$896$$
$$= 5.7\% \times 2.23$$
$$= 12.7\%.$$

Now we can combine Equations 3-1 and 3-2 to form the *Extended Du Pont Equation*, which shows how the profit margin, the assets turnover ratio, and the equity multiplier combine to determine the ROE:

$$\text{ROE} = (\text{Profit margin})\,(\text{Total assets turnover})\,(\text{Equity multiplier})$$
$$= \frac{\text{Net income}}{\text{Sales}} \times \frac{\text{Sales}}{\text{Total assets}} \times \frac{\text{Total assets}}{\text{Common equity}}. \qquad (3\text{-}3)$$

For Allied, we have

$$\text{ROE} = (3.8\%)\,(1.5)\,(2.23)$$
$$= 12.7\%.$$

The 12.7 percent rate of return could, of course, be calculated directly: both Sales and Total assets cancel, leaving Net income/Common equity = $113.5/$896 = 12.7%. However, the Du Pont equation shows how the profit margin, the total assets turnover, and the use of debt interact to determine the return on equity.[13]

Allied's management can use the Du Pont system to analyze ways of improving performance. Focusing on the left, or "profit margin," side of its modified Du Pont chart, Allied's marketing people can study the effects of raising sales prices (or lowering them to increase volume), of moving into new products or markets with higher margins, and so on. The company's cost accountants can study various expense items and, working with engineers, purchasing agents, and other

---

[11]Expressed algebraically,

$$\text{Debt ratio} = \frac{D}{A} = \frac{A - E}{A} = \frac{A}{A} - \frac{E}{A} = 1 - \frac{1}{\text{Equity multiplier}}.$$

Here D is debt, E is equity, A is total assets, and A/E is the equity multiplier. This equation ignores preferred stock.

[12]Note that we could also find the ROE by "grossing up" the ROA, that is, by dividing the ROA by the common equity fraction: ROE = ROA/Equity fraction = 5.7%/0.448 = 12.7%. The two procedures are algebraically equivalent.

[13]Another ratio that is frequently used is the following:

$$\text{Rate of return on investors' capital} = \frac{\text{Net income} + \text{Interest}}{\text{Debt} + \text{Equity}}.$$

The numerator shows the dollar returns to investors, the denominator shows the total amount of money investors have put up, and the ratio itself shows the rate of return on all investors' capital. This ratio is especially important in the public utility industries, where regulators are concerned about the companies' using their monopoly positions to earn excessive returns on investors' capital. In fact, regulators try to set utility prices (service rates) at levels that will force the return on investors' capital to equal a company's cost of capital as defined in Chapter 9.

operating personnel, seek ways to hold down costs. On the "turnover" side, Allied's financial analysts, working with both production and marketing people, can investigate ways to reduce the investment in various types of assets. At the same time, the treasury staff can analyze the effects of alternative financing strategies, seeking to hold down interest expense and the risk of debt while still using leverage to increase the rate of return on equity.

As a result of such an analysis, Ellen Jackson, Allied's president, recently announced a series of moves designed to cut operating costs by more than 20 percent per year. Jackson also announced that the company intends to concentrate its capital in markets where profit margins are reasonably high, and that if competition increases in certain of its product markets (such as the low-price end of the canned fruit market), Allied will withdraw from those markets. Allied is seeking a high return on equity, and Jackson recognizes that if competition drives profit margins too low in a particular market, it will be impossible to earn high returns on the capital invested to serve that market. Therefore, if it is to achieve a high ROE, Allied may have to develop new products and shift capital into new areas. The company's future depends on this type of analysis, and the Du Pont system can help it achieve success.

Jackson herself and Allied's other executives have a strong incentive for improving the company's financial performance, because their compensation is based to a large extent on how well the company does. Allied's executives receive a salary which is sufficient to cover their living costs, but their compensation package also includes "performance shares" which will be awarded if and only if the company meets or exceeds target levels for earnings and the stock price. These target levels are based on Allied's performance relative to other food companies. So, if Allied does well, then Jackson and the other executives—and the stockholders—will also do well. But if things deteriorate, Jackson could be looking for a new job.

SELF-TEST QUESTIONS

Explain how the extended, or modified, Du Pont equation and chart can be used to reveal the basic determinants of ROE.

What is the equity multiplier?

How can management use the Du Pont system to analyze ways of improving the firm's performance?

COMPARATIVE RATIOS AND "BENCHMARKING"

Benchmarking
The process of comparing a particular company with a group of "benchmark" companies.

Ratio analysis involves comparisons because a company's ratios are compared with those of other firms in the same industry, that is, to industry average figures. However, like most firms, Allied's managers go one step further—they also compare their ratios with those of a smaller set of leading food companies. This technique is called **benchmarking**, and the companies used for the comparison are called *benchmark companies*. Allied's management benchmarks against Campbell Soup, a leading manufacturer of canned soups and fruit and vegetable juices; Dean Foods, a processor of canned and frozen vegetables; Dole Food Company, a processor of fruits and vegetables; H.J. Heinz, which makes ketchup and other products; Flowers Industries, a producer of bakery and snack-food goods; Sara Lee, a manufacturer of baked goods; and Morningstar Group, a manufacturer of

INDUSTRY PRACTICE

ROE IS SOARING TO RECORD HEIGHTS

Historically, the average ROE for U.S. corporations has ranged from 10 percent to 13 percent. However, during the last few years ROEs have risen sharply, and in early 1996 the average for the *Fortune* 500 was about 15 percent. Even more incredible, the average ROE for the 30 companies in the Dow Jones Industrial Average was a startling 20.5 percent.

What explains these high ROEs? To answer this question, *Fortune*'s writers used the Du Pont equation to analyze the companies. They noted that ROE can rise for one of three reasons: higher profit margins, greater efficiency in the use of assets (as measured by the total assets turnover ratio), or increased leverage (as measured by the equity multiplier).

According to *Fortune*, each of these factors contributed to the increase in ROE. Write-offs associated with corporate restructurings, along with stock buy-back programs, reduced common equity and thereby increased the equity multiplier. At the same time, asset turnover increased as firms became more efficient in their use of assets. For example, as we will discuss more fully in Chapter 16, many companies adopted just-in-time inventory systems, which reduced the amount of inventory needed to support a given level of sales. This increased inventory turnover and thus total assets turnover.

However, the most important reason for the rise in ROE was a truly dramatic increase in profit margins. Profit margins were relatively constant from 1960 through 1989, but during the 1990s, sales increased at

a much faster rate than costs, causing profit margins to soar. Indeed, widening margins explain about half of the recent increase in ROEs.

Are ROEs likely to remain at their current high levels? Probably not, according to *Fortune*. Much of the recent increase in margins can be attributed to aggressive cost-cutting, but as firms continue to cut costs and improve efficiencies, there is less room for improvement. Also, part of the increase in ROE occurred because the economy was relatively strong for a number of years. Once the economy turns down, the average ROE will probably decline as well. Finally, high rates of return will attract new capital, rising capacity will lead to price-cutting, and eventually rates of return will fall to a level more consistent with "normal" profits.

ON THE WWW

An article entitled, "What's Driving Return on Equity?" appeared in the April 1996 Fortune. *It discusses the three parts of the extended Du Pont equation and how each helps explain the recent run-up in stock prices. The article can be found on the Internet at http://pathfinder.com/ @@aJxbDwYAeEIVw0rD/fortune/ magazine/1996/960429/ return.html. It illustrates how real-world events can be analyzed using financial ratios.*

refrigerated food products. The ratios are calculated for each company, and then the ratios are listed in descending order as shown below for the profit margin on sales as reported by *Value Line* for 1997:

	PROFIT MARGIN
Campbell Soup	10.1%
Heinz	7.2
Sara Lee	4.9
Morningstar	3.8
Allied Food Products	**3.8**
Dole Food Company	3.8
Flowers Industries	2.5
Dean Foods	1.7

The benchmarking setup makes it easy for Allied's management to see exactly where they stand relative to their competition. As the data show, Allied is ranked about in the middle with respect to its profit margin, so the company has room for improvement. Other ratios can be analyzed similarly.

Comparative ratios are available from a number of sources. One useful set is compiled by Dun & Bradstreet (D&B), which provides various ratios calculated for a large number of industries; nine of these ratios are shown for a small sample of industries in Table 3-3. Useful ratios can also be found in the *Annual Statement Studies* published by Robert Morris Associates, which is the national association of bank loan officers. The U.S. Commerce Department's *Quarterly Financial Report*, which is found in most libraries, gives a set of ratios for

TABLE 3-3   Dun & Bradstreet Ratios for Selected Industries: Upper Quartile, Median, and Lower Quartile[a]

SIC CODES, LINE OF BUSINESS, AND NUMBER OF CONCERNS REPORTING	QUICK RATIO	CURRENT RATIO	TOTAL LIABILITIES TO NET WORTH	DAYS SALES OUTSTANDING	NET SALES TO INVENTORY	TOTAL ASSETS TO NET SALES	RETURN ON NET SALES	RETURN ON TOTAL ASSETS	RETURN ON NET WORTH
	×	×	%	DAYS	×	%	%	%	%
2879	2.3	4.7	24.2	22.7	8.8	58.8	4.2	6.4	8.1
Agricultural chemicals	1.1	2.0	67.7	54.4	6.2	75.8	2.0	2.6	3.9
(45)	0.6	1.1	159.1	78.6	3.4	108.9	−1.5	−1.5	−2.6
3724	1.8	3.3	42.5	47.8	11.6	49.3	7.3	13.2	25.5
Aircraft parts, including	1.1	2.0	90.4	61.0	6.2	75.9	2.8	3.7	10.4
engines (62)	0.7	1.5	260.1	70.5	4.0	96.8	0.2	−0.1	0.2
2051	1.8	2.9	33.8	19.7	53.7	25.5	5.4	15.1	45.4
Bakery products	1.0	1.6	99.7	24.1	35.6	33.4	2.9	7.4	16.5
(116)	0.6	0.9	184.9	30.3	20.4	49.0	0.8	2.8	3.4
2086	1.7	3.3	27.5	22.3	25.1	33.9	5.6	12.4	24.8
Beverages	0.9	1.6	61.2	29.2	17.6	47.8	2.5	5.2	14.1
(91)	0.5	1.1	145.0	42.7	12.6	65.0	0.2	0.8	4.9
3312	1.7	2.6	52.5	34.0	19.1	32.6	7.6	15.5	47.3
Blast furnaces and steel	1.0	1.8	135.8	43.4	8.5	57.0	4.7	8.4	21.0
mills (244)	0.7	1.3	318.0	57.0	6.2	86.8	1.8	2.8	8.3
2731	2.3	4.9	23.6	36.3	9.6	43.2	11.5	17.6	35.2
Book publishing	1.2	2.3	83.9	59.5	4.9	65.2	5.1	5.9	16.1
(317)	0.7	1.5	188.9	92.2	2.8	103.1	1.1	1.4	4.0

SOURCE: Industry Norms and Key Business Ratios, 1995–96 Edition, Dun & Bradstreet Credit Services.

[a]The median and quartile ratios can be illustrated by an example. The median quick ratio for agricultural chemical manufacturers, as shown in this table, is 1.1. To obtain this figure, the ratios of current assets less inventories to current debt for each of the 45 concerns were arranged in a graduated series, with the largest ratio at the top and the smallest at the bottom. The median ratio of 1.1 is the ratio halfway between the top and the bottom. The ratio of 2.3, representing the upper quartile, is one-quarter of the way down from the top (or halfway between the top and the median). The ratio 0.6, representing the lower quartile, is one-quarter of the way up from the bottom (or halfway between the median and the bottom). SIC codes are "Standard Industrial Classification" codes used by the U.S. government to classify companies.

manufacturing firms by industry group and size of firm. Trade associations and individual firms' credit departments also compile industry average financial ratios. Finally, financial statement data for thousands of publicly owned corporations are available on magnetic tapes and diskettes, and since brokerage houses, banks, and other financial institutions have access to these data, security analysts can and do generate comparative ratios tailored to their specific needs.

Each of the data-supplying organizations uses a somewhat different set of ratios designed for its own purposes. For example, D&B deals mainly with small firms, many of which are proprietorships, and it sells its services primarily to banks and other lenders. Therefore, D&B is concerned largely with the creditor's viewpoint, and its ratios emphasize current assets and liabilities, not market value ratios. So, when you select a comparative data source, you should be sure that your emphasis is similar to that of the agency whose ratios you plan to use. Additionally, there are often definitional differences in the ratios presented by different sources, so before using a source, be sure to verify the exact definitions of the ratios to ensure consistency with your own work.

SELF-TEST QUESTIONS ??????

Differentiate between trend analysis and comparative ratio analysis.

Why is it useful to conduct comparative ratio analysis?

What is benchmarking, and how does it differ from comparative ratio analysis?

USES AND LIMITATIONS OF RATIO ANALYSIS

As noted earlier, ratio analysis is used by three main groups: (1) *managers,* who employ ratios to help analyze, control, and thus improve their firms' operations; (2) *credit analysts,* such as bank loan officers or bond rating analysts, who analyze ratios to help ascertain a company's ability to pay its debts; and (3) *stock analysts,* who are interested in a company's efficiency, risk, and growth prospects. In later chapters we will look more closely at the basic factors which underlie each ratio, and at that point you will get a better idea about how to interpret and use ratios. Note, though, that while ratio analysis can provide useful information concerning a company's operations and financial condition, it does have limitations that necessitate care and judgment. Some potential problems are listed below:

1. Many large firms operate different divisions in different industries, and for such companies it is difficult to develop a meaningful set of industry averages for comparative purposes. Therefore, ratio analysis is more useful for small, narrowly focused firms than for large, multidivisional ones.

2. Most firms want to be better than average, so merely attaining average performance is not necessarily good. As a target for high-level performance, it is best to focus on the industry leaders' ratios. Benchmarking helps in this regard.

3. Inflation may have badly distorted firms' balance sheets — recorded values are often substantially different from "true" values. Further, since inflation affects both depreciation charges and inventory costs, profits are also affected. Thus, a ratio analysis for one firm over time, or a comparative analysis of firms of different ages, must be interpreted with judgment.

4. Seasonal factors can also distort a ratio analysis. For example, the inventory turnover ratio for a food processor will be radically different if the balance sheet figure used for inventory is the one just before versus just after the close of the canning season. This problem can be minimized by using monthly averages for inventory (and receivables) when calculating turnover ratios.

5. Firms can employ **"window dressing" techniques** to make their financial statements look stronger. To illustrate, a Chicago builder borrowed on a two-year

"Window Dressing" Techniques
Techniques employed by firms to make their financial statements look better than they really are.

basis on December 29, 1997, held the proceeds of the loan as cash for a few days, and then paid off the loan ahead of time on January 2, 1998. This improved his current and quick ratios, and made his year-end 1997 balance sheet look good. However, the improvement was strictly window dressing; a week later the balance sheet was back at the old level.

6. Different accounting practices can distort comparisons. As noted earlier, inventory valuation and depreciation methods can affect financial statements and thus distort comparisons among firms. Also, if one firm leases a substantial amount of its productive equipment, then its assets may appear low relative to sales because leased assets often do not appear on the balance sheet. At the same time, the liability associated with the lease obligation may not be shown as a debt. Therefore, leasing can artificially improve both the turnover and the debt ratios. However, the accounting profession has taken steps to reduce this problem.

7. It is difficult to generalize about whether a particular ratio is "good" or "bad." For example, a high current ratio may indicate a strong liquidity position, which is good, or excessive cash, which is bad (because excess cash in the bank is a nonearning asset). Similarly, a high fixed assets turnover ratio may denote either a firm that uses its assets efficiently or one that is undercapitalized and cannot afford to buy enough assets.

8. A firm may have some ratios that look "good" and others that look "bad," making it difficult to tell whether the company is, on balance, strong or weak. However, statistical procedures can be used to analyze the *net effects* of a set of ratios. Many banks and other lending organizations use statistical procedures to analyze firms' financial ratios, and, on the basis of their analyses, classify companies according to their probability of getting into financial trouble.[14]

Ratio analysis is useful, but analysts should be aware of these problems and make adjustments as necessary. Ratio analysis conducted in a mechanical, unthinking manner is dangerous, but used intelligently and with good judgment, it can provide useful insights into a firm's operations. Your judgment in interpreting a set of ratios is bound to be weak at this point, but it will improve as you go through the remainder of the book.

SELF-TEST QUESTIONS   ???????

List three types of users of ratio analysis. Would these different types of users emphasize the same or different types of ratios?

List several potential problems with ratio analysis.

LOOKING BEYOND THE NUMBERS

Hopefully, working through this chapter has helped your understanding of financial statements and your ability to interpret accounting numbers. These

---

[14]The technique used is discriminant analysis. For a discussion, see Edward I. Altman, "Financial Ratios, Discriminant Analysis, and the Prediction of Corporate Bankruptcy," *Journal of Finance,* September 1968, 589–609, or Eugene F. Brigham and Louis C. Gapenski, *Intermediate Financial Management,* 5th ed., 1996, Chapter 26.

SMALL BUSINESS

FINANCIAL ANALYSIS IN THE SMALL FIRM

Financial ratio analysis is especially useful for small businesses, and readily available sources provide comparative data by size of firm. For example, Robert Morris Associates provides comparative ratios for a number of small-firm classes, down to a size range of zero to $250,000 in annual sales. Nevertheless, analyzing a small firm's statements presents some unique problems. We examine here some of those problems from the standpoint of a bank loan officer, one of the most frequent users of ratio analysis.

When evaluating a small-business credit prospect, a banker is essentially making a prediction about the company's ability to repay its debt. In making this prediction, the banker will be especially concerned about indicators of liquidity and about continuing prospects for profitability. Bankers like to do business with a new customer if it appears that loans can be paid off on time and that the company will remain in business and therefore continue to be a customer for some years to come. Thus, both short-run and long-run viability are of interest to the banker. Note too that the banker's perceptions about the business are important to the owner-manager, because the bank will probably be the firm's primary source of funds.

The first problem the banker is likely to encounter is that, unlike the bank's bigger customers, the small firm may not have audited financial statements. Further, the statements that are available may have been produced on an irregular basis (for example, in some months or quarters but not in others). If the firm is young, it may have historical financial statements for only one year, or perhaps none at all. Also, the finan-cial statements may not have been produced by a reputable accounting firm but by the owner's brother-in-law.

The poor quality of its financial data may therefore be a hinderance for a small business that is attempting to establish a banking relationship. This could keep the firm from getting credit even though it is really on solid financial ground. Therefore, it is in the owner's interest to make sure that the firm's financial data are credible, even if it is more expensive to do so. Furthermore, if the banker is uncomfortable with the data, the firm's management should also be uncomfortable: Because many managerial decisions depend on the numbers in the firm's accounting statements, those numbers should be as accurate as possible.

For a given set of financial ratios, a small firm may be riskier than a larger one. Small firms often produce a single product, rely heavily on a single customer, or both. For example, several years ago a company called Yard Man Inc. manufactured and sold lawn equipment. Most of Yard Man's sales were to Sears, so most of its revenues and profits were due to its Sears account. When Sears decided to drop Yard Man as a supplier, the company was left without its most important customer. Yard Man is no longer in business. Because large firms typically have a broad customer base, they are not as exposed to the sudden loss of a large portion of their business.

A similar danger applies to a single-product company. Just as the loss of a key customer can be disastrous for a small business, so can a shift in the tides of consumer interest in a particular fad. For example, Coleco manufactured and sold the extremely popular Cabbage Patch dolls. The phenomenal popularity of the dolls was a great boon for Coleco. However, the public is fickle—one can never predict when such a fad will die out, leaving the company with a great deal of capacity to make a product that no one will buy, and with a large amount of overvalued inventory. Exactly that situation hit Coleco, and it was forced into bankruptcy.

Extending credit to a small company, especially to a small owner-managed company, often involves yet another risk that is less of a problem for larger firms — dependence on a single key individual whose unexpected death could cause the company to fail. Similarly, if the company is family owned and managed, there is typically one key decision maker, even though several other family members may be involved in helping to manage the company. In the case of the family business, the loss of the top person may not wipe out the company, but it often creates the equally serious problem of who will assume the leadership role. The loss of a key family member is often a highly emotional event, and it is not at all unusual for it to be followed by an ugly and protracted struggle for control of the business. It is in the family's interest, and certainly in the creditors' interests, to see that a plan of management succession is clearly specified before trouble arises. If no good plan can be worked out, perhaps the firm should be forced to carry "key person insurance," payable to the bank and used to retire the loan in the event of the key person's death.

In summary, to determine the creditworthiness of a small firm, the financial analyst must "look beyond the ratios" and analyze the viability of the firm's products, customers, management, and market. Still, ratio analysis is the first step in a sound credit analysis.

important and basic skills are necessary when making business decisions, when evaluating performance, and when forecasting likely future developments.

While it is important to understand and interpret financial statements, sound financial analysis involves more than just calculating and interpreting numbers. Good analysts recognize that certain qualitative factors must be considered when evaluating a company. These factors, as summarized by the American Association of Individual Investors (AAII), are as follows:

1. *Are the company's revenues tied to one key customer?* If so, the company's performance may dramatically decline if the customer goes elsewhere. On the other hand, if the relationship is firmly entrenched, this might actually stabilize sales.

2. *To what extent are the company's revenues tied to one key product?* Companies that rely on a single product may be more efficient and more focused, but a lack of diversification does increase risk. If revenues come from several different products, the overall bottom line will be less affected by a drop in the demand for any one product.

3. *To what extent does the company rely on a single supplier?* Depending on a single supplier may lead to unanticipated shortages, which is something that investors and potential creditors need to assess.

4. *What percentage of the company's business is generated overseas?* Companies with a large percentage of overseas business are often able to realize higher growth and larger profit margins. However, firms with large overseas operations find that the value of their operations depends in large part on the value of the local currency. Thus, fluctuations in currency markets create additional risks for firms with large overseas operations.

5. *Competition.* Generally, increased competition lowers prices and profit margins. In forecasting future performance, it is important to assess both the likely actions of the current competition and the likelihood of new competitors in the future.

6. *Future prospects.* Does the company invest heavily in research and development? If so, its future prospects may depend critically on the success of new products in the pipeline. For example, the market's assessment of a computer company depends on what next year's products look like. Likewise, investors in pharmaceutical companies are interested in knowing whether the company has developed any "breakthrough" drugs that may be marketable in the years ahead.

7. *Legal and regulatory environment.* Changes in laws and regulations have important implications for many industries. For example, when forecasting the future of tobacco companies, it is crucial that an analyst factor in the effects of proposed regulations and pending or likely lawsuits. Likewise, when assessing banks, telecommunications firms, and electric utilities, analysts need to forecast both the extent to which these industries will be regulated in the years ahead and the ability of individual firms to respond to changes in regulation.

SELF-TEST QUESTION

What are some qualitative factors analysts should consider when evaluating a company's likely future financial performance?

SUMMARY

The primary purpose of this chapter was to discuss techniques used by investors and managers to analyze financial statements. The key concepts covered are listed below.

- **Financial statement analysis** generally begins with the calculation of a set of **financial ratios** designed to reveal the relative strengths and weaknesses of a company as compared with other companies in the same industry, and to show whether its financial position has been improving or deteriorating over time.
- **Liquidity ratios** show the relationship of a firm's current assets to its current liabilities, and thus its ability to meet maturing debts.
- Two commonly used liquidity ratios are the **current ratio** and the **quick,** or **acid test, ratio.**
- **Asset management ratios** measure how effectively a firm is managing its assets.
- Asset management ratios include **inventory turnover, days sales outstanding, fixed assets turnover,** and **total assets turnover.**
- **Debt management ratios** reveal (1) the extent to which the firm is financed with debt and (2) its likelihood of defaulting on its debt obligations.
- Debt management ratios include the **debt ratio, times-interest-earned ratio,** and **fixed charge coverage ratio.**
- **Profitability ratios** show the combined effects of liquidity, asset management, and debt management policies on operating results.
- Profitability ratios include the **profit margin on sales,** the **basic earning power ratio,** the **return on total assets,** and the **return on common equity.**
- **Market value ratios** relate the firm's stock price to its earnings and book value per share, and they give management an indication of what investors think of the company's past performance and future prospects.
- Market value ratios include the **price/earnings ratio** and the **market/book ratio.**
- **Trend analysis,** where one plots a ratio over time, is important, because it reveals whether the firm's ratios are improving or deteriorating over time.
- The **Du Pont system** is designed to show how the profit margin on sales, the assets turnover ratio, and the use of debt interact to determine the rate of return on equity. The firm's management can use the Du Pont system to analyze ways of improving the firm's performance.
- **Benchmarking** is the process of comparing a particular company with a group of "benchmark" companies.
- In analyzing a small firm's financial position, ratio analysis is a useful starting point. However, the analyst must also (1) examine the quality of the financial data, (2) ensure that the firm is sufficiently diversified to withstand shifts in customers' buying habits, and (3) determine whether the firm has a plan for the succession of its management.

Ratio analysis has limitations, but used with care and judgment, it can be very helpful.

QUESTIONS

3-1 Financial ratio analysis is conducted by four groups of analysts: managers, equity investors, long-term creditors, and short-term creditors. What is the primary emphasis of each of these groups in evaluating ratios?

3-2 Why would the inventory turnover ratio be more important when analyzing a grocery chain than an insurance company?

3-3 Over the past year, M. D. Ryngaert & Co. has realized an increase in its current ratio and a drop in its total assets turnover ratio. However, the company's sales, quick ratio, and fixed assets turnover ratio have remained constant. What explains these changes?

3-4 Profit margins and turnover ratios vary from one industry to another. What differences would you expect to find between a grocery chain such as Safeway and a steel company? Think particularly about the turnover ratios, the profit margin, and the Du Pont equation.

3-5 How does inflation distort ratio analysis comparisons, both for one company over time (trend analysis) and when different companies are compared? Are only balance sheet items or both balance sheet and income statement items affected?

3-6 If a firm's ROE is low and management wants to improve it, explain how using more debt might help.

3-7 How might (a) seasonal factors and (b) different growth rates distort a comparative ratio analysis? Give some examples. How might these problems be alleviated?

3-8 Why is it sometimes misleading to compare a company's financial ratios with other firms which operate in the same industry?

3-9 Indicate the effects of the transactions listed in the following table on total current assets, current ratio, and net income. Use $(+)$ to indicate an increase, $(-)$ to indicate a decrease, and (0) to indicate either no effect or an indeterminate effect. Be prepared to state any necessary assumptions, and assume an initial current ratio of more than 1.0. (Note: A good accounting background is necessary to answer some of these questions; if yours is not strong, just answer the questions you can handle.)

	TOTAL CURRENT ASSETS	CURRENT RATIO	EFFECT ON NET INCOME
a. Cash is acquired through issuance of additional common stock.	_____	_____	_____
b. Merchandise is sold for cash.	_____	_____	_____
c. Federal income tax due for the previous year is paid.	_____	_____	_____
d. A fixed asset is sold for less than book value.	_____	_____	_____
e. A fixed asset is sold for more than book value.	_____	_____	_____
f. Merchandise is sold on credit.	_____	_____	_____
g. Payment is made to trade creditors for previous purchases.	_____	_____	_____
h. A cash dividend is declared and paid.	_____	_____	_____
i. Cash is obtained through short-term bank loans.	_____	_____	_____
j. Short-term notes receivable are sold at a discount.	_____	_____	_____
k. Marketable securities are sold below cost.	_____	_____	_____
l. Advances are made to employees.	_____	_____	_____
m. Current operating expenses are paid.	_____	_____	_____

	TOTAL CURRENT ASSETS	CURRENT RATIO	EFFECT ON NET INCOME
n. Short-term promissory notes are issued to trade creditors in exchange for past due accounts payable.	_____	_____	_____
o. Ten-year notes are issued to pay off accounts payable.	_____	_____	_____
p. A fully depreciated asset is retired.	_____	_____	_____
q. Accounts receivable are collected.	_____	_____	_____
r. Equipment is purchased with short-term notes.	_____	_____	_____
s. Merchandise is purchased on credit.	_____	_____	_____
t. The estimated taxes payable are increased.	_____	_____	_____

SELF-TEST PROBLEMS (Solutions Appear in Appendix B)

ST-1
Key terms

Define each of the following terms:
a. Liquidity ratios: current ratio; quick, or acid test, ratio
b. Asset management ratios: inventory turnover ratio; days sales outstanding (DSO); fixed assets turnover ratio; total assets turnover ratio
c. Financial leverage: debt ratio; times-interest-earned (TIE) ratio; fixed charge coverage ratio
d. Profitability ratios: profit margin on sales; basic earning power (BEP) ratio; return on total assets (ROA); return on common equity (ROE)
e. Market value ratios: price/earnings (P/E) ratio; market/book (M/B) ratio; book value per share
f. Trend analysis; comparative ratio analysis; benchmarking
g. Du Pont chart; Du Pont equation
h. "Window dressing"; seasonal effects on ratios

ST-2
Debt ratio

K. Billingsworth & Co. had earnings per share of $4 last year, and it paid a $2 dividend. Total retained earnings increased by $12 million during the year, while book value per share at year-end was $40. Billingsworth has no preferred stock, and no new common stock was issued during the year. If Billingsworth's year-end debt (which equals its total liabilities) was $120 million, what was the company's year-end debt/assets ratio?

ST-3
Ratio analysis

The following data apply to A.L. Kaiser & Company (millions of dollars):

Cash and marketable securities	$100.00
Fixed assets	$283.50
Sales	$1,000.00
Net income	$50.00
Quick ratio	2.0×
Current ratio	3.0×
DSO	40 days
ROE	12%

Kaiser has no preferred stock — only common equity, current liabilities, and long-term debt.
a. Find Kaiser's (1) accounts receivable (A/R), (2) current liabilities, (3) current assets, (4) total assets, (5) ROA, (6) common equity, and (7) long-term debt.
b. In Part a, you should have found Kaiser's accounts receivable (A/R) = $111.1 million. If Kaiser could reduce its DSO from 40 days to 30 days while holding other things constant, how much cash would it generate? If this cash were used to buy back common stock (at book value), thus reducing the amount of common equity, how would this affect (1) the ROE, (2) the ROA, and (3) the total debt/total assets ratio?

STARTER PROBLEMS

3-1
Liquidity ratios

Ace Industries has current assets equal to $3 million. The company's current ratio is 1.5, and its quick ratio is 1.0. What is the firm's level of current liabilities? What is the firm's level of inventories?

3-2
Days sales outstanding

Baker Brothers has a DSO of 40 days. The company's average daily sales are $20,000. What is the level of its accounts receivable? Assume there are 360 days in a year.

3-3
Debt ratio

Bartley Barstools has an equity multiplier of 2.4. The company's assets are financed with some combination of long-term debt and common equity. What is the company's debt ratio?

3-4
Du Pont analysis

Doublewide Dealers has an ROA of 10 percent, a 2 percent profit margin, and a return on equity equal to 15 percent. What is the company's total assets turnover? What is the firm's equity multiplier?

EXAM-TYPE PROBLEMS

The problems included in this section are set up in such a way that they could be used as multiple-choice exam problems.

3-5
Ratio calculations

Assume you are given the following relationships for the Brauer Corporation:

Sales/total assets	1.5×
Return on assets (ROA)	3%
Return on equity (ROE)	5%

Calculate Brauer's profit margin and debt ratio.

3-6
Liquidity ratios

The Petry Company has $1,312,500 in current assets and $525,000 in current liabilities. Its initial inventory level is $375,000, and it will raise funds as additional notes payable and use them to increase inventory. How much can Petry's short-term debt (notes payable) increase without pushing its current ratio below 2.0? What will be the firm's quick ratio after Petry has raised the maximum amount of short-term funds?

3-7
Ratio calculations

The Kretovich Company had a quick ratio of 1.4, a current ratio of 3.0, an inventory turnover of 6 times, total current assets of $810,000, and cash and marketable securities of $120,000 in 1997. What were Kretovich's annual sales and its DSO for that year?

3-8
Times-interest-earned ratio

The H.R. Pickett Corporation has $500,000 of debt outstanding, and it pays an interest rate of 10 percent annually. Pickett's annual sales are $2 million, its average tax rate is 30 percent, and its net profit margin on sales is 5 percent. If the company does not maintain a TIE ratio of at least 5 times, its bank will refuse to renew the loan, and bankruptcy will result. What is Pickett's TIE ratio?

3-9
Return on equity

Midwest Packaging's ROE last year was only 3 percent, but its management has developed a new operating plan designed to improve things. The new plan calls for a total debt ratio of 60 percent, which will result in interest charges of $300,000 per year. Management projects an EBIT of $1,000,000 on sales of $10,000,000, and it expects to have a total assets turnover ratio of 2.0. Under these conditions, the tax rate will be 34 percent. If the changes are made, what return on equity will the company earn?

3-10
Return on equity

Central City Construction Company, which is just being formed, needs $1 million of assets, and it expects to have a basic earning power ratio of 20 percent. Central City will own no securities, so all of its income will be operating income. If it chooses to, Central City can finance up to 50 percent of its assets with debt, which will have an 8 percent interest rate. Assuming a 40 percent federal-plus-state tax rate on all taxable income, what is the *difference* between its expected ROE if Central City finances with 50 percent debt versus its expected ROE if it finances entirely with common stock?

3-11
Conceptual: Return on equity

Which of the following statements is most correct? (Hint: Work Problem 3-10 before answering 3-11, and consider the solution setup for 3-10 as you think about 3-11.)
a. If a firm's expected basic earning power (BEP) is constant for all of its assets and exceeds the interest rate on its debt, then adding assets and financing them with debt will raise the firm's expected rate of return on common equity (ROE).
b. The higher its tax rate, the lower a firm's BEP ratio will be, other things held constant.

c. The higher the interest rate on its debt, the lower a firm's BEP ratio will be, other things held constant.

d. The higher its debt ratio, the lower a firm's BEP ratio will be, other things held constant.

e. Statement a is false, but b, c, and d are all true.

3-12
Return on equity

Lloyd and Daughters Inc. has sales of $200,000, a net income of $15,000, and the following balance sheet:

Cash	$ 10,000	Accounts payable	$ 30,000
Receivables	50,000	Other current liabilities	20,000
Inventories	150,000	Long-term debt	50,000
Net fixed assets	90,000	Common equity	200,000
Total assets	$300,000	Total liabilities and equity	$300,000

a. The company's new owner thinks that inventories are excessive and can be lowered to the point where the current ratio is equal to the industry average, 2.5×, without affecting either sales or net income. If inventories are sold off and not replaced so as to reduce the current ratio to 2.5×, if the funds generated are used to reduce common equity (stock can be repurchased at book value), and if no other changes occur, by how much will the ROE change?

b. Now suppose we wanted to take this problem and modify it for use on an exam, that is, to create a new problem which you have not seen to test your knowledge of this type of problem. How would your answer change if (1) We doubled all the dollar amounts? (2) We stated that the target current ratio was 3×? (3) We stated that the target was to achieve an inventory turnover ratio of 2× rather than a current ratio of 2.5×? (Hint: Compare the ROE obtained with an inventory turnover ratio of 2× to the original ROE obtained before any changes are considered.) (4) We said that the company had 10,000 shares of stock outstanding, and we asked how much the change in Part a would increase EPS? (5) What would your answer to (4) be if we changed the original problem to state that the stock was selling for twice book value, so common equity would not be reduced on a dollar-for-dollar basis?

c. Now explain how we could have set the problem up to have you focus on changing accounts receivable, or fixed assets, or using the funds generated to retire debt (we would give you the interest rate on outstanding debt), or how the original problem could have stated that the company needed *more* inventories and it would finance them with new common equity or with new debt.

PROBLEMS

3-13
Ratio analysis

Data for Barry Computer Company and its industry averages follow.
a. Calculate the indicated ratios for Barry.
b. Construct the extended Du Pont equation for both Barry and the industry.
c. Outline Barry's strengths and weaknesses as revealed by your analysis.
d. Suppose Barry had doubled its sales as well as its inventories, accounts receivable, and common equity during 1997. How would that information affect the validity of your ratio analysis? (Hint: Think about averages and the effects of rapid growth on ratios if averages are not used. No calculations are needed.)

BARRY COMPUTER COMPANY: BALANCE SHEET AS OF DECEMBER 31, 1997 (IN THOUSANDS)

Cash	$ 77,500	Accounts payable	$ 129,000
Receivables	336,000	Notes payable	84,000
Inventories	241,500	Other current liabilities	117,000
Total current assets	$ 655,000	Total current liabilities	$ 330,000
Net fixed assets	292,500	Long-term debt	256,500
		Common equity	361,000
Total assets	$ 947,500	Total liabilities and equity	$ 947,500

BARRY COMPUTER COMPANY: INCOME STATEMENT FOR YEAR ENDED DECEMBER 31, 1997 (IN THOUSANDS)

Sales		$1,607,500
Cost of goods sold		
Materials	$717,000	
Labor	453,000	
Heat, light, and power	68,000	
Indirect labor	113,000	
Depreciation	41,500	1,392,500
Gross profit		$ 215,000
Selling expenses		115,000
General and administrative expenses		30,000
Earnings before interest and taxes (EBIT)		$ 70,000
Interest expense		24,500
Earnings before taxes (EBT)		$ 45,500
Federal and state income taxes (40%)		18,200
Net income		$ 27,300

RATIO	BARRY	INDUSTRY AVERAGE
Current assets/current liabilities	_____	2.0×
Days sales outstanding	_____	35 days
Sales/inventories	_____	6.7×
Sales/total assets	_____	3.0×
Net income/sales	_____	1.2%
Net income/total assets	_____	3.6%
Net income/common equity	_____	9.0%
Total debt/total assets	_____	60.0%

3-14
Balance sheet analysis

Complete the balance sheet and sales information in the table that follows for Hoffmeister Industries using the following financial data:

Debt ratio: 50%
Quick ratio: 0.80×
Total assets turnover: 1.5×
Days sales outstanding: 36 days
Gross profit margin on sales: (Sales − Cost of goods sold)/Sales = 25%
Inventory turnover ratio: 5×

BALANCE SHEET

Cash	_____		Accounts payable	_____
Accounts receivable	_____		Long-term debt	60,000
Inventories	_____		Common stock	_____
Fixed assets	_____		Retained earnings	97,500
Total assets	$300,000		Total liabilities and equity	_____
Sales	_____		Cost of goods sold	_____

3-15
Du Pont analysis

The Ferri Furniture Company, a manufacturer and wholesaler of high-quality home furnishings, has been experiencing low profitability in recent years. As a result, the board of directors has replaced the president of the firm with a new president, Helen Adams, who has asked you to make an analysis of the firm's financial position using the Du Pont chart. The most recent industry average ratios, and Ferri's financial statements, are as follows:

INDUSTRY AVERAGE RATIOS

Current ratio	2×	Sales/fixed assets	6×
Debt/total assets	30%	Sales/total assets	3×
Times-interest-earned	7×	Profit margin on sales	3%
Sales/inventory	10×	Return on total assets	9%
Days sales outstanding	24 days	Return on common equity	12.9%

FERRI FURNITURE COMPANY: BALANCE SHEET AS OF DECEMBER 31, 1997 (MILLIONS OF DOLLARS)

Cash	$ 45	Accounts payable	$ 45
Marketable securities	33	Notes payable	45
Net receivables	66	Other current liabilities	21
Inventories	159	Total current liabilities	$111
Total current assets	$303	Long-term debt	24
		Total liabilities	$135
Gross fixed assets	225		
Less depreciation	78	Common stock	114
Net fixed assets	$147	Retained earnings	201
		Total stockholders' equity	$315
Total assets	$450	Total liabilities and equity	$450

FERRI FURNITURE COMPANY: INCOME STATEMENT FOR YEAR ENDED DECEMBER 31, 1997 (MILLIONS OF DOLLARS)

Net sales	$795.0
Cost of goods sold	660.0
Gross profit	$135.0
Selling expenses	73.5
Depreciation expense	12.0
Earnings before interest and taxes	$ 49.5
Interest expense	4.5
Earnings before taxes (EBT)	45.0
Taxes (40%)	18.0
Net income	$ 27.0

a. Calculate those ratios that you think would be useful in this analysis.
b. Construct an extended Du Pont equation for Ferri, and compare the company's ratios to the industry average ratios.
c. Do the balance sheet accounts or the income statement figures seem to be primarily responsible for the low profits?
d. Which specific accounts seem to be most out of line in relation to other firms in the industry?
e. If Ferri had a pronounced seasonal sales pattern, or if it grew rapidly during the year, how might that affect the validity of your ratio analysis? How might you correct for such potential problems?

3-16

Ratio analysis

The Corrigan Corporation's forecasted 1998 financial statements follow, along with some industry average ratios.

a. Calculate Corrigan's 1998 forecasted ratios, compare them with the industry average data, and comment briefly on Corrigan's projected strengths and weaknesses.

b. What do you think would happen to Corrigan's ratios if the company initiated cost-cutting measures that allowed it to hold lower levels of inventory and substantially decreased the cost of goods sold? No calculations are necessary. Think about which ratios would be affected by changes in these two accounts.

CORRIGAN CORPORATION: FORECASTED BALANCE SHEET AS OF DECEMBER 31, 1998

Cash	$ 72,000
Accounts receivable	439,000
Inventories	894,000
Total current assets	$1,405,000
Land and building	238,000
Machinery	132,000
Other fixed assets	61,000
Total assets	$1,836,000
Accounts and notes payable	$ 432,000
Accruals	170,000
Total current liabilities	$ 602,000
Long-term debt	404,290
Common stock	575,000
Retained earnings	254,710
Total liabilities and equity	$1,836,000

CORRIGAN CORPORATION: FORECASTED INCOME STATEMENT FOR 1998

Sales	$4,290,000
Cost of goods sold	3,580,000
Gross operating profit	$ 710,000
General administrative and selling expenses	236,320
Depreciation	159,000
Miscellaneous	134,000
Earnings before taxes (EBT)	$ 180,680
Taxes (40%)	72,272
Net income	$ 108,408
Per-Share Data	
EPS	$4.71
Cash dividends	$0.95
P/E ratio	5×
Market price (average)	$23.57
Number of shares outstanding	23,000

INDUSTRY FINANCIAL RATIOS (1998)[a]

Quick ratio	1.0×
Current ratio	2.7×
Inventory turnover[b]	7.0×
Days sales outstanding	32 days
Fixed assets turnover[b]	13.0×
Total assets turnover[b]	2.6×
Return on assets	9.1%
Return on equity	18.2%
Debt ratio	50.0%
Profit margin on sales	3.5%
P/E ratio	6.0×

[a]Industry average ratios have been constant for the past 4 years.
[b]Based on year-end balance sheet figures.

I N T E G R A T E D   C A S E

D'LEON INC., PART II

3-17 Financial Statement Analysis Part I of this case, presented in Chapter 2, discussed the situation that D'Leon Inc., a regional snack foods producer, was in after an expansion program. D'Leon had increased plant capacity and undertaken a major marketing campaign in an attempt to "go national." Thus far, sales have not been up to the forecasted level, costs have been higher than were projected, and a large loss occurred in 1997 rather than the expected profit. As a result, its managers, directors, and investors are concerned about the firm's survival.

Donna Jamison was brought in as assistant to Fred Campo, D'Leon's chairman, who had the task of getting the company back into a sound financial position. D'Leon's 1996 and 1997 balance sheets and income statements, together with projections for 1998, are given in Tables IC3-1 and IC3-2. In addition, Table IC3-3 gives the company's 1996 and 1997 financial ratios, together with industry average data. The 1998 projected financial statement data represent Jamison's and Campo's best guess for 1998 results, assuming that some new financing is arranged to get the company "over the hump."

Jamison examined monthly data for 1997 (not given in the case), and she detected an improving pattern during the year. Monthly sales were rising, costs were falling, and large losses in the early months had turned to a small profit by December. Thus, the annual data look somewhat worse than final monthly data. Also, it appears to be taking longer for the advertising program to get the message across, for the new sales offices to generate sales, and for the new manufacturing facilities to operate efficiently. In other words, the lags between spending money and deriving benefits were longer than D'Leon's managers had anticipated. For these reasons, Jami-

son and Campo see hope for the company — provided it can survive in the short run.

Jamison must prepare an analysis of where the company is now, what it must do to regain its financial health, and what actions should be taken. Your assignment is to help her answer the following questions. Provide clear explanations, not yes or no answers.

a. Why are ratios useful? What are the five major categories of ratios?
b. Calculate D'Leon's 1998 current and quick ratios based on the projected balance sheet and income statement data. What can you say about the company's liquidity position in 1996, 1997, and as projected for 1998? We often think of ratios as being useful (1) to managers to help run the business, (2) to bankers for credit analysis, and (3) to stockholders for stock valuation. Would these different types of analysts have an equal interest in the liquidity ratios?
c. Calculate the 1998 inventory turnover, days sales outstanding (DSO), fixed assets turnover, and total assets turnover. How does D'Leon's utilization of assets stack up against other firms in its industry?
d. Calculate the 1998 debt, times-interest-earned, and fixed charge coverage ratios. How does D'Leon compare with the industry with respect to financial leverage? What can you conclude from these ratios?
e. Calculate the 1998 profit margin, basic earning power (BEP), return on assets (ROA), and return on equity (ROE). What can you say about these ratios?
f. Calculate the 1998 price/earnings ratio and market/book ratio. Do these ratios indicate that investors are expected to have a high or low opinion of the company?
g. Use the extended Du Pont equation to provide a summary and overview of D'Leon's financial condition as projected

TABLE IC 3-1   Balance Sheets

	1998E	1997	1996
Assets			
Cash	$ 85,632	$ 7,282	$ 57,600
Accounts receivable	878,000	632,160	351,200
Inventories	1,716,480	1,287,360	715,200
Total current assets	$2,680,112	$1,926,802	$1,124,000
Gross fixed assets	1,197,160	1,202,950	491,000
Less accumulated depreciation	380,120	263,160	146,200
Net fixed assets	$ 817,040	$ 939,790	$ 344,800
Total assets	$3,497,152	$2,866,592	$1,468,800
Liabilities and Equity			
Accounts payable	$ 436,800	$ 524,160	$ 145,600
Notes payable	600,000	720,000	200,000
Accruals	408,000	489,600	136,000
Total current liabilities	$1,444,800	$1,733,760	$ 481,600
Long-term debt	500,000	1,000,000	323,432
Common stock	1,680,936	460,000	460,000
Retained earnings	(128,584)	(327,168)	203,768
Total equity	$1,552,352	$ 132,832	$ 663,768
Total liabilities and equity	$3,497,152	$2,866,592	$1,468,800

NOTE: "E" indicates estimated. The 1998 data are forecasts.

for 1998. What are the firm's major strengths and weaknesses?

h. Use the following simplified 1998 balance sheet to show, in general terms, how an improvement in the DSO would tend to affect the stock price. For example, if the company could improve its collection procedures and thereby lower its DSO from 44.9 days to the 32-day industry average without affecting sales, how would that change "ripple through" the financial statements (shown in thousands below) and influence the stock price?

Accounts receivable	$ 878	Debt	$1,945
Other current assets	1,802		
Net fixed assets	817	Equity	1,552
Total assets	$3,497	Liabilities plus equity	$3,497

i. Does it appear that inventories could be adjusted, and, if so, how should that adjustment affect D'Leon's profitability and stock price?

j. In 1997, the company paid its suppliers much later than the due dates, and it was not maintaining financial ratios at levels called for in its bank loan agreements. Therefore, suppliers could cut the company off, and its bank could refuse to renew the loan when it comes due in 90 days. On the basis of data provided, would you, as a credit manager, continue to sell to D'Leon on credit? (You could demand cash on delivery, that is, sell on terms of COD, but that might cause D'Leon to stop buying from your company.) Similarly, if you were the bank loan officer, would you recommend renewing the loan or demand its repayment? Would your actions be influenced if, in early 1998, D'Leon showed you its 1998 projections plus proof that it was going to raise over $1.2 million of new equity capital?

k. In hindsight, what should D'Leon have done back in 1996?

l. What are some potential problems and limitations of financial ratio analysis?

m. What are some qualitative factors analysts should consider when evaluating a company's likely future financial performance?

TABLE IC 3 - 2	Income Statements		

	1998E	1997	1996
Sales	$7,035,600	$5,834,400	$3,432,000
Cost of goods sold	5,728,000	5,728,000	2,864,000
Other expenses	680,000	680,000	340,000
Depreciation	116,960	116,960	18,900
Total operating costs	$6,524,960	$6,524,960	$3,222,900
EBIT	$ 510,640	($ 690,560)	$ 209,100
Interest expense	88,000	176,000	62,500
EBT	$ 422,640	($ 866,560)	$ 146,600
Taxes (40%)	169,056	(346,624)	58,640
Net income	$ 253,584	($ 519,936)	$ 87,960
EPS	$1.014	($5.199)	$0.880
DPS	$0.220	$0.110	$0.220
Book value per share	$6.209	$1.328	$6.638
Stock price	$12.17	$2.25	$8.50
Shares outstanding	250,000	100,000	100,000
Tax rate	40.00%	40.00%	40.00%
Lease payments	40,000	40,000	40,000
Sinking fund payments	0	0	0

NOTE: "E" indicates estimated. The 1998 data are forecasts.

TABLE IC 3 - 3	Ratio Analysis		

	1998E	1997	1996	INDUSTRY AVERAGE
Current		1.1×	2.3×	2.7×
Quick		0.4×	0.8×	1.0×
Inventory turnover		4.5×	4.8×	6.1×
Days sales outstanding (DSO)		39.0	36.8	32.0
Fixed assets turnover		6.2×	10.0×	7.0×
Total assets turnover		2.0×	2.3×	2.6×
Debt ratio		95.4%	54.8%	50.0%
TIE		−3.9×	3.3×	6.2×
Fixed charge coverage		−3.0×	2.4×	5.1×
Profit margin		−8.9%	2.6%	3.5%
Basic earning power		−24.1%	14.2%	19.1%
ROA		−18.1%	6.0%	9.1%
ROE		−391.4%	13.3%	18.2%
Price/earnings		−0.4×	9.7×	14.2×
Market/book		1.7×	1.3×	2.4×
Book value per share		$1.33	$6.64	n.a.

NOTE: "E" indicates estimated. The 1998 data are forecasts.

COMPUTER-RELATED PROBLEM

Work the problem in this section only if you are using the computer problem diskette.

3-18

Ratio analysis

Use the computerized model in the File C3 to solve this problem.

a. Refer back to Problem 3-16. Suppose Corrigan Corporation is considering installing a new computer system which would provide tighter control of inventories, accounts receivable, and accounts payable. If the new system is installed, the following data are projected (rather than the data given in Problem 3-16) for the indicated balance sheet and income statement accounts:

Accounts receivable	$ 395,000
Inventories	700,000
Other fixed assets	150,000
Accounts and notes payable	275,000
Accruals	120,000
Cost of goods sold	3,450,000
Administrative and selling expenses	248,775
P/E ratio	6×

How do these changes affect the projected ratios and the comparison with the industry averages? (Note that any changes to the income statement will change the amount of retained earnings; therefore, the model is set up to calculate 1998 retained earnings as 1997 retained earnings plus net income minus dividends paid. The model also adjusts the cash balance so that the balance sheet balances.)

b. If the new computer were even more efficient than Corrigan's management had estimated, and thus caused the cost of goods sold to decrease by $125,000 from the projections in Part a, what effect would that have on the company's financial position?

c. If the new computer were less efficient than Corrigan's management had estimated, and caused the cost of goods sold to increase by $125,000 from the projections in Part a, what effect would that have on the company's financial position?

d. Change, one by one, the other items in Part a to see how each change affects the ratio analysis. Then think about, and write a paragraph describing, how computer models like this one can be used to help make better decisions about the purchase of such things as a new computer system.

CHAPTER 4

THE FINANCIAL ENVIRONMENT: MARKETS, INSTITUTIONS, AND INTEREST RATES

Financial managers and investors do not operate in a vacuum — they make decisions within a large and complex financial environment. This environment includes financial markets and institutions, tax and regulatory policies, and the state of the economy. The environment both dictates the available financial alternatives and affects the outcomes of various decisions. Therefore, it is crucial that financial managers and investors have a good understanding of the environment in which they operate.

Good financial decisions require an understanding of the current and future direction of the economy, interest rates, and the stock market — but trying to figure out what is going to happen is no trivial matter. One tool analysts use to forecast the future direction of the economy and interest rates is the yield curve. As you will see later in this chapter, the yield curve is a graph that shows the relationship between short-term and long-term interest rates. Studies indicate that if long-term rates are considerably higher than short-term rates, future inflation and interest rates are likely to increase. On the other hand, if long-term rates are lower than short-term rates, this suggests that an economic downturn is coming.

Management's assessment of future inflation has a profound effect on financing decisions. If management is convinced that inflation will not be a problem, it will probably rely on short-term funds to raise new capital. However, if inflation seems likely to accelerate, this sug- gests higher interest rates in the future, so management will be inclined to "lock in" current rates by using long-term debt.

For example, JCPenney recently issued $600 million of long-term debt in three parts: $200 million matured in 12 years and had a cost of 7.38 percent, $200 million had a 20-year maturity and cost 7.65 percent, and $200 million matured in 30 years and had a cost of 6.90 percent. The 30-year portion also gives investors an option to sell the bonds back to the company if interest rates rise, which explains the lower cost of these bonds.

In a press release, Penney indicated that it planned to use the $600 million to pay off some of its outstanding commercial paper. (Commercial paper is a short-term security that financially strong companies use to borrow from the public.) At the time of the Penney issue, the commercial paper rate was 5.5 percent. Why would a company issue long-term debt at more than 7 percent to pay off short-term debt that cost only 5.5 percent? Clearly, Penney was afraid interest rates would rise in the future, which would drive up the cost of funds when it comes time to roll over, or replace, the short-term commercial paper. By locking in long-term rates today, the company protected itself against an increase in interest rates. Of course, if rates remain at current levels or decline, Penney's decision will turn out to be a mistake. We will find out in the years ahead if Penney made a good decision.

Financial managers need to understand the environment and markets within which businesses operate. Therefore, this chapter describes the markets where capital is raised, securities are traded, and stock prices are established, as well as the institutions which operate in these markets. In the process, we shall also explore the principal factors that determine the level of interest rates in the economy.

THE FINANCIAL MARKETS

Businesses, individuals, and governments often need to raise capital. For example, suppose Carolina Power & Light (CP&L) forecasts an increase in the demand for electricity in North Carolina, and the company decides to build a new power plant. Because CP&L almost certainly will not have the $2 billion or so necessary to pay for the plant, the company will have to raise this capital in the financial markets. Or suppose Mr. Fong, the proprietor of a San Francisco hardware store, decides to expand into appliances. Where will he get the money to buy the initial inventory of TV sets, washers, and freezers? Similarly, if the Johnson family wants to buy a home that costs $100,000, but they have only $20,000 in savings, how can they raise the additional $80,000? If the city of New York wants to borrow $200 million to finance a new sewer plant, or the federal government needs more than $100 billion to cover its projected 1997 deficit, they too need access to the capital markets.

On the other hand, some individuals and firms have incomes which are greater than their current expenditures, so they have funds available to invest. For example, Carol Hawk has an income of $36,000, but her expenses are only $30,000, and in 1997 Ford Motor Company had accumulated more than $19 billion of excess cash, which it needs to invest.

TYPES OF MARKETS

People and organizations wanting to borrow money are brought together with those having surplus funds in the *financial markets*. Note that "markets" is plural — there are a great many different financial markets in a developed economy such as ours. Each market deals with a somewhat different type of instrument in terms of the instrument's maturity and the assets backing it. Also, different markets serve different types of customers, or operate in different parts of the country. Here are some of the major types of markets:

1. *Physical asset markets* (also called "tangible" or "real" asset markets) are those for such products as wheat, autos, real estate, computers, and machinery. *Financial asset markets,* on the other hand, deal with stocks, bonds, notes, mortgages, and other *claims on real assets*, as well as with *derivative securities* whose values are *derived* from changes in the prices of other assets.

2. *Spot markets* and *futures markets* are terms that refer to whether the assets are being bought or sold for "on-the-spot" delivery (literally, within a few days) or for delivery at some future date, such as six months or a year into the future.

Money Markets
The financial markets in which funds are borrowed or loaned for short periods (less than one year).

3. **Money markets** are the markets for short-term, highly liquid debt securities. The New York and London money markets have long been the world's

Capital Markets
The financial markets for stocks and for long-term debt (one year or longer).

Primary Markets
Markets in which corporations raise capital by issuing new securities.

Secondary Markets
Markets in which securities and other financial assets are traded among investors after they have been issued by corporations.

largest, but Tokyo is rising rapidly. **Capital markets** are the markets for long-term debt and corporate stocks. The New York Stock Exchange, where the stocks of the largest U.S. corporations are traded, is a prime example of a capital market. There is no hard and fast rule on this, but when describing debt markets, "short term" generally means less than one year, "intermediate term" means one to five years, and "long term" means more than five years.

4. *Mortgage markets* deal with loans on residential, commercial, and industrial real estate, and on farmland, while *consumer credit markets* involve loans on autos and appliances, as well as loans for education, vacations, and so on.

5. *World, national, regional,* and *local markets* also exist. Thus, depending on an organization's size and scope of operations, it may be able to borrow all around the world, or it may be confined to a strictly local, even neighborhood, market.

6. **Primary markets** are the markets in which corporations raise new capital. If Microsoft were to sell a new issue of common stock to raise capital, this would be a primary market transaction. The corporation selling the newly created stock receives the proceeds from the sale in a primary market transaction. **Secondary markets** are markets in which existing, already outstanding, securities are traded among investors. Thus, if Jane Doe decided to buy 1,000 shares of AT&T stock, the purchase would occur in the secondary market. The New York Stock Exchange is a secondary market, since it deals in outstanding, as opposed to newly issued, stocks and bonds. Secondary markets also exist for mortgages, various other types of loans, and other financial assets. The corporation whose securities are being traded is not involved in a secondary market transaction and, thus, does not receive any funds from such a sale.

7. *Private markets*, where transactions are worked out directly between two parties, are differentiated from *public markets*, where standardized contracts are traded on organized exchanges. Bank loans and private placements of debt with insurance companies are examples of private market transactions. Since these transactions are private, they may be structured in any manner that appeals to the two parties. By contrast, securities that are issued in public markets (for example, common stock and corporate bonds) are ultimately held by a large number of individuals. Public securities must have fairly standardized contractual features, both to appeal to a broad range of investors and also because public investors cannot afford the time to study unique, nonstandardized contracts. Their diverse ownership also ensures that public securities are relatively liquid. Private market securities are, therefore, more tailor-made but less liquid, whereas public market securities are more liquid but subject to greater standardization.

Other classifications could be made, but this breakdown is sufficient to show that there are many types of financial markets. Also, note that the distinctions among markets are often blurred and unimportant, except as a general point of reference. For example, it makes little difference if a firm borrows for 11, 12, or 13 months, hence, whether we have a "money" or "capital" market transaction. You should recognize the big differences among types of markets, but don't get hung up trying to distinguish them at the boundaries.

A healthy economy is dependent on efficient transfers of funds from people who are net savers to firms and individuals who need capital. Without efficient transfers, the economy simply could not function: Carolina Power & Light could not raise capital, so Raleigh's citizens would have no electricity; the Johnson

TABLE 4-1 Summary of Major Market Instruments, Market Participants, and Security Characteristics

INSTRUMENT (1)	MARKET (2)	MAJOR PARTICIPANTS (3)	SECURITY CHARACTERISTICS		
			RISKINESS (4)	ORIGINAL MATURITY (5)	INTEREST RATE ON 1/3/97[a] (6)
U.S. Treasury bills	Money	Sold by U.S. Treasury to finance federal expenditures	Default-free	91 days to 1 year	5.0%
Banker's acceptances	Money	A firm's promise to pay, guaranteed by a bank	Low degree of risk if guaranteed by a strong bank	Up to 180 days	5.3
Commercial paper	Money	Issued by financially secure firms to large investors	Low default risk	Up to 270 days	5.5
Negotiable certificates of deposit (CDs)	Money	Issued by major money-center commercial banks to large investors	Default risk depends on the strength of the issuing bank	Up to 1 year	5.4
Money market mutual funds	Money	Invest in Treasury bills, CDs, and commercial paper; held by individuals and businesses	Low degree of risk	No specific maturity (instant liquidity)	4.9
Eurodollar market time deposits	Money	Issued by banks outside U.S.	Default risk depends on the strength of the issuing bank	Up to 1 year	5.4
Consumer credit loans	Money	Issued by banks/credit unions/finance companies to individuals	Risk is variable	Variable	Variable
U.S. Treasury notes and bonds	Capital	Issued by U.S. government	No default risk, but price will decline if interest rates rise	2 to 30 years	6.7

[a]The yield reported on money market mutual funds is from *The Wall Street Journal*. All other data are from the *Federal Reserve Statistical Release*. Money market rates assume a 3-month maturity. The corporate bond rate is for AAA-rated bonds.

ON THE WWW
Students can access current and historical interest rates and economic data as well as regional economic data for the states of Arkansas, Illinois, Indiana, Kentucky, Mississippi, Missouri, and Tennessee from the Federal Reserve Economic Data (FRED) site at http://www.stls.frb.org/fred/.

family would not have adequate housing; Carol Hawk would have no place to invest her savings; and so on. Obviously, the level of employment and productivity, hence our standard of living, would be much lower. Therefore, it is absolutely essential that our financial markets function efficiently — not only quickly, but also at a low cost.[1]

Table 4-1 gives a listing of the most important instruments traded in the various financial markets. The instruments are arranged from top to bottom in ascending order of typical length of maturity. As we go through the book, we will look in much more detail at many of the instruments listed in Table 4-1. For example, we will see that there are many varieties of corporate bonds, ranging

[1]As the countries of the former Soviet Union and other Eastern European nations move toward capitalism, just as much attention must be paid to the establishment of cost-efficient financial markets as to electrical power, transportation, communications, and other infrastructure systems. Economic efficiency is simply impossible without a good system for allocating capital within the economy.

| TABLE 4-1 | *continued* |

			SECURITY CHARACTERISTICS		
INSTRUMENT (1)	MARKET (2)	MAJOR PARTICIPANTS (3)	RISKINESS (4)	ORIGINAL MATURITY (5)	INTEREST RATE ON 1/3/97[a] (6)
Mortgages	Capital	Borrowings from commercial banks and S&Ls by individuals and businesses	Risk is variable	Up to 30 years	7.7%
State and local government bonds	Capital	Issued by state and local governments to individuals and institutional investors	Riskier than U.S. government securities, but exempt from most taxes	Up to 30 years	5.7
Corporate bonds	Capital	Issued by corporations to individuals and institutional investors	Riskier than U.S. government securities, but less risky than preferred and common stocks; varying degree of risk within bonds depending on strength of issuer	Up to 40 years[b]	7.4
Leases	Capital	Similar to debt in that firms can lease assets rather than borrow and then buy the assets	Risk similar to corporate bonds	Generally 3 to 20 years	Similar to bond yields
Preferred stocks	Capital	Issued by corporations to individuals and institutional investors	Riskier than corporate bonds, but less risky than common stock	Unlimited	6 to 8%
Common stocks[c]	Capital	Issued by corporations to individuals and institutional investors	Risky	Unlimited	10 to 15%

[b]Just recently, a few corporations have issued 100-year bonds; however, the majority have issued bonds with maturities less than 40 years.
[c]Common stocks are expected to provide a "return" in the form of dividends and capital gains rather than interest. Of course, if you buy a stock, your *actual* return may be considerably higher or lower than your *expected* return.

from "plain vanilla" bonds to bonds that are convertible into common stocks to bonds whose interest payments vary depending on the inflation rate. Still, the table gives an idea of the characteristics and costs of the instruments traded in the major financial markets.

RECENT TRENDS

Financial markets have experienced tremendous change during the 1980s and 1990s. Technological advances in computers and telecommunications, along with the globalization of banking and commerce, have led to deregulation, and this has increased competition throughout the world. The result is a much more efficient, internationally linked market, but one that is far more complex than we had a few years ago. While these developments have been largely positive, they have also created problems for policy makers. At a recent conference, Federal

Reserve Board Chairman Alan Greenspan stated that modern financial markets "expose national economies to shocks from new and unexpected sources, and with little if any lag." He went on to say that central banks must develop new ways to evaluate and limit risks to the financial system. Large amounts of capital move quickly around the world in response to changes in interest and exchange rates, and these movements can disrupt local institutions and economies.

With globalization has come the need for greater cooperation among regulators at the international level. Various committees are currently working to improve coordination, but the task is not easy. Factors that complicate coordination include (1) the differing structures of the various nations' banking and securities industries, (2) the trend in Europe toward financial service conglomerates, and (3) a reluctance on the part of individual countries to give up control over their national monetary policies. Still, regulators are unanimous about the need to close the gaps in the supervision of worldwide markets.

Derivative
Any financial asset whose value is derived from the value of some other "underlying" asset.

Another important trend in recent years has been the increased use of **derivatives**. A derivative is any security whose value is *derived* from the price of some other "underlying" asset. An option to buy IBM stock is a derivative, as is a contract to buy Japanese yen six months from now. The value of the IBM option depends on the price performance of IBM's stock, and the value of the Japanese yen "future" depends on the exchange rate between yen and dollars. The market for derivatives has grown faster than any other market in recent years, providing corporations with additional opportunities but also exposing them to new risks.

Derivatives can be used either to reduce risks or as speculative investments, which increase risk. As an example of a risk-reducing usage, suppose an importer's net income tends to fall whenever the dollar falls relative to the yen. That company could reduce its risk by purchasing derivatives which increase in value whenever the dollar declines. This would be called a *hedging operation,* and its purpose is to reduce risk exposure. Speculation, on the other hand, is done in the hope of high returns, but it raises risk exposure. For example, Procter & Gamble recently disclosed that it lost $150 million on derivative investments, and Orange County (California) went bankrupt as a result of derivatives speculation.

How does the introduction of derivative products influence the financial markets? The size and complexity of derivatives transactions concern regulators, academics, and members of Congress. Fed Chairman Greenspan noted that, in theory, derivatives should allow companies to manage risk better, but he stated that it is not clear whether recent innovations have "increased or decreased the inherent stability of the financial system." The use of derivatives will be discussed more fully in Chapter 19.

SELF-TEST QUESTIONS   ??????

Distinguish between physical asset markets and financial asset markets.

What is the difference between spot and futures markets?

Distinguish between money and capital markets.

What is the difference between primary and secondary markets?

Differentiate between private and public markets.

Why are financial markets essential for a healthy economy?

What are derivatives, and how is their value determined?

FINANCIAL INSTITUTIONS

Transfers of capital between savers and those who need capital take place in the three different ways diagrammed in Figure 4-1:

1. *Direct transfers* of money and securities, as shown in the top section, occur when a business sells its stocks or bonds directly to savers, without going through any type of financial institution. The business delivers its securities to savers, who in turn give the firm the money it needs.

2. As shown in the middle section, transfers may also go through an *investment banking house* such as Merrill Lynch, which serves as a middleman and facilitates the issuance of securities. The company sells its stocks or bonds to the investment bank, which, in turn, sells these same securities to savers. The businesses' securities and the savers' money merely "pass through" the investment banking house. However, the investment bank does buy and hold the securities for a period of time, so it is taking a risk — it may not be able to resell them to savers for as much as it paid. Because new securities are involved and the corporation receives the proceeds of the sale, this is a primary market transaction.

3. Transfers can also be made through a *financial intermediary* such as a bank or mutual fund. Here the intermediary obtains funds from savers and gives the savers in exchange its own securities. The intermediary then uses this money to purchase and then hold a business's securities. For example, a saver might give dollars to a bank, receiving from it a certificate of deposit, and then the bank might lend the money to a small business in the form of a mortgage loan. Thus, intermediaries literally create new forms of capital — in this case,

F I G U R E   4 - 1   Diagram of the Capital Formation Process

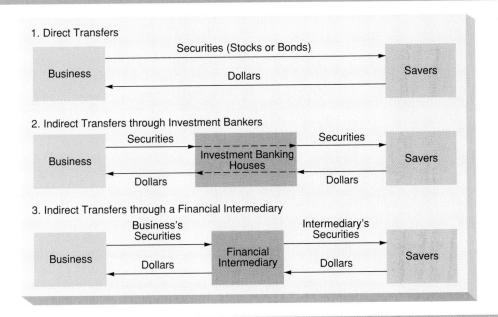

certificates of deposit, which are both safer and more liquid than mortgages and thus are better securities for most savers to hold. The existence of intermediaries greatly increases the efficiency of money and capital markets.

In our example, we assume that the entity needing capital is a business, and specifically a corporation, but it is easy to visualize the demander of capital as a home purchaser, a government unit, and so on.

Investment Banking House
An organization that underwrites and distributes new investment securities and helps businesses obtain financing.

Direct transfers of funds from savers to businesses are possible and do occur on occasion, but it is generally more efficient for a business to enlist the services of an **investment banking house.** Merrill Lynch, Salomon Brothers, Dean Witter, and Goldman Sachs are examples of financial service corporations which offer investment banking services. Such organizations (1) help corporations design securities with features that are currently attractive to investors, (2) buy these securities from the corporation, and (3) resell them to savers. Although the securities are sold twice, this process is really one primary market transaction, with the investment banker acting as a facilitator to help transfer capital from savers to businesses.

Financial Intermediaries
Specialized financial firms that facilitate the transfer of funds from savers to demanders of capital.

The **financial intermediaries** shown in the third section of Figure 4-1 do more than simply transfer money and securities between firms and savers — they literally create new financial products. Since the intermediaries are generally large, they gain economies of scale in analyzing the creditworthiness of potential borrowers, in processing and collecting loans, and in pooling risks and thus helping individual savers diversify, that is, "not put all their financial eggs in one basket." Further, a system of specialized intermediaries can enable savings to do more than just draw interest. For example, individuals can put money into banks and get both interest income and a convenient way of making payments (checking), or put money into life insurance companies and get both interest income and protection for their beneficiaries.

In the United States and other developed nations, a set of specialized, highly efficient financial intermediaries has evolved. The situation is changing rapidly, however, and different types of institutions are performing services that were formerly reserved for others, causing institutional distinctions to become blurred. Still, there is a degree of institutional identity, and here are the major classes of intermediaries:

1. *Commercial banks,* the traditional "department stores of finance," serve a wide variety of savers and borrowers. Historically, commercial banks were the major institutions which handled checking accounts and through which the Federal Reserve System expanded or contracted the money supply. Today, however, several other institutions also provide checking services and significantly influence the money supply. Conversely, commercial banks are providing an ever-widening range of services, including stock brokerage services and insurance.

   Note that commercial banks are quite different from investment banks. Commercial banks lend money, whereas investment banks help companies raise capital from other parties. Prior to 1933, commercial banks offered investment banking services, but the Glass-Steagall Act, which was passed in 1933, prohibited commercial banks from engaging in investment banking. Thus, the Morgan Bank was broken up into two separate organizations, one of which is now the Morgan Guaranty Trust Company, a commercial bank, while the other is Morgan Stanley, a major investment banking house. Note also that Japanese and European banks can offer both commercial and investment banking services. This hinders U.S. banks in global competition, so efforts are being made to get the Glass-Steagall Act repealed or modified.

2. *Savings and loan associations (S&Ls),* which have traditionally served individual savers and residential and commercial mortgage borrowers, take the funds of many small savers and then lend this money to home buyers and other types of borrowers. Because the savers obtain a degree of liquidity that would be absent if they made the mortgage loans directly, perhaps the most significant economic function of the S&Ls is to "create liquidity" which would otherwise be lacking. Also, the S&Ls have more expertise in analyzing credit, setting up loans, and making collections than individual savers, so they reduce the costs and increase the availability of real estate loans. Finally, the S&Ls hold large, diversified portfolios of loans and other assets and thus spread risks in a manner that would be impossible if small savers were making mortgage loans directly. Because of these factors, savers benefit by being able to invest in more liquid, better managed, and less risky assets, whereas borrowers benefit by being able to obtain more capital, and at a lower cost, than would otherwise be possible.

In the 1980s, the S&L industry experienced severe problems when (1) short-term interest rates paid on savings accounts rose well above the returns being earned on the existing mortgages held by S&Ls and (2) commercial real estate suffered a severe slump, resulting in high mortgage default rates. Together, these events forced many S&Ls to either merge with stronger institutions or close their doors.

3. *Mutual savings banks,* which are similar to S&Ls, operate primarily in the northeastern states, accept savings primarily from individuals, and lend mainly on a long-term basis to home buyers and consumers.

4. *Credit unions* are cooperative associations whose members are supposed to have a common bond, such as being employees of the same firm. Members' savings are loaned only to other members, generally for auto purchases, home improvement loans, and home mortgages. Credit unions are often the cheapest source of funds available to individual borrowers.

5. *Pension funds* are retirement plans funded by corporations or government agencies for their workers and administered primarily by the trust departments of commercial banks or by life insurance companies. Pension funds invest primarily in bonds, stocks, mortgages, and real estate.

6. *Life insurance companies* take savings in the form of annual premiums; invest these funds in stocks, bonds, real estate, and mortgages; and finally make payments to the beneficiaries of the insured parties. In recent years, life insurance companies have also offered a variety of tax-deferred savings plans designed to provide benefits to the participants when they retire.

7. *Mutual funds* are corporations which accept money from savers and then use these funds to buy stocks, long-term bonds, or short-term debt instruments issued by businesses or government units. These organizations pool funds and thus reduce risks by diversification. They also achieve economies of scale in analyzing securities, managing portfolios, and buying and selling securities. Different funds are designed to meet the objectives of different types of savers. Hence, there are bond funds for those who desire safety, stock funds for savers who are willing to accept significant risks in the hope of higher returns, and still other funds that are used as interest-bearing checking accounts (the **money market funds**). There are literally thousands of different mutual funds with dozens of different goals and purposes.

Mutual funds have grown more rapidly than any other institution in recent years, in large part because of a change in the way corporations provide

Money Market Fund
A mutual fund that invests in short-term, low-risk securities and allows investors to write checks against their accounts.

for employees' retirement. Before the 1980s, most corporations said, in effect, "Come work for us, and when you retire, we will give you a retirement income based on the salary you were earning during the last five years before you retired." The company was then responsible for setting aside funds each year to make sure that it had the money available to pay the agreed-upon retirement benefits. That situation is changing rapidly. Today, new employees are likely to be told, "Come work for us, and we will give you some money each payday which you can invest for your future retirement. You can't get the money until you retire (without paying a huge tax penalty), but if you invest wisely, you can retire in comfort." Most employees know they don't know how to invest wisely, so they turn their retirement funds over to a mutual fund. Hence, mutual funds are growing rapidly. Excellent information on the objectives and past performance of the various funds are provided in publications such as *Value Line Investment Survey* and *Morningstar Mutual Funds*, which are available in most libraries.

Financial institutions have historically been heavily regulated, with the primary purpose of this regulation being to ensure the safety of the institutions and thus to protect investors. However, these regulations—which have taken the form of prohibitions on nationwide branch banking, restrictions on the types of assets the institutions can buy, ceilings on the interest rates they can pay, and limitations on the types of services they can provide—have tended to impede the free flow of capital and thus have hurt the efficiency of our capital markets. Recognizing this fact, Congress has authorized some major changes, and more are on the horizon.

Financial Service Corporation
A firm which offers a wide range of financial services, including investment banking, brokerage operations, insurance, and commercial banking.

The result of the ongoing regulatory changes has been a blurring of the distinctions between the different types of institutions. Indeed, the trend in the United States today is toward huge **financial service corporations,** which own banks, S&Ls, investment banking houses, insurance companies, pension plan operations, and mutual funds, and which have branches across the country and even around the world. Examples of financial service corporations, most of which started in one area but have now diversified to cover most of the financial spectrum, include Transamerica, Merrill Lynch, American Express, Citicorp, Fidelity, and Prudential.

SELF-TEST QUESTIONS

Identify three different ways capital is transferred between savers and borrowers.

What is the difference between a commercial bank and an investment bank?

Distinguish between investment banking houses and financial intermediaries.

List the major types of intermediaries and briefly describe each's function.

THE STOCK MARKET

As noted earlier, secondary markets are those in which outstanding, previously issued securities are traded. By far the most active secondary market, and the most important one to financial managers, is the *stock market*. Here the prices of firms' stocks are established. Since the primary goal of financial management is to maximize the firm's stock price, a knowledge of the stock market is important to anyone involved in managing a business.

THE STOCK EXCHANGES

There are two basic types of stock markets: (1) *organized exchanges,* which include the New York Stock Exchange (NYSE), the American Stock Exchange (AMEX), and several regional exchanges, and (2) the less formal *over-the-counter market.* Since the organized exchanges have actual physical market locations and are easier to describe and understand, we consider them first.

Organized Security Exchanges
Formal organizations having tangible physical locations that conduct auction markets in designated ("listed") securities. The two major U.S. stock exchanges are the New York Stock Exchange (NYSE) and the American Stock Exchange (AMEX).

The **organized security exchanges** are tangible physical entities. Each of the larger ones occupies its own building, has a limited number of members, and has an elected governing body — its board of governors. Members are said to have "seats" on the exchange, although everybody stands up. These seats, which are bought and sold, give the holder the right to trade on the exchange. There are more than 1,300 seats on the New York Stock Exchange, and recently NYSE seats were selling for about $1.5 million.

Most of the larger investment banking houses operate *brokerage departments,* and they own seats on the exchanges and designate one or more of their officers as members. The exchanges are open on all normal working days, with the members meeting in a large room equipped with telephones and other electronic equipment that enable each member to communicate with his or her firm's offices throughout the country.

Like other markets, security exchanges facilitate communication between buyers and sellers. For example, Merrill Lynch (the largest brokerage firm) might receive an order in its Atlanta office from a customer who wants to buy 100 shares of AT&T stock. Simultaneously, Dean Witter's Denver office might receive an order from a customer wishing to sell 100 shares of AT&T. Each broker communicates by wire with the firm's representative on the NYSE. Other brokers throughout the country are also communicating with their own exchange members. The exchange members with *sell orders* offer the shares for sale, and they are bid for by the members with *buy orders.* Thus, the exchanges operate as *auction markets.*[2]

---

[2]The NYSE is actually a modified auction market, wherein people (through their brokers) bid for stocks. Originally — about 200 years ago — brokers would literally shout, "I have 100 shares of Erie for sale; how much am I offered?" and then sell to the highest bidder. If a broker had a buy order, he or she would shout, "I want to buy 100 shares of Erie; who'll sell at the best price?" The same general situation still exists, although the exchanges now have members known as *specialists* who facilitate the trading process by keeping an inventory of shares of the stocks in which they specialize. If a buy order comes in at a time when no sell order arrives, the specialist will sell off some inventory. Similarly, if a sell order comes in, the specialist will buy and add to inventory. The specialist sets a *bid price* (the price the specialist will pay for the stock) and an *asked price* (the price at which shares will be sold out of inventory). The bid and asked prices are set at levels designed to keep the inventory in balance. If many buy orders start coming in because of favorable developments or sell orders come in because of unfavorable events, the specialist will raise or lower prices to keep supply and demand in balance. Bid prices are somewhat lower than asked prices, with the difference, or *spread,* representing the specialist's profit margin.

Special facilities are available to help institutional investors such as mutual funds or pension funds sell large blocks of stock without depressing their prices. In essence, brokerage houses which cater to institutional clients will purchase blocks (defined as 10,000 or more shares) and then resell the stock to other institutions or individuals. Also, when a firm has a major announcement which is likely to cause its stock price to change sharply, it will ask the exchanges to halt trading in its stock until the announcement has been made and digested by investors. Thus, when Texaco announced that it planned to acquire Getty Oil, trading was halted for one day in both Texaco and Getty stocks.

THE OVER-THE-COUNTER MARKET

Over-the-Counter Market
A large collection of brokers and dealers, connected electronically by telephones and computers, that provides for trading in unlisted securities.

In contrast to the organized security exchanges, the **over-the-counter market** is a nebulous, intangible organization. An explanation of the term "over-the-counter" will help clarify exactly what this market is. As noted above, the exchanges operate as auction markets — buy and sell orders come in more or less simultaneously, and exchange members match these orders. If a stock is traded less frequently, perhaps because it is the stock of a new or a small firm, few buy and sell orders come in, and matching them within a reasonable length of time would be difficult. To avoid this problem, some brokerage firms maintain an inventory of such stocks — they buy when individual investors want to sell and sell when investors want to buy. At one time, the inventory of securities was kept in a safe, and the stocks, when bought and sold, were literally passed over the counter.

Today, the over-the-counter market is defined to include all facilities that are needed to conduct security transactions not conducted on the organized exchanges. These facilities consist of (1) the relatively few *dealers* who hold inventories of over-the-counter securities and who are said to "make a market" in these securities; (2) the thousands of brokers who act as *agents* in bringing the dealers together with investors; and (3) the computers, terminals, and electronic networks that provide a communications link between dealers and brokers. The dealers who make a market in a particular stock continuously quote a price at which they are willing to buy the stock (the *bid price*) and a price at which they will sell shares (the *asked price*). Each dealer's prices, which are adjusted as supply and demand conditions change, can be read off computer screens all across the country. The *spread* between bid and asked prices represents the dealer's markup, or profit.

Brokers and dealers who make up the over-the-counter market are members of a self-regulating body known as the *National Association of Securities Dealers (NASD)*, which licenses brokers and oversees trading practices. The computerized trading network used by NASD is known as the NASD Automated Quotation System (NASDAQ), and *The Wall Street Journal* and other newspapers provide information on NASDAQ transactions.

In terms of numbers of issues, the majority of stocks are traded over the counter, and trading volume is greater on NASDAQ stocks than on the NYSE. However, because the stocks of most large companies are listed on the exchanges, more than half of the dollar volume of stock trading takes place on the exchanges. In recent years, many large companies — including Microsoft, Intel, MCI, and Apple — have elected to remain NASDAQ stocks, so the over-the-counter market is growing faster than the exchanges.

SOME TRENDS IN SECURITY TRADING PROCEDURES

From the NYSE's inception in 1792 until the 1970s, the vast majority of all stock trading occurred on the Exchange and was conducted by member firms. The NYSE established a set of minimum brokerage commission rates, and no member firm could charge a commission lower than the set rate. This was a monopoly, pure and simple. However, on May 1, 1975, the Securities and Exchange Commission (SEC), with strong prodding from the Antitrust Division of the Justice Department, forced the NYSE to abandon its fixed commissions. Commission rates declined dramatically, falling in some cases as much as 95 percent from former levels.

INDUSTRY PRACTICE

AN EXPENSIVE BEER FOR THE NASD

A few summers ago, two professors met for a beer at an academic conference. During their conversation, the professors, William Christie of Vanderbilt University and Paul Schultz of Ohio State University, decided it would be interesting to see how prices are set for NASDAQ stocks. The results of their study were startling to many, and they produced a real firestorm in the investment community.

When looking through data on the bid/asked spreads set by NASDAQ market makers, Christie and Schultz found that the market makers routinely avoided posting quotes which had "odd-eighth fractions," that is, $\frac{1}{8}$, $\frac{3}{8}$, $\frac{5}{8}$, and $\frac{7}{8}$. For example, if a market maker were to use odd-eighth quotes, he might offer to buy a stock for $10\frac{1}{2}$ a share or sell it for $10\frac{5}{8}$, thus providing a "spread," or profit, of $\frac{1}{8}$ point ($10\frac{5}{8} - 10\frac{1}{2} = \frac{1}{8}$). The spread between the two prices is the market maker's compensation for providing a market and taking the risk associated with holding an inventory of a given stock. Note that if he or she avoided odd-eighths fractions, then the offer price would be $10\frac{3}{4}$ (which is $10\frac{6}{8}$), so the spread would be $10\frac{6}{8} - 10\frac{1}{2} = \frac{1}{4}$, or twice as high as if he or she made an odd-eighths quote.

What amazed Christie and Schultz was the fact that this practice was so widespread — even for widely followed stock such as Apple Computer and Lotus Development. The professors concluded that the evidence strongly suggests that there had to be tacit collusion among NASDAQ dealers designed to keep spreads artificially high. The National Association of Security Dealers (NASD) originally denied the accusations. Others have come forward to provide a justification for the practice.

The publicity surrounding the study led the Securities and Exchange Commission (SEC) to investigate. Without admitting guilt, the NASD recently settled with the SEC, and, as part of the agreement, the dealers agreed to spend $100 million during the next five years to improve their enforcement practices — which explains why the professors' beers turned out to be so expensive for the NASD!

SOURCE: William Christie, "An Expensive Beer for the N.A.S.D.," *The New York Times*, August 25, 1996, Sec. 3, 12.

These changes were a boon to the investing public, but not to the brokerage industry. Several "full-service" brokerage houses went bankrupt, and others were forced to merge with stronger firms. The number of brokerage houses has declined from literally thousands in the 1960s to a much smaller number of large, strong, nationwide companies, many of which are units of diversified financial service corporations. Deregulation has also spawned a number of "discount brokers," some of which are affiliated with commercial banks or mutual fund investment companies.[3]

There has also been a rise in "third market" activities, where large financial institutions trade both listed and unlisted stocks among themselves on a 24-hour basis. Buyers and sellers in this market are located all around the globe — New York, San Francisco, Tokyo, Singapore, Zurich, and London — and this makes the 24-hour trading day a necessity. The exchanges have resisted extending their trading hours because it would inconvenience members, but competition will eventually force all major exchanges to operate around the clock. Today, institutional investors, and even some individuals, can trade by computer at any time, day or night.

---

[3]Full-service brokers give investors information on different stocks and make recommendations as to which stocks to buy. Discount brokers do not give advice — they merely execute orders. Some brokerage houses (institutional houses) cater primarily to institutional investors such as pension funds and insurance companies, while others cater to individual investors and are called "retail houses." Large firms such as Merrill Lynch generally have both retail and institutional brokerage operations.

THE COST OF MONEY

Capital in a free economy is allocated through the price system. *The interest rate is the price paid to borrow debt capital. With equity capital, investors expect to receive dividends and capital gains, and these are the components whose sum is the cost of equity money.* The factors which affect the supply of and the demand for investment capital, hence the cost of money, are discussed in this section.

The four most fundamental factors affecting the cost of money are (1) **production opportunities,** (2) **time preferences for consumption,** (3) **risk,** and (4) **inflation**. To see how these factors operate, visualize an isolated island community where the people live on fish. They have a stock of fishing gear which permits them to survive reasonably well, but they would like to have more fish. Now suppose Mr. Crusoe had a bright idea for a new type of fishnet that would enable him to double his daily catch. However, it would take him a year to perfect his design, to build his net, and to learn how to use it efficiently, and Mr. Crusoe would probably starve before he could put his new net into operation. Therefore, he might suggest to Ms. Robinson, Mr. Friday, and several others that if they would give him one fish each day for a year, he would return two fish a day during all of the next year. If someone accepted the offer, then the fish which Ms. Robinson or one of the others gave to Mr. Crusoe would constitute *savings;* these savings would be *invested* in the fishnet; and the extra fish the net produced would constitute a *return on the investment*.

Obviously, the more productive Mr. Crusoe thought the new fishnet would be, the more he could afford to offer potential investors for their savings. In this example, we assume that Mr. Crusoe thought he would be able to pay, and thus he offered, a 100 percent rate of return — he offered to give back two fish for every one he received. He might have tried to attract savings for less — for example, he might have decided to offer only 1.5 fish next year for every one he received this year, which would represent a 50 percent rate of return to Ms. Robinson and the other potential savers.

How attractive Mr. Crusoe's offer appeared to a potential saver would depend in large part on the saver's *time preference for consumption*. For example, Ms. Robinson might be thinking of retirement, and she might be willing to trade fish today for fish in the future on a one-for-one basis. On the other hand, Mr. Friday might have a wife and several young children and need his current fish, so he might be unwilling to "lend" a fish today for anything less than three fish next year. Mr. Friday would be said to have a high time preference for current consumption and Ms. Robinson a low time preference. Note also that if the entire population were living right at the subsistence level, time preferences for current consumption would necessarily be high, aggregate savings would be low, interest rates would be high, and capital formation would be difficult.

The *risk* inherent in the fishnet project, and thus in Mr. Crusoe's ability to repay the loan, would also affect the return investors would require: the higher the perceived risk, the higher the required rate of return. Also, in a more

Production Opportunities
The returns available within an economy from investments in productive (cash-generating) assets.

Time Preferences for Consumption
The preferences of consumers for current consumption as opposed to saving for future consumption.

Risk
In a financial market context, the chance that an investment will not provide the expected return.

Inflation
The tendency of prices to increase over time.

complex society there are many businesses like Mr. Crusoe's, many goods other than fish, and many savers like Ms. Robinson and Mr. Friday. Therefore, people use money as a medium of exchange rather than barter with fish. When money is used, its value in the future, which is affected by *inflation*, comes into play: the higher the expected rate of inflation, the larger the required return. We discuss this point in detail later in the chapter.

Thus, we see that the interest rate paid to savers depends in a basic way (1) on the rate of return producers expect to earn on invested capital, (2) on savers' time preferences for current versus future consumption, (3) on the riskiness of the loan, and (4) on the expected future rate of inflation. Producers' expected returns on their business investments set an upper limit on how much they can pay for savings, while consumers' time preferences for consumption establish how much consumption they are willing to defer, hence how much they will save at different rates of interest offered by producers.[4] Higher risk and higher inflation also lead to higher interest rates.

SELF-TEST QUESTIONS

What is the price paid to borrow money called?

What is the "price" of equity capital?

What four fundamental factors affect the cost of money?

INTEREST RATE LEVELS

Capital is allocated among borrowers by interest rates: Firms with the most profitable investment opportunities are willing and able to pay the most for capital, so they tend to attract it away from inefficient firms or from those whose products are not in demand. Of course, our economy is not completely free in the sense of being influenced only by market forces. Thus, the federal government has agencies which help designated individuals or groups obtain credit on favorable terms. Among those eligible for this kind of assistance are small businesses, certain minorities, and firms willing to build plants in areas with high unemployment. Still, most capital in the U.S. economy is allocated through the price system.

Figure 4-2 shows how supply and demand interact to determine interest rates in two capital markets. Markets A and B represent two of the many capital markets in existence. The going interest rate, which can be designated as either k or i, but for purposes of our discussion is designated as k, is initially 10 percent for the low-risk securities in Market A.[5] Borrowers whose credit is strong enough to borrow in this market can obtain funds at a cost of 10 percent, and investors who want to put their money to work without much risk can obtain a 10 percent return. Riskier borrowers must obtain higher-cost funds in Market B. Investors

---

[4]The term "producers" is really too narrow. A better word might be "borrowers," which would include corporations, home purchasers, people borrowing to go to college, or even people borrowing to buy autos or to pay for vacations. Also, the wealth of a society and its demographics influence its people's ability to save and thus their time preferences for current versus future consumption.

[5]The letter "k" is the traditional symbol for interest rates, but "i" is used frequently today because this term corresponds to the interest rate key on most financial calculators. Therefore, in Chapter 6, when we discuss calculators, the term "i" will be used for interest rate.

FIGURE　4 - 2　Interest Rates as a Function of Supply and Demand for Funds

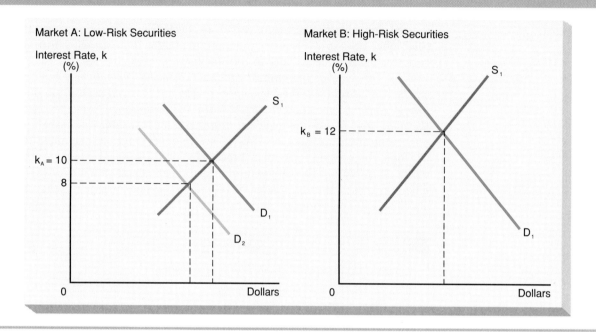

who are more willing to take risks invest in Market B, expecting to earn a 12 percent return but also realizing that they might actually receive much less.

If the demand for funds declines, as it typically does during business recessions, the demand curves will shift to the left, as shown in Curve D_2 in Market A. The market-clearing, or equilibrium, interest rate in this example declines to 8 percent. Similarly, you should be able to visualize what would happen if the Federal Reserve tightened credit: The supply curve, S_1, would shift to the left, and this would raise interest rates and lower the level of borrowing in the economy.

Capital markets are interdependent. For example, if Markets A and B were in equilibrium before the demand shift to D_2 in Market A, then investors were willing to accept the higher risk in Market B in exchange for a *risk premium* of $12\% - 10\% = 2\%$. After the shift to D_2, the risk premium would initially increase to $12\% - 8\% = 4\%$. Immediately, though, this much larger premium would induce some of the lenders in Market A to shift to Market B, which would, in turn, cause the supply curve in Market A to shift to the left (or up) and that in Market B to shift to the right. The transfer of capital between markets would raise the interest rate in Market A and lower it in Market B, thus bringing the risk premium back closer to the original 2 percent.

There are many capital markets in the United States. U.S. firms also invest and raise capital throughout the world, and foreigners both borrow and lend in the United States. There are markets for home loans; farm loans; business loans; federal, state, and local government loans; and consumer loans. Within each category, there are regional markets as well as different types of submarkets. For example, in real estate there are separate markets for first and second mortgages and for loans on single-family homes, apartments, office buildings, shopping

FIGURE   4-3   Long- and Short-Term Interest Rates, 1959–1996

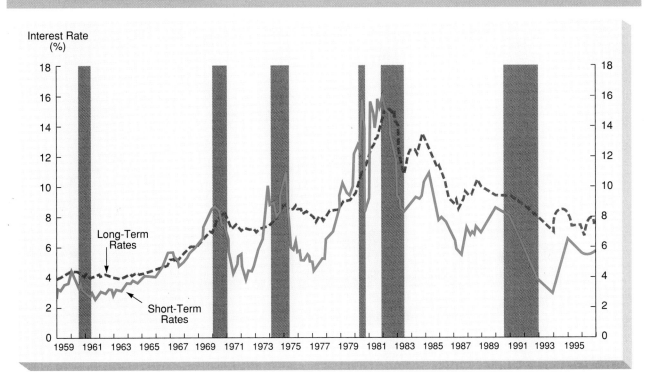

NOTES:

a. The shaded areas designate business recessions.

b. Short-term rates are measured by four- to six-month loans to very large, strong corporations, and long-term rates are measured by AAA corporate bonds.

SOURCE: *Federal Reserve Bulletin.*

centers, vacant land, and so on. Within the business sector there are dozens of types of debt and also several different markets for common stocks.

There is a price for each type of capital, and these prices change over time as shifts occur in supply and demand conditions. Figure 4-3 shows how long- and short-term interest rates to business borrowers have varied since the late 1950s. Notice that short-term interest rates are especially prone to rise during booms and then fall during recessions. (The shaded areas of the chart indicate recessions.) When the economy is expanding, firms need capital, and this demand for capital pushes rates up. Also, inflationary pressures are strongest during business booms, and that also exerts upward pressure on rates. Conditions are reversed during recessions such as the one in 1991 and 1992. Slack business reduces the demand for credit, the rate of inflation falls, and the result is a drop in interest rates. Furthermore, the Federal Reserve often lowers rates during recessions to help stimulate the economy.

These tendencies do not hold exactly — the period after 1984 is a case in point. The price of oil fell dramatically in 1985 and 1986, reducing inflationary pressures on other prices and easing fears of serious long-term inflation. Earlier, these fears had pushed interest rates to record levels. The economy from 1984 to 1987 was fairly strong, but the declining fears about inflation more than offset the

FIGURE 4-4 Relationship between Annual Inflation Rates and Long-Term Interest Rates, 1959–1996

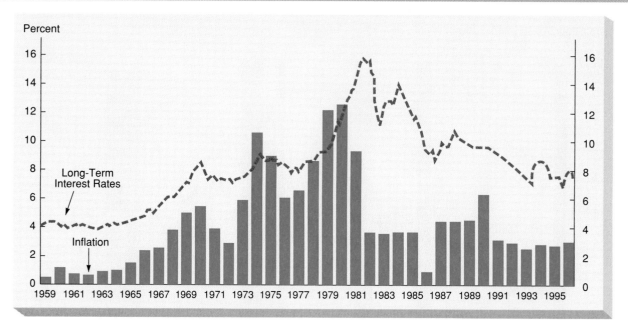

NOTES:

a. Interest rates are those on AAA long-term corporate bonds.

b. Inflation is measured as the annual rate of change in the Consumer Price Index (CPI).

SOURCE: *Federal Reserve Bulletin.*

normal tendency of interest rates to rise during good economic times, and the net result was lower interest rates.[6]

The relationship between inflation and long-term interest rates is highlighted in Figure 4-4, which plots rates of inflation along with long-term interest rates. In the late 1950s and early 1960s, inflation averaged 1 percent per year, and interest rates on high-quality, long-term bonds averaged 5 percent. Then the Vietnam War heated up, leading to an increase in inflation, and interest rates began an upward climb. When the war ended in the early 1970s, inflation dipped a bit, but then the 1973 Arab oil embargo led to rising oil prices, much higher inflation rates, and sharply higher interest rates.

Inflation peaked at about 13 percent in 1980, but interest rates continued to increase into 1981 and 1982, and they remained quite high until 1985, because people were afraid inflation would start to climb again. Thus, the "inflationary psychology" created during the 1970s persisted to the mid-1980s.

Gradually, though, people began to realize that the Federal Reserve was serious about keeping inflation down, that global competition was keeping U.S. auto producers and other corporations from raising prices as they had in the past, and that constraints on corporate price increases were diminishing labor unions'

---

[6]Short-term rates are responsive to current economic conditions, whereas long-term rates primarily reflect long-run expectations for inflation. As a result, short-term rates are sometimes above and sometimes below long-term rates. The relationship between long-term and short-term rates is called the *term structure of interest rates,* and it is discussed later in the chapter.

ability to push through cost-increasing wage hikes. As these realizations set in, interest rates declined, and the "current real rate of interest," which is the difference between the current interest rate and the current inflation rate, declined as shown in Figure 4-4.

In recent years, inflation has been running at less than 3 percent a year. However, long-term interest rates have been volatile, because investors are not sure if inflation is truly under control or is getting ready to jump back to the higher levels of the 1980s. In the years ahead, we can be sure that the level of interest rates will vary (1) with changes in the current rate of inflation and (2) with changes in expectations about future inflation.

SELF-TEST QUESTIONS ??????

How are interest rates used to allocate capital among firms?

What happens to market-clearing, or equilibrium, interest rates in a capital market when the demand for funds declines? What happens when inflation increases or decreases?

Why does the price of capital change during booms and recessions?

How does risk affect interest rates?

THE DETERMINANTS OF MARKET INTEREST RATES

In general, the quoted (or nominal) interest rate on a debt security, k, is composed of a real risk-free rate of interest, k*, plus several premiums that reflect inflation, the riskiness of the security, and the security's marketability (or liquidity). This relationship can be expressed as follows:

$$\text{Quoted interest rate} = k = k^* + IP + DRP + LP + MRP$$
$$= k_{RF} \quad + DRP + LP + MRP. \tag{4-1}$$

Here

k = the quoted, or nominal, rate of interest on a given security.[7] There are many different securities, hence many different quoted interest rates.

k* = the real risk-free rate of interest. k* is pronounced "k-star," and it is the rate that would exist on a riskless security if zero inflation were expected.

k_{RF} = k* + IP, and it is the quoted risk-free rate of interest on a security such as a U.S. Treasury bill, which is very liquid and also free of most risks. Note that k_{RF} includes the premium for expected inflation, because k_{RF} = k* + IP.

IP = inflation premium. IP is equal to the average expected inflation rate over the life of the security. The expected future inflation rate is not necessarily equal to the current inflation rate, so IP is not necessarily equal to current inflation as reported in Figure 4-4.

---

[7]The term *nominal* as it is used here means the *stated* rate as opposed to the *real* rate, which is adjusted to remove inflation effects. If you bought a 10-year Treasury bond in January 1997, the quoted, or nominal, rate would be about 6.5 percent, but if inflation averages 3 percent over the next 10 years, the real rate would be about 6.5% − 3% = 3.5%.

DRP = default risk premium. This premium reflects the possibility that the is-suer will not pay interest or principal at the stated time and in the stated amount. DRP is zero for U.S. Treasury securities, but it rises as the riski-ness of issuers increases.

LP = liquidity, or marketability, premium. This is a premium charged by lend-ers to reflect the fact that some securities cannot be converted to cash on short notice at a "reasonable" price. LP is very low for Treasury secu-rities and for securities issued by large, strong firms, but it is relatively high on securities issued by very small firms.

MRP = maturity risk premium. As we will explain later, longer-term bonds, even Treasury bonds, are exposed to a significant risk of price declines, and a maturity risk premium is charged by lenders to reflect this risk.

As noted above, since $k_{RF} = k^* + IP$, we can rewrite Equation 4-1 as follows:

$$\text{Nominal, or quoted, rate} = k = k_{RF} + DRP + LP + MRP.$$

We discuss the components whose sum makes up the quoted, or nominal, rate on a given security in the following sections.

The Real Risk-Free Rate of Interest, k*

Real Risk-Free Rate of Interest, k*
The rate of interest that would exist on default-free U.S. Treasury securities if no inflation were expected.

The **real risk-free rate of interest, k*,** is defined as the interest rate that would exist on a riskless security if no inflation were expected, and it may be thought of as the rate of interest on *short-term* U.S. Treasury securities in an inflation-free world. The real risk-free rate is not static — it changes over time depending on economic conditions, especially (1) on the rate of return corporations and other borrowers expect to earn on productive assets and (2) on people's time pref-erences for current versus future consumption. Borrowers' expected returns on real asset investments set an upper limit on how much they can afford to pay for borrowed funds, while savers' time preferences for consumption establish how much consumption they are willing to defer, hence the amount of funds they will lend at different interest rates. It is difficult to measure the real risk-free rate precisely, but most experts think that k* has fluctuated in the range of 1 to 4 percent in recent years.[8]

The Nominal, or Quoted, Risk-Free Rate of Interest, k$_{RF}$

Nominal (Quoted) Risk-Free Rate, k$_{RF}$
The rate of interest on a security that is free of all risk; k$_{RF}$ is proxied by the T-bill rate or the T-bond rate. k$_{RF}$ includes an inflation premium.

The **nominal,** or **quoted, risk-free rate, k$_{RF}$,** is the real risk-free rate plus a pre-mium for expected inflation: $k_{RF} = k^* + IP$. To be strictly correct, the risk-free rate should mean the interest rate on a totally risk-free security — one that has no risk of default, no maturity risk, no liquidity risk, and no risk of loss if infla-tion increases. There is no such security, hence there is no observable truly

---

[8]The real rate of interest as discussed here is different from the *current* real rate as discussed in connection with Figure 4-4. The current real rate is the current interest rate minus the current (or latest past) inflation rate, while the real rate, without the word "current," is the current interest rate minus the *expected future* inflation rate. For example, suppose the current quoted rate for short-term Treasury bills is 6 percent, inflation during the latest year was 3 percent, and inflation expected for the coming year is 5 percent. Then the *current* real rate would be 6% − 3% = 3%, but the *expected* real rate would be 6% − 5% = 1%. In the press, the term "real rate" generally means the current real rate, but in economics and finance, hence in this book unless otherwise noted, the real rate means the one based on *expected* inflation rates.

risk-free rate. However, there is one security that is free of most risks — a U.S. Treasury bill (T-bill), which is a short-term security issued by the U.S. government. Treasury bonds (T-bonds), which are longer-term government securities, are free of default and liquidity risks, but T-bonds are exposed to some risk due to changes in the general level of interest rates.

If the term "risk-free rate" is used without either the modifier "real" or the modifier "nominal," people generally mean the quoted (nominal) rate, and we will follow that convention in this book. Therefore, when we use the term risk-free rate, k_{RF}, we mean the nominal risk-free rate, which includes an inflation premium equal to the average expected inflation rate over the life of the security. In general, we use the T-bill rate to approximate the short-term risk-free rate, and the T-bond rate to approximate the long-term risk-free rate. So, whenever you see the term "risk-free rate," assume that we are referring either to the quoted U.S. T-bill rate or to the quoted T-bond rate.

INFLATION PREMIUM (IP)

Inflation has a major impact on interest rates because it erodes the purchasing power of the dollar and lowers the real rate of return on investments. To illustrate, suppose you saved $1,000 and invested it in a Treasury bill that matures in one year and pays a 5 percent interest rate. At the end of the year, you will receive $1,050 — your original $1,000 plus $50 of interest. Now suppose the inflation rate during the year is 10 percent, and it affects all items equally. If gas had cost $1 per gallon at the beginning of the year, it would cost $1.10 at the end of the year. Therefore, your $1,000 would have bought $1,000/$1 = 1,000 gallons at the beginning of the year, but only $1,050/$1.10 = 955 gallons at the end. In *real terms,* you would be worse off — you would receive $50 of interest, but it would not be sufficient to offset inflation. You would thus be better off buying 1,000 gallons of gas (or some other storable asset such as land, timber, apartment buildings, wheat, or gold) than buying the Treasury bill.

Investors are well aware of all this, so when they lend money, they build in an **inflation premium (IP)** equal to the average expected inflation rate over the life of the security. As discussed previously, for a short-term, default-free U.S. Treasury bill, the actual interest rate charged, k_{T-bill}, would be the real risk-free rate, k^*, plus the inflation premium (IP):

$$k_{T-bill} = k_{RF} = k^* + IP.$$

Therefore, if the real risk-free rate of interest were $k^* = 3\%$, and if inflation were expected to be 4 percent (and hence IP = 4%) during the next year, then the quoted rate of interest on one-year T-bills would be 7 percent. In August 1996, the expected one-year inflation rate was about 3 percent, and the yield on one-year T-bills was about 5.6 percent. This implies that the real risk-free rate on short-term securities at that time was 2.6 percent.

It is important to note that the inflation rate built into interest rates is the *inflation rate expected in the future,* not the rate experienced in the past. Thus, the latest reported figures might show an annual inflation rate of 3 percent, but that is for a past period. If people on the average expect a 6 percent inflation rate in the future, then 6 percent would be built into the current interest rate. Note also that the inflation rate reflected in the quoted interest rate on any security is the *average rate of inflation expected over the security's life.* Thus, the inflation rate built into a 1-year bond is the expected inflation rate for the next year, but

Inflation Premium (IP)
A premium equal to expected inflation that investors add to the real risk-free rate of return.

the inflation rate built into a 30-year bond is the average rate of inflation expected over the next 30 years.[9]

Expectations for future inflation are closely, but not perfectly, correlated with rates experienced in the recent past. Therefore, if the inflation rate reported for last month increased, people would tend to raise their expectations for future inflation, and this change in expectations would cause an increase in interest rates.

Note that Germany, Japan, and Switzerland have had lower inflation rates than the United States, hence their interest rates have generally been lower than ours. Italy and most South American countries have experienced high inflation, and that is reflected in their interest rates.

DEFAULT RISK PREMIUM (DRP)

The risk that a borrower will *default* on a loan, which means not pay the interest or the principal, also affects the market interest rate on a security: the greater the default risk, the higher the interest rate. Treasury securities have no default risk, hence they carry the lowest interest rates on taxable securities in the United States. For corporate bonds, the higher the bond's rating, the lower its default risk, and, consequently, the lower its interest rate.[10] Here are some representative interest rates on long-term bonds during July 1996:

	RATE	DRP
U.S. Treasury	7.1%	—
AAA	7.5	0.4%
AA	7.6	0.5
A	7.8	0.7
BBB	8.1	1.0
BB+	8.7	1.6

Default Risk Premium (DRP)
The difference between the interest rate on a U.S. Treasury bond and a corporate bond of equal maturity and marketability.

The difference between the quoted interest rate on a T-bond and that on a corporate bond with similar maturity, liquidity, and other features is the **default risk premium (DRP).** Therefore, if the bonds listed above were otherwise similar, the default risk premium would be DRP = 7.5% − 7.1% = 0.4 percentage point for AAA corporate bonds, 7.6% − 7.1% = 0.5 percentage point for AA, 7.8% − 7.1% = 0.7 percentage point for A corporate bonds, and so forth. Default risk premiums vary somewhat over time, but the July 1996 figures are representative of levels in recent years.

[9]To be theoretically precise, we should use a *geometric average*. Also, since millions of investors are active in the market, it is impossible to determine exactly the consensus expected inflation rate. Survey data are available, however, which give us a reasonably good idea of what investors expect over the next few years. For example, in 1980 the University of Michigan's Survey Research Center reported that people expected inflation during the next year to be 11.9 percent and that the average rate of inflation expected over the next 5 to 10 years was 10.5 percent. Those expectations led to record-high interest rates. However, the economy cooled in 1981 and 1982, and, as Figure 4-4 showed, actual inflation dropped sharply after 1980. This led to gradual reductions in the *expected future* inflation rate. In August 1996, as we write this, the expected future inflation rate is about 3 percent. As inflationary expectations change, so do quoted market interest rates.

[10]Bond ratings, and bonds' riskiness in general, are discussed in detail in Chapter 7. For now, merely note that bonds rated AAA are judged to have less default risk than bonds rated AA, while AA bonds are less risky than A bonds, and so on. Ratings are designated AAA or Aaa, AA or Aa, and so forth, depending on the rating agency. In this book, the designations are used interchangeably.

INDUSTRY PRACTICE

A NEW, TRULY RISKLESS TREASURY BOND

Investors who purchase bonds must constantly worry about inflation. If inflation turns out to be greater than expected, bonds will provide a lower-than-expected real return. To protect themselves against expected increases in inflation, investors build an inflation risk premium into their required rate of return. This raises borrowers' costs.

In January 1997, inflation was running below 3 percent a year, yet long-term Treasury rates were 6.8 percent. A considerable portion of the 6.8 percent rate is attributed to the market's fear that inflation will rise in the years ahead. Therefore, long-term rates should decline if investors can be convinced that inflation is under control. Indeed, the actions taken by the Federal Reserve in recent years have been designed primarily to convince the bond market that the Fed was not going to tolerate rising inflation.

In order to provide investors with an inflation-protected bond, and also to reduce the cost of debt to the government, on January 29, 1997, the U.S. Treasury issued $7 billion of ten-year inflation-indexed bonds. The bonds will pay an interest rate of 3.45 percent, plus an additional amount sufficient to offset inflation, at the end of each year. For example, if inflation as measured by the CPI during the year ending January 28, 1998, turns out to be 3.00 percent, then the holder of one of these bonds would receive two benefits. First, he or she would receive $34.50 of interest, which is 3.45 percent of the bond's initial stated, or "par," value of $1,000. Second, the stated value of the bond would be increased by the inflation rate, to $1,000(1.03) = $1,030, causing the holder's wealth to rise by another $30 dollars. Thus, the total return during the first year would be $34.50 of interest plus $30 of "capital gains," or $64.50 in total, and the total rate of return would be $64.50/$1,000 = 6.45%.

Interest during the second year would be figured as the coupon rate of 3.45 percent times the inflation-adjusted par value, or 0.0345($1,030) = $35.54. Thus, the cash income provided by the bond would rise by exactly enough to cover inflation, producing a real, inflation-adjusted rate of 3.45 percent. Further, since the principal would also rise by the inflation rate, it too would be protected from inflation.

This same adjustment process will continue each year until the bonds mature in January 2007, at which time they will pay the adjusted maturity value, which would be $1,343.92 if inflation continues at the rate of 3 percent per year.

The 3.45 percent rate was set at the auction — interested investors notified the Treasury of how many bonds they were willing to buy at different interest rates. Obviously, potential buyers would buy more bonds if the rate were set relatively high, fewer at a lower rate. Thus Mr. X might indicate that he would buy $1 million of the bonds if the rate was set at 3 percent, $2 million if the rate was 3.5 percent, $3 million at 4 percent, and so on. When the bidding was closed, the Treasury determined that to sell the entire issue, the coupon rate would have to be set at 3.4 percent — that was the lowest rate that would clear the market.

Federal Reserve Board Chairman Greenspan lobbied in favor of the indexed bonds on the grounds that they would help him and the Fed make better estimates of investors' expectations about inflation. He did not explain his reasoning (to our knowledge), but it might have gone something like this:

♦ We know that interest rates in general are determined as follows:

$$k_{RF} = k^* + IP + MRP + DRP + LP.$$

♦ For Treasury bonds, DRP and LP are essentially zero, so for a ten-year bond the rate is

$$k_{RF} = k^* + IP + MRP.$$

The reason the MRP is not zero is that if inflation increases, interest rates will rise and the price of the bonds will decline. Therefore, "regular" ten-year bonds are exposed to maturity risk, hence a maturity risk premium is built into their market interest rate.

♦ The indexed bonds are protected against inflation — if inflation increases, then so will their dollar returns, and as a result, their price will not decline in real terms. Therefore, indexed bonds should have no MRP, hence their market return is

$$k_{RF} = k^* + 0 + 0 = k^*.$$

In other words, the market rate on indexed bonds is the real rate.

♦ The difference between the yield on a regular ten-year bond and that on an indexed bond is the sum of the ten-year bonds' IP and MRP. The yield on regular ten-year bonds was 6.80 percent when the indexed bonds were issued, and the indexed bonds' yield was 3.45 percent. The difference, 3.35 percent, is the average expected inflation rate over the next ten years plus the MRP for ten-year bonds.

♦ The ten-year MRP is about 1.0 percent, and it has been relatively stable in recent years. Therefore, the expected rate of inflation in January 1997 was about 3.45% - 1.00% = 2.45%.

The interest received and the increase in principal are taxed each year as interest income, even though cash from the appreciation will not be received until the bond matures. Therefore, these bonds are especially suitable for individual retirement accounts (IRAs), which are not taxed until funds are withdrawn.

SOURCE: "Inflation Notes Will Offer Fed Forecast Tool," *The Wall Street Journal*, February 3, 1997, C1.

LIQUIDITY PREMIUM (LP)

Liquidity Premium (LP)
A premium added to the equilibrium interest rate on a security if that security cannot be converted to cash on short notice and at close to "fair market value."

A "liquid" asset can be converted to cash quickly and at a "fair market value." Financial assets are generally more liquid than real assets. Because liquidity is important, investors include **liquidity premiums (LP)** when market rates of securities are established. Although it is difficult to accurately measure liquidity premiums, a differential of at least two and probably four or five percentage points exists between the least liquid and the most liquid financial assets of similar default risk and maturity.

MATURITY RISK PREMIUM (MRP)

Interest Rate Risk
The risk of capital losses to which investors are exposed because of changing interest rates.

Maturity Risk Premium (MRP)
A premium which reflects interest rate risk.

U.S. Treasury securities are free of default risk in the sense that one can be virtually certain that the federal government will pay interest on its bonds and will also pay them off when they mature. Therefore, the default risk premium on Treasury securities is essentially zero. Further, active markets exist for Treasury securities, so their liquidity premiums are also close to zero. Thus, as a first approximation, the rate of interest on a Treasury bond should be the risk-free rate, k_{RF}, which is equal to the real risk-free rate, k^*, plus an inflation premium, IP. However, an adjustment is needed for long-term Treasury bonds. The prices of long-term bonds decline sharply whenever interest rates rise, and since interest rates can and do occasionally rise, all long-term bonds, even Treasury bonds, have an element of risk called **interest rate risk.** As a general rule, the bonds of any organization, from the U.S. government to Continental Airlines, have more interest rate risk the longer the maturity of the bond.[11] Therefore, a **maturity risk premium (MRP),** which is higher the longer the years to maturity, must be included in the required interest rate.

The effect of maturity risk premiums is to raise interest rates on long-term bonds relative to those on short-term bonds. This premium, like the others, is difficult to measure, but (1) it varies somewhat over time, rising when interest rates are more volatile and uncertain, then falling when interest rates are more stable, and (2) in recent years, the maturity risk premium on 30-year T-bonds appears to have generally been in the range of one or two percentage points.[12]

Reinvestment Rate Risk
The risk that a decline in interest rates will lead to lower income when bonds mature and funds are reinvested.

We should mention that although long-term bonds are heavily exposed to interest rate risk, short-term bills are heavily exposed to **reinvestment rate risk.** When short-term bills mature and the funds are reinvested, or "rolled over," a decline in interest rates would necessitate reinvestment at a lower rate, and this would result in a decline in interest income. To illustrate, suppose you had $100,000 invested in one-year T-bills, and you lived on the income. In 1981, short-term rates were about 15 percent, so your income would have been about $15,000. However, your income would have declined to about $9,000 by 1983, and to just

---

[11]For example, if someone had bought a 30-year Treasury bond for $1,000 in 1972, when the long-term interest rate was 7 percent, and held it until 1981, when long-term T-bond rates were about 14.5 percent, the value of the bond would have declined to about $514. That would represent a loss of almost half the invested capital, and it demonstrates that long-term bonds, even U.S. Treasury bonds, are not riskless. However, had the investor purchased short-term T-bills in 1972 and subsequently reinvested the principal each time the bills matured, he or she would still have had $1,000. This point will be discussed in detail in Chapter 7.

[12]The MRP for long-term bonds has averaged 1.5 percent over the last 70 years. See *Stocks, Bonds, Bills, and Inflation: 1997 Yearbook* (Chicago: Ibbotson Associates, 1997).

$5,600 by 1996. Had you invested your money in long-term T-bonds, your income (but not the value of the principal) would have been stable.[13] Thus, although "investing short" preserves one's principal, the interest income provided by short-term T-bills is less stable than the interest income on long-term bonds.

SELF-TEST QUESTIONS ?????

Write out an equation for the nominal interest rate on any debt security.

Distinguish between the *real* risk-free rate of interest, k*, and the *nominal,* or *quoted,* risk-free rate of interest, k_{RF}.

How is inflation dealt with when interest rates are determined by investors in the financial markets?

Does the interest rate on a T-bond include a default risk premium? Explain.

Distinguish between liquid and illiquid assets, and identify some assets that are liquid and some that are illiquid.

Briefly explain the following statement: "Although long-term bonds are heavily exposed to interest rate risk, short-term bills are heavily exposed to reinvestment rate risk. The maturity risk premium reflects the net effects of these two opposing forces."

INVESTING OVERSEAS

Country Risk
The risk that arises from investing or doing business in a particular country.

In addition to inflation and liquidity, investors should consider other risk factors before investing overseas. First there is **country risk**, which refers to the risk that arises from investing or doing business in a particular country. This risk depends on the country's economic, political, and social environment. Countries with stable economic, social, political, and regulatory systems provide a safer climate for investment, and therefore less country risk, than less stable nations. Examples of country risk include the risk associated with changes in tax rates, regulations, currency conversion, and exchange rates. Country risk also includes the risk that property will be expropriated without adequate compensation, as well as new host country stipulations about local production, sourcing or hiring practices, and damage or destruction of facilities due to internal strife.

A second thing to keep in mind when investing overseas is that more often than not the security will be denominated in a currency other than the dollar, which means that the value of your investment will depend on what happens to exchange rates. This is known as *exchange rate risk.* For example, if a U.S. investor purchases a Japanese bond, interest will probably be paid in Japanese yen, which must then be converted into dollars if the investor wants to spend his or

---

[13]Long-term bonds also have some reinvestment rate risk. If one is saving and investing for some future purpose, say, to buy a house or for retirement, then to actually earn the quoted rate on a long-term bond, the interest payments must be reinvested at the quoted rate. However, if interest rates fall, the interest payments must be reinvested at a lower rate; thus, the realized return would be less than the quoted rate. Note, though, that reinvestment rate risk is lower on a long-term bond than on a short-term bond because only the interest payments (rather than interest plus principal) on the long-term bond are exposed to reinvestment rate risk. Zero coupon bonds, which are discussed in Chapter 7, are completely free of reinvestment rate risk during their life.

GLOBAL PERSPECTIVES

MEASURING COUNTRY RISK

Various forecasting services measure the level of country risk in different countries and provide indexes that measure factors such as each country's expected economic performance, access to world capital markets, political stability, and level of internal conflict. Country risk analysts use sophisticated models to measure it, thus providing corporate managers and overseas investors with a way to judge both the relative and absolute risk of investing in a given country. A sample of recent country risk estimates compiled by *Euromoney* are presented in the following table. The higher the country's score, the lower its esti-

mated country risk. The maximum possible score is 100.

The countries with the least amount of country risk all have strong, market-based economies, ready access to worldwide capital markets, relatively little social unrest, and a stable political climate. Luxembourgs's top ranking may surprise many, but this ranking is the result of the country's strong economic performance and its status as a tax haven for foreign investment. Some may also be surprised that the United States was not ranked number one. Even though the U.S. economy has been quite strong in recent years, the economies of some other countries have been even stronger (e.g., Luxembourg, Switzer-

land, and Singapore). Also, the United States typically does not receive the highest ranking with respect to political risk — this likely stems from the ongoing uncertainty about whether there will be major shifts in tax and regulatory policies within the United States. Note, though, that there is really not much difference between 98.55 and 97.17 — none of the top five countries have much country risk.

Arguably, there are fewer surprises when looking at the bottom five. Each of these countries has considerable social and political unrest, and none have embraced a market-based economic system. Clearly, an investment in any of these countries is a risky proposition.

Top Five Countries (Least Amount of Country Risk)

RANK	COUNTRY	TOTAL SCORE (MAXIMUM POSSIBLE = 100)
1	Luxembourg	98.55
2	Switzerland	98.45
3	Singapore	98.38
4	Japan	97.19
5	United States	97.17

Bottom Five Countries (Greatest Amount of Country Risk)

RANK	COUNTRY	TOTAL SCORE (MINIMUM POSSIBLE = 0)
174	Cuba	11.72
175	North Korea	8.02
176	Surinam	6.80
177	Iraq	5.50
178	Afghanistan	5.07

her money in the United States. If the yen weakens relative to the dollar, then it will buy fewer dollars, hence the investor will receive fewer dollars when it comes time to convert. Alternatively, if the yen strengthens relative to the dollar, the investor will earn higher dollar returns. It therefore follows that the effective rate of return on a foreign investment will depend on both the performance of the foreign security and on what happens to exchange rates over the life of the investment.

In Chapter 18, we will discuss exchange rates in considerably more detail. However, at this point we can mention two factors which can lead to exchange rate fluctuations. First, changes in relative inflation will lead to changes in exchange rates. If expected inflation increases more within some foreign country than in the United States, the value of that country's currency is likely to fall. Second, an increase in country risk will also cause that country's currency to fall. Consequently, inflation risk, country risk, and exchange rate risk are all interrelated.

SELF-TEST QUESTIONS

What is country risk?

Identify two factors which can cause exchange rates to fluctuate.

THE TERM STRUCTURE OF INTEREST RATES

A study of Figure 4-3 reveals that at certain times such as in 1996, short-term interest rates were lower than long-term rates, whereas at times such as in 1980 and 1981, short-term rates were higher than long-term rates. The relationship between long- and short-term rates, which is known as the **term structure of interest rates,** is important to corporate treasurers, who must decide whether to borrow by issuing long- or short-term debt, and to investors, who must decide whether to buy long- or short-term bonds. Thus, it is important to understand (1) how long- and short-term rates are related to each other and (2) what causes shifts in their relative positions.

Term Structure of Interest Rates
The relationship between bond yields and maturities.

To begin, we can look up in a source such as *The Wall Street Journal* or the *Federal Reserve Bulletin* the interest rates on Treasury bonds of various maturities at a given point in time. For example, the tabular section of Figure 4-5 presents interest rates for different maturities on two dates. The set of data for a given date, when plotted on a graph such as that in Figure 4-5, is called the **yield curve** for that date. The yield curve changes both in position and in slope over time. In March 1980, all rates were relatively high, and short-term rates were higher than long-term rates, causing the yield curve to be *downward sloping.* However, by July 1996, all rates had fallen, and short-term rates were lower than long-term rates, so the yield curve at that time was *upward sloping.* Had we drawn the yield curve during January 1982, it would have been essentially horizontal, for long-term and short-term bonds on that date had about the same rate of interest. (See Figure 4-3.)

Yield Curve
A graph showing the relationship between bond yields and maturities.

Figure 4-5 shows yield curves for U.S. Treasury securities, but we could have constructed them for corporate bonds. For example, we could have developed yield curves for AT&T, Exxon, Continental Airlines, or any other company that borrows money over a range of maturities. Had we constructed such curves and plotted them on Figure 4-5, the corporate yield curves would have been above those for Treasury securities because the corporate yields would include default risk premiums. However, the corporates would have had the same general shape as the Treasury curves. Also, the riskier the corporation, the higher its yield curve, so Continental, which is in a relatively weak financial position, would have had a yield curve substantially higher than that of Exxon, which has a top bond rating.

Historically, in most years long-term rates have been above short-term rates, so the yield curve usually slopes upward. For this reason, people often call an

F I G U R E   4 - 5   U.S. Treasury Bond Interest Rates on Different Dates

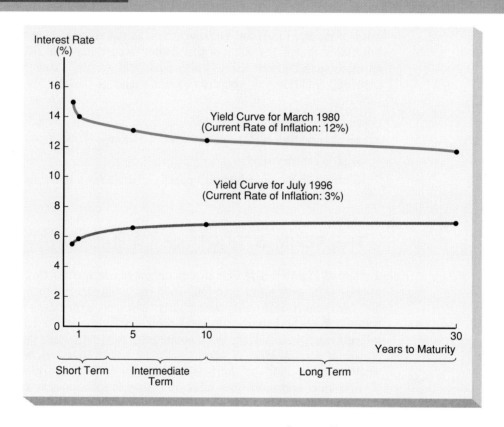

TERM TO MATURITY	INTEREST RATE	
	MARCH 1980	JULY 1996
6 months	15.0%	5.5%
1 year	14.0	5.9
5 years	13.5	6.6
10 years	12.8	6.9
30 years	12.3	7.0

"Normal" Yield Curve
An upward-sloping yield curve.

Inverted ("Abnormal") Yield Curve
A downward-sloping yield curve.

upward-sloping yield curve a **"normal" yield curve** and a yield curve which slopes downward an **inverted,** or **"abnormal," yield curve.** Thus, in Figure 4-5 the yield curve for March 1980 was inverted, but the one for July 1996 was normal. We explain in detail in the next section why an upward slope is the normal situation, but briefly, the reason is that short-term securities have less interest rate risk than longer-term securities, hence smaller MRPs. Therefore, short-term rates are normally lower than long-term rates.

SELF-TEST QUESTIONS

What is a yield curve, and what information would you need to draw this curve?

Distinguish between the shapes of a "normal" yield curve and an "abnormal" yield curve, and explain when each might exist.

WHAT DETERMINES THE SHAPE OF THE YIELD CURVE?[14]

The shape of the yield curve depends on two key factors: (1) expectations about future inflation and (2) perceptions about the relative riskiness of securities with different maturities.

Some academics and practitioners contend that this second factor — relative maturities — is considerably less important than expectations about future rates. They argue that the market is dominated by large bond traders who buy and sell securities of different maturities each day, that these traders focus only on short-term returns, and that they are less concerned with risk. According to this view, a bond trader is just as willing to buy a 30-year bond to pick up a short-term profit as he would be to buy a three-month security. Strict proponents of this view argue that the shape of the yield curve is therefore determined only by market expectations about future interest rates, thus their position has been called the *pure expectations theory* of the term structure of interest rates.

A majority of academics and practitioners would argue, however, that risks associated with changing rates do matter, and, moreover, that the market views long-term securities as riskier than short-term securities. This view is often referred to as the *liquidity preference theory*. The rationales for each of these theories are described below.

EXPECTATIONS THEORY

Expectations Theory
A theory which states that the shape of the yield curve depends on investors' expectations about future interest rates.

The **expectations theory**, sometimes referred to as the *pure expectations theory*, states that the yield curve depends on expectations about future interest rates. To begin, the expectations theory holds that long-term interest rates are a weighted average of current and expected future short-term interest rates. For example, if one-year Treasury bills currently yield 7 percent, but one-year bills are expected to yield 7.5 percent a year from now, investors will expect to earn an average of 7.25 percent over the next two years:[15]

$$\frac{7\% + 7.5\%}{2} = 7.25\%.$$

According to the expectations theory, this implies that a two-year Treasury note purchased today should also yield 7.25 percent. Similarly, if 10-year bonds yield 9 percent today, and if 5-year bonds are expected to yield 7.5 percent 10 years from now, then investors will expect to earn 9 percent for 10 years and 7.5 percent for 5 years, for an average return of 8.5 percent over the next 15 years:

$$\frac{9\% + 9\% + \ldots + 9\% + 7.5\% + \ldots + 7.5\%}{15} = \frac{10(9\%) + 5(7.5\%)}{15} = 8.5\%.$$

Consequently, a 15-year bond should yield this same return, 8.5 percent.

To understand the logic behind this averaging process, ask yourself what would happen if long-term yields were *not* an average of expected short-term yields.

---

[14]This section is relatively technical, but instructors can omit it without loss of continuity.

[15]Technically, we should be using geometric averages rather than arithmetic averages, but the differences are not material in this example. For a discussion of this point, see Robert C. Radcliffe, *Investment: Concepts, Analysis, and Strategy,* 5th ed. (Reading, MA: Addison-Wesley, 1997), Chapter 5.

For example, suppose two-year bonds yielded only 7 percent, not the 7.25 percent calculated above. Bond traders would be able to earn a profit by adopting the following trading strategy:

1. Borrow money for two years at a cost of 7 percent.
2. Invest the money in a series of one-year bonds. The expected return over the two-year period would be (7.0 + 7.5)/2 = 7.25%.

In this case, bond traders would rush to borrow money (demand funds) in the two-year market and invest (or supply funds) in the one-year market. Recall from Figure 4-2 that an increase in the demand for funds raises interest rates, whereas an increase in the supply of funds reduces interest rates. Therefore, bond traders' actions would push up the two-year yield but reduce the yield on one-year bonds. The net effect would be to bring about a market equilibrium in which two-year rates were a weighted average of expected future one-year rates.

The pure expectations theory assumes that investors establish bond prices and interest rates strictly on the basis of expectations for interest rates. This means that they are indifferent with respect to maturity in the sense that they do not view long-term bonds as being riskier than short-term bonds. Therefore, according to the pure expectations theory, the maturity risk premium (MRP) is equal to zero.

Moreover, according to the pure expectations theory, k_t, the nominal interest rate on Treasury securities, is determined as the sum of the real risk-free rate, k^*, plus an inflation premium, IP. Therefore, the nominal rate on a U.S. Treasury bond that matures in t years would be found as follows:

$$k_t = k^* + IP_t.$$

Here IP_t is found as the average inflation rate over the t years until the bond matures. The real risk-free rate tends to be fairly constant over time, so changes in interest rates are driven largely by changes in expected inflation. Note also that under the pure expectations theory, the MRP is assumed to be zero, and for Treasury securities the default risk premium (DRP) and liquidity premium (LP) are also zero.

To illustrate the pure expectations theory, suppose that in late December 1996 the real risk-free rate of interest was expected to remain constant at 3 percent ($k^* = 3\%$). Also, assume that the expected inflation rates for the next three years were as follows:

	EXPECTED ANNUAL (1-YEAR) INFLATION RATE	EXPECTED AVERAGE INFLATION RATE FROM 1996 TO INDICATED YEAR
1997	3%	3%/1 = 3.0%
1998	5%	(3% + 5%)/2 = 4.0%
1999	7%	(3% + 5% + 7%)/3 = 5.0%

Given these expectations, the following pattern of interest rates should exist:

	REAL RISK-FREE RATE (k^*)	+	INFLATION PREMIUM, WHICH IS EQUAL TO THE AVERAGE EXPECTED INFLATION RATE (IP_t)	=	NOMINAL TREASURY BOND RATE FOR EACH MATURITY ($k_{T\text{-BOND}}$)
1-year bond:	3%	+	3.0%	=	6.0%
2-year bond:	3%	+	4.0%	=	7.0%
3-year bond:	3%	+	5.0%	=	8.0%

Had the pattern of expected inflation rates been reversed, with inflation expected to fall from 7 percent to 5 percent and then to 3 percent, the following situation would have existed:

	REAL RISK-FREE RATE		AVERAGE EXPECTED INFLATION RATE		TREASURY BOND RATE FOR EACH MATURITY
1-year bond	3%	+	7.0%	=	10.0%
2-year bond	3%	+	6.0%	=	9.0%
3-year bond	3%	+	5.0%	=	8.0%

These hypothetical data are plotted in Figure 4-6. As you can see, an upward-sloping yield curve occurs when interest rates are expected to increase in the future. This increase could be due to an increase in expected inflation (as is the case in the example above) or to an increase in the expected real risk-free rate. By contrast, a downward-sloping yield curve occurs when interest rates are expected to decline.

In practice, we can never actually observe the marginal investor's expected inflation rate or the real risk-free rate. However, if the pure expectations theory were correct, we could "back out" of the yield curve the bond market's best guess about future interest rates. If, for example, you observe that Treasury securities with one- and two-year maturities yield 7 percent and 8 percent, respectively, this information can be used to calculate the market's forecast of what one-year rates will yield one year from now. If the pure expectations theory is correct, the rate on two-year bonds is the average of the current one-year rate and the one-year rate expected a year from now. Since the current one-year rate is 7 percent,

FIGURE   4-6   Hypothetical Example of the Term Structure of Interest Rates

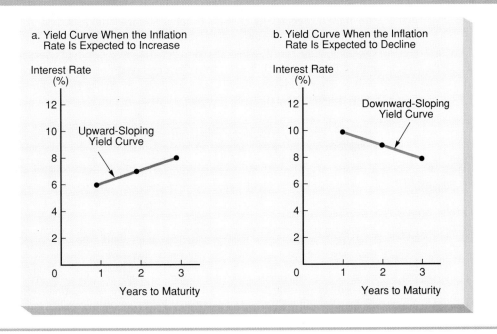

a. Yield Curve When the Inflation Rate Is Expected to Increase

b. Yield Curve When the Inflation Rate Is Expected to Decline

this implies that the one-year rate one year from now is expected to be 9 percent:

$$\text{2-year yield} = 8\% = \frac{7\% + X\%}{2}$$

$$X = 16\% - 7\% = 9\% = \text{1-year yield expected next year.}$$

LIQUIDITY PREFERENCE THEORY

Liquidity Preference Theory
The theory that lenders, other things held constant, would prefer to make short-term loans rather than long-term loans; hence, they will lend short-term funds at lower rates than long-term funds.

The pure expectations theory assumes that the maturity risk premium (MRP) is zero. However, convincing evidence suggests that there is a positive maturity risk premium — investors require higher rates of return on longer-term bonds, other things held constant.[16]

This has given rise to the **liquidity preference theory,** which states that long-term bonds normally yield more than short-term bonds for two reasons: (1) Investors generally prefer to hold short-term securities because such securities are more liquid in the sense that they can be converted to cash with little danger of loss of principal. Investors will, therefore, generally accept lower yields on short-term securities, and this leads to relatively low short-term rates. (2) Borrowers, on the other hand, generally prefer long-term debt because short-term debt exposes them to the risk of having to repay the debt under adverse conditions. Accordingly, borrowers are willing to pay a higher rate, other things held constant, for long-term funds than for short-term funds, and this also leads to relatively low short-term rates. Thus, lender and borrower preferences both operate to cause short-term rates to be lower than long-term rates. Taken together, these two sets of preferences imply that under normal conditions (1) a positive maturity risk premium (MRP) exists and (2) the MRP increases with years to maturity, causing the yield curve to be upward sloping.

It is important to understand that the liquidity preference theory does not imply that expectations do not matter. Indeed, most proponents of the liquidity preference theory would agree that expectations about future interest rates are the most important factor explaining the shape of the yield curve, but they reject the *pure* expectations theory. Since evidence suggests that there is a positive maturity risk premium, both expectations and liquidity preferences affect interest rates. As a result, when the slope of the yield curve changes, this could imply either that the market now thinks rates are going to be different in the future versus what it previously thought, that the maturity risk premium has changed, or that both events have occurred.

SELF-TEST QUESTIONS ??????

What are the two primary factors that explain the shape of the yield curve?

Why might the yield curve slope *downward* at a particular point in time?

---

[16]Some analysts subscribe to another theory, the *market segmentation theory,* which argues that long- and short-term bonds trade in separate markets and that there is little or no connection between the yields on short- and long-term bonds. Proponents of this theory suggest that the yield curve is explained by the relative supply and demand of long- and short-term securities — if the demand for long-term capital is strong relative to the supply of such capital, while the reverse holds in the short-term market, then the yield curve will be upward sloping. While supply and demand conditions are clearly important, most researchers today argue that the actions of bond traders, who buy and sell bonds of different maturities all day, arbitrage away any yield differentials caused by market imperfections and thus ensure that markets are not highly segmented.

OTHER FACTORS THAT INFLUENCE INTEREST RATE LEVELS

In addition to inflationary expectations and liquidity preferences, other factors also influence both the general level of interest rates and the shape of the yield curve. The four most important factors are (1) Federal Reserve policy; (2) the level of the federal budget deficit; (3) international factors, including the foreign trade balance and interest rates in other countries; and (4) the level of business activity.

FEDERAL RESERVE POLICY

As you probably learned in your economics courses, (1) the money supply has a major effect on both the level of economic activity and the inflation rate, and (2) in the United States, the Federal Reserve Board controls the money supply. If the Fed wants to stimulate the economy, as it did in 1995, it increases growth in the money supply. The initial effect of such an action is to cause interest rates to decline. However, a larger money supply may also lead to an increase in the expected inflation rate, which, in turn, could push interest rates up. The reverse holds if the Fed tightens the money supply.

To illustrate, in 1981 inflation was quite high, so the Fed tightened up the money supply. The Fed deals primarily in the short-term end of the market, so this tightening had the direct effect of pushing short-term rates up sharply. At the same time, the very fact that the Fed was taking strong action to reduce inflation led to a decline in expectations for long-run inflation, which led to a decline in long-term bond yields.

In 1991, the situation was just the reverse. To combat the recession, the Fed took steps to reduce interest rates. Short-term rates fell, and long-term rates also dropped, but not as sharply. These lower rates benefitted heavily indebted businesses and individual borrowers, and home mortgage refinancings put additional billions of dollars into consumers' pockets. Savers, of course, lost out, but the net effect of lower interest rates was a stronger economy. Lower rates encourage businesses to borrow for investment, stimulate the housing market, and bring down the value of the dollar relative to other currencies, which helps U.S. exporters and thus lowers the trade deficit.

During periods when the Fed is actively intervening in the markets, the yield curve may be temporarily distorted. Short-term rates will be temporarily "too low" if the Fed is easing credit, and "too high" if it is tightening credit. Long-term rates are not affected as much by Fed intervention. For example, the fear of rising inflation led the Federal Reserve to increase short-term interest rates six times during 1994. While short-term rates rose by nearly 4 percentage points, long-term rates increased by only 1.5 percentage points.

FEDERAL DEFICITS

If the federal government spends more than it takes in from tax revenues, it runs a deficit, and that deficit must be covered either by borrowing or by printing money (increasing the money supply). If the government borrows, this added demand for funds pushes up interest rates. If it prints money, this increases expectations for future inflation, which also drives up interest rates. Thus, the larger the federal deficit, other things held constant, the higher the level of interest rates. Whether long- or short-term rates are more affected depends on how the deficit is financed, so we cannot state, in general, how deficits will affect the slope of the yield curve.

INTERNATIONAL FACTORS

Businesses and individuals in the United States buy from and sell to people and firms in other countries. If we buy more than we sell (that is, if we import more than we export), we are said to be running a *foreign trade deficit*. When trade deficits occur, they must be financed, and the main source of financing is debt. In other words, if we import $200 billion of goods but export only $100 billion, we run a trade deficit of $100 billion, and we would probably borrow the $100 billion.[17] Therefore, the larger our trade deficit, the more we must borrow, and as we increase our borrowing, this drives up interest rates. Also, foreigners are willing to hold U.S. debt if and only if the rate paid on this debt is competitive with interest rates in other countries. Therefore, if the Federal Reserve attempts to lower interest rates in the United States, causing our rates to fall below rates abroad, then foreigners will sell U.S. bonds, those sales will depress bond prices, and the result will be higher U.S. rates. Thus, if the trade deficit is large relative to the size of the overall economy, it may hinder the Fed's ability to combat a recession by lowering interest rates.

The United States has been running annual trade deficits since the mid-1970s, and the cumulative effect of these deficits is that the United States has become the largest debtor nation of all time. As a result, our interest rates are very much influenced by interest rates in other countries around the world (higher rates abroad lead to higher U.S. rates). Because of all this, U.S. corporate treasurers — and anyone else who is affected by interest rates — must keep up with developments in the world economy.

BUSINESS ACTIVITY

Figure 4-3, presented earlier, can be examined to see how business conditions influence interest rates. Here are the key points revealed by the graph:

1. Because inflation increased from 1959 to 1981, the general tendency during that period was toward higher interest rates. However, since the 1981 peak, the trend has generally been downward.

2. Until 1966, short-term rates were almost always below long-term rates. Thus, in those years the yield curve was almost always "normal" in the sense that it was upward sloping.

3. The shaded areas in the graph represent recessions, during which (1) both the demand for money and the rate of inflation tend to fall and (2) the Federal Reserve tends to increase the money supply in an effort to stimulate the economy. As a result, there is a tendency for interest rates to decline during recessions. Currently, in January 1997, we are in a period of relatively stable, but slow, growth. The Fed is reluctant to lower interest rates because it is afraid that action would speed up the economy too much and lead to higher inflation. At the same time, the Fed does not want to raise rates, because that

---

[17]The deficit could also be financed by selling assets, including gold, corporate stocks, entire companies, and real estate. The United States has financed its massive trade deficits by all of these means in recent years, but the primary method has been by borrowing from foreigners.

might drive the economy into a recession. Therefore, interest rates are currently relatively stable.

4. During recessions, short-term rates decline more sharply than long-term rates. This occurs because (1) the Fed operates mainly in the short-term sector, so its intervention has the strongest effect there, and (2) long-term rates reflect the average expected inflation rate over the next 20 to 30 years, and this expectation generally does not change much, even when the current inflation rate is low because of a recession or high because of a boom. So, short-term rates are more volatile than long-term rates.

SELF-TEST QUESTIONS ??????

Other than inflationary expectations and liquidity preferences, name some additional factors which influence interest rates, and explain the effects of each.

How does the Fed stimulate the economy? How does the Fed affect interest rates? Does the Fed have complete control over U.S. interest rates; that is, can it set rates at any level it chooses?

INTEREST RATE LEVELS AND STOCK PRICES

Interest rates have two effects on corporate profits: (1) Because interest is a cost, the higher the interest rate, the lower a firm's profits, other things held constant. (2) Interest rates affect the level of economic activity, and economic activity affects corporate profits. Interest rates obviously affect stock prices because of their effects on profits, but perhaps even more important, they have an effect due to competition in the marketplace between stocks and bonds. If interest rates rise sharply, investors can get higher returns in the bond market, which induces them to sell stocks and to transfer funds from the stock market to the bond market. Selling stock in response to rising interest rates obviously depress stock prices. Of course, the reverse occurs if interest rates decline. Indeed, the bull market of December 1991, when the Dow Jones Industrial Index rose 10 percent in less than a month, was caused almost entirely by a sharp drop in long-term interest rates.

The experience of Kansas City Power, the electric utility serving western Missouri and eastern Kansas, can be used to illustrate the effects of interest rates on stock prices. In 1983, the firm's stock sold for $9.50 per share, and, since the firm paid a $1.17 dividend, the dividend yield was $1.17/$9.50 = 12.3%. Kansas City Power's bonds at the time also yielded about 12.3 percent. Thus, if someone had saved $100,000 and invested it in either the stock or the bonds, his or her annual income would have been about $12,300. (The investor might also have expected the stock price to grow over time, providing some capital gains, but that point is not relevant to this example.)

By 1996, interest rates were lower, and Kansas City Power's bonds were yielding only 8 percent. If the stock still yielded 12.3 percent, investors would be much more inclined to invest in the stock than in the bonds. Thus, investment money would flow into the stock rather than the bonds, and the stock price would be bid up. Indeed, this is exactly what happened. Kansas City Power's stock sold for $25 in early 1996, a gain of 163 percent over the period. Meanwhile, the dividend increased from $1.17 to $1.56, or by only 33 percent. Thus, the major factor in the stock price rise was not the growth in dividends but, rather, the fact that interest rates had fallen. The $25 stock price produced a dividend yield of $1.56/$25 = 6.2%, which was in line with the firm's current bond yield.

SELF-TEST QUESTION

In what two ways do changes in interest rates affect stock prices?

INTEREST RATES AND BUSINESS DECISIONS

The yield curve for July 1996, shown earlier in Figure 4-5, indicates how much the U.S. government had to pay in 1996 to borrow money for one year, five years, ten years, and so on. A business borrower would have had to pay somewhat more, but assume for the moment that we are back in July 1996 and that the yield curve for that year also applies to your company. Now suppose your company has decided (1) to build a new plant with a 30-year life which will cost $1 million and (2) to raise the $1 million by selling an issue of debt (or borrowing) rather than by selling stock. If you borrowed in 1996 on a short-term basis — say, for one year — your interest cost for that year would be only 5.9 percent, or $59,000. On the other hand, if you used long-term (30-year) financing, your cost would be 7.0 percent, or $70,000. Therefore, at first glance, it would seem that you should use short-term debt.

However, this could prove to be a horrible mistake. If you use short-term debt, you will have to renew your loan every year, and the rate charged on each new loan will reflect the then-current short-term rate. Interest rates could return to their March 1980 levels, in which case you would be paying 14 percent, or $140,000, per year. These high interest payments would cut into, and perhaps eliminate, your profits. Your reduced profitability could easily increase your firm's risk to the point where its bond rating would be lowered, causing lenders to increase the risk premium built into the interest rate they charge. That would force you to pay an even higher rate, which would further reduce your profitability, worrying lenders even more, and making them reluctant to renew your loan. If your lenders refused to renew the loan and demanded its repayment, as they would have every right to do, you might have to sell assets at a loss, which could lead to bankruptcy.

On the other hand, if you used long-term financing in 1996, your interest costs would remain constant at $70,000 per year, so an increase in interest rates in the economy would not hurt you. You might even be able to buy up some of your bankrupt competitors at bargain prices — bankruptcies increase dramatically when interest rates rise, primarily because many firms do use too much short-term debt.

Does all this suggest that firms should always avoid short-term debt? Not necessarily. If inflation falls over the next few years, so will interest rates. If you had borrowed on a long-term basis for 7.0 percent in July 1996, your company would be at a major disadvantage if it was locked into 7.0 percent debt while its competitors (who used short-term debt in 1996 and thus rode interest rates down in subsequent years) had a borrowing cost of only 3 or 4 percent.

Financing decisions would be easy if we could develop accurate forecasts of future interest rates. Unfortunately, predicting interest rates with consistent accuracy is somewhere between difficult and impossible—people who make a living by selling interest rate forecasts say it is difficult, but many others say it is impossible.

Even if it is difficult to predict future interest rate *levels,* it is easy to predict that interest rates will *fluctuate*—they always have, and they always will. This being the case, sound financial policy calls for using a mix of long- and short-term debt, as well as equity, to position the firm so that it can survive in any interest rate environment. Further, the optimal financial policy depends in an important way on the nature of the firm's assets—the easier it is to sell off assets to generate cash, the more feasible it is to use large amounts of short-term debt. This makes it more feasible for a firm to finance its current assets than its fixed assets with short-term debt. We will return to this issue later in the book, when we discuss working capital policy.

Changes in interest rates also have implications for savers. For example, if you had a 401(k) plan—and someday you probably will—you would probably want to invest some of your money in a bond mutual fund. You could choose a fund that had an average maturity of 25 years, 20 years, and so on, down to only a few months (a money market fund). How would your choice affect your investment results, hence your retirement income? First, the annual interest income earned by the plan would be affected. For example, if the yield curve were upward sloping, as it normally is, you would earn more interest if you chose a fund that held long-term bonds. Note, though, that if you chose a long-term fund and interest rates then rose, the market value of the bonds in the fund would decline. For example, as we will see in Chapter 7, if you had $100,000 in a fund whose average bond had a maturity of 25 years and a coupon rate of 6 percent, and if interest rates then rose from 6 percent to 10 percent, the market value of your fund would decline from $100,000 to about $64,000. Of course, if rates declined, your fund would increase in value. In any event, your choice of maturity would have a major effect on your investment performance, hence your future income.

SELF-TEST QUESTIONS

If short-term interest rates are lower than long-term rates, why might a borrower still choose to finance with long-term debt?

Explain the following statement: "The optimal financial policy depends in an important way on the nature of the firm's assets."

SUMMARY

In this chapter, we discussed the nature of financial markets, the types of institutions that operate in these markets, how interest rates are determined, and some of the ways in which interest rates affect business decisions. The key concepts covered are listed below.

♦ There are many different types of **financial markets.** Each market serves a different region or deals with a different type of security.

♦ **Physical asset markets,** also called tangible or real asset markets, are those for such products as wheat, autos, and real estate.

♦ **Financial asset markets** deal with stocks, bonds, notes, mortgages, and other claims on real assets.

♦ **Spot markets** and **futures markets** are terms that refer to whether the assets are being bought or sold for "on-the-spot" delivery or for delivery at some future date.

♦ **Money markets** are the markets for debt securities with maturities of less than one year.

♦ **Capital markets** are the markets for long-term debt and corporate stocks.

♦ **Primary markets** are the markets in which corporations raise new capital.

♦ **Secondary markets** are markets in which existing, already outstanding, securities are traded among investors.

♦ Securities firms have been busy developing new financial products called **derivatives,** which is a security whose value is derived from the price of some other "underlying" asset.

♦ Transfers of capital between borrowers and savers take place (1) by **direct transfers** of money and securities; (2) by transfers through **investment banking houses,** which act as middlemen; and (3) by transfers through **financial intermediaries,** which create new securities.

♦ Among the major classes of intermediaries are **commercial banks, savings and loan associations, mutual savings banks, credit unions, pension funds, life insurance companies,** and **mutual funds.**

♦ One result of ongoing regulatory changes has been a blurring of the distinctions between the different financial institutions. The trend in the United States has been toward **financial service corporations** which offer a wide range of financial services, including investment banking, brokerage operations, insurance, and commercial banking.

♦ The **stock market** is an especially important market because this is where stock prices (which are used to "grade" managers' performances) are established.

♦ There are two basic types of stock markets — the **organized exchanges** and the **over-the-counter market.**

♦ Capital is allocated through the price system — a price must be paid to "rent" money. Lenders charge **interest** on funds they lend, while equity investors receive **dividends and capital gains** in return for letting firms use their money.

♦ Four fundamental factors affect the cost of money: (1) **production opportunities**, (2) **time preferences for consumption**, (3) **risk**, and (4) **inflation**.

♦ The **risk-free rate of interest, k_{RF}** is defined as the real risk-free rate, k^*, plus an inflation premium, IP, hence $k_{RF} = k^* + IP$.

♦ The **nominal** (or **quoted) interest rate** on a debt security, **k,** is composed of the real risk-free rate, k^*, plus premiums that reflect inflation (IP), default risk (DRP), liquidity (LP), and maturity risk (MRP):

$$k = k^* + IP + DRP + LP + MRP.$$

♦ If the **real risk-free rate of interest and the various premiums were constant over time,** interest rates would be stable. However, both the real rate and the premiums — especially the premium for expected inflation — **do change over time, causing market interest rates to change.** Also, Federal Reserve intervention to increase or decrease the money supply, as well as international currency flows, lead to fluctuations in interest rates.

♦ The relationship between the yields on securities and the securities' maturities is known as the **term structure of interest rates,** and the **yield curve** is a graph of this relationship.

♦ The shape of the yield curve depends on two key factors: (1) **expectations about future inflation** and (2) **perceptions about the relative riskiness of securities with different maturities.**

♦ The yield curve is normally **upward sloping** — this is called a **normal yield curve.** However, the curve can slope downward (an **inverted yield curve**) if the inflation rate is expected to decline.

♦ A number of theories have been proposed to explain the shape of the yield curve at any point in time. These theories include the **expectations theory** and the **liquidity preference theory.**

♦ **Interest rate levels have a profound effect on stock prices.** Higher interest rates (1) slow down the economy, (2) increase interest expenses and thus lower corporate profits, and (3) cause investors to sell stocks and transfer funds to the bond market. Thus, higher interest rates depress stock prices.

♦ Because interest rate levels are difficult if not impossible to predict, **sound financial policy** calls for using a mix of short- and long-term debt, and also for positioning the firm to survive in any future interest rate environment.

QUESTIONS

4-1 What are financial intermediaries, and what economic functions do they perform?

4-2 Suppose interest rates on residential mortgages of equal risk were 7 percent in California and 9 percent in New York. Could this differential persist? What forces might tend to equalize rates? Would differentials in borrowing costs for businesses of equal risk located in California and New York be more or less likely to exist than differentials in residential mortgage rates? Would differentials in the cost of money for New York and California firms be more likely to exist if the firms being compared were very large or if they were very small? What are the implications of all this for the pressure now being put on Congress to permit banks to engage in nationwide branching?

4-3 What would happen to the standard of living in the United States if people lost faith in the safety of our financial institutions? Why?

4-4 How does a cost-efficient capital market help to reduce the prices of goods and services?

4-5 Which fluctuate more, long-term or short-term interest rates? Why?

4-6 Suppose you believe that the economy is just entering a recession. Your firm must raise capital immediately, and debt will be used. Should you borrow on a long-term or a short-term basis? Why?

4-7 Suppose the population of Area Y is relatively young while that of Area O is relatively old, but everything else about the two areas is equal.
a. Would interest rates likely be the same or different in the two areas? Explain.
b. Would a trend toward nationwide branching by banks and savings and loans, and the development of nationwide diversified financial corporations, affect your answer to Part a?

4-8 Suppose a new process was developed which could be used to make oil out of seawater. The equipment required is quite expensive, but it would, in time, lead to very low prices for gasoline, electricity, and other types of energy. What effect would this have on interest rates?

4-9 Suppose a new and much more liberal Congress and administration were elected, and their first order of business was to take away the independence of the Federal Reserve System, and to force the Fed to greatly expand the money supply. What effect would this have
a. On the level and slope of the yield curve immediately after the announcement?
b. On the level and slope of the yield curve that would exist two or three years in the future?

4-10   It is a fact that the federal government (1) encouraged the development of the savings and loan industry; (2) virtually forced the industry to make long-term, fixed-interest-rate mortgages; and (3) forced the savings and loans to obtain most of their capital as deposits that were withdrawable on demand.

a. Would the savings and loans have higher profits in a world with a "normal" or an inverted yield curve?

b. Would the savings and loan industry be better off if the individual institutions sold their mortgages to federal agencies and then collected servicing fees or if the institutions held the mortgages that they originated?

4-11   Suppose interest rates on Treasury bonds rose from 7 to 14 percent as a result of higher interest rates in Europe. What effect would this have on the price of an average company's common stock?

SELF-TEST PROBLEMS   (Solutions Appear in Appendix B)

ST-1
Key terms

Define each of the following terms:

a. Money market; capital market
b. Primary market; secondary market
c. Private markets; public markets
d. Derivatives
e. Investment banker; financial service corporation
f. Financial intermediary
g. Mutual fund; money market fund
h. Organized security exchanges; over-the-counter market
i. Production opportunities; time preferences for consumption
j. Real risk-free rate of interest, k^*; nominal risk-free rate of interest, k_{RF}
k. Inflation premium (IP)
l. Default risk premium (DRP)
m. Liquidity; liquidity premium (LP)
n. Interest rate risk; maturity risk premium (MRP)
o. Reinvestment rate risk
p. Term structure of interest rates; yield curve
q. "Normal" yield curve; inverted ("abnormal") yield curve
r. Expectations theory
s. Liquidity preference theory
t. Foreign trade deficit

ST-2
Inflation rates

Assume that it is now January 1, 1998. The rate of inflation is expected to be 4 percent throughout 1998. However, increased government deficits and renewed vigor in the economy are then expected to push inflation rates higher. Investors expect the inflation rate to be 5 percent in 1999, 6 percent in 2000, and 7 percent in 2001. The real risk-free rate, k^*, is expected to remain at 2 percent over the next 5 years. Assume that no maturity risk premiums are required on bonds with 5 years or less to maturity. The current interest rate on 5-year T-bonds is 8 percent.

a. What is the average expected inflation rate over the next 4 years?
b. What should be the prevailing interest rate on 4-year T-bonds?
c. What is the implied expected inflation rate in 2002, or Year 5, given that Treasury bonds which mature in that year yield 8 percent?

STARTER PROBLEMS

4-1
Expected rate of interest

The real risk-free rate of interest is 3 percent. Inflation is expected to be 2 percent this year and 4 percent during the next 2 years. Assume that the maturity risk premium is zero. What is the yield on 2-year Treasury securities? What is the yield on 3-year Treasury securities?

4-2
Default risk premium

A Treasury bond which matures in 10 years has a yield of 6 percent. A 10-year corporate bond has a yield of 8 percent. Assume that the liquidity premium on the corporate bond is 0.5 percent. What is the default risk premium on the corporate bond?

4-3
Expected rate of interest

One-year Treasury securities yield 5 percent. The market anticipates that 1 year from now, 1-year Treasury securities will yield 6 percent. If the pure expectations hypothesis is correct, what should be the yield today for 2-year Treasury securities?

4-4
Maturity risk premium

The real risk-free rate is 3 percent, and inflation is expected to be 3 percent for the next 2 years. A 2-year Treasury security yields 6.2 percent. What is the maturity risk premium for the 2-year security?

EXAM-TYPE PROBLEMS

The problems included in this section are set up in such a way that they could be used as multiple-choice exam problems.

4-5
Expected rate of interest

Interest rates on 1-year Treasury securities are currently 5.6 percent, while 2-year Treasury securities are yielding 6 percent. If the pure expectations theory is correct, what does the market believe will be the yield on 1-year securities 1 year from now?

4-6
Expected rate of interest

Interest rates on 4-year Treasury securities are currently 7 percent, while interest rates on 6-year Treasury securities are currently 7.5 percent. If the pure expectations theory is correct, what does the market believe that 2-year securities will be yielding 4 years from now?

4-7
Expected rate of interest

The real risk-free rate is 3 percent. Inflation is expected to be 3 percent this year, 4 percent next year, and then 3.5 percent thereafter. The maturity risk premium is estimated to be $0.0005 \times (t - 1)$, where t = number of years to maturity. What is the nominal interest rate on a 7-year Treasury bill?

4-8
Expected rate of interest

Suppose the annual yield on a 2-year Treasury bond is 4.5 percent, while that on a 1-year bond is 3 percent. k* is 1 percent, and the maturity risk premium is zero.
a. Using the expectations theory, forecast the interest rate on a 1-year bond during the second year. (Hint: Under the expectations theory, the yield on a 2-year bond is equal to the average yield on 1-year bonds in Years 1 and 2.)
b. What is the expected inflation rate in Year 1? Year 2?

4-9
Expected rate of interest

Assume that the real risk-free rate is 2 percent and that the maturity risk premium is zero. If the nominal rate of interest on 1-year bonds is 5 percent and that on comparable-risk 2-year bonds is 7 percent, what is the 1-year interest rate that is expected for Year 2? What inflation rate is expected during Year 2? Comment on why the average interest rate during the 2-year period differs from the 1-year interest rate expected for Year 2.

4-10
Maturity risk premium

Assume that the real risk-free rate, k*, is 3 percent and that inflation is expected to be 8 percent in Year 1, 5 percent in Year 2, and 4 percent thereafter. Assume also that all Treasury bonds are highly liquid and free of default risk. If 2-year and 5-year Treasury bonds both yield 10 percent, what is the difference in the maturity risk premiums (MRPs) on the two bonds; that is, what is MRP_5 minus MRP_2?

4-11
Interest rates

Due to a recession, the inflation rate expected for the coming year is only 3 percent. However, the inflation rate in Year 2 and thereafter is expected to be constant at some level above 3 percent. Assume that the real risk-free rate is k* = 2% for all maturities and that the expectations theory fully explains the yield curve, so there are no maturity premiums. If 3-year Treasury bonds yield 2 percentage points more than 1-year bonds, what inflation rate is expected after Year 1?

PROBLEMS

4-12
Yield curves

Suppose you and most other investors expect the inflation rate to be 7 percent next year, to fall to 5 percent during the following year, and then to remain at a rate of 3 percent thereafter. Assume that the real risk-free rate, k*, will remain at 2 percent and that maturity risk premiums on Treasury securities rise from zero on very short-term bonds (those that mature in a few days) to a level of 0.2 percentage point for 1-year securities. Furthermore, maturity risk premiums increase 0.2 percentage point for each year to maturity, up to a limit of 1.0 percentage point on 5-year or longer-term T-bonds.
a. Calculate the interest rate on 1-, 2-, 3-, 4-, 5-, 10-, and 20-year Treasury securities, and plot the yield curve.

b. Now suppose Exxon, an AAA-rated company, had bonds with the same maturities as the Treasury bonds. As an approximation, plot an Exxon yield curve on the same graph with the Treasury bond yield curve. (Hint: Think about the default risk premium on Exxon's long-term versus its short-term bonds.)

c. Now plot the approximate yield curve of Long Island Lighting Company, a risky nuclear utility.

4-13
Yield curves

The following yields on U.S. Treasury securities were taken from *The Wall Street Journal* in September 1996:

TERM	RATE
6 months	5.5%
1 year	5.9
2 years	6.2
3 years	6.4
4 years	6.6
5 years	6.7
10 years	6.9
20 years	7.2
30 years	7.2

Plot a yield curve based on these data. (Note: If you looked the data up in the *Journal*, you would find that some of the bonds will show very low yields. These are "flower" bonds, which are generally owned by older people and are associated with funerals because they can be turned in and used at par value to pay estate taxes. Thus, flower bonds always sell at close to par and have a yield which is close to the coupon yield, irrespective of the "going rate of interest." Flower bonds no longer are issued; the last one was issued in 1971 with a coupon of 3.5 percent and a maturity date of November 1998. Also, the yields quoted in the *Journal* are not for the same point in time for all bonds, so random variations will appear. An interest rate series that is purged of flower bonds and random variations, and hence provides a better picture of the true yield curve, is known as the "constant maturity series"; this series can be obtained from the *Federal Reserve Bulletin*.)

4-14
Inflation and interest rates

In late 1980, the U.S. Commerce Department released new figures which showed that inflation was running at an annual rate of close to 15 percent. At the time, the prime rate of interest was 21 percent, a record high. However, many investors expected the new Reagan administration to be more effective in controlling inflation than the Carter administration had been. Moreover, many observers believed that the extremely high interest rates and generally tight credit, which resulted from the Federal Reserve System's attempts to curb the inflation rate, would shortly bring about a recession, which, in turn, would lead to a decline in the inflation rate and also in the interest rate. Assume that at the beginning of 1981, the expected inflation rate for 1981 was 13 percent; for 1982, 9 percent; for 1983, 7 percent; and for 1984 and thereafter, 6 percent.

a. What was the average expected inflation rate over the 5-year period 1981–1985? (Use the arithmetic average.)

b. What average *nominal* interest rate would, over the 5-year period, be expected to produce a 2 percent real risk-free rate of return on 5-year Treasury securities?

c. Assuming a real risk-free rate of 2 percent and a maturity risk premium which starts at 0.1 percent and increases by 0.1 percent each year, estimate the interest rate in January 1981 on bonds that mature in 1, 2, 5, 10, and 20 years, and draw a yield curve based on these data.

d. Describe the general economic conditions that could be expected to produce an upward-sloping yield curve.

e. If the consensus among investors in early 1981 had been that the expected inflation rate for every future year was 10 percent (that is, $I_t = I_{t+1} = 10\%$ for t = 1 to ∞), what do you think the yield curve would have looked like? Consider all the factors that are likely to affect the curve. Does your answer here make you question the yield curve you drew in Part c?

INTEGRATED CASE

SMYTH BARRY & COMPANY

4-15 Financial Markets, Institutions, and Taxes   Assume that you recently graduated with a degree in finance and have just reported to work as an investment advisor at the brokerage firm of Smyth Barry & Co. Your first assignment is to explain the nature of the U.S. financial markets to Michelle Varga, a professional tennis player who has just come to the United States from Mexico. Varga is a highly ranked tennis player who expects to invest substantial amounts of money through Smyth Barry. She is also very bright, and, therefore, she would like to understand in general terms what will happen to her money. Your boss has developed the following set of questions which you must ask and answer to explain the U.S. financial system to Varga.

a. What is a market? How are physical asset markets differentiated from financial markets?

b. Differentiate between money markets and capital markets.

c. Differentiate between a primary market and a secondary market. If Apple Computer decided to issue additional common stock, and Varga purchased 100 shares of this stock from Merrill Lynch, the underwriter, would this transaction be a primary market transaction or a secondary market transaction? Would it make a difference if Varga purchased previously outstanding Apple stock in the over-the-counter market?

d. Describe the three primary ways in which capital is transferred between savers and borrowers.

e. Securities can be traded on organized exchanges or in the over-the-counter market. Define each of these markets, and describe how stocks are traded in each of them.

f. What do we call the price that a borrower must pay for debt capital? What is the price of equity capital? What are the four most fundamental factors that affect the cost of money, or the general level of interest rates, in the economy?

g. What is the real risk-free rate of interest (k^*) and the nominal risk-free rate (k_{RF})? How are these two rates measured?

h. Define the terms inflation premium (IP), default risk premium (DRP), liquidity premium (LP), and maturity risk premium (MRP). Which of these premiums is included when determining the interest rate on (1) short-term U.S. Treasury securities, (2) long-term U.S. Treasury securities, (3) short-term corporate securities, and (4) long-term corporate securities? Explain how the premiums would vary over time and among the different securities listed above.

i. Varga is also interested in investing in countries other than the United States. Describe the various types of risks that arise when investing overseas.

j. What is the term structure of interest rates? What is a yield curve? At any given time, how would the yield curve facing an AAA-rated company compare with the yield curve for U.S. Treasury securities? At any given time, how would the yield curve facing a BB-rated company compare with the yield curve for U.S. Treasury securities? Draw a graph to illustrate your answer.

k. Two main theories have been advanced to explain the shape of the yield curve: (1) the expectations theory and (2) the liquidity preference theory. Briefly describe each of these theories. Do economists regard one as being "true"?

l. Suppose most investors expect the inflation rate to be 5 percent next year, 6 percent the following year, and 8 percent thereafter. The real risk-free rate is 3 percent. The maturity risk premium is zero for bonds that mature in 1 year or less, 0.1 percent for 2-year bonds, and then the MRP increases by 0.1 percent per year thereafter for 20 years, after which it is stable. What is the interest rate on 1-year, 10-year, and 20-year Treasury bonds? Draw a yield curve with these data. Is your yield curve consistent with the expectations theory or with the liquidity preference theory?

PART

FUNDAMENTAL CONCEPTS IN FINANCIAL MANAGEMENT

CHAPTER 5
RISK AND RATES OF RETURN

APPENDIX 5A
CALCULATING BETA COEFFICIENTS

CHAPTER 6
TIME VALUE OF MONEY

APPENDIX 6A
CONTINUOUS COMPOUNDING
AND DISCOUNTING

CHAPTER 5

RISK AND RATES OF RETURN

NO PAIN NO GAIN

If someone had invested $1,000 in a portfolio of large-company stocks in 1925 and then reinvested all dividends received, their investment would have grown to $1,114,000 by 1995. Over the same time period, a portfolio of small-company stocks would have grown even more, to $3,822,000. But if instead they had invested in long-term government bonds, the value of their portfolio would have been only $34,000, and a measly $13,000 for short-term bonds.

Given these numbers, why would anyone invest in bonds? The answer is, "Because bonds are less risky." While common stocks have over the past 70 years produced considerably higher returns, (1) we cannot be sure that the past is prologue to the future, and (2) stock values are more likely to experience sharp declines than bonds, so one has a greater chance of losing money on a stock investment. For example, in 1990 the average small-company stock lost 21.6 percent of its value, and large-company stocks lost 3.2 percent. Bonds, though, provided positive returns that year, as they almost always do.

Of course, some stocks are riskier than others, and even in years when the overall stock market is up, many individual stocks go down. Therefore, putting all your money into one stock is extremely risky. According to a recent *Business Week* article, the single best weapon against risk is diversification: "By spreading your money around, you're not tied to the fickleness of a given market, stock, or industry. . . . Correlation, in portfolio-manager speak, helps you diversify properly because it describes how closely two investments track each other. If they move in tandem, they're likely to suffer from the same bad news. So, you should combine assets with low correlations."

U.S. investors tend to think of "the stock market" as the U.S. stock market. However, U.S. stocks amount to only 35 percent of the value of all stocks. Foreign markets have been quite profitable, and they are not perfectly correlated with U.S. markets. Therefore, global diversification offers U.S. investors an opportunity to raise returns and at the same time reduce risk. However, foreign investing brings some risks of its own, most notably "exchange rate risk," which is the danger that exchange rate shifts will decrease the number of dollars a foreign currency will buy.

Although the central thrust of the *Business Week* article was on ways to measure and then reduce risk, it did point out that some newly created instruments which are actually extremely risky have been marketed as low-risk investments to naive investors. For example, several mutual funds have advertised that their portfolios "contain only securities backed by the U.S. government" but then failed to highlight that the funds themselves are using financial leverage, are investing in "derivatives," or are taking some other action which boosts current yields but exposes investors to huge risks.

When you finish this chapter, you should understand what risk is, how it is measured, and what actions can be taken to minimize it or at least to ensure that you are adequately compensated for bearing it.

SOURCES: "Figuring Risk: It's Not So Scary," *Business Week*, November 1, 1993, 154–155; "T-Bill Trauma and the Meaning of Risk," *The Wall Street Journal*, February 12, 1993, C1; *Stocks, Bonds, Bills, and Inflation: 1996 Yearbook* (Chicago: Ibbotson Associates, 1996).

We will now take an in-depth look at how investment risk is measured and how it affects investment returns. We start from the basic premise that investors like returns and dislike risk. Therefore, people will invest in riskier assets only if they expect to receive higher returns. In this chapter, we define precisely what the term *risk* means as it relates to investments, examine procedures managers use to measure risk, and discuss the relationship between risk and return. Then, in Chapters 6, 7, and 8, we extend these relationships to show how risk and return interact to determine security prices. Business executives should understand these concepts and think about them as they plan the actions which will shape their firms' futures.

As you will see, risk can be measured in different ways, and different conclusions about an asset's riskiness can be reached depending on the measure used. This can be confusing, but it will help if you remember the following:

1. All financial assets are expected to produce *cash flows,* and the riskiness of an asset is judged in terms of the riskiness of its cash flows.

2. The riskiness of an asset can be considered in two ways: (1) on a *stand-alone basis,* where the asset's cash flows are analyzed by themselves, or (2) in a *portfolio context,* where the cash flows from a number of assets are combined, and then the consolidated cash flows are analyzed.[1] There is an important difference between stand-alone and portfolio risk, and an asset which has a great deal of risk if held by itself may be much less risky if it is held as part of a larger portfolio.

3. In a portfolio context, an asset's risk can be divided into two components: (1) a *diversifiable risk component,* which can be diversified away and hence is of little concern to diversified investors, and (2) a *market risk component,* which reflects the risk of a general stock market decline and which cannot be eliminated by diversification, hence *does* concern investors. Only market risk is *relevant* — diversifiable risk is irrelevant because it can be eliminated.

4. An asset with a high degree of relevant (market) risk must provide a relatively high expected rate of return to attract investors. Investors in general are *averse to risk,* so they will not buy risky assets unless those assets have high expected returns.

5. In this chapter, we focus on *financial assets* such as stocks and bonds, but the concepts discussed here also apply to *physical assets* such as machines, trucks, or even whole plants. We apply risk analysis to physical assets in Chapter 12.

STAND-ALONE RISK

Risk
The chance that some unfavorable event will occur.

Risk is defined in *Webster's* as "a hazard; a peril; exposure to loss or injury." Thus, risk refers to the chance that some unfavorable event will occur. If you

---

[1]A *portfolio* is a collection of investment securities. If you owned some General Motors stock, some Exxon stock, and some IBM stock, you would be holding a three-stock portfolio. Because diversification lowers risk, most stocks are held in portfolios.

engage in skydiving, you are taking a chance with your life — skydiving is risky. If you bet on the horses, you are risking your money. If you invest in speculative stocks (or, really, *any* stock), you are taking a risk in the hope of making an appreciable return.

An asset's risk can be analyzed in two ways: (1) on a stand-alone basis, where the asset is considered in isolation, and (2) on a portfolio basis, where the asset is held as one of a number of assets in a portfolio. Thus, an asset's **stand-alone risk** is the risk an investor would face if he or she held only this one asset. Obviously, most assets are held in portfolios, but it is necessary to understand stand-alone risk in order to understand risk in a portfolio context.

To illustrate the riskiness of financial assets, suppose an investor buys $100,000 of short-term Treasury bills with an expected return of 5 percent. In this case, the rate of return on the investment, 5 percent, can be estimated quite precisely, and the investment is defined as being essentially *risk free*. However, if the $100,000 were invested in the stock of a company just being organized to prospect for oil in the mid-Atlantic, then the investment's return could not be estimated precisely. One might analyze the situation and conclude that the *expected* rate of return, in a statistical sense, is 20 percent, but the investor should also recognize that the *actual* rate of return could range from, say, $+1,000$ percent to -100 percent. Because there is a significant danger of actually earning much less than the expected return, the stock would be relatively risky.

No investment will be undertaken unless the expected rate of return is high enough to compensate the investor for the perceived risk of the investment. In our example, it is clear that few if any investors would be willing to buy the oil company's stock if its expected return were the same as that of the T-bill.

Naturally, a risky investment might not actually produce its expected rate of return — if assets always produced their expected returns, they would not be risky.

Investment risk, then, is related to the probability of actually earning less than the expected return — the greater the chance of a low or negative return, the riskier the investment. However, risk can be defined more precisely, and it is useful to do so.

PROBABILITY DISTRIBUTIONS

An event's *probability* is defined as the chance that the event will occur. For example, a weather forecaster might state, "There is a 40 percent chance of rain today and a 60 percent chance that it will not rain." If all possible events, or outcomes, are listed, and if a probability is assigned to each event, the listing is called a **probability distribution.** For our weather forecast, we could set up the following probability distribution:

OUTCOME (1)	PROBABILITY (2)
Rain	0.4 = 40%
No rain	0.6 = 60
	1.0 = 100%

The possible outcomes are listed in Column 1, while the probabilities of these outcomes, expressed both as decimals and as percentages, are given in Column 2. Notice that the probabilities must sum to 1.0, or 100 percent.

Probabilities can also be assigned to the possible outcomes (or returns) from an investment. If you buy a bond, you expect to receive interest on the bond, and

---

Stand-Alone Risk
The risk an investor would face if he or she held only one asset. Stand-alone risk is one part of "total risk," with the other part being risk which can be eliminated through diversification.

Probability Distribution
A listing of all possible outcomes, or events, with a probability (chance of occurrence) assigned to each outcome.

TABLE 5 - 1 Probability Distributions for Martin Products and U.S. Electric

DEMAND FOR THE COMPANY'S PRODUCTS	PROBABILITY OF THIS DEMAND OCCURRING	RATE OF RETURN ON STOCK IF THIS DEMAND OCCURS	
		MARTIN PRODUCTS	U.S. ELECTRIC
Strong	0.3	100%	20%
Normal	0.4	15	15
Weak	0.3	(70)	10
	1.0		

those interest payments will provide you with a rate of return on your investment. The possible outcomes from this investment are (1) that the issuer will make the interest payments or (2) that the issuer will default on the interest payments. The higher the probability of default, the riskier the bond, and the higher the risk, the higher the required rate of return. If you invest in a stock instead of buying a bond, you will again expect to earn a return on your money. A stock's return will come from dividends plus capital gains. Again, the riskier the stock — which means the higher the probability that the firm will fail to pay the expected dividends or that the stock price will decline rather than increase as you expected — the higher the expected return must be to induce you to invest in the stock.

With this in mind, consider the possible rates of return (dividend yield plus capital gain or loss) that you might earn next year on a $10,000 investment in the stock of either Martin Products Inc. or U.S. Electric Company. Martin manufactures and distributes computer terminals and equipment for the rapidly growing data transmission industry. Because it faces intense competition, its new products may or may not be competitive in the marketplace, so its future earnings cannot be predicted very well. Indeed, some new company could develop better products and literally bankrupt Martin. U.S. Electric, on the other hand, supplies an essential service, and because it has city franchises which protect it from competition, its sales and profits are relatively stable and predictable.

The rate-of-return probability distributions for the two companies are shown in Table 5-1. There is a 30 percent chance of strong demand, in which case both companies will have high earnings, pay high dividends, and enjoy capital gains. There is a 40 percent probability of normal demand and moderate returns, and there is a 30 percent probability of weak demand, which will mean low earnings and dividends as well as capital losses. Notice, however, that Martin Products' rate of return could vary far more widely than that of U.S. Electric. There is a fairly high probability that the value of Martin's stock will drop substantially, resulting in a 70 percent loss, while there is no chance of a loss for U.S. Electric.[2]

---

[2]It is, of course, completely unrealistic to think that any stock has no chance of a loss. Only in hypothetical examples could this occur. To illustrate, the price of Columbia Gas's stock dropped from $34.50 to $20.00 in just three hours on June 19, 1991. All investors were reminded that any stock is exposed to some risk of loss, and those investors who bought Columbia Gas on June 18 learned that lesson the hard way.

| **T A B L E   5 - 2** | Calculation of Expected Rates of Return: Payoff Matrix |

		MARTIN PRODUCTS		**U.S. ELECTRIC**	
DEMAND FOR THE COMPANY'S PRODUCTS (1)	**PROBABILITY OF THIS DEMAND OCCURRING (2)**	**RATE OF RETURN IF THIS DEMAND OCCURS (3)**	**PRODUCT: (2) × (3) = (4)**	**RATE OF RETURN IF THIS DEMAND OCCURS (5)**	**PRODUCT: (2) × (5) = (6)**
Strong	0.3	100%	30%	20%	6%
Normal	0.4	15	6	15	6
Weak	0.3	(70)	(21)	10	3
	1.0		$\hat{k} = 15\%$		$\hat{k} = 15\%$

EXPECTED RATE OF RETURN

Expected Rate of Return, $\hat{k}$
The rate of return expected to be realized from an investment; the weighted average of the probability distribution of possible results.

If we multiply each possible outcome by its probability of occurrence and then sum these products, as in Table 5-2, we have a *weighted average* of outcomes. The weights are the probabilities, and the weighted average is the **expected rate of return, $\hat{k}$,** called "k-hat."[3] The expected rates of return for both Martin Products and U.S. Electric are shown in Table 5-2 to be 15 percent. This type of table is known as a *payoff matrix.*

The expected rate of return calculation can also be expressed as an equation which does the same thing as the payoff matrix table:[4]

$$\text{Expected rate of return} = \hat{k} = P_1k_1 + P_2k_2 + \cdots + P_nk_n$$

$$= \sum_{i=1}^{n} P_ik_i. \qquad (5\text{-}1)$$

Here k_i is the *i*th possible outcome, P_i is the probability of the *i*th outcome, and n is the number of possible outcomes. Thus, $\hat{k}$ is a weighted average of the possible outcomes (the k_i values), with each outcome's weight being its probability of occurrence. Using the data for Martin Products, we obtain its expected rate of return as follows:

$$\hat{k} = P_1(k_1) + P_2(k_2) + P_3(k_3)$$
$$= 0.3(100\%) + 0.4(15\%) + 0.3(-70\%)$$
$$= 15\%.$$

---

[3]In Chapters 7 and 8, we will use k_d and k_s to signify the returns on bonds and stocks, respectively. However, this distinction is unnecessary in this chapter, so we just use the general term, k, to signify the expected return on an investment.

[4]The second form of the equation is simply a shorthand expression in which sigma (Σ) means "sum up," or add the values of n factors. If i = 1, then $P_ik_i = P_1k_1$; if i = 2, then $P_ik_i = P_2k_2$; and so on until i = n, the last possible outcome. The symbol $\sum_{i=1}^{n}$ simply says, "Go through the following process: First, let i = 1 and find the first product; then let i = 2 and find the second product; then continue until each individual product up to i = n has been found, and then add these individual products to find the expected rate of return."

U.S. Electric's expected rate of return is also 15 percent:

$$\hat{k} = 0.3(20\%) + 0.4(15\%) + 0.3(10\%)$$
$$= 15\%.$$

We can graph the rates of return to obtain a picture of the variability of possible outcomes; this is shown in the Figure 5-1 bar charts. The height of each bar signifies the probability that a given outcome will occur. The range of probable returns for Martin Products is from −70 to +100 percent, with an expected return of 15 percent. The expected return for U.S. Electric is also 15 percent, but its range is much narrower.

Thus far, we have assumed that only three situations can exist: strong, normal, and weak demand. Actually, of course, demand could range from a deep depression to a fantastic boom, and there are an unlimited number of possibilities in between. Suppose we had the time and patience to assign a probability to each possible level of demand (with the sum of the probabilities still equaling 1.0) and to assign a rate of return to each stock for each level of demand. We would have a table similar to Table 5-1, except that it would have many more entries in each column. This table could be used to calculate expected rates of return as shown previously, and the probabilities and outcomes could be approximated by continuous curves such as those presented in Figure 5-2. Here we have changed the assumptions so that there is essentially a zero probability that Martin Products' return will be less than −70 percent or more than 100 percent, or that U.S.

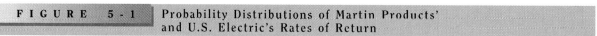

FIGURE 5-1 Probability Distributions of Martin Products' and U.S. Electric's Rates of Return

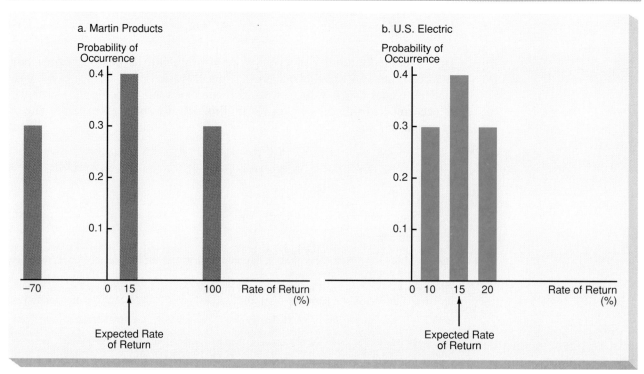

FIGURE 5-2 Continuous Probability Distributions of Martin Products' and U.S. Electric's Rates of Return

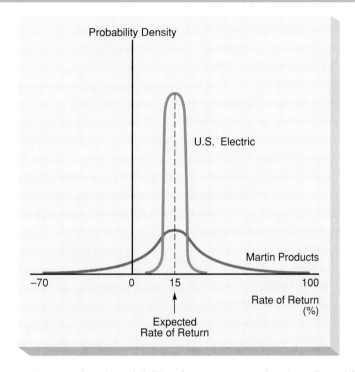

NOTE: The assumptions regarding the probabilities of various outcomes have been changed from those in Figure 5-1. There the probability of obtaining exactly 15 percent was 40 percent; here it is *much smaller* because there are many possible outcomes instead of just three. With continuous distributions, it is more appropriate to ask what the probability is of obtaining at least some specified rate of return than to ask what the probability is of obtaining exactly that rate. This topic is covered in detail in statistics courses.

Electric's return will be less than 10 percent or more than 20 percent, but virtually any return within these limits is possible.

The tighter, or more peaked, the probability distribution, the more likely it is that the actual outcome will be close to the expected value, and, consequently, the less likely it is that the actual return will end up far below the expected return. Thus, the tighter the probability distribution, the lower the risk assigned to a stock. Since U.S. Electric has a relatively tight probability distribution, its *actual return* is likely to be closer to its 15 percent *expected return* than is that of Martin Products.

MEASURING STAND-ALONE RISK: THE STANDARD DEVIATION

Risk is a difficult concept to grasp, and a great deal of controversy has surrounded attempts to define and measure it. However, a common definition, and one that is satisfactory for many purposes, is stated in terms of probability distributions such as those presented in Figure 5-2: *The tighter the probability distribution of expected future returns, the smaller the risk of a given investment.* According to

Standard Deviation, σ
A statistical measure of the variability of a set of observations.

this definition, U.S. Electric is less risky than Martin Products because there is a smaller chance that its actual return will end up far below its expected return.

To be most useful, any measure of risk should have a definite value — we need a measure of the tightness of the probability distribution. One such measure is the **standard deviation,** the symbol for which is **σ,** pronounced "sigma." The smaller the standard deviation, the tighter the probability distribution, and, accordingly, the lower the riskiness of the stock. To calculate the standard deviation, we proceed as shown in Table 5-3, taking the following steps:

1. Calculate the expected rate of return:

$$\text{Expected rate of return} = \hat{k} = \sum_{i=1}^{n} P_i k_i.$$

For Martin, we previously found $\hat{k} = 15\%$.

2. Subtract the expected rate of return ($\hat{k}$) from each possible outcome (k_i) to obtain a set of deviations about $\hat{k}$ as shown in Column 1 of Table 5-3:

$$\text{Deviation}_i = k_i - \hat{k}.$$

Variance, σ²
The square of the standard deviation.

3. Square each deviation, then multiply the result by the probability of occurrence for its related outcome, and then sum these products to obtain the **variance** of the probability distribution as shown in Columns 2 and 3 of the table:

$$\text{Variance} = \sigma^2 = \sum_{i=1}^{n} (k_i - \hat{k})^2 P_i. \qquad (5\text{-}2)$$

4. Finally, find the square root of the variance to obtain the standard deviation:

$$\text{Standard deviation} = \sigma - \sqrt{\sum_{i=1}^{n} (k_i - \hat{k})^2 P_i}. \qquad (5\text{-}3)$$

Thus, the standard deviation is essentially a weighted average of the deviations from the expected value, and it provides an idea of how far above or below the expected value the actual value is likely to be. Martin's standard deviation is seen in Table 5-3 to be $\sigma = 65.84\%$. Using these same procedures, we find U.S. Electric's standard deviation to be 3.87 percent. Martin Products has the larger standard deviation, which indicates a greater variation of returns and thus a greater chance that the expected return will not be realized. Therefore, Martin Products is a riskier investment than U.S. Electric when held alone.

TABLE 5-3	Calculating Martin Products' Standard Deviation	
$k_i - \hat{k}$ (1)	$(k_i - \hat{k})^2$ (2)	$(k_i - \hat{k})^2 P_i$ (3)
$100 - 15 = \quad 85$	7,225	$(7,225)(0.3) = 2,167.5$
$15 - 15 = \quad 0$	0	$(0)(0.4) = \quad 0.0$
$-70 - 15 = -85$	7,225	$(7,225)(0.3) = \underline{2,167.5}$
		$\text{Variance} = \sigma^2 = \underline{4,335.0}$

$$\text{Standard deviation} = \sigma = \sqrt{\sigma^2} = \sqrt{4,335} = 65.84\%.$$

If a probability distribution is normal, the *actual* return will be within ± 1 standard deviation of the *expected* return 68.26 percent of the time. Figure 5-3 illustrates this point, and it also shows the situation for $\pm 2\sigma$ and $\pm 3\sigma$. For Martin Products, $\hat{k} = 15\%$ and $\sigma = 65.84\%$, whereas $\hat{k} = 15\%$ and $\sigma = 3.87\%$ for U.S. Electric. Thus, if the two distributions were normal, there would be a 68.26 percent probability that Martin's actual return would be in the range of 15 ± 65.84 percent, or from -50.84 to 80.84 percent. For U.S. Electric, the 68.26 percent range is 15 ± 3.87 percent, or from 11.13 to 18.87 percent. With such a small σ, there is only a small probability that U.S. Electric's return would be significantly less than expected, so the stock is not very risky. For the average firm listed on the New York Stock Exchange, σ has generally been in the range of 35 to 40 percent in recent years.[5]

ON THE WWW

Wilshire Associates provides a download site for various returns series for indexes such as the Wilshire 5000 and the Wilshire 4500 at http://wilshire.com/home/ products/w5hist.htm in comma delimited ASCII format, making them easy to bring into any spreadsheet.

MEASURING STAND-ALONE RISK: THE COEFFICIENT OF VARIATION

If a choice has to be made between two investments which have the same expected returns but different standard deviations, most people would choose the one with the lower standard deviation and, therefore, the lower risk. Similarly, given a choice between two investments with the same risk (standard deviation) but different expected returns, investors would generally prefer the investment with the higher expected return. To most people, this is common sense — return is "good," risk is "bad," and, consequently, investors want as much return and as

---

[5]In the example, we described the procedure for finding the mean and standard deviation when the data are in the form of a known probability distribution. If only sample returns data over some past period are available, the standard deviation of returns can be estimated using this formula:

$$\text{Estimated } \sigma = S = \sqrt{\frac{\sum\limits_{t=1}^{n} (\bar{k}_t - \bar{k}_{Avg})^2}{n - 1}}. \tag{5-3a}$$

Here $\bar{k}_t$ ("k bar t") denotes the past realized rate of return in Period t, and $\bar{k}_{Avg}$ is the average annual return earned during the last n years. Here is an example:

YEAR	k_t
1995	15%
1996	−5
1997	20

$$\bar{k}_{Avg} = \frac{(15 - 5 + 20)}{3} = 10.0\%$$

$$\text{Estimated } \sigma \text{ (or S)} = \sqrt{\frac{(15 - 10)^2 + (-5 - 10)^2 + (20 - 10)^2}{3 - 1}}$$

$$= \sqrt{\frac{350}{2}} = 13.2\%.$$

The historical σ is often used as an estimate of the future σ. Much less often, and generally incorrectly, $\bar{k}_{Avg}$ for some past period is used as an estimate of k, the expected future return. Because past variability is likely to be repeated, σ may be a good estimate of future risk, but it is much less reasonable to expect that the past *level* of return (which could have been as high as $+100\%$ or as low as -50%) is the best expectation of what investors think will happen in the future.

Equation 5-3a is built into all financial calculators, and it is very easy to use. We simply enter the rates of return and press the key marked S (or S_x) to get the standard deviation. Note, though, that calculators have no built-in formula for finding σ where probabilistic data are involved; there you must go through the process outlined in Table 5-3 and Equation 5-3.

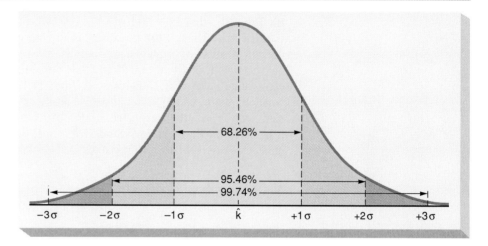

NOTES:
a. The area under the normal curve always equals 1.0, or 100 percent. *Thus, the areas under any pair of normal curves drawn on the same scale, whether they are peaked or flat, must be equal.*
b. Half of the area under a normal curve is to the left of the mean, indicating that there is a 50 percent probability that the actual outcome will be less than the mean, and half is to the right of k, indicating a 50 percent probability that it will be greater than the mean.
c. Of the area under the curve, 68.26 percent is within $\pm 1\sigma$ of the mean, indicating that the probability is 68.26 percent that the actual outcome will be within the range $k - 1\sigma$ to $k + 1\sigma$.
d. Procedures exist for finding the probability of other ranges. These procedures are covered in statistics courses.
e. For a normal distribution, the larger the value of σ, the greater the probability that the actual outcome will vary widely from, and hence perhaps be far below, the expected, or most likely, outcome. *Since the probability of having the actual result turn out to be far below the expected result is one definition of risk, and since σ measures this probability, we can use σ as a measure of risk.* This definition may not be a good one, however, if we are dealing with an asset held in a diversified portfolio. This point is covered later in the chapter.

Coefficient of Variation (CV)
Standardized measure of the risk per unit of return; calculated as the standard deviation divided by the expected return.

little risk as possible. But how do we choose between two investments when one has the higher expected return but the other has the lower standard deviation? To help answer this question, we use another measure of risk, the **coefficient of variation (CV),** which is the standard deviation divided by the expected return:

$$\text{Coefficient of variation} = CV = \frac{\sigma}{\hat{k}}. \qquad (5\text{-}4)$$

The coefficient of variation shows the risk per unit of return, and it provides a more meaningful basis for comparison when the expected returns on two alternatives are not the same. Since U.S. Electric and Martin Products have the same expected return, the coefficient of variation is not really necessary in this case. The firm with the larger standard deviation, Martin, must have the larger coefficient of variation when the means are equal. In fact, the coefficient of variation for Martin is 65.84/15 = 4.39 and that for U.S. Electric is 3.87/15 = 0.26. Thus, Martin is almost 17 times riskier than U.S. Electric on the basis of this criterion.

For a case where the coefficient of variation is necessary, consider Projects X and Y, which have different expected rates of return and different standard

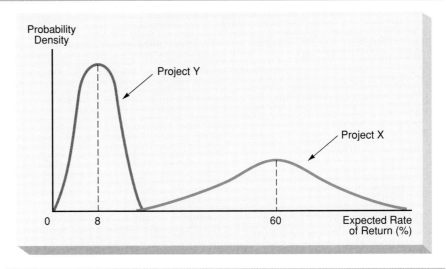

FIGURE 5-4 Comparison of Probability Distributions and Rates of Return for Projects X and Y

deviations. The situation with Projects X and Y is graphed in Figure 5-4. Project X has a 60 percent expected rate of return and a 15 percent standard deviation, while Project Y has an 8 percent expected return but only a 3 percent standard deviation. Is Project X riskier, on a relative basis, because it has the larger standard deviation? If we calculate the coefficients of variation for these two projects, we find that Project X has a coefficient of variation of 15/60 = 0.25, and Project Y has a coefficient of variation of 3/8 = 0.375. Thus, we see that Project Y actually has more risk per unit of return than Project X, in spite of the fact that X's standard deviation is larger. Therefore, even though Project Y has the lower standard deviation, according to the coefficient of variation it is riskier than Project X.

Project Y has the smaller standard deviation, hence the more peaked probability distribution, but it is clear from the graph that the chances of a really low return are higher for Y than for X because X's expected return is so high. Because the coefficient of variation captures the effects of both risk and return, it is a better measure for evaluating risk in situations where investments have substantially different expected returns.

RISK AVERSION AND REQUIRED RETURNS

Suppose you have worked hard and saved $1 million, which you now plan to invest. You can buy a 5 percent U.S. Treasury note, and at the end of one year you will have a sure $1.05 million, which is your original investment plus $50,000 in interest. Alternatively, you can buy stock in R&D Enterprises. If R&D's research programs are successful, your stock will increase in value to $2.1 million. However, if the research is a failure, the value of your stock will go to zero, and you will be penniless. You regard R&D's chances of success or failure as being 50-50, so the expected value of the stock investment is 0.5($0) + 0.5($2,100,000)

I N D U S T R Y   P R A C T I C E

THE TRADE-OFF BETWEEN RISK AND RETURN

The table accompanying this box, re-printed from Ibbotson Associates' *1996 Yearbook,* documents the historical trade-off between risk and return for different classes of investments from 1926 through 1995. As the table shows, those assets that produced the highest average returns also had the highest standard deviations and the widest ranges of returns. For example, small-company stocks had the highest average annual return, 17.7 percent, but their standard deviation of returns, 34.4 percent, was also the highest. By contrast, U.S. Treasury bills had the lowest standard deviation, 3.3 percent, but they also had the lowest average return, 3.8 percent.

When deciding among alternative investments, one needs to be aware of the trade-off between risk and return. While there is certainly no guarantee that history will repeat itself, returns observed in the past are a good starting point for estimating investments' returns in the future. Likewise, the standard deviations of past returns provide useful insights into the risks of different investments. For T-bills, however, the standard deviation needs to be interpreted carefully. Note that the table shows that Treasury bills have a positive standard deviation, which indicates some risk. However, if you invested in a one-year Treasury bill and held it for the full year, your realized return would be the same regardless of what happened to the economy that year, and thus the stan-

dard deviation of your return would be zero. So, why does the table show a 3.3 percent standard deviation for T-bills, which indicates a nonzero risk? In fact, a T-bill is risk-less *if you hold it for one year*, but if you invest in a rolling portfolio of one-year T-bills and hold it for a number of years, your investment income will vary depending on what happens to the level of interest rates in each year. So, while you can be sure of the return you will earn on a T-bill in a given year, you cannot be sure of the return you will earn on a portfolio of T-bills over a period of time.

SOURCE: *Stocks, Bonds, Bills, and Inflation: 1996 Yearbook* (Chicago: Ibbotson Associates, 1996), Table 2-1, 33.

= $1,050,000. Subtracting the $1 million cost of the stock leaves an expected profit of $50,000, or an expected (but risky) 5 percent rate of return:

$$\text{Expected rate of return} = \frac{\text{Expected ending value} - \text{Cost}}{\text{Cost}}$$

$$= \frac{\$1,050,000 - \$1,000,000}{\$1,000,000}$$

$$= \frac{\$50,000}{\$1,000,000} = 5\%.$$

Thus, you have a choice between a sure $50,000 profit (representing a 5 percent rate of return) on the Treasury note and a risky expected $50,000 profit (also representing a 5 percent expected rate of return) on the R&D Enterprises stock.

Summary Statistics of Annual Total Returns, 1926–1995

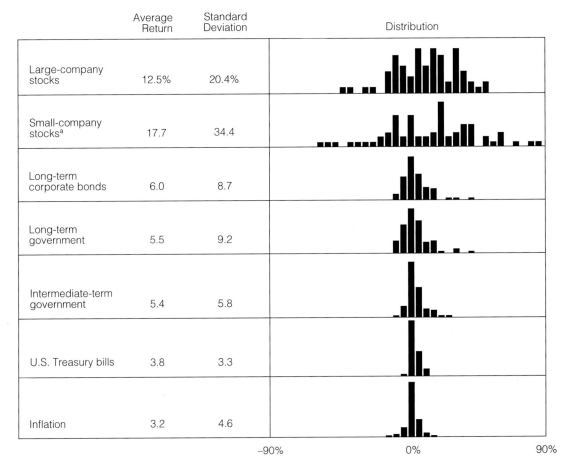

	Average Return	Standard Deviation	Distribution
Large-company stocks	12.5%	20.4%	
Small-company stocks[a]	17.7	34.4	
Long-term corporate bonds	6.0	8.7	
Long-term government	5.5	9.2	
Intermediate-term government	5.4	5.8	
U.S. Treasury bills	3.8	3.3	
Inflation	3.2	4.6	

–90%   0%   90%

[a]The small-company total return in 1933 was 142.9 percent.

SOURCE: *Stocks, Bonds, Bills, and Inflation: 1996 Yearbook* (Chicago: Ibbotson Associates, 1996).

Risk Aversion
Risk-averse investors dislike risk and require higher rates of return as an inducement to buy riskier securities.

Which one would you choose? *If you choose the less risky investment, you are risk averse. Most investors are indeed risk averse, and certainly the average investor is risk averse with regard to his or her "serious money." Because this is a well-documented fact, we shall assume* **risk aversion** *throughout the remainder of the book.*

What are the implications of risk aversion for security prices and rates of return? The answer is that, other things held constant, the higher a security's risk, the lower its price and the higher its required return. To see how risk aversion affects security prices, consider again U.S. Electric and Martin Products stocks. Suppose each stock sold for $100 per share and each had an expected rate of return of 15 percent. Investors are averse to risk, so under these conditions there would be a general preference for U.S. Electric. People with money to invest would bid for U.S. Electric rather than Martin stock, and Martin's stockholders would start selling their stock and using the money to buy U.S. Electric stock. Buying pressure would drive up the price of U.S. Electric's stock, and selling pressure would simultaneously cause Martin's price to decline.

These price changes, in turn, would cause changes in the expected rates of return on the two securities. Suppose, for example, that U.S. Electric's stock price was bid up from $100 to $150, whereas Martin's stock price declined from $100 to $75. This would cause U.S. Electric's expected return to fall to 10 percent, while Martin's expected return would rise to 20 percent. The difference in returns, 20% − 10% = 10%, is a **risk premium, RP,** which represents the additional compensation investors require for assuming the additional risk of Martin stock.

Risk Premium, RP
The difference between the expected rate of return on a given risky asset and that on a less risky asset.

This example demonstrates a very important principle: *In a market dominated by risk-averse investors, riskier securities must have higher expected returns, as estimated by the marginal investor, than less risky securities, for if this situation does not hold, buying and selling in the market will force it to occur.* We will consider the question of how much higher the returns on risky securities must be later in the chapter, after we see how diversification affects the way risk should be measured. Then, in Chapters 7 and 8, we will see how risk-adjusted rates of return affect the prices investors are willing to pay for different securities.

SELF-TEST QUESTIONS

What does "investment risk" mean?

Set up an illustrative probability distribution for an investment.

What is a payoff matrix?

Which of the two stocks graphed in Figure 5-2 is less risky? Why?

How does one calculate the standard deviation?

Which is a better measure of risk if assets have different expected returns: (1) the standard deviation or (2) the coefficient of variation? Explain.

Explain the following statement: "Most investors are risk averse."

How does risk aversion affect rates of return?

RISK IN A PORTFOLIO CONTEXT

In the preceding section, we considered the riskiness of assets held in isolation. Now we analyze the riskiness of assets held in portfolios. As we shall see, an asset held as part of a portfolio is less risky than the same asset held in isolation. Accordingly, most financial assets are held as parts of portfolios. Banks, pension funds, insurance companies, mutual funds, and other financial institutions are required by law to hold diversified portfolios. Even individual investors — at least those whose security holdings constitute a significant part of their total wealth — generally hold portfolios, not the stock of only one firm. This being the case, from an investor's standpoint the fact that a particular stock goes up or down is not very important; *what is important is the return on his or her portfolio, and the portfolio's risk. Logically, then, the risk and return of an individual security should be analyzed in terms of how that security affects the risk and return of the portfolio in which it is held.*

To illustrate, Payco American is a collection agency company which operates nationwide through 37 offices. The company is not well known, its stock is not very liquid, its earnings have fluctuated quite a bit in the past, and it doesn't pay a dividend. All this suggests that Payco is risky and that its required rate of return, k, should be relatively high. However, Payco's required rate of return in 1997, and all other years, was quite low in relation to those of most other companies. This indicates that investors regard Payco as being a low-risk company in spite of its uncertain profits. The reason for this counterintuitive fact has to do with diversification and its effect on risk. Payco's earnings rise during recessions, whereas most other companies' earnings tend to decline when the economy slumps. Therefore, adding Payco to a portfolio of "normal" stocks tends to stabilize returns on the entire portfolio.

PORTFOLIO RETURNS

Expected Return on a Portfolio, $\hat{k}_p$
The weighted average of the expected returns on the assets held in the portfolio.

The **expected return on a portfolio, $\hat{k}_p$,** is simply the weighted average of the expected returns on the individual assets in the portfolio, with the weights being the fraction of the total portfolio invested in each asset:

$$\hat{k}_p = w_1\hat{k}_1 + w_2\hat{k}_2 + \cdots + w_n\hat{k}_n \qquad (5\text{-}5)$$

$$= \sum_{i=1}^{n} w_i\hat{k}_i.$$

Here the $\hat{k}_i$'s are the expected returns on the individual stocks, the w_i's are the weights, and there are n stocks in the portfolio. Note (1) that w_i is the fraction of the portfolio's dollar value invested in Stock i (that is, the value of the investment in Stock i divided by the total value of the portfolio) and (2) that the w_i's must sum to 1.0.

Assume that in August 1997, a security analyst estimated that the following returns could be expected on the stocks of four large companies:

	EXPECTED RETURN, $\hat{k}$
Microsoft	14%
General Electric	13
Arctic Oil	20
Citicorp	18

If we formed a $100,000 portfolio, investing $25,000 in each stock, the expected portfolio return would be 16.25%:

$$\hat{k}_p = w_1\hat{k}_1 + w_2\hat{k}_2 + w_3\hat{k}_3 + w_4\hat{k}_4$$

$$= 0.25(14\%) + 0.25(13\%) + 0.25(20\%) + 0.25(18\%)$$

$$= 16.25\%.$$

Realized Rate of Return, $\bar{k}$
The return that was actually earned during some past period. The actual return ($\bar{k}$) usually turns out to be different from the expected return ($\hat{k}$).

Of course, after the fact and a year later, the actual **realized rates of return, $\bar{k}$,** on the individual stocks — the $\bar{k}_i$, or "k-bar," values — will almost certainly be different from their expected values, so $\bar{k}_p$ will be different from $\hat{k}_p = 16.25\%$. For example, Microsoft stock might double in price and provide a return of $+100\%$, whereas Citicorp stock might have a terrible year, fall sharply, and have a return of -75%. Note, though, that those two events would be somewhat offsetting, so the portfolio's return might still be close to its expected return, even though the individual stocks' actual returns were far from their expected returns.

FIGURE 5-5 Rate of Return Distributions for Two Perfectly Negatively Correlated Stocks (r = −1.0) and for Portfolio WM

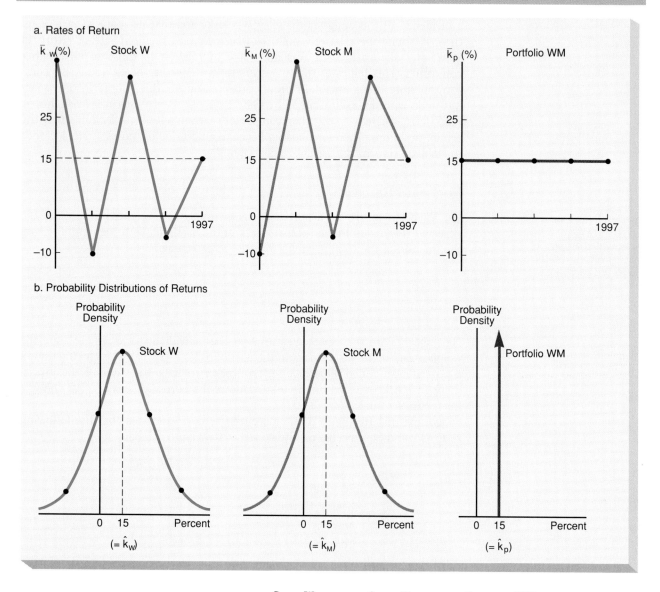

YEAR	STOCK W ($\bar{k}_W$)	STOCK M ($\bar{k}_M$)	PORTFOLIO WM ($\bar{k}_p$)
1993	40.0%	(10.0%)	15.0%
1994	(10.0)	40.0	15.0
1995	35.0	(5.0)	15.0
1996	(5.0)	35.0	15.0
1997	15.0	15.0	15.0
Average return	15.0%	15.0%	15.0%
Standard deviation	22.6%	22.6%	0.0%

PORTFOLIO RISK

As we just saw, the expected return on a portfolio is simply the weighted average of the expected returns on the individual assets in the portfolio. However, unlike returns, the riskiness of a portfolio, σ_p, is generally *not* the weighted average of the standard deviations of the individual assets in the portfolio; the portfolio's risk will be *smaller* than the weighted average of the assets' σ's. In fact, it is theoretically possible to combine stocks which are individually quite risky as measured by their standard deviations and to form a portfolio which is completely riskless, with $\sigma_p = 0$.

To illustrate the effect of combining assets, consider the situation in Figure 5-5. The bottom section gives data on rates of return for Stocks W and M individually, and also for a portfolio invested 50 percent in each stock. The three top graphs show plots of the data in a time series format, and the lower graphs show the probability distributions of returns, assuming that the future is expected to be like the past. The two stocks would be quite risky if they were held in isolation, but when they are combined to form Portfolio WM, they are not risky at all. (Note: These stocks are called W and M because the graphs of their returns in Figure 5-5 resemble a W and an M.)

The reason Stocks W and M can be combined to form a riskless portfolio is that their returns move countercyclically to each other — when W's returns fall, those of M rise, and vice versa. The tendency of two variables to move together is called **correlation,** and the **correlation coefficient, r,** measures this tendency.[6] In statistical terms, we say that the returns on Stocks W and M are *perfectly negatively correlated,* with $r = -1.0$.

The opposite of perfect negative correlation, with $r = -1.0$, is *perfect positive correlation,* with $r = +1.0$. Returns on two perfectly positively correlated stocks (M and M') would move up and down together, and a portfolio consisting of two such stocks would be exactly as risky as the individual stocks. This point is illustrated in Figure 5-6, where we see that the portfolio's standard deviation is equal to that of the individual stocks. *Thus, diversification does nothing to reduce risk if the portfolio consists of perfectly positively correlated stocks.*

Figures 5-5 and 5-6 demonstrate that when stocks are perfectly negatively correlated ($r = -1.0$), all risk can be diversified away, but when stocks are perfectly positively correlated ($r = +1.0$), diversification does no good whatsoever. In reality, most stocks are positively correlated, but not perfectly so. On average, the correlation coefficient for the returns on two randomly selected stocks would be about $+0.6$, and for most pairs of stocks, r would lie in the range of $+0.5$ to $+0.7$. *Under such conditions, combining stocks into portfolios reduces risk but does not eliminate it completely.* Figure 5-7 illustrates this point with two stocks whose correlation coefficient is $r = +0.67$. The portfolio's average return is 15 percent, which is exactly the same as the average return for each of the two stocks, but its standard deviation is 20.6 percent, which is less than the standard deviation of either stock. Thus, the portfolio's risk is *not* an average of the risks of its individual stocks — diversification has reduced, but not eliminated, risk.

Correlation
The tendency of two variables to move together.

Correlation Coefficient, r
A measure of the degree of relationship between two variables.

---

[6]The *correlation coefficient, r,* can range from $+1.0$, denoting that the two variables move up and down in perfect synchronization, to -1.0, denoting that the variables always move in exactly opposite directions. A correlation coefficient of zero indicates that the two variables are not related to each other — that is, changes in one variable are *independent* of changes in the other.

It is easy to calculate correlation coefficients with a financial calculator. Simply enter the returns on the two stocks and then press a key labeled "r." For W and M, $r = -1.0$.

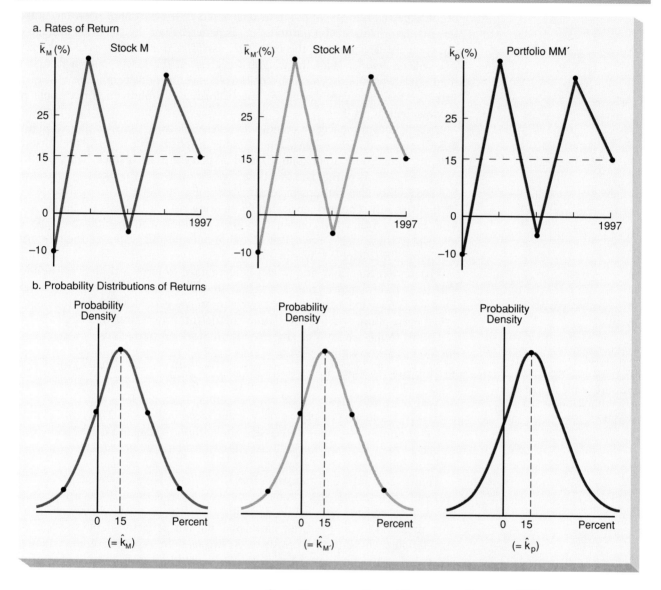

FIGURE 5-6 Rate of Return Distributions for Two Perfectly Positively Correlated Stocks (r = +1.0) and for Portfolio MM'

a. Rates of Return

b. Probability Distributions of Returns

YEAR	STOCK M ($\bar{k}_M$)	STOCK M' ($\bar{k}_M'$)	PORTFOLIO MM' ($\bar{k}_p$)
1993	(10.0%)	(10.0%)	(10.0%)
1994	40.0	40.0	40.0
1995	(5.0)	(5.0)	(5.0)
1996	35.0	35.0	35.0
1997	15.0	15.0	15.0
Average return	15.0%	15.0%	15.0%
Standard deviation	22.6%	22.6%	22.6%

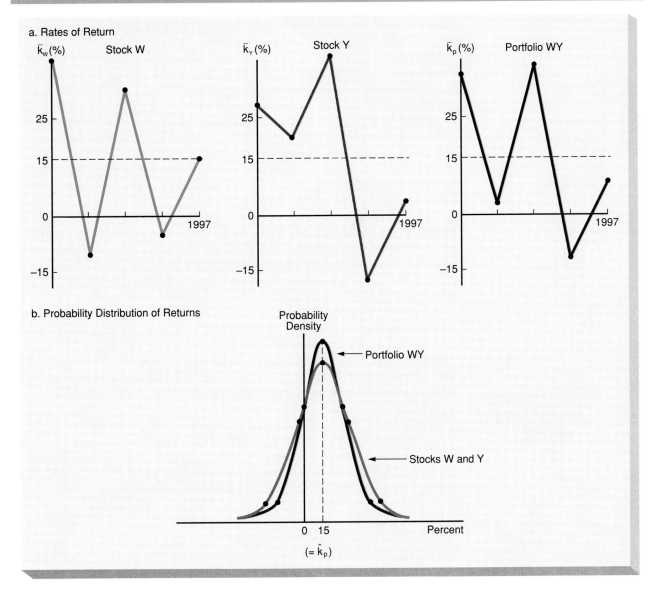

FIGURE 5-7 Rate of Return Distributions for Two Partially Correlated Stocks (r = +0.67) and for Portfolio WY

YEAR	STOCK W ($\bar{k}_W$)	STOCK Y ($\bar{k}_Y$)	PORTFOLIO WY ($\bar{k}_p$)
1993	40.0%	28.0%	34.0%
1994	(10.0)	20.0	5.0
1995	35.0	41.0	38.0
1996	(5.0)	(17.0)	(11.0)
1997	15.0	3.0	9.0
Average return	15.0%	15.0%	15.0%
Standard deviation	22.6%	22.6%	20.6%

From these two-stock portfolio examples, we have seen that in one extreme case (r = −1.0), risk can be completely eliminated, while in the other extreme case (r = +1.0), diversification does nothing to limit risk. Between these extremes, combining two stocks into a portfolio reduces, but does not eliminate, the riskiness inherent in the individual stocks.

What would happen if we included more than two stocks in the portfolio? *As a rule, the riskiness of a portfolio will decline as the number of stocks in the portfolio increases.* If we added enough partially correlated stocks, could we completely eliminate risk? In general, the answer is no, but the extent to which adding stocks to a portfolio reduces its risk depends on the *degree of correlation* among the stocks: The smaller the positive correlation coefficients, the lower the risk in a large portfolio. If we could find a set of stocks whose correlations were zero or negative, all risk could be eliminated. *In the real world, where the correlations among the individual stocks are generally positive but less than +1.0, some, but not all, risk can be eliminated.*

To test your understanding, would you expect to find higher correlations between the returns on two companies in the same or in different industries? For example, would the correlation of returns on Ford's and General Motors' stocks be higher, or would the correlation coefficient be higher between either Ford or GM and AT&T, and how would those correlations affect the risk of portfolios containing them?

Answer: Ford's and GM's returns have a correlation coefficient of about 0.9 with one another because both are affected by auto sales, but their correlation is only about 0.6 with that of AT&T.

Implications: A two-stock portfolio consisting of Ford and GM would be less well diversified than a two-stock portfolio consisting of Ford or GM, plus AT&T. Thus, to minimize risk, portfolios should be diversified across industries.

Before leaving this section we should issue a warning — in the real world, it is *impossible* to find stocks like W and M, whose returns are expected to be perfectly negatively correlated. *Therefore, it is impossible to form completely riskless stock portfolios.* Diversification can reduce risk, but it cannot eliminate it. The real world is closer to the situation depicted in Figure 5-7.

DIVERSIFIABLE RISK VERSUS MARKET RISK

As noted earlier, it is difficult if not impossible to find stocks whose expected returns are not positively correlated — most stocks tend to do well when the national economy is strong and badly when it is weak.[7] Thus, even very large portfolios end up with a substantial amount of risk, but not as much risk as if all the money were invested in only one stock.

To see more precisely how portfolio size affects portfolio risk, consider Figure 5-8, which shows how portfolio risk is affected by forming larger and larger portfolios of randomly selected New York Stock Exchange stocks. Standard deviations are plotted for an average one-stock portfolio, a two-stock portfolio, and so on, up to a portfolio consisting of all 2,000-plus common stocks that were listed on

---

[7]It is not too hard to find a few stocks that happened to have risen because of a particular set of circumstances in the past while most other stocks were declining, but it is much harder to find stocks that could logically be *expected* to go up in the future when other stocks are falling. Payco American, the collection agency discussed earlier, may be one of those rare exceptions.

F I G U R E   5 - 8   Effects of Portfolio Size on Portfolio Risk for Average Stocks

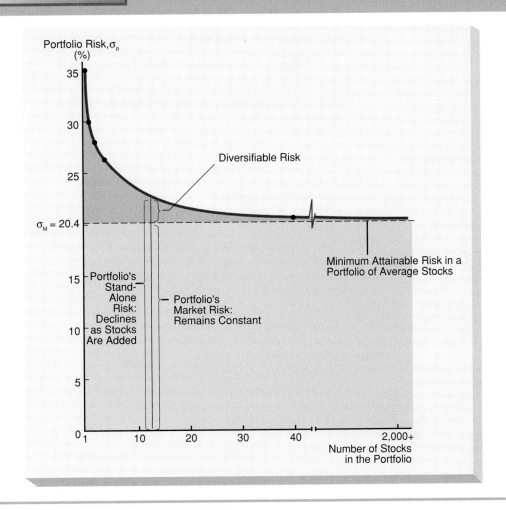

the NYSE at the time the data were graphed. The graph illustrates that, in general, the riskiness of a portfolio consisting of large-company stocks tends to decline and to approach some limit as the size of the portfolio increases. According to data accumulated in recent years, σ_1, the standard deviation of a one-stock portfolio (or an average stock), is approximately 35 percent. A portfolio consisting of all stocks, which is called the **market portfolio,** would have a standard deviation, σ_M, of about 20.4 percent, which is shown as the horizontal dashed line in Figure 5-8.

Market Portfolio
A portfolio consisting of all stocks.

Thus, almost half of the riskiness inherent in an average individual stock can be eliminated if the stock is held in a reasonably well-diversified portfolio, which is one containing 40 or more stocks. Some risk always remains, however, so it is virtually impossible to diversify away the effects of broad stock market movements that affect almost all stocks.

That part of the risk of a stock which *can* be eliminated is called *diversifiable risk,* while that part which *cannot* be eliminated is called *market risk.*[8] The fact

---

[8]Diversifiable risk is also known as *company-specific,* or *unsystematic,* risk. Market risk is also known as *nondiversifiable,* or *systematic,* or *beta,* risk; it is the risk that remains after diversification.

Diversifiable Risk
That part of a security's risk associated with random events; it *can* be eliminated by proper diversification.

Market Risk
That part of a security's risk that *cannot* be eliminated by diversification.

Capital Asset Pricing Model (CAPM)
A model based on the proposition that any stock's required rate of return is equal to the risk-free rate of return plus a risk premium which reflects only the risk remaining after diversification.

Relevant Risk
The risk of a security that cannot be diversified away, or its *market risk*. This reflects a security's contribution to the riskiness of a portfolio.

that a large part of the riskiness of any individual stock can be eliminated is vitally important.

Diversifiable risk is caused by such random events as lawsuits, strikes, successful and unsuccessful marketing programs, winning or losing a major contract, and other events that are unique to a particular firm. Since these events are random, their effects on a portfolio can be eliminated by diversification—bad events in one firm will be offset by good events in another. **Market risk,** on the other hand, stems from factors which systematically affect most firms: war, inflation, recessions, and high interest rates. Since most stocks will tend to be negatively affected by these factors, market risk cannot be eliminated by diversification.

We know that investors demand a premium for bearing risk; that is, the higher the riskiness of a security, the higher its expected return must be to induce investors to buy (or to hold) it. However, if investors are primarily concerned with the riskiness of their *portfolios* rather than the risk of the individual securities in the portfolio, how should the riskiness of an individual stock be measured? One answer is provided by the **Capital Asset Pricing Model (CAPM),** an important tool used to analyze the relationship between risk and rates of return.[9] The primary conclusion of the CAPM is this: *The relevant riskiness of an individual stock is its contribution to the riskiness of a well-diversified portfolio.* In other words, the riskiness of General Electric's stock to a doctor who has a portfolio of 40 stocks or to a trust officer managing a 150-stock portfolio is the contribution the GE stock makes to the portfolio's riskiness. The stock might be quite risky if held by itself, but if half of its risk can be eliminated by diversification, then its **relevant risk,** which is its *contribution to the portfolio's risk,* is much smaller than its stand-alone risk.

A simple example will help make this point clear. Suppose you are offered the chance to flip a coin once; if a head comes up, you win $20,000, but if it comes up tails, you lose $16,000. This is a good bet—the expected return is $0.5(\$20,000) + 0.5(-\$16,000) = \$2,000$. However, it is a highly risky proposition, because you have a 50 percent chance of losing $16,000. Thus, you might well refuse to make the bet. Alternatively, suppose you were offered the chance to flip a coin 100 times, and you would win $200 for each head but lose $160 for each tail. It is possible that you would flip all heads and win $20,000, and it is also possible that you would flip all tails and lose $16,000, but the chances are very high that you would actually flip about 50 heads and about 50 tails, winning a net of about $2,000. Although each individual flip is a risky bet, collectively you have a low-risk proposition because most of the risk has been diversified away. This is the idea behind holding portfolios of stocks rather than just one stock, except that with stocks all of the risk cannot be eliminated by diversification—those risks related to broad, systematic changes in the stock market will remain.

Are all stocks equally risky in the sense that adding them to a well-diversified portfolio would have the same effect on the portfolio's riskiness? The answer is no. Different stocks will affect the portfolio differently, so different securities have different degrees of relevant risk. How can the relevant risk of an individual stock

[9]Indeed, the 1990 Nobel Prize was awarded to the developers of the CAPM, Professors Harry Markowitz and William F. Sharpe. The CAPM is a relatively complex subject, and only its basic elements are presented in this text. For a more detailed discussion, see any standard investments textbook.

The basic concepts of the CAPM were developed specifically for common stocks, and, therefore, the theory is examined first in this context. However, it has become common practice to extend CAPM concepts to capital budgeting and to speak of firms' having "portfolios of tangible assets and projects." In Chapter 12, we discuss the implications of the CAPM for capital budgeting and corporate diversification.

GLOBAL PERSPECTIVES

THE BENEFITS OF DIVERSIFYING OVERSEAS

The size of the global stock market has grown steadily over the last several decades, and it passed the $15 trillion mark during 1995. U.S. stocks account for approximately 41 percent of this total, whereas the Japanese and European markets constitute roughly 25 and 26 percent, respectively. The rest of the world makes up the remaining 8 percent. Although the U.S. equity market has long been the world's biggest, its share of the world total has decreased steadily over time.

The expanding universe of securities available internationally suggests the possibility of achieving a better risk-return trade-off than could be obtained by investing solely in U.S. securities. So, investing overseas might lower risk without sacrificing expected returns. The potential benefits of diversification are due to the facts that the correlation between the returns on U.S. and international securities is fairly low, and returns in developing nations are often quite high.

Figure 5-8, presented earlier, demonstrated that an investor can significantly reduce the risk of his or her portfolio by holding a large number of stocks. The figure accompanying this box suggests that investors may be able to reduce risk even further by holding a large portfolio of stocks from all around the world, given the fact that the returns of domestic and international stocks are not perfectly correlated.

Despite the apparent benefits from investing overseas, the typical U.S. investor still dedicates less than 10 percent of his or her portfolio to foreign stocks — even though foreign stocks represent roughly 60 percent of the worldwide equity market. Researchers and practitioners alike have struggled to understand this reluctance to invest overseas. One explanation is that investors prefer domestic stocks because they have lower transaction costs. However, this explanation is not completely convincing, given that recent studies have found that investors buy and sell their overseas stocks more frequently than they trade their domestic stocks. Other explanations for the domestic bias focus on the additional risks from investing overseas (for example, exchange rate risk) or suggest that the typical U.S. investor is uninformed about international investments and/or views international investments as being extremely risky or uncertain. More recently, other analysts have argued that as world capital markets have become more integrated, the correlation of returns between different countries has increased, hence that the benefits from international diversification have declined.

Whatever the reason for the general reluctance to hold international assets, it is a safe bet that in the years ahead U.S. investors will dedicate more and more of their portfolios to overseas investments.

SOURCE: Kenneth Kasa, "Measuring the Gains from International Portfolio Diversification," *Federal Reserve Bank of San Francisco Weekly Letter,* Number 94-14, April 8, 1994.

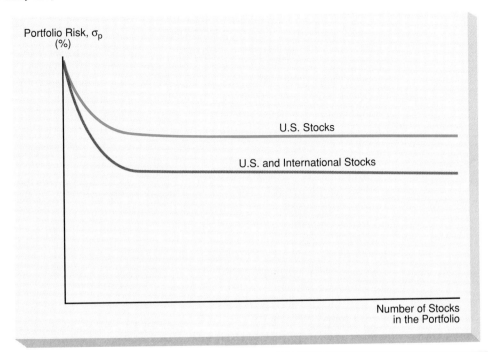

be measured? As we have seen, all risk except that related to broad market movements can, and presumably will, be diversified away. After all, why accept risk that can be easily eliminated? *The risk that remains after diversifying is market risk, or the risk that is inherent in the market, and it can be measured by the degree to which a given stock tends to move up or down with the market.* In the next section, we develop a measure of a stock's market risk, and then, in a later section, we introduce an equation for determining the required rate of return on a stock, given its market risk.

THE CONCEPT OF BETA

Beta Coefficient, b
A measure of the extent to which the returns on a given stock move with the stock market.

The tendency of a stock to move up and down with the market is reflected in its **beta coefficient, b**. Beta is a key element of the CAPM. An *average-risk stock* is defined as one that tends to move up and down in step with the general market as measured by some index such as the Dow Jones Industrials, the S&P 500, or the New York Stock Exchange Index. Such a stock will, *by definition*, have a beta, b, of 1.0, which indicates that, in general, if the market moves up by 10 percent, the stock will also move up by 10 percent, while if the market falls by 10 percent, the stock will likewise fall by 10 percent. A portfolio of such b = 1.0 stocks will move up and down with the broad market averages, and it will be just as risky as the averages. If b = 0.5, the stock is only half as volatile as the market — it will rise and fall only half as much — and a portfolio of such stocks will be half as risky as a portfolio of b = 1.0 stocks. On the other hand, if b = 2.0, the stock is twice as volatile as an average stock, so a portfolio of such stocks will be twice as risky as an average portfolio. The value of such a portfolio could double — or halve — in a short time, and if you held such a portfolio, you could quickly go from millionaire to pauper.

Figure 5-9 graphs the relative volatility of three stocks. The data below the graph assume that in 1995 the "market," defined as a portfolio consisting of all stocks, had a total return (dividend yield plus capital gains yield) of $k_M = 10\%$, and Stocks H, A, and L (for High, Average, and Low risk) also all had returns of 10 percent. In 1996, the market went up sharply, and the return on the market portfolio was $\bar{k}_M = 20\%$. Returns on the three stocks also went up: H soared to 30 percent; A went up to 20 percent, the same as the market; and L only went up to 15 percent. Now, suppose that the market dropped in 1997, and the market return was $\bar{k}_M = -10\%$. The three stocks' returns also fell, H plunging to −30 percent, A falling to −10 percent, and L going down only to $\bar{k}_L = 0\%$. Thus, the three stocks all moved in the same direction as the market, but H was by far the most volatile; A was just as volatile as the market; and L was less volatile.

Beta measures a stock's volatility relative to an average stock, which by definition has b = 1.0, and a stock's beta can be calculated by plotting a line like those in Figure 5-9. The slopes of the lines show how each stock moves in response to a movement in the general market — *indeed, the slope coefficient of such a "regression line" is defined as a beta coefficient.* (Procedures for actually calculating betas are described in Appendix 5A.) Betas for literally thousands of companies are calculated and published by Merrill Lynch, Value Line, and numerous other organizations, and the beta coefficients of some well-known companies are shown in Table 5-4. Most stocks have betas in the range of 0.50 to 1.50, and the average for all stocks is 1.0 by definition.

Theoretically, it is possible for a stock to have a negative beta. In this case, the stock's returns would tend to rise whenever the returns on other stocks fall. In practice, we have never seen a stock with a negative beta. For example, *Value*

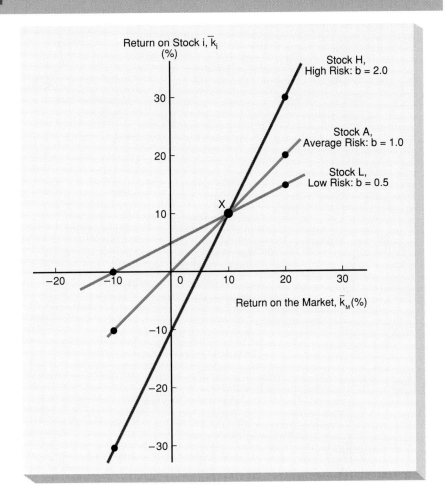

| FIGURE | 5 - 9 | Relative Volatility of Stocks H, A, and L |

YEAR	$\overline{k}_H$	$\overline{k}_A$	$\overline{k}_L$	$\overline{k}_M$
1995	10%	10%	10%	10%
1996	30	20	15	20
1997	(30)	(10)	0	(10)

NOTE: These three stocks plot exactly on their regression lines. This indicates that they are exposed only to market risk. Mutual funds which concentrate on stocks with betas of 2, 1, and 0.5 would have patterns similar to those shown in the graph.

Line follows more than 1,700 stocks, and not one has a negative beta. Keep in mind, though, that a stock in a given year may move counter to the overall market, even though the stock's beta is positive. If a stock has a positive beta, we would *expect* its return to increase whenever the overall stock market rises. However, company-specific factors may cause the stock's realized return to decline, even though the market's return is positive.

If a stock whose beta is greater than 1.0 is added to a b = 1.0 portfolio, then the portfolio's beta, and consequently its riskiness, will increase. Conversely, if a

TABLE 5-4 Illustrative List of Beta Coefficients

STOCK	BETA
America Online	2.10
Bally Entertainment	1.55
Microsoft Corp.	1.20
General Electric	1.15
Procter & Gamble	1.05
Coca-Cola	1.00
Heinz	0.90
IBM	0.90
Energen Corp.[a]	0.70
Empire District Electric	0.55

[a]Energen is a gas distribution company. It has a monopoly in much of Alabama, and its rates are adjusted every three months so as to keep its profits relatively constant.

SOURCE: *Value Line*, August 16, 1996.

stock whose beta is less than 1.0 is added to a b = 1.0 portfolio, the portfolio's beta and risk will decline. *Thus, since a stock's beta measures its contribution to the riskiness of a portfolio, beta is the theoretically correct measure of the stock's riskiness.*

The preceding analysis of risk in a portfolio context is part of the Capital Asset Pricing Model (CAPM), and we can summarize our discussion to this point as follows:

1. A stock's risk consists of two components, market risk and diversifiable risk.
2. Diversifiable risk can be eliminated by diversification, and most investors do indeed diversify, either by holding large portfolios or by purchasing shares in a mutual fund. We are left, then, with market risk, which is caused by general movements in the stock market and which reflects the fact that most stocks are systematically affected by events like war, recessions, and inflation. Market risk is the only relevant risk to a rational, diversified investor because such an investor would eliminate diversifiable risk.
3. Investors must be compensated for bearing risk — the greater the riskiness of a stock, the higher its required return. However, compensation is required only for risk which cannot be eliminated by diversification. If risk premiums existed on stocks due to diversifiable risk, well-diversified investors would start buying those securities (which would not be especially risky to such investors) and bidding up their prices, and the stocks' final (equilibrium) expected returns would reflect only nondiversifiable market risk.

    If this point is not clear, an example may help clarify it. Suppose half of Stock A's risk is market risk (it occurs because Stock A moves up and down with the market), while the other half of A's risk is diversifiable. You hold only Stock A, so you are exposed to all of its risk. As compensation for bearing so much risk, you want a risk premium of 8 percent over the 10 percent T-bond rate. Thus, your required return is $k_A = 10\% + 8\% = 18\%$. But suppose other investors, including your professor, are well diversified; they also hold Stock A, but they have eliminated its diversifiable risk and thus are exposed to only half as much risk as you. Therefore, their risk premium will be only half as large as yours, and their required rate of return will be $k_A = 10\% + 4\% = 14\%$.

    If the stock were yielding more than 14 percent in the market, diversified investors, including your professor, would buy it. If it were yielding 18 percent, you would be willing to buy it, but well-diversified investors would have bid its price up and its yield down, hence you could not buy it at a price low enough to provide you with an 18 percent return. In the end, you would have to accept a 14 percent return or else keep your money in the bank. Thus, risk premiums in a market populated by diversified investors can reflect only market risk.

4. The market risk of a stock is measured by its beta coefficient, which is an index of the stock's relative volatility. Some benchmark betas follow:

    $b = 0.5$: Stock is only half as volatile, or risky, as the average stock.

    $b = 1.0$: Stock is of average risk.

    $b = 2.0$: Stock is twice as risky as the average stock.

5. *Since a stock's beta coefficient determines how the stock affects the riskiness of a diversified portfolio, beta is the most relevant measure of any stock's risk.*

PORTFOLIO BETA COEFFICIENTS

A portfolio consisting of low-beta securities will itself have a low beta, because the beta of a portfolio is a weighted average of the individual securities' betas:

$$b_p = w_1 b_1 + w_2 b_2 + \cdots + w_n b_n$$

$$= \sum_{i=1}^{n} w_i b_i. \qquad (5\text{-}6)$$

Here b_p is the beta of the portfolio, and it shows how volatile the portfolio is in relation to the market; w_i is the fraction of the portfolio invested in the ith stock; and b_i is the beta coefficient of the ith stock. For example, if an investor holds a $100,000 portfolio consisting of $33,333.33 invested in each of three stocks, and if each of the stocks has a beta of 0.7, then the portfolio's beta will be $b_p = 0.7$:

$$b_p = 0.3333(0.7) + 0.3333(0.7) + 0.3333(0.7) = 0.7.$$

Such a portfolio will be less risky than the market, so it should experience relatively narrow price swings and have relatively small rate-of-return fluctuations. In terms of Figure 5-9, the slope of its regression line would be 0.7, which is less than that for a portfolio of average stocks.

    Now suppose one of the existing stocks is sold and replaced by a stock with $b_i = 2.0$. This action will increase the beta of the portfolio from $b_{p1} = 0.7$ to $b_{p2} = 1.13$:

$$b_{p2} = 0.3333(0.7) + 0.3333(0.7) + 0.3333(2.0)$$

$$= 1.13.$$

Had a stock with $b_i = 0.2$ been added, the portfolio beta would have declined from 0.7 to 0.53. Adding a low-beta stock, therefore, would reduce the riskiness of the portfolio. Consequently, adding new stocks to a portfolio can change the riskiness of that portfolio.

SELF-TEST QUESTIONS

Explain the following statement: "An asset held as part of a portfolio is generally less risky than the same asset held in isolation."

What is meant by *perfect positive correlation, perfect negative correlation,* and *zero correlation?*

In general, can the riskiness of a portfolio be reduced to zero by increasing the number of stocks in the portfolio? Explain.

What is an average-risk stock? What will be its beta?

Why is beta the theoretically correct measure of a stock's riskiness?

If you plotted the returns on a particular stock versus those on the Dow Jones Index over the past five years, what would the slope of the regression line you obtained indicate about the stock's market risk?

THE RELATIONSHIP BETWEEN RISK AND RATES OF RETURN

In the preceding section, we saw that under the CAPM theory, beta is the appropriate measure of a stock's relevant risk. Now we must specify the relationship between risk and return: For a given level of risk as measured by beta, what rate of return will investors require to compensate them for bearing that risk? To begin, let us define the following terms:

$\hat{k}_i$ = *expected* rate of return on the ith stock.

k_i = *required* rate of return on the ith stock. Note that if $\hat{k}_i$ is less than k_i, you would not purchase this stock, or you would sell it if you owned it. If $\hat{k}_i$ were greater than k_i, you would want to buy the stock, because it looks like a bargain. You would be indifferent if $\hat{k}_i = k_i$.

$\bar{k}$ = realized, after-the-fact return. One obviously does not know $\bar{k}$ at the time they are considering the purchase of a stock.

k_{RF} = risk-free rate of return. In this context, k_{RF} is generally measured by the return on long-term U.S. Treasury bonds.

b_i = beta coefficient of the ith stock. The beta of an average stock is $b_A = 1.0$.

k_M = required rate of return on a portfolio consisting of all stocks, which is called the *market portfolio.* k_M is also the required rate of return on an average ($b_A = 1.0$) stock.

$RP_M = (k_M - k_{RF})$ = risk premium on "the market," and also on an average ($b = 1.0$) stock. This is the additional return over the risk-free rate required to compensate an average investor for assuming an average amount of risk. Average risk means a stock whose $b_i = b_A = 1.0$.

$$RP_i = (k_M - k_{RF})b_i = (RP_M)b_i = \text{risk premium on the } i\text{th stock.}$$

The stock's risk premium will be less than, equal to, or greater than the premium on an average stock, RP_M, depending on whether its beta is less than, equal to, or greater than 1.0. If $b_i = b_A = 1.0$, then $RP_i = RP_M$.

Market Risk Premium, RP_M
The additional return over the risk-free rate needed to compensate investors for assuming an average amount of risk.

The **market risk premium, RP_M,** shows the premium investors require for bearing the risk of an average stock, and it depends on the degree of risk aversion that investors on average have.[10] Let us assume that at the current time, Treasury bonds yield $k_{RF} = 6\%$ and an average share of stock has a required return of $k_M = 11\%$. Therefore, the market risk premium is 5 percent:

$$RP_M = k_M - k_{RF} = 11\% - 6\% = 5\%.$$

It follows that if one stock were twice as risky as another, its risk premium would be twice as high, while if its risk were only half as much, its risk premium would be half as large. Further, we can measure a stock's relative riskiness by its beta coefficient. If we know the market risk premium, RP_M, and the stock's risk as measured by its beta coefficient, b_i, we can find the stock's risk premium as the product $(RP_M)b_i$. For example, if $b_i = 0.5$ and $RP_M = 5\%$, then RP_i is 2.5 percent:

$$\text{Risk premium for Stock i} = RP_i = (RP_M)b_i \qquad (5\text{-}7)$$
$$= (5\%)(0.5)$$
$$= 2.5\%.$$

As the discussion in Chapter 4 implied, the required return for any investment can be expressed in general terms as

$$\text{Required return} = \text{Risk-free return} + \text{Premium for risk.}$$

Here the risk-free return includes a premium for expected inflation, and we assume that the assets under consideration have similar maturities and liquidity. Under these conditions, the required return for Stock i can be written as follows:

$$\text{SML Equation:} \quad \begin{pmatrix} \text{Required return} \\ \text{on Stock i} \end{pmatrix} = \begin{pmatrix} \text{Risk-free} \\ \text{rate} \end{pmatrix} + \begin{pmatrix} \text{Market risk} \\ \text{premium} \end{pmatrix}\begin{pmatrix} \text{Stock i's} \\ \text{beta} \end{pmatrix}$$

$$k_i = k_{RF} + (k_M - k_{RF})b_i \qquad (5\text{-}8)$$
$$= k_{RF} + (RP_M)b_i$$
$$= 6\% + (11\% - 6\%)(0.5)$$
$$= 6\% + 5\%(0.5)$$
$$= 8.5\%.$$

Equation 5-8 is called the Security Market Line (SML).

---

[10]This concept, as well as other aspects of the CAPM, is discussed in more detail in Chapter 3 of Brigham and Gapenski, *Intermediate Financial Management*. It should be noted that the risk premium of an average stock, $k_M - k_{RF}$, cannot be measured with great precision because it is impossible to obtain precise values for the expected future return on the market, k_M. However, empirical studies suggest that where long-term U.S. Treasury bonds are used to measure k_{RF} and where k_M is an estimate of the expected return on the S&P 400 Industrial Stocks, the market risk premium varies somewhat from year to year, and it has generally ranged from 4 to 8 percent during the last 20 years.

Chapter 3 of *Intermediate Financial Management* also discusses the assumptions embodied in the CAPM framework. Some of these are unrealistic, and because of this the theory does not hold exactly.

If some other Stock j were riskier than Stock i and had $b_j = 2.0$, then its required rate of return would be 16 percent:

$$k_j = 6\% + (5\%)2.0 = 16\%.$$

An average stock, with $b = 1.0$, would have a required return of 11 percent, the same as the market return:

$$k_A = 6\% + (5\%)1.0 = 11\% = k_M.$$

Security Market Line (SML)
The line on a graph that shows the relationship between risk as measured by beta and the required rate of return for individual securities. Equation 5-8 is the equation for the SML.

As noted above, Equation 5-8 is called the **Security Market Line (SML)** equation, and it is often expressed in graph form, as in Figure 5-10, which shows the SML when $k_{RF} = 6\%$ and $k_M = 11\%$. Note the following points:

1. Required rates of return are shown on the vertical axis, while risk as measured by beta is shown on the horizontal axis. This graph is quite different from the one shown in Figure 5-9, where the returns on individual stocks were plotted on the vertical axis and returns on the market index were shown on the horizontal axis. The slopes of the three lines in Figure 5-9 were used to calculate the three stocks' betas, and those betas were then plotted as points on the horizontal axis of Figure 5-10.

2. Riskless securities have $b_i = 0$; therefore, k_{RF} appears as the vertical axis intercept in Figure 5-10. If we could construct a portfolio which had a beta of zero, it would have an expected return equal to the risk-free rate.

FIGURE 5-10 The Security Market Line (SML)

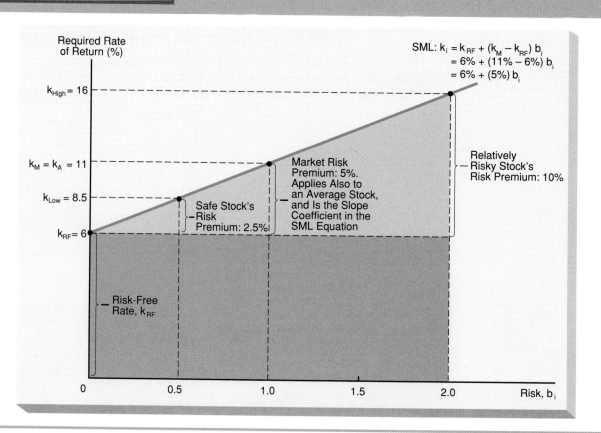

3. The slope of the SML (5% in Figure 5-10) reflects the degree of risk aversion in the economy — the greater the average investor's aversion to risk, then (1) the steeper the slope of the line, (2) the greater the risk premium for all stocks, and (3) the higher the required rate of return on all stocks.[11] These points are discussed further in a later section.

4. The values we worked out for stocks with $b_i = 0.5$, $b_i = 1.0$, and $b_i = 2.0$ agree with the values shown on the graph for k_{Low}, $k_{Average}$, and k_{High}.

Both the Security Market Line and a company's position on it change over time due to changes in interest rates, investors' aversion to risk, and individual companies' betas. Such changes are discussed in the following sections.

THE IMPACT OF INFLATION

As we learned in Chapter 4, interest amounts to "rent" on borrowed money, or the price of money. Thus, k_{RF} is the price of money to a riskless borrower. We also learned that the risk-free rate as measured by the rate on U.S. Treasury securities is called the *nominal,* or *quoted, rate,* and it consists of two elements: (1) a *real inflation-free rate of return, k*,* and (2) an *inflation premium, IP,* equal to the anticipated rate of inflation.[12] Thus, $k_{RF} = k^* + IP$. The real rate on long-term Treasury bonds has historically ranged from 2 to 4 percent, with a mean of about 3 percent. Therefore, if no inflation were expected, long-term Treasury bonds would yield about 3 percent. However, as the expected rate of inflation increases, a premium must be added to the real risk-free rate of return to compensate investors for the loss of purchasing power that results from inflation. Therefore, the 6 percent k_{RF} shown in Figure 5-10 might be thought of as consisting of a 3 percent real risk-free rate of return plus a 3 percent inflation premium: $k_{RF} = k^* + IP = 3\% + 3\% = 6\%$.

If the expected inflation rate rose by 2 percent, to $3\% + 2\% = 5\%$, this would cause k_{RF} to rise to 8 percent. Such a change is shown in Figure 5-11. Notice that under the CAPM, the increase in k_{RF} leads to an *equal* increase in the rate of return on all risky assets, because the same inflation premium is built into the required rate of return of both riskless and risky assets.[13] For example, the rate of return on.an average stock, k_M, increases from 11 to 13 percent. Other risky securities' returns also rise by two percentage points.

---

[11]Students sometimes confuse beta with the slope of the SML. This is a mistake. The slope of any straight line is equal to the "rise" divided by the "run," or $(Y_1 - Y_0)/(X_1 - X_0)$. Consider Figure 5-10. If we let $Y = k$ and $X = $ beta, and we go from the origin to $b = 1.0$, we see that the slope is $(k_M - k_{RF})/(b_M - b_{RF}) = (11\% - 6\%)/(1 - 0) = 5\%$. Thus, the slope of the SML is equal to $(k_M - k_{RF})$, the market risk premium. In Figure 5-10, $k_i = 6\% + 5\%b_i$, so a doubling of beta (for example, from 1.0 to 2.0) would produce a 5 percentage point increase in k_i.

[12]Long-term Treasury bonds also contain a maturity risk premium, MRP. Here we include the MRP in k^* to simplify the discussion.

[13]Recall that the inflation premium for any asset is equal to the average expected rate of inflation over the asset's life. Thus, in this analysis we must assume either that all securities plotted on the SML graph have the same life or else that the expected rate of future inflation is constant.

It should also be noted that k_{RF} in a CAPM analysis can be proxied by either a long-term rate (the T-bond rate) or a short-term rate (the T-bill rate). Traditionally, the T-bill rate was used, but in recent years there has been a movement toward use of the T-bond rate because there is a closer relationship between T-bond yields and stocks than between T-bill yields and stocks. See *Stocks, Bonds, Bills, and Inflation: 1997 Yearbook* (Chicago: Ibbotson Associates, 1997) for a discussion.

FIGURE 5-11 | Shift in the SML Caused by an Increase in Inflation

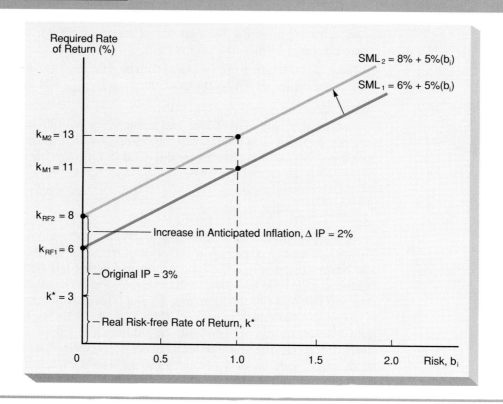

CHANGES IN RISK AVERSION

The slope of the Security Market Line reflects the extent to which investors are averse to risk — the steeper the slope of the line, the greater the average investor's risk aversion. Suppose investors were indifferent to risk; that is, they were not risk averse. If k_{RF} were 6 percent, then risky assets would also provide an expected return of 6 percent, because if there were no risk aversion, there would be no risk premium, and the SML would graph as a horizontal line. As risk aversion increases, so does the risk premium, and this causes the slope of the SML to become steeper.

Figure 5-12 illustrates an increase in risk aversion. The market risk premium rises from 5 to 7.5 percent, causing k_M to rise from $k_{M1} = 11\%$ to $k_{M2} = 13.5\%$. The returns on other risky assets also rise, and the effect of this shift in risk aversion is more pronounced on riskier securities. For example, the required return on a stock with $b_i = 0.5$ increases by only 1.25 percentage points, from 8.5 to 9.75 percent, whereas that on a stock with $b_i = 1.5$ increases by 3.75 percentage points, from 13.5 to 17.25 percent.

CHANGES IN A STOCK'S BETA COEFFICIENT

As we shall see later in the book, a firm can influence its market risk, hence its beta, through changes in the composition of its assets and also through its use of debt. A company's beta can also change as a result of external factors such as increased competition in its industry, the expiration of basic patents, and the like.

FIGURE   5 - 1 2   Shift in the SML Caused by Increased Risk Aversion

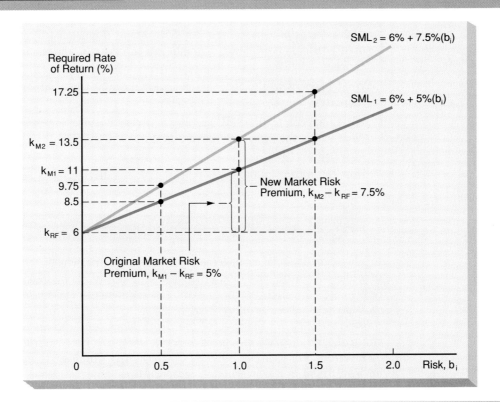

When such changes occur, the required rate of return also changes, and, as we shall see in Chapter 8, this will affect the firm's stock price. For example, consider Allied Food Products, with a beta of 1.40. Now suppose some action occurred which caused Allied's beta to increase from 1.40 to 2.00. If the conditions depicted in Figure 5-10 held, Allied's required rate of return would increase from 13 to 16 percent:

$$k_1 = k_{RF} + (k_M - k_{RF})b_i$$
$$= 6\% + (11\% - 6\%)1.40$$
$$= 13\%$$

to

$$k_2 = 6\% + (11\% - 6\%)2.0$$
$$= 16\%.$$

As we shall see in Chapter 8, this change would have a dramatic impact on Allied's stock.

SELF-TEST QUESTIONS

Differentiate among the expected rate of return ($\hat{k}$), the required rate of return (k), and the realized, after-the-fact return ($\bar{k}$) on a stock. Which would have to be larger to get you to buy the stock, $\hat{k}$ or k? Would $\hat{k}$, k, and $\bar{k}$ typically be the same or different?

What are the differences between the relative volatility graph (Figure 5-9), where "betas are made," and the SML graph (Figure 5-10), where "betas are used"? Discuss both how the graphs are constructed and the information they convey.

What happens to the SML graph in Figure 5-10 when inflation increases or decreases?

What happens to the SML graph when risk aversion increases or decreases? What would the SML look like if investors were indifferent to risk, that is, had zero risk aversion?

How can a firm influence its market risk as reflected in its beta?

PHYSICAL ASSETS VERSUS SECURITIES

In a book on financial management for business firms, why do we spend so much time discussing the riskiness of stocks? Why not begin by looking at the riskiness of such business assets as plant and equipment? *The reason is that, for a management whose primary goal is stock price maximization, the overriding consideration is the riskiness of the firm's stock, and the relevant risk of any physical asset must be measured in terms of its effect on the stock's risk as seen by investors.* For example, suppose Goodyear Tire Company is considering a major investment in a new product, recapped tires. Sales of recaps, hence earnings on the new operation, are highly uncertain, so on a stand-alone basis the new venture appears to be quite risky. However, suppose returns in the recap business are negatively correlated with Goodyear's regular operations — when times are good and people have plenty of money, they buy new tires, but when times are bad, they tend to buy more recaps. Therefore, returns would be high on regular operations and low on the recap division during good times, but the opposite would occur during recessions. The result might be a pattern like that shown earlier in Figure 5-5 for Stocks W and M. Thus, what appears to be a risky investment when viewed on a stand-alone basis might not be very risky when viewed within the context of the company as a whole.

This analysis can be extended to the corporation's stockholders. Because Goodyear's stock is owned by diversified stockholders, the real issue each time management makes an asset investment is this: How will this investment affect the risk of our stockholders? Again, the stand-alone risk of an individual project may look quite high, but viewed in the context of the project's effect on stockholders' risk, it may not be very large. We will address this issue again in Chapter 11, where we examine the effects of capital budgeting on companies' beta coefficients and thus on stockholders' risks.

SELF-TEST QUESTIONS

Explain the following statement: "The stand-alone risk of an individual project may be quite high, but viewed in the context of a project's effect on stockholders, the project's true risk may not be very large."

How would the correlation between returns on a project and returns on the firm's other assets affect the project's risk?

SOME CONCERNS ABOUT BETA AND THE CAPM

The Capital Asset Pricing Model (CAPM) is more than just an abstract theory described in textbooks — it is also widely used by analysts, investors, and corporations. However, despite the CAPM's intuitive appeal, a number of recent studies have raised concerns about its validity. In particular, a recent study by Eugene Fama of the University of Chicago and Kenneth French of Yale found no historical relationship between stocks' returns and their market betas, confirming a position long held by a number of professors and stock market analysts.

If beta does not determine returns, what does? Fama and French found two variables which are consistently related to stock returns: (1) the firm's size and (2) its market/book ratio. After adjusting for other factors, they found that smaller firms have provided relatively high returns, and that returns are higher on stocks with low market/book ratios. By contrast, after controlling for size of firm and market/book ratios, they found no relationship between a stock's beta and its return.

As an alternative to the traditional CAPM, researchers and practitioners have begun to look to more general multi-beta models that encompass the CAPM and address its shortcomings. The multi-beta model is an attractive generalization of the traditional CAPM model's insight that market risk — risk that cannot be diversified away — underlies the pricing of assets. In the multi-beta model, market risk is measured relative to a set of risk factors that determine the behavior of asset returns, whereas the CAPM gauges risk only relative to the market return. It is important to note that the risk factors in the multi-beta model are all non-diversifiable sources of risk. Empirical research investigating the relationship between economic risk factors and security returns is ongoing, but it has discovered several systematic empirical risk factors, including the bond default premium, the bond term structure premium, and inflation.

Practitioners and academicians have long recognized the limitations of the CAPM, and they are constantly looking for ways to improve it. The multi-beta model is a potential step in that direction. Although the CAPM represents a significant step forward in security pricing theory, it does have some deficiencies when applied in practice, hence estimates of k_i found through use of the SML may be subject to considerable error.

SELF-TEST QUESTION

Are there any reasons to question the validity of the CAPM? Explain.

VOLATILITY VERSUS RISK

Before closing this chapter, we should note that volatility does not necessarily imply risk. For example, suppose a company's sales and earnings fluctuate widely from month to month, from year to year, or in some other manner. Does this imply that the company is risky in either the stand-alone or portfolio sense? If the fluctuations follow seasonal or cyclical patterns, as for an ice cream distributor or a steel company, they can be predicted, hence volatility would not signify much in the way of risk. If the ice cream company's earnings dropped about as much as they normally did in the winter, this would not concern investors, so the company's stock price would not be affected. Similarly, if the steel company's earnings fell during a recession, this would not be a surprise, so the company's stock price would not fall nearly as much as its earnings. Therefore, earnings volatility does not necessarily imply investment risk.

Now consider some other company, say, Wal-Mart. In 1995 Wal-Mart's earnings declined for the first time in its history. That decline worried investors — they were concerned that Wal-Mart's era of rapid growth had ended. The result was that Wal-Mart's stock price declined more than its earnings. Again, we conclude that while a downturn in earnings does not necessarily imply risk, it could, depending on conditions.

Now let's consider stock price volatility as opposed to earnings volatility. Is stock price volatility more likely to imply risk than earnings volatility? The answer is a loud yes! Stock prices vary because investors are uncertain about the future, especially about future earnings. So, if you see a company whose stock price fluctuates relatively widely (which will result in a high beta), you can bet that its future earnings are relatively unpredictable. Thus, biotech companies have less predictable earnings than electric utilities, biotechs' stock prices are volatile, and they have relatively high betas.

To conclude, keep two points in mind: (1) Earnings volatility does not necessarily signify risk — you have to think about the cause of the volatility before reaching any conclusion as to whether earnings volatility indicates risk. (2) Stock price volatility *does* signify risk (except for stocks that are negatively correlated with the market, which are few and far between).

SELF-TEST QUESTIONS

Does earnings volatility necessarily imply risk? Explain.

Is stock price volatility more likely to imply risk than earnings volatility? Explain.

SUMMARY

The primary goals of this chapter were (1) to show how risk is measured in financial analysis and (2) to explain how risk affects rates of return. The key concepts covered are listed below.

♦ **Risk** can be defined as the chance that some unfavorable event will occur.

♦ The riskiness of an asset's cash flows can be considered on a **stand-alone basis** (each asset by itself) or in a **portfolio context,** where the investment is combined with other assets and its risk is reduced through **diversification.**

♦ Most rational investors hold **portfolios of assets,** and they are more concerned with the riskiness of their portfolios than with the riskiness of individual assets.

♦ The **expected return** on an investment is the mean value of its probability distribution of returns.

♦ The **greater the probability** that the actual return will be far below the expected return, the **greater the stand-alone risk** associated with an asset.

♦ The average investor is **risk averse,** which means that he or she must be compensated for holding risky assets. Therefore, riskier assets have higher required returns than less risky assets.

♦ An asset's risk consists of (1) **diversifiable risk,** which can be eliminated by diversification, plus (2) **market risk,** which cannot be eliminated by diversification.

♦ The **relevant risk** of an individual asset is its contribution to the riskiness of a well-diversified **portfolio,** which is the asset's **market risk.** Since market risk cannot be eliminated by diversification, investors must be compensated for bearing it.

♦ A stock's **beta coefficient, b,** is a measure of its market risk. Beta measures the extent to which the stock's returns move relative to the market.

♦ A **high-beta stock** is more volatile than an average stock, while a **low-beta stock** is less volatile than an average stock. An **average stock** has b = 1.0.

♦ The **beta of a portfolio** is a **weighted average** of the betas of the individual securities in the portfolio.

♦ The **Security Market Line (SML)** equation shows the relationship between a security's market risk and its required rate of return. The return required for any security i is equal to the **risk-free rate** plus the **market risk premium** times the **security's beta:** $k_i = k_{RF} + (k_M - k_{RF})b_i$.

♦ Even though the expected rate of return on a stock is generally equal to its required return, a number of things can happen to cause the required rate of return to change: (1) **the risk-free rate can change** because of changes in anticipated inflation, (2) **a stock's beta can change,** and (3) **investors' aversion to risk can change.**

♦ Because returns on assets in different countries are not perfectly correlated, **global diversification** may result in lower risk for multinational companies and globally diversified portfolios.

In the next three chapters, we will see how a security's rate of return affects its value. Then, in the remainder of the book, we will examine the ways in which a firm's management can influence a stock's riskiness and hence its price.

QUESTIONS

5-1 The probability distribution of a less risky expected return is more peaked than that of a riskier return. What shape would the probability distribution have for (a) completely certain returns and (b) completely uncertain returns?

5-2 Security A has an expected return of 7 percent, a standard deviation of expected returns of 35 percent, a correlation coefficient with the market of −0.3, and a beta coefficient of −0.5. Security B has an expected return of 12 percent, a standard deviation of returns of 10 percent, a correlation with the market of 0.7, and a beta coefficient of 1.0. Which security is riskier? Why?

5-3 Suppose you owned a portfolio consisting of $250,000 worth of long-term U.S. government bonds.
a. Would your portfolio be riskless?
b. Now suppose you hold a portfolio consisting of $250,000 worth of 30-day Treasury bills. Every 30 days your bills mature, and you reinvest the principal ($250,000) in a new batch of bills. Assume that you live on the investment income from your portfolio and that you want to maintain a constant standard of living. Is your portfolio truly riskless?
c. Can you think of any asset that would be completely riskless? Could someone develop such an asset? Explain.

5-4 A life insurance policy is a financial asset. The premiums paid represent the investment's cost.

a. How would you calculate the expected return on a life insurance policy?

b. Suppose the owner of a life insurance policy has no other financial assets — the person's only other asset is "human capital," or lifetime earnings capacity. What is the correlation coefficient between returns on the insurance policy and returns on the policyholder's human capital?

c. Life insurance companies have to pay administrative costs and sales representatives' commissions; hence, the expected rate of return on insurance premiums is generally low, or even negative. Use the portfolio concept to explain why people buy life insurance in spite of negative expected returns.

5-5 If investors' aversion to risk increased, would the risk premium on a high-beta stock increase more or less than that on a low-beta stock? Explain.

5-6 If a company's beta were to double, would its expected return double?

5-7 Is it possible to construct a portfolio of stocks which has an expected return equal to the risk-free rate?

SELF-TEST PROBLEMS (Solutions Appear in Appendix B)

ST-1
Key terms

Define the following terms, using graphs or equations to illustrate your answers wherever feasible:

a. Stand-alone risk; risk; probability distribution

b. Expected rate of return, $\hat{k}$

c. Continuous probability distribution

d. Standard deviation, σ; variance, σ^2; coefficient of variation, CV

e. Risk aversion; realized rate of return, $\bar{k}$

f. Risk premium for Stock i, RP_i; market risk premium, RP_M

g. Capital Asset Pricing Model (CAPM)

h. Expected return on a portfolio, $\hat{k}_p$; market portfolio

i. Correlation coefficient, r; correlation

j. Market risk; diversifiable risk; relevant risk

k. Beta coefficient, b; average stock's beta, b_A

l. Security Market Line (SML); SML equation

m. Slope of SML as a measure of risk aversion

ST-2
Realized rates of return

Stocks A and B have the following historical returns:

YEAR	STOCK A'S RETURNS, k_A	STOCK B'S RETURNS, k_B
1993	(10.00%)	(3.00%)
1994	18.50	21.29
1995	38.67	44.25
1996	14.33	3.67
1997	33.00	28.30

a. Calculate the average rate of return for each stock during the period 1993 through 1997. Assume that someone held a portfolio consisting of 50 percent of Stock A and 50 percent of Stock B. What would have been the realized rate of return on the portfolio in each year from 1993 through 1997? What would have been the average return on the portfolio during this period?

b. Now calculate the standard deviation of returns for each stock and for the portfolio. Use Equation 5-3a in Footnote 5.

c. Looking at the annual returns data on the two stocks, would you guess that the correlation coefficient between returns on the two stocks is closer to 0.9 or to −0.9?

d. If you added more stocks at random to the portfolio, which of the following is the most accurate statement of what would happen to σ_p?

(1) σ_p would remain constant.

(2) σ_p would decline to somewhere in the vicinity of 21 percent.

(3) σ_p would decline to zero if enough stocks were included.

ST-3
Beta and required rate of return

ECRI Corporation is a holding company with four main subsidiaries. The percentage of its business coming from each of the subsidiaries, and their respective betas, are as follows:

SUBSIDIARY	PERCENTAGE OF BUSINESS	BETA
Electric utility	60%	0.70
Cable company	25	0.90
Real estate	10	1.30
International/special projects	5	1.50

a. What is the holding company's beta?
b. Assume that the risk-free rate is 6 percent and the market risk premium is 5 percent. What is the holding company's required rate of return?
c. ECRI is considering a change in its strategic focus; it will reduce its reliance on the electric utility subsidiary, so the percentage of its business from this subsidiary will be 50 percent. At the same time, ECRI will increase its reliance on the international/special projects division, so the percentage of its business from that subsidiary will rise to 15 percent. What will be the shareholders' required rate of return if they adopt these changes?

STARTER PROBLEMS

5-1
Expected return

A stock's expected return has the following distribution:

DEMAND FOR THE COMPANY'S PRODUCTS	PROBABILITY OF THIS DEMAND OCCURRING	RATE OF RETURN IF THIS DEMAND OCCURS
Weak	0.1	(50)%
Below average	0.2	(5)
Average	0.4	16
Above average	0.2	25
Strong	0.1	60
	1.0	

Calculate the stock's expected return, standard deviation, and coefficient of variation.

5-2
Portfolio beta

An individual has $35,000 invested in a stock which has a beta of 0.8 and $40,000 invested in a stock with a beta of 1.4. If these are the only two investments in her portfolio, what is her portfolio's beta?

5-3
Expected and required rates of return

Assume that the risk-free rate is 5 percent and the market risk premium is 6 percent. What is the expected return for the overall stock market? What is the required rate of return on a stock that has a beta of 1.2?

5-4
Required rate of return

Assume that the risk-free rate is 6 percent and the expected return on the market is 13 percent. What is the required rate of return on a stock that has a beta of 0.7?

EXAM-TYPE PROBLEMS

The problems included in this section are set up in such a way that they could be used as multiple-choice exam problems.

5-5
Expected returns

The market and Stock J have the following probability distributions:

PROBABILITY	k_M	k_j
0.3	15%	20%
0.4	9	5
0.3	18	12

a. Calculate the expected rates of return for the market and Stock J.
b. Calculate the standard deviations for the market and Stock J.
c. Calculate the coefficients of variation for the market and Stock J.

5-6
Expected returns

Stocks X and Y have the following probability distributions of expected future returns:

PROBABILITY	X	Y
0.1	(10%)	(35%)
0.2	2	0
0.4	12	20
0.2	20	25
0.1	38	45

a. Calculate the expected rate of return, $\hat{k}$, for Stock Y. ($\hat{k}_X = 12\%$.)
b. Calculate the standard deviation of expected returns for Stock X. (That for Stock Y is 20.35 percent.) Now calculate the coefficient of variation for Stock Y. Is it possible that most investors might regard Stock Y as being *less* risky than Stock X? Explain.

5-7
Required rate of return

Suppose $k_{RF} = 5\%$, $k_M = 10\%$, and $k_A = 12\%$.
a. Calculate Stock A's beta.
b. If Stock A's beta were 2.0, what would be A's new required rate of return?

5-8
Required rate of return

Suppose $k_{RF} = 9\%$, $k_M = 14\%$, and $b_i = 1.3$.
a. What is k_i, the required rate of return on Stock i?
b. Now suppose k_{RF} (1) increases to 10 percent or (2) decreases to 8 percent. The slope of the SML remains constant. How would this affect k_M and k_i?
c. Now assume k_{RF} remains at 9 percent but k_M (1) increases to 16 percent or (2) falls to 13 percent. The slope of the SML does not remain constant. How would these changes affect k_i?

5-9
Portfolio beta

Suppose you hold a diversified portfolio consisting of a $7,500 investment in each of 20 different common stocks. The portfolio beta is equal to 1.12. Now, suppose you have decided to sell one of the stocks in your portfolio with a beta equal to 1.0 for $7,500 and to use these proceeds to buy another stock for your portfolio. Assume the new stock's beta is equal to 1.75. Calculate your portfolio's new beta.

5-10
Portfolio required return

Suppose you are the money manager of a $4 million investment fund. The fund consists of 4 stocks with the following investments and betas:

STOCK	INVESTMENT	BETA
A	$ 400,000	1.50
B	600,000	(0.50)
C	1,000,000	1.25
D	2,000,000	0.75

If the market required rate of return is 14 percent and the risk-free rate is 6 percent, what is the fund's required rate of return?

5-11
Portfolio beta

You have a $2 million portfolio consisting of a $100,000 investment in each of 20 different stocks. The portfolio has a beta equal to 1.1. You are considering selling $100,000 worth of one stock which has a beta equal to 0.9 and using the proceeds to purchase another stock which has a beta equal to 1.4. What will be the new beta of your portfolio following this transaction?

5-12
Required rate of return

Stock R has a beta of 1.5, Stock S has a beta of 0.75, the expected rate of return on an average stock is 13 percent, and the risk-free rate of return is 7 percent. By how much does the required return on the riskier stock exceed the required return on the less risky stock?

PROBLEMS

5-13
Expected returns

Suppose you won the Florida lottery and were offered (1) $0.5 million or (2) a gamble in which you would get $1 million if a head were flipped but zero if a tail came up.
a. What is the expected value of the gamble?
b. Would you take the sure $0.5 million or the gamble?

c. If you choose the sure $0.5 million, are you a risk averter or a risk seeker?

d. Suppose you actually take the sure $0.5 million. You can invest it in either a U.S. Treasury bond that will return $537,500 at the end of a year or a common stock that has a 50-50 chance of being either worthless or worth $1,150,000 at the end of the year.

(1) What is the expected dollar profit on the stock investment? (The expected profit on the T-bond investment is $37,500.)

(2) What is the expected rate of return on the stock investment? (The expected rate of return on the T-bond investment is 7.5 percent.)

(3) Would you invest in the bond or the stock?

(4) Exactly how large would the expected profit (or the expected rate of return) have to be on the stock investment to make *you* invest in the stock, given the 7.5 percent return on the bond?

(5) How might your decision be affected if, rather than buying one stock for $0.5 million, you could construct a portfolio consisting of 100 stocks with $5,000 invested in each? Each of these stocks has the same return characteristics as the one stock — that is, a 50-50 chance of being worth either zero or $11,500 at year-end. Would the correlation between returns on these stocks matter?

5-14
Security Market Line

The Kish Investment Fund, in which you plan to invest some money, has total capital of $500 million invested in five stocks:

STOCK	INVESTMENT	STOCK'S BETA COEFFICIENT
A	$160 million	0.5
B	120 million	2.0
C	80 million	4.0
D	80 million	1.0
E	60 million	3.0

The beta coefficient for a fund like Kish Investment can be found as a weighted average of the fund's investments. The current risk-free rate is 6 percent, whereas market returns have the following estimated probability distribution for the next period:

PROBABILITY	MARKET RETURN
0.1	7%
0.2	9
0.4	11
0.2	13
0.1	15

a. What is the estimated equation for the Security Market Line (SML)? (Hint: First determine the expected market return.)

b. Compute the fund's required rate of return for the next period.

c. Suppose Bridget Nelson, the president, receives a proposal for a new stock. The investment needed to take a position in the stock is $50 million, it will have an expected return of 15 percent, and its estimated beta coefficient is 2.0. Should the new stock be purchased? At what expected rate of return should the fund be indifferent to purchasing the stock?

5-15
Realized rates of return

Stocks A and B have the following historical returns:

YEAR	STOCK A'S RETURNS, k_A	STOCK B'S RETURNS, k_B
1993	(18.00%)	(14.50%)
1994	33.00	21.80
1995	15.00	30.50
1996	(0.50)	(7.60)
1997	27.00	26.30

a. Calculate the average rate of return for each stock during the period 1993 through 1997.
b. Assume that someone held a portfolio consisting of 50 percent of Stock A and 50 percent of Stock B. What would have been the realized rate of return on the portfolio in each year from 1993 through 1997? What would have been the average return on the portfolio during this period?
c. Calculate the standard deviation of returns for each stock and for the portfolio.
d. Calculate the coefficient of variation for each stock and for the portfolio.
e. If you are a risk-averse investor, would you prefer to hold Stock A, Stock B, or the portfolio? Why?

5-16

Financial calculator needed; expected and required rates of return

You have observed the following returns over time:

YEAR	STOCK X	STOCK Y	MARKET
1993	14%	13%	12%
1994	19	7	10
1995	−16	−5	−12
1996	3	1	1
1997	20	11	15

Assume that the risk-free rate is 6 percent and the market risk premium is 5 percent. (Hint: See Appendix 5A.)
a. What are the betas of Stocks X and Y?
b. What are the required rates of return for Stocks X and Y?
c. What is the required rate of return for a portfolio consisting of 80 percent of Stock X and 20 percent of Stock Y?
d. If Stock X's expected return is 22 percent, is Stock X under- or overvalued?

INTEGRATED CASE

MERRILL FINCH INC.

5-17 Risk and Return Assume that you recently graduated with a major in finance, and you just landed a job as a financial planner with Merrill Finch Inc., a large financial services corporation. Your first assignment is to invest $100,000 for a client. Because the funds are to be invested in a business at the end of 1 year, you have been instructed to plan for a 1-year holding period. Further, your boss has restricted you to the following investment alternatives, shown with their probabilities and associated outcomes. (Disregard for now the items at the bottom of the data; you will fill in the blanks later.)

RETURNS ON ALTERNATIVE INVESTMENTS

				ESTIMATED RATE OF RETURN			
STATE OF THE ECONOMY	PROBABILITY	T-BILLS	HIGH TECH	COLLECTIONS	U.S. RUBBER	MARKET PORTFOLIO	2-STOCK PORTFOLIO
Recession	0.1	8.0%	(22.0%)	28.0%	10.0%*	(13.0%)	3.0%
Below average	0.2	8.0	(2.0)	14.7	(10.0)	1.0	
Average	0.4	8.0	20.0	0.0	7.0	15.0	10.0
Above average	0.2	8.0	35.0	(10.0)	45.0	29.0	
Boom	0.1	8.0	50.0	(20.0)	30.0	43.0	15.0
$\hat{k}$				1.7%	13.8%	15.0%	
σ		0.0		13.4	18.8	15.3	3.3
CV				7.9	1.4	1.0	0.3
b				−0.86	0.68		

*Note that the estimated returns of U.S. Rubber do not always move in the same direction as the overall economy. For example, when the economy is below average, consumers purchase fewer tires than they would if the economy was stronger. However, if the economy is in a flat-out recession, a large number of consumers who were planning to purchase a new car may choose to wait and instead purchase new tires for the car they currently own. Under these circumstances, we would expect U.S. Rubber's stock price to be higher if there is a recession than if the economy was just below average.

Merrill Finch's economic forecasting staff has developed probability estimates for the state of the economy, and its security analysts have developed a sophisticated computer program which was used to estimate the rate of return on each alternative under each state of the economy. High Tech Inc. is an electronics firm; Collections Inc. collects past-due debts; and U.S. Rubber manufactures tires and various other rubber and plastics products. Merrill Finch also maintains an "index fund" which owns a market-weighted fraction of all publicly traded stocks; you can invest in that fund, and thus obtain average stock market results. Given the situation as described, answer the following questions.

a. (1) Why is the T-bill's return independent of the state of the economy? Do T-bills promise a completely risk-free return? (2) Why are High Tech's returns expected to move with the economy whereas Collections' are expected to move counter to the economy?

b. Calculate the expected rate of return on each alternative and fill in the blanks on the row for $\hat{k}$ in the table above.

c. You should recognize that basing a decision solely on expected returns is only appropriate for risk-neutral individuals. Since your client, like virtually everyone, is risk averse, the riskiness of each alternative is an important aspect of the decision. One possible measure of risk is the standard deviation of returns. (1) Calculate this value for each alternative, and fill in the blank on the row for σ in the table above. (2) What type of risk is measured by the standard deviation? (3) Draw a graph which shows *roughly* the shape of the probability distributions for High Tech, U.S. Rubber, and T-bills.

d. Suppose you suddenly remembered that the coefficient of variation (CV) is generally regarded as being a better measure of stand-alone risk than the standard deviation when the alternatives being considered have widely differing expected returns. Calculate the missing CVs, and fill in the blanks on the row for CV in the table above. Does the CV produce the same risk rankings as the standard deviation?

e. Suppose you created a 2-stock portfolio by investing $50,000 in High Tech and $50,000 in Collections. (1) Calculate the expected return (k_p), the standard deviation (σ_p), and the coefficient of variation (CV_p) for this portfolio and fill in the appropriate blanks in the table above. (2) How does the riskiness of this 2-stock portfolio compare with the riskiness of the individual stocks if they were held in isolation?

f. Suppose an investor starts with a portfolio consisting of one randomly selected stock. What would happen (1) to the riskiness and (2) to the expected return of the portfolio as more and more randomly selected stocks were added to the

portfolio? What is the implication for investors? Draw a graph of the two portfolios to illustrate your answer.

g. (1) Should portfolio effects impact the way investors think about the riskiness of individual stocks? (2) If you decided to hold a 1-stock portfolio, and consequently were exposed to more risk than diversified investors, could you expect to be compensated for all of your risk; that is, could you earn a risk premium on that part of your risk that you could have eliminated by diversifying?

h. The expected rates of return and the beta coefficients of the alternatives as supplied by Merrill Finch's computer program are as follows:

SECURITY	RETURN ($\hat{k}$)	RISK (BETA)
High Tech	17.4%	1.29
Market	15.0	1.00
U.S. Rubber	13.8	0.68
T-bills	8.0	0.00
Collections	1.7	(0.86)

(1) What is a beta coefficient, and how are betas used in risk analysis? (2) Do the expected returns appear to be related to each alternative's market risk? (3) Is it possible to choose among the alternatives on the basis of the information developed thus far? Use the data given at the start of the problem to construct a graph which shows how the T-bill's, High Tech's, and Collections' beta coefficients are calculated. Then discuss what betas measure and how they are used in risk analysis.

i. (1) Write out the Security Market Line (SML) equation, use it to calculate the required rate of return on each alternative, and then graph the relationship between the expected and required rates of return. (2) How do the expected rates of return compare with the required rates of return? (3) Does the fact that Collections has an expected return which is less than the T-bill rate make any sense? (4) What would be the market risk and the required return of a 50-50 portfolio of High Tech and Collections? Of High Tech and U.S. Rubber?

j. (1) Suppose investors raised their inflation expectations by 3 percentage points over current estimates as reflected in the 8 percent T-bill rate. What effect would higher inflation have on the SML and on the returns required on high- and low-risk securities? (2) Suppose instead that investors' risk aversion increased enough to cause the market risk premium to increase by 3 percentage points. (Inflation remains constant.) What effect would this have on the SML and on returns of high- and low-risk securities?

COMPUTER-RELATED PROBLEM

Work the problem in this section only if you are using the computer problem diskette.

5-18

Realized rates of return

Using the computerized model in the File C5, rework Problem 5-15, assuming that a third stock, Stock C, is available for inclusion in the portfolio. Stock C has the following historical returns:

YEAR	STOCK C'S RETURNS, k_C
1993	32.00%
1994	(11.75)
1995	10.75
1996	32.25
1997	(6.75)

a. Calculate (or read from the computer screen) the average return, standard deviation, and coefficient of variation for Stock C.

b. Assume that the portfolio now consists of 33.33 percent of Stock A, 33.33 percent of Stock B, and 33.33 percent of Stock C. How does this affect the portfolio return, standard deviation, and coefficient of variation versus when 50 percent was invested in A and in B?

c. Make some other changes in the portfolio, making sure that the percentages sum to 100 percent. For example, enter 25 percent for Stock A, 25 percent for Stock B, and 50 percent for Stock C. (Note that the program will not allow you to enter a zero for the percentage in Stock C.) Notice that $\hat{k}_p$ remains constant and that σ_p changes. Why do these results occur?

d. In Problem 5-15, the standard deviation of the portfolio decreased only slightly, because Stocks A and B were highly positively correlated with one another. In this problem, the addition of Stock C causes the standard deviation of the portfolio to decline dramatically, even though $\sigma_C = \sigma_A = \sigma_B$. What does this indicate about the correlation between Stock C and Stocks A and B?

e. Would you prefer to hold the portfolio described in Problem 5-15 consisting only of Stocks A and B or a portfolio that also included Stock C? If others react similarly, how might this affect the stocks' prices and rates of return?

CALCULATING BETA COEFFICIENTS

The CAPM is an *ex ante* model, which means that all of the variables represent before-the-fact, *expected* values. In particular, the beta coefficient used in the SML equation should reflect the expected volatility of a given stock's return versus the return on the market during some *future* period. However, people generally calculate betas using data from some *past* period, and then assume that the stock's relative volatility will be the same in the future as it was in the past.

To illustrate how betas are calculated, consider Figure 5A-1. The data at the bottom of the figure show the historical realized returns for Stock J and for the market over the last five years. The data points have been plotted on the scatter diagram, and a regression line has been drawn. If all the data points had fallen on a straight line, as they did in Figure 5-9 in Chapter 5, it would be easy to draw an accurate line. If they do not, as in Figure 5A-1, then you must fit the line either "by eye" as an approximation or with a calculator.

Recall what the term *regression line,* or *regression equation,* means: The equation Y = a + bX + e is the standard form of a simple linear regression. It states that the dependent variable, Y, is equal to a constant, a, plus b times X, where b is the slope coefficient and X is the independent variable, plus an error term, e. Thus, the rate of return on the stock during a given time period (Y) depends on what happens to the general stock market, which is measured by $X = \bar{k}_M$.

Once the data have been plotted and the regression line has been drawn on graph paper, we can estimate its intercept and slope, the a and b values in Y = a + bX. The intercept, a, is simply the point where the line cuts the vertical axis. The slope coefficient, b, can be estimated by the "rise-over-run" method. This involves calculating the amount by which $\bar{k}_J$ increases for a given increase in $\bar{k}_M$. For example, we observe in Figure 5A-1 that $\bar{k}_J$ increases from −8.9 to +7.1 percent (the rise) when $\bar{k}_M$ increases from 0 to 10.0 percent (the run). Thus, b, the beta coefficient, can be measured as follows:

$$b = \text{Beta} = \frac{\text{Rise}}{\text{Run}} = \frac{\Delta Y}{\Delta X} = \frac{7.1 - (-8.9)}{10.0 - 0.0} = \frac{16.0}{10.0} = 1.6.$$

Note that rise over run is a ratio, and it would be the same if measured using any two arbitrarily selected points on the line.

The regression line equation enables us to predict a rate of return for Stock J, given a value of $\bar{k}_M$. For example, if $\bar{k}_M = 15\%$, we would predict $\bar{k}_J = -8.9\% + 1.6(15\%) = 15.1\%$. However, the actual return would probably differ from the predicted return. This deviation is the error term, e_J, for the year, and it varies randomly from year to year depending on company-specific factors. Note, though, that the higher the correlation coefficient, the closer the points lie to the regression line, and the smaller the errors.

In actual practice, monthly, rather than annual, returns are generally used for $\bar{k}_J$ and $\bar{k}_M$, and five years of data are often employed; thus, there would be $5 \times 12 = 60$ data points on the scatter diagram. Also, in practice one would use the *least squares method* for finding the regression coefficients a and b; this procedure minimizes the squared values of the error terms. It is discussed in statistics courses.

FIGURE   5A-1   Calculating Beta Coefficients

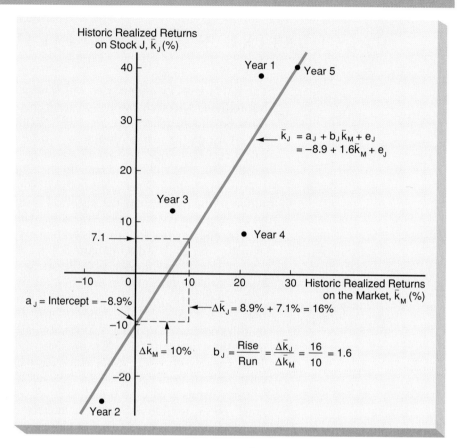

Year	Market ($\bar{k}_M$)	Stock J ($\bar{k}_J$)
1	23.8%	38.6%
2	(7.2)	(24.7)
3	6.6	12.3
4	20.5	8.2
5	30.6	40.1
Average $\bar{k}$	14.9%	14.9%
$\sigma_{\bar{k}}$	15.1%	26.5%

The least squares value of beta can be obtained quite easily with a financial calculator. The procedures that follow explain how to find the values of beta and the slope using either a Texas Instruments, a Hewlett-Packard, or a Sharp financial calculator.

Texas Instruments BA, BA-II, or MBA Calculator

1. Press **2nd** **Mode** until "STAT" shows in the display.
2. Enter the first X value ($\bar{k}_M = 23.8$ in our example), press **x≤y**, and then enter the first Y value ($\bar{k}_J = 38.6$) and press **Σ+**.

3. Repeat Step 2 until all values have been entered.

4. Press **2nd** **b/a** to find the value of Y at X = 0, which is the value of the Y intercept (a), −8.9219, and then press **x≤y** to display the value of the slope (beta), 1.6031.

5. You could also press **2nd** **Corr** to obtain the correlation coefficient, r, which is 0.9134.

Putting it all together, you should have this regression line:

$$\bar{k}_J = -8.92 + 1.60\bar{k}_M$$
$$r = 0.9134.$$

HEWLETT-PACKARD 10B[1]

1. Press **■** **Clear all** to clear your memory registers.

2. Enter the first X value ($\bar{k}_M$ = 23.8 in our example), press **INPUT**, and then enter the first Y value ($\bar{k}_J$ = 38.6) and press **Σ+**. Be *sure* to enter the X variable first.

3. Repeat Step 2 until all values have been entered.

4. To display the vertical axis intercept, press 0 **■** **ŷ,m**. Then −8.9219 should appear.

5. To display the beta coefficient, b, press **■** **SWAP**. Then 1.6031 should appear.

6. To obtain the correlation coefficient, press **■** **x̂,r** and then **■** **SWAP** to get r = 0.9134.

Putting it all together, you should have this regression line:

$$\bar{k}_J = -8.92 + 1.60\bar{k}_M$$
$$r = 0.9134.$$

SHARP EL-733

1. Press **2nd F** **Mode** until "STAT" shows in the lower right corner of the display.

2. Press **2nd F** **CA** to clear all memory registers.

3. Enter the first X value ($\bar{k}_M$ = 23.8 in our example) and press **(x,y)**. (This is the RM key; do not press the second F key at all.) Then enter the first Y value ($\bar{k}_J$ = 38.6), and press **DATA**. (This is the M+ key; again, do not press the second F key.)

4. Repeat Step 3 until all values have been entered.

5. Press **2nd F** **a** to find the value of Y at X = 0, which is the value of the Y intercept (a), −8.9219, and then press **2nd F** **b** to display the value of the slope (beta), 1.6031.

6. You can also press **2nd F** **r** to obtain the correlation coefficient, r, which is 0.9134.

---

[1]The Hewlett-Packard 17B calculator is even easier to use. If you have one, see Chapter 9 of the *Owner's Manual.*

Putting it all together, you should have this regression line:

$$\bar{k}_J = -8.92 + 1.60\bar{k}_M$$

$$r = 0.9134.$$

PROBLEMS

5A-1

Beta coefficients and rates of return

You are given the following set of data:

	HISTORICAL RATES OF RETURN ($\bar{k}$)	
YEAR	STOCK Y ($\bar{k}_Y$)	NYSE ($\bar{k}_M$)
1	3.0%	4.0%
2	18.2	14.3
3	9.1	19.0
4	(6.0)	(14.7)
5	(15.3)	(26.5)
6	33.1	37.2
7	6.1	23.8
8	3.2	(7.2)
9	14.8	6.6
10	24.1	20.5
11	18.0	30.6
Mean	9.8%	9.8%
$\sigma_{\bar{k}}$	13.8	19.6

a. Construct a scatter diagram graph (*on graph paper*) showing the relationship between returns on Stock Y and the market as in Figure 5A-1; then draw a freehand approximation of the regression line. What is the approximate value of the beta coefficient? (If you have a calculator with statistical functions, use it to calculate beta.)

b. Give a verbal interpretation of what the regression line and the beta coefficient show about Stock Y's volatility and relative riskiness as compared with other stocks.

c. Suppose the scatter of points had been more spread out but the regression line was exactly where your present graph shows it. How would this affect (1) the firm's risk if the stock were held in a one-asset portfolio and (2) the actual risk premium on the stock if the CAPM held exactly? How would the degree of scatter (or the correlation coefficient) affect your confidence that the calculated beta will hold true in the years ahead?

d. Suppose the regression line had been downward sloping and the beta coefficient had been negative. What would this imply about (1) Stock Y's relative riskiness and (2) its probable risk premium?

e. Construct an illustrative probability distribution graph of returns (see Figure 5-7) for portfolios consisting of (1) only Stock Y, (2) 1 percent each of 100 stocks with beta coefficients similar to that of Stock Y, and (3) all stocks (that is, the distribution of returns on the market). Use as the expected rate of return the arithmetic mean as given previously for both Stock Y and the market, and assume that the distributions are normal. Are the expected returns "reasonable" — that is, is it reasonable that $\hat{k}_Y = \hat{k}_M = 9.8\%$?

f. Now, suppose that in the next year, Year 12, the market return was 27 percent, but Firm Y increased its use of debt, which raised its perceived risk to investors. Do you think that the return on Stock Y in Year 12 could be approximated by this historical characteristic line?

$$\hat{k}_Y = 3.8\% + 0.62(\hat{k}_M) = 3.8\% + 0.62(27\%) = 20.5\%.$$

g. Now, suppose $\bar{k}_Y$ in Year 12, after the debt ratio was increased, had actually been 0 percent. What would the new beta be, based on the most recent 11 years of data (that is, Years 2 through 12)? Does this beta seem reasonable — that is, is the change in beta consistent with the other facts given in the problem?

5A-2

Security Market Line

You are given the following historical data on market returns, $\bar{k}_M$, and the returns on Stocks A and B, $\bar{k}_A$ and $\bar{k}_B$:

YEAR	$\bar{k}_M$	$\bar{k}_A$	$\bar{k}_B$
1	29.00%	29.00%	20.00%
2	15.20	15.20	13.10
3	(10.00)	(10.00)	0.50
4	3.30	3.30	7.15
5	23.00	23.00	17.00
6	31.70	31.70	21.35

k_{RF}, the risk-free rate, is 9 percent. Your probability distribution for k_M for next year is as follows:

PROBABILITY	k_M
0.1	(14%)
0.2	0
0.4	15
0.2	25
0.1	44

a. Determine graphically the beta coefficients for Stocks A and B.
b. Graph the Security Market Line, and give its equation.
c. Calculate the required rates of return on Stocks A and B.
d. Suppose a new stock, C, with $\hat{k}_C = 18$ percent and $b_C = 2.0$, becomes available. Is this stock in equilibrium; that is, does the required rate of return on Stock C equal its expected return? Explain. If the stock is not in equilibrium, explain how equilibrium will be restored.

CHAPTER 6

TIME VALUE OF MONEY[1]

© Paul Aresu/FPG International

[1]This chapter was written on the assumption that most students will have financial calculators. Calculators are relatively inexpensive, and students who cannot use them run the risk of being deemed obsolete and uncompetitive before they even graduate. Therefore, the chapter has been written to include a discussion of financial calculator solutions along with the regular calculator and tabular solutions. Those sections which require the use of financial calculators are identified, and instructors may choose to permit students to skip them.

Note also that tutorials on how to use several Hewlett-Packard, Texas Instruments, and Sharp calculators are provided in the *Technology Supplement* to this book, which is available to adopting instructors and which may be copied for distribution to purchasers of the book.

Your reaction to the question in the title of this vignette is probably, "First things first! I'm worried about getting a job, not retiring!" But an awareness of the retirement situation could help you land a job because (1) this is an important issue today, (2) employers prefer to hire people who know the issues, and (3) professors often test students on the time value of money with problems related to saving for some future purpose, including retirement. So read on.

A recent *Fortune* article began with some interesting facts: (1) The U.S. savings rate is the lowest of any industrial nation. (2) The ratio of U.S. workers to retirees, which was 17 to 1 in 1950, is now down to 3.2 to 1, and it will decline to less than 2 to 1 after the Year 2000. (3) With so few people paying into the Social Security System, and so many drawing funds out, Social Security may soon be in serious trouble. The article concluded that even people making $85,000 per year will have trouble maintaining a reasonable standard of living after they retire, and many of today's college students will have to support their parents.

If Ms. Jones, who earns $85,000, retires in 1996, expects to live for another 20 years after retirement, and needs 80 percent of her pre-retirement income, she would require $68,000 during 1996. However, if inflation amounts to 5 percent per year, her income requirement would increase to $110,765 in 10 years and to $180,424 in 20 years. If inflation were 7 percent, her Year 20 requirement would jump to $263,139! How much wealth would Ms. Jones need at retirement to maintain her standard of living, and how much would she have to save during each working year to accumulate that wealth?

The answer depends on a number of factors, including the rate she could earn on savings, the inflation rate, and when her savings program began. Also, the answer would depend on how much she will get from Social Security and from her corporate retirement plan, if she has one. (She should not count on much from Social Security unless she is really down and out.) Note, too, that her plans could be upset if the inflation rate increased, if the return on her savings changed, or if she lived beyond 20 years.

Fortune and other organizations have done studies relating to the retirement issue, using the tools and techniques described in this chapter. The general conclusion is that most Americans have been putting their heads in the sand — many of us have been ignoring what is almost certainly going to be a huge personal and social problem. But if you study this chapter carefully, you can avoid the trap that seems to be catching so many people.

In Chapter 1, we saw that the primary goal of financial management is to maximize the value of the firm's stock. We also saw that stock values depend in part on the timing of the cash flows investors expect to receive from an investment — a dollar expected soon is worth more than a dollar expected in the distant future. Therefore, it is essential that financial managers have a clear understanding of the time value of money and its impact on the value of the firm. These concepts are discussed in this chapter, where we show how the timing of cash flows affects asset values and rates of return.

The principles of time value analysis have many applications, ranging from setting up schedules for paying off loans to decisions about whether to acquire new equipment. *In fact, of all the concepts used in finance, none is more important than the time value of money, or discounted cash flow (DCF) analysis.* Since this concept is used throughout the remainder of the book, it is vital that you understand the material in this chapter before you move on to other topics.

TIME LINES

Time Line
An important tool used in time value of money analysis; it is a graphical representation used to show the timing of cash flows.

One of the most important tools in time value analysis is the **time line,** which is used by analysts to help visualize what is happening in a particular problem and then to help set up the problem for solution. To illustrate the time line concept, consider the following diagram:

Time 0 is today; Time 1 is one period from today, or the end of Period 1; Time 2 is two periods from today, or the end of Period 2; and so on. Thus, the numbers above the tick marks represent end-of-period values. Often the periods are years, but other time intervals such as semiannual periods, quarters, months, or even days can be used. If each period on the time line represents a year, the interval from the tick mark corresponding to 0 to the tick mark corresponding to 1 would be Year 1, the interval from 1 to 2 would be Year 2, and so on. Note that each tick mark corresponds to the end of one period as well as the beginning of the next period. In other words, the tick mark at Time 1 represents the *end* of Year 1, and it also represents the *beginning* of Year 2 because Year 1 has just passed.

Cash flows are placed directly below the tick marks, and interest rates are shown directly above the time line. Unknown cash flows, which you are trying to find in the analysis, are indicated by question marks. Now consider the following time line:

Outflow
A cash deposit, cost, or amount paid. Has a minus sign.

Inflow
A cash receipt.

Here the interest rate for each of the three periods is 5 percent; a single amount (or lump sum) cash **outflow** is made at Time 0; and the Time 3 value is an unknown **inflow.** Since the initial $100 is an outflow (an investment), it has a minus sign. Since the Period 3 amount is an inflow, it does not have a minus sign, which implies a plus sign. Note that no cash flows occur at Times 1 and 2. Note also that we generally do not show dollar signs on time lines to reduce clutter.

Now consider the following situation, where a $100 cash outflow is made today, and we will receive an unknown amount at the end of Time 2:

Here the interest rate is 5 percent during the first period, but it rises to 10 percent during the second period. If the interest rate is constant in all periods, we show it only in the first period, but if it changes, we show all the relevant rates on the time line.

Time lines are essential when you are first learning time value concepts, but even experts use time lines to analyze complex problems. We will be using time lines throughout the book, and you should get into the habit of using them when you work problems.

SELF-TEST QUESTION

Draw a three-year time line to illustrate the following situation: (1) An outflow of $10,000 occurs at Time 0. (2) Inflows of $5,000 then occur at the end of Years 1, 2, and 3. (3) The interest rate during all three years is 10 percent.

FUTURE VALUE

Compounding
The arithmetic process of determining the final value of a cash flow or series of cash flows when compound interest is applied.

A dollar in hand today is worth more than a dollar to be received in the future because, if you had it now, you could invest it, earn interest, and end up with more than one dollar in the future. The process of going from today's values, or present values (PVs), to future values (FVs) is called **compounding.** To illustrate, suppose you deposit $100 in a bank that pays 5 percent interest each year. How much would you have at the end of one year? To begin, we define the following terms:

PV = present value, or beginning amount, in your account. Here PV = $100.

i = interest rate the bank pays on the account per year. The interest earned is based on the balance at the beginning of each year, and we assume that it is paid at the end of the year. Here $i = 5\%$, or, expressed as a decimal, $i = 0.05$. Throughout this chapter, we designate the interest rate as i (or I) because that symbol is used on most financial calculators. Note, though, that in later chapters we use the symbol k to denote interest rates because k is used more often in the financial literature.

INT = dollars of interest you earn during the year = Beginning amount $\times$ i. Here INT = $100(0.05) = 5.

FV_n = future value, or ending amount, of your account at the end of n years. Whereas PV is the value now, or the *present value*, FV_n is the value n years into the *future*, after the interest earned has been added to the account.

n = number of periods involved in the analysis. Here n = 1.

In our example, n = 1, so FV_n can be calculated as follows:

$$FV_n = FV_1 = PV + INT$$
$$= PV + PV(i)$$
$$= PV(1 + i).$$
$$= \$100(1 + 0.05) = \$100(1.05) = \$105.$$

Future Value (FV)
The amount to which a cash flow or series of cash flows will grow over a given period of time when compounded at a given interest rate.

Thus, the **future value (FV)** at the end of one year, FV_1, equals the present value multiplied by 1 plus the interest rate, so you will have $105 after one year.

What would you end up with if you left your $100 in the account for five years? Here is a time line set up to show the amount at the end of each year:

	0	1	2	3	4	5
	5%					
Initial deposit:	−100	$FV_1 = ?$	$FV_2 = ?$	$FV_3 = ?$	$FV_4 = ?$	$FV_5 = ?$
Interest earned:		5.00	5.25	5.51	5.79	6.08
Amount at the end of each period = FV_n:		105.00	110.25	115.76	121.55	**127.63**

Note the following points: (1) You start by depositing $100 in the account — this is shown as an outflow at t = 0. (2) You earn $100(0.05) = $5 of interest during the first year, so the amount at the end of Year 1 (or t = 1) is $100 + $5 = $105. (3) You start the second year with $105, earn $5.25 on the now larger amount, and end the second year with $110.25. Your interest during Year 2, $5.25, is higher than the first year's interest, $5, because you earned $5(0.05) = $0.25 interest on the first year's interest. (4) This process continues, and because the beginning balance is higher in each succeeding year, the annual interest earned increases. (5) The total interest earned, $27.63, is reflected in the final balance at t = 5, $127.63.

Note that the value at the end of Year 2, $110.25, is equal to

$$FV_2 = FV_1(1 + i)$$
$$= PV(1 + i)(1 + i)$$
$$= PV(1 + i)^2$$
$$= \$100(1.05)^2 = \$110.25.$$

Continuing, the balance at the end of Year 3 is

$$FV_3 = FV_2(1 + i)$$
$$= PV(1 + i)^3$$
$$= \$100(1.05)^3 = \$115.76,$$

and

$$FV_5 = \$100(1.05)^5 = \$127.63.$$

In general, the future value of an initial lump sum at the end of n years can be found by applying Equation 6-1:

$$FV_n = PV(1 + i)^n. \qquad (6\text{-}1)$$

Equation 6-1 and most other time value of money equations can be solved in four ways: numerically with a regular calculator, with interest tables, with a financial calculator, or with a computer spreadsheet program. Most advanced work in financial management will be done on a computer, but when learning basic concepts it is best to use one (or more) of the other methods.

Numerical Solution

One can use a regular calculator and either multiply (1 + i) by itself n − 1 times or else use the exponential function to raise (1 + i) to the *n*th power. With most calculators, you would enter 1 + i = 1.05 and multiply it by itself four times, or else enter 1.05, then press the y^x (exponential) function key, and then enter 5. In either case, your answer would be 1.2763 (if you set your calculator to display four decimal places), which you would multiply by $100 to get the final answer, $127.6282, which would be rounded to $127.63.

In certain problems, it is extremely difficult to arrive at a solution using a regular calculator. We will tell you this when we have such a problem, and in these cases we will not show a numerical solution. Also, at times we show the numerical solution just below the time line, as a part of the diagram, rather than in a separate section.

Interest Tables (Tabular Solution)

Future Value Interest Factor for i and n (FVIF$_{i,n}$)
The future value of $1 left on deposit for n periods at a rate of i percent per period.

The **Future Value Interest Factor for i and n (FVIF$_{i,n}$)** is defined as $(1 + i)^n$, and these factors can be found by using a regular calculator as discussed above and then put into tables. Table 6-1 is illustrative, while Table A-3 in Appendix A at the back of the book contains FVIF$_{i,n}$ values for a wide range of i and n values.

Since $(1 + i)^n = \text{FVIF}_{i,n}$, Equation 6-1 can be rewritten as follows:

$$FV_n = PV(\text{FVIF}_{i,n}). \tag{6-1a}$$

To illustrate, the FVIF for our five-year, 5 percent interest problem can be found in Table 6-1 by looking down the first column to Period 5, and then looking across that row to the 5 percent column, where we see that FVIF$_{5\%,5}$ = 1.2763. Then, the value of $100 after five years is found as follows:

$$FV_n = PV(\text{FVIF}_{i,n})$$
$$= \$100(1.2763) = \$127.63.$$

Before financial calculators became readily available (in the 1980s), such tables were used extensively, but they are rarely used today in the real world.

Financial Calculator Solution

Equation 6-1 and a number of other equations have been programmed directly into financial calculators, and these calculators can be used to find future values. Note that calculators have five keys which correspond to the five most commonly used time value of money variables:

Here

N = the number of periods. Some calculators use n rather than N.

I = interest rate per period. Some calculators use i or I/YR rather than I.

PV = present value.

PMT = payment. This key is used only if the cash flows involve a series of equal, or constant, payments (an annuity). If there are no periodic payments in a particular problem, then PMT = 0.

FV = future value.

On some financial calculators, these keys are actually buttons on the face of the calculator, while on others they are shown on a screen after going into the time value of money (TVM) menu.

TABLE 6 - 1	Future Value Interest Factors: $FVIF_{i,n} = (1 + i)^n$		
PERIOD (n)	4%	5%	6%
1	1.0400	1.0500	1.0600
2	1.0816	1.1025	1.1236
3	1.1249	1.1576	1.1910
4	1.1699	1.2155	1.2625
5	1.2167	1.2763	1.3382
6	1.2653	1.3401	1.4185

In this chapter, we will deal with equations which involve only four of the variables at any one time — three of the variables will be known, and the calculator will then solve for the fourth (unknown) variable. In the next chapter, when we deal with bonds, we will use all five variables in the bond valuation equation.[2]

To find the future value of $100 after five years at 5 percent using a financial calculator, note that we must solve Equation 6-1:

$$FV_n = PV(1 + i)^n. \qquad (6\text{-}1)$$

The equation has four variables, FV_n, PV, i, and n. If we know any three, we can solve for the fourth. In our example, we enter $N = 5, I = 5, PV = 100$, and $PMT = 0$. Then, when we press the FV key, we get the answer, $FV = 127.63$ (rounded to two decimal places).[3]

Many financial calculators require that all cash flows be designated as either inflows or outflows, with outflows being entered as negative numbers. In our illustration, you deposit, or put in, the initial amount (which is an outflow to you) and you take out, or receive, the ending amount (which is an inflow to you). If your calculator requires that you follow this sign convention, the PV would be entered as -100. (If you entered 100, then the FV would appear as -127.63.) Also, on some calculators you are required to press a "Compute" key before pressing the FV key.

Sometimes the convention of changing signs can be confusing. For example, if you have $100 in the bank now and want to find out how much you will have after five years if your account pays 5 percent interest, the calculator will give you a negative answer, in this case -127.63, because the calculator assumes you are going to withdraw the funds. This sign convention should cause you no problem if you think about what you are doing.

We should also note that financial calculators permit you to specify the number of decimal places that are displayed. Twelve significant digits are

---

[2]The equation programmed into the calculators actually has five variables, one for each key. In this chapter, the value of one of the variables is always zero. It is a good idea to get into the habit of inputting a zero for the unused variable (whose value is automatically set equal to zero when you clear the calculator's memory); if you forget to clear your calculator, inputting a zero will help you avoid trouble.

[3]Here we assume that compounding occurs once each year. Most calculators have a setting which can be used to designate the number of compounding periods per year. For example, the HP-10B comes preset with payments at 12 per year. You would need to change it to 1 per year to get $FV=127.63$. With the HP-10B, you would do this by typing 1, pressing the gold key, and then pressing the P/YR key.

actually used in the calculations, but we generally use two places for answers when working with dollars or percentages and four places when working with decimals. The nature of the problem dictates how many decimal places should be displayed.

Technology has progressed to the point where the only efficient way to solve most time value of money problems is with a financial calculator or a computer spreadsheet. However, you must understand the concepts behind the calculations and know how to set up time lines in order to work complex problems. This is true for stock and bond valuation, capital budgeting, lease analysis, and many other important types of problems.

PROBLEM FORMAT

To help you understand the various types of time value problems, we generally use a standard format in this chapter. First, we state the problem in words. Next, we diagram the problem on a time line. Then, beneath the time line, we show the equation that must be solved. Finally, we present three alternative procedures for solving the equation to obtain the answer: (1) use a regular calculator to obtain a numerical solution, (2) use the tables, or (3) use a financial calculator. Generally, the financial calculator solution is the most efficient.

To illustrate the format, consider the five-year, 5 percent example:

Time Line:

```
0        1       2        3        4        5
|   5%   |       |        |        |        |
-100                                       FV = ?
```

Equation:

$$FV_n = PV(1 + i)^n = \$100(1.05)^5.$$

 1. Numerical Solution:

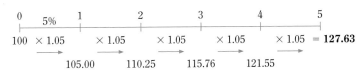

```
0        1        2         3         4         5
|   5%   |        |         |         |         |
100  × 1.05   × 1.05    × 1.05    × 1.05    × 1.05  = 127.63
       →         →          →         →          →
      105.00    110.25    115.76    121.55
```

Using a regular calculator, raise 1.05 to the 5th power and multiply by $100 to get $FV_5 = \$127.63$.

 2. Tabular Solution:

Look up $FVIF_{5\%,5}$ in Table 6-1 or Table A-3 at the end of the book, and then multiply by $100:

$$FV_5 = \$100(FVIF_{5\%,5}) = \$100(1.2763) = \$127.63.$$

 3. Financial Calculator Solution:

Inputs:	5	5	−100	0	
	N	I	PV	PMT	FV
Output:					= 127.63

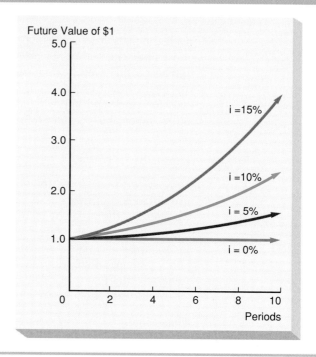

Note that the calculator diagram tells you to input N = 5, I = 5, PV = −100, and PMT = 0, and then to press the FV key to get the answer, 127.63. Interest rates are entered as percentages (5), not decimals (0.05). Also, note that in this particular problem, the PMT key does not come into play, as no constant series of payments is involved.[4] Finally, you should recognize that small rounding differences will often occur among the various solution methods because tables use fewer significant digits (4) than do calculators (12), and also because rounding sometimes is done at intermediate steps in long problems.

GRAPHIC VIEW OF THE COMPOUNDING PROCESS: GROWTH

Figure 6-1 shows how $1 (or any other lump sum) grows over time at various interest rates. The data used to plot the curves could be obtained from Table A-3, or it could be generated with a calculator or computer. The higher the rate of interest, the faster the rate of growth. The interest rate is, in fact, a growth rate: If a sum is deposited and earns 5 percent interest, then the funds on deposit will grow at a rate of 5 percent per period. Note also that time value concepts can be applied to anything that is growing — sales, population, earnings per share, or whatever.

---

[4]We input PMT = 0, but if you cleared the calculator before you started, the PMT register would already have been set to 0.

INDUSTRY PRACTICE

THE POWER OF COMPOUND INTEREST

You are 21 years old and have just graduated from college. After reading the introduction to this chapter, you decide to start saving immediately for your retirement. Your goal is to have $1 million when you retire at age 65. Assuming you earn a 10 percent annual rate on your savings, how much must you save at the end of each year in order to reach your goal?

The answer is $1,532.24, but this amount depends critically on the rate earned on your savings. If rates drop to 8 percent, your required annual savings would rise to $2,801.52, while if rates rise to 12 percent, you would only need to put away $825.21 per year.

What if you are like most of us and wait until later to worry about retirement? If you wait until age 40, you will need to save $10,168 per year to reach your $1 million goal, assuming you earn 10 percent, and $13,679 if you earn only 8 percent. If you wait until age 50 and then earn 8 percent, your required savings will be $36,830 per year.

While $1 million may seem like a lot of money, it won't be when you get ready to retire. If inflation averages 5 percent a year over the next 44 years, your $1 million nest egg will be worth only $116,861 in today's dollars. At an 8 percent rate of return, and assuming you live for 20 years after retirement, your annual retirement income in today's dollars would be $11,903 before taxes. So after celebrating graduation and your new job, start saving!

SELF-TEST QUESTIONS

Explain what is meant by the following statement: "A dollar in hand today is worth more than a dollar to be received next year."

What is compounding? What is "interest on interest"?

Explain the following equation: $FV_1 = PV + INT$.

Set up a time line that shows the following situation: (1) Your initial deposit is $100. (2) The account pays 5 percent interest annually. (3) You want to know how much money you will have at the end of three years.

Write out an equation which you could use to solve the preceding problem.

What are the five TVM (time value of money) input keys on a financial calculator? List them (horizontally) in the proper order.

PRESENT VALUE

Opportunity Cost Rate
The rate of return on the best available alternative investment of equal risk.

Suppose you have some extra cash, and you have a chance to buy a low-risk security which will pay $127.63 at the end of five years. Your local bank is currently offering 5 percent interest on five-year certificates of deposit (CDs), and you regard the security as being exactly as safe as a CD. The 5 percent rate is defined as your **opportunity cost rate,** or the rate of return you could earn on alternative investments of similar risk. How much should you be willing to pay for the security?

From the future value example presented in the previous section, we saw that an initial amount of $100 invested at 5 percent per year would be worth $127.63 at the end of five years. As we will see in a moment, you should be indifferent to the choice between $100 today and $127.63 at the end of five years. The $100 is

Present Value (PV)
The value today of a future cash flow or series of cash flows.

Fair (Equilibrium) Value
The price at which investors are indifferent between buying or selling a security.

Discounting
The process of finding the present value of a cash flow or a series of cash flows; discounting is the reverse of compounding.

defined as the **present value, or PV**, of $127.63 due in five years when the opportunity cost rate is 5 percent. If the price of the security were less than $100, you should buy it, because its price would then be less than the $100 you would have to spend on a similar-risk alternative to end up with $127.63 after five years. Conversely, if the security cost more than $100, you should not buy it, because you would have to invest only $100 in a similar-risk alternative to end up with $127.63 after five years. If the price were exactly $100, then you should be indifferent — you could either buy the security or turn it down. Therefore, $100 is defined as the security's **fair, or equilibrium, value**.

In general, *the present value of a cash flow due n years in the future is the amount which, if it were on hand today, would grow to equal the future amount.* Since $100 would grow to $127.63 in five years at a 5 percent interest rate, $100 is the present value of $127.63 due in five years when the opportunity cost rate is 5 percent.

Finding present values is called **discounting,** and it is simply the reverse of compounding — if you know the PV, you can compound to find the FV, while if you know the FV, you can discount to find the PV. When discounting, you would follow these steps:

Time Line:

$$
\begin{array}{ccccccccccc}
0 & & 1 & & 2 & & 3 & & 4 & & 5 \\
\vdash & \!\!5\% & \dashv & & \dashv & & \dashv & & \dashv & & \dashv \\
PV = ? & & & & & & & & & & 127.63
\end{array}
$$

Equation:

To develop the discounting equation, we begin with the future value equation, Equation 6-1:

$$FV_n = PV(1 + i)^n = PV(FVIF_{i,n}). \qquad \textbf{(6-1)}$$

Next, we solve it for PV in several equivalent forms:

$$PV = \frac{FV_n}{(1 + i)^n} = FV_n\left(\frac{1}{1 + i}\right)^n = FV_n(PVIF_{i,n}). \qquad \textbf{(6-2)}$$

The last form of Equation 6-2 recognizes that the interest factor $PVIF_{i,n}$ is equal to the term in parentheses in the second version of the equation.

1. Numerical Solution:

$$
\begin{array}{ccccccccccc}
0 & & 1 & & 2 & & 3 & & 4 & & 5 \\
\vdash & \!\!5\% & \dashv & & \dashv & & \dashv & & \dashv & & \dashv \\
-100 = & \leftarrow & 105.00 & \leftarrow & 110.25 & \leftarrow & 115.76 & \leftarrow & 121.55 & \leftarrow & 127.63 \\
& & \div 1.05 & & \div 1.05 & & \div 1.05 & & \div 1.05 & & \div 1.05
\end{array}
$$

Divide $127.63 by 1.05 five times, or by $(1.05)^5$, to find PV = $100.

2. Tabular Solution:

Present Value Interest Factor for i and n (PVIF$_{i,n}$)
The present value of $1 due n periods in the future discounted at i percent per period.

The term in parentheses in Equation 6-2 is called the **Present Value Interest Factor for i and n, or PVIF$_{i,n}$**, and Table A-1 in Appendix A contains present value interest factors for selected values of i and n. The value of $PVIF_{i,n}$ for i = 5% and n = 5 is 0.7835, so the present value of $127.63 to be received after five years when the appropriate interest rate is 5 percent is $100:

$$PV = \$127.63(PVIF_{5\%,5}) = \$127.63(0.7835) = \$100.$$

3. Financial Calculator Solution:

Inputs: 5   5   0   127.63

[N]   [I]   [PV]   [PMT]   [FV]

Output: = −100

Enter N = 5, I = 5, PMT = 0, and FV = 127.63, and then press PV to get PV = −100. This is the easy way!

GRAPHIC VIEW OF THE DISCOUNTING PROCESS

Figure 6-2 shows how the present value of $1 (or any other sum) to be received in the future diminishes as the years to receipt and the interest rate increase. Again, the data used to plot the curves could be obtained either with a calculator or from Table A-1, and the graph shows (1) that the present value of a sum to be received at some future date decreases and approaches zero as the payment date is extended further into the future, and (2) that the rate of decrease is greater the higher the interest (discount) rate. At relatively high interest rates, funds due in the future are worth very little today, and even at a relatively low discount rate, the present value of a sum due in the very distant future is quite small. For example, at a 20 percent discount rate, $1 million due in 100 years is worth approximately 1 cent today. (However, 1 cent would grow to almost $1 million in 100 years at 20 percent.)

SELF-TEST QUESTIONS   ??????

What is meant by the term "opportunity cost rate"?

What is discounting? How is it related to compounding?

How does the present value of an amount to be received in the future change as the time is extended and as the interest rate increases?

SOLVING FOR INTEREST RATE AND TIME

At this point, you should realize that compounding and discounting are related to one another, and that we have been dealing with one equation in two different forms:

FV Form:

$$FV_n = PV(1 + i)^n. \qquad (6\text{-}1)$$

PV Form:

$$PV = \frac{FV_n}{(1 + i)^n} = FV_n\left(\frac{1}{1 + i}\right)^n. \qquad (6\text{-}2)$$

There are four variables in these equations — PV, FV, i, and n — and if you know the values of any three, you (or your financial calculator) can find the value of the fourth. Thus far, we have always given you the interest rate (i) and the number of years (n), plus either the PV or the FV. In many situations, though, you will need to solve for either i or n, as we discuss below.

F I G U R E   6 - 2 Relationships among Present Value, Interest Rates, and Time

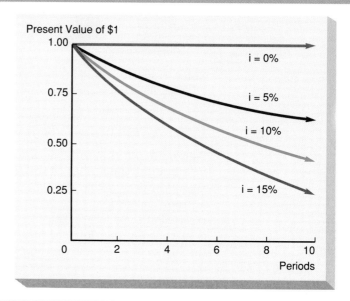

SOLVING FOR i

Suppose you can buy a security at a price of $78.35 which will pay you $100 after five years. Here we know PV, FV, and n, but we do not know i, the interest rate you would earn on the investment. Problems such as this are solved as follows:

Time Line:

Equation:

$$FV_n = PV(1 + i)^n \qquad \text{(6-1)}$$

$100 = $78.35(1 + i)^5$. Solve for i.

1. Numerical Solution:

Go through a trial-and-error process in which you insert different values of i into Equation 6-1 until you find a value which "works" in the sense that the right-hand side of the equation equals $100. The solution value is i = 0.05, or 5 percent. The trial-and-error procedure is extremely tedious and inefficient for most time value problems, so no one in the real world uses it.

2. Tabular Solution:

$$FV_n = PV(1 + i)^n = PV(FVIF_{i,n})$$

$$\$100 = \$78.35(FVIF_{i,5})$$

$$FVIF_{i,5} = \$100/\$78.35 = 1.2763.$$

Find the value of the FVIF as shown above, and then look across the Period 5 row in Table A-3 until you find FVIF = 1.2763. This value is in the 5% column, so the interest rate at which $78.35 grows to $100 over five years is 5 percent. This procedure can be used only if the interest rate is in the table; therefore, it will not work for fractional interest rates or where n is not a whole number. Approximation procedures can be used, but they are laborious and inexact.

3. Financial Calculator Solution:

Inputs:	5		−78.35	0	100
	N	I	PV	PMT	FV
Output:		= 5.0			

Enter N = 5, PV = −78.35, PMT = 0, and FV = 100, and then press I to get I = 5%. This procedure can be used for any interest rate or for any value of n, including fractional values.

SOLVING FOR n

Suppose you know that a security will provide a return of 5 percent per year, that it will cost $78.35, and that you will receive $100 at maturity, but you do not know when the security matures. Thus, you know PV, FV, and i, but you do not know n, the number of periods. Here is the situation:

Time Line:

```
0        1        2          n − 1      n = ?
├──5%──┼────────┼── · · · ──┼──────────┤
−78.35                                  100
```

Equation:

$$FV_n = PV(1 + i)^n \qquad\qquad \textbf{(6-1)}$$

$100 = $78.35(1.05)^n$. Solve for n.

1. Numerical Solution:

Again, you could go through a trial-and-error process wherein you substituted different values for n into the equation. You would find (eventually) that n = 5 "works," so 5 is the number of years it takes for $78.35 to grow to $100 if the interest rate is 5 percent.

2. Tabular Solution:

$$FV_n = PV(1 + i)^n = PV(FVIF_{i,n})$$
$$\$100 = \$78.35(FVIF_{5\%,n})$$
$$FVIF_{5\%,n} = \$100/\$78.35 = 1.2763.$$

Now look down the 5% column in Table A-3 until you find FVIF = 1.2763. This value is in Row 5, which indicates that it takes five years for $78.35 to grow to $100 at a 5 percent interest rate.

3. Financial Calculator Solution:

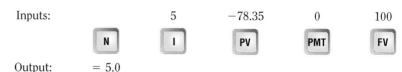

Inputs: 5   −78.35   0   100

N	I	PV	PMT	FV

Output: = 5.0

Enter I = 5, PV = −78.35, PMT = 0, and FV = 100, and then press N to get N = 5.

SELF-TEST QUESTIONS

??????

Assuming that you are given PV, FV, and the time period, n, write out an equation that can be used to determine the interest rate, i.

Assuming that you are given PV, FV, and the interest rate, i, write out an equation that can be used to determine the time period, n.

Explain how a financial calculator can be used to solve for i and n.

FUTURE VALUE OF AN ANNUITY

Annuity
A series of payments of an equal amount at fixed intervals for a specified number of periods.

Ordinary (Deferred) Annuity
An annuity whose payments occur at the end of each period.

Annuity Due
An annuity whose payments occur at the beginning of each period.

An **annuity** is a series of equal payments made at fixed intervals for a specified number of periods. For example, $100 at the end of each of the next three years is a three-year annuity. The payments are given the symbol PMT, and they can occur at either the beginning or the end of each period. If the payments occur at the *end* of each period, as they typically do, the annuity is called an **ordinary**, or **deferred, annuity.** If payments are made at the *beginning* of each period, the annuity is an **annuity due.** Since ordinary annuities are more common in finance, when the term "annuity" is used in this book, you should assume that the payments occur at the end of each period unless otherwise noted.

ORDINARY ANNUITIES

FVA$_n$
The future value of an annuity over n periods.

An ordinary, or deferred, annuity consists of a series of equal payments made at the *end* of each period. If you deposit $100 at the end of each year for three years in a savings account that pays 5 percent interest per year, how much will you have at the end of three years? To answer this question, we must find the future value of the annuity, **FVA$_n$**. Each payment is compounded out to the end of Period n, and the sum of the compounded payments is the future value of the annuity, FVA$_n$.

Time Line:

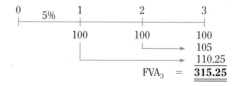

Here we show the regular time line as the top portion of the diagram, but we also show how each cash flow is compounded to produce the value FVA$_n$ in the lower portion of the diagram.

Equation:

$$FVA_n = PMT(1 + i)^{n-1} + PMT(1 + i)^{n-2} + PMT(1 + i)^{n-3} + \cdots + PMT(1 + i)^0$$

$$= PMT \sum_{t=1}^{n} (1 + i)^{n-t}. \qquad (6\text{-}3)$$

Each term in Equation 6-3 represents the compounded amount of an annuity payment, and the superscript in each term indicates the number of periods the payment earns interest. In other words, because the first annuity payment was made at the end of Period 1, interest would be earned in Periods 2 through n only; thus, compounding would be for $n - 1$ periods rather than n periods. Compounding for the second annuity payment would be for Period 3 through Period n, or $n - 2$ periods, and so on. The last annuity payment is made at the same time the computation is made, so there is no time for interest to be earned. The second form of Equation 6-3 is just a shorthand version of the first.

1. Numerical Solution:

The lower section of the time line shows the numerical solution. The future value of each cash flow is found, and those FVs are summed to find the FV of the annuity, $315.25. This is a tedious process for long annuities.

2. Tabular Solution:

Future Value Interest Factor for an Annuity (FVIFA$_{i,n}$)
The future value interest factor for an annuity of n periods compounded at i percent.

The summation term in Equation 6-3 is called the **Future Value Interest Factor for an Annuity (FVIFA$_{i,n}$):**[5]

$$FVIFA_{i,n} = \sum_{t=1}^{n} (1 + i)^{n-t}. \qquad (6\text{-}3a)$$

FVIFAs have been calculated for various combinations of i and n, and Table A-4 in Appendix A contains a set of FVIFA factors. To find the answer to the three-year, $100 annuity problem, first refer to Table A-4 and look down the 5% column to the third period; the FVIFA is 3.1525. Thus, the future value of the $100 annuity is $315.25:

$$FVA_n = PMT(FVIFA_{i,n})$$

$$FVA_3 = \$100(FVIFA_{5\%,3}) = \$100(3.1525) = \$315.25.$$

3. Financial Calculator Solution:

Inputs:	3	5	0	−100	
	N	**I**	**PV**	**PMT**	**FV**
Output:					= 315.25

Note that in annuity problems, the PMT key is used in conjunction with the N and I keys, plus either the PV or the FV key, depending on whether you are

---

[5]Another form for Equation 6-3a is as follows:

$$FVIFA_{i,n} = \frac{(1 + i)^n - 1}{i}.$$

This form is found by applying the algebra of geometric progressions. This equation is useful in situations where the required values of i and n are not in the tables and no financial calculator is available.

trying to find the PV or the FV of the annuity. In our example, you want the FV, so press the FV key to get the answer, $315.25. Since there is no initial payment, we input PV = 0.

Annuities Due

Had the three $100 payments in the previous example been made at the *beginning* of each year, the annuity would have been an *annuity due*. On the time line, each payment would be shifted to the left one year; therefore, each payment would be compounded for one extra year.

1. Time Line and Numerical Solution:

```
0        1        2        3
|---5%---|--------|--------|
100      100      100
                       →  105
                  →  110.25
             →  115.76
          FVA₃ (Annuity due)  =  331.01
```

Again, the time line is shown at the top of the diagram, and the values as calculated with a regular calculator are shown under Year 3. The payments occur earlier, so more interest is earned. Therefore, the future value of the annuity due is larger — $331.01 versus $315.25 for the ordinary annuity.

2. Tabular Solution:

In an annuity due, each payment is compounded for one additional period, so the future value of the entire annuity is equal to the future value of an ordinary annuity compounded for one additional period. Here is the tabular solution:

$$FVA_n \text{ (Annuity due)} = PMT(FVIFA_{i,n})(1 + i) \tag{6-3b}$$
$$= \$100(3.1525)(1.05) = \$331.01.$$

3. Financial Calculator Solution:

Most financial calculators have a switch, or key, marked "DUE" or "BEG" that permits you to switch from end-of-period payments (ordinary annuity) to beginning-of-period payments (annuity due). When the beginning mode is activated, the display will normally show the word "BEGIN." Thus, to deal with annuities due, switch your calculator to "BEGIN" and proceed as before:

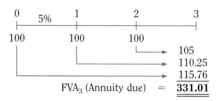

BEGIN

	N	I	PV	PMT	FV
Inputs:	3	5	0	−100	
Output:					= 331.01

Enter N = 3, I = 5, PV = 0, PMT = −100, and then press FV to get the answer, $331.01. *Since most problems specify end-of-period cash flows, you should always switch your calculator back to "END" mode after you work an annuity due problem.*

What is the difference between an ordinary annuity and an annuity due?

How do you modify the equation for determining the value of an ordinary annuity to find the value of an annuity due?

Which annuity has the greater *future* value: an ordinary annuity or an annuity due? Why?

Explain how financial calculators can be used to solve future value of annuity problems.

PRESENT VALUE OF AN ANNUITY

Suppose you were offered the following alternatives: (1) a three-year annuity with payments of $100 or (2) a lump sum payment today. You have no need for the money during the next three years, so if you accept the annuity, you would deposit the payments in a bank account that pays 5 percent interest per year. Similarly, the lump sum payment would be deposited into a bank account. How large must the lump sum payment today be to make it equivalent to the annuity?

ORDINARY ANNUITIES

If the payments come at the end of each year, then the annuity is an ordinary annuity, and it would be set up as follows:

Time Line:

```
        0      5%  1        2        3
        |----------|--------|--------|
                   100      100      100
95.24   ←──────────┘         |        |
90.70   ←───────────────────┘         |
86.38   ←─────────────────────────────┘
PVA₃  = 272.32
```

The regular time line is shown at the top of the diagram, and the numerical solution values are shown in the left column. The PV of the annuity, **PVAₙ,** is $272.32.

PVA_n
The present value of an annuity of n periods.

Equation:

The general equation used to find the PV of an ordinary annuity is shown below:[6]

$$PVA_n = PMT\left(\frac{1}{1+i}\right)^1 + PMT\left(\frac{1}{1+i}\right)^2 + \cdots + PMT\left(\frac{1}{1+i}\right)^n$$

$$= PMT \sum_{t=1}^{n} \left(\frac{1}{1+i}\right)^t. \tag{6-4}$$

---

[6]The summation term is called the PVIFA, and, using the geometric progression solution process, its value is found to be

$$PVIFA_{i,n} = \sum_{t=1}^{n}\left(\frac{1}{1+i}\right)^t = \frac{1 - \dfrac{1}{(1+i)^n}}{i} = \frac{1}{i} - \frac{1}{i(1+i)^n}.$$

This form of the equation is useful for dealing with annuities when the values for i and n are not in the tables and no financial calculator is available.

1. Numerical Solution:

The present value of each cash flow is found and then summed to find the PV of the annuity. This procedure is shown in the lower section of the time line diagram, where we see that the PV of the annuity is $272.32.

2. Tabular Solution:

Present Value Interest Factor for an Annuity (PVIFA$_{i,n}$)
The present value interest factor for an annuity of n periods discounted at i percent.

The summation term in Equation 6-4 is called the **Present Value Interest Factor for an Annuity (PVIFA$_{i,n}$),** and values for the term at different values of i and n are shown in Table A-2 at the back of the book. Here is the equation:

$$PVA_n = PMT(PVIFA_{i,n}). \tag{6-4a}$$

To find the answer to the three-year, $100 annuity problem, simply refer to Table A-2 and look down the 5% column to the third period. The PVIFA is 2.7232, so the present value of the $100 annuity is $272.32:

$$PVA_n = PMT(PVIFA_{i,n})$$
$$PVA_3 = \$100(PVIFA_{5\%,3}) = \$100(2.7232) = \$272.32.$$

3. Financial Calculator Solution:

Output: = 272.32

Enter N = 3, I = 5, PMT = −100, and FV = 0, and then press the PV key to find the PV, $272.32.

One especially important application of the annuity concept relates to loans with constant payments, such as mortgages and auto loans. With such loans, called *amortized loans,* the amount borrowed is the present value of an ordinary annuity, and the payments constitute the annuity stream. We will examine constant payment loans in more depth in a later section of this chapter.

ANNUITIES DUE

Had the three $100 payments in the preceding example been made at the beginning of each year, the annuity would have been an *annuity due.* Each payment would be shifted to the left one year, so each payment would be discounted for one less year. Here is the time line setup:

1. Time Line and Numerical Solution:

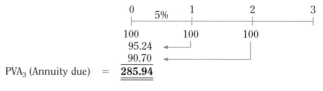

Again, we find the PV of each cash flow and then sum these PVs to find the PV of the annuity due. This procedure is illustrated in the lower section of the time line diagram. Since the cash flows occur sooner, the PV of the annuity due exceeds that of the ordinary annuity, $285.94 versus $272.32.

2. Tabular Solution:

In an annuity due, each payment is discounted for one less period. Since its payments come in faster, an annuity due is more valuable than an ordinary annuity, and this higher value is found by multiplying the PV of an ordinary annuity by $(1 + i)$:

$$PVA_n \text{ (Annuity due)} = PMT(PVIFA_{i,n})(1 + i) \quad \text{(6-4b)}$$
$$= \$100(2.7232)(1.05) = \$285.94.$$

3. Financial Calculator Solution:

Switch to the beginning-of-period mode, and then enter N = 3, I = 5, PMT = −100, and FV = 0, and then press PV to get the answer, $285.94. *Again, since most problems deal with end-of-period cash flows, don't forget to switch your calculator back to the "END" mode.*

SELF-TEST QUESTIONS

Which annuity has the greater present value: an ordinary annuity or an annuity due? Why?

Explain how financial calculators can be used to find the present value of annuities.

PERPETUITIES

Perpetuity
A stream of equal payments expected to continue forever.

Most annuities call for payments to be made over some finite period of time — for example, $100 per year for three years. However, some annuities go on indefinitely, or perpetually, and these annuities are called **perpetuities.** The present value of a perpetuity is found by applying Equation 6-5.[7]

$$PV(\text{Perpetuity}) = \frac{\text{Payment}}{\text{Interest rate}} = \frac{PMT}{i}. \quad \text{(6-5)}$$

Consol
A perpetual bond issued by the British government to consolidate past debts; in general, any perpetual bond.

Perpetuities can be illustrated by some British securities issued after the Napoleonic Wars. In 1815, the British government sold a huge bond issue and used the proceeds to pay off many smaller issues that had been floated in prior years to pay for the wars. Since the purpose of the bonds was to consolidate past debts, the bonds were called **consols.** Suppose each consol promised to pay $100 per year in perpetuity. (Actually, interest was stated in pounds.) What would each

---

[7]The derivation of Equation 6-5 is given in Appendix 4A of Eugene F. Brigham and Louis C. Gapenski, *Intermediate Financial Management,* 5th ed. (Forth Worth, Tex.: Dryden Press, 1996).

INDUSTRY PRACTICE

THE $40 MILLION MAN

If you are a football fan, you've probably heard of Steve Young, the MVP quarterback of the San Francisco 49ers. Young first became famous in 1984, when he graduated from college and signed a contract with the L.A. Express, a team in the now-defunct United States Football League (USFL).

Under the terms of his contract, the Express agreed to pay Young a mind-boggling $40 million. Even in the sports industry, where million dollar contracts are commonplace, the size of Young's contract caught everyone's attention. Why would the Express be willing to pay $40 million to a rookie quarterback who had not yet thrown a pass as a professional?

The time value of money provides most of the answer. Although Young's contract was for four years, the actual payments were spread out over a period of 43 years. Over the first four years, Young was to receive $5.9 million in cash as salary and bonuses. Then, starting in 1990, Young's contract called for the commencement of $34.5 million in deferred compensation in the form of a series of rising annuities, beginning with $200,000 per year through 1999 and rising to a final annuity payment of $3.173 million in the year 2027.

Given that the deferred payments were not to be received for several years, the Express was able to provide for the annuities at a cost considerably less than $34.5 million. Overall, the present value of Young's contract was estimated to be worth about $5.5 million — not too shabby, but a far cry from $40 million.

Also in 1984, Herschel Walker, one of the big stars of the USFL, signed a four-year contract with the New Jersey Generals. While Walker's contract was for "only" $6 million, most of it was paid in up-front money. This led Donald Trump, owner of the Generals, to comment:

> You have to bring the contract down to present value . . . . I know numbers, and if I had my choice between Herschel's contract and Steve Young's contract, I'd take Herschel's.

Less than two years later, the Express and the USFL were struggling, and Young was able to buy out the remaining years of his contract. He signed with the Tampa Bay Buccaneers in the National Football League, and he was later traded to the 49ers. He continues to be well paid, but his current contract is considerably less interesting than his first one.

bond be worth if the opportunity cost rate, or discount rate, was 5 percent? The answer is $2,000:

$$\text{PV (Perpetuity)} = \frac{\$100}{0.05} = \$2,000 \text{ if } i = 5\%.$$

Suppose the interest rate rose to 10 percent; what would happen to the consol's value? The value would drop to $1,000:

$$\text{PV (Perpetuity)} = \frac{\$100}{0.10} = \$1,000 \text{ at } i = 10\%.$$

We see that the value of a perpetuity changes dramatically when interest rates change. Perpetuities are discussed further in Chapter 8.

SELF-TEST QUESTIONS

What happens to the value of a perpetuity when interest rates increase? What happens when interest rates decrease? Why do these changes occur?

UNEVEN CASH FLOW STREAMS

The definition of an annuity includes the words *constant payment* — in other words, annuities involve payments that are equal in every period. Although many financial decisions do involve constant payments, other important decisions involve uneven, or nonconstant, cash flows; for example, common stocks typically pay an increasing stream of dividends over time, and fixed asset investments such as new equipment normally do not generate constant cash flows. Consequently, it is necessary to extend our time value discussion to include **uneven cash flow streams.**

Throughout the book, we will follow convention and reserve the term **payment (PMT)** for annuity situations where the cash flows are equal amounts, and we will use the term **cash flow (CF)** to denote uneven cash flows. Financial calculators are set up to follow this convention, so if you are dealing with uneven cash flows, you will need to use the "cash flow register."

Uneven Cash Flow Stream
A series of cash flows in which the amount varies from one period to the next.

Payment (PMT)
This term designates equal cash flows coming at regular intervals.

Cash Flow (CF)
This term designates uneven cash flows.

PRESENT VALUE OF AN UNEVEN CASH FLOW STREAM

The PV of an uneven cash flow stream is found as the sum of the PVs of the individual cash flows of the stream. For example, suppose we must find the PV of the following cash flow stream, discounted at 6 percent:

0		1	2	3	4	5	6	7
	6%							
PV = ?		100	200	200	200	200	0	1,000

The PV will be found by applying this general present value equation:

$$PV = CF_1\left(\frac{1}{1+i}\right)^1 + CF_2\left(\frac{1}{1+i}\right)^2 + \cdots + CF_n\left(\frac{1}{1+i}\right)^n$$

$$= \sum_{t=1}^{n} CF_t\left(\frac{1}{1+i}\right)^t = \sum_{t=1}^{n} CF_t(PVIF_{i,t}). \tag{6-6}$$

We could find the PV of each individual cash flow using the numerical, tabular, or financial calculator methods, and then sum these values to find the present value of the stream. Here is what the process would look like:

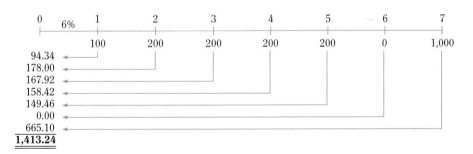

All we did was to apply Equation 6-6, show the individual PVs in the left column of the diagram, and then sum these individual PVs to find the PV of the entire stream.

The present value of a cash flow stream can always be found by summing the present values of the individual cash flows as shown above. However, cash flow regularities within the stream may allow the use of shortcuts. For example, notice that Cash Flows 2 through 5 represent an annuity. We can use that fact to solve the problem in a slightly different manner:

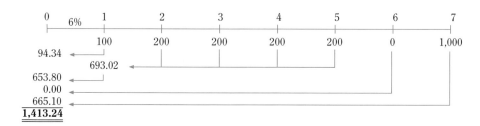

Cash flows during Years 2 to 5 represent an ordinary annuity, and we find its PV at Year 1 (one period before the first payment). This PV ($693.02) must then be discounted back one more period to get its Year 0 value, $653.80.

Problems involving uneven cash flows can be solved in one step with most financial calculators. First, you input the individual cash flows, in chronological order, into the cash flow register. Cash flows are usually designated CF_0, CF_1, CF_2, CF_3, and so on. Next, you enter the interest rate. At this point, you have substituted in all the known values of Equation 6-6, so you only need to press the NPV key to find the present value of the stream. The calculator has been programmed to find the PV of each cash flow and then to sum these values to find the PV of the entire stream. To input the cash flows for this problem, enter 0 (because $CF_0 = 0$), 100, 200, 200, 200, 200, 0, 1000 in that order into the cash flow register, enter $I = 6$, and then press NPV to obtain the answer, $1,413.19. This answer differs slightly from the long-form solution because of rounding differences.

Two points should be noted. First, when dealing with the cash flow register, the calculator uses the term "NPV" rather than "PV." The N stands for "net," so NPV is the abbreviation for "Net Present Value," which is simply the net present value of a series of positive and negative cash flows. Our example has no negative cash flows, but if it did, we would simply input them with negative signs.[8]

The second point to note is that annuities can be entered into the cash flow register more efficiently by using the N_j key. (On some calculators, you are prompted to enter the number of times the cash flow occurs, and on still other calculators, the procedures for inputting data, as we discuss next, may be different. You should consult your calculator manual or our *Technology Supplement* to determine the appropriate steps for your specific calculator.) In this illustration, you would enter $CF_0 = 0$, $CF_1 = 100$, $CF_2 = 200$, $N_j = 4$ (which tells the calculator that the 200 occurs 4 times), $CF_6 = 0$, and $CF_7 = 1000$. Then enter $I = 6$ and press the NPV key, and 1,413.19 will appear in the display. Also, note that amounts entered into the cash flow register remain in the register until they are cleared. Thus, if you had previously worked a problem with eight cash flows, and then moved to a problem with only four cash flows, the calculator would simply add the cash flows from the second problem to those of the first problem. Therefore, you must be sure to clear the cash flow register before starting a new problem.

---

[8]To input negative numbers, type in the positive number, then press the $+/-$ key to change the sign to negative. If you begin by typing the minus sign, you make the mistake of subtracting the negative number from the last number that was entered in the calculator.

FUTURE VALUE OF AN UNEVEN CASH FLOW STREAM

Terminal Value
The future value of an uneven cash flow stream.

The future value of an uneven cash flow stream (sometimes called the **terminal value**) is found by compounding each payment to the end of the stream and then summing the future values:

$$FV_n = CF_1(1 + i)^{n-1} + CF_2(1 + i)^{n-2} + \cdots + CF_n(1 + i)^{n-t}$$

$$= \sum_{t=1}^{n} CF_t(1 + i)^{n-t} = \sum_{t=1}^{n} CF_t(FVIF_{i,n-t}). \qquad (6\text{-}7)$$

The future value of our illustrative uneven cash flow stream is $2,124.92:

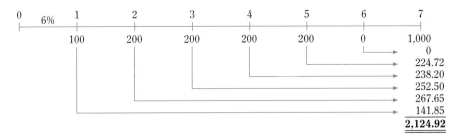

Some financial calculators have a net future value (NFV) key which, after the cash flows and interest rate have been entered, can be used to obtain the future value of an uneven cash flow stream. In any event, it is easy enough to compound the individual cash flows to the terminal year and then sum them to find the FV of the stream. Also, we are generally more interested in the present value of an asset's cash flow stream than in the future value because the present value represents today's value, which is used to find the fair value of the asset. Finally, note that the cash flow stream's net present value can be used to find its net future value: NFV = NPV $(1 + i)^n$. Thus, in our example, you could find the PV of the stream, then find the FV of that PV, compounded for n periods at i percent. In the illustrative problem, find PV = 1,413.19 using the cash flow register and I = 6%. Then enter N = 7, I = 6, PV = −1,413.19, and PMT = 0, and then press FV to find FV = 2,124.92, which equals the NFV shown on the time line above.

SOLVING FOR i WITH UNEVEN CASH FLOW STREAMS

It is relatively easy to solve for i numerically or with the tables when the cash flows are lump sums or annuities. However, it is *extremely difficult* to solve for i if the cash flows are uneven, because then you would have to go through many tedious trial-and-error calculations. With a financial calculator, though, it is easy to find the value of i. Simply input the CF values into the cash flow register and then press the IRR key. IRR stands for "internal rate of return," which is the percentage return on an investment. We will defer further discussion of this calculation for now, but we will take it up later, in our discussion of capital budgeting methods in Chapter 10.[9]

---

[9]To obtain an IRR solution, at least one of the cash flows must have a negative sign, indicating that it is an investment. Since none of the CFs in our example were negative, the cash flow stream has no IRR. However, had we input a cost for CF_0, say, −$1,000, we could have obtained an IRR, which would be the rate of return earned on the $1,000 investment. Here IRR = 13.96%.

SELF-TEST QUESTIONS

Give two examples of financial decisions that would typically involve uneven cash flows. (Hint: Think about a bond or a stock which you plan to hold for five years.)

What is meant by the term "terminal value"?

SEMIANNUAL AND OTHER COMPOUNDING PERIODS

Annual Compounding
The arithmetic process of determining the final value of a cash flow or series of cash flows when interest is added once a year.

Semiannual Compounding
The arithmetic process of determining the final value of a cash flow or series of cash flows when interest is added twice a year.

In all of our examples thus far, we have assumed that interest is compounded once a year, or annually. This is called **annual compounding.** Suppose, however, that you put $100 into a bank which states that it pays a 6 percent annual interest rate but that interest is credited each six months. This is called **semiannual compounding.** How much would you have accumulated at the end of one year, two years, or some other period under semiannual compounding? Note that virtually all bonds pay interest semiannually, most stocks pay dividends quarterly, and most mortgages, student loans, and auto loans require monthly payments. Therefore, it is essential that you understand how to deal with nonannual compounding.

To illustrate semiannual compounding, assume that $100 is placed into an account at an interest rate of 6 percent and left there for three years. First, consider again what would happen under *annual* compounding:

1. Time Line, Equation, and Numerical Solution:

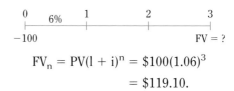

$$FV_n = PV(1 + i)^n = \$100(1.06)^3$$
$$= \$119.10.$$

2. Tabular Solution:

$$FV_3 = \$100(FVIF_{6\%,3}) = \$100(1.1910) = \$119.10.$$

3. Financial Calculator Solution:

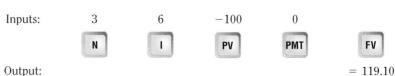

Inputs:	3	6	−100	0	
	N	I	PV	PMT	FV
Output:					= 119.10

The above calculations are for *annual* compounding, but our bank account pays *semiannually*, which is more frequent than once a year. Whenever payments occur more frequently than once a year, or when interest is stated to be compounded more than once a year, then you must convert the stated interest rate to a "periodic rate" and the number of years to "number of periods," as follows:

$$\text{Periodic rate} = \text{Stated rate/Number of payments per year.}$$

$$\text{Number of periods} = \text{Number of years} \times \text{Periods per year.}$$

In our example, where we must find the value of $100 after three years when the stated interest rate is 6 percent, compounded semiannually (or twice a year), you would begin by making the following conversions:

$$\text{Periodic rate} = 6\%/2 = 3\%.$$

$$\text{Periods} = N = 3 \times 2 = 6.$$

In this situation, the investment will earn 3 percent every six months over six periods, not 6 percent per year for three years. As we shall see, there is a significant difference between these two procedures.

You should make the conversions as your first step when working on such a problem *because calculations must be done using the appropriate number of periods and periodic rate, not the number of years and stated rate.* Periodic rates and number of periods, not yearly rates and number of years, should normally be shown on time lines and entered into your calculator whenever you are dealing with anything other than one payment per year (or annual compounding).[10]

With this background, we can now find the value of $100 after three years if it is held in an account that pays a stated rate of 6 percent, but with semiannual compounding. Here is the time line:

Time Line:

```
0        1        2        3        4        5        6   6-month periods
|   3%   |        |        |        |        |        |
-100                                               FV = ?
```

1. Equation and Numerical Solution:

$$FV_n = PV(1 + i)^n = \$100(1.03)^6$$
$$= \$100(1.1941) = \$119.41.$$

Here i = rate per period = annual rate/compounding periods per year = $6\%/2 = 3\%$, and n = the total number of periods = years × periods per year = $3 \times 2 = 6$.

2. Tabular Solution:

$$FV_6 = \$100(FVIF_{3\%,6}) = \$100(1.1941) = \$119.41.$$

Look up FVIF for 3%, 6 periods in Table A-3 and complete the arithmetic.

3. Financial Calculator Solution:

Inputs:	6	3	-100	0	
	N	**I**	**PV**	**PMT**	**FV**
Output:					= 119.41

Enter N = years × periods per year = $3 \times 2 = 6$, I = annual rate/periods per year = $6/2 = 3$, PV = -100, and PMT = 0. Then press FV to find the answer, $119.41 versus $119.10 under annual compounding. The FV is larger under semiannual compounding because interest on interest is being earned more frequently.

---

[10]With some financial calculators, you can enter the annual (nominal) rate and the number of compounding periods rather than make the conversion we recommend. We prefer making the conversion because it is easier to see the problem setup in a time line, and also because it is easy to forget to readjust your calculator after you change its settings and to then make an error on the next problem because of the incorrect setting.

Throughout the world economy, different compounding periods are used for different types of investments. For example, bank accounts generally pay interest daily; most bonds pay interest semiannually; and stocks generally pay dividends quarterly.[11] If we are to properly compare securities with different compounding periods, we need to put them on a common basis. This requires us to distinguish between **nominal, or quoted, interest rates** and **effective, or equivalent, annual rates.**[12]

The nominal, or quoted, or stated, interest rate in our example is 6 percent. *The effective (or equivalent) annual rate (EAR, also called EFF%) is defined as that rate which would produce the same ending (future) value if annual compounding had been used.* In our example, the effective annual rate is the once-a-year rate which would produce an FV of $119.41 at the end of Year 3. Here is a time line of the situation:

```
0    EAR (or EFF%)  1              2              3 Years
|                   |              |              |
-100                                              119.41
```

Our task now is to find the effective annual rate, EAR or EFF%, that is equivalent to 6 percent with semiannual compounding.

We can determine the effective annual rate, given the nominal rate and the number of compounding periods per year, by solving this equation:

$$\text{Effective annual rate} = \text{EAR (or EFF\%)} = \left(1 + \frac{i_{Nom}}{m}\right)^m - 1.0. \quad \textbf{(6-8)}$$

Here i_{Nom} is the nominal, or quoted, interest rate, and m is the number of compounding periods per year. For example, to find the effective annual rate if the nominal rate is 6 percent and semiannual compounding is used, we have[13]

$$\begin{aligned}
\text{Effective annual rate} = \text{EAR (or EFF\%)} &= \left(1 + \frac{0.06}{2}\right)^2 - 1.0 \\
&= (1.03)^2 - 1.0 \\
&= 1.0609 - 1.0 = 0.0609 = 6.09\%.
\end{aligned}$$

The points made about semiannual compounding can be generalized as follows. When compounding occurs more frequently than once a year, we can use a modified version of Equation 6-1 to find the future value of any lump sum:

$$\text{Annual compounding: } FV_n = PV(1 + i)^n. \quad \textbf{(6-1)}$$

$$\text{More frequent compounding: } FV_n = PV\left(1 + \frac{i_{Nom}}{m}\right)^{mn}. \quad \textbf{(6-9)}$$

---

[11]Some banks and savings and loans even pay interest compounded *continuously*. Continuous compounding is discussed in Appendix 6A.

[12]The term *nominal rate* as it is used here has a different meaning than the way it was used in Chapter 4. There, nominal interest rates referred to stated market rates as opposed to real (zero inflation) rates. In this chapter, the term *nominal rate* means the stated, or quoted, annual rate as opposed to the effective annual rate. In both cases, though, *nominal* means *stated*, or *quoted*, as opposed to some adjusted rate.

[13]Most financial calculators are programmed to find the EAR or, given the EAR, to find the nominal rate. This is called "interest rate conversion," and you simply enter the nominal rate and the number of compounding periods per year and then press the EFF% key to find the effective annual rate.

Here i_{Nom} is the nominal, or quoted, rate, m is the number of times compounding occurs per year, and n is the number of years. For example, when banks pay daily interest, the value of m is set at 365 and Equation 6-9 is applied.[14]

To illustrate further the effects of compounding more frequently than annually, consider the interest rate charged on credit cards. Many banks charge 1.5 percent per month, and, in their advertising, they state that the **Annual Percentage Rate (APR)** is $1.5 \times 12 = 18$ percent. However, the "true" rate is the effective annual rate of 19.6 percent:

Annual Percentage Rate (APR)
The periodic rate × the number of periods per year.

$$\text{Effective annual rate} = \text{EAR (or EFF\%)} = \left(1 + \frac{0.18}{12}\right)^{12} - 1$$

$$= (1.015)^{12} - 1.0$$

$$= 0.196 = 19.6\%.$$

Semiannual and other compounding periods can also be used for discounting, and for both lump sums and annuities. First, consider the case where we want to find the PV of an ordinary annuity of $100 per year for three years when the interest rate is 8 percent, *compounded annually*:

Time Line:

1. Numerical Solution:

Find the PV of each cash flow and sum them. The PV of the annuity is $257.71.

2. Tabular Solution:

$$PVA_n = PMT(PVIFA_{i,n})$$

$$= \$100(PVIFA_{8\%,3}) = \$100(2.5771) = \$257.71.$$

3. Financial Calculator Solution:

Inputs: 3   8   100   0

[N]   [I]   [PV]   [PMT]   [FV]

Output: = −257.71

Now, let's change the situation to *semiannual compounding*, where the annuity calls for payments of $50 each six months rather than $100 per year, and the rate is 8 percent, compounded semiannually. Here is the time line:

Time Line:

0	4%	1	2	3	4	5	6	6-month periods
PV = ?		50	50	50	50	50	50	

---

[14]To illustrate, the future value of $1 invested at 10 percent for 1 year under daily compounding is $1.1052:

$$FV_n = \$1\left(1 + \frac{0.10}{365}\right)^{365(1)} = \$1(1.105156) = \$1.1052.$$

Note also that banks sometimes use 360 as the number of days per year for this and other calculations.

1. Numerical Solution:

Find the PV of each cash flow by discounting at 4 percent. Treat each tick mark on the time line as a period, so there would be six periods. The PV of the annuity is $262.11 versus $257.71 under annual compounding.

2. Tabular Solution:

$$PVA_n = PMT(PVIFA_{i,n})$$
$$= \$50(PVIFA_{4\%,6}) = \$50(5.2421) = \$262.11.$$

3. Financial Calculator Solution:

Inputs: 6   4   50   0
            N   I   PV   PMT   FV
Output: = −262.11

The semiannual payments come in sooner, so the $50 semiannual annuity is more valuable than the $100 annual annuity.

SELF-TEST QUESTIONS

What changes must you make in your calculations to determine the future value of an amount that is being compounded at 8 percent semiannually versus one being compounded annually at 8 percent?

Why is semiannual compounding better than annual compounding from a saver's standpoint? What about a borrower's standpoint?

Define the terms "annual percentage rate," "effective (or equivalent) annual rate," and "nominal interest rate."

How does the term "nominal rate" as used in this chapter differ from the term as it was used in Chapter 4?

COMPARISON OF DIFFERENT TYPES OF INTEREST RATES

People in finance often work with three types of interest rates: nominal rates, i_{Nom}; periodic rates, i_{PER}; and effective annual rates, EAR or EFF%. Therefore, it is essential that you understand what each one is and when it should be used.

1. **Nominal, or quoted, rate.** This is the rate that is quoted by banks, brokers, and other financial institutions. So, if you talk with a banker, broker, mortgage lender, auto finance company, or student loan officer about rates, the nominal rate is the one he or she will normally quote you. However, to be meaningful, the quoted nominal rate must also include the number of compounding periods per year. For example, a bank might offer 8.5 percent, compounded quarterly, on CDs, or a mutual fund might offer 8 percent, compounded monthly, on its money market account.

   The nominal rate is also called the Annual Percentage Rate (APR). If a credit card issuer quotes an APR rate of 18 percent, monthly, this means an interest rate of 1.5 percent per month, and an APR = 12(1.5%) = 18%.

Nominal rates can be compared with one another, *but only if the instruments being compared use the same number of compounding periods per year.* Thus, you could compare the quoted yields on two bonds if they both pay interest semiannually. However, to compare an 8.5 percent, annual payment CD with an 8 percent, daily payment money market fund, we would need to put both instruments on an *effective (or equivalent) annual rate (EAR)* basis as discussed later in this section.

Note that the nominal rate is never shown on a time line, and it is never used as an input in a financial calculator (unless compounding occurs only once a year, in which case i_{Nom} = periodic rate = EAR). If more frequent compounding occurs, you should use the periodic rate as discussed below.

2. **Periodic rate, i_{PER}.** This is the rate charged by a lender or paid by a borrower each period. It can be a rate per year, per six-month period, per quarter, per month, per day, or per any other time interval. For example, a bank might charge 1.5 percent per month on its credit card loans, or a finance company might charge 3 percent per quarter on consumer loans. We find the periodic rate as follows:

$$\text{Periodic rate, } i_{PER} = i_{Nom}/m, \qquad \text{(6-10)}$$

which implies that

$$\text{Nominal annual rate} = i_{Nom} = (\text{Periodic rate})(m). \qquad \text{(6-11)}$$

Here i_{Nom} is the nominal annual rate and m is the number of compounding periods per year. To illustrate, consider a finance company loan at 3 percent per quarter:

$$\text{Nominal annual rate} = i_{Nom} = (\text{Periodic rate})(m) = (3\%)(4) = 12\%,$$

or

$$\text{Periodic rate} = i_{Nom}/m = 12\%/4 = 3\% \text{ per quarter.}$$

If there is only one payment per year, or if interest is added only once a year, then m = 1, and the periodic rate is equal to the nominal rate.

The periodic rate is the rate which is generally shown on time lines and used in calculations.[15] To illustrate use of the periodic rate, suppose you make the following eight quarterly payments of $100 each into an account which pays 12 percent, compounded quarterly. How much would you have after two years?

---

[15]The only exception is in situations where (1) annuities are involved and (2) the payment periods do not correspond to the compounding periods. If an annuity is involved and if its payment periods do not correspond to the compounding periods — for example, if you are making quarterly payments into a bank account to build up a specified future sum, but the bank pays interest on a daily basis — then the calculations are more complicated. For such problems, one can proceed in two alternative ways. (1) Determine the periodic (daily) interest rate by dividing the nominal rate by 360 (or 365 if the bank uses a 365-day year), then compound each payment over the exact number of days from the payment date to the terminal point, and then sum the compounded payments to find the future value of the annuity. This is what would generally be done in the real world. Using a computer, it would be a simple process. (2) Calculate the EAR based on daily compounding, then find the corresponding nominal rate based on quarterly compounding (because the annuity payments are made quarterly), then find the quarterly periodic rate, and then use that rate with standard annuity procedures. The second procedure is faster with a calculator, but hard to explain and generally not used in practice given the ready availability of computers.

Time Line and Equation:

```
0   3%   1     2     3     4     5     6     7     8   Quarters
├─────────┼─────┼─────┼─────┼─────┼─────┼─────┼─────┤
       -100  -100  -100  -100  -100  -100  -100  -100
                                                   FV = ?
```

$$FVA_n = \sum_{t=1}^{n} PMT(1 + i)^{n-t} = \sum_{t=1}^{8} \$100(1.03)^{8-t}.$$

1. Numerical Solution:

Compound each $100 payment at 12/4 = 3 percent for the appropriate number of periods, and then sum these individual FVs to find the FV of the payment stream, $889.23.

2. Tabular Solution:

Look up FVIFA for 3%, 8 periods, in Table A-4, and complete the arithmetic:

$$FVA_n = PMT(FVIFA_{i,n})$$

$$= \$100(FVIFA_{3\%,8}) = \$100(8.8923) = \$889.23.$$

3. Financial Calculator Solution:

Inputs: 8   3   0   -100

            [N]   [I]   [PV]   [PMT]   [FV]

Output: = 889.23

Input N = 2 × 4 = 8, I = 12/4 = 3, PV = 0, and PMT = -100, and then press the FV key to get FV = $889.23.

3. **Effective (or equivalent) annual rate (EAR).** This is the annual rate which produces the same result as if we had compounded at a given periodic rate m times per year. The EAR is found as follows:

$$EAR \text{ (or EFF\%)} = \left(1 + \frac{i_{Nom}}{m}\right)^m - 1.0. \qquad \textbf{(6-8)}$$

You could also use the interest conversion feature of a financial calculator.

In the EAR equation, i_{Nom}/m is the periodic rate, and m is the number of periods per year. For example, suppose you could borrow using either a credit card which charges 1 percent per month or a bank loan with a 12 percent quoted nominal interest rate that is compounded quarterly. Which should you choose? To answer this question, the cost rate of each alternative must be expressed as an EAR:

Credit card loan: $EAR = (1 + 0.01)^{12} - 1.0 = (1.01)^{12} - 1.0$

$$= 1.126825 - 1.0 = 0.126825 = 12.6825\%.$$

Bank loan: $EAR = (1 + 0.03)^4 - 1.0 = (1.03)^4 - 1.0$

$$= 1.125509 - 1.0 = 0.125509 = 12.5509\%.$$

Thus, the credit card loan is slightly more costly than the bank loan. This result should have been intuitive to you — both loans have the same 12 percent nominal rate, yet you would have to make monthly payments on the credit card versus quarterly payments under the bank loan.

The EAR rate generally is not used in calculations. Rather, it is used to compare the effective cost or rate of return on loans or investments when payment periods differ, as in the credit card versus bank loan example.

SELF-TEST QUESTIONS   ??????

Define the nominal (or quoted) rate, the periodic rate, and the effective annual rate.

How are the nominal rate, the periodic rate, and the effective annual rate related?

What is the one situation where all three of these rates will be the same?

Which rate should generally be shown on time lines and used in calculations?

FRACTIONAL TIME PERIODS[16]

In all the examples used thus far in the chapter, we have assumed that payments occur at either the beginning or the end of periods, but not at some date *within* a period. However, we often encounter situations that require compounding or discounting over fractional periods. For example, suppose you deposited $100 in a bank that pays 10 percent interest, compounded annually. How much would be in your account after nine months, or 0.75 percent of the way through the year? The answer is $100; since interest is added only at the end of the year, no interest would have been added after only nine months. Years ago, before computers made daily compounding easy, banks really did compound interest annually, but today they generally credit interest daily.

Now let's ask a more realistic question: If a bank adds interest to your account daily, that is, uses daily compounding, and the nominal rate is 10 percent with a 360-day year, how much will be in your account after nine months? The answer is $107.79:[17]

$$\text{Periodic rate} = i_{PER} = 0.10/360 = 0.00027778 \text{ per day.}$$

$$\text{Number of days} = 0.75(360) = 270.$$

$$\text{Ending amount} = \$100(1.00027778)^{270} = \$107.79.$$

Now suppose you borrow $100 from a bank which charges 10 percent per year "simple interest," which means annual rather than daily compounding, but you borrow the $100 for only 270 days. How much interest will you have to pay for the use of $100 for 270 days? Here we would calculate a daily interest rate, i_{PER}, as above, but multiply by 270 rather than use it as an exponent:

$$\text{Interest owed} = \$100(0.00027778)(270) = \$7.50 \text{ interest charged.}$$

You would owe the bank a total of $107.50 after 270 days. This is the procedure most banks actually use to calculate interest on loans.

---

[16]This section is relatively technical, and it can be omitted without loss of continuity.

[17]Here we assumed a 360-day year, and we also assumed that the nine months all have 30 days. In real-world calculations, the bank's computer (and many financial calculators) would have a built-in calendar, and if you input the beginning and ending dates, the computer or calculator would tell you the exact number of days, taking account of 30-day months, 31-day months, and 28- or 29-day months.

Finally, let's consider a somewhat different situation. Say an Internet access firm had 100 customers at the end of 1997, and its customer base is expected to grow steadily at the rate of 10 percent per year. What is the estimated customer base nine months into the new year? This problem would be set up exactly like the bank account with daily compounding, and the estimate would be 107.79 customers, rounded to 108.

The most important thing in problems like these, as in all time value problems, is to be careful! Think about what is involved in a logical, systematic manner, draw a time line if it would help you visualize the situation, and then apply the appropriate equations.

AMORTIZED LOANS

Amortized Loan
A loan that is repaid in equal payments over its life.

One of the most important applications of compound interest involves loans that are paid off in installments over time. Included are automobile loans, home mortgage loans, student loans, and most business loans other than very short-term loans and long-term bonds. If a loan is to be repaid in equal periodic amounts (monthly, quarterly, or annually), it is said to be an **amortized loan.**[18]

To illustrate, suppose a firm borrows $1,000, and the loan is to be repaid in three equal payments at the end of each of the next three years. (In this case, there is only one payment per year, so years = periods and the stated rate = periodic rate.) The lender charges a 6 percent interest rate on the loan balance that is outstanding at the beginning of each year. The first task is to determine the amount the firm must repay each year, or the constant annual payment. To find this amount, recognize that the $1,000 represents the present value of an annuity of PMT dollars per year for three years, discounted at 6 percent:

Time Line and Equation:

$$
\begin{array}{c|c|c|c}
0 & 1 & 2 & 3 \\
\hline
6\% & & & \\
1{,}000 & \text{PMT} & \text{PMT} & \text{PMT}
\end{array}
$$

$$PV = \frac{PMT}{(1+i)^1} + \frac{PMT}{(1+i)^2} + \frac{PMT}{(1+i)^3} = \sum_{t=1}^{3} \frac{PMT}{(1+i)^t}$$

$$\$1{,}000 = \sum_{t=1}^{3} \frac{PMT}{(1.06)^t}.$$

Here we know everything except PMT, so we can solve the equation for PMT.

1. Numerical Solution:

You could follow the trial-and-error procedure, inserting values for PMT in the equation until you found a value that "worked" and caused the right side of the equation to equal $1,000. This would be a tedious process, but you would eventually find PMT = $374.11.

---

[18]The word *amortized* comes from the Latin *mors*, meaning "death," so an amortized loan is one that is "killed off" over time.

2. Tabular Solution:

Substitute in known values and look up PVIFA for 6%, 3 periods in Table A-2:

$$PVA_n = PMT(PVIFA_{i,n})$$
$$\$1,000 = PMT(PVIFA_{6\%,3}) = PMT(2.6730)$$
$$PMT = \$1,000/2.6730 = \$374.11.$$

3. Financial Calculator Solution:

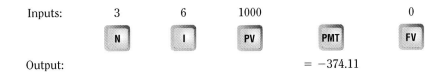

Inputs:	3	6	1000		0
	N	I	PV	PMT	FV
Output:				= −374.11	

Enter N = 3, I = 6, PV = 1000, and FV = 0, and then press the PMT key to find PMT = −$374.11.

Therefore, the firm must pay the lender $374.11 at the end of each of the next three years, and the percentage cost to the borrower, which is also the rate of return to the lender, will be 6 percent.

Each payment consists partly of interest and partly of repayment of principal. This breakdown is given in the **amortization schedule** shown in Table 6-2. The interest component is largest in the first year, and it declines as the outstanding balance of the loan decreases. For tax purposes, a business borrower or home-owner reports the interest component shown in Column 3 as a deductible cost each year, while the lender reports this same amount as taxable income.

Financial calculators are programmed to calculate amortization tables—you simply enter the input data, and then press one key to get each entry in Table 6-2. If you have a financial calculator, it is worthwhile to read the appropriate section of the calculator manual and learn how to use its amortization feature. With a spreadsheet such as *Excel* or *Lotus*, it is easy to set up and print out a full amortization schedule.

Amortization Schedule
A table showing precisely how a loan will be repaid. It gives the required payment on each payment date and a breakdown of the payment, showing how much is interest and how much is repayment of principal.

TABLE 6-2 | **Loan Amortization Schedule, 6 Percent Interest Rate**

YEAR	BEGINNING AMOUNT (1)	PAYMENT (2)	INTEREST[a] (3)	REPAYMENT OF PRINCIPAL[b] (2) − (3) = (4)	REMAINING BALANCE (1) − (4) = (5)
1	$1,000.00	$ 374.11	$ 60.00	$ 314.11	$685.89
2	685.89	374.11	41.15	332.96	352.93
3	352.93	374.11	21.18	352.93	0.00
		$1,122.33	$122.33	$1,000.00	

[a]Interest is calculated by multiplying the loan balance at the beginning of the year by the interest rate. Therefore, interest in Year 1 is $1,000(0.06) = $60; in Year 2 it is $685.89(0.06) = $41.15; and in Year 3 it is $352.93(0.06) = $21.18.

[b]Repayment of principal is equal to the payment of $374.11 minus the interest charge for each year.

SUMMARY

Financial decisions often involve situations in which someone pays money at one point in time and receives money at some later time. Dollars that are paid or received at two different points in time are different, and this difference is recognized and accounted for by *time value of money (TVM) analysis*. We summarize below the types of TVM analysis and the key concepts covered in this chapter, using the data shown in Figure 6-3 to illustrate the various points. Refer to the figure constantly, and try to find in it an example of the points covered as you go through this summary.

♦ **Compounding** is the process of determining the **future value (FV)** of a cash flow or a series of cash flows. The compounded amount, or future value, is equal to the beginning amount plus the interest earned.

♦ Future value: $FV_n = PV(1 + i)^n = PV(FVIF_{i,n})$.
(single payment)
Example: $1,000 compounded for 1 year at 4 percent:

$$FV_1 = \$1,000(1.04)^1 = \$1,040.$$

♦ **Discounting** is the process of finding the **present value (PV)** of a future cash flow or a series of cash flows; discounting is the reciprocal of compounding.

♦ Present value: $PV = \dfrac{FV_n}{(1 + i)^n} = FV_n\left(\dfrac{1}{1 + i}\right)^n = FV_n(PVIF_{i,n})$.
(single payment)

Example: $1,000 discounted back for 2 years at 4 percent:

$$PV = \frac{\$1,000}{(1.04)^2} = \$1,000\left(\frac{1}{1.04}\right)^2 = \$1,000(0.9246) = \$924.60.$$

♦ An **annuity** is defined as a series of equal periodic payments (PMT) for a specified number of periods.

F I G U R E   6 - 3 | **Illustration for Chapter Summary (i = 4%, Annual Compounding)**

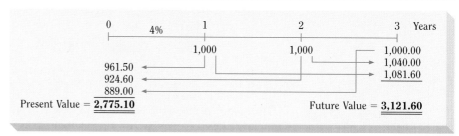

♦ Future value:
(annuity)

$$FVA_n = PMT(1 + i)^{n-1} + PMT(1 + i)^{n-2} + PMT(1 + i)^{n-3} \cdots + PMT(1 + i)^0$$

$$= PMT \sum_{t=1}^{n} (1 + i)^{n-t}$$

$$= PMT(FVIFA_{i,n}).$$

Example: FVA of 3 payments of $1,000 when i = 4%:

$$FVA_3 = \$1,000(3.1216) = \$3,121.60.$$

♦ Present value: $PVA_n = \dfrac{PMT}{(1 + i)^1} + \dfrac{PMT}{(1 + i)^2} + \cdots + \dfrac{PMT}{(1 + i)^n}$
(annuity)

$$= PMT \sum_{t=1}^{n} \left[\frac{1}{1 + i} \right]^t$$

$$= PMT(PVIFA_{i,n}).$$

Example: PVA of 3 payments of $1,000 when i = 4% per period:

$$PVA_3 = \$1,000(2.7751) = \$2,775.10.$$

♦ An annuity whose payments occur at the *end* of each period is called an **ordinary annuity.** The formulas above are for ordinary annuities.

♦ If each payment occurs at the beginning of the period rather than at the end, then we have an **annuity due.** In Figure 6-3, the payments would be shown at Years 0, 1, and 2 rather than at Years 1, 2, and 3. The PV of each payment would be larger, because each payment would be discounted back one year less, so the PV of the annuity would also be larger. Similarly, the FV of the annuity due would also be larger because each payment would be compounded for an extra year. The following formulas can be used to convert the PV and FV of an ordinary annuity to an annuity due:

PVA (annuity due) = PVA of an ordinary annuity $\times$ (1 + i).

Example: PVA of 3 beginning-of-year payments of $1,000 when i = 4%:

PVA (annuity due) = $1,000(2.7751)(1.04) = $2,886.10.

FVA (annuity due) = FVA of an ordinary annuity $\times$ (1 + i).

Example: FVA of 3 beginning-of-year payments of $1,000 when i = 4%:

FVA (annuity due) = $1,000(3.1216)(1.04) = $3,246.46.

♦ If the time line in Figure 6-3 were extended out forever so that the $1,000 payments went on forever, we would have a **perpetuity** whose value could be found as follows:

$$\text{Value of perpetuity} = \frac{PMT}{i} = \frac{\$1,000}{0.04} = \$25,000.$$

♦ If the cash flows in Figure 6-3 were unequal, we could not use the annuity formulas. To find the PV or FV of an uneven series, find the PV or FV of each individual cash flow and then sum them. Note, though, that if some of the cash flows constitute an annuity, then the annuity formula can be used to calculate the present value of that part of the cash flow stream.

♦ **Financial calculators** have built-in programs which perform all of the operations discussed in this chapter. It would be useful for you to buy such a calculator and to learn how to use it.

♦ TVM calculations generally involve equations which have four variables, and if you know three of the values, you (or your calculator) can solve for the fourth.

♦ If you know the cash flows and the PV (or FV) of a cash flow stream, you can **determine the interest rate.** For example, in the Figure 6-3 illustration, if you were given the information that a loan called for 3 payments of $1,000 each, and that the loan had a value today of PV = $2,775.10, then you could find the interest rate that caused the sum of the PVs of the payments to equal $2,775.10. Since we are dealing with an annuity, you could proceed as follows:

a. With a financial calculator, enter N = 3, PV = 2,775.10, PMT = −1,000, FV = 0, and then press the I key to find I = 4%.

b. To use the tables, first recognize that PVA_n = $2,775.10 = $1,000($PVIFA_{i,3}$). Then solve for $PVIFA_{i,3}$:

$$PVIFA_{i,3} = \$2,775.10/\$1,000 = 2.7751.$$

Look up 2.7751 in Table A-2, in the third row. It is in the 4% column, so the interest rate must be 4 percent. If the factor did not appear in the table, this would indicate that the interest rate was not a whole number. In that case, you could not use this procedure to find the exact rate. In practice, though, this is not a problem, because in business people use financial calculators or computers to find interest rates.

♦ Thus far in the summary, we have assumed that payments are made, and interest is earned, annually. However, many contracts call for more frequent payments; for example, mortgage and auto loans call for monthly payments, and most bonds pay interest semiannually. Similarly, most banks compute interest daily. When compounding occurs more frequently than once a year, this fact must be recognized. We can use the Figure 6-3 example to illustrate semiannual compounding. First, recognize that the 4 percent stated rate is a nominal rate which must be converted to a periodic rate, and the number of years must be converted to periods:

$$i_{PER} = \text{Stated rate/Periods per year} = 4\%/2 = 2\%.$$

$$\text{Periods} = \text{Years} \times \text{Periods per year} = 3 \times 2 = 6.$$

The periodic rate and number of periods would be used for calculations and shown on time lines.

If the $1,000 per-year payments were actually payable as $500 each 6 months, you would simply redraw Figure 6-3 to show 6 payments of $500 each, but you would also need to use a **periodic interest rate** of 4%/2 = 2% for determining the PV or FV of the payments.

♦ If we are comparing the costs of loans which require payments more than once a year, or the rates of return on investments which make payments more frequently, then the comparisons should be based on **equivalent** (or **effective**) rates of return using this formula:

$$\text{Effective annual rate} = \text{EAR (or EFF\%)} = \left(1 + \frac{i_{Nom}}{m}\right)^m - 1.0.$$

For semiannual compounding, the effective annual rate is 4.04 percent:

$$\left(1 + \frac{0.04}{2}\right)^2 - 1.0 = (1.02)^2 - 1.0 = 1.0404 - 1.0 = 0.0404 = 4.04\%.$$

♦ The general equation for finding the future value for any number of compounding periods per year is:

$$FV_n = PV\left(1 + \frac{i_{Nom}}{m}\right)^{mn},$$

where

i_{Nom} = quoted interest rate.

m = number of compounding periods per year.

n = number of years.

♦ An **amortized loan** is one that is paid off in equal payments over a specified period. An **amortization schedule** shows how much of each payment constitutes interest, how much is used to reduce the principal, and the unpaid balance at each point in time.

The concepts covered in this chapter will be used throughout the remainder of the book. For example, in Chapters 7 and 8, we will apply present value concepts to the process of valuing bonds and stocks, and we will see that the market prices of securities are established by determining the present values of the cash flows they are expected to provide. In later chapters, the same basic concepts are applied to corporate decisions involving expenditures on capital assets, to the types of capital that should be used to pay for assets, to leasing decisions, and so forth.

QUESTIONS

6-1 What is an *opportunity cost rate*? How is this rate used in time value analysis, and where is it shown on a time line? Is the opportunity rate a single number which is used in all situations?

6-2 An *annuity* is defined as a series of payments of a fixed amount for a specific number of periods. Thus, $100 a year for 10 years is an annuity, but $100 in Year 1, $200 in Year 2, and $400 in Years 3 through 10 does *not* constitute an annuity. However, the second series *contains* an annuity. Is this statement true or false?

6-3 If a firm's earnings per share grew from $1 to $2 over a 10-year period, the *total growth* would be 100 percent, but the *annual growth rate* would be *less than* 10 percent. True or false? Explain.

6-4 Would you rather have a savings account that pays 5 percent interest compounded semi-annually or one that pays 5 percent interest compounded daily? Explain.

6-5 To find the present value of an uneven series of cash flows, you must find the PVs of the individual cash flows and then sum them. Annuity procedures can never be of use, even if some of the cash flows constitute an annuity (for example, $100 each for Years 3, 4, 5, and 6), because the entire series is not an annuity. Is this statement true or false? Explain.

6-6 The present value of a perpetuity is equal to the payment on the annuity, PMT, divided by the interest rate, i: PV = PMT/i. What is the *sum,* or future value, of a perpetuity of PMT dollars per year? (Hint: The answer is infinity, but explain why.)

SELF-TEST PROBLEMS   (Solutions Appear in Appendix B)

ST-1
Key terms
Define each of the following terms:

a. PV; i; INT; FV_n; n; PVA_n; FVA_n; PMT; m; i_{Nom}

b. $FVIF_{i,n}$; $PVIF_{i,n}$; $FVIFA_{i,n}$; $PVIFA_{i,n}$

c. Opportunity cost rate

d. Annuity; lump sum payment; cash flow; uneven cash flow stream

e. Ordinary (deferred) annuity; annuity due

f. Perpetuity; consol

g. Outflow; inflow; time line

h. Compounding; discounting

i. Annual, semiannual, quarterly, monthly, and daily compounding

j. Effective annual rate (EAR); nominal (quoted) interest rate; Annual Percentage Rate (APR); periodic rate

k. Amortization schedule; principal component versus interest component of a payment; amortized loan

l. Terminal value

ST-2
Future value

Assume that it is now January 1, 1998. On January 1, 1999, you will deposit $1,000 into a savings account that pays 8 percent.

a. If the bank compounds interest annually, how much will you have in your account on January 1, 2002?

b. What would your January 1, 2002, balance be if the bank used quarterly compounding rather than annual compounding?

c. Suppose you deposited the $1,000 in 4 payments of $250 each on January 1 of 1999, 2000, 2001, and 2002. How much would you have in your account on January 1, 2002, based on 8 percent annual compounding?

d. Suppose you deposited 4 equal payments in your account on January 1 of 1999, 2000, 2001, and 2002. Assuming an 8 percent interest rate, how large would each of your payments have to be for you to obtain the same ending balance as you calculated in Part a?

ST-3
Time value of money

Assume that it is now January 1, 1998, and you will need $1,000 on January 1, 2002. Your bank compounds interest at an 8 percent annual rate.

a. How much must you deposit on January 1, 1999, to have a balance of $1,000 on January 1, 2002?

b. If you want to make equal payments on each January 1 from 1999 through 2002 to accumulate the $1,000, how large must each of the 4 payments be?

c. If your father were to offer either to make the payments calculated in Part b ($221.92) or to give you a lump sum of $750 on January 1, 1999, which would you choose?

d. If you have only $750 on January 1, 1999, what interest rate, compounded annually, would you have to earn to have the necessary $1,000 on January 1, 2002?

e. Suppose you can deposit only $186.29 each January 1 from 1999 through 2002, but you still need $1,000 on January 1, 2002. What interest rate, with annual compounding, must you seek out to achieve your goal?

f. To help you reach your $1,000 goal, your father offers to give you $400 on January 1, 1999. You will get a part-time job and make 6 additional payments of equal amounts each 6 months thereafter. If all of this money is deposited in a bank which pays 8 percent, compounded semiannually, how large must each of the 6 payments be?

g. What is the effective annual rate being paid by the bank in Part f?

h. *Reinvestment rate risk* was defined in Chapter 4 as being the risk that maturing securities (and coupon payments on bonds) will have to be reinvested at a lower rate of interest than they were previously earning. Is there a reinvestment rate risk involved in the preceding analysis? If so, how might this risk be eliminated?

ST-4
Effective annual rates

Bank A pays 8 percent interest, compounded quarterly, on its money market account. The managers of Bank B want its money market account to equal Bank A's effective annual rate, but interest is to be compounded on a monthly basis. What nominal, or quoted, rate must Bank B set?

STARTER PROBLEMS

6-1
Future value

If you deposit $10,000 in a bank account which pays 10 percent interest annually, how much money will be in your account after 5 years?

6-2
Present value

What is the present value of a security which promises to pay you $5,000 in 20 years? Assume that you can earn 7 percent if you were to invest in other securities of equal risk.

6-3
Time for a lump sum to double

If you deposit money today into an account which pays 6.5 percent interest, how long will it take for you to double your money?

6-4
Effective rate of interest

Your parents are planning to retire in 18 years. They currently have $250,000, and they would like to have $1,000,000 when they retire. What annual rate of interest would they have to earn on their $250,000 in order to reach their goal, assuming they save no more money?

6-5
Future value of an annuity

What is the future value of a 5-year ordinary annuity which promises to pay you $300 each year? The rate of interest is 7 percent.

6-6
Future value of an annuity due

What is the future value of a 5-year annuity due which promises to pay you $300 each year? Assume that all payments are reinvested at 7 percent a year, until Year 5.

6-7
Future value of an annuity

What is the future value of a 5-year annuity due which promises to pay you $300 each year? Assume that all payments are reinvested at 7 percent a year, until Year 4.

6-8
Present and future value of a cash flow stream

An investment pays you $100 at the end of each of the next 3 years. The investment will then pay you $200 at the end of Year 4, $300 at the end of Year 5, and $500 at the end of Year 6. If the rate of interest earned on the investment is 8 percent, what is its present value? What is its future value?

6-9
Comparison of interest rates

An investment pays you 9 percent interest, compounded quarterly. What is the periodic rate of interest? What is the nominal rate of interest? What is the effective rate of interest?

6-10
Loan amortization and effective interest rate

You are thinking about buying a car, and a local bank is willing to lend you $20,000 to buy the car. Under the terms of the loan, it will be fully amortized over 5 years (60 months), and the nominal rate of interest will be 12 percent, with interest paid monthly. What would be the monthly payment on the loan? What would be the effective rate of interest on the loan?

EXAM-TYPE PROBLEMS

The problems included in this section are set up in such a way that they could be used as multiple-choice exam problems.

6-11
Present value comparison

Which amount is worth more at 14 percent, compounded annually: $1,000 in hand today or $2,000 due in 6 years?

6-12
Growth rates

Shalit Corporation's 1997 sales were $12 million. Sales were $6 million 5 years earlier (in 1992).
a. To the nearest percentage point, at what rate have sales been growing?
b. Suppose someone calculated the sales growth for Shalit Corporation in Part a as follows: "Sales doubled in 5 years. This represents a growth of 100 percent in 5 years, so, dividing 100 percent by 5, we find the growth rate to be 20 percent per year." Explain what is wrong with this calculation.

6-13
Expected rate of return

Washington-Atlantic invests $4 million to clear a tract of land and to set out some young pine trees. The trees will mature in 10 years, at which time Washington-Atlantic plans to sell the forest at an expected price of $8 million. What is Washington-Atlantic's expected rate of return?

6-14
Effective rate of interest

Your broker offers to sell you a note for $13,250 that will pay $2,345.05 per year for 10 years. If you buy the note, what interest rate (to the closest percent) will you be earning?

6-15
Effective rate of interest

A mortgage company offers to lend you $85,000; the loan calls for payments of $8,273.59 per year for 30 years. What interest rate is the mortgage company charging you?

6-16
Required lump sum payment

To complete your last year in business school and then go through law school, you will need $10,000 per year for 4 years, starting next year (that is, you will need to withdraw the first $10,000 one year from today). Your rich uncle offers to put you through school, and he will deposit in a bank paying 7 percent interest, compounded annually, a sum of money that is sufficient to provide the 4 payments of $10,000 each. His deposit will be made today.
a. How large must the deposit be?
b. How much will be in the account immediately after you make the first withdrawal? After the last withdrawal?

6-17
Repaying a loan

While you were a student in college, you borrowed $12,000 in student loans at an interest rate of 9 percent, compounded annually. If you repay $1,500 per year, how long, to the nearest year, will it take you to repay the loan?

6-18
Reaching a financial goal

You need to accumulate $10,000. To do so, you plan to make deposits of $1,250 per year, with the first payment being made a year from today, in a bank account which pays 12 percent interest, compounded annually. Your last deposit will be less than $1,250 if less is needed to round out to $10,000. How many years will it take you to reach your $10,000 goal, and how large will the last deposit be?

6-19
Present value of a perpetuity

What is the present value of a perpetuity of $100 per year if the appropriate discount rate is 7 percent? If interest rates in general were to double and the appropriate discount rate rose to 14 percent, what would happen to the present value of the perpetuity?

6-20
Financial calculator needed; PV and effective annual rate

Assume that you inherited some money. A friend of yours is working as an unpaid intern at a local brokerage firm, and her boss is selling some securities which call for 4 payments, $50 at the end of each of the next 3 years, plus a payment of $1,050 at the end of Year 4. Your friend says she can get you some of these securities at a cost of $900 each. Your money is now invested in a bank that pays an 8 percent nominal (quoted) interest rate, but with quarterly compounding. You regard the securities as being just as safe, and as liquid, as your bank deposit, so your required effective annual rate of return on the securities is the same as that on your bank deposit. You must calculate the value of the securities to decide whether they are a good investment. What is their present value to you?

6-21
Loan amortization

Assume that your aunt sold her house on December 31, and that she took a mortgage in the amount of $10,000 as part of the payment. The mortgage has a quoted (or nominal) interest rate of 10%, but it calls for payments every 6 months, beginning on June 30, and the mortgage is to be amortized over 10 years. Now, one year later, your aunt must file Schedule B of her tax return with the IRS, informing them of the interest that was included in the 2 payments made during the year. (This interest will be income to your aunt and a deduction to the buyer of the house.) To the closest dollar, what is the total amount of interest that was paid during the first year?

6-22
Loan amortization

Your company is planning to borrow $1,000,000 on a 5-year, 15%, annual payment, fully amortized term loan. What fraction of the payment made at the end of the second year will represent repayment of principal?

6-23
Nonannual compounding

a. It is now January 1, 1998. You plan to make 5 deposits of $100 each, one every 6 months, with the first payment being made *today*. If the bank pays a nominal interest rate of 12 percent, but uses semiannual compounding, how much will be in your account after 10 years?

b. Ten years from today you must make a payment of $1,432.02. To prepare for this payment, you will make 5 equal deposits, beginning today and for the next 4 quarters, in a bank that pays a nominal interest rate of 12 percent, quarterly compounding. How large must each of the 5 payments be?

6-24
Nominal rate of return

As the manager of Oaks Mall Jewelry, you want to sell on credit, giving customers 3 months in which to pay. However, you will have to borrow from the bank to carry the accounts payable. The bank will charge a nominal 15 percent, but with monthly compounding. You want to quote a nominal rate to your customers (all of whom are expected to pay on time) which will exactly cover your financing costs. What nominal annual rate should you quote to your credit customers?

6-25
Financial calculator needed; required annuity payments

Assume that your father is now 50 years old, that he plans to retire in 10 years, and that he expects to live for 25 years after he retires, that is, until he is 85. He wants a fixed retirement income that has the same purchasing power at the time he retires as $40,000 has today (he realizes that the real value of his retirement income will decline year by year after he retires). His retirement income will begin the day he retires, 10 years from today, and he will then get 24 additional annual payments. Inflation is expected to be 5 percent per year from today forward; he currently has $100,000 saved up; and he expects to earn a return on his savings of 8 percent per year, annual compounding. To the nearest dollar, how much must he save during each of the next 10 years (with deposits being made at the end of each year) to meet his retirement goal?

6-26
Value of an annuity

The prize in last week's Florida lottery was estimated to be worth $35 million. If you were lucky enough to win, the state will pay you $1.75 million per year over the next 20 years. Assume that the first installment is received immediately.

a. If interest rates are 8 percent, what is the present value of the prize?
b. If interest rates are 8 percent, what is the future value after 20 years?
c. How would your answers change if the payments were received at the end of each year?

6-27

Future value of an annuity

Your client is 40 years old and wants to begin saving for retirement. You advise the client to put $5,000 a year into the stock market. You estimate that the market's return will be, on average, 12 percent a year. Assume the investment will be made at the end of the year.
a. If the client follows your advice, how much money will she have by age 65?
b. How much will she have by age 70?

6-28

Present value

You are serving on a jury. A plaintiff is suing the city for injuries sustained after falling down an uncovered manhole. In the trial, doctors testified that it will be 5 years before the plaintiff is able to return to work. The jury has already decided in favor of the plaintiff. You are the foreman of the jury and propose that the jury gives the plaintiff an award to cover the following items:
(1) The present value of 2 years of back-pay ($34,000 in 1996, and $36,000 in 1997). Assume that it is January 1, 1998, and that all salary is received at year end.
(2) The present value of 5 years of future salary (1998–2002). Assume that the plaintiff's salary would increase at a rate of 3 percent a year.
(3) $100,000 for pain and suffering.
(4) $20,000 for court costs.
Assume an interest rate of 7 percent. What should be the size of the settlement?

6-29

Future value

You just started your first job, and you want to buy a house within 3 years. You are currently saving for the down payment. You plan to save $5,000 the first year. You also anticipate that the amount you save each year will rise by 10 percent a year as your salary increases over time. Interest rates are assumed to be 7 percent, and all savings occur at year end. How much money will you have for a down payment in 3 years?

6-30

Required annuity payment

A 15-year security has a price of $340.4689. The security pays $50 at the end of each of the next 5 years, and then it pays a different fixed cash flow amount at the end of each of the following 10 years. Interest rates are 9 percent. What is the annual cash flow amount between Years 6 and 15?

6-31

Financial calculator needed; nonannual compounding

An investment pays $20 semiannually for the next 2 years. The investment has a 7 percent nominal interest rate, and interest is compounded quarterly. What is the future value of the investment?

PROBLEMS

6-32

Present and future values for different periods

Find the following values, *using the equations,* and then work the problems using a financial calculator or the tables to check your answers. Disregard rounding differences. (Hint: If you are using a financial calculator, you can enter the known values, and then press the appropriate key to find the unknown variable. Then, without clearing the TVM register, you can "override" the variable which changes by simply entering a new value for it and then pressing the key for the unknown variable to obtain the second answer. This procedure can be used in Parts b and d, and in many other situations, to see how changes in input variables affect the output variable.) Assume that compounding/discounting occurs once a year.
a. An initial $500 compounded for 1 year at 6 percent.
b. An initial $500 compounded for 2 years at 6 percent.
c. The present value of $500 due in 1 year at a discount rate of 6 percent.
d. The present value of $500 due in 2 years at a discount rate of 6 percent.

6-33

Present and future values for different interest rates

Use the tables or a financial calculator to find the following values. See the hint for Problem 6-32. Assume that compounding/discounting occurs once a year.
a. An initial $500 compounded for 10 years at 6 percent.
b. An initial $500 compounded for 10 years at 12 percent.
c. The present value of $500 due in 10 years at a 6 percent discount rate.
d. The present value of $1,552.90 due in 10 years at a 12 percent discount rate and at a 6 percent rate. Give a verbal definition of the term *present value,* and illustrate it using a time line with data from this problem. As a part of your answer, explain why present values are dependent upon interest rates.

6-34

Time for a lump sum to double

To the closest year, how long will it take $200 to double if it is deposited and earns the following rates? [Notes: (1) See the hint for Problem 6-32. (2) This problem cannot be solved exactly with some financial calculators. For example, if you enter PV = −200, FV = 400, and I = 7 in an HP-12C, and then press the N key, you will get 11 years for

Part a. The correct answer is 10.2448 years, which rounds to 10, but the calculator rounds up. However, the HP-10B and HP-17B give the correct answer. You should look up FVIF = \$400/\$200 = 2 in the tables for Parts a, b, and c, but figure out Part d.] Assume that compounding occurs once a year.
a. 7 percent.
b. 10 percent.
c. 18 percent.
d. 100 percent.

6-35
Future value of an annuity

Find the *future value* of the following annuities. The first payment in these annuities is made at the *end* of Year 1; that is, they are *ordinary annuities*. (Note: See the hint to Problem 6-32. Also, note that you can leave values in the TVM register, switch to "BEG," press FV, and find the FV of the annuity due.) Assume that compounding occurs once a year.
a. \$400 per year for 10 years at 10 percent.
b. \$200 per year for 5 years at 5 percent.
c. \$400 per year for 5 years at 0 percent.
d. Now rework Parts a, b, and c assuming that payments are made at the *beginning* of each year; that is, they are *annuities due*.

6-36
Present value of an annuity

Find the *present value* of the following *ordinary annuities* (see note to Problem 6-35). Assume that discounting occurs once a year.
a. \$400 per year for 10 years at 10 percent.
b. \$200 per year for 5 years at 5 percent.
c. \$400 per year for 5 years at 0 percent.
d. Now rework Parts a, b, and c assuming that payments are made at the *beginning* of each year; that is, they are *annuities due*.

6-37
Uneven cash flow stream

a. Find the present values of the following cash flow streams. The appropriate interest rate is 8 percent, compounded annually. (Hint: It is fairly easy to work this problem dealing with the individual cash flows. However, if you have a financial calculator, read the section of the manual which describes how to enter cash flows such as the ones in this problem. This will take a little time, but the investment will pay huge dividends throughout the course. Note that if you do work with the cash flow register, you must enter $CF_0 = 0$.)

Year	Cash Stream A	Cash Stream B
1	\$100	\$300
2	400	400
3	400	400
4	400	400
5	300	100

b. What is the value of each cash flow stream at a 0 percent interest rate, compounded annually?

6-38
Effective rate of interest

Find the interest rates, or rates of return, on each of the following:
a. You *borrow* \$700 and promise to pay back \$749 at the end of 1 year.
b. You *lend* \$700 and receive a promise to be paid \$749 at the end of 1 year.
c. You borrow \$85,000 and promise to pay back \$201,229 at the end of 10 years.
d. You borrow \$9,000 and promise to make payments of \$2,684.80 per year for 5 years.

6-39
Future value for various compounding periods

Find the amount to which \$500 will grow under each of the following conditions:
a. 12 percent compounded annually for 5 years.
b. 12 percent compounded semiannually for 5 years.
c. 12 percent compounded quarterly for 5 years.
d. 12 percent compounded monthly for 5 years.

6-40
Present value for various compounding periods

Find the present value of \$500 due in the future under each of the following conditions:
a. 12 percent nominal rate, semiannual compounding, discounted back 5 years.
b. 12 percent nominal rate, quarterly compounding, discounted back 5 years.
c. 12 percent nominal rate, monthly compounding, discounted back 1 year.

6-41
Future value of an annuity for various compounding periods

Find the future values of the following ordinary annuities:
a. FV of \$400 each 6 months for 5 years at a nominal rate of 12 percent, compounded semiannually.

b. FV of $200 each 3 months for 5 years at a nominal rate of 12 percent, compounded quarterly.

c. The annuities described in Parts a and b have the same amount of money paid into them during the 5-year period, and both earn interest at the same nominal rate, yet the annuity in Part b earns $101.60 more than the one in Part a over the 5 years. Why does this occur?

6-42
Effective versus nominal interest rates

The First City Bank pays 7 percent interest, compounded annually, on time deposits. The Second City Bank pays 6 percent interest, compounded quarterly.

a. Based on effective, or equivalent, interest rates, in which bank would you prefer to deposit your money?

b. Could your choice of banks be influenced by the fact that you might want to withdraw your funds during the year as opposed to at the end of the year? In answering this question, assume that funds must be left on deposit during the entire compounding period in order for you to receive any interest.

6-43
Amortization schedule

a. Set up an amortization schedule for a $25,000 loan to be repaid in equal installments at the end of each of the next 5 years. The interest rate is 10 percent, compounded annually.

b. How large must each annual payment be if the loan is for $50,000? Assume that the interest rate remains at 10 percent, compounded annually, and that the loan is paid off over 5 years.

c. How large must each payment be if the loan is for $50,000, the interest rate is 10 percent, compounded annually, and the loan is paid off in equal installments at the end of each of the next 10 years? This loan is for the same amount as the loan in Part b, but the payments are spread out over twice as many periods. Why are these payments not half as large as the payments on the loan in Part b?

6-44
Effective rates of return

Assume that AT&T's pension fund managers are considering two alternative securities as investments: (1) Security Z (for zero intermediate year cash flows), which costs $422.41 today, pays nothing during its 10-year life, and then pays $1,000 after 10 years or (2) Security B, which has a cost today of $1,000 and which pays $80 at the end of each of the next 9 years and then $1,080 at the end of Year 10.

a. What is the rate of return on each security?

b. Assume that the interest rate AT&T's pension fund managers can earn on the fund's money falls to 6 percent, compounded annually, immediately after the securities are purchased and is expected to remain at that level for the next 10 years. What would the price of each security change to, what would the fund's profit be on each security, and what would be the percentage profit (profit divided by cost) for each security?

c. Assuming that the cash flows for each security had to be reinvested at the new 6 percent market interest rate, (1) what would be the value attributable to each security at the end of 10 years and (2) what "actual, after-the-fact" rate of return would the fund have earned on each security? (Hint: The "actual" rate of return is found as the interest rate which causes the PV of the compounded Year 10 amount to equal the original cost of the security.)

d. Now assume all the facts as given in Parts b and c, except assume that the interest rate *rose* to 12 percent rather than fell to 6 percent. What would happen to the profit figures as developed in Part b and to the "actual" rates of return as determined in Part c? Explain your results.

6-45
Required annuity payments

A father is planning a savings program to put his daughter through college. His daughter is now 13 years old. She plans to enroll at the university in 5 years, and it should take her 4 years to complete her education. Currently, the cost per year (for everything — food, clothing, tuition, books, transportation, and so forth) is $12,500, but a 5 percent annual inflation rate in these costs is forecasted. The daughter recently received $7,500 from her grandfather's estate; this money, which is invested in a bank account paying 8 percent interest, compounded annually, will be used to help meet the costs of the daughter's education. The rest of the costs will be met by money the father will deposit in the savings account. He will make 6 equal deposits to the account, one deposit in each year from now until his daughter starts college. These deposits will begin today and will also earn 8 percent interest, compounded annually.

a. What will be the present value of the cost of 4 years of education at the time the daughter becomes 18? [Hint: Calculate the future value of the cost (at 5%) for each year of her education, then discount 3 of these costs back (at 8%) to the year in which she turns 18, then sum the 4 costs.]

b. What will be the value of the $7,500 which the daughter received from her grandfather's estate when she starts college at age 18? (Hint: Compound for 5 years at an 8 percent annual rate.)

c. If the father is planning to make the first of 6 deposits today, how large must each deposit be for him to be able to put his daughter through college? (Hint: An annuity due assumes interest is earned on all deposits; however, the 6th deposit earns no interest — therefore, the deposits are an ordinary annuity.)

INTEGRATED CASE

FIRST NATIONAL BANK

6-46 Time Value of Money Analysis Assume that you are nearing graduation and that you have applied for a job with a local bank, First National Bank. As part of the bank's evaluation process, you have been asked to take an examination which covers several financial analysis techniques. The first section of the test addresses time value of money analysis. See how you would do by answering the following questions.

a. Draw time lines for (1) a $100 lump sum cash flow at the end of Year 2, (2) an ordinary annuity of $100 per year for 3 years, and (3) an uneven cash flow stream of −$50, $100, $75, and $50 at the end of Years 0 through 3.

b. (1) What is the future value of an initial $100 after 3 years if it is invested in an account paying 10 percent, annual compounding?

(2) What is the present value of $100 to be received in 3 years if the appropriate interest rate is 10 percent, annual compounding?

c. We sometimes need to find how long it will take a sum of money (or anything else) to grow to some specified amount. For example, if a company's sales are growing at a rate of 20 percent per year, how long will it take sales to double?

d. What is the difference between an ordinary annuity and an annuity due? What type of annuity is shown below? How would you change it to the other type of annuity?

e. (1) What is the future value of a 3-year ordinary annuity of $100 if the appropriate interest rate is 10 percent, annual compounding?

(2) What is the present value of the annuity?

(3) What would the future and present values be if the annuity were an annuity due?

f. What is the present value of the following uneven cash flow stream? The appropriate interest rate is 10 percent, compounded annually.

g. What annual interest rate will cause $100 to grow to $125.97 in 3 years?

h. (1) Will the future value be larger or smaller if we compound an initial amount more often than annually, for example, every 6 months, or *semiannually*, holding the stated interest rate constant? Why?

(2) Define (a) the stated, or quoted, or nominal, rate, (b) the periodic rate, and (c) the effective annual rate (EAR).

(3) What is the effective annual rate corresponding to a nominal rate of 10 percent, compounded semiannually? Compounded quarterly? Compounded daily?

(4) What is the future value of $100 after 3 years under 10 percent semiannual compounding? Quarterly compounding?

i. When will the effective annual rate be equal to the nominal (quoted) rate?

j. (1) What is the value at the end of Year 3 of the following cash flow stream if the quoted interest rate is 10 percent, compounded semiannually?

(2) What is the PV of the same stream?

(3) Is the stream an annuity?

(4) An important rule is that you should *never* show a nominal rate on a time line or use it in calculations unless what condition holds? (Hint: Think of annual compounding, when i_{Nom} = EAR = i_{PER}.) What would be wrong with your answer to Parts j (1) and j (2) if you used the nominal rate, 10 percent, rather than the periodic rate, $i_{Nom}/2$ = 10%/2 = 5%?

k. (1) Construct an amortization schedule for a $1,000, 10 percent, annual compounding loan with 3 equal installments.

(2) What is the annual interest expense for the borrower, and the annual interest income for the lender, during Year 2?

Parts l through o require a financial calculator.

l. Suppose on January 1, 1997, you deposit $100 in an account that pays a nominal, or quoted, interest rate of 10 percent, with interest added (compounded) 365 times per year. How much would you have in your account on October 1, or after 9 months (273 days)?

m. Now, suppose you left your money in the bank for 21 months. Thus, on January 1, 1997, you deposit $100 in an account that pays 10 percent, daily compounding, with a 365-day year. How much would be in your account on October 1, 1998, or 273 + 365 = 638 days later?

n. Suppose someone offered to sell you a note calling for the payment of $1,000 15 months from today (456 days). They offer to sell it to you for $850. You have $850 in a bank time deposit which pays a 7 percent nominal rate with daily (365 days per year) compounding, and you plan to leave the money in the bank unless you buy the note. The note is not risky — you are sure it will be paid on schedule. Should you buy the note? Check the decision in three ways: (1) by comparing your future value if you buy the note versus leaving your money in the bank, (2) by comparing the PV of the note with your current bank account, and (3) by comparing the EAR on the note versus that of the bank account.

o. Suppose the note discussed in Part n had a cost of $850, but called for 5 quarterly payments of $190 each, with the first payment due in 3 months rather than $1,000 at the end of 15 months. Would it be a good investment for you? (Assume that today is January 1, 1997, and that the first payment will be due April 1, 1997.)

COMPUTER-RELATED PROBLEM

Work the problem in this section only if you are using the computer problem diskette.

6-47

Amortization schedule

Use the computerized model in the File C6 to solve this problem.

a. Set up an amortization schedule for a $30,000 loan to be repaid in equal installments at the end of each of the next 20 years at an interest rate of 10 percent, compounded annually. What is the annual payment?

b. Set up an amortization schedule for a $60,000 loan to be repaid in 20 equal installments at an interest rate of 10 percent, compounded annually. What is the annual payment?

c. Set up an amortization schedule for a $60,000 loan to be repaid in 20 equal installments at an interest rate of 20 percent, compounded annually. What is the annual payment?

CONTINUOUS COMPOUNDING AND DISCOUNTING

In Chapter 6 we dealt only with situations where interest is added at discrete intervals—annually, semiannually, monthly, and so forth. In some instances, though, it is possible to have instantaneous, or *continuous,* growth. In this appendix, we discuss present value and future value calculations when the interest rate is compounded continuously.

CONTINUOUS COMPOUNDING

Continuous Compounding
A situation in which interest is added continuously rather than at discrete points in time.

The relationship between discrete and **continuous compounding** is illustrated in Figure 6A-1. Panel a shows the annual compounding case, where interest is added once a year; Panel b shows the situation when compounding occurs twice a year; and Panel c shows interest being earned continuously. As the graphs show, the more frequent the compounding period, the larger the final compounded amount because interest is earned on interest more often.

Equation 6-9 in the chapter can be applied to any number of compounding periods per year:

$$\text{More frequent compounding: } FV_n = PV \left(1 + \frac{i_{\text{Nom}}}{m} \right)^{mn}. \qquad \textbf{(6-9)}$$

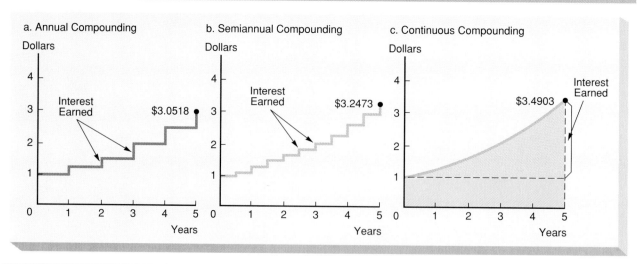

FIGURE 6A-1 Annual, Semiannual, and Continuous Compounding: Future Value with i = 25%

a. Annual Compounding
Dollars
Interest Earned $3.0518

b. Semiannual Compounding
Dollars
Interest Earned $3.2473

c. Continuous Compounding
Dollars
$3.4903   Interest Earned

To illustrate, let PV = \$100, i = 10%, and n = 5. At various compounding periods per year, we obtain the following future values at the end of five years:

$$\text{Annual: } FV_5 = \$100\left(1 + \frac{0.10}{1}\right)^{1(5)} = \$100(1.10)^5 = \$161.05.$$

$$\text{Semiannual: } FV_5 = \$100\left(1 + \frac{0.10}{2}\right)^{2(5)} = \$100(1.05)^{10} = \$162.89.$$

$$\text{Monthly: } FV_5 = \$100\left(1 + \frac{0.10}{12}\right)^{12(5)} = \$100(1.0083)^{60} = \$164.53.$$

$$\text{Daily: } FV_5 = \$100\left(1 + \frac{0.10}{365}\right)^{365(5)} = \$164.86.$$

We could keep going, compounding every hour, every minute, every second, and so on. At the limit, we could compound every instant, or *continuously*. The equation for continuous compounding is

$$FV_n = PV(e^{in}). \tag{6A-1}$$

Here e is the value 2.7183. . . . If \$100 is invested for five years at 10 percent compounded continuously, then FV_5 is calculated as follows:[1]

$$\text{Continuous: } FV_5 = \$100[e^{0.10(5)}] = \$100(2.7183. . .)^{0.5}$$
$$= \$164.87.$$

CONTINUOUS DISCOUNTING

Equation 6A-1 can be transformed into Equation 6A-2 and used to determine present values under continuous discounting:

$$PV = \frac{FV_n}{e^{in}} = FV_n(e^{-in}). \tag{6A-2}$$

Thus, if \$1,649 is due in ten years, and if the appropriate *continuous* discount rate, i, is 5 percent, then the present value of this future payment is

$$PV = \frac{\$1,649}{(2.7183. . .)^{0.5}} = \frac{\$1,649}{1.649} = \$1,000.$$

----

[1]Calculators with exponential functions can be used to evaluate Equation 6A-1. For example, with an HP-10B you would type .5, then press the e^x key to get 1.6487, and then multiply by \$100 to get \$164.87.

FINANCIAL ASSETS

CHAPTER 7
BONDS AND THEIR VALUATION

APPENDIX 7A
ZERO COUPON BONDS

APPENDIX 7B
BANKRUPTCY AND REORGANIZATION

CHAPTER 8
STOCKS AND THEIR VALUATION

CHAPTER 7

BONDS AND
THEIR VALUATION

DISNEY AMAZES INVESTORS

Interest rates plunged in 1993, and corporate borrowers scrambled to lock in low rates by selling long-term bonds. The outer limit for most long-term bonds had been 40 years — investors were unwilling to assume that companies could repay debts due farther in the future, so maturities had to be limited to 40 years to avoid prohibitive risk premiums.

When interest rates took this nosedive, investors found many of their old, high-yielding bonds either maturing or being called, and they were forced to reinvest their money at new, much lower interest rates. This caused their incomes to plunge — this held true for individual retirees and pension funds, both of which invest heavily in the bond market.

How can investors protect themselves against a drop in rates? And how can a corporate borrower lock in a low rate and thus be protected against a later rise in interest rates? The answer, in both cases, is to use longer-term bonds.

Recognizing all this, a large pension fund approached Morgan Stanley & Co., a leading investment banking firm, and asked about the availability of extremely long-term bonds. This fund wanted to lengthen the average maturity of its portfolio, and 100-year bonds would do the trick. However, almost no 100-year bonds existed; two railroads had sold such bonds in the 1800s, but the dollar amounts were too small to make much difference to a large fund. Morgan Stanley seized the opportunity and immediately began to call clients who might be interested in selling long-term bonds to lock in the low current rates. Within a week, Disney had agreed to sell $150 million worth of 7.5 percent, 100-year bonds, buyers were clamoring for them, and the offering "flew out the window."

Soon after the Disney issue, Coca-Cola announced its own 100-year issue, which was also well received. The quick sellout of these issues provided clear evidence that at least some investors have an interest in holding 100-year bonds, but others have their doubts. According to Glenn Murphy, chief investment officer of Travelers Asset Management, the Disney issue will ultimately be a "historic artifact, a curiosity." And William Gross, head of fixed-income investment at Pacific Investment Management, noting the ups and downs of entertainment companies, stated, "It's crazy. Look at the path of Coney Island over the last 50 years and see what happens to amusement parks."

Even if Disney continues to do well and pays interest and principal as they come due, these bonds could still produce headaches for investors. A relatively small 1 percentage point increase in interest rates would cause the value of the Disney bond to fall from its $1,000 offering price to $882, and if long-term interest rates return to the level they were ten years ago, the bond's value would drop to just $538.

Since the Disney and Coke issues, there has been a slow but steady stream of these "century bonds" — Bell South Telecommunications, Columbia/HCA Healthcare Corporation, and the Port Authority of New York and New Jersey are examples. However, not all issues have been successful. Late in 1995, News America Finance Inc. issued $600 million in 50-year bonds and $150 million in 100-year bonds. In both cases, the company's lead underwriter, Goldman Sachs, had a hard time finding interested buyers. Arguably, the fact that the company's credit quality was considerably weaker than the prior issuers of 100-year bonds made the News America bonds a tough sell. Describing this issue, one analyst, Stephen Clark of Technical Data, stated, "This is a borderline-junk credit on a company in an industry that is changing dramatically. Super long debt is usually issued by companies known for their stability and the staying power of their products, like Coca-Cola or Disney."

If you had some extra money, would you be willing to invest in Disney's bonds? How might the terms on the Disney bonds affect the company's stock price? If you were running a business and needed debt capital, would Disney's decision to use 100-year debt affect the way you thought about financing your own company? When you finish this chapter, you should at least know how to think about these questions.

SOURCES: "Disney Amazes Investors with Sale of 100-Year Bonds," *The Wall Street Journal,* July 21, 1993, C1; "T-Bill Trauma and the Meaning of Risk," *The Wall Street Journal,* February 12, 1993, C1.

Bonds are one of the most important types of securities. If you skim through *The Wall Street Journal,* you will see references to a wide variety of bonds. This variety may seem confusing, but there are actually just a few characteristics which distinguish the various types of bonds. Also, you should note that any bond can be valued using the principles discussed in Chapter 6.

While bonds are often viewed as relatively safe investments, one can certainly lose money on them. Indeed, "riskless" long-term U.S. Treasury bonds declined by more than 20 percent during 1994, and "safe" Mexican government bonds declined by 25 percent in just one day, December 27, 1994. Investors who had regarded bonds as being riskless, or at least fairly safe, learned a sad lesson. However, it is also possible to rack up impressive gains in the bond market. In 1995, U.S. Treasury bonds produced a 17.4 percent total return, and high-quality corporate bonds did even better — their total return was nearly 21 percent.

In this chapter, we will discuss the types of bonds companies and government agencies issue, the terms that are contained in bond contracts, and the types of risks to which both bond investors and issuers are exposed.

WHO ISSUES BONDS?

Bond
A long-term debt instrument.

A **bond** is a long-term contract under which a borrower agrees to make payments of interest and principal, on specific dates, to the holders of the bond. For example, on January 2, 1998, Allied Food Products borrowed $50 million by selling 50,000 individual bonds for $1,000 each. Allied received the $50 million, and in exchange it promised to make annual interest payments and to repay the $50 million on a specified maturity date.

Investors have many choices when investing in bonds, but bonds are classified into four main types: Treasury, corporate, municipal, and foreign. Each type differs with respect to expected return and degree of risk.

Treasury Bonds
Bonds issued by the federal government, sometimes referred to as government bonds.

Corporate Bonds
Bonds issued by corporations.

Municipal Bonds
Bonds issued by state and local governments.

Foreign Bonds
Bonds issued by either foreign governments or foreign corporations.

ON THE WWW

An excellent site for information on many types of bonds is Bonds Online, which can be found at http://www.bonds-online.com/index.html. The site has a great deal of information about corporates, municipals, treasuries, and bond funds. It includes free bond searches, through which the user specifies the attributes desired in a bond and then the search returns the publicly traded bonds meeting the criteria. The site also includes a downloadable bond calculator and an excellent glossary of bond terminology. Registration is required to use the bond searches, but it is free.

Treasury bonds, sometimes referred to as government bonds, are issued by the federal government.[1] It is reasonable to assume that the federal government will make good on its promised payments, so these bonds have no default risk. However, Treasury bond prices decline when interest rates rise, so they are not free of all risks.

Corporate bonds, as the name implies, are issued by corporations. Unlike Treasury bonds, corporate bonds are exposed to default risk — if the issuing company gets into trouble, it may be unable to make the promised interest and principal payments. Different corporate bonds have different levels of default risk, depending on the issuing company's characteristics and on the terms of the specific bond. Default risk is often referred to as "credit risk," and, as we saw in Chapter 4, the larger the default or credit risk, the higher the interest rate the issuer must pay.

Municipal bonds, or "munis," are issued by state and local governments. Like corporate bonds, munis have default risk. However, munis offer one major advantage over all other bonds: As we discussed in Chapter 2, the interest earned on most municipal bonds is exempt from federal taxes, and also from state taxes if the holder is a resident of the issuing state. Consequently, municipal bonds carry interest rates that are considerably lower than those on corporate bonds with the same default risk.

Foreign bonds are issued by foreign governments or foreign corporations. Foreign corporate bonds are, of course, exposed to default risk, and so are some foreign government bonds. An additional risk exists if the bonds are denominated in a currency other than that of the investor's home currency. For example, if you purchase corporate bonds denominated in Japanese yen, you will lose money — even if the company does not default on its bonds — if the Japanese yen falls relative to the dollar.

SELF-TEST QUESTIONS

What is a bond?

What are the four main types of bonds?

Why are U.S. Treasury bonds not riskless?

To what types of risk are investors of foreign bonds exposed?

KEY CHARACTERISTICS OF BONDS

Although all bonds have some common characteristics, they do not always have the same contractual features. For example, most corporate bonds have provisions for early repayment (call features), but these provisions can be quite different for different bonds. Differences in contractual provisions, and in the underlying strength of the companies backing the bonds, lead to major differences in bonds' risks, prices, and expected returns. To understand bonds, it is important that you understand the following terms.

---

[1]The U.S. Treasury actually calls its debt issues "bills," "notes," or "bonds." T-bills generally have maturities of 1 year or less at the time of issue, notes generally have original maturities of 2 to 7 years, and bond maturities extend out to 30 years. There are technical differences between bills, notes, and bonds, but they are not important for our purposes, so we generally call all Treasury securities "bonds." Note too that a 30-year T-bond at the time of issue becomes a 1-year bond 29 years later.

PAR VALUE

Par Value
The face value of a stock or bond.

The **par value** is the stated face value of the bond; for illustrative purposes we generally assume a par value of $1,000, although any multiple of $1,000 (for example, $5,000) can be used. The par value generally represents the amount of money the firm borrows and promises to repay on the maturity date.

COUPON INTEREST RATE

Coupon Payment
The specified number of dollars of interest paid each period, generally each six months.

Coupon Interest Rate
The stated annual rate of interest on a bond.

Allied's bonds require the company to pay a fixed number of dollars of interest each year (or, more typically, each six months). When this **coupon payment,** as it is called, is divided by the par value, the result is the **coupon interest rate.** For example, Allied's bonds have a $1,000 par value, and they pay $100 in interest each year. The bond's coupon interest is $100, so its coupon interest rate is $100/$1,000 = 10 percent. The $100 is the yearly "rent" on the $1,000 loan. This payment, which is fixed at the time the bond is issued, remains in force during the life of the bond.[2] Typically, at the time a bond is issued, its coupon payment is set at a level which will enable the bond to be issued at or near its par value.

Floating Rate Bond
A bond whose interest rate fluctuates with shifts in the general level of interest rates.

In some cases, a bond's coupon payment may vary over time. These **floating rate bonds** work as follows. The coupon rate is set for, say, the initial six-month period, after which it is adjusted every six months based on some market rate. Some corporate issues have been tied to the Treasury bond rate, while other issues have been tied to other rates. Many additional provisions can be included in floating rate issues; for example, some are convertible to fixed rate debt, whereas others have upper and lower limits ("caps" and "floors") on how high or low the yield can go.

Floating rate debt is popular with investors who are worried about the risk of rising interest rates, since the coupon received increases whenever market rates rise. This causes the market value of the debt to be stabilized, and it also provides lenders such as banks with income which is better geared to their own obligations. (Banks' deposit costs rise with interest rates, so the income on floating rate loans rises just when banks' deposit costs are rising.) Moreover, floating rate debt appeals to corporations that want to issue long-term debt without committing themselves to paying a historically high interest rate for the entire life of the loan. Of course, if interest rates move even higher after a floating rate bond has been issued, the borrower would have been better off issuing conventional, fixed rate debt.

Zero Coupon Bond
A bond that pays no annual interest but is sold at a discount below par, thus providing compensation to investors in the form of capital appreciation.

Some bonds pay no coupons at all, but are offered at a substantial discount below their par values and hence provide capital appreciation rather than interest income. These securities are called **zero coupon bonds** *("zeros").* Other bonds pay some coupon interest, but not enough to be issued at par. In general, any bond originally offered at a price significantly below its par value is called an **original issue discount bond (OID).** Corporations first used zeros in a major way in 1981. In recent years IBM, Alcoa, JCPenney, ITT, Cities Service, GMAC, Martin-Marietta, and many other companies have used zeros to raise billions of

Original Issue Discount Bond
Any bond originally offered at a price below its par value.

---

[2]Incidentally, some time ago most bonds literally had a number of small (1/2- by 2-inch), dated coupons attached to them, and on each interest payment date, the owner would clip off the coupon for that date and either cash it at his or her bank or mail it to the company's paying agent, who would then mail back a check for the interest. A 30-year, semiannual bond would start with 60 coupons, whereas a 5-year annual payment bond would start with only 5 coupons. Today, new bonds must be *registered* — no physical coupons are involved, and interest checks are mailed automatically to the registered owners of the bonds. Even so, people continue to use the terms *coupon* and *coupon interest rate* when discussing registered bonds.

dollars. Some of the details associated with issuing or investing in zero coupon bonds are discussed more fully in Appendix 7A.

MATURITY DATE

Maturity Date
A specified date on which the par value of a bond must be repaid.

Original Maturity
The number of years to maturity at the time a bond is issued.

Bonds generally have a specified **maturity date** on which the par value must be repaid. Allied's bonds, which were issued on January 2, 1998, will mature on January 1, 2013; thus, they had a 15-year maturity at the time they were issued. Most bonds have **original maturities** (the maturity at the time the bond is issued) ranging from 10 to 40 years, but any maturity is legally permissible.[3] Of course, the effective maturity of a bond declines each year after it has been issued. Thus, Allied's bonds had a 15-year original maturity, but in 1999, a year later, they will have a 14-year maturity, and so on.

CALL PROVISIONS

Call Provision
A provision in a bond contract that gives the issuer the right to redeem the bonds under specified terms prior to the normal maturity date.

Most corporate bonds contain a **call provision,** which gives the issuing corporation the right to call the bonds for redemption.[4] The call provision generally states that the company must pay the bondholders an amount greater than the par value if they are called. The additional sum, which is termed a *call premium,* is typically set equal to one year's interest if the bonds are called during the first year, and the premium declines at a constant rate of INT/N each year thereafter, where INT = annual interest and N = original maturity in years. For example, the call premium on a $1,000 par value, 10-year, 10 percent bond would generally be $100 if it were called during the first year, $90 during the second year (calculated by reducing the $100, or 10 percent, premium by one-tenth), and so on. However, bonds are often not callable until several years (generally 5 to 10) after they were issued. This is known as a *deferred call,* and the bonds are said to have *call protection.*

Suppose a company sold bonds when interest rates were relatively high. Provided the issue is callable, the company could sell a new issue of low-yielding securities if and when interest rates drop. It could then use the proceeds of the new issue to retire the high-rate issue and thus reduce its interest expense. This process is called a *refunding operation,* and it is discussed in greater detail in Appendix 11B.

The call privilege is valuable to the firm but potentially detrimental to the investor, especially if the bonds were issued in a period when interest rates were cyclically high. Accordingly, the interest rate on a new issue of callable bonds will exceed that on a new issue of noncallable bonds. For example, on August 30, 1997, Pacific Timber Company sold a bond issue yielding 9.5 percent; these bonds were callable immediately. On the same day, Northwest Milling Company sold an issue of similar risk and maturity which yielded 9.2 percent; its bonds were noncallable for ten years. Investors were apparently willing to accept a 0.3 percent lower interest rate on Northwest's bonds for the assurance that the 9.2 percent interest rate would be earned for at least ten years. Pacific, on the other hand, had to incur a 0.3 percent higher annual interest rate to obtain the option of calling the bonds in the event of a subsequent decline in interest rates.

---

[3]In July 1993, Walt Disney Co., attempting to lock in a low interest rate, issued the first 100-year bonds to be sold by any borrower in modern times. Soon after, Coca-Cola became the second company to stretch the meaning of "long-term bond" by selling $150 million worth of 100-year bonds.

[4]A majority of municipal bonds also contain call provisions. Call provisions have been included with Treasury bonds, although this occurs less frequently.

SINKING FUNDS

Sinking Fund Provision
A provision in a bond contract that requires the issuer to retire a portion of the bond issue each year.

Some bonds also include a **sinking fund provision** that facilitates the orderly retirement of the bond issue. Typically, the sinking fund requires the firm to retire a portion of the bonds each year. On rare occasions the firm may be required to deposit money with a trustee, which invests the funds and then uses the accumulated sum to retire the bonds when they mature. Usually, though, the sinking fund is used to buy back a certain percentage of the issue each year. A failure to meet the sinking fund requirement causes the bond issue to be thrown into default, which may force the company into bankruptcy. Obviously, a sinking fund can constitute a significant cash drain on the firm.

In most cases, the firm is given the right to handle the sinking fund in either of two ways:

1. The company can call in for redemption (at par value) a certain percentage of the bonds each year; for example, it might be able to call 5 percent of the total original amount of the issue at a price of $1,000 per bond. The bonds are numbered serially, and those called for redemption are determined by a lottery administered by the trustee.

2. The company may buy the required number of bonds on the open market.

The firm will choose the least-cost method. If interest rates have risen, causing bond prices to fall, it will buy bonds in the open market at a discount; if interest rates have fallen, it will call the bonds. Note that a call for sinking fund purposes is quite different from a refunding call as discussed above. A sinking fund call typically requires no call premium,[5] but only a small percentage of the issue is normally callable in any one year.

Although sinking funds are designed to protect bondholders by ensuring that an issue is retired in an orderly fashion, you should recognize that sinking funds at times work to the detriment of bondholders. For example, suppose the bond carries a 10 percent interest rate, but yields on similar bonds have fallen to 7.5 percent. A sinking fund call at par would require an investor to give up a bond that pays $100 of interest and then to reinvest in a bond that pays only $75 per year. This obviously disadvantages those bondholders whose bonds are called. On balance, however, bonds that have a sinking fund are regarded as being safer than those without such a provision, so at the time they are issued sinking fund bonds have lower coupon rates than otherwise similar bonds without sinking funds.

OTHER FEATURES

Convertible Bond
A bond that is exchangeable, at the option of the holder, for common stock of the issuing firm.

Warrant
A long-term option to buy a stated number of shares of common stock at a specified price.

Several other types of bonds are used sufficiently often to warrant mention. First, **convertible bonds** are bonds that are convertible into shares of common stock, at a fixed price, at the option of the bondholder. Convertibles have a lower coupon rate than nonconvertible debt, but they offer investors a chance for capital gains in exchange for the lower coupon rate. Bonds issued with **warrants** are similar to convertibles. Warrants are options which permit the holder to buy stock for a stated price, thereby providing a capital gain if the price of the stock rises. Bonds that are issued with warrants, like convertibles, carry lower coupon rates than straight bonds. Convertibles and warrants will be discussed later in Chapter 20.

---

[5]Some sinking funds require the issuer to pay a call premium.

Income Bond
A bond that pays interest only if the interest is earned.

Indexed (Purchasing Power) Bond
A bond that has interest payments based on an inflation index so as to protect the holder from inflation.

Another type of bond is an **income bond**, which pays interest only if the interest is earned. Thus, these securities cannot bankrupt a company, but from an investor's standpoint they are riskier than "regular" bonds. Yet another bond is the **indexed,** or **purchasing power, bond,** which is popular in Brazil, Israel, and a few other countries plagued by high rates of inflation. Indexed bonds have also been issued in Great Britain. The interest rate paid on these bonds is based on an inflation index such as the consumer price index, so the interest paid rises automatically when the inflation rate rises, thus protecting the bondholders against inflation. The British bonds' interest rate is set equal to the British inflation rate plus 3 percent. Thus, these bonds provide a "real return" of 3 percent. In January 1997, the U.S. Treasury issued indexed bonds, and the real rate on these bonds was 3.45 percent on the issue date.

SELF-TEST QUESTIONS

Define floating rate bonds and zero coupon bonds.

What are the two ways a sinking fund can be handled? Which method will be chosen by the firm if interest rates have risen? If interest rates have fallen?

What is the difference between a call for sinking fund purposes and a refunding call?

Are securities that provide for a sinking fund regarded as being riskier than those without this type of provision? Explain.

Why is a call provision advantageous to a bond issuer? When will the issuer initiate a refunding call? Why?

Define convertible bonds, bonds with warrants, income bonds, and indexed bonds.

Why do bonds with warrants and convertible bonds have lower coupons than similarly rated bonds that do not have these features?

What problem was solved by the introduction of long-term floating rate debt, and how is the rate on such bonds determined?

BOND VALUATION

The value of any financial asset — a stock, a bond, a lease, or even a physical asset such as an apartment building or a piece of machinery — is simply the present value of the cash flows the asset is expected to produce.

The cash flows from a specific bond depend on its contractual features as described above. For a standard coupon-bearing bond such as the one issued by Allied Foods, the cash flows consist of interest payments (10 percent) during the 15-year life of the bond, plus a return of the principal amount borrowed (generally the $1,000 par value) when the bond matures. In the case of a floating rate bond, the interest payments depend on the level of interest rates over time. In the case of a zero coupon bond, there are no interest payments, only the return of principal when the bond matures. For a "regular" bond, here is the situation:

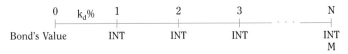

Here

k_d = the bond's market rate of interest = 10%. This is the discount rate that is used to calculate the present value of the bond's cash flows. Note that k_d is *not* the coupon interest rate, and it is equal to the coupon rate only if (as in this case) the bond is selling at par. Generally, the coupon rate is set at k_d when the bond is issued, so most bonds sell at par, hence have k_d = coupon rate only at the time of issue. Thereafter, interest rates as measured by k_d will fluctuate, but the coupon rate is fixed, so k_d will equal the coupon rate only by chance. We used the term "i" or "I" to designate the interest rate in Chapter 6 because those terms are used on financial calculators, but "k," with the subscript "d" to designate the rate on a debt security, is normally used in finance.[6]

N = the number of years before the bond matures = 15. Note that N declines each year after the bond has been issued, so a bond that had a maturity of 15 years when it was issued (original maturity = 15) will have N = 14 after one year, N = 13 after two years, and so on. Note also that at this point we assume that the bond pays interest once a year, or annually, so N is measured in years. Later on, we will deal with semiannual payment bonds, which pay interest each six months.

INT = dollars of interest paid each year = Coupon rate × Par value = 0.10($1,000) = $100. In calculator terminology, INT = PMT = 100. If the bond had been a semiannual payment bond, the payment would have been $50 each six months. The payment would be zero if Allied had issued zero coupon bonds, and it would vary if the bond was a "floater."

M = the par, or maturity, value of the bond = $1,000. This amount must be paid off at maturity.

We can now redraw the time line to show the numerical values for all variables except the bond's value:

The following general equation can be solved to find the value of any bond:

$$\begin{matrix} \text{Bond's} \\ \text{value} \end{matrix} = V_B = \frac{INT}{(1 + k_d)^1} + \frac{INT}{(1 + k_d)^2} + \cdots + \frac{INT}{(1 + k_d)^N} + \frac{M}{(1 + k_d)^N}$$

$$= \sum_{t=1}^{N} \frac{INT}{(1 + k_d)^t} + \frac{M}{(1 + k_d)^N}. \tag{7-1}$$

Equation 7-1 can also be rewritten for use with the tables:

$$V_B = INT(PVIFA_{k_d,N}) + M(PVIF_{k_d,N}). \tag{7-2}$$

---

[6]The appropriate interest rate on debt securities was discussed in Chapter 4. The bond's riskiness, liquidity, and years to maturity, as well as supply and demand conditions in the capital markets, all influence the interest rate on bonds.

Inserting values for our particular bond, we have

$$V_B = \sum_{t=1}^{15} \frac{\$100}{(1.10)^t} + \frac{\$1,000}{(1.10)^{15}}$$

$$= \$100(PVIFA_{10\%,15}) + \$1,000(PVIF_{10\%,15}).$$

Notice that the cash flows consist of an annuity of N years plus a lump sum payment at the end of Year N, and this fact is reflected in Equations 7-1 and 7-2. Further, Equation 7-1 can be solved by the three procedures discussed in Chapter 6: (1) numerically, (2) using the tables, and (3) with a financial calculator.

Numerical Solution:

Simply discount each cash flow back to the present and sum these PVs to find the bond's value; see Figure 7-1 for an example. This procedure is not very efficient, especially if the bond has many years to maturity.

Tabular Solution:

Simply look up the appropriate PVIFA and PVIF values in Tables A-1 and A-2 at the end of the book, insert them into the equation, and complete the arithmetic:

$$V_B = \$100(7.6061) + \$1,000(0.2394)$$

$$= \$760.61 + \$239.40 \approx \$1,000.$$

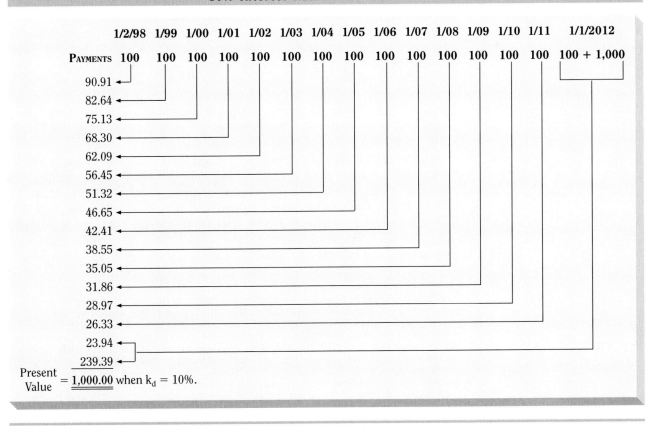

FIGURE   7 - 1   Time Line for Allied Food Products' Bonds, 10% Interest Rate

Present Value = 1,000.00 when k_d = 10%.

There is a one cent rounding difference, which results from the fact that the tables only go to four decimal places.

Financial Calculator Solution:

In Chapter 6, we worked problems where only four of the five time value of money (TVM) keys were used, but all five keys are used with bonds. Here is the setup:

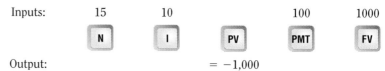

Inputs: 15   10   100   1000
           N   I   PV   PMT   FV

Output: = −1,000

Simply input N = 15, I = k = 10, INT = PMT = 100, M = FV = 1000, and then press the PV key to find the value of the bond, $1,000. Since the PV is an outflow to the investor, it is shown with a negative sign. The calculator is programmed to solve Equation 7-1: It finds the PV of an annuity of $100 per year for 15 years, discounted at 10 percent, then it finds the PV of the $1,000 maturity payment, and then it adds these two PVs to find the value of the bond.

CHANGES IN BOND VALUES OVER TIME

At the time a coupon bond is issued, the coupon is generally set at a level that will cause the market price of the bond to equal its par value. If a lower coupon were set, investors would not be willing to pay $1,000 for the bond, while if a higher coupon were set, investors would clamor for the bond and bid its price up over $1,000. Investment bankers can judge quite precisely the coupon rate that will cause a bond to sell at its $1,000 par value.

A bond that has just been issued is known as a *new issue*. (Investment bankers classify a bond as a new issue for about one month after it has first been issued.) Once the bond has been on the market for a while, it is classified as an *outstanding bond,* also called a *seasoned issue.* Newly issued bonds generally sell very close to par, but the prices of seasoned bonds vary widely from par. Except for floating rate bonds, coupon payments are constant, so when economic conditions change, a bond with a $100 coupon that sold at par when it was issued will sell for more or less than $1,000 thereafter.

Allied's bonds with a 10 percent coupon rate were originally issued at par. If k_d remained constant at 10 percent, what would the value of the bond be one year after it was issued? Now the term to maturity is only 14 years — that is, N = 14. With a financial calculator, just override N = 15 with N = 14, press the PV key, and you find a value of $1,000. If we continued, setting N = 13, N = 12, and so forth, we would see that the value of the bond will remain at $1,000 as long as the going interest rate remains constant at the coupon rate, 10 percent.[7]

---

[7]The bond prices quoted by brokers are calculated as described. However, if you bought a bond between interest payment dates, you would have to pay the basic price plus accrued interest. Thus, if you purchased an Allied bond six months after it was issued, your broker would send you an invoice stating that you must pay $1,000 as the basic price of the bond plus $50 interest, representing one-half the annual interest of $100. The seller of the bond would receive $1,050. If you bought the bond the day before its interest payment date, you would pay $1,000 + (364/365)($100) = $1,099.73. Of course, you would receive an interest payment of $100 at the end of the next day. See Self-Test Problem 2 for a detailed discussion of bond quotations between interest payment dates.

Throughout the chapter, we assume that bonds are being evaluated immediately after an interest payment date. The more expensive financial calculators such as the HP-17B have a built-in calendar which permits the calculation of exact values between interest payment dates.

Now suppose interest rates in the economy fell after the Allied bonds were issued, and, as a result, k_d *fell below the coupon rate*, decreasing from 10 to 5 percent. Both the coupon interest payments and the maturity value remain constant, but now 5 percent values for PVIF and PVIFA would have to be used in Equation 7-2. The value of the bond at the end of the first year would be $1,494.96:

$$V_B = \$100(\text{PVIFA}_{5\%,14}) + \$1,000(\text{PVIF}_{5\%,14})$$
$$= \$100(9.8986) + \$1,000(0.5051)$$
$$= \$989.86 + \$505.10$$
$$= \$1,494.96.$$

With a financial calculator, just change $k_d = I$ from 10 to 5, and then press the PV key to get the answer, $1,494.93. Thus, if k_d fell *below* the coupon rate, the bond would sell above par, or at a *premium*.

The arithmetic of the bond value increase should be clear, but what is the logic behind it? The fact that k_d has fallen to 5 percent means that if you had $1,000 to invest, you could buy new bonds like Allied's (every day some 10 to 12 companies sell new bonds), except that these new bonds would pay $50 of interest each year rather than $100. Naturally, you would prefer $100 to $50, so you would be willing to pay more than $1,000 for an Allied bond to obtain its higher coupons. All investors would react similarly, and as a result, the Allied bonds would be bid up in price to $1,494.96, at which point they would provide the same rate of return to a potential investor as the new bonds, 5 percent.

Assuming that interest rates remain constant at 5 percent for the next 14 years, what would happen to the value of an Allied bond? It would fall gradually from $1,494.96 at present to $1,000 at maturity, when Allied will redeem each bond for $1,000. This point can be illustrated by calculating the value of the bond 1 year later, when it has 13 years remaining to maturity. With a financial calculator, merely input the values for N, I, PMT, and FV, now using N = 13, and press the PV key to find the value of the bond, $1,469.68. Thus, the value of the bond will have fallen from $1,494.96 to $1,469.66, or by $25.30. If you were to calculate the value of the bond at other future dates, the price would continue to fall as the maturity date approached.

Notice that if you purchased the bond at a price of $1,494.96 and then sold it one year later with k_d still at 5 percent, you would have a capital loss of $25.30, or a total return of $100.00 − $25.30 = $74.70. Your percentage rate of return would consist of an *interest yield* (also called a *current yield*) plus a *capital gains yield,* calculated as follows:

Interest, or current, yield =	$100/$1,494.96	= 0.0669 =	6.69%
Capital gains yield =	−$25.30/$1,494.96	= −0.0169 =	−1.69%
Total rate of return, or yield =	$74.70/$1,494.96	= 0.0500 =	5.00%

Had interest rates risen from 10 to 15 percent during the first year after issue rather than fallen, then you would enter N = 14, I = 15, PMT = 100, and FV = 1000, and then press the PV key to find the value of the bond, $713.78. In this case, the bond would sell at a *discount* of $286.22 below its par value:

$$\text{Discount} = \text{Price} - \text{Par value} = \$713.78 - \$1,000.00$$
$$= -\$286.22.$$

The total expected future yield on the bond would again consist of a current yield and a capital gains yield, but now the capital gains yield would be *positive*. The total yield would be 15 percent. To see this, calculate the price of the bond with 13 years left to maturity, assuming that interest rates remain at 15 percent. With a calculator, enter N = 13, I = 15, PMT = 100, and FV = 1000, and then press PV to obtain the bond's value, $720.84.

Notice that the capital gain for the year is the difference between the bond's value at Year 2 (with 13 years remaining) and the bond's value at Year 1 (with 14 years remaining), or $720.84 − $713.78 = $7.06. The interest yield, capital gains yield, and total yield are calculated as follows:

$$\text{Interest, or current, yield} = \$100/\$713.78 = 0.1401 = 14.01\%$$
$$\text{Capital gains yield} = \$7.06/\$713.78 = 0.0099 = \underline{0.99\%}$$
$$\text{Total rate of return, or yield} = \$107.06/\$713.78 = 0.1500 = \underline{15.00\%}$$

Figure 7-2 graphs the value of the bond over time, assuming that interest rates in the economy (1) remain constant at 10 percent, (2) fall to 5 percent and then remain constant at that level, or (3) rise to 15 percent and remain constant at

FIGURE 7-2 Time Path of the Value of a 10% Coupon, $1,000 Par Value Bond When Interest Rates Are 5%, 10%, and 15%

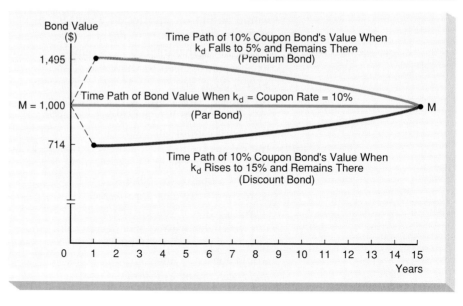

YEAR	$k_d = 5\%$	$k_d = 10\%$	$k_d = 15\%$
0	—	$1,000	—
1	$1,494.96	1,000	$ 713.75
.	.	.	.
.	.	.	.
.	.	.	.
15	1,000	1,000	1,000

NOTE: The curves for 5% and 15% have a slight bow.

that level. Of course, if interest rates do *not* remain constant, then the price of the bond will fluctuate. However, regardless of what future interest rates do, the bond's price will approach $1,000 as it nears the maturity date (barring bankruptcy, in which case the bond's value might fall dramatically).

Figure 7-2 illustrates the following key points:

Discount Bond
A bond that sells below its par value; occurs whenever the going rate of interest *rises above* the coupon rate.

Premium Bond
A bond that sells above its par value; occurs whenever the going rate of interest *falls below* the coupon rate.

1. Whenever the going rate of interest, k_d, is equal to the coupon rate, a *fixed-rate* bond will sell at its par value. Normally, the coupon rate is set equal to the going rate when a bond is issued, causing it to sell at par initially.

2. Interest rates do change over time, but the coupon rate remains fixed after the bond has been issued. Whenever the going rate of interest *rises above* the coupon rate, a fixed-rate bond's price will fall *below* its par value. Such a bond is called a **discount bond.**

3. Whenever the going rate of interest *falls below* the coupon rate, a fixed-rate bond's price will rise *above* its par value. Such a bond is called a **premium bond.**

4. Thus, an *increase* in interest rates will cause the prices of outstanding bonds to *fall,* whereas a *decrease* in rates will cause bond prices to *rise.*

5. The market value of a bond will always approach its par value as its maturity date approaches, provided the firm does not go bankrupt.

These points are very important, for they show that bondholders may suffer capital losses or make capital gains, depending on whether interest rates rise or fall after the bond was purchased. And, as we saw in Chapter 4, interest rates do indeed change over time.

SELF-TEST QUESTIONS

What is meant by the terms "new issue" and "seasoned issue"?

Explain, verbally, the following equation:

$$V_B = \sum_{t=1}^{N} \frac{INT}{(1 + k_d)^t} + \frac{M}{(1 + k_d)^N}.$$

Explain what happens to the price of a fixed-rate bond if (1) interest rates rise above the bond's coupon rate or (2) interest rates fall below the bond's coupon rate.

What is a "discount bond"? A "premium bond"?

Why do the prices of fixed-rate bonds fall if expectations for inflation rise?

BOND YIELDS

If you examine the bond market table of *The Wall Street Journal* or a price sheet put out by a bond dealer, you will typically see information regarding each bond's maturity date, price, and coupon interest rate. You will also see the bond's reported yield. Unlike the coupon interest rate, which is fixed, the bond's yield varies from day to day depending on current market conditions. Moreover, the yield can be calculated in three different ways, and three "answers" can be obtained. These different yields are described in the following sections.

YIELD TO MATURITY

Yield to Maturity (YTM)
The rate of return earned on a bond if it is held to maturity.

Suppose you were offered a 14-year, 10 percent annual coupon, $1,000 par value bond at a price of $1,494.96. What rate of interest would you earn on your investment if you bought the bond and held it to maturity? This rate is called the bond's **yield to maturity (YTM),** and it is the interest rate generally discussed by investors when they talk about rates of return. The yield to maturity is generally the same as the market rate of interest, k_d, and to find it, all you need to do is solve Equation 7-1 for k_d:

$$V_B = \$1,494.96 = \frac{\$100}{(1 + k_d)^1} + \cdots + \frac{\$100}{(1 + k_d)^{14}} + \frac{\$1,000}{(1 + k_d)^{14}}.$$

You could substitute values for k_d until you find a value that "works" and forces the sum of the PVs on the right side of the equal sign to equal $1,494.96.

Finding k_d = YTM by trial-and-error would be a tedious, time-consuming process, but as you might guess, it is easy with a financial calculator.[8] Here is the setup:

Simply enter N = 14, PV = −1494.96, PMT = 100, and FV = 1000, and then press the I key. The answer, 5 percent, will then appear.

The yield to maturity is identical to the total rate of return discussed in the preceding section. The yield to maturity can also be viewed as the bond's *promised rate of return,* which is the return that investors will receive if all the promised payments are made. However, the yield to maturity equals the *expected rate of return* only if (1) the probability of default is zero and (2) the bond cannot be called. If there is some default risk, or if the bond may be called, then there is some probability that the promised payments to maturity will not be received, in which case the calculated yield to maturity will differ from the expected return.

The YTM for a bond that sells at par consists entirely of an interest yield, but if the bond sells at a price other than its par value, the YTM will consist of the interest yield plus a positive or negative capital gains yield. Note also that a bond's yield to maturity changes whenever interest rates in the economy change, and this is almost daily. One who purchases a bond and holds it until it matures will receive the YTM that existed on the purchase date, but the bond's calculated YTM will change frequently between the purchase date and the maturity date.

YIELD TO CALL

If you purchased a bond that was callable and the company called it, you would not have the option of holding it until it matured. Therefore, the yield to

---

[8]A few years ago, bond traders all had specialized tables called *bond tables* that gave yields on bonds of different maturities selling at different premiums and discounts. Because calculators are so much more efficient (and accurate), bond tables are no longer used.

Also, one could use the compound interest tables at the back of this book (Tables A-1 and A-2) to find PVIF factors which force the following equation to an equality:

$$V_B = \$1,494.96 = \$100(\text{PVIFA}_{k_d,14}) + \$1,000(\text{PVIF}_{k_d,14}).$$

Factors for 5 percent would "work," indicating that 5 percent is the bond's YTM. This procedure can be used only if the YTM works out to a whole number percentage.

maturity would not be earned. For example, if Allied's 10 percent coupon bonds were callable, and if interest rates fell from 10 percent to 5 percent, then the company could call in the 10 percent bonds, replace them with 5 percent bonds, and save $100 − $50 = $50 interest per bond per year. This would be beneficial to the company, but not to its bondholders.

If current interest rates are well below an outstanding bond's coupon rate, then a callable bond is likely to be called, and investors will estimate its expected rate of return as the **yield to call (YTC)** rather than as the yield to maturity. To calculate the YTC, solve this equation for k_d:

$$\text{Price of bond} = \sum_{t=1}^{N} \frac{\text{INT}}{(1 + k_d)^t} + \frac{\text{Call price}}{(1 + k_d)^N}. \qquad (7\text{-}3)$$

Here N is the number of years until the company can call the bond; call price is the price the company must pay in order to call the bond (it is often set equal to the par value plus one year's interest); and k_d is the YTC.

To illustrate, suppose Allied's bonds had a provision that permitted the company, if it desired, to call the bonds ten years after the issue date at a price of $1,100. Suppose further that interest rates had fallen, and one year after issuance the going interest rate had declined, causing the price of the bonds to rise to $1,494.96. Here is the time line and the setup for finding the bond's YTC with a financial calculator:

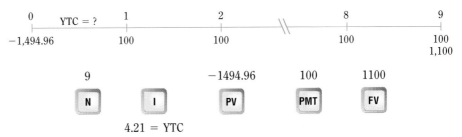

The YTC is 4.21 percent — this is the return you would earn if you bought the bond at a price of $1,494.96 and it was called nine years from today. (The bond could not be called until ten years after issuance, and one year has gone by, so there are nine years left until the first call date.)

Do you think Allied *will* call the bonds when they become callable? Allied's action would depend on what the going interest rate is when the bonds become callable. If the going rate remains at k_d = 5%, then Allied could save 10% − 5% = 5%, or $50 per bond per year, by calling them and replacing the 10 percent bonds with a new 5 percent issue. There would be costs to the company to refund the issue, but the interest savings would probably be worth the cost, so Allied would probably refund the bonds. Therefore, you would probably earn YTC = 4.21% rather than YTM = 5% if you bought the bonds under the indicated conditions.

The analysis used to decide whether or not to call a bond is covered in detail in Appendix 11B. In the balance of this chapter, we assume that bonds are not callable unless otherwise noted, but some of the end-of-chapter problems deal with yield to call.

CURRENT YIELD

If you examine brokerage house reports on bonds, you will often see reference to a bond's **current yield.** The current yield is the annual interest payment divided

---

Yield to Call (YTC)
The rate of return earned on a bond if it is called before its maturity date.

Current Yield
The annual interest payment on a bond divided by the bond's current price.

GLOBAL PERSPECTIVES

DRINKING YOUR COUPONS

Chateau Teyssier, an English vineyard, was looking for some cash to purchase some additional vines and to modernize its production facilities. Their solution? With the assistance of a leading underwriter, Matrix Securities, the vineyard recently issued 375 bonds, each costing 2,650 British pounds. The issue raised nearly 1 million pounds, which is roughly $1.5 million.

What makes these bonds interesting is that, instead of getting paid with something boring like money, these bonds pay their investors back with wine. Each June until 2002, when the bond matures, investors will receive their "coupons." Between 1997 and 2001, each bond will provide six cases of the vineyard's rose or claret. Starting in 1998 and continuing through maturity in 2002, investors will also receive four cases of its prestigious Saint Emilion

Grand Cru. Then, in 2002, they will get their money back.

The bonds are not without risk. The vineyard's owner, Jonathan Malthus, acknowledges that the quality of the wine, "is at the mercy of the gods."

SOURCE: Steven Irvine, "My Wine Is My Bond, and I Drink My Coupons," *Euromoney*, July 1996, 7. Used with permission.

---

by the bond's current price. For example, if Allied's bonds with a 10 percent coupon were currently selling at $985, the bond's current yield would be 10.15 percent ($100/$985).

Unlike the yield to maturity, the current yield does not represent the return that investors should expect to receive from holding the bond. The current yield provides information regarding the amount of cash income that a bond will generate in a given year, but since it does not take account of capital gains or losses that will be realized if the bond is held until maturity (or call), it does not provide an accurate measure of the bond's total expected return.

The fact that the current yield does not provide an accurate measure of a bond's total return can be illustrated with a zero coupon bond. Since zeros pay no annual income, they always have a current yield of zero. This indicates that the bond will not provide any cash interest income, but since the bond will appreciate in value over time, its total return clearly exceeds zero.

SELF-TEST QUESTIONS

Describe the difference between the yield to maturity and the yield to call.

How does a bond's current yield differ from its total return?

Could the current yield exceed the total return?

BONDS WITH SEMIANNUAL COUPONS

Although some bonds pay interest annually, the vast majority actually pay interest semiannually. To evaluate semiannual payment bonds, we must modify the valuation models (Equations 7-1 and 7-2) as follows:

1. Divide the annual coupon interest payment by 2 to determine the amount of interest paid each six months.

2. Multiply the years to maturity, N, by 2 to determine the number of semiannual periods.

3. Divide the nominal (quoted) interest rate, k_d, by 2 to determine the periodic (semiannual) interest rate.

By making these changes, we obtain the following equation for finding the value of a bond that pays interest semiannually:

$$V_B = \sum_{t=1}^{2N} \frac{INT/2}{(1 + k_d/2)^t} + \frac{M}{(1 + k_d/2)^{2N}} \qquad (7\text{-}1a)$$

To illustrate, assume now that Allied Food Products' bonds pay $50 interest each six months rather than $100 at the end of each year. Thus, each interest payment is only half as large, but there are twice as many of them. The coupon rate is thus "10 percent, semiannual payments." This is the nominal, or quoted, rate.[9]

When the going (nominal) rate of interest is 5 percent with semiannual compounding, the value of this 15-year bond is found as follows:

Inputs:	30	2.5		50	1000
	N	I	PV	PMT	FV
Output:			= −1,523.26		

Enter N = 30, k = I = 2.5, PMT = 50, FV = 1000, and then press the PV key to obtain the bond's value, $1,523.26. The value with semiannual interest payments is slightly larger than $1,518.98, the value when interest is paid annually. This higher value occurs because interest payments are received somewhat faster under semiannual compounding.

SELF-TEST QUESTION

Describe how the annual bond valuation formula is changed to evaluate semi-annual coupon bonds. Then, write out the revised formula.

ASSESSING THE RISKINESS OF A BOND

INTEREST RATE RISK

As we saw in Chapter 4, interest rates go up and down over time, and an increase in interest rates leads to a decline in the value of outstanding bonds. This risk of a decline in bond values due to rising interest rates is called **interest rate risk.** To illustrate, suppose you bought some 10 percent Allied bonds at a price of $1,000, and interest rates in the following year rose to 15 percent. As we saw before, the price of the bonds would fall to $713.75, so you would have a loss of

Interest Rate Risk
The risk of a decline in a bond's price due to an increase in interest rates.

---

[9]In this situation, the nominal coupon rate of "10 percent, semiannually," is the rate that bond dealers, corporate treasurers, and investors generally would discuss. Of course, the *effective annual rate* would be higher than 10 percent at the time the bond was issued:

$$EAR = EFF\% = \left(1 + \frac{k_{Nom}}{m}\right)^m - 1 = \left(1 + \frac{0.10}{2}\right)^2 - 1 = (1.05)^2 - 1 = 10.25\%.$$

Note also that 10 percent with annual payments is different than 10 percent with semiannual payments. Thus, we have assumed a change in effective rates in this section from the situation in the preceding section, where we assumed 10 percent with annual payments.

$286.25 per bond.[10] Interest rates can and do rise, and rising rates cause a loss of value for bondholders. Thus, people or firms who invest in bonds are exposed to risk from changing interest rates.

One's exposure to interest rate risk is higher on bonds with long maturities than on those maturing in the near future.[11] This point can be demonstrated by showing how the value of a 1-year bond with a 10 percent annual coupon fluctuates with changes in k_d, and then comparing these changes with those on a 14-year bond as calculated previously. The 1-year bond's values at different interest rates are shown below:

Value at $k_d = 5\%$:

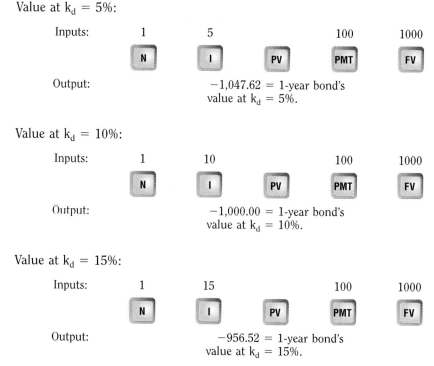

Inputs: 1   5   100   1000
           N   I   PV   PMT   FV

Output: −1,047.62 = 1-year bond's
                             value at $k_d = 5\%$.

Value at $k_d = 10\%$:

Inputs: 1   10   100   1000
           N   I   PV   PMT   FV

Output: −1,000.00 = 1-year bond's
                             value at $k_d = 10\%$.

Value at $k_d = 15\%$:

Inputs: 1   15   100   1000
           N   I   PV   PMT   FV

Output: −956.52 = 1-year bond's
                             value at $k_d = 15\%$.

You would obtain the first value with a financial calculator by entering N = 1, I = 5, PMT = 100, and FV = 1000, and then pressing PV to get $1,047.62. With everything still in your calculator, enter I = 10 to override the old I = 5, and press PV to find the bond's value at $k_d = I = 10$; it is $1,000. Then enter I = 15 and press the PV key to find the last bond value, $956.52.

---

[10]You would have an *accounting* (and tax) loss only if you sold the bond; if you held it to maturity, you would not have such a loss. However, even if you did not sell, you would still have suffered a *real economic loss in an opportunity cost sense* because you would have lost the opportunity to invest at 15 percent and would be stuck with a 10 percent bond in a 15 percent market. In an economic sense, "paper losses" are just as bad as realized accounting losses.

[11]Actually, a bond's maturity and coupon rate both affect interest rate risk. Low coupons mean that most of the bond's return will come from repayment of principal, whereas on a high coupon bond with the same maturity, more of the cash flows will come in during the early years due to the relatively large coupon payments. A measurement called "duration," which finds the average number of years the bond's PV of cash flows remain outstanding, has been developed to combine maturity and coupons. A zero coupon bond, which has no interest payments and whose payments all come at maturity, has a duration equal to the bond's maturity. Coupon bonds all have durations that are shorter than maturity, and the higher the coupon rate, the shorter the duration. Bonds with longer duration are exposed to more interest rate risk. A discussion of duration would go beyond the scope of this book, but see any investments text for a discussion of the concept.

| FIGURE 7 - 3 | Value of Long- and Short-Term 10% Annual Coupon Bonds at Different Market Interest Rates |

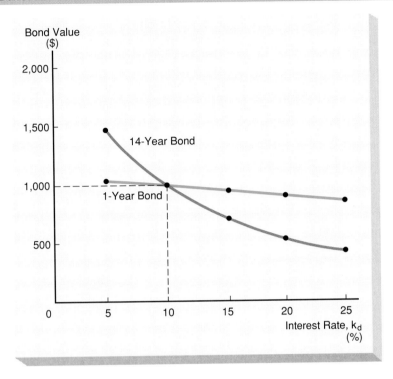

| | VALUE OF | |
CURRENT MARKET INTEREST RATE, k_d	1-YEAR BOND	14-YEAR BOND
5%	$1,047.62	$1,494.93
10	1,000.00	1,000.00
15	956.52	713.78
20	916.67	538.94
25	880.00	426.39

NOTE: Bond values were calculated using a financial calculator assuming annual, or once-a-year, compounding.

The values of the 1-year and 14-year bonds at several current market interest rates are summarized and plotted in Figure 7-3. Notice how much more sensitive the price of the 14-year bond is to changes in interest rates. At a 10 percent interest rate, both the 14-year and the 1-year bonds are valued at $1,000. When rates rise to 15 percent, the 14-year bond falls to $713.78, but the 1-year bond only falls to $956.52.

For bonds with similar coupons, this differential sensitivity to changes in interest rates always holds true — the longer the maturity of the bond, the more its price changes in response to a given change in interest rates. Thus, even if the risk of default on two bonds is exactly the same, the one with the longer maturity is typically exposed to more risk from a rise in interest rates.[12]

The logical explanation for this difference in interest rate risk is simple. Suppose you bought a 14-year bond that yielded 10 percent, or $100 a year. Now suppose interest rates on comparable-risk bonds rose to 15 percent. You would be stuck with only $100 of interest for the next 14 years. On the other hand, had you bought a 1-year bond, you would have a low return for only 1 year. At the end of the year, you would get your $1,000 back, and you could then reinvest it and receive 15 percent, or $150 per year, for the next 13 years. Thus, interest rate risk reflects the length of time one is committed to a given investment.

REINVESTMENT RATE RISK

As we saw in the preceding section, an *increase* in interest rates will hurt bondholders because it will lead to a decline in the value of a bond portfolio. But can a *decrease* in interest rates also hurt bondholders? The answer is yes, because if interest rates fall, a bondholder will probably suffer a reduction in his or her income. For example, consider a retiree who has a portfolio of bonds and lives off the income they produce. The bonds, on average, have a coupon rate of 10 percent. Now suppose interest rates decline to 5 percent. Many of the bonds will be called, and as calls occur, the bondholder will have to replace 10 percent bonds with 5 percent bonds. Even bonds that are not callable will mature, and when they do, they will have to be replaced with lower-yielding bonds. Thus, our retiree will suffer a reduction of income.

Reinvestment Rate Risk
The risk that a decline in interest rates will lead to a decline in income from a bond portfolio.

The risk of an income decline due to a drop in interest rates is called **reinvestment rate risk,** and its importance has been demonstrated to all bondholders in recent years as a result of the sharp drop in rates since the mid-1980s. Reinvestment rate risk is obviously high on callable bonds. It is also high on short maturity bonds, because the shorter the maturity of a bond, the fewer the years when the relatively high old interest rate will be earned, and the sooner the funds will have to be reinvested at the new low rate. Thus, retirees whose primary holdings were short-term securities, such as bank CDs and short-term bonds, were hurt badly by the recent decline in rates, but holders of long-term bonds are still enjoying their old high rates.

COMPARING INTEREST RATE AND REINVESTMENT RATE RISK

Notice that interest rate risk relates to the *value* of the bonds in a portfolio, while reinvestment rate risk relates to the *income* the portfolio produces. If you hold long-term bonds, you will face interest rate risk, that is, the value of your bonds will decline if interest rates rise, but you will not face much reinvestment rate risk, so your income will be stable. On the other hand, if you hold short-term bonds, you will not be exposed to much interest rate risk, so the value of your portfolio will be stable, but you will be exposed to reinvestment rate risk, and your income will fluctuate with changes in interest rates.

[12]If a 10-year bond were plotted in Figure 7-3, its curve would lie between those of the 14-year bond and the 1-year bond. The curve of a 1-month bond would be almost horizontal, indicating that its price would change very little in response to an interest rate change, but a 100-year bond (or a perpetuity) would have a very steep slope. Also, zero coupon bond prices are quite sensitive to interest rate changes, and the longer the maturity of the zero, the greater its price sensitivity. Therefore, 30-year zero coupon bonds have a huge amount of interest rate risk.

We see, then, that no fixed-rate bond can be considered totally riskless — even most Treasury bonds are exposed to both interest rate and reinvestment rate risk.[13] One can minimize interest rate risk by holding short-term bonds or minimize reinvestment rate risk by holding long-term bonds, but the actions that lower one type of risk increase the other. Bond portfolio managers try to balance these two risks, but some risk generally remains in any bond.

SELF-TEST QUESTIONS

Differentiate between interest rate risk and reinvestment rate risk.

To which type of risk are holders of long-term bonds more exposed? Short-term bondholders?

DEFAULT RISK

Another important risk associated with bonds is default risk. If the issuer defaults, investors receive less than the promised return on the bond. Therefore, investors need to assess a bond's default risk before making a purchase. Recall from Chapter 4 that the quoted interest rate includes a default risk premium — the greater the default risk, the higher the bond's yield to maturity. The default risk on Treasury securities is zero, but default risk can be substantial for corporate and municipal bonds.

Suppose two bonds have the same promised stream of cash flows, coupon rate, maturity, liquidity, and inflation exposure, but different levels of default risk. Investors will naturally pay less for the bond with the greater chance of default. As a result, bonds with higher default risk will have higher interest rates: $k_d = k^* + IP + DRP + LP + MRP$.

If its default risk changes, this will affect the price of a bond. For example, if the default risk of the Allied bonds increases, the bonds' price will fall and the yield to maturity ($YTM = k_d$) will increase.

In this section we consider some issues related to default risk. First, we show that corporations can influence the default risk of their bonds by changing the type of bonds they issue. Second we discuss bond ratings, which are used to measure default risk. Third, we describe the "junk bond market," which is the market for bonds with a relatively high probability of default. Finally, we consider bankruptcy and reorganization, which affect how much an investor can expect to recover if a default occurs.

VARIOUS TYPES OF CORPORATE BONDS

Default risk is influenced by both the financial strength of the issuer and the terms of the bond contract, especially whether collateral has been pledged to secure the bond. Some of the types of bonds corporations issue are described below.

MORTGAGE BONDS. Under a **mortgage bond**, the corporation pledges certain assets as security for the bond. To illustrate, in 1996, Billingham Corporation

Mortgage Bond
A bond backed by fixed assets. *First mortgage bonds* are senior in priority to claims of *second mortgage bonds*.

---

[13]Note, though, that indexed Treasury bonds are essentially riskless, but they pay a relatively low real rate. Also, risks have not disappeared — they are simply transferred from bondholders to taxpayers.

needed $10 million to build a major regional distribution center. Bonds in the amount of $4 million, secured by a *first mortgage* on the property, were issued. (The remaining $6 million was financed with equity capital.) If Billingham defaults on the bonds, the bondholders can foreclose on the property and sell it to satisfy their claims.

If Billingham chose to, it could issue *second mortgage bonds* secured by the same $10 million of assets. In the event of liquidation, the holders of these second mortgage bonds would have a claim against the property, but only after the first mortgage bondholders had been paid off in full. Thus, second mortgages are sometimes called *junior mortgages,* because they are junior in priority to the claims of *senior mortgages,* or *first mortgage bonds.*

Indenture
A formal agreement between the issuer of a bond and the bondholders.

All mortgage bonds are subject to an **indenture,** which is a legal document that spells out in detail the rights of both the bondholders and the corporation. The indentures of many major corporations were written 20, 30, 40, or more years ago. These indentures are generally "open ended," meaning that new bonds can be issued from time to time under the existing indenture. However, the amount of new bonds that can be issued is virtually always limited to a specified percentage of the firm's total "bondable property," which generally includes all land, plant, and equipment.

For example, Savannah Electric Company can issue first mortgage bonds totaling up to 60 percent of its fixed assets. If its fixed assets totaled $1 billion, and if it had $500 million of first mortgage bonds outstanding, it could, by the property test, issue another $100 million of bonds (60% of $1 billion = $600 million).

At times, Savannah Electric has been unable to issue any new first mortgage bonds because of another indenture provision: its times-interest-earned (TIE) ratio was below 2.5, the minimum coverage that it must have if it sells new bonds. Thus, although Savannah Electric passed the property test, it failed the coverage test, so it could not issue first mortgage bonds. Savannah Electric then had to finance with junior bonds. Since first mortgage bonds would have carried lower rates of interest than junior long-term debt, this restriction was a costly one.

Savannah Electric's neighbor, Georgia Power Company, has more flexibility under its indenture — its interest coverage requirement is only 2.0. In hearings before the Georgia Public Service Commission, it was suggested that Savannah Electric should change its indenture coverage to 2.0 so that it could issue more first mortgage bonds. However, this was simply not possible — the holders of the outstanding bonds would have to approve the change, and it is inconceivable that they would vote for a change that would seriously weaken their position.

Debenture
A long-term bond that is not secured by a mortgage on specific property.

DEBENTURES. A **debenture** is an unsecured bond, and as such it provides no lien against specific property as security for the obligation. Debenture holders are, therefore, general creditors whose claims are protected by property not otherwise pledged. In practice, the use of debentures depends both on the nature of the firm's assets and on its general credit strength. An extremely strong company such as AT&T will tend to use debentures; it simply does not need to put up property as security for its debt. Debentures are also issued by weak companies which have already pledged most of their assets as collateral for mortgage loans. In this latter case, the debentures are relatively risky, and they will bear a high interest rate.

SUBORDINATED DEBENTURES. The term *subordinate* means "below," or "inferior to," and, in the event of bankruptcy, subordinated debt has claims on assets only

TABLE 7 - 1	Moody's and S&P Bond Ratings

	INVESTMENT GRADE				JUNK BONDS			
Moody's	Aaa	Aa	A	Baa	Ba	B	Caa	C
S&P	AAA	AA	A	BBB	BB	B	CCC	D

NOTE: Both Moody's and S&P use "modifiers" for bonds rated below triple-A. S&P uses a plus and minus system; thus, A+ designates the strongest A-rated bonds and A− the weakest. Moody's uses a 1, 2, or 3 designation, with 1 denoting the strongest and 3 the weakest; thus, within the double-A category, Aa1 is the best, Aa2 is average, and Aa3 is the weakest.

Subordinated Debentures
A bond having a claim on assets only after the senior debt has been paid off in the event of liquidation.

after senior debt has been paid off. **Subordinated debentures** may be subordinated either to designated notes payable (usually bank loans) or to all other debt. In the event of liquidation or reorganization, holders of subordinated debentures cannot be paid until all senior debt, as named in the debentures' indenture, has been paid. Precisely how subordination works, and how it strengthens the position of senior debtholders, is explained in detail in Appendix 7B.

BOND RATINGS

Since the early 1900s, bonds have been assigned quality ratings that reflect their probability of going into default. The three major rating agencies are Moody's Investors Service (Moody's), Standard & Poor's Corporation (S&P), and Fitch Investors Service. Moody's and S&P rating designations are shown in Table 7-1.[14] The triple- and double-A bonds are extremely safe. Single-A and triple-B bonds are also strong enough to be called **investment grade bonds,** and they are the lowest-rated bonds that many banks and other institutional investors are permitted by law to hold. Double-B and lower bonds are speculative, or **junk bonds.** These bonds have a significant probability of going into default. A later section discusses junk bonds in more detail.

Investment Grade Bonds
Bonds rated triple-B or higher; many banks and other institutional investors are permitted by law to hold only investment grade bonds.

Junk Bond
A high-risk, high-yield bond.

BOND RATING CRITERIA. Bond ratings are based on both qualitative and quantitative factors, some of which are listed below:

1. Various ratios, including the debt ratio, the times-interest-earned ratio, the fixed charge coverage ratio, and the current ratio. The better the ratios, the higher the bond's rating.
2. Mortgage provisions: Is the bond secured by a mortgage? If it is, and if the property has a high value in relation to the amount of bonded debt, the bond's rating is enhanced.
3. Subordination provisions: Is the bond subordinated to other debt? If so, it will be rated at least one notch below the rating it would have if it were not subordinated. Conversely, a bond with other debt subordinated to it will have a somewhat higher rating.

[14]In the discussion to follow, reference to the S&P code is intended to imply the Moody's and Fitch's codes as well. Thus, triple-B bonds mean both BBB and Baa bonds; double-B bonds mean both BB and Ba bonds; and so on.

4. Guarantee provisions: Some bonds are guaranteed by other firms. If a weak company's debt is guaranteed by a strong company (usually the weak company's parent), the bond will be given the strong company's rating.

5. Sinking fund: Does the bond have a sinking fund to ensure systematic repayment? This feature is a plus factor to the rating agencies.

6. Maturity: Other things the same, a bond with a shorter maturity will be judged less risky than a longer-term bond, and this will be reflected in the ratings.

7. Stability: Are the issuer's sales and earnings stable?

8. Regulation: Is the issuer regulated, and could an adverse regulatory climate cause the company's economic position to decline? Regulation is especially important for utilities, railroads, and telephone companies.

9. Antitrust: Are any antitrust actions pending against the firm that could erode its position?

10. Overseas operations: What percentage of the firm's sales, assets, and profits are from overseas operations, and what is the political climate in the host countries?

11. Environmental factors: Is the firm likely to face heavy expenditures for pollution control equipment?

12. Product liability: Are the firm's products safe? The tobacco companies today are under pressure, and so are their bond ratings.

13. Pension liabilities: Does the firm have unfunded pension liabilities that could pose a future problem?

14. Labor unrest: Are there potential labor problems on the horizon that could weaken the firm's position? As this is written, a number of airlines face this problem, and it has caused their ratings to be lowered.

15. Accounting policies: If a firm uses relatively conservative accounting policies, its reported earnings will be of "higher quality" than if it uses less conservative procedures. Thus, conservative accounting policies are a plus factor in bond ratings.

Representatives of the rating agencies have consistently stated that no precise formula is used to set a firm's rating; all the factors listed, plus others, are taken into account, but not in a mathematically precise manner. Statistical studies have borne out this contention, for researchers who have tried to predict bond ratings on the basis of quantitative data have had only limited success, indicating that the agencies use subjective judgment when establishing a firm's rating.[15]

IMPORTANCE OF BOND RATINGS.   Bond ratings are important both to firms and to investors. First, because a bond's rating is an indicator of its default risk, the rating has a direct, measurable influence on the bond's interest rate and the firm's cost of debt capital. Second, most bonds are purchased by institutional investors rather than individuals, and many institutions are restricted to investment-grade securities. Thus, if a firm's bonds fall below BBB, it will have a difficult time selling new bonds because many potential purchasers will not be allowed to buy them.

---

[15]See Ahmed Belkaoui, *Industrial Bonds and the Rating Process* (London: Quorum Books, 1983).

As a result of their higher risk and more restricted market, lower-grade bonds have higher required rates of return, k_d, than high-grade bonds. Figure 7-4 illustrates this point. In each of the years shown on the graph, U.S. government bonds have had the lowest yields, AAAs have been next, and BBB

FIGURE 7-4 | Yields on Selected Long-Term Bonds, 1959–1996

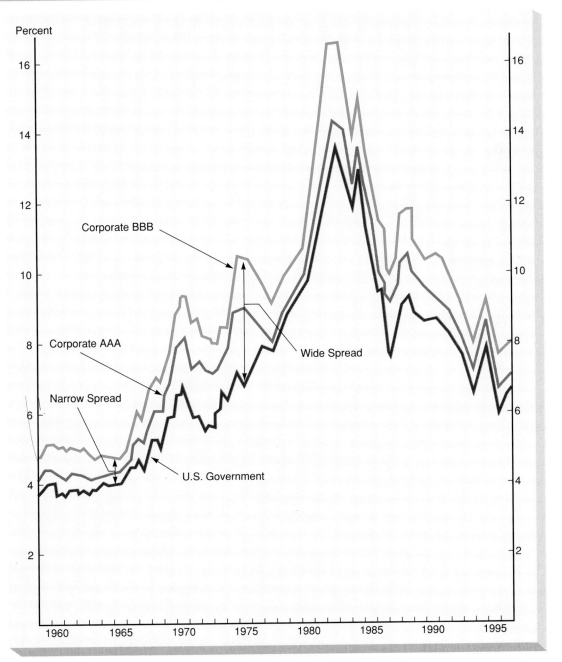

SOURCES: Federal Reserve Board, *Historical Chart Book,* 1983, and *Federal Reserve Bulletin,* various issues.

F I G U R E   7 - 5   Relationship between Bond Ratings and Bond Yields, 1963 and 1996

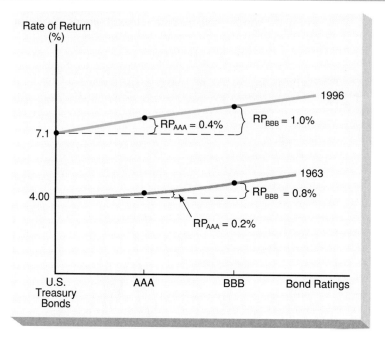

	LONG-TERM GOVERNMENT BONDS (DEFAULT-FREE) (1)	AAA CORPORATE BONDS (2)	BBB CORPORATE BONDS (3)	RISK PREMIUMS	
				AAA (4) = (2) − (1)	BBB (5) = (3) − (1)
June 1963	4.0%	4.2%	4.8%	0.2%	0.8%
July 1996	7.1	7.5	8.1	0.4	1.0

RP_{AAA} = risk premium on AAA bonds.

RP_{BBB} = risk premium on BBB bonds.

SOURCES: *Federal Reserve Bulletin,* December 1963, and *Federal Reserve Statistical Release,* August 1996.

bonds have had the highest yields. The figure also shows that the gaps between yields on the three types of bonds vary over time, indicating that the cost differentials, or risk premiums, fluctuate from year to year. This point is highlighted in Figure 7-5, which gives the yields on the three types of bonds and the risk premiums for AAA and BBB bonds in June 1963 and July 1996.[16]

[16]The term *risk premium* ought to reflect only the difference in expected (and required) returns between two securities that results from differences in their risk. However, the differences between *yields to maturity* on different types of bonds consist of (1) a true risk premium; (2) a liquidity premium, which reflects the fact that U.S. Treasury bonds are more readily marketable than most corporate bonds; (3) a call premium, because most Treasury bonds are not callable whereas corporate bonds are; and (4) an expected loss differential, which reflects the probability of loss on the corporate bonds. As an example of the last point, suppose the yield to maturity on a BBB bond was 8 percent versus 7 percent on government bonds, but there was a 5 percent probability of total default loss on the corporate bond. In this case, the expected return on the BBB bond would be 0.95(8%) + 0.05(0%) = 7.6%, and the risk premium would be 0.6 percent, not the full 1 percentage point difference in "promised" yields to maturity. Because of all these points, the risk premiums given in Figure 7-5 overstate somewhat the true (but unmeasurable) theoretical risk premiums.

SANTA FE BONDS FINALLY MATURE AFTER 114 YEARS

In 1995, Santa Fe Pacific Company made the final payment on some outstanding bonds that were originally issued in 1881! While the bonds were paid off in full, their history has been anything but routine.

Since the bonds were issued in 1881, investors have seen Santa Fe go through two bankruptcy reorganizations, two depressions, several recessions, two world wars, and the collapse of the gold standard. Through it all, the company remained intact, although ironically it did agree to be acquired by Burlington Northern just prior to the bonds' maturity.

When the bonds were issued by the Santa Fe railroad company in 1881, they had a 6 percent coupon. After a promising start, competition in the railroad business, along with the Depression of 1893, dealt a crippling one-two punch to the company's fortunes. After two bankruptcy reorganizations — and two new management teams — the company got back on its feet, and in 1895 it replaced the original bonds with new 100-year bonds. The new bonds, sanctioned by the Bankruptcy Court, matured in 1995 and carried a 4 percent coupon. However, they also had a wrinkle that was in effect until 1900 — the company could skip the coupon payment if, in management's opinion, earnings were not sufficiently high to service the debt. After 1900, the company could no longer just ignore the coupon, but it did have the option of deferring the payments if management deemed deferral necessary. In the late 1890s, Santa Fe did skip the interest, and the bonds sold at an all-time low of $285 (28.5% of par) in 1896. The bonds reached a peak in 1946, when they sold for $1,312.50 in the strong, low interest rate economy after World War II.

Interestingly, the bonds' principal payment was originally pegged to the price of gold, meaning that the principal received at maturity would increase if the price of gold increased. This type of contract was declared invalid in 1933 by President Roosevelt and Congress, and the decision was upheld by the Supreme Court in a 5-4 vote. If just one Supreme Court justice had gone the other way, then, due to an increase in the price of gold, the bonds would have been worth $18,626 rather than $1,000 when they matured in 1995!

In many ways, the saga of the Santa Fe bonds is a testament to the stability of the U.S. financial system. On the other hand, it signifies the many types of risks that investors face when they purchase long-term bonds. Investors in the 100-year bonds recently issued by Disney and Coca-Cola, among others, should perhaps take note.

Note first that the risk-free rate, or vertical axis intercept, rose more than 3 percentage points from 1963 to 1996, primarily reflecting the increase in realized and anticipated inflation. Second, the slope of the line has increased since 1963, indicating an increase in investors' risk aversion. Thus, the penalty for having a low credit rating varies over time. Occasionally, as in 1963, the penalty is quite small, but at other times it is large. These slope differences reflect investors' aversion to risk.

CHANGES IN RATINGS. Changes in a firm's bond rating affect both its ability to borrow long-term capital and the cost of that capital. Rating agencies review outstanding bonds on a periodic basis, occasionally upgrading or downgrading a bond as a result of its issuer's changed circumstances. For example, the September 4, 1996, issue of *Standard & Poor's CreditWeek* reported that Tribune Co.'s senior debt had been downgraded from A+ to A. This downgrading reflected the higher debt burden the company will have in 1997 following its acquisition of Renaissance Communications Corp. While the Renaissance acquisition bolsters Tribune's business position and diversifies its advertising market exposure, it comes at the expense of a marked increase in debt relative to the firm's projected cash flows. In the same issue, *CreditWeek* upgraded the subordinated debt of Specialty Equipment Companies, which provides McDonald's with ice cream machines and grills, from B− to B, to reflect Specialty's improving financial ratios.

JUNK BONDS

Prior to the 1980s, fixed-income investors such as pension funds and insurance companies were generally unwilling to buy risky bonds, so it was almost impossible for risky companies to raise capital in the public bond markets. Then, in the late 1970s, Michael Milken of the investment banking firm Drexel Burnham Lambert, relying on historical studies which showed that risky bonds yielded more than enough to compensate for their risk, began to convince institutional investors of the merits of purchasing risky debt. Thus was born the "junk bond," a high-risk, high-yield bond issued to finance a leveraged buyout, a merger, or a troubled company.[17] For example, Public Service of New Hampshire financed construction of its troubled Seabrook nuclear plant with junk bonds, and junk bonds were used by Ted Turner to finance the development of CNN and Turner Broadcasting. In junk bond deals, the debt ratio is generally extremely high, so the bondholders must bear as much risk as stockholders normally would. The bonds' yields reflect this fact — a promised return of 25 percent per annum was required to sell the Public Service of New Hampshire bonds.

The emergence of junk bonds as an important type of debt is another example of how the investment banking industry adjusts to and facilitates new developments in capital markets. In the 1980s, mergers and takeovers increased dramatically. People like T. Boone Pickens and Henry Kravitz thought that certain old-line, established companies were run inefficiently and were financed too conservatively, and they wanted to take these companies over and restructure them. Michael Milken and his staff at Drexel Burnham Lambert began an active campaign to persuade certain institutions (often S&Ls) to purchase high-yield bonds. Milken developed expertise in putting together deals that were attractive to the institutions yet apparently feasible in the sense that projected cash flows were sufficient to meet the required interest payments. The fact that interest on the bonds was tax deductible, combined with the much higher debt ratios of the restructured firms, also increased after-tax cash flows and helped make the deals appear feasible.

The development of junk bond financing has done much to reshape the U.S. financial scene. The existence of these securities led directly to the loss of independence of Gulf Oil and hundreds of other companies, and it led to major shake-ups in such companies as CBS, Union Carbide, and USX (formerly U.S. Steel). It also caused Drexel Burnham Lambert to leap from essentially nowhere in the 1970s to become the most profitable investment banking firm during the 1980s.

The phenomenal growth of the junk bond market was impressive, but controversial. In 1989, Drexel Burnham Lambert was forced into bankruptcy, and "junk bond king" Michael Milken, who had earned $500 million two years earlier, was sent to jail. These events led to the collapse of the junk bond market in the early 1990s. Since then, however, the junk bond market has rebounded, and junk bonds seem to be here to stay as an important form of corporate financing.

BANKRUPTCY AND REORGANIZATION

During recessions, bankruptcies normally rise, and the most recent recession (in 1991–1992) was no exception. The 1991–1992 casualties included Pan Am, Carter Hawley Hale Stores, Continental Airlines, R. H. Macy & Company, Zale

---

[17]Another type of junk bond is one that was highly rated when it was issued but whose rating has fallen because its issuer corporation has fallen on hard times. Such bonds are called "fallen angels."

Corporation, and McCrory Corporation. Because of its importance, at least a brief discussion of bankruptcy is warranted within the chapter, and a more detailed discussion is presented in Appendix 7B.

When a business becomes *insolvent,* it does not have enough cash to meet its interest and principal payments. A decision must then be made whether to dissolve the firm through *liquidation* or to permit it to *reorganize* and thus stay alive. These issues are addressed in Chapters 7 and 11 of the federal bankruptcy statutes, and the final decision is made by a federal bankruptcy court judge.

The decision to force a firm to liquidate versus permit it to reorganize depends on whether the value of the reorganized firm is likely to be greater than the value of the firm's assets if they are sold off piecemeal. In a reorganization, a committee of unsecured creditors is appointed by the court to negotiate with management on the terms of a potential reorganization. The reorganization plan may call for a *restructuring* of the firm's debt, in which case the interest rate may be reduced, the term to maturity lengthened, or some of the debt may be exchanged for equity. The point of the restructuring is to reduce the financial charges to a level that the firm's cash flows can support. Of course, the common stockholders also have to give up something — they normally see their position diluted as a result of additional shares being given to debtholders in exchange for accepting a reduced amount of debt principal and interest. A trustee may be appointed by the court to oversee the reorganization, but generally the existing management is allowed to retain control.

Liquidation occurs if the company is deemed to be too far gone to be saved — if it is worth more dead than alive. If the bankruptcy court orders a liquidation, assets are sold off and the cash obtained is distributed as specified in Chapter 7 of the Bankruptcy Act. Here is the priority of claims:

1. Secured creditors are entitled to the proceeds of the sale of the specific property that was used to support their loans.
2. The trustee's costs of administering and operating the bankrupt firm are next in line.
3. Expenses incurred after bankruptcy was filed come next.
4. Wages due workers, up to a limit of $2,000 per worker, follow.
5. Claims for unpaid contributions to employee benefit plans are next. This amount, together with wages, cannot exceed $2,000 per worker.
6. Unsecured claims for customer deposits up to $900 per customer are sixth in line.
7. Federal, state, and local taxes due come next.
8. Unfunded pension plan liabilities are next. (Limitations exist as specified in Appendix 7B.)
9. General unsecured creditors are ninth on the list.
10. Preferred stockholders come next, up to the par value of their stock.
11. Common stockholders are finally paid, if anything is left, which is rare.

Appendix 7B provides an illustration of how a firm's assets are distributed after it has been liquidated. For now, you should know (1) that the federal bankruptcy statutes govern both reorganization and liquidation, (2) that bankruptcies occur frequently, and (3) that a priority of the specified claims must be followed when distributing the assets of a liquidated firm.

SELF-TEST QUESTIONS

Differentiate between mortgage bonds and debentures.

Name the major rating agencies, and list some factors that affect bond ratings.

Why are bond ratings important both to firms and to investors?

For what purposes have junk bonds typically been used?

Differentiate between a Chapter 7 liquidation and a Chapter 11 reorganization. When would each be used?

List the priority of claims for the distribution of a liquidated firm's assets.

BOND MARKETS

Corporate bonds are traded primarily in the over-the-counter market. Most bonds are owned by and traded among the large financial institutions (for example, life insurance companies, mutual funds, and pension funds, all of which deal in very large blocks of securities), and it is relatively easy for the over-the-counter bond dealers to arrange the transfer of large blocks of bonds among the relatively few holders of the bonds. It would be much more difficult to conduct similar operations in the stock market among the literally millions of large and small stockholders, so a higher percentage of stock trades occur on the exchanges.

Information on bond trades in the over-the-counter market is not published, but a representative group of bonds is listed and traded on the bond division of the NYSE. Figure 7-6 gives a section of the bond market page of *The Wall Street Journal* for trading on September 18, 1996. A total of 310 issues were traded on that date, but we show only the bonds of Cleveland Electric Company. Note that Cleveland Electric had three different bonds that were traded on September 18; the company actually had more than ten bond issues outstanding, but most of them did not trade on that date.

The bonds of Cleveland Electric and other companies can have various denominations, but for convenience we generally think of each bond as having a par value of $1,000—this is how much per bond the company borrowed and

| FIGURE 7-6 | NYSE Bond Market Transactions, September 18, 1996 |

CORPORATION BONDS

VOLUME $22,786,000

BONDS	CUR YLD	VOL	CLOSE	NET CHG.
ClevEl 8¾05	8.9	477	98	. . .
ClevEl 8⅜11	9.0	145	93¼	− ⅜
ClevEl 8⅜12	9.0	106	93½	− ⅛

SOURCE: *The Wall Street Journal,* September 19, 1996, C20.

how much it must someday repay. However, since other denominations are possible, for trading and reporting purposes bonds are quoted as percentages of par. Looking at the first bond listed in the data in Figure 7-7, we see that there is an 8¾ just after the company's name; this indicates that the bond is of the series which pays 8¾ percent interest, or 0.0875($1,000) = $87.50 of interest per year. The 8¾ percent is the bond's *coupon rate*. The Cleveland Electric bonds, and all the others listed in the *Journal,* pay interest semiannually, so all rates are nominal, not EAR rates. The 05 which comes next indicates that this bond matures and must be repaid in the year 2005; it is not shown in the figure, but this bond was issued in 1970, so it had a 35-year original maturity. The 8.9 in the second column is the bond's current yield: Current yield = $87.50/$980 = 8.93%, rounded to 8.9 percent. The 477 in the third column indicates that 477 of these bonds were traded on September 18, 1996. Since the price shown in the fourth column is expressed as a percentage of par, the bond closed at 98 percent, which translates to $980, the same as the previous day's close.

Coupon rates are generally set at levels which reflect the "going rate of interest" on the day a bond is issued. If the rates were set lower, investors simply would not buy the bonds at the $1,000 par value, so the company could not borrow the money it needed. Thus, bonds generally sell at their par values on the day they are issued, but bond prices fluctuate thereafter as interest rates change.

FIGURE 7-7 Cleveland Electric 8.75%, 35-Year Bond: Market Value as Interest Rates Change

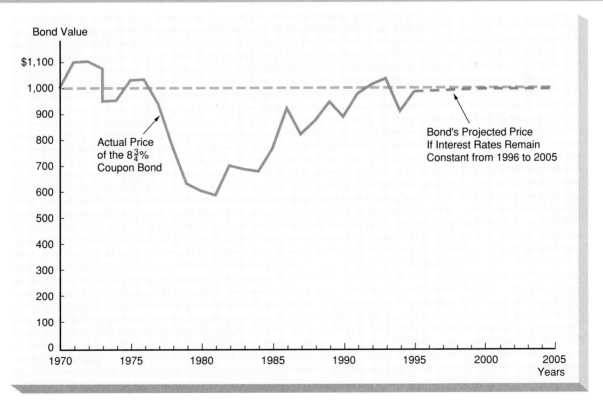

NOTE: The line from 1996 to 2005 appears linear, but it actually has a slight curve.

The Cleveland bonds initially sold at par, rose above par in the early 1970s when interest rates dipped below 8.75 percent, hit a low in 1981, and rose after 1981 due to (1) the general decline in interest rates and (2) the fact that bond values approach their par values as their maturity date approaches.

SELF-TEST QUESTIONS

Why do most bond trades occur in the over-the-counter market?

If a bond issue is to be sold at par, how will its coupon rate be determined?

SUMMARY

This chapter described the different types of bonds governments and corporations issue, explained how bond prices are established, and discussed how investors go about estimating the rates of return they can expect to earn. The key concepts covered are summarized below.

♦ A **bond** is a long-term promissory note issued by a business or governmental unit. The issuer receives money in exchange for promising to make interest payments and to repay the principal on a specified future date.

♦ Some recent innovations in long-term financing include **zero coupon bonds,** which pay no annual interest but which are issued at a discount; **floating rate debt,** whose interest payments fluctuate with changes in the general level of interest rates; and **junk bonds,** which are high-risk, high-yield instruments issued by firms which use a great deal of financial leverage.

♦ A **call provision** gives the issuing corporation the right to redeem the bonds prior to maturity under specified terms, usually at a price greater than the maturity value (the difference is a **call premium**). A firm will typically call a bond if interest rates fall substantially below the coupon rate.

♦ A **sinking fund** is a provision which requires the corporation to retire a portion of the bond issue each year. The purpose of the sinking fund is to provide for the orderly retirement of the issue. A sinking fund typically requires no call premium.

♦ The **value of a bond** is found as the present value of an **annuity** (the interest payments) plus the present value of a lump sum (the **principal**). The bond is evaluated at the appropriate periodic interest rate over the number of periods for which interest payments are made.

♦ The equation used to find the value of an annual coupon bond is:

$$V_B = \sum_{t=1}^{N} \frac{INT}{(1 + k_d)^t} + \frac{M}{(1 + k_d)^N}.$$

An adjustment to the formula must be made if the bond pays interest **semi-annually**: divide INT and k_d by 2, and multiply N by 2.

♦ The return earned on a bond held to maturity is defined as the bond's **yield to maturity (YTM).** If the bond can be redeemed before maturity, it is **callable,** and the return investors receive if it is called is defined as the **yield to call (YTC).** The YTC is found as the present value of the interest payments received while the bond is outstanding plus the present value of the call price (the par value plus a call premium).

♦ The longer the maturity of a bond, the more its price will change in response to a given change in interest rates; this is called **interest rate risk.** However, bonds with short maturities expose investors to high **reinvestment rate risk,** which is the risk that income will decline because cash flows received from bonds will be rolled over at lower interest rates.

♦ Corporate and municipal bonds have **default risk.** If an issuer defaults, investors receive less than the promised return on the bond. Therefore, investors should evaluate a bond's default risk before making a purchase.

♦ There are many different types of bonds. They include **mortgage bonds, debentures, convertibles, bonds with warrants, income bonds,** and **purchasing power (indexed) bonds.** The return required on each type of bond is determined by the bond's riskiness.

♦ Bonds are assigned **ratings** which reflect the probability of their going into default. The highest rating is AAA, and they go down to D. The higher a bond's rating, the lower its risk and its interest rate.

Two related issues are discussed in detail in Appendixes 7A and 7B: zero coupon bonds and bankruptcy. In recent years many companies have used zeros to raise billions of dollars, while bankruptcy is an important consideration for both companies that issue debt and investors.

QUESTIONS

7-1 Is it true that the following equation can be used to find the value of an N-year bond that pays interest once a year?

$$V_B = \sum_{t=1}^{N} \frac{\text{Annual interest}}{(1 + k_d)^t} + \frac{\text{Par value}}{(1 + k_d)^N}.$$

7-2 "The values of outstanding bonds change whenever the going rate of interest changes. In general, short-term interest rates are more volatile than long-term interest rates. Therefore, short-term bond prices are more sensitive to interest rate changes than are long-term bond prices." Is this statement true or false? Explain.

7-3 The rate of return you would get if you bought a bond and held it to its maturity date is called the bond's yield to maturity. If interest rates in the economy rise after a bond has been issued, what will happen to the bond's price and to its YTM? Does the length of time to maturity affect the extent to which a given change in interest rates will affect the bond's price?

7-4 If you buy a *callable* bond and interest rates decline, will the value of your bond rise by as much as it would have risen if the bond had not been callable? Explain.

7-5 A sinking fund can be set up in one of two ways:
(1) The corporation makes annual payments to the trustee, who invests the proceeds in securities (frequently government bonds) and uses the accumulated total to retire the bond issue at maturity.
(2) The trustee uses the annual payments to retire a portion of the issue each year, either calling a given percentage of the issue by a lottery and paying a specified price per bond or buying bonds on the open market, whichever is cheaper.
Discuss the advantages and disadvantages of each procedure from the viewpoint of both the firm and its bondholders.

7-6 Indicate whether each of the following actions will increase or decrease a bond's yield to maturity:
a. A bond's price increases.
b. The company's bonds are downgraded by the rating agencies.
c. A change in the bankruptcy code makes it more difficult for bondholders to receive payments in the event a firm declares bankruptcy.
d. The economy enters a recession.
e. The bonds become subordinated to another debt issue.

SELF-TEST PROBLEMS (Solutions Appear in Appendix B)

ST-1
Key terms

Define each of the following terms:
a. Bond; Treasury bond; corporate bond; municipal bond; foreign bond
b. Par value; maturity date
c. Coupon payment; coupon interest rate
d. Floating rate bond
e. Premium bond; discount bond
f. Current yield (on a bond); yield to maturity (YTM); yield to call (YTC)
g. Reinvestment rate risk; interest rate risk
h. Default risk
i. Mortgage bond
j. Debenture; subordinated debenture
k. Convertible bond; warrant; income bond; indexed, or purchasing power, bond
l. Call provision; sinking fund; indenture
m. Zero coupon bond; original issue discount bond (OID)
n. Junk bond; investment grade bonds

ST-2
Bond valuation

The Pennington Corporation issued a new series of bonds on January 1, 1974. The bonds were sold at par ($1,000), have a 12 percent coupon, and mature in 30 years, on December 31, 2003. Coupon payments are made semiannually (on June 30 and December 31).
a. What was the YTM of Pennington's bonds on January 1, 1974?
b. What was the price of the bond on January 1, 1979, 5 years later, assuming that the level of interest rates had fallen to 10 percent?
c. Find the current yield and capital gains yield on the bond on January 1, 1979, given the price as determined in Part b.
d. On July 1, 1997, Pennington's bonds sold for $916.42. What was the YTM at that date?
e. What were the current yield and capital gains yield on July 1, 1997?
f. Now, assume that you purchased an outstanding Pennington bond on March 1, 1997, when the going rate of interest was 15.5 percent. How large a check must you have written to complete the transaction? This is a hard question! (Hint: $PVIFA_{7.75\%,13} = 8.0136$ and $PVIF_{7.75\%,13} = 0.3789$.)

ST-3
Sinking fund

The Vancouver Development Company has just sold a $100 million, 10-year, 12 percent bond issue. A sinking fund will retire the issue over its life. Sinking fund payments are of equal amounts and will be made *semiannually*, and the proceeds will be used to retire bonds as the payments are made. Bonds can be called at par for sinking fund purposes, or the funds paid into the sinking fund can be used to buy bonds in the open market.
a. How large must each semiannual sinking fund payment be?
b. What will happen, under the conditions of the problem thus far, to the company's debt service requirements per year for this issue over time?
c. Now suppose Vancouver Development set up its sinking fund so that *equal annual amounts,* payable at the end of each year, are paid into a sinking fund trust held by a bank, with the proceeds being used to buy government bonds that pay 9 percent interest. The payments, plus accumulated interest, must total $100 million at the end of 10 years, and the proceeds will be used to retire the bonds at that time. How large must the annual sinking fund payment be now?
d. What are the annual cash requirements for covering bond service costs under the trusteeship arrangement described in Part c? (Note: Interest must be paid on Vancouver's outstanding bonds but not on bonds that have been retired.)
e. What would have to happen to interest rates to cause the company to buy bonds on the open market rather than call them under the original sinking fund plan?

STARTER PROBLEMS

7-1
Bond valuation

Callaghan Motors' bonds have 10 years remaining to maturity. Interest is paid annually, the bonds have a $1,000 par value, and the coupon interest rate is 8 percent. The bonds have a yield to maturity of 9 percent. What is the current market price of these bonds?

7-2
Yield to maturity;
Financial calculator needed

Wilson Wonders' bonds have 12 years remaining to maturity. Interest is paid annually, the bonds have a $1,000 par value, and the coupon interest rate is 10 percent. The bonds sell at a price of $850. What is their yield to maturity?

7-3

Yield to maturity and call;
Financial calculator needed

Thatcher Corporation's bonds will mature in 10 years. The bonds have a face value of $1,000 and an 8 percent coupon rate, paid semiannually. The price of the bonds is $1,100. The bonds are callable in 5 years at a call price of $1,050. What is the yield to maturity? What is the yield to call?

7-4

Current yield

Heath Foods' bonds have 7 years remaining to maturity. The bonds have a face value of $1,000 and a yield to maturity of 8 percent. They pay interest annually and have a 9 percent coupon rate. What is their current yield?

7-5

Bond valuation;
Financial calculator needed

Nungesser Corporation has issued bonds which have a 9 percent coupon rate, payable semiannually. The bonds mature in 8 years, have a face value of $1,000, and a yield to maturity of 8.5 percent. What is the price of the bonds?

EXAM-TYPE PROBLEMS

The problems included in this section are set up in such a way that they could be converted to multiple-choice exam problems.

7-6

Bond valuation

The Garraty Company has two bond issues outstanding. Both bonds pay $100 annual interest plus $1,000 at maturity. Bond L has a maturity of 15 years, and Bond S a maturity of 1 year.
a. What will be the value of each of these bonds when the going rate of interest is (1) 5 percent, (2) 8 percent, and (3) 12 percent? Assume that there is only one more interest payment to be made on Bond S.
b. Why does the longer-term (15-year) bond fluctuate more when interest rates change than does the shorter-term bond (1-year)?

7-7

Yield to maturity

The Heymann Company's bonds have 4 years remaining to maturity. Interest is paid annually; the bonds have a $1,000 par value; and the coupon interest rate is 9 percent.
a. What is the yield to maturity at a current market price of (1) $829 or (2) $1,104?
b. Would you pay $829 for one of these bonds if you thought that the appropriate rate of interest was 12 percent — that is, if k_d = 12%? Explain your answer.

7-8

Yield to call

Six years ago, The Singleton Company sold a 20-year bond issue with a 14 percent annual coupon rate and a 9 percent call premium. Today, Singleton called the bonds. The bonds originally were sold at their face value of $1,000. Compute the realized rate of return for investors who purchased the bonds when they were issued and who surrender them today in exchange for the call price.

7-9

Bond yields;
Financial calculator needed

A 10-year, 12 percent semiannual coupon bond, with a par value of $1,000, may be called in 4 years at a call price of $1,060. The bond sells for $1,100. (Assume that the bond has just been issued.)
a. What is the bond's yield to maturity?
b. What is the bond's current yield?
c. What is the bond's capital gain or loss yield?
d. What is the bond's yield to call?

7-10

Yield to maturity;
Financial calculator needed

You just purchased a bond which matures in 5 years. The bond has a face value of $1,000, and has an 8 percent annual coupon. The bond has a current yield of 8.21 percent. What is the bond's yield to maturity?

7-11

Current yield;
Financial calculater needed

A bond which matures in 7 years sells for $1,020. The bond has a face value of $1,000 and a yield to maturity of 10.5883 percent. The bond pays coupons semiannually. What is the bond's current yield?

7-12

Nominal interest rate

Lloyd Corporation's 14 percent coupon rate, semiannual payment, $1,000 par value bonds, which mature in 30 years, are callable 5 years from now at a price of $1,050. The bonds sell at a price of $1,353.54, and the yield curve is flat. Assuming that interest rates in the economy are expected to remain at their current level, what is the best estimate of Lloyd's nominal interest rate on new bonds?

PROBLEMS

7-13

Bond valuation

Suppose Ford Motor Company sold an issue of bonds with a 10-year maturity, a $1,000 par value, a 10 percent coupon rate, and semiannual interest payments.
a. Two years after the bonds were issued, the going rate of interest on bonds such as these fell to 6 percent. At what price would the bonds sell?
b. Suppose that, 2 years after the initial offering, the going interest rate had risen to 12 percent. At what price would the bonds sell?

c. Suppose that the conditions in Part a existed — that is, interest rates fell to 6 percent 2 years after the issue date. Suppose further that the interest rate remained at 6 percent for the next 8 years. What would happen to the price of the Ford Motor Company bonds over time?

7-14
Bond reporting

Look up the prices of American Telephone & Telegraph's (AT&T) bonds in *The Wall Street Journal* (or some other newspaper which provides this information).
a. If AT&T were to sell a new issue of $1,000 par value long-term bonds, approximately what coupon interest rate would it have to set on the bonds if it wanted to bring them out at par?
b. If you had $10,000 and wanted to invest it in AT&T, what return would you expect to get if you bought AT&T's bonds?

7-15
Discount bond valuation

Assume that in February 1968 the Los Angeles Airport authority issued a series of 3.4 percent, 30-year bonds. Interest rates rose substantially in the years following the issue, and as they did, the price of the bonds declined. In February 1981, 13 years later, the price of the bonds had dropped from $1,000 to $650. In answering the following questions, assume that the bond requires annual interest payments.
a. Each bond originally sold at its $1,000 par value. What was the yield to maturity of these bonds when they were issued?
b. Calculate the yield to maturity in February 1981.
c. Assume that interest rates stabilized at the 1981 level and stayed there for the remainder of the life of the bonds. What would have been the bonds' price in February 1996, when they had 2 years remaining to maturity?
d. What will the price of the bonds be the day before they mature in 1998? (Disregard the last interest payment.)
e. In 1981, the Los Angeles Airport bonds were classified as "discount bonds." What happens to the price of a discount bond as it approaches maturity? Is there a "built-in capital gain" on such bonds?
f. The coupon interest payment divided by the market price of a bond is called the bond's *current yield*. Assuming the conditions in Part c, what would have been the current yield of a Los Angeles Airport bond (1) in February 1981 and (2) in February 1996? What would have been its capital gains yields and total yields (total yield equals yield to maturity) on those same two dates?

7-16
Yield to call

It is now January 1, 1998, and you are considering the purchase of an outstanding Racette Corporation bond that was issued on January 1, 1996. The Racette bond has a 9.5 percent annual coupon and a 30-year original maturity (it matures on December 31, 2025). There is a 5-year call protection (until December 31, 2000), after which time the bond can be called at 109 (that is, at 109 percent of par, or $1,090). Interest rates have declined since the bond was issued, and the bond is now selling at 116.575 percent of par, or $1,165.75. You want to determine both the yield to maturity and the yield to call for this bond. (Note: The yield to call considers the effect of a call provision on the bond's probable yield. In the calculation, we assume that the bond will be outstanding until the call date, at which time it will be called. Thus, the investor will have received interest payments for the call-protected period and then will receive the call price — in this case, $1,090 — on the call date.)
a. What is the yield to maturity in 1998 for the Racette bond? What is its yield to call?
b. If you bought this bond, which return do you think you would actually earn? Explain your reasoning.
c. Suppose the bond had sold at a discount. Would the yield to maturity or the yield to call have been more relevant?

7-17
Interest rate sensitivity;
Financial calculator needed

A bond trader purchased each of the following bonds at a yield to maturity of 8 percent. Immediately after she purchased the bonds, interest rates fell to 7 percent. What is the percentage change in the price of each bond after the decline in interest rates? Fill in the following table:

	PRICE @ 8%	PRICE @ 7%	PERCENTAGE CHANGE
10-year, 10% annual coupon	_____	_____	_____
10-year zero	_____	_____	_____
5-year zero	_____	_____	_____
30-year zero	_____	_____	_____
$100 perpetuity	_____	_____	_____

7-18

Bond valuation;
Financial calculator needed

An investor has two bonds in his portfolio. Each bond matures in 4 years, has a face value of $1,000, and has a yield to maturity equal to 9.6 percent. One bond, Bond C, pays an annual coupon of 10 percent, the other bond, Bond Z, is a zero coupon bond.

a. Assuming that the yield to maturity of each bond remains at 9.6 percent over the next 4 years, what will be the price of each of the bonds at the following time periods? Fill in the following table:

t	PRICE OF BOND C	PRICE OF BOND Z
0	_____	_____
1	_____	_____
2	_____	_____
3	_____	_____
4	_____	_____

b. Plot the time path of the prices for each of the two bonds.

INTEGRATED CASE

WESTERN MONEY MANAGEMENT INC., PART I

7-19 Bond Valuation   Robert Black and Carol Alvarez are vice-presidents of Western Money Management and codirectors of the company's pension fund management division. A major new client, the California League of Cities, has requested that Western present an investment seminar to the mayors of the represented cities, and Black and Alvarez, who will make the actual presentation, have asked you to help them by answering the following questions. Because the Walt Disney Company operates in one of the league's cities, you are to work Disney into the presentation. (See the vignette which opened the chapter for information on Disney.)

a. What are the key features of a bond?

b. What are call provisions and sinking fund provisions? Do these provisions make bonds more or less risky?

c. How is the value of any asset whose value is based on expected future cash flows determined?

d. How is the value of a bond determined? What is the value of a 10-year, $1,000 par value bond with a 10 percent annual coupon if its required rate of return is 10 percent?

e. (1) What would be the value of the bond described in Part d if, just after it had been issued, the expected inflation rate rose by 3 percentage points, causing investors to require a 13 percent return? Would we now have a discount or a premium bond? (If you do not have a financial calculator, $PVIF_{13\%,10} = 0.2946$; $PVIFA_{13\%,10} = 5.4262$.)

(2) What would happen to the bond's value if inflation fell, and k_d declined to 7 percent? Would we now have a premium or a discount bond?

(3) What would happen to the value of the 10-year bond over time if the required rate of return remained at 13 percent, or if it remained at 7 percent? (Hint: With a financial calculator, enter PMT, I, FV, and N, and then change (override) N to see what happens to the PV as the bond approaches maturity.)

f. (1) What is the yield to maturity on a 10-year, 9 percent, annual coupon, $1,000 par value bond that sells for $887.00? That sells for $1,134.20? What does the fact that a bond sells at a discount or at a premium tell you about the relationship between k_d and the bond's coupon rate?

(2) What are the total return, the current yield, and the capital gains yield for the discount bond? (Assume the bond is held to maturity and the company does not default on the bond.)

g. What is *interest rate (or price) risk?* Which bond has more interest rate risk, an annual payment 1-year bond or a 30-year bond? Why?

h. What is *reinvestment rate risk?* Which has more reinvestment rate risk, a 1-year bond or a 10-year bond?

i. How does the equation for valuing a bond change if semiannual payments are made? Find the value of a 10-year, semiannual payment, 10 percent coupon bond if nominal $k_d = 13\%$. (Hint: $PVIF_{6.5\%,20} = 0.2838$ and $PVIFA_{6.5\%,20} = 11.0185$.)

j. Suppose you could buy, for $1,000, either a 10 percent, 10-year, annual payment bond or a 10 percent, 10-year, semiannual payment bond. They are equally risky. Which would you prefer? If $1,000 is the proper price for the semiannual bond, what is the equilibrium price for the annual payment bond?

k. Suppose a 10-year, 10 percent, semiannual coupon bond with a par value of $1,000 is currently selling for $1,135.90, producing a nominal yield to maturity of 8 percent. However, the bond can be called after 5 years for a price of $1,050.

(1) What is the bond's *nominal yield to call (YTC)?*

(2) If you bought this bond, do you think you would be more likely to earn the YTM or the YTC? Why?

l. Disney's bonds were issued with a yield to maturity of 7.5 percent. Does the yield to maturity represent the promised or expected return on the bond?

m. Disney's bonds were rated AA− by S&P. Would you consider these bonds investment grade or junk bonds?

n. What factors determine a company's bond rating?

o. If Disney were to default on the bonds, would the company be immediately liquidated? Would the bondholders be assured of receiving all of their promised payments?

COMPUTER-RELATED PROBLEM

Work the problem in this section only if you are using the computer problem diskette.

7-20

Yield to call

Use the computerized model in the File C7 to solve this problem.

a. Refer back to Problem 7-16. Suppose that on January 1, 1999, the Racette bond is selling for $1,200. What does this indicate about the level of interest rates in 1999 as compared with interest rates a year earlier? What will be the yield to maturity and the yield to call on the Racette bond on this date? Note that the bond now has 27 years remaining until maturity and 2 years until it can be called. Which rate should an investor expect to receive if he or she buys the bond on this date?

b. Suppose that instead of increasing the price, the Racette bond falls to $800 on January 1, 1999. What will be the yield to maturity and the yield to call on this date? Which rate should an investor expect to receive?

APPENDIX 7A

ZERO COUPON BONDS

To understand how zeros are used and analyzed, consider the zeros that are going to be issued by Vandenberg Corporation, a shopping center developer. Vandenberg is developing a new shopping center in San Diego, California, and it needs $50 million. The company does not anticipate major cash flows from the project for about five years. However, Pieter Vandenberg, the president, plans to sell the center once it is fully developed and rented, which should take about five years. Therefore, Vandenberg wants to use a financing vehicle that will not require cash outflows for five years, and he has decided on a five-year zero coupon bond, with a maturity value of $1,000.

Vandenberg Corporation is an A-rated company, and A-rated zeros with five-year maturities yield 6 percent at this time (five-year coupon bonds also yield 6 percent). The company is in the 40 percent federal-plus-state tax bracket. Pieter Vandenberg wants to know the firm's after-tax cost of debt if it uses 6 percent, five-year maturity zeros, and he also wants to know what the bond's cash flows will be. Table 7A-1 provides an analysis of the situation, and the following numbered paragraphs explain the table itself.

1. The information in the "Basic Data" section, except the issue price, was given in the preceding paragraph, and the information in the "Analysis" section was calculated using the known data. The maturity value of the bond is always set at $1,000 or some multiple thereof.

T A B L E   7 A - 1 | Analysis of a Zero Coupon Bond

Basic Data

Maturity value	$1,000
k_d	6.00%, annual compounding
Maturity	5 years
Corporate tax rate	40.00%
Issue price	$747.26

Analysis

	0	1	2	3	4	5 Years
		6%				
(1) Year-end accrued value	$747.26	$792.10	$839.62	$890.00	$943.40	$1,000.00
(2) Interest deduction		44.84	47.52	50.38	53.40	56.60
(3) Tax savings (40%)		17.94	19.01	20.15	21.36	22.64
(4) Cash flow to Vandenberg	+747.26	+17.94	+19.01	+20.15	+21.36	−977.36
After-tax cost of debt	3.60%					

Face value of bonds the company must issue to raise $50 million = Amount needed/Issue price as % of par
= $50,000,000/0.74726
≈ $66,911,000.

2. The issue price is the PV of $1,000, discounted back five years at the rate k_d = 6%, annual compounding. Using the tables, we find PV = $1,000(0.7473) = $747.30. Using a financial calculator, we input N = 5, I = 6, PMT = 0, and FV = 1000, then press the PV key to find PV = $747.26. Note that $747.26, compounded annually for five years at 6 percent, will grow to $1,000 as shown by the time line on Line 1 in Table 7A-1.

3. The accrued values as shown on Line 1 in the analysis section represent the compounded value of the bond at the end of each year. The accrued value for Year 0 is the issue price; the accrued value for Year 1 is found as $747.26(1.06) = $792.10; the accrued value at the end of Year 2 is $747.26(1.06)^2 = $839.62; and, in general, the value at the end of any Year n is

$$\text{Accrued value at the end of Year n} = \text{Issue price} \times (1 + k_d)^n. \quad \textbf{(7A-1)}$$

4. The interest deduction as shown on Line 2 represents the increase in accrued value during the year. Thus, interest in Year 1 = $792.10 − $747.26 = $44.84. In general,

$$\text{Interest in Year n} = \text{Accrued value}_n - \text{Accrued value}_{n-1}. \quad \textbf{(7A-2)}$$

This method of calculating taxable interest is specified in the Tax Code.

5. The company can deduct interest each year, even though the payment is not made in cash. This deduction lowers the taxes that would otherwise be paid, producing the following savings:

$$\text{Tax savings} = (\text{Interest deduction})(T). \quad \textbf{(7A-3)}$$
$$= \$44.84(0.4)$$
$$= \$17.94 \text{ in Year 1.}$$

6. Line 4 represents cash flows on a time line; it shows the cash flow at the end of Years 0 through 5. At Year 0, the company receives the $747.26 issue price. The company also has positive cash inflows equal to the tax savings during Years 1 through 4. Finally, in Year 5, it must pay the $1,000 maturity value, but it gets one more interest tax savings for the year. Therefore, the net cash flow in Year 5 is −$1,000 + $22.64 = −$977.36.

7. Next, we can determine the after-tax cost (or after-tax yield to maturity) of issuing the bonds. Since the cash flow stream is uneven, the after-tax yield to maturity is found by entering the after-tax cash flows, shown in Line 4 of Table 7A-1, into the cash flow register and then pressing the IRR key on the financial calculator. The IRR is the after-tax cost of zero coupon debt to the company. Conceptually, here is the situation:

$$\sum_{t=0}^{n} \frac{CF_n}{(1 + k_{d(AT)})^n} = 0. \quad \textbf{(7A-4)}$$

$$\frac{\$747.26}{(1 + k_{d(AT)})^0} + \frac{\$17.94}{(1 + k_{d(AT)})^1} + \frac{\$19.01}{(1 + k_{d(AT)})^2} + \frac{\$20.15}{(1 + k_{d(AT)})^3} + \frac{\$21.36}{(1 + k_{d(AT)})^4} + \frac{-\$977.36}{(1 + k_{d(AT)})^5} = 0.$$

The value $k_{d(AT)}$ = 0.036 = 3.6%, found with a financial calculator, produces the equality, and it is the cost of this debt. (Input in the cash flow register CF_0 = 747.26, CF_1 = 17.94, and so forth, out to CF_5 = −977.36. Then press the IRR key to find k_d = 3.6%.)

8. Note that $k_d(1 - T) = 6\%(0.6) = 3.6\%$. As we will see in Chapter 9, the cost of capital for regular coupon debt is found using the formula $k_d(1 - T)$. Thus,

there is symmetrical treatment for tax purposes for zero coupon and regular coupon debt; that is, both types of debt use the same after-tax cost formula. This was Congress's intent, and it is why the Tax Code specifies the treatment set forth in Table 7A-1.[1]

Not all original issue discount bonds (OIDs) have zero coupons. For example, Vandenberg might have sold an issue of five-year bonds with a 5 percent coupon at a time when other bonds with similar ratings and maturities were yielding 6 percent. Such bonds would have had a value of $957.88:

$$\text{Bond value} = \sum_{t=1}^{5} \frac{\$50}{(1.06)^t} + \frac{\$1,000}{(1.06)^5} = \$957.88.$$

If an investor had purchased these bonds at a price of $957.88, the yield to maturity would have been 6 percent. The discount of $1,000 − $957.88 = $42.12 would have been amortized over the bond's five-year life, and it would have been handled by both Vandenberg and the bondholders exactly as the discount on the zeros was handled.

Thus, zero coupon bonds are just one type of original issue discount bond. Any nonconvertible bond whose coupon rate is set below the going market rate at the time of its issue will sell at a discount, and it will be classified (for tax and other purposes) as an OID bond.

Shortly after corporations began to issue zeros, investment bankers figured out a way to create zeros from U.S. Treasury bonds, which at the time were issued only in coupon form. In 1982, Salomon Brothers bought $1 billion of 12 percent, 30-year Treasuries. Each bond had 60 coupons worth $60 each, which represented the interest payments due every six months. Salomon then in effect clipped the coupons and placed them in 60 piles; the last pile also contained the now "stripped" bond itself, which represented a promise of $1,000 in the year 2012. These 60 piles of U.S. Treasury promises were then placed with the trust department of a bank and used as collateral for "zero coupon U.S. Treasury Trust Certificates," which are, in essence, zero coupon Treasury bonds. Treasury zeros are, of course, safer than corporate zeros, so they are very popular with pension fund managers. In response to this demand, the Treasury has also created its own "Strips" program, which allows investors to purchase zeros electronically.

Corporate (and municipal) zeros are generally callable at the option of the issuer, just like coupon bonds, after some stated call protection period. The call price is set at a premium over the accrued value at the time of the call. Stripped U.S. Treasury bonds (Treasury zeros) generally are not callable because the Treasury normally sells noncallable bonds. Thus, Treasury zeros are completely protected against reinvestment risk (the risk of having to invest cash flows from a bond at a lower rate because of a decline in interest rates).

---

[1]The purchaser of a zero coupon bond must calculate interest income on the bond in the same manner as the issuer calculates the interest deduction. Thus, in Year 1, a buyer of a bond would report interest income of $44.84 and would pay taxes in the amount of T(Interest income), even though no cash was received. T, of course, would be the bondholder's personal tax rate. Because of the tax situation, most zero coupon bonds are bought by pension funds and other tax-exempt entities. Individuals do, however, buy taxable zeros for their Individual Retirement Accounts (IRAs). Also, state and local governments issue "tax-exempt muni zeros," which are purchased by individuals in high tax brackets.

Note too that we have analyzed the bond as if the cash flows accrued annually. Generally, to facilitate comparisons with semiannual payment coupon bonds, the analysis is conducted on a semiannual basis.

PROBLEMS

7A-1
Zero coupon bonds

A company has just issued 4-year zero coupon bonds with a maturity value of $1,000 and a yield to maturity of 9 percent. The company's tax rate is 40 percent. What is the after-tax cost of debt for the company?

7A-2
Zero coupon bonds

An investor in the 28 percent bracket purchases the bond discussed in Problem 7A-1. What is the investor's after-tax return?

7A-3
Zero coupon bonds and EAR

Assume that the city of Tampa sold tax-exempt (muni), zero coupon bonds 5 years ago. The bonds had a 25-year maturity and a maturity value of $1,000 when they were issued, and the interest rate built into the issue was a nominal 10 percent, but with semiannual compounding. The bonds are now callable at a premium of 10 percent over the accrued value. What effective annual rate of return would an investor who bought the bonds when they were issued and who still owns them earn if they are called today?

BANKRUPTCY AND REORGANIZATION

In the event of bankruptcy, debtholders have a prior claim to a firm's income and assets over the claims of both common and preferred stockholders. Further, different classes of debtholders are treated differently in the event of bankruptcy. Since bankruptcy is a fairly common occurrence, and since it affects both the bankrupt firm and its customers, suppliers, and creditors, it is important to know who gets what if a firm fails. These topics are discussed in this appendix.[1]

FEDERAL BANKRUPTCY LAWS

Bankruptcy actually begins when a firm is unable to meet scheduled payments on its debt or when the firm's cash flow projections indicate that it will soon be unable to meet payments. As the bankruptcy proceedings go forward, the following central issues arise:

1. Does the firm's inability to meet scheduled payments result from a temporary cash flow problem, or does it represent a permanent problem caused by asset values having fallen below debt obligations?

2. If the problem is a temporary one, then an agreement which stretches out payments may be worked out to give the firm time to recover and to satisfy everyone. However, if basic long-run asset values have truly declined, economic losses will have occurred. In this event, who should bear the losses?

3. Is the company "worth more dead than alive" — that is, would the business be more valuable if it were maintained and continued in operation or if it were liquidated and sold off in pieces?

4. Who should control the firm while it is being liquidated or rehabilitated? Should the existing management be left in control, or should a trustee be placed in charge of operations?

These are the primary issues that are addressed in the federal bankruptcy statutes.

Our bankruptcy laws were first enacted in 1898, modified substantially in 1938, changed again in 1978, and further fine-tuned in 1984. The 1978 Act, which provides the basic laws which govern bankruptcy today, was a major revision designed to streamline and expedite proceedings, and it consists of eight odd-numbered chapters, the even-numbered chapters of the earlier Act having been deleted. Chapters 1, 3, and 5 of the 1978 Act contain general provisions applicable to the other chapters; Chapter 7 details the procedures to be followed when liquidating a firm; Chapter 9 deals with financially distressed municipalities; Chapter 11 is the business reorganization chapter; Chapter 13 covers the adjustment of debts for "individuals with regular income"; and Chapter 15 sets up a system of trustees who help administer proceedings under the Act.

This appendix was coauthored by Arthur L. Herrmann of the University of Hartford.

[1]Much of the current work in this area is based on writings by Edward I. Altman. For a summary of his work, and that of others, see Edward I. Altman, "Bankruptcy and Reorganization," in *Handbook of Corporate Finance,* Edward I. Altman, ed. (New York: Wiley, 1986), Chapter 19.

Chapters 11 and 7 are the most important ones for financial management purposes. When you read in the paper that McCrory Corporation or some other company has "filed for Chapter 11," this means that the company is bankrupt and is trying to reorganize under Chapter 11 of the Act. If a reorganization plan cannot be worked out, then the company will be liquidated as prescribed in Chapter 7 of the Act.

The 1978 Act is quite flexible, and it provides a great deal of scope for informal negotiations between a company and its creditors. Under this Act, a case is opened by the filing of a petition with a federal district bankruptcy court. The petition may be either voluntary or involuntary — that is, it may be filed either by the firm's management or by its creditors. A committee of unsecured creditors is then appointed by the court to negotiate with management for a reorganization, which may include the restructuring of debt and other claims against the firm. (A "restructuring" could involve lengthening the maturity of debt, lowering the interest rate on it, reducing the principal amount owed, exchanging common or preferred stock for debt, or some combination of these actions.) A trustee may be appointed by the court if that is deemed to be in the best interests of the creditors and stockholders; otherwise, the existing management will retain control. If no fair and feasible reorganization can be worked out under Chapter 11, the firm will be liquidated under the procedures spelled out in Chapter 7.

FINANCIAL DECISIONS IN BANKRUPTCY

When a business becomes insolvent, a decision must be made whether to dissolve the firm through *liquidation* or to keep it alive through *reorganization*. To a large extent, this decision depends on a determination of the value of the firm if it is rehabilitated versus the value of its assets if they are sold off individually. The procedure that promises higher returns to the creditors and owners will be adopted. However, the "public interest" will also be considered, and this generally means attempting to salvage the firm, even if the salvaging effort may be costly to bondholders. For example, the bankruptcy court kept Eastern Airlines alive, at the cost of millions of dollars which could have been paid to bondholders, until it was obvious even to the judge that Eastern could not be saved. Note, too, that if the decision is made to reorganize the firm, the courts and possibly the SEC will be called upon to determine the fairness and the feasibility of the proposed reorganization plan.

STANDARD OF FAIRNESS. The basic doctrine of *fairness* states that claims must be recognized in the order of their legal and contractual priority. Carrying out this concept of fairness in a reorganization (as opposed to a liquidation) involves the following steps.

1. Future sales must be estimated.
2. Operating conditions must be analyzed so that the future earnings and cash flows can be predicted.
3. A capitalization (or discount) rate to be applied to these future cash flows must be determined.
4. This capitalization rate must then be applied to the estimated cash flows to obtain a present value figure, which is the indicated value for the reorganized company.

5. Provisions for the distribution of the restructured firm's securities to its claimants must be made.

STANDARD OF FEASIBILITY. The primary test of *feasibility* in a reorganization is whether the fixed charges after reorganization can be covered by cash flows. Adequate coverage generally requires an improvement in operating earnings, a reduction of fixed charges, or both. Among the actions that generally must be taken are the following:

1. Debt maturities are usually lengthened, interest rates may be scaled back, and some debt may be converted into equity.
2. When the quality of management has been substandard, a new team must be given control of the company.
3. If inventories have become obsolete or depleted, they must be replaced.
4. Sometimes the plant and equipment must be modernized before the firm can operate on a competitive basis.

LIQUIDATION PROCEDURES

If a company is too far gone to be reorganized, it must be liquidated. Liquidation should occur if a business is worth more dead than alive, or if the possibility of restoring it to financial health is so remote that the creditors would face a high risk of even greater losses if operations were continued.

Chapter 7 of the Bankruptcy Act is designed to do three things: (1) provide safeguards against the withdrawal of assets by the owners of the bankrupt firm, (2) provide for an equitable distribution of the assets among the creditors, and (3) allow insolvent debtors to discharge all of their obligations and to start over unhampered by a burden of prior debt.

The distribution of assets in a liquidation under Chapter 7 of the Bankruptcy Act is governed by the following priority of claims:

1. **Secured creditors, who are entitled to the proceeds of the sale of specific property pledged for a lien or a mortgage.** If the proceeds do not fully satisfy the secured creditors' claims, the remaining balance is treated as a general creditor claim. (See Item 9.)
2. **Trustee's costs to administer and operate the bankrupt firm.**
3. **Expenses incurred after an involuntary case has begun but before a trustee is appointed.**
4. **Wages due workers if earned within three months prior to the filing of the petition of bankruptcy.** The amount of wages is limited to $2,000 per person.
5. **Claims for unpaid contributions to employee benefit plans that were to have been paid within six months prior to filing.** However, these claims, plus wages in Item 4, are not to exceed the $2,000 per employee limit.
6. **Unsecured claims for customer deposits, not to exceed a maximum of $900 per individual.**
7. **Taxes due to federal, state, county, and any other government agency.**
8. **Unfunded pension plan liabilities.** Unfunded pension plan liabilities have a claim above that of the general creditors for an amount up to 30 percent of

the common and preferred equity; any remaining unfunded pension claims rank with the general creditors.

9. **General, or unsecured, creditors.** Holders of trade credit, unsecured loans, the unsatisfied portion of secured loans, and debenture bonds are classified as *general creditors*. Holders of subordinated debt also fall into this category, but they must turn over required amounts to the holders of senior debt, as discussed later in this section.

10. **Preferred stockholders, who can receive an amount up to the par value of the issue.**

11. **Common stockholders, who receive any remaining funds.**

To illustrate how this priority system works, consider the balance sheet of Chiefland Inc., shown in Table 7B-1. The assets have a book value of $90 million. The claims are indicated on the right side of the balance sheet. Note that the debentures are subordinate to the notes payable to banks. Chiefland had filed for reorganization under Chapter 11, but since no fair and feasible reorganization could be arranged, the trustee is liquidating the firm under Chapter 7. The firm also has $15 million of unfunded pension liabilities.[2]

The assets as reported in the balance sheet in Table 7B-1 are greatly overstated; they are, in fact, worth about half of the $90 million at which they are carried. The following amounts are realized on liquidation:

Proceeds from sale of current assets	$41,950,000
Proceeds from sale of fixed assets	5,000,000
Total receipts	$46,950,000

The allocation of available funds is shown in Table 7B-2. The holders of the first mortgage bonds receive the $5 million of net proceeds from the sale of fixed assets. Note that a $1 million unsatisfied claim of the first mortgage holders remains; this claim is added to those of the other general creditors. Next come the fees and expenses of administration, which are typically about 20 percent of gross proceeds; in this example, they are assumed to be $6 million. Next in priority are wages due workers, which total $700,000; taxes due, which amount to $1.3 million; and unfunded pension liabilities of up to 30 percent of the common plus preferred equity, or $12.9 million. Thus far, the total of claims paid from the $46.95 million is $25.90 million, leaving $21.05 million for the general creditors.

---

[2]Under the federal statutes which regulate pension funds, corporations are required to estimate the amount of money needed to provide for the pensions which have been promised to their employees. This determination is made by professional actuaries, taking into account when employees will retire, how long they are likely to live, and the rate of return that can be earned on pension fund assets. If the assets currently in the pension fund are deemed sufficient to make all required payments, the plan is said to be *fully funded*. If assets in the plan are less than the present value of expected future payments, an *unfunded liability* exists. Under federal laws, companies are given up to 30 years to fund any unfunded liabilities. (Note that if a company were fully funded in 1997, but then agreed in 1998 to double pension benefits, this would immediately create a large unfunded liability, and it would need time to make the adjustment. Otherwise, it would be difficult for companies to agree to increase pension benefits.)

Unfunded pension liabilities, including medical benefits to retirees, represent a time bomb ticking in the bowels of many companies. If a company has a relatively old labor force, and if it has promised them substantial retirement benefits but has not set aside assets in a funded pension fund to cover these benefits, it could experience severe trouble in the future. These unfunded pension benefits could even drive the company into bankruptcy, at which point the pension plan would be subject to the bankruptcy laws.

TABLE 7B-1	Chiefland Inc.: Balance Sheet Just before Liquidation (Thousands of Dollars)		
Current assets	$80,000	Accounts payable	$20,000
Net fixed assets	10,000	Notes payable (to banks)	10,000
		Accrued wages, 1,400 @ $500	700
		U.S. taxes	1,000
		State and local taxes	300
		Current liabilities	$32,000
		First mortgage	6,000
		Second mortgage	1,000
		Subordinated debentures[a]	8,000
		Total long-term debt	$15,000
		Preferred stock	2,000
		Common stock	26,000
		Paid-in capital	4,000
		Retained earnings	11,000
		Total equity	$43,000
Total assets	$90,000	Total liabilities and equity	$90,000

[a]Subordinated to $10 million of notes payable to banks.

NOTE: Unfunded pension liabilities are $15 million; this is not reported on the balance sheet.

The claims of the general creditors total $42.1 million. Since $21.05 million is available, claimants will initially be allocated 50 percent of their claims, as shown in Column 2 of Table 7B-2, before the subordination adjustment. This adjustment requires that the holders of subordinated debentures turn over to the holders of notes payable all amounts received until the notes are satisfied. In this situation, the claim of the notes payable is $10 million, but only $5 million is available; the deficiency is therefore $5 million. After transfer of $4 million from the subordinated debentures, there remains a deficiency of $1 million on the notes. This amount will remain unsatisfied.

Note that 92 percent of the first mortgage, 90 percent of the notes payable, and 93 percent of the unfunded pension fund claims are satisfied, whereas a maximum of 50 percent of unsecured claims will be satisfied. These figures illustrate the usefulness of the subordination provision to the security to which the subordination is made. Because no other funds remain, the claims of the holders of preferred and common stock are completely wiped out. Studies of bankruptcy liquidations indicate that unsecured creditors receive, on the average, about 15 cents on the dollar, whereas common stockholders generally receive nothing.

SOCIAL ISSUES IN BANKRUPTCY PROCEEDINGS

An interesting social issue arose in connection with bankruptcy during the 1980s — the role of bankruptcy in settling labor disputes and product liability suits. Normally, bankruptcy proceedings originate after a company has become so financially weak that it cannot meet its current obligations. However, provisions

TABLE   7B-2   Chiefland Inc.: Order of Priority of Claims

Distribution of Proceeds on Liquidation

1. Proceeds from sale of assets $46,950,000
2. First mortgage, paid from sale of fixed assets .... $ 5,000,000
3. Fees and expenses of administration of bankruptcy 6,000,000
4. Wages due workers earned within three months prior to filing of bankruptcy petition ... 700,000
5. Taxes 1,300,000
6. Unfunded pension liabilities[a] 12,900,000 25,900,000
7. Available to general creditors $21,050,000

Distribution to General Creditors

CLAIMS OF GENERAL CREDITORS	CLAIM[b] (1)	APPLICATION OF 50 PERCENT[c] (2)	AFTER SUBORDINATION ADJUSTMENT[d] (3)	PERCENTAGE OF ORIGINAL CLAIMS RECEIVED[e] (4)
Unsatisfied portion of first mortgage	$ 1,000,000	$ 500,000	$ 500,000	92%
Unsatisfied portion of second mortgage	1,000,000	500,000	500,000	50
Notes payable	10,000,000	5,000,000	9,000,000	90
Accounts payable	20,000,000	10,000,000	10,000,000	50
Subordinated debentures	8,000,000	4,000,000	0	0
Pension plan	2,100,000	1,050,000	1,050,000	93
	$42,100,000	$21,050,000	$21,050,000	

[a]Unfunded pension liabilities are $15,000,000, and common and preferred equity total $43,000,000. Unfunded pension liabilities have a prior claim of up to 30 percent of the equity, or $12,900,000, with the remainder, $2,100,000, being treated as a general creditor claim.

[b]Column 1 is the claim of each class of general creditor. Total claims equal $42.1 million.

[c]From Line 7 in the upper section of the table, we see that $21.05 million is available for general creditors. This sum, divided by the $42.1 million of claims, indicates that general creditors will initially receive 50 percent of their claims; this is shown in Column 2.

[d]The debentures are subordinated to the notes payable, so $4 million is reallocated from debentures to notes payable in Column 3.

[e]Column 4 shows the results of dividing the amount in Column 3 by the original claim amount given in Column 1, except for the first mortgage, for which the $5 million received from the sale of fixed assets is included, and the pension plan, for which the $12.9 million is included.

in the Bankruptcy Act permit a company to file for protection under Chapter 11 if *financial forecasts* indicate that a continuation of business under current conditions will lead to insolvency. These provisions were applied by Frank Lorenzo, the principal stockholder of Continental Airlines, who demonstrated that if Continental continued to operate under its then-current union contract, it would become insolvent in a matter of months. The company then filed a plan of reorganization which included major changes in its union contract. The court found for Continental and allowed the company to abrogate its contract. It then reorganized as a nonunion carrier, and that reorganization turned the company from a money loser into a money maker. (However, in 1990, Continental's financial situation reversed again, partly due to rising fuel prices, and the company once again filed for bankruptcy.) Under pressure from labor, Congress changed the bankruptcy laws after the Continental affair to make it more difficult to use the laws to break union contracts.

The bankruptcy laws have also been used to bring about settlements in major product liability suits, the Manville asbestos case being the first, followed by the Dalkon Shield case. In both instances, the companies were being bombarded by literally thousands of lawsuits, and the very existence of such huge contingent liabilities made continued operations virtually impossible. Further, in both cases, it was relatively easy to prove (1) that if the plaintiffs won, the companies would be unable to pay off the full amounts claimed, (2) that a larger amount of funds would be available if the companies continued to operate than if they were liquidated, (3) that continued operations were possible only if the suits were brought to a conclusion, and (4) that a timely resolution of all the suits was impossible because of the number of suits and the different positions taken by different parties. At any rate, the bankruptcy statutes were used to consolidate all the suits and to reach a settlement under which all the plaintiffs obtained more money than they otherwise would have gotten, and the companies were able to stay in business. The stockholders did not do very well because most of the companies' future cash flows were assigned to the plaintiffs, but, even so, the stockholders probably came out better than they would have if the individual suits had been carried through the jury system to a conclusion.

In the Johns-Manville Corporation case, the decision to reorganize was heavily influenced by the prospect of an imminent series of lawsuits. Johns-Manville, a profitable building supplier, faced increasing liabilities resulting from the manufacture of asbestos. When thousands of its employees and consumers were found to be exposed, Johns-Manville filed for Chapter 11 bankruptcy protection and set up a trust fund for the victims as part of its reorganization plan. Present and future claims for exposure were to be paid out of this fund. However, it was later determined that the trust fund was significantly underfunded due to more and larger claims than had been originally estimated.

We have no opinion about the use of the bankruptcy laws to settle social issues such as labor disputes and product liability suits. However, the examples do illustrate how financial projections can be used to demonstrate the effects of different legal decisions. Financial analysis is being used to an increasing extent in various types of legal work, from antitrust cases to suits against stockbrokers by disgruntled customers, and this trend is likely to continue.

PROBLEMS

7B-1
Bankruptcy distributions

The H. Quigley Marble Company has the following balance sheet:

Current assets	$5,040	Accounts payable	$1,080
Fixed assets	2,700	Notes payable (to bank)	540
		Accrued taxes	180
		Accrued wages	180
		Total current liabilities	$1,980
		First mortgage bonds	900
		Second mortgage bonds	900
		Total mortgage bonds	$1,800
		Subordinated debentures	1,080
		Total debt	$4,860
		Preferred stock	360
		Common stock	2,520
Total assets	$7,740	Total liabilities and equity	$7,740

The debentures are subordinated only to the notes payable. Suppose the company goes bankrupt and is liquidated, with $1,800 being received from the sale of the fixed assets, which were pledged as security for the first and second mortgage bonds, and $2,880 received from the sale of current assets. The trustee's costs total $480. How much will each class of investors receive?

7B-2
Bankruptcy distributions

Southwestern Wear Inc. has the following balance sheet:

Current assets	$1,875,000	Accounts payable	$ 375,000
Fixed assets	1,875,000	Notes payable	750,000
		Subordinated debentures	750,000
		Total debt	$1,875,000
		Common equity	1,875,000
Total assets	$3,750,000	Total liabilities and equity	$3,750,000

The trustee's costs total $281,250, and the firm has no accrued taxes or wages. The debentures are subordinated only to the notes payable. If the firm goes bankrupt, how much will each class of investors receive under each of the following conditions?
a. A total of $2.5 million is received from sale of the assets.
b. A total of $1.875 million is received from sale of the assets.

COMPUTER-RELATED PROBLEM

Work the problem in this section only if you are using the computer problem diskette.

7B-3
Bankruptcy distributions

Use the computerized model in the File C7B to solve this problem.
a. Rework Problem 7B-1, assuming that $960 is received from the sale of fixed assets and $2,040 from the sale of current assets.
b. Rework Problem 7B-1, assuming that $1,680 is received from the sale of fixed assets and $3,720 from the sale of current assets.

CHAPTER 8

STOCKS AND
THEIR VALUATION

A $1,000 investment in Disney in 1970 would have grown to $50,000 by 1996, and the same $1,000 investment in Wal-Mart would have done even better — it would have been worth $700,000! However, as any seasoned investor can tell you, stocks can also fall. For example, if at the start of 1994 you had put $1,000 in Gitano, a previously high-flying NYSE apparel company, you would have ended the year with just $50.

All boats rise with the tide, but the same does not hold for the stock market — regardless of the trend, some individual stocks make huge gains while others experience losses. For example, the Dow Jones Industrial Average rose 26 percent in 1996, but IBM gained 66 percent while Bethlehem Steel lost 36 percent. These are both large, relatively stable companies—price swings were even larger for smaller companies.

By virtually any measure, the stock market has performed extraordinarily well in recent years. As of early 1997, the Dow Jones Industrial Average was just over 6700, up nearly 50 percent in a year and a half. To put this in perspective, the Dow reached 1000 in 1965, then took another 22 years to hit 2000, then four more years to reach 3000, and another four years to get to 4000 in 1995. The market has climbed even faster since then — it took only a year to go from 4000 to 5000, and just a few months to pass 6000.

The recent bull market greatly enhanced the wealth of many people, making it possible for them to take early retirement, to buy expensive homes, and to finance large expenditures such as college tuition. Encouraged by this performance, an increasing number of investors have flocked to the market, and today more than 50 million Americans own stock. Moreover, a rising stock market makes it easier and cheaper for corporations to raise equity capital, which sets the stage for continued economic growth.

Some observers, however, are concerned that many investors do not seem to recognize that the stock market is also risky. There is no guarantee that the market will continue to rise, and even in bull markets, not all stocks go up. Federal Reserve Board Chairman Alan Greenspan made the comment that investors may be pushing stock prices up due to "irrational exuberance." If he is right, the market is due for a fall.

While it is difficult to predict prices with precision, we are not completely in the dark when it comes to valuing stocks and determining those most appropriate for a given investor. After studying this chapter, you should have a reasonably good understanding of the factors that influence stock prices; with that knowledge — and a little luck — you might be able to find the next Disney or Wal-Mart, and avoid being a victim of "irrational exuberance."

In Chapter 7 we examined bonds. In this chapter, we take up two other important securities, common and preferred stocks. The value of a stock is determined using the time value of money concepts presented in Chapter 6. However, valuing any asset requires a knowledge of the asset's characteristics, so we begin with some background information on common stock.

LEGAL RIGHTS AND PRIVILEGES OF COMMON STOCKHOLDERS

The common stockholders are the *owners* of a corporation, and as such they have certain rights and privileges as discussed in this section.

CONTROL OF THE FIRM

Its common stockholders have the right to elect a firm's directors, who, in turn, elect the officers who manage the business. In a small firm, the major stockholder typically assumes the positions of president and chairperson of the board of directors. In a large, publicly owned firm, the managers typically have some stock, but their personal holdings are generally insufficient to give them voting control. Thus, the managements of most publicly owned firms can be removed by the stockholders if they decide the management team is not effective.

State and federal laws stipulate how stockholder control is to be exercised. First, corporations must hold an election of directors periodically, usually once a year, with the vote taken at the annual meeting. Frequently, one-third of the directors are elected each year for a three-year term. Each share of stock has one vote; thus, the owner of 1,000 shares has 1,000 votes for each director.[1] Stockholders can appear at the annual meeting and vote in person, but typically they transfer their right to vote to a second party by means of a **proxy.** Management always solicits stockholders' proxies and usually gets them. However, if earnings are poor and stockholders are dissatisfied, an outside group may solicit the proxies in an effort to overthrow management and take control of the business. This is known as a **proxy fight.**

The question of control has become a central issue in finance in recent years. The frequency of proxy fights has increased, as have attempts by one corporation to take over another by purchasing a majority of the outstanding stock. This latter action is called a **takeover.** Some well-known examples of recent takeover battles include KKR's acquisition of RJR Nabisco, Chevron's acquisition of Gulf Oil, and the QVC/Viacom fight to take over Paramount.

Managers who do not have majority control (more than 50 percent of their firms' stock) are very much concerned about proxy fights and takeovers, and many of them are attempting to get stockholder approval for changes in their corporate charters that would make takeovers more difficult. For example, a number of companies have gotten their stockholders to agree (1) to elect only one-third of the directors each year (rather than electing all directors each year), (2) to require 75 percent of the stockholders (rather than 50 percent) to approve a

Proxy
A document giving one person the authority to act for another, typically the power to vote shares of common stock.

Proxy Fight
An attempt by a person or group to gain control of a firm by getting its stockholders to grant that person or group the authority to vote their shares to place a new management into office.

Takeover
An action whereby a person or group succeeds in ousting a firm's management and taking control of the company.

---

[1]In the situation described, a 1,000-share stockholder could cast 1,000 votes for each of three directors if there were three contested seats on the board. An alternative procedure that may be prescribed in the corporate charter calls for *cumulative voting*. Here the 1,000-share stockholder would get 3,000 votes if there were three vacancies, and he or she could cast all of them for one director. Cumulative voting helps small groups to get representation on the board.

merger, and (3) to vote in a "poison pill" provision which would allow the stockholders of a firm that is taken over by another firm to buy shares in the second firm at a reduced price. The poison pill makes the acquisition unattractive and, thus, wards off hostile takeover attempts. Managements seeking such changes generally cite a fear that the firm will be picked up at a bargain price, but it often appears that managers' concerns about their own positions might be an even more important consideration.

Management moves to make takeovers more difficult have been countered by stockholders, especially large institutional stockholders, who do not want to see barriers erected to protect incompetent managers. To illustrate, the California Public Employees Retirement System (Calpers), which is one of the largest institutional investors, announced plans in early 1994 to conduct a proxy fight with several corporations whose financial performances were poor in Calpers' judgment. Calpers wants companies to give outside (nonmanagement) directors more clout and to force managers to be more responsive to stockholder complaints.

Prior to 1993, SEC rules prohibited large investors such as Calpers from getting together to force corporate managers to institute policy changes. However, the SEC changed its rules in 1993, and now large investors can work together to force management changes. One can anticipate that this ruling will serve to keep managers focused on stockholder concerns, which means the maximization of stock prices.

THE PREEMPTIVE RIGHT

Preemptive Right
A provision in the corporate charter or bylaws that gives common stockholders the right to purchase on a pro rata basis new issues of common stock (or convertible securities).

Common stockholders often have the right, called the **preemptive right,** to purchase any additional shares sold by the firm. In some states, the preemptive right is automatically included in every corporate charter; in others, it is necessary to insert it specifically into the charter.

The purpose of the preemptive right is twofold. First, it enables current stockholders to maintain control. If it were not for this safeguard, the management of a corporation could issue a large number of additional shares and purchase these shares itself. Management could thereby seize control of the corporation and frustrate the will of the current stockholders.

The second, and by far the more important, reason for the preemptive right is to protect stockholders against a dilution of value. For example, suppose 1,000 shares of common stock, each with a price of $100, were outstanding, making the total market value of the firm $100,000. If an additional 1,000 shares were sold at $50 a share, or for $50,000, this would raise the total market value to $150,000. When total market value is divided by new total shares outstanding, a value of $75 a share is obtained. The old stockholders thus lose $25 per share, and the new stockholders have an instant profit of $25 per share. Thus, selling common stock at a price below the market value would dilute its price and transfer wealth from the present stockholders to those who were allowed to purchase the new shares. The preemptive right prevents such occurrences.

SELF-TEST QUESTIONS

Identify some actions that companies have taken to make takeovers more difficult.

What are the two primary reasons for the existence of the preemptive right?

TYPES OF COMMON STOCK

Classified Stock
Common stock that is given a special designation, such as Class A, Class B, and so forth, to meet special needs of the company.

Although most firms have only one type of common stock, in some instances **classified stock** is used to meet the special needs of the company. Generally, when special classifications of stock are used, one type is designated *Class A,* another *Class B,* and so on. Small, new companies seeking funds from outside sources frequently use different types of common stock. For example, when Genetic Concepts went public recently, its Class A stock was sold to the public and paid a dividend, but this stock had no voting rights for five years. Its Class B stock, which was retained by the organizers of the company, had full voting rights for five years, but the legal terms stated that dividends could not be paid on the Class B stock until the company had established its earning power by building up retained earnings to a designated level. The use of classified stock thus enabled the public to take a position in a conservatively financed growth company without sacrificing income, while the founders retained absolute control during the crucial early stages of the firm's development. At the same time, outside investors were protected against excessive withdrawals of funds by the original owners. As is often the case in such situations, the Class B stock was called **founders' shares.**

Founders' Shares
Stock owned by the firm's founders that has sole voting rights but restricted dividends for a specified number of years.

Note that "Class A," "Class B," and so on, have no standard meanings. Most firms have no classified shares, but a firm that does could designate its Class B shares as founders' shares and its Class A shares as those sold to the public, while another could reverse these designations. Still other firms could use stock classifications for entirely different purposes. For example, when General Motors acquired Hughes Aircraft for $5 billion, it paid in part with a new Class H common, GMH, which had limited voting rights and whose dividends are tied to Hughes's performance as a GM subsidiary. The reasons for the new stock were reported to be (1) that GM wanted to limit voting privileges on the new classified stock because of management's concern about a possible takeover and (2) that Hughes employees wanted to be rewarded more directly on Hughes's own performance than would have been possible through regular GM stock.

GM's deal posed a problem for the NYSE, which had a rule against listing any company's common stock if the company had any nonvoting common stock outstanding. GM made it clear that it was willing to delist if the NYSE did not change its rules. The NYSE concluded that such arrangements as GM had made were logical and were likely to be made by other companies in the future, so it changed its rules to accommodate GM. In reality, though, the NYSE had little choice. In recent years, the over-the-counter (OTC) market has proven that it can provide a deep, liquid market for common stocks, and the defection of GM would have hurt the NYSE much more than GM.

SELF-TEST QUESTION

What are some reasons why a company might use classified stock?

THE MARKET FOR COMMON STOCK

Some companies are so small that their common stocks are not actively traded; they are owned by only a few people, usually the companies' managers. Such

Closely Held Corporation
A corporation that is owned by a few individuals who are typically associated with the firm's management.

Publicly Owned Corporation
A corporation that is owned by a relatively large number of individuals who are not actively involved in its management.

Over-the-Counter (OTC) Market
The network of dealers that provides for trading in unlisted securities.

Organized Security Exchange
A formal organization, having a tangible physical location, that facilitates trading in designated ("listed") securities. The two major U.S. security exchanges are the New York Stock Exchange (NYSE) and the American Stock Exchange (AMEX).

firms are said to be *privately owned,* or **closely held, corporations,** and their stock is called *closely held stock.* In contrast, the stocks of most larger companies are owned by a large number of investors, most of whom are not active in management. Such companies are called **publicly owned corporations,** and their stock is called *publicly held stock.*

As we saw in Chapter 4, the stocks of smaller publicly owned firms are not listed on an exchange; they trade in the **over-the-counter (OTC) market,** and the companies and their stocks are said to be *unlisted.* However, larger publicly owned companies generally apply for listing on an **organized security exchange,** and they and their stocks are said to be *listed.* Often companies are first listed on a regional exchange such as the Pacific Coast or Midwest Exchange. Then, as they grow, they move up to the American Stock Exchange (AMEX). Finally, if they grow large enough, they are listed on the "Big Board," the New York Stock Exchange (NYSE). About 7,000 stocks are traded in the OTC market, but in terms of market value of both outstanding shares and daily transactions, the NYSE is most important, having about 55 percent of the business.

A recent study found that institutional investors owned about 46 percent of all publicly held common stocks. Included are pension plans (26 percent), mutual funds (10 percent), foreign investors (6 percent), insurance companies (3 percent), and brokerage firms (1 percent). These institutions buy and sell relatively actively, however, so they account for about 75 percent of all transactions. Thus, institutional investors have a heavy influence on the prices of individual stocks.

TYPES OF STOCK MARKET TRANSACTIONS

We can classify stock market transactions into three distinct types:

Secondary Market
The market in which "used" stocks are traded after they have been issued by corporations.

Primary Market
The market in which firms issue new securities to raise corporate capital.

Going Public
The act of selling stock to the public at large by a closely held corporation or its principal stockholders.

1. **Trading in the outstanding shares of established, publicly owned companies: the secondary market.** Allied Food Products, the company we analyzed in earlier chapters, has 50 million shares of stock outstanding. If the owner of 100 shares sells his or her stock, the trade is said to have occurred in the **secondary market.** Thus, the market for outstanding shares, or *used shares,* is the secondary market. The company receives no new money when sales occur in this market.

2. **Additional shares sold by established, publicly owned companies: the primary market.** If Allied decides to sell (or issue) an additional 1 million shares to raise new equity capital, this transaction is said to occur in the **primary market.**[2]

3. **Initial public offerings by privately held firms: the IPO market.** Several years ago, the Coors Brewing Company, which was owned by the Coors family at the time, decided to sell some stock to raise capital needed for a major expansion program.[3] This type of transaction is called **going public** — whenever stock in a closely held corporation is offered to the public for the first time,

---

[2]Allied has 60 million shares authorized but only 50 million outstanding; thus, it has 10 million authorized but unissued shares. If it had no authorized but unissued shares, management could increase the authorized shares by obtaining stockholders' approval, which would generally be granted without any arguments.

[3]The stock Coors offered to the public was designated Class B, and it was nonvoting. The Coors family retained the founders' shares, called Class A stock, which carried full voting privileges. The company was large enough to obtain an NYSE listing, but at that time the Exchange had a requirement that listed common stocks must have full voting rights, which precluded Coors from obtaining an NYSE listing.

INDUSTRY PRACTICE

A WILD INITIAL DAY OF TRADING

It took General Dynamics, a major defense contractor, 43 years to get the value of its stock to $2.7 million. Netscape Communications accomplished the same feat in about one minute in August 1995, when technology-crazed investors had their first chance to buy Netscape's stock on the open market. Never mind that Netscape had never earned a profit or that it had been giving away its primary product free on the Internet.

Netscape produces *Netscape Navigator*, a "web browser" program that enables users to view information on the World Wide Web, the graphical interface portion of the Internet. The company was founded in April 1994 by James Clark, a noted Silicon Valley pioneer, and Marc Andreesen, a 24-year-old techie from the University of Illinois. The IPO (initial public offering) created a nest egg of $565 million for Mr. Clark, who owned 9.7 million shares of Netscape's stock. Mr. Andreesen's gain of $58 million, while not on par

with Mr. Clark's, was not bad for 16 months' work.

How did this all happen? Until August 1995, Netscape had been a privately owned company, with most of the stock owned by four investors: Clark, Andreesen, James Barksdale, who was brought in from McCaw Cellular to be Netscape's president and chief executive officer, and John Doerr, a Silicon Valley venture capitalist. (A venture capitalist is an investor who makes equity investments in startup firms.) To support development of its *Netscape Navigator* and related software, the company needed additional capital, and its best means of raising new funds was to sell common stock to the public. So, on August 8, 1995, the company raised $140 million by selling 5 million shares of common stock at a price of $28 per share.

Original plans called for issuing 3.5 million shares at $14 per share, but demand was so great during the weeks prior to the sale that both the amount and price were increased. Still, investor demand for the stock was so great that the company could have sold 100 million shares. This

pent-up demand caused a near panic on August 9, the first day the shares were publicly traded. Lucky investors who got stock for $28 saw it open at $71 per share on the over-the-counter market, be bid up to $75, and then drop back to end the day at $58.

More than a year later, Netscape's stock continues to attract attention. First, the stock had a 2-for-1 split in 1996, so its adjusted IPO price was $14 rather than $28. Its price range during the last 12 months was $34 to $86, and its latest close was $42. Netscape is currently in a fierce battle with Microsoft to be the dominant Internet browser company. Those who remain bullish on the stock point to the vast growth potential of Internet-related products, as more and more people throughout the world begin surfing the information superhighway. Bears argue, however, that Netscape's stock is wildly overvalued — they are skeptical about both the profit potential of Internet-related products and Netscape's ability to compete with that 800-pound gorilla named Microsoft.

Initial Public Offering (IPO) Market
The market consisting of stocks of companies that are in the process of going public.

the company is said to be going public. The market for stock that is just being offered to the public is called the **initial public offering (IPO) market.**

IPOs have received a lot of attention in recent years, primarily because a number of "hot" issues have realized spectacular gains — often in the first few minutes of trading. Consider the recent IPO of Boston Rotisserie Chicken, which has since been renamed Boston Market. The company's underwriter, Merrill Lynch, set an offering price of $20 a share. However, because of intense demand for the issue, the stock's price rose 75 percent within the first two hours of trading. By the end of the first day, the stock price had risen by 143 percent, and the company's end-of-the-day market value was $800 million — which was particularly startling, given that the company had recently reported a $5 million loss on only $8.3 million of sales. More recently, shares of the trendy restaurant chain Planet Hollywood rose nearly 50 percent in its first day of trading, and when Netscape first hit the market, its stock's price hit $70 a share versus an offering price of only $28 a share. (See the Industry Practice box above, "A Wild Initial Day of Trading.")

Table 8-1 lists the largest, the best performing, and the worst performing IPOs of 1996, and it shows how they performed from their offering dates

| TABLE 8-1 | Initial Public Offerings of 1996 — And How They Performed |

ISSUER	OFFERING DATE	GLOBAL AMOUNT (MILLIONS)	OFFERING PRICE	U.S. AMOUNT (MILLIONS)	12/31/96 PRICE	PERCENT CHANGE[a]
The Biggest						
Lucent Technologies	4/3/96	$3,025.0	$27.00	$2,647.0	$46.25	+71.3%
Associates First Capital	5/7/96	1,943.0	29.00	1,651.6	44.13	+52.2
Deutsche Telekom	11/17/96	11,334.0	18.89	1,605.7	20.38	+ 7.8
New Holland	10/31/96	999.8	21.50	749.8	20.88	− 2.9
Gulfstream Aerospace	10/9/96	888.0	24.00	710.4	24.13	+ 0.5
Travelers/Aetna Property Casualty	4/22/96	885.9	25.00	708.7	35.38	+41.5
Telefonica Del Peru	7/1/96	962.7	20.50	598.8	18.88	− 7.9
Cameco Corp.	3/13/96	524.3	55.19	524.3	40.00	−27.5
Cia. Anonima Nac'l Tel. de Venezuela	11/21/96	1,026.5	23.00	472.0	28.13	+22.3
Sabre Group Holdings	10/10/96	545.4	27.00	436.3	27.88	+ 3.2

ISSUE	OFFERING DATE	OFFERING PRICE	12/31/96 PRICE	PERCENT CHANGE[a]
The Best Performers				
Cymer	9/18/96	$9.50	$48.13	+406.6%
Outdoor Systems	4/24/96	6.67[b]	28.13	+321.9
Sipex	4/2/96	9.50	32.25	+239.5
Whittman-Hart	5/3/96	8.00[a]	25.63	+220.3
Siebel Systems	6/28/96	8.50[b]	27.00	+217.7
Paravant Computer Systems	6/3/96	1.67[b]	5.25	+215.0
Sykes Enterprises	4/29/96	12.00[b]	37.50	+212.5
Pride Automotive Group	4/24/96	5.00	15.38	+207.5
Sawtek	5/1/96	13.00	39.63	+204.8
Pacific Gateway Exchange	7/19/96	12.00	36.50	+204.2
The Worst Performers				
Cable & Co. Worldwide	6/17/96	$6.00	$0.88	−85.42%
N-Vision	5/30/96	5.00	0.81	−83.75
Kaye Kotts Associates	2/22/96	5.00	0.94	−81.25
Thermo-Mizer Environmental	2/28/96	5.00	0.94	−81.25
Riscorp	2/28/96	19.00	3.63	−80.92
Dignity Partners	2/14/96	12.00	2.63	−78.12
Pioneer Commercial Funding	8/13/96	5.00	1.25	−75.00
Multicom Publishing	6/25/96	6.50	1.63	−75.00
Applewoods	4/11/96	2.50[b]	0.63	−75.00
Infonautics	4/30/96	14.00	3.75	−73.21

SOURCE: "Initial Public Offerings of 1996—And How They Performed," *The Wall Street Journal*, January 2, 1997, R4. © 1996 Dow Jones & Company, Inc. All Rights Reserved Worldwide.

[a]Offer to year-end
[b]Adjusted for splits

through year-end 1996. As the table shows, not all IPOs are as well received as were Netscape and Boston Chicken. Moreover, even if you are able to identify a "hot" issue, it is often difficult to purchase shares in the initial offering. These deals are generally *oversubscribed,* which means that the demand for shares at the offering price exceeds the number of shares issued. In such instances, investment bankers favor large institutional investors (who are their best customers), and small investors find it hard, if not impossible, to get in on the ground floor. They can buy the stock in the after-market, but evidence suggests that if you do not get in on the ground floor, the average IPO underperforms the overall market over the longer run.[4]

Finally, it is important to recognize that firms can go public without raising any additional capital. For example, the Ford Motor Company was once owned exclusively by the Ford family. When Henry Ford died, he left a substantial part of his stock to the Ford Foundation. When the Foundation later sold some of this stock to the general public, the Ford Motor Company went public, even though the company raised no capital in the transaction.

SELF-TEST QUESTIONS

Differentiate between a closely held corporation and a publicly owned corporation.

Differentiate between a listed stock and an unlisted stock.

Differentiate between primary and secondary markets.

What is an IPO?

COMMON STOCK VALUATION

Common stock represents an ownership interest in a corporation, but to the typical investor, a share of common stock is simply a piece of paper characterized by two features:

1. It entitles its owner to dividends, but only if the company has earnings out of which dividends can be paid, and only if management chooses to pay dividends rather than retaining and reinvesting all the earnings. Whereas a bond contains a *promise* to pay interest, common stock provides no such promise — if you own a stock, you may *expect* a dividend, but your expectations may not in fact be met. To illustrate, Long Island Lighting Company (LILCO) had paid dividends on its common stock for more than 50 years, and people expected those dividends to continue. However, when the company encountered severe problems a few years ago, it stopped paying dividends. Note, though, that LILCO continued to pay interest on its bonds; if it had not, then it would have been declared bankrupt, and the bondholders could potentially have taken over the company.

2. Stock can be sold at some future date, hopefully at a price greater than the purchase price. If the stock is actually sold at a price above its purchase price, the investor will receive a *capital gain.* Generally, at the time people buy common stocks, they do expect to receive capital gains; otherwise, they would not

---

[4]See Jay R. Ritter, "The Long-Run Performance of Initial Public Offerings," *Journal of Finance,* March 1991, Vol. 46, No. 1, 3–27.

buy the stocks. However, after the fact, one can end up with capital losses rather than capital gains. LILCO's stock price dropped from $17.50 to $3.75 in one year, so the *expected* capital gain on that stock turned out to be a huge *actual* capital loss.

DEFINITIONS OF TERMS USED IN STOCK VALUATION MODELS

Common stocks provide an expected future cash flow stream, and a stock's value is found in the same manner as the values of other financial assets — namely, as the present value of the expected future cash flow stream. The expected cash flows consist of two elements: (1) the dividends expected in each year and (2) the price investors expect to receive when they sell the stock. The expected final stock price includes the return of the original investment plus an expected capital gain.

We saw in Chapter 1 that managers seek to maximize the values of their firms' stocks. A manager's actions affect both the stream of income to investors and the riskiness of that stream. Therefore, managers need to know how alternative actions are likely to affect stock prices. At this point we develop some models to help show how the value of a share of stock is determined. We begin by defining the following terms:

D_t = dividend the stockholder *expects* to receive at the end of Year t. D_0 is the most recent dividend, which has already been paid; D_1 is the first dividend expected, and it will be paid at the end of this year; D_2 is the dividend expected at the end of two years; and so forth. D_1 represents the first cash flow a new purchaser of the stock will receive. Note that D_0, the dividend which has just been paid, is known with certainty. However, all future dividends are expected values, so the estimate of D_t may differ among investors.[5]

P_0 = actual **market price** of the stock today.

Market Price, P_0
The price at which a stock sells in the market.

Intrinsic Value, $\hat{P}_0$
The value of an asset that, in the mind of a particular investor, is justified by the facts; $\hat{P}_0$ may be different from the asset's current market price, its book value, or both.

$\hat{P}_t$ = expected price of the stock at the end of each Year t (pronounced "P hat t"). $\hat{P}_0$ is the **intrinsic,** or *theoretical*, **value** of the stock today as seen by the particular investor doing the analysis; $\hat{P}_1$ is the price expected at the end of one year; and so on. Note that $\hat{P}_0$ is the intrinsic value of the stock today based on a particular investor's estimate of the stock's expected dividend stream and the riskiness of that stream. Hence, whereas the market price P_0 is fixed and is identical for all investors, $\hat{P}_0$ could differ among investors depending on how optimistic they are regarding the company. The caret, or "hat," is used to indicate that $\hat{P}_t$ is an estimated value. $\hat{P}_0$, the individual investor's estimate of the intrinsic value today, could be above or below P_0, the current stock price, but an investor would buy the stock only if his or her estimate of $\hat{P}_0$ were equal to or greater than P_0.

Since there are many investors in the market, there can be many values for $\hat{P}_0$. However, we can think of a group of "average," or "marginal," investors whose actions actually determine the market price.

[5]Stocks generally pay dividends quarterly, so theoretically we should evaluate them on a quarterly basis. However, in stock valuation, most analysts work on an annual basis because the data generally are not precise enough to warrant refinement to a quarterly model. For additional information on the quarterly model, see Charles M. Linke and J. Kenton Zumwalt, "Estimation Biases in Discounted Cash Flow Analysis of Equity Capital Cost in Rate Regulation," *Financial Management*, Autumn 1984,15–21.

For these marginal investors, P_0 must equal $\hat{P}_0$; otherwise, a disequilibrium would exist, and buying and selling in the market would change P_0 until $P_0 = \hat{P}_0$ for a marginal investor.

Growth Rate, g
The expected rate of growth in dividends per share.

g = expected **growth rate** in dividends as predicted by a marginal investor. If dividends are expected to grow at a constant rate, g is also equal to the expected rate of growth in earnings and in the stock's price. Different investors may use different g's to evaluate a firm's stock, but the market price, P_0, is set on the basis of the g estimated by marginal investors.

Required Rate of Return, k_s
The minimum rate of return on a common stock that a stockholder considers acceptable.

k_s = minimum acceptable, or **required, rate of return** on the stock, considering both its riskiness and the returns available on other investments. Again, this term generally relates to marginal investors. The determinants of k_s include the real rate of return, expected inflation, and risk, as discussed in Chapter 5.

Expected Rate of Return, $\hat{k}_s$
The rate of return on a common stock that a stockholder expects to receive.

$\hat{k}_s$ = **expected rate of return** which an investor who buys the stock expects to receive. $\hat{k}_s$ (pronounced "k hat s") could be above or below k_s, but one would buy the stock only if $\hat{k}_s$ were equal to or greater than k_s.

Actual Realized Rate of Return, $\bar{k}_s$
The rate of return on a common stock actually received by stockholders. $\bar{k}_s$ may be greater or less than $\hat{k}_s$ and/or k_s.

$\bar{k}_s$ = **actual,** or **realized,** *after-the-fact* **rate of return,** pronounced "k bar s." You may *expect* to obtain a return of $\hat{k}_s = 15$ percent if you buy Exxon stock today, but if the market goes down, you may end up next year with an actual realized return that is much lower, perhaps even negative.

Dividend Yield
The expected dividend divided by the current price of a share of stock.

D_1/P_0 = expected **dividend yield** on the stock during the coming year. If the stock is expected to pay a dividend of $D_1 = \$1$ during the next 12 months, and if its current price is $P_0 = \$10$, then the expected dividend yield is $\$1/\$10 = 0.10 = 10\%$.

Capital Gains Yield
The capital gain during a given year divided by the beginning price.

$\dfrac{\hat{P}_1 - P_0}{P_0}$ = expected **capital gains yield** on the stock during the coming year. If the stock sells for $10 today, and if it is expected to rise to $10.50 at the end of one year, then the expected capital gain is $\hat{P}_1 - P_0 = \$10.50 - \$10.00 = \$0.50$, and the expected capital gains yield is $\$0.50/\$10 = 0.05 = 5\%$.

Expected Total Return
The sum of the expected dividend yield and the expected capital gains yield.

Expected total return = $\hat{k}_s$ = expected dividend yield (D_1/P_0) plus expected capital gains yield $[(\hat{P}_1 - P_0)/P_0]$. In our example, the **expected total return** = $\hat{k}_s$ = $10\% + 5\% = 15\%$.

EXPECTED DIVIDENDS AS THE BASIS FOR STOCK VALUES

In our discussion of bonds, we found the value of a bond as the present value of interest payments over the life of the bond plus the present value of the bond's maturity (or par) value:

$$V_B = \frac{INT}{(1 + k_d)^1} + \frac{INT}{(1 + k_d)^2} + \cdots + \frac{INT}{(1 + k_d)^N} + \frac{M}{(1 + k_d)^N}.$$

Stock prices are likewise determined as the present value of a stream of cash flows, and the basic stock valuation equation is similar to the bond valuation equation. What are the cash flows that corporations provide to their stockholders? First, think of yourself as an investor who buys a stock with the intention of holding it (in your family) forever. In this case, all that you (and your heirs) will receive is a stream of dividends, and the value of the stock today is calculated as the present value of an infinite stream of dividends:

$$\text{Value of stock} = \hat{P}_0 = \text{PV of expected future dividends}$$

$$= \frac{D_1}{(1 + k_s)^1} + \frac{D_2}{(1 + k_s)^2} + \cdots + \frac{D_\infty}{(1 + k_s)^\infty}$$

$$= \sum_{t=1}^{\infty} \frac{D_t}{(1 + k_s)^t}. \tag{8-1}$$

What about the more typical case, where you expect to hold the stock for a finite period and then sell it — what will be the value of $\hat{P}_0$ in this case? Unless the company is likely to be liquidated and thus to disappear, *the value of the stock is again determined by Equation 8-1*. To see this, recognize that for any individual investor, the expected cash flows consist of expected dividends plus the expected sale price of the stock. However, the sale price the current investor receives will depend on the dividends some future investor expects. Therefore, for all present and future investors in total, expected cash flows must be based on expected future dividends. Put another way, unless a firm is liquidated or sold to another concern, the cash flows it provides to its stockholders will consist only of a stream of dividends; therefore, the value of a share of its stock must be established as the present value of that expected dividend stream.

The general validity of Equation 8-1 can also be confirmed by asking the following question: Suppose I buy a stock and expect to hold it for one year. I will receive dividends during the year plus the value $\hat{P}_1$ when I sell out at the end of the year. But what will determine the value of $\hat{P}_1$? The answer is that it will be determined as the present value of the dividends expected during Year 2 plus the stock price at the end of that year, which, in turn, will be determined as the present value of another set of future dividends and an even more distant stock price. This process can be continued ad infinitum, and the ultimate result is Equation 8-1.[6]

Equation 8-1 is a generalized stock valuation model in the sense that the time pattern of D_t can be anything: D_t can be rising, falling, or constant, it can be fluctuating randomly, or it can even be zero for several years, and Equation 8-1 will still hold. Often, however, the projected stream of dividends follows a systematic pattern, in which case we can develop a simplified (that is, easier to evaluate) version of the stock valuation model expressed in Equation 8-1. In the following sections, we consider the cases of zero growth, constant growth, and nonconstant growth.

Zero Growth Stock
A common stock whose future dividends are not expected to grow at all; that is, g = 0.

STOCK VALUES WITH ZERO GROWTH

Suppose dividends are not expected to grow at all but to remain constant. Here we have a **zero growth stock,** for which the dividends expected in future years

---

[6]We should note that investors periodically lose sight of the long-run nature of stocks as investments and forget that in order to sell a stock at a profit, one must find a buyer who will pay the higher price. If you analyzed a stock's value in accordance with Equation 8-1, concluded that the stock's market price exceeded a reasonable value, and then bought the stock anyway, then you would be following the "bigger fool" theory of investment — you think that you may be a fool to buy the stock at its excessive price, but you also think that when you get ready to sell it, you can find someone who is an even bigger fool. The bigger fool theory was widely followed in the summer of 1987, just before the stock market lost more than one-third of its value in the October 1987 crash. Many people think it is back in vogue now, in early 1997.

are equal to some constant amount — that is, $D_1 = D_2 = D_3$ and so on. Therefore, we can drop the subscripts on D and rewrite Equation 8-1 as follows:

$$\hat{P}_0 = \frac{D}{(1 + k_s)^1} + \frac{D}{(1 + k_s)^2} + \cdots + \frac{D}{(1 + k_s)^\infty}. \qquad (8\text{-}1a)$$

As we noted in Chapter 6 in connection with the British consol bond and also in our discussion of preferred stocks, a security that is expected to pay a constant amount each year forever is called a perpetuity. *Therefore, a zero growth stock is a perpetuity.*

Although a zero growth stock is expected to provide a constant stream of dividends into the indefinite future, each dividend has a smaller present value than the preceding one, and as N gets very large, the present value of the future dividends approaches zero. To illustrate, suppose D = $1.15 and k_s = 13.4%. We can rewrite Equation 8-1a as follows:

$$\hat{P}_0 = \frac{\$1.15}{(1.134)^1} + \frac{\$1.15}{(1.134)^2} + \frac{\$1.15}{(1.134)^3} + \cdots + \frac{\$1.15}{(1.134)^{50}} + \cdots + \frac{\$1.15}{(1.134)^{100}} + \cdots$$

$$= \$1.01 + \$0.89 + \$0.79 + \cdots + \$0.002 + \cdots + \$0.000004 + \cdots$$

We can also show the zero growth stock in graph form, as in Figure 8-1. The horizontal line shows the constant dividend stream, D_t = $1.15. The descending step function curve shows the present value of each future dividend. If we extended the analysis on out to infinity and then summed the present values of all the future dividends, the sum would be equal to the value of the stock.

As we saw in Chapter 6, the value of any perpetuity is simply the payment divided by the discount rate, so the value of a zero growth stock reduces to this formula:

$$\hat{P}_0 = \frac{D}{k_s}. \qquad (8\text{-}2)$$

Therefore, the value of our illustrative stock is $8.58:

$$\hat{P}_0 = \frac{\$1.15}{0.134} = \$8.58.$$

If you extended Figure 8-1 on out forever and then added up the present value of each individual dividend, you would end up with the intrinsic value of the stock, $8.58.[7] The actual market price of the stock, P_0, could be greater than, less than, or equal to $8.58, depending on other investors' perceptions of the dividend pattern and riskiness of the stock.

We could transpose the $\hat{P}_0$ and the k_s in Equation 8-2 and solve for k_s to produce Equation 8-3:

$$\hat{k}_s = \frac{D}{P_0}. \qquad (8\text{-}3)$$

We could then look up the price of the stock and the latest dividend, P_0 and D, in the newspaper, and D/P_0 would be the rate of return we could expect to earn if

---

[7]If you think that having a stock pay dividends forever is unrealistic, then think of it as lasting only for 50 years. Here you would have an annuity of $1.15 per year for 50 years discounted at 13.4 percent. Enter N = 50, I = 13.4, and PMT = 1.15, and then press PV to find the value of the annuity. It is $8.57, which differs by only a penny from that of the perpetuity. Thus, the dividends from Years 51 to infinity contribute almost nothing to the value of the stock.

FIGURE 8-1 Present Values of Dividends of a Zero Growth Stock
(Perpetuity)

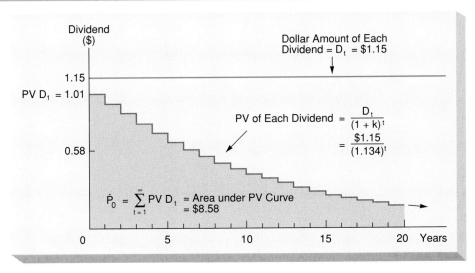

we bought the stock. Since we are dealing with an *expected rate of return,* we put a "hat" on the k value. Thus, if we bought the stock at a price of $8.58 and expected to receive a constant dividend of $1.15, our expected rate of return would be

$$\hat{k}_s = \frac{\$1.15}{\$8.58} = 0.134 = 13.4\%.$$

NORMAL, OR CONSTANT, GROWTH

Although the zero growth model is applicable to a few companies, the earnings and dividends of most companies are expected to increase over time. Expected growth rates vary from company to company, but dividend growth on average is expected to continue in the foreseeable future at about the same rate as that of the nominal gross domestic product (real GDP plus inflation). On this basis, one might expect the dividend of an average, or "normal," company to grow at a rate of 6 to 8 percent a year. Thus, if a **normal,** or **constant, growth** company's last dividend, which has already been paid, was D_0, its dividend in any future Year t may be forecasted as $D_t = D_0(1 + g)^t$, where g is the constant expected rate of growth. For example, if Allied Food Products just paid a dividend of $1.15 (that is, $D_0 = \$1.15$), and if investors expect an 8 percent growth rate, then the estimated dividend one year hence would be $D_1 = \$1.15(1.08) = \$1.24$; D_2 would be $1.34; and the estimated dividend five years hence would be

$$D_t = D_0(1 + g)^t = \$1.15(1.08)^5 = \$1.69.$$

Using this method for estimating future dividends, we can determine the current stock value, $\hat{P}_0$, using Equation 8-1 as set forth previously — in other words, we can find the expected future cash flow stream (the dividends), then calculate the present value of each dividend payment, and finally sum these present values to find the value of the stock. Thus, the intrinsic value of the stock is equal to the present value of its expected future dividends.

Normal (Constant) Growth
Growth which is expected to continue into the foreseeable future at about the same rate as that of the economy as a whole; g is a constant.

If g is constant, Equation 8-1 may be rewritten as follows:[8]

$$\hat{P}_0 = \frac{D_0(1 + g)^1}{(1 + k_s)^1} + \frac{D_0(1 + g)^2}{(1 + k_s)^2} + \cdots + \frac{D_0(1 + g)^\infty}{(1 + k_s)^\infty}$$

$$= \frac{D_0(1 + g)}{k_s - g} = \frac{D_1}{k_s - g}. \tag{8-4}$$

Inserting values into Equation 8-4, we find the value of our illustrative stock to be $23.00:

$$\hat{P}_0 = \frac{\$1.15(1.08)}{0.134 - 0.08} = \frac{\$1.242}{0.054} = \$23.00.$$

Constant Growth Model
Also called the Gordon Model, it is used to find the value of a constant growth stock.

The **constant growth model** as set forth in the last term of Equation 8-4 is often called the Gordon Model, after Myron J. Gordon, who did much to develop and popularize it.

Note that Equation 8-4 is sufficiently general to encompass the zero growth case described earlier: If growth is zero, this is simply a special case of constant growth, and Equation 8-4 is equal to Equation 8-2. Note also that a necessary condition for the derivation of Equation 8-4 is that k_s be greater than g. If the equation is used in situations where k_s is not greater than g, the results will be both wrong and meaningless.

The concept underlying the valuation process for a constant growth stock is graphed in Figure 8-2. Dividends are growing at the rate g = 8%, but because $k_s > g$, the present value of each future dividend is declining. For example, the dividend in Year 1 is $D_1 = D_0(1 + g)^1 = \$1.15(1.08) = \$1.242$. However, the present value of this dividend, discounted at 13.4 percent, is $PV(D_1) = \$1.242/(1.134)^1 = \$1.095$. The dividend expected in Year 2 grows to $\$1.242(1.08) = \$1.341$, but the present value of this dividend falls to $1.04. Continuing, $D_3 = \$1.449$ and $PV(D_3) = \$0.993$, and so on. Thus, the expected dividends are growing, but the present value of each successive dividend is declining, because the dividend growth rate (8%) is less than the rate used for discounting the dividends to the present (13.4%).

If we summed the present values of each future dividend, this summation would be the value of the stock, $\hat{P}_0$. When g is a constant, this summation is equal to $D_1/(k_s - g)$, as shown in Equation 8-4. Therefore, if we extended the lower step function curve in Figure 8-2 on out to infinity and added up the present values of each future dividend, the summation would be identical to the value given by Equation 8-4, $23.00.

Growth in dividends occurs primarily as a result of growth in *earnings per share (EPS)*. Earnings growth, in turn, results from a number of factors, including (1) inflation, (2) the amount of earnings the company retains and reinvests, and (3) the rate of return the company earns on its equity (ROE). Regarding inflation, if output (in units) is stable, but both sales prices and input costs rise at the inflation rate, then EPS will also grow at the inflation

---

[8]The last term in Equation 8-4 is derived in Appendix 4A of Eugene F. Brigham and Louis C. Gapenski, *Intermediate Financial Management,* 5th ed. (Fort Worth, Tex.: Dryden Press, 1996). In essence, Equation 8-4 is the sum of a geometric progression, and the final result is the solution value of the progression.

| FIGURE 8-2 | Present Values of Dividends of a Constant Growth Stock: $D_0 = \$1.15$, $g = 8\%$, $k_s = 13.4\%$ |

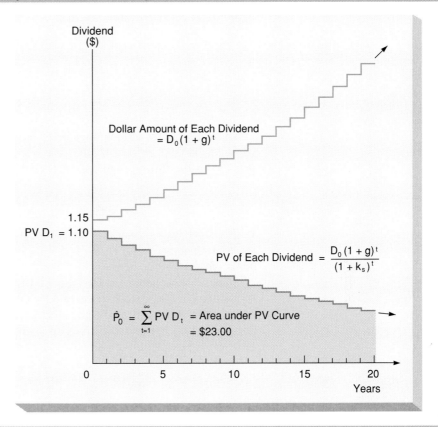

rate. Even without inflation, EPS will also grow as a result of the reinvestment, or plowback, of earnings. If the firm's earnings are not all paid out as dividends (that is, if some fraction of earnings is retained), the dollars of investment behind each share will rise over time, which should lead to growth in earnings and dividends.

Even though a stock's value is derived from expected dividends, this does not necessarily mean that corporations can increase their stock prices by simply raising the current dividend. Shareholders care about *all* dividends, both current and those expected in the future. Moreover, there is a trade-off between current dividends and future dividends. Companies that pay high current dividends necessarily retain and reinvest less of their earnings in the business, and that reduces future earnings and dividends. So, the issue is this: Do shareholders prefer higher current dividends at the cost of lower future dividends, the reverse, or are stockholders indifferent? As we will see in Chapter 14, there is no simple answer to this question. Shareholders prefer to have the company retain earnings, hence pay less current dividends, if it has highly profitable investment opportunities, but they want the company to pay earnings out if investment opportunities are poor. Taxes also play a role, as dividends and capital gains are taxed differently, so dividend policy affects investors' taxes. We will consider dividend policy in detail in Chapter 14.

EXPECTED RATE OF RETURN ON A CONSTANT GROWTH STOCK

We can solve Equation 8-4 for k_s, again using the hat to denote that we are dealing with an expected rate of return:[9]

$$\begin{array}{c} \text{Expected rate} \\ \text{of return} \end{array} = \begin{array}{c} \text{Expected} \\ \text{dividend} \\ \text{yield} \end{array} + \begin{array}{c} \text{Expected growth} \\ \text{rate, or capital} \\ \text{gains yield} \end{array}$$

$$\hat{k}_s = \frac{D_1}{P_0} + g. \qquad (8\text{-}5)$$

Thus, if you buy a stock for a price $P_0 = \$23$, and if you expect the stock to pay a dividend $D_1 = \$1.242$ one year from now and to grow at a constant rate $g = 8\%$ in the future, then your expected rate of return will be 13.4 percent:

$$\hat{k}_s = \frac{\$1.242}{\$23} + 8\% = 5.4\% + 8\% = 13.4\%.$$

In this form, we see that $\hat{k}_s$ is the *expected total return* and that it consists of an *expected dividend yield,* $D_1/P_0 = 5.4\%$, plus an *expected growth rate or capital gains yield,* $g = 8\%$.

Suppose this analysis had been conducted on January 1, 1998, so $P_0 = \$23$ is the January 1, 1998, stock price, and $D_1 = \$1.242$ is the dividend expected at the end of 1998. What is the expected stock price at the end of 1998? We would again apply Equation 8-4, but this time we would use the year-end dividend, $D_2 = D_1 (1 + g) = \$1.242(1.08) = \$1.3414$:

$$\hat{P}_{12/31/98} = \frac{D_{1999}}{k_s - g} = \frac{\$1.3414}{0.134 - 0.08} = \$24.84.$$

Now, notice that $24.84 is 8 percent greater than P_0, the $23 price on January 1, 1998:

$$\$23(1.08) = \$24.84.$$

Thus, we would expect to make a capital gain of $24.84 − $23.00 = $1.84 during 1998, which would provide a capital gains yield of 8 percent:

$$\text{Capital gains yield}_{1998} = \frac{\text{Capital gain}}{\text{Beginning price}} = \frac{\$1.84}{\$23.00} = 0.08 = 8\%.$$

We could extend the analysis on out, and in each future year the expected capital gains yield would always equal g, the expected dividend growth rate.

Continuing, the dividend yield in 1999 could be estimated as follows:

$$\text{Dividend yield}_{1999} = \frac{D_{1999}}{\hat{P}_{12/31/98}} = \frac{\$1.3414}{\$24.84} = 0.054 = 5.4\%.$$

The dividend yield for 2000 could also be calculated, and again it would be 5.4 percent. Thus, *for a constant growth stock,* the following conditions must hold:

1. The dividend is expected to grow forever at a constant rate, g.
2. The stock price is expected to grow at this same rate.

---

[9]The k_s value in Equation 8-4 is a *required* rate of return, but when we transform to obtain Equation 8-5, we are finding an *expected* rate of return. Obviously, the transformation requires that $k_s = \hat{k}_s$. This equality holds if the stock market is in equilibrium, a condition that will be discussed later in the chapter.

3. The expected dividend yield is a constant.

4. The expected capital gains yield is also a constant, and it is equal to g.

5. The expected total rate of return, $\hat{k}_s$, is equal to the expected dividend yield plus the expected growth rate: $\hat{k}_s$ = dividend yield + g.

The term *expected* should be clarified — it means expected in a probabilistic sense, as the statistically expected outcome. Thus, if we say the growth rate is expected to remain constant at 8 percent, we mean that the best prediction for the growth rate in any future year is 8 percent, not that we literally expect the growth rate to be exactly 8 percent in each future year. In this sense, the constant growth assumption is a reasonable one for many large, mature companies.

SUPERNORMAL, OR NONCONSTANT, GROWTH

Firms typically go through *life cycles.* During the early part of their lives, their growth is much faster than that of the economy as a whole; then they match the economy's growth; and finally their growth is slower than that of the economy.[10] Automobile manufacturers in the 1920s and computer software firms such as Microsoft in the 1990s are examples of firms in the early part of the cycle; these firms are called **supernormal,** or **nonconstant, growth** firms. Figure 8-3 illustrates nonconstant growth and also compares it with normal growth, zero growth, and negative growth.[11]

In the figure, the dividends of the supernormal growth firm are expected to grow at a 30 percent rate for three years, after which the growth rate is expected to fall to 8 percent, the assumed average for the economy. The value of this firm, like any other, is the present value of its expected future dividends as determined by Equation 8-1. In the case in which D_t is growing at a constant rate, we simplified Equation 8-1 to $\hat{P}_0 = D_1/(k_s - g)$. In the supernormal case, however, the expected growth rate is not a constant — it declines at the end of the period of supernormal growth.

To find the value of such a stock, or of any nonconstant growth stock when the growth rate will eventually stabilize, we proceed in three steps:

1. Find the PV of the dividends during the period of nonconstant growth.

2. Find the price of the stock at the end of the nonconstant growth period, at which point it has become a constant growth stock, and discount this price back to the present.

3. Add these two components to find the intrinsic value of the stock, $\hat{P}_0$.

Supernormal (Nonconstant) Growth
The part of the life cycle of a firm in which it grows much faster than the economy as a whole.

---

[10] The concept of life cycles could be broadened to *product cycle,* which would include both small startup companies and large companies like Procter & Gamble, which periodically introduce new products that give sales and earnings a boost. We should also mention *business cycles,* which alternately depress and boost sales and profits. The growth rate just after a major new product has been introduced, or just after a firm emerges from the depths of a recession, is likely to be much higher than the "expected long-run average growth rate," which is the proper number for a DCF analysis.

[11] A negative growth rate indicates a declining company. A mining company whose profits are falling because of a declining ore body is an example. Someone buying such a company would expect its earnings, and consequently its dividends and stock price, to decline each year, and this would lead to capital losses rather than capital gains. Obviously, a declining company's stock price will be relatively low, and its dividend yield must be high enough to offset the expected capital loss and still produce a competitive total return. Students sometimes argue that they would not be willing to buy a stock whose price was expected to decline. However, if the annual dividends are large enough to *more than offset* the falling stock price, the stock could still provide a good return.

FIGURE 8-3 Illustrative Dividend Growth Rates

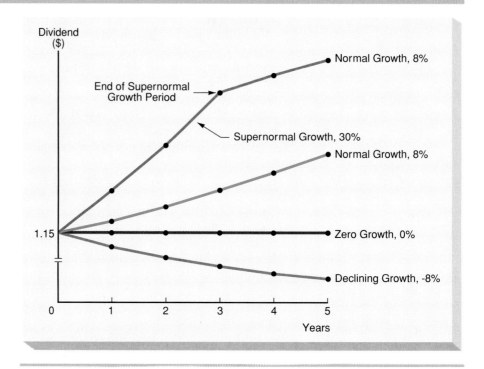

Figure 8-4 can be used to illustrate the process for valuing nonconstant growth stocks, assuming the following five facts exist:

k_s = stockholders' required rate of return = 13.4%. This rate is used to discount the cash flows.

N = years of supernormal growth = 3.

g_s = rate of growth in both earnings and dividends during the supernormal growth period = 30%. (Note: The growth rate during the supernormal growth period could vary from year to year. Also, there could be several different supernormal growth periods, e.g., 30% for three years, then 20% for three years, and then a constant 8%.) This rate is shown directly on the time line.

g_n = rate of normal, constant growth after the supernormal period = 8%. This rate is also shown on the time line, between Periods 3 and 4.

D_0 = last dividend the company paid = $1.15.

The valuation process as diagrammed in Figure 8-4 is explained in the steps set forth below the time line. The value of the supernormal growth stock is calculated to be $39.21.

FIGURE 8-4 | Process for Finding the Value of a Supernormal Growth Stock

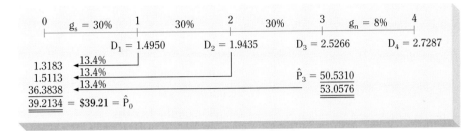

Notes to Figure 8-4:

Step 1. Calculate the dividends expected at the end of each year during the supernormal growth period. Calculate the first dividend, $D_1 = D_0(1 + g_s) = \$1.15(1.30) = \$1.4950$. Here g_s is the growth rate during the three-year supernormal growth period, 30 percent. Show the $1.4950 on the time line as the cash flow at Time 1. Then, calculate $D_2 = D_1(1 + g_s) = \$1.4950(1.30) = \$1.9435$, and then $D_3 = D_2(1 + g_s) = \$1.9435(1.30) = \$2.5266$. Show these values on the time line as the cash flows at Time 2 and Time 3. Note that D_0 is used only to calculate D_1.

Step 2. The price of the stock is the PV of dividends from Time 1 to infinity, so in theory we could project each future dividend, with the normal growth rate, $g_n = 8\%$, used to calculate D_4 and subsequent dividends. However, we know that after D_3 has been paid, which is at Time 3, the stock becomes a constant growth stock. Therefore, we can use the constant growth formula to find $\hat{P}_3$, which is the PV of the dividends from Time 4 to infinity as evaluated at Time 3.

First, we determine $D_4 = \$2.5266(1.08) = \$2.7287$ for use in the formula, and then we calculate $\hat{P}_3$ as follows:

$$\hat{P}_3 = \frac{D_4}{k_s - g_n} = \frac{\$2.7287}{0.134 - 0.08} = \$50.5310.$$

We show this $50.5310 on the time line as a second cash flow at Time 3. The $50.5310 is a Time 3 cash flow in the sense that the owner of the stock could sell it for $50.5310 at Time 3 and also in the sense that $50.5310 is the present value of the dividend cash flows from Time 4 to infinity. Note that the *total cash flow* at Time 3 consists of the sum of $D_3 + \hat{P}_3 = \$2.5266 + \$50.5310 = \$53.0576$.

Step 3. Now that the cash flows have been placed on the time line, we can discount each cash flow at the required rate of return, $k_s = 13.4\%$. We could discount each flow by dividing by $(1.134)^t$, where $t = 1$ for Time 1, $t = 2$ for Time 2, and $t = 3$ for Time 3. This produces the PVs shown to the left below the time line, and the sum of the PVs is the value of the supernormal growth stock, $39.21.

With a financial calculator, you can find the PV of the cash flows as shown on the time line with the cash flow (CFLO) register of your calculator. Enter 0 for CF_0 because you get no cash flow at Time 0, $CF_1 = 1.495$, $CF_2 = 1.9435$, and $CF_3 = 2.5266 + 50.531 = 53.0576$. Then enter I = 13.4, and press the NPV key to find the value of the stock, $39.21.

SELF-TEST QUESTIONS ??????

Explain the following statement: "Whereas a bond contains a promise to pay interest, common stock typically provides an expectation of but no promise of dividends plus capital gains."

What are the two parts of a stock's expected total return?

Write out and explain the valuation model for a zero growth stock.

Write out and explain the valuation model for a constant growth stock.

How does one calculate the capital gains yield and the dividend yield of a stock?

Explain how one would find the value of a supernormal growth stock.

STOCK MARKET EQUILIBRIUM

Recall from Chapter 5 that the required return on Stock X, k_X, can be found using the Security Market Line (SML) equation as it was developed in our discussion of the Capital Asset Pricing Model (CAPM):

$$k_X = k_{RF} + (k_M - k_{RF}) b_X.$$

If the risk-free rate of return is 8 percent, if the required return on an average stock is 12 percent, and if Stock X has a beta of 2, then the marginal investor will require a return of 16 percent on Stock X, calculated as follows:

$$k_X = 8\% + (12\% - 8\%) 2.0$$
$$= 16\%.$$

This 16 percent required return is shown as the point on the SML in Figure 8-5 associated with beta = 2.0.

FIGURE 8 - 5   Expected and Required Returns on Stock X

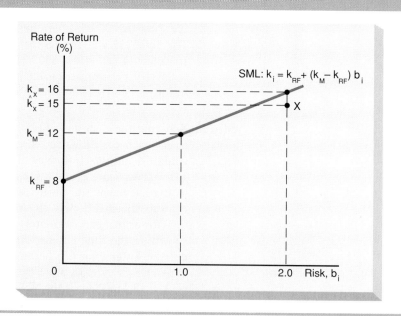

Marginal Investor
A representative investor whose actions reflect the beliefs of those people who are currently trading a stock. It is the marginal investor who determines a stock's price.

The **marginal investor** will want to buy Stock X if its expected rate of return is more than 16 percent, will want to sell it if the expected rate of return is less than 16 percent, and will be indifferent, hence will hold but not buy or sell, if the expected rate of return is exactly 16 percent. Now suppose the investor's portfolio contains Stock X, and he or she analyzes the stock's prospects and concludes that its earnings, dividends, and price can be expected to grow at a constant rate of 5 percent per year. The last dividend was $D_0 = \$2.8571$, so the next expected dividend is

$$D_1 = \$2.8571(1.05) = \$3.$$

Our marginal investor observes that the present price of the stock, P_0, is $30. Should he or she purchase more of Stock X, sell the stock, or maintain the present position?

The investor can calculate Stock X's *expected rate of return* as follows:

$$\hat{k}_X = \frac{D_1}{P_0} + g = \frac{\$3}{\$30} + 5\% = 15\%.$$

This value is plotted on Figure 8-5 as Point X, which is below the SML. Because the expected rate of return is less than the required return, this marginal investor would want to sell the stock, as would most other holders. However, few people would want to buy at the $30 price, so the present owners would be unable to find buyers unless they cut the price of the stock. Thus, the price would decline, and this decline would continue until the stock's price reached $27.27, at which point the market for this security would be in **equilibrium,** defined as the price at which the expected rate of return, 16 percent, is equal to the required rate of return:

Equilibrium
The condition under which the expected return on a security is just equal to its required return, $\hat{k} = k$. Also, $\hat{P}_0 = P_0$, and the price is stable.

$$\hat{k}_X = \frac{\$3}{\$27.27} + 5\% = 11\% + 5\% = 16\% = k_X.$$

Had the stock initially sold for less than $27.27, say, at $25, events would have been reversed. Investors would have wanted to buy the stock because its expected rate of return would have exceeded its required rate of return, and buy orders would have driven the stock's price up to $27.27.

To summarize, in equilibrium two related conditions must hold:

1. A stock's expected rate of return as seen by the marginal investor must equal its required rate of return: $\hat{k}_i = k_i$.

2. The actual market price of the stock must equal its intrinsic value as estimated by the marginal investor: $P_0 = \hat{P}_0$.

Of course, some individual investors may believe that $\hat{k}_i > k$ and $\hat{P}_0 > P_0$, hence they would invest most of their funds in the stock, while other investors may have an opposite view and would sell all of their shares. However, it is the marginal investor who establishes the actual market price, and for this investor, we must have $\hat{k}_i = k_i$ and $P_0 = \hat{P}_0$. If these conditions do not hold, trading will occur until they do hold.

Changes in Equilibrium Stock Prices

Stock prices are not constant — they undergo violent changes at times. For example, on October 19, 1987, the Dow Jones average dropped 508 points, and the average stock lost about 23 percent of its value on that one day. Some individual stocks lost more than 70 percent of their value. Many investors (and companies) were wiped out, and a number of suicides occurred. To see how such changes can occur, assume that Stock X is in equilibrium, selling at a price of $27.27 per share. If all expectations were exactly met, during the next year the price would gradually rise to $28.63, or by 5 percent. However, many different events could occur to cause a change in the equilibrium price of the stock. To illustrate, consider again the set of inputs used to develop Stock X's price of $27.27, along with a new set of assumed input variables:

	VARIABLE VALUE	
	ORIGINAL	NEW
Risk-free rate, k_{RF}	8%	7%
Market risk premium, $k_M - k_{RF}$	4%	3%
Stock X's beta coefficient, b_X	2.0	1.0
Stock X's expected growth rate, g_X	5%	6%
D_0	$2.8571	$2.8571
Price of Stock X	$27.27	?

Now give yourself a test: How would the change in each variable, by itself, affect the price, and what is your guess as to the new stock price?

Every change, taken alone, would lead to an *increase* in the price. The first three changes all lower k_X, which declines from 16 to 10 percent:

$$\text{Original } k_X = 8\% + 4\%(2.0) = 16\%.$$

$$\text{New } k_X = 7\% + 3\%(1.0) - 10\%.$$

Using these values, together with the new g value, we find that $\hat{P}_0$ rises from $27.27 to $75.71.[12]

$$\text{Original } \hat{P}_0 = \frac{\$2.8571(1.05)}{0.16 - 0.05} = \frac{\$3}{0.11} = \$27.27.$$

$$\text{New } \hat{P}_0 = \frac{\$2.8571(1.06)}{0.10 - 0.06} = \frac{\$3.0285}{0.04} = \$75.71.$$

At the new price, the expected and required rates of return will be equal:[13]

$$\hat{k}_X = \frac{\$3.0285}{\$75.71} + 6\% = 10\% = k_X.$$

Evidence suggests that stocks, especially those of large companies, adjust rapidly to disequilibrium situations. Consequently, equilibrium ordinarily exists for any given stock, and required and expected returns are generally equal. Stock prices certainly change, sometimes violently and rapidly, but this simply reflects changing conditions and expectations. There are, of course, times when a stock continues to react for several months to favorable or unfavorable developments, but this does not signify a long adjustment period; rather, it simply indicates that as more new pieces of information about the situation become available, the

---

[12]A price change of this magnitude is by no means rare. The prices of *many* stocks double or halve during a year. For example, during 1996, TSR, a software firm, increased in value by 967 percent. On the other hand, Best Products, a catalog retailer, fell by 99.7 percent.

[13]It should be obvious by now that *actual realized* rates of return are not necessarily equal to expected and required returns. Thus, an investor might have *expected* to receive a return of 15 percent if he or she had bought TSR or Best Products stock in 1996, but, after the fact, the realized return on TSR was far above 15 percent, whereas that on Best Products was far below.

market adjusts to them. The ability of the market to adjust to new information is discussed in the next section.

THE EFFICIENT MARKETS HYPOTHESIS

Efficient Markets Hypothesis (EMH)
The hypothesis that securities are typically in equilibrium — that they are fairly priced in the sense that the price reflects all publicly available information on each security.

A body of theory called the **Efficient Markets Hypothesis (EMH)** holds (1) that stocks are always in equilibrium and (2) that it is impossible for an investor to consistently "beat the market." Essentially, those who believe in the EMH note that there are 100,000 or so full-time, highly trained, professional analysts and traders operating in the market, while there are fewer than 3,000 major stocks. Therefore, if each analyst followed 30 stocks (which is about right, as analysts tend to specialize in the stocks in a specific industry), there would on average be 1,000 analysts following each stock. Further, these analysts work for organizations such as Citibank, Merrill Lynch, Prudential Insurance, and the like, which have billions of dollars available with which to take advantage of bargains. In addition, as a result of SEC disclosure requirements and electronic information networks, as new information about a stock becomes available, these 1,000 analysts generally receive and evaluate it at about the same time. Therefore, the price of a stock will adjust almost immediately to any new development.

LEVELS OF MARKET EFFICIENCY

If markets are efficient, stock prices will rapidly reflect all available information. This raises an important question: What types of information are available and, therefore, incorporated into stock prices? Financial theorists have discussed three forms, or levels, of market efficiency.

WEAK-FORM EFFICIENCY. The *weak form* of the EMH states that all information contained in past price movements is fully reflected in current market prices. If this were true, then information about recent trends in stock prices would be of no use in selecting stocks — the fact that a stock has risen for the past three days, for example, would give us no useful clues as to what it will do today or tomorrow. People who believe that weak-form efficiency exists also believe that "tape watchers" and "chartists" are wasting their time.[14]

For example, after studying the past history of the stock market, a chartist might "discover" the following pattern: If a stock falls three consecutive days, its price typically rises 10 percent the following day. The technician would then conclude that investors could make money by purchasing a stock whose price has fallen three consecutive days.

But if this pattern truly existed, wouldn't other investors also discover it, and if so, why would anyone be willing to sell a stock after it had fallen three consecutive days if they know the stock's price is expected to increase by 10 percent the next day? In other words, if a stock is selling at $40 per share after falling three consecutive days, why would investors sell the stock if they expected it to rise to $44 per share one day later? Those who believe in weak-form efficiency argue that if the stock would really rise to $44 per share tomorrow, its price *today* would actually rise to somewhere near $44 per share immediately, thereby eliminating the trading opportunity. Consequently, weak-form efficiency implies

---

[14]Tape watchers are people who watch the NYSE tape, while chartists plot past patterns of stock price movements. Both are called "technicians," and both believe that they can tell if something is happening to the stock that will cause its price to move up or down in the near future.

that any information that comes from past stock prices is rapidly incorporated into the current stock price.

SEMISTRONG-FORM EFFICIENCY.   The *semistrong form* of the EMH states that current market prices reflect all *publicly available* information. Therefore, if semistrong-form efficiency exists, it would do no good to pore over annual reports or other published data because market prices would have adjusted to any good or bad news contained in such reports back when the news came out. With semistrong-form efficiency, investors should expect to earn the returns predicted by the SML, but they should not expect to do any better unless they have good luck or information that is not publicly available. However, insiders (for example, the presidents of companies) who have information which is not publicly available can earn abnormal returns (returns higher than those predicted by the SML) even under semistrong-form efficiency.

Another implication of semistrong-form efficiency is that whenever information is released to the public, stock prices will respond only if the information is different from what had been expected. If, for example, a company announces a 30 percent increase in earnings, and if that increase is about what analysts had been expecting, the announcement should have little or no effect on the company's stock price. On the other hand, the stock price would probably fall if analysts had expected earnings to increase by more than 30 percent, but it probably would rise if they had expected a smaller increase.

STRONG-FORM EFFICIENCY.   The *strong form* of the EMH states that current market prices reflect all pertinent information, whether publicly available or privately held. If this form holds, even insiders would find it impossible to earn abnormal returns in the stock market.[15]

Many empirical studies have been conducted to test for the three forms of market efficiency. Most of these studies suggest that the stock market is indeed highly efficient in the weak form and reasonably efficient in the semistrong form, at least for the larger and more widely followed stocks. However, the strong-form EMH does not hold, so abnormal profits can be made by those who possess inside information. (See box on page 331.)

IMPLICATIONS OF MARKET EFFICIENCY

What bearing does the EMH have on financial decisions? Since stock prices do seem to reflect public information, most stocks appear to be fairly valued. This does not mean that new developments could not cause a stock's price to soar or to plummet, but it does mean that stocks in general are neither overvalued nor undervalued — they are fairly priced and in equilibrium. However, there are certainly cases in which corporate insiders have information not known to outsiders.

If the EMH is correct, it is a waste of time for most of us to analyze stocks by looking for those that are undervalued. If stock prices already reflect all publicly available information, and hence are fairly priced, one can "beat the market" only

---

[15]Several cases of illegal insider trading have made the news headlines. These cases involved employees of several major investment banking houses and even an employee of the SEC. In the most famous case, Ivan Boesky admitted to making $50 million by purchasing the stock of firms he knew were about to merge. He went to jail, and he had to pay a large fine, but he helped disprove the strong-form EMH.

INDUSTRY PRACTICE

RUN-UPS BEFORE DEALS: CHICANERY OR COINCIDENCE?

Most studies find that markets are not strong-form efficient — the market can be beaten by those with access to inside information. Inside information is particularly valuable when it comes to corporate takeovers.

An article in *Business Week* claimed that one out of every three big mergers in 1994 was preceded by suspicious insider trading. For example, the day before American Home Products launched a $95 per share hostile takeover bid for American Cyana-

mid, there was heavy trading in Cyanamid, and its stock price jumped from $60⅝ to $63 a share. The article went on to document a number of similar cases, all with sharp run-ups in the target firms' stock prices just before merger announcements.

The Securities and Exchange Commission (SEC), which is responsible for policing insider trading, regularly investigates such cases to determine whether there was any illegal insider trading. To be sure, some preannouncement run-ups are undoubtedly legitimate — perhaps a large number of buy orders just randomly came in, or, more likely, perhaps some market professionals

guessed correctly that a merger was likely. However, there are cases in which the evidence strongly suggests information was "leaked" prior to the takeover. Harry C. Johnson, chairman and president of Red Eagle Resources Corporation, which was recently acquired by Lomak Petroleum, put it best after he saw the stock price of his company rise 16 percent the day before the deal was announced: "When there are a lot of people involved in a deal, you have to believe in the tooth fairy to think there can't be leakage."

SOURCE: Adapted from "Insider Trading," *Business Week*, December 12, 1994.

---

by luck, and it is difficult, if not impossible, for anyone to consistently outperform the market averages. Empirical tests have shown that the EMH is, in its weak and semistrong forms, valid. However, people such as corporate officers who have inside information can do better than the averages, and individuals and organizations that are especially good at digging out information on small, new companies also seem to do consistently well. Also, some investors may be able to analyze and react more quickly than others to releases of new information, and these investors may have an advantage over others. However, the buy-sell actions of those investors quickly bring market prices into equilibrium. Therefore, it is generally safe to assume that $\hat{k} = k$, that $\hat{P}_0 = P_0$, and that stocks plot on the SML.[16]

---

[16]Market efficiency also has important implications for managerial decisions, especially those pertaining to common stock issues, stock repurchases, and tender offers. Stocks appear to be fairly valued, so decisions based on the premise that a stock is undervalued or overvalued must be approached with caution. However, managers do have better information about their own companies than outsiders, and this information can legally be used to the companies' (but not the managers') advantage.

We should also note that some Wall Street pros have consistently beaten the market over many years, which is inconsistent with the EMH. An interesting article in the April 3, 1995, issue of *Fortune* (Terence P. Paré, "Yes, You Can Beat the Market") argued strongly against the EMH. Paré suggested that each stock has a fundamental value, but when good or bad news about it is announced, most investors fail to interpret this news correctly. As a result, stocks are generally priced above or below their long-term values.

Think of a graph with stock price on the vertical axis and years on the horizontal axis. A stock's fundamental value might be moving up steadily over time as it retains and reinvests earnings. However, its actual price might fluctuate about the intrinsic value line, overreacting to good or bad news and indicating departures from equilibrium. Successful value investors, according to the article, use fundamental analysis to identify stocks' intrinsic values, and then they buy stocks that are undervalued and sell those that are overvalued.

Paré's argument implies that the market is systematically out of equilibrium and that investors can act on this knowledge to beat the market. That position may turn out to be correct, but it may also be that the superior performance Paré noted simply demonstrates that some people are better at obtaining and interpreting information than others, or have been lucky in the past.

ACTUAL STOCK PRICES AND RETURNS

Our discussion thus far has focused on *expected* stock prices and *expected* rates of return. Anyone who has ever invested in the stock market knows that there can be, and there generally are, large differences between *expected* and *realized* prices and returns.

We can use IBM to illustrate this point. In early 1991, IBM's stock price was about $120 per share. Its 1990 dividend, D_0, was $4.84, but analysts expected the dividend to grow at a constant rate of about 8 percent in the future. Thus, an average investor who bought IBM at a price of $120 expected to earn about 12.4 percent:

$$\hat{k}_s = \frac{\text{Expected dividend}}{\text{yield}} + \frac{\text{Expected growth rate, which is also}}{\text{the expected capital gains yield}}$$

$$= \frac{D_0(1 + g)}{P_0} + g = \frac{\$5.23}{\$120} + 8\%$$

$$= 4.4\% + 8.0\% = 12.4\%.$$

In fact, things did not work out as expected. IBM's share of the computer market in 1991 was weaker than had been predicted, so IBM's earnings did not grow as fast as expected, and its dividend remained at $4.84. So, rather than growing, IBM's stock price declined, and it closed on December 31, 1991, at $89, down $31 for the year. Thus, on a beginning-of-the-year investment of $120, the annual return on IBM for 1991 was -21.8 percent:

$$\bar{k}_s = \text{Actual dividend yield} + \text{Actual capital gains yield}$$

$$= \frac{\$4.84}{\$120} + \frac{-\$31}{\$120} = 4.0\% - 25.8\% = -21.8\%.$$

Many other stocks performed similarly to IBM, or worse, in 1991.

By contrast, IBM's realized returns in recent years have been higher than expected. IBM's shareholders enjoyed a total return of roughly 25 percent in 1995, and they earned 67 percent in 1996. A turnaround of the company's fortunes, combined with a strong overall market, led to these better-than-expected results.

Figure 8-6 shows how the market value of a portfolio of stocks has moved in recent years, and Figure 8-7 shows how total realized returns on the portfolio have varied from year to year. The market trend has been strongly up, but it has gone up in some years and down in others, and the stocks of individual companies have likewise gone up and down.[17] We know from theory that expected

---

[17]If we constructed graphs like Figures 8-6 and 8-7 for individual stocks rather than for a large portfolio, far greater variability would be shown. Also, if we constructed a graph like Figure 8-7 for bonds, it would have the same general shape, but the bars would be somewhat smaller, indicating that gains and losses on bonds are generally smaller than those on stocks. Above-average bond returns occur in years when interest rates decline, and losses on bonds occur only when interest rates rise sharply.

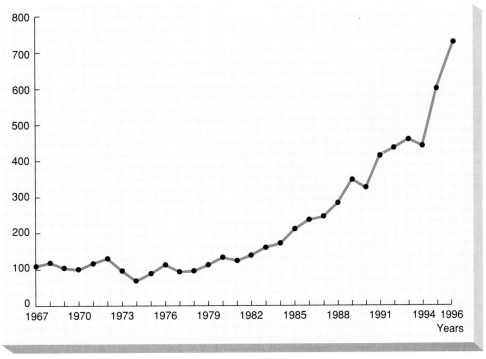

FIGURE 8-6 S&P 500 Index, 1967–1996

SOURCE: Data taken from various issues of *The Wall Street Journal,* "Stock Market Data Bank" section.

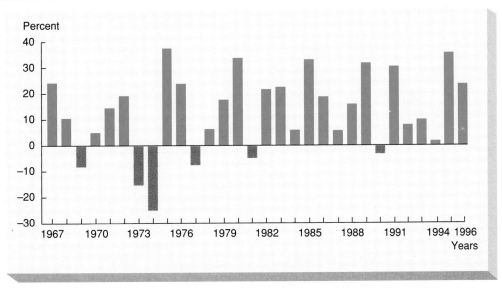

FIGURE 8-7 S&P 500 Index, Total Returns: Dividend Yield + Capital Gain or Loss, 1967–1996

SOURCE: *Stocks, Bonds, Bills, and Inflation: 1997 Yearbook* (Chicago: Ibbotson Associates, 1997).

GLOBAL PERSPECTIVES

INVESTING IN EMERGING MARKETS

Given the possibilities of better diversification and higher returns, U.S. investors have been putting more and more money into foreign stocks. While many investors limit their foreign holdings to developed countries such as Japan, Germany, Canada, and the United Kingdom, others have broadened their portfolios to include emerging markets such as South Korea, Mexico, Singapore, Taiwan, and Russia.

Emerging markets provide opportunities for larger returns, but they also entail greater risks. For example,

Russian stocks rose more than 150 percent in the first half of 1996, as it became apparent that Boris Yeltsin would be reelected president. By contrast, if you had invested in Taiwanese stocks, you would have lost 30 percent in 1995 — a year in which most stock markets performed extremely well.

Stocks in emerging markets are intriguing for two reasons. First, developing nations have the greatest potential for growth. Second, while stock returns in developed countries often move in sync with one another, stocks in emerging markets march to their own drummers. Therefore, the correlation between U.S. stocks and those in emerging markets are

generally lower than between U.S. stocks and those of other developed countries. Thus, correlation data suggest that emerging markets improve the diversification of U.S. investors' portfolios. (Recall from Chapter 5 that the lower the correlation, the better the diversification.)

On the other hand, stocks in emerging markets are often extremely risky, they are less liquid, they involve higher transaction costs, and most U.S. investors do not have ready access to information on the companies involved. To reduce these problems, mutual fund companies have created *country funds,* which invest in "baskets of stocks," for many emerging nations.

returns, as estimated by a marginal investor, are always positive, but in some years, as Figure 8-7 shows, actual returns are negative. Of course, even in bad years some individual companies do well, so "the name of the game" in security analysis is to pick the winners. Financial managers attempt to take actions which will put their companies into the winners' column, but they don't always succeed. In subsequent chapters, we will examine the actions that managers can take to increase the odds of their firms doing relatively well in the marketplace.

INVESTING IN INTERNATIONAL STOCKS

As noted in Chapter 5, the U.S. stock market amounts to only 40 percent of the world stock market, and this is prompting many U.S. investors to hold at least some foreign stocks. Analysts have long touted the benefits of investing overseas, arguing that foreign stocks both improve diversification and provide good growth opportunities. For example, after the U.S. stock market rose an average of 17.5 percent a year during the 1980s, many analysts thought that the U.S. market in the 1990s was due for a correction, and they suggested that investors should increase their holdings of foreign stocks.

To the surprise of many, however, U.S. stocks have outperformed foreign stocks thus far in the 1990s — they have gained about 15 percent a year versus only 3 percent for foreign stocks. Figure 8-8 shows how stocks in different countries performed in 1996. In each case, the lower number in the white box indicates how stocks in that country performed in terms of its local currency, while the upper number shows how the country's stocks performed in terms of the U.S. dollar. For example, in 1996 South African stocks rose by 6.7 percent, but the South African Rand declined more than 20 percent versus the U.S. dollar. Therefore, if U.S. investors had bought South African stocks, they would have made 6.7 percent in Rand terms, but those Rands would have bought 20 percent fewer dollars, so the effective return would have been −16.9 percent. So, the results of

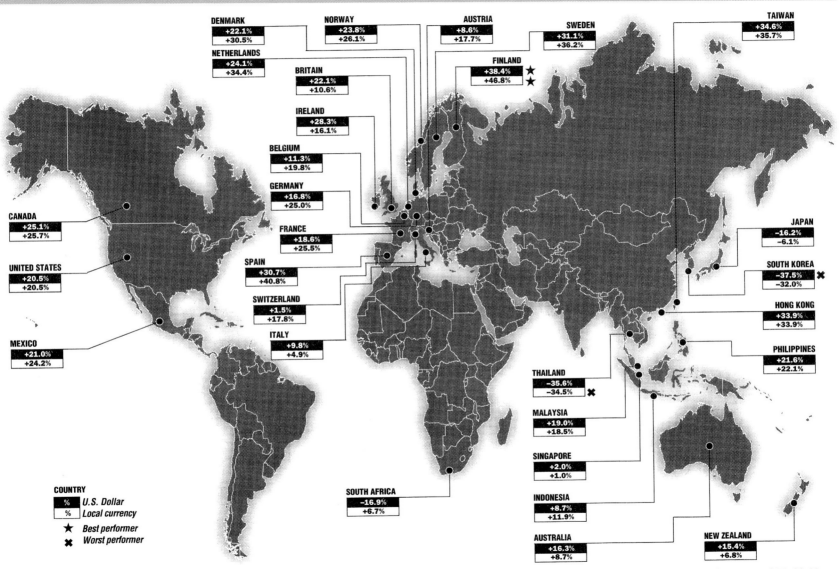

DENMARK
+22.1%
+30.5%

NORWAY
+23.8%
+26.1%

AUSTRIA
+8.6%
+17.7%

SWEDEN
+31.1%
+36.2%

TAIWAN
+34.6%
+35.7%

NETHERLANDS
+24.1%
+34.4%

BRITAIN
+22.1%
+10.6%

FINLAND
+38.4% ★
+46.8% ★

IRELAND
+28.3%
+16.1%

BELGIUM
+11.3%
+19.8%

GERMANY
+16.8%
+25.0%

CANADA
+25.1%
+25.7%

FRANCE
+18.6%
+25.5%

JAPAN
−16.2%
−6.1%

UNITED STATES
+20.5%
+20.5%

SPAIN
+30.7%
+40.8%

SOUTH KOREA
−37.5% ✖
−32.0%

SWITZERLAND
+1.5%
+17.8%

HONG KONG
+33.9%
+33.9%

MEXICO
+21.0%
+24.2%

ITALY
+9.8%
+4.9%

PHILIPPINES
+21.6%
+22.1%

THAILAND
−35.6%
−34.5% ✖

MALAYSIA
+19.0%
+18.5%

SINGAPORE
+2.0%
+1.0%

SOUTH AFRICA
−16.9%
+6.7%

INDONESIA
+8.7%
+11.9%

AUSTRALIA
+16.3%
+8.7%

NEW ZEALAND
+15.4%
+6.8%

COUNTRY
% *U.S. Dollar*
% *Local currency*
★ *Best performer*
✖ *Worst performer*

foreign investments depend in part on what happens to the exchange rate. Indeed, when you invest overseas, you are making two bets: (1) that foreign stocks will increase in their local markets and (2) that the currencies in which you will be paid will rise relative to the dollar.

Despite the fact that U.S. stocks have outperformed foreign stocks in recent years, this by no means suggests that investors should avoid foreign stocks. Foreign investments still improve diversification, and it is inevitable that there will be years when foreign stocks outperform domestic stocks. When this occurs, U.S. investors will be glad they put some of their eggs in overseas markets.

STOCK MARKET REPORTING

Figure 8-9, taken from a daily newspaper, is a section of the stock market page for stocks listed on the NYSE. For each stock, the NYSE report provides specific data on the trading that took place the prior day. Similar information is available for stocks listed on the other exchanges as well as for the larger stocks traded over the counter.

Stocks are listed alphabetically, from AAR Industries to Zweig; the data in Figure 8-9 were taken from the top of the listing. We will examine the data for Abbott Laboratories, AbbotLab, shown about halfway down the table. The two columns on the left show the highest and lowest prices at which the stocks have sold during the past year; Abbott Labs has traded in the range from $48¾ to $38⅛ during the preceding 52 weeks. The figure just to the right of the company's ticker symbol is the dividend; Abbott Labs had a current indicated annual dividend rate of $0.96 per share and a dividend yield (which is the current dividend divided by the closing stock price) of 2 percent. Next comes the ratio of the stock's price to its last 12 months' earnings (the P/E ratio), followed by the volume of trading for the day: 918,100 shares of Abbott Labs stock were traded on September 19, 1996. Following the volume come the high and low prices for the day, and then the closing price. On September 19, Abbott Labs traded as high as $48¾ and as low as $47½, while the last trade was at $48⅜. The last column gives the change from the closing price on the previous day. Abbott Labs' closing price was up ⅞ from the previous day's closing price.

SELF-TEST QUESTIONS

?????

If a stock is *not* in equilibrium, explain how financial markets adjust to bring it into equilibrium.

Explain why expected, required, and realized returns are often different.

What are the key benefits of adding foreign stocks to a portfolio?

When a U.S. investor purchases foreign stocks, what two things is he or she hoping will happen?

PREFERRED STOCK[18]

Preferred stock is a *hybrid* — it is similar to bonds in some respects and to common stock in others. The hybrid nature of preferred stock becomes apparent when we try to classify it in relation to bonds and common stock. Like bonds, preferred

---

[18]Additional information on preferred stock is provided in Chapter 20.

FIGURE 8-9 Stock Market Transactions, September 19, 1996

Quotations as of 5 p.m. Eastern Time
Thursday, September 19, 1996

	52 Weeks Hi	Lo	Stock	Sym	Div	Yld %	PE	Vol 100s	Hi	Lo	Close	Net Chg
			-A-A-A-									
	23⅞	17⅛	AAR	AIR	.48	2.1	21	70	23	22⅞	22⅞	...
s	20⅛	13⅛	ABM Indus	ABM	.35	2.2	16	361	16⅞	15⅞	16¼	– ⅝
	10⅛	9⅛	ACM Gvt Fd	ACG	.90	9.2	...	695	9⅞	9¾	9¾	– ⅛
	7⅞	6⅝	ACM OppFd	AOF	.57	8.3	...	218	7	6⅞	6⅞	...
	9⅛	8⅛	ACM SecFd	GSF	.90	10.0	...	2127	9	8¾	9	+ ⅛
	7¼	6	ACM SpctmFd	SI	.66	10.0	...	852	6⅝	6½	6⅝	+ ⅛
	11¾	9⅝	ACM MgmdInc	ADF	1.26	11.0	...	1358	11½	11⅜	11½	...
	9⅝	8⅜	ACM MgdIncFd	AMF	.90	9.5	...	447	9½	9⅜	9½	...
	13¼	11½	ACM MuniSec	AMU	.90	7.1	...	109	12⅝	12½	12⅝	+ ⅛
	22½	13¾	♣ ACX Tch A	ACX		...	dd	215	16¾	16½	16½	– ⅛
	24¾	13	ADT	ADT		...	dd	17445	20½	20	20¼	– ¼
s	36½	26¼	♣ AFLAC	AFL	.40	1.1	15	2367	35⅛	34	35⅛	+ ⅝
s	31⅝	19¼	AGCO Cp	AG	.04	.2	9	4065	24⅛	23⅜	23⅜	– ⅞
s	21⅛	17⅛	AGL Res	ATG	1.06	5.4	15	378	19⅞	19⅝	19⅝	– ⅜
n	22¾	18½	AJL PepsTr	AJP	1.06e	5.5	...	606	20	19¼	19⅜	– ⅝
	21⅜	18⅜	♣ AMLI Resdntl	AML	1.72	8.4	16	81	20⅝	20⅜	20½	– ⅛
	46⅛	36	♣ AMP	AMP	1.00	2.6	19	5056	39⅜	38⅞	39	– ⅛
	97½	63	AMR	AMR		...	17	6037	81⅜	79⅜	81	+1⅛
	54	47⅛	♣ ARCO Chm	RCM	2.80	5.6	11	92	49⅝	49½	49⅝	...
	50½	36⅜	ASA	ASA	1.20	3.1	...	308	39½	39⅛	39¼	...
	44⅞	35½	ATT Cap	TCC	.44	1.0	14	95	44⅞	44¾	44¾	...
	68⅞	49¼	AT&T Cp	T	1.32	2.3	cc	47224	57⅝	56⅞	57⅛	– ⅝
n	45⅛	42⅜	AT&T Cp wd			...	...	17748	44½	43⅞	44	– ¾
n	29	25¾	AXA ADR	AXA		...	...	478	28¼	27⅞	28¼	+ ¼
s	57⅝	16 5/32	AamesFnl	AAM	.20	.4	25	972	55⅛	54¼	54¼	–1
	48¾	38⅛	AbbotLab	ABT	.96	2.0	21	9181	48¾	47½	48⅜	+ ⅞
	18⅝	12¼	Abitibi g	ABY	.40	...	...	369	13¼	13	13	– ¼
	18⅝	13⅛	♣ AcceptIns	AIF		...	38	115	18⅝	18¼	18¼	– ⅛
	50⅜	32¾	ACE Ltd	ACL	.72	1.5	8	3241	47¼	47	47¼	...
	13⅞	6	AcmeElec	ACE		...	dd	147	7¼	7	7¼	+ ¼
·	19	13¾	AcmeMetals	AMI		...	10	73	15⅞	15¾	15¾	...
	33¾	23½	♣ Acordia	ACO	.80	2.6	18	68	30¾	30⅜	30⅝	+ ⅜
	21⅜	10¾	Acuson	ACN		...	dd	362	17⅞	17½	17⅝	+ ⅛
	19¾	17¾	♣ AdamsExp	ADX	1.66e	8.5	...	231	19⅝	19⅜	19½	...
	34⅛	10¼	♣ AdvMicro	AMD		...	15	10237	14⅝	13¾	14¼	+ ¼
	11⅛	8½	Advest	ADV		...	7	16	10	9⅞	9⅞	– ⅛
s	15⅛	9⅛	Advo	AD		...	dd	444	10½	10¼	10⅜	+ ¼
	13	7⅞	♣ Advocat	AVC		...	11	191	8⅜	8⅛	8¼	– ⅛
	51½	35⅝	AEGON NV	AEG	1.77e	3.5	15	23	49⅞	49¾	49⅞	– ⅛
	6¾	3½	♣ Aeroflex	ARX		...	dd	176	5⅛	5	5	...
	28¾	26¾	AetnaMIPS pfA		2.37	8.7	...	94	27⅜	27⅛	27⅛	...
	78¾	55⅜	Aetna	AET	.20p	...	8	2690	68½	67¾	67⅞	– ¾
n	72⅞	62¼	Aetna pfC		.37p	...	...	112	71⅝	70⅝	70⅞	– ⅝
	20½	10⅞	♣ AgnicoEgl	AEM	.10	.6	...	232	16⅝	16⅜	16½	– ⅛
	19½	13½	AgreeRlty	ADC	1.80	9.5	15	18	19⅛	19	19	– ¼

NOTES: The "pf" following the stock name of the AetnaMIPS listing tells us that this one is a preferred stock rather than a common stock. A "▲" preceding the columns containing a stock's 52-week high and low prices indicates that the price hit a new 52-week high, whereas a "▼" indicates a new 52-week low. An "x" preceding the columns containing the 52-week high and low prices indicates that the stock went ex-dividend that day; this means that someone who buys the stock will not receive the next dividend. An "s" preceding the 52-week high and low prices indicates that the stock was split within the past 52 weeks. (See Chapter 13 for a discussion of stock splits.) ABM Indus. had a stock split during the past 52-week period. An "n" preceding the 52-week high and low prices indicates that the stock is newly issued within the past 52 weeks. There were four stocks in Figure 8-9 that were newly issued within the past 52 weeks. Those companies whose listings are underlined have had large changes in volume compared with average trading volume. An "a" following the dividend column indicates an extra dividend in addition to the regular dividend, while an "f" following the dividend column indicates that the annual dividend was increased on the last declaration date. An "e" following the dividend column indicates that a dividend was declared or paid in the preceding 12 months, but there is no regular dividend rate. A "j" following the dividend column indicates the dividend paid this year; however, at the last dividend meeting a dividend was omitted or deferred. An "m" following the dividend column indicates that the dividend was reduced when the Board last declared the dividend. Finally, a "club" appearing before the company name indicates that *Journal* readers can obtain a copy of the company's annual report.

SOURCE: *The Wall Street Journal,* September 19, 1996, C3.

INDUSTRY PRACTICE

EVALUATING STOCKS THAT DON'T PAY DIVIDENDS

In this chapter, we presented several equations for valuing a firm's common stock. These equations had one common element: they all assumed that the firm is currently paying a dividend. However, many firms, even highly profitable ones, such as Microsoft, have never paid a dividend. If a firm is expected to begin paying dividends in the future, we can modify the equations presented in the chapter and use them to determine the value of the stock.

A new business often expects to have low sales during its first few years of operation as it develops its product. Then, if the product catches on, sales will grow rapidly for several years. For example, Compaq Computer Company had only three employees when it was incorporated in 1982. Its first year was devoted to product development, and 1982 sales were zero. In 1983, however, Compaq began marketing its personal computer, and its sales hit $111 million, a record first-year volume for any new firm. By 1986 Compaq was included in Fortune's 500 largest U.S. industrial firms. Obviously, Compaq has been more successful than most new businesses, but it is common for small firms to have growth rates of 100 percent, 500 percent, or even 1,000 percent during their first few years of operation.

Sales growth brings with it the need for additional assets — Compaq could not have increased sales as it did without also increasing its assets, and asset growth requires an increase in liability and/or equity accounts. Small firms can generally obtain some bank credit, but they must maintain a reasonable balance be-

tween debt and equity. Thus, additional bank borrowings require increases in equity, and getting the equity capital needed to support growth can be difficult for small firms. They have limited access to the capital markets, and, even when they can sell common stock, their owners are reluctant to do so for fear of losing voting control. Therefore, the best source of equity for most small businesses is retained earnings, and for this reason most small firms pay no dividends during their rapid growth years. Eventually, though, successful small firms do pay dividends, and those dividends generally grow rapidly at first but slow down to a sustainable constant rate once the firm reaches maturity.

If a firm currently pays no dividend but is expected to pay dividends in the future, the value of its stock can be found as follows:

1. Estimate when dividends will be paid, the amount of the first dividend, the growth rate during the supernormal growth period, the length of the supernormal period, the long-run (constant) growth rate, and the rate of return required by investors.
2. Use the constant growth model to determine the price of the stock after the firm reaches a stable growth situation.
3. Set out on a time line the cash flows (dividends during the supernormal growth period and the stock price once the constant growth state is reached), and then find the present value of these cash flows. That present value represents the value of the stock today.

To illustrate this process, consider the situation for MarvelLure Inc., a company that was set up in 1996 to produce and market a new high-tech

fishing lure. MarvelLure's sales are currently growing at a rate of 200 percent per year. The company expects to experience a high but declining rate of growth in sales and earnings during the next ten years, after which analysts estimate that it will grow at a steady 10 percent per year. The firm's management has announced that it will pay no dividends for five years, but if earnings materialize as forecasted, it will pay a dividend of $0.20 per share at the end of Year 6, $0.30 in Year 7, $0.40 in Year 8, $0.45 in Year 9, and $0.50 in Year 10. After Year 10, current plans are to increase the dividend by 10 percent per year.

MarvelLure's investment bankers estimate that investors require a 15 percent return on similar stocks. Therefore, we find the value of a share of MarvelLure's stock as follows:

$$P_0 = \frac{\$0}{(1.15)^1} + \cdots + \frac{\$0}{(1.15)^5}$$

$$+ \frac{\$0.20}{(1.15)^6} + \frac{\$0.30}{(1.15)^7}$$

$$+ \frac{\$0.40}{(1.15)^8} + \frac{\$0.45}{(1.15)^9} + \frac{\$0.50}{(1.15)^{10}}$$

$$+ \left(\frac{\$0.50(1.10)}{0.15 - 0.10}\right)\left(\frac{1}{(1.15)^{10}}\right)$$

$$= \$3.30.$$

The last term finds the expected price of the stock in Year 10 and then finds the present value of that price. Thus, we see that the valuation concepts discussed in the chapter can be applied to firms which currently pay no dividends, provided an estimate of future dividends can be made. Clearly, though, these estimates are uncertain, hence stocks such as MarvelLure are very risky.

stock has a par value and a fixed amount of dividends which must be paid before dividends can be paid on the common stock. However, if the preferred dividend is not earned, the directors can omit (or "pass") it without throwing the company into bankruptcy. So, although preferred stock has a fixed payment like bonds, a failure to make this payment will not lead to bankruptcy.

As noted above, preferred stocks entitle their owners to regular, fixed dividend payments. If the payments last forever, the issue is a perpetuity whose value, V_{ps}, is found as follows:

$$V_{ps} = \frac{D_{ps}}{k_{ps}}. \tag{8-6}$$

V_{ps} is the value of the preferred stock, D_{ps} is the preferred dividend, and k_{ps} is the required rate of return. Allied Food Products has preferred stock outstanding which pays a dividend of $10 per year. If the required rate of return on this preferred stock is 10 percent, its value is $100, found by solving Equation 8-6 as follows:

$$V_{ps} = \frac{\$10.00}{0.10} = \$100.00.$$

If we know the current price of a preferred stock and its dividend, we can solve for the rate of return as follows:

$$k_{ps} = \frac{D_{ps}}{V_{ps}}. \tag{8-6a}$$

Some preferred stocks have a stated maturity date, say, 50 years. If Allied's preferred matured in 50 years, paid a $10 annual dividend, and had a required return of 8 percent, then we could find its price as follows: Enter N = 50, I = 8, PMT = 10, and FV = 100. Then press PV to find the price, V_{ps} = $124.47. If k = I = 10%, change I = 8 to I = 10, and find P = V_{ps} = PV = $100. If you know the price of a share of preferred stock, you can solve for I to find the expected rate of return, $\hat{k}_{ps}$.

Most preferred stock pays dividends quarterly. This is true for Allied Food, so we could find the effective rate of return on its preferred stock (perpetual or maturing) as follows:

$$EFF\% = EAR_{ps} = \left(1 + \frac{k_{Nom}}{m}\right)^m - 1 = \left(1 + \frac{0.10}{4}\right)^4 - 1 = 10.38\%.$$

If an investor wanted to compare the returns on Allied's bonds and its preferred stock, it would be best to convert the nominal rates on each security to effective rates and then compare these "equivalent annual rates."

SELF-TEST QUESTIONS   ??????

Explain the following statement: "Preferred stock is a hybrid security."

Is the equation used to value preferred stock more like the one used to evaluate a bond or the one used to evaluate a "normal" common stock?

SUMMARY

Corporate decisions should be analyzed in terms of how alternative courses of action are likely to affect a firm's value. However, it is necessary to know how stock prices are established before attempting to measure how a given decision will affect a specific firm's value. This chapter showed how stock values are determined, and also how investors go about estimating the rates of return they expect to earn. The key concepts covered are summarized below.

♦ A **proxy** is a document which gives one person the power to act for another person, typically the power to vote shares of common stock. A **proxy fight** occurs when an outside group solicits stockholders' proxies in an effort to vote a new management team into office.

♦ A **takeover** occurs when a person or group succeeds in ousting a firm's management and taking control of the company.

♦ Stockholders often have the right to purchase any additional shares sold by the firm. This right, called the **preemptive right,** protects the control of the present stockholders and prevents dilution of their stock's value.

♦ Although most firms have only one type of common stock, in some instances **classified stock** is used to meet the special needs of the company. One type of classified stock is **founders' shares.** This is stock owned by the firm's founders that carries sole voting rights but restricted dividends for a specified number of years.

♦ A **closely held corporation** is one that is owned by a few individuals who are typically associated with the firm's management.

♦ A **publicly owned corporation** is one that is owned by a relatively large number of individuals who are not actively involved in its management.

♦ Whenever stock in a closely held corporation is offered to the public for the first time, the company is said to be **going public.** The market for stock that is just being offered to the public is called the **initial public offering (IPO) market.**

♦ The **value of a share of stock** is calculated as the **present value of the stream of dividends** the stock is expected to provide in the future.

♦ The equation used to find the **value of a constant growth stock** is:

$$\hat{P}_0 = \frac{D_1}{k_s - g}.$$

♦ The **expected total rate of return** from a stock consists of an **expected dividend yield** plus an **expected capital gains yield.** For a constant growth firm, both the expected dividend yield and the expected capital gains yield are constant.

♦ The equation for $\hat{k}_s$, the **expected rate of return on a constant growth stock,** can be expressed as follows:

$$\hat{k}_s = \frac{D_1}{P_0} + g.$$

♦ A **zero growth stock** is one whose future dividends are not expected to grow at all, while a **supernormal growth stock** is one whose earnings and dividends are expected to grow much faster than the economy as a whole over some specified time period and then to grow at the "normal" rate.

◆ To find the **present value of a supernormal growth stock,** (1) find the dividends expected during the supernormal growth period, (2) find the price of the stock at the end of the supernormal growth period, (3) discount the dividends and the projected price back to the present, and (4) sum these PVs to find the current value of the stock, $\hat{P}_0$.

◆ The **Efficient Markets Hypothesis (EMH)** holds (1) that stocks are always in equilibrium and (2) that it is impossible for an investor who does not have inside information to consistently "beat the market." Therefore, according to the EMH, stocks are always fairly valued ($\hat{P}_0 = P_0$), the required return on a stock is equal to its expected return ($k = \hat{k}$), and all stocks' expected returns plot on the SML.

◆ We saw that differences can and do exist between expected and realized returns in the stock and bond markets — only for short-term, risk-free assets are expected and actual (or realized) returns equal.

◆ When U.S. investors purchase foreign stocks, they hope (1) that the stock prices will increase in the local market and (2) that the foreign currencies will rise relative to the U.S. dollar.

◆ **Preferred stock** is a hybrid security having some characteristics of debt and some of equity.

◆ Most preferred stocks are **perpetuities,** and the value of a share of perpetual preferred stock is found as the dividend divided by the required rate of return:

$$V_{ps} = \frac{D_{ps}}{k_{ps}}.$$

◆ **Maturing preferred stock** is evaluated with a formula that is identical in form to the bond value formula.

QUESTIONS

8-1 Two investors are evaluating AT&T's stock for possible purchase. They agree on the expected value of D_1 and also on the expected future dividend growth rate. Further, they agree on the riskiness of the stock. However, one investor normally holds stocks for 2 years, while the other normally holds stocks for 10 years. On the basis of the type of analysis done in this chapter, they should both be willing to pay the same price for AT&T's stock. True or false? Explain.

8-2 A bond that pays interest forever and has no maturity date is a perpetual bond. In what respect is a perpetual bond similar to a no-growth common stock, and to a share of preferred stock?

8-3 If you bought a share of common stock, you would typically expect to receive dividends plus capital gains. Would you expect the distribution between dividend yield and capital gains to be influenced by the firm's decision to pay more dividends rather than to retain and reinvest more of its earnings?

8-4 Is it true that the following expression can be used to find the value of a constant growth stock?

$$\hat{P}_0 = \frac{D_0}{k_s + g}.$$

8-5 It is frequently stated that the primary purpose of the preemptive right is to allow individuals to maintain their proportionate share of the ownership and control of a corporation.

a. How important do you suppose this consideration is for the average stockholder of a firm whose shares are traded on the New York or American Stock Exchanges?

b. Is the preemptive right likely to be of more importance to stockholders of publicly owned or closely held firms? Explain.

SELF-TEST PROBLEMS (Solutions Appear in Appendix B)

ST-1
Key terms

Define each of the following terms:
a. Proxy; proxy fight; takeover
b. Preemptive right
c. Classified stock; founders' shares
d. Closely held corporation; publicly owned corporation
e. Over-the-counter (OTC) market; organized security exchange
f. Secondary market; primary market
g. Going public; initial public offering (IPO) market
h. Intrinsic value (P_0); market price (P_0)
i. Required rate of return, k_s; expected rate of return, $\hat{k}_s$; actual, or realized, rate of return, $\bar{k}_s$
j. Capital gains yield; dividend yield; expected total return
k. Zero growth stock
l. Normal, or constant, growth; supernormal, or nonconstant, growth
m. Equilibrium
n. Efficient Markets Hypothesis (EMH); three forms of EMH
o. Preferred stock

ST-2
Stock growth rates and valuation

You are considering buying the stocks of two companies that operate in the same industry; they have very similar characteristics except for their dividend payout policies. Both companies are expected to earn $6 per share this year. However, Company D (for "dividend") is expected to pay out all of its earnings as dividends, while Company G (for "growth") is expected to pay out only one-third of its earnings, or $2 per share. D's stock price is $40. G and D are equally risky. Which of the following is most likely to be true?
a. Company G will have a faster growth rate than Company D. Therefore, G's stock price should be greater than $40.
b. Although G's growth rate should exceed D's, D's current dividend exceeds that of G, and this should cause D's price to exceed G's.
c. An investor in Stock D will get his or her money back faster because D pays out more of its earnings as dividends. Thus, in a sense, D is like a short-term bond, and G is like a long-term bond. Therefore, if economic shifts cause k_d and k_s to increase, and if the expected streams of dividends from D and G remain constant, both Stocks D and G will decline, but D's price should decline further.
d. D's expected and required rate of return is $\hat{k}_s = k_s = 15\%$. G's expected return will be higher because of its higher expected growth rate.
e. If we observe that G's price is also $40, the best estimate of G's growth rate is 10 percent.

ST-3
Constant growth stock valuation

Ewald Company's current stock price is $36, and its last dividend was $2.40. In view of Ewald's strong financial position and its consequent low risk, its required rate of return is only 12 percent. If dividends are expected to grow at a constant rate, g, in the future, and if k_s is expected to remain at 12 percent, what is Ewald's expected stock price 5 years from now?

ST-4
Supernormal growth stock valuation

Snyder Computer Chips Inc. is experiencing a period of rapid growth. Earnings and dividends are expected to grow at a rate of 15 percent during the next 2 years, at 13 percent in the third year, and at a constant rate of 6 percent thereafter. Snyder's last dividend was $1.15, and the required rate of return on the stock is 12 percent.
a. Calculate the value of the stock today.
b. Calculate $\hat{P}_1$ and $\hat{P}_2$.
c. Calculate the dividend yield and capital gains yield for Years 1, 2, and 3.

STARTER PROBLEMS

8-1
DPS calculation

Warr Corporation just paid a dividend of $1.50 a share (i.e., $D_0 = \$1.50$). The dividend is expected to grow 5 percent a year for the next 3 years, and then 10 percent a year thereafter. What is the expected dividend per share for each of the next 5 years?

8-2
Constant growth valuation

Thomas Brothers is expected to pay a $0.50 per share dividend at the end of the year (i.e., $D_1 = \$0.50$). The dividend is expected to grow at a constant rate of 7 percent a year. The required rate of return on the stock, k_s, is 15 percent. What is the value per share of the company's stock?

8-3
Constant growth valuation

Harrison Clothiers' stock currently sells for $20 a share. The stock just paid a dividend of $1.00 a share (i.e., $D_0 = \$1.00$). The dividend is expected to grow at a constant rate of 10 percent a year. What stock price is expected 1 year from now? What is the required rate of return on the company's stock?

8-4
Preferred stock valuation

Fee Founders has preferred stock outstanding which pays a dividend of $5 at the end of each year. The preferred stock sells for $60 a share. What is the preferred stock's required rate of return?

EXAM-TYPE PROBLEMS

The problems included in this section are set up in such a way that they could be used as multiple-choice exam problems.

8-5
Supernormal growth valuation

A company currently pays a dividend of $2 per share, $D_0 = 2$. It is estimated that the company's dividend will grow at a rate of 20 percent per year for the next 2 years, then the dividend will grow at a constant rate of 7 percent thereafter. The company's stock has a beta equal to 1.2, the risk-free rate is 7.5 percent, and the market risk premium is 4 percent. What would you estimate is the stock's current price?

8-6
Constant growth rate, g

A stock is trading at $80 per share. The stock is expected to have a year-end dividend of $4 per share ($D_1 = 4$) which is expected to grow at some constant rate g throughout time. The stock's required rate of return is 14 percent. If you are an analyst who believes in efficient markets, what would be your forecast of g?

8-7
Constant growth valuation

You are considering an investment in the common stock of Keller Corp. The stock is expected to pay a dividend of $2 a share at the end of the year ($D_1 = \$2.00$). The stock has a beta equal to 0.9. The risk-free rate is 5.6 percent, and the market risk premium is 6 percent. The stock's dividend is expected to grow at some constant rate g. The stock currently sells for $25 a share. Assuming the market is in equilibrium, what does the market believe will be the stock price at the end of 3 years? (That is, what is $\hat{P}_3$?)

8-8
Preferred stock rate of return

What will be the nominal rate of return on a preferred stock with a $100 par value, a stated dividend of 8 percent of par, and a current market price of (a) $60, (b) $80, (c) $100, and (d) $140?

8-9
Declining growth stock valuation

Martell Mining Company's ore reserves are being depleted, so its sales are falling. Also, its pit is getting deeper each year, so its costs are rising. As a result, the company's earnings and dividends are declining at the constant rate of 5 percent per year. If $D_0 = \$5$ and $k_s = 15\%$, what is the value of Martell Mining's stock?

8-10
Rates of return and equilibrium

The beta coefficient for Stock C is $b_c = 0.4$, whereas that for Stock D is $b_D = -0.5$. (Stock D's beta is negative, indicating that its rate of return rises whenever returns on most other stocks fall. There are very few negative beta stocks, although collection agency stocks are sometimes cited as an example.)
a. If the risk-free rate is 9 percent and the expected rate of return on an average stock is 13 percent, what are the required rates of return on Stocks C and D?
b. For Stock C, suppose the current price, P_0, is $25; the next expected dividend, D_1, is $1.50; and the stock's expected constant growth rate is 4 percent. Is the stock in equilibrium? Explain, and describe what will happen if the stock is not in equilibrium.

8-11
Supernormal growth stock valuation

Assume that the average firm in your company's industry is expected to grow at a constant rate of 6 percent and its dividend yield is 7 percent. Your company is about as risky as the average firm in the industry, but it has just successfully completed some R&D work which leads you to expect that its earnings and dividends will grow at a rate of 50 percent $[D_1 = D_0(1 + g) = D_0(1.50)]$ this year and 25 percent the following year, after which growth should match the 6 percent industry average rate. The last dividend paid (D_0) was $1. What is the value per share of your firm's stock?

8-12
Supernormal growth stock valuation

Microtech Corporation is expanding rapidly, and it currently needs to retain all of its earnings, hence it does not pay any dividends. However, investors expect Microtech to begin paying dividends, with the first dividend of $1.00 coming 3 years from today. The dividend should grow rapidly — at a rate of 50 percent per year — during Years 4 and 5. After Year 5, the company should grow at a constant rate of 8 percent per year. If the required return on the stock is 15 percent, what is the value of the stock today?

PROBLEMS

8-13
Preferred stock valuation

Ezzell Corporation issued preferred stock with a stated dividend of 10 percent of par. Preferred stock of this type currently yields 8 percent, and the par value is $100. Assume dividends are paid annually.
a. What is the value of Ezzell's preferred stock?
b. Suppose interest rate levels rise to the point where the preferred stock now yields 12 percent. What would be the value of Ezzell's preferred stock?

8-14
Constant growth stock valuation

Your broker offers to sell you some shares of Bahnsen & Co. common stock that paid a dividend of $2 *yesterday*. You expect the dividend to grow at the rate of 5 percent per year for the next 3 years, and, if you buy the stock, you plan to hold it for 3 years and then sell it.
a. Find the expected dividend for each of the next 3 years; that is, calculate D_1, D_2, and D_3. Note that $D_0 = \$2$.
b. Given that the appropriate discount rate is 12 percent and that the first of these dividend payments will occur 1 year from now, find the present value of the dividend stream; that is, calculate the PV of D_1, D_2, and D_3, and then sum these PVs.
c. You expect the price of the stock 3 years from now to be $34.73; that is, you expect $\hat{P}_3$ to equal $34.73. Discounted at a 12 percent rate, what is the present value of this expected future stock price? In other words, calculate the PV of $34.73.
d. If you plan to buy the stock, hold it for 3 years, and then sell it for $34.73, what is the most you should pay for it?
e. Use Equation 8-4 to calculate the present value of this stock. Assume that $g = 5\%$, and it is constant.
f. Is the value of this stock dependent upon how long you plan to hold it? In other words, if your planned holding period were 2 years or 5 years rather than 3 years, would this affect the value of the stock today, $\hat{P}_0$?

8-15
Return on common stock

You buy a share of The Ludwig Corporation stock for $21.40. You expect it to pay dividends of $1.07, $1.1449, and $1.2250 in Years 1, 2, and 3, respectively, and you expect to sell it at a price of $26.22 at the end of 3 years.
a. Calculate the growth rate in dividends.
b. Calculate the expected dividend yield.
c. Assuming that the calculated growth rate is expected to continue, you can add the dividend yield to the expected growth rate to get the expected total rate of return. What is this stock's expected total rate of return?

8-16
Constant growth stock valuation

Investors require a 15 percent rate of return on Levine Company's stock ($k_s = 15\%$).
a. What will be Levine's stock value if the previous dividend was $D_0 = \$2$ and if investors expect dividends to grow at a constant compound annual rate of (1) −5 percent, (2) 0 percent, (3) 5 percent, and (4) 10 percent?
b. Using data from Part a, what is the Gordon (constant growth) model value for Levine's stock if the required rate of return is 15 percent and the expected growth rate is (1) 15 percent or (2) 20 percent? Are these reasonable results? Explain.
c. Is it reasonable to expect that a constant growth stock would have $g > k_s$?

8-17
Stock reporting

Look up the prices of American Telephone & Telegraph's (AT&T) stock in *The Wall Street Journal* (or some other newspaper which provides this information).
a. What was the stock's price range during the last year?
b. What is AT&T's current dividend? What is its dividend yield?
c. What change occurred in AT&T's stock price the day the newspaper was published?
d. If you had $10,000 and wanted to invest it in AT&T, what return would you expect to get if you bought AT&T's stock? (Hint: Think about capital gains when you answer this question.)

8-18
Supernormal growth stock valuation

It is now January 1, 1998. Wayne-Martin Electric Inc. (WME) has just developed a solar panel capable of generating 200 percent more electricity than any solar panel currently on the market. As a result, WME is expected to experience a 15 percent annual growth rate for the next 5 years. By the end of 5 years, other firms will have developed comparable technology, and WME's growth rate will slow to 5 percent per year indefinitely. Stockholders require a return of 12 percent on WME's stock. The most recent annual dividend (D_0), which was paid yesterday, was $1.75 per share.

a. Calculate WME's expected dividends for 1998, 1999, 2000, 2001, and 2002.

b. Calculate the value of the stock today, P_0. Proceed by finding the present value of the dividends expected at the end of 1998, 1999, 2000, 2001, and 2002 plus the present value of the stock price which should exist at the end of 2002. The year-end 2002 stock price can be found by using the constant growth equation. Notice that to find the December 31, 2002, price, you use the dividend expected in 2003, which is 5 percent greater than the 2002 dividend.

c. Calculate the expected dividend yield, D_1/P_0, the capital gains yield expected in 1998, and the expected total return (dividend yield plus capital gains yield) for 1998. (Assume that $\hat{P}_0 = P_0$, and recognize that the capital gains yield is equal to the total return minus the dividend yield.) Also calculate these same three yields for 2003.

d. How might an investor's tax situation affect his or her decision to purchase stocks of companies in the early stages of their lives, when they are growing rapidly, versus stocks of older, more mature firms? When does WME's stock become "mature" in this example?

e. Suppose your boss tells you she believes that WME's annual growth rate will be only 12 percent during the next 5 years and that the firm's normal growth rate will be only 4 percent. Without doing any calculations, what general effect would these growth-rate changes have on the price of WME's stock?

f. Suppose your boss also tells you that she regards WME as being quite risky and that she believes the required rate of return should be 14 percent, not 12 percent. Again, without doing any calculations, how would the higher required rate of return affect the price of the stock, its capital gains yield, and its dividend yield?

8-19
Supernormal growth stock valuation

Taussig Technologies Corporation (TTC) has been growing at a rate of 20 percent per year in recent years. This same growth rate is expected to last for another 2 years.

a. If $D_0 = \$1.60$, $k = 10\%$, and $g_n = 6\%$, what is TTC's stock worth today? What are its expected dividend yield and capital gains yield at this time?

b. Now assume that TTC's period of supernormal growth is to last another 5 years rather than 2 years. How would this affect its price, dividend yield, and capital gains yield? Answer in words only.

c. What will be TTC's dividend yield and capital gains yield once its period of supernormal growth ends? (Hint: These values will be the same regardless of whether you examine the case of 2 or 5 years of supernormal growth; the calculations are very easy.)

d. Of what interest to investors is the changing relationship between dividend yield and capital gains yield over time?

8-20
Equilibrium stock price

The risk-free rate of return, k_{RF}, is 11 percent; the required rate of return on the market, k_M, is 14 percent; and Upton Company's stock has a beta coefficient of 1.5.

a. If the dividend expected during the coming year, D_1, is $2.25, and if $g = $ a constant 5%, at what price should Upton's stock sell?

b. Now, suppose the Federal Reserve Board increases the money supply, causing the risk-free rate to drop to 9 percent and k_M to fall to 12 percent. What would this do to the price of the stock?

c. In addition to the change in Part b, suppose investors' risk aversion declines; this fact, combined with the decline in k_{RF}, causes k_M to fall to 11 percent. At what price would Upton's stock sell?

d. Now, suppose Upton has a change in management. The new group institutes policies that increase the expected constant growth rate to 6 percent. Also, the new management stabilizes sales and profits, and thus causes the beta coefficient to decline from 1.5 to 1.3. Assume that k_{RF} and k_M are equal to the values in Part c. After all these changes, what is Upton's new equilibrium price? (Note: D_1 goes to $2.27.)

8-21
Beta coefficients

Suppose Chance Chemical Company's management conducts a study and concludes that if Chance expanded its consumer products division (which is less risky than its primary business, industrial chemicals), the firm's beta would decline from 1.2 to 0.9. However, consumer products have a somewhat lower profit margin, and this would cause Chance's constant growth rate in earnings and dividends to fall from 7 to 5 percent.

a. Should management make the change? Assume the following: $k_M = 12\%$; $k_{RF} = 9\%$; $D_0 = \$2$.

b. Assume all the facts as given above except the change in the beta coefficient. How low would the beta have to fall to cause the expansion to be a good one? (Hint: Set $\hat{P}_0$ under the new policy equal to $\hat{P}_0$ under the old one, and find the new beta that will produce this equality.)

INTEGRATED CASE

WESTERN MONEY MANAGEMENT INC., PART II

8-22 Stock Valuation Robert Black and Carol Alvarez are vice-presidents of Western Money Management and codirectors of the company's pension fund management division. A major new client, the California League of Cities, has requested that Western present an investment seminar on common stock valuation to the mayors of the represented cities, and Black and Alvarez, who will make the actual presentation, have asked you to help them by answering the following questions. Because the Walt Disney Company operates in one of the league's cities, you are to work Disney into the presentation.

a. Describe briefly the legal rights and privileges of common stockholders.

b. (1) Write out and explain a formula that can be used to value any stock, regardless of its dividend pattern.

(2) What is a constant growth stock? How are constant growth stocks valued?

(3) What happens if the constant g exceeds k_s? Will many stocks have expected $g > k_s$ in the short run? In the long run (i.e., forever)?

c. Assume that Disney has a beta coefficient of 1.2, that the risk-free rate (the yield on T-bonds) is 6 percent, and that the required rate of return on the market is 11 percent. What is the required rate of return on Disney's stock?

d. Assume that Disney is a constant growth company whose last dividend (D_0, which was paid yesterday) was $0.25, and whose dividend is expected to grow indefinitely at a 6 percent rate.

(1) What would Disney's expected dividend stream be over the next 3 years, and what is the PV of each dividend?

(2) Under these conditions, what would be Disney's current stock price? Note that $g = 6\%$, $k_s = 12\%$.

(3) What should the stock's expected value be 1 year from now?

(4) Calculate the expected dividend yield, the capital gains yield, and the total return during the first year.

e. Now assume that the stock is currently selling at $4.42. What is the expected rate of return on the stock?

f. What would the stock price be if Disney's dividends were expected to have zero growth?

g. Now assume that Disney is expected to experience supernormal dividend growth of 30 percent for the next 3 years, then to fall to a long-run constant growth rate of 10 percent. What would the stock's value be under these conditions? What would its expected dividend yield and capital gains yield be in Year 1? In Year 4?

h. Suppose Disney was expected to experience zero growth during the next 3 years and then to achieve a constant growth rate of 11 percent in the fourth year and thereafter. What would be the stock's value now? What is its expected dividend yield and its capital gains yield in Year 1? In Year 4?

i. Finally, assume that Disney's earnings and dividends are expected to decline by a constant 6 percent per year, that is, $g = -6\%$. Would you or anyone else be willing to buy such a stock? At what price should it sell? What would be the dividend yield and capital gains yield in each year?

j. What does market equilibrium mean?

k. If equilibrium does not exist, how will it be established?

l. What are the various forms of market efficiency? What are the implications of market efficiency?

m. Taylor Company recently issued preferred stock with a constant dividend of $5 a year, at a share price of $50. What is the expected return on the company's preferred stock?

 COMPUTER-RELATED PROBLEM

Work the problem in this section only if you are using the computer problem diskette.

8-23

Supernormal growth stock valuation

Use the model on the computer problem diskette in the File C8 to solve this problem.

a. Refer back to Problem 8-18. Rework Part e, using the computerized model to determine what WME's expected dividends and stock price would be under the conditions given.

b. Suppose your boss tells you that she regards WME as being quite risky and that she believes the required rate of return should be higher than the 12 percent originally specified. Rework the problem under the conditions given in Part e, except change the required rate of return to (1) 13 percent, (2) 15 percent, and (3) 20 percent to determine the effects of the higher required rates of return on WME's stock price.

PART IV

INVESTING IN LONG-TERM ASSETS: CAPITAL BUDGETING

CHAPTER 9
THE COST OF CAPITAL

CHAPTER 10
THE BASICS OF CAPITAL
BUDGETING

CHAPTER 11
CASH FLOW ESTIMATION AND
OTHER TOPICS IN CAPITAL
BUDGETING

APPENDIX 11A
DEPRECIATION

APPENDIX 11B
REFUNDING OPERATIONS

CHAPTER 12
RISK ANALYSIS AND THE OPTIMAL
CAPITAL BUDGET

CHAPTER 9

THE COST OF CAPITAL

FIRST THINGS FIRST

In Chapter 2 we discussed the concept of EVA— Economic Value Added — which is used by an increasing number of companies to measure corporate performance. Developed by the consulting firm Stern Stewart & Company, EVA is designed to measure a corporation's true profitability, and it is calculated as after-tax operating profits less the annual cost of all the capital a firm uses.

The idea behind EVA is quite simple — firms are truly profitable and create value if and only if their income exceeds the cost of all the capital they use to finance operations. The conventional measure of performance, net income, takes into account the cost of debt, which shows up on financial statements as interest expense, but it does not reflect the cost of equity. Therefore, a firm can report positive net income yet still be unprofitable in an economic sense if its net income is less than its cost of equity. EVA corrects this flaw by recognizing that to properly measure a firm's performance, it is necessary to account for the cost of equity capital.

A firm's cost of capital is affected by its financing and investment policies. Thus, the cost of capital is determined in part by the types of capital the firm uses, by its dividend policy, and by the types of investment projects it undertakes (which affects its riskiness).

However, some determinants of the cost of capital are beyond the firm's control. Included in this category are the level of interest rates in the economy, federal and state tax policies, and the firm's regulatory environment.

The four chapters in Part IV discuss how firms decide which potential investments should be undertaken. We begin by estimating how much it will cost to raise the capital used to make investments. Given this estimate, the firm can then evaluate potential projects and accept only those whose expected returns are greater than their costs of capital. That will increase EVA and thus stockholders' wealth.

As you will see in Chapters 10, 11, and 12, deciding whether or not to invest in fixed assets — or *capital budgeting decisions* — involve discounted cash flow analysis. In Chapter 9, we take up the first element in the capital budgeting process, determining the proper discount rate for use in capital budgeting. This discount rate is called the *cost of capital.*

Although the most important use of the cost of capital is in capital budgeting, it is also used for other purposes. For example, the cost of capital is a key factor in decisions relating to the use of debt versus equity capital. The cost of capital is also important in the regulation of electric, gas, and telephone companies. These utilities are natural monopolies in the sense that one firm can supply service at a lower cost than could two or more firms. Since it has a monopoly, your electric or telephone company could, if it were unregulated, exploit you. Therefore, regulators (1) determine the cost of the capital investors have provided the utility and (2) then set rates designed to permit the company to earn its cost of capital, no more and no less.

It should be noted that the cost of capital models and formulas used in this chapter are the same ones we developed in Chapters 7 and 8, where we were concerned with the rates of return investors require on different securities. The same factors that affect required rates of return on securities by investors also determine the cost of capital to a firm, so exactly the same models are used by investors and by corporate treasurers.

THE LOGIC OF THE WEIGHTED AVERAGE COST OF CAPITAL

It is possible to finance a firm entirely with equity funds. In that case, the cost of capital used to analyze capital budgeting decisions should be the company's required return on equity. However, most firms raise a substantial portion of their capital as long-term debt, and many also use preferred stock. For these firms, the cost of capital must reflect the average cost of the various sources of long-term funds used, not just the firms' costs of equity.

Assume that Allied Food Products has a 10 percent cost of debt and a 13.4 percent cost of equity. Further, assume that Allied has made the decision to finance next year's projects with debt. The argument is sometimes made that the cost of capital for these projects is 10 percent because only debt will be used to finance them. However, this position is incorrect. If Allied finances a particular set of projects with debt, the firm will be using up some of its capacity for borrowing in the future. As expansion occurs in subsequent years, Allied will at some point find it necessary to raise additional equity to prevent the debt ratio from becoming too large.

To illustrate, suppose Allied borrows heavily at 10 percent during 1998, using up its debt capacity in the process, to finance projects yielding 11.5 percent. In 1999, it has new projects available that yield 13 percent, well above the return on 1998 projects, but it cannot accept them because they would have to be financed with 13.4 percent equity money. *To avoid this problem, Allied should be viewed as an ongoing concern, and the cost of capital used in capital budgeting should be calculated as a weighted average, or composite, of the various types of funds it generally uses, regardless of the specific financing used to fund a particular project.*

ON THE WWW
Ohio State has a web site with video clips of business professionals discussing various topics of interest in finance. The site can be found at http://www.cob.ohio-state.edu/dept/fin/resources_education/clips.htm. The two video clips relevant to capital budgeting come from Steve Walsh, assistant treasurer of JCPenney: "How We Do Capital Budgeting" and "On the Cost of Capital and Debt." Be forewarned that these files are quite large and are best downloaded using a rapid Internet link.

Why should the cost of capital used in capital budgeting be calculated as a weighted average of the various types of funds the firm generally uses, not the cost of the specific financing used to fund a particular project?

BASIC DEFINITIONS

Capital Component
One of the types of capital used by firms to raise money.

The items on the right side of a firm's balance sheet — various types of debt, preferred stock, and common equity — are called **capital components.** Any increase in total assets must be financed by an increase in one or more of these capital components.

Capital is a necessary factor of production, and like any other factor, it has a cost. The cost of each component is called the *component cost* of that particular type of capital; for example, if Allied can borrow money at 10 percent, its component cost of debt is 10 percent.[1] Throughout this chapter, we concentrate on debt, preferred stock, retained earnings, and new issues of common stock, which are the four major capital structure components; their component costs are identified by the following symbols:

k_d = interest rate on the firm's new debt = before-tax component cost of debt. For Allied, k_d = 10%.

$k_d(1 - T)$ = after-tax component cost of debt, where T is the firm's marginal tax rate. $k_d(1 - T)$ is the debt cost used to calculate the weighted average cost of capital. For Allied, T = 40%, so $k_d(1 - T)$ = 10%(1 − 0.4) = 10%(0.6) = 6.0%.

k_{ps} = component cost of preferred stock. For Allied, k_{ps} = 10.3%.

k_s = component cost of retained earnings (or internal equity). It is identical to the k_s developed in Chapters 5 and 8 and defined there as the required rate of return on common stock. It is generally difficult to estimate k_s, but, as we shall see shortly, for Allied, $k_s \approx 13.4\%$.

k_e = component cost of external equity, or equity obtained by issuing new common stock as opposed to retaining earnings. As we shall see, it is necessary to distinguish between equity raised by retaining earnings and that raised by selling new stock. This is why we distinguish between internal and external equity, k_s and k_e. Further, k_e is always greater than k_s. For Allied, $k_e \approx 14\%$.

WACC = the weighted average cost of capital. If Allied raises new capital to finance asset expansion, and if it is to keep its capital structure in balance (that is, if it is to keep the same percentage of debt, preferred stock, and common equity funds), then it must raise part of its new funds as debt, part as preferred stock, and part as common equity (with equity coming either from retained earnings or from the issuance of new common stock).[2] We will calculate WACC for Allied Food Products shortly.

---

[1]We will see shortly that there is both a before-tax and an after-tax cost of debt; for now, it is sufficient to know that 10 percent is the before-tax component cost of debt.

[2]Firms try to keep their debt, preferred stock, and common equity in optimal proportions; we will learn how they establish these "target" proportions in Chapter 13.

These definitions and concepts are explained in detail in the remainder of the chapter, where we develop a marginal cost of capital (MCC) schedule that can be used in capital budgeting. Later, in Chapter 13, we will extend the analysis to determine the mix of types of capital that will minimize the firm's cost of capital and thereby maximize its value.

Identify the firm's four major capital structure components, and give their respective component cost symbols.

COST OF DEBT, $k_d(1 - T)$

After-tax Cost of Debt, $k_d(1 - T)$
The relevant cost of new debt, taking into account the tax deductibility of interest; used to calculate the WACC.

The **after-tax cost of debt, $k_d(1 - T)$,** is used to calculate the weighted average cost of capital, and it is the interest rate on debt, k_d, less the tax savings that result because interest is deductible. This is the same as k_d multiplied by $(1 - T)$, where T is the firm's marginal tax rate:[3]

$$\text{After-tax component cost of debt} = \text{Interest rate} - \text{Tax savings}$$
$$= k_d - k_d T$$
$$= k_d(1 - T). \tag{9-1}$$

In effect, the government pays part of the cost of debt because interest is deductible. Therefore, if Allied can borrow at an interest rate of 10 percent, and if it has a marginal federal-plus-state tax rate of 40 percent, then its after-tax cost of debt is 6 percent:

$$k_d(1 - T) = 10\%(1.0 - 0.4)$$
$$= 10\%(0.6)$$
$$= 6.0\%.$$

The reason for using the after-tax cost of debt in calculating the weighted average cost of capital is as follows. The value of the firm's stock, which we want to maximize, depends on *after-tax* cash flows. Because interest is a deductible expense, it produces tax savings which reduce the net cost of debt, making the after-tax cost of debt less than the before-tax cost. We are concerned with after-tax cash flows, and since cash flows and rates of return should be placed on a comparable basis, we adjust the interest rate downward to take account of the preferential tax treatment of debt.[4]

---

[3]The federal tax rate for most corporations is 35 percent. However, most corporations are also subject to state income taxes, so the marginal tax rate on most corporate income is about 40 percent. For illustrative purposes, we assume that the effective federal-plus-state tax rate on marginal income is 40 percent. Also, note that the cost of debt is considered in isolation. The effect of debt on the cost of equity, as well as on future increments of debt, is ignored when the weighted cost of a combination of debt and equity is derived in this chapter, but it will be treated in Chapter 13, "Capital Structure and Leverage."

[4]The tax rate is *zero* for a firm with losses. Therefore, for a company that does not pay taxes, the cost of debt is not reduced; that is, in Equation 9-1, the tax rate equals zero, so the after-tax cost of debt is equal to the interest rate.

Note that the cost of debt is the interest rate on *new* debt, not that on already outstanding debt; in other words, we are interested in the *marginal* cost of debt. Our primary concern with the cost of capital is to use it for capital budgeting decisions — for example, would a new machine earn a return greater than the cost of the capital needed to acquire the machine? The rate at which the firm has borrowed in the past is irrelevant — we need the cost of *new capital*.

SELF-TEST QUESTIONS

Why is the after-tax cost of debt rather than the before-tax cost used to calculate the weighted average cost of capital?

Is the relevant cost of debt the interest rate on already *outstanding* debt or that on *new* debt? Why?

COST OF PREFERRED STOCK, k_{ps}

Cost of Preferred Stock, k_{ps}
The rate of return investors require on the firm's preferred stock. k_{ps} is calculated as the preferred dividend, D_{ps}, divided by the net issuing price, P_n.

The component **cost of preferred stock** used to calculate the weighted average cost of capital, k_{ps}, is the preferred dividend, D_{ps}, divided by the net issuing price, P_n, which is the price the firm receives after deducting flotation costs:

$$\text{Component cost of preferred stock} = k_{ps} = \frac{D_{ps}}{P_n}. \quad (9\text{-}2)$$

For example, Allied has preferred stock that pays a $10 dividend per share and sells for $100 per share in the market. If Allied issued new shares of preferred, it would incur an underwriting (or flotation) cost of 2.5 percent, or $2.50 per share, so it would net $97.50 per share. Therefore, Allied's cost of preferred stock is 10.3 percent:

$$k_{ps} = \$10/\$97.50 = 10.3\%.$$

It should also be noted that we have ignored flotation costs (the costs incurred for new issuances) on debt. The reason is that the vast majority of debt (more than 99 percent) is privately placed, hence has no flotation cost. However, if bonds are publicly placed and do involve flotation costs, the solution value of k_d in this formula is used as the after-tax cost of debt:

$$M(1 - F) = \sum_{t=1}^{N} \frac{INT(1 - T)}{(1 + k_d)^t} + \frac{M}{(1 + k_d)^N}.$$

Here F is the percentage amount of the bond flotation cost, N is the number of periods to maturity, INT is the dollars of interest per period, T is the corporate tax rate, M is the maturity value of the bond, and k_d is the after-tax cost of debt adjusted to reflect flotation costs. If we assume that the bond in the example calls for annual payments, that it has a 20-year maturity, and that F = 2%, then the flotation-adjusted, after-tax cost of debt is 6.18 percent versus 6 percent before the flotation adjustment.

Strictly speaking, the after-tax cost of debt should reflect the *expected* cost of debt. While Allied's bonds have a promised return of 10 percent, there is some chance of default, so its bondholders' expected return (and consequently Allied's cost) is a bit less than 10 percent. For a relatively strong company such as Allied, this difference is quite small. Note too that Allied must incur flotation costs when it issues debt, but like the difference between the promised and the expected rate of return, flotation costs are generally small. Finally, note that these two factors tend to offset one another — not including the possibility of default leads to an overstatement of the cost of debt, but not including flotation costs leads to an understatement. For all these reasons, k_d is generally a good approximation of the before-tax cost of debt capital.

No tax adjustments are made when calculating k_{ps} because preferred dividends, unlike interest on debt, are *not* deductible. Therefore, there are no tax savings associated with the use of preferred stock.

SELF-TEST QUESTIONS   ??????

Does the component cost of preferred stock include or exclude flotation costs? Explain.

Is a tax adjustment made to the cost of preferred stock? Why or why not?

COST OF RETAINED EARNINGS, k_s

Cost of Retained Earnings, k_s
The rate of return required by stockholders on a firm's common stock.

The costs of debt and preferred stock are based on the returns investors require on these securities, and so is the cost of retained earnings: The **cost of retained earnings, k_s,** is the rate of return stockholders require on equity capital the firm obtains by retaining earnings.[5]

The reason we must assign a cost of capital to retained earnings involves the *opportunity cost principle.* The firm's after-tax earnings belong to its stockholders. Bondholders are compensated by interest payments, and preferred stockholders by preferred dividends. All earnings remaining after interest and preferred dividends belong to the common stockholders, and these earnings serve to compensate stockholders for the use of their capital. Management may either pay out earnings in the form of dividends or else retain earnings and reinvest them in the business. If management decides to retain earnings, there is an *opportunity cost* involved — stockholders could have received the earnings as dividends and invested this money in other stocks, in bonds, in real estate, or in anything else. Thus, the firm should earn on its retained earnings at least as much as the stockholders themselves could have earned on alternative investments of comparable risk.

What rate of return can stockholders expect to earn on equivalent-risk investments? First, recall from Chapter 8 that stocks are normally in equilibrium, with expected and required rates of return being equal: $\hat{k}_s = k_s$. Thus, we can assume that Allied's stockholders expect to earn a return of k_s on their money. *Therefore, if the firm cannot invest retained earnings and earn at least k_s, it should pay these funds to its stockholders and let them invest directly in other assets that do provide this return.*[6]

Whereas debt and preferred stocks are contractual obligations that have easily determined costs, it is difficult to measure k_s. However, we can employ the principles developed in Chapters 5 and 8 to produce reasonably good cost of equity estimates. Recall that if a stock is in equilibrium, then its required rate of return, k_s, must be equal to its expected rate of return, $\hat{k}_s$. Further, its *required* return is equal to a risk-free rate, k_{RF}, plus a risk premium, RP, whereas the

[5]The term *retained earnings* can be interpreted to mean either the balance sheet item "retained earnings," consisting of all the earnings retained in the business throughout its history, or the income statement item "additions to retained earnings." The income statement item is used in this chapter; for our purpose, *retained earnings* refers to that part of the current year's earnings not paid out in dividends, hence available for reinvestment in the business this year.

[6]Dividends and capital gains are taxed differently, with long-term capital gains being taxed at a lower rate than dividends for many stockholders. That makes it beneficial for companies to retain earnings rather than to pay them out as dividends, and that, in turn, tends to lower the cost of capital for retained earnings. This point is discussed in detail in Chapter 14.

expected return on a constant growth stock is equal to the stock's dividend yield, D_1/P_0, plus its expected growth rate, g:

Required rate of return = Expected rate of return

$$k_s = k_{RF} + RP \quad = \quad D_1/P_0 + g = \hat{k}_s. \qquad (9\text{-}3)$$

Therefore, we can estimate k_s either as $k_s = k_{RF} + RP$ or as $k_s = D_1/P_0 + g$.

THE CAPM APPROACH

One approach to estimating the cost of retained earnings is to use the Capital Asset Pricing Model (CAPM) as developed in Chapter 5, proceeding as follows:

Step 1. Estimate the risk-free rate, k_{RF}, generally taken to be either the U.S. Treasury bond rate or the short-term (30-day) Treasury bill rate.

Step 2. Estimate the stock's beta coefficient, b_i, and use this as an index of the stock's risk. The i signifies the *i*th company's beta.

Step 3. Estimate the expected rate of return on the market, or on an "average" stock, k_M.

Step 4. Substitute the preceding values into the CAPM equation to estimate the required rate of return on the stock in question:

$$k_s = k_{RF} + (k_M - k_{RF})b_i. \qquad (9\text{-}4)$$

Equation 9-4 shows that the CAPM estimate of k_s begins with the risk-free rate, k_{RF}, to which is added a risk premium set equal to the risk premium on an average stock, $k_M - k_{RF}$, scaled up or down to reflect the particular stock's risk as measured by its beta coefficient.

To illustrate the CAPM approach, assume that k_{RF} = 8%, k_M = 13%, and b_i = 0.7 for a given stock. This stock's k_s is calculated as follows:

$$k_s = 8\% + (13\% - 8\%)(0.7)$$
$$= 8\% + (5\%)(0.7)$$
$$= 8\% + 3.5\%$$
$$= 11.5\%.$$

Had b_i been 1.8, indicating that the stock was riskier than average, its k_s would have been

$$k_s = 8\% + (5\%)(1.8)$$
$$= 8\% + 9\%$$
$$= 17\%.$$

For an average stock when k_{RF} is 8 percent and the market risk premium is 5 percent,

$$k_s = k_M = 8\% + (5\%)(1.0) = 13\%.$$

It should be noted that although the CAPM approach appears to yield accurate, precise estimates of k_s, there are actually several problems with it. First, as we saw in Chapter 5, if a firm's stockholders are not well diversified, they may be concerned with *stand-alone risk* rather than just market risk. In that case, the firm's true investment risk would not be measured by its beta, and the CAPM procedure would understate the correct value of k_s. Further, even if the CAPM method is valid, it is hard to obtain correct estimates of the inputs required to make it operational: (1) there is controversy about whether to use long-term or short-term Treasury yields for k_{RF}, (2) it is hard to estimate the beta that investors expect the company to have in the future, and (3) it is difficult to estimate the market risk premium.

BOND-YIELD-PLUS-RISK-PREMIUM APPROACH

Analysts who do not have confidence in the CAPM often use a subjective, ad hoc procedure to estimate a firm's cost of common equity: they simply add a judgmental risk premium of 3 to 5 percentage points to the interest rate on the firm's own long-term debt. It is logical to think that firms with risky, low-rated, and consequently high-interest-rate debt will also have risky, high-cost equity, and the procedure of basing the cost of equity on a readily observable debt cost utilizes this logic. For example, if an extremely strong firm such as Southern Bell had bonds which yielded 8 percent, its cost of equity might be estimated as follows:

$$k_s = \text{Bond yield} + \text{Risk premium} = 8\% + 4\% = 12\%.$$

The bonds of a riskier company such as Continental Airlines might carry a yield of 12 percent, making its estimated cost of equity 16 percent:

$$k_s = 12\% + 4\% = 16\%.$$

Because the 4 percent risk premium is a judgmental estimate, the estimated value of k_s is also judgmental. Empirical work in recent years suggests that the risk premium over a firm's own bond yield has generally ranged from 3 to 5 percentage points, so this method is not likely to produce a precise cost of equity — about all it can do is get us "into the right ballpark."

DIVIDEND-YIELD-PLUS-GROWTH-RATE, OR DISCOUNTED CASH FLOW (DCF), APPROACH

In Chapter 8, we saw that both the price and the expected rate of return on a share of common stock depend, ultimately, on the dividends expected on the stock:

$$P_0 = \frac{D_1}{(1 + k_s)^1} + \frac{D_2}{(1 + k_s)^2} + \cdots$$

$$= \sum_{t=1}^{\infty} \frac{D_t}{(1 + k_s)^t}. \tag{9-5}$$

Here P_0 is the current price of the stock; D_t is the dividend expected to be paid at the end of Year t; and k_s is the required rate of return. If dividends are expected to grow at a constant rate, then, as we saw in Chapter 8, Equation 9-5 reduces to this important formula:

$$P_0 = \frac{D_1}{k_s - g}. \tag{9-6}$$

We can solve for k_s to obtain the required rate of return on common equity, which, for the marginal investor, is also equal to the expected rate of return:

$$k_s = \hat{k}_s = \frac{D_1}{P_0} + \text{Expected g}. \tag{9-7}$$

Thus, investors expect to receive a dividend yield, D_1/P_0, plus a capital gain, g, for a total expected return of $\hat{k}_s$, and in equilibrium this expected return is also equal to the required return, k_s. This method of estimating the cost of equity is called the *discounted cash flow, or DCF, method.* Henceforth, we will assume that equilibrium exists, and we will use the terms k_s and $\hat{k}_s$ interchangeably.

It is easy to determine the dividend yield, but it is difficult to establish the proper growth rate. If past growth rates in earnings and dividends have been relatively stable, and if investors appear to be projecting a continuation of past trends, then g may be based on the firm's historic growth rate. *However, if the company's past growth has been abnormally high or low, either because of its own unique situation or because of general economic fluctuations, then investors will not project the past growth rate into the future.* In this case, g must be estimated in some other manner.

Security analysts regularly make earnings and dividend growth forecasts, looking at such factors as projected sales, profit margins, and competitive factors. For example, *Value Line*, which is available in most libraries, provides growth rate forecasts for 1,700 companies, and Merrill Lynch, Salomon Brothers, and other organizations make similar forecasts. Therefore, someone making a cost of equity estimate can obtain several analysts' forecasts, average them, use the average as a proxy for the growth expectations of investors in general, and then combine this g with the current dividend yield to estimate $\hat{k}_s$ as follows:

$$\hat{k}_s = \frac{D_1}{P_0} + \text{Growth rate as projected by security analysts.}$$

Again, note that this estimate of $\hat{k}_s$ is based on the assumption that g is expected to remain constant in the future.[7]

Another method for estimating g involves first forecasting the firm's average future dividend payout ratio and its complement, the *retention rate,* and then multiplying the retention rate by the company's expected future rate of return on equity (ROE):

$$g = (\text{Retention rate})(\text{ROE}) = (1.0 - \text{Payout rate})(\text{ROE}). \qquad \text{(9-8)}$$

Security analysts often use this procedure when they estimate growth rates. For example, suppose a company is expected to have a constant ROE of 13.4 percent, and it is expected to pay out 40 percent of its earnings and to retain 60 percent. In this case, its forecasted growth rate would be $g = (0.60)(13.4\%) = 8.0\%$.

To illustrate the DCF approach, suppose Allied's stock sells for $23; its next expected dividend is $1.24; and its expected growth rate is 8 percent. Allied's expected and required rate of return, hence its cost of retained earnings, would then be 13.4 percent:

$$\hat{k}_s = k_s = \frac{\$1.24}{\$23} + 8.0\%$$
$$= 5.4\% + 8.0\%$$
$$= 13.4\%.$$

---

[7]Analysts' growth rate forecasts are usually for five years into the future, and the rates provided represent the average growth rate over that five-year horizon. Studies have shown that analysts' forecasts represent the best source of growth rate data for DCF cost of capital estimates. See Robert Harris, "Using Analysts' Growth Rate Forecasts to Estimate Shareholder Required Rates of Return," *Financial Management,* Spring 1986.

Note also that two organizations — IBES and Zacks — collect the forecasts of leading analysts for most larger companies, average these forecasts, and then publish the averages. The IBES and Zacks data are available over the Internet through on-line computer data services.

This 13.4 percent is the minimum rate of return that management must expect to earn to justify retaining earnings and plowing them back into the business rather than paying them out to stockholders as dividends. Put another way, since investors have an *opportunity* to earn 13.4 percent if earnings are paid to them as dividends, then the company's *opportunity cost* of equity from retained earnings is 13.4 percent.

People experienced in estimating equity capital costs recognize that both careful analysis and sound judgment are required. It would be nice to pretend that judgment is unnecessary and to specify an easy, precise way of determining the exact cost of equity capital. Unfortunately, this is not possible — finance is in large part a matter of judgment, and we simply must face that fact.

SELF-TEST QUESTIONS

Why must a cost be assigned to retained earnings?

Name three approaches for estimating the cost of retained earnings.

Identify some problems with the CAPM approach.

What is the reasoning behind the bond-yield-plus-risk-premium approach?

Which of the two components of the constant growth DCF formula, the dividend yield or the growth rate, is more difficult to estimate? Why?

COST OF NEWLY ISSUED COMMON STOCK, OR EXTERNAL EQUITY, k_e

Cost of New Common Equity, k_e
The cost of external equity; based on the cost of retained earnings, but increased for flotation costs.

The **cost of new common equity, k_e**, or external equity, is higher than the cost of retained earnings, k_s, because of flotation costs involved in issuing new common stock. What rate of return must be earned on funds raised by selling stock to make issuing new stock worthwhile? To put it another way, what is the cost of new common stock?

The answer, for a constant growth stock, is found by applying this formula:[8]

$$k_e = \frac{D_1}{P_0(1 - F)} + g. \tag{9-9}$$

---

[8]Equation 9-9 is derived as follows:

Step 1. The old stockholders expect the firm to pay a stream of dividends, D_t, which will be derived from existing assets with a per-share value of P_0. New investors will likewise expect to receive the same stream of dividends, but the funds available to invest in assets will be less than P_0 because of flotation costs. For new investors to receive their expected dividend stream *without impairing the D_t stream of the old investors,* the new funds obtained from the sale of stock must be invested at a return high enough to provide a dividend stream whose present value is equal to the net price the firm will receive:

$$P_n = P_0(1 - F) = \sum_{t=1}^{\infty} \frac{D_t}{(1 + k_e)^t}. \tag{9-10}$$

Here D_t is the dividend stream to new (and old) stockholders, and k_e is the cost of new outside equity.

Step 2. When growth is constant, Equation 9-10 reduces to

$$P_n = P_0(1 - F) = \frac{D_1}{k_e - g}. \tag{9-10a}$$

Step 3. Equation 9-10a can be rearranged to produce Equation 9-9:

$$k_e = \frac{D_1}{P_0(1 - F)} + g.$$

Flotation Cost, F
The percentage cost of issuing new common stock.

Here F is the percentage **flotation cost** incurred in selling the new stock, so $P_0(1 - F)$ is the net price per share received by the company.

Assuming that Allied has a flotation cost of 10 percent, its cost of new outside equity is computed as follows:

$$k_e = \frac{\$1.24}{\$23(1 - 0.10)} + 8.0\%$$

$$= \frac{\$1.24}{\$20.70} + 8.0\%$$

$$= 6.0\% + 8.0\% = 14.0\%.$$

Investors require a return of $k_s = 13.4\%$ on the stock. However, because of flotation costs the company must earn *more* than 13.4 percent on the net funds obtained by selling stock if investors are to receive a 13.4 percent return on the money they put up. Specifically, if the firm earns 14 percent on funds obtained by issuing new stock, then earnings per share will remain at the previously expected level, the firm's expected dividend can be maintained, and, as a result, the price per share will not decline. If the firm earns less than 14 percent, then earnings, dividends, and growth will fall below expectations, causing the stock price to decline. If the firm earns more than 14 percent, the stock price will rise.[9]

The reason for the flotation adjustment can be made clear by a simple example. Suppose Weaver Candy Company has $100,000 of assets and no debt, it earns a 15 percent return (or $15,000) on its assets, and it pays all earnings out as dividends, so its growth rate is zero. The company has 1,000 shares of stock outstanding, so EPS = DPS = $15, and P_0 = $100. Weaver's cost of equity is thus k_s = $15/$100 + 0 = 15%. Now suppose Weaver can get a return of 15 percent on new assets. Should it sell new stock to acquire new assets? If it sold 1,000 new shares of stock to the public for $100 per share, but incurred a 10 percent flotation cost on the issue, it would net $100 − 0.10($100) = $90 per share, or $90,000 in total. It would then invest this $90,000 and earn 15 percent, or $13,500. Its new total earnings would be $15,000 from the old assets plus $13,500 from the new assets, or $28,500 in total, but it would now have 2,000 shares of stock outstanding. Therefore, its EPS and DPS would decline from $15 to $14.25:

$$\text{New EPS and DPS} = \frac{\$28,500}{2,000} = \$14.25.$$

Because its EPS and DPS would fall, the stock price also would fall, from P_0 = $100 to P_1 = $14.25/0.15 = $95.00. This result occurs because while investors put up $100 per share, the company received and invested only $90 per share. Thus, we see that the $90 must earn more than 15 percent to provide investors with a 15 percent return on the $100 they put up. Put another way, dollars raised by selling new stock must "work harder" than dollars raised by retaining earnings.

---

[9]On occasion it is useful to use another equation to calculate the cost of external equity:

$$k_e = \frac{\text{Dividend yield}}{(1 - F)} + g = \frac{D_1/P_0}{(1 - F)} + g. \tag{9-9a}$$

Equation 9-9a is derived algebraically from Equation 9-9, and it is useful when information on dividend yields, but not on dollar dividends and stock prices, is available.

Now suppose Weaver earned a return of k_e based on Equation 9-9 on the $90,000 of new assets:

$$k_e = \frac{D_1}{P_0(1-F)} + g$$

$$= \frac{\$15}{\$100(0.90)} + 0 = 16.667\%.$$

Here is the new situation:

$$\text{New total earnings} = \$15,000 + \$90,000(0.16667)$$
$$= \$15,000 + \$15,000$$
$$= \$30,000.$$

$$\text{New EPS and DPS} = \$30,000/2,000 = \$15.$$
$$\text{New price} = \$15/0.15 = \$100 = \text{Original price.}$$

Thus, if the return on the new assets is equal to k_e as calculated by Equation 9-9, then EPS, DPS, and the stock price will all remain constant. If the return on the new assets exceeds k_e, then EPS, DPS, and P_0 will rise. This confirms the fact that because of flotation costs, the cost of external equity exceeds the cost of equity raised internally from retained earnings.

SELF-TEST QUESTIONS   ??????

Why is the cost of external equity higher than the cost of retained earnings?

How can the DCF model be changed to account for flotation costs?

COMPOSITE, OR WEIGHTED AVERAGE, COST OF CAPITAL, WACC

Target (Optimal) Capital Structure
The percentages of debt, preferred stock, and common equity that will maximize the firm's stock price.

As we shall see in Chapter 13, each firm has an optimal capital structure, defined as that mix of debt, preferred, and common equity that causes its stock price to be maximized. Therefore, a value-maximizing firm will establish a **target (optimal) capital structure** and then raise new capital in a manner that will keep the actual capital structure on target over time. In this chapter, we assume that the firm has identified its optimal capital structure, that it uses this optimum as the target, and that it finances so as to remain constantly on target. How the target is established will be examined in Chapter 13.

Weighted Average Cost of Capital, WACC
A weighted average of the component costs of debt, preferred stock, and common equity.

The target proportions of debt, preferred stock, and common equity, along with the component costs of capital, are used to calculate the firm's **weighted average cost of capital, WACC.** To illustrate, suppose Allied Food has a target capital structure calling for 45 percent debt, 2 percent preferred stock, and 53 percent common equity (retained earnings plus common stock). Its before-tax cost of debt, k_d, is 10 percent; its after-tax cost of debt = $k_d(1-T) = 10\%(0.6) = 6.0\%$; its cost of preferred stock, k_{ps}, is 10.3 percent; its cost of common equity from retained earnings, k_s, is 13.4 percent; its marginal tax rate is 40 percent, and all of

INDUSTRY PRACTICE

HOW MUCH DOES IT COST TO RAISE EXTERNAL CAPITAL?

A recent study by four professors provides some insights into how much it costs U.S. corporations to raise external capital. Using information from the Securities Data Company, they found the average flotation cost for debt and equity issued in the 1990s as presented below.

The common stock flotation costs are for non-IPOs. Costs associated with IPOs are even higher — flotation costs are about 17 percent of gross proceeds for common equity if the amount raised is less than $10 million and about 6 percent if more than $500 million is raised. The data include both utility and nonutility companies. If utilities were excluded, flotation costs would be somewhat higher.

SOURCE: Inmoo Lee, Scott Lochhead, Jay Ritter, and Quanshui Zhao, "The Costs of Raising Capital," *The Journal of Financial Research*, Vol. XIX, No. 1, Spring 1996, 59–74. Reprinted with permission.

AMOUNT OF CAPITAL RAISED (MILLIONS OF DOLLARS)	AVERAGE FLOTATION COST FOR COMMON STOCK (% OF TOTAL CAPITAL RAISED)	AVERAGE FLOTATION COST FOR NEW DEBT (% OF TOTAL CAPITAL RAISED)
2–9.99	13.28	4.39
10–19.99	8.72	2.76
20–39.99	6.93	2.42
40–59.99	5.87	1.32
60–79.99	5.18	2.34
80–99.99	4.73	2.16
100–199.99	4.22	2.31
200–499.99	3.47	2.19
500 and up	3.15	1.64

its new equity will come from retained earnings. Now we can calculate Allied's weighted average cost of capital, WACC, as follows:

$$WACC = w_d k_d (1 - T) + w_{ps} k_{ps} + w_{ce} k_s \qquad (9\text{-}11)$$
$$= 0.45(10\%)(0.6) + 0.02(10.3\%) + 0.53(13.4\%)$$
$$= 10.0\%.$$

Here w_d, w_{ps}, and w_{ce} are the weights used for debt, preferred, and common equity, respectively.

Every dollar of new capital that Allied obtains consists of 45 cents of debt with an after-tax cost of 6 percent, 2 cents of preferred stock with a cost of 10.3 percent, and 53 cents of common equity (all from additions to retained earnings) with a cost of 13.4 percent. The average cost of each whole dollar, WACC, is 10 percent.

The weights could be based either on the accounting values shown on the firm's balance sheet (book values) or on the market values of the different securities. Theoretically, the weights should be based on market values, but if a firm's book value weights are reasonably close to its market value weights, book value weights can be used as a proxy for market value weights. This point is discussed further in Chapter 13, but in the remainder of this chapter, we shall assume that the firm's market values are reasonably close to its book values, and we will use book value capital structure weights.

How does one calculate the weighted average cost of capital? Write out the equation.

MARGINAL COST OF CAPITAL, MCC

The *marginal cost* of any item is the cost of another unit of that item. For example, the marginal cost of labor is the cost of adding one additional worker. The marginal cost of labor may be $25 per person if 10 workers are added but $35 per person if the firm tries to hire 100 new workers, because it will be harder to find 100 people willing and able to do the work. The same concept applies to capital. As the firm tries to attract more new dollars, the cost of each dollar will at some point rise. *Thus, the* **marginal cost of capital (MCC)** *is defined as the cost of the last dollar of new capital the firm raises, and the marginal cost rises as more and more capital is raised during a given period.*

Marginal Cost of Capital (MCC)
The cost of obtaining another dollar of new capital; the weighted average cost of the last dollar of new capital raised.

We can use Allied Food to illustrate the marginal cost of capital concept. The company's target capital structure and other data follow:

Long-term debt	$ 754,000,000	45%
Preferred stock	40,000,000	2
Common equity	896,000,000	53
Total capital	$1,690,000,000	100%

$k_{ps} = 10\%$.

$k_{ps} = 10.3\%$.

$T = 40\%$.

$P_0 = \$23$.

$g = 8\%$, and it is expected to remain constant.

$D_0 = \$1.15 =$ dividends per share in the *last* period. D_0 has already been paid, so someone who purchased this stock today would *not* receive D_0 — rather, he or she would receive D_1, the *next* dividend.

$D_1 = D_0(1 + g) = \$1.15(1.08) = \$1.24$.

$k_s = D_1/P_0 + g = (\$1.24/\$23) + 0.08 = 0.054 + 0.08 = 0.134 = 13.4\%$.

On the basis of these data, the weighted average cost of capital, WACC, is 10 percent:

$$\text{WACC} = \begin{pmatrix}\text{Fraction} \\ \text{of} \\ \text{debt}\end{pmatrix}\begin{pmatrix}\text{Interest} \\ \text{rate}\end{pmatrix}(1 - T) + \begin{pmatrix}\text{Fraction} \\ \text{of} \\ \text{preferred} \\ \text{stock}\end{pmatrix}\begin{pmatrix}\text{Cost} \\ \text{of} \\ \text{preferred} \\ \text{stock}\end{pmatrix} + \begin{pmatrix}\text{Fraction of} \\ \text{common} \\ \text{equity}\end{pmatrix}\begin{pmatrix}\text{Cost} \\ \text{of} \\ \text{equity}\end{pmatrix}$$

$$= \quad (0.45)(10\%)(0.6) \quad + \quad (0.02)(10.3\%) \quad + \quad (0.53)(13.4\%)$$

$$= \quad 2.7\% \quad + \quad 0.2\% \quad + \quad 7.1\%$$

$$= \quad 10.0\%.$$

Note that short-term debt is not included in the capital structure. Allied uses its cost of capital in the capital budgeting process, which involves long-term

INDUSTRY PRACTICE

WACC ESTIMATES FOR SOME LARGE U.S. CORPORATIONS

As noted in Chapter 2, the New York consulting firm of Stern Stewart & Company regularly estimates EVAs and MVAs for large U.S. corporations. To obtain these estimates, Stern Stewart must calculate a WACC for each company. The table below presents some recent WACC estimates as calculated by Stern Stewart for a sample of corporations, along with their debt-to-total-capital ratios.

These estimates suggest that a typical company has a WACC somewhere in the 9 percent to 15 percent range and that the WACC varies considerably depending on (1) the company's risk and (2) the amount of debt it uses. Companies in riskier businesses, such as Intel and Motorola, presumably have higher costs of common equity. Moreover, they tend not to use as much debt. These two factors, in combination, result in higher WACCs than those of companies that operate in more stable businesses, such as Wal-Mart, Heinz, and

BellSouth. We will discuss the effects of capital structure on WACC in more detail in Chapter 13.

Note, though, that riskier companies also have the potential for producing higher returns, and what really matters to shareholders is whether a company is able to generate returns in excess of its cost of capital, thus obtaining a positive EVA.

SOURCE: "Who Are the Real Wealth Creators?", *Fortune*, December 9, 1996, 107.

COMPANY	WACC	BOOK VALUE DEBT RATIO
Intel	14.5%	3%
General Electric	13.5	7
Walt Disney	12.3	33
Coca-Cola	12.0	14
Motorola	11.6	15
AT&T	9.9	39
H.J. Heinz	9.8	47
BellSouth	9.5	33
Exxon	9.4	18
Wal-Mart	9.4	43

assets, and it finances those assets with long-term capital. Thus, current liabilities do not enter the calculation. We will discuss this point in more detail in Chapter 13.[10]

As long as Allied keeps its capital structure on target, and as long as its debt has an after-tax cost of 6 percent, its preferred stock a cost of 10.3 percent, and its common equity a cost of 13.4 percent, then its weighted average cost of capital will be WACC = 10%. Each dollar the firm raises will consist of some long-term debt, some preferred stock, and some common equity, and the cost of the whole dollar will be 10 percent.

A graph which shows how the WACC changes as more and more new capital is raised during a given year is called the **marginal cost of capital schedule.** The graph shown in Figure 9-1 is Allied's MCC schedule. Here the dots represent dollars raised. Because each dollar of new capital has a cost of 10 percent, the

Marginal Cost of Capital (MCC) Schedule
A graph that relates the firm's weighted average cost of each dollar of capital to the total amount of new capital raised.

---

[10]Also see Eugene F. Brigham and Louis C. Gapenski, *Intermediate Financial Management*, 5th ed., Chapter 6.

FIGURE 9-1   Marginal Cost of Capital (MCC) Schedule for Allied Food Products

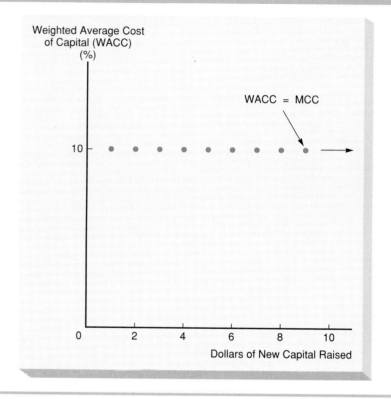

marginal cost of capital (MCC) for Allied is constant at 10 percent under the assumptions we have used thus far.[11]

THE RETAINED EARNINGS BREAK POINT

Could Allied raise an unlimited amount of new capital at the 10 percent cost? The answer is no. As a practical matter, as a company raises larger and larger sums during a given time period, the costs of debt, preferred stock, and common equity begin to rise, and as this occurs, the weighted average cost of each new dollar also rises. Thus, just as corporations cannot hire unlimited numbers of workers at a constant wage, they cannot raise unlimited amounts of capital at a constant cost. At some point, the cost of each new dollar will increase.

Where will this point occur for Allied? As a first step to determining the point at which the MCC begins to rise, recognize that although the company's balance sheet shows total long-term capital of $1,690,000,000, all of this capital was raised in the past, and it has been invested in assets which are being used in operations. New (or marginal) capital presumably will be raised so as to maintain the 45/2/53 debt/preferred/common relationship. Therefore, if Allied wants to raise

---

[11]Allied's MCC schedule in Figure 9-1 would be different (higher) if the company used any capital structure other than 45 percent debt, 2 percent preferred, and 53 percent common equity. This point will be developed in Chapter 13. As a general rule, a different MCC schedule exists for every possible capital structure, and the optimal structure is the one that produces the lowest MCC schedule.

| **T A B L E   9 - 1** | Allied's WACC Using New Retained Earnings and New Common Stock |

I. WACC when Equity Is from New Retained Earnings

	WEIGHT ×	**COMPONENT COST** =	**PRODUCT**
Debt	0.45	6.0%	2.7%
Preferred stock	0.02	10.3	0.2
Common equity (Retained earnings)	0.53	13.4	7.1
	1.00		$WACC_1 = 10.0\%$

II. WACC when Equity Is from Sale of New Common Stock

	WEIGHT ×	**COMPONENT COST** =	**PRODUCT**
Debt	0.45	6.0%	2.7%
Preferred stock	0.02	10.3	0.2
Common equity (New common stock)	0.53	14.0	7.4
	1.00		$WACC_2 = 10.3\%$

$1,000,000 in new capital, it should obtain $450,000 of debt, $20,000 of preferred stock, and $530,000 of common equity. The new common equity could come from two sources: (1) retained earnings, defined as that part of this year's profits which management decides to retain in the business rather than use for dividends (but not earnings retained in the past, for these have already been invested in plant, equipment, inventories, and so on); or (2) proceeds from the sale of new common stock.

The debt will have an interest rate of 10 percent and an after-tax cost of 6 percent, and the preferred stock will have a cost of 10.3 percent. *The cost of common equity will be $k_s = 13.4\%$ as long as the equity is obtained as retained earnings, but it will jump to $k_e = 14\%$ once the company uses up all of its retained earnings and is thus forced to sell new common stock.*

Allied's weighted average cost of capital, when it uses new retained earnings (earnings retained this year, not in the past) and also when it uses new common stock, is shown in Table 9-1. We see that the weighted average cost of each dollar is 10 percent as long as retained earnings are used, but the WACC jumps to 10.3 percent as soon as the firm exhausts its retained earnings and is forced to sell new common stock.

How much new capital can Allied raise before it exhausts its retained earnings and is forced to sell new common stock; that is, where will an increase in the MCC schedule occur? We find this point as follows:[12]

1. Assume that the company expects to have total earnings of $137.8 million in 1998. Further, it has a target payout ratio of 45 percent, so it plans to pay out 45 percent of its earnings as dividends. Thus, the retained earnings for the year are projected to be $137.8(1.0 − 0.45) = $75.8 million.

---

[12]The numbers in this set of calculations are rounded. Since the inputs are estimates, it makes little sense to carry estimates out to very many decimal places — this is "spurious accuracy."

Break Point (BP)
The dollar value of new capital that can be raised before an increase in the firm's weighted average cost of capital occurs.

2. We know that Allied expects to have $75.8 million of retained earnings for the year. We also know that if the company is to remain at its optimal capital structure, it must raise each dollar as 45 cents of debt, 2 cents of preferred, and 53 cents of common equity. Therefore, each 53 cents of retained earnings will support $1 of capital, and the $75.8 million of retained earnings will not be exhausted, hence the WACC will not rise, until $75.8 million of retained earnings, plus some additional amount of debt and preferred stock, have been used up.

3. We now want to know how much *total new capital* — debt, preferred stock, and retained earnings — can be raised before the $75.8 million of retained earnings is exhausted and Allied is forced to sell new common stock. In effect, we are seeking some amount of capital, X, which is called a **break point (BP)** and which represents the total financing that can be done before Allied is forced to sell new common stock.

4. We know that 53 percent, or 0.53, of X, the total capital raised, will be retained earnings, whereas 47 percent will be debt plus preferred. We also know that retained earnings will amount to $75.8 million. Therefore,

$$\text{Retained earnings} = 0.53X = \$75,800,000.$$

5. Solving for X, which is the *retained earnings break point,* we obtain $BP_{RE} = \$143$ million:

$$X = BP_{RE} = \frac{\text{Retained earnings}}{\text{Equity fraction}} = \frac{\$75,800,000}{0.53} = \$143,018,868 \approx 143 \text{ million.}$$

6. Thus, given $75.8 million of retained earnings, Allied can raise a total of $143 million, consisting of 0.53($143 million) = $75.8 million of retained earnings plus 0.02($143 million) = $2.9 million of preferred stock plus 0.45($143 million) = $64.3 million of new debt supported by these new retained earnings, without altering its capital structure (dollars in millions):

New debt supported by retained earnings	$64.3	45%
Preferred stock supported by retained earnings	2.9	2
Retained earnings	75.8	53
Total capital supported by retained earnings, or break point for retained earnings	$143.0	100%

7. The value of X, or $BP_{RE} = \$143$ million, is defined as the *retained earnings break point,* and it is the amount of total capital at which a break, or jump, occurs in the MCC schedule.

Figure 9-2 graphs Allied's marginal cost of capital schedule with the retained earnings break point. Each dollar has a weighted average cost of 10 percent until the company has raised a total of $143 million. This $143 million will consist of $64.3 million of new debt with an after-tax cost of 6 percent, $2.9 million of preferred stock with a cost of 10.3 percent, and $75.8 million of retained earnings with a cost of 13.4 percent. However, if Allied raises one dollar over $143 million, each new dollar will contain 53 cents of equity *obtained by selling new common equity at a cost of 14 percent;* therefore, WACC jumps from 10 percent to 10.3 percent, as calculated back in Table 9-1.

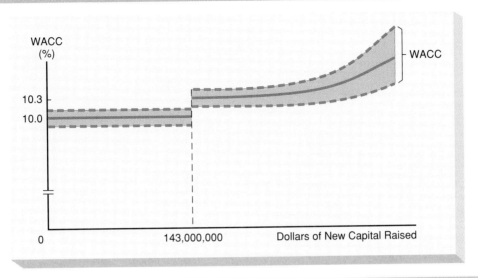

F I G U R E   9 - 2 Marginal Cost of Capital Schedule beyond the
Retained Earnings Break Point for Allied Food Products

Note that we don't really think the MCC jumps by precisely 0.3 percent when
we raise $1 over $143 million. Thus, Figure 9-2 should be regarded as an approximation rather than as a precise representation of reality. We will return to
this point later in the chapter.

THE MCC SCHEDULE BEYOND THE RETAINED EARNINGS BREAK POINT

There is a jump, or break, in Allied's MCC schedule at $143 million of new capi-
tal. Could there be other breaks in the schedule? Yes, there could. The cost of
capital could also rise due to increases in the cost of debt or the cost of preferred
stock, or as a result of further increases in flotation costs as the firm issues more
and more common stock. Some people have asserted that the costs of capital
components other than common stock should not rise. Their argument is that
as long as the capital structure does not change, and presuming that the firm
uses new capital to invest in projects with the same expected return and degree
of risk as its existing projects, investors should be willing to invest unlimited
amounts of additional capital at the same rate. However, this argument is not
borne out in empirical studies. In practice, the demand curve for securities is
downward sloping, so the more securities issued during a given period, (1) the
lower the price received for the securities and (2) the higher the required rate
of return. Therefore, the more new financing required, the higher the firm's
WACC.

As a result of all this, firms face increasing MCC schedules, such as the one
shown in Figure 9-2. Here we have identified a specific retained earnings break
point, but because of estimation difficulties, we have not attempted to identify precisely any additional break points. Moreover, we have (1) shown the MCC schedule to be upward sloping, reflecting a positive relationship between capital raised
and capital costs, and (2) we indicate our inability to measure these costs precisely

by using a band of costs rather than a single line. Note that this band exists over the whole range of capital raised — our component costs are only estimates, these estimates become more uncertain as the firm requires more and more capital, and thus the band widens as the amount of new capital raised increases.

SELF-TEST QUESTIONS   ??????

What is an MCC schedule?

What is the retained earnings break point?

What happens to the MCC schedule beyond the retained earnings break point?

FACTORS THAT AFFECT THE COST OF CAPITAL

The cost of capital is affected by a variety of factors. Some are beyond a firm's control, but others are influenced by its financing and investment policies.

FACTORS THE FIRM CANNOT CONTROL

The two most important factors which are beyond a firm's direct control are the level of interest rates and tax rates.

THE LEVEL OF INTEREST RATES.   If interest rates in the economy rise, the cost of debt increases because firms will have to pay bondholders a higher interest rate to obtain debt capital. Also, recall from our discussion of the CAPM that higher interest rates also increase the costs of common and preferred equity capital. During the early 1990s, interest rates in the United States declined significantly. This reduced the cost of capital for all firms, which encouraged additional investment. Our lower interest rates also enabled U.S. firms to compete more effectively with German and Japanese firms, which in the past had enjoyed relatively low costs of capital.

TAX RATES. Tax rates, which are largely beyond the control of an individual firm (although firms do lobby for more favorable tax treatment), have an important effect on the cost of capital. Tax rates are used in the calculation of the cost of debt for use in the WACC, and there are other less apparent ways in which tax policy affects the cost of capital. For example, lowering the capital gains tax rate relative to the rate on ordinary income would make stocks more attractive, which would reduce the cost of equity relative to that of debt. That would, as we will see in Chapter 13, lead to a change in a firm's optimal capital structure (toward less debt and more equity).

FACTORS THE FIRM CAN CONTROL

A firm can affect its cost of capital through its capital structure policy, its dividend policy, and its investment (capital budgeting) policy.

CAPITAL STRUCTURE POLICY. Until now we have assumed that a firm has a given target capital structure, and we used weights based on that target structure to calculate the WACC. It is clear, though, that a firm can change its capital structure, and such a change can affect its cost of capital. The after-tax cost of debt is lower than the cost of equity. Therefore, if the firm decides to use more debt and less common equity, this change in the weights in the WACC equation will tend to lower the WACC. However, an increase in the use of debt will increase the riskiness of both the debt and the equity, and these increases in component costs will tend to offset the effects of the change in the weights. In Chapter 13, we will discuss this in more depth, and we will demonstrate that a firm's optimal capital structure is the one which minimizes its cost of capital.

DIVIDEND POLICY. Retained earnings is income which has not been paid out as dividends. Therefore, for any given level of earnings, the higher the dividend payout ratio, the lower the amount of retained earnings, hence the further to the left the retained earnings break point in the MCC schedule. As we saw in Figure 9-2, there is a significant increase in the cost of capital beyond the retained earnings break point. Therefore, if the firm's capital budget is such that it must raise capital beyond the break point, it may decide to lower its dividend payout ratio, increase the level of retained earnings, extend outward the retained earnings break point, and thus avoid a sharp increase in its cost of capital. However, as we discuss in Chapter 14, lowering the dividend payout ratio might cause the cost of equity to increase, thus offsetting the benefit of changing the break point. Again, this illustrates why it is more appropriate to think of the MCC schedule as a band rather than as a single line.

INVESTMENT POLICY. When we estimate the cost of capital, we use as the starting point the required rates of return on the firm's outstanding stock and bonds. Those cost rates reflect the riskiness of the firm's existing assets. Therefore, we have implicitly been assuming that new capital will be invested in assets of the same type and with the same degree of risk as is embedded in the existing assets.

This assumption is generally correct, as most firms do invest in assets similar to those it currently operates, but it would be incorrect if the firm dramatically changed its investment policy. For example, if a firm invests in an entirely new line of business, its marginal cost of capital should reflect the riskiness of that new business. To illustrate, ITT Corporation recently sold off its finance company and purchased Caesar's World, a casino gambling firm. This dramatic shift in corporate focus almost certainly affected ITT's cost of capital. Likewise, Disney's purchase of the ABC television network changed the nature and risk of the company in a way that might also influence its cost of capital. The effect of investment policy on capital costs is discussed in detail in Chapter 12, "Risk Analysis and the Optimal Capital Budget."

SELF-TEST QUESTIONS

What two factors which affect the cost of capital are generally beyond the firm's control?

What policies under the firm's control are likely to affect its cost of capital?

Explain how a change in interest rates would affect each component of the weighted average cost of capital.

USING THE MCC IN CAPITAL BUDGETING: A PREVIEW

As noted at the outset of the chapter, the cost of capital is a key element in the capital budgeting process. In essence, capital budgeting consists of these steps:

1. Identify the set of available investment opportunities.
2. Estimate the future cash flows associated with each project.
3. Find the present value of each future cash flow, discounted at the cost of the capital used to finance the project, and sum these PVs to obtain the total PV of each project.
4. Compare each project's PV with its cost, and accept a project if the PV of its future cash inflows exceeds the cost of the project.

As you learned in Chapter 5, the appropriate discount rate for a given cash flow depends on the riskiness of the cash flow — the riskier the cash flow, the higher the discount rate. Therefore, the riskier a capital budgeting project, the higher its cost of capital. In this chapter, we focused on the firm's cost of capital for an *average-risk* project. It should be intuitively clear that firms take on different projects with differing degrees of risk. Part of the capital budgeting process involves assessing the riskiness of each project and assigning it a capital cost based on its relative risk. The cost of capital assigned to an average-risk project should be the marginal cost of capital as determined in this chapter. More risky projects should be assigned higher costs of capital, while less risky projects should be evaluated with a lower cost of capital. We will examine procedures for dealing with project risk in Chapter 12. Basically, though, firms first measure the marginal cost of capital as we did in this chapter, then scale it up or down to reflect individual projects' riskiness.

Another issue that arises is picking the appropriate point on the marginal cost of capital schedule for use in capital budgeting. As we have seen, every dollar raised by Allied Food Products is a weighted average which consists of 45 cents of debt, 2 cents of preferred stock, and 53 cents of common equity (with the equity coming from retained earnings until they have been used up, and then from the issuance of new common stock). Further, we saw that the WACC is constant for a while, but after the firm has exhausted its least expensive sources of capital, the WACC begins to rise. Thus, the firm has an *MCC schedule* which shows its WACC at different amounts of capital raised; Figure 9-2 gave Allied's MCC schedule.

Since its cost of capital depends on how much capital the firm raises, just which cost rate should we use in capital budgeting? Put another way, which of the WACC numbers shown in Figure 9-2 should be used to evaluate an average-risk project? We could use 10.0 percent, 10.3 percent, or some higher number, but which one *should* we use? The answer is based on the concept of marginal analysis as developed in economics. In economics, you learned that firms should expand output to the point where marginal revenue is equal to marginal cost. At that point, the last unit of output exactly covers its cost—further expansion would reduce profits, while the firm would forgo profits at any lower production rate. Therefore, the firm should expand to the point where its marginal revenue equals its marginal cost.

This same type of analysis is applied in capital budgeting. We have already developed the marginal cost curve—it is the MCC schedule. Now we need to develop a schedule that is analogous to the marginal revenue schedule. This is the **Investment Opportunity Schedule (IOS),** which shows the rate of return expected on each potential investment opportunity. As you will see in the next chapter, rates of return on capital projects are found in essentially the same way as rates of returns on stocks and bonds. Thus, we can calculate an expected rate of return on each potential project, and we can then plot those returns on the same graph that shows our marginal cost of capital. Figure 9-3 gives such a graph for Allied Food Products. Projects A, B, and C all have expected rates of return which exceed the cost of the capital that will be used to finance them, but the expected return on Project D is less than its cost of capital. Therefore, Projects A, B, and C should be accepted, and Project D should be rejected.

The WACC at the point where the Investment Opportunity Schedule intersects the MCC curve is defined as "the corporate cost of capital"—this point reflects the marginal cost of capital to the corporation. In our Figure 9-3 example, Allied's corporate cost of capital is WACC = 10.3%, and that is the cost of capital that will be used for Allied in the next two chapters to evaluate its average-risk projects and as the basing point for developing "risk-adjusted costs of capital" for Allied's other projects.

Investment Opportunity Schedule (IOS)
A graph of the firm's investment opportunities ranked in order of the projects' rates of return.

SELF-TEST QUESTIONS

As a general rule, should a firm's cost of capital as determined in this chapter be used to evaluate each and every one of its capital budgeting projects? Explain.

In what respect is marginal analysis in economics analogous to capital budgeting?

Why would it be difficult to identify a firm's cost of capital for use in capital budgeting if you were unsure of how large the capital budget was likely to be?

FIGURE   9 - 3   Combining the MCC and IOS Schedules
to Determine the Optimal Capital Budget

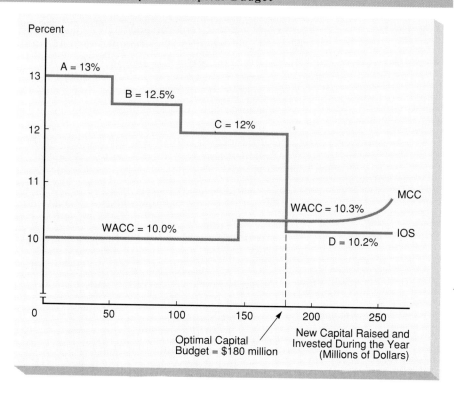

PROJECT	COST (IN MILLIONS)	RATE OF RETURN
A	$50	13.0%
B	50	12.5
C	80	12.0
D	80	10.2

SOME PROBLEM AREAS IN COST OF CAPITAL

A number of difficult issues relating to the cost of capital either have not been mentioned or were glossed over in this chapter. These topics are covered in advanced finance courses, but they deserve some mention now to alert you to potential dangers, as well as to provide you with a preview of some of the matters dealt with in advanced courses.

1. **Depreciation-generated funds.** The largest single source of capital for many firms is depreciation, yet we have not discussed the cost of funds from this source. In brief, depreciation cash flows can either be reinvested or returned to investors (stockholders *and* creditors). The cost of depreciation-generated funds is approximately equal to the weighted average cost of capital which comes from retained earnings and low-cost debt. See Eugene F. Brigham and Louis C. Gapenski, *Intermediate Financial Management,* 5th ed., Chapter 6, for a discussion.

THE COST OF EQUITY CAPITAL FOR SMALL FIRMS

The three equity cost-estimating techniques discussed in this chapter (DCF, Bond-Yield-plus-Risk-Premium, and CAPM) have serious limitations when applied to small firms. Consider first the constant growth model, $k_s = D_1/P_0 + g$. Imagine a small, rapidly growing firm, such as Bio-Technology General (BTG), which will not in the foreseeable future pay dividends. For firms like this, the constant growth model is simply not applicable. In fact, it is difficult to imagine any dividend model that would be of practical benefit for such a firm because of the difficulty of estimating dividends and growth rates.

The second method, which calls for adding a risk premium of 3 to 5 percent to the firm's cost of debt, can be used for some small firms, but problems arise if the firm does not have a publicly traded bond outstanding. BTG, for example, has no public debt outstanding, so we would have trouble using the bond-yield-plus-risk-premium approach for BTG.

The third approach, the CAPM, is often not usable, because if the firm's stock is not publicly traded, then we cannot calculate its beta. For the privately owned firm, we might use the "pure play" CAPM technique, which involves finding a publicly owned firm in the same line of business, estimating that firm's beta, and then using that beta as a replacement for the one of the small business in question.

To illustrate the pure play approach, again consider BTG. The firm is not publicly traded, so we cannot estimate its beta. However, data are available on more established firms, such as Genentech and Genetic Industries, so we could use their betas as representative of the biological and genetic engineering industry. Of course, these firms' betas would have to be subjectively modified to reflect their larger sizes and more established positions, as well as to take ac-

count of the differences in the nature of their products and their capital structures as compared to those of BTG. Still, as long as there are public companies in similar lines of business available for comparison, their betas can be used to help estimate the cost of capital of a firm whose equity is not publicly traded. Note also that a "liquidity premium" as discussed in Chapter 4 would also have to be added to reflect the illiquidity of the small, nonpublic firm's stock.

FLOTATION COSTS FOR SMALL ISSUES

When external equity capital is raised, flotation costs increase the cost of equity capital above that of internal funds. These flotation costs are especially significant for smaller firms, and they can substantially affect capital budgeting decisions involving external equity funds. To illustrate this point, consider a firm that is expected to pay constant dividends forever, hence its growth rate is zero. In this case, if F is the percentage flotation cost, then the cost of equity capital is $k_e = D_1/[P_0(1 - F)]$. The higher the flotation cost, the higher the cost of external equity.

How big is F? Looking at the estimates presented earlier in the Industry Practice box, entitled "How Much Does It Cost to Raise External Capital?", we see that small debt and equity issues have considerably higher flotation costs than large issues. For example, a non-IPO issue of common stock which raises more than $100 million in capital would have a flotation cost of about 3.5 percent. For a firm that is expected to provide a constant 15 percent dividend yield (that is, $D_1/P_0 = 15\%$), the cost of equity would be 15%/(1 − 0.04), or 15.6 percent. However, a similar but smaller firm which raises less than $10 million would have a flotation cost of about 13 percent, which would result in a flotation-adjusted cost of equity capital of 15%/(1 − 0.13) = 17.2 percent, or 1.6 percentage points higher. This differential would be even larger if an

IPO were involved. Therefore, it is clear that a small firm would have to earn considerably more on the same project than a large firm. Small firms are therefore at a substantial disadvantage because of flotation cost effects.

THE SMALL-FIRM EFFECT

A number of researchers have observed that portfolios of small firms' stocks have earned consistently higher average returns than those of large firms' stocks; this is called the "small-firm effect." On the surface, it would seem to be advantageous to the small firm to provide average returns in the stock market that are higher than those of large firms. In reality, however, this is bad news — what the small-firm effect means is that the capital market demands higher returns on stocks of small firms than on the stocks of otherwise similar large firms. Therefore, the basic cost of equity capital is higher for small firms. This compounds the high flotation cost problem noted above.

It may be argued that the stocks of small firms are riskier than those of large firms, and that accounts for the differences in returns. It is true that academic research usually finds that betas are higher for small firms than for large ones. However, the returns for small firms are still larger even after adjusting for the effects of their higher risks as reflected in their beta coefficients.

The small-firm effect is an anomaly in the sense that it is not consistent with the CAPM theory. Still, higher returns reflect a higher cost of capital, so we must conclude that small firms do have higher capital costs than otherwise similar large firms. The manager of a small firm should take this factor into account when estimating his or her firm's cost of equity capital. In general, the cost of equity appears to be about four percentage points higher for small firms (those with market values of less than $20 million) than for large New York Stock Exchange firms with similar risk characteristics.

2. **Privately owned firms.** Our discussion of the cost of equity was related to publicly owned corporations, and we have concentrated on the rate of return required by public stockholders. However, there is a serious question about how one should measure the cost of equity for a firm whose stock is not traded. Tax issues are also especially important in these cases. As a general rule, the same principles of cost of capital estimation apply to both privately held and publicly owned firms, but the problems of obtaining input data are somewhat different for each.

3. **Small businesses.** Small businesses are generally privately owned, making it difficult to estimate their cost of equity. The Small Business box, entitled "The Cost of Equity Capital for Small Firms," discusses this issue.

4. **Measurement problems.** One cannot overemphasize the practical difficulties encountered when estimating the cost of equity. It is very difficult to obtain good input data for the CAPM, for g in the formula $k_s = D_1/P_0 + g$, and for the risk premium in the formula $k_s = $ Bond yield + Risk premium. As a result, we can never be sure just how accurate our estimated cost of capital is.

5. **Costs of capital for projects of differing riskiness.** As we will see in Chapter 12, it is difficult to measure projects' risks, hence to assign risk-adjusted discount rates to capital budgeting projects of differing degrees of riskiness.

6. **Capital structure weights.** In this chapter, we have simply taken as given the target capital structure and used this target to obtain the weights used to calculate k. As we shall see in Chapter 13, establishing the target capital structure is a major task in itself.

Although this listing of problems may appear formidable, the state of the art in cost of capital estimation is really not in bad shape. The procedures outlined in this chapter can be used to obtain cost of capital estimates that are sufficiently accurate for practical purposes, and the problems listed here merely indicate the desirability of refinements. The refinements are not unimportant, but the problems we have identified do not invalidate the usefulness of the procedures outlined in the chapter.

SELF-TEST QUESTION

Identify some problem areas in cost of capital analysis. Do these problems invalidate the cost of capital procedures discussed in the chapter?

SUMMARY

This chapter showed how the MCC schedule is developed for use in the capital budgeting process. The key concepts covered are listed below.

♦ The cost of capital used in capital budgeting is a **weighted average** of the types of capital the firm uses, typically debt, preferred stock, and common equity.

♦ The **component cost of debt** is the **after-tax** cost of new debt. It is found by multiplying the cost of new debt by $(1 - T)$, where T is the firm's marginal tax rate: $k_d(1 - T)$.

♦ The **component cost of preferred stock** is calculated as the preferred dividend divided by the net issuing price, where the net issuing price is the price the firm receives after deducting flotation costs: $k_{ps} = D_{ps}/P_n$.

♦ The **cost of common equity** is the cost of retained earnings as long as the firm has retained earnings, but the cost of equity becomes the cost of new common stock once the firm has exhausted its retained earnings: Cost of equity is thus either k_s or k_e.

♦ The **cost of retained earnings** is the rate of return required by the firm's stockholders, and it can be estimated by three methods: (1) the **CAPM approach,** (2) the **bond-yield-plus-risk-premium approach,** and (3) the **dividend-yield-plus-growth-rate, or DCF, approach.**

♦ To use the **CAPM approach,** one (1) estimates the firm's beta, (2) multiplies this beta by the market risk premium to determine the firm's risk premium, and (3) adds the firm's risk premium to the risk-free rate to obtain the firm's cost of retained earnings: $k_s = k_{RF} + (k_M - k_{RF})b_i$.

♦ The **bond-yield-plus-risk-premium approach** calls for adding a risk premium of from 3 to 5 percentage points to the firm's interest rate on long-term debt: $k_s =$ Bond yield + RP.

♦ To use the **dividend-yield-plus-growth-rate approach,** which is also called the **discounted cash flow (DCF) approach,** one adds the firm's expected growth rate to its expected dividend yield: $k_s = D_1/P_0 + g$.

♦ The **cost of new common equity** is higher than the cost of retained earnings, because the firm must incur **flotation expenses** to sell stock. To find the cost of new common equity, the stock price is first reduced by the flotation expense, then the dividend yield is calculated on the basis of the price the firm will actually receive, and then the expected growth rate is added to this **adjusted dividend yield:** $k_e = D_1/[P_0(1 - F)] + g$.

♦ Each firm has an **optimal capital structure,** defined as that mix of debt, preferred stock, and common equity which minimizes its **weighted average cost of capital (WACC):**

$$\text{WACC} = w_d k_d (1 - T) + w_{ps} k_{ps} + w_{ce} (k_s \text{ or } k_e).$$

♦ The **marginal cost of capital (MCC)** is defined as the cost of the last dollar of new capital that the firm raises. The MCC increases as the firm raises more and more capital during a given period. A graph of the MCC plotted against dollars raised is the **MCC schedule.**

♦ A **break point** will occur in the MCC schedule whenever the amount of equity capital required to finance the firm's capital budget exceeds its retained earnings. At that point, the cost of capital will begin to rise because the firm must use more expensive outside equity.

♦ **Various factors affect a firm's cost of capital.** Some of these factors are determined by the financial environment, but the firm influences others through its financing, investment, and dividend policies.

♦ The **Investment Opportunity Schedule (IOS)** is a graph of the firm's investment opportunities, with the project having the highest return plotted first.

♦ The MCC schedule is combined with the IOS schedule, and the intersection defines the **corporate cost of capital,** which is used to evaluate average-risk capital budgeting projects.

♦ The three equity cost-estimating techniques discussed in this chapter have **serious limitations** when applied to small firms, thus increasing the need for the small-business manager to use judgment.

♦ Stock offerings of less than $1 million have an average flotation cost of 21 percent, while the average flotation cost on large common stock offerings is about 4 percent. As a result, a small firm would have to earn considerably more on the same project than a large firm. Also, the capital market demands higher returns on stocks of small firms than on otherwise similar stocks of large firms — this is called the **small-firm effect.**

The cost of capital as developed in this chapter is used in the following chapters to evaluate capital budgeting projects. In addition, we will extend the concepts developed here in Chapter 13, where we consider the effect of the capital structure on the cost of capital.

QUESTIONS

9-1   In what sense does the marginal cost of capital schedule represent a series of average costs?

9-2   How would each of the following affect a firm's cost of debt, $k_d(1 - T)$; its cost of equity, k_s; and its weighted average cost of capital, WACC? Indicate by a plus (+), a minus (−), or a zero (0) if the factor would raise, lower, or have an indeterminate effect on the item in question. Assume other things are held constant. Be prepared to justify your answer, but recognize that several of the parts probably have no single correct answer; these questions are designed to stimulate thought and discussion.

	EFFECT ON		
	$k_d(1 - T)$	k_s	WACC
a. The corporate tax rate is lowered.	___	___	___
b. The Federal Reserve tightens credit.	___	___	___
c. The firm uses more debt; that is, it increases its debt/assets ratio.	___	___	___
d. The dividend payout ratio is increased.	___	___	___
e. The firm doubles the amount of capital it raises during the year.	___	___	___
f. The firm expands into a risky new area.	___	___	___
g. The firm merges with another firm whose earnings are countercyclical both to those of the first firm and to the stock market.	___	___	___
h. The stock market falls drastically, and the firm's stock falls along with the rest.	___	___	___
i. Investors become more risk averse.	___	___	___
j. The firm is an electric utility with a large investment in nuclear plants. Several states propose a ban on nuclear power generation.	___	___	___

9-3   Suppose a firm estimates its MCC and IOS schedules for the coming year and finds that they intersect at the point 10%, $10 million. What does this intersection point tell us?

SELF-TEST PROBLEMS   (Solutions Appear in Appendix B)

ST-1
Key terms
Define each of the following terms:
a. After-tax cost of debt, $k_d(1 - T)$; capital component cost
b. Cost of preferred stock, k_{ps}

c. Cost of retained earnings, k_s
d. Cost of new common equity, k_e
e. Flotation cost, F
f. Target (optimal) capital structure; capital structure components
g. Weighted average cost of capital, WACC
h. Marginal cost of capital, MCC
i. Marginal cost of capital schedule; break point (BP)
j. Investment opportunity schedule (IOS)

ST-2
Marginal cost of capital

Lancaster Engineering Inc. (LEI) has the following capital structure, which it considers to be optimal:

Debt	25%
Preferred stock	15
Common equity	60
	100%

LEI's expected net income this year is $34,285.72, its established dividend payout ratio is 30 percent, its federal-plus-state tax rate is 40 percent, and investors expect earnings and dividends to grow at a constant rate of 9 percent in the future. LEI paid a dividend of $3.60 per share last year, and its stock currently sells at a price of $60 per share.
  LEI can obtain new capital in the following ways:

♦ *Common:* New common stock has a flotation cost of 10 percent.

♦ *Preferred:* New preferred stock with a dividend of $11 can be sold to the public at a price of $100 per share. The flotation costs are $5 per share.

♦ *Debt:* Debt can be sold at an interest rate of 12 percent.
  Assume that the cost of capital is constant beyond the retained earnings break point.
  a. Find the break point in the MCC schedule.
  b. Determine the cost of each capital structure component.
  c. Calculate the weighted average cost of capital in the intervals between the break in the MCC schedule.
  d. LEI has the following investment opportunities, which are graphed on page 380 as the IOS schedule:

PROJECT	COST AT $t = 0$	RATE OF RETURN
A	$10,000	17.4%
B	20,000	16.0
C	10,000	14.2
D	20,000	13.7
E	10,000	12.0

Add the MCC schedule, which you have already calculated, to this graph.
  e. Using the graph constructed in Part d, which projects should LEI accept? Why?

STARTER PROBLEMS

9-1
Cost of equity

Percy Motors has a target capital structure of 40 percent debt and 60 percent equity. The yield to maturity on the company's outstanding bonds is 9 percent, and the company's tax rate is 40 percent. Percy's CFO has calculated the company's WACC as 9.96 percent. What is the company's cost of equity capital?

9-2
Cost of preferred stock

Tunney Industries can issue perpetual preferred stock at a price of $50 a share. The issue is expected to pay a constant annual dividend of $3.80 a share. The flotation cost on the issue is estimated to be 5 percent. What is the company's cost of preferred stock, k_{ps}?

9-3
Cost of equity

Javits & Sons' common stock is currently trading at $30 a share. The stock is expected to pay a dividend of $3.00 a share at the end of the year ($D_1 = $3.00), and the dividend is

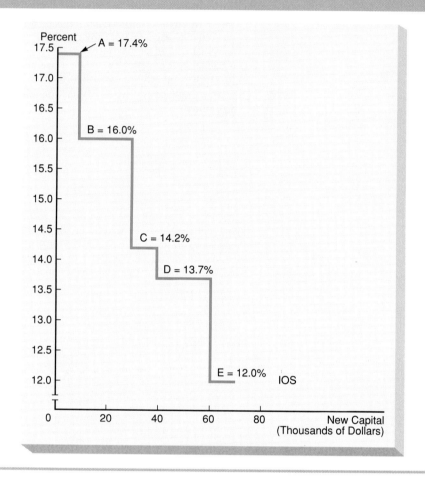

IOS Schedule for Lancaster Engineering Inc.

expected to grow at a constant rate of 5 percent a year. If the company were to issue external equity, it would incur a 10 percent flotation cost. What is the cost of retained earnings? What is the cost of new external equity?

9-4

Retained earnings break point

Boren Brothers has a target capital structure which calls for 70 percent equity and 30 percent debt. The company just reported net income of $700,000, and it has a policy of paying out 40 percent of net income as dividends. How much capital can Boren raise this year without having to sell new common stock, i.e., what is Boren's retained earnings break point?

EXAM-TYPE PROBLEMS

The problems included in this section are set up in such a way that they could be used as multiple-choice exam problems.

9-5

After-tax cost of debt

Calculate the after-tax cost of debt under each of the following conditions:
a. Interest rate, 13 percent; tax rate, 0 percent.
b. Interest rate, 13 percent; tax rate, 20 percent.
c. Interest rate, 13 percent; tax rate, 35 percent.

9-6

After-tax cost of debt

The Heuser Company's currently outstanding 10 percent coupon bonds have a yield to maturity of 12 percent. Heuser believes it could issue at par new bonds that would provide a similar yield to maturity. If its marginal tax rate is 35 percent, what is Heuser's after-tax cost of debt?

9-7
Cost of preferred stock

Trivoli Industries plans to issue some $100 par preferred stock with an 11 percent dividend. The stock is selling on the market for $97.00, and Trivoli must pay flotation costs of 5 percent of the market price. What is the cost of the preferred stock for Trivoli?

9-8
Cost of new common stock

The Evanec Company's next expected dividend, D_1, is $3.18; its growth rate is 6 percent; and the stock now sells for $36. New stock can be sold to net the firm $32.40 per share.
a. What is Evanec's percentage flotation cost, F?
b. What is Evanec's cost of new common stock, k_e?

9-9
Weighted average cost of capital

The Patrick Company's cost of equity is 16 percent. Its before-tax cost of debt is 13 percent, and its average tax rate is 40 percent. The stock sells at book value. Using the following balance sheet, calculate Patrick's after-tax weighted average cost of capital:

ASSETS		LIABILITIES AND EQUITY	
Cash	$ 120		
Accounts receivable	240		
Inventories	360	Long-term debt	$1,152
Plant and equipment, net	2,160	Equity	1,728
Total assets	$2,880	Total liabilities and equity	$2,880

9-10
WACC and percentage of debt financing

Hook Industries has a capital structure which consists solely of debt and common equity. The company estimates that it can issue debt at 11 percent. The company also estimates that its retained earnings are insufficient to finance its capital budget, so it will have to issue new common stock. The company's stock currently pays a $2 dividend per share ($D_0 = 2), and the stock's price is currently $27.50. It is estimated that the company's dividend will grow at a constant rate of 7 percent per year. The tax rate is 35 percent, and the flotation cost is 10 percent. The company estimates that its WACC is 13.95 percent. What percentage of the company's capital structure consists of debt financing?

9-11
Weighted average cost of capital

Midwest Electric Company (MEC) uses only debt and equity. It can borrow unlimited amounts at an interest rate of 10 percent as long as it finances at its target capital structure, which calls for 45 percent debt and 55 percent common equity. Its last dividend was $2, its expected constant growth rate is 4 percent, its stock sells at a price of $25, and new stock would net the company $20 per share after flotation costs. MEC's tax rate is 40 percent, and it expects to have $100 million of retained earnings this year. Two projects are available: Project A has a cost of $200 million and a rate of return of 13 percent, while Project B has a cost of $125 million and a rate of return of 10 percent. All of the company's potential projects are equally risky.
a. What is MEC's cost of equity from newly issued stock?
b. What is MEC's marginal cost of capital, i.e., what WACC cost rate should it use to evaluate capital budgeting projects (these two projects plus any others that might arise during the year, provided the cost of capital schedule remains as it is currently)?

9-12
After-tax cost of debt

A company's 6 percent coupon rate, semiannual payment, $1,000 par value bond which matures in 30 years sells at a price of $515.16. The company's federal-plus-state tax rate is 40 percent. What is the firm's component cost of debt for purposes of calculating the WACC? (Hint: Base your answer on the *nominal* rate.)

9-13
Marginal cost of equity

Patton Paints Corporation has a target capital structure of 40 percent debt and 60 percent common equity. The company expects to have $600,000 of after-tax income during the coming year, and it plans to retain 40 percent of its earnings. The current stock price is $P_0 = 30; the last dividend was $D_0 = 2.00; and the dividend is expected to grow at a constant rate of 7 percent. New stock can be sold at a flotation cost of F = 25 percent. What will be the firm's marginal cost of *equity* capital (not the WACC) if it raises a total of $500,000 of new capital?

PROBLEMS

9-14
Cost of retained earnings

The earnings, dividends, and stock price of Carpetto Technologies Inc. are expected to grow at 7 percent per year in the future. Carpetto's common stock sells for $23 per share, its last dividend was $2.00, and the company will pay a dividend of $2.14 at the end of the current year.

a. Using the discounted cash flow approach, what is its cost of retained earnings?

b. If the firm's beta is 1.6, the risk-free rate is 9 percent, and the average return on the market is 13 percent, what will be the firm's cost of equity using the CAPM approach?

c. If the firm's bonds earn a return of 12 percent, what will k_s be using the bond-yield-plus-risk-premium approach? (Hint: Use the midpoint of the risk premium range.)

d. On the basis of the results of Parts a through c, what would you estimate Carpetto's cost of retained earnings to be?

9-15
Cost of retained earnings

The Bouchard Company's EPS was $6.50 in 1997 and $4.42 in 1992. The company pays out 40 percent of its earnings as dividends, and the stock sells for $36.

a. Calculate the past growth rate in earnings. (Hint: This is a 5-year growth period.)

b. Calculate the *next* expected dividend per share, D_1. ($D_0 = 0.4(\$6.50) = \$2.60$.) Assume that the past growth rate will continue.

c. What is the cost of retained earnings, k_s, for the Bouchard Company?

9-16
Break point calculations

The Heath Company expects earnings of $30 million next year. Its dividend payout ratio is 40 percent, and its debt/assets ratio is 60 percent. Heath uses no preferred stock.

a. What amount of retained earnings does Heath expect next year?

b. At what amount of financing will there be a break point in the MCC schedule?

9-17
Calculation of g and EPS

Sidman Products' stock is currently selling for $60 a share. The firm is expected to earn $5.40 per share this year and to pay a year-end dividend of $3.60.

a. If investors require a 9 percent return, what rate of growth must be expected for Sidman?

b. If Sidman reinvests retained earnings in projects whose average return is equal to the stock's expected rate of return, what will be next year's EPS? [Hint: $g = b(ROE)$, where b = fraction of earnings retained.]

9-18
Weighted average cost of capital

On January 1, 1998, the total assets of the McCue Company were $270 million. The firm's present capital structure, which follows, is considered to be optimal. Assume that there is no short-term debt.

Long-term debt	$135,000,000
Common equity	135,000,000
Total liabilities and equity	$270,000,000

New bonds will have a 10 percent coupon rate and will be sold at par. Common stock, currently selling at $60 a share, can be sold to net the company $54 a share. Stockholders' required rate of return is estimated to be 12 percent, consisting of a dividend yield of 4 percent and an expected growth rate of 8 percent. (The next expected dividend is $2.40, so $2.40/$60 = 4%.) Retained earnings are estimated to be $13.5 million. The marginal corporate tax rate is 40 percent. Assuming that all asset expansion (gross expenditures for fixed assets plus related working capital) is included in the capital budget, the dollar amount of the capital budget, ignoring depreciation, is $135 million.

a. To maintain the present capital structure, how much of the capital budget must Mc-Cue finance by equity?

b. How much of the new equity funds needed will be generated internally? Externally?

c. Calculate the cost of each of the equity components.

d. At what level of capital expenditure will there be a break in McCue's MCC schedule?

e. Calculate the WACC (1) below and (2) above the break in the MCC schedule. (Assume the cost of capital is constant beyond the retained earnings break point.)

f. Plot the MCC schedule. Also, draw in an IOS schedule that is consistent with both the MCC schedule and the projected capital budget. (Any IOS schedule that is consistent will do.)

9-19
Weighted average cost of capital

The following tabulation gives earnings per share figures for the Foust Company during the preceding 10 years. The firm's common stock, 7.8 million shares outstanding, is now

(1/1/98) selling for $65 per share, and the expected dividend at the end of the current year (1998) is 55 percent of the 1997 EPS. Because investors expect past trends to continue, g may be based on the earnings growth rate. (Note that 9 years of growth are reflected in the data.)

YEAR	EPS	YEAR	EPS
1988	$3.90	1993	$5.73
1989	4.21	1994	6.19
1990	4.55	1995	6.68
1991	4.91	1996	7.22
1992	5.31	1997	7.80

The current interest rate on new debt is 9 percent. The firm's marginal tax rate is 40 percent. Its capital structure, considered to be optimal, is as follows:

Debt	$104,000,000
Common equity	156,000,000
Total liabilities and equity	$260,000,000

a. Calculate Foust's after-tax cost of new debt and of common equity, assuming that new equity comes only from retained earnings. Calculate the cost of equity as $k_s = D_1/P_0 + g$.
b. Find Foust's weighted average cost of capital, again assuming that no new common stock is sold and that all debt costs 9 percent.
c. How much can be spent on capital investments before external equity must be sold? (Assume that retained earnings available for 1998 are 45 percent of 1997 earnings. Obtain 1997 earnings by multiplying 1997 EPS by the shares outstanding.)
d. What is Foust's weighted average cost of capital (after the retained earnings break point) if new common stock can be sold to the public at $65 a share to net the firm $58.50 a share? The cost of debt is constant.

9-20
WACC and optimal capital budget

Adams Corporation has four investment projects with the following costs and rates of return:

	COST	RATE OF RETURN
Project 1	$2,000	16.00%
Project 2	3,000	15.00
Project 3	5,000	13.75
Project 4	2,000	12.50

The company estimates that it can issue debt at a before-tax cost of 10 percent, and its tax rate is 30 percent. The company also can issue preferred stock at $50 per share, which pays a constant dividend of $5 per year. The flotation cost on the preferred is $1 per share.

Net income is estimated to be $2,142.86, and the firm plans to maintain its policy of paying out 30 percent as dividends, so retained earnings will equal $1,500. The company's stock currently sells at $40 per share. The year-end dividend, D_1, is expected to be $3.50, and the dividend is expected to grow at a constant rate of 6 percent per year. The flotation cost of issuing new common stock is $4 per share, or 10 percent. The company's capital structure consists of 75 percent common equity, 15 percent debt, and 10 percent preferred stock.

a. What is the retained earnings break point?
b. What is the cost of each of the capital components?
c. What is the WACC, assuming the capital budget is less than the retained earnings break point? What is the WACC, assuming the capital budget exceeds the retained earnings break point?
d. What should be the size of the company's optimal capital budget?

INTEGRATED CASE

COLEMAN TECHNOLOGIES INC.

9-21 Cost of Capital During the last few years, Coleman Technologies has been too constrained by the high cost of capital to make many capital investments. Recently, though, capital costs have been declining, and the company has decided to look seriously at a major expansion program that had been proposed by the marketing department. Assume that you are an assistant to Jerry Lehman, the financial vice-president. Your first task is to estimate Coleman's cost of capital. Lehman has provided you with the following data, which he believes may be relevant to your task:

(1) The firm's tax rate is 40 percent.
(2) The current price of Coleman's 12 percent coupon, semi-annual payment, noncallable bonds with 15 years remaining to maturity is $1,153.72. Coleman does not use short-term interest-bearing debt on a permanent basis. New bonds would be privately placed with no flotation cost.
(3) The current price of the firm's 10 percent, $100 par value, quarterly dividend, perpetual preferred stock is $113.10. Coleman would incur flotation costs of $2.00 per share on a new issue.
(4) Coleman's common stock is currently selling at $50 per share. Its last dividend (D_0) was $4.19, and dividends are expected to grow at a constant rate of 5 percent in the foreseeable future. Coleman's beta is 1.2, the yield on T-bonds is 7 percent, and the market risk premium is estimated to be 6 percent. For the bond-yield-plus-risk-premium approach, the firm uses a 4 percentage point risk premium.
(5) New common stock can be sold at a flotation cost of 15 percent.
(6) Coleman's target capital structure is 30 percent long-term debt, 10 percent preferred stock, and 60 percent common equity.
(7) The firm is forecasting retained earnings of $300,000 for the coming year.

To structure the task somewhat, Lehman has asked you to answer the following questions.

a. (1) What sources of capital should be included when you estimate Coleman's weighted average cost of capital (WACC)?
   (2) Should the component costs be figured on a before-tax or an after-tax basis?
   (3) Should the costs be historical (embedded) costs or new (marginal) costs?
b. What is the market interest rate on Coleman's debt and its component cost of debt?
c. (1) What is the firm's cost of preferred stock?
   (2) Coleman's preferred stock is riskier to investors than its debt, yet the preferred's yield to investors is lower than the yield to maturity on the debt. Does this sug-

gest that you have made a mistake? (Hint: Think about taxes.)
d. (1) Why is there a cost associated with retained earnings?
   (2) What is Coleman's estimated cost of retained earnings using the CAPM approach?
   (3) Why is the T-bond rate a better estimate of the risk-free rate for cost of capital purposes than the T-bill rate?
e. What is the estimated cost of retained earnings using the discounted cash flow (DCF) approach?
f. What is the bond-yield-plus-risk-premium estimate for Coleman's cost of retained earnings?
g. What is your final estimate for k_s?
h. What is Coleman's cost for newly issued common stock, k_e?
i. Explain in words why new common stock has a higher percentage cost than retained earnings.
j. (1) What is Coleman's overall, or weighted average, cost of capital (WACC) when retained earnings are used as the equity component?
   (2) What is the WACC after retained earnings have been exhausted and Coleman uses new common stock with a 15 percent flotation cost?
k. (1) At what amount of new investment would Coleman be forced to issue new common stock? Put another way, what is the largest capital budget the company could support without issuing new common stock? Assume that the 30/10/60 target capital structure will be maintained.
   (2) What is a marginal cost of capital (MCC) schedule? Construct a graph which shows Coleman's MCC schedule.
l. Coleman's director of capital budgeting has identified the three following potential projects:

PROJECT	COST	RATE OF RETURN
A	$700,000	17.0%
B	500,000	15.0
C	800,000	11.5

All of the projects are equally risky, and they are all similar in risk to the company's existing assets.
(1) Plot the IOS schedule on the same graph that contains your MCC schedule. What is the firm's marginal cost of capital for capital budgeting purposes?
(2) What is the dollar size, and the included projects, in Coleman's optimal capital budget? Explain your answer fully.
(3) Would Coleman's MCC schedule remain constant at 12.1 percent beyond $2 million regardless of the amount of capital required?

COMPUTER-RELATED PROBLEM

Work the problem in this section only if you are using the computer problem diskette.

9-22

Marginal cost of capital

Use the model in the File C9 to work this problem.

a. Refer back to Problem 9-20. Now, assume that Adams Corporation changes its capital structure to 45 percent debt, 10 percent preferred stock, and 45 percent common equity. Assume this causes (1) k_d to increase by 2 percentage points, (2) the preferred flotation cost to increase from $1.00 to $3.00, and (3) g to increase from 6 to 7 percent. What happens to the retained earnings break point, the MCC schedule, and the capital budget?

b. Suppose the firm's tax rate falls (1) to 20 percent or (2) to 0 percent. All other input data should remain the same as that assumed in Part a. How does the change in tax rate affect the MCC schedule and the capital budget?

CHAPTER 10

THE BASICS OF
CAPITAL BUDGETING

Just a few years ago, Chrysler was in trouble. Its stock price had plummeted, its bonds had been downgraded, and its future looked bleak. But what a difference a few years can make! Chrysler's stock, which sold for $6 a share in the early 1990s, passed $36 a share in 1997, after the company's directors declared a two-for-one split and raised the dividend. Chrysler's debt rating has improved to investment grade, and the company continues to report strong earnings.

How did the "Chrysler Miracle" come about? First, Chrysler developed a new concept for designing and producing new models. Whereas most other companies have separate design and manufacturing teams, Chrysler combined its two groups into an integrated "platform team." This new approach cut both design time and manufacturing costs, and the result was world leadership in profits per vehicle. Second, because Chrysler was not as well capitalized as its rivals, a shortage of resources forced it to limit model offerings, which turned out to be a blessing in disguise. And third, Chrysler has concentrated on the North American market, which has been stronger than the European and Japanese markets.

Chrysler hired a new chief executive officer in 1992, Robert Eaton, former head of GM's European operations. Eaton is given high marks by most industry watchers, but Chrysler's comeback really began much earlier, under the regime of retired chairman Lee Iacocca. The real test of Eaton's managerial skills will be seen in how Chrysler fares in coming years.

Eaton and his team face some big, important decisions. The company has accumulated more than $8 billion in cash, despite the fact that its capital spending now exceeds $4 billion per year, double the amount spent in 1992. Management plans to use most of this cash for capital expenditures, arguing that to maintain its momentum, new cars must be designed, manufacturing plants must be modernized and expanded, and R&D efforts on electric cars and other innovative products must be continued.

Despite its strong performance, Chrysler recently had to fight off an attack from its largest shareholder, Kirk Kerkorian, who had been pressuring the company to return much of its cash to shareholders — either through higher dividends or stock repurchases. To rebuff Kerkorian's efforts to take over the company, Chrysler was forced to repurchase some of its stock and also to increase the dividend.

In a nutshell, Eaton and Kerkorian disagreed about whether Chrysler's anticipated investments would be able to earn greater returns than what shareholders could expect to earn elsewhere on other investments of equal risk. If it can, then management would be correct to retain and reinvest most of its cash. If not, Kerkorian will turn out to have been right.

In the years ahead, each of Chrysler's investment decisions will require careful analysis, much of it based on the techniques described in this chapter. As you read this chapter, think about how Chrysler — or any other company — could use capital budgeting analysis to make better investment decisions.

In the last chapter, we discussed the cost of capital. Now we turn to investment decisions involving fixed assets, or *capital budgeting*. Here the term *capital* refers to long-term assets used in production, while a *budget* is a plan which details projected inflows and outflows during some future period. Thus, the *capital budget* is an outline of planned investments in fixed assets, and **capital budgeting** is the whole process of analyzing projects and deciding which ones to include in the capital budget.

Capital Budgeting
The process of planning expenditures on assets whose cash flows are expected to extend beyond one year.

Our treatment of capital budgeting is divided into three chapters. This chapter gives an overview and explains the basic techniques used in capital budgeting analysis. Chapter 11 goes on to explain how cash flows are estimated, and then Chapter 12 discusses how risk is dealt with in capital budgeting.

IMPORTANCE OF CAPITAL BUDGETING

A number of factors combine to make capital budgeting perhaps the most important function financial managers and their staffs must perform. First, since the results of capital budgeting decisions continue for many years, the firm loses some of its flexibility. For example, the purchase of an asset with an economic life of ten years "locks in" the firm for a ten-year period. Further, because asset expansion is based on expected future sales, a decision to buy an asset that is expected to last ten years requires a ten-year sales forecast. Finally, a firm's capital budgeting decisions define its strategic direction, because moves into new products, services, or markets must be preceded by capital expenditures.

An erroneous forecast of asset requirements can have serious consequences. If the firm invests too much, it will incur unnecessarily high depreciation and other expenses. On the other hand, if it does not invest enough, two problems may arise. First, its equipment may not be sufficiently modern to enable it to produce competitively. Second, if it has inadequate capacity, it may lose market share to rival firms, and regaining lost customers requires heavy selling expenses, price reductions, or product improvements, all of which are costly.

Timing is also important — capital assets must be available when they are needed. Edward Ford, executive vice-president of Western Design, a decorative tile company, gave the authors an illustration of the importance of capital budgeting. His firm tried to operate near capacity most of the time. During a four-year period, Western experienced intermittent spurts in the demand for its products, which forced it to turn away orders. After these sharp increases in demand, Western would add capacity by renting an additional building, then purchasing and installing the appropriate equipment. It would take six to eight months to get the additional capacity ready, but by then demand had dried up — other firms with available capacity had already taken an increased share of the market. Once Western began to properly forecast demand and plan its capacity requirements a year or so in advance, it was able to maintain and even increase its market share.

Effective capital budgeting can improve both the timing and the quality of asset acquisitions. If a firm forecasts its needs for capital assets in advance, it can purchase and install the assets before they are needed. Unfortunately, many firms do not order capital goods until existing assets are approaching full-capacity usage. If sales increase because of an increase in general market demand, all firms in the industry will tend to order capital goods at about the same time. This results in backlogs, long waiting times for machinery, a deterioration in the quality of the capital equipment, and an increase in costs. The firm that foresees its needs and purchases capital assets during slack periods can avoid these problems. Note, though, that if a firm forecasts an increase in demand and then expands to meet the anticipated demand, but sales do not increase, it will be saddled with excess capacity and high costs, which can lead to losses or even bankruptcy. Thus, an accurate sales forecast is critical.

Capital budgeting typically involves substantial expenditures, and before a firm can spend a large amount of money, it must have the funds lined up — large amounts of money are not available automatically. Therefore, a firm contemplating a major capital expenditure program should plan its financing far enough in advance to be sure funds are available.

SELF-TEST QUESTIONS

Why are capital budgeting decisions so important?

Why is the sales forecast a key element in a capital budgeting decision?

GENERATING IDEAS FOR CAPITAL PROJECTS

The same general concepts that are used in security valuation are also involved in capital budgeting. However, whereas a set of stocks and bonds exists in the securities market, and investors select from this set, *capital budgeting projects are created by the firm*. For example, a sales representative may report that customers are asking for a particular product that the company does not now produce. The sales manager then discusses the idea with the marketing research group to determine the size of the market for the proposed product. If it appears that a significant market does exist, cost accountants and engineers will be asked to estimate production costs. If they conclude that the product can be produced and sold at a sufficient profit, the project will be undertaken.

A firm's growth, and even its ability to remain competitive and to survive, depends on a constant flow of ideas for new products, for ways to make existing products better, and for ways to operate at a lower cost. Accordingly, a well-managed firm will go to great lengths to develop good capital budgeting proposals. For example, the executive vice-president of one very successful corporation indicated that his company takes the following steps to generate projects:

Strategic Business Plan
A long-run plan which outlines in broad terms the firm's basic strategy for the next 5 to 10 years.

> Our R&D department is constantly searching for new products and for ways to improve existing products. In addition, our executive committee, which consists of senior executives in marketing, production, and finance, identifies the products and markets in which our company should compete, and the committee sets long-run targets for each division. These targets, which are spelled out in the corporation's **strategic business plan,** provide a general guide to the operating executives who must meet them. The operating executives then seek new products, set expansion plans for existing products, and look for ways to reduce production and distribution costs. Since bonuses and promotions are based on each unit's ability to meet or exceed its targets, these economic incentives encourage our operating executives to seek out profitable investment opportunities.

While our senior executives are judged and rewarded on the basis of how well their units perform, people further down the line are given bonuses for suggestions which lead to profitable investments. Additionally, a percentage of our corporate profit is set aside for distribution to nonexecutive employees, and we have an Employees' Stock Ownership Plan (ESOP) to provide further incentives. Our objective is to encourage employees at all levels to keep an eye out for good ideas, including those that lead to capital investments.

If a firm has capable and imaginative executives and employees, and if its incentive system is working properly, many ideas for capital investment will be advanced. Some ideas will be good ones, but others will not. Therefore, procedures must be established for screening projects, the primary topic of this chapter.

SELF-TEST QUESTION   ??????

What are some ways firms get ideas for capital projects?

PROJECT CLASSIFICATIONS

Analyzing capital expenditure proposals is not a costless operation — benefits can be gained, but analysis does have a cost. For certain types of projects, a relatively detailed analysis may be warranted; for others, simpler procedures should be used. Accordingly, firms generally categorize projects and then analyze those in each category somewhat differently:

1. **Replacement: maintenance of business.** One category consists of expenditures to replace worn-out or damaged equipment used in the production of profitable products. Replacement projects are necessary if the firm is to continue in business. The only issues here are (a) should this operation be continued and (b) should we continue to use the same production processes? The answers are usually yes, so maintenance decisions are normally made without going through an elaborate decision process.

2. **Replacement: cost reduction.** This category includes expenditures to replace serviceable but obsolete equipment. The purpose here is to lower the costs of labor, materials, and other inputs such as electricity. These decisions are discretionary, and a fairly detailed analysis is generally required.

3. **Expansion of existing products or markets.** Expenditures to increase output of existing products, or to expand retail outlets or distribution facilities in markets now being served, are included here. These decisions are more complex because they require an explicit forecast of growth in demand. Mistakes are more likely, so a more detailed analysis is required. Also, the go/no-go decision is generally made at a higher level within the firm.

4. **Expansion into new products or markets.** These are investments to produce a new product or to expand into a geographic area not currently being served. These projects involve strategic decisions that could change the fundamental nature of the business, and they normally require the expenditure of large sums of money with delayed paybacks. Invariably, a detailed analysis is required, and the final decision is generally made at the very top — by the board of directors as a part of the firm's strategic plan.

5. **Safety and/or environmental projects.** Expenditures necessary to comply with government orders, labor agreements, or insurance policy terms fall into this

category. These expenditures are called *mandatory investments,* and they often involve *nonrevenue-producing projects.* How they are handled depends on their size, with small ones being treated much like the Category 1 projects described above.

6. **Other.** This catch-all includes office buildings, parking lots, executive aircraft, and so on. How they are handled varies among companies.

In general, relatively simple calculations, and only a few supporting documents, are required for replacement decisions, especially maintenance-type investments in profitable plants. A more detailed analysis is required for cost-reduction replacements, for expansion of existing product lines, and especially for investments in new products or areas. Also, within each category projects are broken down by their dollar costs: Larger investments require increasingly detailed analysis and approval at a higher level within the firm. Thus, whereas a plant manager may be authorized to approve maintenance expenditures up to $10,000 on the basis of a relatively unsophisticated analysis, the full board of directors may have to approve decisions which involve either amounts over $1 million or expansions into new products or markets. Statistical data are generally lacking for new-product decisions, so here judgments, as opposed to detailed cost data, are especially important.

ON THE WWW

An interesting study detailing the real-world mechanics of capital budgeting can be found at http:// ashley.ivey.uwo.ca/~dszpiro/ capbud_paper/capbud.html. The study provides an interesting discussion of how capital budgeting is performed in the real world. It is fairly nontechnical.

SELF-TEST QUESTION   ??????

Identify the major project classification categories, and explain how they are used.

SIMILARITIES BETWEEN CAPITAL BUDGETING AND SECURITY VALUATION

Once a potential capital budgeting project has been identified, its evaluation involves the same steps that are used in security analysis:

1. First, the cost of the project must be determined. This is similar to finding the price that must be paid for a stock or bond.

2. Next, management estimates the expected cash flows from the project, including the salvage value of the asset at the end of its expected life. This is similar to estimating the future dividend or interest payment stream on a stock or bond, along with the stock's expected sales price or the bond's maturity value.

3. Third, the riskiness of the projected cash flows must be estimated. This requires information about the probability distribution (uncertainty) of the cash flows.

4. Given the project's riskiness, management determines the cost of capital at which the cash flows should be discounted.

5. Next, the expected cash inflows are put on a present value basis to obtain an estimate of the asset's value to the firm. This is equivalent to finding the present value of a stock's expected future dividends.

6. Finally, the present value of the expected cash inflows is compared with the required outlay, or cost. If the PV of the cash flows exceeds the cost, the project should be accepted. Otherwise, it should be rejected. (Alternatively, if the expected rate of return on the project exceeds its cost of capital, the project is accepted.)

If an individual investor identifies and invests in a stock or bond whose market price is less than its true value, the investor's wealth will increase. Similarly, if a firm identifies (or creates) an investment opportunity with a present value greater than its cost, the value of the firm will increase. Thus, there is a direct link between capital budgeting and stock values: The more effective the firm's capital budgeting procedures, the higher its stock price.

SELF-TEST QUESTION ??????

List the six steps in the capital budgeting process, and compare them with the steps in security valuation.

CAPITAL BUDGETING DECISION RULES

Five key methods are used to rank projects and to decide whether or not they should be accepted for inclusion in the capital budget: (1) payback, (2) discounted payback, (3) net present value (NPV), (4) internal rate of return (IRR), and (5) modified internal rate of return (MIRR). We will explain how each ranking criterion is calculated, and then we will evaluate how well each performs in terms of identifying those projects which will maximize the firm's stock price.

We use the cash flow data shown in Figure 10-1 for Projects S and L to illustrate each method. Also we assume that the projects are equally risky. Note that the cash flows, CF_t, are expected values, and that they have been adjusted to reflect taxes, depreciation, and salvage values. Further, since many projects require an investment in both fixed assets and working capital, the investment outlays

---

FIGURE 1 0 - 1   Net Cash Flows for Projects S and L

YEAR (t)	EXPECTED AFTER-TAX NET CASH FLOWS, CF_t	
	PROJECT S	PROJECT L
0[a]	($1,000)	($1,000)
1	500	100
2	400	300
3	300	400
4	100	600

	0	1	2	3	4
Project S:	−1,000	500	400	300	100

	0	1	2	3	4
Project L:	−1,000	100	300	400	600

[a]CF_0 represents the net investment outlay, or initial cost.

shown as CF_0 include any necessary changes in net working capital.[1] Finally, we assume that all cash flows occur at the end of the designated year. Incidentally, the S stands for *short* and the L for *long:* Project S is a short-term project in the sense that its cash inflows come in sooner than L's.

PAYBACK PERIOD

Payback Period
The length of time required for an investment's net revenues to cover its cost.

The **payback period,** defined as the expected number of years required to recover the original investment, was the first formal method used to evaluate capital budgeting projects. The payback calculation is diagrammed in Figure 10-2, and it is explained below for Project S.

1. Enter $CF_0 = -1000$ in your calculator. (You do not need to use the cash flow register; just have your display show $-1,000$.)
2. Now add $CF_1 = 500$ to find the cumulative cash flow at the end of Year 1. The result is -500.
3. Now add $CF_2 = 400$ to find the cumulative cash flow at the end of Year 2. This is -100.
4. Now add $CF_3 = 300$ to find the cumulative cash flow at the end of Year 3. This is $+200$.
5. We see that by the end of Year 3 the cumulative inflows have more than recovered the initial outflow. Thus, the payback occurred during the third year. If the $300 of inflows come in evenly during Year 3, then the exact payback period can be found as follows:

$$\text{Payback}_S = \text{Year before full recovery} + \frac{\text{Unrecovered cost at start of year}}{\text{Cash flow during year}}$$

$$= 2 + \frac{100}{300} = 2.33 \text{ years.}$$

Applying the same procedure to Project L, we find $\text{Payback}_L = 3.33$ years.

---

[1]The most difficult part of the capital budgeting process is estimating the relevant cash flows. For simplicity, the net cash flows are treated as a given in this chapter, which allows us to focus on the capital budgeting decision rules. However, in Chapter 11 we will discuss cash flow estimation in detail. Also, note that *working capital* is defined as the firm's current assets, and that *net working capital* is current assets minus current liabilities.

FIGURE 10-2   Payback Period for Projects S and L

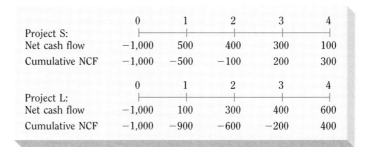

	0	1	2	3	4
Project S:					
Net cash flow	−1,000	500	400	300	100
Cumulative NCF	−1,000	−500	−100	200	300

	0	1	2	3	4
Project L:					
Net cash flow	−1,000	100	300	400	600
Cumulative NCF	−1,000	−900	−600	−200	400

Mutually Exclusive Projects
A set of projects where only one can be accepted.

Independent Projects
Projects whose cash flows are not affected by the acceptance or nonacceptance of other projects.

Discounted Payback Period
The length of time required for an investment's cash flows, discounted at the investment's cost of capital, to cover its cost.

The shorter the payback period, the better. Therefore, if the firm required a payback of three years or less, Project S would be accepted but Project L would be rejected. If the projects were **mutually exclusive,** S would be ranked over L because S has the shorter payback. *Mutually exclusive* means that if one project is taken on, the other must be rejected. For example, the installation of a conveyor-belt system in a warehouse and the purchase of a fleet of forklifts for the same warehouse would be mutually exclusive projects — accepting one implies rejection of the other. **Independent projects** are projects whose cash flows are independent of one another.

Some firms use a variant of the regular payback, the **discounted payback period,** which is similar to the regular payback period except that the expected cash flows are discounted by the project's cost of capital. Thus, the discounted payback period is defined as the number of years required to recover the investment from *discounted* net cash flows. Figure 10-3 contains the discounted net cash flows for Projects S and L, assuming both projects have a cost of capital of 10 percent. To construct Figure 10-3, each cash inflow is divided by $(1 + k)^t = (1.10)^t$, where t is the year in which the cash flow occurs and k is the project's cost of capital. After three years, Project S will have generated $1,011 in discounted cash inflows. Since the cost is $1,000, the discounted payback is just under three years, or, to be precise, 2 + ($214/$225) = 2.95 years. Project L's discounted payback is 3.88 years:

$$\text{Discounted payback}_S = 2.0 + \$214/\$225 = 2.95 \text{ years.}$$

$$\text{Discounted payback}_L = 3.0 + \$360/\$410 = 3.88 \text{ years.}$$

For Projects S and L, the rankings are the same regardless of which payback method is used; that is, Project S is preferred to Project L, and Project S would still be selected if the firm were to require a discounted payback of three years or less. Often, however, the regular and the discounted paybacks produce conflicting rankings.

Note that the payback is a type of "breakeven" calculation in the sense that if cash flows come in at the expected rate until the payback year, then the project will break even. However, the regular payback does not take account of the cost of capital — no cost for the debt or equity used to undertake the project is reflected in the cash flows or the calculation. The discounted payback does take

FIGURE   10 - 3   Projects S and L: Discounted Payback Period

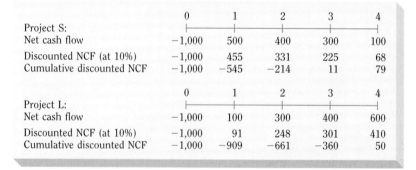

Project S:	0	1	2	3	4
Net cash flow	−1,000	500	400	300	100
Discounted NCF (at 10%)	−1,000	455	331	225	68
Cumulative discounted NCF	−1,000	−545	−214	11	79

Project L:	0	1	2	3	4
Net cash flow	−1,000	100	300	400	600
Discounted NCF (at 10%)	−1,000	91	248	301	410
Cumulative discounted NCF	−1,000	−909	−661	−360	50

account of capital costs — it shows the breakeven year after covering debt and equity costs.

An important drawback of both the payback and discounted payback methods is that they ignore cash flows that are paid or received after the payback period. For example, consider two projects, X and Y, each of which requires an up-front cash outflow of $3,000, so $CF_0 = -\$3,000$. Assume that both projects have a cost of capital of 10 percent. Project X is expected to produce cash inflows of $1,000 each of the next four years, while Project Y will produce no cash flows the first four years but then generate a cash inflow of $1,000,000 five years from now. Common sense suggests that Project Y creates more value for the firm's shareholders, yet its payback and discounted payback make it look worse than Project X. Consequently, both payback methods have serious deficiencies. Therefore, we will not dwell on the finer points of payback analysis.[2]

Although the payback method has some serious faults as a ranking criterion, it does provide information on how long funds will be tied up in a project. Thus, the shorter the payback period, other things held constant, the greater the project's *liquidity*. Also, since cash flows expected in the distant future are generally riskier than near-term cash flows, the payback is often used as one indicator of a project's *riskiness*.

NET PRESENT VALUE (NPV)

Net Present Value (NPV) Method
A method of ranking investment proposals using the NPV, which is equal to the present value of future net cash flows, discounted at the marginal cost of capital.

Discounted Cash Flow (DCF) Techniques
Methods for ranking investment proposals that employ time value of money concepts.

As the flaws in the payback were recognized, people began to search for ways to improve the effectiveness of project evaluations. One such method is the **net present value (NPV) method,** which relies on **discounted cash flow (DCF) techniques.** To implement this approach, we proceed as follows:

1. Find the present value of each cash flow, including both inflows and outflows, discounted at the project's cost of capital.

2. Sum these discounted cash flows; this sum is defined as the project's NPV.

3. If the NPV is positive, the project should be accepted, while if the NPV is negative, it should be rejected. If two projects with positive NPVs are mutually exclusive, the one with the higher NPV should be chosen.

The equation for the NPV is as follows:

$$NPV = CF_0 + \frac{CF_1}{(1+k)^1} + \frac{CF_2}{(1+k)^2} + \cdots + \frac{CF_n}{(1+k)^n}$$

$$= \sum_{t=0}^{n} \frac{CF_t}{(1+k)^t}. \tag{10-1}$$

Here CF_t is the expected net cash flow at Period t, k is the project's cost of capital, and n is its life. Cash outflows (expenditures such as the cost of buying equipment or building factories) are treated as *negative* cash flows. In evaluating Projects S and L, only CF_0 is negative, but for many large projects such as the Alaska Pipeline, an electric generating plant, or IBM's laptop computer project, outflows occur for several years before operations begin and cash flows turn positive.

---

[2]Another capital budgeting technique that was once used widely is the *accounting rate of return (ARR),* which examines a project's contribution to the firm's net income. Although some companies still calculate an ARR, it really has no redeeming features, so we will not discuss it in this text. See Eugene F. Brigham and Louis C. Gapenski, *Intermediate Financial Management,* 5th ed., Chapter 7. Yet another technique which we omit here is the *profitability index,* or *benefit/cost ratio.* Brigham and Gapenski also discuss this method.

At a 10 percent cost of capital, Project S's NPV is $78.82:

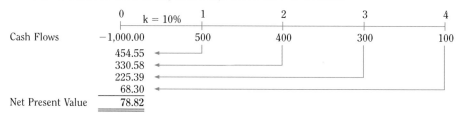

By a similar process, we find $NPV_L = \$49.18$. On this basis, both projects should be accepted if they are independent, but S should be chosen if they are mutually exclusive.

It is not hard to calculate the NPV as was done in the time line by using Equation 10-1 and a regular calculator, along with the interest rate tables. However, it is more efficient to use a financial calculator. Different calculators are set up somewhat differently, but they all have a section of memory called the "cash flow register" which is used for uneven cash flows such as those in Projects S and L (as opposed to equal annuity cash flows). A solution process for Equation 10-1 is literally programmed into financial calculators, and all you have to do is enter the cash flows (being sure to observe the signs), along with the value of k = I. At that point, you have (in your calculator) this equation:

$$NPV_S = -1,000 + \frac{500}{(1.10)^1} + \frac{400}{(1.10)^2} + \frac{300}{(1.10)^3} + \frac{100}{(1.10)^4}.$$

Notice that the equation has one unknown, NPV. Now, all you need to do is to ask the calculator to solve the equation for you, which you do by pressing the NPV button (and, on some calculators, the "compute" button). The answer, 78.82, will appear on the screen.[3]

---

[3]The *Technology Supplement* provided to instructors and available for copying by users explains this and other commonly used calculator applications. For those who do not have the *Supplement,* the steps for two popular calculators, the HP-10B and the HP-17B, are shown below. If you have another type of financial calculator, see its manual or the *Supplement.*

HP-10B:

1. Clear the memory.
2. Enter CF_0 as follows: 1000 +/− CFⱼ .
3. Enter CF_1 as follows: 500 CFⱼ .
4. Repeat the process to enter the other cash flows. Note that CF 0, CF 1, and so forth, flash on the screen as you press the CFⱼ button. If you hold the button down, CF 0 and so forth, will remain on the screen until you release it.
5. Once the CFs have been entered, enter k = I = 10%: 10 I/YR .
6. Now that all of the inputs have been entered, you can press ■ NPV to get the answer, NPV = $78.82.
7. If a cash flow is repeated for several years, you can avoid having to enter the CFs for each year. For example, if the $500 cash flow for Year 1 had also been the CF for Years 2 through 10, making 10 of these $500 cash flows, then after entering 500 CFⱼ the first time, you could enter 10 ■ Nⱼ . This would automatically enter 10 CFs of 500.

HP-17B:

1. Go to the cash flow (CFLO) menu, clear if FLOW(0) = ? does not appear on the screen.
2. Enter CF_0 as follows: 1000 +/− INPUT .
3. Enter CF_1 as follows: 500 INPUT .
4. Now, the calculator will ask you if the 500 is for Period 1 only or if it is also used for several following periods. Since it is only used for Period 1, press INPUT to answer "1." Alternatively, you could press EXIT and then #T? to turn off the prompt for the remainder of the problem. For some problems, you will want to use the repeat feature.

RATIONALE FOR THE NPV METHOD

The rationale for the NPV method is straightforward. An NPV of zero signifies that the project's cash flows are just sufficient to repay the invested capital and to provide the required rate of return on that capital. If a project has a positive NPV, then it is generating more cash than is needed to service its debt and to provide the required return to shareholders, and this excess cash accrues solely to the firm's stockholders. Therefore, if a firm takes on a project with a positive NPV, the position of the stockholders is improved. In our example, shareholders' wealth would increase by $78.82 if the firm takes on Project S, but by only $49.18 if it takes on Project L. Viewed in this manner, it is easy to see why S is preferred to L, and it is also easy to see the logic of the NPV approach.[4]

INTERNAL RATE OF RETURN (IRR)

Internal Rate of Return (IRR) Method
A method of ranking investment proposals using the rate of return on an investment, calculated by finding the discount rate that equates the present value of future cash inflows to the project's cost.

IRR
The discount rate which forces the PV of a project's inflows to equal the PV of its costs.

In Chapter 7 we presented procedures for finding the yield to maturity, or rate of return, on a bond — if you invest in a bond, hold it to maturity, and receive all of the promised cash flows, you will earn the YTM on the money you invested. Exactly the same concepts are employed in capital budgeting when the **internal rate of return (IRR) method** is used. The **IRR** is defined as that discount rate which equates the present value of a project's expected cash inflows to the present value of the project's costs:

$$PV(Inflows) = PV(Investment\ costs),$$

or, equivalently, the rate which forces the NPV to equal zero:

$$CF_0 + \frac{CF_1}{(1 + IRR)^1} + \frac{CF_2}{(1 + IRR)^2} + \cdots + \frac{CF_n}{(1 + IRR)^n} = 0$$

$$NPV = \sum_{t=0}^{n} \frac{CF_t}{(1 + IRR)^t} = 0. \quad (10\text{-}2)$$

For our Project S, here is the time line setup:

	0	IRR	1	2	3	4
Cash Flows	−1,000		500	400	300	100
Sum of PVs for CF$_{1-4}$	1,000					
Net Present Value	0					

$$-1,000 + \frac{500}{(1 + IRR)^1} + \frac{400}{(1 + IRR)^2} + \frac{300}{(1 + IRR)^3} + \frac{100}{(1 + IRR)^4} = 0.$$

5. Enter the remaining CFs, being sure to turn off the prompt or else to specify "1" for each entry.
6. Once the CFs have all been entered, press **EXIT** and then **CALC**.
7. Now enter k = I = 10% as follows: 10 **I%**.
8. Now press **NPV** to get the answer, NPV = $78.82.

[4]This description of the process is somewhat oversimplified. Both analysts and investors anticipate that firms will identify and accept positive NPV projects, and current stock prices reflect these expectations. Thus, stock prices react to announcements of new capital projects only to the extent that such projects were not already expected. In this sense, we may think of a firm's value as consisting of two parts: (1) the value of its existing assets and (2) the value of its "growth opportunities," or projects with positive NPVs.

Thus, we have an equation with one unknown, IRR, and we need to solve for IRR.

Although it is easy to find the NPV without a financial calculator, this is *not* true of the IRR. If the cash flows are constant from year to year, then we have an annuity, and we can use annuity factors as discussed in Chapter 6 to find the IRR. However, if the cash flows are not constant, as is generally the case in capital budgeting, then it is difficult to find the IRR without a financial calculator. Without a calculator, you must solve Equation 10-2 by trial-and-error — try some discount rate (or PVIF factor) and see if the equation solves to zero, and if it does not, try a different discount rate, and continue until you find the rate that forces the equation to equal zero. The discount rate that causes the equation (and the NPV) to equal zero is defined as the IRR. For a realistic project with a fairly long life, the trial-and-error approach is a tedious, time-consuming task.

Fortunately, it is easy to find IRRs with a financial calculator. You follow procedures almost identical to those used to find the NPV. First, you enter the cash flows as shown on the preceding time line into the calculator's cash flow register. In effect, you have entered the cash flows into the equation shown below the time line. Note that we have one unknown, IRR, which is the discount rate that forces the equation to equal zero. The calculator has been programmed to solve for the IRR, and you activate this program by pressing the button labeled "IRR." Then the calculator solves for IRR and displays it on the screen. Here are the IRRs for Projects S and L as found with a financial calculator:[5]

$$IRR_S = 14.5\%$$

$$IRR_L = 11.8\%.$$

Hurdle Rate
The discount rate (cost of capital) which the IRR must exceed if a project is to be accepted.

If both projects have a cost of capital, or **hurdle rate,** of 10 percent, then the internal rate of return rule indicates that if the projects are independent, both should be accepted — they are both expected to earn more than the cost of the capital needed to finance them. If they are mutually exclusive, S ranks higher and should be accepted, while L should be rejected. If the cost of capital is above 14.5 percent, both projects should be rejected.

Notice that the internal rate of return formula, Equation 10-2, is simply the NPV formula, Equation 10-1, solved for the particular discount rate that forces the NPV to equal zero. Thus, the same basic equation is used for both methods, but in the NPV method the discount rate, k, is specified and the NPV is found, whereas in the IRR method the NPV is specified to equal zero, and the interest rate that forces this equality (the IRR) is calculated.

Mathematically, the NPV and IRR methods will always lead to the same accept/reject decisions for independent projects, because if NPV is positive, IRR will exceed k. However, NPV and IRR can give conflicting rankings for mutually exclusive projects. This point will be discussed in more detail in a later section.

RATIONALE FOR THE IRR METHOD

Why is the particular discount rate that equates a project's cost with the present value of its receipts (the IRR) so special? The reason is based on this logic: (1) The IRR on a project is its expected rate of return. (2) If the internal rate of

---

[5]To find the IRR with an HP-10B or HP-17B, repeat the steps given in Footnote 3. Then, with an HP-10B, press ■ IRR/YR , and, after a pause, 14.49, Project S's IRR, will appear. With the HP-17B, simply press IRR% to get the IRR. With both calculators, you would generally want to get both the NPV and the IRR after entering the input data, before clearing the cash flow register. The *Technology Supplement* explains how to find IRR with several other calculators.

return exceeds the cost of the funds used to finance the project, a surplus remains after paying for the capital, and this surplus accrues to the firm's stockholders. (3) Therefore, taking on a project whose IRR exceeds its cost of capital increases shareholders' wealth. On the other hand, if the internal rate of return is less than the cost of capital, then taking on the project imposes a cost on current stockholders. It is this "breakeven" characteristic that makes the IRR useful in evaluating capital projects.

SELF-TEST QUESTIONS ??????

What four capital budgeting ranking methods were discussed in this section? Describe each method, and give the rationale for its use.

What two methods always lead to the same accept/reject decision for independent projects?

What two pieces of information does the payback period convey that are not conveyed by the other methods?

COMPARISON OF THE NPV AND IRR METHODS

In many respects the NPV method is better than IRR, so it is tempting to explain NPV only, to state that it should be used to select projects, and to go on to the next topic. However, the IRR method is familiar to many corporate executives, it is widely entrenched in industry, and it does have some virtues. Therefore, it is important for you to understand the IRR method but also to be able to explain why, at times, a project with a lower IRR may be preferable to one with a higher IRR.

NPV PROFILES

Net Present Value Profile
A graph showing the relationship between a project's NPV and the firm's cost of capital.

A graph which plots a project's NPV against the discount rates is defined as the project's **net present value profile;** profiles for Projects L and S are shown in Figure 10-4. To construct NPV profiles, first note that at a zero discount rate, the NPV is simply the total of the project's undiscounted cash flows. Thus, at a zero discount rate $NPV_S = \$300$, and $NPV_L = \$400$. These values are plotted as the vertical axis intercepts in Figure 10-4. Next, we calculate the projects' NPVs at three discount rates, 5, 10, and 15 percent, and plot these values. The four points plotted on our graph for each project are shown at the bottom of the figure.[6]

Recall that the IRR is defined as the discount rate at which a project's NPV equals zero. Therefore, *the point where its net present value profile crosses the horizontal axis indicates a project's internal rate of return.* Since we calculated IRR_S and IRR_L in an earlier section, we can confirm the validity of the graph.

---

[6]To calculate the points with a financial calculator, enter the cash flows in the cash flow register, enter I = 0, and press the NPV button to find the NPV at a zero cost of capital. Then enter I = 5 to override the zero, and press NPV to get the NPV at 5 percent. Repeat these steps for 10 and 15 percent.

FIGURE   10-4   Net Present Value Profiles: NPVs of Projects S and L at Different Costs of Capital

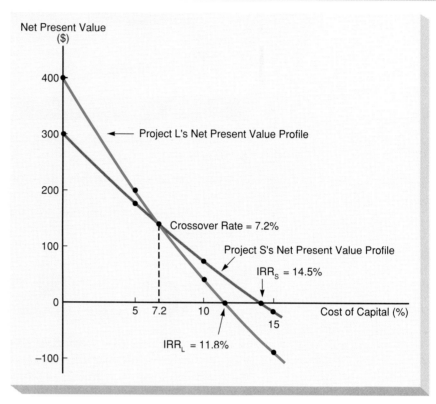

DISCOUNT RATE	NPV$_S$	NPV$_L$
0%	$300.00	$400.00
5	180.42	206.50
10	78.82	49.18
15	(8.33)	(80.14)

When we connect the data points, we have the net present value profiles.[7] NPV profiles can be very useful in project analysis, and we will use them often in the remainder of the chapter.

NPV RANKINGS DEPEND ON THE COST OF CAPITAL

Figure 10-4 shows that the NPV profiles of both Project L and Project S decline as the discount rate increases. But notice in the figure that Project L has the higher NPV at low discount rates, while Project S has the higher NPV if the

---

[7]Notice that the NPV profiles are curved — they are *not* straight lines. NPV approaches the t = 0 cash flow (the cost of the project) as the discount rate increases without limit. The reason is that, at an infinitely high discount rate, the PV of the inflows would be zero, so NPV at (k = ∞) is simply CF$_0$, which in our example is −$1,000. We should also note that under certain conditions the NPV profiles can cross the horizontal axis several times, or never cross it. This point is discussed later in the chapter.

Crossover Rate
The discount rate at which the NPV profiles of two projects cross and, thus, at which the projects' NPVs are equal.

discount rate is greater than the 7.2 percent **crossover rate.** Notice also that Project L's NPV is "more sensitive" to changes in the discount rate than is NPV_S; that is, Project L's net present value profile has the steeper slope, indicating that a given change in k has a larger effect on NPV_L than on NPV_S.

To see why L has the greater sensitivity, recall first that the cash flows from S are received faster than those from L. In a payback sense, S is a short-term project, while L is a long-term project. Next, recall the equation for the NPV:

$$NPV = \frac{CF_0}{(1 + k)^0} + \frac{CF_1}{(1 + k)^1} + \cdots + \frac{CF_n}{(1 + k)^n}.$$

The impact of an increase in the discount rate is much greater on distant than on near-term cash flows. To illustrate, consider the following:

$$\text{PV of \$100 due in 1 year @ k} = 5\%: \frac{\$100}{(1.05)^1} = \$95.24.$$

$$\text{PV of \$100 due in 1 year @ k} = 10\%: \frac{\$100}{(1.10)^1} = \$90.91.$$

$$\text{Percentage decline due to higher k} = \frac{\$95.24 - \$90.91}{\$95.24} = 4.5\%.$$

$$\text{PV of \$100 due in 20 years @ k} = 5\%: \frac{\$100}{(1.05)^{20}} = \$37.69.$$

$$\text{PV of \$100 due in 20 years @ k} = 10\%: \frac{\$100}{(1.10)^{20}} = \$14.86.$$

$$\text{Percentage decline due to higher k} = \frac{\$37.69 - \$14.86}{\$37.69} = 60.6\%.$$

Thus, a doubling of the discount rate causes only a 4.5 percent decline in the PV of a Year 1 cash flow, but the same doubling of the discount rate causes the PV of a Year 20 cash flow to fall by more than 60 percent. Therefore, if a project has most of its cash flows coming in the early years, its NPV will not decline very much if the cost of capital increases, but a project whose cash flows come later will be severely penalized by high capital costs. Accordingly, Project L, which has its largest cash flows in the later years, is hurt badly if the cost of capital is high, while Project S, which has relatively rapid cash flows, is affected less by high capital costs. Therefore, Project L's NPV profile has the steeper slope.

INDEPENDENT PROJECTS

If an *independent* project is being evaluated, then the NPV and IRR criteria always lead to the same accept/reject decision: if NPV says accept, IRR also says accept. To see why this is so, assume that Projects L and S are independent, and then look back at Figure 10-4 and notice (1) that the IRR criterion for acceptance for either project is that the project's cost of capital is less than (or to the left of) the IRR and (2) that whenever a project's cost of capital is less than its IRR, its NPV is positive. Thus, at any cost of capital less than 11.8 percent, Project L will be acceptable by both the NPV and the IRR criteria, while both methods reject the project if the cost of capital is greater than 11.8 percent. Project S — and all other independent projects under consideration — could be analyzed similarly, and it will always turn out that if the IRR method says accept, then so will the NPV method.

MUTUALLY EXCLUSIVE PROJECTS[8]

Now assume that Projects S and L are *mutually exclusive* rather than independent. That is, we can choose either Project S or Project L, or we can reject both, but we cannot accept both projects. Notice in Figure 10-4 that as long as the cost of capital is *greater than* the crossover rate of 7.2 percent, then (1) NPV_S is larger than NPV_L, and (2) IRR_S exceeds IRR_L. Therefore, if k is *greater* than the crossover rate of 7.2 percent, the two methods both lead to the selection of Project S. However, if the cost of capital is *less than* the crossover rate, the NPV method ranks Project L higher, but the IRR method indicates that Project S is better. *Thus, a conflict exists if the cost of capital is less than the crossover rate.* NPV says choose mutually exclusive L, while IRR says take S. Which answer is correct? Logic suggests that the NPV method is better, because it selects the project which adds the most to shareholder wealth.[9]

There are two basic conditions which can cause NPV profiles to cross, and thus conflicts to arise between NPV and IRR: (1) when *project size (or scale) differences* exist, meaning that the cost of one project is larger than that of the other, or (2) when *timing differences* exist, meaning that the timing of cash flows from the two projects differs such that most of the cash flows from one project come in the early years while most of the cash flows from the other project come in the later years, as occurred with our Projects L and S.[10]

When either size or timing differences occur, the firm will have different amounts of funds to invest in the various years, depending on which of the two mutually exclusive projects it chooses. For example, if one project costs more than the other, then the firm will have more money at t = 0 to invest elsewhere if it selects the smaller project. Similarly, for projects of equal size, the one with the larger early cash inflows provides — in our example, Project S — more funds for reinvestment in the early years. Given this situation, the rate of return at which differential cash flows can be invested is a critical issue.

The key to resolving conflicts between mutually exclusive projects is this: How useful is it to generate cash flows sooner rather than later? The value of early cash flows depends on the return we can earn on those cash flows, that is, the rate at which we can reinvest them. *The NPV method implicitly assumes that the rate at which cash flows can be reinvested is the cost of capital, whereas the IRR method assumes that the firm can reinvest at the IRR.* These assumptions are inherent in the mathematics of the discounting process. The cash flows may actually be withdrawn as dividends by the stockholders and spent on beer and pizza, but the NPV method still assumes that cash flows can be reinvested at the cost of capital, while the IRR method assumes reinvestment at the project's IRR.

Which is the better assumption — that cash flows can be reinvested at the cost of capital, or that they can be reinvested at the project's IRR? It can be demonstrated that the best assumption is that projects' cash flows are reinvested at the

---

[8]This section is relatively technical, but it can be omitted without loss of continuity.

[9]The crossover rate is easy to calculate. Simply go back to Figure 10-1, where we set forth the two projects' cash flows, and calculate the difference in those flows in each year. The differences are $CF_S - CF_L = \$0, +\$400, +\$100, -\$100,$ and $-\$500,$ respectively. Enter these values in the cash flow register of a financial calculator, press the IRR button, and the crossover rate, $7.17\% \approx 7.2\%$, appears. Be sure to enter $CF_0 = 0$ or else you will not get the correct answer.

[10]Of course, it is possible for mutually exclusive projects to differ with respect to both scale and timing. Also, if mutually exclusive projects have different lives (as opposed to different cash flow patterns over a common life), this introduces further complications, and for meaningful comparisons, some mutually exclusive projects must be evaluated over a common life. This point will be discussed in Chapter 11.

Reinvestment Rate Assumption
The assumption that cash flows from a project can be reinvested (1) at the cost of capital, if using the NPV method, or (2) at the internal rate of return, if using the IRR method.

cost of capital.[11] Therefore, we conclude that *the best* **reinvestment rate assumption** *is the cost of capital, which is consistent with the NPV method.* This, in turn, leads us to prefer the NPV method, at least for a firm willing and able to obtain capital at a cost reasonably close to its current cost of capital.

We should reiterate that, when projects are independent, the NPV and IRR methods both lead to exactly the same accept/reject decision. However, *when evaluating mutually exclusive projects, especially those that differ in scale and/or timing, the NPV method should be used.*

Multiple IRRs[12]

There is one other situation in which the IRR approach may not be usable — this is when projects with nonnormal cash flows are involved. A project has *normal* cash flows if one or more cash outflows (costs) are followed by a series of cash inflows. If, however, a project calls for a large cash outflow either sometime during or at the end of its life, then the project has *nonnormal* cash flows. Projects with nonnormal cash flows can present unique difficulties when they are evaluated by the IRR method, with the most common problem being the existence of **multiple IRRs.**

Multiple IRRs
The situation where a project has two or more IRRs.

When one solves Equation 10-2 to find the IRR for a project with nonnormal cash flows,

$$\sum_{t=0}^{n} \frac{CF_t}{(1 + IRR)^t} = 0, \qquad \text{(10-2)}$$

it is possible to obtain more than one value of IRR, which means that multiple IRRs occur. Notice that Equation 10-2 is a polynomial of degree n, so it has n different roots, or solutions. All except one of the roots are imaginary numbers when investments have normal cash flows (one or more cash outflows followed by cash inflows), so in the normal case, only one value of IRR appears. However, the possibility of multiple real roots, hence multiple IRRs, arises when the project has nonnormal cash flows (negative net cash flows occur during some year after the project has been placed in operation).

To illustrate this problem, suppose a firm is considering the expenditure of $1.6 million to develop a strip mine (Project M). The mine will produce a cash flow of $10 million at the end of Year 1. Then, at the end of Year 2, $10 million must be expended to restore the land to its original condition. Therefore, the project's expected net cash flows are as follows (in millions of dollars):

	Expected Net Cash Flows	
Year 0	**End of Year 1**	**End of Year 2**
−$1.6	+$10	−$10

These values can be substituted into Equation 10-2 to derive the IRR for the investment:

$$NPV = \frac{-\$1.6 \text{ million}}{(1 + IRR)^0} + \frac{\$10 \text{ million}}{(1 + IRR)^1} + \frac{-\$10 \text{ million}}{(1 + IRR)^2} = 0.$$

---

[11]Again, see Eugene F. Brigham and Louis C. Gapenski, *Intermediate Financial Management,* 5th ed., Chapter 7, for a discussion of this point.

[12]This section is relatively technical, but it can be omitted without loss of continuity.

FIGURE 10-5 NPV Profile for Project M

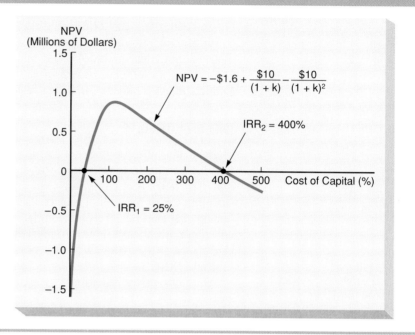

$$NPV = -\$1.6 + \frac{\$10}{(1 + k)} - \frac{\$10}{(1 + k)^2}$$

When solved, we find that NPV = 0 when IRR = 25% and also when IRR = 400%.[13] Therefore, the IRR of the investment is both 25 and 400 percent. This relationship is depicted graphically in Figure 10-5.[14] Note that no dilemma would arise if the NPV method were used; we would simply use Equation 10-1, find the NPV, and use this to evaluate the project. If Project M's cost of capital were 10 percent, then its NPV would be −$0.77 million, and the project should be rejected. If k were between 25 and 400 percent, the NPV would be positive.

One of the authors encountered another example of multiple internal rates of return when a major California bank *borrowed* funds from an insurance company and then used these funds (plus an initial investment of its own) to buy a number of jet engines, which it then leased to a major airline. The bank expected to receive positive net cash flows (lease payments plus tax savings minus interest on the insurance company loan) for a number of years, then several large

---

[13]If you attempted to find the IRR of Project M with many financial calculators, you would get an error message. This same message would be given for all projects with multiple IRRs. However, you can still find Project M's IRRs by first calculating NPVs using several different values for k and then plotting the NPV profile. The intersections with the X-axis give a rough idea of the IRR values. Finally, you can use trial-and-error to find the exact values of k which force NPV = 0.

Note, too, that some calculators, including the HP-10B and 17B, can find the IRR. At the error message, key in a guess, store it, and repress the IRR key. With the HP-10B, type 10 ■ STO ■ IRR, and the answer, 25.00, appears. If you enter as your guess a cost of capital less than the one at which NPV in Figure 10-5 is maximized (about 100%), the lower IRR, 25%, is displayed. If you guess a high rate, say, 150, the higher IRR is shown.

[14]Does Figure 10-5 suggest that the firm should try to *raise* its cost of capital to about 100 percent in order to maximize the NPV of the project? Certainly not. The firm should seek to *minimize* its cost of capital; this will cause its stock price to be maximized. Actions taken to raise the cost of capital might make this particular project look good, but those actions would be terribly harmful to the firm's more numerous projects with normal cash flows. Only if the firm's cost of capital is high in spite of efforts to keep it down will the illustrative project have a positive NPV.

negative cash flows as it repaid the insurance company loan, and, finally, a large inflow from the sale of the engines when the lease expired.

The bank discovered two IRRs and wondered which was correct. It could not ignore the IRR and use the NPV method since the lease was already on the books, and the bank's senior loan committee, as well as Federal Reserve bank examiners, wanted to know the return on the lease. The bank's solution called for calculating and then using the "modified internal rate of return" as discussed in the next section.

The examples just presented illustrate one problem, multiple IRRs, that can arise when the IRR criterion is used with a project that has nonnormal cash flows. Use of the IRR method on projects having nonnormal cash flows could produce other problems such as no IRR or an IRR which leads to an incorrect accept/reject decision. In all such cases, the NPV criterion could be easily applied, and this method leads to conceptually correct capital budgeting decisions.

SELF-TEST QUESTIONS

Describe how NPV profiles are constructed.

What is the crossover rate, and how does it affect the choice between mutually exclusive projects?

What two basic conditions can lead to conflicts between the NPV and IRR methods?

Why is the "reinvestment rate" considered to be the underlying cause of conflicts between the NPV and IRR methods?

If a conflict exists, should the capital budgeting decision be made on the basis of the NPV or the IRR ranking? Why?

Explain the difference between normal and nonnormal cash flows.

What is the "multiple IRR problem," and what condition is necessary for its occurrence?

MODIFIED INTERNAL RATE OF RETURN (MIRR)[15]

In spite of a strong academic preference for NPV, surveys indicate that executives prefer IRR over NPV. Apparently, managers find it intuitively more appealing to evaluate investments in terms of percentage rates of return than dollars of NPV. Given this fact, can we devise a percentage evaluator that is better than the regular IRR? The answer is yes — we can modify the IRR and make it a better indicator of relative profitability, hence better for use in capital budgeting. The new measure is called the **modified IRR,** or **MIRR,** and it is defined as follows:

Modified IRR (MIRR)
The discount rate at which the present value of a project's cost is equal to the present value of its terminal value, where the terminal value is found as the sum of the future values of the cash inflows, compounded at the firm's cost of capital.

$$\text{PV costs} = \text{PV terminal value}$$

$$\sum_{t=0}^{n} \frac{COF_t}{(1 + k)^t} = \frac{\sum_{t=0}^{n} CIF_t(1 + k)^{n-t}}{(1 + MIRR)^n}$$

$$\text{PV costs} = \frac{TV}{(1 + MIRR)^n}. \tag{10-2a}$$

---

[15]Again, this section is relatively technical, but it can be omitted without loss of continuity.

Here COF refers to cash outflows (negative numbers), or the cost of the project, and CIF refers to cash inflows (positive numbers). The left term is simply the PV of the investment outlays when discounted at the cost of capital, and the numerator of the right term is the future value of the inflows, assuming that the cash inflows are reinvested at the cost of capital. The future value of the cash inflows is also called the *terminal value,* or *TV.* The discount rate that forces the PV of the TV to equal the PV of the costs is defined as the MIRR.[16]

If the investment costs are all incurred at t = 0, and if the first operating inflow occurs at t = 1, as is true for the illustrative Projects S and L which we first presented in Figure 10-1, then this equation may be used:

$$\text{Cost} = \frac{TV}{(1 + \text{MIRR})^n} = \frac{\sum_{t=1}^{n} \text{CIF}_t(1 + k)^{n-t}}{(1 + \text{MIRR})^n}. \qquad \text{(10-2b)}$$

We can illustrate the calculation with Project S:

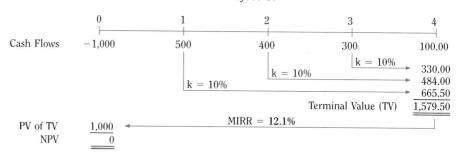

Using the cash flows as set out on the time line, first find the terminal value by compounding each cash inflow at the 10 percent cost of capital. Then enter N = 4, PV = −1000, PMT = 0, FV = 1579.5, and then press the I button to find MIRR$_S$ = 12.1%. Similarly, we find MIRR$_L$ = 11.3%.[17]

The modified IRR has a significant advantage over the regular IRR. MIRR assumes that cash flows from all projects are reinvested at the cost of capital, while the regular IRR assumes that the cash flows from each project are reinvested at the project's own IRR. Since reinvestment at the cost of capital is generally more correct, the modified IRR is a better indicator of a project's true profitability. The MIRR also solves the multiple IRR problem. To illustrate, with k = 10%, Project M (the strip mine project) has MIRR = 5.6% versus its 10 percent cost of capital, so it should be rejected. This is consistent with the decision based on the NPV method, because at k = 10%, NPV = −$0.77 million.

---

[16]There are several alternative definitions for the MIRR. The differences primarily relate to whether negative cash flows which occur after positive cash flows begin should be compounded and treated as part of the TV or discounted and treated as a cost. A related issue is whether negative and positive flows in a given year should be netted or treated separately. For a complete discussion, see William R. McDaniel, Daniel E. McCarty, and Kenneth A. Jessell, "Discounted Cash Flow with Explicit Reinvestment Rates: Tutorial and Extension," *The Financial Review,* August 1988, 369–385, and David M. Shull, "Interpreting Rates of Return: A Modified Rate of Return Approach," *Financial Practice and Education,* Fall 1993, 67–71.

[17]With some calculators, including the HP-17B, you could enter the cash inflows in the cash flow register (being sure to enter CF$_0$ = 0), enter I = 10, and then press the NFV key to find TV = 1,579.50. The HP-10B does not have an NFV key, but you can still use the cash flow register to find TV. Enter the cash flows in the cash flow register (with CF$_0$ = 0), then enter I = 10, then press ■ NPV to find the PV of the inflows, which is 1,078.82. Now, with the regular time value keys, enter N = 4, I = 10, PV = −1078.82, PMT = 0, and press FV to find TV = 1,579.50. Similar procedures can be used with other financial calculators.

Is MIRR as good as NPV for choosing between mutually exclusive projects? If two projects are of equal size and have the same life, then NPV and MIRR will always lead to the same decision. Thus, for any set of projects like our Projects S and L, if $NPV_S > NPV_L$, then $MIRR_S > MIRR_L$, and the kinds of conflicts we encountered between NPV and the regular IRR will not occur. Also, if the projects are of equal size, but differ in lives, the MIRR will always lead to the same decision as the NPV if the MIRRs are both calculated using as the terminal year the life of the longer project. (Just fill in zeros for the shorter project's missing cash flows.) However, if the projects differ in size, then conflicts can still occur. For example, if we were choosing between a large project and a small mutually exclusive one, then we might find $NPV_L > NPV_S$, but $MIRR_S > MIRR_L$.

Our conclusion is that the MIRR is superior to the regular IRR as an indicator of a project's "true" rate of return, or "expected long-term rate of return," but the NPV method is still better for choosing among competing projects because it provides a better indicator of how much each project will increase the value of the firm.

SELF-TEST QUESTIONS

Describe how the modified IRR (MIRR) is calculated.

What is the primary difference between the MIRR and the regular IRR?

What advantages does the MIRR have over the regular IRR for making capital budgeting decisions?

What condition can cause the MIRR and NPV methods to produce conflicting rankings?

CONCLUSIONS ON CAPITAL BUDGETING METHODS

We have discussed five capital budgeting decision methods, comparing the methods against one another and highlighting their relative strengths and weaknesses. In the process, we probably created the impression that "sophisticated" firms should use only one method in the·decision process, NPV. However, virtually all capital budgeting decisions are analyzed by computer, so it is easy to calculate and list all the decision measures: payback and discounted payback, NPV, IRR, and modified IRR (MIRR). In making the accept/reject decision, most large, sophisticated firms such as IBM, GE, and Royal Dutch Petroleum calculate and consider all of the measures, because each one provides decision makers with a somewhat different piece of relevant information.

Payback and discounted payback provide an indication of both the *risk* and the *liquidity* of a project — a long payback means (1) that the investment dollars will be locked up for many years, hence the project is relatively illiquid, and (2) that the project's cash flows must be forecast far out into the future, hence the project is probably quite risky. A good analogy for this is the bond valuation process. An investor should never compare the yields to maturity on two bonds without also considering their terms to maturity, because a bond's riskiness is significantly influenced by its maturity.

NPV is important because it gives a direct measure of the dollar benefit of the project to shareholders, so we regard NPV as the best single measure of *profitability.* IRR also measures profitability, but here it is expressed as a percentage rate of return, which many decision makers prefer. Further, IRR contains information concerning a project's "safety margin." To illustrate, consider the following two projects: Project S (for small) costs $10,000 at t = 0 and is expected to return $16,500 at the end of one year, while Project L (for large) costs $100,000 and has an expected payoff of $115,500 after one year. At a 10 percent cost of capital, both projects have an NPV of $5,000, so by the NPV rule we should be indifferent between them. However, Project S has a much larger margin for error. Even if its realized cash inflow were 39 percent below the $16,500 forecast, the firm would still recover its $10,000 investment. On the other hand, if Project L's inflows fell by only 13 percent from the forecasted $115,500, the firm would not recover its investment. Further, if no inflows were generated at all, the firm would lose only $10,000 with Project S, but $100,000 if it took on Project L.

The NPV provides no information about either of these factors — the "safety margin" inherent in the cash flow forecasts or the amount of capital at risk. However, the IRR does provide "safety margin" information — Project S's IRR is a whopping 65.0 percent, while Project L's IRR is only 15.5 percent. As a result, the realized return could fall substantially for Project S, and it would still make money. Finally, the modified IRR has all the virtues of the IRR, but (1) it incorporates a better reinvestment rate assumption, and (2) it avoids the multiple rate of return problem.

In summary, the different measures provide different types of information to decision makers. Since it is easy to calculate all of them, all should be considered in the decision process. For any specific decision, more weight might be given to one measure than another, but it would be foolish to ignore the information provided by any of the methods.

SELF-TEST QUESTIONS

Describe the advantages and disadvantages of the five capital budgeting methods discussed in this chapter.

Should capital budgeting decisions be made solely on the basis of a project's NPV?

BUSINESS PRACTICES

Harold Bierman published a survey of the capital budgeting methods used by the Fortune 500 industrial companies; here is a summary of his findings:[18]

1. Every single one of the responding firms used some type of DCF method. In 1955, a similar study reported that only 4 percent of large companies used a DCF method. Thus, large firms' usage of DCF methodology has increased dramatically in the last 40 years.

2. The payback period was used by 84 percent of Bierman's surveyed companies. However, no company used it as the primary method, and most companies gave the greatest weight to a DCF method. In 1955, surveys similar to Bierman's found that payback was the most important method.

---

[18]Harold Bierman, "Capital Budgeting in 1993: A Survey," *Financial Management*, Autumn 1993, 24.

3. Currently, 99 percent of the Fortune 500 companies use IRR, while 85 percent use NPV. Thus, most firms actually use both methods.

4. Ninety-three percent of Bierman's companies calculate a weighted average cost of capital as part of their capital budgeting process. A few companies apparently use the same WACC for all projects, but 73 percent adjust the corporate WACC to account for project risk, and 23 percent make adjustments to reflect divisional risk. We will cover risk analysis in capital budgeting in Chapter 12.

5. An examination of surveys done by other authors led Bierman to conclude that there has been a strong trend toward the acceptance of academic recommendations, at least by large companies.

A second 1993 study, conducted by Joe Walker, Richard Burns, and Chad Denson (WBD), focused on small companies.[19] WBD began by noting the same trend toward the use of DCF that Bierman cited, but they reported that only 21 percent of small companies used DCF versus 100 percent for Bierman's large companies. WBD also noted that within their sample, the smaller the firm, the smaller the likelihood that DCF would be used. The focal point of the WBD study was *why* small companies use DCF so much less frequently than large firms. WBD actually based their questionnaire on our box entitled "Capital Budgeting in the Small Firm" on pages 410 and 411, and they concluded that the reasons given in that section do indeed explain why DCF is used infrequently by small firms. The three most frequently cited reasons, according to the survey, were (1) small firms' preoccupation with liquidity, which is best indicated by payback, (2) a lack of familiarity with DCF methods, and (3) a belief that small project sizes make DCF not worth the effort.

The general conclusion one can reach from these studies is that large firms should and do use the procedures we recommend, and that managers of small firms, especially managers with aspirations for future growth, should at least understand DCF procedures well enough to make rational decisions about using or not using them. Moreover, as computer technology makes it easier and less expensive for small firms to use DCF methods, and as more and more of their competitors begin using these methods, survival will necessitate increased DCF usage.

SELF-TEST QUESTIONS

What were Bierman's findings from his survey of capital budgeting methods used by the Fortune 500 companies?

How did the WBD study's findings differ from Bierman's findings?

What general considerations can be reached from these studies?

THE POST-AUDIT

Post-Audit
A comparison of the actual versus the expected results for a given capital project.

An important aspect of the capital budgeting process is the **post-audit,** which involves (1) comparing actual results with those predicted by the project's sponsors and (2) explaining why any differences occurred. For example, many firms

---

[19]Joe Walker, Richard Burns, and Chad Denson, "Why Small Manufacturing Firms Shun DCF," *Journal of Small Business Finance,* 1993, 233–249.

SMALL BUSINESS

CAPITAL BUDGETING IN THE SMALL FIRM

The allocation of capital in small firms is as important as it is in large ones. In fact, given their lack of access to the capital markets, it is often more important in the small firm, because the funds necessary to correct a mistake may not be available. Also, large firms allocate capital to numerous projects, so a mistake on one can be offset by successes with others. Small firms do not have this luxury.

In spite of the importance of capital expenditures to small business, studies of the way decisions are made generally suggest that many small firms use "back-of-the-envelope" analysis, or perhaps no analysis at all. For example, when L. R. Runyon studied 214 firms with net worths of from $500,000 to $1,000,000, he found that almost 70 percent relied upon payback or some other questionable criteria. Only 14 percent used a discounted cash flow analysis, and about 9 percent indicated that they used no formal analysis at all. Studies of larger firms, on the other hand, generally find that most analyze capital budgeting decisions using discounted cash flow techniques.

We are left with a puzzle. Capital budgeting is clearly important to small firms, yet these firms do not use the tools that have been developed to improve these decisions. Why does

this situation exist? One argument is that managers of small firms are simply not well trained; they are unsophisticated. This argument suggests that the managers would use the more sophisticated techniques if they understood them better.

Another argument relates to the fact that management talent is a scarce resource in small firms. That is, even if the managers were exceptionally sophisticated, perhaps demands on them are such that they simply cannot take the time to use elaborate techniques to analyze proposed projects. In other words, small-business managers may be capable of doing careful discounted cash flow analysis, but it would be irrational for them to allocate the time required for such an analysis.

A third argument relates to the cost of analyzing capital projects. To some extent, these costs are fixed; the costs of analysis may be larger for bigger projects, but not by much. To the extent that these costs are indeed fixed, it may not be economical to incur them if the project itself is relatively small. This argument suggests that small firms with small projects may in some cases be making the sensible decision when they rely on management's "gut feeling."

Note also that a major part of the capital budgeting process in large firms involves lower-level analysts' marshalling facts needed by higher-

level decision makers. This step is less necessary in the small firm. Thus, a cursory examination of a small firm's decision process might suggest that capital budgeting decisions are based on snap judgment, but if that judgment is exercised by someone with a total knowledge of the firm and its markets, it could represent a better decision than one based on an elaborate analysis by a lower-level employee in a large firm.

Also, as Runyon reported in his study of manufacturing firms, small firms tend to be cash oriented. They are concerned with basic survival, so they tend to look at expenditures from the standpoint of their near-term effects on cash. This cash and survival orientation leads firms to focus on a relatively short time horizon, and this, in turn, may lead to an emphasis on the payback method. The limitations of payback are well known, but in spite of those limitations, the technique is popular in small business, as it gives the firm a feel for when the cash committed to an investment will be recovered and thus available to repay loans or for new opportunities. Therefore, small firms that are cash oriented and have limited managerial resources may find the payback method appealing. It represents a compromise between the need for extensive analysis on the one hand and the high costs of analysis on the other.

require that the operating divisions send a monthly report for the first six months after a project goes into operation, and a quarterly report thereafter, until the project's results are up to expectations. From then on, reports on the operation are reviewed on a regular basis like those of other operations.

The post-audit has two main purposes:

1. **Improve forecasts.** When decision makers are forced to compare their projections to actual outcomes, there is a tendency for estimates to improve. Conscious or unconscious biases are observed and eliminated; new forecasting methods are sought as the need for them becomes apparent; and people simply tend to do everything better, including forecasting, if they know that their actions are being monitored.

Small firms also face greater uncertainty in the cash flows they might generate beyond the immediate future. Large firms such as AT&T and General Motors have "staying power" — they can make an investment and then ride out business downturns or situations of excess capacity in an industry. Such periods are called "shakeouts," and it is the smaller firms that are generally shaken out. Therefore, most small-business managers are uncomfortable making forecasts beyond a few years. Since discounted cash flow techniques require explicit estimates of cash flows through the life of the project, small-business managers may not take seriously an analysis that hinges on "guesstimate" numbers which, if wrong, could lead to bankruptcy.

THE VALUE OF THE FIRM AND CAPITAL BUDGETING

The single most appealing argument for the use of net present value in capital budgeting is that NPV gives an explicit measure of the effect the investment will have on the firm's value: if NPV is positive, the investment will increase the firm's value and make its owners wealthier. In small firms, however, the stock is often not traded in public markets, so its value cannot be observed. Also, for reasons of control, many small-business owners and managers may not want to broaden ownership by going public.

It is difficult to argue for value-based techniques when the firm's value itself is unobservable. Furthermore, in a closely held firm, the objectives of the individual owner-manager may extend beyond the firm's monetary value. For example, the owner-manager may value the firm's reputation for quality and service and therefore may make an investment that would be rejected on purely economic grounds. In addition, the owner-manager may not hold a well-diversified investment portfolio but may instead have all of his or her eggs in this one basket. In that case, the manager would logically be sensitive to the firm's stand-alone risk, not just to its undiversifiable component. Thus, one project might be viewed as desirable because of its contribution to risk reduction in the firm as a whole, whereas another project with a low beta but high diversifiable risk might be unacceptable, even though in a CAPM framework it would be judged superior.

Another problem faced by a firm that is not publicly traded is that its cost of equity capital is not easily determined — the P_0 term in the cost of equity equation $k = D_1/P_0 + g$ is not observable, nor is its beta.

Since a cost of capital estimate is required to use either the NPV or the IRR method, a small firm in an industry of small firms may simply have no basis for estimating its cost of capital.

CONCLUSIONS

Small firms make less extensive use of DCF techniques than larger firms. This may be a rational decision resulting from a conscious or subconscious conclusion that the costs of sophisticated analyses outweigh their benefits; it may reflect nonmonetary goals of small businesses' owner-managers; or it may reflect difficulties in estimating the cost of capital, which is required for DCF analyses but not for payback. However, non-use of DCF methods may also reflect a weakness in many small firms. We simply do not know. We do know that small businesses must do all they can to compete effectively with big business, and to the extent that a small business fails to use DCF methods because its manager is unsophisticated or uninformed, it may be putting itself at a serious competitive disadvantage.

SOURCE: L. R. Runyon, "Capital Expenditure Decision Making in Small Firms," *Journal of Business Research*, September 1983, 389–397. Reprinted with permission.

---

2. **Improve operations.** Businesses are run by people, and people can perform at higher or lower levels of efficiency. When a divisional team has made a forecast about an investment, its members are, in a sense, putting their reputations on the line. If costs are above predicted levels, sales below expectations, and so on, executives in production, sales, and other areas will strive to improve operations and to bring results into line with forecasts. In a discussion related to this point, one executive made this statement: "You academicians worry only about making good decisions. In business, we also worry about making decisions good."

The post-audit is not a simple process — a number of factors can cause complications. First, we must recognize that each element of the cash flow forecast is subject to uncertainty, so a percentage of all projects undertaken by any reasonably aggressive firm will necessarily go awry. This fact must be considered when appraising the performances of the operating executives who submit capital expenditure requests. Second, projects sometimes fail to meet expectations for reasons beyond the control of the operating executives and for reasons that no one could realistically be expected to anticipate. For example, the 1990–1991 recession adversely affected many projects. Third, it is often difficult to separate the operating results of one investment from those of a larger system. Although some projects stand alone and permit ready identification of costs and revenues, the actual cost savings that result from a new computer system, for example, may be very hard to measure. Fourth, it is often hard to hand out blame or praise because the executives who were responsible for launching a given investment may have moved on by the time the results are known.

Because of these difficulties, some firms tend to play down the importance of the post-audit. However, observations of both businesses and governmental units suggest that the best-run and most successful organizations are the ones that put the greatest emphasis on post-audits. Accordingly, we regard the post-audit as being one of the most important elements in a good capital budgeting system.

SELF-TEST QUESTIONS

What is done in the post-audit?

Identify several purposes of the post-audit.

What are some factors which can cause complications in the post-audit?

USING CAPITAL BUDGETING TECHNIQUES IN OTHER CONTEXTS

The techniques developed in this chapter can help managers make a number of different types of decisions. One example is the use of these techniques when evaluating corporate mergers. Companies frequently decide to acquire other firms to obtain low-cost production facilities, to increase capacity, or to expand into new markets, and the analysis related to such mergers is conceptually similar to that related to regular capital budgeting. Thus, when AT&T decided to go into the cellular telephone business, it had the choice of building facilities from the ground up or acquiring an existing business. AT&T chose to acquire McCaw Cellular. In the analysis related to the merger, AT&T's managers used the techniques employed in regular capital budgeting analysis. We discuss merger analysis in detail in Chapter 21.

Managers also use capital budgeting techniques when deciding whether to downsize personnel or to sell off particular assets or division. Like capital budgeting, such an analysis requires an assessment of how the action will affect the firm's cash flows. In a downsizing, companies typically spend money (i.e., invest) in severance payments to employees who are no longer needed, but the companies then receive benefits in the form of lower future wage costs. When assets are sold, the pattern of cash flows is reversed from those in a typical capital budgeting decision — positive cash flows are realized at the outset, but the firm is sacrificing future cash flows that it would have received if it had continued to use the asset.

So, when deciding whether it makes sense to shed assets, managers compare the cash received with the present value of the lost outflows. If the net present value is positive, the asset sale would increase shareholder value.

Most decisions should be based on whether they contribute to shareholder value, and that, in turn, can be determined by estimating the net present value of a set of cash flows. However, as you will see in the next chapter, the hardest part is coming up with reasonable estimates of those cash flows.

SELF-TEST QUESTION ??????

Give some examples of other decisions that can be analyzed with the capital budgeting techniques developed in this chapter.

SUMMARY

This chapter discussed the capital budgeting process. The key concepts covered are listed below.

- **Capital budgeting** is the process of analyzing potential fixed asset investments. Capital budgeting decisions are probably the most important ones financial managers must make.

- The **payback period** is defined as the number of years required to recover a project's cost. The regular payback method ignores cash flows beyond the payback period, and it does not consider the time value of money. The payback does, however, provide an indication of a project's risk and liquidity, because it shows how long the invested capital will be "at risk."

- The **discounted payback method** is similar to the regular payback method except that it discounts cash flows at the project's cost of capital. It considers the time value of money, but it ignores cash flows beyond the payback period.

- The **net present value (NPV) method** discounts all cash flows at the project's cost of capital and then sums those cash flows. The project is accepted if the NPV is positive.

- The **internal rate of return (IRR)** is defined as the discount rate which forces a project's NPV to equal zero. The project is accepted if the IRR is greater than the cost of capital.

- The NPV and IRR methods make the same accept/reject decisions for **independent projects,** but if projects are **mutually exclusive,** then ranking conflicts can arise. If conflicts arise, the NPV method should be used. The NPV and IRR methods are both superior to the payback, but NPV is superior to IRR.

- The NPV method assumes that cash flows will be reinvested at the firm's cost of capital, while the IRR method assumes reinvestment at the project's IRR. **Reinvestment at the cost of capital is generally a better assumption** in that it is closer to reality.

- The **modified IRR (MIRR) method** corrects some of the problems with the regular IRR. MIRR involves finding the **terminal value (TV)** of the cash inflows, compounded at the firm's cost of capital, and then determining the discount rate which forces the present value of the TV to equal the present value of the outflows.

♦ Sophisticated managers consider all of the project evaluation measures because each measure provides a useful piece of information.

♦ The **post-audit** is a key element of capital budgeting. By comparing actual results with predicted results and then determining why differences occurred, decision makers can improve both their operations and their forecasts of projects' outcomes.

♦ Small firms tend to use the payback method rather than a discounted cash flow method. This may be rational, because (1) the **cost** of conducting a DCF analysis **may outweigh the benefits** for the project being considered, (2) **the firm's cost of capital cannot be estimated accurately,** or (3) the small-business owner may be considering **nonmonetary goals.**

Although this chapter has presented the basic elements of the capital budgeting process, there are many other aspects of this crucial topic. Some of the more important ones are discussed in the following chapter.

QUESTIONS

10-1 How is a project classification scheme (for example, replacement, expansion into new markets, and so forth) used in the capital budgeting process?

10-2 Explain why the NPV of a relatively long-term project, defined as one for which a high percentage of its cash flows are expected in the distant future, is more sensitive to changes in the cost of capital than is the NPV of a short-term project.

10-3 Explain why, if two mutually exclusive projects are being compared, the short-term project might have the higher ranking under the NPV criterion if the cost of capital is high, but the long-term project might be deemed better if the cost of capital is low. Would changes in the cost of capital ever cause a change in the IRR ranking of two such projects?

10-4 In what sense is a reinvestment rate assumption embodied in the NPV, IRR, and MIRR methods? What is the assumed reinvestment rate of each method?

10-5 "If a firm has no mutually exclusive projects, only independent ones, and it also has both a constant cost of capital and projects with normal cash flows in the sense that each project has one or more outflows followed by a stream of inflows, then the NPV and IRR methods will always lead to identical capital budgeting decisions." Discuss this statement. What does it imply about using the IRR method in lieu of the NPV method? If each of the assumptions made in the question were changed (one by one), how would these changes affect your answer?

10-6 Are there conditions under which a firm might be better off if it were to choose a machine with a rapid payback rather than one with a larger NPV?

10-7 A firm has $100 million available for capital expenditures. It is considering investing in one of two projects; each has a cost of $100 million. Project A has an IRR of 20 percent and an NPV of $9 million. It will be terminated at the end of 1 year at a profit of $20 million, resulting in an immediate increase in earnings per share (EPS). Project B, which cannot be postponed, has an IRR of 30 percent and an NPV of $50 million. However, the firm's short-run EPS will be reduced if it accepts Project B, because no revenues will be generated for several years.
a. Should the short-run effects on EPS influence the choice between the two projects?
b. How might situations like the one described here influence a firm's decision to use payback as a part of the capital budgeting process?

SELF-TEST PROBLEMS   (Solutions Appear in Appendix B)

ST-1   Define each of the following terms:
Key terms   a. The capital budget; capital budgeting; strategic business plan

b. Regular payback period; discounted payback period
c. Independent projects; mutually exclusive projects
d. DCF techniques; net present value (NPV) method
e. Internal rate of return (IRR) method
f. Modified internal rate of return (MIRR) method
g. NPV profile; crossover rate
h. Nonnormal cash flow projects; normal cash flow projects; multiple IRRs
i. Project cost of capital, or discount rate
j. Reinvestment rate assumption
k. Post-audit

ST-2

Project analysis

You are a financial analyst for Damon Electronics Company. The director of capital budgeting has asked you to analyze two proposed capital investments, Projects X and Y. Each project has a cost of $10,000, and the cost of capital for each project is 12 percent. The projects' expected net cash flows are as follows:

	EXPECTED NET CASH FLOWS	
YEAR	PROJECT X	PROJECT Y
0	($10,000)	($10,000)
1	6,500	3,500
2	3,000	3,500
3	3,000	3,500
4	1,000	3,500

a. Calculate each project's payback period, net present value (NPV), internal rate of return (IRR), and modified internal rate of return (MIRR).
b. Which project or projects should be accepted if they are independent?
c. Which project should be accepted if they are mutually exclusive?
d. How might a change in the cost of capital produce a conflict between the NPV and IRR rankings of these two projects? Would this conflict exist if k were 5%? (Hint: Plot the NPV profiles.)
e. Why does the conflict exist?

STARTER PROBLEMS

10-1

Payback period

Project K has a cost of $52,125, its expected net cash inflows are $12,000 per year for 8 years, and its cost of capital is 12 percent. What is the project's payback period (to the closest year)? (Hint: Begin by constructing a time line.)

10-2

NPV

Refer to Problem 10-1. What is the project's NPV?

10-3

IRR

Refer to Problem 10-1. What is the project's IRR?

10-4

Discounted payback period

Refer to Problem 10-1. What is the project's discounted payback period?

10-5

MIRR

Refer to Problem 10-1. What is the project's MIRR?

10-6

NPV

Your division is considering two investment projects, each of which requires an up-front expenditure of $15 million. You estimate that the investments will produce the following net cash flows:

YEAR	PROJECT A	PROJECT B
1	$ 5,000,000	$20,000,000
2	10,000,000	10,000,000
3	20,000,000	6,000,000

What are the two projects' net present values, assuming the cost of capital is 10 percent? 5 percent? 15 percent?

10-7
NPV; Financial calculator required

Northwest Utility Corporation has a cost of capital of 11.5 percent, and it has a project with the following net cash flows:

t	NET CASH FLOW
0	−$200
1	235
2	−65
3	300

What is the project's NPV?

EXAM-TYPE PROBLEMS

The problems included in this section are set up in such a way that they could be used as multiple-choice exam problems.

10-8
NPVs, IRRs, and MIRRs for independent projects

Edelman Engineering is considering including two pieces of equipment, a truck and an overhead pulley system, in this year's capital budget. The projects are independent. The cash outlay for the truck is $17,100, and that for the pulley system is $22,430. The firm's cost of capital is 14 percent. After-tax cash flows, including depreciation, are as follows:

YEAR	TRUCK	PULLEY
1	$5,100	$7,500
2	5,100	7,500
3	5,100	7,500
4	5,100	7,500
5	5,100	7,500

Calculate the IRR, the NPV, and the MIRR for each project, and indicate the correct accept/reject decision for each.

10-9
NPVs and IRRs for mutually exclusive projects

B. Davis Industries must choose between a gas-powered and an electric-powered forklift truck for moving materials in its factory. Since both forklifts perform the same function, the firm will choose only one. (They are mutually exclusive investments.) The electric-powered truck will cost more, but it will be less expensive to operate; it will cost $22,000, whereas the gas-powered truck will cost $17,500. The cost of capital that applies to both investments is 12 percent. The life for both types of truck is estimated to be 6 years, during which time the net cash flows for the electric-powered truck will be $6,290 per year and those for the gas-powered truck will be $5,000 per year. Annual net cash flows include depreciation expenses. Calculate the NPV and IRR for each type of truck, and decide which to recommend.

10-10
Capital budgeting methods

Project S costs $15,000 and is expected to produce cash flows of $4,500 per year for 5 years. Project L costs $37,500 and is expected to produce cash flows of $11,100 per year for 5 years. Calculate the two projects' NPVs, IRRs, and MIRRs, assuming a cost of capital of 14 percent. Which project would be selected, assuming they are mutually exclusive, using each ranking method? Which should actually be selected?

10-11
Present value of costs

The Costa Rican Coffee Company is evaluating the within-plant distribution system for its new roasting, grinding, and packing plant. The two alternatives are (1) a conveyor system with a high initial cost but low annual operating costs and (2) several forklift trucks, which cost less but have considerably higher operating costs. The decision to construct the plant has already been made, and the choice here will have no effect on the overall revenues of the project. The cost of capital for the plant is 9 percent, and the projects' expected net costs are listed below:

YEAR	EXPECTED NET CASH COSTS	
	CONVEYOR	FORKLIFT
0	($300,000)	($120,000)
1	(66,000)	(96,000)
2	(66,000)	(96,000)
3	(66,000)	(96,000)
4	(66,000)	(96,000)
5	(66,000)	(96,000)

a. What is the IRR of each alternative?

b. What is the present value of costs of each alternative? Which method should be chosen?

10-12
MIRR and NPV

Your company is considering two mutually exclusive projects, X and Y, whose costs and cash flows are shown below:

YEAR	X	Y
0	($1,000)	($1,000)
1	100	1,000
2	300	100
3	400	50
4	700	50

The projects are equally risky, and their cost of capital is 12 percent. You must make a recommendation, and you must base it on the modified IRR (MIRR). What is the MIRR of the better project?

10-13
NPV and IRR

A company is analyzing two mutually exclusive projects, S and L, whose cash flows are shown below:

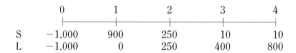

	0	1	2	3	4
S	−1,000	900	250	10	10
L	−1,000	0	250	400	800

The company's cost of capital is 10 percent, and it can get an unlimited amount of capital at that cost. What is the *regular IRR* (not MIRR) of the *better* project? (Hint: Note that the better project may or may not be the one with the higher IRR.)

10-14
MIRR

Project X has a cost of $1,000 at t = 0, and it is expected to produce a uniform cash flow stream for 10 years, i.e., the CFs are the same in Years 1 through 10, and it has a regular IRR of 12 percent. The cost of capital for the project is 10 percent. What is the project's modified IRR (MIRR)?

10-15
NPV and IRR analysis

After discovering a new gold vein in the Colorado mountains, CTC Mining Corporation must decide whether to mine the deposit. The most cost-effective method of mining gold is sulfuric acid extraction, a process that results in environmental damage. To go ahead with the extraction, CTC must spend $900,000 for new mining equipment and pay $165,000 for its installation. The gold mined will net the firm an estimated $350,000 each year over the 5-year life of the vein. CTC's cost of capital is 14 percent. For the purposes of this problem, assume that the cash inflows occur at the end of the year.

a. What is the NPV and IRR of this project?

b. Should this project be undertaken, ignoring environmental concerns?

c. How should environmental effects be considered when evaluating this, or any other, project? How might these effects change your decision in Part b?

10-16
NPV and IRR

John's Publishing Company, a new service that writes term papers for college students, provides 10-page term papers from a list of more than 500 topics. Each paper will cost

$7.50 and is written by a graduate in the topic area. John's will pay $20,000 for the rights to all of the manuscripts. In addition, each author will receive $0.50 in royalties for every paper sold. Marketing expenses are estimated to be a total of $20,000 divided equally between Years 1 and 2, and John's cost of capital is 11 percent. Sales are expected as follows:

YEAR	VOLUME
1	10,000
2	7,000
3	3,000

a. What is the payback period for this investment? Its NPV? Its IRR?
b. What are the ethical implications of this investment?

10-17
NPV and IRR analysis

Sharon Evans, who graduated from the local university 3 years ago with a degree in marketing, is manager of Ann Naylor's store in the Southwest Mall. Sharon's store has 5 years remaining on its lease. Rent is $2,000 per month, 60 payments remain, and the next payment is due in 1 month. The mall's owner plans to sell the property in a year and wants rents at that time to be high so the property will appear more valuable. Therefore, Sharon has been offered a "great deal" (owner's words) on a new 5-year lease. The new lease calls for zero rent for 9 months, then payments of $2,600 per month for the next 51 months. The lease cannot be broken, and Ann Naylor Corporation's cost of capital is 12 percent (or 1 percent per month). Sharon must make a decision. A good one could help her career and move her up in management, but a bad one could hurt her prospects for promotion.
a. Should Sharon accept the new lease? (Hint: Be sure to use 1 percent per month.)
b. Suppose Sharon decided to bargain with the mall's owner over the new lease payment. What new lease payment would make Sharon indifferent between the new and the old leases? (Hint: Find FV of the first 9 payments at t = 9, then treat this as the PV of a 51-period annuity whose payments represent the incremental rent during Months 10 to 60.)
c. Sharon is not sure of the 12 percent cost of capital — it could be higher or lower. At what *nominal cost* of capital would Sharon be indifferent between the two leases? (Hint: Calculate the differences between the two payment streams, and find the IRR of this difference stream.)

PROBLEMS

10-18
NPV and IRR analysis

Cummings Products Company is considering two mutually exclusive investments. The projects' expected net cash flows are as follows:

	EXPECTED NET CASH FLOWS	
YEAR	PROJECT A	PROJECT B
0	($300)	($405)
1	(387)	134
2	(193)	134
3	(100)	134
4	600	134
5	600	134
6	850	134
7	(180)	0

a. Construct NPV profiles for Projects A and B.
b. What is each project's IRR?
c. If you were told that each project's cost of capital was 12 percent, which project should be selected? If the cost of capital was 18 percent, what would be the proper choice?
d. What is each project's MIRR at a cost of capital of 12 percent? At k = 18%? (Hint: Consider Period 7 as the end of Project B's life.)
e. What is the crossover rate, and what is its significance?

10-19
Timing differences

The Northwest Territories Oil Exploration Company is considering two mutually exclusive plans for extracting oil on property for which it has mineral rights. Both plans call for the expenditure of $12,000,000 to drill development wells. Under Plan A, all the oil will be extracted in 1 year, producing a cash flow at t = 1 of $14,400,000. Under Plan B, cash flows will be $2,100,000 per year for 20 years.

a. Construct NPV profiles for Plans A and B, identify each project's IRR, and indicate the approximate crossover rate of return.

b. Suppose a company has a cost of capital of 12 percent, and it can get unlimited capital at that cost. Is it logical to assume that it would take on all available independent projects (of average risk) with returns greater than 12 percent? Further, if all available projects with returns greater than 12 percent have been taken on, would this mean that cash flows from past investments would have an opportunity cost of only 12 percent, because all the firm could do with these cash flows would be to replace money that has a cost of 12 percent? Finally, does this imply that the cost of capital is the correct rate to assume for the reinvestment of a project's cash flows?

10-20
Scale differences

The Parrish Publishing Company is considering two mutually exclusive expansion plans. Plan A calls for the expenditure of $40 million on a large-scale, integrated plant which will provide an expected cash flow stream of $6.4 million per year for 20 years. Plan B calls for the expenditure of $12 million to build a somewhat less efficient, more labor-intensive plant which has an expected cash flow stream of $2.72 million per year for 20 years. Parrish's cost of capital is 10 percent.

a. Calculate each project's NPV and IRR.

b. Graph the NPV profiles for Plan A and Plan B. From the NPV profiles constructed, approximate the crossover rate.

c. Give a logical explanation, based on reinvestment rates and opportunity costs, as to why the NPV method is better than the IRR method when the firm's cost of capital is constant at some value such as 10 percent.

10-21
Multiple rates of return

The Black Hills Uranium Company is deciding whether or not it should open a strip mine, the net cost of which is $2 million. Net cash inflows are expected to be $13 million, all coming at the end of Year 1. The land must be returned to its natural state at a cost of $12 million, payable at the end of Year 2.

a. Plot the project's NPV profile. (Hint: Calculate NPV at k = 0%, 10%, 80%, and 450%, and possibly at other k values.)

b. Should the project be accepted if k = 10%? If k = 20%? Explain your reasoning.

c. Can you think of some other capital budgeting situations in which negative cash flows during or at the other end of the project's life might lead to multiple IRRs?

d. What is the project's MIRR at k = 10%? At k = 20%? Does the MIRR method lead to the same accept/reject decision as the NPV method?

10-22
Payback, NPV, and MIRR

Your division is considering two investment projects, each of which requires an up-front expenditure of $25 million. You estimate that the cost of capital is 10 percent and that the investments will produce the following after-tax cash flows (in millions of dollars):

YEAR	PROJECT A	PROJECT B
1	5	20
2	10	10
3	15	8
4	20	6

a. What is the regular payback period for each of the projects?

b. What is the discounted payback period for each of the projects?

c. If the two projects are independent and the cost of capital is 10 percent, which project or projects should the firm undertake?

d. If the two projects are mutually exclusive and the cost of capital is 5 percent, which project should the firm undertake?

e. If the two projects are mutually exclusive and the cost of capital is 15 percent, which project should the firm undertake?

f. What is the crossover rate?

g. If the cost of capital is 10 percent, what is the modified IRR (MIRR) of each project?

INTEGRATED CASE

ALLIED COMPONENTS COMPANY

10-23 Basics of Capital Budgeting Assume that you recently went to work for Allied Components Company, a supplier of auto repair parts used in the after-market with products from Chrysler, Ford, and other auto makers. Your boss, the chief financial officer (CFO), has just handed you the estimated cash flows for two proposed projects. Project L involves adding a new item to the firm's ignition system line; it would take some time to build up the market for this product, so the cash inflows would increase over time. Project S involves an add-on to an existing line, and its cash flows would decrease over time. Both projects have 3-year lives, because Allied is planning to introduce entirely new models after 3 years.

Here are the projects' net cash flows (in thousands of dollars):

	EXPECTED NET CASH FLOW	
YEAR	PROJECT L	PROJECT S
0	($100)	($100)
1	10	70
2	60	50
3	80	20

Depreciation, salvage values, net working capital requirements, and tax effects are all included in these cash flows.

The CFO also made subjective risk assessments of each project, and he concluded that both projects have risk characteristics which are similar to the firm's average project. Allied's weighted average cost of capital is 10 percent. You must now determine whether one or both of the projects should be accepted.

a. What is capital budgeting? Are there any similarities between a firm's capital budgeting decisions and an individual's investment decisions?

b. What is the difference between independent and mutually exclusive projects? Between projects with normal and non-normal cash flows?

c. (1) What is the payback period? Find the paybacks for Projects L and S.
(2) What is the rationale for the payback method? According to the payback criterion, which project or projects should be accepted if the firm's maximum acceptable payback is 2 years, and if Projects L and S are independent? If they are mutually exclusive?
(3) What is the difference between the regular and discounted payback periods?
(4) What is the main disadvantage of discounted payback? Is the payback method of any real usefulness in capital budgeting decisions?

d. (1) Define the term *net present value (NPV)*. What is each project's NPV?
(2) What is the rationale behind the NPV method? According to NPV, which project or projects should be accepted if they are independent? Mutually exclusive?
(3) Would the NPVs change if the cost of capital changed?

e. (1) Define the term *internal rate of return (IRR)*. What is each project's IRR?
(2) How is the IRR on a project related to the YTM on a bond?
(3) What is the logic behind the IRR method? According to IRR, which projects should be accepted if they are independent? Mutually exclusive?
(4) Would the projects' IRRs change if the cost of capital changed?

f. (1) Draw NPV profiles for Projects L and S. At what discount rate do the profiles cross?
(2) Look at your NPV profile graph without referring to the actual NPVs and IRRs. Which project or projects should be accepted if they are independent? Mutually exclusive? Explain. Are your answers correct at any cost of capital less than 23.6 percent?

g. (1) What is the underlying cause of ranking conflicts between NPV and IRR?
(2) What is the "reinvestment rate assumption," and how does it affect the NPV versus IRR conflict?
(3) Which method is the best? Why?

h. (1) Define the term *modified IRR (MIRR)*. Find the MIRRs for Projects L and S.
(2) What are the MIRR's advantages and disadvantages vis-à-vis the regular IRR? What are the MIRR's advantages and disadvantages vis-à-vis the NPV?

i. As a separate project (Project P), the firm is considering sponsoring a pavilion at the upcoming World's Fair. The pavilion would cost $800,000, and it is expected to result in $5 million of incremental cash inflows during its 1 year of operation. However, it would then take another year, and $5 million of costs, to demolish the site and return it to its original condition. Thus, Project P's expected net cash flows look like this (in millions of dollars):

YEAR	NET CASH FLOWS
0	($0.8)
1	5.0
2	(5.0)

The project is estimated to be of average risk, so its cost of capital is 10 percent.
(1) What is Project P's NPV? What is its IRR? Its MIRR?
(2) Draw Project P's NPV profile. Does Project P have normal or nonnormal cash flows? Should this project be accepted?

COMPUTER-RELATED PROBLEM

Work the problem in this section only if you are using the computer problem diskette.

10-24

NPV and IRR analysis

Use the model in the File C10 to solve this problem.

Gulf Coast Chemical Company (GCCC) is considering two mutually exclusive investments. The projects' expected net cash flows are as follows:

	EXPECTED NET CASH FLOWS	
YEAR	PROJECT A	PROJECT B
0	($46,800)	($63,600)
1	(21,600)	20,400
2	43,200	20,400
3	43,200	20,400
4	43,200	20,400
5	(28,800)	20,400

a. Construct NPV profiles for Projects A and B.
b. Calculate each project's IRR and MIRR. Assume the cost of capital is 13 percent.
c. If the cost of capital for each project is 13 percent, which project should Gulf Coast select? If the cost of capital were 9 percent, what would be the proper choice? If the cost of capital were 15 percent, what would be the proper choice?
d. At what rate do the NPV profiles of the two projects cross?
e. Project A has a large negative outflow in Year 5 associated with ending the project. GCCC's management is confident of Project A's cash flows in Years 0 to 4 but is uncertain about what its Year 5 cash flow will be. (There is no uncertainty about Project B's cash flows.) Under a worst-case scenario, Project A's Year 5 cash flow will be −$36,000, whereas under a best-case scenario, the cash flow will be −$24,000. Redo Parts a, b, and d for each scenario, assuming a 13 percent cost of capital. Press the F10 function key on the computer keyboard to see the new NPV profiles. If the cost of capital for each project is 13 percent, which project should be selected under each scenario?

CHAPTER 11

CASH FLOW ESTIMATION AND OTHER TOPICS IN CAPITAL BUDGETING[1]

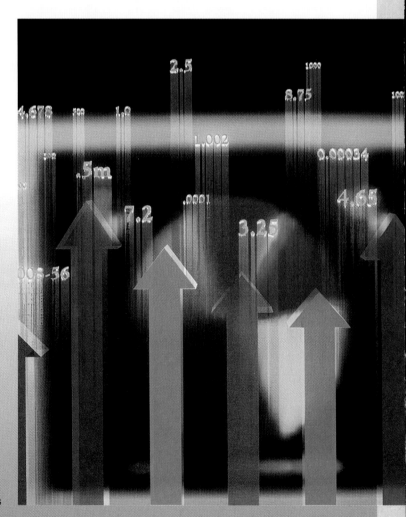

© Cyberimage/Tony Stone Images

---

[1]Parts of this chapter are relatively technical, but all or parts of it can be omitted without loss of continuity if time pressures do not permit full coverage.

LEMONADE VS. COLA

Coca-Cola, Pepsi, and other established soft-drink companies have seen upstarts such as Snapple and Arizona Iced Tea pick up a significant share of their market. Coke and Pepsi are not exactly hurting — they remain by far the dominant players in the soft-drink industry. Still, these companies did not get where they are by rolling over for newcomers, and they are constantly investigating new products and markets.

Iced tea, lemonade, and other fruit drinks are becoming increasingly popular, so Coke and Pepsi are either in these markets or actively considering entry. Coke's product line includes Nestea Iced Tea, Minute Maid, Powerade, and Fruitopia. Pepsi has All Sport, and it has also entered into a partnership with Lipton Iced Tea. Quaker Oats, which makes Gatorade, acquired Snapple but then sold it at a loss.

Whenever these companies contemplate the development of a new product, they must conduct a capital budgeting analysis. Let's say, for example, that Coke is deciding whether it makes sense to produce and market a new lemonade product. Here are some of the factors that it would have to consider:

1. How many people would like the new product well enough to buy it, and how many units would each customer buy per year?
2. What share of the lemonade market could Coke expect to capture?
3. How important would price be; that is, would demand be greatly affected by a small change in price?
4. If Coke did go into the lemonade market, and if it were highly profitable, how long would it take Pepsi and other competitors to follow, and how badly would Coke's prices and sales be hurt?
5. How much would lemonade sales cut into the sales of Coke's other products?
6. How large an investment would be required to set up a plant to produce lemonade and to launch a marketing campaign?
7. What would the production and distribution costs per unit be?
8. If the product were successful in the United States, might this lead to a worldwide expansion, hence to additional profits?

While Coke's track record has been impressive in recent years, this by no means guarantees that Coke would succeed in the lemonade market. Quaker Oats' $1.7 billion acquisition of Snapple illustrates many of the difficulties that arise when making investments in the beverage business — sales of Snapple declined in 1996, leading to the conclusion that Quaker Oats paid way too much for it.

The basic principles of capital budgeting were covered in Chapter 10. Now, we examine some additional issues, including (1) the way cash flows are estimated, (2) replacement decisions, (3) mutually exclusive projects with unequal lives, and (4) the effects of inflation on capital budgeting analysis.

ESTIMATING CASH FLOWS

The most important, but also the most difficult, step in capital budgeting is estimating projects' cash flows — the investment outlays and the annual net cash inflows after a project goes into operation. Many variables are involved, and many individuals and departments participate in the process. For example, the forecasts of unit sales and sales prices are normally made by the marketing group, based on their knowledge of price elasticity, advertising effects, the state of the economy, competitors' reactions, and trends in consumers' tastes. Similarly, the capital outlays associated with a new product are generally obtained from the engineering and product development staffs, while operating costs are estimated by cost accountants, production experts, personnel specialists, purchasing agents, and so forth.

It is difficult to accurately forecast the costs and revenues associated with a large, complex project, so forecast errors can be quite large. For example, when several major oil companies decided to build the Alaska Pipeline, the original cost estimates were in the neighborhood of $700 million, but the final cost was closer to $7 billion. Similar (or even worse) miscalculations are common in forecasts of product design costs, such as the costs to develop a new personal computer. Further, as difficult as plant and equipment costs are to estimate, sales revenues and operating costs over the project's life are even more uncertain. For example, several years ago, Federal Express developed an electronic delivery service system (ZapMail). It used the correct capital budgeting technique, NPV, but it incorrectly estimated the project's cash flows: Projected revenues were too high, projected costs were too low, and virtually no one was willing to pay the price required to cover the project's costs. As a result, cash flows failed to meet the forecasted levels, and Federal Express ended up losing about $200 million on the venture. This example demonstrates a basic truth — if cash flow estimates are not reasonably accurate, any analytical technique, no matter how sophisticated, can lead to poor decisions. Because of its financial strength, Federal Express was able to absorb losses on the project, but the ZapMail venture could have forced a weaker firm into bankruptcy.

The financial staff's role in the forecasting process includes (1) obtaining information from various departments, such as engineering and marketing, (2) ensuring that everyone involved with the forecast uses a consistent set of economic assumptions, and (3) making sure that no biases are inherent in the forecasts. This last point is extremely important, because managers often become emotionally involved with pet projects or develop empire-building complexes, both of which lead to cash flow forecasting biases which make bad projects look good — on paper.

It is almost impossible to overstate the problems one can encounter in cash flow forecasts. It is also difficult to overstate the importance of these forecasts. Still, observing the principles discussed in the next several sections will help minimize forecasting errors.

SELF-TEST QUESTIONS

What is the most important step in a capital budgeting analysis?

What departments are involved in estimating a project's cash flows?

What is the financial staff's role in the forecasting process for capital projects?

IDENTIFYING THE RELEVANT CASH FLOWS

Relevant Cash Flows
The specific cash flows that should be considered in a capital budgeting decision.

The starting point in cash flow estimation is identifying the **relevant cash flows,** defined as the specific set of cash flows that should be considered in the decision at hand. Errors are often made here, but two cardinal rules can help analysts avoid mistakes: (1) Capital budgeting decisions must be based on *cash flows,* not accounting income, and (2) only *incremental cash flows* are relevant to the accept/reject decision. These two rules are discussed in detail in the following sections.

CASH FLOWS VERSUS ACCOUNTING INCOME

In capital budgeting, *annual cash flows, not accounting profits,* are used, and the two are very different. To illustrate, consider Table 11-1, which shows how accounting profits and cash flows are related to each other. We assume that Allied Food Products is planning to start a new division at the end of 1998; that sales and all costs except depreciation represent actual cash flows and will be constant over time; and that the division will use accelerated depreciation, which will cause its reported depreciation charges to decline over time.[2]

The top section of the table shows the situation in the first year of operations, 1999. Accounting profits are $12 million, but the division's net cash flow — money which is available to Allied — is $42 million. The $12 million profit is the return *on the invested capital,* while the $30 million of depreciation is a return *of part of the invested capital.* Therefore, the $42 million cash flow consists of both a return *on* and a return *of* invested capital.

The bottom part of the table shows the situation projected for 2004. Here reported profits have doubled (because of the decline in depreciation), but the net cash flow is lower. Accounting profits are important for some purposes, but for

---

[2]Depreciation procedures are discussed in detail in accounting courses, but we provide a summary and review in Appendix 11A at the end of this chapter. The tables provided in Appendix 11A are used to calculate depreciation charges used in the chapter examples. In some instances, we simplify the depreciation assumptions in order to reduce the arithmetic. Since Congress changes depreciation procedures fairly frequently, it is always necessary to consult the latest tax regulations before developing actual capital budgeting cash flows.

TABLE 11-1	Accounting Profits versus Net Cash Flows (Thousands of Dollars)	

	ACCOUNTING PROFITS	CASH FLOWS
I. 1999 Situation		
Sales	$100,000	$100,000
Costs except depreciation	50,000	50,000
Depreciation	30,000	—
Operating income	$ 20,000	$ 50,000
Federal-plus-state taxes (40%)	8,000	8,000
Net income or net cash flow	$ 12,000	$ 42,000

Net cash flow = Net income plus depreciation = $12,000 + $30,000 = $42,000.

II. 2004 Situation		
Sales	$100,000	$100,000
Costs except depreciation	50,000	50,000
Depreciation	10,000	—
Operating income	$ 40,000	$ 50,000
Federal-plus-state taxes (40%)	16,000	16,000
Net income or net cash flow	$ 24,000	$ 34,000

Net cash flow = Net income plus depreciation = $24,000 + $10,000 = $34,000.

purposes of setting a value on a project, cash flows are what is relevant. Therefore, in capital budgeting, we are interested in net cash flows, defined as

$$\text{Net cash flow} = \text{Net income} + \text{Depreciation}$$
$$= \text{Return } on \text{ capital} + \text{Return } of \text{ capital}, \quad (11\text{-}1)$$

not in accounting profits per se.

Two additional points should be made. First, as we discussed in Chapter 2, net cash flows should be adjusted to reflect all noncash charges, not just depreciation. However, for most firms, depreciation is by far the largest noncash charge. Second, notice that Table 11-1 ignores interest payments, which would be present if the firm used debt. Why are interest payments not reflected in the capital budgeting cash flow analysis? The answer is that interest payments should *not* be included in the estimated cash flows because the effects of debt financing are reflected in the cost of capital used to discount the cash flows. If interest was subtracted from the cash flows, and then the remaining cash flows were discounted, we would be double-counting the cost of debt.

INCREMENTAL CASH FLOWS

Incremental Cash Flow
The net cash flow attributable to an investment project.

In evaluating a project, we focus on those cash flows that occur if and only if we accept the project. These cash flows, called **incremental cash flows,** represent the change in the firm's total cash flow that occurs as a direct result of accepting the project. Four special problems in determining incremental cash flows are discussed next.

Sunk Cost
A cash outlay that has already been incurred and which cannot be recovered regardless of whether the project is accepted or rejected.

Opportunity Cost
The return on the best *alternative* use of an asset, or the highest return that will *not* be earned if funds are invested in a particular project.

Externalities
Effects of a project on cash flows in other parts of the firm.

Cannibalization
Occurs when the introduction of a new product causes sales of existing products to decline.

SUNK COSTS.   A **sunk cost** is an outlay that has already been committed or that has already occurred, hence is not affected by the decision under consideration. Since sunk costs are not incremental costs, they should not be included in the analysis. To illustrate, in 1997, Northeast BankCorp was considering the establishment of a branch office in a newly developed section of Boston. To help with its evaluation, Northeast had, back in 1996, hired a consulting firm to perform a site analysis; the cost was $100,000, and this amount was expensed for tax purposes in 1996. Is this 1996 expenditure a relevant cost with respect to the 1997 capital budgeting decision? The answer is no — the $100,000 is a *sunk cost,* and it will not affect Northeast's future cash flows regardless of whether or not the new branch is built. It often turns out that a particular project has a negative NPV when all the associated costs, including sunk costs, are considered. However, on an incremental basis, the project may be a good one because the *incremental cash flows* are large enough to produce a positive NPV on the *incremental investment*.

OPPORTUNITY COSTS.   A second potential problem relates to **opportunity costs,** which are cash flows that could be generated from an asset the firm already owns provided they are not used for the project in question. To illustrate, Northeast BankCorp already owns a piece of land that is suitable for the branch location. When evaluating the prospective branch, should the cost of the land be disregarded because no additional cash outlay would be required? The answer is no, because there is an *opportunity cost* inherent in the use of the property. In this case, the land could be sold to yield $150,000 after taxes. Use of the site for the branch would require forgoing this inflow, so the $150,000 must be charged as an opportunity cost against the project. Note that the proper land cost in this example is the $150,000 market-determined value, irrespective of whether Northeast originally paid $50,000 or $500,000 for the property. (What Northeast paid would, of course, have an effect on taxes, hence on the after-tax opportunity cost.)

EFFECTS ON OTHER PARTS OF THE FIRM: EXTERNALITIES.   The third potential problem involves the effects of a project on other parts of the firm, which economists call **externalities.** For example, some of Northeast's customers who would use the new branch are already banking with Northeast's downtown office. The loans and deposits, hence profits, generated by these customers would not be new to the bank; rather, they would represent a transfer from the main office to the branch. Thus, the net revenues produced by these customers should not be treated as incremental income in the capital budgeting decision. On the other hand, having a suburban branch would help the bank attract new business to its downtown office, because some people like to be able to bank both close to home and close to work. In this case, the additional revenues that would actually flow to the downtown office should be attributed to the branch. Although they are often difficult to quantify, *externalities* (which can be either positive or negative) should be considered.

When a new project takes sales from an existing product, this is often called **cannibalization.** Naturally, firms do not like to cannibalize their existing products, but it often turns out that if they do not, someone else will. To illustrate, IBM for years refused to provide full support for its PC division because it did not want to steal sales from its highly profitable mainframe business. That turned out to be a huge strategic error, because it allowed Intel, Microsoft, Compaq, and others to become dominant forces in the computer industry. Therefore, when considering externalities, the full implications of the proposed new project should be taken into account.

SHIPPING AND INSTALLATION COSTS. When a firm acquires fixed assets, it often must incur substantial costs for shipping and installing the equipment. These charges are added to the price of the equipment when the project's cost is being determined. Also, the full cost of the equipment, including shipping and installation costs, is used as the *depreciable basis* when depreciation charges are being calculated. Thus, if Northeast BankCorp bought a computer with an invoice price of $100,000, and paid another $10,000 for shipping and installation, then the full cost of the computer, and its depreciable basis, would be $110,000.

SELF-TEST QUESTIONS ??????

Briefly explain the difference between accounting income and net cash flow. Which should be used in capital budgeting? Why?

Explain what the following terms mean, and assess their relevance in capital budgeting: incremental cash flow, sunk cost, opportunity cost, externality, cannibalization, and shipping plus installation costs.

CHANGES IN NET WORKING CAPITAL

Change in Net Working Capital
The increased current assets resulting from a new project, minus the spontaneous increase in accounts payable and accruals.

Normally, additional inventories are required to support a new operation, and expanded sales also lead to additional accounts receivable. Both of these asset increases must be financed. However, payables and accruals will increase spontaneously as a result of the expansion, and this will reduce the cash needed to finance inventories and receivables. The difference between the required increase in current assets and the spontaneous increase in current liabilities is the **change in net working capital.** If this change is positive, as it generally is for expansion projects, this indicates that additional financing, over and above the cost of the fixed assets, will be needed to fund the increase in current assets.

As the project approaches termination, inventories will be sold off and not replaced, and receivables will be collected. As these changes occur, the firm will receive an end-of-project cash inflow that is equal to the net working capital requirement that occurred when the project was begun. Thus, the working capital investment will be returned at the end of the project's life.

SELF-TEST QUESTIONS ??????

How is an increase in net working capital dealt with in capital budgeting?

Does the company get back the dollars it invests in working capital? How?

EVALUATING CAPITAL BUDGETING PROJECTS

Up until this point, we have discussed several important aspects of cash flow analysis, but we have not seen how they affect capital budgeting decisions. Conceptually, these decisions are straightforward: A potential project creates value for the firm's shareholders if and only if the net present value of the incremental cash flows from the project is positive. In practice, however, estimating these cash flows is quite difficult.

In general, the incremental cash flows from a typical project can be classified as follows:

1. *Initial investment outlay.* The initial investment includes the up-front cost of fixed assets associated with the project plus any increases in net working capital.

2. *Operating cash flows over the project's life.* These are the incremental cash inflows over the project's economic life. Annual operating cash flows equal after-tax operating income plus depreciation. Recall (a) that depreciation is added back because it is a noncash expense and (b) that financing costs (including interest expense) are not included because they are accounted for in the discounting process.

3. *Terminal year cash flows.* At the end of a project's life, some extra cash flows are frequently received. These include the after-tax salvage value of the fixed assests, adjusted for taxes if assets are not sold at their book value, plus the return of the net working capital.

For each year of the project's economic life, the *net cash flow* is determined as the sum of the cash flows from each of the three categories. These annual net cash flows, along with the project's cost of capital, are then plotted on a time line and used to calculate the project's NPV and IRR. This procedure is illustrated in the following section.

As we shall see below, the relevant cash flows are different for expansion projects than they are for the replacement of an existing asset.

SELF-TEST QUESTION

What three types of cash flows must be considered when evaluating a proposed project?

EXPANSION PROJECTS

Expansion Project
A project that is intended to increase sales.

An **expansion project** is defined as one where the firm invests in new assets to increase sales. We will illustrate expansion project analysis by examining a project being considered by Brandt-Quigley Corporation (BQC), an Atlanta-based technology company. BQC's research and development department has been applying its expertise in microprocessor technology to develop a small computer designed to control home appliances. Once programmed, the computer will automatically control the heating and air-conditioning systems, security system, hot water heater, and even small appliances such as a coffee maker. By increasing a home's energy efficiency, the computer can save enough on costs to pay for itself within a few years. Developments have now reached the stage where a decision must be made about whether or not to go forward with full-scale production.

BQC's marketing department plans to target sales toward the owners of larger homes; the computer is cost effective only in homes with 2,000 or more square feet of heated/air-conditioned space. The marketing vice-president believes that annual sales would be 20,000 units if the units were priced at $2,000 each, so annual sales are estimated at $40 million. The engineering department has reported that the firm would need additional manufacturing capability, and BQC currently has an option to purchase an existing building, at a cost of $12 million, which would meet this need. The building would be bought and paid for in one year, on December 31, 1998, and for depreciation purposes it would fall into the MACRS 39-year class.

The necessary equipment would be purchased and installed late in 1998, and it would also be paid for on December 31, 1998. The equipment would fall into the MACRS 5-year class, and it would cost $8 million, including transportation and installation.

The project would also require an initial investment of $6 million in net working capital. The initial working capital investment would also be made on December 31, 1998. The project's estimated economic life is four years. At the end of that time, the building is expected to have a market value of $7.5 million and a book value of $10.908 million, whereas the equipment would have a market value of $2 million and a book value of $1.36 million. The production department has estimated that variable manufacturing costs would total 60 percent of sales, and that fixed overhead costs, excluding depreciation, would be $5 million a year. Depreciation expenses would be determined for the year in accordance with the MACRS rates (which are discussed in Appendix 11A).

BQC's marginal federal-plus-state tax rate is 40 percent; its cost of capital is 12 percent; and, for capital budgeting purposes, the company's policy is to assume that operating cash flows occur at the end of each year. Because the plant would begin operations on January 1, 1999, the first operating cash flows would occur on December 31, 1999.

Assume that you are one of the company's financial analysts, and you have been assigned the task of conducting the capital budgeting analysis. For now, assume that the project has the same risk as an average project, and use the corporate weighted average cost of capital, 12 percent.

ANALYSIS OF THE CASH FLOWS

The first step in the analysis is to summarize the investment outlays; this is done in the 1998 column of Table 11-2. For BQC's computer project, the cash outlays consist of the purchase price of the building, the price of the needed equipment, and the required investment in net working capital (NWC), and they total to $26 million.

Having estimated the capital requirements, we must now estimate the cash flows that will occur once production begins; these are set forth in the remaining columns of Table 11-2. The cash flow estimates are based on information provided by BQC's various departments. The depreciation amounts were obtained by multiplying the depreciable basis by the MACRS recovery allowance rates as set forth in Note b to Table 11-2.

The investment in net working capital will be recovered in 2002. Also, estimates of the cash flows from the salvage values are required, and Table 11-3 summarizes this analysis. The building has an estimated salvage value which is less than its book value — it will be sold at a loss for tax purposes. This loss will reduce taxable income and thus will generate a tax savings. In effect, the company will have been depreciating the building too slowly, and it will write off the loss against its ordinary income, saving taxes that it would otherwise have to pay. The equipment, on the other hand, will be sold for more than its book value, and the company will have to pay taxes on the $640,000 profit. In both cases, the book value is calculated as the initial cost minus the accumulated depreciation. The total cash flow from salvage is merely the sum of the net salvage values of the building and equipment components.

TABLE 11-2	BQC Expansion Project Net Cash Flows, 1998–2002 (Thousands of Dollars)				
	1998	**1999**	**2000**	**2001**	**2002**
I. Investment Outlays					
1. Building	($12,000)				
2. Equipment	(8,000)				
3. Increase in NWC[a]	(6,000)				
4. Total net investment	($26,000)				
II. Operating Cash Flows over the Project's Life					
5. Sales revenues		$40,000	$40,000	$40,000	$40,000
6. Variable costs (60% of sales)		24,000	24,000	24,000	24,000
7. Fixed costs		5,000	5,000	5,000	5,000
8. Depreciation (building)[b]		156	312	312	312
9. Depreciation (equipment)[b]		1,600	2,560	1,520	960
10. Operating income before taxes		$ 9,244	$ 8,128	$ 9,168	$ 9,728
11. Taxes on operating income (40%)		3,698	3,251	3,667	3,891
12. Operating income after taxes		$ 5,546	$ 4,877	$ 5,501	$ 5,837
13. Add back depreciation		1,756	2,872	1,832	1,272
14. Operating cash flow		$ 7,302	$ 7,749	$ 7,333	$ 7,109
III. Terminal Year Cash Flows					
15. Return of NWC					6,000
16. Net salvage value (see Table 11-3)	——	——	——	——	10,607
17. Total termination cash flows					16,607
IV. Net Cash Flows					
18. Net cash flow time line (4 + 14 + 17)	($26,000)	$ 7,302	$ 7,749	$ 7,333	$23,716
V. Results					
Net present value (12%)	$ 6,989				
IRR	21.9%				
MIRR	18.9%				
Payback	3.15 years				

[a]NWC = net working capital. These funds will be recovered at the end of the project's operating life, 2002, as inventories are sold off and not replaced and as receivables are collected.

[b]MACRS depreciation expenses were calculated using the following rates:

YEAR	1	2	3	4
Depreciation rates (building)	1.3%	2.6%	2.6%	2.6%
Depreciation rates (equipment)	20.0%	32.0%	19.0%	12.0%

These percentages were multiplied by the depreciable basis ($12,000,000 for the building and $8,000,000 for the equipment) to determine the depreciation expense for each year. Thus, depreciation on the building for 1999 is 0.013(12,000) = $156, while that on the equipment is 0.2(8,000) = $1,600. The allowances have been rounded for ease of computation. See Appendix 11A for a review of MACRS.

T A B L E 1 1 - 3	**Net Salvage Values, Year 2002**	

	BUILDING	**EQUIPMENT**
Initial cost	$12,000,000	$8,000,000
2002 salvage (market) value	7,500,000	2,000,000
2002 book value[a]	10,908,000	1,360,000
Gain (loss) on sale[b]	($ 3,408,000)	$ 640,000
Taxes (40%)	(1,363,200)	256,000
Net salvage value[c]	$ 8,863,200	$1,744,000

Total cash flow from salvage value = $8,863,200 + $1,744,000 = $10,607,200.

[a]The book values equal depreciable basis (initial cost in this case) minus accumulated MACRS depreciation. For the building, accumulated depreciation equals $1,092,000, so book value equals $12,000,000 − $1,092,000 = $10,908,000; for the equipment, accumulated depreciation equals $6,640,000, so book value equals $8,000,000 − $6,640,000 = $1,360,000.

[b]Building: $7,500,000 market value − $10,908,000 book value = −$3,408,000, a loss. This represents a shortfall in depreciation taken versus "true" depreciation, and it is treated as an operating expense for 2002.

Equipment: $2,000,000 market value − $1,360,000 book value = $640,000 profit. Here the depreciation charge exceeds the "true" depreciation, and the difference is called "depreciation recapture." It is taxed as ordinary income in 2002.

[c]Net salvage value equals salvage (market) value minus taxes. For the building, the loss results in a tax credit, so net salvage value = $7,500,000 − (−$1,363,200) = $8,863,200.

MAKING THE DECISION

To summarize the data and prepare for evaluation, we use the "net cash flow" line (Line 18) in Table 11-2 as a time line. Then we show the project's NPV, IRR, MIRR, and payback. The project appears to be acceptable using the NPV, IRR, and MIRR methods, and it also would be acceptable if BQC required a payback of four years or more. Note, however, that the analysis thus far has been based on the assumption that the project has the same risk as the company's average project. If the project were judged to be riskier than average, it would be necessary to increase the cost of capital, which might cause the NPV to become negative and the IRR and MIRR to fall below k.

We should emphasize that capital budgeting decisions are actually based on both quantitative factors such as the calculated NPV, IRR, and MIRR *plus* qualitative, subjective factors such as the firm's strategic long-run plans. Therefore, in actual practice the fact that a calculated NPV is positive does not necessarily mean the project will be accepted, or that a negative NPV automatically leads to rejection. Of course, if managers *knew for certain* that the calculated numbers were correct, they would follow the rules and accept all positive NPV projects. However, the cash flows and cost of capital estimates used to develop the NPV are based on a number of assumptions, and if those assumptions turn out to be incorrect, then the *actual* NPV can turn out to be quite different from the *fore-casted* NPV. Moreover, different members of the management team are likely to think that different assumptions are best, hence disagree on projects' "true" NPVs.

Managers will discuss the assumptions used to generate a project's cash flows at length, and the NPV will be calculated based on different sets of assumptions. The effects of incorrect decisions will also be considered — if the required investment represents a large percentage of the firm's capital, then the

GLOBAL PERSPECTIVES

GE BETS ON EUROPE

The never-ending search for growing and profitable markets has led many U.S. companies to make large investments in foreign countries, especially the rapidly growing markets of Asia and Latin America. Recently, less attention has been paid to Europe as a result of Europe's relatively anemic growth rate, along with the perception, either fair or unfair, that the European market remains stodgy and overregulated, with limited profit potential.

This general attitude notwithstanding, one well-known company, General Electric, has been making huge bets on the European market — more than $10 billion since 1989. Half of this money has been used to invest in new plants and equipment, while the other half has been used to

fund nearly 50 acquisitions. GE's European investments include satellite broadcasting, financial services, and power plants.

Companies that invest overseas face a large set of investment opportunities and have great opportunities for diversification. However, foreign investment exposes them to challenges and risks not faced in the U.S. market. Thus, the profitability of GE's European investments depends on a variety of factors, including the strength of the European economy, exchange rates, and whether European workers and suppliers feel comfortable dealing with GE.

So far, GE's gamble on Europe appears to be paying off. In its most recent fiscal year, GE reported profits of $1 billion from its European subsidiary — or about 15 percent of the company's total annual profit. GE has been particularly successful in its fi-

nancing business. Other areas, including the consumer appliance business, have been considerably less profitable. Overall, though, GE has done well in Europe. Whether it can continue its success in the European market is an open question. However, nobody has questioned GE's resolve. This resolve is reflected in a recent comment to *Fortune* by Sumantra Ghoshal, a London business school professor: "Investing in Europe today requires guts. GE has guts."

SOURCE: "If Europe's Dead, Why Is GE Investing Billions There? At a Time When It's Fashionable to Belittle Europe's Slow Growth, Jack Welch Is Making a Mammoth, Contrarian Bet on the World's Most Mature Market," *Fortune*, September 9, 1996, 114. *Fortune*, ©1996 Time Inc. All rights reserved.

company could be bankrupted if the assumptions turn out to be incorrect, and that fact will enter the final decision. On the other hand, if a number of small, independent projects are involved, forecasting errors might not have serious adverse consequences.

As a result of all this, major capital budgeting decisions are based on qualitative information plus subjective, judgmental factors. We will discuss all this further in the next chapter, when we address the issue of risk.

SELF-TEST QUESTION

What is an expansion project?

REPLACEMENT PROJECT ANALYSIS[3]

Brandt-Quigley's appliance control computer project was used to show how an expansion project is analyzed. All companies, including this one, also make replacement decisions, and the analysis relating to replacements is somewhat different from that for expansion because the cash flows from the old asset must be considered. **Replacement analysis** is illustrated with another BQC example, this time from the company's research and development (R&D) division.

Replacement Analysis
An analysis involving the decision of whether or not to replace an existing asset with a new asset.

---

[3]This section is relatively technical, and if an instructor chooses to do so, it can be omitted without loss of continuity.

A lathe for trimming molded plastics was purchased 10 years ago at a cost of $7,500. The machine had an expected life of 15 years at the time it was purchased, and management originally estimated, and still believes, that the salvage value will be zero at the end of the 15-year life. The machine is being depreciated on a straight line basis; therefore, its annual depreciation charge is $500, and its present book value is $2,500.

The R&D manager reports that a new special-purpose machine can be purchased for $12,000 (including freight and installation), and, over its five-year life, it will reduce labor and raw materials usage sufficiently to cut annual operating costs from $7,000 to $4,000. This reduction in costs will cause before-tax profits to rise by $7,000 − $4,000 = $3,000 per year.

It is estimated that the new machine can be sold for $2,000 at the end of five years; this is its estimated salvage value. The old machine's actual current market value is $1,000, which is below its $2,500 book value. If the new machine is acquired, the old lathe will be sold to another company rather than exchanged for the new machine. The company's marginal federal-plus-state tax rate is 40 percent, and the replacement project is of slightly below-average risk. Net working capital requirements will also increase by $1,000 at the time of replacement. By an IRS ruling, the new machine falls into the 3-year MACRS class, and, since the cash flows are relatively certain, the project's cost of capital is only 11.5 percent versus 12 percent for an average-risk project. Should the replacement be made?

Table 11-4 shows the worksheet format the company uses to analyze replacement projects. Each line is numbered, and a line-by-line description of the table follows.

LINE 1.   The top section of the table, Lines 1 through 5, sets forth the cash flows which occur at (approximately) t = 0, the time the investment is made. Line 1 shows the purchase price of the new machine, including installation and freight charges. Since it is an outflow, it is negative.

LINE 2.   Here we show the price received from the sale of the old equipment.

LINE 3.   Since the old equipment would be sold at less than book value, the sale would create a loss which would reduce the firm's taxable income, and thus its next quarterly income tax payment. The tax saving is equal to (Loss)(T) = ($1,500)(0.40) = $600, where T is the marginal corporate tax rate. The Tax Code defines this loss as an operating loss, because it reflects the fact that inadequate depreciation was taken on the old asset. If there had been a profit on the sale (that is, if the sale price had exceeded book value), Line 3 would have shown a tax liability, a cash outflow. In the actual case, the equipment would be sold at a loss, so no taxes would be paid, and the company would realize a tax savings of $600.[4]

LINE 4.   The investment in additional net working capital (new current asset requirements minus increases in accounts payable and accruals) is shown here. This investment will be recovered at the end of the project's life (see Line 14). No taxes are involved.

---

[4]If the old asset were being exchanged for the new asset, rather than being sold to a third party, the tax consequences would be different. In an exchange of similar assets, no gain or loss is recognized. If the market value of the old asset is greater than its book value, the depreciable basis of the new asset is decreased by the excess amount. Conversely, if the market value of the old asset is less than its book value, the depreciable basis is increased by the shortfall.

TABLE 11-4	Replacement Analysis Worksheet						

	YEAR:	0	1	2	3	4	5
I. Investment Outlay							
1. Cost of new equipment		($12,000)					
2. Market value of old equipment		1,000					
3. Tax savings on sale of old equipment		600					
4. Increase in net working capital		(1,000)					
5. Total net investment		($11,400)					
II. Operating Inflows over the Project's Life							
6. After-tax decrease in costs			$1,800	$1,800	$1,800	$1,800	$1,800
7. Depreciation on new machine			$3,960	$5,400	$1,800	$ 840	$ 0
8. Depreciation on old machine			500	500	500	500	500
9. Change in depreciation $(7 - 8)$			$3,460	$4,900	$1,300	$ 340	($ 500)
10. Tax savings from depreciation (0.4×9)			1,384	1,960	520	136	(200)
11. Net operating cash flows $(6 + 10)$			$3,184	$3,760	$2,320	$1,936	$1,600
III. Terminal Year Cash Flows							
12. Estimated salvage value of new machine							$2,000
13. Tax on salvage value							(800)
14. Return of net working capital							1,000
15. Total termination cash flows							$2,200
IV. Net Cash Flows							
16. Net cash flow time line		($11,400)	$3,184	$3,760	$2,320	$1,936	$3,800

V. Results

NPV: $-$388.77.

IRR: 10.1% versus an 11.5% cost of capital.

MIRR: 10.7% versus an 11.5% cost of capital.

Payback period: 4.1 years.

LINE 5. Here we show the total net cash outflow at the time the replacement is made. The company writes a check for $12,000 to pay for the machine, and another $1,000 is invested in net working capital. However, these outlays are partially offset by proceeds from the sale of the old equipment and a reduced tax bill.

LINE 6. Section II of the table shows the *incremental operating cash flows*, or benefits, that are expected if the replacement is made. The first of these benefits is the reduction in operating costs shown on Line 6. Cash flows increase because operating costs are reduced by $3,000. However, reduced costs also mean higher taxable income, hence higher income taxes. Here is the calculation:

Reduction in costs $= \Delta$ cost $=$	$3,000
Associated increase in taxes $= T(\Delta$ cost$) = 0.4(\$3,000) =$	1,200
Increase in net after-tax cash flows due to cost reduction $= \Delta$ NCF $=$	$1,800

Had the replacement resulted in an increase in sales in addition to the reduction in costs (that is, if the new machine had been both larger and more efficient), then this amount would also be reported on Line 6 (or a separate line could be added). Also, note that the $3,000 cost savings is constant over Years 1 through 5; had the annual savings been expected to change over time, this fact would have to be built into the analysis.

LINE 7.   The depreciable basis of the new machine, $12,000, is multiplied by the appropriate MACRS recovery allowance for 3-year class property (see Table 11A-2) to obtain the depreciation figures shown on Line 7. Note that if you summed across Line 7, the total would be $12,000, the depreciable basis.

LINE 8.   Line 8 shows the $500 straight line depreciation on the old machine.

LINE 9.   The depreciation expense on the old machine as shown on Line 8 can no longer be taken if the replacement is made, but the new machine's depreciation will be available. Therefore, the $500 depreciation on the old machine is subtracted from that on the new machine to show the net change in annual depreciation. The change is positive in Years 1 through 4 but negative in Year 5. The Year 5 negative change in annual depreciation signifies that the purchase of the replacement machine results in a *decrease* in depreciation expense during that year.

LINE 10.   The change in depreciation results in a tax reduction which is equal to the change in depreciation multiplied by the tax rate: Depreciation tax savings = T(Change in depreciation) = 0.40($3,460) = $1,384 for Year 1. Note that the relevant cash flow is the tax savings on the *net change* in depreciation, not just the depreciation on the new equipment. Capital budgeting decisions are based on *incremental* cash flows, and since BQC will lose $500 of depreciation if it replaces the old machine, that fact must be taken into account.

LINE 11.   Here we show the net operating cash flows over the project's five-year life. These flows are found by adding the after-tax cost savings to the depreciation tax savings, or Line 6 + Line 10.

LINE 12.   Part III shows the cash flows associated with the termination of the project. To begin, Line 12 shows the estimated salvage value of the new machine at the end of its five-year life, $2,000.[5]

LINE 13.   Since the book value of the new machine at the end of Year 5 is zero, the company will have to pay taxes of $2,000(0.4) = $800.

LINE 14.   An investment of $1,000 in net working capital was shown as an outflow at t = 0. This investment, like the new machine's salvage value, will be recovered when the project is terminated at the end of Year 5. Accounts receivable will be collected, inventories will be drawn down and not replaced, and the result will be an inflow of $1,000 at t = 5.

---

[5]In this analysis, the salvage value of the old machine is zero. However, if the old machine was expected to have a positive salvage value at the end of five years, replacing the old machine now would eliminate this cash flow. Thus, the after-tax salvage value of the old machine would represent an opportunity cost to the firm, and it would be included as a Year 5 cash outflow in the terminal cash flow section of the worksheet.

LINE 15. Here we show the total cash flows resulting from terminating the project.

LINE 16. Part IV shows, on Line 16, the total net cash flows in a form suitable for capital budgeting evaluation. In effect, Line 16 is a "time line."

Part V of the table, "Results," shows the replacement project's NPV, IRR, MIRR, and payback. Because of the nature of the project, it is less risky than the firm's average project, so a cost of capital of only 11.5 percent is appropriate. However, even at this cost of capital, the NPV is negative. Therefore, the project is not acceptable, hence the old lathe should not be replaced.

The principles of capital budgeting used to analyze replacement projects are also used when firms decide whether it is profitable to call in their existing bonds and replace them with new bonds that have a lower coupon rate. In essence, the costs of the refunding operation (which include the call premium and the flotation costs of issuing new bonds) are compared with the present value of the interest saved if the high-coupon bond is called and replaced with a new, low-coupon bond. Appendix 11B provides a more detailed discussion of the bond refunding decision which highlights its similarity to capital budgeting decisions.

SELF-TEST QUESTION ??????

In a replacement analysis, incremental cash flows in a "new minus old" sense are evaluated. How does this type of analysis differ from that used to evaluate an expansion project?

COMPARING PROJECTS WITH UNEQUAL LIVES[6]

Note that a replacement decision involves comparing two mutually exclusive projects: retaining the old asset versus buying a new one. To simplify matters, in our replacement example we assumed that the new machine had a life equal to the remaining life of the old machine. If, however, we were choosing between two mutually exclusive alternatives with significantly different lives, an adjustment would be necessary. We now discuss two procedures — (1) the replacement chain method and (2) the equivalent annual annuity method — to illustrate the problem and show how to deal with it.

Suppose BQC is planning to modernize its production facilities, and it is considering either a conveyor system (Project C) or some forklift trucks (Project F) for moving materials. Figure 11-1 shows both the expected net cash flows and the NPVs for these two mutually exclusive alternatives. We see that Project C, when discounted at a 12 percent cost of capital, has the higher NPV and thus appears to be the better project.

REPLACEMENT CHAIN (COMMON LIFE) APPROACH

Although the analysis in Figure 11-1 suggests that Project C should be selected, this analysis is incomplete, and the decision to choose Project C is actually

---

[6]This section is relatively technical, and if an instructor chooses to do so, it can be omitted without loss of continuity.

F I G U R E   1 1 - 1 | Expected Net Cash Flows for Projects C and F

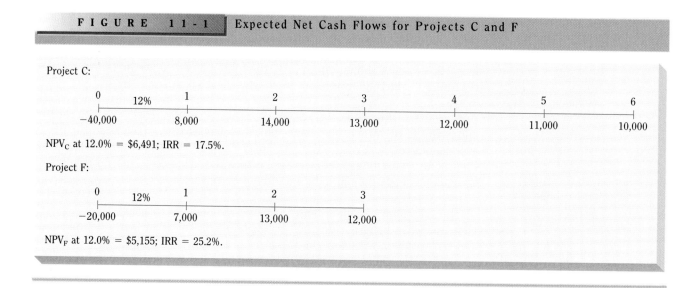

Project C:

0	12%	1	2	3	4	5	6
−40,000		8,000	14,000	13,000	12,000	11,000	10,000

NPV$_C$ at 12.0% = $6,491; IRR = 17.5%.

Project F:

0	12%	1	2	3
−20,000		7,000	13,000	12,000

NPV$_F$ at 12.0% = $5,155; IRR = 25.2%.

---

incorrect. If we choose Project F, we will have an opportunity to make a similar investment in three years, and if cost and revenue conditions continue at the Figure 11-1 levels, this second investment will also be profitable. However, if we choose Project C, we will not have this second investment opportunity. Therefore, to make a proper comparison of Projects C and F, we could apply the **replacement chain (common life) approach;** that is, we could find the NPV of Project F over a six-year period, and then compare this extended NPV with the NPV of Project C over the same six years.

Replacement Chain (Common Life) Approach
A method of comparing projects of unequal lives which assumes that each project can be repeated as many times as necessary to reach a common life span; the NPVs over this life span are then compared, and the project with the higher common life NPV is chosen.

The NPV for Project C as calculated in Figure 11-1 is already over the six-year common life. For Project F, however, we must add in a second project to extend the overall life of the combined projects to six years. Here we assume (1) that Project F's cost and annual cash inflows will not change if the project is repeated in three years and (2) that BQC's cost of capital will remain at 12 percent:

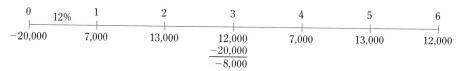

0	12%	1	2	3	4	5	6
−20,000		7,000	13,000	12,000	7,000	13,000	12,000
				−20,000			
				−8,000			

NPV = 12% = $8,824; IRR = 25.2%.

The NPV of this extended Project F is $8,824, and its IRR is 25.2 percent. (The IRR of two Project Fs is the same as the IRR for one Project F.) Since the $8,824 extended NPV of Project F over the common life of six years is greater than the $6,491 NPV of Project C, Project F should be selected.[7]

---

[7]Alternatively, we could recognize that the value of the cash flow stream of two consecutive Project Fs can be summarized by two NPVs: one at Year 0 representing the value of the initial project, and one at Year 3 representing the value of the replication project:

0	12%	1	2	3	4	5	6
5,155				5,155			

NPV = $8,824.

Ignoring rounding differences, the present value of these two cash flows, when discounted at 12 percent, is $8,824, so we again come to the conclusion that Project F should be selected.

EQUIVALENT ANNUAL ANNUITY (EAA) APPROACH

Equivalent Annual Annuity (EAA) Method
A method which calculates the annual payments a project would provide if it were an annuity. When comparing projects of unequal lives, the one with the higher equivalent annual annuity should be chosen.

Although the preceding example illustrates why an extended analysis is necessary if we are comparing mutually exclusive projects with different lives, the arithmetic is generally more complex in practice. For example, one project might have a six-year life versus a ten-year life for the other. This would require a replacement chain analysis over 30 years, the lowest common denominator of the two lives. In such a situation, it is often simpler to use a second procedure, the **equivalent annual annuity (EAA) method**, which involves three steps:

1. Find each project's NPV over its initial life. In Figure 11-1, we found $NPV_C = \$6,491$ and $NPV_F = \$5,155$.

2. There is some constant annuity cash flow (the equivalent annual annuity [EAA]) that has the same present value as a project's calculated NPV. For Project F, here is the time line:

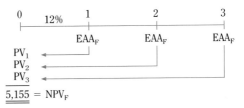

To find the value of EAA_F with a financial calculator, enter N = 3, k = I = 12, PV = −5155, and FV = 0, and solve for PMT. The answer is $2,146. This level cash flow stream, when discounted back three years at 12 percent, has a present value equal to Project F's original NPV, $5,155. The $2,146 is called the project's "equivalent annual annuity (EAA)." The EAA for Project C can be found similarly, and it is $1,579. Thus, Project C has an NPV which is equivalent to an annuity of $1,579 per year, while Project F's NPV is equivalent to an annuity of $2,146.[8]

3. The project with the higher EAA will always have the higher NPV when extended out to any common life. Therefore, since F's EAA is larger than C's, we would choose Project F.

The EAA method is often easier to apply than the replacement chain method, but the replacement chain method is easier to explain to decision makers. Still, the two methods lead to the same decision if consistent assumptions are used.

When should we worry about unequal life analysis? As a general rule, the unequal life issue (1) does not arise for independent projects, but (2) it can arise if mutually exclusive projects with significantly different lives are being compared. However, even for mutually exclusive projects, it is not always appropriate to extend the analysis to a common life. This should only be done if there is a high probability that the projects will actually be repeated at the end of their initial lives.

We should note several potentially serious weaknesses inherent in this type of analysis: (1) If inflation is expected, then replacement equipment will have a higher price. Moreover, both sales prices and operating costs will probably change.

---

[8]Some financial calculators have the EAA feature programmed in. For example, the HP-17B has the function in its cash flow register. One simply keys in the cash flows, enters the interest rate, and then presses the "NUS" key to get the EAA. Hewlett-Packard uses the term NUS (for "net uniform series") in lieu of the term EAA.

Thus, the static conditions built into the analysis would be invalid. (2) Replacements that occur down the road would probably employ new technology, which in turn might change the cash flows. This factor is not built into either replacement chain analysis or the EAA approach. (3) It is difficult enough to estimate the lives of most projects, so estimating the lives of a series of projects is often just a speculation.

In view of these problems, no experienced financial analyst would be too concerned about comparing mutually exclusive projects with lives of, say, eight years and ten years. Given all the uncertainties in the estimation process, such projects would, for all practical purposes, be assumed to have the same life. Still, it is important to recognize that a problem exists if mutually exclusive projects have substantially different lives. When we encounter such problems in practice, we use a computer spreadsheet and build expected inflation and/or possible efficiency gains directly into the cash flow estimates, and then use the replacement chain approach (but not the equivalent annual annuity method). The cash flow estimation is more complicated, but the concepts involved are exactly the same as in our example.

SELF-TEST QUESTIONS

Briefly describe the replacement chain (common life) approach.

Briefly describe the equivalent annual annuity (EAA) approach.

Why is it not always necessary to adjust project cash flow analyses for unequal lives?

DEALING WITH INFLATION

Inflation is a fact of life, and it should be recognized in capital budgeting decisions. Here are some important points about inflation:

1. Recall from Chapter 4 that inflationary expectations are built into interest rates and money costs: $k_i = k^* + IP + LP + MRP + DRP$, with IP being the inflation factor. This factor is reflected in the WACC used to find the NPV and used as the hurdle rate if the IRR or MIRR method is used. Therefore, inflation is reflected in the cost of capital used in a capital budgeting analysis.

2. The NPV method involves finding the PV of each future CF, discounted at the cost of capital, as follows:

$$NPV = \sum_{t=0}^{n} \frac{CF_t}{(1 + k)^t}.$$

The cash flows in the numerator come from a table like Table 11-2, Line 18. Note also that k, which is the WACC, includes a premium for expected inflation, so the higher the expected inflation rate, the larger the value of k, and, other things held constant, the smaller the NPV.

3. If inflation is expected, but this expectation is not built into the forecasted cash flows as shown on Line 18 of Table 11-2, then the calculated NPV will be incorrect — it will be downward biased. To see this, recognize that sales prices over the life of the project are built into the sales revenues shown in Table 11-2, hence into the cash flow projections for BQC's expansion project. If

projected sales prices do not reflect expected inflation, this bias will be present—the denominator of the NPV equation will be increased because expected inflation is automatically built into the cost of capital in the capital market, but the cash flows in the numerator will not be increased. Therefore, the NPV will be biased downward.

It is easy to avoid the inflation bias—simply build inflationary expectations into the cash flows used in the analysis. In other words, when making a table such as Table 11-2, simply reflect expected inflation in the revenue and cost figures, hence in the annual net cash flow forecasts. Then the NPV will be unbiased.

SELF-TEST QUESTIONS

How can inflation cause a downward bias in a project's estimated NPV?

What is the best way of handling inflation in a capital budgeting analysis, and how does this procedure eliminate the potential bias?

SUMMARY

This chapter discussed several issues in capital budgeting. The key concepts covered are listed below.

♦ The most important (and most difficult) step in analyzing a capital budgeting project is **estimating the incremental after-tax cash flows** the project will produce.

♦ **Net cash flows** consist of **net income plus depreciation.** In most situations, net cash flows are estimated by constructing annual cash flow statements.

♦ In determining incremental cash flows, **opportunity costs** (the cash flows forgone by using an asset) must be included, but **sunk costs** (cash outlays that have been made and that cannot be recouped) are not included. Any **externalities** (effects of a project on other parts of the firm) should also be reflected in the analysis.

♦ **Cannibalization** occurs when a new project leads to a reduction in sales of an existing product.

♦ Capital projects often require an additional investment in **net working capital (NWC).** An increase in NWC must be included in the Year 0 initial cash outlay, and then shown as a cash inflow in the final year of the project.

♦ The incremental cash flows from a typical project can be classified into three categories: (1) **initial investment outlay,** (2) **operating cash flows over the project's life,** and (3) **terminal year cash flows.**

♦ **Replacement analysis** is slightly different from that for **expansion projects** because the cash flows from the old asset must be considered in replacement decisions.

♦ If mutually exclusive projects have **unequal lives,** it may be necessary to adjust the analysis to put the projects on an equal life basis. This can be done using either the **replacement chain (common life) approach** or the **equivalent annual annuity (EAA) approach.**

♦ **Inflation effects** must be considered in project analysis. The best procedure is to build inflation directly into the cash flow estimates.

We continue our discussion of capital budgeting analysis in Chapter 12, where we discuss risk analysis and the optimal capital budget.

QUESTIONS

11-1 Cash flows rather than accounting profits are listed in Table 11-2. What is the basis for this emphasis on cash flows as opposed to net income?

11-2 Look at Table 11-4 and answer these questions:
a. Why is the salvage value shown on Line 12 reduced for taxes on Line 13?
b. Why is depreciation on the old machine deducted on Line 8 to get Line 9?
c. What would happen if the new machine permitted a *reduction* in net working capital?
d. Why were the cost savings shown on Line 6 reduced by multiplying the before-tax figure by $(1 - T)$, whereas the change in depreciation figure on Line 9 was multiplied by T?

11-3 Explain why sunk costs should not be included in a capital budgeting analysis, but opportunity costs and externalities should be included.

11-4 Explain how net working capital is recovered at the end of a project's life, and why it is included in a capital budgeting analysis.

11-5 In general, is an explicit recognition of incremental cash flows more important in new project or replacement analysis? Why?

11-6 Why is it true, in general, that a failure to adjust expected cash flows for expected inflation biases the calculated NPV downward?

11-7 Suppose a firm is considering two mutually exclusive projects. One has a life of 6 years and the other a life of 10 years. Would the failure to employ some type of replacement chain analysis bias an NPV analysis against one of the projects? Explain.

SELF-TEST PROBLEMS   (Solutions Appear in Appendix B)

ST-1
Key terms

Define each of the following terms:
a. Cash flow; accounting income; relevant cash flow
b. Incremental cash flow; sunk cost; opportunity cost; externalities; cannibalization
c. Change in net working capital; expansion project
d. Salvage value
e. Replacement analysis
f. Replacement chain (common life) approach
g. Equivalent annual annuity (EAA) method

ST-2
New project analysis

You have been asked by the president of Ellis Construction Company, headquartered in Toledo, to evaluate the proposed acquisition of a new earthmover. The mover's basic price is $50,000, and it will cost another $10,000 to modify it for special use by Ellis Construction. Assume that the mover falls into the MACRS 3-year class. (See Table 11A-2 for MACRS recovery allowance percentages.) It will be sold after 3 years for $20,000, and it will require an increase in net working capital (spare parts inventory) of $2,000. The earthmover purchase will have no effect on revenues, but it is expected to save Ellis $20,000 per year in before-tax operating costs, mainly labor. Ellis's marginal federal-plus-state tax rate is 40 percent.
a. What is the company's net investment if it acquires the earthmover? (That is, what are the Year 0 cash flows?)
b. What are the operating cash flows in Years 1, 2, and 3?
c. What is the terminal year cash flow?
d. If the project's cost of capital is 10 percent, should the earthmover be purchased?

ST-3
Replacement analysis

The Dauten Toy Corporation currently uses an injection molding machine that was purchased 2 years ago. This machine is being depreciated on a straight line basis toward a $500 salvage value, and it has 6 years of remaining life. Its current book value is $2,600, and it can be sold for $3,000 at this time. Thus, the annual depreciation expense is $(\$2,600 - \$500)/6 = \$350$ per year.

Dauten is offered a replacement machine which has a cost of $8,000, an estimated useful life of 6 years, and an estimated salvage value of $800. This machine falls into the MACRS 5-year class. (See Table 11A-2 for MACRS recovery allowance percentages.) The replacement machine would permit an output expansion, so sales would rise by $1,000 per year; even so, the new machine's much greater efficiency would still cause operating expenses to decline by $1,500 per year. The new machine would require that inventories be increased by $2,000, but accounts payable would simultaneously increase by $500. Dauten's marginal federal-plus-state tax rate is 40 percent, and its cost of capital is 15 percent. Should it replace the old machine?

STARTER PROBLEMS

11-1
Investment outlay

Truman Industries is considering an expansion project. The necessary equipment could be purchased for $9 million, and the project would also require an initial $3 million investment in net working capital. The company's tax rate is 40 percent. What is the project's initial investment outlay?

11-2
Operating cash flow

Eisenhower Communications is trying to estimate the first-year operating cash flow (at t = 1) for a proposed project. The financial staff has collected the following information:

Projected sales	$10 million
Operating costs (not including depreciation)	$ 7 million
Depreciation	$ 2 million
Interest expense	$ 2 million

The company faces a 40 percent tax rate. What is the project's operating cash flow for the first year (t = 1)?

11-3
Net salvage value

Kennedy Air Lines is now in the terminal year of a project. The equipment originally cost $20 million, of which 80 percent has been depreciated. Kennedy can sell the used equipment today to another airline for $5 million, and its tax rate is 40 percent. What is the equipment's after-tax net salvage value?

EXAM-TYPE PROBLEMS

The problems included in this section are set up in such a way that they could be used as multiple-choice exam problems.

11-4
Replacement analysis

The Chang Company is considering the purchase of a new machine to replace an obsolete one. The machine being used for the operation has both a book value and a market value of zero; it is in good working order, however, and will last physically for at least another 10 years. The proposed replacement machine will perform the operation so much more efficiently that Chang engineers estimate it will produce after-tax cash flows (labor savings and depreciation) of $9,000 per year. The new machine will cost $40,000 delivered and installed, and its economic life is estimated to be 10 years. It has zero salvage value. The firm's cost of capital is 10 percent, and its marginal tax rate is 35 percent. Should Chang buy the new machine?

11-5
Replacement analysis

Mississippi River Shipyards is considering the replacement of an 8-year-old riveting machine with a new one that will increase earnings before depreciation from $27,000 to $54,000 per year. The new machine will cost $82,500, and it will have an estimated life of 8 years and no salvage value. The new machine will be depreciated over its 5-year MACRS recovery period. (See Table 11A-2 for MACRS recovery allowance percentages.) The applicable corporate tax rate is 40 percent, and the firm's cost of capital is 12 percent. The old machine has been fully depreciated and has no salvage value. Should the old riveting machine be replaced by the new one?

11-6
Unequal lives

Cotner Clothes Inc. is considering the replacement of its old, fully depreciated knitting machine. Two new models are available: Machine 190-3, which has a cost of $190,000, a 3-year expected life, and after-tax cash flows (labor savings and depreciation) of $87,000 per year; and Machine 360-6, which has a cost of $360,000, a 6-year life, and after-tax cash flows of $98,300 per year. Knitting machine prices are not expected to rise, because inflation will be offset by cheaper components (microprocessors) used in the machines.

Assume that Cotner's cost of capital is 14 percent. Should the firm replace its old knitting machine, and, if so, which new machine should it use?

11-7
Unequal lives

Zappe Airlines is considering two alternative planes. Plane A has an expected life of 5 years, will cost $100 million, and will produce net cash flows of $30 million per year. Plane B has a life of 10 years, will cost $132 million, and will produce net cash flows of $25 million per year. Zappe plans to serve the route for 10 years. Inflation in operating costs, airplane costs, and fares is expected to be zero, and the company's cost of capital is 12 percent. By how much would the value of the company increase if it accepted the better project (plane)?

11-8
Unequal lives

The Fernandez Company has the opportunity to invest in one of two mutually exclusive machines which will produce a product it will need for the foreseeable future. Machine A costs $10 million but realizes after-tax inflows of $4 million per year for 4 years. After 4 years, the machine must be replaced. Machine B costs $15 million and realizes after-tax inflows of $3.5 million per year for 8 years, after which it must be replaced. Assume that machine prices are not expected to rise because inflation will be offset by cheaper components used in the machines. If the cost of capital is 10 percent, which machine should the company use? Use both the replacement chain and equivalent annual annuity approaches.

PROBLEMS

11-9
New project analysis

You have been asked by the president of your company to evaluate the proposed acquisition of a spectrometer for the firm's R&D department. The equipment's base price is $140,000, and it would cost another $30,000 to modify it for special use by your firm. The spectrometer, which falls into the MACRS 3-year class, would be sold after 3 years for $60,000. (See Table 11A-2 for MACRS recovery allowance percentages.) Use of the equipment would require an increase in net working capital (spare parts inventory) of $8,000. The spectrometer would have no effect on revenues, but it is expected to save the firm $50,000 per year in before-tax operating costs, mainly labor. The firm's marginal federal-plus-state tax rate is 40 percent.
a. What is the net cost of the spectrometer? (That is, what is the Year 0 net cash flow?)
b. What are the net operating cash flows in Years 1, 2, and 3?
c. What is the terminal year cash flow?
d. If the project's cost of capital is 12 percent, should the spectrometer be purchased?

11-10
New project analysis

The Harris Company is evaluating the proposed acquisition of a new milling machine. The machine's base price is $108,000, and it would cost another $12,500 to modify it for special use by your firm. The machine falls into the MACRS 3-year class, and it would be sold after 3 years for $65,000. (See Table 11A-2 for MACRS recovery allowance percentages.) The machine would require an increase in net working capital (inventory) of $5,500. The milling machine would have no effect on revenues, but it is expected to save the firm $44,000 per year in before-tax operating costs, mainly labor. Harris's marginal tax rate is 35 percent.
a. What is the net cost of the machine for capital budgeting purposes? (That is, what is the Year 0 net cash flow?)
b. What are the net operating cash flows in Years 1, 2, and 3?
c. What is the terminal year cash flow?
d. If the project's cost of capital is 12 percent, should the machine be purchased?

11-11
Replacement analysis

The Erley Equipment Company purchased a machine 5 years ago at a cost of $100,000. The machine had an expected life of 10 years at the time of purchase, and an expected salvage value of $10,000 at the end of the 10 years. It is being depreciated by the straight line method toward a salvage value of $10,000, or by $9,000 per year.

A new machine can be purchased for $150,000, including installation costs. During its 5-year life, it will reduce cash operating expenses by $50,000 per year. Sales are not expected to change. At the end of its useful life, the machine is estimated to be worthless. MACRS depreciation will be used, and the machine will be depreciated over its 3-year class life rather than its 5-year economic life. (See Table 11A-2 for MACRS recovery allowance percentages.)

The old machine can be sold today for $65,000. The firm's tax rate is 35 percent. The appropriate discount rate is 16 percent.
a. If the new machine is purchased, what is the amount of the initial cash flow at Year 0?
b. What incremental operating cash flows will occur at the end of Years 1 through 5 as a result of replacing the old machine?

c. What incremental terminal cash flow will occur at the end of Year 5 if the new machine is purchased?

d. What is the NPV of this project? Should Erley replace the old machine?

11-12
Replacement analysis

The Bigbee Bottling Company is contemplating the replacement of one of its bottling machines with a newer and more efficient one. The old machine has a book value of $600,000 and a remaining useful life of 5 years. The firm does not expect to realize any return from scrapping the old machine in 5 years, but it can sell it now to another firm in the industry for $265,000. The old machine is being depreciated toward a zero salvage value, or by $120,000 per year, using the straight line method.

The new machine has a purchase price of $1,175,000, an estimated useful life and MACRS class life of 5 years, and an estimated salvage value of $145,000. (See Table 11A-2 for MACRS recovery allowance percentages.) It is expected to economize on electric power usage, labor, and repair costs, as well as to reduce the number of defective bottles. In total, an annual savings of $255,000 will be realized if the new machine is installed. The company's marginal tax rate is 35 percent and it has a 12 percent cost of capital.

a. What is the initial cash outlay required for the new machine?

b. Calculate the annual depreciation allowances for both machines, and compute the change in the annual depreciation expense if the replacement is made.

c. What are the operating cash flows in Years 1 through 5?

d. What is the cash flow from the salvage value in Year 5?

e. Should the firm purchase the new machine? Support your answer.

f. In general, how would each of the following factors affect the investment decision, and how should each be treated?

(1) The expected life of the existing machine decreases.

(2) The cost of capital is not constant but is increasing as Bigbee adds more projects into its capital budget for the year.

INTEGRATED CASE

ALLIED FOOD PRODUCTS

11-13 Capital Budgeting and Cash Flow Estimation   After seeing Snapple's success with noncola soft drinks and learning of Coke's and Pepsi's interest, Allied Food Products has decided to consider an expansion of its own in the fruit juice business. The product being considered is fresh lemon juice. Assume that you were recently hired as assistant to the director of capital budgeting, and you must evaluate the new project.

The lemon juice would be produced in an unused building adjacent to Allied's Fort Myers plant; Allied owns the building, which is fully depreciated. The required equipment would cost $200,000, plus an additional $40,000 for shipping and installation. In addition, inventories would rise by $25,000, while accounts payable would go up by $5,000. All of these costs would be incurred at t = 0. By a special ruling, the machinery could be depreciated under the MACRS system as 3-year property.

The project is expected to operate for 4 years, at which time it will be terminated. The cash inflows are assumed to begin 1 year after the project is undertaken, or at t = 1, and to continue out to t = 4. At the end of the project's life (t = 4), the equipment is expected to have a salvage value of $25,000.

Unit sales are expected to total 100,000 cans per year, and the expected sales price is $2.00 per can. Cash operating costs for the project (total operating costs less depreciation) are

expected to total 60 percent of dollar sales. Allied's tax rate is 40 percent, and its weighted average cost of capital is 10 percent. Tentatively, the lemon juice project is assumed to be of equal risk to Allied's other assets.

You have been asked to evaluate the project and to make a recommendation as to whether it should be accepted or rejected. To guide you in your analysis, your boss gave you the following set of questions.

a. Draw a time line which shows when the net cash inflows and outflows will occur, and explain how the time line can be used to help structure the analysis.

b. Allied has a standard form which is used in the capital budgeting process; see Table IC11-1. Part of the table has been completed, but you must replace the blanks with the missing numbers. Complete the table in the following steps:

(1) Fill in the blanks under Year 0 for the initial investment outlay.

(2) Complete the table for unit sales, sales price, total revenues, and operating costs excluding depreciation.

(3) Complete the depreciation data.

(4) Now complete the table down to operating income after taxes, and then down to net cash flows.

(5) Now fill in the blanks under Year 4 for the termination cash flows, and complete the net cash flow line. Discuss working capital. What would have happened if the machinery were sold for less than its book value?

TABLE IC11-1	Allied's Lemon Juice Project (Total Cost in Thousands)				
END OF YEAR:	**0**	**1**	**2**	**3**	**4**
I. Investment Outlay					
Equipment cost					
Installation					
Increase in inventory					
Increase in accounts payable	———				
Total net investment	═══				
II. Operating Cash Flows					
Unit sales (thousands)			100		
Price/unit		$ 2.00	$ 2.00		
Total revenues					$200.0
Operating costs excluding depreciation			$120.0		
Depreciation				36.0	16.8
Total costs		$199.2	$228.0		
Operating income before taxes				$44.0	
Taxes on operating income		0.3			25.3
Operating income after taxes				$26.4	
Depreciation		79.2		36.0	
Operating cash flow	$ 0.0	$ 79.7			$ 54.7
III. Terminal Year Cash Flows					
Return of net working capital					
Salvage value					
Tax on salvage value					
Total termination cash flows					———
IV. Net Cash Flows					
Net cash flow	($260.0)				$ 89.7
Cumulative cash flow for payback:	(260.0)	(180.3)			63.0
Compounded inflows for MIRR:		106.1			89.7
Terminal value of inflows:					
V. Results					
NPV =					
IRR =					
MIRR =					
Payback =					

c. (1) Allied uses debt in its capital structure, so some of the money used to finance the project will be debt. Given this fact, should the projected cash flows be revised to show projected interest charges? Explain.

(2) Suppose you learned that Allied had spent $50,000 to renovate the building last year, expensing these costs. Should this cost be reflected in the analysis? Explain.

(3) Now suppose you learned that Allied could lease its building to another party and earn $25,000 per year. Should that fact be reflected in the analysis? If so, how?

(4) Now assume that the lemon juice project would take away profitable sales from Allied's fresh orange juice business. Should that fact be reflected in your analysis? If so, how?

d. Disregard all the assumptions made in Part c, and assume there was no alternative use for the building over the next 4 years. Now calculate the project's NPV, IRR, MIRR, and regular payback. Do these indicators suggest that the project should be accepted?

e. If this project had been a replacement rather than an expansion project, how would the analysis have changed? Think about the changes that would have to occur in the cash flow table.

f. Assume that inflation is expected to average 5 percent over the next 4 years; that this expectation is reflected in the WACC; and that inflation will increase variable costs and revenues by the same percentage, 5 percent. Does it appear that inflation has been dealt with properly in the analysis? If not, what should be done, and how would the required adjustment affect the decision? You can modify the numbers in the table to quantify your results.

g. In an unrelated analysis, you have also been asked to choose between the following two mutually exclusive projects:

	EXPECTED NET CASH FLOWS	
YEAR	PROJECT S	PROJECT L
0	($100,000)	($100,000)
1	60,000	33,500
2	60,000	33,500
3	—	33,500
4	—	33,500

The projects provide a necessary service, so whichever one is selected is expected to be repeated into the foreseeable future. Both projects are of average risk.

(1) What is each project's initial NPV without replication?
(2) Now construct a time line, and then apply the replacement chain approach to determine the projects' extended NPVs. Which project should be chosen?
(3) Repeat the analysis using the equivalent annual annuity approach.
(4) Now assume that the cost to repeat Project S in Year 2 will increase to $105,000 because of inflationary pressures. How should the analysis be handled now, and which project should be chosen?

COMPUTER-RELATED PROBLEM

Work the problem in this section only if you are using the computer problem diskette.

11-14
Expansion project

Use the computerized model in the File C11 to work this problem.

Golden State Bakers Inc. (GSB) has an opportunity to invest in a new dough machine. GSB needs more productive capacity, so the new machine will not replace an existing machine. The new machine costs $260,000 and will require modifications costing $15,000. It has an expected useful life of 10 years, will be depreciated using the MACRS method over its 5-year class life, and has an expected salvage value of $12,500 at the end of Year 10. (See Table 11A-2 for MACRS recovery allowance percentages.) The machine will require a $22,500 investment in net working capital. It is expected to generate additional sales revenues of $125,000 per year, but its use also will increase annual cash operating expenses by $55,000. GSB's cost of capital is 10 percent, and its marginal tax rate is 40 percent. The machine's book value at the end of Year 10 will be zero, so GSB will have to pay taxes on the $12,500 salvage value.

a. What is the NPV of this expansion project? Should GSB purchase the new machine?
b. Should GSB purchase the new machine if it is expected to be used for only 5 years and then sold for $31,250? (Note that the model is set up to handle a 5-year life; you need only enter the new life and salvage value.)
c. Would the machine be profitable if revenues increased by only $105,000 per year? Assume a 10-year project life and a salvage value of $12,500.
d. Suppose that revenues rose by $125,000 but that expenses rose by $65,000. Would the machine be acceptable under these conditions? Assume a 10-year project life and a salvage value of $12,500.

DEPRECIATION

Suppose a firm buys a milling machine for $100,000 and uses it for five years, after which it is scrapped. The cost of the goods produced by the machine must include a charge for the machine, and this charge is called *depreciation*. In the following sections, we review some of the depreciation concepts covered in accounting courses.

Companies often calculate depreciation one way when figuring taxes and another way when reporting income to investors: many use the *straight line* method for stockholder reporting (or "book" purposes), but they use the fastest rate permitted by law for tax purposes. Under the straight line method used for stockholder reporting, one normally takes the cost of the asset, subtracts its estimated salvage value, and divides the net amount by the asset's useful economic life. For an asset with a 5-year life, which costs $100,000 and has a $12,500 salvage value, the annual straight line depreciation charge is ($100,000 − $12,500)/5 = $17,500. Note, however, as we discuss later in this appendix, that salvage value is *not* considered for tax depreciation purposes.

For tax purposes, Congress changes the permissible tax depreciation methods from time to time. Prior to 1954, the straight line method was required for tax purposes, but in 1954 *accelerated* methods (double-declining balance and sum-of-years'-digits) were permitted. Then, in 1981, the old accelerated methods were replaced by a simpler procedure known as the Accelerated Cost Recovery System (ACRS). The ACRS system was changed again in 1986 as a part of the Tax Reform Act, and it is now known as the *Modified Accelerated Cost Recovery System (MACRS);* a 1993 tax law made further changes in this area.

TAX DEPRECIATION LIFE

For tax purposes, the entire cost of an asset is expensed over its depreciable life. Historically, an asset's depreciable life was determined by its estimated useful economic life; it was intended that an asset would be fully depreciated at approximately the same time that it reached the end of its useful economic life. However, MACRS totally abandoned that practice and set simple guidelines which created several classes of assets, each with a more-or-less arbitrarily prescribed life called a *recovery period* or *class life.* The MACRS class life bears only a rough relationship to the expected useful economic life.

A major effect of the MACRS system has been to shorten the depreciable lives of assets, thus giving businesses larger tax deductions and thereby increasing their cash flows available for investment. Table 11A-1 describes the types of property that fit into the different class life groups, and Table 11A-2 sets forth the MACRS recovery allowance percentages (depreciation rates) for selected classes of investment property.

Consider Table 11A-1 first. The first column gives the MACRS class life, while the second column describes the types of assets which fall into each category. Property in the 27.5- and 39-year categories (real estate) must be depreciated by the straight line method, but 3-, 5-, 7-, and 10-year property (personal property)

TABLE 11A-1	Major Classes and Asset Lives for MACRS

Class	Type of Property
3-year	Certain special manufacturing tools
5-year	Automobiles, light-duty trucks, computers, and certain special manufacturing equipment
7-year	Most industrial equipment, office furniture, and fixtures
10-year	Certain longer-lived types of equipment
27.5-year	Residential rental real property such as apartment buildings
39-year	All nonresidential real property, including commercial and industrial buildings

can be depreciated either by the accelerated method using the rates shown in Table 11A-2 or by an alternate straight line method.[1]

As we saw earlier in the chapter, higher depreciation expenses result in lower taxes, hence higher cash flows. Therefore, since a firm has the choice of using the alternate straight line rates or the accelerated rates shown in Table 11A-2, most elect to use the accelerated rates.

The yearly recovery allowance, or depreciation expense, is determined by multiplying each asset's *depreciable basis* by the applicable recovery percentage shown in Table 11A-2. Calculations are discussed in the following sections.

HALF-YEAR CONVENTION.   Under MACRS, the assumption is generally made that property is placed in service in the middle of the first year. Thus, for 3-year class life property, the recovery period begins in the middle of the year the asset is placed in service and ends three years later. The effect of the *half-year convention* is to extend the recovery period out one more year, so 3-year class life property is depreciated over four calendar years, 5-year property is depreciated over six calendar years, and so on. This convention is incorporated into Table 11A-2's recovery allowance percentages.[2]

DEPRECIABLE BASIS.   The *depreciable basis* is a critical element of MACRS because each year's allowance (depreciation expense) depends jointly on the asset's depreciable basis and its MACRS class life. The depreciable basis under MACRS is equal to the purchase price of the asset plus any shipping and installation costs. The basis is *not* adjusted for *salvage value* (which is the estimated market value of the asset at the end of its useful life) regardless of whether accelerated or the alternate straight line method is used.

[1]As a benefit to very small companies, the Tax Code also permits companies to *expense,* which is equivalent to depreciating over one year, up to $17,500 of equipment. Thus, if a small company bought one asset worth up to $17,500, it could write the asset off in the year it was acquired. This is called "Section 179 expensing." We shall disregard this provision throughout the book.

[2]The half-year convention also applies if the straight line alternative is used, with half of one year's depreciation taken in the first year, a full year's depreciation taken in each of the remaining years of the asset's class life, and the remaining half-year's depreciation taken in the year following the end of the class life. You should recognize that virtually all companies have computerized depreciation systems. Each asset's depreciation pattern is programmed into the system at the time of its acquisition, and the computer aggregates the depreciation allowances for all assets when the accountants close the books and prepare financial statements and tax returns.

TABLE 11A-2 Recovery Allowance Percentage for Personal Property

OWNERSHIP YEAR	CLASS OF INVESTMENT			
	3-YEAR	5-YEAR	7-YEAR	10-YEAR
1	33%	20%	14%	10%
2	45	32	25	18
3	15	19	17	14
4	7	12	13	12
5		11	9	9
6		6	9	7
7			9	7
8			4	7
9				7
10				6
11				3
	100%	100%	100%	100%

NOTES:

a. We developed these recovery allowance percentages based on the 200 percent declining balance method prescribed by MACRS, with a switch to straight line depreciation at some point in the asset's life. For example, consider the 5-year recovery allowance percentages. The straight line percentage would be 20 percent per year, so the 200 percent declining balance multiplier is $2.0(20\%) = 40\% = 0.4$. However, because the half-year convention applies, the MACRS percentage for Year 1 is 20 percent. For Year 2, there is 80 percent of the depreciable basis remaining to be depreciated, so the recovery allowance percentage is $0.40(80\%) = 32\%$. In Year 3, $20\% + 32\% = 52\%$ of the depreciation has been taken, leaving 48%, so the percentage is $0.4(48\%) \approx 19\%$. In Year 4, the percentage is $0.4(29\%) \approx 12\%$. After 4 years, straight line depreciation exceeds the declining balance depreciation, so a switch is made to straight line (this is permitted under the law). However, the half-year convention must also be applied at the end of the class life, and the remaining 17 percent of depreciation must be taken (amortized) over 1.5 years. Thus, the percentage in Year 5 is $17\%/1.5 \approx 11\%$, and in Year 6, $17\% - 11\% = 6\%$. Although the tax tables carry the allowance percentages out to two decimal places, we have rounded to the nearest whole number for ease of illustration.

b. Residential rental property (apartments) is depreciated over a 27.5-year life, whereas commercial and industrial structures are depreciated over 39 years. In both cases, straight line depreciation must be used. The depreciation allowance for the first year is based, pro rata, on the month the asset was placed in service, with the remainder of the first year's depreciation being taken in the 28th or 40th year.

SALE OF A DEPRECIABLE ASSET. If a depreciable asset is sold, the sale price (actual salvage value) minus the then-existing undepreciated book value is added to operating income and taxed at the firm's marginal tax rate. For example, suppose a firm buys a 5-year class life asset for $100,000 and sells it at the end of the fourth year for $25,000. The asset's book value is equal to $100,000(0.11 + 0.06) = $100,000(0.17) = $17,000$. Therefore, $25,000 - $17,000 = $8,000$ is added to the firm's operating income and is taxed.

DEPRECIATION ILLUSTRATION. Assume that Allied Food Products buys a $150,000 machine which falls into the MACRS 5-year class life and places it into service on March 15, 1998. Allied must pay an additional $30,000 for delivery and installation. Salvage value is not considered, so the machine's depreciable basis is $180,000. (Delivery and installation charges are included in the depreciable basis rather than expensed in the year incurred.) Each year's recovery allowance (tax depreciation expense) is determined by multiplying the depreciable basis by the applicable recovery allowance percentage. Thus, the depreciation expense for 1998 is 0.20($180,000) = $36,000, and for 1999 it is 0.32($180,000) = $57,600. Similarly, the depreciation expense is $34,200 for 2000, $21,600 for 2001, $19,800 for 2002, and $10,800 for 2003. The total depreciation expense over the six-year recovery period is $180,000, which is equal to the depreciable basis of the machine.

As noted above, most firms use straight line depreciation for stockholder reporting purposes but MACRS for tax purposes. *For these firms, for capital budgeting, MACRS should be used.* The reason is that, in capital budgeting, we are concerned with cash flows, not reported income. Since MACRS depreciation is used for taxes, this type of depreciation must be used to determine the taxes that will be assessed against a particular project. Only if the depreciation method used for tax purposes is also used for capital budgeting will the analysis produce accurate cash flow estimates.

PROBLEM

11A-1
Depreciation effects

Cate Rzasa, great-granddaughter of the founder of Rzasa Tile Products and current president of the company, believes in simple, conservative accounting. In keeping with her philosophy, she has decreed that the company shall use alternative straight line depreciation, based on the MACRS class lives, for all newly acquired assets. Your boss, the financial vice-president and the only nonfamily officer, has asked you to develop an exhibit which shows how much this policy costs the company in terms of market value. Rzasa is interested in increasing the value of the firm's stock because she fears a family stockholder revolt which might remove her from office. For your exhibit, assume that the company spends $100 million each year on new capital projects, that the projects have on average a 10-year class life, that the company has a 9 percent cost of debt, and that its tax rate is 35 percent. (Hint: Show how much the NPV of projects in an average year would increase if Rzasa used the standard MACRS recovery allowances.)

APPENDIX 11B

REFUNDING OPERATIONS

Refunding decisions actually involve two separate questions: (1) Is it profitable to call an outstanding issue in the current period and replace it with a new issue; and (2) even if refunding is currently profitable, would the firm's expected value be increased even more if the refunding were postponed to a later date? We consider both questions in this appendix.

Note that the decision to refund a security is analyzed in much the same way as a capital budgeting expenditure. The costs of refunding (the investment outlays) are (1) the call premium paid for the privilege of calling the old issue, (2) the costs of selling the new issue, (3) the tax savings from writing off the unexpensed flotation costs on the old issue, and (4) the net interest that must be paid while both issues are outstanding (the new issue is often sold prior to the refunding to ensure that the funds will be available). The annual cash flows, in a capital budgeting sense, are the interest payments that are saved each year plus the net tax savings which the firm receives for amortizing the flotation expenses. For example, if the interest expense on the old issue is $1,000,000, whereas that on the new issue is $700,000, the $300,000 reduction in interest savings constitutes an annual benefit.

The net present value method is used to analyze the advantages of refunding: the future cash flows are discounted back to the present, and then this discounted value is compared with the cash outlays associated with the refunding. The firm should refund the bond only if the present value of the savings exceeds the cost — that is, if the NPV of the refunding operation is positive.

In the discounting process, the after-tax cost of the new debt, k_d, should be used as the discount rate. The reason is that there is relatively little risk to the savings — cash flows in a refunding decision are known with relative certainty, which is quite unlike the situation with cash flows in most capital budgeting decisions.

The easiest way to examine the refunding decision is through an example. McCarty Publishing Company has a $60 million bond issue outstanding that has a 12 percent annual coupon interest rate and 20 years remaining to maturity. This issue, which was sold five years ago, had flotation costs of $3 million that the firm has been amortizing on a straight line basis over the 25-year original life of the issue. The bond has a call provision which makes it possible for the company to retire the issue at this time by calling the bonds in at a 10 percent call premium. Investment bankers have assured the company that it could sell an additional $60 million to $70 million worth of new 20-year bonds at an interest rate of 9 percent. To ensure that the funds required to pay off the old debt will be available, the new bonds will be sold one month before the old issue is called, so for one month, interest will have to be paid on two issues. Current short-term interest rates are 6 percent. Predictions are that long-term interest rates are unlikely to fall below 9 percent.[1] Flotation costs on a new refunding issue will amount to $2,650,000. McCarty's marginal federal-plus-state tax rate is 40 percent. Should the company refund the $60 million of 12 percent bonds?

---

[1]The firm's management has estimated that interest rates will probably remain at their present level of 9 percent or else rise; there is only a 25 percent probability that they will fall further.

The following steps outline the decision process; they are summarized in worksheet form in Table 11B-1. The paragraph numbers below correspond with line numbers in the table.

STEP 1: DETERMINE THE INVESTMENT OUTLAY REQUIRED TO REFUND THE ISSUE.

1. *Call premium on old issue:*

$$\text{Before tax: } 0.10(\$60,000,000) = \$6,000,000.$$
$$\text{After tax: } \$6,000,000(1 - T) = \$6,000,000(0.6)$$
$$= \$3,600,000.$$

Although McCarty must spend $6 million on the call premium, this is a deductible expense in the year the call is made. Because the company is in the 40 percent tax bracket, it saves $2.4 million in taxes; therefore, the after-tax cost of the call is only $3.6 million. This amount is shown on Line 1 of Table 11B-1.

2. *Flotation costs on new issue:*
Flotation costs on the new issue will be $2,650,000. This amount cannot be expensed for tax purposes, so it provides no immediate tax benefit.

TABLE 11B-1	Worksheet for the Bond Refunding Decision	
	AMOUNT BEFORE TAX	**AMOUNT AFTER TAX**
Cost of Refunding at t = 0		
1. Call premium on old bond	$ 6,000,000	$ 3,600,000
2. Flotation costs on new issue	2,650,000	2,650,000
3. Immediate tax savings on old flotation cost expense	(2,400,000)	(960,000)
4. Extra interest paid on old issue	600,000	360,000
5. Interest earned on short-term investment	(300,000)	(180,000)
6. Total after-tax investment		$ 5,470,000
Annual Flotation Cost Tax Effects: t = 1 to 20		
7. Annual tax savings from new issue flotation costs	$ 132,500	$ 53,000
8. Annual lost tax savings from old issue flotation costs	(120,000)	(48,000)
9. Net flotation cost tax savings	$ 12,500	$ 5,000
Annual Interest Savings Due to Refunding: t = 1 to 20		
10. Interest on old bond	$ 7,200,000	$ 4,320,000
11. Interest on new bond	(5,400,000)	(3,240,000)
12. Net interest savings	$ 1,800,000	$ 1,080,000
Refunding NPV		

13. NPV = PV of flotation tax effects + PV of interest savings − Investment
   = $5,000(12.0502) + $1,080,000(12.0502) − $5,470,000
   = $60,251 + $13,014,216 − $5,470,000
   = $13,074,467 − $5,470,000
   = $7,604,467.
Alternatively, using a financial calculator, input N = 20, I = 5.4, PMT = 1085000, FV = 0, and then press PV to find PV = $13,074,425. NPV = $13,074,425 − $5,470,000 = $7,604,425. (Difference due to rounding.)

3. *Flotation costs on old issue:*

The old issue has an unamortized flotation cost of $(20/25)(\$3,000,000) = \$2,400,000$ at this time. If the issue is retired, the unamortized flotation cost may be recognized immediately as an expense, thus creating an after-tax savings of $\$2,400,000(T) = \$960,000$. Because this is a cash inflow, it is shown as a negative outflow on Line 3.

4 and 5. *Additional interest:*

One month's "extra" interest on the old issue, after taxes, costs $360,000:

$$(\text{Dollar amount})(1/12 \text{ of } 12\%)(1 - T) = \text{Interest cost}$$
$$(\$60,000,000)(0.01)(0.6) = \$360,000.$$

However, the proceeds from the new issue can be invested in short-term securities for one month. Thus, $60 million invested at a rate of 6 percent will return $180,000 in after-tax interest:

$$(\$60,000,000)(1/12 \text{ of } 6\%)(1 - T) = \text{Interest earned}$$
$$(\$60,000,000)(0.005)(0.6) = \$180,000.$$

The net after-tax additional interest cost is thus $180,000:

Interest paid on old issue	$360,000
Interest earned on short-term securities	(180,000)
Net additional interest	$180,000

These figures are reflected on Lines 4 and 5 of Table 11B-1.

6. *Total after-tax investment:*

The total investment outlay required to refund the bond issue, which will be financed by debt, is thus $5,470,000:[2]

Call premium	$3,600,000
Flotation costs, new	2,650,000
Flotation costs, old, tax savings	(960,000)
Net additional interest	180,000
Total investment	$5,470,000

This total is shown on Line 6 of Table 11B-1.

STEP 2: CALCULATE THE ANNUAL FLOTATION COST TAX EFFECTS.

7. *Tax savings on flotation costs on the new issue:*

For tax purposes, flotation costs must be amortized over the life of the new bond, or for 20 years. Therefore, the annual tax deduction is

$$\frac{\$2,650,000}{20} = \$132,500.$$

---

[2]The investment outlay (in this case, $5,470,000) is usually obtained by increasing the amount of the new bond issue. In the example given, the new issue would be $65,470,000. However, the interest on the additional debt *should not* be deducted at Step 3 because the $5,470,000 itself will be deducted at Step 4. If additional interest on the $5,470,000 were deducted at Step 3, interest would, in effect, be deducted twice. The situation here is exactly like that in regular capital budgeting decisions. Even though some debt may be used to finance a project, interest on that debt is not subtracted when developing the annual cash flows. Rather, the annual cash flows are *discounted* at the project's cost of capital.

Because McCarty is in the 40 percent tax bracket, it has a tax savings of $132,500(0.4) = $53,000 a year for 20 years. This is an annuity of $53,000 for 20 years, and it is shown on Line 7.

8. *Tax benefits lost on flotation costs on the old issue:*
The firm, however, will no longer receive a tax deduction of $120,000 a year for 20 years, so it loses an after-tax benefit of $48,000 a year. This is shown on Line 8.

9. *Net amortization tax effect:*
The after-tax difference between the amortization tax effects of flotation on the new and old issues is $5,000 a year for 20 years. This is shown on Line 9.

STEP 3: CALCULATE THE ANNUAL INTEREST SAVINGS.

10. *Interest on old bond, after tax:*
The annual after-tax interest on the old issue is $4.32 million:

$$(\$60,000,000)(0.12)(0.6) = \$4,320,000.$$

This is shown on Line 10 of Table 11B-1.

11. *Interest on new bond, after tax:*
The new issue has an annual after-tax cost of $3,240,000:

$$(\$60,000,000)(0.09)(0.6) = \$3,240,000.$$

This is shown on Line 11.

12. *Net annual interest savings:*
Thus, the net annual interest savings is $1,080,000:

Interest on old bonds, after tax	$ 4,320,000
Interest on new bonds, after tax	(3,240,000)
Annual interest savings	$ 1,080,000

This is shown on Line 12.

STEP 4: DETERMINE THE NPV OF THE REFUNDING.

13. *PV of the benefits:*
The PV of the annual after-tax flotation cost benefit of $5,000 a year for 20 years is $60,251, and the PV of the $1,080,000 annual after-tax interest savings for 20 years is $13,014,216:[3]

$$PV = \$5,000(PVIFA_{5.4\%,20})$$
$$= \$5,000(12.0502)$$
$$= \$60,251.$$
$$PV = \$1,080,000(PVIFA_{5.4\%,20})$$
$$= \$1,080,000(12.0502)$$
$$= \$13,014,216.$$

These values are used on Line 13 when finding the NPV of the refunding operation:

Amortization tax effects	$ 60,251
Interest savings	13,014,216
Net investment outlay	(5,470,000)
NPV from refunding	$ 7,604,467

---

[3]The PVIFA for 5.4 percent over 20 years is 12.0502, found with a financial calculator.

Because the net present value of the refunding is positive, it will be profitable to refund the old bond issue.

We can summarize the data shown in Table 11B-1 using a time line (amounts in thousands) as shown below:

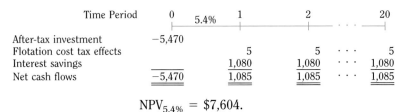

Time Period	0		1	2		20
		5.4%				
After-tax investment	−5,470					
Flotation cost tax effects			5	5	...	5
Interest savings			1,080	1,080	...	1,080
Net cash flows	−5,470		1,085	1,085	...	1,085

$$NPV_{5.4\%} = \$7,604.$$

Several other points should be made. First, because the cash flows are based on differences between contractual obligations, their risk is the same as that of the underlying obligations. Therefore, the present values of the cash flows should be found by discounting at the firm's least risky rate — its after-tax cost of marginal debt. Second, since the refunding operation is advantageous to the firm, it must be disadvantageous to bondholders; they must give up their 12 percent bonds and reinvest in new ones yielding 9 percent. This points out the danger of the call provision to bondholders, and it also explains why bonds without a call feature command higher prices than callable bonds. Third, although it is not emphasized in the example, we assumed that the firm raises the investment required to undertake the refunding operation (the $5,470,000 shown on Line 6 of Table 11B-1) as debt. This should be feasible because the refunding operation will improve the interest coverage ratio, even though a larger amount of debt is outstanding.[4] Fourth, we set up our example in such a way that the new issue had the same maturity as the remaining life of the old one. Often, the old bonds have a relatively short time to maturity (say, 5 to 10 years), whereas the new bonds have a much longer maturity (say, 25 to 30 years). In such a situation, the analysis should be set up similarly to a replacement chain analysis in capital budgeting, which was discussed earlier in the chapter. Fifth, refunding decisions are well suited for analysis with a computer spreadsheet program. The spreadsheet is simple to set up, and once the model has been constructed, it is easy to vary the assumptions (especially the assumption about the interest rate on the refunding issue), and to see how such changes affect the NPV. See Problem 11B-3 for an example.

One final point should be addressed: Although our analysis shows that the refunding would increase the firm's value, would refunding *at this time* truly maximize the firm's expected value? If interest rates continue to fall, the company might be better off waiting, for this could increase the NPV of the refunding operation even more. The mechanics of calculating the NPV in a refunding are easy, but the decision of *when* to refund is not simple at all because it requires a

---

[4]See Ahron R. Ofer and Robert A. Taggart, Jr., "Bond Refunding: A Clarifying Analysis," *Journal of Finance,* March 1977, 21–30, for a discussion of how the method of financing the refunding affects the analysis. Ofer and Taggart prove that if the refunding investment outlay is to be raised as common equity, the before-tax cost of debt is the proper discount rate, whereas if these funds are to be raised as debt, the after-tax cost of debt is the proper discount rate. Since a profitable refunding will virtually always raise the firm's debt-carrying capacity (because total interest charges after the refunding will be lower than before it), it is more logical to use debt than either equity or a combination of debt and equity to finance the operation. Therefore, firms generally do use additional debt to finance refunding operations.

forecast of future interest rates. Thus, the final decision on refunding now versus waiting for a possibly more favorable time is a judgmental decision.

PROBLEMS

11B-1
Refunding analysis

JoAnn Vaughan, financial manager of Gulf Shores Transportation (GST), has been asked by her boss to review GST's outstanding debt issues for possible bond refunding. Five years ago, GST issued $40,000,000 of 11 percent, 25-year debt. The issue, with semiannual coupons, is currently callable at a premium of 11 percent, or $110 for each $1,000 par value bond. Flotation costs on this issue were 6 percent, or $2,400,000.

Vaughan believes that GST could issue 20-year debt today with a coupon rate of 8 percent. The firm has placed many issues in the capital markets during the last 10 years, and its debt flotation costs are currently estimated to be 4 percent of the issue's value. GST's federal-plus-state tax rate is 40 percent.

Help Vaughan conduct the refunding analysis by answering the following questions:

a. What is the total dollar call premium required to call the old issue? Is it tax deductible? What is the net after-tax cost of the call?

b. What is the dollar flotation cost on the new issue? Is it immediately tax deductible? What is the after-tax flotation cost?

c. What amount of old issue flotation costs have not been expensed? Can these deferred costs be expensed immediately if the old issue is refunded? What is the value of the tax savings?

d. What is the net after-tax cash outlay required to refund the old issue?

e. What is the semiannual tax savings which arises from amortizing the flotation costs on the new issue? What is the forgone semiannual tax savings on the old issue flotation costs?

f. What is the semiannual after-tax interest savings that would result from the refunding?

g. Thus far, Vaughan has identified two future cash flows: (1) the net of new issue flotation cost tax savings and old issue flotation cost tax savings which are lost if refunding occurs and (2) after-tax interest savings. What is the sum of these two semiannual cash flows? What is the appropriate discount rate to apply to these future cash flows? What is the present value of these cash flows? (Hint: The $PVIFA_{2.4\%,40} = 25.5309$.)

h. What is the NPV of refunding? Should GST refund now or wait until later?

11B-2
Refunding analysis

Tarpon Technologies is considering whether or not to refund a $75 million, 12 percent coupon, 30-year bond issue that was sold 5 years ago. It is amortizing $5 million of flotation costs on the 12 percent bonds over the issue's 30-year life. Tarpon's investment bankers have indicated that the company could sell a new 25-year issue at an interest rate of 10 percent in today's market. Neither they nor Tarpon's management anticipate that interest rates will fall below 10 percent any time soon, but there is a chance that rates will increase.

A call premium of 12 percent would be required to retire the old bonds, and flotation costs on the new issue would amount to $5 million. Tarpon's marginal federal-plus-state tax rate is 40 percent. The new bonds would be issued 1 month before the old bonds are called, with the proceeds being invested in short-term government securities returning 6 percent annually during the interim period.

a. Perform a complete bond refunding analysis. What is the bond refunding's NPV?

b. What factors would influence Tarpon's decision to refund now rather than later?

 ## COMPUTER-RELATED PROBLEM

Work the problem in this section only if you are using the computer problem diskette.

11B-3
Refunding analysis

Use the computerized model in the File C11B to solve this problem.

a. Refer back to Problem 11B-2. Determine the interest rate on new bonds at which Tarpon would be indifferent to refunding the bond issue. (Hint: You will need to perform this analysis using different rates of interest on new bonds until you find the one which causes the NPV to be zero.)

b. How would the refunding decision be affected if the corporate tax rate were lowered from 40 percent to 35 percent, assuming the rate on new bonds was 10 percent? At what interest rate on new bonds would Tarpon be indifferent to refunding at a 35 percent corporate tax rate?

CHAPTER 12

RISK ANALYSIS AND THE OPTIMAL CAPITAL BUDGET[1]

© Ralph Mercer/Tony Stone Images

---

[1]This chapter is relatively technical, and all or parts of it can be omitted without loss of continuity if time pressures do not permit coverage.

Simplesse, a fat substitute developed by NutraSweet Corporation, was supposed to ensure the company's success and usher in an era of guilt-free gluttony for America's calorie counters and cholesterol watchers. It promised all the taste virtues of real fat but with none of the associated vices. To some, it seemed too good to be true.

Simplesse is a highly processed mixture of whipped egg whites and skim milk intended to simulate not only the taste of fat but also its rich texture, its so-called "mouth-feel." Fat is what makes mayonnaise slippery and potato chips crunchy; it provides the creaminess in Häagen-Dazs ice cream and the gratifying greasiness in a Big Mac. However, consumers recognize the dark side of fat: It tastes great, but it can cause "spare tires" and heart disease.

Unfortunately, Simplesse is temperamental. It curdles when heated too high, which makes it hard to use in cooking. It requires refrigeration, and its shelf life is short. Still, about $100 million went into the development of Simplesse. To justify the expenditure, NutraSweet's managers estimated that Simplesse would provide $444 million in revenues and $20 million in annual profits. Although most of the profits were expected to come from sales to other food companies for use in various food products, to get the ball rolling NutraSweet decided to develop a Simplesse product itself—Simple Pleasures, an imitation ice cream.

The research team's goal was to have Simple Pleasures rival Häagen-Dazs's vanilla flavor. During in-house testing, senior managers would give samples to junior managers and ask, "Doesn't it taste like Häagen-Dazs?" Needless to say, everyone replied, "Yes, it tastes just like Häagen-Dazs." In reality, it tasted more like chalk, and early versions of Simple Pleasures melted too slowly and left a scummy ring around the bowl. To add to the problems, NutraSweet badly underestimated how much it would cost to make and market the product, and how difficult it would be to move from making small batches in the lab to large-scale production runs.

In the end, Simple Pleasures captured about 8 percent of the nonfat ice cream market. The consensus among consumers seems to be that although Simple Pleasures isn't dreadful, it isn't real ice cream. And while it compares favorably in taste and texture with other nonfat ice creams, it is considerably more expensive.

What do NutraSweet's problems have to do with capital budgeting? It is clear that the cash flows associated with new projects are not known with certainty. Indeed, for most projects there is much uncertainty, which means much risk. In this chapter, we discuss procedures that are used to assess risk and incorporate it into the decision process. As you read the chapter, consider how NutraSweet might have used these procedures in its analysis of the Simplesse/Simple Pleasures project.

Up to now we have simply assumed that each project will produce a given set of cash flows, and we then analyzed those cash flows to decide whether to accept or reject the project. Obviously, though, cash flows are not known with certainty, and we don't even know for sure that a project's forecasted "inflows" will be positive. We now turn to risk in capital budgeting, examining the techniques firms use to determine a project's risk and then to decide whether its profit potential is worth the risk. Finally, we explain how the total dollar size of the capital budget is determined.

INTRODUCTION TO PROJECT RISK ANALYSIS

Three separate and distinct types of risk can be identified:

Stand-Alone Risk
The risk an asset would have if it were a firm's only asset and if investors owned only one stock. It is measured by the variability of the asset's expected returns.

Corporate, or Within-Firm, Risk
Risk not considering the effects of stockholders' diversification; it is measured by a project's effect on uncertainty about the firm's future earnings.

Market, or Beta, Risk
That part of a project's risk that cannot be eliminated by diversification; it is measured by the project's beta coefficient.

1. **Stand-alone risk,** which is the project's risk disregarding the fact that it is but one asset within the firm's portfolio of assets and that the firm is but one stock in a typical investor's portfolio of stocks. Stand-alone risk is measured by the variability of the project's expected returns.

2. **Corporate, or within-firm, risk,** which is the project's risk to the corporation, giving consideration to the fact that the project represents only one of the firm's portfolio of assets, hence that some of its risk effects on the firm's profits will be diversified away. Corporate risk is measured by the project's impact on uncertainty about the firm's future earnings.

3. **Market, or beta, risk,** which is the riskiness of the project as seen by a well-diversified stockholder who recognizes that the project is only one of the firm's assets and that the firm's stock is but one small part of the investor's total portfolio. Market risk is measured by the project's effect on the firm's beta coefficient.

As we shall see, a particular project may have high stand-alone risk, yet because of portfolio effects, taking it on may not have much effect on either the firm's risk or that of its owners.

Taking on a project with a high degree of either stand-alone or corporate risk will not necessarily affect the firm's beta. However, if the project has highly uncertain returns, and if those returns are highly correlated with returns on the firm's other assets and with most other assets in the economy, the project will have a high degree of all types of risk. For example, suppose General Motors decides to undertake a major expansion to build electric autos. GM is not sure how its technology will work on a mass production basis, so there are great risks in the venture — its stand-alone risk is high. Management also estimates that the project will do best if the economy is strong, for then people will have more money to spend on the new autos. This means that the project will tend to do well if GM's other divisions do well and will tend to do badly if other divisions do badly. This being the case, the project will also have high corporate risk. Finally, since GM's profits are highly correlated with those of most other firms, the project's beta will also be high. Thus, this project will be risky under all three definitions of risk.

Market risk is important because of its effect on a firm's stock price: Beta affects k, and k affects the stock price. Corporate risk is also important, for these three reasons:

1. Undiversified stockholders, including the owners of small businesses, are more concerned about corporate risk than about market risk.

2. Empirical studies of the determinants of required rates of return (k) generally find that both market and corporate risk affect stock prices. This suggests that investors, even those who are well diversified, consider factors other than market risk when they establish required returns.

3. The firm's stability is important to its managers, workers, customers, suppliers, and creditors, as well as to the community in which it operates. Firms that are in serious danger of bankruptcy, or even of suffering low profits and reduced output, have difficulty attracting and retaining good managers and workers. Also, both suppliers and customers are reluctant to depend on weak firms, and such firms have difficulty borrowing money at reasonable interest rates. These factors tend to reduce risky firms' profitability and hence their stock prices, and this makes corporate risk significant.

For these three reasons, corporate risk is important even if a firm's stockholders are well diversified.

SELF-TEST QUESTIONS

What are the three types of project risk?

Why are (1) market and (2) corporate risk both important?

TECHNIQUES FOR MEASURING STAND-ALONE RISK

Why should a project's stand-alone risk be important to anyone? In theory, this type of risk should be of little or no concern. However, it is actually of great importance for two reasons:

1. It is easier to estimate a project's stand-alone risk than its corporate risk, and it is far easier to measure stand-alone risk than market risk.

2. In the vast majority of cases, all three types of risk are highly correlated — if the general economy does well, so will the firm, and if the firm does well, so will most of its projects. Because of this high correlation, stand-alone risk is generally a good proxy for hard-to-measure corporate and market risk.

The starting point for analyzing a project's stand-alone risk involves determining the uncertainty inherent in its cash flows. This analysis can be handled in a number of ways, ranging from informal judgments to complex economic and statistical analyses involving large-scale computer models. To illustrate what is involved, we shall refer to Brandt-Quigley Corporation's appliance control computer project that we discussed in Chapter 11. Many of the individual cash flows that were shown in Table 11-2 are subject to uncertainty. For example, sales for each year were projected at 20,000 units to be sold at a net price of $2,000 per unit, or $40 million in total. However, actual unit sales will almost certainly be somewhat higher or lower than 20,000, and the sales price will probably turn out to be different from the projected $2,000 per unit. *In effect, the sales quantity and the sales price estimates are really expected values based on probability distributions, as are many of the other values that were shown in Table 11-2.* The distributions could be relatively "tight," reflecting small standard deviations and low risk, or they could be "flat," denoting a great deal of uncertainty about the final value of the variable in question, hence a high degree of stand-alone risk.

The nature of the individual cash flow distributions, and their correlations with one another, determine the nature of the NPV probability distribution and, thus, the project's stand-alone risk. In the following sections, we discuss two techniques for assessing a project's stand-alone risk: (1) sensitivity analysis and (2) scenario analysis.

SENSITIVITY ANALYSIS

Intuitively, we know that many of the variables which determine a project's cash flows are based on a probability distribution rather than being known with certainty. We also know that a change in a key input variable, such as units sold, will cause the NPV to change. **Sensitivity analysis** is a technique which indicates how much NPV will change in response to a given change in an input variable, other things held constant.

Sensitivity Analysis
A risk analysis technique in which key variables are changed one at a time and the resulting changes in the NPV and IRR are observed.

Sensitivity analysis begins with a *base-case* situation, which is developed using the *expected* values for each input. To illustrate, consider the data given back in Table 11-2, in which projected income statements for Brandt-Quigley's computer project were shown. The values used to develop the table, including unit sales, sales price, fixed costs, and variable costs, are the most likely, or base-case, values, and the resulting $6,989,000 NPV shown in Table 11-2 is called the **base-case NPV**. Now we ask a series of "what if" questions: "What if unit sales fall 20 percent below the most likely level?" "What if the sales price per unit falls?" "What if variable costs are 65 percent of dollar sales rather than the expected 60 percent?" Sensitivity analysis is designed to provide the decision maker with answers to questions such as these.

Base-Case NPV
The NPV when sales and other input variables are set equal to their most likely (or base-case) values.

In a sensitivity analysis, each variable is changed by several percentage points above and below the expected value, holding other things constant. Then a new NPV is calculated using each of these values. Finally, the set of NPVs is plotted against the variable that was changed. Figure 12-1 shows the computer project's sensitivity graphs for three key input variables. The table below the graphs gives the NPVs that were used to construct the graphs. The slopes of the lines in the graphs show how sensitive NPV is to changes in each of the inputs: *the steeper the slope, the more sensitive the NPV is to a change in the variable.* In the figure, we see that the project's NPV is very sensitive to changes in variable costs, fairly sensitive to changes in unit sales, and not very sensitive to changes in the cost of capital.

If we were comparing two projects, the one with the steeper sensitivity lines would be riskier, because for that project a relatively small error in estimating a variable such as unit sales would produce a large error in the project's expected NPV. Thus, sensitivity analysis can provide useful insights into the riskiness of a project.

Before we move on, two additional points about sensitivity analysis warrant attention. First, spreadsheet computer models such as *Lotus 1-2-3* or *Microsoft Excel* are ideally suited for performing sensitivity analysis. We used a spreadsheet model to conduct the analyses represented in Figure 12-1; it generated the NPVs and then drew the graphs. Second, we could have plotted all of the sensitivity lines on one graph; this would have facilitated direct comparisons of the sensitivities among different input variables.

FIGURE 12-1 Sensitivity Analysis (Thousands of Dollars)

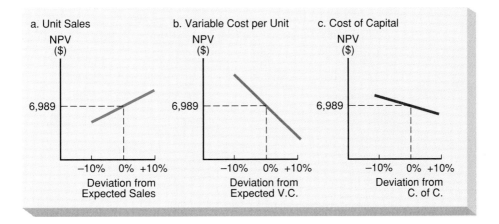

DEVIATION FROM BASE LEVEL (%)	NET PRESENT VALUE		
	UNITS SOLD	VARIABLE COST/UNIT	COST OF CAPITAL
−10	$4,073	$11,362	$8,029
0 (base case)	6,989	6,989	6,989
+10	9,904	2,615	5,996

NOTE: This analysis was performed using a spreadsheet, so the values are slightly different than those that would be obtained using interest factor tables because of rounding differences.

SCENARIO ANALYSIS

Although sensitivity analysis is probably the most widely used risk analysis technique, it does have limitations. Consider, for example, a proposed coal mine project whose NPV is highly sensitive to changes in output, in variable costs, and in sales price. However, if a utility company has contracted to buy a fixed amount of coal at an inflation-adjusted price per ton, the mining venture could be quite safe in spite of its steep sensitivity lines. *In general, a project's stand-alone risk depends on (1) the sensitivity of NPV to changes in key variables and (2) the range of likely values of these variables as reflected in their probability distributions.* Because sensitivity analysis considers only the first factor, it is incomplete.

Scenario analysis is a risk analysis technique that considers both the sensitivity of NPV to changes in key variables and the likely range of variable values. In a scenario analysis, the financial analyst asks operating managers to specify the least "reasonable" set of circumstances (low unit sales, low sales price, high variable cost per unit, high construction cost, and so on) and the most "reasonable" set. The NPVs under the bad and good conditions are then calculated and compared to the expected, or base-case, NPV.

As an example, let us return to the appliance control computer project. Brandt-Quigley's managers are fairly confident of their estimates of all the project's cash flow variables except price and unit sales. Further, they regard a drop in sales below 15,000 units or a rise above 25,000 units as being extremely unlikely. Similarly, they expect the sales price as set in the marketplace to lie

Scenario Analysis
A risk analysis technique in which "bad" and "good" sets of financial circumstances are compared with a most likely, or base-case, situation.

| | **TABLE 12-1** | **Scenario Analysis** | | | |

SCENARIO	PROBABILITY OF OUTCOME (P_i)	SALES VOLUME (UNITS)	SALES PRICE	NPV (THOUSANDS OF DOLLARS)
Worst case	0.25	15,000	$1,500	($ 5,768)
Base case	0.50	20,000	2,000	6,989
Best case	0.25	25,000	2,500	23,390

$$\text{Expected NPV} = \$\ 7,900$$
$$\sigma_{\text{NPV}} = \$10,349$$
$$\text{CV}_{\text{NPV}} = \quad 1.3$$

Worst-Case Scenario
An analysis in which all of the input variables are set at their worst reasonably forecasted values.

Best-Case Scenario
An analysis in which all of the input variables are set at their best reasonably forecasted values.

Base Case
An analysis in which all of the input variables are set at their most likely values.

within the range of $1,500 to $2,500. Thus, 15,000 units at a price of $1,500 defines the lower bound, or the **worst-case scenario,** whereas 25,000 units at a price of $2,500 defines the upper bound, or the **best-case scenario.** Remember that the **base-case** values are 20,000 units at a price of $2,000.

To carry out the scenario analysis, we use the worst-case variable values to obtain the worst-case NPV and the best-case variable values to obtain the best-case NPV.[2] We actually performed the analysis using a spreadsheet model, and Table 12-1 summarizes the results of this analysis. We see that under the base-case forecast, a positive NPV results; the worst case produces a negative NPV; and the best-case results in a very large positive NPV.

We can use the results of the scenario analysis to determine the expected NPV, the standard deviation of NPV, and the coefficient of variation. To begin, we need an estimate of the probabilities of occurrence of the three scenarios, the P_i values. Suppose management estimates that there is a 25 percent probability of the worst-case scenario occurring, a 50 percent probability of the base case, and a 25 percent probability of the best case. Of course, it is *very difficult* to estimate scenario probabilities accurately.

The scenario probabilities and NPVs constitute a probability distribution of returns just like those we dealt with in Chapter 5, except that the returns are measured in dollars instead of percentages (rates of return). The expected NPV (in thousands of dollars) is $7,900:[3]

$$\text{Expected NPV} = \sum_{i=1}^{n} P_i(\text{NPV}_i)$$
$$= 0.25(-\$5,768) + 0.50(\$6,989) + 0.25(\$23,390)$$
$$= \$7,900.$$

---

[2]We could have included worst- and best-case values for fixed and variable costs, income tax rates, salvage values, and so on. For illustrative purposes, we limited the changes to only two variables. Also, note that we are treating sales price and quantity as independent variables; that is, a low sales price could occur when unit sales were low, and a high sales price could be coupled with high unit sales, or vice versa. As we discuss in the next section, it is relatively easy to vary these assumptions if the facts of the situation suggest a different set of conditions.

[3]Note that the expected NPV, $7,900, is *not* the same as the base-case NPV, $6,989 (in thousands). This is because the two uncertain variables, sales volume and sales price, are multiplied together to obtain dollar sales, and this process causes the NPV distribution to be skewed to the right. A big number times another big number produces a very big number, which, in turn, causes the average, or expected value, to increase.

COCA-COLA TAKES ON THE HIGH-RISK, HIGH-RETURN MARKETS OF ASIA

Roughly half the world's population lives in China, India, and Indonesia. Since this region offers tremendous market potential, many U.S. companies are investing heavily in the area. For example, Coca-Cola, facing a relatively flat domestic market (soft-drink sales in the United States have grown by about 4 percent annually over the past decade) has aggressively looked overseas for growth. Over the next five to six years Coke expects to invest $2 billion in the three Asian giants —China, India, and Indonesia. These countries all have young, rapidly growing populations, and many people have yet to try their first Coke. So, while Coke sales in China have grown at a 49 percent annual rate during the past decade, the average Chinese citizen drinks only five Cokes a year. By contrast, per-capita consumption in the United States, at 343 servings a year, is pretty well saturated. Coke expects to capture 40 percent of a rapidly growing soft-drink market in China, and the consulting firm McKinsey & Company thinks Coke sales in China will hit $1 billion by the year 2000.

To be sure, such investments are risky. First, Coke faces political risk in each of the three countries. (See Chapter 4 for a discussion of country risk.) Many Chinese and Indians have a strong aversion to U.S. goods, partly because they fear losing control of their economies to foreigners. China, for example, has indicated that it is considering steps to restrict Coke's expansion. Clearly, Coke is at the mercy of local authorities, and its ability to operate in these markets could always be curtailed by a change in the political leadership or a backlash against American products.

In addition to political risk, the company also faces a host of logistical problems in its Far Eastern operations. Coke likes to distribute its product directly to retailers in order to manage inventory and to control quality, but that's tough, if not impossible, in many underdeveloped markets. In many cases, it must rely on local citizens riding bicycles to deliver its product in the more distant rural areas.

Despite the risks, Coca-Cola thinks the expected returns are worth the risks. At the same time, in a rather interesting way, investing in Coca-Cola has become an indirect way for investors to bet on the rapidly growing Asian markets. Jennifer Salomon, a beverage stock analyst for Salomon Brothers, says Coke tells potential investors, "Why bother investing in all of these different Asian companies when you can have 'one-stop shopping' with us?"

SOURCE: "Coke Pours into Asia: It's Promising Huge Growth in China, India, and Indonesia," *Business Week*, October 28, 1996, 72–77.

The standard deviation of the NPV is $10,349 (in thousands of dollars):

$$\sigma_{NPV} = \sqrt{\sum_{i=1}^{n} P_i(NPV_i - \text{Expected NPV})^2}$$
$$= \sqrt{\begin{array}{l} 0.25(-\$5,768 - \$7,900)^2 + 0.50(\$6,989 - \$7,900)^2 \\ + 0.25(\$23,390 - \$7,900)^2 \end{array}}$$
$$= \$10,349.$$

Finally, the project's coefficient of variation is 1.3:

$$CV_{NPV} = \frac{\sigma_{NPV}}{E(NPV)} = \frac{\$10,349}{\$7,900} = 1.3.$$

Now the project's coefficient of variation can be compared with the coefficient of variation of Brandt-Quigley's "average" project to get an idea of the relative riskiness of the appliance control computer project. Brandt-Quigley's existing projects, on average, have a coefficient of variation of about 1.0, so, on the basis of this stand-alone risk measure, Brandt-Quigley's managers would conclude that the appliance computer project is 30 percent riskier than an "average" project.

Scenario analysis provides useful information about a project's stand-alone risk. However, it is limited in that it only considers a few discrete outcomes

(NPVs), even though there are an infinite number of possibilities. We briefly describe a more complete method of assessing a project's stand-alone risk in the next section.

MONTE CARLO SIMULATION

Monte Carlo Simulation
A risk analysis technique in which probable future events are simulated on a computer, generating estimated rates of return and risk indexes.

Monte Carlo simulation, so named because this type of analysis grew out of work on the mathematics of casino gambling, ties together sensitivities and input variable probability distributions.[4] However, simulation requires a relatively powerful computer, coupled with an efficient financial planning software package, whereas scenario analysis can be done using a PC with a spreadsheet program or even a calculator.

In a simulation analysis, the computer begins by picking at random a value for each variable — sales in units, the sales price, the variable cost per unit, and so on. Then those values are combined, and the project's NPV is calculated and stored in the computer's memory. Next, a second set of input values is selected at random, and a second NPV is calculated. This process is repeated perhaps 1,000 times, generating 1,000 NPVs. These NPVs are then analyzed, and the mean and standard deviation of the set of NPVs is determined. The mean, or average value, is used as a measure of the project's expected profitability, and the standard deviation (or coefficient of variation) is used as a measure of the project's risk.

Monte Carlo simulation is useful, but it is a relatively complex procedure. Therefore, a detailed discussion is best left for advanced finance courses.

ON THE WWW
The are several Monte Carlo simulation software packages available which work as add-ons to popular PC spreadsheet programs. A demo version of one, called @RISK, can be downloaded from http://www.palisade.com/products/risk/index.html.

SELF-TEST QUESTIONS ??????

List two reasons why, in practice, a project's stand-alone risk is important.

Differentiate between sensitivity and scenario analyses. What advantage does scenario analysis have over sensitivity analysis?

What is Monte Carlo simulation?

BETA (OR MARKET) RISK

The types of risk analysis discussed thus far provide insights into a project's risk and thus help managers make better accept/reject decisions. However, we have not yet taken account of portfolio risk. In this section, we show how the CAPM can be used to help overcome this shortcoming. Of course, the CAPM has shortcomings of its own, but it nevertheless offers useful insights into risk analysis in capital budgeting.

To begin, recall from Chapter 5 that the Security Market Line equation expresses the risk/return relationship as follows:

$$k_s = k_{RF} + (k_M - k_{RF})b_i.$$

As an example, consider the case of Erie Steel Company, an integrated steel producer operating in the Great Lakes region. For simplicity, assume that Erie uses only equity capital, so its cost of equity is also its corporate cost of capital, or

---

[4]The use of simulation analysis in capital budgeting was first reported by David B. Hertz, "Risk Analysis in Capital Investments," *Harvard Business Review,* January–February 1964, 95–106.

INDUSTRY PRACTICE

HIGH-TECH CFOs

Recent improvements in technology have made it easier for corporations to utilize complex risk analysis techniques. New software and higher-powered computers enable financial managers to process large amounts of information, so technically astute finance people can consider a broad range of scenarios using computers to estimate the effects of changes in sales, operating costs, interest rates, the overall economy, and even the weather. Given such analysis, financial managers can make better decisions as to which course of action is most likely to generate the optimal trade-off between risk and return.

Done properly, risk analysis can also account for the correlation between various types of risk. For example, if interest rates and currencies tend to move together in a particular way, this tendency can be incorporated into the model. This can enable financial managers to better determine the likelihood and effect of "worst-case" outcomes.

While this type of risk analysis is undeniably useful, it is only as good as the information and assumptions that go into constructing the various models. Also, risk models frequently involve complex calculations, and they generate output which requires financial managers to have a fair amount of mathematical sophistication. However, technology is helping to solve these problems. New programs have been developed recently to present risk analysis output in an intuitive way. For example, Andrew Lo, an MIT finance professor, has developed a program which conveniently summarizes the risk, return, and liquidity profiles of various strategies using a new data visualization process that enables complicated relationships to be plotted along three-dimensional graphs that are easy to interpret. While some old-guard CFOs may bristle at these new approaches, younger and more computer-savvy CFOs are likely to embrace this technology. As Lo puts it: "The video-game generation just loves these 3-D tools."

SOURCE: Adapted from "The CFO Goes 3-D: Higher Math and Savvy Software Are Crucial," *Business Week*, October 28, 1996, 144, 150.

WACC. Erie's beta = b = 1.1; k_{RF} = 8%; and k_M = 12%. Thus, Erie's cost of equity is 12.4 percent:

$$k_s = 8\% + (12\% - 8\%)1.1$$
$$= 8\% + (4\%)1.1$$
$$= 12.4\%.$$

This suggests that investors should be willing to give Erie money to invest in average-risk projects if the company expects to earn 12.4 percent or more on this money. Here again, by average risk we mean projects having risk similar to the firm's existing assets. *Therefore, as a first approximation, Erie should invest in capital projects if and only if these projects have an expected return of 12.4 percent or more.*[5] Erie should use 12.4 percent as its discount rate to determine the NPV of an average-risk project.

Suppose, however, that taking on a particular project would cause a change in Erie's beta coefficient, which, in turn, would change the company's cost of equity. For example, suppose Erie is considering the construction of a fleet of barges to haul iron ore, and barge operations have betas of 1.5 rather than 1.1. Since the firm itself may be regarded as a "portfolio of assets," and since the beta of any portfolio is a weighted average of the betas of its individual assets, taking on the barge project would cause the overall corporate beta to rise to somewhere between the original beta of 1.1 and the barge project's beta of 1.5. The exact value of the new beta would depend on the relative size of the investment in barge operations versus Erie's other assets. If 80 percent of Erie's total funds

---

[5]To simplify things somewhat, we assume that the firm uses only equity capital. If debt is used, the cost of capital used must be a weighted average of the costs of debt and equity. This point was discussed in Chapter 9.

ended up in basic steel operations with a beta of 1.1 and 20 percent in barge operations with a beta of 1.5, the new corporate beta would be 1.18:

$$\text{New beta} = 0.8(1.1) + 0.2(1.5)$$
$$= 1.18.$$

This increase in Erie's beta coefficient would cause its stock price to decline *unless the increased beta were offset by a higher expected rate of return.* Specifically, taking on the new project would cause the overall corporate cost of capital to rise from the original 12.4 percent to 12.72 percent:

$$k_s = 8\% + (4\%)1.18$$
$$= 12.72\%.$$

Therefore, to keep the barge investment from lowering the value of the firm, Erie's overall expected rate of return must also rise from 12.4 to 12.72 percent.

If investments in basic steel must earn 12.4 percent, how much must Erie expect to earn on the barge investment to cause the new overall expected rate of return to equal 12.72 percent? We know that if Erie undertakes the barge investment, it will have 80 percent of its assets invested in basic steel projects earning 12.4 percent and 20 percent in barge operations earning "X" percent, and the average required rate of return will be 12.72 percent. Therefore,

$$0.8(12.4\%) + 0.2X = 12.72\%$$
$$0.2X = 2.8\%$$
$$X = 14\%.$$

Since $X = 14\%$, we see that the barge project must have an expected return of at least 14 percent if the corporation is to earn its new cost of capital.

In summary, if Erie takes on the barge project, its corporate beta will rise from 1.1 to 1.18, its cost of capital will rise from 12.4 to 12.72 percent, and the barge investment must earn 14 percent if the company is to earn its new overall cost of capital.

This line of reasoning leads to the conclusion that if the beta coefficient for each project, b_p, could be determined, then a **project cost of capital, k_p,** for each individual project could be found as follows:

Project Cost of Capital, k_p
The risk-adjusted cost of capital for an individual project.

$$k_p = k_{RF} + (k_M - k_{RF})b_p.$$

Thus, for basic steel projects with $b = 1.1$, Erie should use 12.4 percent as the cost of capital. The barge project, with $b = 1.5$, should be evaluated at a 14 percent cost of capital:

$$k_{Barge} = 8\% + (4\%)1.5$$
$$= 8\% + 6\%$$
$$= 14\%.$$

On the other hand, a low-risk project, such as a new distribution center with a beta of only 0.5, would have a cost of capital of 10 percent:

$$k_{Center} = 8\% + (4\%)0.5$$
$$= 10\%.$$

Figure 12-2 gives a graphic summary of these concepts as applied to Erie Steel. Note the following points:

1. The SML is the same Security Market Line that we developed in Chapter 5. It shows how investors are willing to make trade-offs between risk as measured by beta and expected returns. The higher the beta risk, the higher the rate of return needed to compensate investors for bearing this risk. The SML specifies the nature of this relationship.

2. Erie Steel initially has a beta of 1.1, so its required rate of return on average-risk investments is 12.4 percent.

3. High-risk investments such as the barge line require higher rates of return, whereas low-risk investments such as the distribution center require lower rates of return. If Erie concentrates its new investments in either high- or low-risk projects as opposed to average-risk projects, its corporate beta will rise or fall from the current value of 1.1. Consequently, Erie's required rate of return on common stock will change from its current value of 12.4 percent.

4. If the expected rate of return on a given capital project lies *above* the SML, the expected rate of return on the project is more than enough to compensate for its risk, and the project should be accepted. Conversely, if the project's rate of return lies *below* the SML, it should be rejected. Thus, Project M in Figure 12-2 is acceptable, whereas Project N should be rejected. N has a higher expected return than M, but the differential is not enough to offset its higher risk.

5. For simplicity, the Erie Steel illustration is based on the assumption that the company used no debt financing, which allows us to use the SML to plot the company's cost of capital. The basic concepts presented in the Erie illustration

FIGURE 12-2 Using the Security Market Line Concept in Capital Budgeting

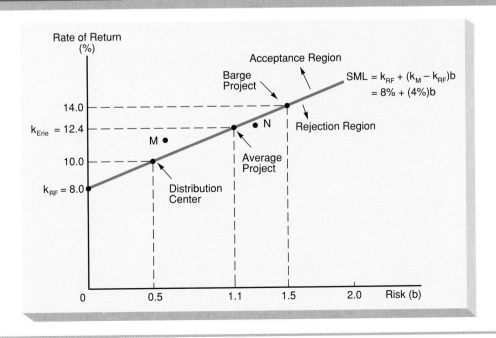

also hold for companies that use debt financing. As we discussed in previous chapters, the discount rate applied in capital budgeting is the firm's weighted average cost of capital. When debt financing is used, the project's cost of equity must be combined with the cost of debt to obtain the project's overall cost of capital.

SELF-TEST QUESTIONS

What is meant by the term "average-risk project"? Based on the CAPM, how would one find the cost of capital for such a project, for a low-risk project, and for a high-risk project?

Complete the following sentence: An increase in a company's beta coefficient would cause its stock price to decline unless its expected rate of return . . .

Explain why you should accept a given capital project if its expected rate of return lies above the SML. What if the expected rate of return lies on the SML? Below the SML?

TECHNIQUES FOR MEASURING BETA RISK

In Chapter 5 we discussed the estimation of betas for stocks, and we indicated the difficulties in estimating beta. The estimation of project betas is even more difficult, and more fraught with uncertainty. However, two approaches have been used to estimate individual assets' betas — the pure play method and the accounting beta method.

THE PURE PLAY METHOD

Pure Play Method
An approach used for estimating the beta of a project in which a firm (1) identifies several companies whose only business is the product in question, (2) calculates the beta for each firm, and then (3) averages the betas to find an approximation to its own project's beta.

In the **pure play method,** the company tries to find several single-product companies in the same line of business as the project being evaluated, and it then averages those companies' betas to determine the cost of capital for its own project. For example, suppose Erie could find three existing single-product firms that operate barges, and suppose also that Erie's management believes its barge project would be subject to the same risks as those firms. Erie could then determine the betas of those firms, average them, and use this average beta as a proxy for the barge project's beta.[6]

The pure play approach can only be used for major assets such as whole divisions, and even then it is frequently difficult to implement because it is often impossible to find pure play proxy firms. However, when IBM was considering going into personal computers, it was able to obtain data on Apple Computer and several other essentially pure play personal computer companies. This is often the case when a firm considers a major investment outside its primary field.

THE ACCOUNTING BETA METHOD

As noted above, it may be impossible to find single-product, publicly traded firms suitable for the pure play approach. If that is the case, we may be able to use the

---

[6]If the pure play firms employ different capital structures than that of Erie, this fact must be dealt with by adjusting the beta coefficients. See Eugene F. Brigham and Louis C. Gapenski, *Intermediate Financial Management,* 5th ed., Chapter 9, for a discussion of this aspect of the pure play method.

Accounting Beta Method
A method of estimating a project's beta by running a regression of the company's return on assets against the average return on assets for a large sample of firms.

accounting beta method. Betas normally are found as described in Appendix 5A — by regressing the returns of a particular company's *stock* against returns on a *stock market index*. However, we could run a regression of the company's *accounting return on assets* against the *average return on assets* for a large sample of companies, such as those included in the S&P 400. Betas determined in this way (that is, by using accounting data rather than stock market data) are called *accounting betas.*

Accounting betas for a totally new project can be calculated only after the project has been accepted, placed in operation, and begun to generate output and accounting results — too late for the capital budgeting decision. However, to the extent management thinks a given project is similar to other projects the firm has undertaken in the past, some other project's accounting beta can be used as a proxy for that of the project in question. In practice, accounting betas are normally calculated for divisions or other large units, not for single assets, and divisional betas are then used for the division's projects.

SELF-TEST QUESTION

Describe the pure play and the accounting beta methods for estimating individual projects' betas.

SHOULD FIRMS DIVERSIFY TO REDUCE RISK?

As we learned in Chapter 5, a security may be risky if held in isolation but not very risky if held as part of a well-diversified portfolio. The same is true of capital budgeting; returns on an individual project may be highly uncertain, but if the project is small relative to the total firm, and if its returns are not highly correlated with the firm's other assets, the project may not be very risky in either the corporate or the beta sense.

Many firms make a serious effort to diversify; often this is a specific objective of the long-run strategic plan. For example, KeyCorp, a bank holding company headquartered in New England, has weathered that region's economic storms be cause it also owns banks in the Pacific Northwest that have been profitable. Similarly, NCNB, a North Carolina–based banking concern that acquired Atlanta–based C&S/Sovran to become NationsBank, the third largest U.S. bank, stated: "We like having textiles and tobacco in North Carolina, citrus growing and tourism in Florida, cattle ranching and oil in Texas." One objective of moves such as those of KeyCorp and NationsBank is to stabilize earnings, reduce corporate risk, and raise the value of the firm's stock.

The wisdom of corporate diversification to reduce risk has been questioned — why should a firm diversify when stockholders can easily diversify themselves? In other words, although it may be true that if the returns on NCNB's and C&S/Sovran's stocks are not perfectly positively correlated, hence merging the companies will reduce their risks somewhat, would it not be just as easy for investors to diversify directly, without the trouble and expense of a merger?

The answer is not simple. Although stockholders could directly obtain some of the risk-reducing benefits through personal diversification, other benefits can be gained only by diversification at the corporate level. For example, a more stable bank might be able to attract a better work force and also obtain funds cheaper than could two less stable banks. More important, there are often spillover effects from mergers. For example, NCNB became expert at cleaning up bad real estate loans after it acquired banks in Texas, and that expertise helped it clean up bad loans at C&S/Sovran. Further, combining the administrative offices of the two banks resulted in economies of scale, lower costs, and, thus, higher profits.

SELF-TEST QUESTIONS

Does a merger that lowers a company's corporate risk by stabilizing earnings necessarily benefit stockholders?

Are there any good reasons why a firm might want to diversify through mergers even though its stockholders could diversify on their own?

PROJECT RISK CONCLUSIONS

We have discussed the three types of risk normally considered in capital budgeting analysis — stand-alone risk, within-firm (or corporate) risk, and market risk — and we have discussed ways of assessing each. However, two important questions remain: (1) Should firms be concerned with stand-alone and corporate risk in their capital budgeting decisions, and (2) what do we do when the stand-alone, within-firm, and market risk assessments lead to different conclusions?

These questions do not have easy answers. From a theoretical standpoint, well-diversified investors should be concerned only with market risk, managers should be concerned only with stock price maximization, and these two factors should lead to the conclusion that market (beta) risk ought to be given virtually all the weight in capital budgeting decisions. However, if investors are not well diversified, if the CAPM does not operate exactly as theory says it should, or if measurement problems keep managers from having confidence in the CAPM approach in capital budgeting, it may be appropriate to give stand-alone and corporate risk more weight than financial theorists suggest. Note also that the CAPM ignores bankruptcy costs, even though such costs can be substantial, and the probability of bankruptcy depends on a firm's corporate risk, not on its beta risk. Therefore, one can easily conclude that even well-diversified investors should want a firm's management to give at least some consideration to a projects's corporate risk instead of concentrating entirely on market risk.

Although it would be nice to reconcile these problems and to measure project risk on some absolute scale, the best we can do in practice is to estimate project risk in a somewhat nebulous, relative sense. For example, we can generally say with a fair degree of confidence that a particular project has more or less stand-alone risk than the firm's average project. Then, assuming that stand-alone and corporate risk are highly correlated (which is typical), the project's stand-alone risk will be a good measure of its corporate risk. Finally, assuming that market risk and corporate risk are highly correlated (as is true for most companies), a project with more corporate risk than average will also have more market risk, and vice versa for projects with low corporate risk.[7]

---

[7]For example, see M. Chapman Findlay III, Arthur E. Gooding, and Wallace Q. Weaver, Jr., "On the Relevant Risk for Determining Capital Expenditure Hurdle Rates," *Financial Management,* Winter 1976, 9–16.

SELF-TEST QUESTIONS

In theory, should a firm be concerned with stand-alone and corporate risk? Should the firm be concerned with these risks in practice?

If a project's stand-alone, corporate, and market risk are highly correlated, would this make the task of measuring risk easier or harder? Explain.

INCORPORATING PROJECT RISK AND CAPITAL STRUCTURE INTO CAPITAL BUDGETING

Capital budgeting can affect a firm's market risk, its corporate risk, or both, but it is extremely difficult to quantify either type of risk. Although it may be possible to reach the general conclusion that one project is riskier than another, it is difficult to develop a really good *quantitative measure* of project risk. This makes it difficult to incorporate differential risk into capital budgeting decisions.

Risk-Adjusted Discount Rate
The discount rate that applies to a particular risky stream of income; the riskier the project's income stream, the higher the discount rate.

Two methods are used to incorporate project risk into capital budgeting. One is called the *certainty equivalent* approach. Here all cash flows that are not known with certainty are scaled down, and the riskier the flows, the lower their certainty equivalent values. The other method, and the one we focus on, is the **risk-adjusted discount rate** approach, under which differential project risk is dealt with by changing the discount rate. Average-risk projects are discounted at the firm's average cost of capital, higher-risk projects are discounted at a higher cost of capital, and lower-risk projects are discounted at a rate below the firm's average cost of capital. Unfortunately, unless one is willing to rely completely on the CAPM, there is no good way of specifying exactly *how much* higher or lower these discount rates should be; given the present state of the art, risk adjustments are necessarily judgmental and somewhat arbitrary.

Capital structure must also be taken into account if a firm finances different assets in different ways. For example, one division might have a lot of real estate which is well suited as collateral for loans, whereas some other division might have most of its capital tied up in research and development, which is not good collateral. As a result, the division with the real estate might have a higher *debt capacity* than the division with the machinery, hence an optimal capital structure which contains a higher percentage of debt. In this case, the financial staff might calculate the cost of capital differently for the two divisions.[8]

Although the process is not exact, many companies use a two-step procedure to develop risk-adjusted discount rates for use in capital budgeting. First, *divisional costs of capital* are established for each of the major operating divisions on the basis of each division's estimated average riskiness and capital structure. Second, within each division all projects are classified into three categories — high risk, average risk, and low risk. Then, each division uses its basic divisional cost of capital for average-risk projects, reduces the divisional cost of capital by one or two percentage points when evaluating low-risk projects, and raises the cost of capital by several percentage points for high-risk projects. For example, if a division's basic cost of capital is estimated to be 10 percent, a 12 percent discount rate might be used for a high-risk project and a 9 percent rate for a low-risk project. Average-risk projects, which constitute about 80 percent of most capital budgets, would be evaluated at the 10 percent divisional cost of

---

[8]We will say more about the optimal capital structure and debt capacity in Chapter 13.

capital. This procedure is far from precise, but it does at least recognize that different divisions have different characteristics, hence different costs of capital, and it also takes account of differential project riskiness within divisions.

SELF-TEST QUESTIONS

How are risk-adjusted discount rates used to incorporate project risk into the capital budget decision process?

Briefly explain the two-step process many companies use to develop risk-adjusted discount rates for use in capital budgeting.

THE OPTIMAL CAPITAL BUDGET

In Chapter 9, we developed the concept of the weighted average cost of capital (WACC). Then, in Chapters 10, 11, and up to this point in Chapter 12, we have discussed how the cost of capital is used in capital budgeting. However, capital budgeting and the cost of capital are actually interrelated — we cannot determine the cost of capital until we determine the size of the capital budget, and we cannot determine the size of the capital budget until we determine the cost of capital. Therefore, as we show in this section, *the cost of capital and the capital budget must be determined simultaneously.* Citrus Grove Corporation, a producer of fruit juices, is used to illustrate the process.

THE INVESTMENT OPPORTUNITY SCHEDULE (IOS)

Investment Opportunity Schedule (IOS)
A graph of the firm's investment opportunities ranked in order of the projects' rates of return.

Consider first Figure 12-3, which provides information on Citrus Grove's potential projects for next year. The tabular data below the graphs show the six projects' cash flows and IRRs. The graph is defined as the firm's **investment opportunity schedule (IOS),** which is a plot of each project's IRR, in descending order, versus the dollars of new capital required to finance it. For example, Project B has an IRR of 20 percent, shown on the vertical axis, and a cost of $100,000, shown on the horizontal axis.[9] Notice that Projects A and B are mutually exclusive. Thus, Citrus Grove has two possible IOS schedules: the one shown in panel a consists of Project B plus C, D, E, and F, and the one shown in panel b consists of Project A plus C, D, E, and F. Beyond $600,000, the two IOS schedules are identical. Thus, the two alternative schedules differ only in that one contains B, and thus ranks C second, while the other contains A, in which case C ranks first because IRR_C is greater than IRR_A. For now, we assume that all six projects have the same risk as Citrus Grove's average project.

THE MARGINAL COST OF CAPITAL (MCC) SCHEDULE

In Chapter 9, we discussed the concept of the weighted average cost of capital (WACC). We saw that the value of the WACC depends on the amount of new capital raised — the WACC will, after some point, rise if more and more capital is raised during a given year. This increase occurs because (1) flotation costs cause the cost of new equity to be higher than the cost of retained earnings and (2) higher

---

[9]Do not be concerned by our use of IRR rather than MIRR or NPV. The fact is, we cannot calculate either MIRR or NPV until we know k, and we are using this analysis to develop a first-approximation estimate of k. Later on, we could switch to MIRR or NPV.

FIGURE 12-3 Citrus Grove Corporation: IOS Schedules

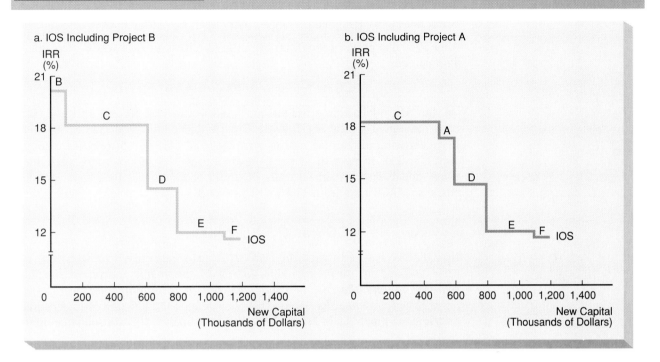

POTENTIAL CAPITAL PROJECTS' CASH FLOWS

YEAR	Aª	Bª	C	D	E	F
0	($100,000)	($100,000)	($500,000)	($200,000)	($300,000)	($100,000)
1	23,150	75,000	143,689	52,138	98,800	58,781
2	50,000	45,000	143,689	52,138	98,800	58,781
3	70,000	10,750	143,689	52,138	98,800	—
4	—	—	143,689	52,138	98,800	—
5	—	—	143,689	52,138	—	—
6	—	—	143,689	52,138	—	—
IRR	17.0%	20.0%	18.2%	14.5%	12.0%	11.5%

ªProjects A and B are mutually exclusive, so only one can be in the final capital budget.

rates of return on debt, preferred stock, and common stock may be required to induce investors to supply additional capital to the firm.

Suppose Citrus Grove's cost of retained earnings is 15 percent, while its cost of new common stock is 16.8 percent. The company's target capital structure calls for 40 percent debt and 60 percent common equity; its marginal federal-plus-state tax rate is 40 percent; and its before-tax cost of debt is 10 percent. Thus, Citrus Grove's WACC using retained earnings as the common equity component is 11.4 percent:

$$\text{WACC}_1 = w_d(k_d)(1 - T) + w_{ce}k_s$$
$$= 0.4(10\%)(0.6) + 0.6(15\%) = 11.4\%.$$

Citrus Grove is forecasting $420,000 of retained earnings during the planning period, hence the firm's retained earnings break point is $700,000:

Break point$_{RE}$ = Retained earnings/Equity fraction = $420,000/0.6 = $700,000.

After $700,000 of new capital has been raised, Citrus Grove's WACC increases to 12.5 percent:

$$WACC_2 = 0.4(10\%)(0.6) + 0.6(16.8\%) \approx 12.5\%.$$

Thus, each dollar has a weighted average cost of 11.4 percent until the company has raised a total of $700,000. This $700,000 will consist of $280,000 of new debt with an after-tax cost of 6 percent and $420,000 of retained earnings with a cost of 15 percent. If the company raises $700,001 or more, each additional dollar will contain 60 cents of equity obtained by selling new common stock, so WACC rises from 11.4 to 12.5 percent.

COMBINING THE MCC AND IOS SCHEDULES

Now that we have estimated the MCC schedule, we can use it to determine the basic discount rate for the capital budgeting process; *that is, we can use the MCC schedule to find the cost of capital for use in determining an average-risk project's net present value.* To do this, we combine the IOS and MCC schedules on the same graph, as in Figure 12-4, and then analyze this consolidated figure.

FINDING THE MARGINAL COST OF CAPITAL. Just how far down its IOS curve should Citrus Grove go? That is, which of the firm's available projects should it accept? *First, Citrus Grove should accept all independent projects that have rates of return in excess of the cost of the capital that will be used to finance them, and it should reject all others.* Projects E and F should be rejected, because they would have to be financed with capital that has a cost of 12.5 percent, and at that cost of capital, we know that these projects must have negative NPVs because their IRRs are below the cost of capital. Therefore, Citrus Grove's capital budget should consist of either A or B, plus C and D, and the firm should raise and invest a total of $800,000.[10]

The preceding analysis, as summarized in Figure 12-4, reveals a very important point: The corporate cost of capital used in the capital budgeting process is determined at the intersection of the IOS and MCC schedules. This cost is called the firm's *marginal cost of capital (MCC),* and if it is used in capital budgeting, then the firm will make correct accept/reject decisions, and its level of investment will be optimal. If the firm uses any other rate for average-risk projects, its capital budget will not be optimal.

If Citrus Grove had fewer good investment opportunities, then its IOS schedule would be shifted to the left, possibly causing the intersection to occur on the $WACC_1 = 11.4\%$ portion of the MCC curve. Then, Citrus Grove's MCC would be 11.4 percent, and average-risk projects would be evaluated at that rate. Conversely, if the firm had more and better investment opportunities, its IOS would be shifted to the right, and if the shift were very far to the right, then the

---

[10]Note that if the MCC schedule cuts through a project, and if that project must be accepted in total or else rejected, then we can calculate the average cost of the capital that will be used to finance the project (some at the higher WACC and some at the lower WACC) and compare that average WACC to the project's IRR.

FIGURE 12 - 4 Citrus Grove Corporation: Combined IOS and MCC Schedules

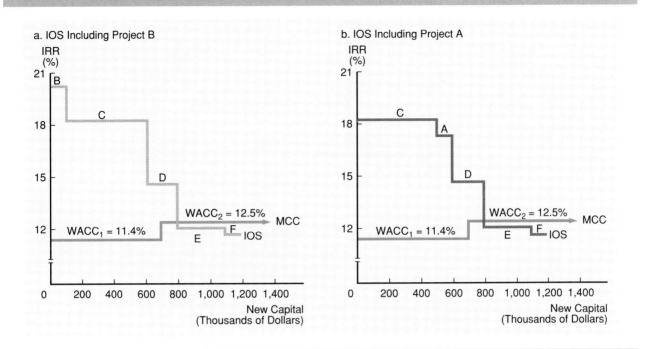

a. IOS Including Project B

b. IOS Including Project A

MCC might rise above 12.5 percent. Thus, we see that the discount rate used for evaluating average-risk projects is influenced by the set of potential projects. We have, of course, abstracted from differential project riskiness in this section, because we assumed that all of Citrus Grove's projects are equally risky.

CHOOSING BETWEEN MUTUALLY EXCLUSIVE PROJECTS. We have not yet completely determined Citrus Grove's optimal capital budget. We know that it should total $800,000, and that Projects C and D should be included, but we do not know which of the mutually exclusive projects, A or B, should be made part of the final budget. How should we choose between A and B? *The project with the higher NPV should be chosen.*

Notice that Figure 12-3 contained the projects' IRRs, but no NPVs or MIRRs. We were not able to determine NPVs or MIRRs at that point because we did not know Citrus Grove's marginal cost of capital. Now, in Figure 12-4, we see that the last dollar raised will cost 12.5 percent, so Citrus Grove's marginal cost of capital is 12.5 percent. Therefore, assuming the projects both have average risk, we can use a 12.5 percent discount rate to find $NPV_A = \$9,247$ and $NPV_B = \$9,772$. Citrus Grove should select Project B because its NPV is higher.

SELF-TEST QUESTIONS

How is a firm's marginal cost of capital for use in capital budgeting determined?

How should a firm choose between mutually exclusive projects?

CAPITAL RATIONING

Under ordinary circumstances, capital budgeting is an application of this classic economic principle: A firm should expand to the point where its marginal return is just equal to its marginal cost. However, under some circumstances a firm may deviate from this principle and place an absolute limit on the size of its capital budget. This is called **capital rationing.** Due to the complexity of this subject, it is best left for advanced finance courses.

Capital Rationing
A situation in which a constraint is placed on the total size of the firm's capital budget.

SELF-TEST QUESTION

Define capital rationing.

ESTABLISHING THE OPTIMAL CAPITAL BUDGET IN PRACTICE

The procedures set forth in the marginal cost of capital section are conceptually correct, and it is important that you understand the logic of this process. However, Citrus Grove (and most other companies) actually uses a more judgmental, less quantitative process for establishing its final capital budget:

Step 1. The financial vice-president obtains a reasonably good fix on the firm's IOS schedule from the director of capital budgeting, and a reasonably good estimate of the MCC schedule from the treasurer. These two schedules are then combined, as in Figure 12-4, to get a reasonably good approximation of the corporation's marginal cost of capital (the cost of capital at the intersection of the IOS and MCC schedules).

Step 2. The corporate MCC is scaled up or down for each division to reflect the division's capital structure and risk characteristics. Citrus Grove, for example, assigns a factor of 0.9 to its stable, low-risk fresh citrus juice division, but a factor of 1.1 to its more risky exotic fruit juice group. Therefore, if the corporate MCC is determined to be 12.5 percent, the cost for the citrus juice division is 0.9(12.5%) = 11.25%, while that for the exotic fruit juice division is 1.1(12.5%) = 13.75%.

Step 3. Each project within each division is classified into one of three groups — high risk, average risk, and low risk — and the same 0.9 and 1.1 factors are used to adjust the divisional MCCs. For example, a low-risk project in the citrus juice division would have a cost of capital of 0.9(11.25%) = 10.13%, rounded to 10 percent, while a high-risk project in the exotic fruit juice division would have a cost of 1.1(13.75%) = 15.13%, rounded to 15 percent.

Step 4. Each project's NPV is then determined, using its risk-adjusted project cost of capital. The optimal capital budget consists of all independent projects with positive risk-adjusted NPVs plus those mutually exclusive projects with the highest positive risk-adjusted NPVs.

These steps implicitly assume that the projects taken on have, on average, about the same debt capacity and risk characteristics, and, consequently, the same weighted average cost of capital as the firm's existing assets. If this is not true, then the corporate MCC determined in Step 1 will not be correct, and it will have to be adjusted. However, given all the measurement errors and uncertainties inherent in the entire cost of capital/capital budgeting process, it would be unrealistic to push the adjustment process very far.

This type of analysis may seem more precise than the data warrant. Nevertheless, the procedure does force the firm to think carefully about each division's relative risk, about the risk of each project within the divisions, and about the relationship between the total amount of capital raised and the cost of that capital. Further, the procedure forces the firm to adjust its capital budget to reflect capital market conditions — if the costs of debt and equity rise, this fact will be reflected in the cost of capital used to evaluate projects, and projects that would be marginally acceptable when capital costs were low would (correctly) be ruled unacceptable when capital costs were high.

SELF-TEST QUESTION

Describe the general procedures that firms follow when establishing their capital budgets.

SUMMARY

This chapter discussed three issues in capital budgeting: (1) assessing risk, (2) incorporating risk into capital budgeting decisions, and (3) determining the optimal capital budget. The key concepts covered are summarized below.

♦ A project's **stand-alone risk** is the risk the project would have if it were the firm's only asset and if the firm's stockholders held only that one stock. Stand-alone risk is measured by the variability of the asset's expected returns, and it is often used as a proxy for both market and corporate risk because (1) market and corporate risk are difficult to measure and (2) the three types of risk are usually highly correlated.

♦ **Within-firm,** or **corporate, risk** reflects the effects of a project on the firm's risk, and it is measured by the project's effect on the firm's earnings variability. Stockholder diversification is not taken into account.

♦ **Market risk** reflects the effects of a project on the riskiness of stockholders, assuming they hold diversified portfolios. In theory, market risk should be the most relevant type of risk.

♦ **Corporate risk** is important because it influences the firm's ability to use low-cost debt, to maintain smooth operations over time, and to avoid crises that might consume management's energy and disrupt employees, customers, suppliers, and the community.

♦ **Sensitivity analysis** is a technique which shows how much a project's NPV or IRR will change in response to a given change in an input variable such as sales, other things held constant.

♦ **Scenario analysis** is a risk analysis technique in which the best- and worst-case NPVs are compared with the project's expected NPV.

♦ **Monte Carlo simulation** is a risk analysis technique in which a computer is used to simulate probable future events and thus to estimate the profitability and riskiness of a project.

♦ The **pure play method** and the **accounting beta method** can be used to estimate betas for large projects or for divisions.

♦ The **risk-adjusted discount rate,** or **project cost of capital,** is the rate used to evaluate a particular project. It is based on the corporate WACC, which is increased for projects which are riskier than the firm's average project but decreased for less risky projects.

♦ **Capital rationing** occurs when management places a constraint on the size of the firm's capital budget during a particular period.

♦ The **investment opportunity schedule (IOS)** is a graph of the firm's investment opportunities, listed in descending order of IRR.

♦ The **marginal cost of capital (MCC) schedule** is a graph of the firm's weighted average cost of capital versus the amount of funds raised.

♦ The MCC schedule is combined with the IOS schedule, and the intersection defines the firm's **marginal cost of capital** for use in capital budgeting.

QUESTIONS

12-1   Define (a) simulation analysis, (b) scenario analysis, and (c) sensitivity analysis. If AT&T were considering two investments, one calling for the expenditure of $200 million to develop a satellite communications system and the other involving the expenditure of $12,000 for a new truck, on which one would the company be more likely to use simulation analysis?

12-2   Distinguish between beta (or market) risk, within-firm (or corporate) risk, and stand-alone risk for a project being considered for inclusion in the capital budget. Which type of risk do you believe should be given the greatest weight in capital budgeting decisions? Explain.

12-3   Suppose Reading Engine Company, which has a high beta as well as a great deal of corporate risk, merged with Simplicity Patterns Inc. Simplicity's sales rise during recessions, when people are more likely to make their own clothes, and, consequently, its beta is negative but its corporate risk is relatively high. What would the merger do to the costs of capital in the consolidated company's locomotive engine division and in its patterns division?

12-4   Suppose a firm estimates its cost of capital for the coming year to be 10 percent. What are reasonable costs of capital for evaluating average-risk projects, high-risk projects, and low-risk projects?

SELF-TEST PROBLEMS   (Solutions Appear in Appendix B)

ST-1   Define each of the following terms:
Key terms
a. Stand-alone risk; corporate (within-firm) risk; market (beta) risk
b. Worst-case scenario; best-case scenario; base case
c. Sensitivity analysis
d. Scenario analysis
e. Monte Carlo simulation analysis
f. Coefficient of variation versus standard deviation
g. Project beta versus corporate beta
h. Pure play method of estimating divisional betas; accounting beta method
i. Corporate diversification versus stockholder diversification
j. Risk-adjusted discount rate; project cost of capital
k. Capital rationing

ST-2
Corporate risk analysis

The staff of Heymann Manufacturing has estimated the following net cash flows and prob-abilities for a new manufacturing process:

	NET CASH FLOWS		
YEAR	P = 0.2	P = 0.6	P = 0.2
0	($100,000)	($100,000)	($100,000)
1	20,000	30,000	40,000
2	20,000	30,000	40,000
3	20,000	30,000	40,000
4	20,000	30,000	40,000
5	20,000	30,000	40,000
5*	0	20,000	30,000

Line 0 gives the cost of the process, Lines 1 through 5 give operating cash flows, and Line 5* contains the estimated salvage values. Heymann's cost of capital for an average-risk project is 10 percent.

a. Assume that the project has average risk. Find the project's expected NPV. (Hint: Use expected values for the net cash flow in each year.)

b. Find the best-case and worst-case NPVs. What is the probability of occurrence of the worst case if the cash flows are perfectly dependent (perfectly positively correlated) over time? If they are independent over time?

c. Assume that all the cash flows are perfectly positively correlated, that is, there are only three possible cash flow streams over time: (1) the worst case, (2) the most likely, or base, case, and (3) the best case, with probabilities of 0.2, 0.6, and 0.2, respectively. These cases are represented by each of the columns in the table. Find the expected NPV, its standard deviation, and its coefficient of variation.

d. The coefficient of variation of Heymann's average project is in the range 0.8 to 1.0. If the coefficient of variation of a project being evaluated is greater than 1.0, 2 percentage points are added to the firm's cost of capital. Similarly, if the coefficient of variation is less than 0.8, 1 percentage point is deducted from the cost of capital. What is the project's cost of capital? Should Heymann accept or reject the project?

ST-3
Optimal capital budget

Wolfe Enterprises has the following capital structure, which it considers to be optimal under the present and forecasted conditions:

Debt	30%
Common equity	70
Total capital	100%

For the coming year, management expects to realize net income of $105,000. The past dividend policy of paying out 50 percent of earnings will continue. Present commitments from its banker will allow the firm to borrow at a rate of 8 percent.

The company's federal-plus-state tax rate is 40 percent, the current market price of its stock is $50 per share, its *last* dividend was $1.85 per share, and its expected constant growth rate is 8 percent. External equity (new common) can be sold at a flotation cost of 15 percent.

The firm has the following investment opportunities for the next period:

PROJECT	COST	IRR
A	$50,000	12%
B	15,000	11
C	20,000	10
D	50,000	9

Management asks you to help them determine what projects (if any) should be under-taken. You proceed with this analysis by following these steps:

a. Calculate the WACC using both retained earnings and new common stock.

b. Graph the IOS and MCC schedules.

c. Which projects should the firm accept?

d. What implicit assumptions about project risk are embodied in this problem? If you learned that Projects A and B were of above-average risk, yet the firm chose the projects which you indicated in Part c, how would this affect the situation?

e. The problem stated that the firm pays out 50 percent of its earnings as dividends. How would the analysis change if the payout ratio were changed to 0 percent? To 100 percent?

STARTER PROBLEMS

12-1

Corporate risk analysis

Huang Industries is considering a proposed project for its capital budget. The company estimates that the project's NPV is $12 million. This estimate assumes that the economy and market conditions will be average over the next few years. The company's CFO, however, forecasts that there is only a 50 percent chance that the economy will be average. Recognizing this uncertainty, she has also performed the following scenario analysis:

ECONOMIC SCENARIO	PROBABILITY OF OUTCOME	NPV
Recession	0.05	($70 million)
Below average	0.20	(25 million)
Average	0.50	12 million
Above average	0.20	20 million
Boom	0.05	30 million

What is the project's expected NPV, its standard deviation, and its coefficient of variation?

12-2

CAPM and beta

Ontario Foods uses the SML to determine the cost of equity capital. Currently, the risk-free rate is 5 percent, the expected return on the market is 10 percent, and Ontario's beta is 1.4. The company is considering a proposed project which has an estimated beta of 0.7. What is the project's cost of equity? If selected, the proposed project would represent 20 percent of the firm's total assets. What would the firm's new beta and cost of equity be if it were to accept the project?

12-3

Optimal capital budget

Midwest Water Works estimates that its retained earnings break point, BP_{RE}, is $5 million, and its WACC is 10 percent if equity comes from retained earnings. However, if the company issues new stock to raise new equity, it estimates that its WACC will rise to 10.5 percent. The company is considering the following seven investment projects:

PROJECT	SIZE	IRR
A	$1 million	12.0%
B	2 million	11.5
C	2 million	11.2
D	2 million	11.0
E	1 million	10.7
F	1 million	10.3
G	1 million	10.2

Assume that each of these projects is independent and that each is just as risky as the firm's existing assets. Which set of projects should be accepted, and what is the firm's optimal capital budget?

12-4

Optimal capital budget

Refer to Problem 12-3. Now assume that Projects C and D are mutually exclusive. Project D has a NPV of $400,000, whereas Project C has a NPV of $350,000. Which set of projects should be accepted, and what is the firm's optimal capital budget?

12-5

Risk-adjusted optimal capital budget

Refer to Problem 12-3. Assume again that each of the projects is independent but that management decides to incorporate project risk differentials. Management judges Projects B, C, D, and E to have average risk, Project A to have high risk, and Projects F and G to have low risk. The company adds 2 percentage points to the cost of capital of those projects that are significantly more risky than average, and it subtracts 2 percentage points from the cost of capital for those that are substantially less risky than average. Which set of projects should be accepted, and what is the firm's optimal capital budget?

EXAM-TYPE PROBLEMS

The problems included in this section are set up in such a way that they could be used as multiple-choice exam problems.

12-6
Risk adjustment

The risk-free rate of return is 9 percent, and the market risk premium is 5 percent. The beta of the project under analysis is 1.4, with expected net cash flows estimated to be $1,500 per year for 5 years. The required investment outlay on the project is $4,500.
a. What is the required risk-adjusted return on the project?
b. Should the project be accepted?

12-7
Divisional required rates of return

Turner Computer Corporation, a producer of office computer equipment, currently has assets of $15 million and a beta of 1.4. The risk-free rate is 8 percent and the market risk premium is 5 percent. Turner would like to expand into the risky home computer market. If the expansion is undertaken, Turner would create a new division with $3.75 million in assets. The new division would have a beta of 1.8.
a. What is Turner's current required rate of return?
b. If the expansion is undertaken, what would be the firm's new beta? What is the new overall required rate of return, and what rate of return must the home computer division produce to leave the new overall required rate of return unchanged?

12-8
Optimal capital budget

The Cuddeback Corporation's present capital structure, which is also its target capital structure, calls for 50 percent debt and 50 percent common equity. The firm has only one potential project, an expansion program with a 10.2 percent IRR and a cost of $20 million but which is completely divisible; that is, Cuddeback can invest any amount up to $20 million. The firm expects to retain $3 million of earnings next year. It can raise up to $5 million in new debt at a before-tax cost of 8 percent, and all debt after the first $5 million will have a cost of 10 percent. The cost of retained earnings is 12 percent, and the firm can sell any amount of new common stock desired at a constant cost of new equity of 15 percent. The firm's marginal federal-plus-state tax rate is 40 percent. What is the firm's optimal capital budget?

12-9
Optimal capital budget

The management of Karp Phosphate Industries (KPI) is planning next year's capital budget. KPI projects its net income at $7,500, and its payout ratio is 40 percent. The company's earnings and dividends are growing at a constant rate of 5 percent; the last dividend, D_0, was $0.90; and the current stock price is $8.59. KPI's new debt will cost 14 percent. If KPI issues new common stock, flotation costs will be 20 percent. KPI is at its optimal capital structure, which is 40 percent debt and 60 percent equity, and the firm's marginal tax rate is 40 percent. KPI has the following independent, indivisible, and equally risky investment opportunities:

PROJECT	COST	IRR
A	$15,000	17%
B	20,000	14
C	15,000	16
D	12,000	15

What is KPI's optimal capital budget?

12-10
Risk-adjusted optimal capital budget

Refer to Problem 12-9. Management now decides to incorporate project risk differentials into the analysis. The new policy is to add 2 percentage points to the cost of capital of those projects significantly more risky than average and to subtract 2 percentage points from the cost of capital of those which are substantially less risky than average. Management judges Project A to be of high risk, Projects C and D to be of average risk, and Project B to be of low risk. No projects are divisible. What is the optimal capital budget after adjustment for project risk?

PROBLEMS

12-11
Risky cash flows

The Butler-Perkins Company (BPC) must decide between two mutually exclusive investment projects. Each project costs $6,750 and has an expected life of 3 years. Annual net cash flows from each project begin 1 year after the initial investment is made and have the following probability distributions:

PROJECT A		PROJECT B	
PROBABILITY	NET CASH FLOWS	PROBABILITY	NET CASH FLOWS
0.2	$6,000	0.2	$ 0
0.6	6,750	0.6	6,750
0.2	7,500	0.2	18,000

BPC has decided to evaluate the riskier project at a 12 percent rate and the less risky project at a 10 percent rate.

a. What is the expected value of the annual net cash flows from each project? What is the coefficient of variation (CV)? (Hint: Use Equation 5-3 from Chapter 5 to calculate the standard deviation of Project A. $\sigma_B = \$5,798$ and $CV_B = 0.76$.)

b. What is the risk-adjusted NPV of each project?

c. If it were known that Project B was negatively correlated with other cash flows of the firm whereas Project A was positively correlated, how would this knowledge affect the decision? If Project B's cash flows were negatively correlated with gross domestic product (GDP), would that influence your assessment of its risk?

12-12
CAPM approach to risk adjustments

Goodtread Rubber Company has two divisions: the tire division, which manufactures tires for new autos, and the recap division, which manufactures recapping materials that are sold to independent tire recapping shops throughout the United States. Since auto manufacturing fluctuates with the general economy, the tire division's earnings contribution to Goodtread's stock price is highly correlated with returns on most other stocks. If the tire division were operated as a separate company, its beta coefficient would be about 1.50. The sales and profits of the recap division, on the other hand, tend to be countercyclical, because recap sales boom when people cannot afford to buy new tires. The recap division's beta is estimated to be 0.5. Approximately 75 percent of Goodtread's corporate assets are invested in the tire division and 25 percent are invested in the recap division.

Currently, the rate of interest on Treasury securities is 9 percent, and the expected rate of return on an average share of stock is 13 percent. Goodtread uses only common equity capital, so it has no debt outstanding.

a. What is the required rate of return on Goodtread's stock?

b. What discount rate should be used to evaluate capital budgeting projects? Explain your answer fully, and, in the process, illustrate your answer with a project which costs $160,000, has a 10-year life, and provides expected after-tax net cash flows of $30,000 per year.

12-13
Scenario analysis

Your firm, Agrico Products, is considering the purchase of a tractor which will have a net cost of $36,000, will increase pre-tax operating cash flows before taking account of depreciation effects by $12,000 per year, and will be depreciated on a straight line basis to zero over 5 years at the rate of $7,200 per year, beginning the first year. (Annual cash flows will be $12,000, before taxes, plus the tax savings that result from $7,200 of depreciation.) The board of directors is having a heated debate about whether the tractor will actually last 5 years. Specifically, Elizabeth Brannigan insists that she knows of some tractors that have lasted only 4 years. Philip Glasgo agrees with Brannigan, but he argues that most tractors do give 5 years of service. Laura Evans says she has known some to last for as long as 8 years.

Given this discussion, the board asks you to prepare a scenario analysis to ascertain the importance of the uncertainty about the tractor's life. Assume a 40 percent marginal federal-plus-state tax rate, a zero salvage value, and a cost of capital of 10 percent. (Hint: Here straight line depreciation is based on the MACRS class life of the tractor and is not affected by the actual life. Also, ignore the half-year convention for this problem.)

INTEGRATED CASE

ALLIED FOOD PRODUCTS, PART II

12-14 Risk Analysis   The Chapter 11 Integrated Case contained the details of a capital budgeting evaluation being conducted by Allied Food Products. Although inflation was considered in the initial analysis, the riskiness of the project was not considered. The expected cash flows, considering inflation as they were estimated in Chapter 11 (in thousands of dollars), are given in the following table. Allied's overall cost of capital (WACC) is 10 percent.

You have been asked to answer the following questions.

a. (1) What are the three levels, or types, of project risk that are normally considered?
   (2) Which type is most relevant?
   (3) Which type is easiest to measure?
   (4) Are the three types of risk generally highly correlated?

b. (1) What is sensitivity analysis?
   (2) Discuss how one would perform a sensitivity analysis on the unit sales, salvage value, and cost of capital for the project. Assume that each of these variables deviates from its base-case, or expected, value by plus and minus 10, 20, and 30 percent. Explain how you would calculate the NPV, IRR, MIRR, and payback for each case. Include a sensitivity diagram, and discuss the results.
   (3) What is the primary weakness of sensitivity analysis? What are its primary advantages?

c. Assume that you are confident about the estimates of all the variables that affect the cash flows except unit sales. If product acceptance is poor, sales would be only 75,000 units a year, while a strong consumer response would produce sales of 125,000 units. In either case, cash costs would still amount to 60 percent of revenues. You believe that there is a 25 percent chance of poor acceptance, a 25 percent chance of excellent acceptance, and a 50 percent chance of average acceptance (the base case).
   (1) What is the worst-case NPV? The best-case NPV?
   (2) Use the worst-, most likely (or base), and best-case NPVs, with their probabilities of occurrence, to find the project's expected NPV, standard deviation, and coefficient of variation.

			YEAR		
	0	**1**	**2**	**3**	**4**
Investment in:					
Fixed assets	($240)				
Net working capital	(20)				
Unit sales (thousands)		100	100	100	100
Sales price (dollars)		$2.100	$2.205	$2.315	$2.431
Total revenues		$210.0	$220.5	$231.5	$243.1
Cash operating costs (60%)		126.0	132.3	138.9	145.9
Depreciation		79.2	108.0	36.0	16.8
Operating income before taxes		$ 4.8	($ 19.8)	$ 56.6	$ 80.4
Taxes on operating income (40%)		1.9	(7.9)	22.6	32.1
Operating income after taxes		$ 2.9	($ 11.9)	$ 34.0	$ 48.3
Plus depreciation		79.2	108.0	36.0	16.8
Operating cash flow		$ 82.1	$ 96.1	$ 70.0	$ 65.1
Salvage value					25.0
Tax on SV (40%)					(10.0)
Recovery of NWC					20.0
Net cash flow	($260)	$ 82.1	$ 96.1	$ 70.0	$100.1
Cumulative cash flows for payback:	(260.0)	(177.9)	(81.8)	(11.8)	88.3
Compounded inflows for MIRR:		109.2	116.3	77.0	100.1
Terminal value of inflows:					402.6

NPV at 10% cost of capital = $15.0
IRR   =   12.6%
MIRR   =   11.6%

d. (1) Assume that Allied's average project has a coefficient of variation (CV) in the range of 1.25 to 1.75. Would the lemon juice project be classified as high risk, average risk, or low risk? What type of risk is being measured here?

(2) Based on common sense, how highly correlated do you think the project would be with the firm's other assets? (Give a correlation coefficient, or range of coefficients, based on your judgment.)

(3) How would this correlation coefficient and the previously calculated σ combine to affect the project's contribution to corporate, or within-firm, risk? Explain.

e. (1) Based on your judgment, what do you think the project's correlation coefficient would be with respect to the general economy and thus with returns on "the market"?

(2) How would correlation with the economy affect the project's market risk?

f. (1) Allied typically adds or subtracts 3 percentage points to the overall cost of capital to adjust for risk. Should the lemon juice project be accepted?

(2) What subjective risk factors should be considered before the final decision is made?

g. (1) Assume for purposes of this problem that Allied's target capital structure is 50 percent debt and 50 percent common equity, its cost of debt is 12 percent, the risk-free rate is 10 percent, the market risk premium is 6 percent, and the firm's tax rate is 40 percent. If your estimate of the new project's beta is 1.2, what is its weighted average cost of capital based on the CAPM?

(2) How does the project's market risk compare with the firm's overall market risk?

(3) How does the project's market risk compare with its stand-alone risk?

(4) Briefly describe two methods that you could conceivably have used to estimate the project's beta. How feasible do you think those procedures would actually be in this case?

(5) What are the advantages and disadvantages of focusing on a project's market risk?

h. As a completely different project, Allied is also evaluating two different systems for disposing of wastes associated with another product, fresh grapefruit juice. Plan W requires more workers but less capital, while Plan C requires more capital but fewer workers. Both systems have 3-year lives. Since the production line choice has no impact on revenues, you will base your decision on the relative costs of the two systems as set forth below:

EXPECTED NET COSTS

YEAR	PLAN W	PLAN C
0	($500)	($1,000)
1	(500)	(300)
2	(500)	(300)
3	(500)	(300)

(1) Assume initially that the two systems are both of average risk. Which one should be chosen?

(2) Now assume that the worker-intensive plan (W) is judged to be riskier than average, because future wage rates are very difficult to forecast. Under this condition, which system should be chosen? Base your answer on the lowest reasonable PV of future costs. (Hint: This is a tricky question; risky *outflows* should be discounted at *low* rates.)

(3) Do the two plans have IRRs?

INTEGRATED CASE

BLUM INDUSTRIES

12-15 Optimal Capital Budget Ron Redwine, financial manager of Blum Industries, is developing the firm's optimal capital budget for the coming year. He has identified the 5 potential projects shown below; none of the projects can be repeated. Projects B and B* are mutually exclusive, while the remainder are independent.

PROJECT	COST	CF_{1-n}	LIFE (n)	IRR	NPV
A	$400,000	$119,326	5	15%	
B	200,000	56,863	5	13	
B*	200,000	35,397	10	12	
C	100,000	27,057	5	11	
D	300,000	79,139	5	10	

The following information was developed for use in determining Blum's weighted average cost of capital (WACC):

Interest rate on new debt	8.0%
Tax rate	40.0%
Debt ratio	60.0%
Current stock price, P_0	$20.00
Last dividend, D_0	$2.00
Expected constant growth rate, g	6.0%
Flotation cost on common, F	19.0%
Expected addition to retained earnings	$200,000.00

Blum adjusts for differential project risk by adding or subtracting 2 percentage points to the firm's marginal cost of capital.

a. Calculate the WACC, and then plot the company's IOS and MCC schedules. What is the firm's marginal cost of capital for capital budgeting purposes?

b. Assume initially that all 5 projects are of average risk. What is Blum's optimal capital budget? Explain your answer.

c. Now assume that the retained earnings break point occurred at $900,000 of new capital. What effect would this have on the firm's MCC schedule and on its optimal capital budget?

d. Return to the situation in Part a, with the $500,000 retained earnings break point. Suppose Project A is reexamined, and it is judged to be a high-risk project, while Projects C and D are, upon reexamination, judged to have low risk. Projects B and B* remain average-risk projects. How would these changes affect Blum's optimal capital budget?

e. In reality, companies like Blum have hundreds of projects to evaluate each year, hence it is generally not practical to draw IOS and MCC schedules which include every potential project. Suppose this situation exists for Blum. Suppose also that the company has 3 divisions, L, A, and H, with low, average, and high risk, respectively, and that the projects within each division can also be grouped into 3 risk categories. Describe how Blum might go about structuring its capital budgeting decision process and choosing its optimal set of projects. For this purpose, assume that Blum's overall WACC is estimated to be 11 percent. As part of your answer, find appropriate divisional and project hurdle rates when differential risk is considered.

COMPUTER-RELATED PROBLEM

Work the problem in this section only if you are using the computer problem diskette.

12-16

Sensitivity analysis

Use the computerized model in the File C12 to solve this problem.

a. Refer back to Problem 12-13. Agrico's board of directors would like to know how sensitive the analysis is to the cost of capital. Assume that the tractor's life is 5 years, and analyze the effects of a change in the cost of capital to 8 percent or to 12 percent. Is the project very sensitive to changes in the cost of capital?

b. The board also would like to determine the sensitivity of the project to changes in the increase in pre-tax operating revenues. The directors believe that the increase will be no less than $8,400 per year and no more than $15,600 per year. Analyze the project at these levels of operating revenue, assuming a 5-year project life and a 10 percent cost of capital.

CAPITAL STRUCTURE AND DIVIDEND POLICY

CHAPTER 13
CAPITAL STRUCTURE
AND LEVERAGE

APPENDIX 13A
DEGREE OF LEVERAGE

CHAPTER 14
DIVIDEND POLICY

CHAPTER 13

CAPITAL STRUCTURE AND LEVERAGE

© John Wilkes/Photonica

When a firm expands, it needs capital, and that capital can come from debt or equity. Debt has two important advantages. First, interest paid is tax deductible, which lowers debt's effective cost. Second, debtholders get a fixed return, so stockholders do not have to share their profits if the business is extremely successful.

However, debt also has disadvantages. First, the higher the debt ratio, the riskier the company, hence the higher its interest rate will be. Second, if a company falls on hard times and operating income is not sufficient to cover interest charges, its stockholders will have to make up the shortfall, and if they cannot, bankruptcy will result. Good times may be just around the corner, but too much debt can keep the company from getting there and thus can wipe out the stockholders.

Kroger, the nation's largest supermarket chain, is a good example of a firm that has used debt wisely. Like many food stores, Kroger has a heavy debt burden, but the assets purchased with that debt have earned more than the cost of the debt, so "debt leverage" has increased the company's profits. As a result, its earnings per share have experienced good growth, and in recent years Kroger's stock has outperformed the overall market.

On the other hand, there are numerous examples of high debt pushing otherwise well-regarded companies into bankruptcy. For example, a few years ago, many of the nation's largest retailers, including Federated Department Stores and R.H. Macy, were forced to declare bankruptcy as a result of their excessive use of debt.

Debt financing has also led to severe problems for many airlines, including U.S. Air. In 1996, U.S. Air had a long-term debt to capitalization ratio of almost 100 percent, hence it was financed almost entirely by debt. Further, its annual interest expense was more than $200 million, considerably more than its average operating income. U.S. Air cannot pay dividends on its common stock, and its very survival is at stake. The airline industry is extremely cyclical, and large amounts of debt put tremendous pressures on a company when earnings turn south.

Companies can finance with either debt or equity. Is one better than the other? If so, should firms be financed either with all debt or all equity? If the best solution is some mix of debt and equity, what is the optimal mix? In this chapter, we discuss the key facets of the debt-versus-equity, or capital structure, decision. As you read the chapter, think about Kroger and U.S. Air, and the ways the concepts we discuss might aid the managers of these and other companies as they make capital structure decisions.

In Chapter 9, when we calculated the weighted average cost of capital for use in capital budgeting, we assumed that the firm had a specific target capital structure. However, the optimal capital structure may change over time, changes in capital structure affect the riskiness and cost of each type of capital, and all this can change the weighted average cost of capital. Moreover, a change in the cost of capital can affect capital budgeting decisions and, ultimately, the firm's stock price.

Many factors influence capital structure decisions, and, as you will see, determining the optimal capital structure is not an exact science. Therefore, even firms in the same industry often have dramatically different capital structures. In this chapter we first consider the effect of capital structure on risk, and then we use these insights to help answer the question of how firms should finance their operations.

🌐 *ON THE WWW*

Two video clips of Steve Walsh, Assistant Treasurer at JCPenney, are available at http:// www.cob.ohio-state.edu/dept/fin/ resources_education/clips.htm. The first clip discusses the cost of capital and debt, while the second clip discusses optimal capital structure at JCPenney relative to the capital structure theory of Modigliani/Miller.

Target Capital Structure
The mix of debt, preferred stock, and common equity with which the firm plans to raise capital.

THE TARGET CAPITAL STRUCTURE

Firms should first analyze a number of factors, then establish a **target capital structure.** This target may change over time as conditions change, but at any given moment, management should have a specific capital structure in mind. If the actual debt ratio is below the target level, expansion capital will probably be raised by issuing debt, whereas if the debt ratio is above the target, equity will probably be used.

Capital structure policy involves a trade-off between risk and return:

♦ Using more debt raises the risk borne by stockholders.

♦ However, using more debt generally leads to a higher expected rate of return.

Higher risk tends to lower a stock's price, but a higher expected rate of return raises it. *Therefore, the optimal capital structure must strike that balance between risk and return which maximizes the firm's stock price.*

Four primary factors influence capital structure decisions.

1. *Business risk,* or the riskiness inherent in the firm's operations if it used no debt. The greater the firm's business risk, the lower its optimal debt ratio.

2. The firm's *tax position.* A major reason for using debt is that interest is deductible, which lowers the effective cost of debt. However, if most of a firm's income is already sheltered from taxes by depreciation tax shields, interest on currently outstanding debt, or tax loss carry-forwards, its tax rate will be low, so additional debt will not be as advantageous as it would be to a firm with a higher effective tax rate.

3. *Financial flexibility,* or the ability to raise capital on reasonable terms under adverse conditions. Corporate treasurers know that a steady supply of capital is necessary for stable operations, which is vital for long-run success. They also know that when money is tight in the economy, or when a firm is experiencing operating difficulties, suppliers of capital prefer to provide funds to companies with strong balance sheets. Therefore, both the potential future need for funds and the consequences of a funds shortage influence the target capital structure — the greater the probable future need for capital, and the worse the consequences of a capital shortage, the stronger the balance sheet should be.

4. *Managerial conservatism or aggressiveness.* Some managers are more aggressive than others, hence some firms are more inclined to use debt in an effort to boost profits. This factor does not affect the true optimal, or value-maximizing, capital structure, but it does influence the manager-determined target capital structure.

These four points largely determine the target capital structure, but operating conditions can cause the actual capital structure to vary from the target. For example, Illinois Power has a target debt ratio of about 45 percent, but large losses associated with a nuclear plant forced it to write down its common equity, and that raised the debt ratio above the target level. The company is now trying to get its equity back up to the target level.

SELF-TEST QUESTIONS

What four factors affect the target capital structure?

In what sense does capital structure policy involve a trade-off between risk and return?

BUSINESS AND FINANCIAL RISK

In Chapter 5, when we examined risk from the viewpoint of the individual investor, we distinguished between *risk on a stand-alone basis,* where an asset's cash flows are analyzed by themselves, and *risk in a portfolio context,* where the cash flows from a number of assets are combined and then the consolidated cash flows are analyzed. In a portfolio context, we saw that an asset's risk can be divided into two components: *diversifiable risk,* which can be diversified away and hence is of little concern to most investors, and *market risk,* which is measured by the beta coefficient and which reflects broad market movements that cannot be eliminated by diversification and therefore is of concern to all investors. Then, in Chapter 12, we examined risk from the viewpoint of the corporation, and we considered how capital budgeting decisions affect the firm's riskiness.

Now we introduce two new dimensions of risk:

1. *Business risk,* which is the riskiness of the firm's assets if it uses no debt.
2. *Financial risk,* which is the additional risk placed on the common stockholders as a result of the decision to use debt.[1]

BUSINESS RISK

Business Risk
The risk associated with projections of a firm's future returns on assets.

Business risk is defined as the uncertainty inherent in projections of future returns on assets (ROA), and it is the single most important determinant of capital structure. Consider Bigbee Electronics Company, a firm that currently uses 100 percent equity. Since the company has no debt, its ROE moves in lock-step with its ROA, and either ROE or ROA can be examined to estimate business risk. Figure 13-1 gives some clues about Bigbee's business risk. The top graph shows the

---

[1]Using preferred stock also adds to financial risk. To simplify matters, in this chapter we shall consider only debt and common equity.

FIGURE 13-1 Bigbee Electronics Company: Trend in ROE, 1987–1997, and Subjective Probability Distribution of ROE, 1997

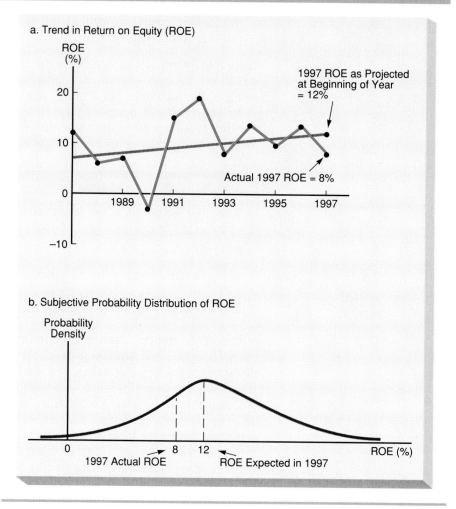

a. Trend in Return on Equity (ROE)

1997 ROE as Projected at Beginning of Year = 12%

Actual 1997 ROE = 8%

b. Subjective Probability Distribution of ROE

1997 Actual ROE

ROE Expected in 1997

trend in ROE (and ROA) from 1987 through 1997; this graph gives both security analysts and Bigbee's management an idea of the extent to which ROE has varied in the past and might vary in the future. The bottom graph shows the beginning-of-year, subjectively estimated probability distribution of Bigbee's ROE for 1997 based on the trend line in the top section of Figure 13-1. The estimate was made at the beginning of 1997, and the expected 12 percent was read from the trend line. As the graphs indicate, the actual ROE in 1997 (8%) fell below the expected value (12%).

Bigbee's past fluctuations in ROE were caused by many factors — booms and recessions in the national economy, successful new products introduced both by Bigbee and by its competitors, labor strikes, a fire in Bigbee's major plant, and so on. Similar events will doubtless occur in the future, and when they do, ROE will rise or fall. Further, there is always the possibility that a long-term disaster will strike, permanently depressing the company's earning power. For example, a competitor might introduce a new product that would permanently lower

Bigbee's earnings.[2] Uncertainty about Bigbee's future ROE is the company's *basic business risk*.

Business risk varies from one industry to another, and also among firms in a given industry. Further, business risk can change over time. For example, the electric utilities were regarded for years as having little business risk, but the introduction of competition in recent years altered their situation, producing sharp declines in ROE for some companies and greatly increasing the industry's business risk. Today, food processors and grocery retailers are frequently cited as examples of industries with low business risk, whereas cyclical manufacturing industries such as steel are regarded as having relatively high business risk. Smaller companies, especially single-product firms, also have relatively high business risk.[3]

Business risk depends on a number of factors, including the following:

1. **Demand (unit sales) variability.** The more stable a firm's unit sales, other things held constant, the lower its business risk. The amount of competition a firm faces is a factor here.

2. **Sales price variability.** Firms whose products are sold in highly volatile markets are exposed to more business risk than similar firms whose output prices are relatively stable. Again, the amount of competition faced is important.

3. **Input price variability.** Firms whose input costs, including product development costs, are highly uncertain are exposed to high business risk.

4. **Ability to adjust output prices for changes in input prices.** Some firms have little difficulty in raising their own output prices when input costs rise, and the greater the ability to adjust output prices, the lower the business risk. This factor is especially important during periods of high inflation.

5. **The extent to which costs are fixed: operating leverage.** If a high percentage of costs are fixed, hence do not decline when demand decreases, this increases the company's business risk. This factor is called *operating leverage,* and it is discussed at length in the next section.

Each of these factors is influenced by the firm's industry characteristics, but each is also controllable to some extent by management. For example, many firms can, through their marketing policies, take actions to stabilize both unit sales and sales prices. However, such stabilization may require either large expenditures on advertising or price concessions to induce customers to commit to purchase fixed quantities at fixed prices in the future. Similarly, firms such as Bigbee Electronics can reduce the volatility of future input costs by negotiating long-term labor and materials supply contracts, but they may have to agree to pay prices above the current market price to obtain these contracts.[4]

---

[2]Two examples of "safe" industries that turned out to be risky are the railroads just before automobiles, airplanes, and trucks took away most of their business, and the telegraph business just before telephones came on the scene. Also, numerous individual companies have been hurt, if not destroyed, by antitrust actions, fraud, or just plain bad management.

[3]We have avoided any discussion of market versus company-specific risk in this section. We note now (1) that any action which increases business risk will generally increase a firm's beta coefficient but (2) that a part of business risk as we define it will generally be company-specific and hence subject to elimination through diversification by the firm's stockholders.

[4]For example, utilities could recently buy coal in the spot market for about $30 per ton, but under a five-year contract, the cost was about $50 per ton. Clearly, the price for reducing uncertainty was high! Hedging with futures and options, discussed in Chapter 19, can also reduce business risk.

OPERATING LEVERAGE

Operating Leverage
The extent to which fixed costs are used in a firm's operations.

As noted above, business risk depends in part on the extent to which a firm's costs are fixed. If fixed costs are high, even a small decline in sales can lead to a large decline in operating profits and ROE. Therefore, other things held constant, the higher a firm's fixed costs, the greater its business risk. Higher fixed costs are generally associated with more highly automated, capital-intensive firms and industries; electric utilities, telephone companies, and airlines are examples.

If a high percentage of a firm's total costs are fixed, the firm is said to have high **operating leverage.** In physics, leverage implies the use of a lever to raise a heavy object with a small amount of force. In politics, people who have leverage can accomplish a great deal with their smallest word or action. *In business terminology, high operating leverage, other things held constant, means that a relatively small change in sales will result in a large change in operating income.*

Figure 13-2 illustrates operating leverage by comparing the results Bigbee can expect with different amounts of operating leverage. Project A calls for a small amount of fixed charges. Here the firm would not have much automated equipment, so its depreciation, maintenance, property taxes, and so on, would be low. However, under Project A the total cost line has a relatively steep slope, indicating that variable costs per unit are higher than they would be if the firm used more leverage. Project B, on the other hand, calls for a higher level of fixed costs. Here the firm uses automated equipment with which one operator can turn out few or many units for a given labor cost. The **breakeven point** is higher under Project B: It occurs at 40,000 units under Project A versus 60,000 units under Project B.

Breakeven Point
The volume of sales at which total costs equal total revenues, causing operating profits (or EBIT) to equal zero.

We can develop a formula to find the breakeven quantity by recognizing that breakeven occurs when operating income (EBIT) is equal to zero, which implies that sales revenues are equal to costs:

$$\text{Sales} = \text{Costs}$$
$$PQ = VQ + F$$
$$PQ - VQ - F = 0. \tag{13-1}$$

Here P is average sales price per unit of output, Q is units of output, V is variable cost per unit, and F is fixed operating costs. We can solve Equation 13-1 for the breakeven quantity, Q_{BE}:

$$Q_{BE} = \frac{F}{P - V}. \tag{13-1a}$$

For Project A,

$$Q_{BE} = \frac{\$20,000}{\$2.00 - \$1.50} = 40,000 \text{ units,}$$

and for Project B,

$$Q_{BE} = \frac{\$60,000}{\$2.00 - \$1.00} = 60,000 \text{ units.}$$

Note that while our example applied the concept of operating leverage to two investment projects, A and B, it can also be applied to entire firms. Firms such as Bigbee Electronics can use different sets of assets to manufacture and sell their output, and different operating setups typically result in different operating leverage. So, the concept of operating leverage can be used to analyze either

FIGURE 13-2 Illustration of Operating Leverage

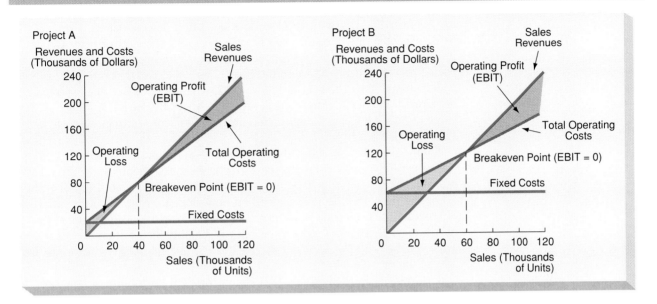

		PROJECT A	PROJECT B
	Price	$2.00	$2.00
	Variable costs	$1.50	$1.00
	Fixed costs	$20,000	$60,000
	Assets	$200,000	$200,000
	Tax rate	40%	40%

				PROJECT A				PROJECT B			
DEMAND	PROBABILITY	UNITS SOLD	DOLLAR SALES	OPERATING COSTS	OPERATING PROFITS (EBIT)	NET INCOME	ROE	OPERATING COSTS	OPERATING PROFITS (EBIT)	NET INCOME	ROE
Terrible	0.05	0	$ 0	$ 20,000	($20,000)	($12,000)	−6.00%	$ 60,000	($ 60,000)	($36,000)	−18.00%
Poor	0.20	40,000	80,000	80,000	0	0	0.00	100,000	(20,000)	(12,000)	−6.00
Normal	0.50	100,000	200,000	170,000	30,000	18,000	9.00	160,000	40,000	24,000	12.00
Good	0.20	160,000	320,000	260,000	60,000	36,000	18.00	220,000	100,000	60,000	30.00
Wonderful	0.05	200,000	400,000	320,000	80,000	48,000	24.00	260,000	140,000	84,000	42.00
Expected values:		100,000	$200,000	$170,000	$30,000	$18,000	9.00%	$160,000	$ 40,000	$24,000	12.00%
Standard deviation:							7.41%				14.82%
Coefficient of variation							0.82				1.23

NOTES a. The federal-plus-state tax rate is 40 percent, so NI = EBIT(1 − Tax rate) = EBIT(0.6).
b. ROE = NI/Equity. The firm has no debt, so Assets = Equity = $200,000.
c. The breakeven sales level for Project B is not shown in the table, but it is 60,000 units or $120,000.
d. The expected values, standard deviations, and coefficients of variation were found using the procedures discussed in Chapter 5.

capital budgeting projects or entire firms. Of course, if a firm takes on many projects with high operating leverage, then the firm itself will end up with a lot of operating leverage.

Our next question is this: How does operating leverage affect a project's or firm's expected rate of return, and the riskiness of the project or firm? Generally, if other things are held constant, using more operating leverage raises the expected rate of return, but it also increases the riskiness of that return. This point is demonstrated by the data in Figure 13-2, where we see that the expected rate of return is higher for the more leveraged Project B, but B's riskiness as measured by either the standard deviation or the coefficient of variation is also higher than that of Project A.

Figure 13-3 demonstrates the same point — it shows that Project B offers a higher expected return, but B entails greater risk. The graphs show the relevant probability distributions. The upper panel plots the probability distribution of sales, and it shows that sales depend on how demand for the project varies, not on whether the project is manufactured by the set of assets acquired under Project A or Project B. Therefore, the same sales probability distribution applies to both production plans. Expected sales are $200,000, but actual sales can range from zero to about $400,000.

The lower section of Figure 13-3 shows the ROE probability distributions for the two projects. Project B has a higher expected level of ROE, but it also entails a much higher probability of large losses. Therefore, Project B, the one with more fixed costs and thus more operating leverage, is riskier. *In general, holding other things constant, the greater the operating leverage, the greater the business risk as measured by variability of EBIT and ROE.*

To what extent can firms control their operating leverage? In many respects, operating leverage is determined by technology. Electric utilities, telephone companies, airlines, steel mills, and chemical companies simply *must* make heavy investments in fixed assets, and, as a result, they have high fixed costs and thus high operating leverage. Grocery stores, on the other hand, have substantially lower fixed costs, hence lower operating leverage. Still, all firms have some control over their operating leverage. For example, an electric utility can expand its generating capacity by building either a nuclear reactor or a gas-fired plant. The nuclear generator would require a larger investment and hence have higher fixed costs, but its variable operating costs would be relatively low. The gas-fired plant, on the other hand, would require a smaller investment and have lower fixed costs, but its variable costs (for gas) would be high. Thus, capital budgeting decisions can influence operating leverage and thus basic business risk.

The concept of operating leverage was in fact originally developed for use in capital budgeting. Alternative methods for making a given product often result in different operating leverage and different breakeven points, and thus different degrees of business risk. Bigbee Electronics and other companies regularly undertake a breakeven analysis as part of their capital budgeting process. Still, once a corporation's operating leverage has been established, this factor influences its capital structure decisions.

FINANCIAL RISK

Financial Leverage
The extent to which fixed-income securities (debt and preferred stock) are used in a firm's capital structure.

Financial Risk
An increase in stockholders' risk, over and above the firm's basic business risk, resulting from the use of financial leverage.

Financial leverage refers to the use of fixed-income securities — debt and preferred stock — and **financial risk** is the additional risk placed on the common stockholders as a result of financial leverage. We can extend the Bigbee Electronics example to illustrate the effects of financial leverage. First, assume that

FIGURE 13-3 Analysis of Business Risk

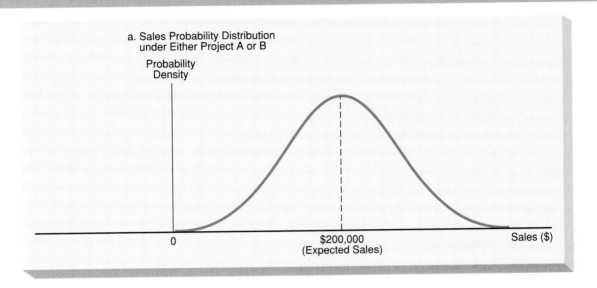

a. Sales Probability Distribution under Either Project A or B

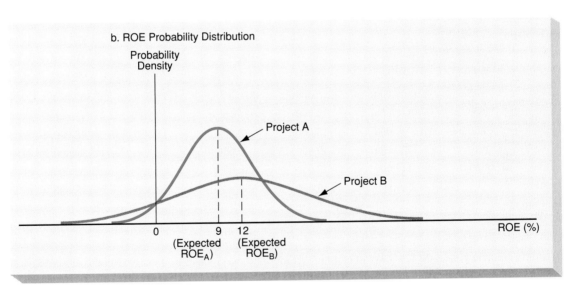

b. ROE Probability Distribution

NOTE: We are using continuous distributions to approximate the discrete distributions contained in Figure 13-2.

the company decided to go with Project B — it decided that the higher expected return was sufficient to compensate for the higher risk. As we know, Project B requires $200,000 of assets, so the company will have to raise $200,000. It could raise the money as common equity, it could borrow the money, or it could use some debt and some equity, with the total coming to $200,000.

For now, assume that only two financing choices are being considered — all equity or 50 percent debt and 50 percent equity. Now consider Table 13-1, which shows how the financing choice will affect Project B's expected return and the risk. The probabilities were taken from the tabular section of Figure 13-2, and they show how demand for the output from the project might vary. The second

TABLE	13-1	Effects of Financial Leverage: Project B Financed with Zero Debt or with 50 Percent Debt

Project B with Zero Debt

DEMAND FOR PRODUCT	PROBABILITY	EBIT	INTEREST	PRE-TAX INCOME	TAXES (40%)	NET INCOME	ROE
Terrible	0.05	($60,000)	$0	($60,000)	($24,000)	($36,000)	−18.00%
Poor	0.20	(20,000)	0	(20,000)	(8,000)	(12,000)	−6.00
Normal	0.50	40,000	0	40,000	16,000	24,000	12.00
Good	0.20	100,000	0	100,000	40,000	60,000	30.00
Wonderful	0.05	140,000	0	140,000	56,000	84,000	42.00
Expected values:		$40,000	$0	$40,000	$16,000	$24,000	12.00%
Standard deviation:							14.82%
Coefficient of variation:							1.23

Project B with 50% Debt

Debt ratio	50.00%
Assets	$200,000
Debt	$100,000
Equity	$100,000
Interest rate:	10.00%

DEMAND FOR PRODUCT	PROBABILITY	EBIT	INTEREST	PRE-TAX INCOME	TAXES (40%)	NET INCOME	ROE
Terrible	0.05	($60,000)	$10,000	($70,000)	($28,000)	($42,000)	−42.00%
Poor	0.20	(20,000)	10,000	(30,000)	(12,000)	(18,000)	−18.00
Normal	0.50	40,000	10,000	30,000	12,000	18,000	18.00
Good	0.20	100,000	10,000	90,000	36,000	54,000	54.00
Wonderful	0.05	140,000	10,000	130,000	52,000	78,000	78.00
Expected values:		$40,000	$10,000	$30,000	$12,000	$18,000	18.00%
Standard deviation:							29.64%
Coefficient of variation:							1.65

Assumptions: 1. The firm can finance the $200,000 cost of the project with all common equity or with $100,000 of equity and $100,000 of debt at an interest rate of 10 percent.
2. Sales and operating costs, hence EBIT, are not affected by the financing decision. Therefore, EBIT under both financing plans is identical, and it is taken from the EBIT column for Project B in Figure 13-2.

column shows the EBIT figures as developed for Project B under the different demand conditions as shown for Project B in the tabular section of Figure 13-2. Note that these probabilities and the EBITs apply regardless of how the firm finances Project B, so they are identical in the top and bottom sections of Table 13-1.

Now focus on the top section of Table 13-1, which shows the situation assuming Bigbee uses no debt and finances Project B entirely with common equity. Since debt is zero, interest is also zero, hence pre-tax income is equal to EBIT. Taxes at 40 percent are deducted to produce net income, which is then divided by the $200,000 of equity to determine the ROE. If demand is terrible, then sales will be zero (from Figure 13-2), and the company will incur a loss of $60,000; this loss can be used to offset income from other sources or carried back to offset prior-year income. In either case the result will be a $24,000 tax credit, so the net loss if demand is terrible will be $36,000. Dividing the loss by the $200,000 of equity results in an ROE of −18 percent. A similar procedure is used to determine the results under other demand conditions, and the probability-weighted average of the resulting ROEs is the expected value, 12 percent. Note that this 12 percent is the same as we found in Figure 13-2 for Project B — since no leverage was used, the ROE remains constant.

Now let's look at the situation if Bigbee decides to use 50 percent debt financing, with the debt costing 10 percent. Demand will not be affected, nor will operating costs, hence the EBIT columns are the same for the zero debt and 50 percent debt cases. However, the company will now have $100,000 of debt with a cost of 10 percent, hence its interest expense will be $10,000. This interest must be paid regardless of the state of the economy — if it is not paid, the company will be forced into bankruptcy, and stockholders will probably be wiped out. Therefore, we show a $10,000 cost in the third column as a fixed number for all demand conditions. The fourth column shows pre-tax income, the fifth the applicable taxes, and the sixth the resulting net income. When the net income figures are divided by the equity investment — which will now be only $100,000 because $100,000 of the $200,000 total requirement was obtained as debt — we find the ROEs under each demand state. If demand is terrible and sales are zero, then a very large loss will be incurred, and the ROE will be −42 percent. However, if demand is wonderful, then ROE will be a wonderful 78 percent. The probability-weighted average is the expected ROE, which is 18 percent if the company uses 50 percent debt.

Typically, financing with debt increases the expected rate of return for an investment, but debt also increases the riskiness of the investment to the owners of the firm, its common stockholders. This situation holds with our example — financial leverage raises the expected ROE from 12 percent to 18 percent, but it also increases the riskiness of the investment as measured by the coefficient of variation from 1.23 to 1.65.

Figure 13-4 graphs the data in Table 13-1. We see in another way that using financial leverage increases the expected ROE, but leverage also flattens out the

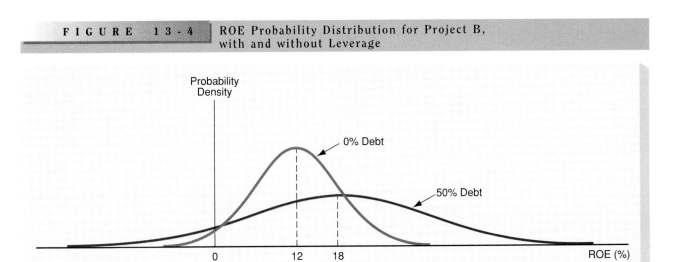

FIGURE 13-4 ROE Probability Distribution for Project B, with and without Leverage

probability distribution and increases the probability of a large loss, thus increasing the risk borne by stockholders.

We can summarize the discussion to this point:

1. Some amount of *business risk* is inherent in all assets other than riskless bonds, and business risk is generally higher if the firm chooses to use more *operating leverage.*

2. The concepts of business risk and operating leverage can be applied to whole firms as well as to investment projects. If a firm accepts a number of capital budgeting projects which have high business risk and operating leverage, then the firm itself will have high business risk and operating leverage. Diversification may mitigate business risk to some extent, but in general taking on a lot of risky projects results in a risky firm.

3. Although using more operating leverage generally increases a firm's or project's risk, higher operating leverage also increases the expected rate of return.

4. Assets, including whole firms, must be financed, and the two basic types of capital are debt or equity. In general, increasing the use of debt increases the expected rate of return, but more debt also means that the firm's stockholders must bear more risk.

5. We see, then, that there are two types of leverage — operating leverage and financial leverage — and they both increase the expected returns to and risks borne by stockholders. Our examples demonstrate these points and, hopefully, make the situation intuitively clear. One can also develop the points algebraically, as we do in Appendix 13A, where we calculate the *degree of operating leverage,* the *degree of financial leverage,* and the *degree of total leverage.*

6. Our focus in this chapter is on capital structure, or the extent to which debt is used to finance assets. We see that as a general proposition, financial leverage raises the expected rate of return, but at the cost of increased risk. So, we are faced with a trade-off: If we use more financial leverage, we increase the expected rate of return, which is good, but we also increase risk, which is bad.

7. This raises two related questions: (1) Is the higher expected rate of return associated with debt sufficient to compensate for the increased risk resulting from its use, and (2) what is the optimal amount of debt for a firm to use? The answer to both questions is essentially the same: If using debt increases the value of the firm, then use it, and the debt ratio that maximizes the firm's value is the optimal capital structure. It is not easy to measure the effects of capital structure on stock prices, but this is the essence of the capital structure decision. In the remainder of the chapter we discuss the types of analysis that financial managers go through when establishing their firms' capital structures.

SELF-TEST QUESTIONS ??????

Explain the difference between business risk and financial risk.

Identify some of the more important factors that affect business risk.

Why does business risk vary from industry to industry?

What is financial risk, and how does it arise?

| TABLE 13 - 2 | Data on Bigbee Electronics Company |

I. Balance Sheet on 12/31/97

Current assets	$100,000	Debt	$ 0
Net fixed assets	100,000	Common equity (10,000 shares)	200,000
Total assets	$200,000	Total liabilities and equity	$200,000

II. Income Statement for 1997

Sales		$200,000
Fixed operating costs	$ 40,000	
Variable operating costs	120,000	160,000
Earnings before interest and taxes (EBIT)		$ 40,000
Interest		0
Earnings before taxes		$ 40,000
Taxes (40%)		16,000
Net income		$ 24,000

III. Other Data

1. Earnings per share = EPS = $24,000/10,000 shares = $2.40.
2. Dividends per share = DPS = $24,000/10,000 shares = $2.40. (Thus, Bigbee pays out all of its earnings as dividends.)
3. Book value per share = $200,000/10,000 shares = $20.
4. Market price per share = P_0 = $20. (Thus, the stock sells at its book value, so M/B = 1.0.)
5. Price/earnings ratio = P/E = $20/$2.40 = 8.33 times.

DETERMINING THE OPTIMAL CAPITAL STRUCTURE

In the preceding section we used one of Bigbee Electronics Company's capital budgeting projects to illustrate operating and financial leverage. We stated, though, that the same leverage concepts and methods of analysis could be applied to entire companies, and in this section we consider Bigbee as a whole. The company has acquired assets over time through the capital budgeting process, those assets have their own unique business risks and operating leverage, and the company's business risk reflects the riskiness of its individual assets.[5]

Bigbee's greatly simplified financial statements are shown in Table 13-2. We have omitted three zeros from the dollar figures and from the number of shares to simplify the arithmetic throughout the chapter. To date, the company has never used debt, but the treasurer is now considering a possible change in the capital structure. If Bigbee does decide to use some debt, how far should it go? *The*

---

[5]The company's business risk is less than the weighted average of the riskiness of its individual assets. Because of diversification effects, some of the riskiness of the individual assets will be eliminated when they are combined into the firm's "portfolio of assets." The extent to which diversification lowers risk depends on how closely returns on the various assets are correlated with each other. See Chapters 5 and 12 for further discussion.

TABLE 13 - 3	Interest Rates for Bigbee with Different Debt/Assets Ratios

AMOUNT BORROWED[a]	DEBT/ASSETS RATIO	INTEREST RATE, k_d, ON ALL DEBT
$ 20,000	10%	8.0%
40,000	20	8.3
60,000	30	9.0
80,000	40	10.0
100,000	50	12.0
120,000	60	15.0

[a]We assume that the firm must borrow in increments of $20,000. We also assume that Bigbee is unable to borrow more than $120,000, which is 60 percent of its $200,000 of assets, because of restrictions in its corporate charter.

answer is that the company should use the amount of debt, or the capital structure, that maximizes the price of its stock.

EBIT/EPS ANALYSIS

Changes in the use of debt will cause changes in earnings per share (EPS) and, consequently, in the stock price. To understand the relationship between financial leverage and EPS, first consider Table 13-3, which shows how Bigbee's cost of debt would vary if it used different percentages of debt. The higher the percentage of debt, the riskier the debt, hence the higher the interest rate lenders will charge.

Now consider Table 13-4, which shows how expected EPS varies with changes in financial leverage. Section I of the table begins with a probability distribution of sales; we assume for simplicity that sales can take on only three values, $100,000, $200,000, or $300,000. In the remainder of Section I, we calculate EBIT at each sales level. We assume that both sales and operating costs are independent of financial leverage, so the three EBIT figures ($0, $40,000, and $80,000) will always remain the same, no matter how much debt Bigbee uses.[6]

Section II of Table 13-4, the zero debt case, calculates Bigbee's earnings per share at each sales level under the assumption that the company continues to use no debt. Net income is divided by the 10,000 shares outstanding to obtain EPS. If sales are as low as $100,000, EPS will be zero, but EPS will rise to $4.80

---

[6]In the real world, capital structure does at times affect EBIT. First, if debt levels are excessive, the firm will probably find it difficult to obtain financing if its earnings are low at a time when interest rates are high. This could lead to stop-start construction and R&D programs, as well as to having to pass up good investment opportunities. Second, a weak financial condition (i.e., too much debt) could cause a firm to lose sales. For example, prior to the time that its huge debt forced Eastern Airlines into bankruptcy, many people refused to buy Eastern tickets because they were afraid the company would go bankrupt and leave them holding unusable tickets. Third, financially strong companies are able to bargain hard with their unions and suppliers, whereas weaker ones may have to give in simply because they do not have the financial resources to carry on the fight. Finally, a company with so much debt that bankruptcy is a serious threat will have difficulty attracting and retaining managers and employees, or it will have to pay premium salaries. People value job security, and financially weak companies simply cannot provide such protection. For all these reasons, it is not totally correct to say that a firm's financial policy has no effect on its operating income.

TABLE 13-4	EPS with Different Amounts of Financial Leverage (Thousands of Dollars, except Per-Share Figures)

I. Calculation of EBIT

Probability of indicated sales	0.2	0.6	0.2
Sales	$100.0	$200.0	$300.0
Fixed costs	40.0	40.0	40.0
Variable costs (60% of sales)	60.0	120.0	180.0
Total costs (except interest)	$100.0	$160.0	$220.0
Earnings before interest and taxes (EBIT)	$ 0.0	$ 40.0	$ 80.0

II. Situation if Debt/Assets (D/A) = 0%

EBIT (from Section I)	$ 0.0	$ 40.0	$ 80.0
Less interest	0.0	0.0	0.0
Earnings before taxes (EBT)	$ 0.0	$ 40.0	$ 80.0
Taxes (40%)	0.0	(16.0)	(32.0)
Net income	$ 0.0	$ 24.0	$ 48.0
Earnings per share (EPS) on 10,000 shares[a]	$ 0.0	$ 2.40	$ 4.80
Expected EPS		$ 2.40	
Standard deviation of EPS		$ 1.52	
Coefficient of variation		0.63	

III. Situation if Debt/Assets (D/A) = 50%

EBIT (from Section I)	$ 0.0	$ 40.0	$ 80.0
Less interest (0.12 × $100,000)	12.0	12.0	12.0
Earnings before taxes (EBT)	($ 12.0)	$ 28.0	$ 68.0
Taxes (40%; tax credit on losses)	4.8	(11.2)	(27.2)
Net income	($ 7.2)	$ 16.8	$ 40.8
Earnings per share (EPS) on 5,000 shares[a]	($ 1.44)	$ 3.36	$ 8.16
Expected EPS		$ 3.36	
Standard deviation of EPS		$ 3.04	
Coefficient of variation		0.90	

[a]The EPS figures can also be obtained using the following formula, in which the numerator amounts to an income statement at a given sales level laid out horizontally:

$$\text{EPS} = \frac{(\text{Sales} - \text{Fixed costs} - \text{Variable costs} - \text{Interest})(1 - \text{Tax rate})}{\text{Shares outstanding}} = \frac{(\text{EBIT} - \text{I})(1 - \text{T})}{\text{Shares outstanding}}.$$

For example, with zero debt and Sales = $200,000, EPS is $2.40:

$$\text{EPS}_{D/A=0} = \frac{(\$200,000 - \$40,000 - \$120,000 - 0)(0.6)}{10,000} = \$2.40.$$

With 50 percent debt and Sales = $200,000, EPS is $3.36:

$$\text{EPS}_{D/A=0.5} = \frac{(\$200,000 - \$40,000 - \$120,000 - \$12,000)(0.6)}{5,000} = \$3.36.$$

The sales level at which EPS will be equal under the two financing policies, or the indifference level of sales, S_I, can be found by setting $\text{EPS}_{D/A=0}$ equal to $\text{EPS}_{D/A=0.5}$ and solving for S_I:

$$\text{EPS}_{D/A=0} = \frac{(S_I - \$40,000 - 0.6S_I - 0)(0.6)}{10,000} = \frac{(S_I - \$40,000 - 0.6S_I - \$12,000)(0.6)}{5,000} = \text{EPS}_{D/A=0.5}.$$

$S_I = \$160,000$.

By substituting this value of sales into either equation, we can find EPS_I, the earnings per share at this indifference point. In our example, $\text{EPS}_I = \$1.44$.

FIGURE 13-5 Probability Distributions of EPS with Different Amounts of Financial Leverage

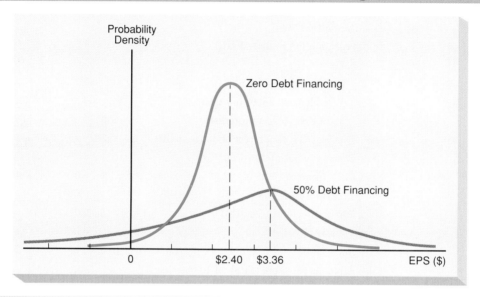

at a sales level of $300,000. The EPS at each sales level is then multiplied by the probability of that sales level to calculate the expected EPS, which is $2.40 if Bigbee uses no debt. We also calculate the standard deviation of EPS and the coefficient of variation as indicators of the firm's risk at a zero debt ratio: $\sigma_{EPS} = \$1.52$, and $CV_{EPS} = 0.63$.[7]

Section III shows the results if Bigbee financed with a debt/assets ratio of 50 percent. In this situation, $100,000 of the $200,000 total capital would be debt. The interest rate on the debt, 12 percent, is taken from Table 13-3. With $100,000 of 12 percent debt outstanding, the company's interest expense in Table 13-4 would be $12,000 per year. This is a fixed cost — it is the same regardless of the level of sales — and it is deducted from the EBIT values as calculated in the top section. Next, taxes are taken out to calculate net income. EPS is then calculated as net income divided by shares outstanding. With debt = 0, there would be 10,000 shares outstanding. However, if half of the equity were replaced by debt (debt = $100,000), there would be only 5,000 shares outstanding, and we must use this fact to determine the EPS figures that would result at each of the three possible sales levels.[8] With a debt/assets ratio of 50 percent, the EPS figure would be −$1.44 if sales were as low as $100,000; it would rise to $3.36 if sales were $200,000; and it would soar to $8.16 if sales were as high as $300,000.

The EPS distributions under the two financial structures are graphed in Figure 13-5, where we use continuous distributions rather than the discrete distributions contained in Table 13-4. Although expected EPS would be much higher

---

[7]See Chapter 5 for a review of procedures for calculating the standard deviation and coefficient of variation. Recall that the advantage of the coefficient of variation is that it permits better comparisons when the expected values of EPS vary, as they do here for the two capital structures.

[8]We assume in this example that the firm could change its capital structure by repurchasing common stock at its book value of $100,000/5,000 shares = $20 per share. However, the firm may actually have to pay a higher price to repurchase its stock on the open market. If Bigbee had to pay $22 per share, then it could repurchase only $100,000/$22 = 4,545 shares, and, in this case, expected EPS would be only $16,800/(10,000 − 4,545) = $16,800/5,455 = $3.08 rather than $3.36.

| FIGURE 13-6 | Relationships among Expected EPS, Risk, and Financial Leverage |

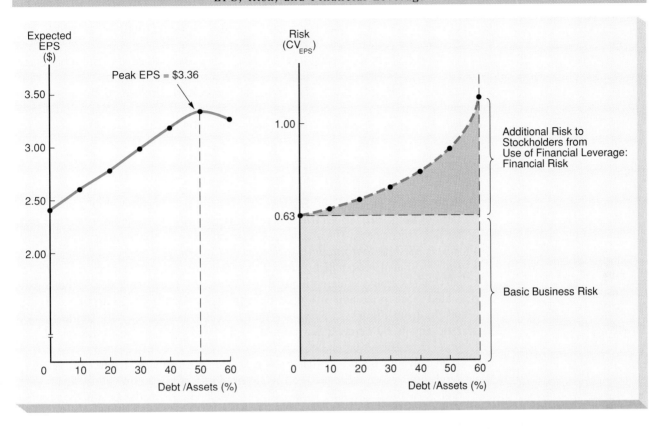

DEBT/ASSETS RATIO	EXPECTED EPS	STANDARD DEVIATION OF EPS	COEFFICIENT OF VARIATION
0%[a]	$2.40[a]	$1.52[a]	0.63[a]
10	2.56	1.69	0.66
20	2.75	1.90	0.69
30	2.97	2.17	0.73
40	3.20	2.53	0.79
50[a]	3.36[a]	3.04[a]	0.90[a]
60	3.30	3.79	1.15

[a]Values for D/A = 0 and D/A = 50 percent are taken from Table 13-4. Values at other D/A ratios were calculated similarly.

if financial leverage were employed, the graph makes it clear that the risk of low, or even negative, EPS would also be higher if debt were used.

Another view of the relationships among expected EPS, risk, and financial leverage is presented in Figure 13-6. The tabular data in the lower section were calculated in the manner set forth in Table 13-4, and the graphs plot these data. Here we see that expected EPS rises until the firm is financed with 50 percent debt. Interest charges rise, but this effect is more than offset by the declining number of shares outstanding as debt is substituted for equity. However, EPS peaks at a debt ratio of 50 percent, beyond which interest rates rise so rapidly that EPS falls in spite of the falling number of shares outstanding.

The right panel of Figure 13-6 shows that risk, as measured by the coefficient of variation of EPS, rises continuously, and at an increasing rate, as debt is substituted for equity.

We see, then, that using leverage has both good and bad effects: higher leverage increases expected earnings per share (in this example, until the D/A ratio equals 50 percent), but it also increases risk. Clearly, Bigbee's debt ratio should not exceed 50 percent, but where, in the range of 0 to 50 percent, should it be set? This issue is discussed in the following sections.

THE EFFECT OF CAPITAL STRUCTURE ON STOCK PRICES AND THE COST OF CAPITAL

As we saw in Figure 13-6, Bigbee's expected EPS is maximized at a debt/assets ratio of 50 percent. Does this mean that Bigbee's optimal capital structure calls for 50 percent debt? The answer is a resounding no — *the optimal capital structure is the one that maximizes the price of the firm's stock, and this generally calls for a debt ratio which is lower than the one that maximizes expected EPS.*

This statement is demonstrated in Table 13-5, which develops Bigbee's estimated stock price and WACC at different debt/assets ratios. Carrying over the results from Figure 13-6, we see that EPS is maximized when the debt/assets ratio equals 50 percent; however, the estimated stock price is maximized at a lower debt level (40 percent debt).

Recall from Chapter 8 that stock prices are positively related to expected dividends but negatively related to the required rate of return on equity. Firms with higher earnings are able to pay higher dividends, so to the extent that higher debt levels raise expected earnings per share, leverage works to increase the stock price. However, higher debt levels also increase the firm's risk, and that raises the cost of equity and works to reduce the stock price. So, even though increasing the debt ratio from 40 to 50 percent raises EPS, the higher EPS is more than offset by the corresponding increase in risk.

Notice from Table 13-5 that increases in the debt/assets ratio raise the cost of both debt and equity. (The cost of debt, k_d, is taken from Table 13-3.) Bondholders recognize that, other things held constant, firms with higher debt levels are more likely to experience financial distress, which explains why increases in the debt/assets ratio raise the cost of debt. Also, recall from Chapter 5 that a stock's beta measures its relative volatility as compared with that of an average stock. The beta coefficients shown in Column 4 of Table 13-5 were estimated by management. It has been demonstrated both theoretically and empirically that a firm's beta increases with its financial leverage. The exact nature of this relationship for a given firm is difficult to estimate, but the values given in Column 4 show management's estimates of the relationship for Bigbee.

Assuming that the risk-free rate of return, k_{RF}, is 6 percent, and that the required return on an average stock, k_M, is 10 percent, we can use the CAPM equation to develop estimates of the required rates of return, k_s, for Bigbee as shown in Column 5. Here we see that k_s is 12 percent if no financial leverage is used, but k_s rises to 16.8 percent if the company finances with 60 percent debt, the maximum permitted by its charter.

Figure 13-7 graphs Bigbee's required rate of return on equity at different debt levels. The figure also shows the composition of Bigbee's required return: the

| TABLE 13-5 | Bigbee's Stock Price and Cost of Capital Estimates with Different Debt/Assets Ratios |

DEBT/ ASSETS (1)	k_d (2)	EXPECTED EPS (AND DPS)[a] (3)	ESTIMATED BETA (4)	$k_s = [k_{RF} + (k_M - k_{RF})b]$[b] (5)	ESTIMATED PRICE[c] (6)	RESULTING P/E RATIO (7)	WEIGHTED AVERAGE COST OF CAPITAL, WACC[d] (8)
0%	—	$ 2.40	1.50	12.0%	$ 20.00	8.33	12.00%
10	8.0%	2.56	1.55	12.2	20.98	8.20	11.46
20	8.3	2.75	1.65	12.6	21.83	7.94	11.08
30	9.0	2.97	1.80	13.2	22.50	7.58	10.86
40	**10.0**	**3.20**	**2.00**	**14.0**	**22.86**	**7.14**	**10.80**
50	12.0	3.36	2.30	15.2	22.11	6.58	11.20
60	15.0	3.30	2.70	16.8	19.64	5.95	12.12

[a]Bigbee pays all of its earnings out as dividends, so EPS = DPS.

[b]We assume that k_{RF} = 6% and k_M = 10%. Therefore, at debt/assets equal to zero, k_s = 6% + (10% − 6%)1.5 = 6% + 6% = 12%. Other values of k_s are calculated similarly.

[c]Since all earnings are paid out as dividends, no retained earnings will be plowed back into the business, and growth in EPS and DPS will be zero. Hence, the zero growth stock price model developed in Chapter 8 can be used to estimate the price of Bigbee's stock. For example, at debt/assets = 0,

$$P_0 = \frac{DPS}{k_s} = \frac{\$2.40}{0.12} = \$20.$$

Other prices were calculated similarly.

[d]Column 8 is found by use of the weighted average cost of capital (WACC) equation developed in Chapter 9:

$$WACC = w_d k_d (1 - T) + w_{ce} k_s$$
$$= (D/A)(k_d)(1 - T) + (1 - D/A)k_s.$$

For example, at D/A = 40%,

$$WACC = 0.4(10\%)(0.6) + 0.6(14.0\%) = 10.80\%.$$

We use book weights here, but market value weights would be theoretically better. See *Intermediate Financial Management*, 5th Edition, Chapter 12, for a discussion of this point.

risk-free rate of 6 percent plus premiums for business and financial risk. As you can see from the graph, the business risk premium does not depend on the debt level — it remains constant at 6 percent at all debt levels. However, the premium for financial risk varies depending on the debt level — the higher the debt level, the greater the risk premium.

The zero growth stock valuation model developed in Chapter 8 is used in Table 13-5, along with the Column 3 values of DPS and the Column 5 values of k_s, to develop the estimated stock prices shown in Column 6. Here we see that the expected stock price first rises with financial leverage, hits a peak of $22.86 at a debt/assets ratio of 40 percent, and then begins to decline. *Thus, Bigbee's optimal capital structure calls for 40 percent debt.*

The price/earnings ratios shown in Column 7 were calculated by dividing the price in Column 6 by the expected earnings given in Column 3. We use the pattern of P/E ratios as a check on the "reasonableness" of the other data. Other things held constant, P/E ratios should decline as a firm's riskiness increases, and that pattern is shown in our illustrative case. Also, at the time Bigbee's data were being analyzed, the P/Es shown here were generally consistent with those

FIGURE 13 - 7   Bigbee's Required Rate of Return
on Equity at Different Debt Levels

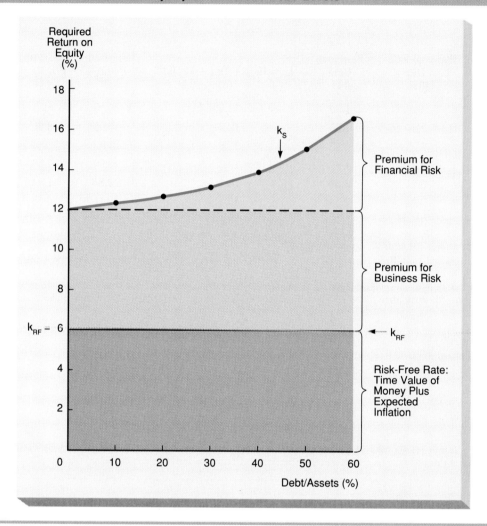

of zero growth companies with varying amounts of financial leverage. Thus, the
data in Column 7 reinforce our confidence in the reasonableness of the estimated
prices shown in Column 6.

Finally, Column 8 shows Bigbee's weighted average cost of capital, WACC, calculated as described in Chapter 9, at the different capital structures. If the company uses zero debt, its capital is all equity, so WACC = k_s = 12%. As the firm
begins to use lower-cost debt, its weighted average cost of capital declines. However, as the debt ratio increases, the costs of both debt and equity rise, and the
increasing costs of the two components begin to offset the fact that larger
amounts of low-cost debt are being used. At 40 percent debt, WACC hits a minimum of 10.8 percent, and it rises after that as the debt ratio is increased.

It can be seen that the capital structure that maximizes the firm's stock price
is also the capital structure that minimizes its WACC. Note too that even

though the component cost of equity is generally higher than that of debt, using only lower-cost debt would not maximize value because of the feedback effects of debt on the costs of debt and equity. If Bigbee were to issue more than 40 percent debt, it would then be relying more on the cheaper source of capital, but this lower cost would be more than offset by the fact that using more debt would raise the costs of both debt and equity. These thoughts were echoed in a recent Annual Report of the Georgia-Pacific Corporation:

> On a market-value basis, our debt-to-capital ratio was 47 percent. By employing this capital structure, we believe that our weighted average cost of capital is nearly optimized — at approximately 10 percent. Although reducing debt significantly would somewhat reduce the marginal cost of debt, significant debt reduction would likely increase our weighted average cost of capital by raising the proportion of higher-cost equity.

The EPS, cost of capital, and stock price data shown in Table 13-5 are plotted in Figure 13-8. As the graph shows, the debt/assets ratio that maximizes Bigbee's expected EPS is 50 percent. However, the expected stock price is maximized, and the cost of capital is minimized, at a 40 percent debt ratio. *Thus, Bigbee's optimal capital structure calls for 40 percent debt and 60 percent equity.* Management should set its target capital structure at these ratios, and if the existing ratios are off target, it should move toward the target when new security offerings are made.

SELF-TEST QUESTIONS ??????

Explain this statement: "Using leverage has both good and bad effects."

Is expected EPS maximized at the optimal capital structure?

LIQUIDITY AND CASH FLOW ANALYSIS

There are some practical difficulties with the types of analyses described thus far in the chapter, including the following:

1. It is virtually impossible to determine exactly how either P/E ratios or equity capitalization rates (k_s values) are affected by different degrees of financial leverage. The best we can do is make educated guesses about these relationships. Therefore, management rarely, if ever, has sufficient confidence in the type of analysis set forth in Table 13-5 and Figure 13-8 to use it as the sole determinant of the target capital structure.

2. A firm's managers may be more or less conservative than the average stockholder, hence management may set a somewhat different target capital structure than the one that would maximize the stock price. The managers of a publicly owned firm would never admit this, for unless they owned voting control, they would quickly be removed from office. However, in view of the uncertainties about what constitutes the value-maximizing capital structure, management could always say that the target capital structure employed is, in its judgment, the value-maximizing structure, and it would be difficult to prove otherwise. Still, if management is far off target, especially on the low

FIGURE 13-8 Effects of Capital Structure on EPS, Cost of Capital, and Stock Price

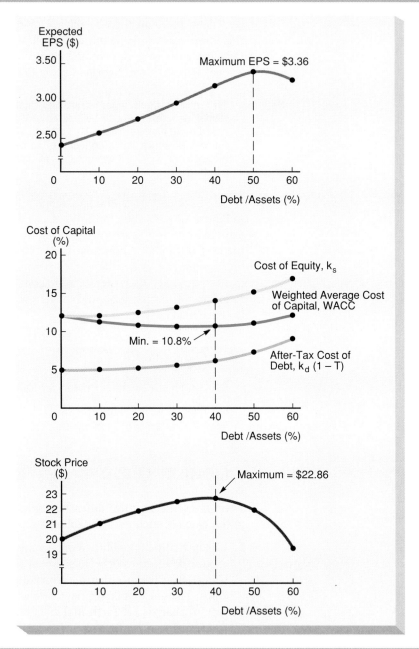

side, then chances are high that some other firm or management group will take the company over, increase its leverage, and thereby raise its value. This point is discussed in more detail later in the chapter.

3. Managers of large firms, especially those which provide vital services such as electricity or telephones, have a responsibility to provide *continuous* service; therefore, they must refrain from using leverage to the point where the firms'

| FIGURE 13-9 | Bigbee's Probability of Default at Different Debt Levels |

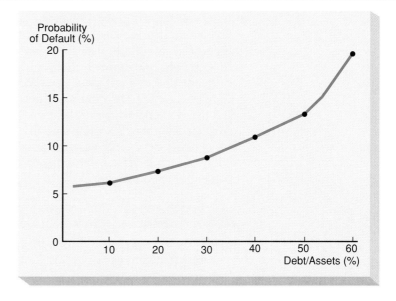

DEBT/ASSETS	EXPECTED TIE[a]	PROBABILITY OF DEFAULT AS MEASURED BY TIE < 1.0
10%	25.0	6.4%
20	12.0	7.4
30	7.4	8.5
40	5.0	10.6
50	3.3	13.6
60	2.2	19.5

[a]TIE = EBIT/Interest. For example, when debt/assets = 50%, TIE = $40,000/$12,000 = 3.3. Data are from Tables 13-3 and 13-4. Probabilities were found using Z tables from any statistics text.

long-run viability is endangered. Long-run viability may conflict with short-run stock price maximization and capital cost minimization.[9]

For all of these reasons, managers are concerned about the effects of financial leverage on the risk of bankruptcy, so an analysis of potential financial distress is an important input in all capital structure decisions. Accordingly, managements give considerable weight to financial strength indicators such as the **times-interest-earned (TIE) ratio.** The lower this ratio, the higher the probability that a firm will default on its debt and be forced into bankruptcy.

The tabular material in the lower section of Figure 13-9 shows Bigbee's expected TIE ratio at several different debt/assets ratios. If the debt/assets ratio were

Times-Interest-Earned (TIE) Ratio
A ratio that measures the firm's ability to meet its annual interest obligations, calculated by dividing earnings before interest and taxes by interest charges: $TIE = \dfrac{EBIT}{I}$.

[9]Recognizing this fact, most public utility commissions require utilities to obtain approval before issuing long-term securities, and Congress has empowered the SEC to supervise the capital structures of public utility holding companies. However, in addition to concern over the firms' safety, which suggests low debt ratios, both managers and regulators recognize a need to keep all costs as low as possible, including the cost of capital. Since a firm's capital structure affects its cost of capital, regulatory commissions and utility managers try to select capital structures that will minimize the cost of capital, subject to the constraint that the firm's financial flexibility not be endangered.

only 10 percent, the expected TIE would be a high 25 times, and the probability of the actual TIE falling below 1.0 would be only 6.4 percent. However, the expected interest coverage ratio would decline rapidly if the debt ratio were increased, and the probability of the actual TIE falling below 1.0 would rise. We must stress that the coverages shown in the table are the *expected* values at different debt ratios, and that the *actual* TIE at any debt ratio would be higher if sales exceeded the expected $200,000 level, but lower if sales fell below $200,000.

Figure 13-9 graphs Bigbee's probability of default at different levels of debt. In Bigbee's case, the TIE ratio has a normal distribution, and we used that fact to find the area under the normal curve to the left of 1.0. This number represents the probability that the company will have a TIE ratio less than 1.0 and thus will not be covering its interest expense. We have defined this area to be the probability of default. As you can see from the graph, the chance of default increases as the debt ratio increases.[10]

SELF-TEST QUESTION

Why do managers give considerable weight to the TIE ratio when they make capital structure decisions? Why not just use the capital structure that maximizes the stock price?

CAPITAL STRUCTURE THEORY

Modern capital structure theory began in 1958, when Professors Franco Modigliani and Merton Miller (hereafter MM) published what has been called the most influential finance article ever written.[11] MM proved, under a very restrictive set of assumptions, that a firm's value is unaffected by its capital structure. Put another way — MM's results suggest that it does not matter how a firm finances its operations, so capital structure is irrelevant. However, MM's study was based on some unrealistic assumptions, including the following:

1. There are no brokerage costs.
2. There are no taxes.
3. There are no bankruptcy costs.
4. Investors can borrow at the same rate as corporations.
5. All investors have the same information as management about the firm's future investment opportunities.
6. EBIT is not affected by the use of debt.

Despite the fact that some of these assumptions are obviously unrealistic, MM's irrelevance result is extremely important. By indicating the conditions under which capital structure is irrelevant, MM also provided us with some clues about

---

[10]Note that cash flows, which include depreciation, can be sufficient to cover required interest payments even though the TIE is less than 1.0. Thus, at least for a while, a firm may be able to avoid bankruptcy even though its operating income is less than its interest charges. However, most debt contracts stipulate that firms must maintain the TIE ratio above some minimum level, say, 2.0 or 2.5, or else they cannot borrow any additional funds, which can severely constrain operations. Such potential constraints, as much as the threat of actual bankruptcy, limit the use of debt.

[11]Franco Modigliani and Merton H. Miller, "The Cost of Capital, Corporation Finance, and the Theory of Investment," *American Economic Review*, June 1958. Modigliani and Miller both won Nobel Prizes for their work.

INDUSTRY PRACTICE

YOGI BERRA ON THE M&M PROPOSITION

When a waitress asked Yogi Berra (Baseball Hall of Fame catcher for the New York Yankees) whether he wanted his pizza cut into four pieces or eight, Yogi replied: "Better make it four, I don't think I can eat eight."[12]

Yogi's quip helps convey the basic insight of Modigliani and Miller. The firm's choice of leverage "slices" the distribution of future cash flows in a way that is like slicing a pizza. M&M recognize that if you fix a company's investment activities, it's like fixing the size of the pizza; no information costs means that everyone sees the same pizza; no taxes means the IRS gets none of the pie; and no "contracting" costs means nothing sticks to the knife.

So, just as the substance of Yogi's meal is unaffected by whether the pizza is sliced into four pieces or eight, the economic substance of the firm is unaffected by whether the liability side of the balance sheet is sliced to include more or less debt.

[12]Lee Green, *Sportswit* (New York: Fawcett Crest, 1984), 228.

SOURCE: "Yogi Berra on the M&M Proposition," *Journal of Applied Corporate Finance*, Vol. 7, no. 4, Winter 1995, 6. Used by permission.

---

what is required for capital structure to be relevant and hence to affect a firm's value. MM's work marked the beginning of modern capital structure research, and subsequent research has focused on relaxing the MM assumptions in order to develop a more realistic theory of capital structure. Research in this area is quite extensive, but the highlights are summarized in the following sections.

THE EFFECT OF TAXES

MM published a follow-up paper in 1963 in which they relaxed the assumption that there are no corporate taxes.[13] The tax code allows corporations to deduct interest payments as an expense, but dividend payments to stockholders are not deductible. This differential treatment encourages corporations to use debt in their capital structures. Indeed, MM demonstrated that if all their other assumptions hold, this differential treatment leads to a situation which calls for 100 percent debt financing.

However, this conclusion was modified several years later by Merton Miller (this time without Modigliani) when he brought in the effects of personal taxes.[14] He noted that all of the income from bonds is generally interest, which is taxed as personal income at rates going up to 39.6 percent, while income from stocks generally comes partly from dividends and partly from capital gains. Further, capital gains are taxed at a maximum rate of 28 percent, and this tax is deferred until the stock is sold and the gain realized. If stock is held until the owner dies, no capital gains tax whatever must be paid. So, on balance, returns on common stocks are taxed at lower effective rates than returns on debt.

Because of the tax situation, Miller argued that investors are willing to accept relatively low before-tax returns on stock relative to the before-tax returns on bonds. (The situation here is similar to that with tax-exempt municipal bonds as discussed in Chapter 7 and preferred stocks held by corporate investors as discussed in Chapter 8.) For example, an investor might require a return of 10 percent on Bigbee's bonds, and if stock income were taxed at the same rate as bond

---

[13]Franco Modigliani and Merton H. Miller, "Corporate Income Taxes and the Cost of Capital: A Correction," *American Economic Review* 53, June 1963, 433–443.

[14]Merton H. Miller, "Debt and Taxes," *Journal of Finance* 32, May 1977, 261–275.

income, the required rate of return on Bigbee's stock might be 16 percent because of the stock's greater risk. However, in view of the favorable treatment of income on the stock, investors might be willing to accept a before-tax return of only 14 percent on the stock.

Thus, as Miller pointed out, (1) the *deductibility of interest* favors the use of debt financing, but (2) the *more favorable tax treatment of income from stocks* lowers the required rate of return on stock and thus favors the use of equity financing. It is difficult to say what the net effect of these two factors is. Most observers believe that interest deductibility has the stronger effect, hence that our tax system still favors the corporate use of debt. However, that effect is certainly reduced by the lower capital gains tax rate.

One can observe changes in corporate financing patterns following major changes in tax rates. For example, in 1993 the top personal tax rate on interest and dividends was raised sharply, but the capital gains tax rate was not increased. This could be expected to result in a greater reliance on equity financing, especially through retained earnings, and that has indeed been the case.

THE EFFECT OF BANKRUPTCY COSTS

MM's irrelevance results also depended on the assumption that there are no bankruptcy costs. However, in practice bankruptcy can be quite costly. Firms in bankruptcy have very high legal and accounting expenses, and they also have a hard time retaining customers, suppliers, and employees. Moreover, bankruptcy often forces a firm to liquidate or sell assets for less than they would be worth if the firm were to continue operating. For example, if a steel manufacturer goes out of business, it might be hard to find buyers for the company's plant and equipment, even though the equipment was quite expensive. Assets such as plant and equipment are often illiquid because they are configured to a company's individual needs and also because they are difficult to disassemble and move.

Note, too, that the *threat of bankruptcy*, not just bankruptcy per se, brings about these problems. Key employees jump ship, suppliers refuse to grant credit, customers seek more stable suppliers, and lenders demand higher interest rates and impose more restrictive loan covenants.

Bankruptcy-related problems are more likely to arise when a firm includes more debt in its capital structure. Therefore, bankruptcy costs discourage firms from pushing their use of debt to excessive levels.

Bankruptcy-related costs have two components: (1) the probability of their occurrence and (2) the costs they would produce given that financial distress has arisen. Firms whose earnings are more volatile, all else equal, face a greater chance of bankruptcy and, therefore, should use less debt than more stable firms. This is consistent with our earlier point that firms with high operating leverage, and thus greater business risk, should limit their use of financial leverage. Likewise, firms which would face high costs in the event of financial distress should rely less heavily on debt. For example, firms whose assets are illiquid and thus would have to be sold at "fire sale" prices should limit their use of debt financing.

TRADE-OFF THEORY

The preceding arguments led to the development of what is called "the trade-off theory of leverage," in which firms trade off the benefits of debt financing (favorable corporate tax treatment) against the higher interest rates and bankruptcy costs. A summary of the trade-off theory is expressed graphically in Figure 13-10. Here are some observations about the figure:

1. The fact that interest is a deductible expense makes debt less expensive than common or preferred stock. In effect, the government pays part of the cost of debt capital, or, to put it another way, debt provides *tax shelter benefits*. As a result, using debt causes more of the firm's operating income (EBIT) to flow through to investors, so the more debt a company uses, the higher its value and stock price. Under the assumptions of the Modigliani-Miller with-taxes paper, a firm's stock price will be maximized if it uses virtually 100 percent debt, and the line labeled "MM Result Incorporating the Effects of Corporate Taxation" in Figure 13-10 expresses their idea of the relationship between stock prices and debt.

2. In the real world, firms rarely use 100 percent debt. One reason is the fact that stocks benefit from the lower capital gains tax. More importantly, firms limit their use of debt to hold down bankruptcy-related costs.

3. There is some threshold level of debt, labeled D_1 in Figure 13-10, below which the probability of bankruptcy is so low as to be immaterial. Beyond D_1, however, bankruptcy-related costs become increasingly important, and they reduce the tax benefits of debt at an increasing rate. In the range from D_1 to D_2, bankruptcy-related costs reduce but do not completely offset the tax benefits of debt, so the firm's stock price rises (but at a decreasing rate) as its debt ratio increases. However, beyond D_2, bankruptcy-related costs exceed the tax benefits, so from this point on increasing the debt ratio lowers the value of the stock. Therefore, D_2 is the optimal capital structure. Of course, D_1 and D_2

FIGURE 13 - 10 Effect of Leverage on the Value of Bigbee's Stock

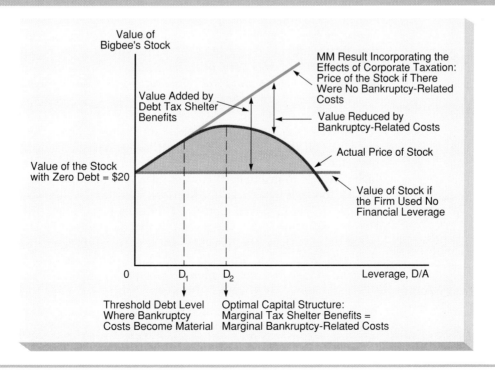

vary from firm to firm, depending on their business risk and bankruptcy costs.

4. While theoretical and empirical work supports the general shape of the curves in Figures 13-8 and 13-10, these graphs must be taken as approximations, not as precisely defined functions. The numbers in Figure 13-8 are shown out to two decimal places, but that is merely for illustrative purposes — the numbers are not nearly that accurate in view of the fact that the data on which the graph is based are judgmental estimates.

5. Another disturbing aspect of capital structure theory as expressed in Figure 13-10 is the fact that many large, successful firms, such as Intel and Microsoft, use far less debt than the theory suggests. This point led to the development of signaling theory, which is discussed below.

SIGNALING THEORY

Symmetric Information
The situation in which investors and managers have identical information about firms' prospects.

Asymmetric Information
The situation in which managers have different (better) information about firms' prospects than do investors.

MM assumed that investors have the same information about a firm's prospects as its managers — this is called **symmetric information.** However, in fact managers often have better information than outside investors. This is called **asymmetric information,** and it has an important effect on the optimal capital structure. To see why, consider two situations, one in which the company's managers know that its prospects are extremely favorable (Firm F) and one in which the managers know that the future looks unfavorable (Firm U).

Suppose, for example, that Firm F's R&D labs have just discovered a nonpatentable cure for the common cold. They want to keep the new product a secret as long as possible to delay competitors' entry into the market. New plants must be built to make the new product, so capital must be raised. How should Firm F's management raise the needed capital? If the firm sells stock, then, when profits from the new product start flowing in, the price of the stock would rise sharply, and the purchasers of the new stock would make a bonanza. The current stockholders (including the managers) would also do well, but not as well as they would have done if the company had not sold stock before the price increased, because then they would not have had to share the benefits of the new product with the new stockholders. *Therefore, one would expect a firm with very favorable prospects to try to avoid selling stock and, rather, to raise any required new capital by other means, including using debt beyond the normal target capital structure.*[15]

Now let's consider Firm U. Suppose its managers have information that new orders are off sharply because a competitor has installed new technology which has improved its products' quality. Firm U must upgrade its own facilities, at a high cost, just to maintain its current sales. As a result, its return on investment will fall (but not by as much as if it took no action, which would lead to a 100 percent loss through bankruptcy). How should Firm U raise the needed capital? Here the situation is just the reverse of that facing Firm F, which did not want to sell stock so as to avoid having to share the benefits of future developments. *A firm with unfavorable prospects would want to sell stock, which would mean bringing in new investors to share the losses!*[16]

---

[15]It would be illegal for Firm F's managers to personally purchase more shares on the basis of their inside knowledge of the new product. They could be sent to jail if they did.

[16]Of course, Firm U would have to make certain disclosures when it offered new shares to the public, but it might be able to meet the legal requirements without fully disclosing management's worst fears.

The conclusion from all this is that firms with extremely bright prospects prefer not to finance through new stock offerings, whereas firms with poor prospects do like to finance with outside equity. How should you, as an investor, react to this conclusion? You ought to say, "If I see that a company plans to issue new stock, this should worry me because I know that management would not want to issue stock if future prospects looked good. However, management would want to issue stock if things looked bad. Therefore, I should lower my estimate of the firm's value, other things held constant, if it issues new stock."

If you gave the above answer, your views are consistent with those of sophisticated portfolio managers of institutions such as Morgan Guaranty Trust, Prudential Insurance, and so forth. *In a nutshell, the announcement of a stock offering is generally taken as a* **signal** *that the firm's prospects as seen by its management are not bright.* This, in turn, suggests that when a firm announces a new stock offering, more often than not, the price of its stock will decline. Empirical studies have shown that this situation does indeed exist.[17]

What are the implications of all this for capital structure decisions? Since issuing stock emits a negative signal and thus tends to depress the stock price, even if the company's prospects are bright, a firm should, in normal times, maintain a **reserve borrowing capacity** which can be used in the event that some especially good investment opportunity comes along. *This means that firms should, in normal times, use more equity and less debt than is suggested by the tax benefit/bankruptcy cost trade-off model expressed in Figure 13-10.*

Signaling/asymmetric information concepts also have implications for the marginal cost of capital (MCC) curve as discussed in Chapter 9. There we saw that the weighted average cost of capital (WACC) jumped when retained earnings were exhausted and the firm was forced to sell new common stock to raise equity. The jump in the WACC, or the break in the MCC schedule, was attributed only to flotation costs. However, if the announcement of a stock sale causes a decline in the price of the stock, then k as measured by $k = D_1/P_0 + g$ will rise because of the decline in P_0. This factor reinforces the effects of flotation costs, and perhaps it is an even more important explanation for the jump in the MCC schedule at the point at which new stock must be issued. For example, assume that $P_0 = \$10$, $D_1 = \$1$, $g = 5\%$, and $F = 10\%$. Therefore, $k_s = 10\% + 5\% = 15\%$, and k_e, the cost of external equity, is 16.1 percent:

$$k_e = \frac{D_1}{P_0(1-F)} + g = \frac{\$1}{\$10(1.0 - 0.10)} + 5\% = 16.1\%.$$

Suppose, however, that the announcement of a stock sale causes the market price of the stock to fall from $P_0 = \$10$ to $P_0 = \$8$. This will increase the costs of both retained earnings (k_s) and external equity:

$$k_s = \frac{D_1}{P_0} + g = \frac{\$1}{\$8} + 5\% = 17.5\%.$$

$$k_e = \frac{D_1}{P_0(1-F)} + g = \frac{\$1}{\$8(0.9)} + 5\% = 18.9\%.$$

This would, of course, have significant implications for capital budgeting. Specifically, it would make it even more difficult for a marginal project to show a positive NPV if the project required the firm to sell stock to raise capital.

Signal
An action taken by a firm's management which provides clues to investors about how management views the firm's prospects.

Reserve Borrowing Capacity
The ability to borrow money at a reasonable cost when good investment opportunities arise. Firms often use less debt than specified by the MM optimal capital structure to ensure that they can obtain debt capital later if they need to.

[17]Paul Asquith and David W. Mullins, Jr., "The Impact of Initiating Dividend Payments on Shareholders' Wealth," *Journal of Business,* January 1983, 77–96.

USING DEBT FINANCING TO CONSTRAIN MANAGERS

In Chapter 1 we stated that agency problems may arise if managers and share-holders have different objectives. Such conflicts are particularly likely when the firm's managers have too much cash at their disposal. Managers often use such cash to finance their pet projects or for perquisites such as nicer offices, corporate jets, and tickets to sporting events, all of which may do little to maximize stock prices.[18] By contrast, managers with limited "free cash flow" are less able to make wasteful expenditures.

Firms can reduce excess cash flow in a variety of ways. One way is to funnel some of it back to shareholders through higher dividends or stock repurchases. Another alternative is to shift the capital structure toward more debt in the hope that higher debt service requirements will force managers to become more disciplined. If debt is not serviced as required, the firm will be forced into bankruptcy, in which case its managers would likely lose their jobs. Therefore, a manager is less likely to buy an expensive new corporate jet if the firm has large debt service requirements which could cost the manager his or her job.

A leveraged buyout (LBO) is one way to reduce excess cash flow. Recall from Chapter 1 that in an LBO debt is used to finance the purchase of a company's shares, after which the firm "goes private." Many leveraged buyouts, which were especially common during the late 1980s, were designed specifically to reduce corporate waste. As noted, high debt payments force managers to conserve cash by eliminating unnecessary expenditures.

Of course, increasing debt and reducing free cash flow has its downside: It increases the risk of bankruptcy. One professor has argued that adding debt to a firm's capital structure is like putting a dagger into the steering wheel of a car.[19] The dagger—which points toward your stomach—motivates you to drive more carefully, but you may get stabbed if someone runs into you, even if you are being careful. The analogy applies to corporations in the following sense: Higher debt forces managers to be more careful with shareholders' money, but even well-run firms could face bankruptcy (get stabbed) if some event beyond their control such as a war, an earthquake, a strike, or a recession occurs. To complete the analogy, the capital structure decision comes down to deciding how big a dagger stockholders should use to keep managers in line.

If you find our discussion of capital structure theory imprecise and somewhat confusing, you are not alone. In truth, no one knows how to identify precisely a firm's optimal capital structure, or how to measure the effects of capital structure on stock prices and the cost of capital. In practice, capital structure decisions must be made using a combination of judgment and numerical analysis. Still, an understanding of the theoretical issues presented here can help you make better judgments on capital structure issues.[20]

---

[18] If you don't believe corporate managers can waste money, read Bryan Burrough, *Barbarians at the Gate* (New York: Harper & Row, 1990), the story of the takeover of RJR-Nabisco.

[19] Ben Bernake, "Is There Too Much Corporate Debt?" Federal Reserve Bank of Philadelphia *Business Review,* September/October 1989, 3–13.

[20] One of the authors can report firsthand the usefulness of financial theory in the actual establishment of corporate capital structures. In recent years, he has served as a consultant to several of the regional telephone companies established as a result of the breakup of AT&T, as well as to several large electric utilities. On the basis of finance theory and computer models which simulated results under a range of conditions, the companies were able to specify "optimal capital structure ranges" with at least a reasonable degree of confidence. Without finance theory, setting a target capital structure would have amounted to little more than throwing darts.

Why did MM with taxes lead to 100 percent equity?

How would an increase in corporate taxes affect firms' capital structure decisions? What about personal taxes?

Explain how "asymmetric information" and "signals" affect capital structure decisions.

What is meant by *reserve borrowing capacity,* and why is it important to firms?

How can the use of debt serve to discipline managers?

CHECKLIST FOR CAPITAL STRUCTURE DECISIONS

In addition to the types of analysis discussed above, firms generally consider the following factors when making capital structure decisions:

1. **Sales stability.** A firm whose sales are relatively stable can safely take on more debt and incur higher fixed charges than a company with unstable sales. Utility companies, because of their stable demand, have historically been able to use more financial leverage than industrial firms.

2. **Asset structure.** Firms whose assets are suitable as security for loans tend to use debt rather heavily. General-purpose assets which can be used by many businesses make good collateral, whereas special-purpose assets do not. Thus, real estate companies are usually highly leveraged, whereas companies involved in technological research are not.

3. **Operating leverage.** Other things the same, a firm with less operating leverage is better able to employ financial leverage because it will have less business risk. (This is discussed in greater detail in Appendix 13A.)

4. **Growth rate.** Other things the same, faster-growing firms must rely more heavily on external capital (see Chapter 15). Further, the flotation costs involved in selling common stock exceed those incurred when selling debt, which encourages them to rely more heavily on debt. At the same time, however, rapidly growing firms often face greater uncertainty, which tends to reduce their willingness to use debt.

5. **Profitability.** One often observes that firms with very high rates of return on investment use relatively little debt. Although there is no theoretical justification for this fact, one practical explanation is that very profitable firms such as Intel, Microsoft, and Coca-Cola simply do not need to do much debt financing. Their high rates of return enable them to do most of their financing with internally generated funds.

6. **Taxes.** Interest is a deductible expense, and deductions are most valuable to firms with high tax rates. Therefore, the higher a firm's tax rate, the greater the advantage of debt.

7. **Control.** The effect of debt versus stock on a management's control position can influence capital structure. If management currently has voting control (over 50 percent of the stock) but is not in a position to buy any more stock, it may choose debt for new financings. On the other hand, management may decide to use equity if the firm's financial situation is so weak that the use

of debt might subject it to serious risk of default, because if the firm goes into default, the managers will almost surely lose their jobs. However, if too little debt is used, management runs the risk of a takeover. Thus, control considerations could lead to the use of *either* debt or equity, because the type of capital that best protects management will vary from situation to situation. In any event, if management is at all insecure, it will consider the control situation.

8. **Management attitudes.** Since no one can prove that one capital structure will lead to higher stock prices than another, management can exercise its own judgment about the proper capital structure. Some managements tend to be more conservative than others, and thus use less debt than the average firm in their industry, whereas aggressive managements use more debt in the quest for higher profits.

9. **Lender and rating agency attitudes.** Regardless of managers' own analyses of the proper leverage factors for their firms, lenders' and rating agencies' attitudes frequently influence financial structure decisions. In the majority of cases, the corporation discusses its capital structure with lenders and rating agencies and gives much weight to their advice. For example, one large utility was recently told by Moody and Standard & Poor that its bonds would be downgraded if it issued more bonds. This influenced its decision to finance its expansion with common equity.

10. **Market conditions.** Conditions in the stock and bond markets undergo both long- and short-run changes that can have an important bearing on a firm's optimal capital structure. For example, during a recent credit crunch, the junk bond market dried up, and there was simply no market at a "reasonable" interest rate for any new long-term bonds rated below triple B. Therefore, low-rated companies in need of capital were forced to go to the stock market or to the short-term debt market, regardless of their target capital structures. When conditions eased, however, these companies sold bonds to get their capital structures back on target.

11. **The firm's internal condition.** A firm's own internal condition can also have a bearing on its target capital structure. For example, suppose a firm has just successfully completed an R&D program, and it forecasts higher earnings in the immediate future. However, the new earnings are not yet anticipated by investors, hence are not reflected in the stock price. This company would not want to issue stock — it would prefer to finance with debt until the higher earnings materialize and are reflected in the stock price. Then it could sell an issue of common stock, retire the debt, and return to its target capital structure. This point was discussed earlier in connection with asymmetric information and signaling.

12. **Financial flexibility.** An astute corporate treasurer made this statement to the authors:

> Our company can earn a lot more money from good capital budgeting and operating decisions than from good financing decisions. Indeed, we are not sure exactly how financing decisions affect our stock price, but we know for sure that having to turn down a promising venture because funds are not available will reduce our long-run profitability. For this reason, my primary goal as treasurer is to always be in a position to raise the capital needed to support operations.
>
> We also know that when times are good, we can raise capital with either stocks or bonds, but when times are bad, suppliers of capital are much more willing to

make funds available if we give them a secured position, and this means debt. Further, when we sell a new issue of stock, this sends a negative "signal" to investors, so stock sales by a mature company such as ours are not desirable.

Putting all these thoughts together gives rise to the goal of *maintaining financial flexibility,* which, from an operational viewpoint, means *maintaining adequate reserve borrowing capacity.* Determining an "adequate" reserve borrowing capacity is judgmental, but it clearly depends on the factors discussed in the chapter, including the firm's forecasted need for funds, predicted capital market conditions, management's confidence in its forecasts, and the consequences of a capital shortage.

SELF-TEST QUESTIONS

How does sales stability affect the target capital structure?

How does the type of assets used affect a firm's capital structure?

How do taxes affect the target capital structure?

How do lender and rating agency attitudes affect capital structure?

How does the firm's internal condition affect its actual capital structure?

What is "financial flexibility," and is it increased or decreased by a high debt ratio?

VARIATIONS IN CAPITAL STRUCTURES

As might be expected, wide variations in the use of financial leverage occur both across industries and among the individual firms in each industry. Table 13-6

| TABLE 13-6 | Capital Structure Percentages, 1996: Six Industries Ranked by Common Equity Ratios[a] |

INDUSTRY	COMMON EQUITY RATIO[b] (1)	LONG-TERM DEBT RATIO (2)	TIMES-INTEREST-EARNED RATIO (3)	RETURN ON EQUITY (4)
Computers	76.34%	23.66%	7.8×	10.3%
Pharmaceuticals	74.07	25.93	16.2	29.2
Aerospace and defense[c]	70.92	29.08	4.1	8.1
Steel	68.03	31.97	6.3	16.4
Utilities[d]	48.13	51.87	3.0	12.1
Airlines	27.55	72.45	2.2	17.2

NOTES: [a]Capital structure ratios are calculated as a percentage of total capital, where total capital is defined as long-term debt plus equity.

[b]These ratios are based on accounting (or book) values. Stated on a market-value basis, the equity percentages would rise because most stocks sell at prices that are much higher than their book values. Capital is defined as long-term debt plus equity.

[c]This industry was going through changes related to downsizing in the defense budget which caused the low 1996 ROE.

[d]Utility data were given by region. These numbers represent an average of the data given for the four regions.

SOURCE: *Dow Jones News Retrieval,* 1997. Data collected through year-end 1996.

GLOBAL PERSPECTIVES

TAKING A LOOK AT GLOBAL CAPITAL STRUCTURES

To what extent does capital structure vary across different countries? The following table, which is taken from a recent study by Raghuram Rajan and Luigi Zingales, both of the University of Chicago, shows the median debt ratios of firms in the largest industrial countries.

Rajan and Zingales also show that there is considerable variation in capital structure among firms within each of the seven countries. However, they also show that capital structures for the firms in each country are generally determined by a similar set of factors: firm size, profitability, market-to-book ratio, and the ratio of fixed assets to total assets. All in all, the Rajan-Zingales study suggests that the points developed in this chapter apply to firms all around the world.

SOURCE: Raghuram G. Rajan and Luigi Zingales, "What Do We Know about Capital Structure? Some Evidence from International Data," *The Journal of Finance*, Vol. 50, no. 5, December 1995, 1421–1460. Used with permission.

Median Percentage of Debt to Total Assets in Different Countries

COUNTRY	BOOK VALUE DEBT RATIO
Canada	32%
France	18
Germany	11
Italy	21
Japan	21
United Kingdom	10
United States	25

illustrates differences for selected industries; the ranking is in descending order of the ratio of common equity to total capital, as shown in Column 1.[21]

Computer and pharmaceutical companies do not use much debt (their ratios of common equity to total capital are high) because the uncertainties inherent in industries that are cyclical, oriented toward research, or subject to huge product liability suits render the heavy use of debt unwise. The airline and utility companies, on the other hand, use debt relatively heavily. The utilities have traditionally used large amounts of debt, particularly long-term debt, because their fixed assets make good security for mortgage bonds, and also because their relatively stable sales make it safe for them to carry more debt than would be true for firms with more business risk.

Particular attention should be given to the times-interest-earned (TIE) ratio because it gives an indication of how safe the debt is and how vulnerable the company is to financial distress. TIE ratios depend on three factors: (1) the percentage of debt, (2) the interest rate on the debt, and (3) the company's profitability. Generally, the least leveraged industries, such as the pharmaceutical industry, have the highest coverage ratios, whereas the utility industry, which finances heavily with debt, has a low average coverage ratio.

---

[21]Information on capital structures and financial strength is available from a multitude of sources. We used the *Dow Jones News Retrieval* system to develop Table 13-6, but published sources include *The Value Line Investment Survey, Robert Morris Association Annual Studies,* and *Dun & Bradstreet Key Business Ratios.*

Wide variations also exist among firms within given industries. For example, although the average ratio of common equity to total capital in 1996 for the pharmaceutical industry was 74.1 percent, Merck's ratio was 89.7 percent, whereas American Home Product had a ratio of only 50.2 percent. Thus, factors unique to individual firms, including managerial attitudes, play an important role in setting target capital structures.

SELF-TEST QUESTION ??????

Why do wide variations in the use of financial leverage occur both across industries and among the individual firms in each industry?

SUMMARY

In this chapter, we examined the effects of financial leverage on stock prices, earnings per share, and the cost of capital. The key concepts covered are summarized below.

♦ A firm's **optimal capital structure** is that mix of debt and equity which maximizes the stock price. At any point in time, management has a specific **target capital structure** in mind, presumably the optimal one, although this target may change over time.

♦ Several factors influence a firm's capital structure. These include the firm's (1) **business risk,** (2) **tax position,** (3) need for **financial flexibility,** and (4) **managerial conservatism or aggressiveness.**

♦ **Business risk** is the uncertainty about projections of future returns on assets. A firm will have little business risk if the demand for its products is stable, if the prices of its inputs and products remain relatively constant, if it can adjust its prices freely if costs increase, and if a high percentage of its costs are variable and hence will decrease if sales decrease. Other things the same, the lower a firm's business risk, the higher its optimal debt ratio.

♦ **Financial leverage** is the extent to which fixed-income securities (debt and preferred stock) are used in a firm's capital structure. **Financial risk** is the added risk borne by stockholders as a result of financial leverage.

♦ **Modigliani and Miller** developed a **trade-off theory of capital structure.** They showed that debt is useful because interest is **tax deductible,** but also that debt brings with it costs associated with actual or potential bankruptcy. Under MM's theory, the optimal capital structure strikes a balance between the tax benefits of debt and the costs associated with bankruptcy.

♦ An alternative (or, really, complementary) theory of capital structure relates to the **signals** given to investors by a firm's decision to use debt versus stock to raise new capital. A stock issue sets off a negative signal, while using debt is a positive, or at least a neutral, signal. As a result, companies try to avoid having to issue stock by maintaining a **reserve borrowing capacity,** and this means using less debt in "normal" times than the MM trade-off theory would suggest.

♦ A firm's owners may have it use a relatively large amount of debt to constrain the managers. **A high debt ratio raises the threat of bankruptcy,** which carries a cost but which also forces managers to be more careful and less wasteful with shareholders' money. Many corporate takeovers and leveraged buyouts in recent years were designed to improve efficiency by reducing the free cash flow available to managers.

Although it is theoretically possible to determine a firm's optimal capital structure, as a practical matter we cannot estimate it with precision. Accordingly, financial executives generally treat the optimal capital structure as a range — for example, 40 to 50 percent debt — rather than as a precise point, such as 45 percent. The concepts discussed in this chapter help managers understand the factors they should consider when they set the target capital structure ranges for their firms.

QUESTIONS

13-1 Explain why the following statement is true: "Other things the same, firms with relatively stable sales are able to carry relatively high debt ratios."

13-2 Why do public utilities pursue a different financial policy than retail firms?

13-3 Why is EBIT generally considered to be independent of financial leverage? Why might EBIT actually be influenced by financial leverage at high debt levels?

13-4 If a firm went from zero debt to successively higher levels of debt, why would you expect its stock price to first rise, then hit a peak, and then begin to decline?

13-5 Why is the debt level that maximizes a firm's expected EPS generally higher than the one that maximizes its stock price?

13-6 When the Bell System was broken up, the old AT&T was split into a new AT&T plus seven regional telephone companies. The specific reason for forcing the breakup was to increase the degree of competition in the telephone industry. AT&T had a monopoly on local service, long distance, and the manufacture of all the equipment used by telephone companies, and the breakup was expected to open most of these markets to competition. In the court order that set the terms of the breakup, the capital structures of the surviving companies were specified, and much attention was given to the increased competition telephone companies could expect in the future. Do you think the optimal capital structure after the breakup should be the same as the pre-breakup optimal capital structure? Explain your position.

13-7 Assume that you are advising the management of a firm that is about to double its assets to serve its rapidly growing market. It must choose between a highly automated production process and a less automated one, and it must also choose a capital structure for financing the expansion. Should the asset investment and financing decisions be jointly determined, or should each decision be made separately? How would these decisions affect one another? How could the leverage concept be used to help management analyze the situation?

13-8 Your firm's R&D department has been working on a new process which, if it works, can produce oil from coal at a cost of about $5 per barrel versus a current market price of $20 per barrel. The company needs $10 million of external funds at this time to complete the research. The results of the research will be known in about a year, and there is about a 50-50 chance of success. If the research is successful, your company will need to raise a substantial amount of new money to put the idea into production. Your economists forecast that although the economy will be depressed next year, interest rates will be high because of international monetary problems. You must recommend how the currently needed $10 million should be raised — as debt or as equity. How would the potential impact of your project influence your decision?

13-9 Explain how profits or losses will be magnified for a firm with high operating leverage as opposed to a firm with lower operating leverage.

13-10 What data are necessary to construct a breakeven analysis?

13-11 What would be the effect of each of the following on a firm's breakeven point?
a. An increase in the sales price with no change in unit costs.
b. A change from straight line depreciation to the MACRS method with no change in the beginning amount of fixed assets.
c. A reduction in variable labor costs; other things are held constant.

13-12 If Congress considers a change in the tax code which will increase personal tax rates but reduce corporate tax rates, what effect would this tax code change have on the average company's capital structure decision?

13-13 Which of the following are likely to encourage a firm to increase the amount of debt in its capital structure?
a. The corporate tax rate increases.
b. The personal tax rate increases.
c. The firm's assets become less liquid.
d. Changes in the bankruptcy code make bankruptcy less costly.
e. The firm's earnings become more volatile.

SELF-TEST PROBLEMS (Solutions Appear in Appendix B)

ST-1
Key terms

Define each of the following terms:
a. Target capital structure; optimal capital structure; target range
b. Business risk; financial risk
c. Financial leverage; operating leverage; breakeven point
d. Times-interest-earned (TIE) ratio
e. Symmetric information; asymmetric information
f. Trade-off theory; signaling theory
g. Reserve borrowing capacity

ST-2
Financial leverage

Gentry Motors Inc., a producer of turbine generators, is in this situation: EBIT = $4 million; tax rate = T = 35%; debt outstanding = D = $2 million; k_d = 10%; k_s = 15%; shares of stock outstanding = N_0 = 600,000; and book value per share = $10. Since Gentry's product market is stable and the company expects no growth, all earnings are paid out as dividends. The debt consists of perpetual bonds.
a. What are Gentry's earnings per share (EPS) and its price per share (P_0)?
b. What is Gentry's weighted average cost of capital (WACC)?
c. Gentry can increase its debt by $8 million, to a total of $10 million, using the new debt to buy back and retire some of its shares at the current price. Its interest rate on debt will be 12 percent (it will have to call and refund the old debt), and its cost of equity will rise from 15 percent to 17 percent. EBIT will remain constant. Should Gentry change its capital structure?
d. If Gentry did not have to refund the $2 million of old debt, how would this affect things? Assume that the new and the still outstanding debt are equally risky, with k_d = 12%, but that the coupon rate on the old debt is 10 percent.
e. What is Gentry's TIE coverage ratio under the original situation and under the conditions in Part c of this question?

ST-3
Operating leverage and breakeven analysis

Olinde Electronics Inc. produces stereo components which sell for P = $100. Olinde's fixed costs are $200,000; 5,000 components are produced and sold each year; EBIT is currently $50,000; and Olinde's assets (all equity financed) are $500,000. Olinde estimates that it can change its production process, adding $400,000 to investment and $50,000 to fixed operating costs. This change will (1) reduce variable costs per unit by $10 and (2) increase output by 2,000 units, but (3) the sales price on all units will have to be lowered to $95 to permit sales of the additional output. Olinde has tax loss carry-forwards that cause its tax rate to be zero. Olinde uses no debt, and its average cost of capital is 10 percent.
a. Should Olinde make the change?
b. Would Olinde's breakeven point increase or decrease if it made the change?
c. Suppose Olinde were unable to raise additional equity financing and had to borrow the $400,000 to make the investment at an interest rate of 10 percent. Use the Du Pont equation to find the expected ROA of the investment. Should Olinde make the change if debt financing must be used?

STARTER PROBLEMS

13-1
Breakeven quantity

A company estimates that its fixed operating costs are $500,000, and its variable costs are $3.00 per unit sold. Each unit produced sells for $4.00. What is the company's breakeven point? In other words, how many units must it sell before its operating income becomes positive?

13-2
Optimal capital structure

Jackson Trucking Company is trying to determine its optimal capital structure. The company's CFO believes the optimal debt ratio is somewhere between 20 percent and 50 percent. Her staff has compiled the following projections for the company's EPS and stock price for various debt levels:

DEBT RATIO	PROJECTED EPS	PROJECTED STOCK PRICE
20%	$3.20	$35.00
30	3.45	36.50
40	3.75	36.25
50	3.50	35.50

Assuming that the firm uses only debt and common equity, what is Jackson's optimal capital structure? At what debt ratio is the company's WACC minimized?

EXAM-TYPE PROBLEMS

The problems included in this section are set up in such a way that they could be used as multiple-choice exam problems.

13-3
Breakeven analysis

The Shipley Corporation produces tea kettles, which it sells for $15 each. Fixed costs are $700,000 for up to 400,000 units of output. Variable costs are $10 per kettle.
a. What is the firm's gain or loss at sales of 125,000 units? Of 175,000 units?
b. What is the breakeven point? Illustrate by means of a chart.

13-4
Breakeven analysis

The Weaver Watch Company manufactures ladies' watches which are sold through discount houses. Each watch is sold for $25; the fixed costs are $140,000 for 30,000 watches or less; variable costs are $15 per watch.
a. What is the firm's gain or loss at sales of 8,000 watches? Of 18,000 watches?
b. What is the breakeven point? Illustrate by means of a chart.
c. What happens to the breakeven point if the selling price rises to $31? What is the significance of the change to the financial manager?
d. What happens to the breakeven point if the selling price rises to $31 but variable costs rise to $23 a unit?

13-5
Breakeven analysis

The following relationships exist for Shome Industries, a manufacturer of electronic components. Each unit of output is sold for $45; the fixed costs are $175,000; variable costs are $20 per unit.
a. What is the firm's gain or loss at sales of 5,000 units? Of 12,000 units?
b. What is the breakeven point?

13-6
Financial leverage effects

A company currently has assets of $5 million. The firm is 100 percent equity financed. The company currently has net income of $1 million, and it pays out 40 percent of its net income as dividends. Both net income and dividends are expected to grow at a constant rate of 5 percent per year. There are 200,000 shares of stock outstanding, and it is estimated that the current cost of capital is 13.40 percent.
   The company is considering a recapitalization where it will issue $1 million in debt and use the proceeds to repurchase stock. Investment bankers have estimated that if the company goes through with the recapitalization, its before-tax cost of debt will be 11 percent, and the cost of equity will rise to 14.5 percent. The company has a 40 percent federal-plus-state tax rate.
a. What is the current share price of the stock (before the recapitalization)?
b. Assuming that the company maintains the same payout ratio, what will be its stock price following the recapitalization?

13-7
Financial leverage effects

The firms HL and LL are identical except for their leverage ratios and interest rates on debt. Each has $20 million in assets, earned $4 million before interest and taxes in 1997, and has a 40 percent federal-plus-state tax rate. Firm HL, however, has a leverage ratio (D/TA) of 50 percent and pays 12 percent interest on its debt, whereas LL has a 30 percent leverage ratio and pays only 10 percent interest on debt.
a. Calculate the rate of return on equity (net income/equity) for each firm.
b. Observing that HL has a higher return on equity, LL's treasurer decides to raise the leverage ratio from 30 to 60 percent, which will increase LL's interest rate on all debt to 15 percent. Calculate the new rate of return on equity for LL.

13-8
Financial leverage effects

The Neal Company wishes to calculate next year's return on equity under different leverage ratios. Neal's total assets are $14 million, and its federal-plus-state tax rate is 40 percent. The company is able to estimate next year's earnings before interest and taxes for three possible states of the world: $4.2 million with a 0.2 probability, $2.8 million with a 0.5 probability, and $700,000 with a 0.3 probability. Calculate Neal's expected return on equity, standard deviation, and coefficient of variation for each of the following leverage ratios, and evaluate the results:

LEVERAGE (DEBT/TOTAL ASSETS)	INTEREST RATE
0%	—
10	9%
50	11
60	14

13-9
Breakeven analysis

A Los Angeles company offers patient-ordered magnetic resonance scans to examine hearts. Traditionally, this test is ordered by physicians; however, in this case, patients solicit the exam without medical intervention and receive results without medical interpretation.

The magnetic resonance machine (MRM) costs $2,500,000, and the company estimates that the machine's installation will cost $46,000. The procedure requires a nurse who is paid $50 per hour, a technician who is paid $30 per hour, and a physician who is paid $150 per hour. Patients are billed $900 for the procedure, compared with $700 for a traditional x-ray series.
a. How many patients must the company treat to break even?
b. Is the $200 cost differential ethical, considering no medical interpretation is given?

PROBLEMS

13-10
Risk analysis

a. Given the following information, calculate the expected value for Firm C's EPS. $E(EPS_A) = \$5.10$, and $\sigma_A = \$3.61$; $E(EPS_B) = \$4.20$, and $\sigma_B = \$2.96$; and $\sigma_C = \$4.11$.

	PROBABILITY				
	0.1	0.2	0.4	0.2	0.1
Firm A: EPS_A	($1.50)	$1.80	$5.10	$8.40	$11.70
Firm B: EPS_B	(1.20)	1.50	4.20	6.90	9.60
Firm C: EPS_C	(2.40)	1.35	5.10	8.85	12.60

b. Discuss the relative riskiness of the three firms' (A, B, and C) earnings.

13-11
Degree of leverage

Wingler Communications Corporation (WCC) supplies headphones to airlines for use with movie and stereo programs. The headphones sell for $288 per set, and this year's sales are expected to be 45,000 units. Variable production costs for the expected sales under present production methods are estimated at $10,200,000, and fixed production (operating) costs at present are $1,560,000. WCC has $4,800,000 of debt outstanding at an interest rate of 8 percent. There are 240,000 shares of common stock outstanding, and there is no preferred stock. The dividend payout ratio is 70 percent, and WCC is in the 40 percent federal-plus-state tax bracket.

The company is considering investing $7,200,000 in new equipment. Sales would not increase, but variable costs per unit would decline by 20 percent. Also, fixed operating costs would increase from $1,560,000 to $1,800,000. WCC could raise the required capital by borrowing $7,200,000 at 10 percent or by selling 240,000 additional shares at $30 per share.
a. What would be WCC's EPS (1) under the old production process, (2) under the new process if it uses debt, and (3) under the new process if it uses common stock?
b. At what unit sales level would WCC have the same EPS, assuming it undertakes the investment and finances it with debt or with stock? (Hint: V = variable cost per unit = $8,160,000/45,000$, and EPS = $[(PQ - VQ - F - I)(1 - T)]/N$. Set $EPS_{Stock} = EPS_{Debt}$ and solve for Q.)
c. At what unit sales level would EPS = 0 under the three production/financing setups — that is, under the old plan, the new plan with debt financing, and the new plan with

stock financing? (Hint: Note that $V_{Old} = \$10,200,000/45,000$, and use the hints for Part c, setting the EPS equation equal to zero.)

d. On the basis of the analysis in Parts a through c, and given that operating leverage is lower under the new setup, which plan is the riskiest, which has the highest expected EPS, and which would you recommend? Assume here that there is a fairly high probability of sales falling as low as 25,000 units, and determine EPS_{Debt} and EPS_{Stock} at that sales level to help assess the riskiness of the two financing plans.

13-12
Financing alternatives

The Severn Company plans to raise a net amount of $270 million to finance new equipment and working capital in early 1998. Two alternatives are being considered: Common stock may be sold to net $60 per share, or bonds yielding 12 percent may be issued. The balance sheet and income statement of the Severn Company prior to financing are as follows:

THE SEVERN COMPANY: BALANCE SHEET AS OF DECEMBER 31, 1997 (MILLIONS OF DOLLARS)

Current assets	$ 900.00	Accounts payable	$ 172.50
Net fixed assets	450.00	Notes payable to bank	255.00
		Other current liabilities	225.00
		Total current liabilities	$ 652.50
		Long-term debt (10%)	300.00
		Common stock, $3 par	60.00
		Retained earnings	337.50
Total assets	$1,350.00	Total liabilities and equity	$1,350.00

THE SEVERN COMPANY: INCOME STATEMENT FOR YEAR ENDED DECEMBER 31, 1997 (MILLIONS OF DOLLARS)

Sales	$2,475.00
Operating costs	2,227.50
Earnings before interest and taxes (10%)	$ 247.50
Interest on short-term debt	15.00
Interest on long-term debt	30.00
Earnings before taxes	$ 202.50
Federal-plus-state taxes (40%)	81.00
Net income	$ 121.50

The probability distribution for annual sales is as follows:

PROBABILITY	ANNUAL SALES (MILLIONS OF DOLLARS)
0.30	$2,250
0.40	2,700
0.30	3,150

Assuming that EBIT is equal to 10 percent of sales, calculate earnings per share under both the debt financing and the stock financing alternatives at each possible level of sales. Then calculate expected earnings per share and σ_{EPS} under both debt and stock financing. Also, calculate the debt ratio and the times-interest-earned (TIE) ratio at the expected sales level under each alternative. The old debt will remain outstanding. Which financing method do you recommend?

13-13
Breakeven and operating leverage

a. Given the following graphs, calculate the total fixed costs, variable costs per unit, and sales price for Firm A. Firm B's fixed costs are $120,000, its variable costs per unit are $4, and its sales price is $8 per unit.

b. Which firm has the higher operating leverage at any given level of sales? Explain.

c. At what *sales level*, in units, do both firms earn the same operating profit?

Breakeven Charts for Problem 13-13

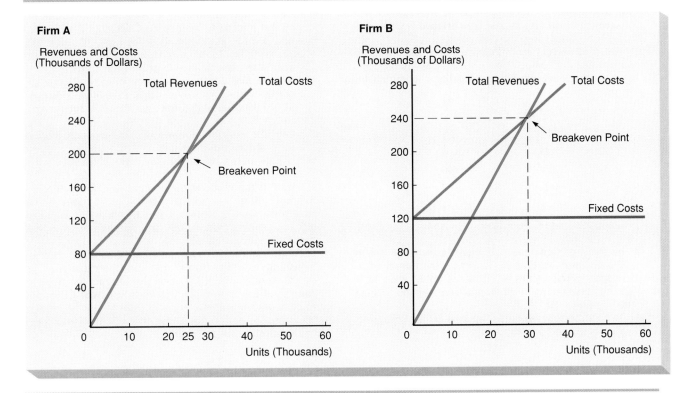

Firm A

Revenues and Costs
(Thousands of Dollars)

Total Revenues   Total Costs

Breakeven Point

Fixed Costs

Units (Thousands)

Firm B

Revenues and Costs
(Thousands of Dollars)

Total Revenues   Total Costs

Breakeven Point

Fixed Costs

Units (Thousands)

INTEGRATED CASE

CAMPUS DELI INC.

13-14 Optimal Capital Structure Assume that you have just been hired as business manager of Campus Deli (CD), which is located adjacent to the campus. Sales were $1,350,000 last year; variable costs were 60 percent of sales; and fixed costs were $40,000. Therefore, EBIT totaled $500,000. Because the university's enrollment is capped, EBIT is expected to be constant over time. Since no expansion capital is required, CD pays out all earnings as dividends. Assets are $2 million, and 100,000 shares are outstanding. The management group owns about 50 percent of the stock, which is traded in the over-the-counter market.

CD currently has no debt — it is an all-equity firm — and its 100,000 shares outstanding sell at a price of $20 per share, which is also the book value. The firm's federal-plus-state tax rate is 40 percent. On the basis of statements made in your finance text, you believe that CD's shareholders would be better off if some debt financing were used. When you suggested this to your new boss, she encouraged you to pursue the idea, but to provide support for the suggestion.

You then obtained from a local investment banker the fol-

lowing estimates of the costs of debt and equity at different debt levels (in thousands of dollars):

AMOUNT BORROWED	k_d	k_s
$ 0	10.0%	15.0%
250	10.0	15.5
500	11.0	16.5
750	13.0	18.0
1,000	16.0	20.0

If the firm were recapitalized, debt would be issued, and the borrowed funds would be used to repurchase stock. Stockholders, in turn, would use funds provided by the repurchase to buy equities in other fast-food companies similar to CD. You plan to complete your report by asking and then answering the following questions.

a. (1) What is business risk? What factors influence a firm's business risk?

(2) What is operating leverage, and how does it affect a firm's business risk?

b. (1) What is meant by the terms "financial leverage" and "financial risk"?

(2) How does financial risk differ from business risk?

c. Now, to develop an example which can be presented to CD's management as an illustration, consider two hypothetical firms, Firm U, with zero debt financing, and Firm L, with $10,000 of 12 percent debt. Both firms have $20,000 in total assets and a 40 percent federal-plus-state tax rate, and they have the following EBIT probability distribution for next year:

PROBABILITY	EBIT
0.25	$2,000
0.50	3,000
0.25	4,000

(1) Complete the partial income statements and the firms' ratios in Table IC13-1.

(2) Be prepared to discuss each entry in the table and to explain how this example illustrates the impact of financial leverage on expected rate of return and risk.

d. With the above points in mind, now consider the optimal capital structure for CD.

(1) To begin, define the terms "optimal capital structure" and "target capital structure."

(2) Describe briefly, without using numbers, the sequence of events that would occur if CD decided to recapitalize and to increase its use of debt.

(3) Assume that shares could be repurchased at the current market price of $20 per share. Calculate CD's expected EPS and TIE at debt levels of $0, $250,000, $500,000, $750,000, and $1,000,000. How many shares would remain after recapitalization under each scenario?

(4) What would be the new stock price if CD recapitalizes with $250,000 of debt? $500,000? $750,000? $1,000,000? Recall that the payout ratio is 100 percent, so g = 0.

(5) Considering only the levels of debt discussed, what is CD's optimal capital structure?

(6) Is EPS maximized at the debt level which maximizes share price? Why?

(7) What is the WACC at the optimal capital structure?

e. Suppose you discovered that CD had more business risk than you originally estimated. Describe how this would affect the analysis. What if the firm had less business risk than originally estimated?

f. What are some factors a manager should consider when establishing his or her firm's target capital structure?

g. Put labels on Figure IC13-1, and then discuss the graph as you might use it to explain to your boss why CD might want to use some debt.

h. How does the existence of asymmetric information and signaling affect capital structure?

TABLE IC13-1 Income Statements and Ratios

	FIRM U			FIRM L		
Assets	$20,000	$20,000	$20,000	$20,000	$20,000	$20,000
Equity	$20,000	$20,000	$20,000	$10,000	$10,000	$10,000
Probability	0.25	0.50	0.25	0.25	0.50	0.25
Sales	$ 6,000	$ 9,000	$12,000	$ 6,000	$ 9,000	$12,000
Operating costs	4,000	6,000	8,000	4,000	6,000	8,000
Earnings before interest and taxes	$ 2,000	$ 3,000	$ 4,000	$ 2,000	$ 3,000	$ 4,000
Interest (12%)	0	0	0	1,200		1,200
Earnings before taxes	$ 2,000	$ 3,000	$ 4,000	$ 800	$	$ 2,800
Taxes (40%)	800	1,200	1,600	320		1,120
Net income	$ 1,200	$ 1,800	$ 2,400	$ 480	$	$ 1,680
Basic earning power (BEP = EBIT/Assets)	10.0%	15.0%	20.0%	10.0%	%	20.0%
ROE	6.0%	9.0%	12.0%	4.8%	%	16.8%
TIE	∞	∞	∞	1.7×	×	3.3×
Expected basic earning power		15.0%			%	
Expected ROE		9.0%			10.8%	
Expected TIE		∞			2.5×	
σ_{BEP}		3.5%			%	
σ_{ROE}		2.1%			4.2%	
σ_{TIE}		0			0.6×	

F I G U R E   I C 1 3 - 1   Relationship between Capital Structure and Stock Price

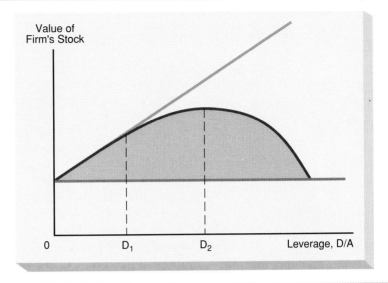

COMPUTER-RELATED PROBLEM

Work the problem in this section only if you are using the computer problem diskette.

13-15

Effects of financial leverage

Use the model in File C13 to work this problem.

a. Rework Problem 13-12, assuming that the old long-term debt will not remain outstanding but, rather, that it must be refinanced at the new long-term interest rate of 12 percent. What effect does this have on the decision to refinance?

b. What would be the effect on the refinancing decision if the rate on long-term debt fell to 5 percent or rose to 20 percent, assuming that all long-term debt must be refinanced?

c. Which financing method would be recommended if the stock price (1) rose to $105 or (2) fell to $30? (Assume that all debt will have an interest rate of 12 percent.)

d. With $P_0 = \$60$ and $k_d = 12\%$, change the sales probability distribution to the following:

ALTERNATIVE 1		ALTERNATIVE 2	
SALES	PROBABILITY	SALES	PROBABILITY
$2,250	0	$ 0	0.3
2,700	1.0	2,700	0.4
3,150	0	7,500	0.3

What are the implications of these changes?

DEGREE OF LEVERAGE

In our discussion of operating leverage earlier in the chapter, we made no mention of financial leverage, and when we discussed financial leverage, operating leverage was assumed to be given. Actually, the two types of leverage are interrelated. For example, if a firm *reduced* its operating leverage, this would probably lead to an *increase* in its optimal use of financial leverage. On the other hand, if it decided to *increase* its operating leverage, its optimal capital structure would probably call for *less* debt.

The theory of finance has not been developed to the point where we can actually specify simultaneously the optimal levels of operating and financial leverage. However, we can see how operating and financial leverage interact through an analysis of the *degree of leverage concept.*

DEGREE OF OPERATING LEVERAGE (DOL)

The *degree of operating leverage (DOL)* is defined as the percentage change in operating income (or EBIT) that results from a given percentage change in sales:

$$\text{DOL} = \frac{\text{Percentage change in EBIT}}{\text{Percentage change in sales}} = \frac{\dfrac{\Delta \text{EBIT}}{\text{EBIT}}}{\dfrac{\Delta Q}{Q}}. \tag{13A-1}$$

In effect, the DOL is an index number which measures the effect of a change in sales on operating income, or EBIT.

DOL can also be calculated by using Equation 13A-2, which is derived from Equation 13A-1:

$$\text{DOL}_Q = \text{Degree of operating leverage at Point Q}$$

$$= \frac{Q(P - V)}{Q(P - V) - F}, \tag{13A-2}$$

or, based on dollar sales rather than units,

$$\text{DOL}_S = \frac{S - VC}{S - VC - F}. \tag{13A-2a}$$

Here Q is the initial units of output, P is the average sales price per unit of output, V is the variable cost per unit, F is fixed operating costs, S is initial sales in dollars, and VC is total variable costs. Equation 13A-2 is normally used to analyze a single product, such as IBM's PC, whereas Equation 13A-2a is used to evaluate an entire firm with many types of products, where "quantity in units" and "sales price" are not meaningful.

Equation 13A-2 is developed from Equation 13A-1 as follows. The change in units of output is defined as ΔQ. In equation form, EBIT $= Q(P - V) - F$, where Q is units sold, P is the price per unit, V is the variable cost per unit, and F is the total fixed costs. Since both price and fixed costs are constant, the change in

EBIT is ΔEBIT = ΔQ(P − V). The initial EBIT is Q(P − V) − F, so the percentage change in EBIT is

$$\%\Delta\text{EBIT} = \frac{\Delta Q(P - V)}{Q(P - V) - F}.$$

The percentage change in output is $\Delta Q/Q$, so the ratio of the percentage change in EBIT to the percentage change in output is

$$\text{DOL} = \frac{\dfrac{\Delta Q(P - V)}{Q(P - V) - F}}{\dfrac{\Delta Q}{Q}} = \left(\frac{\Delta Q(P - V)}{Q(P - V) - F}\right)\left(\frac{Q}{(\Delta Q)}\right) = \frac{Q(P - V)}{Q(P - V) - F}. \quad \textbf{(13A-2)}$$

Applying Equation 13A-2a to data for Bigbee Electronics at a sales level of $200,000 as shown back in Table 13-4, we find its degree of operating leverage to be 2.0:

$$\text{DOL}_{\$200,000} = \frac{\$200,000 - \$120,000}{\$200,000 - \$120,000 - \$40,000}$$

$$= \frac{\$80,000}{\$40,000} = 2.0.$$

Thus, an X percent increase in sales will produce a 2X percent increase in EBIT. For example, a 50 percent increase in sales, starting from sales of $200,000, will result in a 2(50%)= 100% increase in EBIT. This situation is confirmed by examining Section I of Table 13-4, where we see that a 50 percent increase in sales, from $200,000 to $300,000, causes EBIT to double. Note, however, that if sales decrease by 50 percent, then EBIT will decrease by 100 percent; this is again confirmed by Table 13-4, as EBIT decreases to $0 if sales decrease to $100,000.

Note also that the DOL is specific to the initial sales level; thus, if we evaluated DOL from a sales base of $300,000, it would be different from the DOL at $200,000 of sales:

$$\text{DOL}_{\$300,000} = \frac{\$300,000 - \$180,000}{\$300,000 - \$180,000 - \$40,000}$$

$$= \frac{\$120,000}{\$80,000} = 1.5.$$

In general, if a firm is operating at close to its breakeven point, the degree of operating leverage will be high, but DOL declines the higher the base level of sales is above breakeven sales. Looking back at the top section of Table 13-4, we see that the company's breakeven point (before consideration of financial leverage) is at sales of $100,000. At that level, DOL is infinite:

$$\text{DOL}_{\$100,000} = \frac{\$100,000 - \$60,000}{\$100,000 - \$60,000 - \$40,000}$$

$$= \frac{\$40,000}{0} = \text{undefined but} \approx \text{infinity.}$$

When evaluated at higher and higher sales levels, DOL progressively declines.

DEGREE OF FINANCIAL LEVERAGE (DFL)

Operating leverage affects earnings *before* interest and taxes (EBIT), whereas financial leverage affects earnings *after* interest and taxes, or the earnings available to common stockholders. In terms of Table 13-4, operating leverage affects the top section, whereas financial leverage affects the lower sections. Thus, if Bigbee decided to use more operating leverage, its fixed costs would be higher than $40,000, its variable cost ratio would be lower than 60 percent of sales, and its EBIT would be more sensitive to changes in sales. *Financial leverage takes over where operating leverage leaves off, further magnifying the effects on earnings per share of changes in the level of sales.* For this reason, operating leverage is sometimes referred to as *first-stage leverage* and financial leverage as *second-stage leverage.*

The *degree of financial leverage (DFL)* is defined as the percentage change in earnings per share that results from a given percentage change in earnings before interest and taxes (EBIT), and it is calculated as follows:

$$DFL = \frac{\text{Percentage change in EPS}}{\text{Percentage change in EBIT}}$$

$$= \frac{EBIT}{EBIT - I}. \tag{13A-3}$$

Equation 13A-3 is developed as follows:

1. Recall that $EBIT = Q(P - V) - F$.

2. Earnings per share are found as $EPS = [(EBIT - I)(1 - T)]/N$, where I is interest paid, T is the corporate tax rate, and N is the number of shares outstanding.

3. I is a constant, so $\Delta I = 0$; hence, ΔEPS, the change in EPS, is

$$\Delta EPS = \frac{(\Delta EBIT - \Delta I)(1 - T)}{N} = \frac{\Delta EBIT(1 - T)}{N}.$$

4. The percentage change in EPS is the change in EPS divided by the original EPS:

$$\frac{\dfrac{\Delta EBIT(1 - T)}{N}}{\dfrac{(EBIT - I)(1 - T)}{N}} = \left[\frac{\Delta EBIT(1 - T)}{N}\right]\left[\frac{N}{(EBIT - I)(1 - T)}\right] = \frac{\Delta EBIT}{EBIT - I}.$$

5. The degree of financial leverage is the percentage change in EPS over the percentage change in EBIT:

$$DFL = \frac{\dfrac{\Delta EBIT}{EBIT - I}}{\dfrac{\Delta EBIT}{EBIT}} = \left(\frac{\Delta EBIT}{EBIT - I}\right)\left(\frac{EBIT}{\Delta EBIT}\right) = \frac{EBIT}{EBIT - I}. \tag{13A-3}$$

6. This equation must be modified if the firm has preferred stock outstanding.

Applying Equation 13A-3 to data for Bigbee at sales of $200,000 and an EBIT of $40,000, the degree of financial leverage with a 50 percent debt ratio is

$$DFL_{S=\$200,000,\ D=50\%} = \frac{\$40,000}{\$40,000 - \$12,000}$$

$$= 1.43.$$

Therefore, a 100 percent increase in EBIT would result in a 1.43(100%) = 143 percent increase in earnings per share. This may be confirmed by referring to the lower section of Table 13-4, where we see that a 100 percent increase in EBIT, from \$40,000 to \$80,000, produces a 143 percent increase in EPS:

$$\%\Delta\text{EPS} = \frac{\Delta\text{EPS}}{\text{EPS}_0} = \frac{\$8.16 - \$3.36}{\$3.36} = \frac{\$4.80}{\$3.36} = 1.43 = 143\%.$$

If no debt were used, the degree of financial leverage would by definition be 1.0, so a 100 percent increase in EBIT would produce exactly a 100 percent increase in EPS. This can be confirmed from the data in Section II of Table 13-4.

Combining Operating and Financial Leverage (DTL)

Thus far, we have seen:

1. That the greater the use of fixed operating costs as measured by the degree of operating leverage, the more sensitive EBIT will be to changes in sales, and

2. That the greater the use of debt as measured by the degree of financial leverage, the more sensitive EPS will be to changes in EBIT.

Therefore, if a firm uses a considerable amount of both operating and financial leverage, then even small changes in sales will lead to wide fluctuations in EPS.

Equation 13A-2 for the degree of operating leverage can be combined with Equation 13A-3 for the degree of financial leverage to produce the equation for the *degree of total leverage (DTL)*, which shows how a given change in sales will affect earnings per share. Here are three equivalent equations for DTL:

$$\text{DTL} = (\text{DOL})(\text{DFL}). \tag{13A-4}$$

$$\text{DTL} = \frac{Q(P - V)}{Q(P - V) - F - I}. \tag{13A-4a}$$

$$\text{DTL} = \frac{S - VC}{S - VC - F - I}. \tag{13A-4b}$$

Equation 13A-4 is simply a definition, while Equations 13A-4a and 13A-4b are developed as follows:

1. Recognize that EBIT = $Q(P - V) - F$, and then rewrite Equation 13A-3 as follows:

$$\text{DFL} = \frac{\text{EBIT}}{\text{EBIT} - I} = \frac{Q(P - V) - F}{Q(P - V) - F - I} = \frac{S - VC - F}{S - VC - F - I}. \tag{13A-3a}$$

2. The degree of total leverage is equal to the degree of operating leverage times the degree of financial leverage, or Equation 13A-2 times Equation 13A-3a:

$$\text{DTL} = (\text{DOL})(\text{DFL}) \tag{13A-4}$$

$$= (\text{Equation 13A-2})(\text{Equation 13A-3a})$$

$$= \left[\frac{Q(P - V)}{Q(P - V) - F}\right]\left[\frac{Q(P - V) - F}{Q(P - V) - F - I}\right]$$

$$= \frac{Q(P - V)}{Q(P - V) - F - I} \tag{13A-4a}$$

$$= \frac{S - VC}{S - VC - F - I}. \tag{13A-4b}$$

Applying Equation 13A-4b to data for Bigbee at sales of $200,000, we can substitute data from Table 13-4 into Equation 13A-4b to find the degree of total leverage if the debt ratio is 50 percent:

$$DTL_{\$200,000,\ 50\%} = \frac{\$200,000 - \$120,000}{\$200,000 - \$120,000 - \$40,000 - \$12,000}$$

$$= \frac{\$80,000}{\$28,000} = 2.86.$$

Equivalently, using Equation 13A-4, we get the same result:

$$DTL_{\$200,000,\ 50\%} = (2.00)(1.43) = 2.86.$$

We can use the degree of total leverage (DTL) number to find the new earnings per share (EPS_1) for any given percentage increase in sales (%Δ Sales), proceeding as follows:

$$EPS_1 = EPS_0 + EPS_0[(DTL)(\%\Delta Sales)]$$

$$= EPS_0[1.0 + (DTL)(\%\Delta Sales)]. \qquad (13A\text{-}5)$$

For example, a 50 percent (or 0.5) increase in sales, from $200,000 to $300,000, would cause EPS_0 ($3.36 as shown in Section III of Table 13-4) to increase to $8.16:

$$EPS_1 = \$3.36[1.0 + (2.86)(0.5)]$$

$$= \$3.36(2.43)$$

$$= \$8.16.$$

This figure agrees with the one for EPS shown in Table 13-4.

The degree of leverage concept is useful primarily for the insights it provides regarding the joint effects of operating and financial leverage on earnings per share. The concept can be used to show the management of a business, for example, that a decision to automate a plant and to finance the new equipment with debt would result in a situation wherein a 10 percent decline in sales would produce a 50 percent decline in earnings, whereas with a different operating and financial leverage package, a 10 percent sales decline would cause earnings to decline by only 20 percent. Having the alternatives stated in this manner gives decision makers a better idea of the ramifications of alternative actions.[1]

PROBLEMS

13A-1
Degree of operating leverage

Grant Grocers has sales of $1,000,000. The company's fixed costs total $250,000, and its variable costs are 60 percent of sales. What is the company's degree of operating leverage? If sales increased 20 percent, what would be the percentage increase in EBIT?

---

[1]The degree of leverage concept is also useful for investors. If firms in an industry are ranked by degree of total leverage, an investor who is optimistic about prospects for the industry might favor those firms with high leverage, and vice versa if industry sales are expected to decline. However, it is very difficult to separate fixed from variable costs. Accounting statements simply do not make this breakdown, so an analyst must make the separation in a judgmental manner. Note that costs are really fixed, variable, and "semivariable," for if times get tough enough, firms will sell off depreciable assets and thus reduce depreciation charges (a fixed cost), lay off "permanent" employees, reduce salaries of the remaining personnel, and so on. For this reason, the degree of leverage concept is generally more useful for thinking about the general nature of the relationship than for developing precise numbers, and any numbers developed should be thought of as approximations rather than as exact specifications.

13A-2

Degree of financial leverage

Arthur Johnson Inc.'s operating income is $500,000, the company's interest expense is $200,000, and its tax rate is 40 percent. What is the company's degree of financial leverage? If the company were able to double its operating income, what would be the percentage increase in net income?

13A-3

Degree of leverage

A company currently has $2 million in sales. Its variable costs equal 70 percent of its sales, its fixed costs are $100,000, and its annual interest expense is $50,000.

a. What is the company's degree of operating leverage?

b. If this company's operating income (EBIT) rises by 10 percent, how much will its net income increase?

c. If the company's sales increase 10 percent, how much will the company's net income increase?

13A-4

Operating leverage effects

The Hastings Corporation will begin operations next year to produce a single product at a price of $12 per unit. Hastings has a choice of two methods of production: Method A, with variable costs of $6.75 per unit and fixed operating costs of $675,000; and Method B, with variable costs of $8.25 per unit and fixed operating costs of $401,250. To support operations under either production method, the firm requires $2,250,000 in assets, and it has established a debt ratio of 40 percent. The cost of debt is $k_d = 10$ percent. The tax rate is irrelevant for the problem, and fixed *operating* costs do not include interest.

a. The sales forecast for the coming year is 200,000 units. Under which method would EBIT be more adversely affected if sales did not reach the expected levels? (Hint: Compare DOLs under the two production methods.)

b. Given the firm's present debt, which method would produce the greater percentage increase in earnings per share for a given increase in EBIT? (Hint: Compare DFLs under the two methods.)

c. Calculate DTL under each method, and then evaluate the firm's risk under each method.

d. Is there some debt ratio under Method A which would produce the same DTL_A as the DTL_B that you calculated in Part c? (Hint: Let $DTL_A = DTL_B = 2.90$ as calculated in Part c, solve for I, and then determine the amount of debt that is consistent with this level of I. Conceivably, debt could be *negative,* which implies holding liquid assets rather than borrowing.)

CHAPTER 14

DIVIDEND POLICY

At 9:02 on the morning of January 26, 1993, the financial news wire carried this one-sentence announcement: "IBM slashes the quarterly dividend on its common from $4.84 to $2.16." Shortly thereafter, IBM provided this additional information.

> The Board of Directors took this action only after serious deliberation and careful consideration of both IBM's earnings and the investment required for the long-term development of the Company's businesses, as well as IBM's intention to pay an appropriate return to shareholders. After weighing all factors, and taking into account the need to maintain IBM's strong financial position, the Board decided to act now in the best long-term interests of the Company and its shareholders.

IBM's dividend cut—the first ever for the company—reduced the annual dividend from $4.84 to $2.16. The $4.84 amount had been established in 1989, and the dividend growth rate prior to 1989 had averaged 7 percent per year.

Many analysts and investors had been expecting a dividend cut because IBM had been hammered by the shift from mainframe computing to personal computers. So, IBM was trapped with most of its resources devoted to poor-selling products. Meanwhile, nimbler companies such as Microsoft and Intel were earning record profits from the software and microchip businesses that IBM, in effect, gave them in the 1980s. The end result was that IBM set a record for corporate losses in 1992, saw a 60 percent drop in its stock price, and was forced to make a 53 percent dividend cut.

IBM's problems mounted in 1993, and it cut the dividend again, from $2.16 to $1.00. However, in 1994 a new management team began to turn things around, and earnings per share has steadily improved. After losing money in 1993, the company had an earnings per share of $4.92 in 1994 and $11.00 in 1995. With profitability restored, IBM now faces two related questions: (1) How much of its free cash flow should it pass on to stockholders, and (2) should it provide this cash to stockholders by raising the dividend or by repurchasing stock? Thus far, IBM's board has authorized repurchases of more than $10 billion in common stock, and it also raised the dividend from $1.00 to $1.40. Further, most analysts expect to see the dividend continue to increase as earnings grow. For example, *Value Line* forecasts a dividend of $3 on earnings of $15.50 in 1999. These prospects lifted the stock price from a 1993 low of $40.75 to a 1997 high of $170. Since then, however, IBM's stock has retreated, but *Value Line* still forecasts a price of more than $200 by 1999. What really happens remains to be seen.

This chapter discusses the many facets of dividend policy. As you read the chapter, put yourself in the shoes of an IBM board member. If the board saw the company's problems on the horizon a few years earlier, why didn't it cut the dividend then? Also, if things looked so bleak, why didn't the board eliminate the dividend instead of just cutting it? Finally, if IBM continues to improve, should the dividend be raised, should more shares be repurchased, or should the company do some of each? By the end of the chapter, you should have a good idea of both how dividend policy decisions are made and the dilemma faced by IBM's board.

Successful companies earn income. That income can then be reinvested in operating assets, used to acquire securities, used to retire debt, or distributed to stockholders. If the decision is made to distribute income to stockholders, three key issues arise: (1) What percentage should be distributed? (2) Should the distribution be as cash dividends, or should the cash be passed on to shareholders by buying back some of the stock they hold? (3) How stable should the distribution be; that is, should the funds paid out from year to year be stable and dependable, which stockholders would probably prefer, or be allowed to vary with the firms' cash flows and investment requirements, which would probably be better from the firm's standpoint? These three issues are the primary focus of this chapter, but we also consider two related issues, stock dividends and stock splits.

ON THE WWW

An excellent source of recent dividend news releases for major corporations is available at the Web site of Corporate Financials Online *at http://www.cfonews.com/. By clicking on any of the companies preceded by a blue dot, students can see a screen that will allow them to access a company's most recent dividend announcements.*

DIVIDENDS VERSUS CAPITAL GAINS: WHAT DO INVESTORS PREFER?

When deciding how much cash to distribute to stockholders, financial managers must keep in mind that the firm's objective is to maximize shareholder value. Consequently, the **target payout ratio** — defined as the percentage of net income to be paid out as cash dividends — should be based in large part on investors' preferences for dividends versus capital gains: do investors prefer (1) to have the firm distribute income as cash dividends or (2) to have it either repurchase stock or else plow the earnings back into the business, both of which should result in capital gains? This preference can be considered in terms of the constant growth stock valuation model:

Target Payout Ratio
The percentage of net income paid out as cash dividends.

$$\hat{P}_0 = \frac{D_1}{k_s - g}.$$

If the company increases the payout ratio, it raises D_1. This increase in the numerator, taken alone, would cause the stock price to rise. However, if D_1 is raised, then less money will be available for reinvestment, that will cause the expected growth rate to decline, and that would tend to lower the stock's price. Thus, any change in payout policy will have two opposing effects. Therefore, the firm's **optimal dividend policy** must strike a balance between current dividends and future growth so as to maximize the stock price.

Optimal Dividend Policy
The dividend policy that strikes a balance between current dividends and future growth and maximizes the firm's stock price.

In this section we examine three theories of investor preference: (1) the dividend irrelevance theory, (2) the "bird-in-the-hand" theory, and (3) the tax preference theory.

DIVIDEND IRRELEVANCE THEORY

It has been argued that dividend policy has no effect on either the price of a firm's stock or its cost of capital. If dividend policy has no significant effects,

Dividend Irrelevance Theory
The theory that a firm's dividend policy has no effect on either its value or its cost of capital.

then it would be *irrelevant*. The principal proponents of the **dividend irrelevance theory** are Merton Miller and Franco Modigliani (MM).[1] They argued that the firm's value is determined only by its basic earning power and its business risk. In other words, MM argued that the value of the firm depends only on the income produced by its assets, not on how this income is split between dividends and retained earnings.

To understand MM's argument that dividend policy is irrelevant, recognize that any shareholder can construct his or her own dividend policy. For example, if a firm does not pay dividends, a shareholder who wants a 5 percent dividend can "create" it by selling 5 percent of his or her stock. Conversely, if a company pays a higher dividend than an investor desires, the investor can use the unwanted dividends to buy additional shares of the company's stock. If investors could buy and sell shares and thus create their own dividend policy without incurring costs, then the firm's dividend policy would truly be irrelevant. Note, though, that investors who want additional dividends must incur brokerage costs to sell shares, and investors who do not want dividends must first pay taxes on the unwanted dividends and then incur brokerage costs to purchase shares with the after-tax dividends. Since taxes and brokerage costs certainly exist, dividend policy may well be relevant.

In developing their dividend theory, MM made a number of assumptions, especially the absence of taxes and brokerage costs. Obviously, taxes and brokerage costs do exist, so the MM irrelevance theory may not be true. However, MM argued (correctly) that all economic theories are based on simplifying assumptions, and that the validity of a theory must be judged by empirical tests, not by the realism of its assumptions. We will discuss empirical tests of MM's dividend irrelevance theory shortly.

BIRD-IN-THE-HAND THEORY

The principal conclusion of MM's dividend irrelevance theory is that dividend policy does not affect the required rate of return on equity, k_s. This conclusion has been hotly debated in academic circles. In particular, Myron Gordon and John Lintner argued that k_s decreases as the dividend payout is increased because investors are less certain of receiving the capital gains which are supposed to result from retaining earnings than they are of receiving dividend payments.[2] Gordon and Lintner said, in effect, that investors value a dollar of expected dividends more highly than a dollar of expected capital gains because the dividend yield component, D_1/P_0, is less risky than the g component in the total expected return equation, $k_s = D_1/P_0 + g$.

Bird-in-the-Hand Theory
MM's name for the theory that a firm's value will be maximized by setting a high dividend payout ratio.

MM disagreed. They argued that k_s is independent of dividend policy, which implies that investors are indifferent between D_1/P_0 and g and, hence, between dividends and capital gains. MM called the Gordon-Lintner argument the **bird-in-the-hand** fallacy because, in MM's view, most investors plan to reinvest their dividends in the stock of the same or similar firms, and, in any event, the riskiness of the firm's cash flows to investors in the long run is determined by the riskiness of operating cash flows, not by dividend payout policy.

---

[1]Merton H. Miller and Franco Modigliani, "Dividend Policy, Growth, and the Valuation of Shares," *Journal of Business,* October 1961, 411–433.

[2]Myron J. Gordon, "Optimal Investment and Financing Policy," *Journal of Finance,* May 1963, 264–272, and John Lintner, "Dividends, Earnings, Leverage, Stock Prices, and the Supply of Capital to Corporations," *Review of Economics and Statistics,* August 1962, 243–269.

TAX PREFERENCE THEORY

There are three tax-related reasons for thinking that investors might prefer a low dividend payout to a high payout: (1) Recall from Chapter 2 that long-term capital gains are taxed at a maximum rate of 28 percent, whereas dividend income is taxed at effective rates which go up to 39.6 percent. Therefore, wealthy investors (who own most of the stock and receive most of the dividends) might prefer to have companies retain and plow earnings back into the business. Earnings growth would presumably lead to stock price increases, and lower-taxed capital gains would be substituted for higher-taxed dividends. (2) Taxes are not paid on the gain until a stock is sold. Due to time value effects, a dollar of taxes paid in the future has a lower effective cost than a dollar paid today. (3) If a stock is held by someone until he or she dies, no capital gains tax is due at all — the beneficiaries who receive the stock can use the stock's value on the death day as their cost basis and thus completely escape the capital gains tax.

Because of these tax advantages, investors may prefer to have companies retain most of their earnings. If so, investors would be willing to pay more for low-payout companies than for otherwise similar high-payout companies.

ILLUSTRATION OF THE THREE DIVIDEND POLICY THEORIES

Figure 14-1 illustrates the three alternative dividend policy theories: (1) Miller and Modigliani's dividend irrelevance theory, (2) Gordon and Lintner's bird-in-the-hand theory, and (3) the tax preference theory. To understand the three theories, consider the case of Hardin Electronics, which has from its inception plowed all earnings back into the business and thus has never paid a dividend. Hardin's management is now reconsidering its dividend policy, and it wants to adopt the policy that will maximize its stock price.

Consider first the data presented below the graph. Columns 1 through 4 show three alternative payout policies: (1) Retain all earnings and pay out nothing, which is the present policy, (2) pay out 50 percent of earnings, and (3) pay out 100 percent of earnings. In the example, we assume that the company will have a 15 percent ROE regardless of which payout policy it follows, so with a book value per share of $30, EPS will be 0.15($30) = $4.50 under all payout policies.[3] Given an EPS of $4.50, dividends per share are shown in Column 3 under each payout policy.

Under the assumption of a constant ROE, the growth rate shown in Column 4 will be g = (% Retained)(ROE), and it will vary from 15 percent at a zero payout to zero at a 100 percent payout. For example, if Hardin pays out 50 percent of its earnings, then its dividend growth rate will be g = 0.5(15%) = 7.5%.

Columns 5, 6, and 7 show how the situation would look if MM's irrelevance theory were correct. Under this theory, neither the stock price nor the cost of equity would be affected by the payout policy — the stock price would remain constant at $30, and k_s would be stable at 15 percent. Note that k_s is found as the sum of the growth rate in Column 4 plus the dividend yield in Column 6.

---

[3]When the three theories were developed, it was assumed that a company's investment opportunities would be held constant and that if the company increased its dividends, its capital budget could be funded by selling common stock. Conversely, if a high-payout company lowered its payout to the point where earnings exceeded good investment opportunities, it was assumed that the company would repurchase shares. Transactions costs were assumed to be immaterial. We maintain those assumptions in our example.

| FIGURE 14-1 | Dividend Irrelevance, Bird-in-the-Hand, and Tax Preference Dividend Theories |

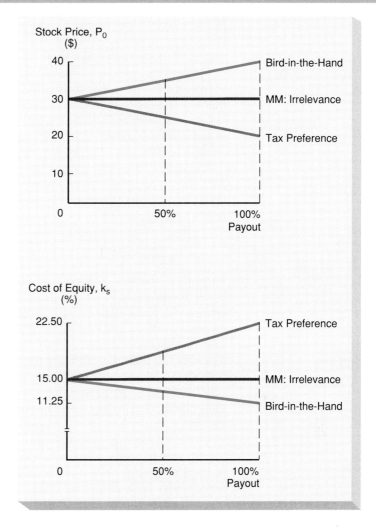

| ALTERNATIVE PAYOUT POLICIES | | | | POSSIBLE SITUATIONS (ONLY ONE CAN BE TRUE) | | | | | | | | |
| | | | | MM: IRRELEVANCE | | | BIRD-IN-THE-HAND | | | TAX PREFERENCE | | |
PERCENT PAYOUT (1)	PERCENT RETAINED (2)	DPS (3)	g (4)	P_0 (5)	D/P_0 (6)	k_s (7)	P_0 (8)	D/P_0 (9)	k_s (10)	P_0 (11)	D/P_0 (12)	k_s (13)
0%	100%	$0.00	15.0%	$30	0.0%	15.0%	$30	0.00%	15.00%	$30	0.0%	15.0%
50	50	2.25	7.5	30	7.5	15.0	35	6.43	13.93	25	9.0	16.5
100	0	4.50	0.0	30	15.0	15.0	40	11.25	11.25	20	22.5	22.5

NOTES:

1. Book value = Initial market value = $30 per share.
2. ROE = 15%.
3. EPS = $30(0.15) = $4.50.
4. g = (% retained)(ROE) = (% retained)(15%). Example: At payout = 50%, g = 0.5(15%) = 7.5%.
5. k_s = Dividend yield + Growth rate.

Columns 8, 9, and 10 show the situation if the bird-in-the-hand theory were true. Under this theory, investors prefer dividends, and the more of its earnings the company pays out, the higher its stock price and the lower its cost of equity. In our example, the bird-in-the-hand theory indicates that adopting a 100 percent payout policy would cause the stock price to rise from $30 to $40, and the cost of equity would decline from 15 percent to 11.25 percent.

Finally, Columns 11, 12, and 13 show the situation if the tax preference theory were correct. Under this theory, investors prefer companies which retain earnings and thus provide returns in the form of lower-taxed capital gains rather than higher-taxed dividends. If the tax preference theory were correct, then an increase in the dividend payout ratio from its current zero level would cause the stock price to decline and the cost of equity to rise.

The data in the table are plotted to produce the two graphs shown in Figure 14-1. The upper graph shows how the stock price would react to dividend policy under each of the theories, and the lower graph shows how the cost of equity would be affected.

USING EMPIRICAL EVIDENCE TO DECIDE WHICH THEORY IS BEST

These three theories offer contradictory advice to corporate managers, so which, if any, should we believe? The most logical way to proceed is to test the theories empirically. Many such tests have been conducted, but their results have been unclear. There are two reasons for this: (1) For a valid statistical test, things other than dividend policy must be held constant; that is, the sample companies must differ only in their dividend policies, and (2) we must be able to measure with a high degree of accuracy each sample firm's cost of equity. Neither of these two conditions holds: We cannot find a set of publicly owned firms that differ only in their dividend policies, nor can we obtain precise estimates of the cost of equity.

Therefore, no one can establish a clear relationship between dividend policy and the cost of equity. Investors cannot be seen to uniformly prefer either higher or lower dividends. Nevertheless, *individual* investors do have strong preferences. Some prefer high dividends, while others prefer all capital gains. These differences among individuals help explain why it is difficult to reach any definitive conclusions regarding the optimal dividend payout. Even so, both evidence and logic suggest that investors prefer firms which follow a *stable, predictable* dividend policy (regardless of the payout level). We will consider the issue of dividend stability later in the chapter.

SELF-TEST QUESTIONS

Differentiate among the dividend irrelevance theory, the bird-in-the-hand theory, and the tax preference theory. Use a graph such as Figure 14-1 to illustrate your answer.

What did Modigliani and Miller assume about taxes and brokerage costs when they developed their dividend irrelevance theory?

How did the bird-in-the-hand theory get its name?

In what sense does MM's theory represent a middle-ground position between the other two theories?

What have been the results of empirical tests of the dividend theories?

OTHER DIVIDEND POLICY ISSUES

Before we discuss how dividend policy is set in practice, we must examine two other theoretical issues that could affect our views toward dividend policy: (1) the *information content,* or *signaling, hypothesis* and (2) the *clientele effect.*

INFORMATION CONTENT, OR SIGNALING, HYPOTHESIS

When MM set forth their dividend irrelevance theory, they assumed that everyone — investors and managers alike — has identical information regarding the firm's future earnings and dividend. In reality, however, different investors have different views on both the level of future dividend payments and the uncertainty inherent in those payments, and managers have better information about future prospects than public stockholders.

It has been observed that an increase in the dividend is often accompanied by an increase in the price of a stock, while a dividend cut generally leads to a stock price decline. This could indicate that investors, in the aggregate, prefer dividends to capital gains. However, MM argued differently. They noted the well-established fact that corporations are reluctant to cut dividends, hence do not raise dividends unless they anticipate higher earnings in the future. Thus, MM argued that a higher-than-expected dividend increase is a "signal" to investors that the firm's management forecasts good future earnings.[4] Conversely, a dividend reduction, or a smaller-than-expected increase, is a signal that management is forecasting poor earnings in the future. Thus, MM argued that investors' reactions to changes in dividend policy do not necessarily show that investors prefer dividends to retained earnings. Rather, they argue that price changes following dividend actions simply indicate that there is an important **information, or signaling, content** in dividend announcements.

Like most other aspects of dividend policy, empirical studies of signaling have had mixed results. There is clearly some information content in dividend announcements. However, it is difficult to tell whether the stock price changes that follow increases or decreases in dividends reflect only signaling effects or both signaling and dividend preference. Still, signaling effects should definitely be considered when a firm is contemplating a change in dividend policy.

Information Content (Signaling) Hypothesis
The theory that investors regard dividend changes as signals of management's earnings forecasts.

CLIENTELE EFFECT

As we indicated earlier, different groups, or *clienteles*, of stockholders prefer different dividend payout policies. For example, retired individuals and university endowment funds generally prefer cash income, so they may want the firm to pay out a high percentage of its earnings. Such investors (and pension funds) are often in low or even zero tax brackets, so taxes are of no concern. On the other hand, stockholders in their peak earning years might prefer reinvestment,

---

[4]Stephen Ross has suggested that managers can use capital structure as well as dividends to give signals concerning firms' future prospects. For example, a firm with good earnings prospects can carry more debt than a similar firm with poor earnings prospects. This theory, called *incentive signaling*, rests on the premise that signals with cash-based variables (either debt interest or dividends) cannot be mimicked by unsuccessful firms because such firms do not have the future cash-generating power to maintain the announced interest or dividend payment. Thus, investors are more likely to believe a glowing verbal report when it is accompanied by a dividend increase or a debt-financed expansion program. See Stephen A. Ross, "The Determination of Financial Structure: The Incentive-Signaling Approach," *The Bell Journal of Economics,* Spring 1977, 23–40.

because they have less need for current investment income and would simply reinvest dividends received, after first paying income taxes on those dividends.

If a firm retains and reinvests income rather than paying dividends, those stockholders who need current income would be disadvantaged. The value of their stock might increase, but they would be forced to go to the trouble and expense of selling off some of their shares to obtain cash. Also, some institutional investors (or trustees for individuals) would be legally precluded from selling stock and then "spending capital." On the other hand, stockholders who are saving rather then spending dividends might favor the low dividend policy, for the less the firm pays out in dividends, the less these stockholders will have to pay in current taxes, and the less trouble and expense they will have to go through to reinvest their after-tax dividends. Therefore, investors who want current investment income should own shares in high dividend payout firms, while investors with no need for current investment income should own shares in low dividend payout firms. For example, investors seeking high cash income might invest in electric utilities, which averaged a 79 percent payout from 1991 through 1995, while those favoring growth could invest in the semiconductor industry, which paid out only 7 percent.

To the extent that stockholders can switch firms, a firm can change from one dividend payout policy to another and then let stockholders who do not like the new policy sell to other investors who do. However, frequent switching would be inefficient because of (1) brokerage costs, (2) the likelihood that stockholders who are selling will have to pay capital gains taxes, and (3) a possible shortage of investors who like the firm's newly adopted dividend policy. Thus, management should be hesitant to change its dividend policy, because a change might cause current shareholders to sell their stock, forcing the stock price down. Such a price decline might be temporary, but it might also be permanent — if few new investors are attracted by the new dividend policy, then the stock price would remain depressed. Of course, the new policy might attract an even larger clientele than the firm had before, in which case the stock price would rise.

Clientele Effect
The tendency of a firm to attract a set of investors who like its dividend policy.

Evidence from several studies suggests that there is in fact a **clientele effect**.[5] MM and others have argued that one clientele is as good as another, so the existence of a clientele effect does not necessarily imply that one dividend policy is better than any other. MM may be wrong, though, and neither they nor anyone else can prove that the aggregate makeup of investors permits firms to disregard clientele effects. This issue, like most others in the dividend arena, is still up in the air.

SELF-TEST QUESTION

Define (1) information content and (2) the clientele effect, and explain how they affect dividend policy.

DIVIDEND STABILITY

As we noted at the beginning of the chapter, the stability of dividends is also important. Profits and cash flows vary over time, as do investment opportunities.

---

[5]For example, see R. Richardson Pettit, "Taxes, Transactions Costs and the Clientele Effect of Dividends," *The Journal of Financial Economics,* December 1977, 419–436.

Taken alone, this suggests that corporations should vary their dividends over time, increasing them when cash flows are large and the need for funds is low and lowering them when cash is in short supply relative to investment opportunities. However, many stockholders rely on dividends to meet expenses, and they would be seriously inconvenienced if the dividend stream were unstable. Further, reducing dividends to make funds available for capital investment could send incorrect signals, and that could drive down stock prices. Thus, maximizing its stock price requires a firm to balance its internal needs for funds against the needs and desires of its stockholders.

How should this balance be struck; that is, how stable and dependable should a firm attempt to make its dividends? It is impossible to give a definitive answer to this question, but the following points are relevant:

1. Virtually every publicly owned company makes a five- to ten-year financial forecast of earnings and dividends. Such forecasts are never made public — they are used for internal planning purposes only. However, security analysts construct similar forecasts and do make them available to investors; see *Value Line* for an example. Further, virtually every internal five- to ten-year corporate forecast we have seen for a "normal" company projects a trend of higher earnings and dividends. Both managers and investors know that economic conditions may cause actual results to differ from forecasted results, but "normal" companies expect to grow.

2. Years ago, when inflation was not persistent, the term "stable dividend policy" meant a policy of paying the same dollar dividend year after year. AT&T was a prime example of a company with a stable dividend policy — it paid $9 per year ($2.25 per quarter) for 25 straight years. Today, though, most companies and stockholders expect earnings to grow over time as a result of retained earnings and inflation. Further, dividends are normally expected to grow more or less in line with earnings. Thus, today a "stable dividend policy" generally means increasing the dividend at a reasonably steady rate. For example, Rubbermaid made this statement in a recent annual report:

   > Dividends per share were increased . . . for the 34th consecutive year. . . . Our goal is to increase sales, earnings, and earnings per share by 15% per year, while achieving a 21% return on beginning shareholders' equity. It is also the Company's objective to pay approximately 30% of current year's earnings as dividends, which will permit us to retain sufficient capital to provide for future growth.

   Rubbermaid used the word "approximately" in discussing its payout ratio, because even if earnings vary a bit from the target level, the company still planned to increase the dividend by the target growth rate. Even though Rubbermaid did not mention the dividend growth rate in the statement, analysts can calculate the growth rate and see that it is the same 15 percent as indicated for sales and earnings:

   $$g = b(ROE)$$
   $$= (1 - Payout)(ROE)$$
   $$= 0.7(21\%) \approx 15\%.$$

Here b is the fraction of earnings that are retained, or 1.0 minus the payout ratio.

Companies with volatile earnings and cash flows would be reluctant to make a commitment to increase the dividend each year, so they would not make such a detailed statement. Even so, most companies would like to be able to exhibit the kind of stability Rubbermaid has shown, and they try to come as close to it as they can.

Dividend stability has two components: (1) How dependable is the growth rate, and (2) can we count on at least receiving the current dividend in the future? The most stable policy, from an investor's standpoint, is that of a firm whose dividend growth rate is predictable — such a company's total return (dividend yield plus capital gains yield) would be relatively stable over the long run, and its stock would be a good hedge against inflation. The second most stable policy is where stockholders can be reasonably sure that the current dividend will not be reduced — it may not grow at a steady rate, but management will probably be able to avoid cutting the dividend. The least stable situation is where earnings and cash flows are so volatile that investors cannot count on the company to maintain the current dividend over a typical business cycle.

3. Most observers believe that dividend stability is desirable. Assuming this position is correct, investors prefer stocks that pay more predictable dividends to stocks which pay the same average amount of dividends but in a more erratic manner. This means that the cost of equity will be minimized, and the stock price maximized, if a firm stabilizes its dividends as much as possible.

SELF-TEST QUESTIONS

??????

What does the term "stable dividend policy" mean?

What are the two components of dividend stability?

ESTABLISHING THE DIVIDEND POLICY IN PRACTICE

In the preceding sections we saw that investors may or may not prefer dividends to capital gains, but that they do prefer predictable to unpredictable dividends. Given this situation, how should firms set their basic dividend policies? For example, how should a company like Rubbermaid establish the specific percentage of earnings it will pay out? Rubbermaid's target is 30 percent, but why not 40 percent, 50 percent, or some other percentage? In this section, we describe how firms actually set their dividend policies.

SETTING THE TARGET PAYOUT RATIO: THE RESIDUAL DIVIDEND MODEL[6]

When deciding how much cash should be distributed to stockholders, two points should be kept in mind: (1) The overriding objective is to maximize shareholder value, and (2) the cash flows produced by the firm belong to its shareholders. Management should refrain from retaining income unless it can be reinvested to produce returns higher than shareholders could themselves earn by investing the cash in investments of equal risk. On the other hand, recall from Chapter 9 that

---

[6]The term "payout ratio" can be interpreted in two ways: (1) the conventional way, where the payout ratio means the percentage of net income to common paid out as cash dividends, or (2) the percentage of net income distributed to stockholders as dividends and through share repurchases. In this section, we assume that no repurchases occur. Increasingly, though, firms are using the residual model to determine "distributions to shareholders" and then making a separate decision as to the form of that distribution. Further, an increasing percentage of the distribution is in the form of repurchases.

internal equity (retained earnings) is cheaper than external equity (new common stock). This encourages firms to retain earnings because this adds to the equity base and thus reduces the likelihood that the firm will have to raise external equity at a later date to fund future investment projects.

When establishing a dividend policy, one size does not fit all. Some firms produce a lot of cash but have a limited number of investment opportunities — this is true for firms in profitable but mature industries where few opportunities for growth exist. Such firms typically distribute a large percentage of their cash to shareholders, thereby attracting investment clienteles which prefer high dividends. Other firms generate little or no excess cash but have many good investment opportunities — this is often true of new firms in rapidly growing industries. Such firms often distribute little or no cash to their shareholders but enjoy rising earnings and stock prices, thereby attracting investors who prefer capital gains.

As Table 14-1 suggests, dividend payouts and dividend yields for large corporations vary considerably. Generally, firms in stable, cash-producing industries such as utilities, financial services, and tobacco pay relatively high dividends, whereas companies in rapidly growing industries such as computer and cable TV tend to pay lower dividends.

Residual Dividend Model
A model in which the dividend paid is set equal to the actual earnings minus the amount of retained earnings necessary to finance the firm's optimal capital budget.

For a given firm, the optimal payout ratio is a function of four factors: (1) investors' preferences for dividends versus capital gains, (2) the firm's investment opportunities, (3) its target capital structure, and (4) the availability and cost of external capital. The last three elements are combined in what we call the **residual dividend model.** Under this model a firm follows these four steps when deciding its target payout ratio: (1) It determines the optimal capital budget; (2) it determines the amount of equity needed to finance that budget, given its target capital structure; (3) it uses retained earnings to meet equity requirements

TABLE 14-1	Dividend Payouts		
COMPANY	**INDUSTRY**	**DIVIDEND PAYOUT**	**DIVIDEND YIELD**
I. Companies That Pay High Dividends			
Northeast Utilities	Utility	81.0%	7.7%
Santa Fe Pacific Pipeline	Petroleum pipeline	78.0	8.8
RJR Nabisco Holdings	Tobacco/food	77.0	6.2
Bankers Trust	Banking	64.0	5.1
Philip Morris	Consumer products/tobacco	57.0	5.2
Mellon Bank	Banking	48.0	4.6
II. Companies That Pay Low or No Dividends			
McDonald's	Fast-food restaurants	16.0%	0.6%
Intel	Semiconductors	4.0	0.2
Compaq Computer	Computers	0.0	0.0
Apple Computer	Computers	0.0	0.0
Microsoft	Computer software	0.0	0.0
Health Management Association	Health care services	0.0	0.0

SOURCE: *Value Line Investment Survey,* various 1996 issues.

to the extent possible; and (4) it pays dividends only if more earnings are available than are needed to support the optimal capital budget. The word *residual* implies "leftover," and the residual policy implies that dividends are paid out of "leftover" earnings.

Most firms have a target capital structure that calls for at least some debt, so new financing is done partly with debt and partly with equity. As long as the firm finances with the optimal mix of debt and equity, and provided it uses only internally generated equity (retained earnings), then the marginal cost of each new dollar of capital will be minimized. Internally generated equity is available for financing a certain amount of new investment, but beyond that amount, the firm must turn to more expensive new common stock. At the point where new stock must be sold, the cost of equity, and consequently the marginal cost of capital, rises.

These concepts, which were developed in Chapter 12, are illustrated in Figure 14-2 with data from the Texas and Western (T&W) Transport Company. T&W has an initial marginal cost of capital of 10 percent. However, this cost rate assumes that all new equity comes from retained earnings. Therefore, MCC = 10% as long as retained earnings are available, but MCC begins to rise at the point where new stock must be sold.

T&W has $60 million of net income and a 40 percent optimal debt ratio. Provided it does not pay any cash dividends, T&W can make net investments (investments in addition to asset replacements financed from depreciation) of $100 million, consisting of $60 million from retained earnings plus $40 million of new debt supported by the retained earnings, at a 10 percent marginal cost of capital. Therefore, its MCC will be constant at 10 percent up to $100 million of capital if it retains all of its earnings. Beyond $100 million, the MCC will rise because the firm must use more expensive new common stock.

FIGURE 14-2 Texas and Western Transport Company: Marginal Cost of Capital

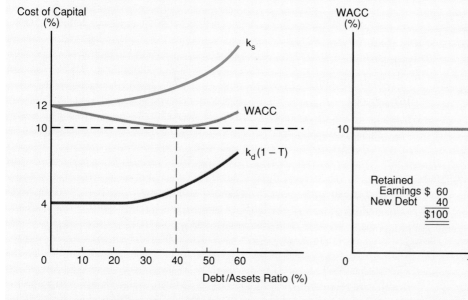
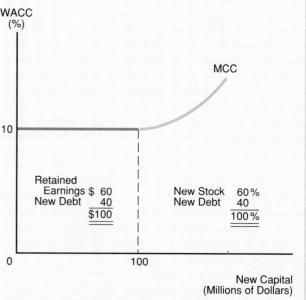

| FIGURE 14-3 | Texas and Western Transport Company: Investment Opportunity Schedules |

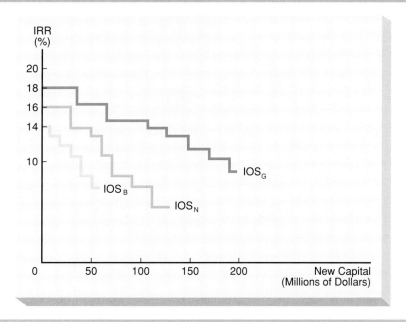

Of course, if T&W does not retain all of its earnings, then its MCC will begin to rise before $100 million. For example, if T&W retains only $30 million, its MCC will begin to rise at $50 million: $30 million of retained earnings + $20 million of debt.

Now suppose T&W's director of capital budgeting constructs investment opportunity schedules under three economic scenarios and plots them on a graph. The investment opportunity schedules for three different states of the economy—good (IOS_G), normal (IOS_N), and bad (IOS_B)—are shown in Figure 14-3. T&W can invest the most money, and earn the highest rates of return, when the investment opportunities are as given by IOS_G.

In Figure 14-4, we combine the investment opportunity schedules with the cost of capital schedule that would exist if the company retained all of its earnings. The point where the relevant IOS curve cuts the MCC curve defines the proper level of new investment. If investment opportunities are relatively bad (IOS_B), the optimal level of investment is $40 million; if opportunities are normal (IOS_N), $70 million should be invested; and if opportunities are relatively good (IOS_G), T&W should make new investments in the amount of $150 million.[7]

Consider the situation in which IOS_G is the appropriate schedule. T&W should raise and invest $150 million. It has $60 million of earnings and a 40 percent target debt ratio. Thus, if it retained all of its earnings, it could finance $100 million, consisting of $60 million of retained earnings plus $40 million of new debt, at an average cost of 10 percent. The additional $50 million would include external equity and thus would have a higher cost. If T&W paid out part of its

---

[7]Figure 14-4 shows one MCC schedule and three IOS schedules for three possible sets of investment opportunities. Actually, both the MCC and the IOS schedules would normally change from year to year as interest rates and stock prices change. Figure 14-4 is designed to illustrate a point, not to duplicate reality. In reality, there would be one MCC and one IOS schedule for each year, but those schedules would change from year to year.

FIGURE 14-4   Texas and Western Transport Company:
Interrelationships between Cost of Capital,
Investment Opportunities, and New Investment

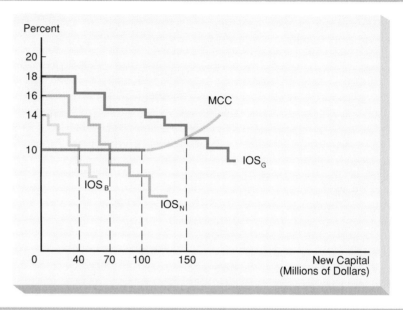

earnings in dividends, it would have to use costly new common stock earlier than need be, so its MCC curve would rise earlier than it otherwise would. This suggests that under the conditions of IOS_G, T&W should retain all of its earnings. According to the residual policy, T&W's payout ratio should, in this case, be zero.

Under the conditions of IOS_N, however, T&W should invest only $70 million. How should this investment be financed? First, notice that if T&W retained all of its earnings, $60 million, it would need to sell only $10 million of new debt. However, if T&W retained $60 million and sold only $10 million of new debt, it would move away from its target capital structure. To stay on target, T&W must finance 60 percent of the required $70 million with equity — retained earnings — and 40 percent with debt. This means that it would retain only $42 million and sell $28 million of new debt. Since T&W would retain only $42 million of its $60 million total earnings, it would have to distribute the residual, $18 million, to its stockholders. Thus, its optimal payout ratio would be $18/$60 = 30% if IOS_N prevailed.

Under the conditions of IOS_B, T&W should invest only $40 million. Because it has $60 million in earnings, it could finance the entire $40 million out of retained earnings and still have $20 million available for dividends. Should this be done? Under our assumptions, this would not be a good decision because it would force T&W away from its optimal capital structure. To stay at the 40 percent target debt/assets ratio, T&W must retain $24 million of earnings and sell $16 million of debt. When the $24 million of retained earnings is subtracted from the $60 million of total earnings, T&W would be left with a residual of $36 million, which is the amount that should be paid out in dividends. Thus, under IOS_B, the payout ratio as prescribed by the residual policy would be $36/$60 = 60 percent.

Since both the IOS and earnings level will surely vary from year to year, strict adherence to the residual dividend policy would result in dividend instability — one year the firm might declare zero dividends because investment opportunities were good, but the next year it might pay a large dividend because investment opportunities were poor. Similarly, fluctuating earnings would also lead to variable dividends even if investment opportunities were stable. Thus, following the residual dividend policy would be optimal only if investors were not bothered by fluctuating dividends. However, since investors prefer stable, dependable dividends, k_s would be higher, and the stock price lower, if the firm followed the residual model in a strict sense rather than attempting to stabilize its dividends over time. Therefore, firms should

1. Estimate what their MCC and IOS schedules are likely to look like, on average, over the next five or so years.

2. Use the forecasted MCC and IOS information to find the residual model payout ratio and dollars of dividends during the planning period.

3. Then set a *target payout ratio* based on the projected data.

Thus, firms should use the residual policy to help set their long-run target payout ratios, but not as a guide to the payout in any one year.

Companies use the residual dividend model as discussed above to help understand the determinants of an optimal dividend policy, but they typically use a computerized financial forecasting model when setting the target payout ratio. Most larger corporations forecast their financial statements over the next five to ten years. Information on projected capital expenditures and working capital requirements is entered into the model, along with sales forecasts, profit margins, depreciation, and the other elements required to forecast cash flows. The target capital structure is also specified, and the model shows the amount of debt and equity that will be required to meet the capital budgeting requirements while maintaining the target capital structure.

Then, dividend payments are introduced. Naturally, the higher the payout ratio, the greater the required external equity. Most companies then use the model to find a dividend pattern over the forecast period (generally five years) that will provide sufficient equity to support the capital budget without having to sell new common stock or move the capital structure ratios outside the optimal range. The end result might include a statement, in a memo from the financial vice-president to the chairman of the board, such as the following:

> We forecasted the total market demand for our products, what our share of the market is likely to be, and our required investments in capital assets and working capital. Using this information, we developed projected balance sheets and income statements for the period 1998–2002.
>
> Our 1997 dividends totaled $50 million, or $2 per share. On the basis of projected earnings, cash flows, and capital requirements, we can increase the dividend by 8 percent per year. This is consistent with a payout ratio of 42 percent, on average, over the forecast period. Any faster dividend growth rate (or higher payout) would require us to sell common stock, cut the capital budget, or raise the debt ratio. Any slower growth rate would lead to a buildup of the common equity ratio. Therefore, I recommend that the Board increase the dividend for 1998 by 8 percent, to $2.16, and that it plan for similar increases in the future.
>
> Events over the next five years will undoubtedly lead to differences between our forecasts and actual results. If and when changes occur, we will want to reexamine our position. However, I am confident that we can meet any random cash shortfalls by increasing our borrowings — we have unused debt capacity which gives us flexibility in this regard.
>
> We ran the corporate model under several recession scenarios. If the economy really crashes, our earnings will not cover the dividend. However, in all "reasonable" scenarios cash flows do cover the dividend. I know the Board does not want to push the dividend up to a level where we would have to cut it under bad economic conditions. Our model runs indicate, though, that the $2.16 dividend can be maintained under

any reasonable set of forecasts. Only if we increased the dividend to over $3 would we be seriously exposed to the danger of having to cut the dividend.

I might also note that *Value Line* and most other analysts' reports are forecasting that our dividends will grow in the 6 percent to 8 percent range. Thus, if we go to $2.16, we will be at the high end of the range, which should give our stock a boost. With takeover rumors so widespread, getting the stock up a bit would make us all breathe a little easier.

Finally, we considered distributing cash to shareholders through a stock repurchase program. Here we would reduce the dividend payout ratio and use the funds so generated to buy our stock on the open market. Such a program has several advantages, but it would also have drawbacks. I do not recommend that we institute a stock repurchase program at this time. However, if our free cash flows exceed our forecasts, I would recommend that we use these surpluses to buy back stock. Also, I plan to continue looking into a regular repurchase program, and I may recommend such a program in the future.

This company, like Rubbermaid, has very stable operations, so it can plan its dividends with a fairly high degree of confidence. Other companies, especially those in cyclical industries, have difficulty maintaining in bad times a dividend that is really too low in good times. Such companies set a very low "regular" dividend and then supplement it with an "extra" dividend when times are good. General Motors, Ford, and other auto companies have followed the **low-regular-dividend-plus-extras** policy in the past. Each company announced a low regular dividend that it was sure could be maintained "through hell or high water," and stockholders could count on receiving this dividend under all conditions. Then when times were good and profits and cash flows were high, the companies paid a clearly designated extra dividend. Investors recognized that the extras might not be maintained in the future, so they did not interpret them as a signal that the companies' earnings were going up permanently, nor did they take the elimination of the extra as a negative signal. In recent years, however, the auto companies and other companies have replaced the "extras" in their low-regular-dividend-plus-extras policy with stock repurchases.

Low-Regular-Dividend-Plus-Extras
The policy of announcing a low, regular dividend that can be maintained no matter what, and then when times are good paying a designated "extra" dividend.

EARNINGS, CASH FLOWS, AND DIVIDENDS

We normally think of earnings as being the primary determinant of dividends, but in reality cash flows are even more important. This situation is revealed in Figure 14-5, which gives data for Chevron Corporation from 1972 through 1996. Chevron's dividends increased steadily from 1972 to 1981; during that period both earnings and cash flows were rising, as was the price of oil. After 1981, oil prices declined sharply, pulling earnings down. Cash flows, though, remained well above the dividend requirement.

Chevron acquired Gulf Oil in 1984, and it issued over $10 billion of debt to finance the acquisition. Interest on the debt hurt earnings immediately after the merger, as did certain write-offs connected with the merger. Further, Chevron's management wanted to pay off the new debt as fast as possible. All of this influenced the company's decision to hold the dividend constant from 1982 through 1987. Earnings improved dramatically in 1988, and the dividend has increased more or less steadily since then. Note that the dividend was increased in 1991 in spite of the weak earnings and cash flow resulting from the Persian Gulf War.

Now look at Columns 4 and 6, which show payout ratios based on earnings and on cash flows. The earnings payout is quite volatile — dividends ranged from 26 percent to 113 percent of earnings. The cash flow payout, on the other hand, is much more stable — it ranged from 19 percent to 33 percent of cash flows.

FIGURE 14-5 Chevron: Earnings, Cash Flows, and Dividends, 1972–1996

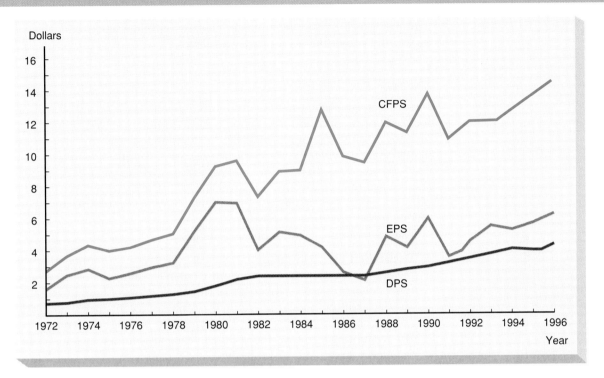

YEAR (1)	DIVIDENDS PER SHARE (2)	EARNINGS PER SHARE (3)	EARNINGS PAYOUT (4)	CASH FLOW PER SHARE (5)	CASH FLOW PAYOUT (6)
1972	$0.73	$1.61	45%	$ 2.72	27%
1973	0.78	2.49	31	3.68	21
1974	0.96	2.86	34	4.36	22
1975	1.00	2.28	44	4.00	25
1976	1.08	2.59	42	4.22	26
1977	1.18	2.98	40	4.68	25
1978	1.28	3.24	40	5.06	25
1979	1.45	5.22	28	7.29	20
1980	1.80	7.02	26	9.26	19
1981	2.20	6.96	32	9.61	23
1982	2.40	4.03	60	7.35	33
1983	2.40	5.15	47	8.93	27
1984	2.40	4.94	49	9.00	27
1985	2.40	4.19	57	12.76	19
1986	2.40	2.63	91	9.86	24
1987	2.40	2.13	113	9.47	25
1988	2.55	4.86	52	11.97	21
1989	2.80	4.16	67	11.33	25
1990	2.95	6.02	49	13.75	21
1991	3.25	3.69	88	11.14	29
1992	3.30	4.70	70	12.88	26
1993	3.50	5.60	62	13.12	27
1994	3.70	5.20	71	12.66	29
1995	3.70	6.20	60	13.80	27
1996 (est.)	4.00	7.00	57	15.00	27

NOTE: For consistency, data have not been adjusted for a two-for-one split in 1994.

SOURCE: *Value Line Investment Survey,* various issues.

Further, the correlation between dividends and cash flows was 0.93 versus only 0.48 between dividends and earnings. Thus, dividends clearly depend more on cash flows, which reflect the company's *ability* to pay dividends, than on current earnings, which are heavily influenced by accounting practices and which do not necessarily reflect the ability to pay dividends.

PAYMENT PROCEDURES

Dividends are normally paid quarterly, and, if conditions permit, the dividend is increased once each year. For example, Katz Corporation paid $0.50 per quarter in 1997, or at an annual rate of $2.00. In common financial parlance, we say that in 1997 Katz's *regular quarterly dividend* was $0.50, and its *annual dividend* was $2.00. In late 1997, Katz's board of directors met, reviewed projections for 1998, and decided to keep the 1998 dividend at $2.00. The directors announced the $2 rate, so stockholders could count on receiving it unless the company experiences unanticipated operating problems.

The actual payment procedure is as follows:

Declaration Date
The date on which a firm's directors issue a statement declaring a dividend.

1. **Declaration date.** On the **declaration date** — say, on November 10 — the directors meet and declare the regular dividend, issuing a statement similar to the following: "On November 10, 1997, the directors of Katz Corporation met and declared the regular quarterly dividend of 50 cents per share, payable to holders of record on December 12, payment to be made on January 2, 1998." For accounting purposes, the declared dividend becomes an actual liability on the declaration date. If a balance sheet were constructed, the amount ($0.50) × (Number of shares outstanding) would appear as a current liability, and retained earnings would be reduced by a like amount.

Holder-of-Record Date
If the company lists the stockholder as an owner on this date, then the stockholder receives the dividend.

2. **Holder-of-record date.** At the close of business on the **holder-of-record date**, December 12, the company closes its stock transfer books and makes up a list of shareholders as of that date. If Katz Corporation is notified of the sale before 5 P.M. on December 12, then the new owner receives the dividend. However, if notification is received on or after December 13, the previous owner gets the dividend check.

3. **Ex-dividend date.** Suppose Jean Buyer buys 100 shares of stock from John Seller on December 8. Will the company be notified of the transfer in time to list Buyer as the new owner and thus pay the dividend to her? To avoid conflict, the securities industry has set up a convention under which the right to the dividend remains with the stock until four business days prior to the holder-of-record date; on the fourth day before that date, the right to the dividend no longer goes with the shares. The date when the right to the dividend leaves the stock is called the **ex-dividend date.** In this case, the ex-dividend date is four days prior to December 12, or December 8:

Ex-Dividend Date
The date on which the right to the current dividend no longer accompanies a stock; it is usually four working days prior to the holder-of-record date.

Dividend goes with stock	December 7 Buyer would receive the dividend
- -	- -
Ex-dividend date:	December 8 Seller would receive the dividend
- -	- -
	December 9
	December 10
	December 11
Holder-of-record date:	December 12

Therefore, if Buyer is to receive the dividend, she must buy the stock on or before December 7. If she buys it on December 8 or later, Seller will receive the dividend because he will be the official holder of record.

Katz's dividend amounts to $0.50, so the ex-dividend date is important. Barring fluctuations in the stock market, one would normally expect the price of a stock to drop by approximately the amount of the dividend on the ex-dividend date. Thus, if Katz closed at $30½ on December 7, it would probably open at about $30 on December 8.[8]

Payment Date
The date on which a firm actually mails dividend checks.

4. **Payment date.** The company actually mails the checks to the holders of record on January 2, the **payment date**.

SELF-TEST QUESTIONS ??????

Explain the logic of the residual dividend model, the steps a firm would take to implement it, and why it is more likely to be used to establish a long-run payout target than to set the actual year-by-year payout ratio.

How do firms use planning models to help set dividend policy?

Which are more critical to the dividend decision, earnings or cash flow? Explain.

Explain the procedures used to actually pay the dividend.

Why is the ex-dividend date important to investors?

CHANGING DIVIDEND POLICIES

From our previous discussion, it is obvious that firms should try to establish a rational dividend policy and then stick with it. Dividend policy can be changed, but this can cause problems because such changes can inconvenience the firm's existing stockholders, send unintended signals, and convey the impression of dividend instability, all of which can have negative implications for stock prices. Still, economic circumstances do change, and occasionally such changes dictate that a firm should alter its dividend policy.

---

[8]December 7, 1997, is a Sunday. Therefore, the buyer would actually have to purchase the stock on Friday, December 5, to receive the dividend. Also, tax effects cause the price decline on average to be less than the full amount of the dividend. Suppose you were an investor in the 40 percent federal-plus-state tax bracket. If you bought Katz's stock on December 5, you would receive the dividend, but you would almost immediately pay 40 percent of it out in taxes. Thus, you would want to wait until December 8 to buy the stock if you thought you could get it for $0.50 less per share. Your reaction, and those of others, would influence stock prices around dividend payment dates. Here is what would happen:

1. Other things held constant, a stock's price should rise during the quarter, with the daily price increase (for Katz) equal to $0.50/90 = $0.005556. Therefore, if the price started at $30 just after its last ex-dividend date, it would rise to $30.50 on December 7.

2. In the absence of taxes, the stock's price would fall to $30 on December 8 and then start up as the next dividend accrual period began. Thus, over time, if everything else were held constant, the stock's price would follow a sawtooth pattern if it were plotted on a graph.

3. Because of taxes, the stock's price would neither rise by the full amount of the dividend nor fall by the full dividend amount when it goes ex-dividend.

4. The amount of the rise and subsequent fall would depend on the average investor's marginal tax rate.

See Edwin J. Elton and Martin J. Gruber, "Marginal Stockholder Tax Rates and the Clientele Effect," *Review of Economics and Statistics*, February 1970, 68–74, for an interesting discussion of all this.

One of the most striking examples of a dividend policy change occurred in May 1994, when FPL Group, a utility holding company whose primary subsidiary is Florida Power & Light, announced a cut in its quarterly dividend from $0.62 per share to $0.42. At the same time, FPL stated it would buy back 10 million of its common shares over the next three years to bolster its stock price.[9] Here is the text of the letter to its stockholders in which FPL announced these changes:

Dear Shareholder,

Over the past several years, we have been working hard to enhance shareholder value by aligning our strategy with a rapidly changing business environment. . . . The Energy Policy Act of 1992 has brought permanent changes to the electric industry. Although we have taken effective and sometimes painful steps to prepare for these changes, one critical problem remains. Our dividend payout ratio of 90 percent — the percentage of our earnings paid to shareholders as dividends — is far too high for a growth company. It is well above the industry average, and it has limited the growth in the price of our stock.

To meet the challenges of this competitive marketplace and to ensure the financial strength and flexibility necessary for success, the Board of Directors has announced a change in our financial strategy that includes the following milestones:

♦ A new dividend policy that provides for paying out 60 to 65 percent of prior years' earnings. This means a reduction in the quarterly dividend from 62 to 42 cents per share beginning with the next payment.

♦ The authorization to repurchase 10 million shares of common stock over the next three years, including at least 4 million shares in the next year.

♦ An earlier dividend evaluation beginning in February 1995 to more closely link dividend rates to annual earnings.

We believe this financial strategy will enhance long-term share value and will facilitate both earnings per share and dividend growth to about 5 percent per year over the next several years.

Adding to shareholder wealth in this manner should be increasingly significant given recent changes in the tax law, which have made capital gains more attractive than dividend income.

. . . We take this action from a position of strength. We are not being forced into a defensive position by expectations of poor financial performance. Rather, it is a strategic decision to align our dividend policy and your total return as a shareholder with the growth characteristics of our company.

We appreciate your understanding and support, and we will continue to provide updates on our progress in forthcoming shareholder reports.

Several analysts called the FPL decision a watershed event for the electric utility industry. Furthermore, many analysts believe that other utilities will follow FPL's lead. FPL saw its circumstances changing — its core electric business is moving from a regulated monopoly environment to one of increasing competition, and the new environment requires a stronger balance sheet and more financial flexibility than is consistent with a 90 percent payout policy.

What did the market think about FPL's dividend policy change? The company's stock price fell by 14 percent the day the announcement was made. In the past, hundreds of dividend cuts followed by sharply lower earnings had conditioned investors to expect the worst when a company reduces it dividend — this is the signaling effect discussed earlier. However, over the next few months, as they understood FPL's actions better, analysts began to praise the decision and to

---

[9]For a complete discussion of the FPL decision, see Dennis Soter, Eugene Brigham, and Paul Evanson, "The Dividend Cut Heard 'Round the World: The Case of FPL," *Journal of Applied Corporate Finance*, Spring 1996, 4–15. Also, note that stock repurchases are discussed in a later section.

recommend the stock. As a result, FPL's stock outperformed the average utility and soon exceeded the pre-announcement price. The policy change was painful to FPL's stockholders in the short run, but it was clearly the proper move, and it is proving to be beneficial to stockholders in the longer run.

SELF-TEST QUESTIONS

Why do companies change their dividend policies?

What is the best strategy for announcing dividend policy changes?

DIVIDEND REINVESTMENT PLANS

Dividend Reinvestment Plan (DRP)
A plan that enables a stockholder to automatically reinvest dividends received back into the stock of the paying firm.

During the 1970s, most large companies instituted **dividend reinvestment plans (DRPs or DRIPs)**, whereby stockholders can automatically reinvest their dividends in the stock of the paying corporation.[10] Today most larger companies offer DRIPs, and although participation rates vary considerably, about 25 percent of the average firm's shareholders are enrolled. There are two types of DRIPs: (1) plans which involve only "old stock" that is already outstanding and (2) plans which involve newly issued stock. In either case, the stockholder must pay taxes on the amount of the dividends, even though stock rather than cash is received.

Under both types of DRIPs, stockholders choose between continuing to receive dividend checks or having the company use the dividends to buy more stock in the corporation. Under the "old stock" type of plan, if a stockholder elects reinvestment, a bank, acting as trustee, takes the total funds available for reinvestment, purchases the corporation's stock on the open market, and allocates the shares purchased to the participating stockholders' accounts on a pro rata basis. The transactions costs of buying shares (brokerage costs) are low because of volume purchases, so these plans benefit small stockholders who do not need cash dividends for current consumption.

The "new stock" type of DRIP invests the dividends in newly issued stock, hence these plans raise new capital for the firm. AT&T, Xerox, Union Carbide, and many other companies have had new stock plans in effect in recent years, using them to raise substantial amounts of new equity capital. No fees are charged to stockholders, and many companies offer stock at a discount of 3 percent to 5 percent below the actual market price. The companies offer discounts as a trade-off against flotation costs that would be incurred if new stock had been issued through investment bankers rather than through the dividend reinvestment plans.

One interesting aspect of DRIPs is that they are forcing corporations to reexamine their basic dividend policies. A high participation rate in a DRIP suggests that stockholders might be better off if the firm simply reduced cash dividends, which would save stockholders some personal income taxes. Quite a few firms are surveying their stockholders to learn more about their preferences and to find out how they would react to a change in dividend policy. A more rational approach to basic dividend policy decisions may emerge from this research.

Note that companies start or stop using new stock DRIPs depending on their need for equity capital. Thus, both Union Carbide and AT&T recently stopped

---

[10]See Richard H. Pettway and R. Phil Malone, "Automatic Dividend Reinvestment Plans," *Financial Management*, Winter 1973, 11–18, for an excellent discussion of the subject.

offering a new stock DRIP with a 5 percent discount because their needs for equity capital declined, but about the same time Xerox began such a plan.

Some companies have expanded their DRIPs by moving to "open enrollment," whereby anyone can purchase the firm's stock directly and thus bypass brokers' commissions. Exxon not only allows investors to buy their initial shares at no fee but also lets them pick up additional shares through automatic bank account withdrawals. Several plans, including Mobil's, offer dividend reinvestment for individual retirement accounts, and some, such as U.S. West, allow participants to invest weekly or monthly rather than on the quarterly dividend schedule. In all of these plans, and many others, stockholders can invest more than the dividends they are foregoing — they simply send a check to the company and buy shares without a brokerage commission. According to First Chicago Trust, which handles the paperwork for 13 million shareholder DRIP accounts, at least half of all DRIPs will offer open enrollment, extra purchases, and other expanded services within the next few years.

SELF-TEST QUESTIONS

What are dividend reinvestment plans?

What are their advantages and disadvantages from both the stockholders' and the firm's perspectives?

SUMMARY OF FACTORS INFLUENCING DIVIDEND POLICY

In earlier sections, we described both the major theories of investor preference and some issues concerning the effects of dividend policy on the value of a firm. We also discussed the residual dividend model for setting a firm's long-run target payout ratio. In this section, we discuss several other factors that affect the dividend decision. These factors may be grouped into four broad categories: (1) constraints on dividend payments, (2) investment opportunities, (3) availability and cost of alternative sources of capital, and (4) effects of dividend policy on k_s. Each of these categories has several subparts, which we discuss in the following paragraphs.

CONSTRAINTS

1. **Bond indentures.** Debt contracts often limit dividend payments to earnings generated after the loan was granted. Also, debt contracts often stipulate that no dividends can be paid unless the current ratio, times-interest-earned ratio, and other safety ratios exceed stated minimums.

2. **Preferred stock restrictions.** Typically, common dividends cannot be paid if the company has omitted its preferred dividend. The preferred arrearages must be satisfied before common dividends can be resumed.

3. **Impairment of capital rule.** Dividend payments cannot exceed the balance sheet item "retained earnings." This legal restriction, known as the *impairment of capital rule,* is designed to protect creditors. Without the rule, a company that is in trouble might distribute most of its assets to stockholders

and leave its debtholders out in the cold. (*Liquidating dividends* can be paid out of capital, but they must be indicated as such, and they must not reduce capital below the limits stated in debt contracts.)

4. **Availability of cash.** Cash dividends can be paid only with cash. Thus, a shortage of cash in the bank can restrict dividend payments. However, the ability to borrow can offset this factor.

5. **Penalty tax on improperly accumulated earnings.** To prevent wealthy individuals from using corporations to avoid personal taxes, the tax code provides for a special surtax on improperly accumulated income. Thus, if the IRS can demonstrate that a firm's dividend payout ratio is being deliberately held down to help its stockholders avoid personal taxes, the firm is subject to heavy penalties. This factor is generally relevant only to privately owned firms.

INVESTMENT OPPORTUNITIES

1. **Location of the IOS schedule.** If a firm's "typical" IOS schedule as shown earlier in Figure 14-4 is far to the right, this will tend to produce a low target payout ratio, and vice versa if the IOS is far to the left.

2. **Possibility of accelerating or delaying projects.** The ability to accelerate or to postpone projects will permit a firm to adhere more closely to a stable dividend policy.

ALTERNATIVE SOURCES OF CAPITAL

1. **Cost of selling new stock.** If a firm needs to finance a given level of investment, it can obtain equity by retaining earnings or by issuing new common stock. If flotation costs (including any negative signaling effects of a stock offering) are high, k_e will be well above k_s, making it better to set a low payout ratio and to finance through retention rather than through sale of new common stock. On the other hand, a high dividend payout ratio is more feasible for a firm whose flotation costs are low. Flotation costs differ among firms — for example, the flotation percentage is generally higher for small firms, so they tend to set low payout ratios.

2. **Ability to substitute debt for equity.** A firm can finance a given level of investment with either debt or equity. As noted above, low stock flotation costs permit a more flexible dividend policy because equity can be raised either by retaining earnings or by selling new stock. A similar situation holds for debt policy: if the firm can adjust its debt ratio without raising costs sharply, it can pay the expected dividend, even if earnings fluctuate, by using a variable debt ratio. The shape of the average cost of capital curve (in the left-hand panel of Figure 14-2) determines the practical extent to which the debt ratio can be varied. If the average cost of capital curve is relatively flat over a wide range, then a higher payout ratio is more feasible than if the curve had a sharp V shape.

3. **Control.** If management is concerned about maintaining control, it may be reluctant to sell new stock, hence the company may retain more earnings than it otherwise would. However, if stockholders want higher dividends and a proxy fight looms, then the dividend will be increased. This factor motivated Chrysler to raise its dividend in 1996.

Effects of Dividend Policy on k_s

The effects of dividend policy on k_s may be considered in terms of four factors: (1) stockholders' desire for current versus future income, (2) perceived riskiness of dividends versus capital gains, (3) the tax advantage of capital gains over dividends, and (4) the information content of dividends (signaling). Since we discussed each of these factors in detail earlier, we need only note here that the importance of each factor in terms of its effect on k_s varies from firm to firm depending on the makeup of its current and possible future stockholders.

It should be apparent from our discussion thus far that dividend policy decisions are truly exercises in informed judgment, not decisions that can be quantified precisely. Even so, to make rational dividend decisions, financial managers must take account of all the points discussed in the preceding sections.

SELF-TEST QUESTIONS ??????

Identify the four broad sets of factors which affect dividend policy.

What constraints affect dividend policy?

How do investment opportunities affect dividend policy?

How does the availability and cost of outside capital affect dividend policy?

OVERVIEW OF THE DIVIDEND POLICY DECISION

In many ways, our discussion of dividend policy parallels our discussion of capital structure: We have presented the relevant theories and issues, and we have listed some additional factors that influence dividend policy, but we have not come up with any hard-and-fast guidelines that managers can follow. It should be apparent from our discussion that dividend policy decisions are exercises in informed judgment, not decisions that can be based on a precise mathematical model.

In practice, dividend policy is not an independent decision — the dividend decision is made jointly with capital structure and capital budgeting decisions. The underlying reason for this joint decision process is asymmetric information, which influences managerial actions in two ways:

1. In general, managers do not want to issue new common stock. First, new common stock involves issuance costs — commissions, fees, and so on — and those costs can be avoided by using retained earnings to finance the firm's equity needs. Also, as we discussed in Chapter 13, asymmetric information causes investors to view new common stock issues as negative signals and thus lowers expectations regarding the firm's future prospects. The end result is that the announcement of a new stock issue usually leads to a decrease in the stock price. Considering the total costs involved, including both issuance and asymmetric information costs, managers strongly prefer to use retained earnings as their primary source of new equity.

2. Dividend changes provide signals about managers' beliefs as to their firms' future prospects. Thus, dividend reductions, or worse yet, omissions, generally

have a significant negative effect on a firm's stock price. Since managers recognize this, they try to set dollar dividends low enough so that there is only a remote chance that the dividend will have to be reduced in the future. Of course, unexpectedly large dividend increases can be used to provide positive signals.

The effects of asymmetric information suggest that, to the extent possible, managers should avoid both new common stock sales and dividend cuts, because both actions tend to lower stock prices. Thus, in setting dividend policy, managers should begin by considering the firm's future investment opportunities relative to its projected internal sources of funds. The firm's target capital structure also plays a part, but because the optimal capital structure is a *range*, firms can vary their actual capital structures somewhat from year to year. Since it is best to avoid issuing new common stock, the target long-term payout ratio should be designed to permit the firm to meet all of its equity capital requirements with retained earnings. In effect, managers should use the residual dividend model to set dividends, but in a long-term framework. Finally, the current dollar dividend should be set so that there is an extremely low probability that the dividend, once set, will ever have to be lowered or omitted.

Of course, the dividend decision is made during the planning process, so there is uncertainty about future investment opportunities and operating cash flows. Thus, the actual payout ratio in any year will probably be above or below the firm's long-range target. However, the dollar dividend should be maintained, or increased as planned, unless the firm's financial condition deteriorates to the point where the planned policy simply cannot be maintained. A steady or increasing stream of dividends over the long run signals that the firm's financial condition is under control. Further, investor uncertainty is decreased by stable dividends, so a steady dividend stream reduces the negative effect of a new stock issue, should one become absolutely necessary.

In general, firms with superior investment opportunities should set lower payouts, hence retain more earnings, than firms with poor investment opportunities. The degree of uncertainty also influences the decision. If there is a great deal of uncertainty in the forecasts of **free cash flows**, which are defined here as the firm's operating cash flows minus mandatory equity investments, then it is best to be conservative and to set a lower current dollar dividend. Also, firms with postponable investment opportunities can afford to set a higher dollar dividend, because, in times of stress, investments can be postponed for a year or two, thus increasing the cash available for dividends. Finally, firms which have a flat WACC curve, when WACC is plotted against the debt ratio as in the left panel of Figure 14-4, can also afford to set a higher payout ratio, because they can, in times of stress, more easily issue additional debt to maintain the capital budgeting program without having to cut dividends or issue stock.

Firms have only one opportunity to set the dividend payment from scratch. Therefore, today's dividend decisions are constrained by policies that were set in the past, hence setting a policy for the next five years necessarily begins with a review of the current situation.

Although we have outlined a rational process for managers to use when setting their firms' dividend policies, dividend policy still remains one of the most judgmental decisions that firms must make. For this reason, dividend policy is always set by the board of directors — the financial staff analyzes the situation and makes a recommendation, but the board makes the final decision.

Free Cash Flows
The firm's operating cash flows less mandatory equity investments.

STOCK DIVIDENDS AND STOCK SPLITS

Stock dividends and stock splits are related to the firm's cash dividend policy. The rationale for stock dividends and splits can best be explained through an example. We will use Porter Electronic Controls Inc., a $700 million electronic components manufacturer, for this purpose. Since its inception, Porter's markets have been expanding, and the company has enjoyed growth in sales and earnings. Some of its earnings have been paid out in dividends, but some are also retained each year, causing its earnings per share and stock price to grow. The company began its life with only a few thousand shares outstanding, and, after some years of growth, each of Porter's shares had a very high EPS and DPS. When a "normal" P/E ratio was applied, the derived market price was so high that few people could afford to buy a "round lot" of 100 shares. This limited the demand for the stock and thus kept the total market value of the firm below what it would have been if more shares, at a lower price, had been outstanding. To correct this situation, Porter "split its stock," as described in the next section.

STOCK SPLITS

Stock Split
An action taken by a firm to increase the number of shares outstanding, such as doubling the number of shares outstanding by giving each stockholder two new shares for each one formerly held.

Although there is little empirical evidence to support the contention, there is nevertheless a widespread belief in financial circles that an *optimal price range* exists for stocks. "Optimal" means that if the price is within this range, the price/earnings ratio, hence the firm's value, will be maximized. Many observers, including Porter's management, believe that the best range for most stocks is from $20 to $80 per share. Accordingly, if the price of Porter's stock rose to $80, management would probably declare a two-for-one **stock split,** thus doubling the number of shares outstanding, halving the earnings and dividends per share, and thereby lowering the stock price. Each stockholder would have more shares, but each share would be worth less. If the post-split price were $40, Porter's stockholders would be exactly as well off as they were before the split. However, if the stock price were to stabilize above $40, stockholders would be better off. Stock splits can be of any size — for example, the stock could be split two-for-one, three-for-one, one-and-a-half-for-one, or in any other way.[11]

STOCK DIVIDENDS

Stock Dividend
A dividend paid in the form of additional shares of stock rather than in cash.

Stock dividends are similar to stock splits in that they "divide the pie into smaller slices" without affecting the fundamental position of the current stockholders. On a 5 percent stock dividend, the holder of 100 shares would receive an additional 5 shares (without cost); on a 20 percent stock dividend, the same holder

---

[11]*Reverse splits,* which reduce the shares outstanding, can even be used. For example, a company whose stock sells for $5 might employ a one-for-five reverse split, exchanging one new share for five old ones and raising the value of the shares to about $25, which is within the optimal price range. LTV Corporation did this after several years of losses had driven its stock price down below the optimal range.

would receive 20 new shares; and so on. Again, the total number of shares is increased, so earnings, dividends, and price per share all decline.

If a firm wants to reduce the price of its stock, should it use a stock split or a stock dividend? Stock splits are generally used after a sharp price run-up to produce a large price reduction. Stock dividends used on a regular annual basis will keep the stock price more or less constrained. For example, if a firm's earnings and dividends were growing at about 10 percent per year, its stock price would tend to go up at about that same rate, and it would soon be outside the desired trading range. A 10 percent annual stock dividend would maintain the stock price within the optimal trading range. Note, though, that small stock dividends create bookkeeping problems and unnecessary expenses, so firms today use stock splits far more often than stock dividends.[12]

PRICE EFFECTS

If a company splits its stock or declares a stock dividend, will this increase the market value of its stock? Several empirical studies have sought to answer this question, and here is a summary of their findings.[13]

1. On average, the price of a company's stock rises shortly after it announces a stock split or dividend.

2. However, these price increases are more the result of the fact that investors take stock splits/dividends as signals of higher future earnings and dividends than of a desire for stock dividends/splits per se. Since only companies whose managements think things look good tend to split their stocks, the announcement of a stock split is taken as a signal that earnings and cash dividends are likely to rise. Thus, the price increases associated with stock splits/dividends are probably the result of signals of favorable prospects for earnings and dividends, not a desire for stock splits/dividends per se.

3. If a company announces a stock split or dividend, its price will tend to rise. However, if during the next few months it does not announce an increase in earnings and dividends, then its stock price will drop back to the earlier level.

4. As we noted earlier, brokerage commissions are generally higher in percentage terms on lower-priced stocks. This means that it is more expensive to trade low-priced than high-priced stocks, and this, in turn, means that stock splits may reduce the liquidity of a company's shares. This particular piece of evidence suggests that stock splits/dividends might actually be harmful, although

---

[12]Accountants treat stock splits and stock dividends somewhat differently. For example, in a two-for-one stock split, the number of shares outstanding is doubled and the par value is halved, and that is about all there is to it. With a stock dividend, a bookkeeping entry is made transferring "retained earnings" to "common stock." For example, if a firm had 1,000,000 shares outstanding, if the stock price was $10, and if it wanted to pay a 10 percent stock dividend, then (1) each stockholder would be given one new share of stock for each ten shares held, and (2) the accounting entries would involve showing 100,000 more shares outstanding and transferring 100,000($10) = $1,000,000 from "retained earnings" to "common stock." The retained earnings transfer limits the size of stock dividends, but that is not important because companies can always split their stock in any way they choose.

[13]See Eugene F. Fama, Lawrence Fisher, Michael C. Jensen, and Richard Roll, "The Adjustment of Stock Prices to New Information," *International Economic Review*, February 1969, 1–21; Mark S. Grinblatt, Ronald M. Masulis, and Sheridan Titman, "The Valuation Effects of Stock Splits and Stock Dividends," *Journal of Financial Economics*, December 1984, 461–490; C. Austin Barker, "Evaluation of Stock Dividends," *Harvard Business Review*, July–August 1958, 99–114; and Copeland op.cit, 115–141.

a lower price does mean that more investors can afford to trade in round lots (100 shares), which carry lower commissions than do odd lots (less than 100 shares).

What do we conclude from all this? From a pure economic standpoint, stock dividends and splits are just additional pieces of paper. However, they provide management with a relatively low-cost way of signaling that the firm's prospects look good. Further, we should note that since few large, publicly owned stocks sell at prices above several hundred dollars, we simply do not know what the effect would be if Microsoft, Xerox, Hewlett-Packard, and other highly successful firms had never split their stocks, and consequently had sold at prices in the thousands or even tens of thousands of dollars. All in all, it probably makes sense to employ stock dividends/splits when a firm's prospects are favorable, especially if the price of its stock has gone beyond the normal trading range.[14]

SELF-TEST QUESTIONS

What are stock dividends and stock splits?

What impact do stock dividends and splits have on stock prices? Why?

In what situations should managers consider the use of stock dividends?

In what situations should they consider the use of stock splits?

STOCK REPURCHASES

Several years ago, a *Fortune* article entitled "Beating the Market by Buying Back Stock" discussed the fact that during a one-year period, more than 600 major corporations repurchased significant amounts of their own stock. It also gave illustrations of some specific companies' repurchase programs and their effects on stock prices. The article's conclusion was that "buy-backs have made a mint for shareholders who stay with the companies carrying them out."

In addition, we noted earlier that both IBM and FPL recently cut their dividends but simultaneously instituted programs to repurchase shares of their stocks. Thus they substituted share repurchases for cash dividends as a way to distribute funds to stockholders. IBM and FPL are not alone — during 1995 Philip Morris, GE, Disney, Citicorp, Merck, and more than 800 other companies took similar actions, and the dollars used to repurchase shares approximately matched the amount paid out as dividends.

Stock Repurchase
A transaction in which a firm buys back shares of its own stock, thereby decreasing shares outstanding, increasing EPS, and, often, increasing the stock price.

Why are stock repurchase programs becoming so popular? The short answer is that they enhance shareholder value: A more complete answer is given in the remainder of this section, where we explain what a **stock repurchase** is, how it is carried out, and how the financial manager should analyze a possible repurchase program.

There are two principal types of repurchases: (1) situations where the firm has cash available for distribution to its stockholders, and it distributes this cash by repurchasing shares rather than by paying cash dividends, and (2) situations

---

[14]It is interesting to note that Berkshire Hathaway, which is controlled by billionaire Warren Buffett, one of the most successful financiers of the twentieth century, has never had a stock split, and its stock sold on the NYSE for $35,900 per share in early 1997. But, in response to investment trusts that were being formed to sell fractional units of the stock, Buffett created a new class of Berkshire Hathaway stock (Class B) worth about $1/30$ of a Class A (regular) share.

INDUSTRY PRACTICE

STOCK REPURCHASES: AN EASY WAY TO BOOST STOCK PRICES?

Looking for a way to boost your company's stock price? Why not buy back some of your company's shares? That reflects the thinking of an increasing number of financial managers. By mid-1996, a record 850 companies had indicated that they would repurchase shares, up from 655 announcements over the same time period in 1995 and 535 in 1994. Moreover, repurchase programs are increasing in size — during 1995 and the first half of 1996, 37 companies have announced buybacks that exceed $1 billion.

The buyback rage is in some ways surprising. Given the recent performance of the stock market, it has become quite expensive to buy back shares. Nevertheless, the market's response to a buyback announcement is usually positive. For example, in mid-1996 Reebok announced that it would buy back one-third of its outstanding shares, and on the announcement day, the stock price rose 10 percent. Reebok's experience is not unique. A recent study found (1) that the average company's stock rose 3.5 percent the day a buyback was announced and (2) that companies which repurchase shares outperform the market over a four-year period following the announcement.[15]

Why are buybacks so popular with investors? The general view is that financial managers are signaling to the investment community a belief that the stock is undervalued, hence that the company thinks it own stock is an attractive investment. In this respect, stock repurchases have the opposite effect of stock issuances, which are thought to signal that the firm's stock is overvalued. Buybacks also help assure investors that the company is not wasting its shareholders' money by investing in subpar investments. Michael O'Neill, the CFO of BankAmerica, puts it this way: "We look very hard internally, but if we don't have a profitable use for capital, we think we should return it to shareholders."

Despite all the recent hoopla surrounding buybacks, many analysts stress that in some instances they have a downside: If a firm's stock is actually overvalued, buying back shares at the inflated price will harm the remaining stockholders. In this regard, buybacks should not be viewed as a gimmick to boost stock prices in the short run, but should be used only if they are part of a well-thought-out strategy for investment and for distributing cash to stockholders. Indeed, buybacks do not always succeed — Disney, for example, announced a buyback in April 1996, and its stock price fell more than 10 percent in the next six months.

[15]David Ikenberry, Josef Lakonishok, and Theo Vermaelen, "Market Under-Reaction to Open Market Share Repurchases," *Rice University Working Paper*, June 1994.

SOURCE: Adapted from "Buybacks Make News, But Do They Make Sense?" *BusinessWeek*, August 12, 1996, 76.

---

where the firm concludes that its capital structure is too heavily weighted with equity, and then it sells debt and uses the proceeds to buy back its stock.

Stock that has been repurchased by a firm is called *treasury stock*. If some of the outstanding stock is repurchased, fewer shares will remain outstanding. Assuming that the repurchase does not adversely affect the firm's future earnings, the earnings per share on the remaining shares will increase, resulting in a higher market price per share. As a result, capital gains will have been substituted for dividends.

THE EFFECTS OF STOCK REPURCHASES

Many companies have been repurchasing their stock in recent years. Until the 1980s, most repurchases amounted to a few million dollars, but in 1985, Phillips Petroleum announced plans for the largest repurchase on record — 81 million of its shares with a market value of $4.1 billion. Other large repurchases have been made by Texaco, IBM, CBS, Coca-Cola, Teledyne, Atlantic Richfield, Goodyear, and Xerox. Indeed, since 1985, more shares have been repurchased than issued.

The effects of a repurchase can be illustrated with data on American Development Corporation (ADC). The company expects to earn $4.4 million in 1998, and 50 percent of this amount, or $2.2 million, has been allocated for distribution to common shareholders. There are 1.1 million shares outstanding, and the market price is $20 a share. ADC believes that it can either use the $2.2 million to re-purchase 100,000 of its shares through a tender offer at $22 a share or else pay a cash dividend of $2 a share.[16]

The effect of the repurchase on the EPS and market price per share of the remaining stock can be analyzed in the following way:

1. Current EPS $= \dfrac{\text{Total earnings}}{\text{Number of shares}} = \dfrac{\$4.4 \text{ million}}{1.1 \text{ million}} = \$4$ per share.

2. P/E ratio $= \dfrac{\$20}{\$4} = 5\times$.

3. EPS after repurchasing 100,000 shares $= \dfrac{\$4.4 \text{ million}}{1 \text{ million}} = \$4.40$ per share.

4. Expected market price after repurchase $= (\text{P/E})(\text{EPS}) = (5)(\$4.40)$
$$= \$22 \text{ per share.}$$

It should be noted from this example that investors would receive before-tax benefits of $2 per share in any case, either in the form of a $2 cash dividend or a $2 increase in the stock price. This result would occur because we assumed, first, that shares could be repurchased at exactly $22 a share and, second, that the P/E ratio would remain constant. If shares could be bought for less than $22, the operation would be even better for *remaining* stockholders, but the reverse would hold if ADC had to pay more than $22 a share. Furthermore, the P/E ratio might change as a result of the repurchase operation, rising if investors viewed it favorably and falling if they viewed it unfavorably. Some factors that might affect P/E ratios are considered next.

ADVANTAGES OF REPURCHASES

The advantages of repurchases are as follows:

1. Repurchase announcements are viewed as positive signals by investors because the repurchase is often motivated by management's belief that the firm's shares are undervalued.

2. The stockholders have a choice when the firm distributes cash by repurchasing stock — they can sell or not sell. With a cash dividend, on the other hand, stockholders must accept a dividend payment and pay the tax. Thus, those stockholders who need cash can sell back some of their shares, while those who do not want additional cash can simply retain their stock. From a tax standpoint, a repurchase permits both types of stockholders to get what they want.

---

[16]Stock repurchases are generally made in one of three ways: (1) A publicly owned firm can simply buy its own stock through a broker on the open market. (2) It can make a *tender offer,* under which it permits stockholders to send in (that is, "tender") their shares to the firm in exchange for a speci-fied price per share. In this case, it generally indicates that it will buy up to a specified number of shares within a particular time period (usually about two weeks); if more shares are tendered than the company wishes to purchase, purchases are made on a pro rata basis. (3) The firm can purchase a block of shares from one large holder on a negotiated basis. If a negotiated purchase is employed, care must be taken to ensure that this one stockholder does not receive preferential treatment over other stockholders or that any preference given can be justified by "sound business reasons." Tex-aco's management was sued by stockholders who were unhappy over the company's repurchase of about $600 million of stock from the Bass Brothers' interests at a substantial premium over the mar-ket price. The suit charged that Texaco's management, afraid the Bass Brothers would attempt a take-over, used the buyback to get them off its back. Such payments have been dubbed "greenmail."

3. A third advantage is that a repurchase can remove a large block of stock that is "overhanging" the market and keeping the price per share down.

4. Dividends are "sticky" in the short run because managements are reluctant to raise the dividend if the increase cannot be maintained in the future— managements dislike cutting cash dividends because of the negative signal a cut gives. Hence, if the excess cash flow is thought to be only temporary, management may prefer to make the distribution in the form of a share repurchase rather than to declare an increased cash dividend that cannot be maintained.

5. Companies can use the residual model to set a *target cash distribution* level, then divide the distribution into a *dividend component* and a *repurchase component*. The dividend payout ratio will be relatively low, but the dividend itself will be relatively secure, and it will grow as a result of the declining number of shares outstanding. The company has more flexibility in adjusting the total distribution than it would if the entire distribution were in the form of cash dividends, because repurchases can be varied from year to year without giving off adverse signals. This procedure, which is what FPL did, has much to recommend it, and it is a primary reason for the dramatic increase in the volume of share repurchases.

6. Repurchases can be used to produce large-scale changes in capital structures. For example, several years ago Consolidated Edison decided to repurchase $400 million of its common stock in order to increase its debt ratio. The repurchase was necessary because even if the company financed its capital budget only with debt, it would still have taken years to get the debt ratio up to the target level. Con Ed used the repurchase to produce a rapid change in its capital structure.

DISADVANTAGES OF REPURCHASES

Disadvantages of repurchases include the following:

1. Stockholders may not be indifferent between dividends and capital gains, and the price of the stock might benefit more from cash dividends than from repurchases. Cash dividends are generally dependable, but repurchases are not. Further, if a firm announced a regular, dependable repurchase program, the improper accumulation tax might become a threat.

2. The *selling* stockholders may not be fully aware of all the implications of a repurchase, or they may not have all pertinent information about the corporation's present and future activities. However, firms generally announce repurchase programs before embarking on them to avoid potential stockholder suits.

3. The corporation may pay too high a price for the repurchased stock, to the disadvantage of remaining stockholders. If its shares are not actively traded, and if the firm seeks to acquire a relatively large amount of its stock, then the price may be bid above its equilibrium level and then fall after the firm ceases its repurchase operations.

CONCLUSIONS ON STOCK REPURCHASES

When all the pros and cons on stock repurchases have been totaled, where do we stand? Our conclusions may be summarized as follows:

1. Because of the lower capital gains tax rate and the deferred tax on capital gains, repurchases have a significant tax advantage over dividends as a way to

GLOBAL PERSPECTIVES

SHARE REPURCHASES ARE LESS COMMON OVERSEAS

While stock repurchases have become quite common in the United States, they are considerably less common, and often illegal, overseas. During the 1990s, 50 European companies have announced stock buyback programs — in contrast to more than 800 U.S. companies an-nouncing buyback plans during just the first eight months of 1996. More-over, most of the European buybacks have occurred in one country — Great Britain. Even in England, where buybacks are allowed and are fairly common, regulators still view them with some skepticism. For ex-ample, England recently closed a tax loophole which had encouraged buybacks — this change led Reuters to cancel a proposed buyback.

Nevertheless, there are some indi-cations that buybacks may become more common overseas. Germany and France are taking steps to elimi-nate laws which prohibit buybacks. Likewise, regulators in other Euro-pean and Asian countries are slowly beginning to reconsider their long-held opposition to buybacks.

SOURCE: "Business This Week: Taking Cred-its," *The Economist*, October 12, 1996, 5; "Share Repurchases," *The Economist*, July 2, 1994, 70.

---

distribute income to stockholders. This advantage is reinforced by the fact that repurchases provide cash to stockholders who want cash but allow those who do not need current cash to delay its receipt. On the other hand, dividends are more dependable and are thus better suited for those who need a steady source of income.

2. Because of signaling effects, companies should not vary their dividends — this would lower investors' confidence in a company and adversely affect its cost of equity and its stock price. However, cash flows vary over time, as do investment opportunities, so the "proper" dividend in the residual model sense varies. To get around this problem, a company can set its dividend at a level low enough to keep dividend payments from constraining operations and then use repurchases on a more or less regular basis to distribute excess cash. Such a procedure would provide regular, dependable dividends plus additional cash flow to those stockholders who want it.

3. Repurchases are also useful when a firm wants to make a large shift in its capital structure within a short period of time, or wants to distribute cash from a one-time event such as the sale of a division.

In an earlier edition of this book, we argued that companies ought to be doing more repurchasing and paying out less cash as dividends than they were. Increases in the size and frequency of repurchases in recent years suggest that companies have reached this same conclusion.

SELF-TEST QUESTIONS

Explain how repurchases can (1) help stockholders hold down taxes and (2) help firms change their capital structures.

What is treasury stock?

What are three ways a firm can repurchase its stock?

What are some advantages and disadvantages of stock repurchases?

How can stock repurchases help a company operate in accordance with the residual dividend model?

SUMMARY

Dividend policy involves the decision to pay out earnings versus retaining them for reinvestment in the firm. The key concepts covered in the chapter are listed below.

♦ **Dividend policy** involves three issues: (1) What fraction of earnings should be distributed, on average, over time? (2) Should the distribution be in the form of cash dividends or stock repurchases? (3) Should the firm maintain a steady, stable dividend growth rate?

♦ The **optimal dividend policy** strikes a balance between current dividends and future growth so as to maximize the firm's stock price.

♦ Miller and Modigliani developed the **dividend irrelevance theory,** which holds that a firm's dividend policy has no effect on either the value of its stock or its cost of capital.

♦ The **bird-in-the-hand theory** holds that the firm's value will be maximized by a high dividend payout ratio, because investors regard cash dividends as being less risky than potential capital gains.

♦ The **tax preference theory** states that because long-term capital gains are subject to less onerous taxes than dividends, investors prefer to have companies retain earnings rather than pay them out as dividends.

♦ **Empirical tests** of the three theories **have been inconclusive.** Therefore, academicians cannot tell corporate managers how a given change in dividend policy will affect stock prices and capital costs.

♦ Dividend policy should take account of the **information content of dividends (signaling)** and the **clientele effect.** The information content, or signaling, effect relates to the fact that investors regard an unexpected dividend change as a signal of management's forecast of future earnings. The clientele effect suggests that a firm will attract investors who like the firm's dividend payout policy. Both factors should be considered by firms that are considering a change in dividend policy.

♦ In practice, most firms try to follow a policy of paying a **steadily increasing dividend.** This policy provides investors with stable, dependable income, and departures from it give investors signals about management's expectations for future earnings.

♦ Most firms use the **residual dividend model** to set the long-run target payout ratio at a level which will permit the firm to satisfy its equity requirements with retained earnings.

♦ **Legal constraints, investment opportunities, availability and cost of funds from other sources,** and **taxes** are also considered when firms establish dividend policies.

♦ A **dividend reinvestment plan (DRP or DRIP)** allows stockholders to have the company automatically use dividends to purchase additional shares of stock. DRIPs are popular because they allow stockholders to acquire additional shares without incurring brokerage fees.

♦ A **stock split** increases the number of shares outstanding. Normally, splits reduce the price per share in proportion to the increase in shares because splits merely "divide the pie into smaller slices." However, firms generally split their stocks only if (1) the price is quite high and (2) management thinks the future is bright. Therefore, stock splits are often taken as positive signals and thus boost stock prices.

♦ A **stock dividend** is a dividend paid in additional shares of stock rather than in cash. Both stock dividends and splits are used to keep stock prices within an "optimal" trading range.

♦ Under a **stock repurchase plan,** a firm buys back some of its outstanding stock, thereby decreasing the number of shares, which should increase both EPS and the stock price. Repurchases are useful for making major changes in capital structure, as well as for distributing temporary excess cash.

QUESTIONS

14-1   How would each of the following changes tend to affect aggregate (that is, the average for all corporations) payout ratios, other things held constant? Explain your answers.
a. An increase in the personal income tax rate.
b. A liberalization of depreciation for federal income tax purposes — that is, faster tax write-offs.
c. A rise in interest rates.
d. An increase in corporate profits.
e. A decline in investment opportunities.
f. Permission for corporations to deduct dividends for tax purposes as they now do interest charges.
g. A change in the tax code so that both realized and unrealized capital gains in any year were taxed at the same rate as dividends.

14-2   Discuss the pros and cons of having the directors formally announce what a firm's dividend policy will be in the future.

14-3   Most firms would like to have their stock selling at a high P/E ratio, and they would also like to have extensive public ownership (many different shareholders). Explain how stock dividends or stock splits may help achieve these goals.

14-4   What is the difference between a stock dividend and a stock split? As a stockholder, would you prefer to see your company declare a 100 percent stock dividend or a two-for-one split? Assume that either action is feasible.

14-5   "The cost of retained earnings is less than the cost of new outside equity capital. Consequently, it is totally irrational for a firm to sell a new issue of stock and to pay dividends during the same year." Discuss this statement.

14-6   Would it ever be rational for a firm to borrow money in order to pay dividends? Explain.

14-7   "Executive salaries have been shown to be more closely correlated to the size of the firm than to its profitability. If a firm's board of directors is controlled by management instead of by outside directors, this might result in the firm's retaining more earnings than can be justified from the stockholders' point of view." Discuss the statement, being sure (a) to use Figure 14-4 in your answer and (b) to explain the implied relationship between dividend policy and stock prices.

14-8   Modigliani and Miller (MM) on the one hand and Gordon and Lintner (GL) on the other have expressed strong views regarding the effect of dividend policy on a firm's cost of capital and value.
a. In essence, what are the MM and GL views regarding the effect of dividend policy on the cost of capital and stock prices?
b. How does the tax preference theory differ from the views of MM and GL?
c. According to the text, which of the theories, if any, has received statistical confirmation from empirical tests?
d. How could MM use the *information content,* or *signaling, hypothesis* to counter their opponents' arguments? If you were debating MM, how would you counter them?
e. How could MM use the *clientele effect* concept to counter their opponents' arguments? If you were debating MM, how would you counter them?

14-9   More NYSE companies had stock dividends and stock splits during 1983 and 1984 than ever before. What events in these years could have made stock splits and stock dividends so popular? Explain the rationale that a financial vice-president might give his or her board of directors to support a stock split/dividend recommendation.

14-10 One position expressed in the financial literature is that firms set their dividends as a residual after using income to support new investment.

a. Explain what a residual dividend policy implies, illustrating your answer with a graph showing how different conditions could lead to different dividend payout ratios.

b. Think back to Chapter 13, where we considered the relationship between capital structure and the cost of capital. If the WACC-versus-debt-ratio plot was shaped like a sharp V, would this have a different implication for the importance of setting dividends according to the residual policy than if the plot was shaped like a shallow bowl (or a flattened U)?

c. Assume that Companies A and B both have IOS schedules that intersect their MCC schedules at a point which, under the residual policy, calls for a 30 percent payout. In both cases, a 30 percent payout would require a cut in the annual dividend from $3 to $1.50. One company cuts its dividend, whereas the other does not. One company has a relatively steep IOS curve, whereas the other has a relatively flat one. Explain which company probably has the steeper curve.

14-11 Indicate whether the following statements are true or false. If the statement is false, explain why.

a. If a firm repurchases its stock in the open market, the shareholders who tender the stock are subject to capital gains taxes.

b. If you own 100 shares in a company's stock and the company's stock splits two for one, you will own 200 shares in the company following the split.

c. Some dividend reinvestment plans increase the amount of equity capital available to the firm.

d. The tax code encourages companies to pay a large percentage of their net income in the form of dividends.

e. If your company has established a clientele of investors who prefer large dividends, the company is unlikely to adopt a residual dividend policy.

f. If a firm follows a residual dividend policy, holding all else constant, its dividend payout will tend to rise whenever the firm's investment opportunities improve.

SELF-TEST PROBLEMS (Solutions Appear in Appendix B)

ST-1

Key terms

Define each of the following terms:

a. Optimal dividend policy

b. Dividend irrelevance theory; bird-in-the-hand theory; tax preference theory

c. Information content, or signaling, hypothesis; clientele effect

d. Residual dividend model

e. Extra dividend

f. Declaration date; holder-of-record date; ex-dividend date; payment date

g. Dividend reinvestment plan (DRIP)

h. Stock split; stock dividend

i. Stock repurchase

ST-2

Alternative dividend policies

Components Manufacturing Corporation (CMC) has an all-common-equity capital structure. It has 200,000 shares of $2 par value common stock outstanding. When CMC's founder, who was also its research director and most successful inventor, retired unexpectedly to the South Pacific in late 1997, CMC was left suddenly and permanently with materially lower growth expectations and relatively few attractive new investment opportunities. Unfortunately, there was no way to replace the founder's contributions to the firm. Previously, CMC found it necessary to plow back most of its earnings to finance growth, which averaged 12 percent per year. Future growth at a 5 percent rate is considered realistic, but that level would call for an increase in the dividend payout. Further, it now appears that new investment projects with at least the 14 percent rate of return required by CMC's stockholders ($k_s = 14\%$) would amount to only $800,000 for 1998 in comparison to a projected $2,000,000 of net income. If the existing 20 percent dividend payout were continued, retained earnings would be $1.6 million in 1998, but, as noted, investments which yield the 14 percent cost of capital would amount to only $800,000.

The one encouraging thing is that the high earnings from existing assets are expected to continue, and net income of $2 million is still expected for 1998. Given the dramatically changed circumstances, CMC's management is reviewing the firm's dividend policy.

a. Assuming that the acceptable 1998 investment projects would be financed entirely by earnings retained during the year, calculate DPS in 1998, assuming that CMC uses the residual dividend model.

b. What payout ratio does your answer to Part a imply for 1998?

c. If a 60 percent payout ratio is maintained for the foreseeable future, what is your estimate of the present market price of the common stock? How does this compare with the market price that should have prevailed under the assumptions existing just before the news about the founder's retirement? If the two values of P_0 are different, comment on why.

d. What would happen to the price of the stock if the old 20 percent payout were continued? Assume that if this payout is maintained, the average rate of return on the retained earnings will fall to 7.5 percent and the new growth rate will be

$$g = (1.0 - \text{Payout ratio})(\text{ROE})$$
$$= (1.0 - 0.2)(7.5\%)$$
$$= (0.8)(7.5\%) = 6.0\%.$$

STARTER PROBLEMS

14-1
Residual dividend model

Axel Telecommunications has a target capital structure which consists of 70 percent debt and 30 percent equity. The company anticipates that its capital budget for the upcoming year will be $3,000,000. If Axel reports net income of $2,000,000 and it follows a residual dividend payout policy, what will be its dividend payout ratio?

14-2
Stock split

Gamma Medical's stock trades at $90 a share. The company is contemplating a 3-for-2 stock split. Assuming that the stock split will have no effect on the market value of its equity, what will be the company's stock price following the stock split?

14-3
Stock repurchases

Beta Industries has net income of $2,000,000 and it has 1,000,000 shares of common stock outstanding. The company's stock currently trades at $32 a share. Beta is considering a plan where it will use available cash to repurchase 20 percent of its shares in the open market. The repurchase is expected to have no effect on either net income or the company's P/E ratio. What will be its stock price following the stock repurchase?

EXAM-TYPE PROBLEMS

The problems included in this section are set up in such a way that they could be used as multiple-choice exam problems.

14-4
External equity financing

Northern Pacific Heating and Cooling Inc. has a 6-month backlog of orders for its patented solar heating system. To meet this demand, management plans to expand production capacity by 40 percent with a $10 million investment in plant and machinery. The firm wants to maintain a 40 percent debt-to-total-assets ratio in its capital structure; it also wants to maintain its past dividend policy of distributing 45 percent of last year's net income. In 1997, net income was $5 million. How much external equity must Northern Pacific seek at the beginning of 1998 to expand capacity as desired?

14-5
Residual dividend policy

Petersen Company has a capital budget of $1.2 million. The company wants to maintain a target capital structure which is 60 percent debt and 40 percent equity. The company forecasts that its net income this year will be $600,000. If the company follows a residual dividend policy, what will be its payout ratio?

14-6
Dividend payout

The Wei Corporation expects next year's net income to be $15 million. The firm's debt ratio is currently 40 percent. Wei has $12 million of profitable investment opportunities, and it wishes to maintain its existing debt ratio. According to the residual dividend model, how large should Wei's dividend payout ratio be next year?

14-7
Stock split

After a 5-for-1 stock split, the Strasburg Company paid a dividend of $0.75 per new share, which represents a 9 percent increase over last year's pre-split dividend. What was last year's dividend per share?

14-8
Dividend payout

The Welch Company's optimal capital structure calls for 50 percent debt and 50 percent common equity. The interest rate on its debt is a constant 10 percent; its cost of common equity from retained earnings is 14 percent; the cost of equity from new stock is 16 percent; and its federal-plus-state tax rate is 40 percent. Welch has the following investment opportunities:

Project A: Cost = $5 million; IRR = 20%.

Project B: Cost = $5 million; IRR = 12%.

Project C: Cost = $5 million; IRR = 9%.

Welch expects to have net income of $7,287,500. If Welch bases its dividends on the residual model, what will its payout ratio be?

PROBLEMS

14-9
Alternative dividend policies

In 1997 the Keenan Company paid dividends totaling $3,600,000 on net income of $10.8 million. 1997 was a normal year, and for the past 10 years, earnings have grown at a constant rate of 10 percent. However, in 1998, earnings are expected to jump to $14.4 million, and the firm expects to have profitable investment opportunities of $8.4 million. It is predicted that Keenan will not be able to maintain the 1998 level of earnings growth — the high 1998 earnings level is attributable to an exceptionally profitable new product line introduced that year — and the company will return to its previous 10 percent growth rate. Keenan's target debt ratio is 40 percent.
a. Calculate Keenan's total dividends for 1998 if it follows each of the following policies:
   (1) Its 1998 dividend payment is set to force dividends to grow at the long-run growth rate in earnings.
   (2) It continues the 1997 dividend payout ratio.
   (3) It uses a pure residual dividend policy (40 percent of the $8.4 million investment is financed with debt).
   (4) It employs a regular-dividend-plus-extras policy, with the regular dividend being based on the long-run growth rate and the extra dividend being set according to the residual policy.
b. Which of the preceding policies would you recommend? Restrict your choices to the ones listed, but justify your answer.
c. Assume that investors expect Keenan to pay total dividends of $9,000,000 in 1998 and to have the dividend grow at 10 percent after 1998. The stock's total market value is $180 million. What is the company's cost of equity?
d. What is Keenan's long-run average return on equity? [Hint: g = (Retention rate)(ROE) = (1.0 − Payout rate)(ROE).]
e. Does a 1998 dividend of $9,000,000 seem reasonable in view of your answers to Parts c and d? If not, should the dividend be higher or lower?

14-10
Dividend policy and capital structure

Buena Vista City Tobacco Company has for many years enjoyed a moderate but stable growth in sales and earnings. However, cigar consumption, and consequently Buena Vista's sales, have been falling recently, primarily because of an increasing awareness of the dangers of smoking to health. Anticipating further declines in tobacco sales for the future, Buena Vista's management hopes eventually to move almost entirely out of the tobacco business and into a newly developed, diversified product line in growth-oriented industries. The company is especially interested in the prospects for pollution-control devices because its research department has already done much work on the problems of filtering smoke. Right now, the company estimates that an investment of $15 million is necessary to purchase new facilities and to begin operations on these products, but the investment could be earning a return of about 18 percent within a short time. The only other available investment opportunity totals $6 million and is expected to return about 10.4 percent.
The company is expected to pay a $3.00 dividend on its 3 million outstanding shares, the same as its dividend last year. The directors might, however, change the dividend if there are good reasons for doing so. Total earnings after taxes for the year are expected to be $14.25 million; the common stock is currently selling for $56.25; the firm's target debt

ratio (debt/assets ratio) is 45 percent; and its federal-plus-state tax rate is 40 percent. The costs of various forms of financing are as follows:

New bonds, $k_d = 11\%$. This is a before-tax rate.

New common stock sold at $56.25 per share will net $51.25.

Required rate of return on retained earnings, $k_s = 14\%$.

a. Calculate Buena Vista's expected payout ratio, the break point at which MCC rises, and its marginal cost of capital above and below the point of exhaustion of retained earnings at the current payout. (Hint: k_s is given, and D_1/P_0 can be found. Then, knowing k_s and D_1/P_0, g can be determined.)
b. How large should Buena Vista's capital budget be for the year?
c. What is an appropriate dividend policy for Buena Vista? How should the capital budget be financed?
d. How might risk factors influence Buena Vista's cost of capital, capital structure, and dividend policy?
e. What assumptions, if any, do your answers to the preceding parts make about investors' preferences for dividends versus capital gains (in other words, what are investors' preferences regarding the D_1/P_0 and g components of k_s)?

INTEGRATED CASE

SOUTHEASTERN STEEL COMPANY

14-11 Dividend Policy   Southeastern Steel Company (SSC) was formed 5 years ago to exploit a new continuous-casting process. SSC's founders, Donald Brown and Margo Valencia, had been employed in the research department of a major integrated-steel company, but when that company decided against using the new process (which Brown and Valencia had developed), they decided to strike out on their own. One advantage of the new process was that it required relatively little capital in comparison with the typical steel company, so Brown and Valencia have been able to avoid issuing new stock, and thus they own all of the shares. However, SSC has now reached the stage where outside equity capital is necessary if the firm is to achieve its growth targets yet still maintain its target capital structure of 60 percent equity and 40 percent debt. Therefore, Brown and Valencia have decided to take the company public. Until now, Brown and Valencia have paid themselves reasonable salaries but routinely reinvested all after-tax earnings in the firm, so dividend policy has not been an issue. However, before talking with potential outside investors, they must decide on a dividend policy.

Assume that you were recently hired by Arthur Adamson & Company (AA), a national consulting firm, which has been asked to help SSC prepare for its public offering. Martha Millon, the senior AA consultant in your group, has asked you to make a presentation to Brown and Valencia in which you review the theory of dividend policy and discuss the following questions.

a. (1) What is meant by the term "dividend policy"?
   (2) The terms "irrelevance," "bird in the hand," and "tax preference" have been used to describe three major

theories regarding the way dividend policy affects a firm's value. Explain what these terms mean, and briefly describe each theory.
   (3) What do the three theories indicate regarding the actions management should take with respect to dividend policy?
   (4) Explain the relationships between dividend policy, stock price, and the cost of equity under each dividend policy theory by constructing two graphs such as those shown in Figure 14-1. Dividend payout should be placed on the X axis.
   (5) What results have empirical studies of the dividend theories produced? How does all this affect what we can tell managers about dividend policy?
b. Discuss (1) the information content, or signaling, hypothesis, (2) the clientele effect, and (3) their effects on dividend policy.
c. (1) Assume that SSC has an $800,000 capital budget planned for the coming year. You have determined that its present capital structure (60 percent equity and 40 percent debt) is optimal, and its net income is forecasted at $600,000. Use the residual dividend model approach to determine SSC's total dollar dividend and payout ratio. In the process, explain what the residual dividend model is, and use a graph to illustrate your answer. Then, explain what would happen if net income were forecasted at $400,000, or at $800,000.
   (2) In general terms, how would a change in investment opportunities affect the payout ratio under the residual payment policy?
   (3) What are the advantages and disadvantages of the residual policy? (Hint: Don't neglect signaling and clientele effects.)

d. What is a dividend reinvestment plan (DRIP), and how does it work?

e. Describe the series of steps that most firms take in setting dividend policy in practice.

f. What are stock repurchases? Discuss the advantages and disadvantages of a firm's repurchasing its own shares.

g. What are stock dividends and stock splits? What are the advantages and disadvantages of stock dividends and stock splits?

COMPUTER-RELATED PROBLEM

Work the problem in this section only if you are using the computer problem diskette.

14-12

Dividend policy and capital structure

Use the model in the File C14 to work this problem.

Refer back to Problem 14-10. Assume that Buena Vista's management is considering a change in the firm's capital structure to include more debt; thus, management would like to analyze the effects of an increase in the debt ratio to 60 percent. The treasurer believes that such a move would cause lenders to increase the required rate of return on new bonds to 12 percent, and that k_s would rise to 14.5 percent.

a. How would this change affect the optimal capital budget?

b. If k_s rose to 16 percent, would the low-return project be acceptable?

c. Would the project selection be affected if the dividend was reduced to $1.88 from $3.00, still assuming $k_s = 16$ percent?

FINANCIAL PLANNING AND WORKING CAPITAL MANAGEMENT

CHAPTER 15

FINANCIAL FORECASTING

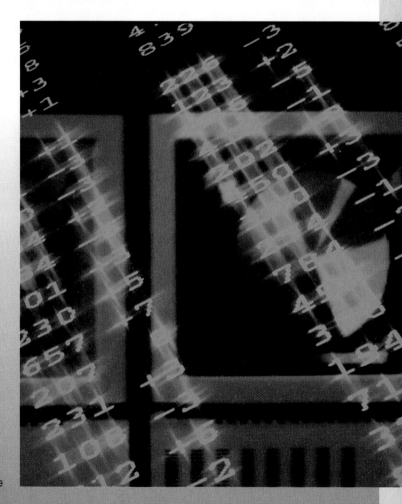

In mid-February 1997, corporations were reporting earnings for 1996. Simultaneously, security analysts were issuing their forecasts of earnings for 1997. Stock prices were extremely volatile, moving up with a good earnings surprise — that is, where reported EPS was higher than analysts had been expecting — and down with unpleasant surprises. Corporate executives know that these reactions will occur, so they generally try to give analysts early warnings when unpleasant surprises are likely to occur. The logic is that unpleasant surprises increase uncertainty about the future, so a stock will react less negatively to low earnings if the drop is anticipated than if it is a complete surprise.

Corporate finance staffs also review their own internal plans and forecasts during February. Firms' formal plans are generally completed in the fall of the prior year and then go into effect at the start of the year, so in February, information starts coming in that indicates how the year is shaping up.

Zacks Investment Research is one organization which keeps track of analysts' earnings forecasts. Generally, at least eight to ten analysts publish forecasts for each major corporation. Zacks tallies these forecasts and publishes the mean estimates, which form the basis for many investors' expectations, hence the basis for stock prices.

Corporate financial staffs pay close attention to how their competitors are doing — this is called "benchmarking" — and executives' salaries and bonuses are generally based on how a company has done in comparison with its benchmark competitors. Since the Zacks report gives an early indication of how the competition is doing, it is closely scrutinized by financial executives and their staffs. If a company's financial position does not appear to be shaping up well, then the midnight oil will be burned in an attempt to improve it.

Well-run companies generally base their operating plans on a set of forecasted financial statements. The process begins with a sales forecast for the next five or so years. Then the assets required to meet the sales targets are determined, and a decision is made concerning how to finance the required assets. At that point, income statements and balance sheets can be projected, and earnings and dividends per share, as well as a set of key ratios, can be forecasted.

Once the "base-case" forecasted statements and ratios have been prepared, top managers will ask questions such as these: Are the forecasted results as good as we can do, and if not, how might we change our operating plans to produce better earnings and a higher stock price? How sure are we that we will be able to achieve the projected results? For example, if our base-case forecast assumes a reasonably strong economy, but a recession occurs, what would happen, and would we be better off under an alternative operating plan?

In this chapter, we explore the financial planning process. Then, in the remaining chapters of Part VI, we will see how working capital management fits into the overall planning process.

SALES FORECASTS

Sales Forecast
A forecast of a firm's unit and dollar sales for some future period; it is generally based on recent sales trends plus forecasts of the economic prospects for the nation, region, industry, and so forth.

The **sales forecast** generally starts with a review of sales during the past five to ten years, expressed in a graph such as that in Figure 15-1. The first part of the graph shows five years of historical sales for Allied Food Products, the diversified food processor and distributor whose financial statements were first presented back in Chapter 2. The graph could have contained ten years of sales data, but Allied typically focuses on sales figures for the latest five years because the firm's studies have shown that its future growth is more closely related to recent events than to the distant past.

Allied had its ups and downs during the period from 1993 to 1997. In 1995, poor weather in California's fruit-producing regions resulted in low production, which caused 1995 sales to fall below the 1994 level. Then, a bumper crop in 1996 pushed sales up by 15 percent, an unusually high growth rate for a mature food processor. Based on a regression analysis, Allied's forecasters determined that the average annual growth rate in sales over the past five years was 9.9 percent. On the basis of this historical sales trend, on planned new-product introductions, and on Allied's forecast for the economy, the firm's planning committee projects a 10 percent sales growth rate during 1998, to sales of $3,300 million. Here are some of the factors Allied considered in developing its sales forecast:

1. Allied Food Products is divided into three divisions: canned foods, frozen foods, and packaged foods such as dried fruits. Sales growth is seldom the same for each of the divisions, so to begin the forecasting process, divisional projections are made on the basis of historical growth, and then the divisional forecasts are combined to produce a "first approximation" corporate sales forecast.

2. Next, the level of economic activity in each of the company's marketing areas is forecasted — for example, how strong will the economies be in each of Allied's six domestic and two foreign distribution territories, and what population changes are forecasted in each area?

3. Allied's planning committee also looks at the firm's probable market share in each distribution territory. Consideration is given to such factors as the firm's

F I G U R E   1 5 - 1 **Allied Food Products: 1998 Sales Projection (Millions of Dollars)**

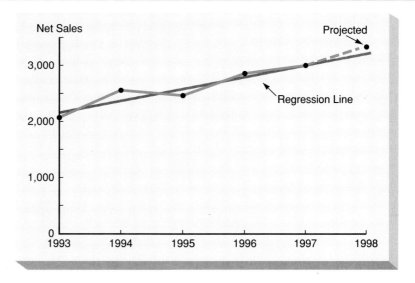

YEAR	SALES
1993	$2,058
1994	2,534
1995	2,472
1996	2,850
1997	3,000
1998	3,300 (Projected)

production and distribution capacity, its competitors' capacities, new-product introductions that are planned by Allied or its competitors, and potential changes in shelf-space allocations, which are vital for food sales. Pricing strategies are also considered — for example, does the company have plans to raise prices to boost margins, or to lower prices to increase market share and take advantage of economies of scale? Obviously, such factors could greatly affect future sales. In addition, Allied's export sales are affected by exchange rates, governmental policies, and the like.

4. Allied's planners must also consider the effects of inflation on prices. Over the next five years, the inflation rate is expected to average 3 to 4 percent, and Allied plans to increase prices, on average, by a like amount. In addition, the firm expects to expand its market share in certain products, resulting in a 4 percent growth rate in unit sales. The combination of unit sales growth and increases in sales prices has resulted in historical revenue growth rates in the 8 to 10 percent range, and this same situation is expected in the future.

5. Advertising campaigns, promotional discounts, credit terms, and the like also affect sales, so probable developments for these items are also factored in.

6. Forecasts are made for each division, both in the aggregate and on an individual product basis. The individual product sales forecasts are summed, and

this sum is compared with the aggregated division forecasts. Differences are reconciled, and the end result is a sales forecast for the company as a whole but with breakdowns by the three divisions and by individual products.

If the sales forecast is off, the consequences can be serious. First, if the market expands *more* than Allied has geared up for, the company will not be able to meet demand. Its customers will end up buying competitors' products, and Allied will lose market share. On the other hand, if its projections are overly optimistic, Allied could end up with too much plant, equipment, and inventory. This would mean low turnover ratios, excessive costs for depreciation and storage, and, possibly, write-offs of spoiled inventory. All of this would result in low profits, a low rate of return on equity, and a depressed stock price. If Allied had financed the expansion with debt, its problems would, of course, be compounded. Thus, an accurate sales forecast is critical to profitability.[1]

SELF-TEST QUESTIONS   ??????

How do past trends affect a sales forecast?

List some factors that should be considered when developing a sales forecast.

Briefly explain why an accurate sales forecast is critical to profitability.

FINANCIAL STATEMENT FORECASTING: THE CONSTANT RATIO METHOD

Constant Ratio Method
A method of forecasting future financial statements, and future financial requirements, that assumes certain financial ratios will remain constant.

Once sales have been forecasted, we must forecast future balance sheets and income statements. The simplest technique, and the one that is most useful for explaining the mechanics of financial statement forecasting, is the **constant ratio method.** The steps in this procedure are described below for Allied Food Products.

STEP 1. FORECASTED INCOME STATEMENT

The income statement for the coming year is forecasted in order to obtain an estimate of reported income and the amount of retained earnings the company will generate during the year. This requires assumptions about the operating cost ratio, the tax rate, interest charges, and the dividend payout ratio. In the simplest case, the assumption is made that all costs will increase at the same rate as sales; in more complicated situations, specific costs will be forecasted separately. Still, the primary objective of this part of the forecast is to determine how much income the company will earn and retain for reinvestment during the forecasted year.

Table 15-1 shows Allied's actual 1997 and forecasted 1998 income statements. To begin, we assume that sales and costs will grow by 10 percent in 1998 over the 1997 levels. Therefore, we show the factor $(1 + g) = 1.10$ in the first three rows of Column 2, and in the same rows of Column 3 we show the forecasted

---

[1]A sales forecast is actually the *expected value of a probability distribution* of possible levels of sales. Because any sales forecast is subject to a greater or lesser degree of uncertainty, financial planners are often just as interested in the degree of uncertainty inherent in the sales forecast (the standard deviation in sales) as in the expected value of sales.

TABLE 15-1	Allied Food Products: Actual 1997 and Projected 1998 Income Statements (Millions of Dollars)

	ACTUAL 1997 (1)	FORECAST BASIS (2)	1998 FORECAST (3)
1. Sales	$3,000	$\times 1.10^a$	$3,300
2. Costs except depreciation	2,616	$\times 1.10$	2,878
3. Depreciation	100	$\times 1.10$	110
4. Total operating costs	$2,716		$2,988
5. EBIT	$ 284		$ 312
6. Less interest	88	$\rightarrow$	88^b
7. Earnings before taxes (EBT)	$ 196		$ 224
8. Taxes (40%)	78		89
9. NI before preferred dividends	$ 118		$ 135
10. Dividends to preferred	4	$\rightarrow$	4^b
11. NI available to common	$ 114		$ 131
12. Dividends to common	$ 58		$ 63^c$
13. Addition to retained earnings	$ 56		$ 68

$^a\times 1.10$ indicates "times $1 + g$"; used for items which grow proportionally with sales. Here $g = 0.10$.

^{b}1997 amount carried over for forecast. Indicated in Column 2 by an arrow.

^{c}Dividends are projected. See text for explanation.

1998 sales, operating costs, and depreciation. EBIT is found by subtraction, while the interest charges in Column 3 are simply carried over from Column 1.

Earnings before taxes (EBT) are then calculated, as is net income before preferred dividends. Preferred dividends are carried over from the 1997 column, and they will remain constant unless Allied decides to issue additional preferred stock in 1998. Net income available to common is calculated, and then the 1998 dividends are forecasted as follows: The 1997 dividend per share is $1.15, and this dividend is expected to be increased by about 8 percent, to $1.25. Since there are 50 million shares outstanding, the projected dividends are $1.25(50,000,000) = $62.5 million, rounded to $63 million.

As the last part of the forecasted income statement, the $63 million projected dividends are subtracted from the $131 million projected net income to determine the projection of retained earnings, $131 − $63 = $68 million.

STEP 2. FORECAST THE BALANCE SHEET

If Allied's sales are to increase, then its assets must also grow. Since the company was operating at full capacity in 1997, each asset account must increase if the higher sales level is to be attained: More cash will be needed for transactions, higher sales will lead to higher receivables, additional inventory will have to be stocked, and new plant and equipment must be added.

Further, if Allied's assets are to increase, its liabilities and equity must also increase — the additional assets must be financed in some manner. **Spontaneously generated funds** will be provided by accounts payable and accruals. For

Spontaneously Generated Funds
Funds that are obtained automatically from routine business transactions.

example, as sales increase, so will Allied's purchases of raw materials, and these larger purchases will spontaneously lead to higher levels of accounts payable. Similarly, a higher level of operations will require more labor, while higher sales should result in higher taxable income. Therefore, accrued wages and taxes will both increase. In general, these spontaneous liability accounts will increase at the same rate as sales.

Retained earnings will also increase, but not at the same rate as sales: the new balance for retained earnings will be the old level plus the addition to retained earnings, which we calculated in Step 1. Also, notes payable, long-term bonds, preferred stock, and common stock will not rise spontaneously with sales — rather, the projected levels of these accounts will depend on financing decisions that we will discuss later.

In summary, (1) higher sales must be supported by additional assets, (2) some of the asset increases can be financed by spontaneous increases in accounts payable and accruals and by retained earnings, and (3) any shortfall must be financed from external sources, using some combination of debt, preferred stock, and common stock.

Table 15-2 contains Allied's actual 1997 and projected 1998 balance sheets. The mechanics of the balance sheet forecast are similar to those used to develop the forecasted income statement. First, those balance sheet accounts that are expected to increase directly with sales are multiplied by 1.10 to obtain the initial 1998 forecasts. Thus, 1998 cash is projected to be $10(1.10) = $11 million, accounts receivable are projected to be $375(1.10) ≈ $412 million, and so on. Note that Allied was operating its fixed assets at full capacity in 1997, so its net plant and equipment must also increase by the 10 percent sales growth rate.

Once the individual asset accounts have been forecasted, they can be summed to complete the asset side of the balance sheet. Thus, total current assets as forecasted for 1998 are $11 + $412 + $677 = $1,100 million, and total assets equal $2,200 million.

Next, the spontaneously increasing liabilities (accounts payable and accruals) are forecasted and shown in Column 3, the first-pass forecast. Then, those liability and equity accounts whose values reflect conscious management decisions — notes payable, long-term bonds, preferred stock, and common stock — are initially set at their 1997 levels. Thus, 1998 notes payable are initially set at $110 million, the long-term bond account is forecasted at $754 million, and so on. The 1998 value for the retained earnings (RE) account is obtained by adding the projected addition to retained earnings as developed in the 1998 income statement (see Table 15-1) to the 1997 ending balance:

$$1998 \text{ RE} = 1997 \text{ RE} + 1998 \text{ forecasted addition to RE}$$
$$= \$766 + \$68 = \$834 \text{ million.}$$

The forecast of total assets as shown in Column 3 (first-pass forecast) of Table 15-2 is $2,200 million, which indicates that Allied must add $200 million of new assets in 1998 to support the higher sales level. However, the forecasted liability and equity accounts as shown in the lower portion of Column 3 rise by only $88 million, to $2,088 million. Since the balance sheet must balance, Allied must raise an additional $2,200 − $2,088 = $112 million, which we designate as **Additional Funds Needed (AFN).** The AFN will be raised by borrowing from the bank as notes payable, by issuing long-term bonds, and by selling new common stock.

Additional Funds Needed (AFN)
Funds that a firm must raise externally through borrowing or by selling new common or preferred stock.

| TABLE 15-2 | Allied Food Products: Actual 1997 and Projected 1998 Balance Sheets (Millions of Dollars) |

	ACTUAL 1997 (1)	1 + SALES g (2)	FIRST PASS (3)	AFN[a] (4)	SECOND PASS (5)
			1998 FORECAST		
Cash	$ 10	×1.10[b]	$ 11	→	$ 11
Accounts receivable	375	×1.10	412	→	412
Inventories	615	×1.10	677	→	677
Total current assets	$1,000		$1,100		$1,100
Net plant and equipment	1,000	×1.10	1,100	→	1,100
Total assets	$2,000		$2,200		$2,200
Accounts payable	$ 60	×1.10	$ 66	→	$ 66
Notes payable	110	→	110[c]	+ 28	138
Accruals	140	×1.10	154	→	154
Total current liabilities	$ 310		$ 330		$ 358
Long-term bonds	754	→	754[c]	+ 28	782
Total debt	$1,064		$1,084		$1,140
Preferred stock	40	→	40[c]	→	40
Common stock	130	→	130[c]	+ 56	186
Retained earnings	766	+68[d]	834	→	834
Total common equity	$ 896		$ 964		$1,020
Total liabilities and equity	$2,000		$2,088	+112	$2,200
Additional funds needed (AFN)			$ 112		

[a]AFN stands for "Additional Funds Needed." This figure is determined at the bottom of Column 3, and Column 4 shows how the required $112 of AFN will be raised.

[b]×1.10 indicates "times 1 + g"; used for items which grow proportionally with sales. Here g = 0.10.

[c]Indicates a 1997 amount carried over as the first-pass forecast. Arrows also indicate items whose values are carried over from one pass to another.

[d]From Table 15-1, Line 13.

STEP 3. RAISING THE ADDITIONAL FUNDS NEEDED

Allied's financial staff will base the financial mix on several factors, including the firm's target capital structure, the effect of short-term borrowing on its current ratio, conditions in the debt and equity markets, and restrictions imposed by existing debt agreements. Allied's financial staff, after considering all of the relevant factors, decided on the following financing mix to raise the additional $112 million:

	AMOUNT OF NEW CAPITAL		
	PERCENT	DOLLARS (MILLIONS)	INTEREST RATE
Notes payable	25%	$ 28	8%
Long-term bonds	25	28	10
Common stock	50	56	—
	100%	$112	

These amounts, which are shown in Column 4 of Table 15-2, are added to the initially forecasted account totals as shown in Column 3 to generate the second-pass balance sheet. Thus, in Column 5 the notes payable account increases to $110 + $28 = $138 million, long-term bonds rise to $754 + $28 = $782 million, and common stock increases to $130 + $56 = $186 million.

A COMPLICATION: FINANCING FEEDBACKS

Our projected financial statements are incomplete in one sense—they do not reflect the fact that interest must be paid on the debt used to help finance the AFN, and dividends must be paid on the shares issued to raise the equity part of the AFN. These payments would lower the net income and retained earnings shown in the projected statements. One could take account of these "financing feedback effects" by adding columns to Tables 15-1 and 15-2, and then making further adjustments. The adjustments are not difficult, but they do involve a good bit of arithmetic. In view of the fact that all of the data are based on forecasts, and since the adjustments add substantially to the work but relatively little to the accuracy of the forecasts, we leave them to later finance courses.[2]

ANALYSIS OF THE FORECAST

The 1998 forecast as developed above is only the first part of Allied's total forecasting process. We must go on to analyze the projected statements to determine whether the forecast meets the firm's financial targets as set forth in the five-year financial plan. If the statements do not meet the targets, then elements of the forecast must be changed.

Table 15-3 shows Allied's key ratios for 1997 plus the projected 1998 ratios, along with the latest industry average ratios. (The table also shows some "revised" data, which we will discuss later. Disregard the revised data for now.) The firm's financial condition at the close of 1997 was weak, with many ratios being well below the industry averages. For example, Allied's current ratio was only 3.2 versus 4.2 for an average food processor. The preliminary forecast for 1998, which assumes that Allied's past practices will continue into the future, is also relatively weak, and this condition will persist unless management takes action to improve things.

Allied actually decided to take three steps to improve its financial condition: (1) It will lay off some workers and close certain operations. These steps should lower operating costs (excluding depreciation) from the current 87.2 percent of sales to 86 percent. (2) By screening credit customers more closely and by being more aggressive in collecting past-due accounts, the days sales outstanding on receivables can be reduced from 45 to 42.5 days. (3) Finally, management thinks the inventory turnover ratio can be raised from 4.9 to 6 times through the use of tighter inventory controls.[3]

These proposed operational changes were then used to create a revised set of forecasted statements for 1998. We do not show the new financial statements,

---

[2]For a thorough discussion of financing feedbacks, see Eugene F. Brigham and Louis C. Gapenski, *Intermediate Financial Management*, 5th ed., Chapter 19.

[3]We will discuss receivables and inventory management in detail in Chapter 16.

TABLE 15-3	Projected AFN and Key Ratios

	1997	1998 FORECAST[a]	INDUSTRY AVERAGE	REVISED[b] 1998
AFN		$112		($64)
Current ratio	3.2	3.1	4.2	3.6
Inventory turnover	4.9	4.9	9.0	6.0
Days sales outstanding	45.0	45.0	36.0	42.5
Total assets turnover	1.5	1.5	1.8	1.6
Debt ratio[c]	55.2%	51.8%	40.0%	51.6%
Profit margin	3.8%	4.0%	5.0%	4.8%
Return on assets	5.7%	6.0%	9.0%	7.7%
Return on equity	12.7%	12.8%	15.0%	15.9%

[a]The forecasted ratios are based on Tables 15-1 and 15-2.
[b]The "Revised" data show ratios after policy changes related to asset levels as discussed later have been incorporated into the forecast.
[c]Includes preferred stock.

but their impact on the key ratios is shown in the last column of Table 15-3. Here are the highlights of the revised forecast:

1. Reducing operating costs from 87.2 to 86 percent of sales lowered Allied's forecasted cost figures on Rows 2 and 4 of Table 15-1. These changes, when worked on through the statement, resulted in a profit margin improvement from 4.0 to 4.8 percent, which is closer to the industry average.

2. The increase in the profit margin results in an increase in projected retained earnings. Further, by tightening inventory controls and reducing the days sales outstanding, Allied projects a reduction in inventories and receivables. Taken together, these actions resulted in a *negative* AFN of $64 million, which means that Allied would actually generate $64 million more from internal operations during 1998 than it needs for new assets. This $64 million of surplus funds could be used to reduce short-term debt, which would lead to a decrease in the forecasted debt ratio from 51.8 to 51.6 percent. The debt ratio would still be well above the industry average, but this is a step in the right direction.

3. The indicated changes would also affect Allied's current ratio, which would improve from 3.1 to 3.6.

4. These actions would also raise the rate of return on assets from 6.0 to 7.7 percent, and they would boost the return on equity from 12.8 to 15.9 percent, which would even exceed the industry average.

Although Allied's managers believe that the revised forecast is achievable, they cannot be sure of this. Accordingly, they want to know how variations in sales would affect the forecast. Therefore, a spreadsheet model was run using several different sales growth rates, and the results were analyzed to see how the ratios would change under different growth scenarios. To illustrate, if the sales growth rate increased from 10 to 20 percent, the additional funding requirement would change dramatically, from a $64 million *surplus* to an $83 million *shortfall*.

The spreadsheet model was also used to evaluate dividend policy. If Allied decided to reduce its dividend growth rate, then additional funds would be generated, and these funds could be invested in plant, equipment, and inventories, used to reduce debt, or used to repurchase stock.

The model was also used to evaluate financing alternatives. For example, Allied could use the forecasted $64 million of surplus funds to retire long-term bonds rather than to reduce short-term debt. Under this financing alternative, the current ratio would drop from 3.6 to 2.9, but the total debt ratio would still decline, and the interest coverage ratio would rise.

Forecasting is an iterative process, both in the way the financial statements are generated and the way the financial plan is developed. For planning purposes, the financial staff develops a preliminary forecast based on a continuation of past policies and trends. This provides a starting point, or "baseline" forecast. Next, the model is modified to see what effects alternative operating plans would have on the firm's earnings and financial condition. This results in a revised forecast. Then alternative operating plans are examined under different sales growth scenarios, and the model is used to evaluate both dividend policy and capital structure decisions.

The model can also be used to analyze alternative working capital policies — that is, to see the effects of changes in cash management, credit policy, inventory policy, and the use of different types of short-term credit. We will examine Allied's working capital policy within the framework of the company's financial model in the following chapters, but in the remainder of this chapter, we consider some other aspects of the financial forecasting process.

SELF-TEST QUESTIONS

What is the AFN, and how is it estimated?

What is a financing feedback, and how do feedbacks affect the estimated AFN?

THE AFN FORMULA

Most firms forecast their capital requirements by constructing pro forma income statements and balance sheets as described above. However, when the ratios are expected to remain constant, then the following formula is sometimes used to forecast financial requirements:

$$\begin{matrix} \text{Additional} & \text{Required} & \text{Spontaneous} & \text{Increase in} \\ \text{funds} & = \text{increase} & - \text{increase in} & - \text{retained} \\ \text{needed} & \text{in assets} & \text{liabilities} & \text{earnings} \\ \text{AFN} & = (A^*/S_0)\Delta S & - (L^*/S_0)\Delta S & - MS_1(1-d). \end{matrix}$$ (15-1)

Here

AFN = additional funds needed.

A* = assets that are tied directly to sales, hence which must increase if sales are to increase. Note that A designates total assets and A* designates those assets that must increase if sales are to increase. When the firm is operating at full capacity, as is the case here, A* = A. Often, though, A* and A are not equal, and the equation must be modified or else the projected financial statement method must be used.

S_0 = sales during the last year.

A^*/S_0 = percentage of required assets to sales, which also shows the required dollar increase in assets per \$1 increase in sales. A^*/S_0 = \$2,000/\$3,000 = 0.6667 for Allied. Thus, for every \$1 increase in sales, assets must increase by about 67 cents.

L^* = liabilities that increase spontaneously. L^* is normally much less than total liabilities (L).

L^*/S_0 = liabilities that increase spontaneously as a percentage of sales, or spontaneously generated financing per \$1 increase in sales. L^*/S_0 = (\$60 + \$140)/\$3,000 = 0.0667 for Allied. Thus, every \$1 increase in sales generates about 7 cents of spontaneous financing.

S_1 = total sales projected for next year. Note that S_0 designates last year's sales, and S_1 = \$3,300 million for Allied.

ΔS = change in sales = $S_1 - S_0$ = \$3,300 million − \$3,000 million = \$300 million for Allied.

M = profit margin, or profit per \$1 of sales. M = \$114/\$3,000 = 0.0380 for Allied. So, Allied earns 3.8 cents on each dollar of sales.

d = percentage of earnings paid out in common dividends, or the dividend payout ratio; d = \$58/\$114 = 0.5088 for Allied.

Inserting values for Allied into Equation 15-1, we find the additional funds needed to be \$118 million:

$$\text{AFN} = \begin{array}{c}\text{Required}\\ \text{asset}\\ \text{increase}\end{array} - \begin{array}{c}\text{Spontaneous}\\ \text{liability}\\ \text{increase}\end{array} - \begin{array}{c}\text{Increase}\\ \text{in retained}\\ \text{earnings}\end{array}$$

$$= 0.667(\Delta S) - 0.067(\Delta S) - 0.038(S_1)(1 - 0.509)$$

$$= 0.667(\$300 \text{ million}) - 0.067(\$300 \text{ million}) - 0.038(\$3,300 \text{ million})(0.491)$$

$$= \$200 \text{ million} - \$20 \text{ million} - \$62 \text{ million}$$

$$= \$118 \text{ million}.$$

To increase sales by \$300 million, the formula suggests that Allied must increase assets by \$200 million. The \$200 million of new assets must be financed in some manner. Of the total, \$20 million will come from a spontaneous increase in liabilities, while another \$62 million will be obtained from retained earnings. The remaining \$118 million must be raised from external sources. This value is an approximation, but it is only slightly different from the AFN figure (\$112 million) we developed in Table 15-2.[4]

Inherent in the formula are the assumptions (1) that each asset item must increase in direct proportion to sales increases, (2) that accounts payable and accruals also grow at the same rate as sales, (3) and that the profit margin is constant. Obviously, these assumptions do not always hold, so the formula does not always produce reliable results. Therefore, the formula is used primarily to get a rough-and-ready forecast of financial requirements, and as a supplement to the projected financial statement method.

---

[4]If Table 15-2 had been extended to include financing feedbacks, the forecasted AFN would have been \$119 million, which is very close to the formula AFN.

RELATIONSHIP BETWEEN SALES GROWTH AND FINANCIAL REQUIREMENTS

The faster Allied's growth rate in sales, the greater its need for additional financing. We can use Equation 15-1, which is plotted in Figure 15-2, to demonstrate this relationship. The tabular data show Allied's additional financial requirements at various growth rates, and these data are plotted in the graph. The figure illustrates four important points:

1. **Financial feasibility.** At low growth rates, Allied needs no external financing, and it even generates surplus cash. However, if the company grows faster than

---

FIGURE   15 - 2   Relationship between Growth in Sales and Financial Requirements, Assuming $S_0 = \$3,000$ (Millions of Dollars)

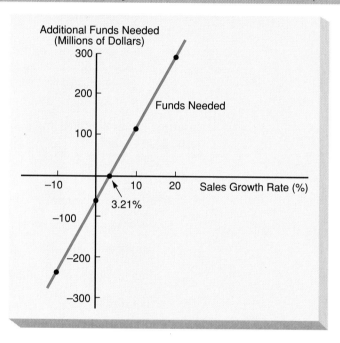

GROWTH RATE IN SALES (1)	INCREASE (DECREASE) IN SALES, ΔS (2)	FORECASTED SALES, S_1 (3)	ADDITIONAL FUNDS NEEDED (4)
20%	$600	$3,600	$293
10	300	3,300	118
3.21	96	3,096	0
0	0	3,000	−56
−10	−300	2,700	−230

Explanation of Columns:
Column 1: Assumed growth rate in sales, g.
Column 2: Increase (decrease) in sales, $\Delta S = g(S_0) = g(\$3,000)$.
Column 3: Forecasted sales, $S_1 = S_0 + g(S_0) = S_0(1 + g) = \$3,000(1 + g)$.
Column 4: Additional funds needed $= 0.667(\Delta S) - 0.067(\Delta S) - 0.019(S_1)$.

3.21 percent, it must raise capital from outside sources.[5] Further, the faster the growth rate, the greater the capital requirements. If management foresees difficulties in raising the required capital, it should reconsider the feasibility of the expansion plans.

2. **Effect of dividend policy on financing needs.** Dividend policy as reflected in the payout ratio (d in Equation 15-1) also affects external capital requirements — the higher the payout ratio, the smaller the addition to retained earnings, hence the greater the need for external capital. Therefore, if Allied foresees difficulties in raising capital, it should consider reducing the dividend payout ratio. This would lower (or shift to the right) the line in Figure 15-2, indicating smaller external capital requirements at all growth rates. However, before changing its dividend policy, management should consider the effects of such a decision on the stock price, as discussed in Chapter 14.

   Notice that the line in Figure 15-2 does *not* pass through the origin. Thus, at low growth rates (below 3.21 percent), surplus funds will be produced, because new retained earnings plus spontaneous funds will exceed the required asset increases. Only if the dividend payout ratio were 100 percent, meaning that the firm did not retain any of its earnings, would the "funds needed" line pass through the origin.

Capital Intensity Ratio
The amount of assets required per dollar of sales (A^*/S_0).

3. **Capital intensity.** The amount of assets required per dollar of sales, A^*/S_0 in Equation 15-1, is often called the **capital intensity ratio.** This ratio has a major effect on capital requirements. If the capital intensity ratio is low, sales can grow rapidly without much outside capital. However, if the firm is capital intensive, even a small growth in output will require a great deal of new outside capital.

4. **Profit margin.** The profit margin, M, is also an important determinant of the funds-required equation — the higher the margin, the lower the funds requirements. In terms of the graph, an increase in the profit margin would cause the line to shift down, and its slope would also become less steep. Because of the relationship between profit margins and additional capital requirements, some very rapidly growing firms do not need much external capital. For example, for many years, Xerox grew at a rapid rate with very little borrowing or stock sales. However, as the company lost patent protection and as competition intensified in the copier industry, Xerox's profit margin declined, its needs for external capital rose, and it began to borrow from banks and other sources.

SELF-TEST QUESTIONS ???????

Under certain conditions a formula can be used to forecast AFN. Give the formula and briefly explain it.

How do the following factors affect external capital requirements?
a. Dividend payout ratio.
b. Capital intensity.
c. Profit margin.

---

[5]We found the 3.21 percent growth rate by setting AFN equal to zero, substituting gS_0 for ΔS and $S_0 + g(S_0)$ for S_1 in the AFN equation, and then solving the equation $0 = 0.667(g)(S_0) - 0.067(g)(S_0) - 0.038(S_0 + gS_0)(1 - 0.509)$ for g. The g that solved this equation was about 0.0321, or 3.21 percent.

FORECASTING FINANCIAL REQUIREMENTS WHEN THE BALANCE SHEET RATIOS ARE SUBJECT TO CHANGE

Both the AFN formula and the projected financial statement method as we used it assume that the ratios of assets and liabilities to sales (A^*/S_0 and L^*/S_0) remain constant over time. This, in turn, requires the assumption that each "spontaneous" asset and liability item increases at the same rate as sales. In graph form, this implies the type of relationship shown in Panel a of Figure 15-3, a relationship that is (1) linear and (2) passes through the origin. Under those conditions, if the company's sales increase from $200 million to $400 million, or by 100 percent, inventory will also increase by 100 percent, from $100 million to $200 million.

FIGURE 15-3 Four Possible Ratio Relationships (Millions of Dollars)

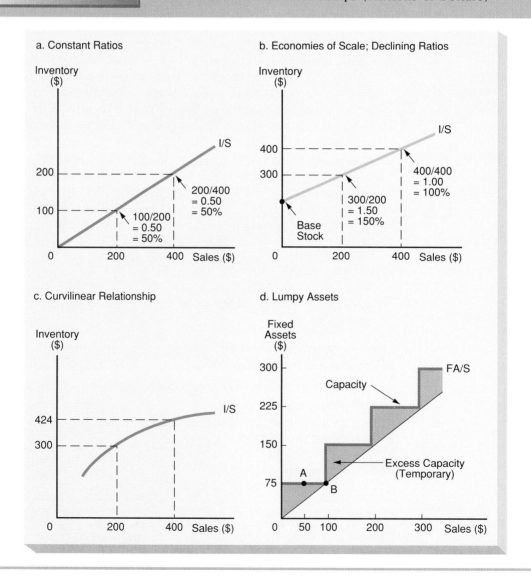

The assumption of constant ratios and identical growth rates is appropriate at times, but there are times when it is incorrect. Three such conditions are described in the following sections.

ECONOMIES OF SCALE

There are economies of scale in the use of many kinds of assets, and when economies occur, the ratios are likely to change over time as the size of the firm increases. For example, firms often need to maintain base stocks of different inventory items, even if current sales are quite low. As sales expand, inventories grow less rapidly than sales, so the ratio of inventory to sales (I/S) declines. This situation is depicted in Panel b of Figure 15-3. Here we see that the inventory/sales ratio is 1.5, or 150 percent, when sales are $200 million, but the ratio declines to 1.0 when sales climb to $400 million.

The relationship used to illustrate economies of scale is linear, but nonlinear relationships often exist. Indeed, if the firm uses one popular model for establishing inventory levels (the EOQ model), its inventories will rise with the square root of sales. This situation is shown in Panel c of Figure 15-3, which shows a curved line whose slope decreases at higher sales levels. In this situation, very large sales increases would require very few additional inventories.

LUMPY ASSETS

Lumpy Assets
Assets that cannot be acquired in small increments but must be obtained in large, discrete units.

In many industries, technological considerations dictate that if a firm is to be competitive, it must add fixed assets in large, discrete units; such assets are often referred to as **lumpy assets.** In the paper industry, for example, there are strong economies of scale in basic paper mill equipment, so when a paper company expands capacity, it must do so in large, lumpy increments. This type of situation is depicted in Panel d of Figure 15-3. Here we assume that the minimum economically efficient plant has a cost of $75 million, and that such a plant can produce enough output to reach a sales level of $100 million. If the firm is to be competitive, it simply must have at least $75 million of fixed assets.

Lumpy assets have a major effect on the fixed assets/sales (FA/S) ratio at different sales levels and, consequently, on financial requirements. At Point A in Panel d, which represents a sales level of $50 million, the fixed assets are $75 million, so the ratio FA/S = $75/$50 = 1.5. Sales can expand by $50 million, out to $100 million, with no additions to fixed assets. At that point, represented by Point B, the ratio FA/S = $75/$100 = 0.75. However, since the firm is operating at capacity (sales of $100 million), even a small increase in sales would require a doubling of plant capacity, so a small projected sales increase would bring with it a very large financial requirement.[6]

---

[6]Several other points should be noted about Panel d of Figure 15-3. First, if the firm is operating at a sales level of $100 million or less, any expansion that calls for a sales increase above $100 million would require a *doubling* of the firm's fixed assets. A much smaller percentage increase would be involved if the firm were large enough to be operating a number of plants. Second, firms generally go to multiple shifts and take other actions to minimize the need for new fixed asset capacity as they approach Point B. However, these efforts can go only so far, and eventually a fixed asset expansion will be required. Third, firms often make arrangements to share excess capacity with other firms in their industry. For example, the situation in the electric utility industry is very much like that depicted in Panel d. However, electric companies often build jointly owned plants, or else they "take turns" building plants, and then they buy power from or sell power to other utilities to avoid building new plants that may be underutilized.

EXCESS ASSETS DUE TO FORECASTING ERRORS

Panels a, b, c, and d of Figure 15-3 all focus on target, or projected, relationships between sales and assets. Actual sales, however, are often different from projected sales, and the actual asset/sales ratio for a given period may be quite different from the planned ratio. To illustrate, the firm depicted in Panel b of Figure 15-3 might, when its sales are at $200 million and its inventories at $300 million, project a sales expansion to $400 million and then increase its inventories to $400 million in anticipation of the sales expansion. However, suppose an unforeseen economic downturn were to hold sales to only $300 million. Actual inventories would then be $400 million, but inventories of only $350 million would be needed to support actual sales of $300 million. Thus, inventories would be $50 million larger than needed. In that situation, if the firm were making its forecast for the following year, it should recognize that sales could expand by $100 million with no increase whatever in inventories, but that any sales expansion beyond $100 million would require additional financing to increase inventories.

SELF-TEST QUESTION ???????

Describe three conditions under which the assumption that each "spontaneous" asset and liability item increases at the same rate as sales is *not* correct.

OTHER TECHNIQUES FOR FORECASTING FINANCIAL STATEMENTS

If any of the conditions noted above apply (economies of scale, excess capacity, or lumpy assets), the A^*/S_0 ratio will not be a constant, and the constant growth forecasting methods as discussed thus far should not be used. Rather, other techniques must be used to forecast asset levels and additional financing requirements. Two of these methods — linear regression and excess capacity adjustments — are discussed in the following sections.

SIMPLE LINEAR REGRESSION

If we assume that the relationship between a certain type of asset and sales is linear, then we can use simple linear regression techniques to estimate the requirements for that type of asset for any given sales increase. For example, Allied's sales, inventories, and receivables during the last five years are shown in the lower section of Figure 15-4, and each current asset item is plotted in the upper section as a scatter diagram versus sales. Estimated regression equations determined using a financial calculator are also shown with each graph. For example, the estimated relationship between inventories and sales (in millions of dollars) is

$$\text{Inventories} = -\$35.7 + 0.186(\text{Sales}).$$

The plotted points are not very close to the regression line, which indicates a low degree of correlation. In fact, the correlation coefficient between inventories and sales is 0.71, indicating that there is only a moderate linear relationship between these two variables. Still, management regards the regression relationship as providing a reasonable basis for forecasting target inventory levels.

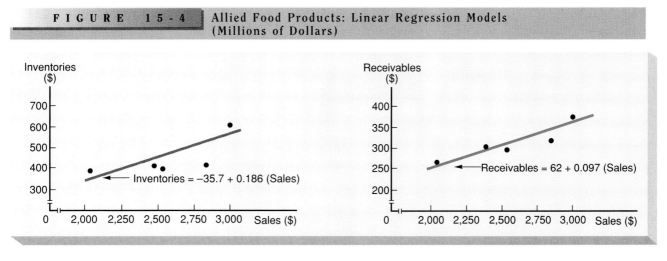

FIGURE 15-4	Allied Food Products: Linear Regression Models (Millions of Dollars)

YEAR	SALES	INVENTORIES	ACCOUNTS RECEIVABLE
1993	$2,058	$387	$268
1994	2,534	398	297
1995	2,472	409	304
1996	2,850	415	315
1997	3,000	615	375

We can use the estimated relationship between inventories and sales to forecast 1998 inventory levels. Since 1998 sales are projected at $3,300 million, 1998 inventories should be $578 million:

$$\text{Inventories} = -\$35.7 + 0.186(\$3,300) = \$578 \text{ million.}$$

This is $99 million less than the preliminary forecast based on the projected financial statement method. The difference occurs because the projected financial statement method assumed that the ratio of inventories to sales would remain constant, when in fact it will probably decline. Note also that although our graphs show linear relationships, we could have easily used a nonlinear regression model had such a relationship been indicated.

After analyzing the regression results, Allied's managers decided that a new forecast of AFN should be developed in which a lower days sales outstanding and a higher inventory turnover ratio are assumed. Management recognized that the 1997 levels of these accounts were above the industry averages, hence that the preliminary results projected for 1998 are unnecessarily too high. When simple linear regression was used to forecast the receivables and inventories accounts, this caused the 1998 levels to reflect both the average relationships of these accounts to sales over the five-year period and also the trend in the variables' values. The projected financial statement method assumed that the nonoptimal 1997 relationships would continue in 1998 and beyond.

EXCESS CAPACITY ADJUSTMENTS

Consider again the Allied Food Products example set forth in Tables 15-1 and 15-2, but now assume that excess capacity exists in fixed assets. Specifically, assume that fixed assets in 1997 were being utilized to only 96 percent of capacity. If fixed assets had been used to full capacity, 1997 sales could have been as high as $3,125 million, versus the $3,000 million in actual sales:

$$\begin{matrix}\text{Full} \\ \text{capacity} \\ \text{sales}\end{matrix} = \frac{\text{Actual sales}}{\begin{matrix}\text{Percentage of capacity} \\ \text{at which fixed assets} \\ \text{were operated}\end{matrix}} = \frac{\$3,000 \text{ million}}{0.96} = \$3,125 \text{ million.} \quad \textbf{(15-2)}$$

This suggests that Allied's Fixed assets/Sales ratio should be 32 percent:

$$\text{Target fixed assets/Sales ratio} = \frac{\text{Actual fixed assets}}{\text{Full capacity sales}} \quad \textbf{(15-3)}$$

$$= \frac{\$1,000}{\$3,125} = 0.32 = 32\%.$$

Therefore, if sales are to increase to $3,300 million, then fixed assets would have to increase to $1,056 million:

$$\begin{matrix}\text{Required level} \\ \text{of fixed assets}\end{matrix} = (\text{Target fixed assets/Sales ratio})\,(\text{Projected sales}) \quad \textbf{(15-4)}$$

$$= 0.32(\$3,300) = \$1,056 \text{ million.}$$

We previously forecasted that Allied would need to increase fixed assets at the same rate as sales, or by 10 percent. That meant an increase from $1,000 million to $1,100 million, or by $100 million. Now we see that the actual required increase is only from $1,000 million to $1,056 million, or by $56 million. Thus, the capacity-adjusted forecast is $100 million − $56 million = $44 million less than the earlier forecast. With a smaller fixed asset requirement, the projected AFN would decline from an estimated $112 million to $112 million − $44 million = $68 million.

Note also that when excess capacity exists, sales can grow to the capacity sales as determined above with no increase whatever in fixed assets, but sales beyond that level will require fixed asset additions as calculated in our example. The same situation could occur with respect to inventories, and the required additions would be determined in exactly the same manner as for fixed assets. Theoretically, the same situation could occur with other types of assets, but as a practical matter, excess capacity normally exists primarily with respect to fixed assets and inventories.

SELF-TEST QUESTIONS   ??????

Would it be more important to use the regression method of forecasting asset requirements if the true situation were like that in Panel a or that in Panel b of Figure 15-3?

If excess capacity exists, how will that affect the AFN?

COMPUTERIZED FINANCIAL PLANNING MODELS

Although financial forecasting as described in this chapter can be done with a calculator, virtually all corporate forecasts are made using computerized forecasting models. Many computerized financial forecasting models are based on a spreadsheet program such as *Lotus 1-2-3* or *Microsoft Excel*. Spreadsheet models have two major advantages over pencil-and-paper calculations. First, it is much faster to construct a spreadsheet model than to make a "by hand" forecast if the forecast period extends beyond two or three years. Second, and more important, a spreadsheet model can recompute the projected financial statements and ratios almost instantaneously when one of the input variables is changed, thus making it easy for managers to determine the effects of changes in variables such as sales.

We developed the forecasts for Allied using a five-year financial planning model based on a spreadsheet model which uses five years of historical data. We used the spreadsheet's linear regression capability to develop Allied's historical sales growth rate and the historical relationships between accounts receivable, inventories, and sales. Other input data include forecasted sales growth rates, the financing mix to apply to any additional funds needed, the cost rates on incremental debt financing, and the tax rate. The model calculates projected financial statements for five years, including financing feedback effects, along with some key financial ratios. Thus, it was quite easy to examine the effects of alternative assumptions on Allied's forecasts.[7]

SELF-TEST QUESTION

Why are computerized planning models playing an increasingly important role in corporate management?

SUMMARY

This chapter described in broad outline how firms project their financial statements and determine their capital requirements. The key concepts covered are listed below.

♦ Management establishes a **target balance sheet** on the basis of ratio analysis.

♦ **Financial forecasting** generally begins with a forecast of the firm's sales, in terms of both units and dollars, for some future period.

---

[7]It is becoming increasingly easy for companies to develop planning models as a result of the dramatic recent improvements in computer hardware and software. *Lotus 1-2-3* and *Excel* are the most widely used systems, although many companies also employ more complex and elaborate modeling systems. Increasingly, a knowledge of *Lotus 1-2-3, Excel,* or some similar spreadsheet program is becoming a requirement for getting even an entry-level job in many corporations. Indeed, surveys indicate that the probability of a business student getting an attractive job offer increases dramatically if he or she has a working knowledge of spreadsheets. In addition, starting salaries are materially higher for those students who have such a knowledge.

Note also that we have concentrated on long-run, or strategic, financial planning. Within the framework of the long-run strategic plan, firms also develop short-run financial plans. For example, in Table 15-2, we saw that Allied Food Products expects to need $112 million by the end of 1998, and that it plans to raise this capital by using short-term debt, long-term debt, and common stock. However, we do not know when during the year the funds will be needed, or when Allied will obtain each of its different types of capital. To address these issues, the firm must develop a short-run financial plan, the centerpiece of which is the *cash budget,* which is a projection of cash inflows and outflows on a daily, weekly, or monthly basis during the coming year (or other budget period). We will discuss cash budgeting in Chapter 16, where we consider cash and marketable securities.

♦ The **projected,** or **pro forma, financial statement method** and the **formula method** are used to forecast financial requirements.

♦ A firm can determine its **additional funds needed (AFN)** by estimating the amount of new assets necessary to support the forecasted level of sales and then subtracting from that amount the spontaneous funds that will be generated from operations. The firm can then plan to raise the AFN through bank borrowing, by issuing securities, or both.

♦ The **higher a firm's sales growth rate,** the **greater** will be its need for additional financing. Similarly, the **larger a firm's dividend payout ratio,** the **greater** its need for additional funds.

♦ Adjustments must be made if **economies of scale** exist in the use of assets, if **excess capacity** exists, or if assets must be added in **lumpy increments.**

♦ **Linear regression** and **excess capacity adjustments** can be used to forecast asset requirements in situations in which assets cannot be expected to grow at the same rate as sales.

The type of forecasting described in this chapter is important for several reasons. First, if the projected operating results are unsatisfactory, management can "go back to the drawing board," reformulate its plans, and develop more reasonable targets for the coming year. Second, it is possible that the funds required to meet the sales forecast simply cannot be obtained; if so, it is obviously better to know this in advance and to scale back the projected level of operations than to suddenly run out of cash and have operations grind to a halt. And third, even if the required funds can be raised, it is desirable to plan for their acquisition well in advance.

QUESTIONS

15-1 Certain liability and net worth items generally increase spontaneously with increases in sales. Put a check (✔) by those items that typically increase spontaneously:

Accounts payable	_____
Notes payable to banks	_____
Accrued wages	_____
Accrued taxes	_____
Mortgage bonds	_____
Common stock	_____
Retained earnings	_____

15-2 The following equation can, under certain assumptions, be used to forecast financial requirements:

$$AFN = (A^*/S_0)(\Delta S) - (L^*/S_0)(\Delta S) - MS_1(1 - d).$$

Under what conditions does the equation give satisfactory predictions, and when should it *not* be used?

15-3 Assume that an average firm in the office supply business has a 6 percent after-tax profit margin, a 40 percent debt/assets ratio, a total assets turnover of 2 times, and a dividend payout ratio of 40 percent. Is it true that if such a firm is to have *any* sales growth (g > 0), it will be forced either to borrow or to sell common stock (that is, it will need some nonspontaneous, external capital even if g is very small)?

15-4 Is it true that computerized corporate planning models were a fad during the 1980s but, because of a need for flexibility in corporate planning, they have been dropped by most firms in the 1990s?

15-5 Suppose a firm makes the following policy changes. If the change means that external, nonspontaneous financial requirements (AFN) will increase, indicate this by a (+); indicate a decrease by a (−); and indicate indeterminate or no effect by a (0). Think in terms of the immediate, short-run effect on funds requirements.

a. The dividend payout ratio is increased. _____

b. The firm contracts to buy, rather than make, certain components used in its products. _____

c. The firm decides to pay all suppliers on delivery, rather than after a 30-day delay, to take advantage of discounts for rapid payment. _____

d. The firm begins to sell on credit (previously all sales had been on a cash basis). _____

e. The firm's profit margin is eroded by increased competition; sales are steady. _____

f. Advertising expenditures are stepped up. _____

g. A decision is made to substitute long-term mortgage bonds for short-term bank loans. _____

h. The firm begins to pay employees on a weekly basis (previously it had paid at the end of each month). _____

SELF-TEST PROBLEMS (Solutions Appear in Appendix B)

ST-1
Key terms

Define each of the following terms:

a. Sales forecast
b. Projected financial statement method
c. Spontaneously generated funds
d. Dividend payout ratio
e. Pro forma financial statement
f. Additional funds needed (AFN); AFN formula
g. Capital intensity ratio
h. Lumpy assets
i. Financing feedback

ST-2
Growth rate

Weatherford Industries Inc. has the following ratios: $A^*/S_0 = 1.6$; $L^*/S_0 = 0.4$; profit margin = 0.10; and dividend payout ratio = 0.45, or 45 percent. Sales last year were $100 million. Assuming that these ratios will remain constant, use the AFN formula to determine the maximum growth rate Weatherford can achieve without having to employ nonspontaneous external funds.

ST-3
Additional funds needed

Suppose Weatherford's financial consultants report (1) that the inventory turnover ratio is sales/inventory = 3 times versus an industry average of 4 times and (2) that Weatherford could reduce inventories and thus raise its turnover to 4 without affecting sales, the profit margin, or the other asset turnover ratios. Under these conditions, use the AFN formula to determine the amount of additional funds Weatherford would require during each of the next 2 years if sales grew at a rate of 20 percent per year.

STARTER PROBLEMS

Carter Corporation's sales are expected to increase from $5 million in 1997 to $6 million in 1998, or by 20 percent. Its assets totaled $3 million at the end of 1997. Carter is at full capacity, so its assets must grow at the same rate as projected sales. At the end of 1997, current liabilities were $1 million, consisting of $250,000 of accounts payable, $500,000 of notes payable, and $250,000 of accruals. The after-tax profit margin is forecasted to be 5 percent, and the forecasted payout ratio is 70 percent. Use this information to answer Problems 15-1, 15-2, and 15-3.

15-1
AFN formula

Use the AFN formula to forecast Carter's additional funds needed for the coming year.

15-2
AFN formula

What would the additional funds needed be if the company's year-end 1997 assets had been $4 million? Assume that all other numbers are the same. Why is this AFN different from the one you found in Problem 15-1? Is the company's "capital intensity" the same or different?

15-3
AFN formula

Return to the assumption that the company had $3 million in assets at the end of 1997, but now assume that the company pays no dividends. Under these assumptions, what would be the additional funds needed for the coming year? Why is this AFN different from the one you found in Problem 15-1?

Exam-Type Problems

The problems included in this section are set up in such a way that they could be used as multiple-choice exam problems.

15-4
Long-term financing needed

At year-end 1997, total assets for Ambrose Inc. were $1.2 million and accounts payable were $375,000. Sales, which in 1997 were $2.5 million, are expected to increase by 25 percent in 1998. Total assets and accounts payable are proportional to sales, and that relationship will be maintained. Ambrose typically uses no current liabilities other than accounts payable. Common stock amounted to $425,000 in 1997, and retained earnings were $295,000. Ambrose plans to sell new common stock in the amount of $75,000. The firm's profit margin on sales is 6 percent; 40 percent of earnings will be paid out as dividends.
a. What was Ambrose's total debt in 1997?
b. How much new, long-term debt financing will be needed in 1998? (Hint: AFN − New stock = New long-term debt.)

15-5
Additional funds needed

The Flint Company's sales are forecasted to increase from $1,000 in 1997 to $2,000 in 1998. Here is the December 31, 1997, balance sheet:

Cash	$ 100	Accounts payable	$ 50
Accounts receivable	200	Notes payable	150
Inventory	200	Accruals	50
Total current assets	$ 500	Total current liabilities	$ 250
Net fixed assets	500	Long-term debt	400
		Common stock	100
		Retained earnings	250
Total assets	$1,000	Total liabilities and equity	$1,000

Flint's fixed assets were used to only 50 percent of capacity during 1997, but its current assets were at their proper levels. All assets except fixed assets increase at the same rate as sales, and fixed assets would also increase at the same rate if the current excess capacity did not exist. Flint's after-tax profit margin is forecasted to be 5 percent, and its payout ratio will be 60 percent. What is Flint's additional funds needed (AFN) for the coming year?

15-6
Sales increase

Pierce Furnishings generated $2.0 million in sales during 1997, and its year-end total assets were $1.5 million. Also, at year-end 1997, current liabilities were $500,000, consisting of $200,000 of notes payable, $200,000 of accounts payable, and $100,000 of accruals. Looking ahead to 1998, the company estimates that its assets must increase by 75 cents for every $1 increase in sales. Pierce's profit margin is 5 percent, and its payout ratio is 60 percent. How large a sales increase can the company achieve without having to raise funds externally?

Problems

15-7
Pro forma statements and ratios

Tozer Computers makes bulk purchases of small computers, stocks them in conveniently located warehouses, and ships them to its chain of retail stores. Tozer's balance sheet as of December 31, 1997, is shown here (millions of dollars):

Cash	$ 3.5	Accounts payable	$ 9.0
Receivables	26.0	Notes payable	18.0
Inventory	58.0	Accruals	8.5
Total current assets	$ 87.5	Total current liabilities	$ 35.5
Net fixed assets	35.0	Mortgage loan	6.0
		Common stock	15.0
		Retained earnings	66.0
Total assets	$122.5	Total liabilities and equity	$122.5

Sales for 1997 were $350 million, while net income for the year was $10.5 million. Tozer paid dividends of $4.2 million to common stockholders. The firm is operating at full capacity. Assume that all ratios remain constant.

a. If sales are projected to increase by $70 million, or 20 percent, during 1998, use the AFN equation to determine Tozer's projected external capital requirements.

b. Construct Tozer's pro forma balance sheet for December 31, 1998. Assume that all external capital requirements are met by bank loans and are reflected in notes payable.

c. Now calculate the following ratios, based on your projected December 31, 1998, balance sheet. Tozer's 1997 ratios and industry average ratios are shown here for comparison:

	TOZER COMPUTERS		INDUSTRY AVERAGE
	12/31/98	12/31/97	12/31/97
Current ratio	_____	2.5×	3×
Debt/total assets	_____	33.9%	30%
Rate of return on equity	_____	13.0%	12%

d. Now assume that Tozer grows by the same $70 million but that the growth is spread over 5 years — that is, that sales grow by $14 million each year.
   (1) Calculate total additional financial requirements over the 5-year period. (Hint: Use 1997 ratios, $\Delta S = \$70$, but *total* sales for the 5-year period.)
   (2) Construct a pro forma balance sheet as of December 31, 2002, using notes payable as the balancing item.
   (3) Calculate the current ratio, total debt/total assets ratio, and rate of return on equity as of December 31, 2002. [Hint: Be sure to use *total sales*, which amount to $1,960 million, to calculate retained earnings, but 2002 profits to calculate the rate of return on equity — that is, return on equity = (2002 profits)/(12/31/02 equity).]

e. Do the plans outlined in Parts b and/or d seem feasible to you? That is, do you think Tozer could borrow the required capital, and would the company be raising the odds on its bankruptcy to an excessive level in the event of some temporary misfortune?

15-8
Additional funds needed

Cooley Textile's 1997 financial statements are shown below.

COOLEY TEXTILE: BALANCE SHEET AS OF DECEMBER 31, 1997 (THOUSANDS OF DOLLARS)

Cash	$ 1,080	Accounts payable	$ 4,320
Receivables	6,480	Accruals	2,880
Inventory	9,000	Notes payable	2,100
Total current assets	$16,560	Total current liabilities	$ 9,300
Net fixed assets	12,600	Mortgage bonds	3,500
		Common stock	3,500
		Retained earnings	12,860
Total assets	$29,160	Total liabilities and equity	$29,160

COOLEY TEXTILE: INCOME STATEMENT FOR DECEMBER 31, 1997 (THOUSANDS OF DOLLARS)

Sales	$36,000
Operating costs	32,440
Earnings before interest and taxes	$ 3,560
Interest	560
Earnings before taxes	$ 3,000
Taxes (40%)	1,200
Net income	$ 1,800
Dividends (45%)	$810
Addition to retained earnings	$990

Suppose 1998 sales are projected to increase by 15 percent over 1997 sales. Determine the additional funds needed. Assume that the company was operating at full capacity in 1997, that it cannot sell off any of its fixed assets, and that any required financing will be borrowed as notes payable. Also, assume that assets, spontaneous liabilities, and operating costs are expected to increase by the same percentage as sales. Use the projected financial statement method to develop a pro forma balance sheet and income statement for December 31, 1998. Use the pro forma income statement to determine the addition to retained earnings.

15-9

Excess capacity

Krogh Lumber's 1997 financial statements are shown below.

KROGH LUMBER: BALANCE SHEET AS OF DECEMBER 31, 1997 (THOUSANDS OF DOLLARS)

Cash	$ 1,800	Accounts payable	$ 7,200
Receivables	10,800	Notes payable	3,472
Inventory	12,600	Accruals	2,520
Total current assets	$25,200	Total current liabilities	$13,192
		Mortgage bonds	5,000
		Common stock	2,000
Net fixed assets	21,600	Retained earnings	26,608
Total assets	$46,800	Total liabilities and equity	$46,800

KROGH LUMBER: INCOME STATEMENT FOR DECEMBER 31, 1997 (THOUSANDS OF DOLLARS)

Sales	$36,000
Operating costs	30,783
Earnings before interest and taxes	$ 5,217
Interest	1,017
Earnings before taxes	$ 4,200
Taxes (40%)	1,680
Net income	$ 2,520
Dividends (60%)	$1,512
Addition to retained earnings	1,008

a. Assume that the company was operating at full capacity in 1997 with regard to all items *except* fixed assets; fixed assets in 1997 were being utilized to only 75 percent of capacity. By what percentage could 1998 sales increase over 1997 sales without the need for an increase in fixed assets?

b. Now suppose 1998 sales increase by 25 percent over 1997 sales. How much additional external capital will be required? Assume that Krogh cannot sell any fixed assets. (Hint: Use the projected financial statement method to develop a pro forma balance sheet and income statement as in Tables 15-1 and 15-2.) Assume that any required financing is borrowed as notes payable. Use a pro forma income statement to determine the addition to retained earnings. (Another hint: Notes payable = $6,021.)

c. Suppose the industry average DSO and inventory turnover ratio are 90 days and 3.33, respectively, and that Krogh Lumber matches these figures in 1998 and then uses the funds released to reduce equity. (It pays a special dividend out of retained earnings.) What would this do to the rate of return on year-end 1998 equity? Use the balance sheet and income statement as developed in Part b.

15-10

Additional funds needed

Morrissey Technologies Inc.'s 1997 financial statements are shown below.

MORRISSEY TECHNOLOGIES INC.: BALANCE SHEET AS OF DECEMBER 31, 1997

Cash	$ 180,000	Accounts payable	$ 360,000
Receivables	360,000	Notes payable	156,000
Inventory	720,000	Accruals	180,000
Total current assets	$1,260,000	Total current liabilities	$ 696,000
Fixed assets	1,440,000	Common stock	1,800,000
		Retained earnings	204,000
Total assets	$2,700,000	Total liabilities and equity	$2,700,000

MORRISSEY TECHNOLOGIES INC.: INCOME STATEMENT FOR DECEMBER 31, 1997

Sales	$3,600,000
Operating costs	3,279,720
EBIT	$ 320,280
Interest	20,280
EBT	$ 300,000
Taxes (40%)	120,000
Net income	$ 180,000
Per Share Data:	
Common stock price	$24.00
Earnings per share (EPS)	$ 1.80
Dividends per share (DPS)	$ 1.08

a. Suppose that in 1998 sales increase by 10 percent over 1997 sales and that 1998 DPS will increase to $1.12. Construct the pro forma financial statements using the projected financial statement method. Use AFN as the balancing item. How much additional capital will be required? Assume the firm operated at full capacity in 1997.
b. If the profit margin were to remain at 5 percent and the dividend payout rate were to remain at 60 percent, at what growth rate in sales would the additional financing requirements be exactly zero? (Hint: Set AFN equal to zero and solve for g.)

15-11
External financing requirements

The 1997 balance sheet and income statement for the Lewis Company are shown below.

LEWIS COMPANY: BALANCE SHEET AS OF DECEMBER 31, 1997 (THOUSANDS OF DOLLARS)

Cash	$ 80	Accounts payable	$ 160
Accounts receivable	240	Accruals	40
Inventory	720	Notes payable	252
Total current assets	$1,040	Total current liabilities	$ 452
Fixed assets	3,200	Long-term debt	1,244
		Total debt	$1,696
		Common stock	1,605
		Retained earnings	939
Total assets	$4,240	Total liabilities and equity	$4,240

LEWIS COMPANY: INCOME STATEMENT FOR DECEMBER 31, 1997 (THOUSANDS OF DOLLARS)

Sales	$8,000
Operating costs	7,450
EBIT	$ 550
Interest	150
EBT	$ 400
Taxes (40%)	160
Net income	$ 240
Per Share Data:	
Common stock price	$16.96
Earnings per share (EPS)	$ 1.60
Dividends per share (DPS)	$ 1.04

a. The firm operated at full capacity in 1997. It expects sales to increase by 20 percent during 1998 and expects 1998 dividends per share to increase to $1.10. Use the projected financial statement method to determine how much outside financing is required, developing the firm's pro forma balance sheet and income statement, and use AFN as the balancing item.

b. If the firm must maintain a current ratio of 2.3 and a debt ratio of 40 percent, how much financing will be obtained using notes payable, long-term debt, and common stock?

INTEGRATED CASE

NEW WORLD CHEMICALS INC.

15-12 Financial Forecasting Sue Wilson, the new financial manager of New World Chemicals (NWC), a California producer of specialized chemicals for use in fruit orchards, must prepare a financial forecast for 1998. NWC's 1997 sales were $2 billion, and the marketing department is forecasting a 25 percent increase for 1998. Wilson thinks the company was operating at full capacity in 1997, but she is not sure about this. The 1997 financial statements, plus some other data, are given in Table IC15-1.

Assume that you were recently hired as Wilson's assistant, and your first major task is to help her develop the forecast. She asked you to begin by answering the following set of questions.

a. Assume (1) that NWC was operating at full capacity in 1997 with respect to all assets, (2) that all assets must grow proportionally with sales, (3) that accounts payable and accruals will also grow in proportion to sales, and (4) that the 1997 profit margin and dividend payout will be maintained. Under these conditions, what will the company's financial requirements be for the coming year? Use the AFN equation to answer this question.

b. Now estimate the 1998 financial requirements using the projected financial statement approach. Assume (1) that each type of asset, as well as payables, accruals, and fixed and variable costs, grow at the same rate as sales; (2) that the payout ratio is held constant at 30 percent; and (3) that external funds needed are financed 50 percent by notes payable and 50 percent by long-term debt (no new common stock will be issued.

c. Why do the two methods produce somewhat different AFN forecasts? Which method provides the more accurate forecast?

d. Calculate NWC's forecasted ratios, and compare them with the company's 1997 ratios and with the industry averages. How does NWC compare with the average firm in its industry, and is the company expected to improve during the coming year?

e. Suppose you now learn that NWC's 1997 receivables and inventory were in line with required levels, given the firm's credit and inventory policies, but that excess capacity existed with regard to fixed assets. Specifically, fixed assets were operated at only 75 percent of capacity.
(1) What level of sales could have existed in 1997 with the available fixed assets? What would the fixed assets/sales

ratio have been if NWC had been operating at full capacity?
(2) How would the existence of excess capacity in fixed assets affect the additional funds needed during 1998?

f. Without actually working out the numbers, how would you expect the ratios to change in the situation where excess capacity in fixed assets exists? Explain your reasoning.

g. Based on comparisons between NWC's days sales outstanding (DSO) and inventory turnover ratios with the industry average figures, does it appear that NWC is operating efficiently with respect to its inventory and accounts receivable? If the company were able to bring these ratios into line with the industry averages, what effect would this have on its AFN and its financial ratios? (Note: Inventory and receivables will be discussed in detail in Chapter 16.)

h. The relationship between sales and the various types of assets is important in financial forecasting. The financial statement method, under the assumption that each asset item grows at the same rate as sales, leads to an AFN forecast that is reasonably close to the forecast using the AFN equation. Explain how each of the following factors would affect the accuracy of financial forecasts based on the AFN equation: (1) excess capacity; (2) base stocks of assets, such as shoes in a shoe store; (3) economies of scale in the use of assets; and (4) lumpy assets.

i. (1) How could regression analysis be used to detect the presence of the situations described above and then to improve the financial forecasts? Plot a graph of the following data, which is for a typical well-managed company in NWC's industry, to illustrate your answer.

YEAR	SALES	INVENTORIES
1995	$1,280	$118
1996	1,600	138
1997	2,000	162
1998E	2,500	192

(2) On the same graph that plots the above data, draw a line which shows how the regression line would have to appear to justify the use of the AFN formula and the projected financial statement forecasting method. As a

T A B L E I C 1 5 - 1	Financial Statements and Other Data on NWC (Millions of Dollars)

A. 1997 Balance Sheet

Cash and securities	$ 20	Accounts payable and accruals	$ 100
Accounts receivable	240	Notes payable	100
Inventory	240	Total current liabilities	$ 200
Total current assets	$ 500	Long-term debt	100
Net fixed assets	500	Common stock	500
		Retained earnings	200
Total assets	$ 1,000	Total liabilities and equity	$1,000

B. 1997 Income Statement

Sales	$2,000.00
Less: Variable costs	1,200.00
Fixed costs	700.00
Earnings before interest and taxes	$ 100.00
Interest	16.00
Earnings before taxes	$ 84.00
Taxes (40%)	33.60
Net income	$ 50.40
Dividends (30%)	15.12
Addition to retained earnings	$ 35.28

C. Key Ratios	**NWC**	**INDUSTRY**	**COMMENT**
Basic earnings power	10.00%	20.00%	
Profit margin	2.52	4.00	
Return on equity	7.20	15.60	
Days sales outstanding (360 days)	43.20 days	32.00 days	
Inventory turnover	8.33×	11.00×	
Fixed assets turnover	4.00	5.00	
Total assets turnover	2.00	2.50	
Debt/assets	30.00%	36.00%	
Times interest earned	6.25×	9.40×	
Current ratio	2.50	3.00	
Payout ratio	30.00%	30.00%	

part of your answer, show the growth rate in inventory that results from a 10 percent increase in sales from a sales level of (a) $200 and (b) $2,000 based on both the actual regression line and a *hypothetical* regression line which is linear and which goes through the origin.

j. How would changes in these items affect the AFN? (1) The dividend payout ratio, (2) the profit margin, (3) the capital intensity ratio, and (4) if NWC begins buying from its suppliers on terms which permit it to pay after 60 days rather than after 30 days. (Consider each item separately and hold all other things constant.)

COMPUTER-RELATED PROBLEM

Work the problem in this section only if you are using the computer problem diskette.

15-13

Forecasting

Use the model in File C15 to solve this problem. Pettijohn Industries' 1997 financial statements are shown below.

PETTIJOHN INDUSTRIES: BALANCE SHEET AS OF DECEMBER 31, 1997 (MILLIONS OF DOLLARS)

Cash	$ 4.0	Accounts payable	$ 8.0
Receivables	12.0	Notes payable	5.0
Inventory	16.0	Total current liabilities	$13.0
Total current assets	$32.0	Long-term debt	12.0
Net fixed assets	40.0	Common stock	20.0
		Retained earnings	27.0
Total assets	$72.0	Total liabilities and equity	$72.0

PETTIJOHN INDUSTRIES: INCOME STATEMENT FOR DECEMBER 31, 1997 (MILLIONS OF DOLLARS)

Sales	$80.0
Operating costs	71.3
EBIT	$ 8.7
Interest	2.0
EBT	$ 6.7
Taxes (40%)	2.7
Net income	$ 4.0
Dividends (40%)	$1.60
Addition to retained earnings	$2.40

Assume that the firm has no excess capacity in fixed assets, that the average interest rate for debt is 12 percent, and that the projected annual sales growth rate for the next 5 years is 15 percent.

a. Pettijohn plans to finance its additional funds needed with 50 percent short-term debt and 50 percent long-term debt. Using the projected financial statement method, prepare the pro forma financial statements for 1998 through 2002, and then determine (1) additional funds needed, (2) the current ratio, (3) the debt ratio, and (4) the return on equity.

b. Sales growth could be 5 percentage points above or below the projected 15 percent. Determine the effect of such variances on AFN and the key ratios.

c. Perform an analysis to determine the sensitivity of AFN and the key ratios for the year 2002 to changes in the dividend payout ratio as specified in the following, assuming sales grow at a constant 15 percent. What happens to AFN if the dividend payout ratio (1) is raised from 40 to 70 percent or (2) is lowered from 40 to 20 percent?

CHAPTER 16

MANAGING CURRENT ASSETS

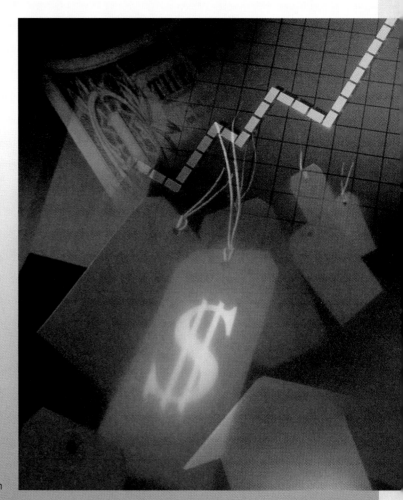

© Ralph Mercer/Gamma Liaison

Core Industries Inc. is a $200 million electrical equipment manufacturer whose stock is listed on the NYSE. The stock traded in the range of $12 to $17 per share during most of the 1980s, but during the recession of 1990, earnings plunged and the stock dropped to $4. Then Core's directors made several key managerial changes, including the chief financial officer (CFO), and things improved dramatically.

At an annual meeting of stockholders, the new CFO, Ray Steben, kicked off the presentations, informing stockholders that while sales had increased by 12 percent, profits jumped 29 percent and the stock price 79 percent.

What caused this dramatic improvement? According to Steben, the improvement resulted primarily from the company's renewed focus on stockholder value and better working capital management:

> These strong sales and earnings figures are further evidence that shareholder value will continue to be focused upon, and your management will be stewards of the capital entrusted to it. Return on beginning equity jumped from 7.2 percent to 13.3 percent, a level not exceeded since 1981. As you know, our stated objective is to better 15 percent. Return on average capital employed improved almost 50 percent, from 4.5 percent to 6.8 percent. And the company was considerably more efficient in its use of

BETTER WORKING CAPITAL MANAGEMENT LIFTS STOCK PRICE

working capital. As a direct result of a companywide program, operating working capital was reduced from $0.50 to $0.40 per dollar of sales. Operating working capital is basically receivables and inventory less payables and accruals. The cash freed up by this program was used to reduce debt and to invest in operations and acquisitions that will return better than our cost of capital.

Following Steben's address, Core's president, Dave Zimmer, elaborated on Core's improvement and the ways management planned to keep the momentum going in the coming years. Like Steben, Zimmer stressed the improvement in working capital management, especially the fact that capital previously locked up in excessive inventories and receivables had been freed up and was now earning returns for stockholders. Zimmer also informed the stockholders that "your top management has placed a significant portion of its compensation at risk both through the annual bonus plan and the new, long-term incentive plan." He then explained that EVA will be used to tie management's compensation directly to stock price performance, so managers will do well only if stockholders do well.

Since the focus on EVA and working capital began, Core has continued to perform well. It has continued to improve the ratio of working capital to sales, and this has led to continued increases in earnings. So, the stock price has continued to move up nicely.

While generally pleased with its recent performance, Core's management has been resolute in its desire to continue improving operations. It plans to continue shrinking working capital, and as noted, it has also taken steps to implement the Economic Value Added (EVA) concept discussed in Chapter 2. An expert on EVA, Mark MacGuidwin, was brought in, and employees throughout the corporation are now compensated based on the EVA of their division.

Clearly, Core Industries' operations have been improved, and like other manufacturers, this improvement centered on streamlining working capital to improve efficiency. The result has been a higher stock price.

About 60 percent of a typical financial manager's time is devoted to working capital management, and many students' first jobs will involve working capital. This is particularly true in smaller businesses, where most new jobs in the United States are being created.

Working capital policy involves two basic questions: (1) What is the appropriate amount of current assets for the firm to carry, both in total and for each specific account, and (2) how should current assets be financed? This chapter addresses current asset holdings, and Chapter 17 addresses their financing.

WORKING CAPITAL TERMINOLOGY

We begin our discussion of working capital policy by reviewing some basic definitions and concepts:

Working Capital
A firm's investment in short-term assets — cash, marketable securities, inventory, and accounts receivable.

Net Working Capital
Current assets minus current liabilities.

1. **Working capital,** sometimes called *gross working capital,* simply refers to current assets used in operations.
2. **Net working capital** is defined as current assets minus current liabilities.
3. The *current ratio,* which was discussed in Chapter 3, is calculated by dividing current assets by current liabilities, and it is intended to measure liquidity. However, a high current ratio does not ensure that a firm will have the cash required to meet its needs. If inventories cannot be sold, or if receivables cannot be collected in a timely manner, then the apparent safety reflected in a high current ratio could be illusory.
4. The *quick ratio,* or *acid test,* also attempts to measure liquidity, and it is found by subtracting inventories from current assets and then dividing by current liabilities. The quick ratio removes inventories from current assets because they are the least liquid of current assets. Therefore, the quick ratio is an "acid test" of a company's ability to meet its current obligations.
5. The best and most comprehensive picture of a firm's liquidity position is shown by its *cash budget.* This statement, which forecasts cash inflows and outflows, focuses on what really counts, namely, the firm's ability to generate sufficient cash inflows to meet its required cash outflows. We will discuss cash budgeting in detail later in the chapter.

Working Capital Policy
Basic policy decisions regarding (1) target levels for each category of current assets and (2) how current assets will be financed.

6. **Working capital policy** refers to the firm's policies regarding (1) target levels for each category of current assets and (2) how current assets will be financed.
7. *Working capital management* involves both setting working capital policy and carrying out that policy in day-to-day operations.

The term *working capital* originated with the old Yankee peddler, who would load up his wagon with goods and then go off on his route to peddle his wares. The merchandise was called working capital because it was what he actually sold, or "turned over," to produce his profits. The wagon and horse were his fixed assets. He generally owned the horse and wagon, so they were financed with "equity" capital, but he borrowed the funds to buy the merchandise. These borrowings were called *working capital loans,* and they had to be repaid after each trip to demonstrate to the bank that the credit was sound. If the peddler was able to repay the loan, then the bank would make another loan, and banks that followed this procedure were said to be employing "sound banking practices."

SELF-TEST QUESTIONS

Why is the quick ratio also called an acid test?

How did the term "working capital" originate?

ALTERNATIVE CURRENT ASSET INVESTMENT POLICIES

Relaxed Current Asset Investment Policy
A policy under which relatively large amounts of cash, marketable securities, and inventories are carried and under which sales are stimulated by a liberal credit policy, resulting in a high level of receivables.

Restricted Current Asset Investment Policy
A policy under which holdings of cash, securities, inventories, and receivables are minimized.

Moderate Current Asset Investment Policy
A policy that is between the relaxed and restricted policies.

Figure 16-1 shows three alternative policies regarding the total amount of current assets carried. Essentially, these policies differ with regard to the amount of current assets carried to support any given level of sales, hence in the turnover of those assets. The line with the steepest slope represents a **relaxed current asset investment** (or "fat cat") **policy,** where relatively large amounts of cash, marketable securities, and inventories are carried, and where sales are stimulated by the use of a credit policy that provides liberal financing to customers and a corresponding high level of receivables. Conversely, with the **restricted current asset investment** (or "lean-and-mean") **policy,** the holdings of cash, securities, inventories, and receivables are minimized. Under the restricted policy, current assets are turned over more frequently, so each dollar of current assets is forced to "work harder." The **moderate current asset investment policy** is between the two extremes. Core Industries, as discussed in the opening vignette, recently brought in a new management team which switched from a relaxed to a restricted policy, with good results.

Under conditions of certainty — when sales, costs, lead times, payment periods, and so on, are known for sure — all firms would hold only minimal levels of current assets. Any larger amounts would increase the need for external funding without a corresponding increase in profits, while any smaller holdings would involve late payments to suppliers along with lost sales due to inventory shortages and an overly restrictive credit policy.

However, the picture changes when uncertainty is introduced. Here the firm requires some minimum amount of cash and inventories based on expected payments, expected sales, expected order lead times, and so on, plus additional holdings, or *safety stocks,* which enable it to deal with departures from the expected values. Similarly, accounts receivable levels are determined by credit terms, and the tougher the credit terms, the lower the receivables for any given level of sales. With a restricted current asset investment policy, the firm would hold minimal safety stocks of cash and inventories, and it would have a tight credit policy even though this meant running the risk of losing sales. A restricted, lean-and-mean current asset investment policy generally provides the highest expected return on this investment, but it entails the greatest risk, while the reverse is true under a relaxed policy. The moderate policy falls in between the two extremes in terms of expected risk and return.

FIGURE   16-1 Alternative Current Asset Investment Policies
(Millions of Dollars)

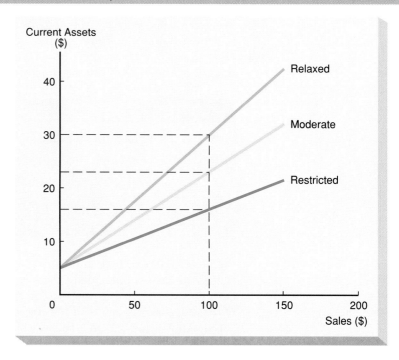

POLICY	CURRENT ASSETS TO SUPPORT SALES OF $100	TURNOVER OF CURRENT ASSETS
Relaxed	$30	3.3×
Moderate	23	4.3×
Restricted	16	6.3×

NOTE: The sales/current assets relationship is shown here as being linear, but the relationship is often curvilinear.

Changing technology can lead to dramatic changes in the optimal current asset investment policy. For example, if new technology makes it possible for a manufacturer such as Core Industries to speed up the production of a given product from ten days to five days, then its work-in-progress inventory can be cut in half. Similarly, retailers such as Wal-Mart or Home Depot have installed systems under which bar codes on all merchandise are read at the cash register. The information on the sale is electronically transmitted to a computer which maintains a record of the inventory of each item, and the computer automatically transmits orders to suppliers' computers when stocks fall to prescribed levels. With such a system, inventories will be held at optimal levels; orders will reflect exactly what styles, colors, and sizes consumers are buying; and the firm's profits will be maximized.

MANAGING THE COMPONENTS OF WORKING CAPITAL

Working capital consists of four main components: cash, marketable securities, inventory, and accounts receivable. The remainder of this chapter will focus on the issues involved with managing each of these components. As you will see, a

INDUSTRY PRACTICE

EVA AND WORKING CAPITAL

Economic Value Added (EVA) provides a useful way of thinking about working capital — this is the approach taken by Core Industries, the company discussed at the beginning of this chapter. The EVA formula is as follows:

$$EVA = [EBIT \times (1 - T)] - (WACC \times \text{Total capital}).$$

If a company such as Core can reduce inventories, cash holdings, or receivables without seriously affecting operating income, then cash will be freed up. This cash can then be used to pay off debt or to repurchase stock, both of which reduce capital. If capital is reduced, then financing costs will decline, and this will raise EVA. Many firms have reported that when division managers and other operating people think about working capital in these terms, they find ways to reduce it, because their compensation depends on their divisions' EVAs.

We can also think of working capital management in terms of ROE and the Du Pont equation:

$$ROE = \frac{\text{Profit}}{\text{margin}} \times \frac{\text{Total assets turnover}}{} \times \frac{\text{Leverage}}{\text{factor}}$$

$$= \frac{\text{Net income}/}{\text{Sales}} \times \frac{\text{Sales}/}{\text{Total assets}} \times \frac{\text{Assets}/}{\text{Equity}}.$$

If working capital and hence total assets can be reduced without seriously affecting the profit margin, this will increase the total assets turnover and, consequently, ROE.

---

common thread underlies all current asset management. For each type of asset, firms face a fundamental trade-off: current assets (that is, working capital) are necessary to conduct business, and the greater the holdings of current assets, the smaller the danger of running out, hence the lower the firm's operating risk. However, holding working capital is costly — if inventories are too large, then the firm will have assets which earn a zero or even negative return if storage and spoilage costs are high. And, of course, firms must acquire capital to buy assets such as inventory, this capital has a cost, and this increases the downward drag from excessive inventories (or receivables or even cash). So, there is pressure to hold the amount of working capital to the minimum consistent with running the business without interruption.

Firms typically follow a cycle in which they purchase inventory, sell goods on credit, and then collect accounts receivable. This cycle is referred to as the cash conversion cycle, and it is discussed in detail in Appendix 16A. Sound working capital policy is designed to minimize the time between cash expenditures on materials and the collection of cash on sales.

SELF-TEST QUESTIONS ??????

Identify and explain three alternative current asset investment policies.

What are the principal components of working capital?

What are the reasons for not wanting to hold too little working capital? For not wanting to hold too much?

What is the fundamental trade-off that managers face when managing working capital?

THE CONCEPT OF ZERO WORKING CAPITAL

At first glance, it might seem that working capital management is not as important as capital budgeting, dividend policy, and other decisions that determine

ON THE WWW

An article entitled "Cutting Working Capital" can be found at http://www.sbc1.com/sbc/info/PreviousOAAB.html. The article is reprinted from Small Business News and provides an excellent discussion of the advantages and pitfalls of cutting working capital.

a firm's long-term direction. However, in today's world of intense global competition, working capital management is receiving increasing attention from managers striving for peak efficiency. In fact, the goal of many leading companies today—including American Standard, Campbell Soup, General Electric, Quaker Oats, and Whirlpool—is *zero working capital.* Proponents of the zero working capital concept claim that a movement toward this goal not only generates cash but also speeds up production and helps businesses make more timely deliveries and operate more efficiently. The concept has its own definition of working capital: Inventories + Receivables − Payables. The rationale here is (1) that inventories and receivables are the keys to making sales, but (2) that inventories can be financed by suppliers through accounts payable.

On average, companies use 20 cents of working capital for each dollar of sales. So, on average, working capital is turned over five times per year. Reducing working capital and thus increasing turnover has two major financial benefits. First, every dollar freed up by reducing inventories or receivables, or by increasing payables, results in a one-time contribution to cash flow. Second, a movement toward zero working capital permanently raises a company's earnings. Like all capital, funds invested in working capital cost money, so reducing those funds yields permanent savings in capital costs. In addition to the financial benefits, reducing working capital forces a company to produce and deliver faster than its competitors, which helps it gain new business and charge premium prices for providing good service. As inventories disappear, warehouses can be sold off, both labor and handling equipment needs are reduced, and obsolete and/or out-of-style goods are minimized.

To illustrate the benefits of striving for zero working capital, in just one year Campbell Soup pared its working capital by $80 million. It used the cash to develop new products and to buy companies in Britain, Australia, and other countries. Equally important, the company expects to increase annual profits by $50 million over the next few years by lowering overtime labor and storage costs.

The most important factor in moving toward zero working capital is increased speed. If the production process is fast enough, companies can produce items as they are ordered rather than having to forecast demand and build up large inventories that are managed by bureaucracies. The best companies are able to start production after an order is received yet still meet customer delivery requirements. This system is known as *demand flow,* or *demand-based management,* and it builds on the just-in-time method of inventory control which we will discuss later in this chapter. (See the Industry Practice box entitled "American Standard Embraces Demand Flow Management.") However, demand flow management is broader than just-in-time, because it requires that all elements of a production system operate quickly and efficiently.

ON THE WWW

American Standard provides a detailed discussion of how they are applying demand flow production concepts to reengineered manufacturing and office processes in an attempt to achieve zero working capital. The site can be accessed at http://www.teamflow.com/AmerStd.html.

Achieving zero working capital requires that every order and part move at maximum speed, which generally means replacing paper with electronic data. Then, orders streak from the processing department to the plant, flexible production lines produce each product every day, and finished goods flow directly from the production line onto waiting trucks or rail cars. Instead of cluttering plants or warehouses with inventories, products move directly into the pipeline. As efficiency rises, working capital dwindles.

Clearly, it is not possible for most firms to achieve zero working capital and infinitely efficient production. Still, a focus on minimizing receivables and inventories while maximizing payables will help a firm lower its investment in working capital and achieve financial and production economies.

INDUSTRY PRACTICE

AMERICAN STANDARD EMBRACES DEMAND FLOW MANAGEMENT

The recent history of New Jersey based American Standard provides an interesting illustration of how demand flow management can dramatically improve corporate performance. Fighting off a hostile bid from Black and Decker, American Standard's management undertook a leveraged buyout in 1988. The resulting debt load and a weak economy devastated the company, so in 1989,

the newly promoted CEO, Emmanuel Kampouris, began looking for ways to improve the company's profitability.

Kampouris decided that demand flow management would improve efficiency. So far, the strategy has paid off handsomely. The company has dramatically reduced the time it takes to produce a wide variety of products. For example, bathroom fixtures, which had taken three weeks to produce, are now ready for sale in less than four days. As a result, working capital as a percentage of sales has shrunk dramatically. Sales have

risen, but inventories have fallen, and inventory turnover has increased sharply.

American Standard's achievements have drawn the attention of many companies, including General Electric. After implementing its own demand flow management, GE succeeded in reducing inventories in some of its plants by up to 30 percent.

SOURCE: "American Standard Wises Up," *Business Week*, November 18, 1996, 70–74.

SELF-TEST QUESTION

??????

What is the basic idea of zero working capital, and how is working capital defined in this concept?

CASH MANAGEMENT

Approximately 1.5 percent of the average industrial firm's assets are held in the form of cash, which is defined as demand deposits plus currency. Cash is often called a "nonearning asset." It is needed to pay for labor and raw materials, to buy fixed assets, to pay taxes, to service debt, to pay dividends, and so on. However, cash itself (and also most commercial checking accounts) earns no interest. Thus, the goal of the cash manager is to minimize the amount of cash the firm must hold for use in conducting its normal business activities, yet, at the same time, to have sufficient cash (1) to take trade discounts, (2) to maintain its credit rating, and (3) to meet unexpected cash needs. We begin our analysis with a discussion of the reasons for holding cash.

RATIONALE FOR HOLDING CASH

Firms hold cash for two primary reasons:

Transactions Balance
A cash balance associated with payments and collections; the balance necessary for day-to-day operations.

1. **Transactions.** Cash balances are necessary in business operations. Payments must be made in cash, and receipts are deposited in the cash account. Cash balances associated with routine payments and collections are known as **transactions balances.**

2. **Compensation to banks for providing loans and services**. A bank makes money by lending out funds that have been deposited with it, so the larger its deposits, the better the bank's profit position. If a bank is providing services to a

Compensating Balance
A bank balance that a firm must maintain to compensate the bank for services rendered or for granting a loan.

Precautionary Balance
A cash balance held in reserve for random, unforeseen fluctuations in cash inflows and outflows.

Speculative Balance
A cash balance that is held to enable the firm to take advantage of any bargain purchases that might arise.

Trade Discount
A price reduction that suppliers offer customers for early payment of bills.

customer, it may require the customer to leave a minimum balance on deposit to help offset the costs of providing the services. Also, banks may require borrowers to hold deposits at the bank. Both types of deposits are defined as **compensating balances,** and they are discussed in detail later in this chapter.

Two other reasons for holding cash have been noted in the finance and economics literature: for *precaution* and for *speculation.* Cash inflows and outflows are unpredictable, with the degree of predictability varying among firms and industries. Therefore, firms need to hold some cash in reserve for random, unforeseen fluctuations in inflows and outflows. These "safety stocks" are called **precautionary balances,** and the less predictable the firm's cash flows, the larger such balances should be. However, if the firm has easy access to borrowed funds — that is, if it can borrow on short notice — its need for precautionary balances is reduced. Also, as we note later in this chapter, firms that would otherwise need large precautionary balances tend to hold highly liquid marketable securities rather than cash per se. Marketable securities serve many of the purposes of cash, but they provide greater interest income than bank deposits.

Some cash balances may be held to enable the firm to take advantage of bargain purchases that might arise; these funds are called **speculative balances.** However, firms today are more likely to rely on reserve borrowing capacity and/or marketable securities portfolios than on cash per se for speculative purposes.

The cash accounts of most firms can be thought of as consisting of transactions, compensating, precautionary, and speculative balances. However, we cannot calculate the amount needed for each purpose, sum them, and produce a total desired cash balance, because the same money often serves more than one purpose. For instance, precautionary and speculative balances can also be used to satisfy compensating balance requirements. Firms do, however, consider all four factors when establishing their target cash positions.

ADVANTAGES OF HOLDING ADEQUATE CASH AND NEAR-CASH ASSETS

In addition to the four motives just discussed, sound working capital management requires that an ample supply of cash and near-cash assets be maintained for several specific reasons:

1. It is essential that the firm have sufficient cash and near-cash assets to take **trade discounts.** Suppliers frequently offer customers discounts for early payment of bills. As we will see in the next chapter, the cost of not taking discounts is very high, so firms should have enough cash to permit payment of bills in time to take discounts.

2. Adequate holdings of cash and near-cash assets can help the firm maintain its credit rating by keeping its current and acid test ratios in line with those of other firms in its industry. A strong credit rating enables the firm both to purchase goods from suppliers on favorable terms and to maintain an ample line of low-cost credit with its bank.

3. Cash and near-cash assets are useful for taking advantage of favorable business opportunities, such as special offers from suppliers or the chance to acquire another firm.

4. The firm should have sufficient cash and near-cash assets to meet such emergencies as strikes, fires, or competitors' marketing campaigns, and to weather seasonal and cyclical downturns.

Why is cash management important?

What are the two primary motives for holding cash?

What are the two secondary motives for holding cash as noted in the finance and economics literature?

THE CASH BUDGET

Cash Budget
A table showing cash flows (receipts, disbursements, and cash balances) for a firm over a specified period.

The firm estimates its needs for cash as a part of its general budgeting, or forecasting, process. First, it forecasts sales, its fixed asset and inventory requirements, and the times when payments must be made. This information is combined with projections about when accounts receivable will be collected, tax payment dates, dividend and interest payment dates, and so on. All of this information is summarized in the **cash budget,** which shows the firm's projected cash inflows and outflows over some specified period. Generally, firms use a monthly cash budget forecasted over the next year, plus a more detailed daily or weekly cash budget for the coming month. The monthly cash budgets are used for planning purposes, and the daily or weekly budgets for actual cash control.

The cash budget provides more detailed information concerning a firm's future cash flows than do the forecasted financial statements. In the previous chapter, we developed Allied Food Products' 1998 forecasted financial statements. Allied's projected 1998 sales were $3,300 million, resulting in a net cash flow from operations of $162 million. When all expenditures and financing flows are considered, Allied's cash account is projected to increase by $1 million in 1998. Does this mean that Allied will not have to worry about cash shortages during 1998? To answer this question, we must construct Allied's cash budget for 1998.

To simplify the example, we will only consider Allied's cash budget for the last half of 1998. Further, we will not list every cash flow but rather focus on the operating cash flows. Allied's sales peak is in September, shortly after the majority of its raw food inputs have been harvested. All sales are made on terms of 2/10, net 40, meaning that a 2 percent discount is allowed if payment is made within 10 days, and, if the discount is not taken, the full amount is due in 40 days. However, like most companies, Allied finds that some of its customers delay payment up to 90 days. Experience has shown that payment on 20 percent of Allied's dollar sales is made during the month in which the sale is made — these are the discount sales. On 70 percent of sales, payment is made during the month immediately following the month of sale, and on 10 percent of sales payment is made in the second month following the month of sale.

The costs to Allied of foodstuffs, spices, preservatives, and packaging materials average 70 percent of the sales prices of the finished products. These purchases are generally made one month before the firm expects to sell the finished products, but Allied's purchase terms with its suppliers allow it to delay payments for 30 days. Accordingly, if July sales are forecasted at $300 million, then purchases during June will amount to $210 million, and this amount will actually be paid in July.

Such other cash expenditures as wages and rent are also built into the cash budget, and Allied must make estimated tax payments of $30 million on September 15 and $20 million on December 15. Also, a $100 million payment for a new

Target Cash Balance
The desired cash balance that a firm plans to maintain in order to conduct business.

plant must be made in October. Assuming that Allied's **target cash balance** is $10 million, and that it projects $15 million to be on hand on July 1, 1998, what will its monthly cash surpluses or shortfalls be for the period from July to December?

The monthly cash flows are shown in Table 16-1. Section I of the table provides a worksheet for calculating both collections on sales and payments on purchases. Line 1 gives the sales forecast for the period from May through December. (May and June sales are necessary to determine collections for July and August.) Next, Lines 2 through 5 show cash collections. Line 2 shows that 20 percent of the sales during any given month are collected during that month. Customers who pay in the first month, however, take the discount, so the cash collected in the month of sale is reduced by 2 percent; for example, collections during July for the $300 million of sales in that month will be 20 percent times sales times 1.0 minus the 2 percent discount = $(0.20)($300)(0.98) \approx 59 million. Line 3 shows the collections on the previous month's sales, or 70 percent of sales in the preceding month; for example, in July, 70 percent of the $250 million June sales, or $175 million, will be collected. Line 4 gives collections from sales two months earlier, or 10 percent of sales in that month; for example, the July collections for May sales are $(0.10)($200) = 20 million. The collections during each month are summed and shown on Line 5; thus, the July collections represent 20 percent of July sales (minus the discount) plus 70 percent of June sales plus 10 percent of May sales, or $254 million in total.

Next, payments for purchases of raw materials are shown. July sales are forecasted at $300 million, so Allied will purchase $210 million of materials in June (Line 6) and pay for these purchases in July (Line 7). Similarly, Allied will purchase $280 million of materials in July to meet August's forecasted sales of $400 million.

With Section I completed, Section II can be constructed. Cash from collections is shown on Line 8. Lines 9 through 14 list payments made during each month, and these payments are summed on Line 15. The difference between cash receipts and cash payments (Line 8 minus Line 15) is the net cash gain or loss during the month. For July there is a net cash loss of $11 million, as shown on Line 16.

In Section III, we first determine the cash balance Allied would have at the start of each month, assuming no borrowing is done. This is shown on Line 17. Allied will have $15 million on hand on July 1. The beginning cash balance (Line 17) is then added to the net cash gain or loss during the month (Line 16) to obtain the cumulative cash that would be on hand if no financing were done (Line 18). At the end of July, Allied forecasts a cumulative cash balance of $4 million in the absence of borrowing.

The target cash balance, $10 million, is then subtracted from the cumulative cash balance to determine the firm's borrowing requirements, shown in parentheses, or its surplus cash. Because Allied expects to have cumulative cash, as shown on Line 18, of only $4 million in July, it will have to borrow $6 million to bring the cash account up to the target balance of $10 million. Assuming that this amount is indeed borrowed, loans outstanding will total $6 million at the end of July. (Allied did not have any loans outstanding on July 1.) The cash surplus or required loan balance is given on Line 20; a positive value indicates a cash surplus, whereas a negative value indicates a loan requirement. Note that the surplus cash or loan requirement shown on Line 20 is a *cumulative amount*. Allied must borrow $6 million in July. Then, it has an additional cash shortfall during August of $37 million as reported on Line 16, so its total loan requirement at the end of August is $6 + $37 = $43 million, as reported on Line 20.

TABLE 16-1 Allied Food Products: Cash Budget (Millions of Dollars)

	MAY	JUN	JUL	AUG	SEP	OCT	NOV	DEC
I. COLLECTIONS AND PURCHASES WORKSHEET								
(1) Sales (gross)[a]	$200	$250	$300	$400	$500	$350	$250	$200
Collections								
(2) During month of sale: (0.2)(0.98)(month's sales)			59	78	98	69	49	39
(3) During first month after sale: 0.7(previous month's sales)			175	210	280	350	245	175
(4) During second month after sale: 0.1(sales 2 months ago)			20	25	30	40	50	35
(5) Total collections (2 + 3 + 4)			$254	$313	$408	$459	$344	$249
Purchases								
(6) 0.7(next month's sales)		$210	$280	$350	$245	$175	$140	
(7) Payments (prior month's purchases)			$210	$280	$350	$245	$175	$140
II. CASH GAIN OR LOSS FOR MONTH								
(8) Collections (from Section I)			$254	$313	$408	$459	$344	$249
(9) Payments for purchases (from Section I)			$210	$280	$350	$245	$175	$140
(10) Wages and salaries			30	40	50	40	30	30
(11) Rent			15	15	15	15	15	15
(12) Other expenses			10	15	20	15	10	10
(13) Taxes					30			20
(14) Payment for plant construction						100		
(15) Total payments			$265	$350	$465	$415	$230	$215
(16) Net cash gain (loss) during month (Line 8 − Line 15)			($ 11)	($ 37)	($ 57)	$ 44	$114	$ 34
III. LOAN REQUIREMENT OR CASH SURPLUS								
(17) Cash at start of month if no borrowing is done[b]			$ 15	$ 4	($ 33)	($ 90)	($ 46)	$ 68
(18) Cumulative cash: cash at start +gain or −loss = Line 16 + Line 17			$ 4	($ 33)	($ 90)	($ 46)	$ 68	$102
(19) Target cash balance			10	10	10	10	10	10
(20) Cumulative surplus cash or loans outstanding to maintain $10 target cash balance: (Line 18 − Line 19)[c]			($ 6)	($ 43)	($100)	($ 56)	$ 58	$ 92

[a]Although the budget period is July through December, sales and purchases data for May and June are needed to determine collections and payments during July and August.

[b]The amount shown on Line 17 for July, the $15 balance (in millions), is on hand initially. The values shown for each of the following months on Line 17 are equal to the cumulative cash as shown on Line 18 for the preceding month; for example, the $4 shown on Line 17 for August is taken from Line 18 in the July column.

[c]When the target cash balance of $10 (Line 19) is deducted from the cumulative cash balance (Line 18), a resulting negative figure on Line 20 (shown in parentheses) represents a required loan, whereas a positive figure represents surplus cash. Loans are required from July through October, and surpluses are expected during November and December. Note also that firms can borrow or pay off loans on a daily basis, so the $6 borrowed during July would be done on a daily basis, as needed, and during October the $100 loan that existed at the beginning of the month would be reduced daily to the $56 ending balance, which, in turn, would be completely paid off during November.

Allied's arrangement with the bank permits it to increase its outstanding loans on a daily basis, up to a prearranged maximum, just as you could increase the amount you owe on a credit card. Allied will use any surplus funds it generates to pay off its loans, and because the loan can be paid down at any time, on a daily basis, the firm will never have both a cash surplus and an outstanding loan balance.

This same procedure is used in the following months. Sales will peak in September, accompanied by increased payments for purchases, wages, and other items. Receipts from sales will also go up, but the firm will still be left with a $57 million net cash outflow during the month. The total loan requirement at the end of September will hit a peak of $100 million, the cumulative cash plus the target cash balance. The $100 million can also be found as the $43 million needed at the end of August plus the $57 million cash deficit for September.

Sales, purchases, and payments for past purchases will fall sharply in October, but collections will be the highest of any month because they will reflect the high September sales. As a result, Allied will enjoy a healthy $44 million net cash gain during October. This net gain can be used to pay off borrowings, so loans outstanding will decline by $44 million, to $56 million.

Allied will have an even larger cash surplus in November, which will permit it to pay off all of its loans. In fact, the company is expected to have $58 million in surplus cash by the month's end, and another cash surplus in December will swell the excess cash to $92 million. With such a large amount of unneeded funds, Allied's treasurer will certainly want to invest in interest-bearing securities or to put the funds to use in some other way.

Here are some additional points about cash budgets:

1. For simplicity, our illustrative budget for Allied omitted many important cash flows that are anticipated for 1998, such as dividends, proceeds from stock and bond sales, and fixed asset additions. Some of these are projected to occur in the first half of the year, but those that are projected for the July–December period could easily be added to the table. The final cash budget should contain all projected cash inflows and outflows, and it should be consistent with the forecasted financial statements.

2. Our cash budget does not reflect interest on loans or income from investing surplus cash. This refinement could easily be added.

3. If cash inflows and outflows are not uniform during the month, we could seriously understate the firm's peak financing requirements. The data in Table 16-1 show the situation expected on the last day of each month, but on any given day during the month, it could be quite different. For example, if all payments had to be made on the fifth of each month, but collections came in uniformly throughout the month, the firm would need to borrow much larger amounts than those shown in Table 16-1. In this case, we would prepare a cash budget which determined requirements on a daily basis.

4. Since depreciation is a noncash charge, it does not appear on the cash budget other than through its effect on taxable income, hence on taxes paid.

5. Since the cash budget represents a forecast, all the values in the table are *expected* values. If actual sales, purchases, and so on, are different from the forecasted levels, then the projected cash deficits and surpluses will also be incorrect. Thus, Allied might end up needing to borrow larger amounts than are indicated on Line 20, so it should arrange a line of credit in excess of that amount. For example, if Allied's monthly sales turn out to be only 80 percent

of their forecasted levels, its maximum cumulative borrowing requirement will turn out to be $126 million rather than $100 million, a 26 percent increase from the expected figure.

6. Spreadsheet programs are particularly well suited for constructing and analyzing cash budgets, especially with respect to the sensitivity of cash flows to changes in sales levels, collection periods, and the like. We could change any assumption, say, the projected monthly sales or the lag before customers pay, and the cash budget would automatically and instantly be recalculated. This would show us exactly how the firm's borrowing requirements would change if conditions changed. Also, with a spreadsheet model, it is easy to add features like interest paid on loans, interest earned on marketable securities, and so on. We have written such a model for the computer-related problem at the end of the chapter.

7. Finally, we should note that the target cash balance probably will be adjusted over time, rising and falling with seasonal patterns and with long-term changes in the scale of the firm's operations. Thus, Allied will probably plan to maintain larger cash balances during August and September than at other times, and as the company grows, so will its required cash balance. Also, the firm might even set the target cash balance at zero — this could be done if it carried a portfolio of marketable securities which could be sold to replenish the cash account, or if it had an arrangement with its bank that permitted it to borrow any funds needed on a daily basis. In that event, the cash budget would simply stop with Line 18, and the amounts on that line would represent projected loans outstanding or surplus cash. Note, though, that most firms would find it difficult to operate with a zero-balance bank account, just as you would, and the costs of such an operation would in most instances offset the costs associated with maintaining a positive cash balance. Therefore, most firms do set a positive target cash balance.

Statistics are not available on whether transactions balances or compensating balances actually control most firms' target cash balances, but compensating balance requirements do often dominate, especially during periods of high interest rates and tight money.[1]

SELF-TEST QUESTIONS

What is the purpose of a cash budget?

What are the three major sections of a cash budget?

Suppose a firm's cash flows do not occur uniformly throughout the month. What impact would this have on the accuracy of the forecasted borrowing requirements?

How could uncertainty be handled in a cash budget?

Does depreciation appear in a cash budget? Explain.

---

[1]This point was underscored by an incident that occurred at a professional finance meeting. A professor presented a scholarly paper that used operations research techniques to determine "optimal cash balances" for a sample of firms. He then reported that the firms' actual cash balances greatly exceeded their optimal balances, suggesting inefficiency and the need for more refined techniques. The discussant of the paper made her comments short and sweet. She reported that she had written each of the sample firms and asked them why they had so much cash; they had uniformly replied that their cash holdings were set by compensating balance requirements. Thus, the model might have been useful to determine the optimal cash balance in the absence of compensating balance requirements, but it was precisely those requirements that determined actual balances.

CASH MANAGEMENT TECHNIQUES

Cash management has changed significantly over the last 20 years for two reasons. First, from the early 1970s to the mid-1980s, there was an upward trend in interest rates which increased the opportunity cost of holding cash. This encouraged financial managers to search for more efficient ways of managing cash. Second, technological developments, particularly computerized electronic funds transfer mechanisms, changed the way cash is managed.

Most cash management activities are performed jointly by the firm and its banks. Effective cash management encompasses proper management of cash inflows and outflows, which entails (1) synchronizing cash flows, (2) using float, (3) accelerating collections, (4) getting available funds to where they are needed, and (5) controlling disbursements. Most business is conducted by large firms, many of which operate regionally, nationally, or even globally. They collect cash from many sources and make payments from a number of different cities or even countries. For example, companies such as IBM, General Motors, and Hewlett-Packard have manufacturing plants all around the world, even more sales offices, and bank accounts in virtually every city where they do business. Their collection points follow sales patterns. Some disbursements are made from local offices, but most are made in the cities where manufacturing occurs, or else from the home office. Thus, a major corporation might have hundreds or even thousands of bank accounts, and since there is no reason to think that inflows and outflows will balance in each account, a system must be in place to transfer funds from where they come in to where they are needed, to arrange loans to cover net corporate shortfalls, and to invest net corporate surpluses without delay. We discuss the most commonly used techniques for accomplishing these tasks in the following sections.

CASH FLOW SYNCHRONIZATION

If you as an individual were to receive income once a year, you would probably put it in the bank, draw down your account periodically, and have an average balance during the year equal to about half your annual income. If you received income monthly instead of once a year, you would operate similarly, but now your average balance would be much smaller. If you could arrange to receive income daily and to pay rent, tuition, and other charges on a daily basis, and if you were confident of your forecasted inflows and outflows, then you could hold a very small average cash balance.

Exactly the same situation holds for businesses — by improving their forecasts and by arranging things so that cash receipts coincide with cash requirements, firms can reduce their transactions balances to a minimum. Recognizing all this, utility companies, oil companies, credit card companies, and so on, arrange to bill customers, and to pay their own bills, on regular "billing cycles" throughout the month. This **synchronization of cash flows** provides cash when it is needed and thus enables firms to reduce cash balances, decrease bank loans, lower interest expenses, and boost profits.

Synchronized Cash Flows
A situation in which inflows coincide with outflows, thereby permitting a firm to hold low transactions balances.

SPEED UP THE CHECK-CLEARING PROCESS

When a customer writes and mails a check, this *does not* mean that the funds are immediately available to the receiving firm. Most of us have been told by

Check Clearing
The process of converting a check that has been written and mailed into cash in the payee's account.

someone that "the check is in the mail," and we have also deposited a check in our account and then been told that we cannot write our own checks against this deposit until the **check-clearing** process has been completed. Our bank must first make sure that the check we deposited is good and the funds are available before it will give us cash.

In practice, it may take a long time for a firm to process incoming checks and obtain the use of the money. A check must first be delivered through the mail and then be cleared through the banking system before the money can be put to use. Checks received from customers in distant cities are especially subject to delays because of mail time and also because more parties are involved. For example, assume that we receive a check and deposit it in our bank. Our bank must send the check to the bank on which it was drawn. Only when this latter bank transfers funds to our bank are the funds available for us to use. Checks are generally cleared through the Federal Reserve System or through a clearinghouse set up by the banks in a particular city. Of course, if the check is deposited in the same bank on which it was drawn, that bank merely transfers funds by bookkeeping entries from one depositor to another. The length of time required for checks to clear is thus a function of the distance between the payer's and the payee's banks. In the case of private clearinghouses, it can range from one to three days. Checks are generally cleared through the Federal Reserve System in about two days, but mail delays can slow down things on each end of the Fed's involvement in the process.

USING FLOAT

Float is defined as the difference between the balance shown in a firm's (or individual's) checkbook and the balance on the bank's records. Suppose a firm writes, on average, checks in the amount of $5,000 each day, and it takes six days for these checks to clear and to be deducted from the firm's bank account. This will cause the firm's own checkbook to show a balance $30,000 smaller than the balance on the bank's records; this difference is called **disbursement float.** Now suppose the firm also receives checks in the amount of $5,000 daily, but it loses four days while they are being deposited and cleared. This will result in $20,000 of **collections float.** In total, the firm's **net float** — the difference between the $30,000 positive disbursement float and the $20,000 negative collections float — will be $10,000.

Disbursement Float
The value of the checks which we have written but which are still being processed and thus have not been deducted from our account balance by the bank.

Collections Float
The amount of checks that we have received but which have not yet been credited to our account.

Net Float
The difference between our checkbook balance and the balance shown on the bank's books.

If the firm's own collection and clearing process is more efficient than that of the recipients of its checks — which is generally true of larger, more efficient firms — then the firm could actually show a *negative* balance on its own books but have a *positive* balance on its bank records. Some firms indicate that they *never* have positive book cash balances. One large manufacturer of construction equipment stated that while its account, according to its bank's records, shows an average cash balance of about $20 million, its *book* cash balance is *minus* $20 million — it has $40 million of net float. Obviously, the firm must be able to forecast its disbursements and collections accurately in order to make such heavy use of float.

E. F. Hutton provides an example of pushing cash management too far. Hutton, a leading brokerage firm at the time, did business with banks across the country, and it had to keep compensating balances in these banks. The sizes of the required compensating balances were known, and any excess funds in these banks were sent electronically, on a daily basis, to New York and San Francisco banks, where they were immediately invested in interest-bearing securities.

However, rather than waiting to see what the end-of-day balances actually were, Hutton began estimating inflows and outflows, and it transferred out for investment the *estimated* end-of-day excess. But then Hutton got greedy and began *kiting* checks. Hutton deliberately overestimated its deposits and underestimated clearings of its own checks, thereby deliberately overstating its estimated end-of-day balances. As a result, Hutton was chronically overdrawn at its local banks, and it was in effect earning interest on funds which really belonged to those local banks. It is entirely proper to forecast what your bank will have recorded as your balance and then to make decisions based on the estimate, even if that balance is different from the balance your own books show. However, it is illegal to forecast an overdrawn situation but then to tell the bank that you expect to have a positive balance.[2]

Delays that cause float arise because it takes time for checks (1) to travel through the mail (mail float), (2) to be processed by the receiving firm (processing float), and (3) to clear through the banking system (clearing, or availability, float). Basically, the size of a firm's net float is a function of its ability to speed up collections on checks received and to slow down collections on checks written. Efficient firms go to great lengths to speed up the processing of incoming checks, thus putting the funds to work faster, and they try to stretch their own payments out as long as possible.

ACCELERATION OF RECEIPTS

Financial managers have searched for ways to collect receivables faster since credit transactions began. Although cash collection is the financial manager's responsibility, the speed with which checks are cleared depends on the banking system. Several techniques are now used both to speed collections and to get funds where they are needed. Included are (1) lockbox plans established close to customers and (2) requiring large customers to pay by wire or automatic debit.

Lockbox Plan
A procedure used to speed up collections and reduce float through the use of post office boxes in payers' local areas.

LOCKBOXES.   A **lockbox plan** is one of the oldest cash management tools. In a lockbox system, incoming checks are sent to post office boxes rather than to corporate headquarters. For example, a firm headquartered in New York City might have its West Coast customers send their payments to a box in San Francisco, its customers in the Southwest send their checks to Dallas, and so on, rather than having all checks sent to New York City. Several times a day a local bank will collect the contents of the lockbox and deposit the checks into the company's local account. The bank then provides the firm with a daily record of the receipts collected, usually via an electronic data transmission system in a format that permits on-line updating of the firm's accounts receivable records.

A lockbox system reduces the time required for a firm to receive incoming checks, to deposit them, and to get them cleared through the banking system so

---

[2]A question raised during the Hutton investigation was this: "Why didn't the banks recognize that Hutton was systematically overdrawing its account and call the company to task?" The answer is that some banks, with tight controls, did exactly that — they refused to let Hutton get away with the practice. Other banks were lax. Still other banks apparently let Hutton get away with being chronically overdrawn out of fear of losing its business: Hutton used its economic muscle to force the banks to let it get away with an illegal act. In many people's opinion, the banks were as much at fault as Hutton. Still, in business dealings, honesty is presumed, and Hutton was dishonest in its dealings with the banks. This dishonesty severely damaged Hutton's reputation, cost the company profits totaling hundreds of millions of dollars, cost its top managers their jobs, and contributed to the ultimate demise of the company.

the funds are available for use. Lockbox services can often increase the availability of funds by two to five days over the "regular" system.

PAYMENT BY WIRE OR AUTOMATIC DEBIT. Firms are increasingly demanding payments of larger bills by wire, or even by automatic electronic debits, whereby funds are automatically deducted from one account and added to another. This is, of course, the ultimate in a speeded-up collection process, and computer technology is making such a process increasingly feasible and efficient.

SELF-TEST QUESTIONS

??????

What is float? How do firms use float to increase cash management efficiency?

What are some methods firms can use to accelerate receipts?

MARKETABLE SECURITIES

Marketable Securities
Securities that can be sold on short notice.

Realistically, the management of cash and marketable securities cannot be separated — management of one implies management of the other. In the first part of the chapter, we focused on cash management. Now, we turn to **marketable securities.**

Marketable securities typically provide much lower yields than operating assets. For example, recently Chrysler held a $8.7 billion portfolio of short-term marketable securities that yielded about 6 percent, but its operating assets provided a return of about 14 percent. Why would a company such as Chrysler have such large holdings of low-yielding assets?

In many cases, companies hold marketable securities for the same reasons they hold cash. Although these securities are not the same as cash, in most cases they can be converted to cash on very short notice (often just a few minutes) with a single telephone call. Moreover, while cash and most commercial checking accounts yield nothing, marketable securities provide at least a modest return. For this reason, many firms hold at least some marketable securities in lieu of larger cash balances, liquidating part of the portfolio to increase the cash account when cash outflows exceed inflows. In such situations, the marketable securities could be used as a substitute for transactions balances, for precautionary balances, for speculative balances, or for all three. In most cases, the securities are held primarily for precautionary purposes — most firms prefer to rely on bank credit to make temporary transactions or to meet speculative needs, but they may still hold some liquid assets to guard against a possible shortage of bank credit.

A few years ago, Chrysler had essentially no cash — it was incurring huge losses, and those losses had drained its cash account. Then a new management team took over, improved operations, and began generating positive cash flows. By 1996, Chrysler's cash (and marketable securities) was up to $8.7 billion, and analysts were forecasting a further buildup over the next year or so to more than $10 billion. Management indicated, in various statements, that the cash hoard was necessary to enable the company to weather the next downturn in auto sales.

Although setting the target cash balance is, to a large extent, judgmental, analytical rules can be applied to help formulate better judgments. For example, years ago William Baumol recognized that the trade-off between cash and marketable securities is similar to the one firms face when setting the optimal level of inventory.[3] Baumol applied the EOQ inventory model to determine the optimal level of cash balances.[4] He suggested that cash holdings should be higher if costs are high and the time to liquidate marketable securities is long, but that those holdings should be lower if interest rates are low. His logic was that if it is expensive and time consuming to convert securities to cash, and if securities do not earn much because interest rates are low, then it does not pay to hold securities as opposed to cash. It does pay to hold securities if interest rates are high and the securities can be converted to cash quickly and cheaply.

SELF-TEST QUESTIONS

Why might a company hold low-yielding marketable securities when it could earn a much higher return on operating assets?

Why would a low interest rate environment lead to larger cash balances?

How might improvements in telecommunications technology affect the level of corporations' cash balances?

INVENTORY

Inventories, which may be classified as (1) *supplies,* (2) *raw materials,* (3) *work-in-process,* and (4) *finished goods,* are an essential part of virtually all business operations. As is the case with accounts receivable, inventory levels depend heavily upon sales. However, whereas receivables build up *after* sales have been made, inventory must be acquired *ahead* of sales. This is a critical difference, and the necessity of forecasting sales before establishing target inventory levels makes inventory management a difficult task. Also, since errors in the establishment of inventory levels quickly lead either to lost sales or to excessive carrying costs, inventory management is as important as it is difficult.

Inventory management techniques are covered in depth in production management courses. Still, since financial managers have a responsibility both for raising the capital needed to carry inventory and for the firm's overall profitability, we need to cover the financial aspects of inventory management here. Two examples will make clear the types of issues involved in inventory management, and the financial problems poor inventory control can cause.

RETAIL CLOTHING STORE

Chicago Discount Clothing (CDC) must order swimsuits for summer sales in January, and it must take delivery by April to be sure of having enough suits to meet the heavy May–June demand. Bathing suits come in many styles, colors, and sizes, and if CDC stocks incorrectly, either in total or in terms of the style-color-size distribution, then the store will have trouble. It will lose potential sales if it stocks too few suits, and it will be forced to lower prices and take losses if it stocks too many or the wrong types.

---

[3]William J. Baumol, "The Transactions Demand for Cash: An Inventory Theoretic Approach," *Quarterly Journal of Economics,* November 1952, 545–556.

[4]A more complete description of the Economic Ordering Quantity (EOQ) model can be found in Eugene F. Brigham and Louis C. Gapenski, *Intermediate Financial Management,* 5th ed., Chapter 22.

The effects of inventory changes on the balance sheet are important. For simplicity, assume that CDC has a $10,000 base stock of inventory which is financed by common stock. Its balance sheet is as follows:

Inventory (base stock)	$10,000	Common stock	$10,000
Total assets	$10,000	Total claims	$10,000

Now it anticipates that it will sell $5,000 of swimsuits (at cost) this summer. Dollar sales will actually be greater than $5,000, since CDC makes about $200 in profits for every $1,000 of inventory sold. CDC finances its seasonal inventory with bank loans, so its pre-summer balance sheet would look like this:

Inventory (seasonal)	$ 5,000	Notes payable to bank	$ 5,000
Inventory (base stock)	10,000	Common stock	10,000
Total assets	$15,000	Total claims	$15,000

If everything works out as planned, sales will be made, inventory will be converted to cash, the bank loan will be retired, and the company will earn a profit. The balance sheet, after a successful season, might look like this:

Cash	$ 1,000	Notes payable to bank	$ 0
Inventory (seasonal)	0	Common stock	10,000
Inventory (base stock)	10,000	Retained earnings	1,000
Total assets	$11,000	Total claims	$11,000

The company is now in a highly liquid position and is ready to begin a new season.

But suppose the season had not gone well, and CDC had only sold $1,000 of its inventory. As fall approached, the balance sheet would look like this:

Cash	$ 200	Notes payable to bank	$ 4,000
Inventory (seasonal)	4,000	Common stock	10,000
Inventory (base stock)	10,000	Retained earnings	200
Total assets	$14,200	Total claims	$14,200

Now suppose the bank insists on repayment of the $4,000 outstanding on the loan, and it wants cash, not swimsuits. But if the swimsuits did not sell well in the summer, how will out-of-style suits sell in the fall? Assume that CDC is forced to mark the suits down to half their cost (not half the selling price) in order to sell them to raise cash to repay the bank loan. Here is the result:

Cash	$ 2,200	Notes payable to bank	$ 4,000
Inventory (base stock)	10,000	Common stock	10,000
		Retained earnings	(1,800)
Total assets	$12,200	Total claims	$12,200

At this point, CDC is in serious trouble. It does not have the cash to pay off the loan, and the firm's shareholders have lost $1,800 of their equity. If the bank will not extend the loan, and if other sources of cash are not available, CDC will have to mark down its base stock prices in an effort to stimulate sales, and if this does not work, CDC could be forced into bankruptcy. Clearly, poor inventory decisions can spell trouble.

APPLIANCE MANUFACTURER

Now consider a different situation, that of Housepro Corporation, an appliance manufacturer. Here is its inventory position, in millions of dollars:

Raw materials	$ 200
Work-in-process	200
Finished goods	600
Total inventory	$1,000

Suppose Housepro anticipates that the economy is about to get much stronger and that the demand for appliances will rise sharply. If it is to share in the expected boom, Housepro will have to increase production. This means it will have to increase inventory, and, since the inventory buildup must precede sales, additional financing will be required — some liability account, perhaps notes payable, will have to be increased in order to finance the inventory buildup.

Proper inventory management requires close coordination among the sales, purchasing, production, and finance departments. The sales/marketing department is generally the first to spot changes in demand. These changes must be worked into the company's purchasing and manufacturing schedules, and the financial manager must arrange any financing needed to support the inventory buildup. Lack of coordination among departments, poor sales forecasts, or both, can lead to disaster.

SELF-TEST QUESTIONS

Why is good inventory management essential to a firm's success?

What departments should be involved in inventory decisions?

INVENTORY COSTS

The twin goals of inventory management are (1) to ensure that the inventories needed to sustain operations are available, but (2) to hold the costs of ordering and carrying inventories to the lowest possible level. Table 16-2 gives a listing of the typical costs associated with inventory, divided into three categories: carrying costs, ordering and receiving costs, and the costs that are incurred if the firm runs short of inventory.

Inventory is costly to store; therefore, there is always pressure to reduce inventory as part of firms' overall cost-containment strategies. A recent article in *Fortune* highlights the fact that an increasing number of corporations are taking drastic steps to control inventory costs.[5] For example, Trane Corporation, which makes air conditioners, recently adopted the just-in-time inventory procedures described in the next section.

In the past, Trane produced parts on a steady basis, stored them as inventory, and had them ready whenever the company received an order for a batch of air conditioners. However, the company reached the point where its inventory covered an area equal to three football fields, and it still sometimes took as long as 15 days to fill an order. To make matters worse, occasionally some of the

---

[5]Shawn Tully, "Raiding a Company's Hidden Cash," *Fortune*, August 22, 1994, 82–87.

TABLE 16-2 Costs Associated with Inventory

	APPROXIMATE ANNUAL COST AS A PERCENTAGE OF INVENTORY VALUE
I. Carrying Costs	
Cost of capital tied up	12.0%
Storage and handling costs	0.5
Insurance	0.5
Property taxes	1.0
Depreciation and obsolescence	12.0
Total	26.0%
II. Ordering, Shipping, and Receiving Costs	
Cost of placing orders, including production and set-up costs	Varies
Shipping and handling costs	2.5%
III. Costs of Running Short	
Loss of sales	Varies
Loss of customer goodwill	Varies
Disruption of production schedules	Varies

NOTE: These costs vary from firm to firm, from item to item, and also over time. The figures shown are U.S. Department of Commerce estimates for an average manufacturing firm. Where costs vary so widely that no meaningful numbers can be assigned, the term "Varies" is reported.

necessary components simply could not be located, while in other instances the components were located but found to have been damaged from long storage.

Then Trane adopted a new inventory policy — it began producing components only after an order is received, and then sending the parts directly from the machines which make them to the final assembly line. The net effect: Inventories fell nearly 40 percent even as sales increased by 30 percent.

However, as Table 16-2 indicates, there are costs associated with holding too little inventory, and these costs can be severe. Generally, if a business carries small inventories, it must reorder frequently. This increases ordering costs. Even more important, firms can miss out on profitable sales, and also suffer a loss of goodwill which can lead to lower future sales. So, it is important to have enough inventory on hand to meet customer demands.

Suppose IBM has developed a new line of notebook computers. How much inventory should it produce and have on hand when the marketing campaign is launched? If it fails to produce enough inventory, retailers and customers are likely to be frustrated because they cannot immediately purchase the highly advertised product. Rather than wait, many customers will purchase a notebook computer elsewhere. On the other hand, if IBM has too much inventory, it will incur unnecessarily high carrying costs. In addition, computers become obsolete quickly, so if inventory levels are high but sales are mediocre, the company may have to discount the notebooks to sell them. Apart from reducing the profit margin on this year's line of computers, these discounts may push down computer prices in general, thereby reducing profit margins on the company's other products as well.

INVENTORY CONTROL SYSTEMS

Inventory management requires the establishment of an *inventory control system.* Inventory control systems run the gamut from very simple to extremely complex, depending on the size of the firm and the nature of its inventory. For example, one simple control procedure is the **red-line method** — inventory items are stocked in a bin, a red line is drawn around the inside of the bin at the level of the reorder point, and the inventory clerk places an order when the red line shows. The **two-bin method** has inventory items stocked in two bins. When the working bin is empty, an order is placed and inventory is drawn from the second bin. These procedures work well for parts such as bolts in a manufacturing process, or for many items in retail businesses.

COMPUTERIZED SYSTEMS

Most companies today employ **computerized inventory control systems.** The computer starts with an inventory count in memory. As withdrawals are made, they are recorded by the computer, and the inventory balance is revised. When the reorder point is reached, the computer automatically places an order, and when the order is received, the recorded balance is increased. As we noted earlier, retailers such as Wal-Mart have carried this system quite far — each item has a bar code, and, as an item is checked out, the code is read, a signal is sent to the computer, and the inventory balance is adjusted at the same time the price is fed into the cash register tape. When the balance drops to the reorder point, an order is placed. In Wal-Mart's case, the order goes directly from its computers to those of its suppliers.

A good inventory control system is dynamic, not static. A company such as Wal-Mart or General Motors stocks hundreds of thousands of different items. The sales (or use) of individual items can rise or fall quite separately from rising or falling overall corporate sales. As the usage rate for an individual item begins to rise or fall, the inventory manager must adjust its balance to avoid running short or ending up with obsolete items. If the change in the usage rate appears to be permanent, the safety stock level should be reconsidered, and the computer model used in the control process should be reprogrammed.

JUST-IN-TIME SYSTEMS

An approach to inventory control called the **just-in-time (JIT) system** was developed by Japanese firms but has gained popularity throughout the world. Toyota provides a good example of the just-in-time system. Eight of Toyota's ten

Red-Line Method
An inventory control procedure in which a red line is drawn around the inside of an inventory-stocked bin to indicate the reorder point level.

Two-Bin Method
An inventory control procedure in which an order is placed when one of two inventory-stocked bins is empty.

Computerized Inventory Control System
A system of inventory control in which a computer is used to determine reorder points and to adjust inventory balances.

Just-in-Time (JIT) System
A system of inventory control in which a manufacturer coordinates production with suppliers so that raw materials or components arrive just as they are needed in the production process.

factories, along with most of Toyota's suppliers, dot the countryside around Toyota City. Delivery of components is tied to the speed of the assembly line, and parts are generally delivered no more than a few hours before they are used. The just-in-time system reduces the need for Toyota and other manufacturers to carry large inventories, but it requires a great deal of coordination between the manufacturer and its suppliers, both in the timing of deliveries and the quality of the parts. It also requires that component parts be perfect; otherwise, a few bad parts could stop the entire production line. Therefore, JIT inventory management has been developed in conjunction with total quality management (TQM).

Not surprisingly, U.S. automobile manufacturers were among the first domestic firms to move toward just-in-time systems. Ford has been restructuring its production system with a goal of increasing its inventory turnover from 20 times a year to 30 or 40 times. Of course, just-in-time systems place considerable pressure on suppliers. GM formerly kept a ten-day supply of seats and other parts made by Lear Siegler; now GM sends in orders at four- to eight-hour intervals and expects immediate shipment. A Lear Siegler spokesman stated, "We can't afford to keep things sitting around either," so Lear Siegler has had to be tougher on its own suppliers.

Just-in-time systems are also being adopted by smaller firms. In fact, some production experts say that small companies are better positioned than large ones to use just-in-time methods, because it is easier to redefine job functions and to educate people in small firms. One small-firm example is Fireplace Manufacturers Inc., a manufacturer of prefabricated fireplaces. The company was recently having cash flow problems, and it was carrying $1.1 million in inventory to support annual sales of about $8 million. The company went to a just-in-time system, trimmed its raw material and work-in-process inventory to $750,000, and freed up $350,000 of cash, even as sales doubled.

The close coordination required between the parties using JIT procedures has led to an overall reduction of inventory throughout the production-distribution system, and to a general improvement in economic efficiency. This point is made by companies such as Wal-Mart and Toyota, and it is borne out by economic statistics, which show that inventory as a percentage of sales has been declining since the use of just-in-time procedures began.

OUT-SOURCING

Out-Sourcing
The practice of purchasing components rather than making them in-house.

Another important development related to inventory is **out-sourcing,** which is the practice of purchasing components rather than making them in-house. Thus, if GM arranged to buy radiators, axles, and other parts from suppliers rather than making them itself, it would be increasing its use of out-sourcing. Out-sourcing is often combined with just-in-time systems to reduce inventory levels. However, perhaps the major reason for out-sourcing has nothing to do with inventory policy — a bureaucratic, unionized company like GM can often buy parts from a smaller, nonunionized supplier at a lower cost than if it made them itself.

THE RELATIONSHIP BETWEEN PRODUCTION SCHEDULING AND INVENTORY LEVELS

A final point relating to inventory levels is *the relationship between production scheduling and inventory levels.* A firm such as a greeting card manufacturer has highly seasonal sales. Such a firm could produce on a steady, year-round

INDUSTRY PRACTICE

KEEPING INVENTORY LEAN

What do just-in-time (JIT) inventory methods and supercomputers have in common? The answer is that both are being used, in a coordinated manner, to keep U.S. business inventories remarkably lean. Recent statistics show that retail, wholesale, and factory inventories — taken together and adjusted for inflation — amount to just 1.4 times monthly sales, the lowest reading on record. And leaner inventories mean lower inventory carrying costs for businesses, hence greater profits.

JIT became the watchword for many U.S. manufacturers in the mid-1980s, as they began to adopt this Japanese method of inventory delivery. JIT involves redesigning production so that parts and raw materials flow into the factory just as they are needed, thus allowing manufacturers to save the cost of carrying inventories. Large firms, including General Motors, Campbell Soup, Motorola, Hewlett-Packard, and Intel, as well as dozens of small firms such as Omark Industries, an Oregon manufacturer of power saw chains, have converted to JIT. A recent survey of 385 manufacturing plants in the United States found that more than 16 percent were "extremely skilled" in JIT procedures, and another 44 percent had plans under way to "excel" in JIT operations. Importantly, the inventory turnover ratios of plants using JIT procedures were twice as high as those for the survey groups as a whole.

Large corporations started the just-in-time trend in the United States, but Robert W. Hall of Indiana University, who has written several books on the subject, says smaller companies are actually better positioned to adopt the method. Hall points out that small firms usually have only one plant to convert, and they usually have simpler accounting and planning systems. Also, their management groups are smaller and can make faster decisions than can larger firms. Another advantage for many small firms is that smaller, nonunionized labor forces make it easier to redesign job functions.

Worker attitudes toward these changes have generally been the greatest stumbling block for companies — large or small — that convert to JIT methods. One company president says employee acceptance depends on management. "It's just a matter of managers getting their mind-sets correct." This can be difficult, though, since managers must give up the security of large inventories and trust their suppliers more than they ever have before. It is essential for managers to work closely with suppliers to ensure that parts or materials get to the plant at the right time and in the right sequence for the assembly line.

Cadbury Schweppes PLC, the London food and beverage producer, has inventory levels that are a fraction of what they were in the mid-1980s as a result of "closer cooperation with a smaller but better informed set of suppliers." The Schweppes unit gets 80 percent of its glass containers from a single supplier, as compared with 30 percent seven years ago. The firm's director of purchasing commented, "We used to play one off against the other and keep them guessing, but now we work very closely together, providing sales forecasts and other data we once kept to ourselves." By working in this way, the Schweppes unit has been able to reduce its inventory carrying costs, including financing and warehousing costs, dramatically.

When a company adopts the JIT method, it is essential that managers be concerned not only with their own problems but also with those faced by their suppliers. Xerox, for instance, went into the new system with the idea that "this was an inventory reduction program for our benefit," according to the materials manager for the copier division, "and we treated it that way, asking suppliers to hold inventories without compensation. Suppliers protested, and good relationships built over many years began to deteriorate." To improve the

---

basis, or it could let production rise and fall with sales. If it established a level production schedule, its inventory would rise sharply during periods when sales were low and then decline during peak sales periods, but the average inventory held would be substantially higher than if production rose and fell with sales.

Our discussions of just-in-time systems, out-sourcing, and production scheduling all point out the necessity of coordinating inventory policy with manufacturing/procurement policies. Companies try to minimize *total production and distribution costs,* and inventory costs are just one part of total costs. Still, they are an important cost, and financial managers should be aware of the determinants of inventory costs and how they can be minimized.

situation, Xerox reorganized its production and ordering schedules so suppliers could plan better. It also formed classes about JIT for the suppliers. One supplier, Rockford Dynatorq, reduced the time needed to make one brake part from three and a half weeks to just one day with the help of Xerox. Rockford's inventory dropped by 10 percent in just six months.

Improvement in quality control is a common by-product of JIT. First, with smaller inventories it is more critical than ever that there be few unusable units. In addition, many wasteful procedures are also discovered when manufacturers reevaluate their production processes for JIT conversion. Costs that add nothing to a product's value are incurred every time an item is moved, inspected, or stored in inventory, and JIT helps trim these costs.

Retailers such as Kmart, Wal-Mart, and Dayton Hudson are using a sophisticated approach to maintaining lean inventories and reducing carrying costs. These firms are using supercomputers, extraordinarily powerful parallel computers, to help managers decide what to buy, where to stock it, and when to cut prices. Wayne Hood, a retail analyst with Prudential Securities, states that "Technology like this is absolutely critical . . . It's going to separate the winners from the losers in retailing in the 1990s. Companies that don't invest in technology — even in hard times — won't make it."

The parallel design of these supercomputers, where thousands of small processors work as one instead of having two to four large processors as in mainframe computers, permits retailing managers to quickly access data. For example, managers can obtain data on-line instantly from every register, in every store, during the last year: What was sold, when, and what were the colors, styles, sizes, and prices? These managers can then act on this information. Mainframe computers would choke on this terabyte (a trillion characters of information) of data. In addition to having the capability of accessing such information, the supercomputers are less costly than the mainframes.

Supercomputers have been especially effective in managing seasonal inventory items. Seasonal merchandise, such as Christmas and Valentine's Day items, have high profit margins, so it is bad to have them go out of stock. But they also have a "death date" — a time at which they must be completely sold out. Therefore, such items need to be tightly managed. By using supercomputers, Kmart was able to determine that it sold 50 percent of its Valentine inventory in a particular store in the last two days, hence that there was no need to panic and mark down prices to move the stock. Thus, the store managers were able to avoid unnecessary price cuts, and this increased the stores' profits.

It is apparent from firms' statements and from reported statistics that the trend to lower inventory levels represents a long-term, serious commitment. According to Geoffrey Moore, a Columbia University economist, the trend toward leaner inventories will reduce the volatility of U.S. business cycles because with smaller stockpiles of inventories, inventory draw-downs during recessions cannot last as long. Therefore, production must pick up sooner than would be the case if initial inventories were larger. Thus, it appears that JIT procedures, combined with supercomputers, will lower companies' costs and help stabilize the economy. But they will also make life increasingly difficult for smaller, less efficient firms.

SOURCES: "Small Manufacturers Shifting to 'Just-in-Time' Techniques," *The Wall Street Journal*, December 21, 1987; "Having a Hard Time," *Fortune*, June 9, 1986; "General Motors' Little Engine That Could," *Business Week*, August 3, 1987; "Firms' Inventories Are Remarkably Lean," *The Wall Street Journal*, November 3, 1992; "Supercomputers Manage Holiday Stock," *The Wall Street Journal*, December 23, 1992.

SELF-TEST QUESTIONS ??????

Describe some inventory control systems that are used in practice.

What are just-in-time systems? What are their advantages? Why is quality especially important if a JIT system is used?

What is out-sourcing?

Describe the relationship between production scheduling and inventory levels.

RECEIVABLES MANAGEMENT

Account Receivable
A balance due from a customer.

Firms would, in general, rather sell for cash than on credit, but competitive pressures force most firms to offer credit. Thus, goods are shipped, inventories are reduced, and an **account receivable** is created.[6] Eventually, the customer will pay the account, at which time (1) the firm will receive cash and (2) its receivables will decline. Carrying receivables has both direct and indirect costs, but it also has an important benefit — increased sales.

Receivables management begins with the decision of whether or not to grant credit. In this section, we discuss the manner in which receivables build up, and we also discuss several alternative ways to monitor receivables. A monitoring system is important, because without it receivables will build up to excessive levels, cash flows will decline, and bad debts will offset the profits on sales. Corrective action is often needed, and the only way to know whether the situation is getting out of hand is with a good receivables control system.

THE ACCUMULATION OF RECEIVABLES

The total amount of accounts receivable outstanding at any given time is determined by two factors: (1) the volume of credit sales and (2) the average length of time between sales and collections. For example, suppose Boston Lumber Company (BLC), a wholesale distributor of lumber products, opens a warehouse on January 1 and, starting the first day, makes sales of $1,000 each day. For simplicity, we assume that all sales are on credit, and customers are given ten days to pay. At the end of the first day, accounts receivable will be $1,000; they will rise to $2,000 by the end of the second day; and by January 10, they will have risen to 10($1,000) = $10,000. On January 11, another $1,000 will be added to receivables, but payments for sales made on January 1 will reduce receivables by $1,000, so total accounts receivable will remain constant at $10,000. In general, once the firm's operations have stabilized, this situation will exist:

$$\frac{\text{Accounts}}{\text{receivable}} = \frac{\text{Credit sales}}{\text{per day}} \times \frac{\text{Length of}}{\text{collection period}} \quad (16\text{-}1)$$

$$= \ \$1,000 \ \times \ 10 \text{ days} \ = \$10,000.$$

If either credit sales or the collection period changes, such changes will be reflected in accounts receivable.

Notice that the $10,000 investment in receivables must be financed. To illustrate, suppose that when the warehouse opened on January 1, BLC's shareholders had put up $800 as common stock and used this money to buy the goods sold the first day. The $800 of inventory will be sold for $1,000, so BLC's gross profit on the $800 investment is $200, or 25 percent. In this situation, the beginning balance sheet would be as follows:[7]

---

[6]Whenever goods are sold on credit, two accounts are created — an asset item entitled *accounts receivable* appears on the books of the selling firm, and a liability item called *accounts payable* appears on the books of the purchaser. At this point, we are analyzing the transaction from the viewpoint of the seller, so we are concentrating on the variables under its control, in this case, the receivables. We will examine the transaction from the viewpoint of the purchaser in Chapter 17, where we discuss accounts payable as a source of funds and consider their cost relative to the cost of funds obtained from other sources.

[7]Note that the firm would need other assets such as cash, fixed assets, and a permanent stock of inventory. Also, overhead costs and taxes would have to be deducted, so retained earnings would be less than the figures shown here. We abstract from these details here so that we may focus on receivables.

Inventories	$800	Common stock	$800
Total assets	$800	Total liabilities and equity	$800

At the end of the day, the balance sheet would look like this:

Accounts receivable	$1,000	Common stock	$ 800
Inventories	0	Retained earnings	200
Total assets	$1,000	Total liabilities and equity	$1,000

To remain in business, BLC must replenish inventories. To do so requires that $800 of goods be purchased, and this requires $800 in cash. Assuming that BLC borrows the $800 from the bank, the balance sheet at the start of the second day will be as follows:

Accounts receivable	$1,000	Notes payable to bank	$ 800
Inventories	800	Common stock	800
		Retained earnings	200
Total assets	$1,800	Total liabilities and equity	$1,800

At the end of the second day, the inventories will have been converted to receivables, and the firm will have to borrow another $800 to restock for the third day.

This process will continue, provided the bank is willing to lend the necessary funds, until the beginning of the 11th day, when the balance sheet reads as follows:

Accounts receivable	$10,000	Notes payable to bank	$ 8,000
Inventories	800	Common stock	800
		Retained earnings	2,000
Total assets	$10,800	Total liabilities and equity	$10,800

From this point on, $1,000 of receivables will be collected every day, and $800 of these funds can be used to purchase new inventories.

This example makes it clear (1) that accounts receivable depend jointly on the level of credit sales and the collection period, (2) that any increase in receivables must be financed in some manner, but (3) that the entire amount of receivables does not have to be financed because the profit portion ($200 of each $1,000 of sales) does not represent a cash outflow. In our example, we assumed bank financing, but, as we demonstrate in Chapter 17, there are many alternative ways to finance current assets.

MONITORING THE RECEIVABLES POSITION

Investors — both stockholders and bank loan officers — should pay close attention to accounts receivable management, for, as we shall see, one can be misled by reported financial statements and later suffer serious losses on an investment.

When a credit sale is made, the following events occur: (1) Inventories are reduced by the cost of goods sold, (2) accounts receivable are increased by the sales price, and (3) the difference is profit, which is added to retained earnings. If the sale is for cash, then the cash from the sale has actually been received by the firm, but if the sale is on credit, the firm will not receive the cash from the sale unless and until the account is collected. Firms have been known to encourage "sales" to very weak customers in order to report high profits. This could boost the firm's stock price, at least until credit losses begin to lower earnings, at which time the stock price will fall. Analyses along the lines suggested in the following sections will detect any such questionable practice, as well as any unconscious deterioration in the quality of accounts receivable. Such early detection could help both investors and bankers avoid losses.[8]

DAYS SALES OUTSTANDING (DSO). Suppose Super Sets Inc., a television manufacturer, sells 200,000 television sets a year at a price of $198 each. Further, assume that all sales are on credit with the following terms: if payment is made within 10 days, customers will receive a 2 percent discount; otherwise the full amount is due within 30 days. Finally, assume that 70 percent of the customers take discounts and pay on Day 10, while the other 30 percent pay on Day 30.

Super Sets's **days sales outstanding (DSO),** sometimes called the *average collection period (ACP),* is 16 days:

$$DSO = ACP = 0.7(10 \text{ days}) + 0.3(30 \text{ days}) = 16 \text{ days}.$$

Super Sets's *average daily sales (ADS),* assuming a 360-day year, is $110,000:

$$ADS = \frac{\text{Annual sales}}{360} = \frac{(\text{Units sold})(\text{Sales price})}{360} \tag{16-2}$$

$$= \frac{200,000(\$198)}{360} = \frac{\$39,600,000}{360} = \$110,000.$$

Super Sets's accounts receivable, assuming a constant, uniform rate of sales throughout the year, will at any point in time be $1,760,000:

$$\text{Receivables} = (\text{ADS})(\text{DSO}) \tag{16-3}$$

$$= (\$110,000)(16) = \$1,760,000.$$

Note also that its DSO, or average collection period, is a measure of the average length of time it takes Super Sets's customers to pay off their credit purchases, and the DSO is often compared with an industry average DSO. For example, if all television manufacturers sell on the same credit terms, and if the industry average DSO is 25 days versus Super Sets's 16 days, then Super Sets either has a higher percentage of discount customers or else its credit department is exceptionally good at ensuring prompt payment.

Finally, note that if you know both the annual sales and the receivables balance, you can calculate DSO as follows:

$$DSO = \frac{\text{Receivables}}{\text{Sales per day}} = \frac{\$1,760,000}{\$110,000} = 16 \text{ days}.$$

The DSO can also be compared with the firm's own credit terms. For example, suppose Super Sets's DSO had been averaging 35 days. With a 35-day DSO, some customers would obviously be taking more than 30 days to pay their bills. In fact, if many customers were paying within 10 days to take advantage of the discount, the others must, on average, be taking much longer than 35 days. One way to check this possibility is to use an aging schedule as described in the next section.

Days Sales Outstanding (DSO) The average length of time required to collect credit sales.

---

[8]Accountants are increasingly interested in these matters. Investors have sued several of the major accounting firms for substantial damages when (1) profits were overstated and (2) it could be shown that the auditors should have conducted an analysis along the lines described here and then reported the results to stockholders in their audit opinion.

Aging Schedule
A report showing how long accounts receivable have been outstanding.

AGING SCHEDULES. An **aging schedule** breaks down a firm's receivables by age of account. Table 16-3 contains the December 31, 1997, aging schedules of two television manufacturers, Super Sets and Wonder Vision. Both firms offer the same credit terms, and both show the same total receivables. However, Super Sets's aging schedule indicates that all of its customers pay on time — 70 percent pay on Day 10 while 30 percent pay on Day 30. Wonder Vision's schedule, which is more typical, shows that many of its customers are not abiding by its credit terms — some 27 percent of its receivables are more than 30 days past due, even though Wonder Vision's credit terms call for full payment by Day 30.

Aging schedules cannot be constructed from the type of summary data reported in financial statements; they must be developed from the firm's accounts receivable ledger. However, well-run firms have computerized their accounts receivable records, so it is easy to determine the age of each invoice, to sort electronically by age categories, and thus to generate an aging schedule.

Management should constantly monitor both the DSO and the aging schedule to detect trends, to see how the firm's collection experience compares with its credit terms, and to see how effectively the credit department is operating in comparison with other firms in the industry. If the DSO starts to lengthen, or if the aging schedule begins to show an increasing percentage of past-due accounts, then the firm's credit policy may need to be tightened.

Although a change in the DSO or the aging schedule should signal the firm to investigate its credit policy, a deterioration in either of these measures does not necessarily indicate that the firm's credit policy has weakened. In fact, if a firm experiences sharp seasonal variations, or if it is growing rapidly, then both the aging schedule and the DSO may be distorted. To see this point, note that the DSO is calculated as follows:

$$DSO = \frac{\text{Accounts receivable}}{\text{Sales}/360}.$$

Since receivables at a given point in time reflect sales in the last month or so, but sales as shown in the denominator of the equation are for the last 12 months, a seasonal increase in sales will increase the numerator more than the denominator, hence will raise the DSO. This will occur even if customers are still paying exactly as before. Similar problems arise with the aging schedule if sales fluctuate widely. Therefore, a change in either the DSO or the aging schedule should

TABLE 16-3 Aging Schedules

Age of Account (Days)	Super Sets Value of Account	Percentage of Total Value	Wonder Vision Value of Account	Percentage of Total value
0–10	$1,232,000	70%	$ 825,000	47%
11–30	528,000	30	460,000	26
31–45	0	0	265,000	15
46–60	0	0	179,000	10
Over 60	0	0	31,000	2
Total receivables	$1,760,000	100%	$1,760,000	100%

be taken as a signal to investigate further, but not necessarily as a sign that the firm's credit policy has weakened. Still, days sales outstanding and the aging schedule are useful tools for reviewing the credit department's performance.[9]

SELF-TEST QUESTIONS　　　??????

Explain how a new firm's receivables balance is built up over time.

Define days sales outstanding (DSO). What can be learned from it? How is it affected by sales fluctuations?

What is an aging schedule? What can be learned from it? How is it affected by sales fluctuations?

CREDIT POLICY

The success or failure of a business depends primarily on the demand for its products — as a rule, the higher its sales, the larger its profits and the higher its stock price. Sales, in turn, depend on a number of factors, some exogenous but others under the firm's control. The major controllable determinants of demand are sales prices, product quality, advertising, and the firm's **credit policy.** Credit policy, in turn, consists of these four variables:

Credit Policy
A set of decisions that include a firm's credit period, credit standards, collection procedures, and discounts offered.

1. *Credit period,* which is the length of time buyers are given to pay for their purchases.
2. *Credit standards,* which refer to the required financial strength of acceptable credit customers.
3. *Collection policy,* which is measured by its toughness or laxity in attempting to collect on slow-paying accounts.
4. *Discounts* given for early payment, including the discount percentage and how rapidly payment must be made to qualify for the discount.

The credit manager is responsible for administering the firm's credit policy. However, because of the pervasive importance of credit, the credit policy itself is normally established by the executive committee, which usually consists of the president plus the vice-presidents of finance, marketing, and production.

SELF-TEST QUESTION　　　??????

What are the four credit policy variables?

SETTING THE CREDIT PERIOD AND STANDARDS

Credit Terms
A statement of the credit period and any discounts offered — for example, 2/10, net 30.

Credit Period
The length of time for which credit is granted.

A firm's regular **credit terms,** which include the **credit period** and *discount,* might call for sales on a 2/10, net 30 basis to all "acceptable" customers. Here customers who pay within 10 days would be given a 2 percent discount, and others

---

[9]See Eugene F. Brigham and Louis C Gapenski, *Intermediate Financial Management,* 5th ed., Chapter 23, for a more complete discussion of the problems with the DSO and aging schedule and ways to correct for them.

would be required to pay within 30 days. Its *credit standards* would be applied to determine which customers qualify for the regular credit terms, and the amount of credit available to each customer.

CREDIT STANDARDS

Credit Standards
Standards that stipulate the required financial strength that an applicant must demonstrate to be granted credit.

Credit standards refer to the financial strength and creditworthiness a customer must exhibit in order to qualify for credit. If a customer does not qualify for the regular credit terms, it can still purchase from the firm, but under more restrictive terms. For example, a firm's "regular" credit terms might call for payment after 30 days, and these terms might be extended to all qualified customers. The firm's credit standards would be applied to determine which customers qualified for the regular credit terms, and how much credit each should receive. The major factors considered when setting credit standards relate to the likelihood that a given customer will pay slowly or perhaps end up as a bad debt loss.

Setting credit standards requires a measurement of *credit quality,* which is defined in terms of the probability of a customer's default. The probability estimate for a given customer is, for the most part, a subjective judgment. Nevertheless, credit evaluation is a well-established practice, and a good credit manager can make reasonably accurate judgments of the probability of default by different classes of customers.

Managing a credit department requires fast, accurate, and up-to-date information. To help get such information, the National Association of Credit Management (a group with 43,000 member firms) persuaded TRW, a large credit-reporting agency, to develop a computer-based telecommunications network for the collection, storage, retrieval, and distribution of credit information. A typical business credit report would include the following pieces of information:

1. A summary balance sheet and income statement.
2. A number of key ratios, with trend information.
3. Information obtained from the firm's suppliers telling whether it pays promptly or slowly, and whether it has recently failed to make any payments.
4. A verbal description of the physical condition of the firm's operations.
5. A verbal description of the backgrounds of the firm's owners, including any previous bankruptcies, lawsuits, divorce settlement problems, and the like.
6. A summary rating, ranging from A for the best credit risks down to F for those that are deemed likely to default.

Although a great deal of credit information is available, it must still be processed in a judgmental manner. Computerized information systems can assist in making better credit decisions, but, in the final analysis, most credit decisions are really exercises in informed judgment.[10]

---

[10]Credit analysts use procedures ranging from highly sophisticated, computerized "credit-scoring" systems, which actually calculate the statistical probability that a given customer will default, to informal procedures, which involve going through a checklist of factors that should be considered when processing a credit application. The credit-scoring systems use various financial ratios such as the current ratio and the debt ratio (for businesses) and income, years with the same employer, and the like (for individuals) to determine the statistical probability of default. Credit is then granted to those with low default probabilities. The informal procedures often involve examining the "5 C's of Credit": character, capacity, capital, collateral, and conditions. Character is obvious; capacity is a subjective estimate of ability to repay; capital means how much net worth the borrower has; collateral means assets pledged to secure the loan; and conditions refers to business conditions, which affect ability to repay.

What are credit terms?

What is credit quality, and how is it assessed?

SETTING THE COLLECTION POLICY

Collection Policy
The procedures that a firm follows to collect accounts receivable.

Collection policy refers to the procedures the firm follows to collect past-due accounts. For example, a letter might be sent to customers when a bill is 10 days past due; a more severe letter, followed by a telephone call, would be sent if payment is not received within 30 days; and the account would be turned over to a collection agency after 90 days.

The collection process can be expensive in terms of both out-of-pocket expenditures and lost goodwill — customers dislike being turned over to a collection agency. However, at least some firmness is needed to prevent an undue lengthening of the collection period and to minimize outright losses. A balance must be struck between the costs and benefits of different collection policies.

Changes in collection policy influence sales, the collection period, and the bad debt loss percentage. All of this should be taken into account when setting the credit policy.

How does collection policy influence sales, the collection period, and the bad debt loss percentage?

CASH DISCOUNTS

Cash Discount
A reduction in the price of goods given to encourage early payment.

The last element in the credit policy decision, the use of **cash discounts** for early payment, is analyzed by balancing the costs and benefits of different cash discounts. For example, a firm might decide to change its credit terms from "net 30," which means that customers must pay within 30 days, to "2/10, net 30," where a 2 percent discount is given if payment is made in ten days. This change should produce two benefits: (1) It should attract new customers who consider the discount to be a price reduction, and (2) the discount should cause a reduction in the days sales outstanding, because some existing customers will pay more promptly in order to get the discount. Offsetting these benefits is the dollar cost of the discounts. The optimal discount percentage is established at the point where the marginal costs and benefits are exactly offsetting.

Seasonal Dating
Terms used to induce customers to buy early by not requiring payment until the purchaser's selling season, regardless of when the goods are shipped.

If sales are seasonal, a firm may use **seasonal dating** on discounts. For example, Slimware Inc., a swimsuit manufacturer, sells on terms of 2/10, net 30, May 1 dating. This means that the effective invoice date is May 1, even if the sale was made back in January. The discount may be taken up to May 10; otherwise, the full amount must be paid on May 30. Slimware produces throughout the year, but retail sales of bathing suits are concentrated in the spring and early summer. By offering seasonal dating, the company induces some of its customers to stock up early, saving Slimware some storage costs and also "nailing down sales."

SELF-TEST QUESTIONS ??????

How can cash discounts be used to influence sales volume and the DSO?

What is seasonal dating?

OTHER FACTORS INFLUENCING CREDIT POLICY

In addition to the factors discussed in previous sections, two other points should be made regarding credit policy.

PROFIT POTENTIAL

We have emphasized the costs of granting credit. *However, if it is possible to sell on credit and also to impose a carrying charge on the receivables that are outstanding, then credit sales can actually be more profitable than cash sales.* This is especially true for consumer durables (autos, appliances, and so on), but it is also true for certain types of industrial equipment. Thus, GM's General Motors Acceptance Corporation (GMAC) unit, which finances automobiles, is highly profitable, as is Sears' credit subsidiary.[11] Some encyclopedia companies even lose money on cash sales but more than make up these losses from the carrying charges on their credit sales. Obviously, such companies would rather sell on credit than for cash!

The carrying charges on outstanding credit are generally about 18 percent on a nominal basis: 1.5 percent per month, so $1.5\% \times 12 = 18\%$. This is equivalent to an effective annual rate of $(1.015)^{12} - 1.0 = 19.6\%$. Having receivables outstanding that earn more than 18 percent is highly profitable unless there are too many bad debt losses.

LEGAL CONSIDERATIONS

It is illegal, under the Robinson-Patman Act, for a firm to charge prices that discriminate between customers unless these differential prices are cost-justified. The same holds true for credit — it is illegal to offer more favorable credit terms to one customer or class of customers than to another, unless the differences are cost-justified.

SELF-TEST QUESTION ??????

How do profit potential and legal considerations affect a firm's credit policy?

---

[11]Companies that do a large volume of sales financing typically set up subsidiary companies called *captive finance companies* to do the actual financing. Thus, General Motors, Chrysler, and Ford all have captive finance companies, as do Sears, IBM, and General Electric.

SUMMARY

This chapter discussed the management of current assets, particularly cash, marketable securities, inventory, and receivables. The key concepts are listed below.

♦ **Working capital** refers to current assets, and **net working capital** is defined as current assets minus current liabilities. **Working capital policy** refers to decisions relating to current assets and their financing.

♦ Under a **relaxed current asset policy,** a firm would hold relatively large amounts of each type of current asset. Under a **restricted current asset policy,** the firm would hold minimal amounts of these items.

♦ A policy which strives for **zero working capital** not only generates cash but also speeds up production and helps businesses operate more efficiently. This concept has its own definition of working capital: Inventories + Receivables − Payables. The rationale is that inventories and receivables are the keys to making sales, and that inventories can be financed by suppliers through accounts payable.

♦ The **primary goal of cash management** is to reduce the amount of cash held to the minimum necessary to conduct business.

♦ The **transactions balance** is the cash necessary to conduct day-to-day business, whereas the **precautionary balance** is a cash reserve held to meet random, unforeseen needs. A **compensating balance** is a minimum checking account balance that a bank requires as compensation either for services provided or as part of a loan agreement. Firms also hold **speculative balances,** which allow them to take advantage of bargain purchases. Note, though, that borrowing capacity and marketable security holdings both reduce the need for precautionary and speculative balances.

♦ A **cash budget** is a schedule showing projected cash inflows and outflows over some period. The cash budget is used to predict cash surpluses and deficits, and it is the primary cash management planning tool.

♦ **Cash management techniques** generally fall into five categories: (1) synchronizing cash flows, (2) using float, (3) accelerating collections, (4) determining where and when funds will be needed, and (5) controlling disbursements.

♦ **Disbursement float** is the amount of funds associated with checks written by a firm that are still in process and hence have not yet been deducted from the firm's bank account.

♦ **Collections float** is the amount of funds associated with checks written to a firm that have not been cleared, hence are not yet available for the firm's use.

♦ **Net float** is the difference between disbursement float and collections float, and it also is equal to the difference between the balance in the firm's own checkbook and the balance on the bank's records. The larger the net float, the smaller the cash balance the firm must maintain, so net float is good.

♦ Two techniques that can be used to speed up collections are (1) **lockboxes** and (2) **wire transfers.**

♦ Firms can reduce their cash balances by holding **marketable securities,** which can be sold on short notice at close to their quoted prices. Marketable securities serve both as a substitute for cash and as a temporary investment for funds that will be needed in the near future. Safety is the primary consideration when selecting marketable securities.

♦ **Inventory management** involves determining how much inventory to hold, when to place orders, and how many units to order.

♦ **Inventory** can be grouped into four categories: (1) supplies, (2) raw materials, (3) work-in-process, and (4) finished goods.

♦ **Inventory costs** can be divided into three types: carrying costs, ordering costs, and stock-out costs. In general, carrying costs increase as the level of inventory rises, but ordering costs and stock-out costs decline with larger inventory holdings.

♦ Firms use inventory control systems such as the **red-line method** and the **two-bin method,** as well as **computerized inventory control systems,** to help them keep track of actual inventory levels and to ensure that inventory levels are adjusted as sales change. **Just-in-time (JIT) systems** are used to hold down inventory costs and, simultaneously, to improve the production process.

♦ When a firm sells goods to a customer on credit, an **account receivable** is created.

♦ A firm can use an **aging schedule** and the **days sales outstanding (DSO)** to help keep track of its receivables position and to help avoid an increase in bad debts.

♦ A firm's **credit policy** consists of four elements: (1) credit period, (2) discounts given for early payment, (3) credit standards, and (4) collection policy. The first two, when combined, are called the **credit terms.**

♦ Two major sources of external credit information are **credit associations,** which are local groups that meet frequently and correspond with one another to exchange information on credit customers, and **credit-reporting agencies,** which collect credit information and sell it for a fee.

♦ Additional factors that influence a firm's overall credit policy are (1) **profit potential** and (2) **legal considerations.**

♦ The basic objective of the credit manager is to increase profitable sales by extending credit to worthy customers and therefore adding value to the firm.

Working capital policy involves two basic issues. The first, determining the appropriate level for each type of current asset, was addressed in this chapter. The second, how current assets should be financed, will be addressed in Chapter 17.

QUESTIONS

16-1 Assuming the firm's sales volume remained constant, would you expect it to have a higher cash balance during a tight-money period or during an easy-money period? Why?

16-2 What are the two principal reasons for holding cash? Can a firm estimate its target cash balance by summing the cash held to satisfy each of the two?

16-3 Explain how each of the following factors would probably affect a firm's target cash balance if all other factors were held constant.
   a. The firm institutes a new billing procedure which better synchronizes its cash inflows and outflows.
   b. The firm develops a new sales forecasting technique which improves its forecasts.
   c. The firm reduces its portfolio of U.S. Treasury bills.
   d. The firm arranges to use an overdraft system for its checking account.
   e. The firm borrows a large amount of money from its bank and also begins to write far more checks than it did in the past.
   f. Interest rates on Treasury bills rise from 5 percent to 10 percent.

16-4 Why would a lockbox plan make more sense for a firm that makes sales all over the United States than for a firm with the same volume of business but concentrated in its home city?

16-5 Is it true that when one firm sells to another on credit, the seller records the transaction as an account receivable while the buyer records it as an account payable and that, disregarding discounts, the receivable typically exceeds the payable by the amount of profit on the sale?

16-6 What are the four elements of a firm's credit policy? To what extent can firms set their own credit policies as opposed to having to accept policies that are dictated by "the competition"?

16-7 Suppose that a firm makes a purchase and receives the shipment on February 1. The terms of trade as stated on the invoice read "2/10, net 40, May 1 dating." What is the latest date on which payment can be made and the discount still be taken? What is the date on which payment must be made if the discount is not taken?

16-8 a. What is the days sales outstanding (DSO) for a firm whose sales are $2,880,000 per year and whose accounts receivable are $312,000? (Use 360 days per year.)
b. Is it true that if this firm sells on terms of 3/10, net 40, its customers probably all pay on time?

16-9 Is it true that if a firm calculates its days sales outstanding, it has no need for an aging schedule?

16-10 Firm A had no credit losses last year, but 1 percent of Firm B's accounts receivable proved to be uncollectible and resulted in losses. Should Firm B fire its credit manager and hire A's?

16-11 Indicate by a (+), (−), or (0) whether each of the following events would probably cause accounts receivable (A/R), sales, and profits to increase, decrease, or be affected in an indeterminant manner:

	A/R	SALES	PROFITS
The firm tightens its credit standards.			
The terms of trade are changed from 2/10, net 30, to 3/10, net 30.			
The terms are changed from 2/10, net 30, to 3/10, net 40.			
The credit manager gets tough with past-due accounts.			

16-12 A firm can reduce its investment in inventory by having its suppliers hold raw materials inventory and its customers hold finished goods inventory. Explain actions a firm can take which would result in larger inventory for its suppliers and customers and smaller inventory for itself. What are the limitations of such actions?

SELF-TEST PROBLEMS (Solutions Appear in Appendix B)

ST-1
Key terms
Define each of the following terms:
a. Working capital; net working capital; working capital policy
b. Relaxed current asset investment policy; restricted current asset investment policy; moderate current asset investment policy
c. Transactions balance; compensating balance; precautionary balance; speculative balance
d. Cash budget; target cash balance
e. Trade discounts
f. Synchronized cash flows
g. Check clearing; net float; disbursement float; collections float
h. Lockbox plan
i. Marketable securities
j. Red-line method; two-bin method; computerized inventory control system
k. Just-in-time system; out-sourcing

l. Account receivable; days sales outstanding

m. Aging schedule

n. Credit policy; credit period; credit standards; collection policy; credit terms

o. Cash discounts

p. Seasonal dating

ST-2
Working capital policy

The Calgary Company is attempting to establish a current assets policy. Fixed assets are $600,000, and the firm plans to maintain a 50 percent debt-to-assets ratio. The interest rate is 10 percent on all debt. Three alternative current asset policies are under consideration: 40, 50, and 60 percent of projected sales. The company expects to earn 15 percent before interest and taxes on sales of $3 million. Calgary's effective federal-plus-state tax rate is 40 percent. What is the expected return on equity under each alternative?

ST-3
Float

The Upton Company is setting up a new checking account with Howe National Bank. Upton plans to issue checks in the amount of $1 million each day and to deduct them from its own records at the close of business on the day they are written. On average, the bank will receive and clear the checks at 5 P.M. the third day after they are written; for example, a check written on Monday will be cleared on Thursday afternoon. The firm's agreement with the bank requires it to maintain a $500,000 average compensating balance; this is $250,000 greater than the cash balance the firm would otherwise have on deposit. It makes a $500,000 deposit at the time it opens the account.

a. Assuming that the firm makes deposits at 4 P.M. each day (and the bank includes them in that day's transactions), how much must it deposit daily in order to maintain a sufficient balance once it reaches a steady state? Indicate the required deposit on Day 1, Day 2, Day 3, if any, and each day thereafter, assuming that the company will write checks for $1 million on Day 1 and each day thereafter.

b. How many days of float does Upton have?

c. What ending daily balance should the firm try to maintain (1) on the bank's records and (2) on its own records?

STARTER PROBLEMS

16-1
Net float

On a typical day, Troan Corporation writes $10,000 in checks. It generally takes 4 days for those checks to clear. Each day the firm typically receives $10,000 in checks that take 3 days to clear. What is the firm's average net float?

16-2
Cash management

Williams & Sons last year reported sales of $10 million and an inventory turnover ratio of 2. The company is now adopting a just-in-time inventory system. If the new system is able to reduce the firm's inventory level and increase the firm's inventory turnover ratio to 5, while maintaining the same level of sales, how much cash will be freed up?

16-3
Receivables investment

Medwig Corporation has a DSO of 17 days. The company averages $3,500 in credit sales each day. What is the company's average accounts receivable?

EXAM-TYPE PROBLEMS

The problems included in this section are set up in such a way that they could be used as multiple-choice exam problems.

16-4
Lockbox system

I. Malitz and Associates Inc. operates a mail-order firm doing business on the West Coast. Malitz receives an average of $325,000 in payments per day. On average, it takes 4 days from the time customers mail checks until Malitz receives and processes them. Malitz is considering the use of a lockbox system to reduce collection and processing float. The system will cost $6,500 per month and will consist of 10 local depository banks and a concentration bank located in San Francisco. Under this system, customers' checks should be received at the lockbox locations 1 day after they are mailed, and daily totals will be transferred to San Francisco using wire transfers costing $9.75 each. Assume that Malitz has an opportunity cost of 10 percent and that there are $52 \times 5 = 260$ working days, hence 260 transfers from each lockbox location, in a year.

a. What is the total annual cost of operating the lockbox system?

b. What is the benefit of the lockbox system to Malitz?

c. Should Malitz initiate the system?

16-5
Receivables investment

McDowell Industries sells on terms of 3/10, net 30. Total sales for the year are $900,000. Forty percent of the customers pay on the 10th day and take discounts; the other 60 percent pay, on average, 40 days after their purchases.
a. What is the days sales outstanding?
b. What is the average amount of receivables?
c. What would happen to average receivables if McDowell toughened up on its collection policy with the result that all nondiscount customers paid on the 30th day?

PROBLEMS

16-6
Working capital policy

The Rentz Corporation is attempting to determine the optimal level of current assets for the coming year. Management expects sales to increase to approximately $2 million as a result of an asset expansion presently being undertaken. Fixed assets total $1 million, and the firm wishes to maintain a 60 percent debt ratio. Rentz's interest cost is currently 8 percent on both short-term and longer-term debt (which the firm uses in its permanent structure). Three alternatives regarding the projected current asset level are available to the firm: (1) a tight policy requiring current assets of only 45 percent of projected sales, (2) a moderate policy of 50 percent of sales in current assets, and (3) a relaxed policy requiring current assets of 60 percent of sales. The firm expects to generate earnings before interest and taxes at a rate of 12 percent on total sales.
a. What is the expected return on equity under each current asset level? (Assume a 40 percent effective federal-plus-state tax rate.)
b. In this problem, we have assumed that the level of expected sales is independent of current asset policy. Is this a valid assumption?
c. How would the overall riskiness of the firm vary under each policy?

16-7
Net float

The Stendardi-Stephens Company (SSC) is setting up a new checking account with National Bank. SSC plans to issue checks in the amount of $1.6 million each day and to deduct them from its own records at the close of business on the day they are written. On average, the bank will receive and clear (that is, deduct from the firm's bank balance) the checks at 5 P.M. the fourth day after they are written; for example, a check written on Monday will be cleared on Friday afternoon. The firm's agreement with the bank requires it to maintain a $1.2 million average compensating balance; this is $400,000 greater than the cash balance the firm would otherwise have on deposit. It makes a $1.2 million deposit at the time it opens the account.
a. Assuming that the firm makes deposits at 4 P.M. each day (and the bank includes them in that day's transactions), how much must it deposit daily in order to maintain a sufficient balance once it reaches a steady state? Indicate the required deposit on Day 1, Day 2, Day 3, Day 4, if any, and each day thereafter, assuming that the company will write checks for $1.6 million on Day 1 and each day thereafter.
b. How many days of float does SSC carry?
c. What ending daily balance should the firm try to maintain (1) on the bank's records and (2) on its own records?
d. Explain how net float can help increase the value of the firm's common stock.

16-8
Lockbox system

The Hardin-Gehr Corporation (HGC) began operations 5 years ago as a small firm serving customers in the Detroit area. However, its reputation and market area grew quickly, so that today HGC has customers throughout the entire United States. Despite its broad customer base, HGC has maintained its headquarters in Detroit and keeps its central billing system there. HGC's management is considering an alternative collection procedure to reduce its mail time and processing float. On average, it takes 5 days from the time customers mail payments until HGC is able to receive, process, and deposit them. HGC would like to set up a lockbox collection system, which it estimates would reduce the time lag from customer mailing to deposit by 3 days — bringing it down to 2 days. HGC receives an average of $1,400,000 in payments per day.
a. How many days of collection float now exist (HGC's customers' disbursement float) and what would it be under the lockbox system? What reduction in cash balances could HGC achieve by initiating the lockbox system?
b. If HGC has an opportunity cost of 10 percent, how much is the lockbox system worth on an annual basis?
c. What is the maximum monthly charge HGC should pay for the lockbox system?

16-9

Cash budgeting

Dorothy Koehl recently leased space in the Southside Mall and opened a new business, Koehl's Doll Shop. Business has been good, but Koehl has frequently run out of cash. This has necessitated late payment on certain orders, which, in turn, is beginning to cause a problem with suppliers. Koehl plans to borrow from the bank to have cash ready as needed, but first she needs a forecast of just how much she must borrow. Accordingly, she has asked you to prepare a cash budget for the critical period around Christmas, when needs will be especially high.

Sales are made on a cash basis only. Koehl's purchases must be paid for during the following month. Koehl pays herself a salary of $4,800 per month, and the rent is $2,000 per month. In addition, she must make a tax payment of $12,000 in December. The current cash on hand (on December 1) is $400, but Koehl has agreed to maintain an average bank balance of $6,000 — this is her target cash balance. (Disregard till cash, which is insignificant because Koehl keeps only a small amount on hand in order to lessen the chances of robbery.)

The estimated sales and purchases for December, January, and February are shown below. Purchases during November amounted to $140,000.

	SALES	PURCHASES
December	$160,000	$40,000
January	40,000	40,000
February	60,000	40,000

a. Prepare a cash budget for December, January, and February.

b. Now, suppose Koehl were to start selling on a credit basis on December 1, giving customers 30 days to pay. All customers accept these terms, and all other facts in the problem are unchanged. What would the company's loan requirements be at the end of December in this case? (Hint: The calculations required to answer this question are minimal.)

16-10

Cash budgeting

Helen Bowers, owner of Helen's Fashion Designs, is planning to request a line of credit from her bank. She has estimated the following sales forecasts for the firm for parts of 1998 and 1999:

May 1998	$180,000
June	180,000
July	360,000
August	540,000
September	720,000
October	360,000
November	360,000
December	90,000
January 1999	180,000

Collection estimates obtained from the credit and collection department are as follows: collections within the month of sale, 10 percent; collections the month following the sale, 75 percent; collections the second month following the sale, 15 percent. Payments for labor and raw materials are typically made during the month following the one in which these costs have been incurred. Total labor and raw materials costs are estimated for each month as follows:

May 1998	$ 90,000
June	90,000
July	126,000
August	882,000
September	306,000
October	234,000
November	162,000
December	90,000

General and administrative salaries will amount to approximately $27,000 a month; lease payments under long-term lease contracts will be $9,000 a month; depreciation charges will be $36,000 a month; miscellaneous expenses will be $2,700 a month; income tax payments of $63,000 will be due in both September and December; and a progress payment of $180,000 on a new design studio must be paid in October. Cash on hand on July 1 will amount to $132,000, and a minimum cash balance of $90,000 will be maintained throughout the cash budget period.

a. Prepare a monthly cash budget for the last 6 months of 1998.

b. Prepare an estimate of the required financing (or excess funds) — that is, the amount of money Bowers will need to borrow (or will have available to invest) — for each month during that period.

c. Assume that receipts from sales come in uniformly during the month (that is, cash receipts come in at the rate of 1/30 each day), but all outflows are paid on the 5th of the month. Will this have an effect on the cash budget — in other words, would the cash budget you have prepared be valid under these assumptions? If not, what can be done to make a valid estimate of peak financing requirements? No calculations are required, although calculations can be used to illustrate the effects.

d. Bowers produces on a seasonal basis, just ahead of sales. Without making any calculations, discuss how the company's current ratio and debt ratio would vary during the year assuming all financial requirements were met by short-term bank loans. Could changes in these ratios affect the firm's ability to obtain bank credit?

INTEGRATED CASE

SKI EQUIPMENT INC.

16-11 Managing Current Assets Dan Barnes, financial manager of Ski Equipment Inc. (SKI), is excited, but apprehensive. The company's founder recently sold his 51 percent controlling block of stock to Kent Koren, who is a big fan of EVA (Economic Value Added). EVA is found by taking the after-tax operating profit and then subtracting the dollar cost of all the capital the firm uses:

$$EVA = EBIT (1 - T) - \text{Capital costs}$$

$$= EBIT (1 - T) - WACC \text{ (Capital employed).}$$

If EVA is positive, then the firm is creating value. On the other hand, if EVA is negative, the firm is not covering its cost of capital, and stockholders' value is being eroded. Koren rewards managers handsomely if they create value, but those whose operations produce negative EVAs are soon looking for work. Koren frequently points out that if a company can generate its current level of sales with less assets, it would need less capital. That would, other things held constant, lower capital costs and increase its EVA.

Shortly after he took control of SKI, Kent Koren met with SKI's senior executives to tell them of his plans for the company. First, he presented some EVA data which convinced everyone that SKI had not been creating value in recent

years. He then stated, in no uncertain terms, that this situation must change. He noted that SKI's designs of skis, boots, and clothing are acclaimed throughout the industry, but something is seriously amiss elsewhere in the company. Costs are too high, prices are too low, or the company employs too much capital, and he wants SKI's managers to correct the problem or else.

Barnes has long felt that SKI's working capital situation should be studied — the company may have the optimal amounts of cash, securities, receivables, and inventories, but it may also have too much or too little of these items. In the past, the production manager resisted Dan's efforts to question his holdings of raw materials inventories, the marketing manager resisted questions about finished goods, the sales staff resisted questions about credit policy (which affects accounts receivable), and the treasurer did not want to talk about her cash and securities balances. Koren's speech made it clear that such resistance would no longer be tolerated.

Dan also knows that decisions about working capital cannot be made in a vacuum. For example, if inventories could be lowered without adversely affecting operations, then less capital would be required, the dollar cost of capital would decline, and EVA would increase. However, lower raw materials inventories might lead to production slowdowns and higher costs, while lower finished goods inventories might lead to the loss of profitable sales. So, before inventories

TABLE IC 16-1 Selected Ratios: SKI and Industry Average

	SKI	INDUSTRY
Current	1.75	2.25
Quick	0.83	1.20
Debt/assets	58.76%	50.00%
Turnover of cash and securities	16.67	22.22
Days sales outstanding	45.00	32.00
Inventory turnover	4.82	7.00
Fixed assets turnover	11.35	12.00
Total assets turnover	2.08	3.00
Profit margin on sales	2.07%	3.50%
Return on equity (ROE)	10.45%	21.00%

are changed, it will be necessary to study operating as well as financial effects. The situation is the same with regard to cash and receivables.

a. Dan plans to use the ratios in Table IC16-1 as the starting point for discussions with SKI's operating executives. He wants everyone to think about the pros and cons of changing each type of current asset and how changes would interact to affect profits and EVA. Based on the Table IC16-1 data, does SKI seem to be following a relaxed, moderate, or restricted working capital policy?

b. How can one distinguish between a relaxed but rational working capital policy and a situation where a firm simply has a lot of current assets because it is inefficient? Does SKI's working capital policy seem appropriate?

c. What might SKI do to reduce its cash and securities without harming operations?

d. What is "float," and how is it affected by the firm's cash manager (treasurer)?

In an attempt to better understand SKI's cash position, Dan developed a cash budget. Data for the first 2 months of the year are shown in Table IC16-2. (Note that Dan's preliminary cash budget does not account for interest income or interest expense.) He has the figures for the other months, but they are not shown in Table IC16-2.

e. Should depreciation expense be explicitly included in the cash budget? Why or why not?

f. In his preliminary cash budget, Dan has assumed that all sales are collected and, thus, that SKI has no bad debts. Is this realistic? If not, how would bad debts be dealt with in a cash budgeting sense? (Hint: Bad debts will affect collections but not purchases.)

g. Dan's cash budget for the entire year, although not given here, is based heavily on his forecast for monthly sales. Sales are expected to be extremely low between May and September but then increase dramatically in the fall and winter. November is typically the firm's best month, when SKI ships equipment to retailers for the holiday season. Interestingly, Dan's forecasted cash budget indicates that the company's cash holdings will exceed the targeted cash balance every month except for October and November, when shipments will be high but collections will not be coming in until later. Based on the ratios in Table IC16-1, does it appear that SKI's target cash balance is appropriate? In addition to possibly lowering the target cash balance, what actions might SKI take to better improve its cash management policies, and how might that affect its EVA?

h. What reasons might SKI have for maintaining a relatively high amount of cash?

i. What are the three categories of inventory costs? If the company takes steps to reduce its inventory, what effect would this have on the various costs of holding inventory?

j. Is there any reason to think that SKI may be holding too much inventory? If so, how would that affect EVA and ROE?

k. If the company reduces its inventory without adversely affecting sales, what effect should this have on the company's cash position (1) in the short run and (2) in the long run? Explain in terms of the cash budget and the balance sheet.

l. Dan knows that SKI sells on the same credit terms as other firms in its industry. Use the ratios presented in Table IC16-1 to explain whether SKI's customers pay more or less promptly than those of its competitors. If there are differences, does that suggest that SKI should tighten or loosen its credit policy? What four variables make up a firm's credit policy, and in what direction should each be changed by SKI?

m. Does SKI face any risks if it tightens its credit policy?

n. If the company reduces its DSO without seriously affecting sales, what effect would this have on its cash position (1) in the short run and (2) in the long run? Answer in terms of the cash budget and the balance sheet. What effect should this have on EVA in the long run?

TABLE IC16-2 | **SKI's Cash Budget for January and February**

	NOV	DEC	JAN	FEB	MAR	APR
I. COLLECTIONS AND PURCHASES WORKSHEET						
(1) Sales (gross)	$71,218	$68,212	$65,213	$52,475	$42,909	$30,524
Collections						
(2) During month of sale (0.2)(0.98)(month's sales)			12,781.75	10,285.10		
(3) During first month after sale (0.7)(previous month's sales)			47,748.40	45,649.10		
(4) During second month after sale (0.1)(sales 2 months ago)			7,121.80	6,821.20		
(5) Total collections (Lines 2 + 3 + 4)			$67,651.95	$62,755.40		
Purchases						
(6) (0.85)(forecasted sales 2 months from now)		$44,603.75	$36,472.65	$25,945.40		
(7) Payments (1-month lag)			44,603.75	36,472.65		
II. CASH GAIN OR LOSS FOR MONTH						
(8) Collections (from Section I)			$67,651.95	$62,755.40		
(9) Payments for purchases (from Section I)			44,603.75	36,472.65		
(10) Wages and salaries			6,690.56	5,470.90		
(11) Rent			2,500.00	2,500.00		
(12) Taxes						
(13) Total payments			$53,794.31	$44,443.55		
(14) Net cash gain (loss) during month (Line 8 − Line 13)			$13,857.64	$18,311.85		
III. CASH SURPLUS OR LOAN REQUIREMENT						
(15) Cash at beginning of month if no borrowing is done			$3,000.00	$16,857.64		
(16) Cumulative cash (cash at start, + gain or − loss = Line 14 + Line 15)			16,857.64	35,169.49		
(17) Target cash balance			1,500.00	1,500.00		
(18) Cumulative surplus cash or loans outstanding to maintain $1,500 target cash balance (Line 16 − Line 17)			$15,357.64	$33,669.49		

 COMPUTER-RELATED PROBLEM

Work the problem in this section only if you are using the computer problem diskette.

16-12
Cash budgeting

Use the model in the File C16 to solve this problem.
a. Refer back to Problem 16-10. Suppose that by offering a 2 percent cash discount for paying within the month of sale, the credit manager of Helen's Fashion Designs has revised the collection percentages to 50 percent, 35 percent, and 15 percent, respectively. How will this affect the loan requirements?
b. Return the payment percentages to their base-case values: 10 percent, 75 percent, and 15 percent, respectively, and the discount to zero percent. Now suppose sales fall to

only 70 percent of the forecasted level. Production is maintained, so cash outflows are unchanged. How does this affect Bowers's financial requirements?

c. Return sales to the forecasted level (100%), and suppose collections slow down to 3 percent, 10 percent, and 87 percent for the 3 months, respectively. How does this affect financial requirements? If Bowers went to a cash-only sales policy, how would that affect requirements, other things held constant?

THE CASH CONVERSION CYCLE

As we noted earlier in the chapter, the concept of working capital management originated with the old Yankee peddler, who would borrow to buy inventory, sell the inventory to pay off the bank loan, and then repeat the cycle. That concept has been applied to more complex businesses, where it is used to analyze the effectiveness of a firm's working capital management.

We can illustrate the process with data from Real Time Computer Corporation (RTC), which in early 1997 introduced a new super-minicomputer that can perform 500 million instructions per second and that will sell for $250,000. The effects of this new product on RTC's working capital position were analyzed in terms of the following five steps:

1. RTC will order and then receive the materials it needs to produce the 100 computers it expects to sell. Because RTC and most other firms purchase materials on credit, this transaction will create an account payable. However, the purchase will have no immediate cash flow effect.

2. Labor will be used to convert the materials into finished computers. However, wages will not be fully paid at the time the work is done, so, like accounts payable, accrued wages will also build up.

3. The finished computers will be sold, but on credit. Therefore, sales will create receivables, not immediate cash inflows.

4. At some point before cash comes in, RTC must pay off its accounts payable and accrued wages. This outflow must be financed.

5. The cycle will be completed when RTC's receivables have been collected. At that time, the company can pay off the credit that was used to finance production, and it can then repeat the cycle.

The *cash conversion cycle* model, which focuses on the length of time between when the company makes payments and when it receives cash inflows, formalizes the steps outlined above.[1] The following terms are used in the model:

1. *Inventory conversion period,* which is the average time required to convert materials into finished goods and then to sell those goods. Note that the inventory conversion period is calculated by dividing inventory by sales per day. For example, if average inventories are $2 million and sales are $10 million, then the inventory conversion period is 72 days:

$$\text{Inventory conversion period} = \frac{\text{Inventory}}{\text{Sales per day}} \qquad (16A\text{-}1)$$

$$= \frac{\$2,000,000}{\$10,000,000/360}$$

$$= 72 \text{ days}.$$

---

[1]See Verlyn D. Richards and Eugene J. Laughlin, "A Cash Conversion Cycle Approach to Liquidity Analysis," *Financial Management,* Spring 1980, 32–38.

Thus, it takes an average of 72 days to convert materials into finished goods and then to sell those goods.

2. *Receivables collection period,* which is the average length of time required to convert the firm's receivables into cash, that is, to collect cash following a sale. The receivables collection period is also called the *days sales outstanding (DSO),* and it is calculated by dividing accounts receivable by the average credit sales per day. If receivables are $666,667 and sales are $10 million, the receivables collection period is

$$\frac{\text{Receivables}}{\text{collection period}} = \text{DSO} = \frac{\text{Receivables}}{\text{Sales/360}} \tag{16A-2}$$

$$= \frac{\$666,667}{\$10 \text{ million}/360} = 24 \text{ days.}$$

Thus, it takes 24 days after a sale to convert the receivables into cash.

3. *Payables deferral period,* which is the average length of time between the purchase of materials and labor and the payment of cash for them. For example, if the firm on average has 30 days to pay for labor and materials, if its cost of goods sold are $8 million per year, and if its accounts payable average $666,667, then its payables deferral period can be calculated as follows:

$$\frac{\text{Payables}}{\text{deferral}} = \frac{\text{Payables}}{\text{Purchases per day}}$$
$$\text{period}$$

$$= \frac{\text{Payables}}{\text{Cost of goods sold}/360} \tag{16A-3}$$

$$= \frac{\$666,667}{\$8,000,000/360}$$

$$= 30 \text{ days.}$$

The calculated figure is consistent with the stated 30-day payment period.

4. *Cash conversion cycle,* which nets out the three periods just defined and which therefore equals the length of time between the firm's actual cash expenditures to pay for productive resources (materials and labor) and its own cash receipts from the sale of products (that is, the length of time between paying for labor and materials and collecting on receivables). The cash conversion cycle thus equals the average length of time a dollar is tied up in current assets.

We can now use these definitions to analyze the cash conversion cycle. First, the concept is diagrammed in Figure 16A-1. Each component is given a number, and the cash conversion cycle can be expressed by this equation:

$$
\begin{array}{ccccccc}
(1) & + & (2) & - & (3) & = & (4) \\
\text{Inventory} & & \text{Receivables} & & \text{Payables} & & \text{Cash} \\
\text{conversion} & + & \text{collection} & - & \text{deferral} & = & \text{conversion .} \\
\text{period} & & \text{period} & & \text{period} & & \text{cycle}
\end{array} \tag{16A-4}
$$

To illustrate, suppose it takes Real Time an average of 72 days to convert raw materials to computers and then to sell them, and another 24 days to collect on receivables. However, 30 days normally elapse between receipt of raw

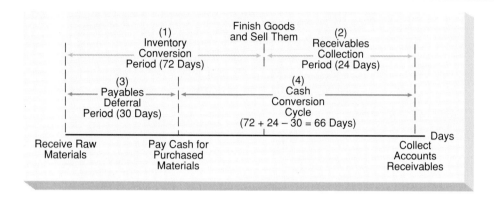

materials and payment for them. In this case, the cash conversion cycle would be 66 days:

$$72 \text{ days} + 24 \text{ days} - 30 \text{ days} = 66 \text{ days}.$$

To look at it another way,

Cash inflow delay   − Payment delay = Net delay

$$(72 \text{ days} + 24 \text{ days}) - \quad 30 \text{ days} \quad = 66 \text{ days}.$$

Given these data, RTC knows when it starts producing a computer that it will have to finance the manufacturing costs for a 66-day period. The firm's goal should be to shorten its cash conversion cycle as much as possible without hurting operations. This would improve profits, because the longer the cash conversion cycle, the greater the need for external financing, and that financing has a cost.

The cash conversion cycle can be shortened (1) by reducing the inventory conversion period by processing and selling goods more quickly, (2) by reducing the receivables collection period by speeding up collections, or (3) by lengthening the payables deferral period by slowing down the firm's own payments. To the extent that these actions can be taken *without increasing costs or depressing sales,* they should be carried out.

We can illustrate the benefits of shortening the cash conversion cycle by looking again at Real Time Computer Corporation. Suppose RTC must spend $200,000 on materials and labor to produce one computer, and it takes three days to produce a computer. Thus, it must invest $200,000/3 = $66,667 for each day's production. This investment must be financed for 66 days — the length of the cash conversion cycle — so the company's working capital financing needs will be 66 × $66,667 = $4.4 million. If RTC could reduce the cash conversion cycle to 56 days, say, by deferring payment of its accounts payable an additional 10 days, or by speeding up either the production process or the collection of its receivables, it could reduce its working capital financing requirements by $666,667. We see, then, that actions which affect the inventory conversion period, the receivables collection period, and the payables deferral period all affect the cash conversion cycle, hence they influence the firm's need for current assets and current asset financing. You should keep the cash conversion cycle concept in mind as you go through the other chapters on working capital management.

PROBLEMS

16A-1
Working capital investment

The Prestopino Corporation is a leading U.S. producer of automobile batteries. Prestopino turns out 1,500 batteries a day at a cost of $6 per battery for materials and labor. It takes the firm 22 days to convert raw materials into a battery. Prestopino allows its customers 40 days in which to pay for the batteries, and the firm generally pays its suppliers in 30 days.

a. What is the length of Prestopino's cash conversion cycle?

b. At a steady state in which Prestopino produces 1,500 batteries a day, what amount of working capital must it finance?

c. By what amount could Prestopino reduce its working capital financing needs if it was able to stretch its payables deferral period to 35 days?

d. Prestopino's management is trying to analyze the effect of a proposed new production process on the working capital investment. The new production process would allow Prestopino to decrease its inventory conversion period to 20 days and to increase its daily production to 1,800 batteries. However, the new process would cause the cost of materials and labor to increase to $7. Assuming the change does not affect the receivables collection period (40 days) or the payables deferral period (30 days), what will be the length of the cash conversion cycle and the working capital financing requirement if the new production process is implemented?

16A-2
Cash conversion cycle

The Zocco Corporation has an inventory conversion period of 75 days, a receivables collection period of 38 days, and a payables deferral period of 30 days.

a. What is the length of the firm's cash conversion cycle?

b. If Zocco's annual sales are $3,375,000 and all sales are on credit, what is the firm's investment in accounts receivable?

c. How many times per year does Zocco turn over its inventory?

16A-3
Working capital cash flow cycle

The Christie Corporation is trying to determine the effect of its inventory turnover ratio and days sales outstanding (DSO) on its cash flow cycle. Christie's 1997 sales (all on credit) were $150,000, and it earned a net profit of 6 percent, or $9,000. It turned over its inventory 6 times during the year, and its DSO was 36 days. The firm had fixed assets totaling $40,000. Christie's payables deferral period is 40 days.

a. Calculate Christie's cash conversion cycle.

b. Assuming Christie holds negligible amounts of cash and marketable securities, calculate its total assets turnover and ROA.

c. Suppose Christie's managers believe that the inventory turnover can be raised to 8 times. What would Christie's cash conversion cycle, total assets turnover, and ROA have been if the inventory turnover had been 8 for 1997?

CHAPTER 17

FINANCING
CURRENT ASSETS

The last chapter discussed steps Core Industries has taken to improve its working capital management. Core reduced its cash, receivables, and inventories, and the result was lower operating costs and higher profits. Even so, Core still has substantial holdings of current assets, and the funds invested in these assets must be obtained from some source. This involves "working capital financing policy," the focus of the current chapter.

Most firms use several types of short-term debt to finance their working capital requirements. Included are bank loans, trade credit, commercial paper, and accruals. However, companies structure their current liabilities in a manner that depends on the nature of their business. For example, the sales of Toys R Us are very seasonal— nearly half of all sales occur in the final three months of the year. To meet holiday demands, Toys R Us must dramatically increase its inventories during the summer and early fall. This inventory buildup must be financed until after Christmas, when collections bring cash into the till

SOUND WORKING CAPITAL POLICY REQUIRES APPROPRIATE FINANCING

and debts can be reduced. The company finances the buildup with trade credit, loans from U.S. and foreign banks, commercial paper, and the sale of marketable securities built up during the slack season.

Short-term credit is generally cheaper than long-term capital, but it is a riskier, less dependable source of financing. Interest rates can increase dramatically, and changes in a company's financial position can affect both the cost and availability of short-term credit.

Core Industries finances its working capital in several ways. First, it uses trade credit and accruals because such credit is essentially free. In addition, it uses bank loans, including a five-year, $50 million revolving credit agreement. Currently, Core is highly liquid, and it is in a good position to finance internal growth, to acquire other companies, or both.

After you have completed this chapter, you will have a better understanding of the various ways corporations finance their current assets, and of the costs associated with each type of financing.

In the last chapter, we discussed the first step in working capital management — determining the optimal level for each type of current asset. Now we turn to the second step — financing current assets. We begin with a discussion of alternative financing policies.

ALTERNATIVE CURRENT ASSET FINANCING POLICIES

Most businesses experience seasonal and/or cyclical fluctuations. For example, construction firms have peaks in the spring and summer, retailers peak around Christmas, and the manufacturers who supply both construction companies and retailers follow similar patterns. Similarly, virtually all businesses must build up current assets when the economy is strong, but they then sell off inventories and reduce receivables when the economy slacks off. Still, current assets rarely drop to zero — companies have some **permanent current assets,** which are the current assets on hand at the low point of the cycle. Then, as sales increase during the upswing, current assets must be increased, and these additional current assets are defined as **temporary current assets.** The manner in which the permanent and temporary current assets are financed is called the firm's *current asset financing policy.*

MATURITY MATCHING, OR "SELF-LIQUIDATING," APPROACH

The **maturity matching,** or **"self-liquidating," approach** calls for matching asset and liability maturities as shown in Panel a of Figure 17-1. This strategy minimizes the risk that the firm will be unable to pay off its maturing obligations. To illustrate, suppose a company borrows on a one-year basis and uses the funds obtained to build and equip a plant. Cash flows from the plant (profits plus depreciation) would not be sufficient to pay off the loan at the end of only one year, so the loan would have to be renewed. If for some reason the lender refused to renew the loan, then the company would have problems. Had the plant been financed with long-term debt, however, the required loan payments would have been better matched with cash flows from profits and depreciation, and the problem of renewal would not have arisen.

At the limit, a firm could attempt to match exactly the maturity structure of its assets and liabilities. Inventory expected to be sold in 30 days could be financed with a 30-day bank loan; a machine expected to last for 5 years could be financed with a 5-year loan; a 20-year building could be financed with a 20-year mortgage bond; and so forth. Actually, of course, two factors prevent this exact maturity matching: (1) there is uncertainty about the lives of assets, and (2) some common equity must be used, and common equity has no maturity. To illustrate the uncertainty factor, a firm might finance inventories with a 30-day loan, expecting to sell the inventories and then use the cash to retire the loan. But if sales were slow, the cash would not be forthcoming, and the use of short-term credit could end up causing a problem. Still, if a firm makes an attempt to match asset and liability maturities, we would define this as a moderate current asset financing policy.

Permanent Current Assets
Current assets that a firm must carry even at the trough of its cycles.

Temporary Current Assets
Current assets that fluctuate with seasonal or cyclical variations in sales.

Maturity Matching, or "Self-Liquidating," Approach
A financing policy that matches asset and liability maturities. This is a moderate policy.

FIGURE 17-1 Alternative Current Asset Financing Policies

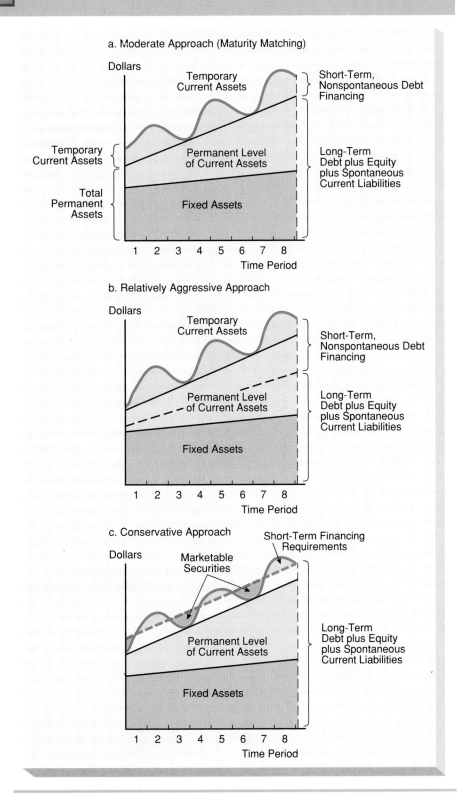

a. Moderate Approach (Maturity Matching)

b. Relatively Aggressive Approach

c. Conservative Approach

AGGRESSIVE APPROACH

Panel b of Figure 17-1 illustrates the situation for a relatively aggressive firm which finances all of its fixed assets with long-term capital and part of its permanent current assets with short-term, nonspontaneous credit. Note that we used the term "relatively" in the title for Panel b because there can be different *degrees* of aggressiveness. For example, the dashed line in Panel b could have been drawn *below* the line designating fixed assets, indicating that all of the permanent current assets and part of the fixed assets were financed with short-term credit; this would be a highly aggressive, extremely nonconservative position, and the firm would be very much subject to dangers from rising interest rates as well as to loan renewal problems. However, short-term debt is often cheaper than long-term debt, and some firms are willing to sacrifice safety for the chance of higher profits.

CONSERVATIVE APPROACH

Panel c of Figure 17-1 has the dashed line *above* the line designating permanent current assets, indicating that permanent capital is being used to finance all permanent asset requirements and also to meet some of the seasonal needs. In this situation, the firm uses a small amount of short-term, nonspontaneous credit to meet its peak requirements, but it also meets a part of its seasonal needs by "storing liquidity" in the form of marketable securities. The humps above the dashed line represent short-term financing, while the troughs below the dashed line represent short-term security holdings. Panel c represents a very safe, conservative current asset financing policy.

Chrysler, which in 1996 had $8.7 billion of cash and marketable securities, fits the Panel c pattern. Its chairman, Robert Eaton, stated that these liquid assets will be needed during the next recession, and he cited as evidence the fact that Chrysler had an operating cash deficit of more than $4 billion during the 1991–1992 recession. However, some of Chrysler's stockholders, notably Lee Iacocca and Kirk Kerkorian, argued that only $2 billion was necessary. They felt that Chrysler could borrow funds in the future if need be, so the extra $6.7 billion should be redeployed to earn more than the 3 percent after taxes it was getting. The Chrysler example illustrates the fact that there is no clear, precise answer to the question of how much cash and securities a firm should hold.

SELF-TEST QUESTIONS

What is meant by the term "permanent current assets"?

What is meant by the term "temporary current assets"?

What is meant by the term "current asset financing policy"?

What are three alternative current asset financing policies? Is one best?

ADVANTAGES AND DISADVANTAGES OF SHORT-TERM FINANCING

The three possible financing policies described above were distinguished by the relative amounts of short-term debt used under each policy. The aggressive policy called for the greatest use of short-term debt, while the conservative policy called for the least. Maturity matching fell in between. Although short-term credit is generally riskier than long-term credit, using short-term funds does have some significant advantages. The pros and cons of short-term financing are considered in this section.

SPEED

A short-term loan can be obtained much faster than long-term credit. Lenders will insist on a more thorough financial examination before extending long-term credit, and the loan agreement will have to be spelled out in considerable detail because a lot can happen during the life of a 10- to 20-year loan. Therefore, if funds are needed in a hurry, the firm should look to the short-term markets.

FLEXIBILITY

If its needs for funds are seasonal or cyclical, a firm may not want to commit itself to long-term debt for three reasons: (1) Flotation costs are higher for long-term debt than for short-term credit. (2) Although long-term debt can be repaid early, provided the loan agreement includes a prepayment provision, prepayment penalties can be expensive. Accordingly, if a firm thinks its need for funds will diminish in the near future, it should choose short-term debt. (3) Long-term loan agreements always contain provisions, or covenants, which constrain the firm's future actions. Short-term credit agreements are generally less restrictive.

COST OF LONG-TERM VERSUS SHORT-TERM DEBT

The yield curve is normally upward sloping, indicating that interest rates are generally lower on short-term debt. Thus, under normal conditions, interest costs at the time the funds are obtained will be lower if the firm borrows on a short-term rather than a long-term basis.

RISKS OF LONG-TERM VERSUS SHORT-TERM DEBT

Even though short-term rates are often lower than long-term rates, short-term credit is riskier for two reasons: (1) If a firm borrows on a long-term basis, its interest costs will be relatively stable over time, but if it uses short-term credit, its interest expense will fluctuate widely, at times going quite high. For example, the rate banks charge large corporations for short-term debt more than tripled over a two-year period in the 1980s, rising from 6.25 to 21 percent. Many firms that had borrowed heavily on a short-term basis simply could not meet their rising interest costs, and as a result, bankruptcies hit record levels during that period. (2) If a firm borrows heavily on a short-term basis, a temporary recession may render it unable to repay this debt. If the borrower is in a weak financial position, the lender may not extend the loan, which could force the firm into bankruptcy. Braniff Airlines, which failed during a credit crunch in the 1980s, is an example.

Another good example of the riskiness of short-term debt is provided by Transamerica Corporation, a major financial services company. Transamerica's chairman, Mr. Beckett, described how his company was moving to reduce its dependency on short-term loans whose costs vary with short-term interest rates. According to Beckett, Transamerica had reduced its variable-rate (short-term) loans by about $450 million over a two-year period. "We aren't going to go through the enormous increase in debt expense again that had such a serious impact on earnings," he said. The company's earnings fell sharply because money rates rose to record highs. "We were almost entirely in variable-rate debt," he said, but currently "about 65 percent is fixed rate and 35 percent variable. We've come a long way, and we'll keep plugging away at it." Transamerica's earnings were badly depressed by the increase in short-term rates, but other companies were even less fortunate — they simply could not pay the rising interest charges, and this forced them into bankruptcy.

SELF-TEST QUESTION   ??????

What are the advantages and disadvantages of short-term debt over long-term debt?

SOURCES OF SHORT-TERM FINANCING

Statements about the flexibility, cost, and riskiness of short-term versus long-term debt depend, to a large extent, on the type of short-term credit that is actually used. There are numerous sources of short-term funds, and in the following sections we describe four major types: (1) accruals, (2) accounts payable (trade credit), (3) bank loans, and (4) commercial paper.

ACCRUALS

Accruals
Continually recurring short-term liabilities, especially accrued wages and accrued taxes.

Firms generally pay employees on a weekly, biweekly, or monthly basis, so the balance sheet will typically show some accrued wages. Similarly, the firm's own estimated income taxes, Social Security and income taxes withheld from employee payrolls, and sales taxes collected are generally paid on a weekly, monthly, or quarterly basis, hence the balance sheet will typically show some accrued taxes along with accrued wages.

These **accruals** increase automatically, or spontaneously, as a firm's operations expand. Further, this type of debt is "free" in the sense that no explicit interest is paid on funds raised through accruals. However, a firm cannot ordinarily control its accruals: The timing of wage payments is set by economic forces and industry custom, while tax payment dates are established by law. Thus, firms use all the accruals they can, but they have little control over the levels of these accounts.

SELF-TEST QUESTIONS   ??????

What types of short-term credit are classified as accruals?

What is the cost of accruals?

How much control do financial managers have over the dollar amount of accruals?

Trade Credit
Debt arising from credit sales and recorded as an account receivable by the seller and as an account payable by the buyer.

ACCOUNTS PAYABLE (TRADE CREDIT)

Firms generally make purchases from other firms on credit, recording the debt as an *account payable*. Accounts payable, or **trade credit,** is the largest single category of short-term debt, representing about 40 percent of the current liabilities of the average nonfinancial corporation. The percentage is somewhat larger for smaller firms: Because small companies often do not qualify for financing from other sources, they rely especially heavily on trade credit.[1]

Trade credit is a "spontaneous" source of financing in the sense that it arises from ordinary business transactions. For example, suppose a firm makes average purchases of $2,000 a day on terms of net 30, meaning that it must pay for goods 30 days after the invoice date. On average, it will owe 30 times $2,000, or $60,000, to its suppliers. If its sales, and consequently its purchases, were to double, then its accounts payable would also double, to $120,000. So, simply by growing, the firm would spontaneously generate an additional $60,000 of financing. Similarly, if the terms under which it bought were extended from 30 to 40 days, its accounts payable would expand from $60,000 to $80,000. Thus, lengthening the credit period, as well as expanding sales and purchases, generates additional financing.

THE COST OF TRADE CREDIT

Firms that sell on credit have a *credit policy* that includes certain *terms of credit*. For example, Microchip Electronics sells on terms of 2/10, net 30, meaning that it gives its customers a 2 percent discount if they pay within 10 days of the invoice date, but the full invoice amount is due and payable within 30 days if the discount is not taken.

Note that the true price of Microchip's products is the net price, or 0.98 times the list price, because any customer can purchase an item at that price as long as the customer pays within 10 days. Now consider Personal Computer Company (PCC), which buys its memory chips from Microchip. One commonly used memory chip is listed at $100, so the "true" price to PCC is $98. Now if PCC wants an additional 20 days of credit beyond the 10-day discount period, it must incur a finance charge of $2 per chip for that credit. Thus, the $100 list price consists of two components:

$$\text{List price} = \$98 \text{ true price} + \$2 \text{ finance charge.}$$

The question PCC must ask before it turns down the discount to obtain the additional 20 days of credit from Microchip is this: Could we obtain credit under better terms from some other lender, say, a bank? In other words, could 20 days of credit be obtained for less than $2 per chip?

PCC buys an average of $11,760,000 of memory chips from Microchip each year at the net, or true, price. This amounts to $11,760,000/360 = $32,666.67 per day. For simplicity, assume that Microchip is PCC's only supplier. If PCC decides not to take the additional trade credit — that is, if it pays on the 10th day and takes the discount — its payables will average 10($32,666.67) = $326,667. Thus, PCC will be receiving $326,667 of credit from Microchip.

Now suppose PCC decides to take the additional 20 days credit and thus must pay the finance charge. Since PCC will now pay on the 30th day, its accounts

---

[1]In a credit sale, the seller records the transaction as a receivable, the buyer as a payable. We examined accounts receivable as an asset in Chapter 16. Our focus in this chapter is on accounts payable, a liability item. We might also note that if a firm's accounts payable exceed its receivables, it is said to be *receiving net trade credit,* whereas if its receivables exceed its payables, it is *extending net trade credit.* Smaller firms frequently receive net credit; larger firms generally extend it.

payable will increase to 30($32,666.67) = $980,000.[2] Microchip will now be supplying PCC with an additional $980,000 − $326,667 = $653,333 of credit, which PCC could use to build up its cash account, to pay off debt, to expand inventories, or even to extend credit to its own customers, hence increasing its own accounts receivable.

The additional trade credit offered by Microchip has a cost — PCC must pay a finance charge equal to the 2 percent discount it is foregoing. PCC buys $11,760,000 of chips at the true price, and the added finance charges increase the total cost to $11,760,000/0.98 = $12 million. Therefore, the annual financing cost is $12,000,000 − $11,760,000 = $240,000. Dividing the $240,000 financing cost by the $653,333 of additional credit, we find the nominal annual cost rate of the additional trade credit to be 36.7 percent:

$$\text{Nominal annual cost} = \frac{\$240,000}{\$653,333} = 36.7\%.$$

If PCC can borrow from its bank (or from other sources) at an interest rate less than 36.7 percent, it should take discounts and forgo the additional trade credit.

The following equation can be used to calculate the nominal cost, on an annual basis, of not taking discounts, illustrated with terms of 2/10, net 30:

$$\frac{\text{Nominal annual cost}}{} = \frac{\text{Discount percent}}{100 - \frac{\text{Discount}}{\text{percent}}} \times \frac{360 \text{ days}}{\text{Days credit is outstanding} - \frac{\text{Discount}}{\text{period}}}. \quad (17\text{-}1)$$

$$= \frac{2}{98} \times \frac{360}{20} = 2.04\% \times 18 = 36.7\%.$$

The numerator of the first term, Discount percent, is the cost per dollar of credit, while the denominator in this term, 100 − Discount percent, represents the funds made available by not taking the discount. Thus, the first term, 2.04%, is the cost per period for the trade credit. The denominator of the second term is the number of days of extra credit obtained by not taking the discount, so the entire second term shows how many times each year the cost is incurred, 18 times in this example.

The nominal annual cost formula does not take account of compounding, and in effective annual interest terms, the cost of trade credit is even higher. The discount amounts to interest, and with terms of 2/10, net 30, the firm gains use of the funds for 30 − 10 = 20 days, so there are 360/20 = 18 "interest periods" per year. Remember that the first term in Equation 17-1, (Discount percent)/(100 − Discount percent) = 0.02/0.98 = 0.0204, is the periodic interest rate. This rate is paid 18 times each year, so the effective annual cost of trade credit is

$$\text{Effective annual rate} = (1.0204)^{18} - 1.0 = 1.439 - 1.0 = 43.9\%.$$

Thus, the 36.7 percent nominal cost calculated with Equation 17-1 understates the true cost.

Notice, however, that the cost of trade credit can be reduced by paying late. Thus, if PCC could get away with paying in 60 days rather than in the specified

---

[2]A question arises here: Should accounts payable reflect gross purchases or purchases net of discounts? Generally accepted accounting principles permit either treatment if the difference is not material, but if the discount is material, then the transaction must be recorded net of discounts, or at "true" prices. Then, the higher payment that results from not taking discounts is reported as an additional expense called "discounts lost." *Thus, we show accounts payable net of discounts even if the company does not expect to take discounts.*

30 days, then the effective credit period would become $60 - 10 = 50$ days, the number of times the discount would be lost would fall to $360/50 = 7.2$, and the nominal cost would drop from 36.7 percent to $2.04\% \times 7.2 = 14.7\%$. The effective annual rate would drop from 43.9 to 15.7 percent:

$$\text{Effective annual rate} = (1.0204)^{7.2} - 1.0 = 1.157 - 1.0 = 15.7\%.$$

Stretching Accounts Payable
The practice of deliberately paying late.

In periods of excess capacity, firms may be able to get away with deliberately paying late, or **stretching accounts payable.** However, they will also suffer a variety of problems associated with being branded a "slow payer." These problems are discussed later in the chapter.

The costs of the additional trade credit from forgoing discounts under some other purchase terms are shown below:

CREDIT TERMS	COST OF ADDITIONAL CREDIT IF THE CASH DISCOUNT IS NOT TAKEN	
	NOMINAL COST	EFFECTIVE COST
1/10, net 20	36.4%	43.6%
1/10, net 30	18.2	19.8
2/10, net 20	73.5	106.9
3/15, net 45	37.1	44.1

As these figures show, the cost of not taking discounts can be substantial. Incidentally, throughout the chapter, we assume that payments are made either on the *last day* for taking discounts or on the *last day* of the credit period, unless otherwise noted. It would be foolish to pay, say, on the 5th day or on the 20th day if the credit terms were 2/10, net 30.[3]

EFFECTS OF TRADE CREDIT ON THE FINANCIAL STATEMENTS

A firm's policy with regard to taking or not taking discounts can have a significant effect on its financial statements. To illustrate, assume that PCC is just beginning its operations. On the first day, it makes net purchases of $32,666.67. This amount is recorded on its balance sheet under accounts payable.[4] The second day it buys another $32,666.67. The first day's purchases are not yet paid for, so at the end of the second day, accounts payable total $65,333.34. Accounts payable increase by another $32,666.67 on the third day, for a total of $98,000, and after ten days, accounts payable are up to $326,667.

If PCC takes discounts, then on the 11th day it will have to pay for the $32,666.67 of purchases made on the first day, which will reduce accounts

---

[3] A financial calculator can also be used to determine the cost of trade credit. If the terms of credit are 2/10, net 30, this implies that for every $100 of goods purchased at the full list price, the customer has the choice of paying the full amount in 30 days or else paying $98 in 10 days. If a customer decides not to take the discount, then it is in effect borrowing $98, the amount it would otherwise have to pay, from Day 11 to Day 30, or for 20 days. It will then have to pay $100, which is the $98 loan plus a $2 financing charge, at the end of the 20-day loan period. To calculate the interest rate, enter $N = 1$, $PV = 98$, $PMT = 0$, $FV = -100$, and then press I to obtain 2.04 percent. This is the rate for 20 days. To calculate the effective annual interest rate on a 360-day basis, enter $N = 20/360 = 0.05556$, $PV = 98$, $PMT = 0$, $FV = -100$, and then press I to obtain 43.86 percent. The $20/360 = 0.05556$ is the fraction of a year the "loan" is outstanding, and the 43.86 percent is the annualized cost of not taking discounts.

[4] Inventories also increase by $32,666.67, but we are not now concerned with inventories. Again, note that both inventories and receivables are recorded net of discounts regardless of whether discounts are taken.

payable. However, it will buy another $32,666.67, which will increase payables. Thus, after the 10th day of operations, PCC's balance sheet will level off, showing a balance of $326,667 in accounts payable, assuming the company pays on the 10th day and takes discounts.

Now suppose PCC decides not to take discounts. In this case, on the 11th day it will add another $32,666.67 to payables, but it will not pay for the purchases made on the 1st day. Thus, the balance sheet figure for accounts payable will rise to 11($32,666.67) = $359,333.37. This buildup will continue through the 30th day, at which point payables will total 30($32,666.67) = $980,000. On the 31st day, PCC will buy another $32,666.67 of goods, which will increase accounts payable, but it will also pay for the purchases made the 1st day, which will reduce payables. Thus, its accounts payable will stabilize at $980,000 after 30 days if it does not take discounts.

The top section of Table 17-1 shows PCC's balance sheet, after it reaches a steady state, under the two trade credit policies. Total assets are unchanged by this policy decision, and we also assume that the accruals and common equity accounts are unchanged. The differences show up in accounts payable and notes payable; when PCC elects to take discounts and thus gives up some of the trade

T A B L E 1 7 - 1	PCC's Financial Statements with Different Trade Credit Policies		
	TAKE DISCOUNTS; BORROW FROM BANK (1)	DO NOT TAKE DISCOUNTS; USE MAXIMUM TRADE CREDIT (2)	DIFFERENCE (1) − (2)
I. Balance Sheets			
Cash	$ 500,000	$ 500,000	$ 0
Receivables	1,000,000	1,000,000	0
Inventories	2,000,000	2,000,000	0
Fixed assets	2,980,000	2,980,000	0
Total assets	$ 6,480,000	$ 6,480,000	$ 0
Accounts payable	$ 326,667	$ 980,000	$−653,333
Notes payable (10%)	653,333	0	+653,333
Accruals	500,000	500,000	0
Common equity	5,000,000	5,000,000	0
Total claims	$ 6,480,000	$ 6,480,000	$ 0
II. Income Statements			
Sales	$15,000,000	$15,000,000	$ 0
Less: Purchases	11,760,000	11,760,000	0
Labor	2,000,000	2,000,000	0
Interest	65,333	0	+65,333
Discounts lost	0	240,000	−240,000
Earnings before taxes (EBT)	$ 1,174,667	$ 1,000,000	$+174,667
Taxes (40%)	469,867	400,000	−69,867
Net income	$ 704,800	$ 600,000	$+104,800

credit it otherwise could have obtained, it will have to raise $653,333 from some other source. It could have sold more common stock, or it could have used long-term bonds, but it chose to use bank credit, which has a 10 percent cost and is reflected in the notes payable account.

The bottom section of Table 17-1 shows PCC's income statement under the two policies. If the company does not take discounts, then its interest expense will be zero, but it will have a $240,000 expense for discounts lost. On the other hand, if it does take discounts, it will incur an interest expense of $65,333, but it will avoid the cost of discounts lost. Since discounts lost exceed the interest expense, the take-discounts policy results in a higher net income and, thus, in a higher stock price.

COMPONENTS OF TRADE CREDIT: FREE VERSUS COSTLY

Free Trade Credit
Credit received during the discount period.

Costly Trade Credit
Credit taken in excess of free trade credit, whose cost is equal to the discount lost.

On the basis of the preceding discussion, trade credit can be divided into two components: (1) **free trade credit,** which involves credit received during the discount period and which for PCC amounts to 10 days' net purchases, or $326,667, and (2) **costly trade credit,** which involves credit in excess of the free trade credit and whose cost is an implicit one based on the forgone discounts.[5] PCC could obtain $653,333, or 20 days' net purchases, of nonfree trade credit at a nominal cost of 37 percent. *Firms should always use the free component, but they should use the costly component only after analyzing the cost of this capital to make sure that it is less than the cost of funds which could be obtained from other sources.* Under the terms of trade found in most industries, the costly component is relatively expensive, so stronger firms will avoid using it.

We noted earlier that firms sometimes can and do deviate from the stated credit terms, thus altering the percentage cost figures cited earlier. For example, a California manufacturing firm that buys on terms of 2/10, net 30, makes a practice of paying in 15 days (rather than 10), but it still takes discounts. Its treasurer simply waits until 15 days after receipt of the goods to pay, then writes a check for the invoiced amount less the 2 percent discount. The company's suppliers want its business, so they tolerate this practice. Similarly, a Wisconsin firm that also buys on terms of 2/10, net 30, does not take discounts, but it pays in 60 rather than in 30 days, thus "stretching" its trade credit. As we saw earlier, both practices reduce the calculated cost of trade credit. Neither of these firms is "loved" by its suppliers, and neither could continue these practices in times when suppliers were operating at full capacity and had order backlogs, but these practices can and do reduce the costs of trade credit during times when suppliers have excess capacity.

SELF-TEST QUESTIONS ??????

What is trade credit?

What is the difference between free trade credit and costly trade credit?

What is the formula for finding the nominal annual cost of trade credit? What is the formula for the effective annual cost rate of trade credit?

How does the cost of costly trade credit generally compare with the cost of short-term bank loans?

---

[5]There is some question as to whether any credit is really "free," because the supplier will have a cost of carrying receivables which must be passed on to the customer in the form of higher prices. Still, if suppliers sell on standard terms such as 2/10, net 30, and if the base price cannot be negotiated downward for early payment, then for all intents and purposes, the ten days of trade credit is indeed "free."

SHORT-TERM BANK LOANS

Commercial banks, whose loans generally appear on firms' balance sheets as notes payable, are second in importance to trade credit as a source of short-term financing.[6] The banks' influence is actually greater than it appears from the dollar amounts because banks provide *nonspontaneous* funds. As a firm's financing needs increase, it requests additional funds from its bank. If the request is denied, the firm may be forced to abandon attractive growth opportunities. The key features of bank loans are discussed in the following paragraphs.

MATURITY

Although banks do make longer-term loans, *the bulk of their lending is on a short-term basis* — about two-thirds of all bank loans mature in a year or less. Bank loans to businesses are frequently written as 90-day notes, so the loan must be repaid or renewed at the end of 90 days. Of course, if a borrower's financial position has deteriorated, the bank may refuse to renew the loan. This can mean serious trouble for the borrower.

PROMISSORY NOTE

Promissory Note
A document specifying the terms and conditions of a loan, including the amount, interest rate, and repayment schedule.

When a bank loan is approved, the agreement is executed by signing a **promissory note.** The note specifies (1) the amount borrowed; (2) the interest rate; (3) the repayment schedule, which can call for either a lump sum or a series of installments; (4) any collateral that might have to be put up as security for the loan; and (5) any other terms and conditions to which the bank and the borrower have agreed. When the note is signed, the bank credits the borrower's checking account with the funds, so on the borrower's balance sheet both cash and notes payable increase.

COMPENSATING BALANCES

Compensating Balance
A minimum checking account balance that a firm must maintain with a commercial bank, generally equal to 10 to 20 percent of the amount of loans outstanding.

Banks sometimes require borrowers to maintain an average demand deposit (checking account) balance equal to from 10 to 20 percent of the face amount of the loan. This is called a **compensating balance,** and such balances raise the effective interest rate on the loans. For example, if a firm needs $80,000 to pay off outstanding obligations, but if it must maintain a 20 percent compensating balance, then it must borrow $100,000 to obtain a usable $80,000. If the stated annual interest rate is 8 percent, the effective cost is actually 10 percent: $8,000 interest divided by $80,000 of usable funds equals 10 percent.[7]

---

[6]Although commercial banks remain the primary source of short-term loans, other sources are available. For example, GE Capital Corporation (GECC) had several billion dollars in commercial loans outstanding. Firms such as GECC, which was initially established to finance consumers' purchases of GE's durable goods, often find business loans to be more profitable than consumer loans.

[7]Note, however, that the compensating balance may be set as a minimum monthly *average,* and if the firm would maintain this average anyway, the compensating balance requirement would not raise the effective interest rate. Also, note that these *loan* compensating balances are added to any compensating balances that the firm's bank may require for *services performed,* such as clearing checks.

INFORMAL LINE OF CREDIT

Line of Credit
An informal arrangement in which a bank agrees to lend up to a specified maximum amount of funds during a designated period.

A **line of credit** is an informal agreement between a bank and a borrower indicating the maximum credit the bank will extend to the borrower. For example, on December 31, a bank loan officer might indicate to a financial manager that the bank regards the firm as being "good" for up to $80,000 during the forthcoming year, provided the borrower's financial condition does not deteriorate. If on January 10 the financial manager signs a promissory note for $15,000 for 90 days, this would be called "taking down" $15,000 of the total line of credit. This amount would be credited to the firm's checking account at the bank, and before repayment of the $15,000, the firm could borrow additional amounts up to a total of $80,000 outstanding at any one time.

REVOLVING CREDIT AGREEMENT

Revolving Credit Agreement
A formal, committed line of credit extended by a bank or other lending institution.

A **revolving credit agreement** is a formal line of credit often used by large firms. To illustrate, in 1997 Texas Petroleum Company negotiated a revolving credit agreement for $100 million with a group of banks. The banks were formally committed for four years to lend the firm up to $100 million if the funds were needed. Texas Petroleum, in turn, paid an annual commitment fee of ¼ of 1 percent on the unused balance of the commitment to compensate the banks for making the commitment. Thus, if Texas Petroleum did not take down any of the $100 million commitment during a year, it would still be required to pay a $250,000 annual fee, normally in monthly installments of $20,833.33. If it borrowed $50 million on the first day of the agreement, the unused portion of the line of credit would fall to $50 million, and the annual fee would fall to $125,000. Of course, interest would also have to be paid on the money Texas Petroleum actually borrowed. As a general rule, the interest rate on "revolvers" is pegged to the prime rate, the T-bill rate, or some other market rate, so the cost of the loan varies over time as interest rates change.[8] Texas Petroleum's rate was set at prime plus 0.5 percentage point.

Note that a revolving credit agreement is very similar to an informal line of credit, but with an important difference: The bank has a *legal obligation* to honor a revolving credit agreement, and it receives a commitment fee. Neither the legal obligation nor the fee exists under the informal line of credit.

SELF-TEST QUESTION

??????

Explain how a firm that expects to need funds during the coming year might make sure the needed funds will be available.

THE COST OF BANK LOANS

The cost of bank loans varies for different types of borrowers at any given point in time and for all borrowers over time. Interest rates are higher for riskier

---

[8]Each bank sets its own prime rate, but, because of competitive forces, most banks' prime rates are identical. Further, most banks follow the rate set by the large New York City banks.

In recent years many banks have been lending to the very strongest companies at rates below the prime rate. As we discuss later in this chapter, larger firms have ready access to the commercial paper market, and if banks want to do business with these larger companies, they must match, or at least come close to, the commercial paper rate.

Prime Rate
A published interest rate charged by commercial banks to large, strong borrowers.

borrowers, and rates are also higher on smaller loans because of the fixed costs involved in making and servicing loans. If a firm can qualify as a "prime credit" because of its size and financial strength, it can borrow at the **prime rate,** which at one time was the lowest rate banks charged. Rates on other loans are generally scaled up from the prime rate, but loans to very large, strong customers are made at rates below prime. Thus, loans to smaller, riskier borrowers are generally stated to carry an interest rate of "prime *plus* some number of percentage points," but loans to larger, less risky borrowers may have a rate stated as "prime *minus* some percentage points."

Bank rates vary widely over time depending on economic conditions and Federal Reserve policy. When the economy is weak, then (1) loan demand is usually slack, (2) inflation is low, and (3) the Fed also makes plenty of money available to the system. As a result, rates on all types of loans are relatively low. Conversely, when the economy is booming, loan demand is typically strong, the Fed restricts the money supply, and the result is high interest rates. As an indication of the kinds of fluctuations that can occur, the prime rate during 1980 rose from 11 percent to 21 percent in just four months, and it rose from 6 to 9 percent during 1994. The prime rate is currently (April 1997) 8.50 percent. Interest rates on other bank loans also vary, generally moving with the prime rate.

The terms on a short-term bank loan to a business are spelled out in the promissory note. Here are the key elements contained in most promissory notes:

1. **Interest only versus amortized.** Loans are either *interest-only,* meaning that only interest is paid during the life of the loan, and the principal is repaid when the loan matures, or *amortized,* meaning that some of the principal is repaid on each payment date. Amortized loans are called *installment loans.*

2. **Collateral.** If a short-term loan is secured by some specific collateral, generally accounts receivable or inventories, this fact is indicated in the note. If the collateral is to be kept on the premises of the borrower, then a form called a *UCC-1* (Uniform Commercial Code-1) is filed with the secretary of the state in which the collateral resides, along with a *Security Agreement* (also part of the Uniform Commercial Code) which describes the nature of the agreement. These filings prevent the borrower from using the same collateral to secure loans from different lenders, and they spell out conditions under which the lender can seize the collateral.

3. **Loan guarantees.** If the borrower is a small corporation, its bank will probably insist that the larger stockholders *personally guarantee* the loan. Banks have often seen a troubled company's owner divert assets from the company to some other entity he or she owned, so banks protect themselves by insisting on personal guarantees. However, stockholder guarantees are virtually impossible to get in the case of larger corporations which have many stockholders. Also, guarantees are unnecessary for proprietorships or partnerships because here the owners are already personally liable for the business's debts.

4. **Nominal, or stated, interest rate.** The interest rate can be either *fixed* or *floating.* If it floats, it is generally indexed to the bank's prime rate, to the T-bill rate, or to the London Inter-Bank Offer Rate (LIBOR). Most loans of any size ($25,000 and up) have floating rates if their maturities are greater than 90 days. The note will also indicate whether the bank uses a *360- or 365-day year* for purposes of calculating interest; most banks use a 360-day year.

5. **Frequency of interest payments.** If the note is on an interest-only basis, it will indicate *how frequently interest must be paid.* Interest is typically calculated on a daily basis but paid monthly.

6. **Maturity.** Long-term loans always have specific maturity dates. A short-term loan may or may not have a specified maturity. For example, a loan may mature in 30 days, 90 days, 6 months, or 1 year, or it may call for "payment on demand," in which case the loan can remain outstanding as long as the borrower wants to continue using the funds and the bank agrees. Banks virtually never call demand notes unless the borrower's creditworthiness deteriorates, so some "short-term loans" remain outstanding for years, with the interest rate floating with rates in the economy.

7. **Discount interest.** Most loans call for interest to be paid after it has been earned, but *discount loans* require that interest be paid in advance. If the loan is on a discount basis, the borrower actually receives less than the face amount of the loan, and this increases the loan's effective cost. We discuss discount loans in a later section.

8. **Add-on basis installment loans.** Auto loans and other types of consumer installment loans are generally set up on an "add-on basis," which means that interest charges over the life of the loan are calculated and then added to the face amount of the loan. Thus, the borrower signs a note for the funds received plus the interest. The add-on feature also raises the effective cost of a loan, as we demonstrate in a later section.

9. **Other cost elements.** As noted above, some loans require compensating balances, and revolving credit agreements often require commitment fees. Both of these conditions will be spelled out in the loan agreement, and both raise the effective cost of a loan above its stated nominal rate.

REGULAR, OR SIMPLE, INTEREST

Regular, or Simple, Interest
The situation when interest is not compounded, that is, interest is not earned on interest.

In this and the following sections, we explain how to calculate the effective cost of different bank loans. For illustrative purposes, we assume a loan of $10,000 at a nominal interest rate of 12 percent, with a 365-day year.

For business loans, the most common procedure is called **regular,** or **simple, interest,** based on an interest-only loan. We begin by dividing the nominal interest rate, 12 percent in this case, by 365 (or 360 in some cases) to get the rate per day:

$$\text{Interest rate per day} = \frac{\text{Nominal rate}}{\text{Days in year}} \tag{17-2}$$

$$= 0.12/365 = 0.00032876712.$$

This rate is then multiplied by the actual number of days during the specific payment period, and then times the amount of the loan. For example, if the loan is interest-only, with monthly payments, then the interest payment for January would be $101.92:

$$\text{Interest charge for period} = (\text{Days in period})(\text{Rate per day})(\text{Amount of loan}) \tag{17-3}$$

$$= (31 \text{ days})(0.00032876712)($10,000) = $101.92.$$

If interest were payable quarterly, and if there were 91 days in the particular quarter, then the interest payment would be $299.18. The annual interest would be

365 × 0.00032876712 × $10,000 = $1,200.00. Note that if the bank had based the interest calculation on a 360-day year, as most banks do, the interest charges would have been slightly higher, and the annual charge would have been $1,216.67. Obviously, banks use a 360-day year to boost their earnings.

The effective interest rate on a loan depends on how frequently interest must be paid — the more frequently, the higher the effective rate. We demonstrate this point with two time lines, one for interest paid once a year and one for quarterly payments:

Interest paid annually:

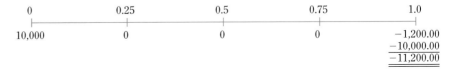

The borrower gets $10,000 at t = 0 and pays $11,200 at t = 1. With a financial calculator, enter N = 1, PV = 10000, PMT = 0, and FV = −11200, and then press I to get the effective cost of the loan, 12 percent.

Interest paid quarterly:

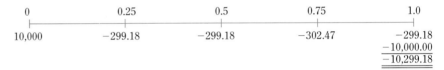

Note that the third quarter has 92 days. We enter the data in the cash flow register of a financial calculator (being sure to use the +/− key to enter −299.18), and we find the periodic rate to be 2.9999 percent. The effective annual rate is 12.55 percent:

$$\text{Effective annual rate, quarterly} = (1 + 0.029999)^4 - 1 = 12.55\%.$$

Had the loan called for interest to be paid monthly, the effective rate would have been 12.68 percent, and if interest had been paid daily, the rate would have been 12.75 percent. These rates would be higher if the bank used a 360-day year.

In these examples, we assumed that the loan matured in one year but that interest was paid at various times during the year. The rates we calculated would have been exactly the same as the ones above even if the loan had matured on each interest payment date. In other words, the effective rate on a monthly payment loan would be 12.68 percent regardless of whether it matured after one month, six months, one year, or ten years, providing the stated rate remains at 12 percent.

DISCOUNT INTEREST

Discount Interest
Interest that is calculated on the face amount of a loan but is paid in advance.

In a **discount interest** loan, the bank deducts the interest in advance (*discounts* the loan). Thus, the borrower receives less than the face value of the loan. On a one-year, $10,000 loan with a 12 percent (nominal) rate, discount basis, the interest is $10,000(0.12) = $1,200. Therefore, the borrower obtains the use of only $10,000 − $1,200 = $8,800. If the loan were for less than a year, the interest charge (the discount) would be lower; in our example, it would be $600 if the loan were for six months, hence the amount received would be $9,400.

INDUSTRY PRACTICE

THE TRAVAILS OF JAMESWAY

The recent travails of Jamesway Corporation, a retailer which operates primarily in the northeastern United States, provides a vivid illustration of the difficulty of maintaining an inexpensive source of funds. After 28 profitable years, Jamesway's financial position deteriorated as a result of unforeseen problems when it implemented a new automated merchandise ordering system. Order errors led to excessive inventory buildup, which, in turn, required the firm to mark down its goods and to book large losses.

Jamesway's lead lender, which had been providing the company with short-term credit to finance its inventories, cut its line of credit in half. The problems were exacerbated because a considerable amount of long-term debt was coming due in the near future. This situation caused suppliers to restrict credit to Jamesway, squeezing it still further. In the end, the company was unable to finance the purchase of inventory needed for the "Back-to-School" and Christmas holiday seasons, and it was forced to declare bankruptcy.

After working out a plan of reorganization, the company emerged from bankruptcy in early 1995. Needless to say, a key element of the reorganization plan was to obtain a firmly committed line of credit.

The effective rate on a discount loan is always higher than the rate on an otherwise similar simple interest loan. To illustrate, consider the situation for a discounted 12 percent loan for one year:

Discount interest, paid annually:

0	0.25	0.5	0.75	1.0
10,000	0	0	0	−10,000
−1,200				
8,800				

With a financial calculator, enter N = 1, PV = 8800, PMT = 0, and FV = −10000, and then press I to get the effective cost of the loan, 13.64 percent.[9]

If a discount loan matures in less than a year, say, after one quarter, we have this situation:

Discount interest, one quarter:

0	0.25	0.5	0.75	1.0
10,000	−10,000	0	0	0
−300				
9,700				

---

[9]Note that the firm actually receives less than the face amount of the loan:

Funds received = Face amount of loan (1.0 − Nominal interest rate).

We can solve for the face amount as follows:

$$\text{Face amount of loan} = \frac{\text{Funds received}}{1.0 - \text{Nominal rate (decimal)}}.$$

Therefore, if the borrowing firm actually requires $10,000 of cash, it must borrow $11,363.64:

$$\text{Face value} = \frac{\$10,000}{1.0 - 0.12} = \frac{\$10,000}{0.88} = \$11,363.64.$$

Now, the borrower will receive $11,363.64 − 0.12($11,363.64) = $10,000. Increasing the face value of the loan does not change the effective rate of 13.64 percent on the $10,000 of usable funds.

Enter N = 1, PV = 9700, PMT = 0, and FV = −10000, and then press I to find the periodic rate, 3.092784 percent per quarter, which corresponds to an effective annual rate of 12.96 percent. Thus, shortening the period of a discount loan lowers the effective rate of interest. This occurs because there is a delay in paying interest relative to a longer-term discount loan ($300 paid each quarter rather than $1,200 paid up front).

EFFECTS OF COMPENSATING BALANCES

If the bank requires a compensating balance, and if the amount of the required balance exceeds the amount the firm would normally hold on deposit, then the excess must be deducted at t = 0 and then added back when the loan matures. This has the effect of raising the effective rate on the loan. To illustrate, here is the setup for a one-year discount loan, with a 20 percent compensating balance which the firm would not otherwise hold on deposit:

Discount interest, paid annually, with 20 percent compensating balance:

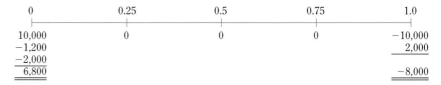

Note that the bank initially gives, and the borrower gets, $10,000 at time 0. However, the bank takes out the $1,200 of interest in advance, and the company must leave $2,000 in the bank as a compensating balance, hence the borrower's effective net cash flow at t = 0 is $6,800. At t = 1, the borrower must repay the $10,000, but $2,000 is already in the bank (the compensating balance), so the company must repay a net amount of $8,000.

With a financial calculator, enter N = 1, PV = 6800, PMT = 0, and FV = −8000, and then press I to get the effective cost of the discount loan with a compensating balance, 17.65 percent.

INSTALLMENT LOANS: ADD-ON INTEREST

Add-On Interest
Interest that is calculated and added to funds received to determine the face amount of an installment loan.

Lenders typically charge **add-on interest** on automobile and other types of installment loans. The term "add-on" means that the interest is calculated and then added to the amount received to determine the loan's face value. To illustrate, suppose you borrow $10,000 on an add-on basis at a nominal rate of 12 percent to buy a car, with the loan to be repaid in 12 monthly installments. At a 12 percent add-on rate, you will pay a total interest charge of $10,000(0.12) = $1,200. However, since the loan is paid off in monthly installments, you have the use of the full $10,000 for only the first month, and the outstanding balance declines until, during the last month, only $1/12$ of the original loan will still be outstanding. Thus, you are paying $1,200 for the use of only about half the loan's face amount, as the average usable funds is only about $5,000. Therefore, we can calculate the approximate annual rate as follows:

$$\text{Approximate annual rate}_{\text{Add-on}} = \frac{\text{Interest paid}}{(\text{Amount received})/2} \qquad \textbf{(17-4)}$$

$$= \frac{\$1,200}{\$10,000/2} = 24.0\%.$$

To determine the effective rate of an add-on loan, we proceed as follows:

1. The total amount to be repaid is $10,000 of principal, plus $1,200 of interest, or $11,200.

2. The monthly payment is $11,200/12 = $933.33.

3. You are, in effect, paying off a 12-period annuity of $933.33 in order to receive $10,000 today, so $10,000 is the present value of the annuity. Here is the time line:

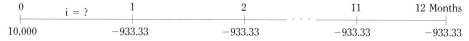

4. With a financial calculator, enter N = 12, PV = 10000, PMT = −933.33, FV = 0, and then press I to obtain 1.7880 percent. However, this is a monthly rate.

5. The effective annual rate is found as follows:[10]

$$\text{Effective annual rate}_{\text{Add-on}} = (1 + k_d)^n - 1.0$$
$$= (1.01788)^{12} - 1.0$$
$$= 1.2370 - 1.0 = 23.7\%.$$

Annual Percentage Rate (APR)
A rate reported by banks and other lenders on loans when the effective rate exceeds the nominal rate of interest.

The **annual percentage rate (APR),** which by law the bank is required to state in bold print on all "consumer loan" agreements, would be 21.46 percent:

$$\text{APR rate} = (\text{Periods per year})(\text{Rate per period})$$
$$= 12(1.7880\%) = 21.46\%.$$

Prior to the passage of the truth in lending laws in the 1970s, most banks would have called this a 12 percent loan, period. The truth in lending laws apply primarily to consumer as opposed to business loans.

SELF-TEST QUESTIONS ??????

What are some different ways banks can calculate interest on loans?

What is a compensating balance? What effect does a compensating balance requirement have on the effective interest rate on a loan?

CHOOSING A BANK

Individuals whose only contact with their bank is through the use of its checking services generally choose a bank for the convenience of its location and the competitive cost of its services. However, a business that borrows from banks must look at other criteria, and a potential borrower seeking a banking relationship should recognize that important differences exist among banks. Some of these differences are considered next.

---

[10]Note that if an installment loan is paid off ahead of schedule, additional complications arise. For the classic discussion of this point, see Dick Bonker, "The Rule of 78," *Journal of Finance*, June 1976, 877–888.

WILLINGNESS TO ASSUME RISKS

Banks have different basic policies toward risk. Some are inclined to follow relatively conservative lending practices, while others engage in what are properly termed "creative banking practices." These policies reflect partly the personalities of bank officers and partly the characteristics of the bank's deposit liabilities. Thus, a bank with fluctuating deposit liabilities in a static community will tend to be a conservative lender, while a bank whose deposits are growing with little interruption may follow more liberal credit policies. Similarly, a large bank with broad diversification over geographic regions and across industries can obtain the benefit of combining and averaging risks. Thus, marginal credit risks that might be unacceptable to a small or specialized bank can be pooled by a branch banking system to reduce the overall risk of a group of marginal accounts.[11]

ADVICE AND COUNSEL

Some bank loan officers are active in providing counsel and in stimulating development loans to firms in their early and formative years. Certain banks have specialized departments which make loans to firms expected to grow and thus to become more important customers. The personnel of these departments can provide valuable counseling to customers: The bankers' experience with other firms in growth situations may enable them to spot, and then to warn their customers about, developing problems.

LOYALTY TO CUSTOMERS

Banks differ in their support of borrowers in bad times. This characteristic is referred to as the degree of *loyalty* of the bank. Some banks may put great pressure on a business to liquidate its loans when the firm's outlook becomes clouded, whereas others will stand by the firm and work diligently to help it get back on its feet. An especially dramatic illustration of this point was Bank of America's bailout of Memorex Corporation. The bank could have forced Memorex into bankruptcy, but instead it loaned the company additional capital and helped it survive a bad period. Memorex's stock price subsequently rose from $1.50 to $68, so Bank of America's help was indeed beneficial.

SPECIALIZATION

Banks differ greatly in their degrees of loan specialization. Larger banks have separate departments that specialize in different kinds of loans — for example, real estate loans, farm loans, and commercial loans. Within these broad categories, there may be a specialization by line of business, such as steel, machinery, cattle, or textiles. The strengths of banks are also likely to reflect the nature of the business and the economic environment in which they operate. For example,

---

[11]Bank deposits are insured by a federal agency, and banks are required to pay premiums to cover the cost of this insurance. Logically, riskier banks should pay higher premiums, but to date political forces have limited the use of risk-based insurance premiums. As an alternative, banks with riskier loan portfolios are required to have more equity capital per dollar of deposits than less risky banks. The savings and loan industry, until the 1980s, had federal insurance, no differential capital requirements, and lax regulations. As a result, some S&L operators wrote very high interest rate, but very risky, loans using low-cost, insured deposits. If the loans paid off, the S&L owners would get rich. If they went into default, the taxpayers would have to pay off the deposits. Those government policies ended up costing taxpayers more than $100 billion.

some California banks have become specialists in lending to electronics companies, while many Midwestern banks are agricultural specialists. A sound firm can obtain more creative cooperation and more active support by going to a bank that has experience and familiarity with its particular type of business. Therefore, a bank that is excellent for one firm may be unsatisfactory for another.

MAXIMUM LOAN SIZE

The size of a bank can be an important factor. Since the maximum loan a bank can make to any one customer is limited to 15 percent of the bank's capital accounts (capital stock plus retained earnings), it is generally not appropriate for large firms to develop borrowing relationships with small banks.

MERCHANT BANKING

The term "merchant bank" was originally applied to banks which not only made loans but also provided customers with equity capital and financial advice. Prior to 1933, U.S. commercial banks performed all types of merchant banking functions. However, about one-third of the U.S. banks failed during the Great Depression, in part because of these activities, so in 1933 the Glass-Steagall Act was passed in an effort to reduce banks' exposure to risk. In recent years, commercial banks have been attempting to get back into merchant banking, in part because their foreign competitors offer such services, and U.S. banks compete with foreign banks for multinational corporations' business. Currently, the larger banks, often through subsidiaries, are being permitted to get back into merchant banking, at least to a limited extent. This trend will probably continue, and if it does, corporations will need to consider a bank's ability to provide a full range of commercial and merchant banking services when choosing a bank.

OTHER SERVICES

Banks can also provide cash management services, assist with electronic funds transfers, help firms obtain foreign exchange, and the like, and the availability of such services should be taken into account when selecting a bank. Also, if the firm is a small business whose manager owns most of its stock, the bank's willingness and ability to provide trust and estate services should also be considered.

SELF-TEST QUESTION

What are some factors that should be considered when choosing a bank?

COMMERCIAL PAPER

Commercial Paper
Unsecured, short-term promissory notes of large firms, usually issued in denominations of $100,000 or more and having an interest rate somewhat below the prime rate.

Commercial paper is a type of unsecured promissory note issued by large, strong firms and sold primarily to other business firms, to insurance companies, to pension funds, to money market mutual funds, and to banks. Although the amount of commercial paper outstanding is smaller than bank loans outstanding, this form of financing has grown in the last several years. In early 1996, there was approximately $720 billion of commercial paper outstanding, versus about $960 billion of bank loans. Much of this commercial paper outstanding is issued by financial institutions.

MATURITY AND COST

Maturities of commercial paper generally vary from one to nine months, with an average of about five months.[12] The interest rate on commercial paper fluctuates with supply and demand conditions — it is determined in the marketplace, varying daily as conditions change. Recently, commercial paper rates have ranged from 1½ to 3 percentage points below the stated prime rate, and about ⅛ to ½ of a percentage point above the T-bill rate. For example, on March 3, 1997, the average rate on three-month commercial paper was 5.43 percent, the stated prime rate was 8.25 percent, and the three-month T-bill rate was 5.21 percent.

USE OF COMMERCIAL PAPER

The use of commercial paper is restricted to a comparatively small number of very large concerns that are exceptionally good credit risks. Dealers prefer to handle the paper of firms whose net worth is $100 million or more and whose annual borrowing exceeds $10 million. One potential problem with commercial paper is that a debtor who is in temporary financial difficulty may receive little help because commercial paper dealings are generally less personal than are bank relationships. Thus, banks are generally more able and willing to help a good customer weather a temporary storm than is a commercial paper dealer. On the other hand, using commercial paper permits a corporation to tap a wide range of credit sources, including financial institutions outside its own area and industrial corporations across the country, and this can reduce interest costs.

SELF-TEST QUESTIONS

What is commercial paper?

What types of companies can use commercial paper to meet their short-term financing needs?

How does the cost of commercial paper compare with the cost of short-term bank loans? With the cost of Treasury bills?

USE OF SECURITY IN SHORT-TERM FINANCING

Thus far, we have not addressed the question of whether or not short-term loans should be secured. Commercial paper is never secured, but other types of loans can be secured if this is deemed necessary or desirable. Other things held constant, it is better to borrow on an unsecured basis, since the bookkeeping costs of **secured loans** are often high. However, firms often find that they can borrow only if they put up some type of collateral to protect the lender, or that by using security they can borrow at a much lower rate.

Several different kinds of collateral can be employed, including marketable stocks or bonds, land or buildings, equipment, inventory, and accounts receivable. Marketable securities make excellent collateral, but few firms that need loans also hold portfolios of stocks and bonds. Similarly, real property (land and buildings) and equipment are good forms of collateral, but they are generally used as

Secured Loan
A loan backed by collateral, often inventories or receivables.

---

[12]The maximum maturity without SEC registration is 270 days. Also, commercial paper can only be sold to "sophisticated" investors; otherwise, SEC registration would be required even for maturities of 270 days or less.

security for long-term loans rather than for working capital loans. Therefore, most secured short-term business borrowing involves the use of accounts receivable and inventories as collateral.

To understand the use of security, consider the case of a Chicago hardware dealer who wanted to modernize and expand his store. He requested a $200,000 bank loan. After examining his business's financial statements, the bank indicated that it would lend him a maximum of $100,000 and that the interest rate would be 10 percent, discount interest, for an effective rate of 11.1 percent. The owner had a substantial personal portfolio of stocks, and he offered to put up $300,000 of high-quality stocks to support the $200,000 loan. The bank then granted the full $200,000 loan, and at the prime rate of 8.25 percent, simple interest. The store owner might also have used his inventories or receivables as security for the loan, but processing costs would have been high. Procedures for using accounts receivable and inventories as security for short-term credit are described in Appendix 17A.[13]

SELF-TEST QUESTIONS ??????

What is a secured loan?

What are some types of current assets that are pledged as security for short-term loans?

SUMMARY

This chapter examined the types of credit that can be used to finance current assets. The key concepts covered are listed below.

◆ **Permanent current assets** are those current assets that the firm holds even during slack times, whereas **temporary current assets** are the additional current assets that are needed during seasonal or cyclical peaks. The methods used to finance permanent and temporary current assets define the firm's **current asset financing policy.**

◆ A **moderate** approach to current asset financing involves matching, to the extent possible, the maturities of assets and liabilities, so that temporary current assets are financed with short-term nonspontaneous debt, and permanent current assets and fixed assets are financed with long-term debt or equity, plus spontaneous debt. Under an **aggressive** approach, some permanent current assets, and perhaps even some fixed assets, are financed with short-term debt. A **conservative** approach would be to use long-term capital to finance all permanent assets and some of the temporary current assets.

◆ The advantages of short-term credit are (1) the **speed** with which short-term loans can be arranged, (2) increased **flexibility,** and (3) the fact that short-term **interest rates** are generally **lower** than long-term rates. The principal disadvantage of short-term credit is the **extra risk** the borrower must bear because (1) the lender can demand payment on short notice and (2) the cost of the loan will increase if interest rates rise.

---

[13]The term "asset-based financing" is often used as a synonym for "secured financing." In recent years, accounts receivable have been used as security for long-term bonds, and this permits corporations to borrow from lenders such as pension funds rather than being restricted to banks and other traditional short-term lenders.

- ♦ **Short-term credit** is defined as any liability originally scheduled for payment within one year. The four major sources of short-term credit are (1) accruals, (2) accounts payable, (3) loans from commercial banks and finance companies, and (4) commercial paper.

- ♦ **Accruals,** which are continually recurring short-term liabilities, represent free, spontaneous credit.

- ♦ **Accounts payable,** or **trade credit,** is the largest category of short-term debt. Trade credit arises spontaneously as a result of credit purchases. Firms should use all the **free trade credit** they can obtain, but they should use **costly trade credit** only if it is less expensive than other forms of short-term debt. Suppliers often offer discounts to customers who pay within a stated discount period. The following equation may be used to calculate the nominal cost, on an annual basis, of not taking discounts:

$$\frac{\text{Nominal}}{\text{cost}} = \frac{\text{Discount percent}}{100 - \frac{\text{Discount}}{\text{percent}}} \times \frac{360}{\frac{\text{Days credit}}{\text{is outstanding}} - \frac{\text{Discount}}{\text{period}}}.$$

- ♦ **Bank loans** are an important source of short-term credit. Interest on bank loans may be quoted as **simple interest, discount interest,** or **add-on interest.** The effective rate on a bank loan always exceeds the quoted nominal rate except for a simple interest loan where the interest is paid once a year.

- ♦ When a bank loan is approved, a **promissory note** is signed. It specifies: (1) the amount borrowed, (2) the percentage interest rate, (3) the repayment schedule, (4) the collateral, and (5) any other conditions to which the parties have agreed.

- ♦ Banks sometimes require borrowers to maintain **compensating balances,** which are deposit requirements set at between 10 and 20 percent of the loan amount. Compensating balances raise the effective interest rate on bank loans.

- ♦ **A line of credit** is an informal agreement between the bank and the borrower indicating the maximum amount of credit the bank will extend to the borrower.

- ♦ A **revolving credit agreement** is a formal line of credit often used by large firms; it involves a **commitment fee.**

- ♦ **Commercial paper** is unsecured short-term debt issued by large, financially strong corporations. Although the cost of commercial paper is lower than the cost of bank loans, it can be used only by large firms with exceptionally strong credit ratings.

- ♦ Sometimes a borrower will find that it is necessary to borrow on a **secured basis,** in which case the borrower pledges assets such as real estate, securities, equipment, inventories, or accounts receivable as collateral for the loan.

QUESTIONS

17-1 How does the seasonal nature of a firm's sales influence its decision regarding the amount of short-term credit to use in its financial structure?

17-2 What are the advantages of matching the maturities of assets and liabilities? What are the disadvantages?

17-3 From the standpoint of the borrower, is long-term or short-term credit riskier? Explain. Would it ever make sense to borrow on a short-term basis if short-term rates were above long-term rates?

17-4 If long-term credit exposes a borrower to less risk, why would people or firms ever borrow on a short-term basis?

17-5 "Firms can control their accruals within fairly wide limits; depending on the cost of accruals, financing from this source will be increased or decreased." Discuss.

17-6 Is it true that both trade credit and accruals represent a spontaneous source of capital for financing growth? Explain.

17-7 Is it true that most firms are able to obtain some free trade credit and that additional trade credit is often available, but at a cost? Explain.

17-8 The availability of bank credit is often more important to a small firm than to a large one. Why?

17-9 What kinds of firms use commercial paper? Could Mama and Papa Gus's Corner Grocery borrow using this form of credit?

17-10 Given that commercial paper interest rates are generally lower than bank loan rates to a given borrower, why might firms which are capable of selling commercial paper also use bank credit?

17-11 Suppose a firm can obtain funds by borrowing at the prime rate or by selling commercial paper.
a. If the prime rate is 8.25 percent, what is a reasonable estimate for the cost of commercial paper?
b. If a substantial cost differential exists, why might a firm like this one actually borrow some of its funds in each market?

SELF-TEST PROBLEMS (Solutions Appear in Appendix B)

ST-1
Key terms

Define each of the following terms:
a. Permanent current assets; temporary current assets
b. Moderate current asset financing policy; aggressive current asset financing policy; conservative current asset financing policy
c. Maturity matching, or "self-liquidating," approach
d. Accruals
e. Trade credit; stretching accounts payable; free trade credit; costly trade credit
f. Promissory note; line of credit; revolving credit agreement
g. Prime rate
h. Simple interest; discount interest; add-on interest
i. Compensating balance (CB)
j. Commercial paper
k. Secured loan

ST-2
Current asset financing

Vanderheiden Press Inc. and the Herrenhouse Publishing Company had the following balance sheets as of December 31, 1997 (thousands of dollars):

	VANDERHEIDEN PRESS	HERRENHOUSE PUBLISHING
Current assets	$100,000	$ 80,000
Fixed assets (net)	100,000	120,000
Total assets	$200,000	$200,000
Current liabilities	$ 20,000	$ 80,000
Long-term debt	80,000	20,000
Common stock	50,000	50,000
Retained earnings	50,000	50,000
Total liabilities and equity	$200,000	$200,000

Earnings before interest and taxes for both firms are $30 million, and the effective federal-plus-state tax rate is 40 percent.
a. What is the return on equity for each firm if the interest rate on current liabilities is 10 percent and the rate on long-term debt is 13 percent?
b. Assume that the short-term rate rises to 20 percent. While the rate on new long-term debt rises to 16 percent, the rate on existing long-term debt remains unchanged. What

would be the return on equity for Vanderheiden Press and Herrenhouse Publishing under these conditions?

c. Which company is in a riskier position? Why?

STARTER PROBLEMS

17-1
Cost of trade credit

What is the nominal and effective cost of trade credit (on a 360-day basis) under the credit terms of 3/15, net 30?

17-2
Cost of trade credit

A large retailer obtains merchandise under the credit terms of 1/15, net 45, but routinely takes 60 days to pay its bills. Given that the retailer is an important customer, suppliers allow the firm to stretch its credit terms. What is the retailer's effective cost of trade credit (on a 360-day basis)?

17-3
Accounts payable

A chain of appliance stores, APP Corporation, purchases inventory with a net price of $500,000 each day. The company purchases the inventory under the credit terms of 2/15, net 40. APP always takes the discount, but takes the full 15 days to pay its bills. What is the average accounts payable for APP?

17-4
Cost of bank loan

On March 1, Minnerly Motors obtained a business loan from a local bank. The loan is a $25,000 interest-only loan with a nominal rate of 11 percent. Interest is calculated on a simple interest basis with a 365-day year. What is Minnerly's interest charge for the first month (assuming 31 days in the month)?

17-5
Cost of bank loan

Mary Jones recently obtained an automobile loan from a local bank. The loan is for $15,000 with a nominal interest rate of 11 percent. However, this is an installment loan, so the bank also charges add-on interest. Mary must make monthly payments on the loan, and the loan is to be repaid in 1 year. What is the effective annual rate on the loan (assuming a 365-day year)?

EXAM-TYPE PROBLEMS

The problems included in this section are set up in such a way that they could be used as multiple-choice exam problems.

17-6
Cost of trade credit

Calculate the nominal annual cost of nonfree trade credit under each of the following terms. Assume payment is made either on the due date or on the discount date.
a. 1/15, net 20.
b. 2/10, net 60.
c. 3/10, net 45.
d. 2/10, net 45.
e. 2/15, net 40.

17-7
Cost of trade credit

a. If a firm buys under terms of 3/15, net 45, but actually pays on the 20th day and *still takes the discount*, what is the nominal cost of its nonfree trade credit?
b. Does it receive more or less credit than it would if it paid within 15 days?

17-8
Cost of bank loans

Del Hawley, owner of Hawley's Hardware, is negotiating with First City Bank for a $50,000, 1-year loan. First City has offered Hawley the following alternatives. Calculate the effective annual interest rate for each alternative. Which alternative has the lowest effective annual interest rate?
a. A 12 percent annual rate on a simple interest loan, with no compensating balance required and interest due at the end of the year.
b. A 9 percent annual rate on a simple interest loan, with a 20 percent compensating balance required and interest again due at the end of the year.
c. An 8.75 percent annual rate on a discounted loan, with a 15 percent compensating balance.
d. Interest is figured as 8 percent of the $50,000 amount, *payable at the end of the year,* but the $50,000 is repayable in monthly installments during the year.

17-9
Cost of trade credit

Grunewald Industries sells on terms of 2/10, net 40. Gross sales last year were $4.5 million, and accounts receivable averaged $437,500. Half of Grunewald's customers paid on the 10th day and took discounts. What are the nominal and effective costs of trade credit to Grunewald's nondiscount customers? (Hint: Calculate sales/day based on a 360-day year;

then get average receivables of discount customers; then find the DSO for the nondiscount customers.)

17-10
Effective cost of short-term credit

The D. J. Masson Corporation needs to raise $500,000 for 1 year to supply working capital to a new store. Masson buys from its suppliers on terms of 3/10, net 90, and it currently pays on the 10th day and takes discounts, but it could forgo discounts, pay on the 90th day, and get the needed $500,000 in the form of costly trade credit. Alternatively, Masson could borrow from its bank on a 12 percent discount interest rate basis. What is the effective annual interest rate of the lower-cost source?

17-11
Effective cost of short-term credit

Yonge Corporation must arrange financing for its working capital requirements for the coming year. Yonge can (a) borrow from its bank on a simple interest basis (interest payable at the end of the loan) for 1 year at a 12 percent nominal rate; (b) borrow on a 3-month, but renewable, loan at an 11.5 percent nominal rate; (c) borrow on an installment loan basis at a 6 percent add-on rate with 12 end-of-month payments; or (d) obtain the needed funds by no longer taking discounts and thus increasing its accounts payable. Yonge buys on terms of 1/15, net 60. What is the effective annual cost (*not* the nominal cost) of the *least expensive* type of credit, assuming 360 days per year?

PROBLEMS

17-12
Cash discounts

Suppose a firm makes purchases of $3.6 million per year under terms of 2/10, net 30, and takes discounts.
a. What is the average amount of accounts payable net of discounts? (Assume that the $3.6 million of purchases is net of discounts — that is, gross purchases are $3,673,469, discounts are $73,469, and net purchases are $3.6 million. Also, use 360 days in a year.)
b. Is there a cost of the trade credit the firm uses?
c. If the firm did not take discounts but it did pay on the due date, what would be its average payables and the cost of this nonfree trade credit?
d. What would its cost of not taking discounts be if it could stretch its payments to 40 days?

17-13
Trade credit versus bank credit

The Thompson Corporation projects an increase in sales from $1.5 million to $2 million, but it needs an additional $300,000 of current assets to support this expansion. The money can be obtained from the bank at an interest rate of 13 percent, discount interest; no compensating balance is required. Alternatively, Thompson can finance the expansion by no longer taking discounts, thus increasing accounts payable. Thompson purchases under terms of 2/10, net 30, but it can delay payment for an additional 35 days — paying in 65 days and thus becoming 35 days past due — without a penalty because of its suppliers' current excess capacity problems.
a. Based strictly on effective, or equivalent, annual interest rate comparisons, how should Thompson finance its expansion?
b. What additional qualitative factors should Thompson consider before reaching a decision?

17-14
Bank financing

The Raattama Corporation had sales of $3.5 million last year, and it earned a 5 percent return, after taxes, on sales. Recently, the company has fallen behind in its accounts payable. Although its terms of purchase are net 30 days, its accounts payable represent 60 days' purchases. The company's treasurer is seeking to increase bank borrowings in order to become current in meeting its trade obligations (that is, to have 30 days' payables outstanding). The company's balance sheet is as follows (thousands of dollars):

Cash	$ 100	Accounts payable	$ 600
Accounts receivable	300	Bank loans	700
Inventory	1,400	Accruals	200
Current assets	$1,800	Current liabilities	$1,500
Land and buildings	600	Mortgage on real estate	700
Equipment	600	Common stock, $0.10 par	300
		Retained earnings	500
Total assets	$3,000	Total liabilities and equity	$3,000

a. How much bank financing is needed to eliminate the past-due accounts payable?

b. Would you as a bank loan officer make the loan? Why?

17-15

Cost of bank loans

Gifts Galore Inc. borrowed $1.5 million from National City Bank. The loan was made at a simple annual interest rate of 9 percent a year for 3 months. A 20 percent compensating balance requirement raised the effective interest rate.

a. The nominal interest rate on the loan was 11.25 percent. What is the true effective rate?

b. What would be the effective cost of the loan if the note required discount interest?

c. What would be the nominal annual interest rate on the loan if National City Bank required Gifts Galore to repay the loan and interest in 3 equal monthly installments?

17-16

Short-term financing analysis

Malone Feed and Supply Company buys on terms of 1/10, net 30, but it has not been taking discounts and has actually been paying in 60 rather than 30 days. Malone's balance sheet follows (thousands of dollars):

Cash	$ 50	Accounts payable[a]	$ 500
Accounts receivable	450	Notes payable	50
Inventory	750	Accruals	50
Current assets	$1,250	Current liabilities	$ 600
		Long-term debt	150
Fixed assets	750	Common equity	1,250
Total assets	$2,000	Total liabilities and equity	$2,000

[a]Stated net of discounts.

Now, Malone's suppliers are threatening to stop shipments unless the company begins making prompt payments (that is, paying in 30 days or less). The firm can borrow on a 1-year note (call this a current liability) from its bank at a rate of 15 percent, discount interest, with a 20 percent compensating balance required. (Malone's $50,000 of cash is needed for transactions; it cannot be used as part of the compensating balance.)

a. Determine what action Malone should take by calculating (1) the cost of nonfree trade credit and (2) the cost of the bank loan.

b. Assume that Malone forgoes discounts and then borrows the amount needed to become current on its payables from the bank. How large will the bank loan be?

c. Based on your conclusion in Part b, construct a pro forma balance sheet. (Hint: You will need to include an account entitled "prepaid interest" under current assets.)

17-17

Alternative financing arrangements

Suncoast Boats Inc. estimates that because of the seasonal nature of its business, it will require an additional $2 million of cash for the month of July. Suncoast Boats has the following 4 options available for raising the needed funds:

(1) Establish a 1-year line of credit for $2 million with a commercial bank. The commitment fee will be 0.5 percent per year on the unused portion, and the interest charge on the used funds will be 11 percent per annum. Assume that the funds are needed only in July, and that there are 30 days in July and 360 days in the year.

(2) Forgo the trade discount of 2/10, net 40, on $2 million of purchases during July.

(3) Issue $2 million of 30-day commercial paper at a 9.5 percent per annum interest rate. The total transactions fee, including the cost of a backup credit line, on using commercial paper is 0.5 percent of the amount of the issue.

(4) Issue $2 million of 60-day commercial paper at a 9 percent per annum interest rate, plus a transactions fee of 0.5 percent. Since the funds are required for only 30 days, the excess funds ($2 million) can be invested in 9.4 percent per annum marketable securities for the month of August. The total transactions cost of purchasing and selling the marketable securities is 0.4 percent of the amount of the issue.

a. What is the dollar cost of each financing arrangement?

b. Is the source with the lowest expected cost necessarily the one to select? Why or why not?

I N T E G R A T E D   C A S E

BATS AND BALLS INC.

17-18 Working Capital Financing Policy Bats and Balls (B&B) Inc., a baseball equipment manufacturer, is a small company with seasonal sales. Each year before the baseball season, B&B purchases inventory which is financed through a combination of trade credit and short-term bank loans. At the end of the season, B&B uses sales revenues to repay its short-term obligations. The company is always looking for ways to become more profitable, and senior management has asked one of its employees, Ann Taylor, to review the company's current asset financing policies. Putting together her report, Ann is trying to answer each of the following questions:

a. B&B tries to match the maturity of its assets and liabilities. Describe how B&B could adopt either a more aggressive or more conservative financing policy.

b. What are the advantages and disadvantages of using short-term credit as a source of financing?

c. Is it likely that B&B could make significantly greater use of accruals?

d. Assume that B&B buys on terms of 1/10, net 30, but that it can get away with paying on the 40th day if it chooses not to take discounts. Also, assume that it purchases $3 million of components per year, net of discounts. How much free trade credit can the company get, how much costly trade credit can it get, and what is the percentage cost of the costly credit? Should B&B take discounts?

e. Would it be feasible for B&B to finance with commercial paper?

f. Suppose B&B decided to raise an additional $100,000 as a 1-year loan from its bank, for which it was quoted a rate of 8 percent. What is the effective annual cost rate assuming (1) simple interest, (2) discount interest, (3) discount interest with a 10 percent compensating balance, and (4) add-on interest on a 12-month installment loan? For the first three of these assumptions, would it matter if the loan were for 90 days, but renewable, rather than for a year?

g. How large would the loan actually be in each of the cases in Part f?

h. What are the pros and cons of borrowing on a secured versus an unsecured basis? If inventories or receivables are to be used as collateral, how would the loan be handled?

COMPUTER-RELATED PROBLEM

Work the problem in this section only if you are using the computer problem diskette.

17-19
Working capital financing

Three companies — Aggressive, Moderate, and Conservative — have different working capital management policies as implied by their names. For example, Aggressive employs only minimal current assets, and it finances almost entirely with current liabilities plus equity. This restricted approach has a dual effect. It keeps total assets low, which tends to increase return on assets; but because of stock-outs and credit rejections, total sales are reduced, and because inventory is ordered more frequently and in smaller quantities, variable costs are increased. Condensed balance sheets for the three companies follow:

	AGGRESSIVE	MODERATE	CONSERVATIVE
Current assets	$225,000	$300,000	$450,000
Fixed assets	300,000	300,000	300,000
Total assets	$525,000	$600,000	$750,000
Current liabilities (12%)	$300,000	$150,000	$ 75,000
Long-term debt (10%)	0	150,000	300,000
Total debt	$300,000	$300,000	$375,000
Equity	225,000	300,000	375,000
Total liabilities and equity	$525,000	$600,000	$750,000
Current ratio	0.75:1	2:1	6:1

The cost of goods sold functions for the three firms are as follows:

$$\text{Cost of goods sold} = \text{Fixed costs} + \text{Variable costs.}$$

Aggressive: Cost of goods sold = $300,000 + 0.70(Sales).

Moderate: Cost of goods sold = $405,000 + 0.65(Sales).

Conservative: Cost of goods sold = $577,500 + 0.60(Sales).

Because of the working capital differences, sales for the three firms under different economic conditions are expected to vary as follows:

	AGGRESSIVE	MODERATE	CONSERVATIVE
Strong economy	$1,800,000	$1,875,000	$1,950,000
Average economy	1,350,000	1,500,000	1,725,000
Weak economy	1,050,000	1,200,000	1,575,000

a. Construct income statements for each company for strong, average, and weak economies using the following format:

> Sales
> Less cost of goods sold
> Earnings before interest and taxes (EBIT)
> Less interest expense
> Earnings before taxes (EBT)
> Less taxes (40%)
> Net income

b. Compare the basic earning power (EBIT/assets) and return on equity for the companies. Which company is best in a strong economy? In an average economy? In a weak economy?

c. Suppose that, with sales at the average-economy level, short-term interest rates rose to 20 percent. How would this affect the three firms?

d. Suppose that because of production slowdowns caused by inventory shortages, the aggressive company's variable cost ratio rose to 80 percent. What would happen to its ROE? Assume a short-term interest rate of 12 percent.

e. What considerations for management of working capital are indicated by this problem?

SECURED SHORT-TERM FINANCING

This appendix discusses procedures for using accounts receivable and inventories as security for short-term loans. As noted earlier in the chapter, secured loans involve quite a bit of paperwork and other administrative costs, which make them relatively expensive. However, this is often the only type of financing available to weaker firms.

ACCOUNTS RECEIVABLE FINANCING

Accounts receivable financing involves either the pledging of receivables or the selling of receivables (called factoring). The *pledging of accounts receivable,* or putting accounts receivable up as security for a loan, is characterized by the fact that the lender not only has a claim against the receivables but also has *recourse* to the borrower: If the person or firm that bought the goods does not pay, the selling firm must take the loss. Therefore, the risk of default on the pledged accounts receivable remains with the borrower. The buyer of the goods is not ordinarily notified about the pledging of the receivables, and the financial institution that lends on the security of accounts receivable is generally either a commercial bank or one of the large industrial finance companies.

Factoring, or selling accounts receivable, involves the purchase of accounts receivable by the lender, generally without recourse to the borrower, which means that if the purchaser of the goods does not pay for them, the lender rather than the seller of the goods takes the loss. Under factoring, the buyer of the goods is typically notified of the transfer and is asked to make payment directly to the financial institution. Since the factoring firm assumes the risk of default on bad accounts, it must make the credit check. Accordingly, factors provide not only money, but also a credit department for the borrower. Incidentally, the same financial institutions that make loans against pledged receivables also serve as factors. Thus, depending on the circumstances and the wishes of the borrower, a financial institution will provide either form of receivables financing.

PROCEDURE FOR PLEDGING ACCOUNTS RECEIVABLE.
The financing of accounts receivable is initiated by a legally binding agreement between the seller of the goods and the financing institution. The agreement sets forth in detail the procedures to be followed and the legal obligations of both parties. Once the working relationship has been established, the seller periodically takes a batch of invoices to the financing institution. The lender reviews the invoices and makes credit appraisals of the buyers. Invoices of companies that do not meet the lender's credit standards are not accepted for pledging.

The financial institution seeks to protect itself at every phase of the operation. First, selection of sound invoices is one way the lender safeguards itself. Second, if the buyer of the goods does not pay the invoice, the lender still has recourse against the seller. Third, additional protection is afforded the lender because the loan will generally be less than 100 percent of the pledged receivables; for example, the lender may advance the selling firm only 75 percent of the amount of the pledged invoices.

PROCEDURE FOR FACTORING ACCOUNTS RECEIVABLE. The procedures used in factoring are somewhat different from those for pledging. Again, an agreement between the seller and the factor specifies legal obligations and procedural arrangements. When the seller receives an order from a buyer, a credit approval slip is written and immediately sent to the factoring company for a credit check. If the factor approves the credit, shipment is made and the invoice is stamped to notify the buyer to make payment directly to the factoring company. If the factor does not approve the sale, the seller generally refuses to fill the order; if the sale is made anyway, the factor will not buy the account.

The factor normally performs three functions: (1) credit checking, (2) lending, and (3) risk bearing. However, the seller can select various combinations of these functions by changing provisions in the factoring agreement. For example, a small- or medium-sized firm may have the factor perform the risk-bearing function and thus avoid having to establish a credit department. The factor's service is often less costly than a credit department that would have excess capacity for the firm's credit volume. At the same time, if the selling firm uses someone who is not really qualified for the job to perform credit checking, then that person's lack of education, training, and experience could result in excessive losses.

The seller may have the factor perform the credit-checking and risk-taking functions without performing the lending function. The following procedure illustrates the handling of a $10,000 order under this arrangement. The factor checks and approves the invoices. The goods are shipped on terms of net 30. Payment is made to the factor, who remits to the seller. If the buyer defaults, however, the $10,000 must still be remitted to the seller, and if the $10,000 is never paid, the factor sustains a $10,000 loss. Note that in this situation, the factor does not remit funds to the seller until either they are received from the buyer of the goods or the credit period has expired. Thus, the factor does not supply any credit.

Now consider the more typical situation in which the factor performs the lending, risk-bearing, and credit-checking functions. The goods are shipped, and even though payment is not due for 30 days, the factor immediately makes funds available to the seller. Suppose $10,000 worth of goods are shipped. Further, assume that the factoring commission for credit checking and risk bearing is 2.5 percent of the invoice price, or $250, and that the interest expense is computed at a 9 percent annual rate on the invoice balance, or $75.[1] The selling firm's accounting entry is as follows:

Cash	$9,175	
Interest expense	75	
Factoring commission	250	
Reserve due from factor on collection of account	500	
Accounts receivable		$10,000

---

[1]Since the interest is only for one month, we multiply 1/12 of the quoted rate (9 percent) by the $10,000 invoice price:

$$(1/12)(0.09)(\$10,000) = \$75.$$

The effective annual interest rate is above 9 percent because (1) the term is for less than one year and (2) a discounting procedure is used and the borrower does not get the full $10,000. In many instances, however, the factoring contract calls for interest to be calculated on the invoice price minus the factoring commission and the reserve account.

The $500 due from the factor upon collection of the account is a reserve established by the factor to cover disputes between the seller and buyers over damaged goods, goods returned by the buyers to the seller, and the failure to make an outright sale of goods. The reserve is paid to the selling firm when the factor collects on the account.

Factoring is normally a continuous process instead of the single cycle just described. The firm that sells the goods receives an order; it transmits this order to the factor for approval; upon approval, the firm ships the goods; the factor advances the invoice amount minus withholdings to the seller; the buyer pays the factor when payment is due; and the factor periodically remits any excess in the reserve to the seller of the goods. Once a routine has been established, a continuous circular flow of goods and funds takes place between the seller, the buyers of the goods, and the factor. Thus, once the factoring agreement is in force, funds from this source are *spontaneous* in the sense that an increase in sales will automatically generate additional credit.

Cost of Receivables Financing. Both accounts receivable pledging and factoring are convenient and advantageous, but they can be costly. The credit-checking and risk-bearing fee is 1 to 3 percent of the amount of invoices accepted by the factor, and it may be even more if the buyers are poor credit risks. The cost of money is reflected in the interest rate (usually 2 to 3 percentage points over the prime rate) charged on the unpaid balance of the funds advanced by the factor.

Evaluation of Receivables Financing. It cannot be said categorically that accounts receivable financing is always either a good or a poor way to raise funds. Among the advantages is, first, the flexibility of this source of financing: As the firm's sales expand, more financing is needed, but a larger volume of invoices, and hence a larger amount of receivables financing, is generated automatically. Second, receivables can be used as security for loans that would not otherwise be granted. Third, factoring can provide the services of a credit department that might otherwise be available only at a higher cost.

Accounts receivable financing also has disadvantages. First, when invoices are numerous and relatively small in dollar amount, the administrative costs involved may be excessive. Second, since receivables represent the firm's most liquid noncash assets, some trade creditors may refuse to sell on credit to a firm that factors or pledges its receivables on the grounds that this practice weakens the position of other creditors.

Future Use of Receivables Financing. We may make a prediction at this point: In the future, accounts receivable financing will increase in relative importance. Computer technology is rapidly advancing toward the point where credit records of individuals and firms can be kept on disks and magnetic tapes. For example, one device used by retailers consists of a box which, when an individual's magnetic credit card is inserted, gives a signal that the credit is "good" and that a bank is willing to "buy" the receivable created as soon as the store completes the sale. The cost of handling invoices will be greatly reduced over present-day costs because the new systems will be so highly automated. This will make it possible to use accounts receivable financing for very small sales, and it will reduce the cost of all receivables financing. The net result will be a marked expansion of accounts receivable financing. In fact, when consumers use credit cards such as MasterCard or Visa, the seller is in effect factoring receivables. The seller receives the amount of the purchase, minus a percentage fee, the next working day. The buyer receives 30 days' (or so) credit, at which time he or she remits payment directly to the credit card company or sponsoring bank.

INVENTORY FINANCING

A substantial amount of credit is secured by business inventories. If a firm is a relatively good credit risk, the mere existence of the inventory may be a sufficient basis for receiving an unsecured loan. However, if the firm is a relatively poor risk, the lending institution may insist upon security in the form of a *lien* against the inventory. Methods for using inventories as security are discussed in this section.

BLANKET LIENS.   The *inventory blanket lien* gives the lending institution a lien against all the borrower's inventories. However, the borrower is free to sell inventories, and thus the value of the collateral can be reduced below the level that existed when the loan was granted.

TRUST RECEIPTS.   Because of the inherent weakness of the blanket lien, another procedure for inventory financing has been developed — the *security instrument* (also called the *trust receipt),* which is an instrument acknowledging that the goods are held in trust for the lender. Under this method, the borrowing firm, as a condition for receiving funds from the lender, signs and delivers a trust receipt for the goods. The goods can be stored in a public warehouse or held on the premises of the borrower. The trust receipt states that the goods are held in trust for the lender or are segregated on the borrower's premises on the lender's behalf, and that any proceeds from the sale of the goods must be transmitted to the lender at the end of each day. Automobile dealer financing is one of the best examples of trust receipt financing.

One defect of trust receipt financing is the requirement that a trust receipt be issued for specific goods. For example, if the security is autos in a dealer's inventory, the trust receipts must indicate the cars by registration number. In order to validate its trust receipts, the lending institution must send someone to the borrower's premises periodically to see that the auto numbers are correctly listed because auto dealers who are in financial difficulty have been known to sell cars backing trust receipts and then use the funds obtained for other operations rather than to repay the bank. Problems are compounded if the borrower has a number of different locations, especially if they are separated geographically from the lender. To offset these inconveniences, *warehousing* has come into wide use as a method of securing loans with inventory.

WAREHOUSE RECEIPTS.   *Warehouse receipt financing* is another way to use inventory as security. It is a method of financing which uses inventory as a security and which requires public notification, physical control of the inventory, and supervision by a custodian of the field warehousing concern. A *public warehouse* is an independent third-party operation engaged in the business of storing goods. Items which must age, such as tobacco and liquor, are often financed and stored in public warehouses. Sometimes a public warehouse is not practical because of the bulkiness of goods and the expense of transporting them to and from the borrower's premises. In such cases, a *field warehouse* may be established on the borrower's grounds. To provide inventory supervision, the lending institution employs a third party in the arrangement, the field warehousing company, which acts as its agent.

Field warehousing can be illustrated by a simple example. Suppose a firm which has iron stacked in an open yard on its premises needs a loan. A field warehousing concern can place a temporary fence around the iron, erect a sign stating "This is a field warehouse supervised by the Smith Field Warehousing Corporation," and then assign an employee to supervise and control the fenced-in inventory.

This example illustrates the three essential elements for the establishment of a field warehouse: (1) public notification, (2) physical control of the inventory, and (3) supervision by a custodian of the field warehousing concern. When the field warehousing operation is relatively small, the third condition is sometimes violated by hiring an employee of the borrower to supervise the inventory. This practice is viewed as undesirable by most lenders because there is no control over the collateral by a person independent of the borrowing firm.[2]

The field warehouse financing operation is best described by an actual case. A California tomato cannery was interested in financing its operations by bank borrowing. It had sufficient funds to finance 15 to 20 percent of its operations during the canning season. These funds were adequate to purchase and process an initial batch of tomatoes. As the cans were put into boxes and rolled into the storerooms, the cannery needed additional funds for both raw materials and labor. Because of the cannery's poor credit rating, the bank decided that a field warehousing operation was necessary to secure its loans.

The field warehouse was established, and the custodian notified the bank of the description, by number, of the boxes of canned tomatoes in storage and under warehouse control. With this inventory as collateral, the lending institution established for the cannery a deposit on which it could draw. From this point on, the bank financed the operations. The cannery needed only enough cash to initiate the cycle. The farmers brought in more tomatoes; the cannery processed them; the cans were boxed; the boxes were put into the field warehouse; field warehouse receipts were drawn up and sent to the bank; the bank established further deposits for the cannery on the basis of the additional collateral, and the cannery could draw on the deposits to continue the cycle.

Of course, the cannery's ultimate objective was to sell the canned tomatoes. As it received purchase orders, it transmitted them to the bank, and the bank directed the custodian to release the inventories. It was agreed that as remittances were received by the cannery, they would be turned over to the bank. These remittances thus paid off the loans.

Note that a seasonal pattern existed. At the beginning of the tomato harvesting and canning season, the cannery's cash needs and loan requirements began to rise, and they reached a peak just as the season ended. It was expected that well before the new canning season began, the cannery would have sold a sufficient volume to pay off the loan. If the cannery had experienced a bad year, the bank might have carried the loan over for another year to enable the company to work off its inventory.

ACCEPTABLE PRODUCTS.   In addition to canned foods, which account for about 17 percent of all field warehouse loans, many other types of products provide a basis

---

[2]This absence of independent control was the main cause of the breakdown that resulted in more than $200 million of losses on loans to the Allied Crude Vegetable Oil Company by Bank of America and other banks. American Express Field Warehousing Company was handling the operation, but it hired men from Allied's own staff as custodians. Their dishonesty was not discovered because of another breakdown — the fact that the American Express touring inspector did not actually take a physical inventory of the warehouses. As a consequence, the swindle was not discovered until losses running into the hundreds of millions of dollars had been suffered.

for field warehouse financing. Some of these are miscellaneous groceries, which represent about 13 percent; lumber products, about 10 percent; and coal and coke, about 6 percent. These products are relatively nonperishable and are sold in well-developed, organized markets. Nonperishability protects the lender if it should have to take over the security. For this reason, a bank would not make a field warehousing loan on perishables such as fresh fish, but frozen fish, which can be stored for a long time, can be field warehoused.

COST OF FINANCING.   The fixed costs of a field warehousing arrangement are relatively high; such financing is therefore not suitable for a very small firm. If a field warehousing company sets up a field warehouse, it will typically set a minimum charge of about $5,000 per year, plus about 1 to 2 percent of the amount of credit extended to the borrower. Furthermore, the financing institution will charge an interest rate of 2 to 3 percentage points over the prime rate. An efficient field warehousing operation requires a minimum inventory of at least $1 million.

EVALUATION OF INVENTORY FINANCING.   The use of inventory financing, especially field warehouse financing, as a source of funds has many advantages. First, the amount of funds available is flexible because the financing is tied to inventory growth, which, in turn, is related directly to financing needs. Second, the field warehousing arrangement increases the acceptability of inventories as loan collateral; some inventories simply would not be accepted by a bank as security without such an arrangement. Third, the necessity for inventory control and safekeeping, as well as the use of specialists in warehousing, often results in improved warehouse practices, which, in turn, save handling costs, insurance charges, theft losses, and so on. Thus, field warehousing companies often save money for firms in spite of the costs of financing that we have discussed. The major disadvantages of field warehousing include the paperwork, physical separation requirements, and, for small firms, the fixed-cost element.

PROBLEMS

17A-1
Receivables financing

Finnerty's Funtime Company manufactures plastic toys. It buys raw materials, manufactures the toys in the spring and summer, and ships them to department stores and toy stores by late summer or early fall. Funtime factors its receivables; if it did not, its October 1997 balance sheet would appear as follows (thousands of dollars):

Cash	$ 40	Accounts payable	$1,200
Receivables	1,200	Notes payable	800
Inventory	800	Accruals	80
Current assets	$2,040	Current liabilities	$2,080
		Mortgages	200
		Common stock	400
Fixed assets	800	Retained earnings	160
Total assets	$2,840	Total liabilities and equity	$2,840

Funtime provides extended credit to its customers, so its receivables are not due for payment until January 31, 1998. Also, Funtime would have been overdue on some $800,000 of its accounts payable if the preceding situation had actually existed.

Funtime has an agreement with a finance company to factor the receivables for the period October 31 through January 31 of each selling season. The factoring company charges a flat commission of 2 percent of the invoice price, plus 6 percent per year interest on the outstanding balance; it deducts a reserve of 8 percent for returned and damaged materials. Interest and commissions are paid in advance. No interest is charged on the reserved funds or on the commission.

   a. Show Funtime's balance sheet on October 31, 1997, including the purchase of all the receivables by the factoring company and the use of the funds to pay accounts payable.

   b. If the $1.2 million is the average level of outstanding receivables, and if they turn over 4 times a year (hence the commission is paid 4 times a year), what are the total dollar costs of receivables financing (factoring) and the effective annual interest rate?

17A-2
Factoring arrangement

Merville Industries needs an additional $500,000, which it plans to obtain through a factoring arrangement. The factor would purchase Merville's accounts receivable and advance the invoice amount, minus a 2 percent commission, on the invoices purchased each month. Merville sells on terms of net 30 days. In addition, the factor charges a 12 percent annual interest rate on the total invoice amount, to be deducted in advance.

   a. What amount of accounts receivable must be factored to net $500,000?

   b. If Merville can reduce credit expenses by $3,500 per month and avoid bad debt losses of 2.5 percent on the factored amount, what is the total dollar cost of the factoring arrangement?

   c. What would be the total cost of the factoring arrangement if Merville's funds needed rose to $750,000? Would the factoring arrangement be profitable under these circumstances?

17A-3
Field warehousing arrangement

Because of crop failures last year, the San Joaquin Packing Company has no funds available to finance its canning operations during the next 6 months. It estimates that it will require $1,200,000 from inventory financing during the period. One alternative is to establish a 6-month, $1,500,000 line of credit with terms of 9 percent annual interest on the used portion, a 1 percent commitment fee on the unused portion, and a $300,000 compensating balance at all times. The other alternative is to use field warehouse financing. The costs of the field warehouse arrangement in this case would be a flat fee of $2,000, plus 8 percent annual interest on all outstanding credit, plus 1 percent of the maximum amount of credit extended.

Expected inventory levels to be financed are as follows:

Month	Amount
July 1998	$ 250,000
August	1,000,000
September	1,200,000
October	950,000
November	600,000
December	0

   a. Calculate the cost of funds from using the line of credit. Be sure to include interest charges and commitment fees. Note that each month's borrowings will be $300,000 greater than the inventory level to be financed because of the compensating balance requirement.

   b. Calculate the total cost of the field warehousing operation.

   c. Compare the cost of the field warehousing arrangement to the cost of the line of credit. Which alternative should San Joaquin choose?

PART

VII

SPECIAL
TOPICS
IN
FINANCIAL
MANAGEMENT

CHAPTER 18
MULTINATIONAL FINANCIAL
MANAGEMENT

CHAPTER 19
DERIVATIVES AND RISK
MANAGEMENT

CHAPTER 20
HYBRID FINANCING: PREFERRED
STOCK, LEASING, WARRANTS,
AND CONVERTIBLES

CHAPTER 21
MERGERS, LBOs, DIVESTITURES,
AND HOLDING COMPANIES

CHAPTER 18

MULTINATIONAL FINANCIAL MANAGEMENT[1]

© Sarah Jones/Masterfile

[1]This chapter was coauthored by Professors Roy Crum of the University of Florida and Subu Venkataraman of Northwestern University.

U.S. FIRMS LOOK OVERSEAS TO ENHANCE SHAREHOLDER VALUE

From the end of World War II until the 1970s, the United States dominated the world economy, but that situation no longer exists. Raw materials, finished goods, services, and money flow freely across most national boundaries, as do innovative ideas and new technologies. World-class U.S. companies are making breakthroughs in foreign labs, obtaining capital from foreign investors, and putting foreign employees on the fast track to the top. Dozens of top U.S. manufacturers, including Dow Chemical, Colgate-Palmolive, Gillette, Hewlett-Packard, and Xerox, sell more of their products outside the United States than they do at home. Service firms are not far behind, as Citicorp, Disney, McDonald's, and Time Warner all receive more than 20 percent of their revenues from foreign sales.

The trend is even more pronounced in profits. In recent years, Coca-Cola and many other companies have made more money in the Pacific Rim and western Europe than in the United States. As U.S. companies begin to reap half or more of their sales and profits from abroad, they are finding it useful to blend into the foreign landscape in order to win product acceptance and avoid political problems.

At the same time, foreign-based multinationals are arriving on American shores in ever greater numbers. Sweden's ABB, the Netherlands's Philips, France's Thomson, and Japan's Fujitsu and Honda are all waging campaigns to be identified as American companies that employ Americans, transfer technology to America, and help the U.S. trade balance and overall economic health. Few Americans know or care that Thomson owns the RCA and General Electric names in consumer electronics or that Philips owns Magnavox.

The emergence of "world companies" raises a host of questions for governments seeking to shape their nations' economic destinies. For example, should domestic firms be favored, or does it make no difference what a company's nationality is as long as it provides domestic jobs? Should a company make an effort to keep jobs in its home country, or should it produce where total production costs are lowest? What nation controls the technology developed by a multinational corporation, particularly if the technology can be used in military applications? What obligations does a multinational company headquartered in a given country have to adhere to rules imposed by its home country with respect to its operations outside the home country? And if a U.S. firm such as Xerox produces copiers in Japan and then ships them to the United States, should they be reflected in the trade deficit in the same way as Toyotas imported from Japan? Keep these questions in mind as you read this chapter. At the end, you should have a better appreciation of both the problems facing governments and the difficult but profitable opportunities facing financial managers of multinational companies.

Managers of multinational companies must deal with a wide range of issues that are not present when a company operates in a single country. In this chapter, we highlight the key differences between multinational and domestic corporations, and we discuss the impact these differences have on the financial management of multinational businesses.

MULTINATIONAL, OR GLOBAL, CORPORATIONS

Multinational, or Global, Corporation
A firm that operates in an integrated fashion in a number of countries.

The term **multinational,** or **global, corporation** is used to describe a firm that operates in an integrated fashion in a number of countries. During the period since World War II, a new and fundamentally different form of international commercial activity has developed, and this has greatly increased worldwide economic and political interdependence. Rather than merely buying resources from and selling goods in foreign nations, multinational firms now make direct investments in fully integrated operations, from extraction of raw materials, through the manufacturing process, to distribution to consumers throughout the world. Today, multinational corporate networks control a large and growing share of the world's technological, marketing, and productive resources.

Companies, both U.S. and foreign, go "global" for six primary reasons:

1. **To seek new markets.** After a company has saturated its home market, growth opportunities are often better in foreign markets. Thus, such homegrown firms as Coca-Cola and McDonald's are aggressively expanding into overseas markets, and foreign firms such as Sony and Toshiba now dominate the U.S. consumer electronics market.

2. **To seek raw materials.** Many U.S. oil companies, such as Exxon, have major subsidiaries around the world to ensure access to the basic resources needed to sustain the companies' primary business line.

3. **To seek new technology.** No single nation holds a commanding advantage in all technologies, so companies are scouring the globe for leading scientific and design ideas. For example, Xerox has introduced more than 80 different office copiers in the United States that were engineered and built by its Japanese joint venture, Fuji Xerox. Similarly, versions of the superconcentrated detergent that Procter & Gamble first formulated in Japan in response to a rival's product are now being marketed under the Ariel name in Europe and under the Cheer and Tide labels in the United States.

4. **To seek production efficiency.** Companies in high-cost countries are shifting production to low-cost countries. For example, GE has production and assembly plants in Mexico, South Korea, and Singapore, and even Japanese manufacturers are shifting some of their production to lower-cost countries in the Pacific Rim. Even BMW and Mercedes-Benz, in response to high production costs in Germany, have built assembly plants in the United States. The ability to shift production from country to country has important implications for labor costs in all countries. For example, when Xerox threatened to move its copier

rebuilding work to Mexico, its union in Rochester agreed to work rule changes and productivity improvements that kept the operation in the United States. Some multinational companies make decisions almost daily on where to shift production. When Dow Chemical saw European demand for a certain solvent declining, the company scaled back production at a German plant and shifted its production to another chemical which had previously been imported from the United States. Relying on complex computer models for making such decisions, Dow runs its plants at peak capacity and thus keeps capital costs down.

5. **To avoid political and regulatory hurdles.** The primary reason Japanese auto companies moved production to the United States was to get around U.S. import quotas. Now Honda, Nissan, Toyota, Mazda, and Mitsubishi are all assembling automobiles or trucks in the United States. One of the factors that prompted U.S. pharmaceutical maker SmithKline and Britain's Beecham to merge was that they wanted to avoid licensing and regulatory delays in their largest markets, Western Europe and the United States. Now Smith-Kline Beecham can identify itself as an inside player in both Europe and the United States. Similarly, when Germany's BASF launched biotechnology research at home, it confronted legal and political challenges from the environmentally conscious Green movement. In response, BASF shifted its cancer and immune system research to two laboratories in Boston suburbs. This location is attractive not only because of its large number of engineers and scientists but also because the Boston area has better resolved controversies involving safety, animal rights, and the environment. "We decided it would be better to have the laboratories located where we have fewer insecurities about what will happen in the future," said Rolf-Dieter Acker, BASF's director of biotechnology research.

6. **To diversify.** By establishing worldwide production facilities and markets, firms can cushion the impact of adverse economic trends in any single country. For example, General Motors softened the blow of poor sales in the United States during the 1990–1991 recession with strong sales by its European subsidiaries. In general, geographic diversification works because the economic ups and downs of different countries are not perfectly correlated. Therefore, companies investing overseas benefit from diversification in the same way that individuals benefit from investing globally.

Over the past 10 to 15 years, there has been an increasing amount of investment in the United States by foreign corporations, and in foreign nations by U.S. corporations. This trend is shown in Figure 18-1, and it is important because of its implications for eroding the traditional doctrine of independence and self-reliance that has been a hallmark of U.S. policy. Just as U.S. corporations with extensive overseas operations are said to use their economic power to exert substantial economic and political influence over host governments in many parts of the world, it is feared that foreign corporations are gaining similar sway over U.S. policy. These developments suggest an increasing degree of mutual influence and interdependence among business enterprises and nations, to which the United States is not immune.

The world economy is quite fluid. Here are a few of the recent events which have dramatically changed the international financial environment:

1. The disintegration of the former Soviet Union and the movement toward market economies in the newly formed countries have created a vast new market for international commerce.

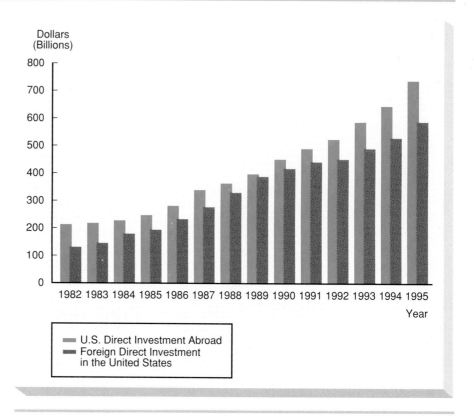

FIGURE 18-1 Direct Investment for the United States, 1982–1995

SOURCE: J. Lowe and S. Vargas, "Direct Investment Positions on a Historical Cost Basis," *Survey of Current Business,* July 1996.

ON THE WWW

The passage of NAFTA (North American Free Trade Agreement) ensures that continued international investment will be made by U.S. corporations. An interesting January 1997 article about the impact of NAFTA on the U.S. economy can be found on the United States Trade Representative's Homepage at http:// www.ustr.gov/agreements/nafta/ information/econ.html. Detailed information on NAFTA can be found on the U.S. Department of Commerce's NAFTA Home Page at http://iepnt1.itaiep.doc.gov/nafta/ nafta2.htm.

2. The reunification of Germany, coupled with the collapse of communism in Eastern Europe, has created significant new opportunities for foreign investment.

3. The European Community and the European Free Trade Association have created a "borderless" region where people, capital, goods, and services move freely among the 19 nations without the burden of tariffs. Negotiations are also under way to create a single "Eurocurrency," which would greatly simplify economic exchange among the participating countries.

4. The North American Free Trade Agreement (NAFTA) has moved the economies of the United States, Canada, and Mexico much closer together, and made them more interdependent.

5. U.S. bank regulations have been loosened dramatically. One key deregulatory feature was the removal of interest rate ceilings, thus allowing banks to attract foreign deposits by raising rates. Another key feature was the removal of barriers to entry by foreign banks, which resulted in more cross-border banking transactions. Still, U.S. commercial and investment banks do not have as much freedom as foreign banks, which has led many U.S. banks to establish subsidiaries in Europe that can offer a wider range of services, hence increase global competition in the financial services industry.

What is a multinational corporation?

Why do companies "go global"?

MULTINATIONAL VERSUS DOMESTIC FINANCIAL MANAGEMENT

In theory, the concepts and procedures discussed in the first 17 chapters are valid for both domestic and multinational operations. However, six major factors distinguish financial management in firms operating entirely within a single country from firms that operate globally:

1. **Different currency denominations.** Cash flows in various parts of a multinational corporate system will be denominated in different currencies. Hence, an analysis of exchange rates must be included in all financial analyses.

2. **Economic and legal ramifications.** Each country has its own unique economic and legal systems, and these differences can cause significant problems when a corporation tries to coordinate and control the worldwide operations of its subsidiaries. For example, differences in tax laws among countries can cause a given economic transaction to have strikingly different after-tax consequences, depending on where the transaction occurred. Similarly, differences in legal systems of host nations, such as the Common Law of Great Britain versus the French Civil Law, complicate matters ranging from the simple recording of business transactions to the role played by the judiciary in resolving conflicts. Such differences can restrict multinational corporations' flexibility in deploying resources, and can even make procedures that are required in one part of the company illegal in another part. These differences also make it difficult for executives trained in one country to operate effectively in another.

3. **Language differences.** The ability to communicate is critical in all business transactions, and here U.S. citizens are often at a disadvantage because we are generally fluent only in English, while European and Japanese businesspeople are usually fluent in several languages, including English. Thus, they can invade our markets more easily than we can penetrate theirs.

4. **Cultural differences.** Even within geographic regions that are considered relatively homogeneous, different countries have unique cultural heritages that shape values and influence the conduct of business. Multinational corporations find that matters such as defining the appropriate goals of the firm, attitudes toward risk, dealings with employees, and the ability to curtail unprofitable operations vary dramatically from one country to the next.

5. **Role of governments.** Most financial models assume the existence of a competitive marketplace in which the terms of trade are determined by the participants. The government, through its power to establish basic ground rules, is involved in the process, but its role is minimal. Thus, the market provides the primary barometer of success and the best clues about what must be done to remain competitive. This view of the process is reasonably correct for the United States and Western Europe, but it does not accurately describe the

situation in most of the world. Frequently, the terms under which companies compete, the actions that must be taken or avoided, and the terms of trade on various transactions are determined not in the marketplace but by direct negotiation between the host government and the multinational corporation. This is essentially a political process, and it must be treated as such. Thus, our traditional financial models have to be recast to include political and other noneconomic aspects of the decision.

6. **Political risk.** A nation is free to place constraints on the transfer of corporate resources and even to expropriate without compensation assets within their boundaries. This is *political risk,* and it tends to be largely a given rather than a variable that can be changed by negotiation. Political risk varies from country to country, and it must be addressed explicitly in any financial analysis. Another aspect of political risk is terrorism against U.S. firms or executives. For example, U.S. and Japanese executives have been kidnapped and held for ransom in several South American countries.

These six factors complicate financial management, and they increase the risks faced by multinational firms. However, prospects for high profits, diversification benefits, and other factors make it worthwhile for firms to accept these risks and learn how to manage them.

SELF-TEST QUESTION ??????

Identify and briefly discuss six major factors that complicate financial management in multinational firms.

EXCHANGE RATES

Exchange Rate
The number of units of a given currency that can be purchased for one unit of another currency.

An **exchange rate** specifies the number of units of a given currency that can be purchased with one unit of another currency. Exchange rates appear in the financial sections of newspapers each day. Selected rates from a recent issue of *The Wall Street Journal* are given in Table 18-1. The values shown in Column 1 are the number of U.S. dollars required to purchase one unit of foreign currency; this is called a *direct quotation*. Direct quotations have a dollar sign in their quotation. Thus, the direct U.S. dollar quotation for the German mark is $0.6418, because one German mark could be bought for 64.18 cents. The exchange rates given in Column 2 represent the number of units of foreign currency that can be purchased for one U.S. dollar; these are called *indirect quotations*. Indirect quotations often begin with the foreign currency's equivalent to the dollar sign. Thus, the indirect quotation for the German mark is M1.5581. (The "M" stands for *Mark*, and it is equivalent to the symbol "$.") Normal practice in the United States is to use indirect quotations (Column 2) for all currencies other than British pounds, for which direct quotations are given. Thus, we speak of the pound as "selling at $1.67" but of the mark as "being at 1.56."

It is also a universal convention on the world's foreign currency exchanges to state all exchange rates except British pounds on a "dollar basis" — that is, as the foreign currency price of one U.S. dollar as reported in Column 2 of Table 18-1. Thus, in all currency trading centers, whether in New York, Frankfurt, London, Tokyo, or anywhere else, the exchange rate for the German mark would be displayed as M1.5581. This convention eliminates confusion when comparing quotations from one trading center with those from another.

TABLE 18-1	Illustrative Exchange Rates

	DIRECT QUOTATION: U.S. DOLLARS REQUIRED TO BUY ONE UNIT OF FOREIGN CURRENCY (1)	**INDIRECT QUOTATION: NUMBER OF UNITS OF FOREIGN CURRENCY PER U.S. DOLLAR** (2)
British pound	$1.6650	0.6006
Canadian dollar	0.7315	1.3671
Dutch guilder	0.5736	1.7435
French franc	0.1902	5.2575
German mark	0.6418	1.5581
Italian lira	0.0006523	1,533.0000
Japanse yen	0.008769	114.0400
Mexican peso	0.12726	7.8580
Spanish peseta	0.007634	130.9900
Swiss franc	0.7465	1.3395

NOTE: Column 2 equals 1.0 divided by Column 1. However, rounding differences do occur.
SOURCE: *The Wall Street Journal*, December 20, 1996.

We can use the data in Table 18-1 to show how one works with exchange rates. Suppose a U.S. tourist on holiday flies from New York to London, then to Paris, then on to Munich, and finally back to New York. When she arrives at London's Heathrow Airport, she goes to the bank to check the foreign exchange listing. The rate she observes for U.S. dollars is $1.6650; this means that £1 will cost her $1.6650. Assume that she exchanges $2,000 for $2,000/$1.6650 = £1,201.20 and enjoys a week's vacation in London, spending £701.20 while there.

At the end of the week she travels to Dover to catch the Hovercraft to Calais on the coast of France and realizes that she needs to exchange her 500 remaining British pounds for French francs. However, what she sees on the board is the direct quotation between pounds and dollars ($1.6650) and the indirect quotation between francs and dollars (FF5.2575). (For our purposes, we assume that the exchange rates in effect at the start of the trip remain in effect throughout our example. This is unrealistic for reasons explained later in this chapter.) The exchange rate between any two currencies is called a *cross rate*. Cross rates are actually calculated on the basis of various currencies relative to the U.S. dollar. For example, the cross rate between British pounds and French francs is computed as follows:

$$\text{Cross rate} = \frac{\text{Dollars}}{\text{Pound}} \times \frac{\text{Francs}}{\text{Dollar}} = \frac{\text{Francs}}{\text{Pound}}$$

$$= 1.6650 \text{ dollars per pound} \times 5.2575 \text{ francs per dollar}$$

$$= 8.7537 \text{ francs per pound.}$$

Therefore, for every British pound she would receive 8.7537 French francs, so she would receive 8.7537 × 500 = 4,376.87 ≈ 4,377 francs.

When she finishes touring in France and arrives in Germany, she again needs to determine a cross rate, this time between French francs and German marks. The dollar-basis quotes she sees, as shown in Table 18-1, are FF5.2575 per dollar and M1.5581 per dollar. To find the cross rate, she must divide the two dollar-basis rates:

$$\text{Cross rate} = \frac{\dfrac{\text{Marks}}{\text{Dollar}}}{\dfrac{\text{Francs}}{\text{Dollar}}} = \frac{\text{Marks}}{\text{Franc}}$$

$$= \frac{\text{M1.5581 per \$}}{\text{FF5.2575 per \$}} = 0.2964 \text{ marks per franc.}$$

Then, if she had FF3,000 remaining, she could exchange them for $0.2964 \times 3{,}000 = \text{M889.20}$, or about 889 marks.

Finally, when her vacation ends and she returns to New York, the quotation she sees is M1.5581, which tells her that she can buy 1.5581 marks for a dollar. She now holds 50 marks, so she wants to know how many U.S. dollars she will receive for her marks. First, she must find the reciprocal of the quoted indirect rate,

$$\frac{1}{\text{M1.5581}} = \$0.6418,$$

which is the direct quote shown in Table 18-1, Column 1. Then she will end up with

$$\$0.6418 \times 50 = \$32.09.$$

In this example, we made three very strong and generally incorrect assumptions. First, we assumed that our traveler had to calculate all the cross rates. For retail transactions, it is customary to display the cross rates directly instead of a series of dollar rates. Second, we assumed that exchange rates remain constant over time. Actually, exchange rates vary every day, often dramatically. We will have more to say about exchange rate fluctuations in the next section. Finally, we assumed that there were no transactions costs involved in exchanging currencies. In reality, small retail exchange transactions such as those in our example usually involve fixed and/or sliding scale fees that can easily consume five or more percent of the transaction amount. However, credit card purchases minimize these fees.

Major business publications such as *The Wall Street Journal* regularly report cross rates among key currencies. The reported cross rates for December 19, 1996, are listed in Table 18-2. When examining the table, note the following points:

1. Column 1 gives indirect quotes for dollars, that is, units of a foreign currency that can be bought with one U.S. dollar. Examples: $1 will buy 5.2575 French francs or 1.5581 German marks. Note the consistency with Table 18-1, Column 2.

2. Other columns show number of units of other currencies that can be bought with one pound, one Swiss franc, etc. Examples: 1 D-mark will buy 0.87741 Canadian dollar, 3.3743 French francs, or 0.64181 U.S. dollar.

3. The rows show direct quotes, that is, number of units of the currency of the country listed in the left column required to buy one unit of the currency

TABLE 18-2	Key Currency Cross Rates Late New York Trading December 19, 1996								

	DOLLAR	POUND	SFRANC	GUILDER	PESO	YEN	LIRA	D-MARK	FFRANC	CDNDLR
Canada	1.3671	2.2762	1.0206	0.78411	0.17398	0.01199	0.00089	0.87741	0.26003	—
France	5.2575	8.7537	3.9250	3.0155	0.66906	0.04610	0.00343	3.3743	—	3.8457
Germany	1.5581	2.5942	1.1632	0.89366	0.19828	0.01366	0.00102	—	0.29636	1.1397
Italy	1533.0	2552.4	1144.5	879.27	195.09	13.443	—	983.89	291.58	1121.4
Japan	114.04	189.88	85.136	65.409	14.513	—	0.07439	73.192	21.691	83.417
Mexico	7.8580	13.084	5.8664	4.5070	—	0.06891	0.00513	5.0433	1.4946	5.7479
Netherlands	1.7435	2.9029	1.3016	—	0.22188	0.01529	0.00114	1.1190	0.33162	1.2753
Switzerland	1.3395	2.2303	—	0.76828	0.17046	0.01175	0.00087	0.85970	0.25478	0.97981
United Kingdom	0.60060	—	0.44838	0.34448	0.07643	0.00527	0.00039	0.38547	0.11424	0.43932
United States	—	1.6650	0.74655	0.57356	0.12726	0.00877	0.00065	0.64181	0.19020	0.73148

SOURCE: "Key Currency Cross Rates," *The Wall Street Journal*, December 20, 1996, C17. ©1996 Dow Jones & Company, Inc. All Rights Reserved Worldwide.

listed in the top row. The bottom row is particularly interesting, as it shows the direct quotes for the U.S. dollar. This row is consistent with Column 1 of Table 18-1. Note too that the values on the bottom row are reciprocals of the values in Column 1. Thus, $1/0.6006 = 1.6650$.

4. Now notice, by reading down the FFranc column, that one French franc was worth $0.29636 \approx 0.2964$ German marks. This is the same cross rate that we calculated for the U.S. tourist in our previous example.

The tie-in with the dollar ensures that all currencies are related to one another in a consistent manner. If this consistency did not exist, currency traders could gain profits by buying undervalued currencies and selling overvalued currencies. This process, known as arbitrage, works to bring about an equilibrium wherein the same relationship described earlier would exist. In fact, currency traders are constantly operating in the market, seeking small inconsistencies from which they can profit. Their existence enables the rest of us to assume that currency markets are in equilibrium and that, at any point in time, cross rates are all internally consistent.

SELF-TEST QUESTIONS

What is an exchange rate?

Explain the difference between direct and indirect quotations.

What is a cross rate?

THE INTERNATIONAL MONETARY SYSTEM

Every nation has a monetary system with a monetary authority. In the United States, the Federal Reserve is our monetary authority, and its task is to hold down inflation while promoting economic growth and raising our national standard of

Fixed Exchange Rate System
The world monetary system in existence after World War II until 1971, under which the value of the U.S. dollar was tied to gold, and the values of the other currencies were pegged to the U.S. dollar.

living. Moreover, if countries are to trade with one another, we must have some sort of system designed to facilitate payments between nations.

From the end of World War II until August 1971, the world was on a **fixed exchange rate system** administered by the International Monetary Fund (IMF). Under this system, the U.S. dollar was linked to gold ($35 per ounce), and other currencies were then tied to the dollar. Exchange rates between other currencies and the dollar were controlled within narrow limits but then adjusted periodically. For example, in 1964 the British pound was adjusted to $2.80 for £1, with a 1 percent permissible fluctuation about this rate.

Fluctuations in exchange rates occur because of changes in the supply of and demand for dollars, pounds, and other currencies. These supply and demand changes have two primary sources. First, changes in the demand for currencies depend on changes in imports and exports of goods and services. For example, U.S. importers must buy British pounds to pay for British goods, whereas British importers must buy U.S. dollars to pay for U.S. goods. If U.S. imports from Great Britain exceeded U.S. exports to Great Britain, there would be a greater demand for pounds than for dollars, and this would drive up the price of the pound relative to that of the dollar. In terms of Table 18-1, the dollar cost of a pound might rise from $1.6650 to $2.0000. The U.S. dollar would be said to be *depreciating,* because a dollar would now be worth fewer pounds, whereas the pound would be *appreciating.* In this example, the root cause of the change would be the U.S. **trade deficit** with Great Britain. Of course, if U.S. exports to Great Britain were greater than U.S. imports from Great Britain, Great Britain would have a trade deficit with the United States.[2]

Trade Deficit
A situation where a country imports more than it exports.

Changes in the demand for a currency, hence exchange rate fluctuations, also depend on capital movements. For example, suppose interest rates in Great Britain were higher than those in the United States. To take advantage of the high British interest rates, U.S. banks, corporations, and even sophisticated individuals would buy pounds with dollars and then use those pounds to purchase high-yielding British securities. These purchases would tend to drive up the price of pounds.[3]

Before August 1971, exchange rate fluctuations were kept within the narrow 1 percent limit by regular intervention of the British government in the market.

---

[2]If the dollar value of the pound moved up from $1.67 to $2.00, this increase in the value of the pound would mean that British goods would now be more expensive in the United States. For example, a box of candy costing £1 in England would rise in price in the United States from about $1.67 to $2.00. Conversely, U.S. goods would become cheaper in England. For example, the British could now buy goods worth $2.00 for £1, whereas before the exchange rate change £1 would buy merchandise worth only $1.67. These price changes would, of course, tend to *reduce* British exports and *increase* imports, and this, in turn, would lower the exchange rate, because people in the United States would be buying fewer pounds to pay for English goods. Before 1971, the 1 percent limit severely constrained the market's ability to reach an equilibrium between trade balances and exchange rates.

[3]Such capital inflows would also tend to drive down British interest rates. If British rates were high in the first place because of efforts by the British monetary authorities to curb inflation, these international currency flows would tend to thwart that effort. This is one of the reasons domestic and international economies are so closely linked.

A good example of this occurred during the summer of 1981. In an effort to curb inflation, the Federal Reserve Board helped push U.S. interest rates to record levels. This, in turn, caused a flow of capital from European nations to the United States. The Europeans were suffering from a severe recession and wanted to keep interest rates down in order to stimulate investment, but U.S. policy made this difficult because of international capital flows. Just the opposite occurred in 1992, when the Fed drove short-term rates down to record lows in the United States to promote growth, while Germany and most other European countries pushed their rates higher to combat the inflationary pressures of reunification. Thus, investment in the United States was dampened as investors moved their money overseas to capture higher interest rates.

Devaluation
The process of officially *reducing* the value of a country's currency relative to other currencies.

Revaluation
The process of officially *increasing* the value of a country's currency relative to other currencies.

Floating Exchange Rates
A system under which exchange rates are not fixed by government policy but are allowed to float up or down in accordance with supply and demand.

When the value of the pound was falling, the Bank of England would step in and buy pounds to push up their price, offering gold or foreign currencies in exchange. Conversely, when the pound rate was too high, the Bank of England would sell pounds. The central banks of other countries operated similarly.

Devaluations and **revaluations** occurred only rarely before 1971. They were usually accompanied by severe international financial repercussions, partly because nations tended to postpone needed measures until economic pressures had built up to explosive proportions. For this and other reasons, the old international monetary system came to a dramatic end in the early 1970s, when the U.S. dollar, the foundation upon which all other currencies were anchored, was cut loose from the gold standard and, in effect, allowed to "float."

The United States and other major trading nations currently operate under a system of **floating exchange rates,** whereby currency prices are allowed to seek their own levels without much governmental intervention. However, the central bank of each country does intervene to some extent, buying and selling its currency to smooth out exchange rate fluctuations.

Each central bank would like to keep its average exchange rate at a level deemed desirable by its government's economic policy. This is important, because exchange rates have a profound effect on the levels of imports and exports, which influence the level of domestic employment. For example, if a country is having a problem with unemployment, its central bank might try to lower interest rates, which would cause capital to flee the country to find higher rates, which would lead to the sale of the currency, which would cause a *decline* in the value of the currency. This would cause its goods to be cheaper in world markets and thus stimulate exports, production, and domestic employment. Conversely, the central bank of a country that is operating at full capacity and experiencing inflation might try to raise the value of its currency to reduce exports and increase imports. Under the current floating rate system, however, such intervention can affect the situation only temporarily, because market forces will prevail in the long run.

Exchange rate fluctuations can have a profound impact on international monetary transactions. For example, in 1985 it cost Honda Motors 2,380,000 yen to build a particular model in Japan and ship it to the United States. The model carried a U.S. sticker price of $12,000. Since the $12,000 sales price was the equivalent of (238 yen per dollar)($12,000) = 2,856,000 yen, which was 20 percent above the 2,380,000 yen cost, the automaker had built a 20 percent markup into the U.S. sales price. However, three years later the dollar had depreciated to 128 yen. Now if the model still sold for $12,000, the yen return to Honda would be only (128 yen per dollar)($12,000) = 1,536,000 yen, and the automaker would be losing about 35 percent on each auto sold. Therefore, the depreciation of the dollar against the yen turned a healthy profit into a huge loss. In fact, for Honda to maintain its 20 percent markup, the model would have to sell in the United States for 2,856,000 yen/128 yen per dollar = $22,312.50. This situation, which had grown even worse by 1996, with 114 yen per dollar, led Honda to build its most popular model, the Accord, in Marysville, Ohio.

The inherent volatility of exchange rates under a floating system increases the uncertainty of the cash flows for a multinational corporation. Because these cash flows are generated in many parts of the world, they are denominated in many different currencies. Since exchange rates can change, the dollar-equivalent value of a company's consolidated cash flows can also fluctuate. For example, Toyota estimates that each one-yen drop in the dollar reduces the company's annual net income by about 10 billion yen. This is known as *exchange rate risk,* and it is a major factor differentiating a global company from a purely domestic one.

Concerns about exchange rate risk have spurred attempts to stabilize currency movements. In 1979, The *European Monetary System (EMS)* was formed. Participants in the EMS agreed to limit fluctuations in their exchange rates so that rates stayed within a prespecified range. It was felt that this arrangement would prevent the frequent disruptions to international trade and economic health that were caused by the vagaries of a floating foreign exchange market. However, efforts to fix exchange rates rather than letting them float have not met with much success. For example, in the 1990s, Britain was forced to withdraw from the exchange rate arrangement of the EMS because of its inability to support the pound. Similarly, in 1995, while facing substantial political and economic turmoil, Mexico attempted to stabilize the peso. However, participants in the foreign exchange market simply sold billions of pesos and forced the Mexican central bank to allow the peso to float.

European nations are now moving toward an alternative to the EMS. Under the *Treaty of Maastricht* (signed in 1991), participants in the *European Monetary Union (EMU)* agreed to take a step beyond merely trying to fix their exchange rates relative to each other. They agreed to move to a common currency, the *Euro,* that will replace the currencies of the member countries. The hope is that such an arrangement will be more successful than the arrangements of the past in terms of creating a stable international economic environment.

Note too that in today's floating exchange rate environment, many countries have chosen to peg their currencies to one or more major currencies. Countries with **pegged exchange rates** establish a fixed exchange rate with some major currency, and then the values of the pegged currencies move together over time. For example, Venezuela pegs its currency to the U.S. dollar at a rate of 0.002107 Bolivar per dollar. Its reason for pegging its currency to the dollar is that a large portion of its revenues are linked to its oil exports, which are typically traded in dollars, and its trading partners feel more comfortable dealing with contracts that can, in essence, be stated in dollar terms. Similarly, Kuwait pegs its currency to a composite of currencies that roughly represents the mix of currencies used by its trading partners to purchase its oil. In other instances, currencies are pegged because of traditional ties — for example, Chad, a former French colony, still pegs its currency to the French franc.[4]

Before closing our discussion of the international monetary system, we should note that not all currencies are **convertible.** A currency is convertible when the nation which issued the currency allows it to be traded in the currency markets and is willing to redeem it at market rates. This means that, except for limited central bank influence, the issuing government loses control over the value of its currency. Lack of convertibility creates major problems for international trade. For example, consider the situation faced by Pepsico when it wanted to open a chain of Pizza Hut restaurants in the Soviet Union. The Russian ruble is not convertible, so Pepsico could not take the profits from its restaurants out of the Soviet Union in the form of dollars. There was no mechanism to exchange the rubles it earned in Russia for dollars, so the investment in the Soviet Union was essentially worthless to the U.S. parent. However, Pepsico arranged to use the ruble profit from the restaurants to buy Russian vodka, which it then shipped to the United States and sold for dollars. Pepsico managed to work things out, but lack of convertibility significantly inhibits the ability of a country to attract foreign investment.

Pegged Exchange Rate
Occurs when a country establishes a fixed exchange rate with another major currency; consequently, values of pegged currencies move together over time.

Convertible Currency
A currency that may be readily exchanged for other currencies.

---

[4]The International Monetary Fund reports each year a full listing of exchange rate arrangements in its *International Monetary Statistics.*

What is the difference between a fixed exchange rate system and a floating rate system? Which system is better? Explain.

What are pegged exchange rates?

What does it mean to say that the dollar is depreciating with respect to the British pound? For a U.S. consumer of British goods, would this be good or bad? How could changes in consumption arrest the decline of the dollar?

What is a convertible currency?

TRADING IN FOREIGN EXCHANGE

ON THE WWW

Current currency future prices are available directly from the Chicago Mercantile Exchange (CME) on their Web site at http:// www.cme.com/market/ hotquote.html. The quotes are updated every ten minutes throughout the trading session. Updated currency spot and forward rates (from 1 to 12 months) are also provided by the Bank of Montreal Treasury Group at http:/ /www.bmo.com/economic/ fxrates.htm.

Importers, exporters, tourists, and governments buy and sell currencies in the foreign exchange market. For example, when a U.S. trader imports automobiles from Germany, payment will probably be made in German marks. The importer buys marks (through its bank) in the foreign exchange market, much as one buys common stocks on the New York Stock Exchange or pork bellies on the Chicago Mercantile Exchange. However, whereas stock and commodity exchanges have organized trading floors, the foreign exchange market consists of a network of brokers and banks based in New York, London, Tokyo, and other financial centers. Most buy and sell orders are conducted by computer and telephone.[5]

SPOT RATES AND FORWARD RATES

Spot Rate
The effective exchange rate for a foreign currency for delivery on (approximately) the current day.

The exchange rates shown earlier in Tables 18-1 and 18-2 are known as **spot rates,** which means the rate paid for delivery of the currency "on the spot" or, in reality, no more than two days after the day of the trade. For most of the world's major currencies, it is also possible to buy (or sell) currencies for delivery at some agreed-upon future date, usually 30, 90, or 180 days from the day the transaction is negotiated. This rate is known as the **forward exchange rate.** For example, if a U.S. firm must make payment to a Japanese firm in 30 days, the U.S. firm's treasurer can buy Japanese yen today for delivery in 30 days, paying the 30-day forward rate of $0.0088 per Japanese yen (which equals 113.50 yen per dollar). Forward rates are analogous to futures prices on commodity exchanges, where contracts are drawn up for wheat or corn to be delivered at agreed-upon prices at some future date. The contract is signed today, and the future dollar cost of the Japanese yen is then known with certainty. Purchasing a forward contract is one technique for eliminating the volatility of future cash flows caused by fluctuations in exchange rates. This technique, which is called "hedging," will be discussed in more detail in Chapter 19.

Forward Exchange Rate
An agreed-upon price at which two currencies will be exchanged at some future date.

Recent forward rates for 30-, 90-, and 180-day delivery, along with the current spot rates for some commonly traded currencies, are given in Table 18-3. If one can obtain *more* of the foreign currency for a dollar in the forward than in the spot market, the forward currency is less valuable than the spot currency, and the forward currency is said to be selling at a **discount.** Thus, because 1 dollar could buy 0.6006 British pound in the spot market but 0.6035 pound in the 180-

Discount on Forward Rate
The situation when the spot rate is less than the forward rate.

---

[5]For a more detailed explanation of exchange rate determination and operations of the foreign exchange market, see Mark Eaker, Frank Fabozzi, and Dwight Grant, *International Corporate Finance* (Fort Worth, TX: Dryden Press, 1996).

		FORWARD RATES			
	SPOT RATE	30 DAYS	90 DAYS	180 DAYS	FORWARD RATE AT A PREMIUM OR DISCOUNT
British pound	0.6006	0.6009	0.6019	0.6035	Discount
Japanese yen	114.0400	113.5000	112.5900	111.1300	Premium
German mark	1.5581	1.5551	1.5493	1.5401	Premium

TABLE 18-3 Selected Spot and Forward Exchange Rates, December 19, 1996 (Number of Units of Foreign Currency per U.S. Dollar)

NOTES:
a. These are representative quotes as provided by a sample of New York banks. Forward rates for other currencies and for other lengths of time can often be negotiated.
b. When it takes more units of a foreign currency to buy one dollar in the future, the value of the foreign currency is less in the forward market than in the spot market, hence the forward rate is at a *discount* to the spot rate.
SOURCE: *The Wall Street Journal,* December 20, 1996.

day forward market, forward pounds sell at a discount as compared with spot pounds. Conversely, since a dollar would buy *fewer* yen in the forward than in the spot market, the forward yen is selling at a **premium.**

Premium on Forward Rate
The situation when the spot rate is greater than the forward rate.

SELF-TEST QUESTIONS

Differentiate between spot and forward exchange rates.

Explain what it means for a forward currency to sell at a discount, and at a premium.

INTEREST RATE PARITY

Market forces determine whether a currency sells at a forward premium or discount, and the relationship between spot and forward exchange rates is summarized in a concept called *interest rate parity.*

Interest Rate Parity
Specifies that investors should expect to earn the same return in all countries after adjusting for risk.

Interest rate parity holds that investors should expect to earn the same return in all countries after adjusting for risk. It recognizes that when you invest in a country other than your home country, you are affected by two forces — returns on the investment itself and changes in the exchange rate. It follows that your overall return will be higher than the investment's stated return if the currency your investment is denominated in appreciates relative to your home currency. Likewise, your overall return will be lower if the overseas currency you are holding declines in value.

Interest rate parity is expressed as follows:

$$\frac{f_t}{e_0} = \frac{(1 + k_h)}{(1 + k_f)}.$$

Here f_t is the t-period forward exchange rate and e_0 is today's spot exchange rate, both expressed in terms of the amount of home currency received per unit of foreign currency, and k_h and k_f are the periodic interest rates in the home country and the foreign country, respectively. If this relationship, which is defined as interest rate parity, does not hold, then currency traders will buy and sell currencies — that is, engage in arbitrage — until it does hold.

To illustrate interest rate parity, consider the case of a U.S. investor who can buy default-free 90-day German bonds that promise a 4 percent nominal return and are denominated in German marks. The 90-day rate, k_f, is 4%/4 = 1% because 90 days is 1/4 of a 360-day year. Assume also that the spot exchange rate is $e_0 = \$0.6418$, which means that you can exchange 0.6418 dollar for one mark, or 1.5581 marks per dollar. Finally, assume that the 90-day forward exchange rate, f_t, is $0.6455, which means that you can exchange one mark for 0.6455 dollar, or receive 1.5493 marks per dollar exchanged, 90 days from now.

The U.S. investor can receive a 4 percent annualized return denominated in marks, but if he or she ultimately wants to consume goods in the United States, those marks must be converted to dollars. The dollar return of the investment depends, therefore, on what happens to exchange rates over the next three months. However, the investor can lock in the dollar return by selling the foreign currency in the forward market. For example, the investor could simultaneously

♦ Convert $1,000 to 1,558.1 marks in the spot market.

♦ Invest the 1,558.1 marks in 90-day German bonds that have a 4 percent annualized return or a 1 percent quarterly return, hence will pay (1,558.1)(1.01) = 1,573.68 marks in 90 days.

♦ Agree today to exchange these 1,573.68 marks 90 days from now at the 90-day forward exchange rate of 1.5493 marks per dollar, or for a total of $1,015.74.

This investment, therefore, has an expected 90-day return of $15.74/$1,000 = 1.57%, which translates into a nominal return of 4(1.57%) = 6.28%. In this case, 4 percent of the expected 6.28 percent return is coming from the bond itself, and 2.28 percent arises because the market believes the mark will strengthen relative to the dollar. Notice that by locking in the forward rate today, the investor has eliminated any exchange rate risk. And, since the German bond is assumed to be default-free, the investor is assured of earning a 6.28 percent dollar return.

Interest rate parity implies that an investment in the United States with the same risk as a German bond should have a return of 6.28 percent. Solving for k_h in the preceding equation, we indeed find that the predicted interest rate in the United States is 6.28 percent.

Interest rate parity shows why a particular currency might be at a forward premium or discount. Notice that a currency is at a forward premium ($f_t > e_0$) whenever domestic interest rates are higher than foreign interest rates ($k_h > k_f$). Discounts prevail if domestic interest rates are lower than foreign interest rates. If these conditions do not hold, then arbitrage will soon force interest rates back to parity.

SELF-TEST QUESTION ??????

Briefly explain interest rate parity, illustrating with an example.

GLOBAL PERSPECTIVES

HUNGRY FOR A BIG MAC? GO TO CHINA!

Purchasing power parity (PPP) implies that the same product will sell for the same price in every country after adjusting for current exchange rates. One problem when testing to see if PPP holds is that it assumes that goods consumed in different countries are of the same quality. For example, if you find that a product is more expensive in Italy than it is in Switzerland, one explanation is that PPP fails to hold, but another explanation is that the product sold in Italy is of a higher quality and therefore deserves a higher price.

One way to test for PPP is to find goods that have the same quality worldwide. With this in mind, the *Economist* magazine occasionally compares the prices of a well-known good whose quality is the same in nearly 80 different countries: the McDonald's Big Mac hamburger.

The table on the next page provides information collected during 1995. The first column shows the price of a Big Mac in the local currency. Column 2 calculates the price of the Big Mac in terms of the U.S. dollar — this is obtained by dividing the local price by the actual exchange rate at that time. For example, a Big Mac costs 18.5 French francs in Paris. Given an exchange rate of 4.80 francs per dollar, this implies that the dollar price of a Big Mac is 18.5 francs/4.80 francs per dollar = $3.85.

The third column backs out the implied exchange rate that would hold under PPP. This is obtained by dividing the price of the Big Mac in each local currency by its U.S. price. For example, a Big Mac costs 8,100 rubles in Russia, and $2.32 in the United States. If PPP holds, the exchange rate should be 3,491 rubles per dollar (8,100 rubles)/($2.32).

Comparing the implied exchange rate to the actual exchange rate in Column 4, we see the extent to which the local currency is under- or overvalued relative to the dollar. Given that the actual exchange rate at the time was 4,985 rubles per dollar, this implies that the ruble was 30 percent undervalued.

The evidence suggests that strict PPP does not hold, but the Big Mac test may shed some insights about where exchange rates are headed. For example, the Big Mac 1995 test suggests that the yen was highly overvalued relative to the dollar, and since that time the dollar has strengthened roughly 30 percent relative to the yen.

One last benefit of the Big Mac test is that it tells us the cheapest places to find a Big Mac. According to the data, if you are looking for a Big Mac, head to China, and avoid Switzerland.

SOURCE: Excerpted from "Big MacCurrencies," *The Economist*, April 15, 1995, 74. Reprinted by permission from *The Economist*.

 ON THE WWW

The full text of the 1996 purchasing power parity article from The Economist, *entitled "McCurrencies: Where's the Beef?", is available at http://economist.iconnet.net/issue/27-04-96/fn1.html. The article, short and entertaining, includes a table similar to the one presented in the textbook, except the data is one year newer, thereby providing the opportunity to observe currency fluctuation in action.*

Purchasing Power Parity
The relationship where the same products cost roughly the same amount in different countries after taking into account the exchange rate.

PURCHASING POWER PARITY

We have discussed exchange rates in some detail, and we have considered the relationship between spot and forward exchange rates, but we have not yet addressed the fundamental question: What determines the level of exchange rates in each country? As it turns out, exchange rates are influenced by a multitude of factors that are difficult to predict, particularly on a day-to-day basis. However, market forces work to ensure that similar goods sell for similar prices in different countries after taking exchange rates into account. This relationship is known as *purchasing power parity.*

Purchasing power parity (PPP), sometimes referred to as the *law of one price,* implies that the level of exchange rates adjusts so that identical goods cost the same amount in different countries. For example, if a pair of tennis shoes costs $150 in the United States and 100 pounds in Britain, PPP would imply that the exchange rate would be $1.50 per pound. Consumers could purchase the shoes in Britain for 100 pounds, or they could exchange their 100 pounds for $150 and then purchase the same shoes in the United States at the same effective cost,

| | BIG MAC PRICES | | | | |
	IN LOCAL CURRENCY (1)	IN DOLLARS (2)	IMPLIED EXCHANGE RATE BASED ON PPP[a] (3)	ACTUAL $ EXCHANGE RATE 7/4/95 (4)	LOCAL CURRENCY UNDER(−)/OVER(+) VALUATION[b](%) (5)
United States[c]	$2.32	2.32	—	—	—
Argentina	Peso 3.00	3.00	1.29	1.00	+29
Australia	A$2.45	1.82	1.06	1.35	−22
Britain	£1.74	2.80	1.33[d]	1.61[d]	+21
Canada	C$2.77	1.99	1.19	1.39	−14
China	Yuan9.00	1.05	3.88	8.54	−55
Denmark	DKr26.75	4.92	11.50	5.43	+112
France	FFr18.5	3.85	7.97	4.80	+66
Germany	DM4.80	3.48	2.07	1.38	+50
Hong Kong	HK$9.50	1.23	4.09	7.73	−47
Italy	Lire4,500	2.64	1,940.00	1,702.00	+14
Japan	¥ 391	4.65	169.00	84.20	+100
Mexico	Peso10.9	1.71	4.70	6.37	−26
Russia	Ruble8,100	1.62	3,491.00	4,985.00	−30
Spain	Ptas355	2.86	153.00	124.00	+23
Switzerland	SFr5.90	5.20	2.54	1.13	+124
Thailand	Baht48.0	1.95	20.70	24.60	−16

NOTES:
[a]Purchasing power parity: local price divided by price in the United States.
[b]Against dollar.
[c]Average of New York, Chicago, San Francisco, and Atlanta.
[d]Dollars per pound.
SOURCE: McDonald's.

assuming no transaction or transportation costs. Here is the equation for purchasing power parity:

$$P_h = (P_f)(e_0),$$

or

$$e_0 = \frac{P_h}{P_f}.$$

Here

P_h = the price of the good in the home country ($150, assuming the United States is the home country).

P_f = the price of the good in the foreign country (100 pounds).

e_0 = the spot market exchange rate, expressed as the number of units of home currency that can be exchanged for one unit of foreign currency ($1.50 per pound).

PPP assumes that market forces will eliminate situations where the same product sells at a different price overseas. For example, if the shoes cost $140 in the

United States, importers/exporters could purchase the shoes in the United States for \$140, sell the shoes for 100 pounds in Britain, exchange the 100 pounds for \$150 in the foreign exchange market, and earn a profit of \$10 on every pair of shoes. This situation violates PPP, because $\$140 = P_h < (P_f)(e_0) = \$150$. Ultimately, this trading activity would increase the demand for shoes in the United States and thus P_h, increase the supply of shoes in Britain and thus reduce P_f, and increase the demand for dollars in the foreign exchange market and thus reduce e_0. Each of these actions works to restore PPP.

Notice that PPP assumes there are no transportation or transaction costs, or regulations, which limit the ability to ship goods between countries. In many cases, these assumptions are incorrect, which explains why PPP is often violated. An additional complication, when empirically testing to see whether PPP holds, is that products in different countries are rarely identical. Frequently, there are real or perceived differences in quality, which can lead to price differences in different countries.

The concepts of interest rate and purchasing power parity are critically important to those engaged in international activities. Companies and investors must anticipate changes in interest rates, inflation, and exchange rates, and they often try to hedge the risks of adverse movements in these factors. The parity relationships are extremely useful in judging and anticipating future conditions.

SELF-TEST QUESTION ??????

What is meant by purchasing power parity? Illustrate it.

INFLATION, INTEREST RATES, AND EXCHANGE RATES

Relative inflation rates, or the rates of inflation in foreign countries compared with that in the home country, have many implications for multinational financial decisions. Obviously, relative inflation rates will greatly influence future production costs at home and abroad. Equally important, inflation has a dominant influence on relative interest rates and exchange rates. Both of these factors influence the methods chosen by multinational corporations for financing their foreign investments, and both have an important effect on the profitability of foreign investments.

The currencies of countries with higher inflation rates than that of the United States by definition depreciate over time against the dollar. Countries where this has occurred include France, Italy, Mexico, and all the South American nations. On the other hand, the currencies of Germany, Switzerland, and Japan, which have had less inflation than the United States, have appreciated against the dollar. *In fact, a foreign currency will, on average, depreciate or appreciate at a percentage rate approximately equal to the amount by which its inflation rate exceeds or is less than our own.*

Relative inflation rates also affect interest rates. The interest rate in any country is largely determined by its inflation rate. Therefore, countries currently experiencing higher rates of inflation than the United States also tend to have higher interest rates. The reverse is true for countries with lower inflation rates.

It is tempting for a multinational corporation to borrow in countries with the lowest interest rates. However, this is not always a good strategy. Suppose, for example, that interest rates in Germany are lower than those in the United States because of Germany's lower inflation rate. A U.S. multinational firm could therefore save interest by borrowing in Germany. However, because of relative inflation rates, the mark will probably appreciate in the future, causing the dollar cost of annual interest and principal payments on German debt to rise over time. Thus, *the lower interest rate could be more than offset by losses from currency appreciation.* Similarly, multinational corporations should not necessarily avoid borrowing in a country such as Brazil, where interest rates have been very high, because future depreciation of the Brazilian cruzeiro could make such borrowing end up being relatively inexpensive.

SELF-TEST QUESTIONS

What effects do relative inflation rates have on relative interest rates?

What happens over time to the currencies of countries with higher inflation rates than that of the United States? To those with lower inflation rates?

Why might a multinational corporation decide to borrow in a country such as Brazil, where interest rates are high, rather than in a country like Germany, where interest rates are low?

INTERNATIONAL MONEY AND CAPITAL MARKETS

One way for U.S. citizens to invest in world markets is to buy the stocks of U.S. multinational corporations that invest directly in foreign countries. Another way is to purchase foreign securities — stocks, bonds, or money market instruments issued by foreign companies. Security investments are known as *portfolio investments,* and they are distinguished from *direct investments* in physical assets by U.S. corporations.

From World War II through the 1960s, the U.S. capital markets dominated world markets. Today, however, the value of U.S. securities represents less than one-fourth the value of all securities. Given this situation, it is important for both corporate managers and investors to have an understanding of international markets. Moreover, these markets often offer better opportunities for raising or investing capital than are available domestically.

EURODOLLAR MARKET

Eurodollar
A U.S. dollar deposited in a bank outside the United States.

A **Eurodollar** is a U.S. dollar deposited in a bank outside the United States. (Although they are called Eurodollars because they originated in Europe, Eurodollars are really any dollars deposited in any part of the world other than the United States.) The bank in which the deposit is made may be a non-U.S. bank, such as Barclay's Bank in London; the foreign branch of a U.S. bank, such as Citibank's Paris branch; or even a foreign branch of a third-country bank, such as Barclay's Munich branch. Most Eurodollar deposits are for $500,000 or more, and they have maturities ranging from overnight to about one year.

The major difference between Eurodollar deposits and regular U.S. time deposits is their geographic locations. The two types of deposits do not involve different currencies — in both cases, dollars are on deposit. However, Eurodollars are outside the direct control of the U.S. monetary authorities, so U.S. banking regulations, including reserve requirements and FDIC insurance premiums, do not apply. The absence of these costs means that the interest rate paid on Eurodollar deposits can be higher than domestic U.S. rates on equivalent instruments.

Although the dollar is the leading international currency, British pounds, German marks, Swiss francs, Japanese yen, and other currencies are also deposited outside their home countries; these *Eurocurrencies* are handled in exactly the same way as Eurodollars.

Eurodollars are borrowed by U.S. and foreign corporations for various purposes, but especially to pay for goods exported from the United States and to invest in U.S. security markets. Also, U.S. dollars are used as an international currency, or international medium of exchange, and many Eurodollars are used for this purpose. It is interesting to note that Eurodollars were actually "invented" by the Soviets in 1946. International merchants did not trust the Soviets or their rubles, so the Soviets bought some dollars (for gold), deposited them in a Paris bank, and then used these dollars to buy goods in the world markets. Others found it convenient to use dollars this same way, and soon the Eurodollar market was in full swing.

Eurodollars are usually held in interest-bearing accounts. The interest rate paid on these deposits depends (1) on the bank's lending rate, as the interest a bank earns on loans determines its willingness and ability to pay interest on deposits, and (2) on rates of return available on U.S. money market instruments. If money market rates in the United States were above Eurodollar deposit rates, these dollars would be sent back and invested in the United States, whereas if Eurodollar deposit rates were significantly above U.S. rates, which is more often the case, more dollars would be sent out of the United States to become Eurodollars. Given the existence of the Eurodollar market and the electronic flow of dollars to and from the United States, it is easy to see why interest rates in the United States cannot be insulated from those in other parts of the world.

Interest rates on Eurodollar deposits (and loans) are tied to a standard rate known by the acronym *LIBOR*, which stands for *London InterBank Offer Rate*. LIBOR is the rate of interest offered by the largest and strongest London banks on dollar deposits of significant size. In December 1996, LIBOR rates were over half a percentage point above domestic U.S. bank rates on time deposits of the same maturity—4.94 percent for three-month CDs versus 5.63 percent for LIBOR CDs. The Eurodollar market is essentially a short-term market; most loans and deposits are for less than one year.

INTERNATIONAL BOND MARKETS

Any bond sold outside the country of the borrower is called an international bond. However, there are two important types of international bonds: foreign bonds and Eurobonds. **Foreign bonds** are bonds sold by a foreign borrower but denominated in the currency of the country in which the issue is sold. For instance, Northern Telcom (a Canadian company) may need U.S. dollars to finance the operations of its subsidiaries in the United States. If it decides to raise the needed capital in the U.S. bond market, the bond will be underwritten by a syndicate of U.S. investment bankers, denominated in U.S. dollars, and sold to U.S. investors in accordance with SEC and applicable state regulations. Except for the foreign origin of the borrower, this bond will be indistinguishable from those issued by equivalent U.S. corporations. Since Northern Telcom is a foreign corporation, however, the bond will be called a foreign bond.

ON THE WWW

Current three-month and six-month LIBOR rates can be obtained from a site maintained by Kuhlmann Commercial Capital at http://www.kuhlmann.com/rates.html. The site also allows the user to view historical charts of the LIBOR rates.

Foreign Bond
A bond sold by a foreign borrower but denominated in the currency of the country in which it is sold.

Eurobond
A bond sold in a country other than the one in whose currency the bond is denominated.

The term **Eurobond** is used to designate any bond issued in one country but denominated in the currency of some other country. Examples include a Ford Motor Company issue denominated in dollars and sold in Germany, or a British firm's sale of mark-denominated bonds in Switzerland. The institutional arrangements by which Eurobonds are marketed are different than those for most other bond issues, with the most important distinction being a far lower level of required disclosure than is usually found for bonds issued in domestic markets, particularly in the United States. Governments tend to be less strict when regulating securities denominated in foreign currencies, because the bonds' purchasers are generally more "sophisticated." The lower disclosure requirements result in lower total transaction costs for Eurobonds.

Eurobonds appeal to investors for several reasons. Generally, they are issued in bearer form rather than as registered bonds, so the names and nationalities of investors are not recorded. Individuals who desire anonymity, whether for privacy reasons or for tax avoidance, like Eurobonds. Similarly, most governments do not withhold taxes on interest payments associated with Eurobonds. If the investor requires an effective yield of 10 percent, a Eurobond that is exempt from tax withholding would need a coupon rate of 10 percent. Another type of bond — for instance, a domestic issue subject to a 30 percent withholding tax on interest paid to foreigners — would need a coupon rate of 14.3 percent to yield an after-withholding rate of 10 percent. Investors who desire secrecy would not want to file for a refund of the tax, so they would prefer to hold the Eurobond.

More than half of all Eurobonds are denominated in dollars. Bonds in Japanese yen, German marks, and Dutch guilders account for most of the rest. Although centered in Europe, Eurobonds are truly international. Their underwriting syndicates include investment bankers from all parts of the world, and the bonds are sold to investors not only in Europe but also in such faraway places as Bahrain and Singapore. Up to a few years ago, Eurobonds were issued solely by multinational firms, by international financial institutions, or by national governments. Today, however, the Eurobond market is also being tapped by purely domestic U.S. firms, because they often find that by borrowing overseas they can lower their debt costs.

INTERNATIONAL STOCK MARKETS

New issues of stock are sold in international markets for a variety of reasons. For example, a non-U.S. firm might sell an equity issue in the United States because it can tap a much larger source of capital than in its home country. Also, a U.S. firm might tap a foreign market because it wants to create an equity market presence to accompany its operations in that country. Large multinational companies also occasionally issue new stock simultaneously in multiple countries. For example, Alcan Aluminum, a Canadian company, recently issued new stock in Canada, Europe, and the United States simultaneously, using different underwriting syndicates in each market.

In addition to new issues, outstanding stocks of large multinational companies are increasingly being listed on multiple international exchanges. For example, Coca-Cola's stock is traded on six stock exchanges in the United States, four stock exchanges in Switzerland, and the Frankfurt stock exchange in Germany. Some foreign stocks are listed in the United States — an example here is Royal Dutch Petroleum, which is listed on the NYSE. U.S. investors can also invest in foreign companies through *American Depository Receipts (ADRs),* which are certificates representing ownership of foreign stock held in trust. About 1,300

ADRs are now available in the United States, with most of them traded on the over-the-counter (OTC) market. However, more and more ADRs are being listed on the New York Stock Exchange, including Germany's Daimler-Benz, England's British Airways, Japan's Honda Motors, and Italy's Fiat Group.

SELF-TEST QUESTIONS ??????

Differentiate between foreign portfolio investments and direct foreign investments.

What are Eurodollars?

Has the development of the Eurodollar market made it easier or more difficult for the Federal Reserve to control U.S. interest rates?

Differentiate between foreign bonds and Eurobonds.

Why do Eurobonds appeal to investors?

MULTINATIONAL CAPITAL BUDGETING

Up to now, we have discussed the general environment in which multinational firms operate. In the remainder of the chapter, we will see how international factors affect key corporate decisions. We begin with capital budgeting. Although the same basic principles of capital budgeting analysis apply to both foreign and domestic operations, there are some key differences. First, cash flow estimation is more complex for overseas investments. Most multinational firms set up separate subsidiaries in each foreign country in which they operate, and the relevant cash flows for the parent company are the dividends and royalties paid by the subsidiaries to the parent. Second, these cash flows must be converted into the parent company's currency, hence they are subject to exchange rate risk. For example, General Motors' German subsidiary may make a profit of 100 million marks in 1998, but the value of this profit to GM will depend on the dollar/mark exchange rate: How many *dollars* will 100 million marks buy?

Repatriation of Earnings
The process of sending cash flows from a foreign subsidiary back to the parent company.

Dividends and royalties are normally taxed by both foreign and home-country governments. Furthermore, a foreign government may restrict the amount of the cash that may be **repatriated** to the parent company. For example, some governments place a ceiling, stated as a percentage of the company's net worth, on the amount of cash dividends that a subsidiary can pay to its parent. Such restrictions are normally intended to force multinational firms to reinvest earnings in the foreign country, although restrictions are sometimes imposed to prevent large currency outflows, which might disrupt the exchange rate.

Whatever the host country's motivation for blocking repatriation of profits, the result is that the parent corporation cannot use cash flows blocked in the foreign country to pay dividends to its shareholders or to invest elsewhere in the business. Hence, from the perspective of the parent organization, *the cash flows relevant for foreign investment analysis are the cash flows that the subsidiary is actually expected to send back to the parent.* The present value of those cash flows is found by applying an appropriate discount rate, and this present value is then compared with the parent's required investment to determine the project's NPV.

In addition to the complexities of the cash flow analysis, *the cost of capital may be different for a foreign project than for an equivalent domestic project, because foreign projects may be more or less risky.* A higher risk could arise from two primary sources — (1) exchange rate risk and (2) political risk. A lower risk might result from international diversification.

Exchange Rate Risk.
The risk that relates to what the basic cash flows will be worth in the parent company's home currency.

Exchange rate risk relates to what the basic cash flows will be worth in the parent company's home currency. The foreign currency cash flows to be turned over to the parent must be converted into U.S. dollars by translating them at expected future exchange rates. An analysis should be conducted to ascertain the effects of exchange rate variations, and, on the basis of this analysis, an exchange rate risk premium should be added to the domestic cost of capital to reflect exchange rate risk. It is sometimes possible to hedge against exchange rate fluctuations, but it may not be possible to hedge completely, especially on long-term projects. If hedging is used, the costs of doing so must be subtracted from the project's cash flows.

Political Risk
Potential actions by a host government which would reduce the value of a company's investment.

Political risk refers to potential actions by a host government which would reduce the value of a company's investment. It includes at one extreme the expropriation without compensation of the subsidiary's assets, but it also includes less drastic actions that reduce the value of the parent firm's investment in the foreign subsidiary, including higher taxes, tighter repatriation or currency controls, and restrictions on prices charged. The risk of expropriation is small in traditionally friendly and stable countries such as Great Britain or Switzerland. However, in Latin America, Africa, the Far East, and Eastern Europe, the risk may be substantial. Past expropriations include those of ITT and Anaconda Copper in Chile, Gulf Oil in Bolivia, Occidental Petroleum in Libya, Enron Corporation in Peru, and the assets of many companies in Iraq, Iran, and Cuba.

Several organizations rate the political risk of countries. For example, International Business Communications, a London company, publishes the *International Country Risk Guide,* which contains individual ratings for political, financial, and economic risk, along with a composite rating for each country. Table 18-4 contains selected portions of a recent report. The political variable — which makes up 50 percent of the composite rating — includes factors such as government corruption and the gap between economic expectations and reality. The

TABLE 18-4 Selected Countries Ranked by Composite Risk

RANK	COUNTRY	POLITICAL RISK	FINANCIAL RISK	ECONOMIC RISK	COMPOSITE RISK
1	Switzerland	93.0	50.0	39.5	91.5
9	United States	78.0	49.0	39.5	83.5
10	Canada	81.0	48.0	37.0	83.0
25	Venezuela	75.0	40.0	36.0	75.5
50	Israel	58.0	33.0	34.5	63.0
75	Panama	47.0	24.0	38.0	54.5
100	Peru	45.0	28.0	21.5	47.5
125	Burma	27.0	9.0	22.5	28.5
129	Liberia	10.0	8.0	12.0	15.0

NOTE: A total of 129 countries are ranked, but only 9 are shown here.
SOURCE: *International Country Risk Guide.*

financial rating looks at such things as the likelihood of losses from exchange controls and loan defaults. The economic rating takes into account such factors as inflation and debt-service costs.

The best, or least risky, score is 100 for political factors and 50 each for the financial and economic factors, and the composite risk is a weighted average of the political, financial, and economic factors. The United States is ranked ninth, below Switzerland, Luxembourg, Norway, Austria, Germany, Netherlands, Brunei, and Japan. Liberia, as shown in Table 18-4, is ranked last.

If a company's management has a serious concern that a given country might expropriate foreign assets, it will probably not make significant investments in that country. However, companies can take steps to reduce the potential loss from expropriation in three major ways: (1) finance the subsidiary with local capital, (2) structure operations so that the subsidiary has value only as a part of the integrated corporate system, and (3) obtain insurance against economic losses from expropriation from a source such as the Overseas Private Investment Corporation (OPIC). In the latter case, insurance premiums would have to be added to the project's cost.

SELF-TEST QUESTIONS

List some key differences in capital budgeting as applied to foreign versus domestic operations.

What are the relevant cash flows for an international investment?

Why might the cost of capital for a foreign project differ from that of an equivalent domestic project? Could it be lower?

What adjustments might be made to the domestic cost of capital for a foreign investment due to exchange rate risk and political risk?

INTERNATIONAL CAPITAL STRUCTURES

Companies' capital structures vary among the large industrial countries. For example, the Organization for Economic Cooperation and Development (OECD) recently reported that, on average, Japanese firms use 85 percent debt to total assets (in book value terms), German firms use 64 percent, and U.S. firms use 55 percent. One problem, however, when interpreting these numbers is that different countries often use very different accounting conventions with regard to (1) reporting assets on a historical- versus a replacement-cost basis, (2) the treatment of leased assets, (3) pension plan funding, and (4) capitalizing versus expensing R&D costs. These differences make it difficult to compare capital structures.

One recent study, by Raghuram Rajan and Luigi Zingales of the University of Chicago, attempts to control for differences in accounting practices. In their study, Rajan and Zingales used a database which covers fewer firms than the OECD but which provides a more complete breakdown of balance sheet data. Rajan and Zingales concluded that differences in accounting practices can explain much of the cross-country variation in capital structures.

Rajan's and Zingales' results are summarized in Table 18-5. There are a number of different ways to measure capital structure. One measure is the average ratio of total liabilities to total assets — this is similar to the measure used by

| TABLE 18-5 | Median Capital Structures among Large Industrialized Countries (Measured in Terms of Book Value) |

COUNTRY	TOTAL LIABILITIES TO TOTAL ASSETS (UNADJUSTED FOR DIFFERENCES IN ACCOUNTING DIFFERENCES) (1)	DEBT TO TOTAL ASSETS (UNADJUSTED FOR ACCOUNTING DIFFERENCES) (2)	TOTAL LIABILITIES TO TOTAL ASSETS (ADJUSTED FOR DIFFERENCES IN ACCOUNTING DIFFERENCES) (3)	DEBT TO TOTAL ASSETS (ADJUSTED FOR ACCOUNTING DIFFERENCES) (4)	TIMES INTEREST EARNED (TIE) RATIO (5)
Canada	56%	32%	48%	32%	1.55×
France	71	25	69	18	2.64
Germany	73	16	50	11	3.20
Italy	70	27	68	21	1.81
Japan	69	35	62	21	2.46
United Kingdom	54	18	47	10	4.79
United States	58	27	52	25	2.41
Mean	64.4%	25.7%	56.6%	19.7%	2.69×
Standard deviation	8.1%	6.9%	9.5%	7.7%	1.07×

SOURCE: Raghuram Rajan and Luigi Zingales: "What Do We Know about Capital Structure? Some Evidence from International Data," *The Journal of Finance*, Vol. 50, No. 5, December 1995, 1421–1460. Used with permission.

the OECD, and it is reported in column 1. Based on this measure, German and Japanese firms appear to be more highly levered than U.S. firms. However, if you look at column 2, where capital structure is measured by interest-bearing debt to total assets, it appears that German firms use *less* leverage than U.S. and Japanese firms. What explains this difference? Rajan and Zingales argue that much of this difference is explained by the way German firms account for pension liabilities. German firms generally include all pension liabilities (and their offsetting assets) on the balance sheet, whereas firms in other countries (including the United States) generally "net out" pension assets and liabilities on their balance sheets. To see the importance of this difference, consider a firm with $10 million in liabilities (not including pension liabilities) and $20 million in assets (not including pension assets). Assume that the firm has $10 million in pension liabilities which are fully funded by $10 million in pension assets. Therefore, net pension liabilities are zero. If this firm were in the United States, it would report a ratio of total liabilities to total assets equal to 50 percent ($10 million/$20 million). By contrast, if this firm operated in Germany, both its pension assets and liabilities would be reported on the balance sheet. The firm would have $20 million in liabilities and $30 million in assets—or a 67 percent ($20 million/$30 million) ratio of total liabilities to total assets. Total debt is the sum of short-term debt and long-term debt and excludes other liabilities including pension liabilities. Therefore, the measure of total debt to total assets provides a more comparable measure of leverage across different countries.

Rajan and Zingales also make a variety of adjustments which attempt to control for other differences in accounting practices. The effect of these adjustments are reported in Columns 3 and 4. Overall, the evidence suggests that companies in Germany and the United Kingdom tend to have less leverage, whereas firms in Canada appear to have more leverage, relative to firms in the United States, France, Italy, and Japan. This conclusion is supported by data in the final column, which shows the average times-interest-earned ratio for firms in a number of different countries. Recall from Chapter 3 that the times-interest-earned ratio is the ratio of operating income (EBIT) to interest expense. This measure indicates how much cash the firm has available to service its interest expense. In general, firms with more leverage have a lower times-interest-earned ratio. The data indicate that this ratio is highest in the United Kingdom and Germany and lowest in Canada.

SELF-TEST QUESTION   ??????

Do international differences in financial leverage exist? Explain.

MULTINATIONAL WORKING CAPITAL MANAGEMENT

CASH MANAGEMENT

The goals of cash management in a multinational corporation are similar to those in a purely domestic corporation: (1) to speed up collections, slow down disbursements, and thus maximize net float; (2) to shift cash as rapidly as possible from those parts of the business where it is not needed to those parts where it is needed; and (3) to maximize the risk-adjusted, after-tax rate of return on temporary cash balances. Multinational companies use the same general procedures for achieving these goals as domestic firms, but because of longer distances and more serious mail delays, such devices as lockbox systems and electronic funds transfers are especially important.

Although multinational and domestic corporations have the same objectives and use similar procedures, multinational corporations face a far more complex task. As noted earlier in our discussion of political risk, foreign governments often place restrictions on transfers of funds out of the country, so although IBM can transfer money from its Salt Lake City office to its New York concentration bank just by pressing a few buttons, a similar transfer from its Buenos Aires office is far more complex. Buenos Aires funds are denominated in australs (Argentina's equivalent of the dollar), so the australs must be converted to dollars before the transfer. If there is a shortage of dollars in Argentina, or if the Argentinean government wants to conserve dollars to purchase strategic materials, then conversion, hence the transfer, may be blocked. Even if no dollar shortage exists in Argentina, the government may still restrict funds outflows if those funds represent profits or depreciation rather than payments for purchased materials or equipment, because many countries, especially those that are less developed, want profits reinvested in the country in order to stimulate economic growth.

Once it has been determined what funds can be transferred, the next task is to get those funds to locations where they will earn the highest returns. Whereas domestic corporations tend to think in terms of domestic securities, multinationals are more likely to be aware of investment opportunities all around the world. Most multinational corporations use one or more global concentration banks, located in money centers such as London, New York, Tokyo, Zurich, or Singapore, and their staffs in those cities, working with international bankers, know of and are able to take advantage of the best rates available anywhere in the world.

CREDIT MANAGEMENT

Like most other aspects of finance, credit management in the multinational corporation is similar to but more complex than that in a purely domestic business. First, granting credit is more risky in an international context because, in addition to the normal risks of default, the multinational corporation must also worry about exchange rate fluctuations between the time a sale is made and the time a receivable is collected. For example, if IBM sold a computer to a Japanese customer for 90 million yen when the exchange rate was 90 yen to the dollar, IBM would obtain 90,000,000/90 = $1,000,000 for the computer. However, if it sold the computer on terms of net/6 months, and if the yen fell against the dollar so that one dollar would now buy 112.5 yen, IBM would end up realizing only 90,000,000/112.5 = $800,000 when it collected the receivable. Hedging can reduce this type of risk, but at a cost.

Offering credit is generally more important for multinational corporations than for purely domestic firms for two reasons. First, much U.S. trade is with poorer, less developed nations, where granting credit is generally a necessary condition for doing business. Second, and in large part as a result of the first point, developed nations whose economic health depends on exports often help their manufacturing firms compete internationally by granting credit to foreign countries. In Japan, for example, the major manufacturing firms have direct ownership ties with large "trading companies" engaged in international trade, as well as with giant commercial banks. In addition, a government agency, the Ministry of International Trade and Industry (MITI), helps Japanese firms identify potential export markets and also helps potential customers arrange credit for purchases from Japanese firms. In effect, the huge Japanese trade surpluses are used to finance Japanese exports, thus helping to perpetuate their favorable trade balance. The United States has attempted to counter with the Export-Import Bank, which is funded by Congress, but the fact that the United States has a large balance of payments deficit is clear evidence that we have been less successful than others in world markets in recent years.

The huge debt which countries such as Brazil, Mexico, and Argentina owe U.S. and other international banks is well known, and this situation illustrates how credit policy (by banks in this case) can go astray. The banks face a particularly sticky problem with these loans, because if a sovereign nation defaults, the banks cannot lay claim to the assets of the country as they could if a corporate customer defaulted. Note too that although the banks' loans to foreign governments are getting most of the headlines, many U.S. multinational corporations are also in trouble as a result of granting credit to business customers in the same countries where bank loans to governments are on shaky ground.

By pointing out the risks in granting credit internationally, we are not suggesting that such credit is bad. Quite the contrary, for the potential gains from international operations far outweigh the risks, at least for companies (and banks) that have the necessary expertise.

INVENTORY MANAGEMENT

As with most other aspects of finance, inventory management in a multinational setting is similar to but more complex than for a purely domestic firm. First, there is the matter of the physical location of inventories. For example, where should Exxon keep its stockpiles of crude oil and refined products? It has refineries and marketing centers located worldwide, and one alternative is to keep items concentrated in a few strategic spots from which they can then be shipped as needs arise. Such a strategy might minimize the total amount of inventories needed and thus might minimize the investment in inventories. Note, though, that consideration will have to be given to potential delays in getting goods from central storage locations to user locations all around the world. Both working stocks and safety stocks would have to be maintained at each user location, as well as at the strategic storage centers. Problems like the Iraqi occupation of Kuwait and the subsequent trade embargo, which brought with it the potential for a shutdown of production of about 25 percent of the world's oil supply, complicate matters further.

Exchange rates also influence inventory policy. If a local currency, say, the Danish krone, were expected to rise in value against the dollar, a U.S. company operating in Denmark would want to increase stocks of local products before the rise in the krone, and vice versa if the krone were expected to fall.

Another factor that must be considered is the possibility of import or export quotas or tariffs. For example, Apple Computer Company was buying certain memory chips from Japanese suppliers at a bargain price. Then U.S. chipmakers accused the Japanese of dumping chips in the U.S. market at prices below cost, so they sought to force the Japanese to raise prices. That led Apple to increase its chip inventory.[6] Then computer sales slacked off, and Apple ended up with an oversupply of obsolete computer chips. As a result, Apple's profits were hurt and its stock price fell, demonstrating once more the importance of careful inventory management.

As mentioned earlier, another danger in certain countries is the threat of expropriation. If that threat is large, inventory holdings will be minimized, and goods will be brought in only as needed. Similarly, if the operation involves extraction of raw materials such as oil or bauxite, processing plants may be moved offshore rather than located close to the production site.

Taxes have two effects on multinational inventory management. First, countries often impose property taxes on assets, including inventories, and when this is done, the tax is based on holdings as of a specific date, say, January 1 or March 1. Such rules make it advantageous for a multinational firm (1) to schedule production so that inventories are low on the assessment date, and (2) if assessment dates vary among countries in a region, to hold safety stocks in different countries at different times during the year.

Finally, multinational firms may consider the possibility of at-sea storage. Oil, chemical, grain, and other companies that deal in a bulk commodity that must be stored in some type of tank can often buy tankers at a cost not much greater — or perhaps even less, considering land cost — than land-based facilities.

---

[6]The term "dumping" warrants explanation, because the practice is so potentially important in international markets. Suppose Japanese chipmakers have excess capacity. A particular chip has a variable cost of $25, and its "fully allocated cost," which is the $25 plus total fixed cost per unit of output, is $40. Now suppose the Japanese firm can sell chips in the United States at $35 per unit, but if it charges $40, it will not make any sales because U.S. chipmakers sell for $35.50. If the Japanese firm sells at $35, it will cover variable cost plus make a contribution to fixed overhead, so selling at $35 makes sense. Continuing, if the Japanese firm can sell in Japan at $40, but U.S. firms are excluded from Japanese markets by import duties or other barriers, the Japanese will have a huge advantage over U.S. manufacturers. This practice of selling goods at lower prices in foreign markets than at home is called "dumping." U.S. firms are required by antitrust laws to offer the same price to all customers and, therefore, cannot engage in dumping.

Loaded tankers can then be kept at sea or at anchor in some strategic location. This eliminates the danger of expropriation, minimizes the property tax problem, and maximizes flexibility with regard to shipping to areas where needs are greatest or prices highest.

This discussion has only scratched the surface of inventory management in the multinational corporation — the task is much more complex than for a purely domestic firm. However, the greater the degree of complexity, the greater the rewards from superior performance, so if you want challenge along with potentially high rewards, look to the international arena.

SELF-TEST QUESTIONS ???????

What are some factors that make cash management especially complicated in a multinational corporation?

Why is granting credit especially risky in an international context?

Why is credit policy especially important for a multinational firm?

SUMMARY

This chapter discussed the most important differences between multinational and domestic financial management. Some of the key concepts are listed below:

♦ **International operations** are becoming increasingly important to individual firms and to the national economy. A **multinational, or global, corporation** is a firm that operates in an integrated fashion in a number of countries.

♦ Companies "go global" for six primary reasons: (1) **to expand their markets,** (2) **to obtain raw materials,** (3) **to seek new technology,** (4) **to lower production costs,** (5) **to avoid trade barriers,** and (6) **to diversify.**

♦ Six major factors distinguish financial management as practiced by domestic firms from that practiced by multinational corporations: (1) **different currency denominations,** (2) **different economic and legal structures,** (3) **languages,** (4) **cultural differences,** (5) **role of governments,** and (6) **political risk.**

♦ When discussing **exchange rates,** the number of U.S. dollars required to purchase one unit of a foreign currency is called a **direct quotation,** while the number of units of foreign currency that can be purchased for one U.S. dollar is an **indirect quotation.**

♦ Financial forecasting is more difficult for multinational firms, because **exchange rate fluctuations** make it difficult to estimate the dollars that overseas operations will produce.

♦ Prior to August 1971, the world was on a **fixed exchange rate system** whereby the U.S. dollar was linked to gold and other currencies were then tied to the dollar. After August 1971, the world monetary system changed to a **floating system** under which major world currency rates float with market forces, largely unrestricted by governmental intervention. The central bank of each country does operate in the foreign exchange market, buying and selling currencies to smooth out exchange rate fluctuations, but only to a limited extent.

♦ **Pegged exchange rates** occur when a country establishes a fixed exchange rate with a major currency. Consequently, the values of pegged currencies move together over time.

- ◆ **Spot rates** are the rates paid for delivery of currency "on the spot," while the **forward exchange rate** is the rate paid for delivery at some agreed-upon future date, usually 30, 90, or 180 days from the day the transaction is negotiated. The forward rate can be at either a **premium** or a **discount** to the spot rate.

- ◆ **Interest rate parity** holds that investors should expect to earn the same return in all countries after adjusting for risk.

- ◆ **Purchasing power parity,** sometimes referred to as the *law of one price,* implies that the level of exchange rates adjusts so that identical goods cost the same in different countries.

- ◆ Granting credit is more risky in an international context because, in addition to the normal risks of default, the multinational firm must worry about **exchange rate changes** between the time a sale is made and the time a receivable is collected.

- ◆ Credit policy is important for a multinational firm for two reasons: (1) Much trade is with less-developed nations, and in such situations granting credit is a necessary condition for doing business. (2) The governments of nations such as Japan whose economic health depends upon exports often help their firms compete by granting credit to foreign customers.

- ◆ Foreign investments are similar to domestic investments, but political risk and exchange rate risk must be considered. **Political risk** is the risk that the foreign government will take some action which will decrease the value of the investment, while **exchange rate risk** is the risk of losses due to fluctuations in the value of the dollar relative to the values of foreign currencies.

- ◆ Investments in **international capital projects** expose firms to exchange rate risk and political risk. The relevant cash flows in international capital budgeting are the dollars which can be turned over to the parent company.

- ◆ **Eurodollars** are U.S. dollars deposited in banks outside the United States. Interest rates on Eurodollars are tied to **LIBOR,** the London interbank offer rate.

- ◆ U.S. firms often find that they can raise long-term capital at a lower cost outside the United States by selling bonds in the **international capital markets.** International bonds may be either **foreign bonds,** which are exactly like regular domestic bonds except that the issuer is a foreign company, or **Eurobonds,** which are bonds sold in a foreign country but denominated in the currency of the issuing company's home country.

QUESTIONS

18-1 Under the fixed exchange rate system, what was the currency against which all other currency values were defined? Why?

18-2 Exchange rates fluctuate under both the fixed exchange rate and floating exchange rate systems. What, then, is the difference between the two systems?

18-3 If the French franc depreciates against the U.S. dollar, can a dollar buy more or fewer French francs as a result?

18-4 If the United States imports more goods from abroad than it exports, foreigners will tend to have a surplus of U.S. dollars. What will this do to the value of the dollar with respect to foreign currencies? What is the corresponding effect on foreign investments in the United States?

18-5 Why do U.S. corporations build manufacturing plants abroad when they could build them at home?

18-6 Should firms require higher rates of return on foreign projects than on identical projects located at home? Explain.

18-7 What is a Eurodollar? If a French citizen deposits $10,000 in Chase Manhattan Bank in New York, have Eurodollars been created? What if the deposit is made in Barclay's Bank in London? Chase Manhattan's Paris branch? Does the existence of the Eurodollar market make the Federal Reserve's job of controlling U.S. interest rates easier or more difficult? Explain.

18-8 Does interest rate parity imply that interest rates are the same in all countries?

18-9 Why might purchasing power parity fail to hold?

SELF-TEST PROBLEM

ST-1
Key terms

Define each of the following terms:
a. Multinational corporation
b. Exchange rate
c. Fixed exchange rate system; floating exchange rates
d. Trade deficit
e. Devaluation; revaluation
f. Exchange rate risk; convertible currency
g. Pegged exchange rates
h. Interest rate parity; purchasing power parity
i. Spot rate; forward exchange rate
j. Discount on forward rate; premium on forward rate
k. Repatriation of earnings; political risk
l. Eurodollar; Eurobond; international bond; foreign bond
m. European currency units (ECUs); Eurocurrencies

STARTER PROBLEMS

18-1
Cross rates

A currency trader observes that in the spot exchange market, one U.S. dollar can be exchanged for 1,498.2 Italian lira or for 111.23 Japanese yen. What is the cross-exchange rate between the yen and the lira; that is, how many yen would you receive for every lira exchanged?

18-2
Interest rate parity

Six-month T-bills have a nominal rate of 7 percent, while default-free Japanese bonds that mature in 6 months have a nominal rate of 5.5 percent. In the spot exchange market, one yen equals $0.009. If interest rate parity holds, what is the 6-month forward exchange rate?

18-3
Purchasing power parity

A television set costs $500 in the United States. The same set costs 2,535 French francs. If purchasing power parity holds, what is the spot exchange rate between the franc and the dollar?

EXAM-TYPE PROBLEMS

The problems included in this section are set up in such a way that they could be used as multiple-choice exam problems.

18-4
Exchange rate

If British pounds sell for $1.50 (U.S.) per pound, what should dollars sell for in pounds per dollar?

18-5
Currency appreciation

Suppose that 1 French franc could be purchased in the foreign exchange market for 20 U.S. cents today. If the franc appreciated 10 percent tomorrow against the dollar, how many francs would a dollar buy tomorrow?

18-6
Cross exchange rates

Suppose the exchange rate between U.S. dollars and the French franc was FF5.9 = $1, and the exchange rate between the dollar and the British pound was £1 = $1.50. What was the exchange rate between francs and pounds?

18-7
Cross exchange rates

Look up the 3 currencies in Problem 18-6 in the foreign exchange section of a current issue of *The Wall Street Journal*. What is the current exchange rate between francs and pounds?

18-8
Foreign investment analysis

After all foreign and U.S. taxes, a U.S. corporation expects to receive 3 pounds of dividends per share from a British subsidiary this year. The exchange rate at the end of the year is expected to be $1.60 per pound, and the pound is expected to depreciate 5 percent against the dollar each year for an indefinite period. The dividend (in pounds) is expected to grow at 10 percent a year indefinitely. The parent U.S. corporation owns 10 million shares of the subsidiary. What is the present value in dollars of its equity ownership of the subsidiary? Assume a cost of equity capital of 15 percent for the subsidiary.

18-9
Exchange gains and losses

You are the vice-president of International InfoXchange, headquartered in Chicago, Illinois. All shareholders of the firm live in the United States. Earlier this month, you obtained a loan of 5 million Canadian dollars from a bank in Toronto to finance the construction of a new plant in Montreal. At the time the loan was received, the exchange rate was 75 U.S. cents to the Canadian dollar. By the end of the month, it has unexpectedly dropped to 70 cents. Has your company made a gain or loss as a result, and by how much?

PROBLEMS

18-10
Exchange rates

Table 18-1 lists foreign exchange rates for December 19, 1996. On that day, how many dollars would be required to purchase 1,000 units of each of the following: German marks, Italian lira, Japanese yen, Mexican pesos, and Swiss francs?

18-11
Exchange rates

Look up the 5 currencies in Problem 18-10 in the foreign exchange section of a current issue of *The Wall Street Journal*.
a. What is the current exchange rate for changing dollars into 1,000 units of marks, lira, yen, pesos, and Swiss francs?
b. What is the percentage gain or loss between the December 19, 1996, exchange rate and the current exchange rate for each of the currencies in Part a?

18-12
Results of exchange rate changes

Early in September 1983, it took 245 Japanese yen to equal $1. More than 13 years later, in December 1996, that exchange rate had fallen to 114 yen to $1. Assume the price of a Japanese-manufactured automobile was $8,000 in September 1983 and that its price changes were in direct relation to exchange rates.
a. Has the price, in dollars, of the automobile increased or decreased during the 13-year period because of changes in the exchange rate?
b. What would the dollar price of the automobile be on December 19, 1996, again assuming that the car's price changes only with exchange rates?

18-13
Spot and forward rates

Boisjoly French Imports has agreed to purchase 15,000 cases of French wine for 16 million francs at today's spot rate. The firm's financial manager, James Desreumaux, has noted the following current spot and forward rates:

	U.S. DOLLAR/FRANC	FRANC/U.S. DOLLAR
Spot	0.16933	5.9055
30-day forward	0.16890	5.9207
90-day forward	0.16807	5.9499
180-day forward	0.16719	5.9812

On the same day, Desreumaux agrees to purchase 15,000 more cases of wine in 3 months at the same price of 16 million francs.
a. What is the price of the wine, in U.S. dollars, if it is purchased at today's spot rate?
b. What is the cost, in dollars, of the second 15,000 cases if payment is made in 90 days and the spot rate at that time equals today's 90-day forward rate?
c. If the exchange rate for the French franc is 5.00 to $1 in 90 days, how much will he have to pay for the wine (in dollars)?

18-14
Interest rate parity

Assume that interest rate parity holds and that 90-day risk-free securities yield 5 percent in the United States and 5.3 percent in Germany. In the spot market 1 mark equals 0.63 dollar.
a. Is the 90-day forward rate trading at a premium or discount relative to the spot rate?
b. What is the 90-day forward rate?

18-15
Interest rate parity

Assume that interest rate parity holds. In both the spot market and the 90-day forward market 1 Japanese yen equals 0.0086 dollar. The 90-day risk-free securities yield 4.6 percent in Japan. What is the yield on 90-day risk-free securities in the United States?

18-16
Purchasing power parity

In the spot market 7.8 pesos can be exchanged for 1 U.S. dollar. A compact disk costs $15 in the United States. If purchasing power parity holds, what should be the price of the same disk in Mexico?

18-17
Purchasing power parity

A chair costs 500 French francs. The same chair also costs 10,000 Japanese yen. If purchasing power parity holds, what should be the exchange rate between the yen and the French franc?

INTEGRATED CASE

CITRUS PRODUCTS INC.

18-18 Multinational Financial Management   Citrus Products Inc. is a medium-sized producer of citrus juice drinks with groves in Indian River County, Florida. Until now, the company has confined its operations and sales to the United States, but its CEO, George Gaynor, wants to expand into Europe. The first step would be to set up sales subsidiaries in Spain and Portugal, then to set up a production plant in Spain, and, finally, to distribute the product throughout the European common market. The firm's financial manager, Ruth Schmidt, is enthusiastic about the plan, but she is worried about the implications of the foreign expansion on the firm's financial management process. She has asked you, the firm's most recently hired financial analyst, to develop a 1-hour tutorial package that explains the basics of multinational financial management. The tutorial will be presented at the next board of directors meeting. To get you started, Schmidt has supplied you with the following list of questions.

a. What is a multinational corporation? Why do firms expand into other countries?

b. What are the six major factors which distinguish multinational financial management from financial management as practiced by a purely domestic firm?

c. Consider the following illustrative exchange rates.

	U.S. DOLLARS REQUIRED TO BUY ONE UNIT OF FOREIGN CURRENCY
Spanish peseta	0.0075
Portuguese escudo	0.0063

  (1) Are these currency prices direct quotations or indirect quotations?

  (2) Calculate the indirect quotations for pesetas and escudos.

  (3) What is a cross rate? Calculate the two cross rates between pesetas and escudos.

  (4) Assume Citrus Products can produce a liter of orange juice and ship it to Spain for $1.75. If the firm wants a 50 percent markup on the product, what should the orange juice sell for in Spain?

  (5) Now, assume Citrus Products begins producing the same liter of orange juice in Spain. The product costs 200 pesetas to produce and ship to Portugal, where it can be sold for 400 escudos. What is the dollar profit on the sale?

  (6) What is exchange rate risk?

d. Briefly describe the current international monetary system. How does the current system differ from the system that was in place prior to August 1971?

e. What is a convertible currency? What problems arise when a multinational company operates in a country whose currency is not convertible?

f. What is the difference between spot rates and forward rates? When is the forward rate at a premium to the spot rate? At a discount?

g. What is interest rate parity? Currently, you can exchange 1 peseta for 0.0080 dollar in the 30-day forward market, and the risk-free rate on 30-day securities is 4 percent in both Spain and the United States. Does interest rate parity hold? If not, which securities offer the highest expected return?

h. What is purchasing power parity? If grapefruit juice costs $2.00 a liter in the United States and purchasing power parity holds, what should be the price of grapefruit juice in Portugal?

i. What impact does relative inflation have on interest rates and exchange rates?

j. Briefly discuss the international capital markets.

k. To what extent do average capital structures vary across different countries?

l. What is the impact of multinational operations on each of the following financial management topics?

  (1) Cash management.

  (2) Capital budgeting decisions.

  (3) Credit management.

  (4) Inventory management.

CHAPTER 19

DERIVATIVES AND RISK MANAGEMENT

USING DERIVATIVES PRUDENTLY TO REDUCE RISK

Corporate financial managers are generally thought of as models of caution, paid to manage a company's finances prudently and conservatively. But recent events at Procter & Gamble, Gibson Greetings, and Metallgesellschaft, a German company, have shaken that image. Each of these companies incurred huge losses on derivatives transactions which were supposedly undertaken to reduce risk.

A look at how P&G got into trouble with risky derivatives shows how tempting it can be for a company to try to magnify its returns, but how difficult it is to predict the risks involved. P&G profited handsomely with derivatives in the early 1990s. Sensing more opportunity for gain, the P&G treasury staff asked Bankers Trust in late 1993 to create a derivative whose returns would depend on both U.S. and German interest rates. Bankers Trust, perhaps the most aggressive dealer in exotic securities, gave P&G three choices. P&G chose the most aggressive, the derivative that promised the greatest reward but entailed the greatest risk.

The transaction involved two complex swaps. P&G was allowed to issue floating rate debt at below-market rates, but, in return, the company had to give Bankers Trust a series of "put options" that gave the bank the right to sell to P&G U.S. Treasury bonds and German government bonds at a fixed price. If interest rates in both countries were constant or fell, there would be no problem for P&G — the bonds would be worth more on the open mar-

ket than the fixed price, so Bankers Trust would not require P&G to buy them. But if rates rose, P&G would have to buy bonds at above-market prices.

Rates climbed rapidly after the deal was struck, causing bond prices to plunge, so P&G was saddled with a rising liability to buy bonds at above-market prices. Bankers Trust said that it advised P&G to cut its losses by closing out the transactions, but P&G wouldn't budge. When the first losses hit, the P&G folks who set the transaction up probably said, "Oh-oh, we have a problem. But let's wait and see what interest rates do before we tell the boss." By the time P&G bit the bullet and closed out the position, it had a pre-tax loss of $157 million.

P&G contended that it was victimized by Bankers Trust, and it sued, contending that the bank did not disclose all the risks involved in the transactions. Said a P&G spokesperson, "These transactions were intended to be hedges. We use swaps to manage and reduce our borrowing costs, not to make money. The swaps turned out to be speculative transactions that were highly leveraged and clearly did not fit our policy." On the other hand, Bankers Trust claimed that P&G is a sophisticated company and that it knew the rules of the game. The lawsuit was finally settled after more than two years of haggling, with Bankers Trust agreeing to cover about 80 percent of P&G's losses. However, the topic of derivative use and abuse has continued to be one of the hottest topics in the financial press.

In this chapter, we will discuss risk management, a topic of increasing importance to financial managers. The term *risk management* can mean many things, but in business it involves identifying events that could have adverse financial consequences and then taking actions to prevent and/or minimize the damage caused by these events. Years ago, corporate risk managers dealt primarily with insurance — they made sure the firm was adequately insured against fire, theft, and other casualties, and that it had adequate liability coverage. More recently, the scope of risk management has been broadened to include such things as controlling the costs of key inputs like petroleum by purchasing oil futures, or protecting against changes in interest rates or exchange rates through dealings in the interest rate or foreign exchange markets. In addition, risk managers try to ensure that actions designed to hedge against risk — as P&G claimed its derivatives transactions were supposed to be — are not actually increasing risks.

Derivatives

Securities whose values are determined by the market price or interest rate of some other asset.

Since perhaps the most important aspect of risk management involves derivative securities, we begin the chapter with a discussion of derivatives. **Derivatives** are securities whose values are determined by the market price (or interest rate) of some other asset. Derivatives include *options,* whose values depend on the price of some underlying stock; *interest rate and exchange rate futures and swaps,* whose values depend on interest rate and exchange rate levels; and *commodity futures,* whose values depend on commodity prices.

BACKGROUND ON DERIVATIVES

An historical perspective is useful when studying derivatives. One of the first formal markets for derivatives was the futures market for wheat. Farmers were concerned about the price they would receive for their wheat when they sold it in the fall, and millers were concerned about the price they would have to pay. The risks faced by both parties could be reduced if they could establish a price earlier in the year. Accordingly, mill agents would go out to the wheat belt and make contracts with farmers which called for the farmers to deliver grain at a predetermined price. Both parties benefited from the transaction in the sense that their risks were reduced. The farmers could concentrate on growing their crop without worrying about the price of grain, and the millers could concentrate on their milling operations. Thus, *hedging with futures* lowered aggregate risk in the economy.

 ON THE WWW

The Chicago Board of Trade has an excellent web site at http://www.cbot.com/menu.htm. Make sure to check out the Visitor's Center for a wealth of information on the history and operation of the exchange.

These early futures dealings were between two parties who arranged transactions between themselves. Soon, though, middlemen came into the picture, and *trading* in futures was established. The Chicago Board of Trade was an early marketplace for this dealing, and *futures dealers* helped make a market in futures contracts. Thus, farmers could sell futures on the exchange, and millers could buy them there. This improved the efficiency and lowered the cost of hedging operations.

Quickly, a third group — *speculators* — entered the scene. As we will see in the next section, most derivatives, including futures, are highly leveraged, meaning that a small change in the value of the underlying asset will produce a large change in the price of the derivative. This leverage appealed to speculators. At first blush, one might think that the appearance of speculators would increase risk, but this is not true. Speculators add capital and players to the market, and this tends to stabilize the market. Of course, derivatives markets are inherently volatile due to the leverage involved, hence risk to the speculators themselves is high. Still their bearing that risk makes the derivatives markets more stable for the hedgers.

Natural Hedges
Situations in which aggregate risk can be reduced by derivatives transactions between two parties.

Natural hedges, defined as situations in which aggregate risk can be reduced by derivatives transactions between two parties (called *counterparties*), exist for many commodities, for foreign currencies, for interest rates on securities with different maturities, and even for common stocks where portfolio managers want to "hedge their bets." Natural hedges occur when futures are traded between cotton farmers and cotton mills, copper mines and copper fabricators, importers and foreign manufacturers for currency exchange rates, electric utilities and coal miners, and oil producers and oil users. In all such situations, hedging reduces aggregate risk and thus benefits the economy.

Hedging can also be done in situations where no natural hedge exists. Here one party wants to reduce some type of risk, and another party agrees to sell a contract which protects the first party from that specific event or situation. Insurance is an obvious example of this type of hedge. Note, though, that with non-symmetric hedges, risks are generally *transferred* rather than *eliminated*. Even here, though, insurance companies can reduce certain types of risk through diversification.

The derivatives markets have grown more rapidly than any other major market in recent years, for a number of reasons. First, analytical techniques such as the Black-Scholes Option Pricing Model, which is discussed in the next section, have been developed to help establish "fair" prices, and having a better basis for pricing hedges makes the counterparties more comfortable with deals. Second, computers and electronic communications make it much easier for counterparties to deal with one another. Third, globalization has greatly increased the importance of currency markets and the need for reducing the exchange rate risks brought on by global trade. Recent trends and developments are sure to continue if not accelerate, so the use of derivatives for risk management purposes is bound to grow.

Note, though, that derivatives do have a potential downside. These instruments are highly leveraged, so small miscalculations can lead to huge losses. Also, they are complicated, hence not well understood by most people. This makes mistakes more likely than with less complex instruments, and it makes it harder for a firm's top management to exercise proper control over derivatives transactions. One 28-year-old, relatively low-level employee, operating in the Far East, entered into transactions that led to the bankruptcy of Britain's oldest bank (Barings Bank), the institution that held the accounts of the Queen of England. P&G's problems were discussed earlier, and Orange County, California, went bankrupt due to its treasurer's speculation in derivatives. Hundreds of other horror stories could be told.

The P&G, Orange County, and Barings Bank affairs make the headlines, causing some people to argue that derivatives should be regulated out of existence to "protect the public." However, derivatives are used far more often to hedge risks than in harmful speculations, but these beneficial transactions never make the headlines. So, while the horror stories point out the need for top managers to exercise control over the personnel who deal with derivatives, they certainly do not justify the elimination of derivatives.

In the balance of this chapter, we discuss how firms can manage risks, and how derivatives are used in risk management.

ON THE WWW

An excellent article about the fiasco in Orange County, entitled "Orange County: Don't Blame Derivatives," can be found on NYU's Stern Business School website at http://equity.stern. nyu.edu/Webzine/Sternbusiness/ Spring95/orange.html. The article, written by Stephen Figlewski and Lawrence J. White, professors at NYU, provides an excellent discussion of what derivatives are, how they work, and why Orange County got into trouble in the first place.

SELF-TEST QUESTIONS

What is a "natural hedge"? Give some examples of natural hedges.

List three reasons the derivatives markets have grown more rapidly than any other major market in recent years.

ORANGE COUNTY BLUES

It was too good to be true. For more than 20 years, the investment fund managed by California's Orange County produced impressive returns. However, this all came to an end in December 1994, when the county announced that the fund had generated more than $2 billion in losses. The county's treasurer, Robert Citron, was forced to resign, and both the county and its fund were declared bankrupt.

What happened? During the 1980s, fund manager Citron had followed a strategy of investing in long-term securities. The trend in interest rates was downward. When rates decline, long-term bond prices rise, so Citron's fund had earned both interest and capital gains. Furthermore, Citron started borrowing at low short-term rates and investing in higher-yielding long-term bonds, which further increased the fund's interest income and capital gains.

Such a strategy works wonderfully during a period of declining rates: The fund's record was outstanding, and Citron was a hero in Orange County. However, Citron's confidence in his ability to beat the market turned to overconfidence, and he failed to display a reasonable degree of prudence. In November 1993, he became convinced that interest rates were poised for another dramatic decline, so he began borrowing heavily and using the money to purchase "high octane" — exceptionally risky — derivative products

whose values were extremely sensitive to changes in interest rates. One of Citron's favorites was a derivative called an "inverse floater," whose interest payments rise when interest rates fall, and vice versa. Another favorite was a complicated derivative product that was designed to go up in value if the yield curve steepened, that is, if long-term rates increased relative to short-term rates.

Citron was betting (1) that interest rates in general were going to decline and (2) that short-term rates were going to decline more than long-term rates. However, his predictions were completely wrong. The economy strengthened in 1994, causing the Fed to raise interest rates dramatically. Further, short-term rates went up almost 4 percentage points versus less than 2 percentage points for long-term rates, so the yield curve flattened instead of growing steeper.

These changes caused the value of inverse floaters and yield curve derivatives to plunge, and the general increase in rates also reduced the value of the "plain vanilla" securities the fund held. Further, the problem was exacerbated because the fund had borrowed on a short-term basis to finance its investments, and its own interest costs rose steadily as interest rates increased.

The fund used its assets (securities) as collateral for its loans. It took in some $7.5 billion in tax receipts, fees, and the like from school districts, cities in the county such as Anaheim (home of Disneyland), and

water districts. This money was "invested" in derivatives and other securities until such time as it was needed for payrolls and the like. In the meantime, its "investments" were used as collateral for loans to buy still more derivatives.

Interestingly, most of the derivatives in which Orange County invested were based on securities issued by the federal government. Those securities could decline in value even though there will be no default on their cash payments. Of course, if the amount of cash received declines, as it would on an inverse floater if interest rates rise, the value of the security will decline, and such a security is certainly not riskless.

Orange County is the fifth largest county in the country — and one of the wealthiest — and it is slowly recovering from Citron's folly. But the losses have had some profound effects on Orange County's citizens. The county's bonds were downgraded from AA to junk, causing its interest rates to soar. Highway projects were canceled, and some employees had to be laid off.

More recently, Orange County has issued new debt. In early 1997, more than a year after the county declared bankruptcy, it sold $880 million in bonds, but at a high cost. Moreover, many problems are still unresolved. For example, the county has filed lawsuits against both its investment banker, Merrill Lynch, and its auditor, KPMG Peat Marwick. The outcome of these lawsuits may not be resolved for several years.

OPTIONS

Option
A contract which gives its holder the right to buy (or sell) an asset at a predetermined price within a specified period of time.

An **option** is a contract which gives its holder the right to buy (or sell) an asset at some predetermined price within a specified period of time. Financial managers should understand option theory both for risk management and also because such an understanding will help them structure warrant and convertible financings.

OPTION TYPES AND MARKETS

There are many types of options and option markets.[1] To illustrate how options work, suppose you owned 100 shares of General Computer Corporation (GCC), which on March 22, 1997, sold for $53.50 per share. You could sell to someone the right to buy your 100 shares at any time during the next four months at a price of, say, $55 per share. The $55 is called the **strike, or exercise, price.** Such options exist, and they are traded on a number of exchanges, with the Chicago Board Options Exchange (CBOE) being the oldest and the largest. This type of option is defined as a **call option,** because the purchaser has a "call" on 100 shares of stock. The seller of an option is called the option *writer.* An investor who "writes" call options against stock held in his or her portfolio is said to be selling *covered options.* Options sold without the stock to back them up are called *naked options.* When the exercise price exceeds the current stock price, a call option is said to be *out-of-the-money.* When the exercise price is below the current price of the stock, the option is *in-the-money.*

You can also buy an option which gives you the right to *sell* a stock at a specified price within some future period — this is called a **put option.** For example, suppose you think GCC's stock price is likely to decline from its current level of $53.50 sometime during the next four months. Table 19-1 provides data on GCC's options. You could buy a four-month put option (the July put option) for $218.75 ($2 3/16 × 100) which would give you the right to sell 100 shares (which you would not necessarily own) at a price of $50 per share ($50 is the strike price). Suppose you bought this 100-share contract for $218.75 and then GCC's stock fell to $45. Your put option would rise in value to ($50 − $45)(100) = $500. After subtracting the $218.75 you paid for the option, your profit (before taxes and commissions) would be $281.25.

Table 19-1 contains an extract from the March 22, 1997, Listed Options Quotations Table as it would appear in a daily newspaper. This extract, which focuses on GCC, U.S. Medical, and Sport World, reflects the trading which occurred on the previous day. Sport World's April $55 call option sold for $0.50. Thus, for $0.50(100) = $50 you could buy options that would give you the right to purchase 100 shares of Sport World stock at a price of $55 per share from March until April, or during the next month.[2] If the stock price stayed below $55 during that period, you would lose your $50, but if it rose to $65, your $50 investment would increase in value to ($65 − $55)(100) = $1,000 in less than 30 days. That translates into a very healthy annualized rate of return. Incidentally, if the stock price did go up, you would not actually exercise your options and buy the stock — rather, you would sell the options, which would then have a value of $1,000 versus the $50 you paid, to another option buyer or back to the original seller.

In addition to options on individual stocks, options are also available on several stock indexes such as the NYSE Index and the S&P 100 Index. Index options permit one to hedge (or bet) on a rise or fall in the general market as well as on individual stocks.

Option trading is one of the hottest financial activities in the United States. The leverage involved makes it possible for speculators with just a few dollars to make a fortune almost overnight. Also, investors with sizable portfolios can sell

---

Strike (Exercise) Price
The price that must be paid for a share of common stock when an option is exercised.

Call Option
An option to buy, or "call," a share of stock at a certain price within a specified period.

Put Option
An option to sell a share of stock at a certain price within a specified period.

---

[1] For an in-depth treatment of options, see Don M. Chance, *An Introduction to Derivatives* (Fort Worth, TX: Dryden, 1995).

[2] Actually, the *expiration date,* which is the last date that the option can be exercised, is the Friday before the third Saturday of the exercise month. Thus, the April options actually have a term one day less than four weeks. Also, note that option contracts are generally written in 100-share multiples.

| TABLE   19-1 | March 22, 1997, Listed Options Quotations |

CLOSING PRICE	STRIKE PRICE	CALLS — LAST QUOTE			PUTS — LAST QUOTE		
		APRIL	MAY	JULY	APRIL	MAY	JULY
General Computer Corporation (GCC)							
53½	50	4¼	4¾	5½	⅝	1⅜	2³⁄₁₆
53½	55	1⁵⁄₁₆	2¹⁄₁₆	3⅛	2⅝	r	4½
53½	60	⁵⁄₁₆	¹¹⁄₁₆	1½	6⅝	r	8
U.S. Medical							
56⅝	55	4¼	5⅛	7	2¼	3¾	r
Sport World							
53⅛	55	½	1⅛	r	2⅛	r	r

NOTE: r means not traded on March 21.

options against their stocks and earn the value of the option (less brokerage commissions), even if the stock's price remains constant. Most importantly, though, options can be used to create *hedges* which protect the value of an individual stock or portfolio. We will discuss hedging strategies in more detail later in the chapter.[3]

Conventional options are generally written for six months or less, but a new type of option called a **Long-term Equity AnticiPation Security (LEAPS)** has been trading in recent years. Like conventional options, LEAPS are listed on exchanges and are tied both to individual stocks and to stock indexes. The major difference is that LEAPS are long-term options, having maturities of up to 2½ years. One-year LEAPS cost about twice as much as the matching three-month option, but because of their much longer time to expiration, LEAPS provide buyers with more potential for gains and offer better long-term protection for a portfolio.

Corporations on whose stocks options are written have nothing to do with the option market. Corporations do not raise money in the option market, nor do they have any direct transactions in it. Moreover, option holders do not vote for corporate directors or receive dividends. There have been studies by the SEC and others as to whether option trading stabilizes or destabilizes the stock market, and whether this activity helps or hinders corporations seeking to raise new capital. The studies have not been conclusive, but option trading is here to stay, and many regard it as the most exciting game in town.

Long-Term Equity AnticiPation Security (LEAPS)
Long-term options that are listed on the exchanges and tied to both individual stocks and to stock indexes.

FACTORS THAT AFFECT THE VALUE OF A CALL OPTION

A study of Table 19-1 provides some insights into call option valuation. First, we see that there are at least three factors which affect a call option's value: (1) The

---

[3]It should be noted that insiders who trade illegally generally buy options rather than stock because the leverage inherent in options increases the profit potential. Note, though, that it is illegal to use insider information for personal gain, and an insider using such information would be taking advantage of the option seller. Insider trading, in addition to being unfair and essentially equivalent to stealing, hurts the economy: Investors lose confidence in the capital markets and raise their required returns because of an increased element of risk, and this raises the cost of capital and thus reduces the level of real investment.

higher the stock's market price in relation to the strike price, the higher will be the call option price. Thus, Sport World's $55 April call option sells for $0.50, whereas U.S. Medical's $55 April option sells for $4.25. This difference arises because U.S. Medical's current stock price is $56⅝ versus only $53⅛ for Sport World. (2) The higher the strike price, the lower the call option price. Thus, all of GCC's call options, regardless of exercise month, decline as the strike price increases. (3) The longer the option period, the higher the option price. This occurs because the longer the time before expiration, the greater the chance that the stock price will climb substantially above the exercise price. Thus, option prices increase as the expiration date is lengthened. Other factors that affect option values, especially the volatility of the underlying stock, are discussed in later sections.

FORMULA VALUE VERSUS OPTION PRICE

How is the actual price of a call option determined in the market? In the next section, we present a widely used model (the Black-Scholes model) for pricing call options, but first it is useful to establish some basic concepts. To begin, we define a call option's **formula value** as follows:

Formula Value
The value of an option calculated as the current stock price minus the strike, or exercise, price.

$$\text{Formula value} = \frac{\text{Current price}}{\text{of the stock}} - \text{Strike price.}$$

For example, if a stock sells for $50 and its option has a strike price of $20, then the formula value is $30. The formula value can be thought of as the value of the option if it was exercised today. Note that the calculated formula value of a call option could be negative, but realistically the minimum "true" value of an option is zero, because no one would exercise an out-of-the-money option. Note also that an option's formula value is only a first approximation value — it merely provides a starting point for finding the actual value of the option.

Now consider Figure 19-1, which presents some data on Space Technology Inc. (STI), a company which recently went public and whose stock price has fluctuated widely during its short history. The third column in the tabular data shows the formula values for STI's call option when the stock was selling at different prices; the fourth column gives the actual market prices for the option; and the fifth column shows the premium of the actual option price over its formula value. At any stock price below $20, the formula value is set at zero, but above $20, each $1 increase in the price of the stock brings with it a $1 increase in the option's formula value. Note, however, that the actual market price of the option lies above the formula value at each price of the common stock, although the premium declines as the price of the stock increases. For example, when the stock sold for $20 and the option had a zero formula value, its actual price, and the premium, was $9. Then, as the price of the stock rose, the *formula value's increase* matched the stock's increase dollar for dollar, but the *market price* of the option climbed less rapidly, causing the premium to decline. The premium was $9 when the stock sold for $20 a share, but it had declined to $1 by the time the stock price had risen to $73 a share. Beyond that point, the premium virtually disappeared.

Why does this pattern exist? Why should a call option ever sell for more than its formula value, and why does the premium decline as the price of the stock increases? The answer lies in part in the speculative appeal of options — they enable someone to gain a high degree of personal leverage when buying securities. To illustrate, suppose STI's option sold for exactly its formula value. Now

FIGURE 19-1 Space Technology Inc.: Option Price and Formula Value

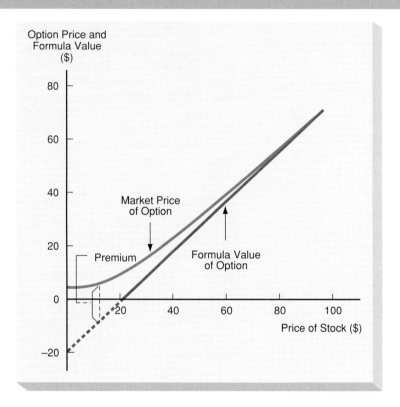

PRICE OF STOCK (1)	STRIKE PRICE (2)	FORMULA VALUE OF OPTION (1) − (2) = (3)	MARKET PRICE OF OPTION (4)	PREMIUM (4) − (3) = (5)
$20.00	$20.00	$ 0.00	$ 9.00	$9.00
21.00	20.00	1.00	9.75	8.75
22.00	20.00	2.00	10.50	8.50
35.00	20.00	15.00	21.00	6.00
42.00	20.00	22.00	26.00	4.00
50.00	20.00	30.00	32.00	2.00
73.00	20.00	53.00	54.00	1.00
98.00	20.00	78.00	78.50	0.50

suppose you were thinking of investing in the company's common stock at a time when it was selling for $21 a share. If you bought a share and the price rose to $42, you would have made a 100 percent capital gain. However, had you bought the option at its formula value ($1 when the stock was selling for $21), your capital gain would have been $22 − $1 = $21 on a $1 investment, or 2,100 percent! At the same time, your total loss potential with the option would be only $1 versus a potential loss of $21 if you purchased the stock. The huge capital gains potential, combined with the loss limitation, is clearly worth something — the exact amount it is worth to investors is the amount of the premium. Note, however, that buying the option is riskier than buying STI's stock, because there is a higher probability of losing money on the option. If STI's stock price remains at $21, you would break even if you bought the stock (ignoring transaction costs), but you would have a 100 percent loss on the option investment.

Why does the premium decline as the price of the stock rises? Part of the answer is that both the leverage effect and the loss protection feature decline at high stock prices. For example, if you were thinking of buying STI stock when its price was $73 a share, the formula value of the option would be $53. If the stock price doubled to $146, you would have a 100 percent gain on the stock. Now note that the formula value of the option would go from $53 to $126, for a percentage gain of 138 percent versus 2,100 percent in the earlier case. Notice also that the potential loss per dollar of potential gain on the option is much greater when the option is selling at high prices. These two factors, the declining leverage impact and the increasing danger of larger losses, help explain why the premium diminishes as the price of the common stock rises.

In addition to the stock price and the exercise price, the price of an option depends on three other factors: (1) the option's term to maturity, (2) the variability of the stock price, and (3) the risk-free rate. We will explain precisely how these factors affect call option prices later, but for now, note these points:

1. The longer a call option has to run, the greater its value and the larger its premium. If an option expires at 4 p.m. today, there is not much chance that the stock price will go way up, so the option must sell at close to its formula value, and its premium must be small. On the other hand, if the expiration date is a year away, the stock price could rise sharply, pulling the option's value up with it.

2. An option on an extremely volatile stock is worth more than one on a very stable stock. If the stock price rarely moves, then there is only a small chance of a large gain. However, if the stock price is highly volatile, the option could easily become very valuable. At the same time, losses on options are limited — you can make an unlimited amount, but you can only lose what you paid for the option. Therefore, a large decline in a stock's price does not have a corresponding bad effect on option holders. As a result of the unlimited upside but limited downside, the more volatile a stock, the higher the value of its options.

3. The payoff on an option will occur in the future, so the value of the option is, in a sense, the present value of an expected future payoff. The higher the discount rate used to find the PV, the lower the value of the call option.

Because of Points 1 and 2, in a graph such as Figure 19-1 the longer an option's life, the higher its market price line would be above the formula value line. Similarly, the more volatile the price of the underlying stock, the higher is the market price line. We will see precisely how these factors, and also the discount rate, affect option values in the following section, where we discuss the Black-Scholes option pricing model.

SELF-TEST QUESTIONS

What is an option? A call option? A put option?

Define a call option's formula value. Why is the actual market price of a call option usually above its formula value?

What are some factors which affect a call option's value?

THE BLACK-SCHOLES OPTION PRICING MODEL (OPM)[4]

The *Black-Scholes Option Pricing Model (OPM)*, developed in 1973, helped give rise to the rapid growth in options trading.[5] This model, which has even been programmed into the permanent memories of some hand-held calculators, is widely used by option traders.

In deriving their option pricing model, Black and Scholes made the following assumptions:

1. The stock underlying the call option provides no dividends or other distributions during the life of the option.
2. There are no transaction costs for buying or selling either the stock or the option.
3. The short-term, risk-free interest rate is known and is constant during the life of the option.
4. Any purchaser of a security may borrow any fraction of the purchase price at the short-term, risk-free interest rate.
5. Short selling is permitted, and the short seller will receive immediately the full cash proceeds of today's price for a security sold short.[6]
6. The call option can be exercised only on its expiration date.
7. Trading in all securities takes place continuously, and the stock price moves randomly.

The derivation of the Black-Scholes model rests on the concept of a riskless hedge. By buying shares of a stock and simultaneously selling call options on that stock, an investor can create a risk-free investment position, where gains on the stock will exactly offset losses on the option. This riskless hedged position must earn a rate of return equal to the risk-free rate; otherwise, an arbitrage opportunity would exist, and people trying to take advantage of this opportunity would drive the price of the option to the equilibrium level as specified by the Black-Scholes model.

The Black-Scholes model consists of the following three equations:

$$V = P[N(d_1)] - Xe^{-k_{RF}t}[N(d_2)]. \tag{19-1}$$

$$d_1 = \frac{\ln(P/X) + [k_{RF} + (\sigma^2/2)]t}{\sigma\sqrt{t}}. \tag{19-2}$$

$$d_2 = d_1 - \sigma\sqrt{t}. \tag{19-3}$$

[4]This section is relatively technical, so it can be omitted without loss of continuity if time pressures do not permit coverage.

[5]See Fischer Black and Myron Scholes, "The Pricing of Options and Corporate Liabilities," *Journal of Political Economy,* May/June 1973, 637–659.

[6]Suppose an investor (or speculator) does not now own any IBM stock. If the investor anticipates a rise in the stock price and consequently buys IBM stock, he or she is said to have *gone long* in IBM. On the other hand, if the investor thinks IBM's stock is likely to fall, he or she could *go short,* or *sell IBM short.* Since the short seller has no IBM stock, he or she would have to borrow the shares sold short from a broker. If the stock price falls, the short seller could, later on, buy shares on the open market and pay back the ones borrowed from the broker. The short seller's profit, before commissions and taxes, would be the difference between the price received from the short sale and the price paid later to purchase the replacement stock.

Here

$$V = \text{current value of the call option.}$$

$$P = \text{current price of the underlying stock.}$$

$$N(d_i) = \text{probability that a deviation less than } d_i \text{ will occur in a standard normal distribution. Thus, } N(d_i) \text{ and } N(d_2) \text{ represent areas under a standard normal distribution function.}$$

$$X = \text{exercise, or strike, price of the option.}$$

$$e \approx 2.7183.$$

$$k_{RF} = \text{risk-free interest rate.}$$

$$t = \text{time until the option expires (the option period).}$$

$$\ln(P/X) = \text{natural logarithm of } P/X.$$

$$\sigma^2 = \text{variance of the rate of return on the stock.}$$

Note that the value of the option is a function of the variables we discussed earlier: (1) P, the stock's price; (2) t, the option's time to expiration; (3) X, the strike price; (4) σ^2, the variance of the underlying stock; and (5) k_{RF}, the risk-free rate. We do not derive the Black-Scholes model — the derivation involves some extremely complicated mathematics that go far beyond the scope of this text. However, it is not difficult to use the model. Under the assumptions set forth previously, if the option price is different from the one found by Equation 19-1, this would provide the opportunity for arbitrage profits, which would force the option price back to the value indicated by the model.[7] As we noted earlier, the Black-Scholes model is widely used by traders, so actual option prices conform reasonably well to values derived from the model.

In essence, the first term of Equation 19-1, $P[N(d_1)]$, can be thought of as the expected present value of the terminal stock price, while the second term, $Xe^{-k_{RF}t}[N(d_2)]$, can be thought of as the present value of the exercise price. However, rather than try to figure out exactly what the equations mean, it is more productive to plug in some numbers to see how changes in the inputs affect the value of an option.

OPM ILLUSTRATION

The current stock price, P, the exercise price, X, and the time to maturity, t, can all be obtained from a newspaper such as *The Wall Street Journal*. The risk-free rate, k_{RF}, is the yield on a Treasury bill with a maturity equal to the option expiration date. The annualized variance of stock returns, σ^2, can be estimated by multiplying the variance of the percentage change in daily stock prices for the past year [that is, the variance of $(P_t - P_{t-1})/P_t$], by 365 days.

Assume that the following information has been obtained:

$$P = \$20.$$

$$X = \$20.$$

$$t = 3 \text{ months or } 0.25 \text{ year.}$$

$$k_{RF} = 12\% = 0.12.$$

$$\sigma^2 = 0.16. \text{ Note that if } \sigma^2 = 0.16, \text{ then } \sigma = \sqrt{0.16} = 0.4.$$

---

[7]*Programmed trading,* in which stocks are bought and options are sold, or vice versa, is an example of arbitrage between stocks and options.

Given this information, we can now use the OPM by solving Equations 19-1, 19-2, and 19-3. Since d_1 and d_2 are required inputs for Equation 19-1, we solve Equations 19-2 and 19-3 first:

$$d_1 = \frac{\ln(\$20/\$20) + [0.12 + (0.16/2)](0.25)}{0.40(0.50)}$$

$$= \frac{0 + 0.05}{0.20} = 0.25.$$

$$d_2 = d_1 - 0.4\sqrt{0.25} = 0.25 - 0.20 = 0.05.$$

Note that $N(d_1) = N(0.25)$ and $N(d_2) = N(0.05)$ represent areas under a standard normal distribution function. From Table A-5 in Appendix A at the end of the book, we see that the value $d_1 = 0.25$ implies a probability of $0.0987 + 0.5000 = 0.5987$, so $N(d_1) = 0.5987$. Similarly, $N(d_2) = 0.5199$. We can use those values to solve Equation 19-1:

$$V = \$20[N(d_1)] - \$20e^{-(0.12)(0.25)}[N(d_2)]$$

$$= \$20[N(0.25)] - \$20(0.9704)[N(0.05)]$$

$$= \$20(0.5987) - \$19.41(0.5199)$$

$$= \$11.97 - \$10.09 = \$1.88.$$

Thus the value of the option, under the assumed conditions, is $1.88. Suppose the actual option price were $2.25. Arbitrageurs could simultaneously sell the option, buy the underlying stock, and earn a riskless profit. Such trading would occur until the price of the option was driven down to $1.88. The reverse would occur if the option sold for less than $1.88. Thus, investors would be unwilling to pay more than $1.88 for the option, and they could not buy it for less, so $1.88 is the *equilibrium value* of the option.

To see how the five OPM factors affect the value of the option, consider Table 19-2. Here the top row shows the base-case input values which were used above to illustrate the OPM and the resulting option value, $V = \$1.88$. In each of the subsequent rows, the boldfaced factor is increased, while the other four are held constant at their base-case levels. The resulting value of the call option is given in the last column. Now let's consider the effects of the changes:

1. **Current stock price.** If the current stock price, P, increases from $20 to $25, the option value increases from $1.88 to $5.81. Thus, the value of the option increases as the stock price increases, but by less than the stock price increase, $3.93 versus $5.00. Note, though, that the percentage increase in the option value, ($5.81 − $1.88)/$1.88 = 209%, far exceeds the percentage increase in the stock price, ($25 − $20)/$20 = 25%.

2. **Exercise price.** If the exercise price, X, increases from $20 to $25, the value of the option declines. Again, the decrease in the option value is less than the exercise price increase, but the percentage change in the option value, ($0.39 − $1.88)/$1.88 = −79%, exceeds the percentage change in the exercise price, ($25 − $20)/$20 = 25%.

3. **Option period.** As the time to expiration increases from $t = 3$ months (or 0.25 year) to $t = 6$ months (or 0.50 year), the value of the option increases from $1.88 to $2.81. This occurs because the value of the option depends on the chances for an increase in the price of the underlying stock, and the longer

T A B L E 1 9 - 2	Effects of OPM Factors on the Value of a Call Option

| | INPUT FACTORS | | | | | |
CASE	P	X	t	k_{RF}	σ^2	V
Base case	$20	$20	0.25	12%	0.16	$1.88
Increase P by $5	**25**	20	0.25	12	0.16	5.81
Increase X by $5	20	**25**	0.25	12	0.16	0.39
Increase t to 6 months	20	20	**0.50**	12	0.16	2.81
Increase k_{RF} to 16%	20	20	0.25	**16**	0.16	1.99
Increase σ^2 to 0.25	20	20	0.25	12	**0.25**	2.27

the option has to go, the higher the stock price may climb. Thus, a six-month option is worth more than a three-month option.

4. **Risk-free rate.** As the risk-free rate increases from 12 to 16 percent, the value of the option increases slightly, from $1.88 to $1.99. Equations 19-1, 19-2, and 19-3 suggest that the principal effect of an increase in k_{RF} is to reduce the present value of the exercise price, $Xe^{-k_{RF}t}$, hence to increase the current value of the option.[8] The risk-free rate also plays a role in determining the values of the normal distribution functions $N(d_1)$ and $N(d_2)$, but this effect is of secondary importance. Indeed, option prices in general are not very sensitive to interest rate changes, at least not to changes within the ranges normally encountered.

5. **Variance.** As the variance increases from the base case 0.16 to 0.25, the value of the option increases from $1.88 to $2.27. Therefore, the riskier the underlying security, the more valuable the option. This result is logical. First, if you bought an option to buy a stock that sells at its exercise price, and if $\sigma^2 = 0$, then there would be a zero probability of the stock going up, hence a zero probability of making money on the option. On the other hand, if you bought an option on a high-variance stock, there would be a fairly high probability that the stock would go way up, hence that you would make a large profit on the option. Of course, a high-variance stock could go way down, but as an option holder, your losses would be limited to the price paid for the option — only the right-hand side of the stock's probability distribution counts. Put another way, an increase in the price of the stock helps options holders more than a decrease hurts them, so the greater the variance, the greater is the value of the option. This makes options on risky stocks more valuable than those on safer, low-variance stocks.

This concludes our discussion of options and option pricing theory. The next section discusses some other types of derivative securities.

---

[8]At this point, you may be wondering why the first term in Equation 19-1, $P[N(d_1)]$, is not discounted. In fact, it has been, because the current stock price, P, already represents the present value of the expected stock price at expiration. In other words, P is a discounted value, and the discount rate used in the market to determine today's stock price includes the risk-free rate. Thus, Equation 19-1 can be thought of as the present value of the end-of-option-period spread between the stock price and the strike price, adjusted for the probability that the stock price will be higher than the strike price.

OTHER TYPES OF DERIVATIVES

Put and call options represent an important class of derivative securities, but there are other types of derivatives, including forward contracts, futures, swaps, structured notes, inverse floaters, and a host of other "exotic" contracts.

FORWARD CONTRACTS VERSUS FUTURES CONTRACTS

Forward Contract
A contract under which one party agrees to buy a commodity at a specific price on a specific future date and the other party agrees to make the sale. Physical delivery occurs.

Futures Contract
Standardized contracts that are traded on exchanges and are "marked to market" daily, but where physical delivery of the underlying asset is virtually never taken.

Forward contracts are agreements where one party agrees to buy a commodity at a specific price on a specific future date and the other party agrees to make the sale. *Goods are actually delivered under forward contracts.* Unless both parties are financially strong, there is a danger that one party will default on the contract, especially if the price of the commodity changes markedly after the agreement is reached.

A **futures contract** is similar to a forward contract, but with three key differences: (1) Futures contracts are "marked to market" on a daily basis, meaning that gains and losses are noted and money must be put up to cover losses. This greatly reduces the risk of default that exists with forward contracts. (2) With futures, physical delivery of the underlying asset is virtually never taken — the two parties simply settle up with cash for the difference between the contracted price and the actual price on the expiration date. (3) Futures contracts are generally standardized instruments that are traded on exchanges, whereas forward contracts are generally tailor-made, are negotiated between two parties, and are not traded after they have been signed.

Futures and forward contracts were originally used for commodities such as wheat, where farmers would sell forward contracts to millers, enabling both parties to lock in prices and thus reduce their risk exposure. Commodities contracts are still important, but today more trading is done in foreign exchange and interest rate futures. To illustrate how foreign exchange futures are used, suppose GE arranges to buy electric motors from a German manufacturer on terms that call for GE to pay 1 million marks in 180 days. GE would not want to give up the free trade credit, but if the mark appreciated against the dollar during the next six months, the dollar cost of the million marks would rise. GE could hedge the transaction by buying a forward contract under which it agreed to buy the million marks in 180 days at a fixed price. This would lock in the dollar cost of the motors. This transaction would probably be conducted through a money center bank, which would try to find a German company (a "counterparty") that needed dollars in six months. Alternatively, GE could buy a futures contract on an exchange.

Interest rate futures represent another huge and growing market. For example, suppose Simonset Corporation decides to build a new plant at a cost of $20 million. It plans to finance the project with 20-year bonds which would carry a 10 percent interest rate if they were issued today. However, the company will not need the money for about six months. Simonset could go ahead and sell 20-year bonds now, locking in the 10 percent rate, but it would have the money before it was needed, so it would have to invest in short-term securities which would yield less than 10 percent. However, if Simonset waits six months to sell the bond issue, interest rates might be higher than they are today, in which case the value of the plant would be reduced, perhaps to the point of making it unprofitable.

One solution to Simonset's dilemma involves *interest rate futures*, which are based on a hypothetical 20-year Treasury bond with an 8 percent semiannual coupon. If interest rates in the economy go up, the value of the hypothetical T-bond will go down, and vice versa. In our example, Simonset is worried about an increase in interest rates. Should rates rise, the hypothetical Treasury bond's value would decline. Therefore, Simonset could sell T-bond futures for delivery in six months to hedge its position. If interest rates rise, Simonset will have to pay more when it issues its own bonds. However, it will make a profit on its futures position because it will have pre-sold the bonds at a higher price than it will have to pay to cover (repurchase) them. Of course, if interest rates decline, Simonset will lose on its futures position, but this will be offset by the fact that it will get to pay a lower interest rate when it issues its bonds.

Our examples show that forward contracts and futures can be used to hedge, or reduce, risks. It has been estimated that more than 95 percent of all transactions are indeed designed as hedges, with banks and futures dealers serving as middlemen between hedging counterparties. Interest rate and exchange rate futures can, of course, be used for speculative as well as hedging purposes. One can buy a T-bond contract on $100,000 of bonds with only $5,000 down, in which case a small change in interest rates will result in a very large gain or loss. Still, the primary motivation behind the vast majority of these transactions is to hedge risks, not to create them.

SWAPS

Swap
Two parties agree to exchange obligations to make specified payment streams.

A **swap** is just what the name implies — two parties agree to swap something, generally obligations to make specified payment streams. Most swaps today involve either interest payments or currencies. To illustrate an interest rate swap, suppose Company S has a 20-year, $100 million floating rate bond issue outstanding, while Company F has a $100 million, 20-year, fixed rate issue outstanding. Thus, each company has an obligation to make a stream of interest payments, but one payment stream is fixed while the other will vary as interest rates change in the future.

Now suppose Company S has stable cash flows, and it wants to lock in its cost of debt. Company F has cash flows that fluctuate with the economy, rising when the economy is strong and falling when it is weak. Recognizing that interest rates also move up and down with the economy, Company F has concluded that it would be better off with variable rate debt. If the companies swapped their payment obligations, an *interest rate swap* would occur. Company S would now have to make a fixed payment stream, which is consistent with its cash inflows, and Company F would have a floating stream, which for it is less risky.

Note, though, that swaps can involve *side payments*. For example, if interest rates had fallen sharply since Company F issued its bonds, then its old payment obligations would be relatively high, and it would have to make a side payment to get S to agree to the swap. Similarly, if the credit risk of one company was higher than that of the other, the stronger company would be concerned about the ability of its weaker "counterparty" to make the required payments. This too would lead to the need for a side payment.

Currency swaps are similar to interest rate swaps. To illustrate, suppose Company A, an American firm, had issued $100 million of dollar-denominated bonds in the United States to fund an investment in Germany. Meanwhile, Company G, a German firm, had issued $100 million of mark-denominated bonds in Germany to make an investment in the United States. Company A would earn marks but be required to make payments in dollars, and Company G would be in a reverse situation. Thus, both companies would be exposed to exchange rate risk. However, both companies' risks would be eliminated if they swapped payment obligations. As with interest rate swaps, differences in interest rates or credit risks would require side payments.

Originally, swaps were arranged between companies by money center banks, which would match up counterparties. Such matching still occurs, but today most swaps are between companies and banks, with the banks then taking steps to ensure that their own risks are hedged. For example, Citibank might arrange a swap with Company A, which would agree to make specified payments in marks to the bank, and the bank would make the dollar payments Company A would otherwise owe. Citibank would charge a fee for setting up the swap, and these charges would reflect the creditworthiness of Company A. To protect itself against exchange rate movements, the bank would hedge its position, either by lining up a German company which needed to make dollar payments or else by using currency futures.

STRUCTURED NOTES

The term **structured note** often means a debt obligation which is derived from some other debt obligation. For example, in the early 1980s, investment bankers began buying large blocks of 30-year, noncallable Treasury bonds and then *stripping* them to create a series of zero coupon bonds. The zero with the shortest maturity was backed by the first interest payment on the T-bond issue, the second shortest zero was backed by the next interest payment, and so forth, on out to a 30-year zero backed by the last interest payment plus the maturity value of the T-bond. Zeros formed by stripping T-bonds were one of the first types of structured notes.

Another important type of structured note is backed by the interest and principal payments on mortgages. In the 1970s, Wall Street firms began to buy large packages of mortgages backed by federal agencies and then place these packages, or "pools," with a trustee. Then bonds called *Collateralized Mortgage Obligations (CMOs),* backed by the mortgage pool held in trust, were sold to pension funds, individuals for their IRA accounts, and other investors who were willing to invest in CMOs but who would not have purchased individual mortgages. This *securitization* of mortgages made billions of dollars of new capital available to home buyers.

CMOs are more difficult to evaluate than straight bonds for several reasons. First, the underlying mortgages can be prepaid at any time, and when this occurs the prepayment proceeds are used to retire part of the CMO debt itself. Therefore, the holder of a CMO is never sure when his or her bond will be called. This situation is further complicated by the fact that when interest rates decline, this causes bond prices to rise. However, declining rates also lead to mortgage prepayments, which cause the CMOs to be called especially rapidly.

It should also be noted that a variety of structured notes can be created, ranging from notes whose cash flows can be predicted with virtual certainty to other notes whose payment streams are highly uncertain. For example, investment bankers can (and do) create notes called *IOs,* (for *Interest Only*), which provide cash flows from the interest component of the mortgage amortization payments, and *POs* (for *Principal Only*), which are paid from the principal repayment stream. In each case, the value of the note is found as the PV of an expected payment stream, but the length and size of the stream are uncertain. Suppose, for example, that you are offered an IO which you expect to provide payments of $100 for ten years (you expect the mortgages to be refinanced after ten years, at which time your payments will cease). Suppose further that you discount the expected payment stream at a rate of 10 percent and determine that the value is $614.46. You have $614.46 to invest, so you buy the IO, expecting to earn 10 percent on your money.

Now suppose interest rates decline. If rates fall, the discount rate would drop, and that would normally imply an increase in the IO's value. However, if rates decline sharply, this would lead to a rash of mortgage refinancings, in which case your payments, which come from interest only, would cease (or be greatly reduced), and the value of your IO would fall sharply. On the other hand, a sharp increase in interest rates would reduce refinancing, lengthen your expected payment stream, and probably increase the value of your IO.

Investment bankers can slice and dice a pool of mortgages into a bewildering array of structured notes, ranging from "plain vanilla" ones with highly predictable cash flows to "exotic" ones (sometimes called "toxic waste") whose risks are almost incalculable but are surely large.

Securitizing mortgages through CMOs serves a useful economic function — it provides an investment outlet for pension funds and others with money to invest, and it makes more money available to homeowners at a reasonable cost. Also, some investors want relatively safe investments, while others are willing to buy more speculative securities for the higher expected returns they provide. Structured notes permit a partitioning of risks to give investors what they want. There are dangers, though. The "toxic waste" is often bought by naive officials managing money for local governments like Orange County, California, when they really ought to be holding only safe securities.

INVERSE FLOATERS

A floating rate note has an interest rate that rises and falls with some interest rate index. For example, the interest rate on a $100,000 note at prime plus 1 percent would be 9 percent when the prime rate is 8 percent, and the note's rate would move up and down with the prime rate. Since both the cash flows associated with the note and the discount rate used to value it rise and fall together, the market value of the note would be relatively stable.

Inverse Floater
A note in which the interest paid moves counter to market rates.

With an **inverse floater,** the rate paid on the note moves counter to market rates. Thus, if interest rates in the economy rose, the interest rate paid on an inverse floater would fall, lowering its cash interest payments. At the same time, the discount rate used to value the inverse floater's cash flows would rise along with other rates. The combined effect of lower cash flows and a higher discount rate would lead to a very large decline in the value of the inverse floater. Thus, inverse floaters are exceptionally vulnerable to increases in interest rates. Of course, if interest rates fall, the value of an inverse floater will soar.

We have discussed the most important types of derivative securities, but certainly not all types. This discussion should, though, give you a good idea of how and why derivatives are created, and how they can be used and misused.

SELF-TEST QUESTION   ??????

Briefly describe the following types of derivative securities:
  (1) Futures and forward contracts.
  (2) Swaps.
  (3) Structured notes.
  (4) Inverse floaters.

RISK MANAGEMENT

Risk Management
Involves the management of unpredictable events that have adverse consequences for the firm.

As businesses become increasingly complex, it is becoming more and more difficult for CEOs and directors to know what problems might lie in wait. Therefore, companies need to have someone systematically look for potential problems and design safeguards to minimize potential damage. With this in mind, most larger firms have designated "risk managers" who report to the chief financial officer, while the CFOs of smaller firms personally assume risk management responsibilities. In any event, **risk management** is becoming increasingly important, and it is something finance students should understand. Therefore, in the remainder of this chapter we discuss the basics of risk management, with particular emphasis on how derivatives can be used to hedge financial risks.

FUNDAMENTALS OF RISK MANAGEMENT

It is useful to begin our discussion of risk management by defining some commonly used terms that describe different risks. Some of these risks can be mitigated, or managed, and that is what risk management is all about.

1. *Pure risks* are risks that offer only the prospect of a loss. Examples include the risk that a plant will be destroyed by fire or that a product liability suit will result in a large judgment against the firm.

2. *Speculative risks* are situations that offer the chance of a gain but might result in a loss. Thus, investments in new projects and marketable securities involve speculative risks.

3. *Demand risks* are associated with the demand for a firm's products or services. Because sales are essential to all businesses, demand risk is one of the most significant risks that firms face.

4. *Input risks* are risks associated with input costs, including both labor and materials. Thus, a company that uses copper as a raw material in its manufacturing process faces the risk that the cost of copper will increase and that it will not be able to pass this increase on to its customers.

5. *Financial risks* are risks that result from financial transactions. As we have seen, if a firm plans to issue new bonds, it faces the risk that interest rates

will rise before the bonds can be brought to market. Similarly, if the firm enters into contracts with foreign customers or suppliers, it faces the risk that fluctuations in exchange rates will result in unanticipated losses.

6. *Property risks* are associated with destruction of productive assets. Thus, the threat of fire, floods, and riots imposes property risks on a firm.

7. *Personnel risks* are risks that result from employees' actions. Examples include the risks associated with employee fraud or embezzlement, or suits based on charges of age or sex discrimination.

8. *Environmental risks* include risks associated with polluting the environment. Public awareness in recent years, coupled with the huge costs of environmental cleanup, has increased the importance of this risk.

9. *Liability risks* are associated with product, service, or employee actions. Examples include the very large judgments assessed against asbestos manufacturers and some health care providers, as well as costs incurred as a result of improper actions of employees, such as driving corporate vehicles in a reckless manner.

10. *Insurable risks* are risks that can be covered by insurance. In general, property, personnel, environmental, and liability risks can be transferred to insurance companies. Note, though, that the *ability* to insure a risk does not necessarily mean that the risk *should be* insured. Indeed, a major function of risk management involves evaluating all alternatives for managing a particular risk, including self-insurance, and then choosing the optimal alternative.

Note that the risk classifications we used are somewhat arbitrary, and different classifications are commonly used in different industries. However, the list does give an idea of the wide variety of risks to which a firm can be exposed.

AN APPROACH TO RISK MANAGEMENT

Firms often use the following process for managing risks.

1. **Identify the risks faced by the firm.** Here the risk manager identifies the potential risks faced by his or her firm.

2. **Measure the potential impact of each risk.** Some risks are so small as to be immaterial, whereas others have the potential for dooming the company. It is useful to segregate risks by potential impact and then to focus on the most serious threats.

3. **Decide how each relevant risk should be handled.** In most situations, risk exposure can be reduced through one of the following techniques:

   a. **Transfer the risk to an insurance company.** Often, it is advantageous to insure against, hence transfer, a risk. However, insurability does not necessarily mean that a risk should be covered by insurance. In many instances, it might be better for the company to *self-insure*, which means bearing the risk directly rather than paying another party to bear it.

   b. **Transfer the function that produces the risk to a third party.** For example, suppose a furniture manufacturer is concerned about potential liabilities arising from its ownership of a fleet of trucks used to transfer products from its manufacturing plant to various points across the country. One way to eliminate this risk would be to contract with a trucking company to do the shipping, thus passing the risks to a third party.

c. **Purchase derivative contracts to reduce risk.** As we indicated earlier, firms use derivatives to hedge risks. Commodity derivatives can be used to reduce input risks. For example, a cereal company may use corn or wheat futures to hedge against increases in grain prices. Similarly, financial derivatives can be used to reduce risks that arise from changes in interest rates and exchange rates.

d. **Reduce the probability of occurrence of an adverse event.** The expected loss arising from any risk is a function of both the probability of occurrence and the dollar loss if the adverse event occurs. In some instances, it is possible to reduce the probability that an adverse event will occur. For example, the probability that a fire will occur can be reduced by instituting a fire prevention program, by replacing old electrical wiring, and by using fire-resistant materials in areas with the greatest fire potential.

e. **Reduce the magnitude of the loss associated with an adverse event.** Continuing with the fire risk example, the dollar cost associated with a fire can be reduced by such actions as installing sprinkler systems, designing facilities with self-contained fire zones, and locating facilities close to a fire station.

f. **Totally avoid the activity that gives rise to the risk.** For example, a company might discontinue a product or service line because the risks outweigh the rewards, as with the recent decision by Dow-Corning to discontinue its manufacture of silicon breast implants.

Note that risk management decisions, like all corporate decisions, should be based on a cost/benefit analysis for each feasible alternative. For example, suppose it would cost $50,000 per year to conduct a comprehensive fire safety training program for all personnel in a high-risk plant. Presumably, this program would reduce the expected value of future fire losses. An alternative to the training program would be to place $50,000 annually in a reserve fund set aside to cover future fire losses. Both alternatives involve expected cash flows, and from an economic standpoint the choice should be made on the basis of the lowest present value of future costs. Thus, the same financial management techniques applied to other corporate decisions can also be applied to risk management decisions. Note, though, that if a fire occurs and a life is lost, the trade-off between fire prevention and expected losses may not sit well with a jury. The same thing holds true for product liability, as Ford, GM, and others have learned.

SELF-TEST QUESTIONS   ??????

Define the following terms:
(1) Pure risks.
(2) Speculative risks.
(3) Demand risks.
(4) Input risks.
(5) Financial risks.
(6) Property risks.
(7) Personnel risks.
(8) Environmental risks.
(9) Liability risks.
(10) Insurable risks.
(11) Self-insurance.

Should a firm insure itself against all of the insurable risks it faces? Explain.

GLOBAL PERSPECTIVES

BARINGS AND SUMITOMO SUFFER LARGE LOSSES IN THE DERIVATIVE MARKETS

Barings, a conservative English Bank with a long, impressive history dating back to its financing of the Louisiana Purchase in the 19th century, collapsed in 1995 when one of its traders lost $1.4 billion in derivatives trades. Nicholas Leeson, a 28-year-old trader in Barings' Singapore office, had speculated in Japanese stock index and interest rate futures without his superiors' knowledge. A lack of internal controls at the bank allowed him to accumulate large losses without being detected. Leeson's losses caught many by surprise, and they provided ammunition to those who argue that trading in derivatives should be more highly regulated if not sharply curtailed.

Most argue that the blame goes beyond Leeson — that both the bank and the exchanges were at fault for failing to provide sufficient oversight. For misreporting his trades, Leeson is currently serving a 6½-year sentence in a Singapore prison. What remained of Barings was ultimately sold to a Dutch banking concern.

Many analysts, including those who argued that the Barings episode was just an unsettling but isolated incident, were startled by a similar case a year and a half after the Barings debacle. In June 1996, Japan's Sumitomo Corporation disclosed that its well-respected chief copper trader, Yasuo Hamanaka, had been conducting unauthorized speculative trades for more than a decade. The cumulative loss on these trades was $2.6 billion. Hamanaka has been indicted on charges of fraud and forgery.

These two events illustrate both the dangers of derivatives and the importance of internal controls. While it is unsettling to learn that the actions of a single, relatively low-level employee can suddenly cripple a giant corporation, these losses should be placed in perspective. The overwhelming majority of firms that use derivatives have been successful in enhancing performance and/or reducing risk. For this reason, most analysts argue that it would be a huge mistake to use the rare instances where fraud occurred to limit a market which has, for the most part, been a resounding success. However, given the volume of business in this market, we can in the future expect to see other problems similar to those encountered by Barings and Sumitomo.

USING DERIVATIVES TO REDUCE RISKS

Firms are subject to numerous risks related to interest rate, stock price, and exchange rate fluctuations in the financial markets. For an investor, one of the most obvious ways to reduce financial risks is to hold a broadly diversified portfolio of stocks and debt securities, including international securities and debt of varying maturities. However, derivatives can also be used to reduce the risks associated with financial and commodity markets.[9]

ON THE WWW

Information from the CBOT on the financial market futures they trade is available at http:// www.cbot.com/trader/tp_fin.htm. The site provides some general information on the various types of financial market instruments which are available and provides information on how to order specific literature or the CBOT's publication catalog.

HEDGING WITH FUTURES

One of the most useful tools for reducing interest rate, exchange rate, and commodity risk is to hedge in the futures markets. Most financial and real asset transactions occur in what is known as the *spot,* or *cash, market,* where the asset is delivered immediately (or within a few days). *Futures,* or *futures contracts,* on the other hand, call for the purchase or sale of an asset at some future date, but at a price which is fixed today.

In 1997, futures contracts were available on more than 30 real and financial assets traded on 14 U.S. exchanges, the largest of which are the Chicago Board of Trade (CBOT) and the Chicago Mercantile Exchange (CME). Futures contracts

---

[9]In Chapter 18, we discussed both the risks involved with holding foreign currencies and procedures for reducing such risks.

Commodity Futures
A contract that is used to hedge against price changes for input materials.

Financial Futures
A contract that is used to hedge against fluctuating interest rates, stock prices, and exchange rates.

are divided into two classes, **commodity futures** and **financial futures.** Commodity futures, which cover oil, various grains, oilseeds, livestock, meats, fibers, metals, and wood, were first traded in the United States in the mid-1800s. Financial futures, which were first traded in 1975, include Treasury bills, notes, bonds, certificates of deposit, Eurodollar deposits, foreign currencies, and stock indexes.

To illustrate how futures contracts work, consider the CBOT's contract on Treasury bonds. The basic contract is for $100,000 of a hypothetical 8 percent coupon, semiannual payment Treasury bond with 20 years to maturity. Table 19-3 shows an extract from the Treasury bond futures table which appeared in the January 24, 1997, issue of *The Wall Street Journal.*

The first column gives the delivery month; the next three columns give the opening, high, and low prices on that contract on that day. The opening price for the March future, 110-31, means 110 plus 31/32, or 110.96875 percent of par. Column 5 gives the settlement price, which is typically the price at the close of trading. Column 6 reports the change in the settlement price from the preceding day — the March contract dropped by 6/32. Columns 7 and 8 give the life-of-contract highs and lows. Finally, Column 9 shows the "open interest," which is the number of contracts outstanding.

To illustrate, we focus on the Treasury bonds for September delivery. The settlement price was 109-30, or 109 plus 30/32 percent of the $100,000 contract value. Thus, the price at which one could buy $100,000 face value of 8 percent, 20-year Treasury bonds to be delivered in September was 109.9375 percent of par, or 1.099375($100,000) = $109,937.50. The contract price declined by 6/32 of 1 percent of $100,000, or by $187.50, from the previous day, so if you had bought the contract yesterday, you would have lost $187.50. Over its life, the contract's price has ranged from 100.5625 to 117.65625, and there were 5,613 contracts outstanding, representing a total value of about $620 million.

 ON THE WWW
You can obtain daily closing prices on Treasury bond futures and other types of futures contracts from the web site of Ira Epstein & Company at http:// www.iepstein.com/quotes.html.

Note that the contract declined by 6/32 of a percent on this particular day. Why would the value of the bond futures contract decline? Since bond prices decline when interest rates rise, we know that interest rates rose on that day. Moreover, we can calculate the implied rates inherent in the futures contracts. (*The Wall Street Journal* formerly provided the implied yields, but now one must calculate them.) Recall that the contract relates to a hypothetical 20-year, semiannual payment, 8 percent coupon bond. The closing price (settlement price) was 109 and 30/32, or 109.9375 percent of par. Using a financial calculator, we can solve for k_d in the following equation:

TABLE 19-3	Futures Prices

TREASURY BONDS (CBOT) — $100,000; PTS. 32NDS OF 100%

DELIVERY MONTH (1)	OPEN (2)	HIGH (3)	LOW (4)	SETTLE (5)	CHANGE (6)	LIFETIME HIGH (7)	LOW (8)	OPEN INTEREST (9)
Mar	110-31	111-07	110-20	110-27	−6	120-00	99-26	469,775
June	110-17	110-23	110-05	110-11	−6	118-21	99-16	27,206
Sept	110-05	110-06	109-24	109-30	−6	117-21	100-18	5,613

SOURCE: *The Wall Street Journal,* January 24, 1997, C14.

$$\$1{,}099.375 = \sum_{t=1}^{40} \frac{\$40}{(1 + k_d/2)^t} + \frac{\$1{,}000}{(1 + k_d/2)^{40}}.$$

The solution value for the six-month rate is 3.532, which is equivalent to a nominal rate of 7.065 percent. Since the price of the bond fell by 6/32 that day, we could find the previous day's closing (settlement) price and its implied interest rate, which would turn out to be 7.048 percent. Therefore, interest rates rose by 1.7 basis points, which was enough to lower the value of the contract by $187.50.

Thus, the futures contract for September delivery of this hypothetical bond sold for $109,937.50 for 100 bonds with a par value of $100,000, which translates to a yield to maturity of about 7.1 percent. This yield reflects investors' beliefs about what the interest rate level will be in September. The spot yield on T-bonds was about 6.7 percent at the time, so the marginal trader in the futures market was predicting a 40-basis-point increase in yields over the next eight months. That prediction could, of course, turn out to be incorrect.

Now suppose that three months later interest rates in the futures market had fallen from the earlier levels, say, from 7.1 to 6.5 percent. Falling interest rates mean rising bond prices, and we could calculate that the September contract would then be worth about $116,656. Thus, the contract's value would have increased by $116,656 − $109,938 = $6,718.

When futures contracts are purchased, the purchaser does not have to put up the full amount of the purchase price; rather, the purchaser is required to post an initial *margin,* which for CBT Treasury bond contracts is $3,000 per $100,000 contract. However, investors are required to maintain a certain value in the margin account, called a *maintenance margin.* If the value of the contract declines, then the owner may be required to add additional funds to the margin account, and the more the contract value falls, the more money must be added. The value of the contract is checked at the end of every working day, and margin account adjustments are made at that time. This is called "marking to market." If an investor purchased our illustrative contract and then sold it later for $116,656, he or she would have made a profit of $6,718 on a $3,000 investment, or a return of over 200 percent in only three months. It is clear, therefore, that futures contracts offer a considerable amount of leverage. Of course, if interest rates had risen, then the value of the contract would have declined, and the investor could easily have lost his or her $3,000, or more. Futures contracts are never settled by delivery of the securities involved. Rather, the transaction is completed by reversing the trade, which amounts to selling the contract back to the original seller.[10] The actual gains and losses on the contract are realized when the futures contract is closed.

Futures contracts and options are similar to one another — so similar that people often confuse the two. Therefore, it is useful to compare the two instruments. A *futures contract* is a definite agreement on the part of one party to buy something on a specific date and at a specific price, and the other party agrees to sell on the same terms. No matter how low or how high the price goes, the two parties must settle the contract at the agreed-upon price. An *option,* on the other hand, merely gives someone the right to buy (call) or sell (put) an asset, but the

---

[10]The buyers and sellers of most financial futures contracts do not actually trade with one another — each trader's contractual obligation is with a futures exchange. This feature helps to guarantee the fiscal integrity of the trade. Incidentally, commodities futures traded on the exchanges are settled in the same way as financial futures, but in the case of commodities much of the contracting is done off the exchange, between farmers and processors, as *forward contracts,* in which case actual deliveries occur.

holder of the option does not have to complete the transaction. Note also that options exist both for individual stocks and for "bundles" of stocks such as those in the S&P and Value Line indexes, but generally not for commodities. Futures, on the other hand, are used for commodities, debt securities, and stock indexes. The two types of instruments can be used for the same purposes. One is not necessarily better or worse than another — they are simply different.

SECURITY PRICE EXPOSURE

Firms are obviously exposed to losses due to changes in security prices when securities are held in investment portfolios, and they are also exposed during times when securities are being issued. In addition, firms are exposed to risk if they use floating rate debt to finance an investment that produces a fixed income stream. Often, these risks can be mitigated by using derivatives. As we discussed earlier, derivatives are securities whose value stems, or is derived, from the values of other assets. Thus, options and futures contracts are derivatives, because their values depend on the prices of some underlying asset. Now we will explore further the use of two types of derivatives, futures and swaps, to help manage certain types of risk.

Speculation
With futures it involves betting on future price movements.

Hedging
Using transactions to lower risk.

FUTURES. Futures are used for both speculation and hedging. **Speculation** involves betting on future price movements, and futures are used because of the leverage inherent in the contract. **Hedging,** on the other hand, is done by a firm or individual to protect against a price change that would otherwise negatively affect profits. For example, rising interest rates and commodity (raw material) prices can hurt profits, as can adverse currency fluctuations. If two parties have mirror-image risks, then they can enter into a transaction that eliminates, as opposed to transfers, risks. This is a "natural hedge." Of course, one party to a futures contract could be a speculator, the other a hedger. Thus, to the extent that speculators broaden the market and make hedging possible, they help decrease risk to those who seek to avoid it.

Long Hedges
Futures contracts are bought in anticipation of (or to guard against) price increases.

Short Hedges
Futures contracts are sold to guard against price declines.

There are two basic types of hedges: (1) **long hedges,** in which futures contracts are bought in anticipation of (or to guard against) price increases, and (2) **short hedges,** where a firm or individual sells futures contracts to guard against price declines. Recall that rising interest rates lower bond prices and thus decrease the value of bond futures contracts. Therefore, if a firm or individual needs to guard against an *increase* in interest rates, a futures contract that makes money if rates rise should be used. That means selling, or going short, on a futures contract. To illustrate, assume that in January Carson Foods is considering a plan to issue $10,000,000 of 20-year bonds in June to finance a capital expenditure program. The interest rate would be 10 percent if the bonds were issued today, and at that rate the project would have a positive NPV. However, interest rates may rise over the next five months, and when the issue is actually sold, the interest rate might be substantially above 10 percent, which would make the project a bad investment. Carson can protect itself against a rise in rates by hedging in the futures market.

In this situation, Carson would be hurt by an increase in interest rates, so it would use a short hedge. It would choose a futures contract on that security most similar to the one it plans to issue, long-term bonds. In this case, Carson would probably hedge with Treasury bond futures. Since it plans to issue $10,000,000 of bonds, it would sell $10,000,000/$100,000 = 100 Treasury bond contracts for delivery in June. Carson would have to put up 100($3,000) = $300,000 in margin money and also pay brokerage commissions. We can see from Table 19-3 that each June contract has a value of 110 plus 11/32 percent, so the total value of the 100 contracts is 1.1034375($100,000)(100) = $11,034,375. Now suppose renewed fears of inflation push the interest rate on Carson's debt up by 100 basis points, to 11 percent, over the next five months. If Carson issued 10 percent coupon bonds, they would bring only $920 per bond, because investors now require an 11 percent return. Thus, Carson would lose $80 per bond times 10,000 bonds, or $800,000, as a result of delaying the financing. However, the increase in interest rates would also bring about a change in the value of Carson's short position in the futures market. Since interest rates have increased, the value of the futures contract would fall, and if the interest rate on the futures contract also increased by the same full percentage point, from 7.029 to 8.029 percent, the contract value would fall to $9,971,288. Carson would then close its position in the futures market by repurchasing for $9,971,288 the contracts which it earlier sold short for $11,034,375, giving it a profit of $1,063,087, less commissions.

Thus, Carson would, if we ignore commissions and the opportunity cost of the margin money, offset the loss on the bond issue. In fact, in our example Carson more than offsets the loss, pocketing an additional $263,087. Of course, if interest rates had fallen, Carson would have lost on its futures position, but this loss would have been offset by the fact that Carson could now sell its bonds with a lower coupon.

If futures contracts existed on Carson's own debt, and interest rates moved identically in the spot and futures markets, then the firm could construct a **perfect hedge,** in which gains on the futures contract would exactly offset losses on the bonds. In reality, it is virtually impossible to construct perfect hedges, because in most cases the underlying asset is not identical to the futures asset, and even when they are, prices (and interest rates) may not move exactly together in the spot and futures markets.

Note too that if Carson had been planning an equity offering, and if its stock tended to move fairly closely with one of the stock indexes, the company could have hedged against falling stock prices by selling short the index future. Even better, if options on Carson's stock were traded in the option market, then it could use options rather than futures to hedge against falling stock prices.

The futures and options markets permit flexibility in the timing of financial transactions, because the firm can be protected, at least partially, against changes that occur between the time a decision is reached and the time when the transaction will be completed. However, this protection has a cost — the firm must pay commisions. Whether or not the protection is worth the cost is a matter of judgment. The decision to hedge also depends on management's risk aversion as well as the company's strength and ability to assume the risk in question. In theory, the reduction in risk resulting from a hedge transaction should have a value exactly equal to the cost of the hedge. Thus, a firm should be indifferent to hedging. However, many firms believe that hedging is worthwhile. Trammell Crow, a large Texas real estate developer, recently used T-bill futures to lock in interest costs on floating rate construction loans, while Dart & Kraft used Eurodollar futures to protect its marketable securities portfolio. Merrill Lynch, Salomon Brothers, and the other investment banking houses hedge in the futures and options markets to protect themselves when they are engaged in major underwritings.

Perfect Hedge
Occurs when the gain or loss on the hedged transaction exactly offsets the loss or gain on the unhedged position.

SWAPS. A *swap* is another method for reducing financial risks. As we noted earlier, a swap is an exchange.[11] In finance, it is an exchange of cash payment obligations, in which each party to the swap prefers the payment type or pattern of the other party. In other words, swaps occur because the counterparties prefer the terms of the other's debt contract, and the swap enables each party to obtain a preferred payment obligation. Generally, one party has a fixed rate obligation and the other a floating rate obligation, or one has an obligation denominated in one currency and the other in another currency.

Major changes have occurred over time in the swaps market. First, standardized contracts have been developed for the most common types of swaps, and this has had two effects: (1) Standardized contracts lower the time and effort involved in arranging swaps, and thus lower transactions costs. (2) The development of standardized contracts has led to a secondary market for swaps, which has increased the liquidity and efficiency of the swaps market. A number of international banks now make markets in swaps and offer quotes on several standard types. Also, as noted above, the banks now take counterparty positions in swaps, so it is not necessary to find another firm with mirror-image needs before a swap transaction can be completed. The bank would generally find a final counterparty for the swap at a later date, so its positioning helps make the swap market more operationally efficient.[12]

To further illustrate a swap transaction, consider the following situation. An electric utility currently has outstanding a five-year floating rate note tied to the prime rate. The prime rate could rise significantly over the period, so the note carries a high degree of interest rate risk. The utility could, however, enter into a swap with a counterparty, say, Citibank, wherein the utility would pay Citibank a fixed series of interest payments over the five-year period, and Citibank would make the company's required floating rate payments. As a result, the utility would have converted a floating rate loan to a fixed rate loan, and the risk of rising interest rates would have been passed from the utility to Citibank. Such a transaction can lower both parties' risks — because banks' revenues rise as interest rates rise, Citibank's risk would actually be lower if it had floating rate obligations.

Longer-term swaps can also be made. Recently, Citibank entered into a 17-year swap in an electricity cogeneration project financing deal. The project's sponsors were unable to obtain fixed rate financing on reasonable terms, and they were afraid that interest rates would increase and make the project unprofitable. The project's sponsors were, however, able to borrow from local banks on a floating rate basis and then arrange a simultaneous swap with Citibank for a fixed rate obligation.

COMMODITY PRICE EXPOSURE

As we noted earlier, futures markets were established for many commodities long before they began to be used for financial instruments. We can use Porter Elec-

---

[11]For more information on swaps, see Clifford W. Smith, Jr., Charles W. Smithson, and Lee Macdonald Wakeman, "The Evolving Market for Swaps," *Midland Corporate Finance Journal,* Winter 1986, 20–32; and Mary E. Ruth and Steve R. Vinson, "Managing Interest Rate Uncertainty amidst Change," *Public Utilities Fortnightly,* December 22, 1988, 28–31.

[12]The role of banks in the global swap market is worrisome to the Federal Reserve and other central banks. When banks take positions in swaps, they are themselves exposed to various risks, and if the counterparties cannot meet their obligations, a bank could suddenly become liable for making two sets of payments. Further, swaps are "off balance sheet" transactions, so it is currently impossible to tell just how large the swap market is or who has what obligation. The fear is that if one large multinational bank gets into trouble, the entire worldwide swap market could collapse like a house of cards. See "Swap Fever: Big Money, Big Risks," *Fortune,* June 1, 1992.

tronics, which uses large quantities of copper as well as several precious metals, to illustrate inventory hedging. Suppose that in May 1997, Porter foresaw a need for 100,000 pounds of copper in March 1998 for use in fulfilling a fixed price contract to supply solar power cells to the U.S. government. Porter's managers are concerned that a strike by Chilean copper miners will occur, which could raise the price of copper in world markets and possibly turn the expected profit on the solar cells into a loss.

Porter could, of course, go ahead and buy the copper that it will need to fulfill the contract, but if it does it will incur substantial carrying costs. As an alternative, the company could hedge against increasing copper prices in the futures market. The New York Commodity Exchange trades standard copper futures contracts of 25,000 pounds each. Thus, Porter could buy four contracts (go long) for delivery in March 1998. Assume that these contracts were trading in May for about $1.00 per pound, and that the spot price at that date was about $1.02 per pound. If copper prices do rise appreciably over the next ten months, the value of Porter's long position in copper futures would increase, thus offsetting some of the price increase in the commodity itself. Of course, if copper prices fall, Porter would lose money on its futures contract, but the company would be buying the copper on the spot market at a cheaper price, so it would make a higher-than-anticipated profit on its sale of solar cells. Thus, hedging in the copper futures market locks in the cost of raw materials and removes some risk to which the firm would otherwise be exposed.

Eastman Kodak uses silver futures to hedge against short-term increases in the price of silver, which is the primary ingredient in black-and-white film. Many other manufacturers, such as Alcoa with aluminum and Archer Daniels Midland with grains, routinely use the futures markets to reduce the risks associated with input price volatility.

THE USE AND MISUSE OF DERIVATIVES

Most of the news stories about derivatives are related to financial disasters. Much less is heard about the benefits of derivatives. However, because of these benefits, more than 90 percent of large U.S. companies use derivatives on a regular basis. Moreover, according to McKinsey & Company, by the year 2000 it will be necessary for all CFOs to understand derivatives to do their job well. Even now, sophisticated investors and analysts are demanding that firms use derivatives to hedge certain risks. For example, Compaq Computer was recently sued by a shareholder group for failing to properly hedge its foreign exchange exposure. The shareholders lost the suit, but Compaq got the message and now uses currency futures to hedge its international operations. In another example, Prudential Securities reduced its earnings estimate for Cone Mills, a North Carolina textile company, because Cone did not sufficiently hedge its exposure to changing cotton prices. These examples lead to one conclusion: if a company can safely and inexpensively hedge its risks, it should do so.

There can, however, be a downside to the use of derivatives. Hedging is invariably cited by authorities as a "good" use of derivatives, whereas speculating with derivatives is often cited as a "bad" use. Some people and organizations can afford to bear the risks involved in speculating with derivatives, but others are either not sufficiently knowledgeable about the risks they are taking or else should not be taking those risks in the first place. Most would agree that the typical corporation should use derivatives only to hedge risks, not to speculate in an effort to increase profits. Hedging allows managers to concentrate on running their core businesses without having to worry about interest rate, currency, and commodity price variability. However, problems can arise quickly when hedges are improperly constructed or when a corporate treasurer, eager to report relatively high returns, uses derivatives for speculative purposes.

One interesting example of a derivatives debacle involved Kashima Oil, a Japanese firm that imports oil. It pays with U.S. dollars but then sells oil in the Japanese market for yen. Kashima began by using currency futures to hedge, but then it started to speculate on dollar-yen price movements, hoping to increase profits. When the currency markets moved against Kashima's speculative position, lax accounting rules permitted it to avoid reporting the losses by simply rolling over the contract. By the time Kashima bit the bullet and closed its position, it had lost $1.5 billion. Other companies have experienced similar problems.

Our position is that derivatives can and should be used to hedge against certain risks, but that the leverage inherent in derivatives contracts makes them potentially dangerous instruments. Also, CFOs, CEOs, and board members should be reasonably knowledgeable about the derivatives their firms use, should establish policies regarding when they can and cannot be used, and should establish audit procedures to ensure that the policies are actually carried out. Moreover, a firm's derivatives position should be reported to stockholders, because stockholders have a right to know when situations such as that involving P&G or Kashima might arise.

SELF-TEST QUESTIONS   ??????

What is a futures contract?

Explain how a company can use the futures market to hedge against rising interest rates.

What is a swap? Describe the mechanics of a fixed rate to floating rate swap.

Explain how a company can use the futures market to hedge against rising raw materials prices.

How should derivatives be used in risk management? What problems can occur?

SUMMARY

This chapter provided an introduction to derivative securities and corporate risk management. The key concepts covered are listed below:

♦ **Derivatives** are securities whose values are determined by the market price or interest rate of some other security.

♦ A **hedge** is a transaction which lowers risk. A **natural hedge** is a transaction between two **counterparties** where both parties' risks are reduced.

♦ **Options** are financial instruments that (1) are created by exchanges rather than firms, (2) are bought and sold primarily by investors, and (3) are of importance to both investors and financial managers.

♦ The two primary types of options are (1) **call options,** which give the holder the right to purchase a specified asset at a given price (the **exercise** or **strike price**) for a given period of time, and (2) **put options,** which give the holder the right to sell an asset at a given price for a given period of time.

♦ A call option's **formula value** is defined as the current price of the stock less the strike price.

♦ The **Black-Scholes Option Pricing Model (OPM)** can be used to estimate the value of a call option.

♦ A **futures contract** is a standardized contract that is traded on an exchange and is "marked to market" daily, but where physical delivery of the underlying asset does not occur.

♦ Under a **forward contract**, one party agrees to buy a commodity at a specific price and a specific future date and the other party agrees to make the sale. Delivery does occur.

♦ A **structured note** is a debt obligation derived from another debt obligation.

♦ A **swap** is an exchange of cash payment obligations. Swaps occur because the parties involved prefer someone else's payment stream.

♦ In general, **risk management** involves the management of unpredictable events that have adverse consequences for the firm.

♦ The three steps in risk management are as follows: (1) **identify** the risks faced by the company, (2) **measure** the potential impacts of these risks, and (3) **decide** how each relevant risk should be dealt with.

♦ In most situations, risk exposure can be dealt with by one or more of the following techniques: (1) **transfer** the **risk** to an insurance company, (2) **transfer** the **function** that produces the risk to a third party, (3) **purchase derivative contracts,** (4) **reduce the probability** of occurrence of an adverse event, (5) **reduce the magnitude** of the loss associated with an adverse event, and (6) totally **avoid** the activity that gives rise to the risk.

♦ **Financial futures** markets permit firms to create **hedge** positions to protect themselves against fluctuating interest rates, stock prices, and exchange rates.

♦ **Commodity futures** can be used to hedge against input price increases.

♦ **Long hedges** involve buying futures contracts to guard against price increases.

♦ **Short hedges** involve selling futures contracts to guard against price declines.

♦ A **perfect hedge** occurs when the gain or loss on the hedged transaction exactly offsets the loss or gain on the unhedged position.

QUESTIONS

19-1 Why do options typically sell at prices higher than their formula values?

19-2 Discuss some of the techniques available to reduce risk exposures.

19-3 Explain how the futures markets can be used to reduce interest rate and input price risk.

19-4 How can swaps be used to reduce the risks associated with debt contracts?

SELF-TEST PROBLEM   (Solution Appears in Appendix B)

ST-1
Key terms
Define each of the following terms:
a. Derivative
b. Option; call option; put option
c. Formula value; strike price
d. Black-Scholes Option Pricing Model
e. Corporate risk management
f. Financial futures; forward contract
g. Hedging; natural hedge; long hedges; short hedges; perfect hedge
h. Swap; structured note
i. Commodity futures

STARTER PROBLEMS

19-1
Options

A call option on the stock of Bedrock Boulders has a market price of $7. The stock sells for $30 a share, and the option has an exercise price of $25 a share.
a. What is the formula value of the call option?
b. What is the premium on the option?

19-2
Options

Which of the following events are likely to increase the market value of a call option on a common stock? Explain.
a. An increase in the stock's price.
b. An increase in the volatility of the stock price.
c. An increase in the risk-free rate.
d. A decrease in the time until the option expires.

EXAM-TYPE PROBLEMS

19-3
Black-Scholes model

Assume you have been given the following information on Purcell Industries:

Current stock price = $15	Exercise price of option = $15
Time to maturity of option = 6 months	Risk-free rate = 10%
Variance of stock price = 0.12	$d_1 = 0.32660$
$d_2 = 0.08165$	$N(d_1) = 0.62795$
$N(d_2) = 0.53252$	

Using the Black-Scholes Option Pricing Model, what would be the value of the option?

19-4
Options

The exercise price on one of Flanagan Company's options is $15, its formula value is $22, and its premium is $5. What are the option's market value and the price of the stock?

19-5
Futures

What is the implied interest rate on a Treasury bond ($100,000) futures contract that settled at 100-16? If interest rates increased by 1 percent, what would be the contract's new value?

PROBLEM

19-6
Hedging

The Zinn Company plans to issue $10,000,000 of 10-year bonds in September to help finance a new research and development laboratory. It is now January, and the current cost of debt to the high-risk biotech company is 11 percent. However, the firm's financial manager is concerned that interest rates will climb even higher in coming months.
a. Use data in Table 19-3 to create a hedge against rising interest rates.
b. Assume that interest rates in general increase by 200 basis points. How well did your hedge perform?
c. What is a perfect hedge? Are most real-world hedges perfect? Explain.

INTEGRATED CASE

TROPICAL SWEETS INC.

19-7 Derivatives and Corporate Risk Management   Assume that you have just been hired as a financial analyst by Tropical Sweets Inc., a mid-sized California company that specializes in creating exotic candies from tropical fruits such as mangoes, papayas, and dates. The firm's CEO, George Yamaguchi, recently returned from an industry corporate executive conference in San Francisco, and one of the sessions he attended was on the pressing need for smaller companies to institute corporate risk management programs. Since no one at Tropical Sweets is familiar with the basics of

derivatives and corporate risk management, Yamaguchi has asked you to prepare a brief report that the firm's executives could use to gain at least a cursory understanding of the topics.

To begin, you gathered some outside materials on derivatives and corporate risk management and used these materials to draft a list of pertinent questions that need to be answered. In fact, one possible approach to the paper is to use a question-and-answer format. Now that the questions have been drafted, you have to develop the answers.
a. What is an option? What is the single most important characteristic of an option?

b. Options have a unique set of terminology. Define the following terms:
   (1) Call option
   (2) Put option
   (3) Exercise price
   (4) Striking, or strike, price
   (5) Option price
   (6) Expiration date
   (7) Formula value
   (8) Covered option
   (9) Naked option
   (10) In-the-money call
   (11) Out-of-the-money call
   (12) LEAP
c. Consider Tropical Sweets' call option with a $25 strike price. The following table contains historical values for this option at different stock prices:

STOCK PRICE	CALL OPTION PRICE
$25	$ 3.00
30	7.50
35	12.00
40	16.50
45	21.00
50	25.50

   (1) Create a table which shows (a) stock price, (b) strike price, (c) formula value, (d) option price, and (e) the premium of option price over formula value.
   (2) What happens to the premium of option price over formula value as the stock price rises? Why?
d. In 1973, Fischer Black and Myron Scholes developed the Black-Scholes Option Pricing Model (OPM).
   (1) What assumptions underlie the OPM?
   (2) Write out the three equations that constitute the model.
   (3) What is the value of the following call option according to the OPM?

Stock price = $27.00

Exercise price = $25.00

Time to expiration = 6 months

Risk-free rate = 6.0%

Stock return variance = 0.11

e. What impact does each of the following call option parameters have on the value of a call option?
   (1) Current stock price
   (2) Exercise price
   (3) Option's term to maturity
   (4) Risk-free rate
   (5) Variability of the stock price
f. What is corporate risk management? Why is it important to all firms?
g. Risks that firms face can be categorized in many ways. Define the following types of risk:
   (1) Speculative risks
   (2) Pure risks
   (3) Demand risks
   (4) Input risks
   (5) Financial risks
   (6) Property risks
   (7) Personnel risks
   (8) Environmental risks
   (9) Liability risks
   (10) Insurable risks
h. What are the three steps of corporate risk management?
i. What are some actions that companies can take to minimize or reduce risk exposures?
j. What is financial risk exposure? Describe the following concepts and techniques that can be used to reduce financial risks:
   (1) Derivatives
   (2) Futures markets
   (3) Hedging
   (4) Swaps
k. Describe how commodity futures markets can be used to reduce input price risk.

 COMPUTER-RELATED PROBLEM

Work the problem in this section only if you are using the computer problem diskette.

19-8
Options

Use the model in File C19 to solve this problem. Considine Software Corporation (CSC) options are actively traded on one of the regional exchanges. CSC's current stock price is $10, with a 0.16 instantaneous variance of returns. The current 6-month risk-free rate is 12 percent.

a. What is the value of CSC's 6-month option with an exercise price of $10 according to the Black-Scholes model?
b. What would be the effect on the option price if CSC redeployed its assets and thereby reduced its variance of returns to 0.09?
c. Assume that CSC returns to its initial asset structure; that is, its stock return variance is 0.16. Now assume that CSC's current stock price is $15. What effect does the stock price increase have on the option value?
d. Return to base-case (Part a) values. Now assume that the strike price is $15. What is the new option value?

CHAPTER 20

HYBRID FINANCING: PREFERRED STOCK, LEASING, WARRANTS, AND CONVERTIBLES

The use of convertible securities — generally bonds or preferred stocks that can be exchanged for common stock of the issuing corporation — has soared during the last decade. In 1995, U.S. firms issued $125 billion of convertibles, a fourfold increase from ten years earlier.

Why do companies use convertibles so heavily? To answer this question, recognize that convertibles virtually always have coupon rates that are lower than would be required on straight, nonconvertible bonds or preferred stocks. Therefore, if a company raises $100 million by issuing convertible bonds, its interest expense is lower than if it financed with nonconvertible debt. But why would investors be willing to buy convertibles given their lower cash payments? The answer lies in the conversion feature — if the price of the issuer's stock rises, the holder of the convertible can exchange it for stock and realize a capital gain. So, convertibles hold down the cash costs of debt by giving investors an opportunity for capital gains which can more than offset the low cash returns.

Convertibles can work out well or badly for investors and companies alike. To illustrate, in 1989 MCI issued $1.3 billion of convertible bonds at a rate 4 percentage points lower than its cost would have been on nonconvertible debt. Investors who purchased the issue expected MCI's stock price to rise, at which point they expected to exchange the debt for stock and earn a capital gain. However, MCI's stock price didn't rise to the point where it was attractive to convert, and when the issue became callable in 1993, MCI called the bonds, eliminated the conversion option, and thus eliminated the possibility of capital gains.

An example with a different result is Hercules Inc.'s $68 million 1990 issue of convertible bonds. The coupon rate was set at 8 percent, 3.5 percentage points less than the 11.5 percent required on the company's nonconvertible debt. Hercules' stock has since soared, and by 1996 a $1,000 investment in the convertibles was worth $2,530, giving investors a return of 22.5 percent per year.

Convertibles are attractive to investors because they offer the opportunity to earn the higher returns associated with stocks, but if things don't go well for the company, the convertibles still have the stability associated with debt. However, things can go awry. For example, in 1994 Boston Chicken, a company whose stock price jumped from $20 to $51 the day it was issued, sold $130 million of convertible bonds. Then the issue was hit with a "double whammy" — the stock price fell, and interest rates rose. This lowered the value of both the underlying bond and the conversion option, and, as a result, the convertibles lost 30 percent of their value.

Like all securities, convertibles expose both issuers and investors to risks but offer rewards. When you finish this chapter, you should have a much better understanding of convertibles, how they are valued, and why a firm might choose to issue a convertible bond rather than either straight debt or common stock.

In this chapter, we examine four sources of long-term capital: *preferred stock,* which is a hybrid security that represents a cross between debt and common equity; *leasing,* which is used by financial managers as an alternative to borrowing to finance fixed assets; *warrants,* which are derivative securities that are issued by firms; and *convertibles,* which are hybrids between debt (or preferred stock) and warrants.

PREFERRED STOCK

Preferred stock is a hybrid — it is similar to bonds in some respects and to common stock in others. Accountants classify preferred stock as equity, hence show it on the balance sheet as an equity account. However, one can view preferred stock as being somewhere between debt and common equity — it imposes a fixed charge and thus increases the firm's financial leverage, yet omitting the preferred dividend does not force a company into bankruptcy. We first describe the basic features of preferred, after which we describe some recent innovations in preferred stock financing.

BASIC FEATURES

Preferred stock has a par (or liquidating) value, often either $25 or $100. The dividend is indicated as a percentage of par, as so many dollars per share, or both ways. For example, several years ago Klondike Power Company sold 150,000 shares of $100 par value perpetual preferred stock for a total of $15 million. This preferred had a stated annual dividend of $12 per share, so the preferred dividend yield was $12/$100 = 0.12, or 12 percent, at the time of issue. The dividend was set when the stock was issued; it will not be changed in the future. Therefore, if the required rate of return on preferred, k_{ps}, changes from 12 percent after the issue date — as it did — then the market price of the preferred stock will go up or down. Currently, k_{ps} for Klondike Power's preferred is 9 percent, and the price of the preferred has risen from $100 to $12/0.09 = $133.33.

If the preferred dividend is not earned, the company does not have to pay it. However, most preferred issues are **cumulative,** meaning that the cumulative total of all unpaid preferred dividends must be paid before dividends can be paid on the common stock. Unpaid preferred dividends are called **arrearages.** Dividends in arrears do not earn interest; thus, arrearages do not grow in a compound interest sense — they only grow from additional nonpayments of the preferred dividend. Also, many preferred stocks accrue arrearages for only a limited number of years, say, three years, meaning that the cumulative feature ceases after three years. However, the dividends in arrears continue in force until they are paid.

Preferred stock normally has no voting rights. However, most preferred issues stipulate that the preferred stockholders can elect a minority of the directors — say, three out of ten — if the preferred dividend is passed (omitted). Jersey Central Power & Light, one of the companies that owned a share of the Three Mile

Cumulative
A protective feature on preferred stock that requires preferred dividends previously not paid to be paid before any common dividends can be paid.

Arrearages
Unpaid preferred dividends.

Island (TMI) nuclear plant, had preferred stock outstanding which could elect a *majority* of the directors if the preferred dividend was passed for four successive quarters. Jersey Central kept paying its preferred dividends even during the dark days following the TMI accident. Had the preferred not been entitled to elect a majority of the directors, the dividend would probably have been passed.

Although nonpayment of preferred dividends will not bankrupt a company, corporations issue preferred with every intention of paying the dividend. Even if passing the dividend does not give the preferred stockholders control of the company, failure to pay a preferred dividend precludes payment of common dividends. In addition, passing the dividend makes it difficult for a firm to raise capital by selling bonds, and virtually impossible to sell more preferred or common stock. However, having preferred stock outstanding does give a firm the chance to overcome its difficulties — if bonds had been used instead of preferred stock, the company might have been forced into bankruptcy before it could straighten out its problems. *Thus, from the viewpoint of the issuing corporation, preferred stock is less risky than bonds.*

Investors, on the other hand, regard preferred stock as being riskier than bonds for two reasons: (1) Preferred stockholders' claims are subordinated to those of bondholders in the event of liquidation, and (2) bondholders are more likely to continue receiving income during hard times than are preferred stockholders. Accordingly, investors require a higher after-tax rate of return on a given firm's preferred stock than on its bonds. However, since 70 percent of preferred dividends is exempt from the corporate tax, preferred stock is attractive to corporate investors. In recent years, high-grade preferred stock, on average, has sold on a lower pre-tax yield basis than have high-grade bonds. As an example, recently Du Pont's preferred stock had a market yield of about 7.0 percent, whereas its bonds provided a yield of 8.3 percent, or 1.3 percentage points *more* than its preferred. The tax treatment accounted for this differential; the *after-tax yield* to corporate investors was greater on the preferred stock than on the bonds.[1]

About half of all preferred stock issued in recent years has been convertible into common stock. For example, Enron Corporation issued preferred stock which stipulated that one share of preferred could be converted into three shares of common, at the option of the preferred stockholder. Convertibles are discussed at length in a later section.

Some preferred stocks are similar to perpetual bonds in that they have no maturity date. However, many preferred shares do have a sinking fund provision, often one which calls for the retirement of 2 percent of the issue each year, meaning that the issue will "mature" in a maximum of 50 years. Also, many preferred issues are callable, and this feature can also limit the life of the preferred.[2]

---

[1]The after-tax yield on an 8.3 percent bond to a corporate investor in the 40 percent marginal tax rate bracket is $8.3\%(1 - T) = 8.3\%(0.6) = 4.98\%$. The after-tax yield on a 7.0 percent preferred stock is $7.0\%(1 - \text{Effective T}) = 7.0\%[1 - (0.30)(0.4)] = 7.0\%(0.88) = 6.16\%$. Also, note that tax law prohibits firms from issuing debt and then using the proceeds to purchase another firm's preferred or common stock. If debt is used for stock purchases, then the 70 percent dividend exclusion is reduced. This provision is designed to prevent firms from engaging in "tax arbitrage," or the use of tax-deductible debt to purchase largely tax-exempt preferred stock.

[2]Prior to the late 1970s, virtually all preferred stock was perpetual, and almost no issues had sinking funds or call provisions. Then, insurance company regulators, worried about the unrealized losses the companies had been incurring on preferred holdings as a result of rising interest rates, put into effect some regulatory changes which essentially mandated that insurance companies buy only limited life preferreds. From that time on, virtually no new preferred has been perpetual. This example illustrates the way securities change as a result of changes in the economic environment.

Nonconvertible preferred stock is virtually all owned by corporations, which can take advantage of the 70 percent dividend exclusion to obtain a higher after-tax yield on preferred stock than on bonds. Individuals should not own preferred stocks (except convertible preferreds) — they can get higher yields on safer bonds, so it is not logical for them to hold preferreds. As a result of this ownership pattern, the volume of preferred stock financing is geared to the supply of money in the hands of insurance companies and other corporate investors. When the supply of such money is plentiful, the prices of preferred stocks are bid up, their yields fall, and investment bankers suggest to companies that they consider issuing preferred stock.

For issuers, preferred stock has a tax *disadvantage* relative to debt because interest expense is deductible while preferred dividends are not. On the other hand, omitting a preferred dividend has less serious consequences than defaulting on an interest payment. Firms with low tax rates may have an incentive to issue preferred stock which can be bought by corporate investors with high tax rates who can take advantage of the 70 percent dividend exclusion. If a firm has a lower tax rate than a potential corporate buyer, the firm might be better off issuing preferred stock than comparable-risk debt. In essence, firms with high tax rates have an incentive to buy preferred stock, and this may lower preferred yields sufficiently to offset the fact that preferred dividends are not tax deductible.[3]

RECENT INNOVATIONS

Two important new types of preferred stock have been developed in recent years: (1) floating, or adjustable rate, preferred, and (2) money market, or market auction, preferred.

Adjustable rate preferred stocks (ARPs), instead of paying fixed dividends, have their dividends tied to the rate on Treasury securities. The ARPs, which are issued mainly by utilities and large commercial banks, were touted as nearly perfect short-term corporate investments since (1) only 30 percent of the dividends are taxable to corporations and (2) the floating rate feature was supposed to keep the issue trading at near par. The new security proved to be so popular as a short-term investment for firms with idle cash that new mutual funds designed just to invest in them sprouted like weeds (shares of the funds, in turn, were purchased by corporations). However, the ARPs still had some price volatility due (1) to changes in the riskiness of the issues (some big banks which had issued ARPs, such as Continental Illinois, ran into serious loan default problems) and (2) to the fact that Treasury yields fluctuated between dividend rate adjustments dates. Thus, the ARPs had too much price instability to be held in the liquid asset portfolios of many corporate investors.

In 1984, investment bankers introduced *money market,* or *market auction, preferred.* Here the underwriter conducts an auction on the issue every seven weeks (to get the 70 percent exclusion from taxable income, buyers must hold the stock at least 46 days). Holders who want to sell their shares can put them up for auction at par value. Buyers then submit bids in the form of the yields they are willing to accept over the next seven-week period. The yield set on the issue for the coming period is the lowest yield sufficient to sell all the shares

Adjustable Rate Preferred Stocks (ARPs)
Preferred stocks whose dividends are tied to the rate on Treasury securities.

[3]For a more rigorous treatment of the tax hypothesis of preferred stock, see Iraj Fooladi and Gordon S. Roberts, "On Preferred Stock," *Journal of Financial Research,* Winter 1986, 319–324. For an example of an empirical test of the hypothesis, see Arthur L. Houston, Jr., and Carol Olson Houston, "Financing with Preferred Stock," *Financial Management,* Autumn 1990, 42–54.

being offered at that auction. The buyers pay the sellers the par value, hence holders are virtually assured that their shares can be sold at par. The issuer then must pay a dividend rate over the next seven-week period as determined by the auction. From the holder's standpoint, market auction preferred is a low-risk, largely tax-exempt, seven-week maturity security which can be sold between auction dates at close to par. However, if there are not enough buyers to match the sellers (in spite of the high yield), then the auction can fail. This has occurred on occasion. For example, a few years ago, an auction of MCorp (a Texas bank holding company) failed to attract enough buyers. Analysts attributed the failure to the downgrading of MCorp's preferred stock from double A to single B, which caused potential buyers to think (correctly, as it turned out) that the company would go bankrupt and not pay any dividends.

Adjustable rate and market auction preferreds are also issued by many nonfinancial corporations. For example, Texas Instruments recently issued $225 million of market auction preferred. About the only thing investors do not like about ARPs and auction market preferreds is that, as stock, they are more vulnerable to an issuer's financial problems than debt would be, as evidenced by the MCorp example.

ADVANTAGES AND DISADVANTAGES OF PREFERRED STOCK

There are both advantages and disadvantages to financing with preferred stock. Here are the major advantages from the issuer's standpoint:

1. In contrast to bonds, the obligation to pay preferred dividends is not contractual, and passing a preferred dividend cannot force a firm into bankruptcy.
2. By issuing preferred stock, the firm avoids the dilution of common equity that occurs when common stock is sold.
3. Since preferred stock sometimes has no maturity, and since preferred sinking fund payments, if present, are typically spread over a long period, preferred issues avoid the cash flow drain from repayment of principal that is inherent in debt issues.

There are two major disadvantages:

1. Preferred stock dividends are not a deductible expense to the issuer, hence the after-tax cost of preferred is typically higher than the after-tax cost of debt. However, the tax advantage of preferreds to corporate purchasers lowers its effective cost.
2. Although preferred dividends can be passed, investors expect them to be paid, and firms intend to pay the dividends if conditions permit. Thus, preferred dividends are considered to be a fixed cost, hence their use, like that of debt, increases the financial risk of the firm and thus its cost of common equity.

SELF-TEST QUESTIONS ??????

Should preferred stock be considered as equity or debt? Explain.

Who are the major purchasers of nonconvertible preferred stock? Why?

Briefly explain the mechanics of adjustable rate and market auction preferred stock.

What are the advantages and disadvantages of preferred stock to the issuer?

LEASING

Firms generally own fixed assets and report them on their balance sheets, but it is the *use* of buildings and equipment that is important, not their ownership per se. One way of obtaining the use of assets is to buy them, but an alternative is to lease them. Prior to the 1950s, leasing was generally associated with real estate — land and buildings. Today, however, it is possible to lease virtually any kind of fixed asset, and, in 1997, about 30 percent of all new capital equipment acquired by businesses was leased.

TYPES OF LEASES

Leasing takes three different forms: (1) *sale-and-leaseback* arrangements, (2) *operating leases,* and (3) straight *financial,* or *capital, leases.*

Sale and Leaseback
An arrangement whereby a firm sells land, buildings, or equipment and simultaneously leases the property back for a specified period under specific terms.

Lessee
The party that uses, rather than the one who owns, the leased property.

Lessor
The owner of the leased property.

SALE AND LEASEBACK.   Under a **sale and leaseback,** a firm that owns land, buildings, or equipment sells the property and simultaneously executes an agreement to lease the property back for a specified period under specific terms. The purchaser could be an insurance company, a commercial bank, a specialized leasing company, or even an individual investor. The sale-and-leaseback plan is an alternative to taking out a mortgage loan.

The firm which is selling the property, or the **lessee,** immediately receives the purchase price put up by the buyer, or the **lessor.**[4] At the same time, the seller-lessee firm retains the use of the property just as if it had borrowed and mortgaged the property to secure the loan. Note that under a mortgage loan arrangement, the financial institution would normally receive a series of equal payments just sufficient to amortize the loan while providing a specified rate of return to the lender on the outstanding balance. Under a sale-and-leaseback arrangement, the lease payments are set up in exactly the same way; the payments are set so as to return the purchase price to the investor-lessor while providing a specified rate of return on the lessor's outstanding investment.

Operating Lease
A lease under which the lessor maintains and finances the property; also called a *service lease.*

OPERATING LEASES.   **Operating leases,** sometimes called *service leases,* provide for both *financing* and *maintenance.* IBM is one of the pioneers of the operating lease contract, and computers and office copying machines, together with automobiles and trucks, are the primary types of equipment involved. Ordinarily, these leases call for the lessor to maintain and service the leased equipment, and the cost of providing maintenance is built into the lease payments.

Another important characteristic of operating leases is the fact that they are frequently *not fully amortized;* in other words, the payments required under the lease contract are not sufficient to recover the full cost of the equipment. However, the lease contract is written for a period considerably shorter than the expected economic life of the leased equipment, and the lessor expects to recover all investment costs through subsequent renewal payments, through subsequent leases to other lessees, or by selling the leased equipment.

A final feature of operating leases is that they frequently contain a *cancellation clause,* which gives the lessee the right to cancel the lease before the expiration of the basic agreement. This is an important consideration for the lessee, for it means that the equipment can be returned if it is rendered obsolete by

---

[4]The term *lessee* is pronounced "less-ee," not "lease-ee," and *lessor* is pronounced "less-or."

T A B L E   2 0 - 1   Balance Sheet Effects of Leasing

BEFORE ASSET INCREASE				AFTER ASSET INCREASE							
FIRMS B AND L				FIRM B, WHICH BORROWS AND BUYS				FIRM L, WHICH LEASES			
Current assets	$ 50	Debt	$ 50	Current assets	$ 50	Debt	$150	Current assets	$ 50	Debt	$ 50
Fixed assets	50	Equity	50	Fixed assets	150	Equity	50	Fixed assets	50	Equity	50
Total	$100		$100	Total	$200		$200	Total	$100		$100
	Debt ratio: 50%				Debt ratio: 75%				Debt ratio: 50%		

technological developments or if it is no longer needed because of a decline in the lessee's business.

Financial Lease
A lease that does not provide for maintenance services, is not cancelable, and is fully amortized over its life; also called a *capital lease.*

FINANCIAL, OR CAPITAL, LEASES.   **Financial leases,** sometimes called *capital leases,* are differentiated from operating leases in three respects: (1) they do *not* provide for maintenance services, (2) they are *not* cancelable, and (3) they *are* fully amortized (that is, the lessor receives rental payments which are equal to the full price of the leased equipment plus a return on the investment). In a typical financial lease arrangement, the firm that will use the equipment (the lessee) selects the specific items it requires and negotiates the price and delivery terms with the manufacturer. The user firm then negotiates terms with a leasing company and, once the lease terms are set, arranges to have the lessor buy the equipment from the manufacturer or the distributor. When the equipment is purchased, the user firm simultaneously executes the lease agreement.

Financial leases are similar to sale-and-leaseback arrangements, the major difference being that the leased equipment is new and the lessor buys it from a manufacturer or a distributor instead of from the user-lessee. A sale and leaseback may thus be thought of as a special type of financial lease, and both sale and leasebacks and financial leases are analyzed in the same manner.[5]

FINANCIAL STATEMENT EFFECTS

Lease payments are shown as operating expenses on a firm's income statement, but under certain conditions, neither the leased assets nor the liabilities under the lease contract appears on the firm's balance sheet. For this reason, leasing is often called **off balance sheet financing.** This point is illustrated in Table 20-1 by the balance sheets of two hypothetical firms, B (for Buy) and L (for Lease). Initially, the balance sheets of both firms are identical, and both have debt ratios of 50 percent. Each firm then decides to acquire fixed assets which cost $100. Firm B borrows $100 to make the purchase, so both an asset and a liability are recorded on its balance sheet, and its debt ratio is increased to 75 percent. Firm L leases the equipment, so its balance sheet is unchanged. The lease may call for

Off Balance Sheet Financing
Financing in which the assets and liabilities involved do not appear on the firm's balance sheet.

---

[5]For a lease transaction to qualify as a lease for *tax purposes,* and thus for the lessee to be able to deduct the lease payments, the life of the lease must not exceed 80 percent of the expected life of the asset, and the lessee cannot be permitted to buy the asset at a nominal value. These conditions are IRS requirements, and they should not be confused with the FASB requirements discussed later in the chapter concerning the capitalization of leases. It is important to consult lawyers and accountants to ascertain whether or not a prospective lease meets current IRS regulations.

fixed charges as high as or even higher than those on the loan, and the obligations assumed under the lease may be equally or more dangerous from the standpoint of financial safety, but the firm's debt ratio remains at 50 percent.

To correct this problem, the Financial Accounting Standards Board issued **FASB #13,** which requires that for an unqualified audit report, firms that enter into financial (or capital) leases must restate their balance sheets to report (1) leased assets as fixed assets and (2) the present value of future lease payments as a liability. This process is called *capitalizing the lease,* and its net effect is to cause Firms B and L to have similar balance sheets, both of which will resemble the one shown for Firm B after the asset increase.[6]

The logic behind FASB #13 is as follows. If a firm signs a lease contract, its obligation to make lease payments is just as binding as if it had signed a loan agreement. The failure to make lease payments can bankrupt a firm just as surely as can the failure to make principal and interest payments on a loan. Therefore, for all intents and purposes, a financial lease is identical to a loan.[7] This being the case, when a firm signs a lease agreement, it has, in effect, raised its "true" debt ratio and thereby has changed its "true" capital structure. Accordingly, if the firm had previously established a target capital structure, and if there is no reason to think that the optimal capital structure has changed, then using lease financing requires additional equity just as does debt financing.

If a disclosure of the lease in the Table 20-1 example were not made, then investors could be deceived into thinking that Firm L's financial position is stronger than it actually is. Even if the lease were disclosed in a footnote, investors might not fully recognize its impact and might not see that Firms B and L are in essentially the same financial position. If this were the case, Firm L would have increased its true amount of debt through a lease arrangement, but its required return on debt, k_d, its required return on equity, k_s, and consequently its weighted average cost of capital, would not have increased as much as those of Firm B, which borrowed directly. Thus, investors would be willing to accept a lower return from Firm L because they would mistakenly view it as being in a stronger financial position than Firm B. These benefits of leasing would accrue to stockholders at the expense of new investors, who were, in effect, being deceived by the fact that the firm's balance sheet did not fully reflect its true liability situation. This is why FASB #13 was issued.

A lease must be classified as a capital lease, and hence be capitalized and shown directly on the balance sheet, if any one of the following conditions exists:

1. Under the terms of the lease, ownership of the property is effectively transferred from the lessor to the lessee.

---

[6]FASB #13, "Accounting for Leases," November 1976, spells out in detail the conditions under which leases must be capitalized, and the procedures for doing so.

[7]There are, however, certain legal differences between loans and leases. In a bankruptcy liquidation, the lessor is entitled to take possession of the leased asset, and, if the value of the asset is less than the required payments under the lease, the lessor can enter a claim (as a general creditor) for one year's lease payments. In a bankruptcy reorganization, the lessor receives the asset plus three years' lease payments, if needed, to bring the value of the asset up to the remaining investment in the lease. Under a secured loan arrangement, on the other hand, the lender has a security interest in the asset, meaning that if it is sold, the lender will be given the proceeds, and the full unsatisfied portion of the lender's claim will be treated as a general creditor obligation (see Appendix 7B). It is not possible to state as a general rule whether a supplier of capital is in a stronger position as a secured creditor or as a lessor. Since one position is usually regarded as being about as good as the other at the time the financial arrangements are being made, a lease is about as risky as a secured term loan from both the lessor-lender's and the lessee-borrower's viewpoints.

2. The lessee can purchase the property or renew the lease at less than a fair market price when the lease expires.

3. The lease runs for a period equal to or greater than 75 percent of the asset's life. Thus, if an asset has a 10-year life and if the lease is written for more than 7.5 years, the lease must be capitalized.

4. The present value of the lease payments is equal to or greater than 90 percent of the initial value of the asset.[8]

These rules, together with strong footnote disclosures for operating leases, are sufficient to ensure that no one will be fooled by lease financing. Thus, leases are recognized to be essentially the same as debt, and they have the same effects as debt on the firm's required rate of return. Therefore, leasing will not generally permit a firm to use more financial leverage than could be obtained with conventional debt.

EVALUATION BY THE LESSEE

Any prospective lease must be evaluated by both the lessee and the lessor. The lessee must determine whether leasing an asset will be less costly than buying it, and the lessor must decide whether or not the lease will provide a reasonable rate of return. Since our focus in this book is primarily on financial management as opposed to investments, we restrict our analysis to that conducted by the lessee.[9]

In the typical case, the events leading to a lease arrangement follow the sequence described in the following list. We should note that a great deal of theoretical literature exists about the correct way to evaluate lease-versus-purchase decisions, and some very complex decision models have been developed to aid in the analysis. The analysis given here, however, leads to the correct decision in every case we have ever encountered.

1. The firm decides to acquire a particular building or piece of equipment. This decision is based on regular capital budgeting procedures, and the decision to acquire the asset is a "done deal" before the lease analysis begins. Therefore, in a lease analysis we are concerned simply with whether to finance the machine by a lease or by a loan.

2. Once the firm has decided to acquire the asset, the next question is how to finance it. Well-run businesses do not have excess cash lying around, so new assets must be financed in some manner.

3. Funds to purchase the asset could be obtained by borrowing, by retaining earnings, or by issuing new stock. Alternatively, the asset could be leased. Because of the FASB #13 capitalization/disclosure provision for leases, a lease would have the same capital structure effect as a loan.

---

[8]The discount rate used to calculate the present value of the lease payments must be the lower of (1) the rate used by the lessor to establish the lease payments or (2) the interest rate which the lessee would have paid for new debt with a maturity equal to that of the lease.

[9]The lessee is typically offered a set of lease terms by the lessor, which is generally a bank, a finance company such as General Electric Capital (the largest U.S. lessor), or some other institutional lender. The lessee can accept or reject the lease, or shop around for a better deal. In this chapter, we take the lease terms as given for purposes of our analysis. See Chapter 17 of Eugene F. Brigham and Louis C. Gapenski, *Intermediate Financial Management,* 5th ed., for a discussion of lease analysis from the lessor's standpoint, including a discussion of how a potential lessee can use such an analysis in bargaining for better terms.

As indicated earlier, a lease is comparable to a loan in the sense that the firm is required to make a specified series of payments, and a failure to make these payments can result in bankruptcy. Thus, it is most appropriate to compare the cost of leasing with that of debt financing.[10] The lease-versus-borrow-and-purchase analysis is illustrated with data on the Mitchell Electronics Company. The following conditions are assumed:

1. Mitchell plans to acquire equipment with a five-year life which has a cost of $10,000,000, delivered and installed.

2. Mitchell can borrow the required $10 million, using a 10 percent loan to be amortized over five years. Therefore, the loan will call for payments of $2,637,974.81 per year, found with a financial calculator as follows: input N = 5, I = 10, PV = − 10000000, and FV = 0, and then press PMT to find the payment, $2,637,974.81.

3. Alternatively, Mitchell can lease the equipment for five years at a rental charge of $2,800,000 per year, payable at the end of the year. The lessor will own the asset at the expiration of the lease.[11] The lease payment schedule is established by the potential lessor, and Mitchell can accept it, reject it, or negotiate.

4. The equipment will definitely be used for five years, at which time its estimated net salvage value will be $715,000. Mitchell plans to continue using the equipment beyond Year 5, so (1) if it purchases the equipment, the company will keep it, and (2) if it leases the equipment, the company will exercise an option to buy it at its estimated salvage value, $715,000.

5. The lease contract stipulates that the lessor will maintain the equipment. However, if Mitchell borrows and buys, it will have to bear the cost of maintenance. This service will be performed by the equipment manufacturer at a fixed contract rate of $500,000 per year, payable at year-end.

6. The equipment falls in the MACRS five-year class life, and Mitchell's effective federal-plus-state tax rate is 40 percent. Also, the depreciable basis is the original cost of $10,000,000.

NPV ANALYSIS. Table 20-2 shows the cash flows that would be incurred each year under the two financing plans. The table is set up to produce two time lines of cash flows, one for owning as shown on Line 5 and one for leasing as shown on Line 10. All cash flows occur at the end of the year.

The top section of the table (Lines 1–6) is devoted to the cost of owning (borrowing and buying). Lines 1–4 show the individual cash flow items. Line 5 is a time line which summarizes the annual net cash flows that Mitchell will incur if it finances the equipment with a loan. The present values of these cash flows are summed to find the *present value of the cost of owning,* which is shown on Line 6 in the Year 0 column. (Note that with a financial calculator, we would input the cash flows as shown on Line 5 into the cash flow register, input the interest rate, I = 6, and then press the NPV key to obtain the PV of owning the equipment.)

[10]The analysis should compare the cost of leasing to the cost of debt financing *regardless* of how the asset is actually financed. The asset may actually be purchased with available cash if it is not leased, but because leasing is a substitute for debt financing, a comparison between the two is still appropriate.

[11]Lease payments can occur at the beginning of the year or at the end of the year. In this example, we assume end-of-year payments, but we demonstrate beginning-of-year payments in Self-Test Problem ST-2.

| **TABLE 20-2** | Mitchell Electronics Company: NPV Lease Analysis (Thousands of Dollars) | | | | | |

	YEAR					
	0	**1**	**2**	**3**	**4**	**5**
I. Cost of Owning						
1. Net purchase price	($10,000)					
2. Maintenance cost		($ 500)	($ 500)	($ 500)	($ 500)	($ 500)
3. Tax savings from maintenance		200	200	200	200	200
4. Tax savings from depreciation		800	1,280	760	480	440
5. Net cash flow	($10,000)	$ 500	$ 980	$ 460	$ 180	$ 140
6. PV cost of owning at 6%	($ 8,023)					
II. Cost of Leasing						
7. Lease payment		($2,800)	($2,800)	($2,800)	($2,800)	($2,800)
8. Tax savings from lease payment		1,120	1,120	1,120	1,120	1,120
9. Cost to exercise option						(715)
10. Net cash flow	$ 0	($1,680)	($1,680)	($1,680)	($1,680)	($2,395)
11. PV cost of leasing at 6%	($ 7,611)					

III. Cost Comparison

12. Net Advantage to Leasing = NAL
= PV cost of owning − PV cost of leasing
= $8,023 − $7,611 = $412 = $412,000.

NOTE: A line-by-line explanation of the table follows:

1. If Mitchell buys the equipment, it will have to spend $10,000,000 at t = 0.
2. If the equipment is owned, Mitchell must pay $500,000 at the end of each year for maintenance.
3. The $500,000 maintenance expense is tax deductible, so it will produce an annual tax savings of (Tax rate)(Maintenance expense) = 0.4($500,000) = $200,000.
4. If Mitchell buys the equipment, it can depreciate it for tax purposes and thus lower taxable income and taxes. The tax savings in each year is equal to (Tax rate)(Depreciation expense) = 0.4(Depreciation expense). As shown in Appendix 11A, the MACRS rates for five-year property are 0.20, 0.32, 0.19, 0.12, and 0.11 in Years 1–5, respectively. To illustrate the calculation of the depreciation tax savings, consider Year 2. The depreciation expense is 0.32($10,000,000) = $3,200,000, and the tax savings is 0.4($3,200,000) = $1,280,000.
5. The net cash flows associated with owning are found by summing Lines 1–4.
6. The PV (in thousands) of the Line 5 cash flows, when discounted at 6 percent, is −$8,023.
7. The annual end-of-year lease payment is $2,800,000.
8. Since the lease payment is tax deductible, a tax savings of (Tax rate)(Lease payment) = 0.4($2,800,000) = $1,120,000 results.
9. Because Mitchell plans to continue to use the equipment after the lease expires, it must exercise the purchase option for $715,000 at the end of Year 5 if it leases.
10. The net cash flows associated with leasing are found by summing Lines 7–9.
11. The PV (in thousands) of the Line 10 cash flows, when discounted at 6 percent, is −$7,611.
12. The net advantage to leasing is merely the difference between the PV cost of owning (in thousands) and the PV cost of leasing (in thousands) = $8,023 − $7,611 = $412. Since the NAL is positive, leasing is favored over borrowing and buying.

Section II of the table calculates the present value cost of leasing. The lease payments are $2,800,000 per year; this rate, which in this example (but not in all cases) includes maintenance, was established by the prospective lessor and then offered to Mitchell Electronics. If Mitchell accepts the lease, the full $2,800,000 will be a deductible expense, so the tax savings is (Tax rate)(Lease payment) $= (0.4)(\$2,800,000) = \$1,120,000$. These amounts are shown on Lines 7 and 8.

Line 9 in the lease section shows the $715,000 which Mitchell expects to pay in Year 5 to purchase the equipment. We include this amount as a cost of leasing because Mitchell will almost certainly want to continue the operation and thus will be forced to purchase the equipment from the lessor. If we had assumed that the operation would not be continued, then no entry would have appeared on this line. However, in that case, we would have included the $715,000, minus applicable taxes, as a Year 5 inflow in the cost of owning analysis, because if the asset were purchased originally, it would be sold after five years. Line 10 shows the net cash flows associated with leasing for each year, and Line 11 shows the PV cost of leasing. (As indicated earlier in the cost of owning analysis, using a financial calculator, we would input the cash flows as shown on Line 10 into the cash flow register, input the interest rate, $I = 6$, and then press the NPV key to obtain the PV cost of leasing the equipment.)

The rate used to discount the cash flows is a critical issue. In Chapter 5, we saw that the riskier a cash flow, the higher the discount rate used to find its present value. This same principle was observed in capital budgeting, and it also applies in lease analysis. Just how risky are the cash flows under consideration here? Most of them are relatively certain, at least when compared with the types of cash flow estimates that were developed in capital budgeting. For example, the maintenance payments are set by contract, as is the lease payment schedule. The depreciation expenses are also established by law and are not subject to change. The tax savings are somewhat uncertain because tax rates may change, although tax rates do not change very often. The residual value is the least certain of the cash flows, but even here the $715,000 cost is set, and Mitchell's management is fairly confident that it will want to acquire the property.

Since the cash flows under both the lease and the borrow-and-purchase alternatives are all reasonably certain, they should be discounted at a relatively low rate. Most analysts recommend that the company's cost of debt be used, and this rate seems reasonable in our example. Further, since all the cash flows are on an after-tax basis, *the after-tax cost of debt, which is 6 percent, should be used.* Accordingly, in Table 20-2, we used a 6 percent discount rate to obtain the present values of the costs of owning and leasing. The financing method that results in the smaller present value of costs is the one that should be selected. The example shown in Table 20-2 indicates that leasing has a net advantage over buying: the present value of the cost of leasing is $412,000 less than that of buying. Therefore, it is to Mitchell's advantage to lease.

FACTORS THAT AFFECT LEASING DECISIONS

The basic method of analysis set forth in Table 20-2 is sufficient to handle most situations. However, two factors warrant additional comments.

ESTIMATED RESIDUAL VALUE. It is important to note that the lessor will own the property upon the expiration of the lease. The estimated end-of-lease value of the property is called the **residual value.** Superficially, it would appear that if residual values are expected to be large, owning would have an advantage over leasing. However, if expected residual values are large — as they may be under inflation for certain types of equipment as well as if real property is involved — then competition among leasing companies will force leasing rates down to the point where potential residual values will be fully recognized in the lease contract rates. Thus,

Residual Value
The value of leased property at the end of the lease term.

the existence of large residual values on equipment is not likely to bias the decision against leasing.

INCREASED CREDIT AVAILABILITY. As noted earlier, leasing is sometimes said to have an advantage for firms that are seeking the maximum degree of financial leverage. First, it is sometimes argued that a firm can obtain more money, and for a longer period, under a lease arrangement than under a loan secured by the asset. Second, because some leases do not appear on the balance sheet, lease financing has been said to give the firm a stronger appearance in a *superficial* credit analysis, thus permitting it to use more leverage than it could if it did not lease. There may be some truth to these claims for smaller firms. However, now that larger firms are required to capitalize major leases and to report them on their balance sheets, this point is of questionable validity.

SELF-TEST QUESTIONS ??????

Define each of these terms: (1) sale-and-leaseback arrangements, (2) operating leases, and (3) financial, or capital, leases.

What is off balance sheet financing, what is FASB #13, and how are the two related?

List the sequence of events, for the lessee, leading to a lease arrangement.

Why is it appropriate to compare the cost of lease financing with that of debt financing? Why does the comparison *not* depend on how the asset will actually be financed if it is not leased?

WARRANTS

Warrant
A long-term option to buy a stated number of shares of common stock at a specified price.

A **warrant** is a certificate issued by a company which gives the warrant holder the right to buy a stated number of shares of the company's stock at a specified price for some specified length of time. Generally, warrants are distributed with debt, and they are used to induce investors to buy a firm's long-term debt at a lower interest rate than would otherwise be required. For example, when Infomatics Corporation, a rapidly growing high-tech company, wanted to sell $50 million of 20-year bonds in 1997, the company's investment bankers informed the financial vice-president that the bonds would be difficult to sell, and that an interest rate of 10 percent would be required. However, as an alternative the bankers suggested that investors would be willing to buy the bonds with a coupon rate of only 8 percent if the company would offer 20 warrants with each $1,000 bond, each warrant entitling the holder to buy one share of common stock at an *exercise price* of $22 per share. The stock was selling for $20 per share at the time, and the warrants would expire in the year 2007 if they had not been exercised previously.

Why would investors be willing to buy Infomatics Corporation's bonds at a yield of only 8 percent in a 10 percent market just because warrants were also offered as part of the package? It is because the warrants are long-term *call options* which have value because their holders can buy the firm's common stock at a fixed price regardless of how high the stock price climbs. This option offsets the low interest rate on the bonds and makes the package of low-yield bonds plus warrants attractive to investors. (See Chapter 19 for a more complete discussion of options.)

INITIAL MARKET PRICE OF BOND WITH WARRANTS

The Infomatics bonds, if they had been issued as straight debt, would have carried a 10 percent interest rate. However, with warrants attached, the bonds were sold to yield 8 percent. Someone buying the bonds at their $1,000 initial offering price would thus be receiving a package consisting of an 8 percent, 20-year bond plus 20 warrants. Since the going interest rate on bonds as risky as those of Infomatics was 10 percent, we can find the straight-debt value of the bonds, assuming an annual coupon for ease of illustration, as follows:

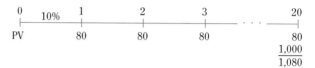

Using a financial calculator, we would input the following data in the TVM register: N = 20, I = 10, PMT = 80, and FV = 1000. Then, we would press the PV key to obtain the answer of $829.73, or approximately $830. Thus, a person buying the bonds in the initial underwriting would pay $1,000 and receive in exchange a straight bond worth about $830 plus 20 warrants presumably worth about $1,000 − $830 = $170:

$$\begin{array}{ccc} \text{Price paid for} & \text{Straight-debt} & \text{Value of} \\ \text{bond with warrants} = & \text{value of bond} + & \text{warrants} \end{array} \qquad \textbf{(20-1)}$$

$$\$1,000 \quad = \quad \$830 \quad + \quad \$170.$$

Since investors receive 20 warrants with each bond, each warrant has an implied value of $170/20 = $8.50.

The key issue in setting the terms in a bond-with-warrants offering is valuing the warrants. The straight-debt value of the bond can be estimated quite accurately. However, it is much more difficult to estimate the value of the warrants. If, when the issue is originally priced, the value estimated for the warrants is greater than their true market value, then the coupon rate on the bonds will be set too low, and it will be difficult to sell the bonds-with-warrants package at its par value. Conversely, if the warrants are undervalued, then the coupon rate will be set too high, the value of the package will quickly rise above $1,000, and investors who buy the issue will end up receiving a windfall profit from Infomatics' stockholders.

USE OF WARRANTS IN FINANCING

Warrants are generally used by small, rapidly growing firms as "sweeteners" when they sell debt or preferred stock. Such firms are frequently regarded by investors as being highly risky. Their bonds can be sold only at extremely high interest rates and with very restrictive indenture provisions. To avoid this, firms such as Infomatics often offer warrants along with the bonds. However, some years ago AT&T raised $1.57 billion by selling bonds with warrants. This was the largest financing of any type ever undertaken by a business firm, and it marked the first use ever of warrants by a large, strong corporation.[12]

---

[12]It is interesting to note that before the AT&T issue, the New York Stock Exchange's stated policy was that warrants could not be listed because they were "speculative" instruments rather than "investment" securities. When AT&T issued warrants, however, the Exchange changed its policy, agreeing to list warrants that met certain requirements. Many other warrants have since been listed. It is

Getting warrants along with bonds enables investors to share in the company's growth, if it does in fact grow and prosper. Therefore, investors are willing to accept a lower bond interest rate and less restrictive indenture provisions. A bond with warrants has some characteristics of debt and some characteristics of equity. It is a hybrid security that provides the financial manager with an opportunity to expand the firm's mix of securities and thus to appeal to a broader group of investors.

Detachable Warrant
A warrant that can be detached from a bond and traded independently of it.

Virtually all warrants today are **detachable warrants.** Thus, after a bond with attached warrants is sold, the warrants can be detached and traded separately from the bond. Further, even after the warrants have been exercised, the bond (with its low coupon rate) remains outstanding. Therefore, the warrants bring in additional funds while leaving interest costs relatively low.

The exercise price on warrants is generally set some 20 to 30 percent above the market price of the stock on the date the bond is issued. If the firm grows and prospers, and if its stock price rises above the exercise price at which shares may be purchased, warrant holders could exercise their warrants and buy stock at the stated price. However, without some incentive, warrants would never be exercised prior to maturity — their value in the open market would be greater than their value if exercised, so holders would hold on rather than exercise. There are three conditions which encourage holders to exercise their warrants: (1) Warrant holders will surely exercise warrants and buy stock if the warrants are about to expire and the market price of the stock is above the exercise price. (2) Warrant holders will exercise voluntarily if the company raises the dividend on the common stock by a sufficient amount. No dividend is earned on the warrant, so it provides no current income. However, if the common stock pays a high dividend, it provides an attractive dividend yield. This induces warrant holders to exercise their option to buy the stock. (3) Warrants sometimes have **stepped-up exercise prices,** which prod owners into exercising them. For example, Williamson Scientific Company has warrants outstanding with an exercise price of $25 until December 31, 2001, at which time the exercise price rises to $30. If the price of the common stock is over $25 just before December 31, 2001, many warrant holders will exercise their options before the stepped-up price takes effect and the value of the warrants falls.

Stepped-Up Exercise Price
An exercise price that is specified to rise if a warrant is exercised after a designated date.

Another desirable feature of warrants is that they generally bring in funds only if funds are needed. If the company grows, it will probably need new equity capital. At the same time, growth will cause the stock price to rise and the warrants to be exercised, providing the firm with additional cash. If the company is not successful and cannot profitably employ additional money, the price of its stock will probably not rise sufficiently to induce exercise of the warrants.

THE COMPONENT COST OF BONDS WITH WARRANTS

When Infomatics issued its debt with warrants, the firm received $50 million, or $1,000 for each bond. Simultaneously, the company assumed an obligation to

---

also interesting to note that, prior to the sale, AT&T's treasury staff, working with Morgan Stanley analysts, estimated the value of the warrants as a part of the underwriting decision. The package was supposed to sell for a total price in the neighborhood of $1,000. The bond value could be determined accurately, so the trick was to estimate the equilibrium value of the warrant under different possible exercise prices and years to expiration, and then to use an exercise price and life which would cause Bond value + Warrant value ≈ $1,000. Using the option pricing model, the AT&T/Morgan Stanley analysts set terms which caused the warrant to sell on the open market at a price that was only 35¢ off from the estimated price.

pay $80 interest for 20 years plus $1,000 at the end of 20 years. The pre-tax cost of the money would have been 10 percent if no warrants had been attached, but each Infomatics bond had 20 warrants, each of which entitles its holder to buy one share of Infomatics stock for $22. What is the percentage cost of the $50 million? As we shall see, the cost is well above the 8 percent coupon rate on the bonds.

Assume that Infomatics' stock price, which is now $20, is expected to grow, and does grow, at 10 percent per year. When the warrants expire ten years from now, the stock price would be $20(1.10)^{10} = $51.87. Assuming the warrants had not been exercised during the ten-year period, the company would then have to issue one share of stock worth $51.87 for each warrant exercised and, in return, Infomatics would receive the exercise price, $22. Thus, a purchaser of the bonds, if he or she holds the complete package, would make a profit in Year 10 of $51.87 − $22 = $29.87 for each common share issued. Since each bond has 20 warrants attached, investors would have a gain of 20($29.87) = $597.40 per bond at the end of Year 10. Here is a time line of the cash flow stream to an investor:

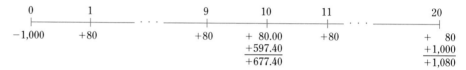

The IRR of this stream is 10.7 percent, which is the investor's overall rate of return on the issue. This return is 70 basis points higher than the return on straight debt. This reflects the fact that the issue is riskier to investors than a straight-debt issue because some of the return is expected to come in the form of stock price appreciation, and that part of the return is relatively risky.

The expected rate of return to investors is, of course, equivalent to the before-tax cost to the company — this was true of common stocks, straight bonds, and preferred stocks, and it is also true of bonds sold with warrants. In thinking about this, note that the investor's Year 10 gain of $597.40 does not just appear out of thin air — the company is giving the warrant holders the right to buy for $22 a share of stock with a market value of $51.87. That dilutes the value of the outstanding stock, so Infomatics' existing shareholders are incurring a cost due to dilution which is exactly equal to the warrant holders' gain.

The cost of warrants can also be considered in terms of the effect on earnings per share (EPS). Suppose Infomatics had 1,000,000 common shares outstanding just prior to the expiration of the warrants. Further, suppose the company earns 13.5 percent on its market value equity. Therefore, its earnings per share are 0.135($51.87) = $7, and its total earnings are 1,000,000($7) = $7,000,000. Now, if there were 100,000 warrants outstanding at expiration, exercise of these warrants would bring in 100,000($22) = $2,200,000 of new equity funds, and the number of shares would increase by 100,000. Assuming that the earning power of the $2.2 million of new assets was also 13.5 percent, then 0.135($2,200,000) = $297,000 of new earnings would be produced, making the new total earnings $7,000,000 + $297,000 = $7,297,000. When the new total earnings is divided by the new total shares outstanding (1,000,000 + 100,000 = 1,100,000), we get a new EPS of $6.63:

New EPS = $7,297,000/1,100,000 = $6.63, versus $7.00.

Thus, exercise of the warrants results in a dilution of EPS from $7 to $6.63, or by $0.37. This $0.37 EPS dilution is a real cost, it is borne by Infomatics' original shareholders, and it must be considered when calculating the cost of the bonds with warrants. The 10.7 percent cost we calculated above takes account of dilution effects.

SELF-TEST QUESTIONS ??????

What is a warrant?

Describe how a new bond issue with warrants is valued.

How are warrants used in corporate financing?

The use of warrants lowers the coupon rate on the corresponding debt issue. Does this mean that the component cost of a debt-plus-warrants package is less than the cost of straight debt? Explain.

CONVERTIBLE SECURITIES

Convertible Security
A security, usually a bond or preferred stock, that is exchangeable at the option of the holder for the common stock of the issuing firm.

Convertible securities are bonds or preferred stocks which, under specified terms and conditions, can be exchanged for common stock at the option of the holder. Unlike the exercise of warrants, which brings in additional funds to the firm, conversion does not provide capital: debt (or preferred stock) is simply replaced on the balance sheet by common stock. Of course, reducing the debt or preferred stock will improve the firm's financial strength and make it easier to raise additional fixed charge capital, but that requires a separate action.

CONVERSION RATIO AND CONVERSION PRICE

Conversion Ratio, CR
The number of shares of common stock that are obtained by converting a convertible bond or share of convertible preferred stock.

Conversion Price, P_c
The effective price paid for common stock obtained by converting a convertible security.

One of the most important provisions of a convertible security is the **conversion ratio, CR,** defined as the number of shares of stock a bondholder will receive upon conversion. Related to the conversion ratio is the **conversion price, P_c,** which is the effective price investors pay for the common stock when conversion occurs. The relationship between the conversion ratio and the conversion price can be illustrated by the Silicon Valley Software Company's convertible debentures, issued at their $1,000 par value in July of 1997. At any time prior to maturity on July 15, 2017, a debenture holder can exchange a bond for 20 shares of common stock; therefore, the conversion ratio, CR, is 20. The bond has a par value of $1,000, so the holder would be relinquishing the right to receive $1,000 at maturity if he or she converts. Dividing the $1,000 par value by the 20 shares received gives a conversion price of $50 a share:

$$\text{Conversion price} = P_c = \frac{\text{Par value of bond given up}}{\text{Shares received}} \tag{20-2}$$

$$= \frac{\$1,000}{\text{CR}} = \frac{\$1,000}{20} = \$50.$$

Conversely, by solving for CR, we obtain the conversion ratio:

$$\text{Conversion ratio} = \text{CR} = \frac{\$1,000}{P_c} \tag{20-3}$$

$$= \frac{\$1,000}{\$50} = 20 \text{ shares.}$$

Once CR is set, the value of P_c is established, and vice versa.

Like a warrant's exercise price, the conversion price is typically set at from 20 to 30 percent above the prevailing market price of the common stock at the time the convertible issue is sold. Exactly how the conversion price is established can best be understood after examining some of the reasons firms use convertibles.

Generally, the conversion price and conversion ratio are fixed for the life of the bond, although sometimes a stepped-up conversion price is used. For example, the 1997 convertible debentures for Breedon Industries are convertible into 12.5 shares until 2007; into 11.76 shares from 2007 until 2017; and into 11.11 shares from 2017 until maturity in 2027. The conversion price thus starts at $80, rises to $85, and then goes to $90. Breedon's convertibles, like most, have a ten-year call-protection period.

Another factor that may cause a change in the conversion price and ratio is a standard feature of almost all convertibles — the clause protecting the convertible against dilution from stock splits, stock dividends, and the sale of common stock at prices below the conversion price. The typical provision states that if common stock is sold at a price below the conversion price, then the conversion price must be lowered (and the conversion ratio raised) to the price at which the new stock was issued. Also, if the stock is split, or if a stock dividend is declared, the conversion price must be lowered by the percentage amount of the stock dividend or split. For example, if Breedon Industries were to have a two-for-one stock split during the first ten years of its convertible's life, the conversion ratio would automatically be adjusted from 12.5 to 25, and the conversion price lowered from $80 to $40. If this protection were not contained in the contract, a company could completely thwart conversion by the use of stock splits and stock dividends. Warrants are similarly protected against dilution.

The standard protection against dilution from selling new stock at prices below the conversion price can, however, get a company into trouble. For example, assume that Breedon's stock was selling for $65 per share at the time the convertible was issued. Further, suppose the market went sour, and Breedon's stock dropped to $50 per share. If Breedon needed new equity to support operations, a new common stock sale would require the company to lower the conversion price on the convertible debentures from $80 to $50. That would raise the value of the convertibles and, in effect, transfer wealth from current shareholders to the convertible holders. This transfer would, de facto, amount to an additional flotation cost on the new common stock issue. Potential problems such as this must be kept in mind by firms considering the use of convertibles or bonds with warrants.

THE COST OF CONVERTIBLE CAPITAL

In the spring of 1997, Silicon Valley Software was evaluating the use of the convertible bond issue described earlier. The issue would consist of 20-year convertible bonds which would sell at a price of $1,000 per bond; this $1,000 would also be the bond's par (and maturity) value. The bonds would pay a 10 percent annual coupon interest rate, or $100 per year. Each bond would be convertible into 20 shares of stock, so the conversion price would be $1,000/20 = $50. The stock was expected to pay a dividend of $2.80 during the coming year, and it sold at $35 per share. Further, the stock price was expected to grow at a constant rate of 8 percent per year. Therefore, $k_s = \hat{k}_s = D_1/P_0 + g = \$2.80/\$35 + 8\% = 16\%$. If the bonds were not made convertible, they would have to offer a yield of 13 percent, given their riskiness and the general level of interest rates. The convertible bonds would not be callable for ten years, after which they could be called at a price of \$1,050, with this price declining by \$5 per year thereafter. If after ten years the conversion value exceeds the call price by at least 20 percent, management would probably call the bonds.

Figure 20-1 shows the expectations of both an average investor and the company.[13]

1. The horizontal line at M = \$1,000 represents the par (and maturity) value. Also, \$1,000 is the price at which the bond is initially offered to the public.

2. The bond is protected against call for ten years. It is initially callable at a price of \$1,050, and the call price declines thereafter by \$5 per year. Thus, the call price is represented by the solid section of the line V_0M''.

3. Since the convertible has a 10 percent coupon rate, and since the yield on a nonconvertible bond of similar risk was stated to be 13 percent, the expected "straight-bond" value of the convertible, B_t, must be less than par. At the time of issue, B_0 is \$789:

$$\begin{array}{c}\text{Pure-debt value at}\\ \text{time of issue}\end{array} = B_0 = \sum_{t=1}^{N} \frac{\text{Coupon interest}}{(1 + k_d)^t} + \frac{\text{Maturity value}}{(1 + k_d)^N} \quad \textbf{(20-4)}$$

$$B_0 = \sum_{t=1}^{20} \frac{\$100}{(1.13)^t} + \frac{\$1,000}{(1.13)^{20}} = \$789.$$

Note, however, that the bond's straight-debt value must be \$1,000 just prior to maturity, so the bond's expected straight-debt value rises over time. B_t follows the line B_0M'' in the graph.

4. The bond's initial **conversion value, C_t,** or the value of the stock the investor would receive if the bonds were converted at t = 0, is \$700: the bond's conversion value is $P_t(CR)$, so at t = 0, conversion value = $P_0(CR)$ = \$35(20 shares) = \$700. Since the stock price is expected to grow at an 8 percent rate, the conversion value should rise over time. For example, in Year 5 it should be $P_5(CR)$ = \$35(1.08)^5(20) = \$1,029. The expected conversion value over time is given by the line C_t in Figure 20-1.

5. The actual market price of the bond can never fall below the higher of its straight-debt value or its conversion value. If the market price dropped below the straight-bond value, those who wanted bonds would recognize the bargain and buy the convertible as a bond. Similarly, if the market price dropped below the conversion value, people would buy the convertibles, exercise them to get stock, and then sell the stock at a profit. Therefore, the higher of the bond value and conversion value curves in the graph represents a *floor price* for the bond. In Figure 20-1, the floor price is represented by the thicker shaded line B_0XC_t.

6. The bond's market value will typically exceed its floor value. It will exceed the straight-bond value because the option to convert is worth something—a 10 percent bond with conversion possibilities is worth more than a 10 percent bond without this option. The convertible's price will also exceed the conversion value because if the stock price declines, the bond value floor will protect the convertible holder. We cannot say exactly where the

Conversion Value, C_t
The value of common stock obtained by converting a convertible security.

---

[13]For a more complete discussion of how the terms of a convertible offering are determined, see M. Wayne Marr and G. Rodney Thompson, "The Pricing of New Convertible Bond Issues," *Financial Management,* Summer 1984, 31–37.

FIGURE 20-1   Silicon Valley Software: Convertible Bond Model

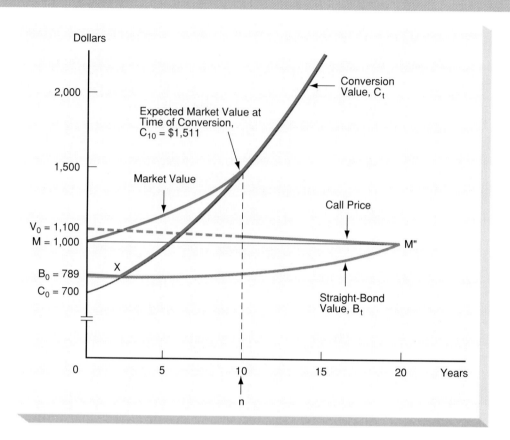

YEAR	PURE-BOND VALUE, B_t	CONVERSION VALUE, C_t	MATURITY VALUE, M	MARKET VALUE	FLOOR VALUE	PREMIUM
0	$ 789	$ 700	$1,000	$1,000	$ 789	$211
1	792	756	$1,000	1,023	792	231
2	795	816	$1,000	1,071	816	255
3	798	882	$1,000	1,147	882	265
4	802	952	$1,000	1,192	952	240
5	806	1,029	$1,000	1,241	1,029	212
6	811	1,111	$1,000	1,293	1,111	182
7	816	1,200	$1,000	1,344	1,200	144
8	822	1,296	$1,000	1,398	1,296	102
9	829	1,399	$1,000	1,453	1,399	54
10	837	1,511	$1,000	1,511	1,511	0
11	846	1,632	$1,000	1,632	1,632	0
.	.	.	.	.	.	.
.	.	.	.	.	.	.
.	.	.	.	.	.	.
20	1,000	3,263	$1,000	3,263	3,263	0

market value line will lie, but as a rule it will be at or above the floor set by the straight-bond and conversion value lines.

7. At some point, the market value line will touch the conversion value line. This convergence will occur for two reasons. First, the stock should pay higher and higher dividends as the years go by, but the interest payments on the convertible are fixed. For example, Silicon's convertibles would pay $100 in interest annually, while the dividends on the 20 shares received upon conversion would initially be 20($2.80) = $56. However, at an 8 percent growth rate, the dividends after ten years would be up to $120.90, while the interest would still be $100. Thus, at some point, rising dividends could be expected to push against the fixed interest payments, causing the premium to disappear and investors to convert voluntarily. Second, once the bond becomes callable, its market price cannot exceed the higher of the conversion value and the call price without exposing investors to the danger of a call. For example, suppose that ten years after issue (when the bonds were callable), the market price of the bonds was $1,600, the conversion value was $1,500, and the call price was $1,050. If the company called the bonds the day after you bought ten bonds for $16,000, you would be forced to convert into stock worth only $15,000, so you would suffer a loss of $100 per bond, or $1,000, in one day. Recognizing this danger, you and other investors would simply not pay much of a premium over the higher of the call price or the conversion value once the bond becomes callable. Therefore, in Figure 20-1, we assume that the market value line hits the conversion value line in Year 10, when the bond becomes callable.

8. We can let n represent the year when investors expect conversion to occur, either voluntarily because of rising dividends or because the company calls the convertibles to strengthen its balance sheet by substituting equity for debt. In our example, we assume that n = 10, the first call date.

9. Since n = 10, the expected market value at Year 10 is $35(1.08)^{10}(20) = $1,511. An investor can find the expected rate of return on the convertible bond, k_c, by finding the IRR of the following cash flow stream:

The solution is k_c = IRR = 12.8 percent.

10. The return on a convertible is expected to come partly from interest income and partly from capital gains; in this case, the total expected return is 12.8 percent, with 10 percent representing interest income and 2.8 percent representing the expected capital gain. The interest component is relatively assured, while the capital gain component is more risky. Had the company issued a straight bond, all of the return would come in the form of interest. Therefore, a convertible's expected return is more risky than that of a straight bond. This leads us to conclude that k_c should be larger than the cost of straight debt, k_d. Thus, it would seem that the expected rate of return on Silicon's convertibles, k_c, should lie between its cost of straight debt, k_d = 13%, and its cost of common stock, k_s = 16%.

11. Investment bankers use the type of model described here, plus a knowledge of the market, to set the terms on convertibles (the conversion ratio and the

INDUSTRY PRACTICE

APPLE COMPUTER ISSUES PRIVATELY PLACED CONVERTIBLE BONDS

In mid-1996 Apple Computer, once a high-flying leader in the computer industry, was fighting to stay alive. The company had recently reported negative earnings, its stock price had steadily fallen in a market where technology stocks were generally rising, and its cash position had weakened just as a lot of its debt was about to mature.

The company clearly needed new capital, but the weak stock price made it costly to issue equity, and its weak ratios made a straight-debt issue too expensive. Therefore, the company decided to issue convertible bonds. The bonds had a five-year maturity, carried a 6 percent coupon, and were convertible at $29.20 a share. At the time, Apple's stock was selling for about $24, and a new issue of straight, nonconvertible debt

would have cost about 11 percent. Apple is saving $33 million in interest per year, and if the issue is converted, then the company would, in effect, have issued stock for $29.20 rather than $24 per share.

The initial response to the offering was positive. Investors, increasingly confident that Apple was taking the necessary steps to improve its performance, liked the downside protection of the fixed payments on the bond and the upside potential of the option to convert, if the company's stock price increased. Apple's original plan was to raise $500 million, but demand was so strong it increased the issue to $660 million.

However, not everyone thought the convertible was a good idea. In an interview with *Fortune* magazine, former junk bond king Michael Milken argued that investors should avoid high-tech companies that issued convertible bonds at a time when the equity market is strong:

It reminds me of the airline and aerospace industries several decades ago. When those industries got into trouble, the stocks did poorly, so no one converted the bonds. Then the companies had to struggle to get out from under the debt burden.

Milken then commented on the Apple deal, terming it "a terrible mistake."

So far, Milken appears to have been correct. As of early 1997, Apple's stock had fallen to $15 per share — roughly 38 percent below where it was just prior to the offering. The convertible bonds themselves have fallen nearly 20 percent. We'll find out in the years ahead whether Apple can turn itself around, and whether these bonds do what was expected of them.

SOURCES: "The Midas of the Eighties Tells Us Where Tomorrow's Wealth Lies," *Fortune*, September 30, 1996, 80; "Apple's Overnight Success Story," *Institutional Investor*, January 1997, 68–69.

---

coupon interest rate) such that the security will just "clear the market" at its $1,000 offering price. In our example, the required conditions do not hold — the calculated rate of return on the convertible is only 12.8 percent, which is less, rather than more, than the 13 percent cost of straight debt. Therefore, the terms on the bond must be made more attractive to investors. Silicon Valley Software would have to increase the coupon interest rate on the convertible above 10 percent, raise the conversion ratio above 20 (and thereby lower the conversion price from $50 to a level closer to the current $35 market price of the stock), or use a combination of these two such that the expected rate of return on the convertible ends up between 13 and 16 percent.[14]

ON THE WEB

A full-text version of the Fortune article, "The Midas of the Eighties Tells Us Where Tomorrow's Wealth Lies," can be found at http://pathfinder.com/@@YRXYqgYA *51KFjSv/fortune/magazine/1996/960930/mlb.html. It is an excellent article on hybrid securities.

USE OF CONVERTIBLES IN FINANCING

Convertibles have two important advantages from the issuer's standpoint. (1) Convertibles, like bonds with warrants, offer a company the chance to sell debt with a low interest rate in exchange for a chance to participate in the company's success if it does well. (2) In a sense, convertibles provide a way to sell common stock at prices higher than those currently prevailing. Some companies actually

---

[14]In this discussion, we ignore the tax advantages to investors associated with capital gains. This factor could explain why k_c is less than k_d.

want to sell common stock, not debt, but feel that the price of their stock is temporarily depressed. Management may know, for example, that earnings are depressed because of startup costs associated with a new project, but they expect earnings to rise sharply during the next year or so, pulling the price of the stock up with them. Thus, if the company sold stock now, it would be giving up more shares than necessary to raise a given amount of money. However, if it set the conversion price 20 to 30 percent above the present market price of the stock, then 20 to 30 percent fewer shares would be given up when the bonds were converted than if stock were sold directly at the current time. Notice, however, that management is counting on the stock's price to rise above the conversion price to make the bonds attractive in conversion. If earnings do not rise and pull the stock price up, hence conversion does not occur, then the company will be saddled with debt in the face of low earnings, which could be disastrous.

How can the company be sure that conversion will occur if the stock price rises above the conversion price? Typically, convertibles contain a call provision that enables the issuing firm to force bondholders to convert. Suppose the conversion price is $50, the conversion ratio is 20, the market price of the common stock has risen to $60, and the call price on the convertible bond is $1,050. If the company calls the bond, bondholders can either convert into common stock with a market value of 20($60) = $1,200 or allow the company to redeem the bond for $1,050. Naturally, bondholders prefer $1,200 to $1,050, so conversion would occur. The call provision therefore gives the company a way to force conversion, provided the market price of the stock is greater than the conversion price. Note, however, that most convertibles have a fairly long period of call protection — ten years is typical. Therefore, if the company wants to be able to force conversion fairly early, then it will have to set a short call-protection period. This will, in turn, require that it set a higher coupon rate or a lower conversion price.

From the standpoint of the issuer, convertibles have three important disadvantages: (1) The use of a convertible security gives the issuer the opportunity to sell stock at a price higher than the price at which it could be sold currently. However, if the stock greatly increases in price, the firm would probably find that it would have been better off if it had used straight debt in spite of its higher cost and then later sold common stock and refunded the debt. (2) Convertibles typically have a low coupon interest rate, and the advantage of this low-cost debt will be lost when conversion occurs. (3) If the company truly wants to raise equity capital, and if the price of the stock does not rise sufficiently after the bond is issued, then the company will be stuck with debt. This debt will, however, have a low coupon rate.

CONVERTIBLES AND AGENCY COSTS

One of the potential agency problems between bondholders and stockholders discussed in Chapter 1 is asset substitution. Stockholders have an "option-related" incentive to take on projects with high upside potential even though they increase the riskiness of the firm. When such an action is taken, there is potential for a wealth transfer between bondholders and stockholders. However, when convertible debt is issued, actions which increase the riskiness of the company may also increase the value of the convertible debt. Thus, some of the gains to shareholders from taking on high-risk projects may be shared with convertible bondholders. This sharing of benefits lowers agency costs. The same general logic applies to warrants.

SELF-TEST QUESTIONS   ??????

What is a conversion ratio? A conversion price? A straight-bond value?

What is meant by a convertible's floor value?

What are the advantages and disadvantages of convertibles to issuers? To investors?

How do convertibles reduce agency costs?

A FINAL COMPARISON OF WARRANTS AND CONVERTIBLES

Convertible debt can be thought of as straight debt with nondetachable warrants. Thus, at first blush, it might appear that debt with warrants and convertible debt are more or less interchangeable. However, a closer look reveals one major and several minor differences between these securities.[15] First, as we discussed previously, the exercise of warrants brings in new equity capital, while the conversion of convertibles results only in an accounting transfer. Second, there is a difference in the flexibility they provide management. Most convertible issues contain a call provision that allows the issuer either to refund the debt or to force conversion, depending on the relationship between the conversion value and call price. However, most warrants are not callable, so firms generally must wait until maturity for the warrants to generate new equity capital. Generally, maturities also differ between warrants and convertibles. Warrants typically have much shorter maturities than convertibles, and warrants typically expire before their accompanying debt matures. Further, warrants often provide for fewer future common shares than do convertibles. Together, these facts suggest that debt-plus-warrant issuers are actually more interested in selling debt than in selling equity.

In general, firms that issue debt with warrants are smaller and riskier than those that issue convertibles. One possible rationale for the use of option securities, especially the use of debt with warrants by small firms, is the difficulty investors have assessing the risk of small companies. If a startup with a new, untested product seeks debt financing, it is very difficult for potential lenders to judge the riskiness of the venture, hence it is difficult to set a fair interest rate. Under these circumstances, many potential investors will be reluctant to invest, making it necessary to set very high interest rates to attract debt capital. By issuing debt with warrants, investors obtain a package that offers upside potential to offset the risks of loss.

Finally, there is a significant difference in issuance costs between debt with warrants and convertible debt. Bonds with warrants typically require issuance costs that are about 120 basis points more than the flotation costs for convertibles. In general, bond-with-warrant financings have underwriting fees that closely reflect the weighted average of the fees associated with debt

---

[15]For a more detailed comparison of warrants and convertibles, see Michael S. Long and Stephen E. Sefcik, "Participation Financing: A Comparison of the Characteristics of Convertible Debt and Straight Bonds Issued in Conjunction with Warrants," *Financial Management*, Autumn 1990, 23–34.

and equity issues, while underwriting costs for convertibles are substantially lower.

What are some differences between debt-with-warrant financing and convertible debt?

Explain how bonds with warrants might help risky firms sell debt securities.

REPORTING EARNINGS WHEN WARRANTS OR CONVERTIBLES ARE OUTSTANDING

If warrants or convertibles are outstanding, a firm could theoretically report earnings per share in one of three ways:

1. *Simple EPS,* where earnings available to common stockholders are divided by the average number of shares actually outstanding during the period.

2. *Primary EPS,* where earnings available are divided by the average number of shares that would have been outstanding if warrants and convertibles "likely to be converted in the near future" had actually been exercised or converted. In calculating primary EPS, earnings are first adjusted by "backing out" the interest on the convertibles, after which the adjusted earnings are divided by the adjusted number of shares. Accountants have a formula which basically compares the conversion or exercise price with the actual market value of the stock to determine the likelihood of conversion when deciding on the need to use this adjustment procedure.

3. *Fully diluted EPS,* which is similar to primary EPS except that *all* warrants and convertibles are assumed to be exercised or converted, regardless of the likelihood of exercise or conversion.

Simple EPS is virtually never reported by firms which have warrants or convertibles likely to be exercised or converted, but the SEC requires that primary and fully diluted earnings be shown. For firms with large amounts of option securities, there can be a substantial difference between the primary and fully diluted EPS figures. The purpose of the provision is, of course, to give investors a more accurate picture of the firm's true profit position.

What are the three possible methods for reporting EPS when warrants and convertibles are outstanding?

Which methods are most used in practice?

Why should investors be concerned about a firm's outstanding warrants and convertibles?

SMALL BUSINESS

LEASE FINANCING FOR SMALL BUSINESSES

Earlier in this chapter, we saw that under certain conditions leasing an asset can be less costly than borrowing to purchase the asset. For the small firm, leasing often offers three additional advantages: (1) it conserves cash, (2) it makes better use of managers' time, and (3) it provides financing quickly.

CONSERVING CASH

Small firms often have limited cash resources. Because many leasing companies do not require the lessee to make even a small down payment, and because leases are often for longer terms and thus require lower payments than bank loans, leasing can help the small firm conserve its cash. Leasing companies also may be willing to work with a company to design a flexible leasing package that will help the lessee preserve its cash during critical times. For example, when Surgicare of Central Jersey opened its first surgical center, the firm did not have sufficient cash to pay for the necessary equipment. Surgicare's options were to borrow at a high interest rate, to sell stock to the public (which is difficult for a startup firm), or to lease the equipment. Surgicare's financial vice-president, John Rutzel, decided to

lease the needed equipment from Copelco Financial Services, a leasing company which specializes in health care equipment. Copelco allowed Surgicare to make very low payments for the first six months, slightly higher payments during the second six months, and level payments thereafter. These unique lease terms "got Surgicare through the startup phase, when cash flow was the critical consideration."

FREEING MANAGERS FOR OTHER TASKS

Most small-business owners find that they never have enough time to get everything done — being in charge of sales, operations, budgeting, and everything else, they are simply spread too thin. If an asset is owned, the firm must maintain it in good working condition and also keep records on its use for tax depreciation purposes. However, leasing assets frees the business's owner of these duties. First, paperwork is reduced because maintenance records, depreciation schedules, and other records do not have to be maintained on leased assets. Second, less time may have to be spent "shopping around" for the right equipment because leasing companies, which generally specialize in a particular industry, can often provide the manager with the information necessary to select the

needed assets. Third, since the assets can be traded in if they become obsolete, the initial choice of equipment is less critical. And fourth, the burden of servicing and repairing the equipment can be passed on to the lessor.

OBTAINING ASSETS QUICKLY AND INEXPENSIVELY

Many new, small firms find that banks are unwilling to lend them money at a reasonable cost. However, because leasing companies retain the ownership of the equipment, they may be more willing to take chances with startup firms. When Ed Lavin started Offset Printing Company, his bank would not lend him the money to purchase the necessary printing presses — the bank wanted to lend only to firms with proven track records. Lavin arranged to lease the needed presses from Eaton Financial, which also advised him on the best type of equipment to meet his needs. Recently, Lavin's firm achieved sales of $250,000, and as his company grew, he expanded by leasing additional equipment. Thus, (1) leasing allowed Lavin to go into business when his bank was unwilling to help, (2) his leasing company provided him with help in selecting equipment, and (3) the leasing company also provided additional capital to meet his expansion needs.

SUMMARY

In this chapter, we discussed preferred stock, leasing, warrants, and convertibles. The key concepts are listed below:

♦ **Preferred stock** is a hybrid — it is similar to bonds in some respects and to common stock in other ways.

♦ The 1980s spawned two innovations in preferred stock financing: (1) **floating,** or **adjustable rate, preferred,** and (2) **money market,** or **market auction, preferred.**

♦ **Leasing** is a means of obtaining the use of an asset without purchasing that asset. The three most important forms of leasing are (1) **sale-and-leaseback** arrangements, under which a firm sells an asset to another party and leases it back for a specified period under specific terms; (2) **operating leases,** under which the lessor both maintains and finances the asset; and (3) **financial leases,** under which the asset is fully amortized over the life of the lease, the lessor does not normally provide maintenance, and the lease is not cancelable.

♦ The **decision to lease or to buy an asset** is made by comparing the financing costs of the two alternatives and choosing the method with the lower PV cost. All cash flows should be discounted at the **after-tax cost of debt,** because the relevant cash flows are relatively certain and are on an after-tax basis.

♦ A **warrant** is a long-term call option issued along with a bond. Warrants are generally detachable from the bond, and they trade separately in the market. When warrants are exercised, the firm receives additional equity capital, and the original bonds remain outstanding.

♦ A **convertible security** is a bond or preferred stock which can be exchanged for common stock at the option of the holder. When a security is converted, debt or preferred stock is replaced with common stock, but no money changes hands.

♦ Warrants and convertibles are **"sweeteners"** which are used to make the underlying debt or preferred stock issue more attractive to investors. Although the coupon rate on the debt is lower when options are involved, the overall cost of the issue is higher than the cost of straight debt because option-related securities are riskier.

QUESTIONS

20-1 For purposes of measuring a firm's leverage, should preferred stock be classified as debt or equity? Does it matter if the classification is being made (a) by the firm's management, (b) by creditors, or (c) by equity investors?

20-2 You are told that one corporation just issued $100 million of preferred stock and another purchased $100 million of preferred stock as an investment. You are also told that one firm has an effective tax rate of 20 percent, whereas the other is in the 35 percent bracket. Which firm is more likely to have bought the preferred? Explain.

20-3 One often finds that a company's bonds have a higher yield than its preferred stock, even though the bonds are considered to be less risky than the preferred to an investor. What causes this yield differential?

20-4 Why would a company choose to issue floating rate as opposed to fixed rate preferred stock?

20-5 Distinguish between operating leases and financial leases. Would a firm be more likely to finance a fleet of trucks or a manufacturing plant with an operating lease?

20-6 One alleged advantage of leasing voiced in the past was that it kept liabilities off the balance sheet, thus making it possible for a firm to obtain more leverage than it otherwise could have. This raised the question of whether or not both the lease obligation and the asset involved should be capitalized and shown on the balance sheet. Discuss the pros and cons of capitalizing leases and related assets.

20-7 Suppose there were no IRS restrictions on what constitutes a valid lease. Explain in a manner that a legislator might understand why some restrictions should be imposed.

20-8 Suppose Congress changed the tax laws in a way that (1) permitted equipment to be depreciated over a shorter period, (2) lowered corporate tax rates, and (3) reinstated the investment tax credit. Discuss how each of these changes would affect the relative use of leasing versus conventional debt in the U.S. economy.

20-9 What effect does the expected growth rate of a firm's stock price (subsequent to issue) have on its ability to raise additional funds through (a) convertibles and (b) warrants?

20-10 a. How would a firm's decision to pay out a higher percentage of its earnings as dividends affect each of the following?
(1) The value of its long-term warrants.

(2) The likelihood that its convertible bonds will be converted.

(3) The likelihood that its warrants will be exercised.

b. If you owned the warrants or convertibles of a company, would you be pleased or displeased if it raised its payout rate from 20 percent to 80 percent? Why?

20-11 Evaluate the following statement: "Issuing convertible securities represents a means by which a firm can sell common stock at a price above the existing market price."

20-12 Suppose a company simultaneously issues $50 million of convertible bonds with a coupon rate of 9 percent and $50 million of pure bonds with a coupon rate of 12 percent. Both bonds have the same maturity. Does the fact that the convertible issue has the lower coupon rate suggest that it is less risky than the pure bond? Would you regard its cost of capital as being lower on the convertible than on the pure bond? Explain. (Hint: Although it might appear at first glance that the convertible's cost of capital is lower, this is not necessarily the case because the interest rate on the convertible understates its cost. Think about this.)

SELF-TEST PROBLEMS (Solutions Appear in Appendix B)

ST-1
Key terms

Define each of the following terms:

a. Cumulative dividends; adjustable rate preferred stock

b. Arrearages

c. Lessee; lessor

d. Sale and leaseback; operating lease; financial lease

e. Off balance sheet financing; FASB #13

f. Residual value

g. Warrant; detachable warrant; stepped-up exercise price

h. Convertible security; conversion ratio, CR; conversion price, P_c; conversion value, C_t

i. Simple EPS; primary EPS; fully diluted EPS

ST-2
Lease analysis

The Olsen Company has decided to acquire a new truck. One alternative is to lease the truck on a 4-year contract for a lease payment of $10,000 per year, with payments to be made at the *beginning* of each year. The lease would include maintenance. Alternatively, Olsen could purchase the truck outright for $40,000, financing with a bank loan for the net purchase price, amortized over a 4-year period at an interest rate of 10 percent per year, payments to be made at the *end* of each year. Under the borrow-to-purchase arrangement, Olsen would have to maintain the truck at a cost of $1,000 per year, payable at year-end. The truck falls into the MACRS 3-year class. It has a salvage value of $10,000, which is the expected market value after 4 years, at which time Olsen plans to replace the truck irrespective of whether it leases or buys. Olsen has a federal-plus-state tax rate of 40 percent.

a. What is Olsen's PV cost of leasing?

b. What is Olsen's PV cost of owning? Should the truck be leased or purchased?

c. The appropriate discount rate for use in Olsen's analysis is the firm's after-tax cost of debt. Why?

d. The salvage value is the least certain cash flow in the analysis. How might Olsen incorporate the higher riskiness of this cash flow into the analysis?

STARTER PROBLEMS

20-1
Leasing

Connors Construction needs a piece of equipment which can either be leased or purchased. The equipment costs $100. One option is to borrow $100 from the local bank and use the money to buy the equipment. The other option is to lease the equipment. If Connors chooses to lease the equipment, it *would not* capitalize the lease on the balance sheet. Below is the company's balance sheet *prior* to the purchase or leasing of the equipment:

Current assets	$300	Debt	$400
Fixed assets	500	Equity	400
Total assets	$800	Total liabilities and equity	$800

What would be the company's debt ratio if it chose to purchase the equipment? What would be the company's debt ratio if it chose to lease the equipment? Would the company's financial risk be different depending on whether the equipment was leased or purchased?

20-2
Warrants

Gregg Company recently issued two types of bonds. The first issue consisted of 20-year straight (no warrants attached) bonds with an 8 percent annual coupon. The second issue consisted of 20-year bonds with a 6 percent annual coupon with warrants attached. Both bonds were issued at par ($1,000). What is the value of the warrants that were attached to the second issue?

20-3
Convertibles

Petersen Securities recently issued convertible bonds with a $1,000 par value. The bonds have a conversion price of $40 a share. What is the bonds' conversion ratio?

EXAM-TYPE PROBLEMS

The problems included in this section are set up in such a way that they could be used as multiple-choice exam problems.

20-4
Lease versus buy

Morris-Meyer Mining Company must install $1.5 million of new machinery in its Nevada mine. It can obtain a bank loan for 100 percent of the required amount. Alternatively, a Nevada investment banking firm which represents a group of investors believes that it can arrange for a lease financing plan. Assume that the following facts apply:

(1) The equipment falls in the MACRS 3-year class.
(2) Estimated maintenance expenses are $75,000 per year.
(3) Morris-Meyer's federal-plus-state tax rate is 40 percent.
(4) If the money is borrowed, the bank loan will be at a rate of 15 percent, amortized in 4 equal installments to be paid at the end of each year.
(5) The tentative lease terms call for end-of-year payments of $400,000 per year for 4 years.
(6) Under the proposed lease terms, the lessee must pay for insurance, property taxes, and maintenance.
(7) Morris-Meyer must use the equipment if it is to continue in business, so it will almost certainly want to acquire the property at the end of the lease. If it does, then under the lease terms, it can purchase the machinery at its fair market value at that time. The best estimate of this market value is the $250,000 salvage value, but it could be much higher or lower under certain circumstances.

To assist management in making the proper lease-versus-buy decision, you are asked to answer the following questions.

a. Assuming that the lease can be arranged, should Morris-Meyer lease, or should it borrow and buy the equipment? Explain.
b. Consider the $250,000 estimated salvage value. Is it appropriate to discount it at the same rate as the other cash flows? What about the other cash flows — are they all equally risky? (Hint: Riskier cash flows are normally discounted at higher rates, but when the cash flows are *costs* rather than *inflows,* the normal procedure must be reversed.)

20-5
Warrants

Pogue Industries Inc. has warrants outstanding that permit its holders to purchase 1 share of stock per warrant at a price of $21. (Refer to Chapter 19 for Parts a, b, and c.)

a. Calculate the formula value of Pogue's warrants if the common stock sells at each of the following prices: $18, $21, $25, and $70.
b. At what approximate price do you think the warrants would actually sell under each condition indicated in Part a? What premium is implied in your price? Your answer will be a guess, but your prices and premiums should bear reasonable relationships to each other.
c. How would each of the following factors affect your estimates of the warrants' prices and premiums in Part b?
   (1) The life of the warrant is lengthened.
   (2) The expected variability (σ_p) in the stock's price decreases.
   (3) The expected growth rate in the stock's EPS increases.
   (4) The company announces the following change in dividend policy: whereas it formerly paid no dividends, henceforth it will pay out *all* earnings as dividends.
d. Assume Pogue's stock now sells for $18 per share. The company wants to sell some 20-year, annual interest, $1,000 par value bonds. Each bond will have 50 warrants, each

exercisable into 1 share of stock at an exercise price of $21. Pogue's pure bonds yield 10 percent. Regardless of your answer to Part b, assume that the warrants will have a market value of $1.50 when the stock sells at $18. What annual coupon interest rate and annual dollar coupon must the company set on the bonds with warrants if they are to clear the market? Round to the nearest dollar or percentage point.

PROBLEMS

20-6

Balance sheet effects of leasing

Two textile companies, McDaniel-Edwards Manufacturing and Jordan-Hocking Mills, began operations with identical balance sheets. A year later, both required additional manufacturing capacity at a cost of $200,000. McDaniel-Edwards obtained a 5-year, $200,000 loan at an 8 percent interest rate from its bank. Jordan-Hocking, on the other hand, decided to lease the required $200,000 capacity from National Leasing for 5 years; an 8 percent return was built into the lease. The balance sheet for each company, before the asset increases, is as follows:

		Debt	$200,000
		Equity	200,000
Total assets	$400,000	Total liabilities and equity	$400,000

a. Show the balance sheet of each firm after the asset increase, and calculate each firm's new debt ratio. (Assume Jordan-Hocking's lease is kept off the balance sheet.)
b. Show how Jordan-Hocking's balance sheet would have looked immediately after the financing if it had capitalized the lease.
c. Would the rate of return (1) on assets and (2) on equity be affected by the choice of financing? How?

20-7

Lease analysis

As part of its overall plant modernization and cost reduction program, the management of Tanner-Woods Textile Mills has decided to install a new automated weaving loom. In the capital budgeting analysis of this equipment, the IRR of the project was found to be 20 percent versus a project required return of 12 percent.

The loom has an invoice price of $250,000, including delivery and installation charges. The funds needed could be borrowed from the bank through a 4-year amortized loan at a 10 percent interest rate, with payments to be made at the end of each year. In the event that the loom is purchased, the manufacturer will contract to maintain and service it for a fee of $20,000 per year paid at the end of each year. The loom falls in the MACRS 5-year class, and Tanner-Woods's marginal federal-plus-state tax rate is 40 percent.

United Automation Inc., maker of the loom, has offered to lease the loom to Tanner-Woods for $70,000 upon delivery and installation (at t = 0) plus 4 additional annual lease payments of $70,000 to be made at the ends of Years 1 through 4. (Note that there are 5 lease payments in total.) The lease agreement includes maintenance and servicing. Actually, the loom has an expected life of 8 years, at which time its expected salvage value is zero; however, after 4 years, its market value is expected to equal its book value of $42,500. Tanner-Woods plans to build an entirely new plant in 4 years, so it has no interest in either leasing or owning the proposed loom for more than that period.

a. Should the loom be leased or purchased?
b. The salvage value is clearly the most uncertain cash flow in the analysis. Assume that the appropriate salvage value pre-tax discount rate is 15 percent. What would be the effect of a salvage value risk adjustment on the decision?
c. The original analysis assumed that Tanner-Woods would not need the loom after 4 years. Now assume that the firm will continue to use it after the lease expires. Thus, if it leased, Tanner-Woods would have to buy the asset after 4 years at the then existing market value, which is assumed to equal the book value. What effect would this requirement have on the basic analysis? (No numerical analysis is required; just verbalize.)

20-8

Convertibles

The Hadaway Company was planning to finance an expansion in the summer of 1997. The principal executives of the company agreed that an industrial company like theirs should finance growth by means of common stock rather than by debt. However, they believed that the price of the company's common stock did not reflect its true worth, so they decided to sell a convertible security. They considered a convertible debenture but feared the burden of fixed interest charges if the common stock did not rise enough to make conversion attractive. They decided on an issue of convertible preferred stock, which would pay a dividend of $1.05 per share.

The common stock was selling for $21 a share at the time. Management projected earnings for 1997 at $1.50 a share and expected a future growth rate of 10 percent a year in 1998 and beyond. It was agreed by the investment bankers and management that the common stock would continue to sell at 14 times earnings, the current price/earnings ratio.

a. What conversion price should be set by the issuer? The conversion rate will be 1.0; that is, each share of convertible preferred can be converted into 1 share of common. Therefore, the convertible's par value (as well as the issue price) will be equal to the conversion price, which, in turn, will be determined as a percentage over the current market price of the common. Your answer will be a guess, but make it a reasonable one.

b. Should the preferred stock include a call provision? Why or why not?

20-9
Financing alternatives

The Howe Computer Company has grown rapidly during the past 5 years. Recently, its commercial bank urged the company to consider increasing its permanent financing. Its bank loan under a line of credit has risen to $150,000, carrying a 10 percent interest rate, and Howe has been 30 to 60 days late in paying trade creditors.

Discussions with an investment banker have resulted in the decision to raise $250,000 at this time. Investment bankers have assured Howe that the following alternatives are feasible (flotation costs will be ignored):

♦ *Alternative 1:* Sell common stock at $10 per share.

♦ *Alternative 2:* Sell convertible bonds at a 10 percent coupon, convertible into 80 shares of common stock for each $1,000 bond (that is, the conversion price is $12.50 per share).

♦ *Alternative 3:* Sell debentures with a 10 percent coupon; each $1,000 bond will have 80 warrants to buy 1 share of common stock at $12.50.

Keith Howe, the president, owns 80 percent of Howe's common stock and wishes to maintain control of the company; 50,000 shares are outstanding. The following are summaries of Howe's latest financial statements:

BALANCE SHEET

		Current liabilities	$200,000
		Common stock, $1 par	50,000
		Retained earnings	25,000
Total assets	$275,000	Total liabilities and equity	$275,000

INCOME STATEMENT

Sales	$550,000
All costs except interest	495,000
EBIT	$ 55,000
Interest	15,000
EBT	$ 40,000
Taxes (40%)	16,000
Net income	$ 24,000
Shares outstanding	50,000
Earnings per share	$0.48
Price/earnings ratio	18×
Market price of stock	$8.64

a. Show the new balance sheet under each alternative. For Alternatives 2 and 3, show the balance sheet after conversion of the debentures or exercise of the warrants. Assume that $150,000 of the funds raised will be used to pay off the bank loan and the rest to increase total assets.

b. Show Keith Howe's control position under each alternative, assuming that he does not purchase additional shares.

c. What is the effect on earnings per share of each alternative if it is assumed that earnings before interest and taxes will be 20 percent of total assets?

d. What will be the debt ratio under each alternative?

e. Which of the three alternatives would you recommend to Keith Howe, and why?

20-10
Convertibles

O'Brien Computers Inc. needs to raise $35 million to begin producing a new microcomputer. O'Brien's straight, nonconvertible debentures currently yield 12 percent. Its stock sells for $38 per share, the last dividend was $2.46, and the expected growth rate is a constant 8 percent. Investment bankers have tentatively proposed that O'Brien raise the $35 million by issuing convertible debentures. These convertibles would have a $1,000 par value, carry an annual coupon rate of 10 percent, have a 20-year maturity, and be convertible into 20 shares of stock. The bonds would be noncallable for 5 years, after which they would be callable at a price of $1,075; this call price would decline by $5 per year in Year 6 and each year thereafter. Management has called convertibles in the past (and presumably will call them again in the future), once they were eligible for call, as soon as their conversion value was about 20 percent above their par value (not their call price).

a. Draw an accurate graph similar to Figure 20-1 representing the expectations set forth in the problem.

b. Suppose the previously outlined projects work out on schedule for 2 years, but then O'Brien begins to experience extremely strong competition from Japanese firms. As a result, O'Brien's expected growth rate drops from 8 percent to zero. Assume that the dividend at the time of the drop is $2.87. The company's credit strength is not impaired, and its value of k_s is also unchanged. What would happen (1) to the stock price and (2) to the convertible bond's price? Be as precise as you can.

INTEGRATED CASE

FISH & CHIPS INC., PART I

20-11 Lease Analysis Martha Millon, financial manager for Fish & Chips Inc., has been asked to perform a lease-versus-buy analysis on a new computer system. The computer costs $1,200,000, and, if it is purchased, Fish & Chips could obtain a term loan for the full amount at a 10 percent cost. The loan would be amortized over the 4-year life of the computer, with payments made at the end of each year. The computer is classified as special purpose, and hence it falls into the MACRS 3-year class. If the computer is purchased, a maintenance contract must be obtained at a cost of $25,000, payable at the beginning of each year.

After 4 years, the computer will be sold, and Millon's best estimate of its residual value at that time is $125,000. Because technology is changing rapidly, however, the residual value is very uncertain.

As an alternative, National Leasing is willing to write a 4-year lease on the computer, including maintenance, for payments of $340,000 at the *beginning* of each year. Fish & Chips' marginal federal-plus-state tax rate is 40 percent. Help Millon conduct her analysis by answering the following questions.

a. (1) Why is leasing sometimes referred to as "off balance sheet" financing?

(2) What is the difference between a capital lease and an operating lease?

(3) What effect does leasing have on a firm's capital structure?

b. (1) What is Fish & Chips' present value cost of owning the computer? (Hint: Set up a table whose bottom line is a "time line" which shows the net cash flows over the period t = 0 to t = 4, and then find the PV of these net cash flows, or the PV cost of owning.)

(2) Explain the rationale for the discount rate you used to find the PV.

c. (1) What is Fish & Chips' present value cost of leasing the computer? (Hint: Again, construct a time line.)

(2) What is the net advantage to leasing? Does your analysis indicate that the firm should buy or lease the computer? Explain.

d. Now assume that Millon believes the computer's residual value could be as low as $0 or as high as $250,000, but she stands by $125,000 as her expected value. She concludes that the residual value is riskier than the other cash flows in the analysis, and she wants to incorporate this differential risk into her analysis. Describe how this could be accomplished. What effect would it have on the lease decision?

e. Millon knows that her firm has been considering moving its headquarters to a new location for some time, and she is concerned that these plans may come to fruition prior to the expiration of the lease. If the move occurs, the company would obtain completely new computers, and hence Millon would like to include a cancellation clause in the lease contract. What effect would a cancellation clause have on the riskiness of the lease?

INTEGRATED CASE

FISH & CHIPS INC., PART II

20-12 Preferred Stock, Warrants, and Convertibles   Martha Millon, financial manager of Fish & Chips Inc., is facing a dilemma. The firm was founded 5 years ago to develop a new fast-food concept, and although Fish & Chips has done well, the firm's founder and chairman believes that an industry shake-out is imminent. To survive, the firm must capture market share now, and this requires a large infusion of new capital.

Because the stock price may rise rapidly, Millon does not want to issue new common stock. On the other hand, interest rates are currently very high by historical standards, and, with the firm's B rating, the interest payments on a new debt issue would be too much to handle if sales took a downturn. Thus, Millon has narrowed her choice to bonds with warrants or convertible bonds. She has asked you to help in the decision process by answering the following questions.

a. How does preferred stock differ from common equity and debt?

b. What is floating rate preferred?

c. How can a knowledge of call options help one understand warrants and convertibles?

d. One of Millon's alternatives is to issue a bond with warrants attached. Fish & Chips' current stock price is $10, and its cost of 20-year, annual coupon debt without warrants is estimated by its investment bankers to be 12 percent. The bankers suggest attaching 50 warrants to each bond, with each warrant having an exercise price of $12.50. It is estimated that each warrant, when detached and traded separately, will have a value of $1.50.

   (1) What coupon rate should be set on the bond with warrants if the total package is to sell for $1,000?

   (2) Suppose the bonds are issued and the warrants immediately trade for $2.50 each. What does this imply about the terms of the issue? Did the company "win" or "lose"?

   (3) When would you expect the warrants to be exercised?

   (4) Will the warrants bring in additional capital when exercised? If so, how much and what type of capital?

   (5) Because warrants lower the cost of the accompanying debt, shouldn't all debt be issued with warrants? What is the expected cost of the bond with warrants if the warrants are expected to be exercised in 5 years, when Fish & Chips' stock price is expected to be $17.50? How would you expect the cost of the bond with warrants to compare with the cost of straight debt? With the cost of common stock?

e. As an alternative to the bond with warrants, Millon is considering convertible bonds. The firm's investment bankers estimate that Fish & Chips could sell a 20-year, 10 percent annual coupon, callable convertible bond for its $1,000 par value, whereas a straight-debt issue would require a 12 percent coupon. Fish & Chips' current stock price is $10, its last dividend was $0.74, and the dividend is expected to grow at a constant rate of 8 percent. The convertible could be converted into 80 shares of Fish & Chips stock at the owner's option.

   (1) What conversion price, P_c, is implied in the convertible's terms?

   (2) What is the straight-debt value of the convertible? What is the implied value of the convertibility feature?

   (3) What is the formula for the bond's conversion value in any year? Its value at Year 0? At Year 10?

   (4) What is meant by the term "floor value" of a convertible? What is the convertible's expected floor value in Year 0? In Year 10?

   (5) Assume that Fish & Chips intends to force conversion by calling the bond when its conversion value is 20 percent above its par value, or at $1.2(\$1,000) = \$1,200$. When is the issue expected to be called? Answer to the closest year.

   (6) What is the expected cost of the convertible to Fish & Chips? Does this cost appear consistent with the riskiness of the issue? Assume conversion in Year 5 at a conversion value of $1,200.

f. Millon believes that the costs of both the bond with warrants and the convertible bond are essentially equal, so her decision must be based on other factors. What are some of the factors that she should consider in making her decision?

COMPUTER-RELATED PROBLEM

Work the problem in this section only if you are using the computer problem diskette.

20-13

Lease versus buy

Use the model in the File C20 to work this problem.

a. Refer back to Problem 20-4. Determine the lease payment at which Morris-Meyer would be indifferent to buying or leasing; that is, find the lease payment which equates the NPV of leasing to that of buying. (Hint: Use trial-and-error.)

b. Using the $400,000 lease payment, what would be the effect if Morris-Meyer's tax rate fell to 20 percent? What would be the effect if the tax rate fell to zero percent? What do these results suggest?

CHAPTER 21

MERGERS, LBOs, DIVESTITURES, AND HOLDING COMPANIES

MICKEY MOUSE LEARNS THE "ABCs" OF MERGING

On July 31, 1995, the mouse roared — Mickey Mouse that is — for that's when Disney's chairman, Michael Eisner, announced that Disney planned to acquire broadcast powerhouse Capital Cities/ABC for almost $19 billion in stock and cash. The acquisition, one of the largest ever, created an unrivaled global entertainment giant, with revenues of about $20 billion.

The deal called for Disney to pay $65 plus one share of Disney stock for each Cap Cities/ABC share, for a total price of about $124 per share. Thomas Murphy, chairman of Cap Cities/ABC, said that the two sides were able to agree only because Disney was willing to include Disney stock in the price, which gave Cap Cities/ABC shareholders a stake in the new company's upside potential. When the deal took place, Cap Cities/ABC shareholders could ask for all stock or all cash rather than accept the primary cash-plus-stock offer. However, they were not guaranteed their choice, because Disney would only issue a maximum of 155 million new shares.

Disney, which had about $3 billion in debt, borrowed another $10 billion to help finance the cash portion of the deal. Although $13 billion is a great deal of debt, it still represents only 20 percent of the market value of the new company, which will generate an annual cash flow of $4.6 billion, far more than enough to service the debt. Interest-ingly, the deal was struck without the help (and cost) of investment bankers. Cap Cities/ABC was counseled by Warren Buffett, its largest stockholder, while Disney had the advice of a longtime Disney investor, Texas billionaire Sid Bass. Investment bankers were only brought in at the end of the negotiations, mostly to provide fairness opinions.

Eisner expects huge synergies to result from the acquisition. Examples include getting more Disney-produced shows on the ABC television network, using Disney's syndication muscle to sell programs produced by ABC, and the joint packaging of the Disney Channel and Cap Cities' ESPN. According to Eisner, the new company will be a "fantastic combination" which has the capability of becoming the "strongest creative company in the world." Warren Buffett, no stranger to mergers and acquisitions, said, "This deal makes more sense than any deal I've ever seen with the possible exception of Cap Cities' acquisition of ABC a decade ago." He added, "It's a wonderful marriage of the number one content company [Disney] and the number one distribution company [Cap Cities/ABC]."

Only time will tell whether the acquisition fulfills the participants' high expectations, but there is no doubt that mergers and acquisitions such as this one will be an important part of the future financial landscape. As you read this chapter, think about the motivations behind Disney's acquisition, and what specific actions had to be taken to establish a price for Cap Cities/ABC and to bring the deal to completion. Also, think about the new compnay's effects on its competitors, and how other firms might feel compelled to undertake mega-mergers of their own.

Most corporate growth occurs by *internal expansion,* which takes place when a firm's existing divisions grow through normal capital budgeting activities. However, the most dramatic examples of growth, and often the largest increases in firms' stock prices, result from *mergers,* the first topic covered in this chapter. *Leveraged buyouts,* or *LBOs,* occur when a firm's stock is acquired by a small group of investors rather than by another operating company. Since LBOs are similar to mergers in many respects, they are also covered in this chapter. Conditions change over time, and, as a result, firms often find it desirable to sell off, or *divest,* major divisions to other firms that can better utilize the divested assets. Divestitures are also discussed in the chapter. Finally, we discuss the *holding company* form of organization, wherein one corporation owns the stock of one or more other companies.

RATIONALE FOR MERGERS

Many reasons have been proposed by financial managers and theorists to account for the high level of U.S. merger activity. The primary motives behind corporate **mergers** are presented in this section.[1]

SYNERGY

Merger
The combination of two firms to form a single firm.

The primary motivation for most mergers is to increase the value of the combined enterprise. If Companies A and B merge to form Company C, and if C's value exceeds that of A and B taken separately, then **synergy** is said to exist. Such a merger should be beneficial to both A's and B's stockholders.[2] Synergistic effects can arise from four sources: (1) *operating economies,* which result from economies of scale in management, marketing, production, or distribution; (2) *financial economies,* including lower transactions costs and better coverage by security analysts; (3) *differential efficiency,* which implies that the management of one firm is more efficient and that the weaker firm's assets will be more productive after the merger; and (4) *increased market power* due to reduced competition. Operating and financial economies are socially desirable, as are mergers that increase managerial efficiency, but mergers that reduce competition are socially undesirable and illegal.[3]

Synergy
The condition wherein the whole is greater than the sum of its parts; in a synergistic merger, the postmerger value exceeds the sum of the separate companies' premerger values.

---

[1]As we use the term, *merger* means any combination that forms one economic unit from two or more previous ones. For legal purposes, there are distinctions among the various ways these combinations can occur, but our focus is on the fundamental economic and financial aspects of mergers.

[2]If synergy exists, then the whole is greater than the sum of the parts. Synergy is also called the "2 plus 2 equals 5 effect." The distribution of the synergistic gain between A's and B's stockholders is determined by negotiation. This point is discussed later in the chapter.

[3]In the 1880s and 1890s, many mergers occurred in the United States, and some of them were obviously directed toward gaining market power rather than increasing efficiency. As a result, Congress passed a series of acts designed to ensure that mergers are not used as a method of reducing competition. The principal acts include the Sherman Act (1890), the Clayton Act (1914), and the Celler Act (1950). These acts make it illegal for firms to combine if the combination tends to lessen competition. The acts are enforced by the antitrust division of the Justice Department and by the Federal Trade Commission.

Lotus Development Corporation was acquired recently by IBM. Lotus had an outstanding group of software developers, and it owned the Notes system for communicating between PC users. However, its marketing was relatively weak, and it had a shortage of capital. IBM, on the other hand, had an outstanding marketing organization and a huge pool of capital, so it was able to increase the market value of Lotus's assets. The recently announced merger between Morgan Stanley and Dean Witter is another synergistic merger. This deal "unites Wall Street with Main Street." Morgan Stanley, an elite investment bank which specializes in underwriting securities for the world's leading corporations, is joining forces with Dean Witter, which has thousands of sales representatives and 40 million retail customers. After the merger, Dean Witter's brokers can distribute securities brought in by Morgan Stanley's investment bankers, and this should help both organizations in the increasingly competitive securities markets.

TAX CONSIDERATIONS

Tax considerations have stimulated a number of mergers. For example, a profitable firm in the highest tax bracket could acquire a firm with large accumulated tax losses. These losses could then be turned into immediate tax savings rather than carried forward and used in the future.[4] Also, mergers can serve as a way of minimizing taxes when disposing of excess cash. If a firm has a shortage of internal investment opportunities compared with its cash flow, it could (1) pay an extra dividend, (2) invest in marketable securities, (3) repurchase its own stock, or (4) purchase another firm. If it pays an extra dividend, its stockholders would have to pay immediate taxes on the distribution. Marketable securities often provide a good temporary parking place for money, but they generally earn a rate of return less than that required by stockholders. A stock repurchase might result in a capital gain for the remaining stockholders, and it might push up the firm's stock price to a level which would be disadvantageous to remaining stockholders. Finally, a repurchase designed solely to avoid dividend payments might be challenged by the IRS. However, using surplus cash to acquire another firm might avoid all these problems, and this has motivated a number of mergers.

PURCHASE OF ASSETS BELOW THEIR REPLACEMENT COST

Sometimes a firm will be touted as an acquisition candidate because the cost of replacing its assets is considerably higher than its market value. For example, in the early 1980s oil companies could acquire reserves cheaper by buying other oil companies than by doing exploratory drilling. Thus, Chevron acquired Gulf Oil to augment its reserves. Similarly, in the 1980s several steel company executives stated that it was cheaper to buy an existing steel company than to construct a new mill. For example, LTV (the fourth largest steel company) acquired Republic Steel (the sixth largest) for $700 million in a merger that created the second largest firm in the industry.

Of course, the true value of any firm is a function of its future earnings power, not the cost of replacing its assets. Thus, acquisitions should be based on the economic value of the acquired assets, not on their replacement cost.

---

[4]Mergers undertaken only to use accumulated tax losses would probably be challenged by the IRS. However, because many factors are present in any given merger, it is hard to prove that a merger was motivated only, or even primarily, by tax considerations.

DIVERSIFICATION

Managers often cite diversification as a reason for mergers. They contend that diversification helps stabilize a firm's earnings and thus benefits its owners. Stabilization of earnings is certainly beneficial to employees, suppliers, and customers, but its value is less certain from the standpoint of stockholders. Why should Firm A acquire Firm B to stabilize earnings when a stockholder in Firm A could sell some of his or her stock in A and use the proceeds to purchase stock in Firm B? In many cases, stockholders can diversify more easily than could the firm.

Of course, if you were the owner-manager of a closely held firm, it might be nearly impossible for you to sell part of your stock to diversify, because that would dilute your ownership and perhaps also generate a large capital gains tax. So, a diversification merger might be the best way to achieve personal diversification.

MANAGERS' PERSONAL INCENTIVES

Financial economists like to think that business decisions are based only on economic considerations, especially maximization of firms' values. However, some business decisions are based more on managers' personal motivations than on economic analyses. Many people, business leaders included, like power, and more power is attached to running a larger corporation than a smaller one. Obviously, no executive would admit that his or her ego was the primary reason behind a merger, but egos do seem to play a prominent role in many mergers.

It has also been observed that executive salaries are highly correlated with company size — the bigger the company, the higher the salaries of its top officers. This too could play a role in corporate acquisition programs.

After most hostile takeovers, the managers of the target companies lose their jobs, or at least their autonomy. Therefore, managers who own less than 51 percent of their firms' stock look to devices that will lessen the chances of a takeover. Mergers can serve as such a device. For example, when Enron was under attack, it arranged to buy Houston Natural Gas, paying for Houston primarily with debt. That merger made Enron much larger, hence harder for any potential acquirer to "digest," and the much higher debt level made it harder for an acquiring company to use debt to buy Enron. Such **defensive mergers** are hard to defend on economic grounds. The managers involved invariably argue that synergy, not a desire to protect their own jobs, motivated the acquisition, but observers suspect that many mergers were designed more to benefit managers than stockholders.

Defensive Merger
A merger designed to make a company less vulnerable to a takeover.

BREAKUP VALUE

Firms can be valued by book value, economic value, or replacement value. Recently, takeover specialists have begun to recognize **breakup value** as another basis for valuation. Analysts estimate a company's breakup value, which is the value of the individual parts of the firm if they were sold off separately. If this value is higher than the firm's current market value, then a takeover specialist could acquire the firm at or even above its current market value, sell it off in pieces, and earn a substantial profit.

Breakup Value
A firm's value if its assets are sold off in pieces.

Define synergy. Is synergy a valid rationale for mergers? Describe several situations that might produce synergistic gains.

Give two examples of how tax considerations can motivate mergers.

Suppose your firm could purchase another firm for only half of its replacement value. Would this be a sufficient justification for the acquisition?

Discuss the merits of diversification as a rationale for mergers.

What is breakup value?

TYPES OF MERGERS

Horizontal Merger
A combination of two firms that produce the same type of good or service.

Vertical Merger
A merger between a firm and one of its suppliers or customers.

Congeneric Merger
A merger of firms in the same general industry, but for which no customer or supplier relationship exists.

Conglomerate Merger
A merger of companies in totally different industries.

Economists classify mergers into four types: (1) horizontal, (2) vertical, (3) congeneric, and (4) conglomerate. A **horizontal merger** occurs when one firm combines with another in its same line of business — for example, when one computer manufacturer acquires another, or when two retail food chains merge. An example of a **vertical merger** would be a steel producer's acquisition of one of its own suppliers, such as an iron or coal mining firm, or an oil producer's acquisition of a petrochemical firm which uses oil as a raw material. *Congeneric* means "allied in nature or action," hence a **congeneric merger** involves related enterprises but not producers of the same product (horizontal) or firms in a producer-supplier relationship (vertical). IBM's acquisition of Lotus is an example of a congeneric merger. A **conglomerate merger** occurs when unrelated enterprises combine, as illustrated by Mobil Oil's acquisition of Montgomery Ward.

Operating economies (and also anticompetitive effects) are at least partially dependent on the type of merger involved. Vertical and horizontal mergers generally provide the greatest synergistic operating benefits, but they are also the ones most likely to be attacked by the Department of Justice as anticompetitive. In any event, it is useful to think of these economic classifications when analyzing prospective mergers.

What are the four economic types of mergers?

LEVEL OF MERGER ACTIVITY

Five major "merger waves" have occurred in the United States. The first was in the late 1800s, when consolidations occurred in the oil, steel, tobacco, and other basic industries. The second was in the 1920s, when the stock market boom helped financial promoters consolidate firms in a number of industries, including utilities, communications, and autos. The third was in the 1960s, when conglomerate mergers were the rage. The fourth began in the 1980s, when LBO firms and others began using junk bonds to finance all manner of acquisitions. The fifth, which involves strategic alliances designed to enable firms to compete better in the global economy, is in progress today.

| TABLE 21-1A | The Five Biggest Mergers Involving U.S. Corporations (Billions of Dollars) |

COMPANY	YEAR	VALUE	PAID THE ACQUIRED FIRM'S STOCKHOLDERS WITH:
AT&T-McCaw Cellular	1994	$18.9	Acquiring firm's stock
Disney-Capital Cities/ABC	1996	18.8	Cash and stock
Time-Warner Communications	1990	14.1	Cash
Chevron-Gulf	1984	13.3	Cash
Philip Morris-Kraft	1988	12.9	Cash

| TABLE 21-1B | Recently Announced (But Not Completed) U.S. Mergers Likely to Join List of Largest Mergers (Billions of Dollars) |

COMPANY	YEAR ANNOUNCED	VALUE	PAID THE ACQUIRED FIRM'S STOCKHOLDERS WITH:
Bell Atlantic/NYNEX	1996	$21.3	Stock
British Telecom/MCI	1996	21.3	Cash and stock
SBC Communications/Pacific Telesis	1996	16.5	Stock
Boeing/McDonnell Douglas	1996	14.0	Stock
WorldCom/MFS Communications	1996	13.4	Stock

As can be seen from Table 21-1, some huge mergers have occurred in recent years, and some even bigger ones are in the works.[5] The table lists only mergers involving U.S. firms, but large mergers are not unique to the United States. For example, in 1996, global drug companies Ciba-Geigy and Sandoz Ltd. announced a merger which was valued at more than $30 billion. In general, the mergers in the 1990s have been significantly different from those of the 1980s. Most 1980s mergers were financial transactions in which buyers sought to buy companies that were selling at less than their true values as a result of incompetent or sluggish management. If a target company could be managed better, if redundant assets could be sold, and if operating and administrative costs could be cut, profits and stock prices would rise. In the 1990s, on the other hand, most of the mergers have been strategic in nature — companies are merging with other companies to enable the consolidated company to better position itself to compete in the world economy. Indeed, many recent mergers have involved companies in the defense, media, computer, and health care industries, all of which are experiencing rapid structural changes and intense competition.

Other differences between the 1980s and the 1990s are the way the mergers were financed and how the target firms' stockholders were compensated. In the 1980s, cash was the preferred method of payment, because large cash payments

---

[5]For detailed reviews of the 1980s merger wave, see Andrei Shleifer and Robert W. Vishny, "The Takeover Wave of the 1980s," *Journal of Applied Corporate Finance,* Fall 1991, 49–56; Edmund Faltermayer, "The Deal Decade: Verdict on the '80s," *Fortune,* August 26, 1991, 58–70; and "The Best and Worst Deals of the '80s: What We Learned from All Those Mergers, Acquisitions, and Takeovers," *Business Week,* January 15, 1990, 52–57.

could convince even the most reluctant shareholder to approve the deal. Moreover, the cash was generally obtained by borrowing, which left the consolidated company with a heavy debt burden, which often led to difficulties. In the 1990s, stock has replaced borrowed cash as the merger currency for two reasons: (1) Many of the 1980s mergers were financed with junk bonds which later went into default. These defaults, along with the demise of Drexel Burnham, the leading junk bond dealer, have made it difficult to arrange debt-financed mergers. (2) During the 1990s, most mergers have been strategic — as between AT&T and McCaw, IBM and Lotus, and Disney and Cap Cities/ABC — where both companies' managers realized that they needed one another. Most of these mergers have been friendly, and stock swaps are easier to arrange in friendly mergers than in hostile ones. Also, both sets of managers have been concerned about the post-merger financial strength of the consolidated company, and the surviving company will obviously be stronger if the deal is financed with stock rather than debt.

Although the larger 1990s mergers have generally been stock-for-stock, many of the smaller mergers have been for cash. Even here, though, things have been different. In the 1980s, companies typically borrowed to get the money to finance cash acquisitions. In the 1990s, corporate cash flows have been very high, so companies have been able to pay for their smaller acquisitions out of cash flow.

Yet another factor in the 1990s has been the increase in cross-border mergers. Many of these mergers have been motivated by large shifts in the value of the world's leading currencies. For example, in the early 1990s, the dollar was weak relative to the yen and the mark. The decline in the dollar made it easier for Japanese and German acquirers to buy U.S. corporations.

SELF-TEST QUESTIONS

What are the five major "merger waves" that have occurred in the United States?

What are some reasons for the current wave?

HOSTILE VERSUS FRIENDLY TAKEOVERS

In the vast majority of merger situations, one firm (generally the larger of the two) simply decides to buy another company, negotiates a price with the management of the target firm, and then acquires the target company. Occasionally, the acquired firm will initiate the action, but it is much more common for a firm to seek acquisitions than to seek to be acquired.[6] Following convention, we call a company that seeks to acquire another firm the **acquiring company** and the one which it seeks to acquire the **target company.**

Once an acquiring company has identified a possible target, it must (1) establish a suitable price, or range of prices, and (2) tentatively set the terms of payment — will it offer cash, its own common stock, bonds, or some combination? Next, the acquiring firm's managers must decide how to approach the target

Acquiring Company
A company that seeks to acquire another firm.

Target Company
A firm that another company seeks to acquire.

---

[6]However, if a firm is in financial difficulty, if its managers are elderly and do not think that suitable replacements are on hand, or if it needs the support (often the capital) of a larger company, then it may seek to be acquired. Thus, when a number of Texas, Ohio, and Maryland financial institutions were in trouble in the 1980s, they lobbied to get their state legislatures to pass laws that would make it easier for them to be acquired. Out-of-state banks then moved in to help salvage the situation and minimize depositor losses.

company's managers. If the acquiring firm has reason to believe that the target's management will approve the merger, then it will simply propose a merger and try to work out some suitable terms. If an agreement is reached, then the two management groups will issue statements to their stockholders indicating that they approve the merger, and the target firm's management will recommend to its stockholders that they agree to the merger. Generally, the stockholders are asked to *tender* (or send in) their shares to a designated financial institution, along with a signed power of attorney which transfers ownership of the shares to the acquiring firm. The target firm's stockholders then receive the specified payment, either common stock of the acquiring company (in which case the target company's stockholders become stockholders of the acquiring company), cash, bonds, or some mix of cash and securities. This is a **friendly merger.**

Friendly Merger
A merger whose terms are approved by the managements of both companies.

The 1995 acquisition of Scott Paper by Kimberly-Clark typifies a friendly merger. After negotiations between the two boards, Kimberly-Clark announced that the managements of the two firms had agreed to the deal. Each Scott shareholder would receive 0.78 share of Kimberly-Clark for each Scott share, a deal worth about $6.8 million. The acquisition combined the Kleenex brand name of Kimberly-Clark with Scott's brands, providing many operating synergies. Furthermore, Scott Paper's strong presence in Europe gave Kimberly-Clark a much better position from which to expand its overseas sales. The merger was approved by the shareholders of both firms, and no antitrust issues were raised. Therefore, the merger was completed in just a few months.

Often, however, the target company's management resists the merger. Perhaps they feel that the price offered is too low, or perhaps they simply want to keep their jobs. In either case, the acquiring firm's offer is said to be *hostile* rather than friendly, and the acquiring firm must make a direct appeal to the target firm's stockholders. In a **hostile merger,** the acquiring company will again make a **tender offer,** and again it will ask the stockholders of the target firm to tender their shares in exchange for the offered price. This time, though, the target firm's managers will urge stockholders not to tender their shares, generally stating that the price offered (cash, bonds, or stocks in the acquiring firm) is too low.

Hostile Merger
A merger in which the target firm's management resists acquisition.

Tender Offer
The offer of one firm to buy the stock of another by going directly to the stockholders, frequently (but not always) over the opposition of the target company's management.

The battle between Shamrock Holdings and Polaroid illustrates a failed hostile merger attempt. It began when Polaroid's stock was trading in the low $30s. At the time, many analysts had declared that Polaroid was a likely takeover candidate because of its sluggish performance but strong brand name. Also, Polaroid was expected to receive a substantial settlement from its successful suit against Eastman Kodak, which had been found guilty of violating Polaroid's instant camera patents.

Shamrock Holdings, the investment vehicle of the Roy E. Disney family, proposed a friendly takeover, was rebuffed, and then made a $45-per-share hostile tender offer. Polaroid responded to the unwanted offer (1) by selling a block of its stock to a newly established employee stock ownership plan (ESOP), (2) by selling another block to a friendly investor (a *white squire*), and (3) by buying back 22 percent of its outstanding shares at $50 a share. To finance all of this, Polaroid added $536 million in bank debt. Additionally, Polaroid restructured its operations by cutting its work force by 15 percent through a voluntary early retirement program. Shamrock responded to these actions (1) by initiating a **proxy fight** to elect a new slate of officers at Polaroid, and (2) by filing a court suit challenging the legitimacy of Polaroid's defensive maneuvers.

Proxy Fight
An attempt to gain control of a firm by soliciting stockholders to vote for a new management team.

After nine months of heated exchanges between the companies, an accord was reached in March 1989. Polaroid agreed to pay Shamrock $20 million in compensation for expenses incurred in the battle, and Shamrock signed an agreement promising not to seek control of Polaroid for ten years. Also, Polaroid agreed to spend $5 million in advertising on Shamrock's radio and television stations and to distribute to shareholders much of its pending award from Kodak. In addition, Shamrock agreed to drop all litigation, as well as its proxy fight. Although defeated, Shamrock ended up making about $35 million before taxes, considering both the cash settlement and the price increase on the Polaroid shares it owned. Stanley P. Gold, Shamrock's president, said that the decision to settle was sealed by Delaware court decisions upholding Polaroid's defenses. "It isn't that I went away quietly; I tried as hard as I could," he said. Polaroid ended up with more debt, although it still had a strong balance sheet, and a $36-per-share stock price. Polaroid's president and CEO said, "The fundamental changes and initiatives put in place during this period made us stronger, despite the pressure." (Note: In December 1996, Polaroid's stock was selling for $40.50, $4.50 below the $45 offered several years earlier. Meanwhile, the market as measured by the Dow Jones industrials had risen more than 70 percent. Were Polaroid's shareholders well served by its managers' resistance to the Shamrock takeover?)

The 1995 battle of Ingersoll-Rand and Clark Equipment illustrates a hostile takeover that succeeded. The battle began in March, when Ingersoll-Rand, an industrial machinery maker, approached Clark, a construction equipment manufacturer, with a proposal to negotiate a friendly acquisition. After Clark's management rebuffed the proposal, Ingersoll-Rand announced a hostile, all-cash tender offer of $77 per share for Clark's stock. The shares, which were selling for just over $50 prior to the offer, immediately jumped to $83 in anticipation of a competing bidder at a higher price. Clark's board rejected the offer, but in view of the high price set on the bid, the board came under intense pressure to negotiate a deal. Adding to the pressure was the fact that Clark, unlike most companies, elected all of its directors each year, so the entire seven-member board ran the risk of being ousted at the next shareholder meeting — only a month away. With the pressure mounting, Clark's board agreed to a sweetened $86-per-share deal only one week after the hostile tender offer was launched.

The Clark acquisition illustrates three points. First, an all-cash offer that is high enough will generally overcome any resistance by the target firm's management. Second, and this appears to be a trend in the 1990s wave, strategic buyers often begin the hostile bidding process with a "preemptive" or "blowout" bid. The idea here is to offer such a high premium over the preannouncement price that (1) no other bidders will be willing to jump into the fray, and (2) it will be impossible for the target company's board to simply reject the bid. Third, if a hostile bid is eventually accepted by the target's board, the deal ends up as "friendly," regardless of the length or acrimony during the hostile phase.

IBM is reported to have negotiated with Lotus for almost two years before launching its hostile tender offer on June 5, 1995. The week before the offer was announced, Lotus's stock sold for $30 per share. IBM offered $60 per share, a 100 percent premium. IBM decided to make a preemptive bid, one so high that Lotus's stockholders would probably tender their stock and that no "white knight" could match or exceed. IBM had a cash hoard in excess of $10 billion, so it was unlikely that its bid could be stopped. On June 11, Lotus's board agreed to the takeover at a price of $64 per share, so again, a hostile offer ended up as a friendly merger.

SELF-TEST QUESTION

??????

What is the difference between a hostile and a friendly merger?

MERGER REGULATION

Prior to the mid-1960s, friendly acquisitions generally took place as simple exchange-of-stock mergers, and proxy fights were the primary weapons used in hostile control battles. However, in the mid-1960s corporate raiders began to operate differently. First, it took a long time to mount a proxy fight — raiders had to first request a list of the target company's stockholders, be refused, and then get a court order forcing management to turn over the list. During that time, the target's management could think through and then implement a strategy to fend off the raider. As a result, management won most proxy fights.

Then raiders began saying to themselves, "If we could bring the decision to a head quickly, before management can take countermeasures, that would greatly increase the probability of a successful takeover." That led the raiders to turn from proxy fights to tender offers, which had a much shorter response time. For example, the stockholders of a company whose stock was selling for $20 might be offered $27 per share and be given two weeks to accept. The raider, meanwhile, would have accumulated a substantial block of the shares in open market purchases, and additional shares might have been purchased by institutional friends of the raider, who promised to tender their shares in exchange for the tip that a raid was to occur.

Faced with a well-planned raid, managements were generally overwhelmed. The stock might actually be worth more than the offered price to other potential bidders, but management simply did not have time to get this message across to stockholders or to find a friendly competing bidder (white knight). This situation seemed unfair, so Congress passed the Williams Act in 1968. This law had two main objectives: (1) to regulate the way acquiring firms can structure takeover offers and (2) to force acquiring firms to disclose more information about their offers. Basically, Congress wanted to put target managements in a better position to defend against hostile offers. Additionally, Congress believed that shareholders needed easier access to information about tender offers — including information on any securities that might be offered in lieu of cash — in order to make rational tender-versus-don't-tender decisions.

The Williams Act placed the following four restrictions on acquiring firms: (1) Acquirers must disclose their current holdings and future intentions within ten days of amassing at least 5 percent of a company's stock. (2) Acquirers must disclose the source of the funds to be used in the acquisition. (3) The target firm's shareholders must be allowed at least 20 days to tender their shares; that is, the offer must be "open" for at least 20 days. (4) If the acquiring firm increases the offer price during the 20-day open period, all shareholders who tendered prior to the new offer must receive the higher price. In total, these restrictions were intended to reduce the acquiring firm's ability to surprise management and to stampede target shareholders into accepting an inadequate offer. Prior to the Williams Act, offers were generally made on a first-come, first-served basis, and they were often accompanied by an implicit threat to lower the bid price after 50 percent of the shares were in hand. The legislation also gave the target more time to mount a defense, and it gave rival bidders and white knights a chance to enter the fray and thus help a target's stockholders obtain a better price.

Many states have also passed laws designed to protect firms in their states from hostile takeovers. At first, these laws focused on disclosure requirements, but by the late 1970s several states had enacted takeover statutes so restrictive that they virtually precluded hostile takeovers. In 1979, MITE Corporation, a Delaware firm, made a hostile tender offer for Chicago Rivet and Machine Co., a publicly held Illinois corporation. Chicago Rivet sought protection under the Illinois Business Takeover Act. The constitutionality of the Illinois act was contested, and the U.S. Supreme Court found the law unconstitutional. The court ruled that the Illinois law put undue burdens on interstate commerce. The opinion also stated that the market for securities is a national market, and even though the issuing firm was incorporated in Illinois, the state of Illinois could not regulate interstate securities transactions.

The Illinois decision effectively eliminated the first generation of state merger regulations. However, the states kept trying to protect their state-headquartered companies, and in 1987 the U.S. Supreme Court upheld an Indiana law which radically changed the rules of the takeover game. Specifically, the Indiana law first defined "control shares" as enough shares to give an investor 20 percent of the vote. It went on to state that when an investor buys control shares, those shares can be voted only after approval by a majority of "disinterested shareholders," defined as those who are neither officers nor inside directors of the company, nor associates of the raider. The law also gives the buyer of control shares the right to insist that a shareholders' meeting be called within 50 days to decide whether the shares may be voted. The Indiana law dealt a major blow to raiders, mainly because it slows down the action. Delaware (the state in which most large companies are incorporated) later passed a similar bill, and so did New York and a number of other important states.

The new state laws also have some features which protect target stockholders from their own managers. Included are limits on the use of golden parachutes, onerous debt-financing plans, and some types of takeover defenses. Since these laws do not regulate tender offers per se, but rather govern the practices of firms in the state, they have withstood all legal challenges to date. But when companies such as IBM offer 100 percent premiums for companies such as Lotus, it is hard for any defense to hold them off.

SELF-TEST QUESTIONS

Is there a need to regulate mergers? Explain.

Do the states play a role in merger regulation, or is it all done at the national level?

ANALYSIS OF A POTENTIAL MERGER

In theory, merger analysis is quite simple. The acquiring firm simply performs an analysis to value the target company and then determines whether the target can be bought at that value or, preferably, for less than the estimated value. The target company, on the other hand, should accept the offer if the price exceeds its value assuming it continued to operate independently. Theory aside, however, some difficult issues are involved. In this section, we first discuss valuing the target firm, which is the initial step in a merger analysis. Then we discuss setting the bid price, postmerger control, and structuring the takeover bid.

Several methodologies are used to value target firms, but we will confine our discussion to the two most common: discounted cash flow and market multiple analysis. However, regardless of the valuation methodology, it is crucial to recognize two facts. First, the target company typically will not continue to operate as a separate entity, but will become part of the acquiring firm's portfolio of assets. Therefore, changes in operations will affect the value of the business and must be considered in the analysis. Second, the goal of merger valuation is to value the target business's equity, or ownership position, because a business is acquired from its owners, not from its creditors. Thus, although we use the phrase "valuing the firm," our focus is on the value of the equity rather than on total value.

DISCOUNTED CASH FLOW ANALYSIS

The *discounted cash flow (DCF)* approach to valuing a business involves the application of capital budgeting procedures to an entire firm rather than to a single project. To apply this method, two key items are needed: (1) pro forma statements that forecast the incremental cash flows expected to result from the merger and (2) a discount rate, or cost of capital, to apply to these projected cash flows.

Financial Merger
A merger in which the firms involved will not be operated as a single unit and from which no operating economies are expected.

Operating Merger
A merger in which operations of the firms involved are integrated in hope of achieving synergistic benefits.

PRO FORMA CASH FLOW STATEMENTS. Obtaining accurate postmerger cash flow forecasts is by far the most important task in a merger analysis. In a pure **financial merger,** in which no synergies are expected, the incremental postmerger cash flows are simply the expected cash flows of the target firm. In an **operating merger,** where the two firms' operations are to be integrated, forecasting future cash flows is more difficult.

Table 21-2 shows the projected cash flow statements for Apex Corporation, which is being considered as a target by Hightech, a large conglomerate. The projected data are for the postmerger period, and all synergistic effects have been included. Apex currently uses 30 percent debt, but if it were acquired, Hightech would increase Apex's debt ratio to 50 percent. Both Hightech and Apex have a 40 percent marginal federal-plus-state tax rate.

Lines 1 through 4 of the table show the operating information that Hightech expects for the Apex subsidiary if the merger takes place, and Line 5 contains the earnings before interest and taxes (EBIT) for each year. Unlike a typical capital budgeting analysis, a merger analysis usually *does* incorporate interest expense into the cash flow forecast, as shown on Line 6. This is done for three reasons: (1) acquiring firms often assume the debt of the target firm, so old debt at different coupon rates is often part of the deal; (2) the acquisition is often financed partially by debt; and (3) if the subsidiary is to grow in the future, new debt will have to be issued over time to support the expansion. Thus, debt associated with a merger is typically more complex than the single issue of new debt associated with a normal capital project, and the easiest way to properly account for the complexities of merger debt is to specifically include each year's expected interest expense in the cash flow forecast. Therefore, we are using what is called the *equity residual method* to value the target firm. Here the estimated net cash flows are a residual which belongs solely to the acquiring firm's shareholders.

Line 7 contains the earnings before taxes (EBT), and Line 8 gives taxes based on Hightech's 40 percent marginal rate. Line 9 lists each year's net income, and depreciation is added back on Line 10 to obtain each year's cash flow as shown on Line 11. Since some of Apex's assets will wear out or become obsolete, and since Hightech plans to expand the Apex subsidiary should the acquisition occur, some equity funds must be retained and reinvested in the business. These retentions, which are not available for transfer to the parent, are shown on Line 12. Finally, we have projected only five years of cash flows, but Hightech would likely operate the Apex subsidiary for many years — in theory, forever. Therefore, we applied the constant growth model to the 2002 cash flow to estimate the value of

| | TABLE | 2 1 - 2 | Projected Postmerger Cash Flow Statements for the Apex Subsidiary as of December 31 (Millions of Dollars) |

	1998	1999	2000	2001	2002
1. Net sales	$105.0	$126.0	$151.0	$174.0	$191.0
2. Cost of goods sold	80.0	94.0	111.0	127.0	137.0
3. Selling and administrative expenses	10.0	12.0	13.0	15.0	16.0
4. Depreciation	8.0	8.0	9.0	9.0	10.0
5. EBIT	$ 7.0	$ 12.0	$ 18.0	$ 23.0	$ 28.0
6. Interest[a]	3.0	4.0	5.0	6.0	6.0
7. EBT	$ 4.0	$ 8.0	$ 13.0	$ 17.0	$ 22.0
8. Taxes (40%)[b]	1.6	3.2	5.2	6.8	8.8
9. Net income	$ 2.4	$ 4.8	$ 7.8	$ 10.2	$ 13.2
10. Plus depreciation	8.0	8.0	9.0	9.0	10.0
11. Cash flow	$ 10.4	$ 12.8	$ 16.8	$ 19.2	$ 23.2
12. Less retentions needed for growth[c]	4.0	4.0	7.0	9.0	12.0
13. Plus terminal value[d]					150.2
14. Net cash flow to Hightech[e]	$ 6.4	$ 8.8	$ 9.8	$ 10.2	$161.4

[a]Interest payments are estimates based on Apex's existing debt, plus additional debt required to increase the debt ratio to 50 percent, plus additional debt required to finance growth.

[b]Hightech will file a consolidated tax return after the merger. Thus, the taxes shown here are the full corporate taxes attributable to Apex's operations: there will be no additional taxes on any cash flows passed from Apex to Hightech.

[c]Some of the cash flows generated by the Apex subsidiary after the merger must be retained to finance asset replacements and growth, while some will be transferred to Hightech to pay dividends on its stock or for redeployment within the corporation.

[d]Apex's available cash flows are expected to grow at a constant 10 percent rate after 2002. The value of all post-2002 cash flows as of December 31, 2002, is estimated by use of the constant growth model to be $150.2 million:

$$V_{2002} = \frac{CF_{2003}}{k_s - g} = \frac{(\$23.2 - \$12.0)(1.10)}{0.182 - 0.10} = \$150.2 \text{ million.}$$

In the next section, we discuss the estimated 18.2 percent cost of equity. The $150.2 million is the PV at the end of 2002 of the stream of cash flows for year 2003 and thereafter.

[e]These are the net cash flows projected to be available to Hightech by virtue of the acquisition. The cash flows could be used for dividend payments to Hightech's stockholders, to finance asset expansion in Hightech's other divisions and subsidiaries, and so on.

all cash flows beyond 2002. (See Note d to Table 21-2.) This "terminal value" represents Apex's projected value at the end of 2002, and it is shown on Line 13.

The net cash flows shown on Line 14 would be available to Hightech's stockholders, and they are the basis of the valuation.[7] Of course, the postmerger cash flows are extremely difficult to estimate, and in a complete merger valuation, just as in a complete capital budgeting analysis, sensitivity, scenario, and simulation analyses should be conducted. Indeed, in a friendly merger the acquiring firm would send a team consisting of literally dozens of accountants, engineers, and so forth, to the target firm's headquarters. They would go over its books,

---

[7]We purposely kept the cash flows relatively simple to help focus on key issues. In an actual merger valuation, the cash flows would be much more complex, normally including such items as additional capital furnished by the acquiring firm, tax loss carry-forwards, tax effects of plant and equipment valuation adjustments, and cash flows from the sale of some of the subsidiary's assets.

estimate required maintenance expenditures, set values on assets such as real estate and petroleum reserves, and the like.

ESTIMATING THE DISCOUNT RATE. The bottom-line net cash flows shown on Line 14 are after interest and taxes, hence they represent equity. Therefore, they should be discounted at the cost of equity rather than at the overall cost of capital. Further, the discount rate used should reflect the riskiness of the cash flows in the table. Therefore, the most appropriate discount rate is Apex's cost of equity, not that of either Hightech or the consolidated postmerger firm.

Although we will not illustrate it here, Hightech could perform a risk analysis on the Table 21-2 cash flows just as it does on any set of capital budgeting flows. Sensitivity analysis, scenario analysis, and/or Monte Carlo simulation could be used to give Hightech's management a feel for the risks involved with the acquisition. Apex is a publicly traded company, so we can assess directly its market risk. Apex's market-determined premerger beta was 1.28. However, this reflects its premerger 30 percent debt ratio, while its postmerger debt ratio will increase to 50 percent. Hightech's investment bankers estimate that Apex's beta will rise to 1.63 if its debt ratio is increased to 50 percent.

We use the Security Market Line to estimate Apex's postmerger cost of equity. If the risk-free rate is 10 percent and the market risk premium is 5 percent, then Apex's cost of equity, k_s, after the merger with Hightech, would be about 18.2 percent:[8]

$$k_s = k_{RF} + (RP_M)b = 10\% + (5\%)1.63 = 18.15\% \approx 18.2\%.$$

VALUING THE CASH FLOWS. The current value of Apex to Hightech is the present value of the cash flows expected from Hightech, discounted at 18.2 percent (in millions of dollars):

$$V_{1997} = \frac{\$6.4}{(1.182)^1} + \frac{\$8.8}{(1.182)^2} + \frac{\$9.8}{(1.182)^3} + \frac{\$10.2}{(1.182)^4} + \frac{\$161.4}{(1.182)^5} \approx \$92.8.$$

Thus, the value of Apex to Hightech is $92.8 million.

MARKET MULTIPLE ANALYSIS

Another method of valuing a target company is *market multiple analysis,* which applies a market-determined multiple to net income, earnings per share, sales, book value, or, for businesses such as cable TV or cellular telephone systems, the number of subscribers. While the DCF method applies valuation concepts in a precise manner, focusing on expected cash flows, market multiple analysis is more ad hoc. To illustrate the concept, note that Apex's forecasted net income is $2.4 million in 1998, and it rises to $13.2 million in 2002, for an average of $7.7 mil-

---

[8]In this example, we used the Capital Asset Pricing Model to estimate Apex's cost of equity, and thus we assumed that investors require a premium for market risk only. We could have also conducted a corporate risk analysis, in which the relevant risk would be the contribution of Apex's cash flows to the total risk of the postmerger firm.

In actual merger situations among large firms, companies almost always hire an investment banker to help develop valuation estimates. For example, when General Electric acquired Utah International, GE hired Morgan Stanley to determine Utah's value. We discussed the valuation process with the Morgan Stanley analyst in charge of the appraisal, and he confirmed that they applied all of the standard procedures discussed in this chapter. Note, though, that merger analysis, like the analysis of any other complex issue, requires judgment, and people's judgments differ as to how much weight to give to different methods in any given situation.

lion over the five-year forecast period. The average P/E ratio for publicly traded companies similar to Apex is 12.

To estimate Apex's value using the market P/E multiple approach, simply multiply its $7.7 million net income by the market multiple of 12 to obtain the value of $7.7(12) = $92.4 million. This is the equity, or ownership, value of the firm. Note that we used the average net income over the coming five years to value Apex. The market P/E multiple of 12 is based on the current year's income of comparable companies, but Apex's current income does not reflect synergistic effects or managerial changes that will be made. By averaging future net income, we are attempting to capture the value added by Hightech to Apex's operations.

Note that earnings (or cash flow) measures other than net income can be used in the market multiple approach. For example, another commonly used measure is *earnings before interest, taxes, depreciation, and amortization (EBITDA).* The procedure would be identical to that just described, except that the market multiple would be price divided by EBITDA rather than earnings per share, and this multiple would be multiplied by Apex's EBITDA.

As noted above, in some businesses such as cable TV and cellular telephone, an important element in the valuation process is the number of customers a company has. The acquirer has an idea of the cost required to obtain a new customer and the average cash flow per customer. For example, telephone companies have been paying about $2,000 per customer for cellular operators. Medical companies such as HMOs have applied similar logic in acquisitions, basing their valuations on the number of people insured.

SETTING THE BID PRICE

Using the DCF valuation results, $92.8 million is the most Hightech could pay for Apex—if it pays more, then Hightech's own value will be diluted. On the other hand, if Hightech can get Apex for less than $92.8 million, Hightech's stockholders will gain value. Therefore, Hightech will bid something less than $92.8 million when it makes an offer for Apex.

Figure 21-1 graphs the merger situation. The $92.8 million is shown as a point on the horizontal axis, and it is the maximum price that Hightech can afford to pay. If Hightech pays less, say, $82.8 million, then its stockholders will gain $10 million from the merger, while if it pays more, its stockholders will lose. What we have, then, is a 45-degree line which cuts the X axis at $92.8 million, and that line shows how much Hightech's stockholders can expect to gain or lose at different acquisition prices.

Now consider the target company, Apex. It has 10 million shares of stock which sell for $6.25, so its value as an independent operating company is presumably $62.5 million. [In making this statement, we assume (1) that the company is being operated as well as possible by its present management, and (2) that the $6.25 market price per share does not include a "speculative merger premium" in addition to the PV of operating cash flows.] If Apex is acquired at a price greater than $62.5 million, its stockholders will gain value, while they will lose value at any lower price. Thus, we can draw another 45-degree line, this one with an upward slope, to show how the merger price affects Apex's stockholders.

The difference between $62.5 and $92.8 million, or $30.3 million, represents synergistic benefits expected from the merger. Here are some points to note:

1. If there were no synergistic benefits, the maximum bid would be equal to the current value of the target company. The greater the synergistic gains, the

F I G U R E   2 1 - 1   A View of Merger Analysis (Millions of Dollars)

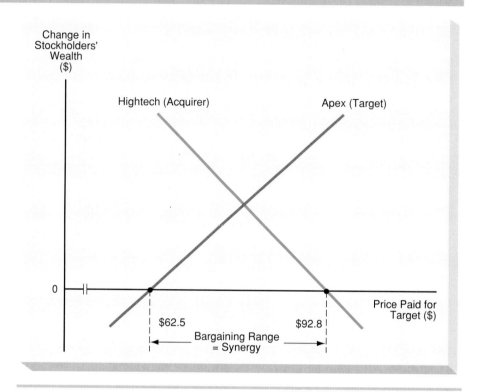

greater the gap between the target's current price and the maximum the acquiring company could pay.

2. The greater the synergistic gains, the more likely a merger is to be consummated.

3. The issue of how to divide the synergistic benefits is critically important. Obviously, both parties will want to get as much as possible. In our example, if Apex's management knew the maximum price that Hightech could pay, it would argue for a price close to $92.8 million. Hightech, on the other hand, would try to get Apex at a price as close to $62.5 million as possible.

4. Where, within the $62.5 to $92.8 million range, will the actual price be set? The answer depends on a number of factors, including whether Hightech offers to pay with cash or securities, the negotiating skills of the two management teams, and, most importantly, the bargaining positions of the two parties as determined by fundamental economic conditions. To illustrate the latter point, suppose there are many companies similar to Apex that Hightech could acquire, but no company other than Hightech that could gain synergies by acquiring Apex. In this case, Hightech would probably make a relatively low, take-it-or-leave-it offer, and Apex would probably take it because some gain is better than none. On the other hand, if Apex has some unique technology or other asset that many companies want, then once Hightech announces its offer, others will probably make competing bids, and the final price will probably be close to or even above $92.8 million. A price above $92.8 million would presumably be paid by some other company which had a better synergistic fit

or, perhaps, whose management was more optimistic about Apex's cash flow potential. In Figure 21-1, this situation would be represented by a line parallel to that for Hightech but shifted to the right of the Hightech line.

5. Hightech would, of course, want to keep its maximum bid secret, and it would plan its bidding strategy carefully and consistently with the situation. If it thought that other bidders would emerge, or that Apex's management might resist in order to preserve their jobs, it might make a high "preemptive" bid in hopes of scaring off competing bids and/or management resistance. On the other hand, it might make a low-ball bid in hopes of "stealing" the company.

We will have more to say about these points in the sections that follow, and you should keep Figure 21-1 in mind as you go through the rest of the chapter.

POSTMERGER CONTROL

The employment/control situation is often of vital interest in a merger analysis. First, consider the situation in which a small, owner-managed firm sells out to a larger concern. The owner-manager may be anxious to retain a high-status position, and he or she may also have developed a camaraderie with the employees and thus be concerned about their retention after the merger. If so, these points would be stressed during the merger negotiations.[9] When a publicly owned firm not controlled by its managers is merged into another company, the acquired firm's management will be worried about its postmerger position. If the acquiring firm agrees to retain the old management, then management may be willing to support the merger and to recommend its acceptance to the stockholders. If the old management is to be removed, then it will probably resist the merger.[10]

SELF-TEST QUESTIONS ??????

What is the difference between an operating merger and a financial merger?

Describe the way postmerger cash flows are estimated in a DCF analysis.

What is the basis for the discount rate in a DCF analysis? Describe how this rate might be estimated.

Describe the market multiple approach.

---

[9]The acquiring firm may also be concerned about this point, especially if the target firm's management is quite good. Indeed, a condition of the merger may be that the management team agree to stay on for a period such as five years after the merger. In this case, the price paid may be contingent on the acquired firm's performance subsequent to the merger. For example, when International Holdings acquired Walker Products, the price paid was an immediate 100,000 shares of International Holdings stock worth $63 per share plus an additional 30,000 shares each year for the next three years, provided Walker Products earned at least $1 million during each of these years. Since Walker's managers owned the stock and would receive the bonus, they had a strong incentive to stay on and help the firm meet its targets.

Finally, if the managers of the target company are highly competent but do not wish to remain on after the merger, the acquiring firm may build into the merger contract a noncompete agreement with the old management. Typically, the acquired firm's principal officers must agree not to affiliate with a new business which is competitive with the one they sold for a specified period, say, five years. Such agreements are especially important with service-oriented businesses.

[10]Managements of firms that are thought to be attractive merger candidates often arrange *golden parachutes* for themselves. Golden parachutes are extremely lucrative retirement plans which take effect if a merger is consummated. Thus, when Bendix was acquired by Allied, Bill Agee, Bendix's chairman, "pulled the ripcord of his golden parachute" and walked away with $4 million. If a golden parachute is large enough, it can also function as a poison pill — for example, where the president of a firm worth $10 million would have to be paid $8 million if the firm is acquired, this will prevent a takeover. Stockholders are increasingly resisting such arrangements, but some still exist.

INDUSTRY PRACTICE

WHEN YOU MERGE YOU COMBINE MORE THAN JUST FINANCIAL STATEMENTS

When corporations merge, they combine more than just their financial statements. Mergers bring together two organizations with different histories and corporate cultures. Deals that look good on paper can fail if the individuals involved are unwilling or unable to work together to generate the potential synergies. Consequently, when analyzing a potential merger, it is important to determine whether the two companies are compatible.

Many deals fall apart because, during the "due diligence" phase, synergistic benefits are revealed to be less than was originally anticipated, so there is little economic rationale for the merger. Other negotiations break off because the two parties cannot agree on the price to be paid for the acquired firm's stock. In addition, merger talks often collapse because of "social issues." These social issues include both the "chemistry" of the companies and their personnel and such basic issues as these: What will be the name of the combined company? Where will headquarters be located? And, most important: Who will run the combined company? Robert Kindler, a partner at Cravath, Swaine & Moore, a prominent New York law firm that specializes in mergers, summarizes the importance of these issues as follows: "Even transactions that make absolute economic sense don't happen unless the social issues work."

Investment bankers, lawyers, and other professionals state that mergers tend to be most successful if there is a clear and well-arranged plan spelling out who will run the company. This issue is straightforward if one firm is clearly dominant and is acquiring the other. However, in cases where there is "a merger of equals," senior personnel issues often become sticky. This situation is made considerably easier if one of the chief executives is at or near the retirement age.

Some analysts believe that social issues often play too large a role, derailing mergers that should take place. In other cases where a merger occurs, concerns about social issues preclude managers from undertaking the necessary changes — like laying off redundant staff — for the deal to benefit shareholders.

SOURCE: "In Many Merger Deals, Ego and Pride Play Big Roles in Which Way Talks Go," *The Wall Street Journal,* August 22, 1996, C1. ©1996 Dow Jones & Company, Inc. All Rights Reserved Worldwide.

What are some factors that acquiring firms consider when they set a bid price? How do control issues affect mergers?

STRUCTURING THE TAKEOVER BID

The acquiring firm's offer to the target's shareholders can be in the form of cash, stock of the acquiring firm, debt of the acquiring firm, or some combination. The structure of the bid affects (1) the capital structure of the postmerger firm, (2) the tax treatment of the acquiring firm and the target's stockholders, (3) the ability of the target firm's stockholders to benefit from future merger-related gains, and (4) the types of federal and state regulations to which the acquiring firm will be subjected. In this section, we discuss how acquiring firms structure their offers.

The form of payment offered to the target's shareholders determines the personal tax treatment of these stockholders. Target shareholders do not have to pay taxes on stock they receive in the transaction provided at least 50 percent of the payment to target shareholders, in total, is in the form of shares (either common or preferred) of the acquiring firm. In such *nontaxable offers,* target shareholders do not realize any capital gains or losses until they sell the equity securities they received. However, capital gains must be taken and treated as income in the transaction year if an offer consists of more than 50 percent cash and/or debt securities. Also, even in "nontaxable deals," capital gains taxes must be paid by stockholders who take cash.

All other things being equal, stockholders prefer nontaxable offers, since they may then postpone capital gains taxes. Furthermore, if the target firm's stockholders receive stock, they will benefit from synergistic gains resulting from the merger. Most target shareholders are thus willing to give up their stock for a lower price in a nontaxable offer than in a taxable offer. As a result, one might expect nontaxable bids to dominate. However, this is not the case — roughly half of all mergers have been taxable, and, as noted in Table 21-1, three of the top five mergers were all-cash deals.

Prior to 1986, if a firm paid more than book value for a target firm's assets in a taxable merger, it could write up those assets, depreciate the marked-up value for tax purposes, and thus lower the postmerger firm's taxes vis-à-vis the taxes of the two firms operating separately. At the same time, the target firm did not have to pay any taxes on the write-up at the time of the merger. Under current law, if the acquiring company writes up the target company's assets for tax purposes, then the target company must pay capital gains taxes in the year the merger occurs. (These taxes can be avoided if the acquiring company elects not to write up acquired assets and depreciates them on their old basis.)

Note also that in 1986 the maximum capital gains tax rate on personal income rose from 20 percent to 28 percent, a 40 percent increase. This, of course, means that target companies' stockholders now net less from a merger than they would have under the old law. When one considers the combined effects of the corporate and personal tax changes, it is clear that the tax treatment of mergers is significantly less favorable today than it was prior to 1987. This means that a lot less money ends up in the pockets of selling stockholders, so they require larger premiums to sell.

Securities laws also have an effect on the construction of the offer. The SEC has oversight over the issuance of new securities, including stock or debt issued in connection with a merger. Therefore, whenever a corporation bids for control of another firm through the exchange of equity or debt, the entire process must take place under the scrutiny of the Securities and Exchange Commission. The time required for such reviews allows target managements to implement defensive tactics and other firms to make competing offers, and as a result, nearly all hostile tender offers are for cash rather than securities.

SELF-TEST QUESTIONS ??????

What are some alternative ways of structuring takeover bids?

How do taxes influence the payment structure?

How do securities laws affect the payment structure?

THE ROLE OF INVESTMENT BANKERS

Investment banks are involved with mergers in a number of ways: (1) they help arrange mergers, (2) they help target companies develop and implement defensive tactics, (3) they help value target companies, (4) they help finance mergers, and (5) they invest in the stocks of potential merger candidates. These merger-related activities have been quite profitable. For example, the investment bankers and lawyers who arranged the Campeau-Federated merger earned fees of about $83 million — First Boston and Wasserstein Perella split $29 million from Campeau, and Goldman Sachs, Hellman & Friedman, and Shearson Lehman Hutton divided up $54 million for representing Federated. No wonder investment banking houses are able to make top offers to finance graduates!

ARRANGING MERGERS

The major investment banking firms have merger and acquisition groups which operate within their corporate finance departments. (Corporate finance departments offer advice, as opposed to underwriting or brokerage services, to business firms.) Members of these groups identify firms with excess cash that might want to buy other firms, companies that might be willing to be bought, and firms that might, for a number of reasons, be attractive to others. Also, if an oil company, for instance, decided to expand into coal mining, then it might enlist the aid of an investment banker to help it acquire a coal company. Similarly, dissident stockholders of firms with poor track records might work with investment bankers to oust management by helping to arrange a merger. Investment bankers are reported to have offered packages of financing to corporate raiders, where the package includes both designing the securities to be used in the tender offer, plus lining up people and firms who will buy the target firm's stock now and then tender it once the final offer is made.

Investment bankers have occasionally taken illegal actions in the merger arena. For one thing, they are reported to have *parked stock* — purchasing it for a raider under a guaranteed buy-back agreement — to help the raider de facto accumulate more than 5 percent of the target's stock without disclosing the position. People have gone to jail for this.

DEVELOPING DEFENSIVE TACTICS

Target firms that do not want to be acquired generally enlist the help of an investment banking firm, along with a law firm that specializes in mergers. Defenses include such tactics as (1) changing the bylaws so that only one-third of the directors are elected each year and/or so that a 75 percent approval (a *supermajority*) versus a simple majority is required to approve a merger; (2) trying to convince the target firm's stockholders that the price being offered is too low; (3) raising antitrust issues in the hope that the Justice Department will intervene; (4) repurchasing stock in the open market in an effort to push the price above that being offered by the potential acquirer; (5) getting a **white knight** who is acceptable to the target firm's management to compete with the potential acquirer; (6) getting a "white squire" who is friendly to current management to buy enough of the target firm's shares to block the merger; and (7) taking a poison pill, as described next.

Poison pills — which occasionally really do amount to committing economic suicide to avoid a takeover — are such tactics as borrowing on terms that require immediate repayment of all loans if the firm is acquired, selling off at bargain prices the assets that originally made the firm a desirable target, granting such lucrative **golden parachutes** to their executives that the cash drain from these payments would render the merger infeasible, and planning defensive mergers which would leave the firm with new assets of questionable value and a huge debt load. Currently, the most popular poison pill is for a company to give its stockholders *stock purchase rights* which allow them to buy at half-price the stock of an acquiring firm, should the firm be acquired. The blatant use of poison pills is constrained by directors' awareness that excessive use could trigger personal suits by stockholders against directors who voted for them, and, per-

White Knight
A company that is acceptable to the management of a firm under threat of a hostile takeover.

Poison Pill
An action which will seriously hurt a company if it is acquired by another.

Golden Parachutes
Large payments made to the managers of a firm if it is acquired.

haps in the near future, by laws that would further limit management's use of pills. Still, investment bankers and antitakeover lawyers are busy thinking up new poison pill formulas, and others are just as busy trying to come up with antidotes.[11]

To illustrate a typical poison pill, consider Chrysler's poison pill share rights purchase plan. Chrysler's stockholders received one full right in the poison pill plan for each share of common stock held. Each right entitles the holder to buy one-hundredth of a share of Chrysler junior participating cumulative preferred stock for $120. However, the primary purpose of the rights is to act as a poison pill. Certain events, as described next, will cause the rights either to "kick in" and hence entitle holders to buy Chrysler common stock at half its market value, or to "flip over" and hence entitle holders to buy common stock in an acquiring entity at half its market value.

A "kick in" will occur if a shareholder acquires 20 percent or more of the firm's common stock. Further, Chrysler's board could trigger the "kick in" if an owner of 10 percent or more of the firm's stock has "adverse" intentions, where "adverse" intentions are defined as any intentions to take actions that are detrimental to the long-term interests of Chrysler and its shareholders. A "kick over" will occur if a hostile takeover occurs, which is any takeover that is not supported by Chrysler's board of directors.

Another takeover defense that is being used is the employee stock ownership plan (ESOP). ESOPs are designed to give lower-level employees an ownership stake in the firm, and current tax laws provide generous incentives for companies to establish such plans and fund them with the firm's common stock. As we discussed earlier, Polaroid used an ESOP to help fend off Shamrock Holdings's hostile takeover attempt. Also, Procter & Gamble recently set up an ESOP that, along with an existing profit-sharing plan, eventually will give employees a 20 percent ownership stake in the company. Since the trustees of ESOPs generally support current management in any takeover attempt, and since up to 85 percent of the votes is often required to complete a merger, an ESOP can provide an effective defense against a hostile tender offer. Procter & Gamble stated that its ESOP was designed primarily to lower its costs by utilizing the plan's tax advantages and to improve employees' retirement security. However, the company also noted that the ESOP would strengthen its defenses against a takeover.

ESTABLISHING A FAIR VALUE

If a friendly merger is being worked out between two firms' managements, it is important to document that the agreed-upon price is a fair one; otherwise, the stockholders of either company may sue to block the merger. Therefore, in most large mergers each side will hire an investment banking firm to evaluate the target company and to help establish the fair price. For example, General Electric employed Morgan Stanley to determine a fair price for Utah International, as did Royal Dutch to help establish the price it paid for Shell Oil. Even if the merger is not friendly, investment bankers may still be asked to help establish a price. If a surprise tender offer is to be made, the acquiring firm will want to know the lowest price at which it might be able to acquire the stock,

---

[11]It has become extremely difficult and expensive for companies to buy "directors' insurance" which protects the board from such contingencies as stockholders' suits, and even when insurance is available it often does not pay for losses if the directors have not exercised due caution and judgment. This exposure is making directors extremely leery of actions that might trigger stockholder suits.

while the target firm may seek help in "proving" that the price being offered is too low.[12]

FINANCING MERGERS

Many mergers are financed with the acquiring company's excess cash. However, if the acquiring company has no excess cash, it will require a source of funds. Perhaps the single most important factor behind the 1980s merger wave was the development of junk bonds for use in financing acquisitions.

Drexel Burnham Lambert was the primary developer of junk bonds, defined as bonds rated below investment grade (BBB/Baa). Prior to Drexel's actions, it was almost impossible to sell low-grade bonds to raise new capital. Drexel then pioneered a procedure under which a target firm's situation would be appraised very closely, and a cash flow projection similar to that in Table 21-2 (but much more detailed) would be developed.

With the cash flows having been forecasted, Drexel's analysts would figure out a debt structure — amount of debt, maturity structure, and interest rate — that could be serviced by the cash flows. With this information, Drexel's junk bond people, operating out of Beverly Hills, would approach financial institutions (savings and loans, insurance companies, pension funds, and mutual funds) with a financing plan, and they would offer a rate of return several percentage points above the rate on more conservative investments. Drexel's early deals worked out well, and the institutions that bought the bonds were quite pleased. These results enabled Drexel to expand its network of investors, which increased its ability to finance larger and larger mergers. T. Boone Pickens, who went after Phillips, Texaco, and several other oil giants, was an early Drexel customer, as was Ted Turner.

To be successful in the mergers and acquisitions (M&A) business, an investment banker must be able to offer a financing package to clients, whether they are acquirers who need capital to take over companies or target companies trying to finance stock repurchase plans or other defenses against takeovers. Drexel was the leading player in the merger financing game during the 1980s, but since Drexel's bankruptcy Merrill Lynch, Morgan Stanley, Salomon Brothers, and others are all vying for the title.

ARBITRAGE OPERATIONS

Arbitrage
The simultaneous buying and selling of the same commodity or security in two different markets at different prices, and pocketing a risk-free return.

Arbitrage generally means simultaneously buying and selling the same commodity or security in two different markets at different prices, and pocketing a risk-free return. However, the major brokerage houses, as well as some wealthy private investors, are engaged in a different type of arbitrage called *risk arbitrage*. The *arbitrageurs,* or "arbs," speculate in the stocks of companies that are likely takeover targets. Vast amounts of capital are required to speculate in a large number of securities and thus reduce risk, and also to make money on narrow spreads.

---

[12]Such investigations must obviously be done in secret, for if someone knew that Company A was thinking of offering, say, $50 per share for Company T, which was currently selling at $35 per share, then huge profits could be made. One of the biggest scandals to hit Wall Street was the disclosure that Ivan Boesky was buying information from Dennis Levine, a senior member of the investment banking house of Drexel Burnham Lambert, about target companies that Drexel was analyzing for others. Purchases based on such insider information would, of course, raise the prices of the stocks and thus force Drexel's clients to pay more than they otherwise would have had to pay. Levine and Boesky, among others, went to jail for their improper use of inside information.

However, the large investment bankers have the wherewithal to play the game. To be successful, arbs need to be able to sniff out likely targets, assess the probability of offers reaching fruition, and move in and out of the market quickly and with low transactions costs.

The risk arbitrage business has been rocked by insider trading scandals. Indeed, the most famous arb of all, Ivan Boesky, was caught buying inside information from executives of some leading investment banking houses and law firms. The Boesky affair slowed down risk arbitrage activity, but with deals such as IBM's offer of $60 per share for Lotus's $30 stock, risk arbitrage is not about to go away.

SELF-TEST QUESTIONS   ??????

What are some defensive tactics that firms can use to resist hostile takeovers?

What is the difference between pure arbitrage and risk arbitrage?

What role did junk bonds play in the merger wave of the 1980s?

WHO WINS: THE EMPIRICAL EVIDENCE

All the recent merger activity has raised two questions: (1) Do corporate acquisitions create value, and, (2) if so, how is the value shared between the parties?

Most researchers agree that takeovers increase the wealth of the shareholders of target firms, for otherwise they would not agree to the offer. However, there is a debate as to whether mergers benefit the acquiring firm's shareholders. In particular, managements of acquiring firms may be motivated by factors other than shareholder wealth maximization. For example, they may want to merge merely to increase the size of the corporations they manage, because increased size usually brings larger salaries plus job security, perquisites, power, and prestige.

The validity of the competing views on who gains from corporate acquisitions can be tested by examining the stock price changes that occur around the time of a merger or takeover announcement. Changes in the stock prices of the acquiring and target firms represent market participants' beliefs about the value created by the merger, and about how that value will be divided between the target and acquiring firms' shareholders. So, examining a large sample of stock price movements can shed light on the issue of who gains from mergers.

One cannot simply examine stock prices around merger announcement dates, because other factors influence stock prices. For example, if a merger was announced on a day when the entire market advanced, the fact that the firm in question's price rose would not necessarily signify that the merger was expected to create value. Hence, studies examine *abnormal returns* associated with merger announcements, where abnormal returns are defined as that part of a stock price change caused by factors other than changes in the general stock market.

Many studies have examined both acquiring and target firms' stock price responses to mergers and tender offers.[13] Jointly, these studies have covered nearly every acquisition involving publicly traded firms from the early 1960s to the present, and they are remarkably consistent in their results: on average, the stock

---

[13]For an excellent summary of the effects of mergers on value, see Michael C. Jensen and Richard S. Ruback, "The Market for Corporate Control: The Scientific Evidence," *Journal of Financial Economics,* April 1983, 5–50.

prices of target firms increase by about 30 percent in hostile tender offers, while in friendly mergers the average increase is about 20 percent. However, for both hostile and friendly deals, the stock prices of acquiring firms, on average, remain constant. Thus, the evidence strongly indicates (1) that acquisitions do create value, but (2) that shareholders of target firms reap virtually all the benefits.

In hindsight, these results are not too surprising. First, target firms' shareholders can always say no, so they are in the driver's seat. Second, takeovers are a competitive game, so if one potential acquiring firm does not offer full value for a potential target, then another firm will generally jump in with a higher bid. Finally, managements of acquiring firms might well be willing to give up all the value created by the merger, because the merger would enhance the acquiring managers' personal positions without harming their shareholders.

It has also been argued that acquisitions may increase shareholder wealth at the expense of bondholders — in particular, concern has been expressed that leveraged buyouts dilute the claims of bondholders. Specific instances can be cited where bonds were downgraded and bondholders did suffer losses, sometimes quite large, as a direct result of an acquisition. However, most studies find no evidence to support the contention that bondholders on average lose in corporate acquisitions.

SELF-TEST QUESTIONS

Explain how researchers can study the effects of mergers on shareholder wealth.

Do mergers create value? If so, who profits from this value?

Do the research results discussed in this section seem logical? Explain.

CORPORATE ALLIANCES

Corporate, or Strategic, Alliance
A cooperative deal that stops short of a merger.

Mergers are one way for two companies to join forces, but many companies are striking cooperative deals, called **corporate,** or **strategic, alliances,** which stop far short of merging. Whereas mergers combine all of the assets of the firms involved, as well as their managerial and technical expertise, alliances allow firms to create combinations that focus on specific business lines that offer the most potential synergies. These alliances take many forms, from simple marketing agreements to joint ownership of worldwide operations.

Joint Venture
A corporate alliance in which two or more independent companies combine their resources to achieve a specific, limited objective.

One form of corporate alliance is the **joint venture,** in which parts of companies are joined to achieve specific, limited objectives.[14] A joint venture is controlled by a management team consisting of representatives of the two (or more) parent companies. Joint ventures have been used often by U.S., Japanese, and European firms to share technology and/or marketing expertise. For example, Whirlpool recently announced a joint venture with the Dutch electronics giant Philips to produce appliances under Philips's brand names in five European countries. By joining with their foreign counterparts, U.S. firms are attempting to gain a stronger foothold in Europe. Although alliances are new to some firms,

---

[14]Cross-licensing, consortia, joint bidding, and franchising are still other ways for firms to combine resources. For more information on joint ventures, see Sanford V. Berg, Jerome Duncan, and Phillip Friedman, *Joint Venture Strategies and Corporate Innovation* (Cambridge, MA: Oelgeschlager, Gunn and Hain, 1982).

they are established practices to others. For example, Corning Glass now obtains over half of its profits from 23 joint ventures, two-thirds of them with foreign companies representing almost all of Europe, as well as Japan, China, South Korea, and Australia.

SELF-TEST QUESTIONS

What is the difference between a merger and a corporate alliance?

What is a joint venture? Give some reasons why joint ventures may be advantageous to the parties involved.

LEVERAGED BUYOUTS

Leveraged Buyout (LBO)
A situation in which a small group of investors (which usually includes the firm's managers) borrows heavily to buy all the shares of a company.

In a **leveraged buyout (LBO)** a small group of investors, usually including current management, acquires a firm in a transaction financed largely by debt. The debt is serviced with funds generated by the acquired company's operations and, often, by the sale of some of its assets. Generally, the acquiring group plans to run the acquired company for a number of years, boost its sales and profits, and then take it public again as a stronger company. Naturally, the acquiring group expects to make a substantial profit from the LBO, but the inherent risks are great due to the heavy use of financial leverage. To illustrate the profit potential, Kohlberg Kravis Roberts & Company (KKR), a leading LBO specialist firm, averaged a spectacular 50 percent annual return on its LBO investments during the 1980s. However, the weak economy and strong stock prices have dampened the returns on LBO investments, so recent activity has been slower than in its heyday of the 1980s.

A good example of an LBO was KKR's buyout of RJR Nabisco. RJR, a leading producer of tobacco and food products with brands such as Winston, Camel, Planters, Ritz, Oreo, and Del Monte, was trading at about $55 a share in October 1988. Then, F. Ross Johnson, the company's chairman and CEO, announced a $75-a-share, or $17.6 billion, offer to outside stockholders in a plan to take the firm private. This deal, if completed, would have been the largest business transaction up to that time. After the announcement, RJR's stock price soared to $77.25, which indicated that investors thought the final price would be even higher than Johnson's opening bid. A few days later KKR offered $90 per share, or $20.6 billion, for RJR. The battle between the two bidders raged until late November, when RJR's board accepted KKR's revised bid of cash and securities worth about $106 a share, for a total value of about $25 billion. Of course, the investment bankers' fees reflected the record size of the deal — the bankers received almost $400 million, with Drexel Burnham Lambert alone getting over $200 million. Johnson lost his job, but he walked away with a multimillion-dollar golden parachute.

KKR wasted no time in restructuring the newly private RJR. In June 1989, RJR sold its five European businesses to France's BSN for $2.5 million. Then, in September RJR sold the tropical fruit portion of its Del Monte foods unit to Polly Peck, a London-based food company, for $875 million. In the same month, RJR sold the Del Monte canned foods business to an LBO group led by Citicorp Venture Capital for $1.48 billion. Next, in October 1990 RJR sold its Baby Ruth, Butterfinger, and Pearson candy businesses to Nestlé, a Swiss company, for $370 million. In total, RJR sold off more than $5 billion worth of businesses in 1990 to help pay down the tremendous debt taken on in the LBO. In addition to asset sales, in 1991 RJR went public again by issuing more than $1 billion in new common stock, which placed about 25 percent of the firm's common stock in public hands. Also, as the firm's credit rating improved due to retirement of some of its debt, RJR issued about $1 billion of new debt at significantly lower rates and used the proceeds to retire even more of its high-cost debt.

The RJR Nabisco story is the classic LBO tale — a company is taken private in a highly leveraged deal, the private firm's high-cost junk debt is reduced through asset sales, and finally the company again goes public, which gives the original LBO dealmakers the opportunity to "cash out." This story, however, did not have a fairytale ending. When KKR finally sold the last of its RJR shares in early 1995, it made a profit of about $60 million on a $3.1 billion investment, hardly a stellar return. The best a KKR spokesman could say about the deal was that "it preserved investors' equity." The transaction was largely financed by outside investors, with KKR putting up only $126 million of the original investment. Even though the return on their investment was the same as that received by outside investors, KKR earned an additional $500 million in transactions, advisor, management, and directors' fees.

Regardless of the outcome of the RJR Nabisco deal, there have been some spectacularly successful LBOs. For example, in an early deal that helped fuel the LBO wave, William Simon and Raymond Chambers bought Gibson Greeting Cards in 1982 for $1 million in equity and $79 million in debt. Less than 18 months later, Simon's personal investment of $330,000 was worth $66 million in cash and stock. However, there have also been some spectacular failures. For example, in 1988 Revco became the first large LBO to file for Chapter 11 bankruptcy. It turned out that sales were nearly $1 billion short of the $3.4 billion forecasted at the time of the drugstore chain's buyout.[15]

SELF-TEST QUESTIONS

What is an LBO?

Have LBOs been profitable in recent years?

What actions do companies typically take to meet the large debt burdens resulting from LBOs?

How do LBOs typically affect bondholders?

DIVESTITURES

Although corporations do more buying than selling of productive facilities, a good bit of selling does occur. In this section, we briefly discuss the major types of divestitures, after which we present some recent examples and rationales for divestitures.

---

[15]For a more detailed discussion of the impact of the RJR LBO on the firm's different classes of investors, see Nancy Mohan and Carl R. Chen, "A Review of the RJR-Nabisco Buyout," *Journal of Applied Corporate Finance,* Summer 1990, 102–108. For interesting discussions of highly leveraged takeovers, see Martin S. Fridson, "What Went Wrong with the Highly Leveraged Deals? (Or, All Variety of Agency Costs)," *Journal of Applied Corporate Finance,* Fall 1991, 57–67; and "The Economic Consequences of High Leverage and Stock Market Pressures on Corporate Management: A Round Table Discussion," *Journal of Applied Corporate Finance,* Summer 1990, 6–57.

GLOBAL PERSPECTIVES

GOVERNMENTS ARE DIVESTING STATE-OWNED BUSINESSES TO SPUR ECONOMIC EFFICIENCY

In many countries governments have traditionally owned or controlled a number of key businesses. When Margaret Thatcher became prime minister of Britain in 1979, she set out to reverse this trend, and soon her officials were devising methods for the government to divest state-owned enterprises. Thatcher coined the term "privatization" to describe the process of transferring productive operations and assets from the public sector to the private sector.

The privatization momentum picked up in the early and mid-1980s, expanding to other countries including France, Germany, Japan, and Singapore. Privatization accelerated fur-ther as the communist countries and authoritarian regimes across Eastern Europe, Asia, and Latin America shifted toward market-based economies.

Telecommunications, electric power, and airlines are examples of industries that have undergone extensive privatization throughout the world. These industries are vitally important to the economic infrastructure of every nation, and for this reason governments have historically been heavily involved in owning and regulating them within their national borders. Generally, the government-owned enterprise was granted monopoly power to supply the service in question and was subsidized in an effort to hold down costs to consumers. However, economists have long argued that government operations are inherently less efficient than are enterprises which are subject to competitive pressures and whose managers are guided by the profit motive. Thus, in recent years there have been numerous privatizations in these important industries, and as governments have sold their interests, competition has led to lower costs and improved service.

In Western Europe, privatizations in the telecommunications industry have been given an extra push by a European Union plan which opened markets to competition. Because most European telecoms were government owned, the resulting privatizations brought to market tens of billions of dollars of telecom stock. Globally, governments have raised hundreds of billions of dollars through privatizations.

The results are not all in, but it is clear that the removal of bureaucrats and politicians from the control of key enterprises often results in increased economic efficiency and a higher standard of living.

TYPES OF DIVESTITURES

Divestiture
The sale of some of a company's operating assets.

Spin-Off
A divestiture in which the stock of a subsidiary is given to the parent company's stockholders.

Liquidation
A liquidation occurs when the assets of a division are sold off piecemeal, rather than as an operating entity.

There are three primary types of **divestitures:** (1) sale of an operating unit to another firm, (2) setting up the business to be divested as a separate corporation and then "spinning it off" to the divesting firm's stockholders, and (3) outright liquidation of assets.

Sale to another firm generally involves the sale of an entire division or unit, usually for cash but sometimes for stock of the acquiring firm. In a **spin-off,** the firm's existing stockholders are given new stock representing separate ownership rights in the division which was divested. The division establishes its own board of directors and officers, and it becomes a separate company. The stockholders end up owning shares of two firms instead of one, but no cash has been transferred. Finally, in a **liquidation** the assets of a division are sold off piecemeal, rather than as an operating entity. To illustrate the different types of divestitures, we present some recent examples in the next section.

DIVESTITURE ILLUSTRATIONS

1. Pepsi recently announced plans to spin off its fast-food business, which includes Pizza Hut, Taco Bell, and Kentucky Fried Chicken. Pepsi originally acquired the chains because it wanted to increase the distribution channels for its soft drinks. Over time, however, Pepsi began to realize that the soft-drink and restaurant businesses were quite different, and synergies between them were less than anticipated. The proposed spin-off is part of Pepsi's attempt to

once again focus on its core business. However, Pepsi will try to maintain these distribution channels by signing long-term contracts which ensure that Pepsi products will be sold exclusively in each of the three spun-off chains. While the terms of the divestiture have not been finalized, the initial response from investors has been positive.

2. In 1987, United Airlines sold its Hilton International Hotels subsidiary to Ladbroke Group PLC of Britain for $1.1 billion. Later, United divested its Hertz rental car unit and its Westin hotel group. The sales culminated a disastrous strategic move by United to build a full-service travel empire. The failed strategy resulted in the firing of Richard J. Ferris, the company's chairman. The move into nonairline travel-related businesses had been viewed by many analysts as a mistake, because there were few synergies to be gained. Further, analysts feared that United's managers, preoccupied by running hotels and rental car companies, would not maintain the company's focus in the highly competitive airline industry. The funds raised by the divestitures were paid out to United's shareholders as a special dividend.

3. IU International, a multimillion-dollar conglomerate that was listed on the NYSE, spun off three major subsidiaries — Gotaas-Larson, an ocean shipping company involved in petroleum transportation; Canadian Utilities, an electric utility; and Echo Bay Mines, a gold mining company. IU kept its distribution and manufacturing operations. IU's management originally acquired and combined several highly cyclical businesses such as ocean shipping and gold mining with stable ones such as utilities in order to gain overall corporate stability through diversification. The strategy worked reasonably well from an operating standpoint, but it failed in the financial markets. IU's diversity kept it from being classified in any particular industrial group, so security analysts did not follow it, hence did not recommend it to investors. (Analysts tend to concentrate on an industry, and they do not like to recommend a company they do not understand.) As a result, IU had a low P/E ratio and a low market price. After the spin-offs, the package of securities rose in value from $10 to $75.

4. AT&T was broken up in 1984 to settle a Justice Department antitrust suit filed in the 1970s.[16] For almost 100 years AT&T had operated as a holding company which owned Western Electric (its manufacturing subsidiary), Bell Labs (its research arm), a huge long-distance network which was operated as a division of the parent company, and 22 Bell operating companies, such as Pacific Telephone, New York Telephone, Southern Bell, and Southwestern Bell. In 1984, AT&T was reorganized into eight separate companies — a slimmed-down AT&T which kept Western Electric, Bell Labs, and the long-distance operations, plus seven new regional telephone holding companies that were created from the 22 old operating telephone companies. The stock of the seven new telephone companies was then spun off to the old AT&T's stockholders. A person who held 100 shares of old AT&T stock owned, after the divestiture, 100 shares of the "new" AT&T plus 10 shares of each of the seven new operating companies. These 170 shares were backed by the same assets that had previously backed 100 shares of old AT&T common.

---

[16]Another forced divestiture involved Du Pont and General Motors. In 1921, GM was in serious financial trouble, and Du Pont supplied capital in exchange for 23 percent of the stock. In the 1950s, the Justice Department won an antitrust suit which required Du Pont to spin off (to Du Pont's stockholders) its GM stock.

The AT&T divestiture resulted from a suit by the Justice Department, which wanted to divide the Bell System into a regulated monopoly segment (the seven regional telephone companies) and a manufacturing/long-distance segment which would be exposed to competition. The breakup was designed to strengthen competition and thus speed up technological change in those parts of the telecommunications industry that are not natural monopolies.

5. After its forced breakup, AT&T lost little time in building itself up. In 1991 it acquired computer maker NCR, and in 1994 it bought McCaw Cellular Communications, a cellular phone operator. Then, in 1995, AT&T made a surprise announcement. Its massive combination of technology assets was not paying off, and AT&T's stock was in the doldrums. Then the company announced that it would split itself into three parts. The surviving AT&T was to include the core $53 billion long-distance and cellular phone businesses. The division which makes the switching equipment used by local and long-distance companies was to be spun off under the name Lucent Technologies. AT&T also planned to spin off its loss-plagued computer business (the former NCR). AT&T shares took off on the announcement, adding more than $6 to the share price and $11 billion to AT&T's total value — more than enough to make up for the purchase of NCR and the ensuing losses. One reason for the breakup was the fact that AT&T and the local telephone companies were entering one another's markets, and the locals were reluctant to buy equipment from a competitor (AT&T). Therefore, Lucent was losing business to other manufacturers. Also, the breakup permitted the managers of each entity to focus exclusively on the problems and opportunities unique to its business. Now they can concentrate on those areas where they have the greatest expertise without distraction from events in other business lines.

6. Some years ago, Woolworth liquidated all of its 336 Woolco discount stores. This made the company, which had had sales of $7.2 billion before the liquidation, 30 percent smaller. Woolco had posted operating losses of $19 million the year before the liquidation, and its losses in the latest six months had climbed to an alarming $21 million. Woolworth's CEO, Edward F. Gibbons, was quoted as saying, "How many losses can you take?" Woolco's problems necessitated a write-off of $325 million, but management believed it was better to go ahead and "bite the bullet" rather than let the losing stores bleed the company to death.

7. As a result of some imprudent loans to oil companies and to developing nations, Continental Illinois, one of the largest U.S. bank holding companies, was threatened with bankruptcy. Continental then sold off several profitable divisions, such as its leasing and credit card operations, to raise funds to cover bad-loan losses. In effect, Continental sold assets in order to stay alive. Ultimately, Continental was bailed out by the Federal Deposit Insurance Corporation and the Federal Reserve, which (a) arranged a $7.5 billion rescue package and (b) provided a blanket guarantee for all of Continental's $40 billion of deposits, which kept deposits in excess of $100,000 from fleeing the bank because of their uninsured status.

As the preceding examples illustrate, the reasons for divestitures vary widely. Sometimes the market feels more comfortable when firms "stick to their knitting"; the Pepsi and United Airlines divestitures are examples. Similarly, IU International demonstrates that there are cases in which a company becomes so complex and diverse that analysts and investors just do not understand it and consequently ignore it. Other companies need cash either to finance expansion in their primary business lines or to reduce a large debt burden, and divestitures can be used to raise this cash; Continental Bank illustrates this point. The divestitures also show that running a business is a dynamic process—conditions change, corporate strategies change in response, and as a result firms alter their asset portfolios by acquisitions and/or divestitures. Some divestitures, such as Woolworth's liquidation of its Woolco stores, are to unload losing assets that would otherwise drag the company down. The first AT&T example is one of the many instances in which a divestiture is the result of an antitrust settlement, and the second AT&T spin-off illustrates a situation where the parts of the business can operate more efficiently alone than together.

SELF-TEST QUESTIONS

What are some reasons companies divest assets?

What are three major motives for divestitures?

HOLDING COMPANIES

Holding Company
A corporation that owns sufficient common stock of another firm to achieve working control over it.

Holding companies date from 1889, when New Jersey became the first state to pass a law permitting corporations to be formed for the sole purpose of owning the stocks of other companies. Many of the advantages and disadvantages of holding companies are identical to those of any large-scale organization. Whether a company is organized on a divisional basis or with subsidiaries kept as separate companies does not affect the basic reasons for conducting a large-scale, multiproduct, multiplant operation. However, as we show next, the use of holding companies to control large-scale operations has some distinct advantages and disadvantages.

ADVANTAGES OF HOLDING COMPANIES

1. **Control with fractional ownership.** Through a holding company operation, a firm may buy 5, 10, or 50 percent of the stock of another corporation. Such fractional ownership may be sufficient to give the holding company effective working control over the operations of the company in which it has acquired stock ownership. Working control is often considered to entail more than 25 percent of the common stock, but it can be as low as 10 percent if the stock is widely distributed. One financier says that the attitude of management is more important than the number of shares owned: "If management thinks you can control the company, then you do." In addition, control on a very slim margin can be held through relationships with large stockholders outside the holding company group.

Operating Company
A subsidiary of a holding company operated as a separate legal entity.

2. **Isolation of risks.** Because the various **operating companies** in a holding company system are separate legal entities, the obligations of any one unit are separate from those of the other units. Therefore, catastrophic losses incurred by one unit of the holding company system may not be translatable into claims on the assets of the other units. However, we should note that while this is a customary generalization, it is not always valid. First, the **parent company** may feel obligated to make good on the subsidiary's debts, even though it is not legally bound to do so, in order to keep its good name and to retain custom-

Parent Company
A holding company; a firm which controls another firm by owning a large block of its stock.

ers. An example of this was American Express's payment of more than $100 million in connection with a swindle that was the responsibility of one of its subsidiaries. Second, a parent company may feel obligated to supply capital to an affiliate in order to protect its initial investment; General Public Utilities' continued support of its subsidiaries' Three Mile Island nuclear plant after the accident at that plant is an example. And, third, when lending to one of the units of a holding company system, an astute loan officer may require a guarantee by the parent holding company. To some degree, therefore, the assets in the various elements of a holding company are not really separate. Still, a catastrophic loss, as could occur if a drug company's subsidiary distributed a batch of toxic medicine, may be avoided.[17]

DISADVANTAGES OF HOLDING COMPANIES

1. **Partial multiple taxation.** Provided the holding company owns at least 80 percent of a subsidiary's voting stock, the IRS permits the filing of consolidated returns, in which case dividends received by the parent are not taxed. However, if less than 80 percent of the stock is owned, then tax returns cannot be consolidated. Firms that own more than 20 percent but less than 80 percent of another corporation can deduct 80 percent of the dividends received, while firms that own less than 20 percent may deduct only 70 percent of the dividends received. This partial double taxation somewhat offsets the benefits of holding company control with limited ownership, but whether the tax penalty is sufficient to offset other possible advantages is a matter that must be decided in individual situations.

2. **Ease of enforced dissolution.** It is relatively easy to require dissolution by disposal of stock ownership of a holding company operation found guilty of antitrust violations. For instance, in the 1950s Du Pont was required to dispose of its 23 percent stock interest in General Motors Corporation, acquired in the early 1920s. Because there was no fusion between the corporations, there were no difficulties from an operating standpoint in requiring the separation of the two companies. However, if complete amalgamation had taken place, it would have been much more difficult to break up the company after so many years, and the likelihood of forced divestiture would have been reduced.

HOLDING COMPANIES AS A LEVERAGING DEVICE

The holding company vehicle has been used to obtain huge degrees of financial leverage. In the 1920s, several tiers of holding companies were established in the electric utility, railroad, and other industries. In those days, an operating company at the bottom of the pyramid might have $100 million of assets, financed by $50 million of debt and $50 million of equity. Then, a first-tier holding company might own the stock of the operating firm as its only asset and be financed with $25 million of debt and $25 million of equity. A second-tier holding company, which owned the stock of the first-tier company, might be financed with $12.5 million of debt and $12.5 million of equity. Such systems were ex-

---

[17]Note, though, that the parent company would still be held accountable for such losses if it were deemed to exercise operating control over the subsidiary. Thus, Union Carbide was held responsible for its subsidiary's Bhopal, India, disaster, and Dow Chemical may be held liable for Dow-Corning's multibillion-dollar silicone breast implant product liability judgment.

SMALL BUSINESS

MERGING AS A MEANS OF EXITING A CLOSELY HELD BUSINESS

Imagine a small family-run business that has achieved success. The entire family fortune may be tied up in the firm, as might be the case if a successful entrepreneur — say, Grandpa — started a business, brought his sons and daughters in as they reached adulthood, and continued to run the enterprise as it grew.

In such a situation, particularly if the firm is valued in the millions, the family's entire financial well-being may depend on the success of this business. As long as Grandpa is healthy and continues to run things, everything is fine. Grandpa may, in fact, be reluctant to sell the business; it gives him something to pass on to his family, and it provides a place for his children and grandchildren to work.

Closely held family businesses are fairly common in the United States, yet for several reasons, maintaining the business in its closely held form may not be in the family's best interests. First, there is the problem of succession. Because at some point Grandpa will retire or die, the issue of who will succeed him is important. Sometimes there is a clear choice for the successor, and everyone agrees with the choice. More often, however, even in families that are very close, the problem of succession can split the family apart. This problem is especially acute if Grandpa dies unexpectedly. At a highly emotional time, a key business decision — the choice of a new president — needs to be made, and the choice is not a simple one. It is, therefore, essential that Grandpa and the other principals set up a plan of succession. If the issue is not resolvable, plans should be made for the outright sale of the business in the event of Grandpa's death.

A second problem is that the business represents the family's primary asset, but family members have no easy way to realize that value when they need cash because the business is not liquid. Sometimes a plan will be made for someone to buy a family member's stock at a predetermined price, such as at its book value per share. This enables the family member to obtain cash, but the price paid probably bears little relation to the market value of the shares. Thus, a family member gives up a valuable asset for the sake of liquidity, taking a potential loss in the process. An alternative is to register the shares and take the company public so that family members can use their equity as they choose. A disadvantage to this approach is the potential loss of control as the number of shares held by the public increases.

A third problem is that as the firm grows, the family may be unable to provide the financial resources necessary to support that growth. If external funds are needed, they will generally be more difficult to obtain in a private, closely held business.

Perhaps an even more serious problem is that, since the family's entire wealth is tied up in a single business, the family holds an *undiversified portfolio*. As was explained in Chapter 5, diversification reduces a portfolio's risk. Thus, the goals of maintaining control and reducing risk through diversification are in conflict. Again, a public offering would allow family members to sell some of their stock and to diversify their own personal portfolios.

Both the diversification motive and family members' liquidity needs often indicate that a business's own-ership structure should be changed. There is, however, another alternative besides going public — that of selling the business outright to another company or of merging it into a larger firm. This alternative is often overlooked by owners of closely held businesses, because it frequently means an immediate and complete loss of control. Selling out deserves special consideration, however, because it can often produce far greater value than can be achieved in a public offering.

With the sale of the business, the family gives up control, yet that control is what makes the firm more valuable in a merger than in a public offering. Merger premiums for public companies often range from 50 to 70 percent over the market price. Therefore, a company worth $10 million in the public market might be acquired for a price of $15 to $17 million in a merger. In contrast, initial public offerings (IPOs) are normally made at below-market prices. Furthermore, if the owners sell a significant amount of their stock in the IPO, the market will take that as a signal that the company's future is dim, and the price will be depressed even more.

What are the disadvantages to a merger? An obvious disadvantage is the loss of control. Also, family members risk losing employment in the firm. In such a case, however, they will have additional wealth to sustain them while they seek other opportunities.

The owners of a closely held family business must consider the costs and benefits of continuing to be closely held versus either going public or being acquired in a merger. Of the three alternatives, the merger alternative is likely to provide the greatest benefits to the family members.

tended to five or six levels. With six holding companies, $100 million of operating assets could be controlled at the top by only $0.78 million of equity, and the operating assets would have to provide enough cash income to support $99.22 million of debt. *Such a holding company system is highly leveraged—its consolidated debt ratio is 99.22 percent, even though each of the individual components shows only a 50 percent debt/assets ratio.* Because of this consolidated leverage, even a small decline in profits at the operating company level could bring the whole system down like a house of cards. This situation existed in the electric utility industry in the 1920s, and the Depression of the 1930s wreaked havoc with the holding companies and led to federal legislation which constrained holding companies in that industry.

SELF-TEST QUESTIONS

What is a holding company?

What are some of the advantages of holding companies? What are some of the disadvantages?

SUMMARY

This chapter included discussions of mergers, divestitures, holding companies, and LBOs. The key concepts covered are listed below:

- A **merger** occurs when two firms combine to form a single company. The primary motives for mergers are (1) synergy, (2) tax considerations, (3) purchase of assets below their replacement costs, (4) diversification, and (5) gaining control over a larger enterprise.
- Mergers can provide economic benefits through **economies of scale** and through putting assets in the hands of **more efficient managers.** However, mergers also have the potential for reducing competition, and for this reason they are carefully regulated by governmental agencies.
- In most mergers, one company (the **acquiring firm**) initiates action to take over another (the **target firm**).
- A **horizontal merger** occurs when two firms in the same line of business combine.
- A **vertical merger** combines a firm with one of its customers or suppliers.
- A **congeneric merger** involves firms in related industries, but where no customer-supplier relationship exists.
- A **conglomerate merger** occurs when firms in totally different industries combine.
- In a **friendly merger,** the managements of both firms approve the merger, whereas in a **hostile merger,** the target firm's management opposes it.
- An **operating merger** is one where the operations of the two firms are combined. A **financial merger** is one where the firms continue to operate separately, hence no operating economies are expected.
- In a **merger analysis,** the key issues to be resolved are (1) the price to be paid for the target firm and (2) the employment/control situation.

♦ Two methods are commonly used to determine the **value of the target firm:** (1) the **discounted cash flow (DCF)** method and (2) the **market multiple** method.

♦ A **joint venture** is a **corporate alliance** in which two or more companies combine some of their resources to achieve a specific, limited objective.

♦ A **divestiture** is the sale of some of a company's operating assets. A divestiture may involve (1) selling an operating unit to another firm, (2) **spinning off** a unit as a separate company, or (3) the outright **liquidation** of a unit's assets.

♦ The **reasons for divestiture** include to settle antitrust suits, to clarify what a company actually does, to enable management to concentrate on a particular type of activity, and to raise capital needed to strengthen the corporation's core business.

♦ A **holding company** is a corporation which owns sufficient stock in another firm to control it. The holding company is also known as the **parent company,** and the companies which it controls are called **subsidiaries,** or **operating companies.**

♦ Advantages to holding company operations include (1) control can often be obtained for a smaller cash outlay, (2) risks may be segregated, and (3) regulated companies can operate separate subsidiaries for their regulated and unregulated businesses.

♦ Disadvantages to holding company operations include (1) tax penalties and (2) the fact that incomplete ownership, if it exists, can lead to control problems.

♦ A **leveraged buyout (LBO)** is a transaction in which a firm's publicly owned stock is acquired in a mostly debt-financed tender offer, and a privately owned, highly leveraged firm results. Often, the firm's own management initiates the LBO.

QUESTIONS

21-1   Four economic classifications of mergers are (1) horizontal, (2) vertical, (3) conglomerate, and (4) congeneric. Explain the significance of these terms in merger analysis with regard to (a) the likelihood of governmental intervention and (b) possibilities for operating synergy.

21-2   Firm A wants to acquire Firm B. Firm B's management agrees that the merger is a good idea. Might a tender offer be used?

21-3   Distinguish between operating mergers and financial mergers.

21-4   In the spring of 1984, Disney Productions' stock was selling for about $3.125 per share (all prices have been adjusted for 4:1 splits in 1986 and 1992). Then Saul Steinberg, a New York financier, began acquiring it, and after he had 12 percent, he announced a tender offer for another 37 percent of the stock — which would bring his holdings up to 49 percent — at a price of $4.22 per share. Disney's management then announced plans to buy Gibson Greeting Cards and Arvida Corporation, paying for them with stock. It also lined up bank credit and (according to Steinberg) was prepared to borrow up to $2 billion and use the funds to repurchase shares at a higher price than Steinberg was offering. All of these efforts were designed to keep Steinberg from taking control. In June, Disney's management agreed to pay Steinberg $4.84 per share, which gave him a gain of about $60 million on a 2-month investment of about $26.5 million.

When Disney's buy-back of Steinberg's shares was announced, the stock price fell almost instantly from $4.25 to $2.875. Many Disney stockholders were irate, and they sued to block the buyout. Also, the Disney affair added fuel to the fire in a Congressional committee that was holding hearings on proposed legislation that would (1) prohibit someone from acquiring more than 10 percent of a firm's stock without making a tender offer for all the remaining shares, (2) prohibit poison pill tactics such as those Disney's management had used to fight off Steinberg, (3) prohibit buy-backs such as the deal eventually offered to Steinberg (greenmail) unless there was an approving vote by stockholders, and (4) prohibit (or substantially curtail) the use of golden parachutes (the one thing Disney's management did not try).

Set forth the arguments for and against this type of legislation. What provisions, if any, should it contain? Also, look up Disney's current stock price to see how its stockholders have actually fared.

21-5 Two large, publicly owned firms are contemplating a merger. No operating synergy is expected. However, since returns on the 2 firms are not perfectly positively correlated, the standard deviation of earnings would be reduced for the combined corporation. One group of consultants argues that this risk reduction is sufficient grounds for the merger. Another group thinks this type of risk reduction is irrelevant because stockholders can themselves hold the stock of both companies and thus gain the risk-reduction benefits without all the hassles and expenses of the merger. Whose position is correct?

SELF-TEST PROBLEM

ST-1
Key terms

Define each of the following terms:
a. Synergy; merger
b. Horizontal merger; vertical merger; congeneric merger; conglomerate merger
c. Friendly merger; hostile merger; defensive merger; tender offer; target company; breakup value; acquiring company
d. Operating merger; financial merger
e. White knight; poison pill; golden parachute; proxy fight
f. Joint venture; corporate alliance
g. Divestiture; spin-off; leveraged buyout (LBO)
h. Holding company; operating company; parent company
i. Arbitrage

STARTER PROBLEMS

The following information is required to work Problems 21-1, 21-2, and 21-3.

Harrison Corporation is interested in acquiring Van Buren Corporation. Assume that the risk-free rate of interest is 5 percent and the market risk premium is 6 percent.

21-1
Valuation

Van Buren currently expects to pay a year-end dividend of $2.00 a share ($D_1 = \$2.00$). Van Buren's dividend is expected to grow at a constant rate of 5 percent a year, and its beta is 0.9. What is the current price of Van Buren's stock?

21-2
Merger valuation

Harrison estimates that if it acquires Van Buren, the year-end dividend will remain at $2.00 a share, but synergies will enable the dividend to grow at a constant rate of 7 percent a year (instead of the current 5 percent). Harrison also plans to increase the debt ratio of what would be its Van Buren subsidiary — the effect of this would be to raise Van Buren's beta to 1.1. What is the per-share value of Van Buren to Harrison Corporation?

21-3
Merger bid

On the basis of your answers to Problems 21-1 and 21-2, if Harrison were to acquire Van Buren, what would be the range of possible prices that it could bid for each share of Van Buren common stock?

EXAM-TYPE PROBLEM

The problem included in this section is set up in such a way that it could be used as a multiple-choice exam problem.

21-4
Merger analysis

Apilado Appliance Corporation is considering a merger with the Vaccaro Vacuum Company. Vaccaro is a publicly traded company, and its current beta is 1.30. Vaccaro has been barely profitable, so it has paid an average of only 20 percent in taxes during the last several years. In addition, it uses little debt, having a debt ratio of just 25 percent.

If the acquisition were made, Apilado would operate Vaccaro as a separate, wholly owned subsidiary. Apilado would pay taxes on a consolidated basis, and the tax rate would therefore increase to 35 percent. Apilado also would increase the debt capitalization in the Vaccaro subsidiary to 40 percent of assets, which would increase its beta to 1.50. Apilado's acquisition department estimates that Vaccaro, if acquired, would produce the following net cash flows to Apilado's shareholders (in millions of dollars):

YEAR	NET CASH FLOWS
1	$1.30
2	1.50
3	1.75
4	2.00
5 and beyond	Constant growth at 6%

These cash flows include all acquisition effects. Apilado's cost of equity is 14 percent, its beta is 1.0, and its cost of debt is 10 percent. The risk-free rate is 8 percent.
a. What discount rate should be used to discount the estimated cash flows? (Hint: Use Apilado's k_s to determine the market risk premium.)
b. What is the dollar value of Vaccaro to Apilado?
c. Vaccaro has 1.2 million common shares outstanding. What is the maximum price per share that Apilado should offer for Vaccaro? If the tender offer is accepted at this price, what will happen to Apilado's stock price?

PROBLEMS

21-5
Capital budgeting analysis

The Stanley Stationery Shoppe wishes to acquire The Carlson Card Gallery for $400,000. Stanley expects the merger to provide incremental earnings of about $64,000 a year for 10 years. Ken Stanley has calculated the marginal cost of capital for this investment to be 10 percent. Conduct a capital budgeting analysis for Stanley to determine whether or not he should purchase The Carlson Card Gallery.

21-6
Merger analysis

TransWorld Communications Inc., a large telecommunications company, is evaluating the possible acquisition of Georgia Cable Company (GCC), a regional cable company. Trans-World's analysts project the following postmerger data for GCC (in thousands of dollars):

		1998	1999	2000	2001
Net sales		$450	$518	$555	$600
Selling and administrative expense		45	53	60	68
Interest		18	21	24	27
Tax rate after merger	35%				
Cost of goods sold as a percent of sales	65%				
Beta after merger	1.50				
Risk-free rate	8%				
Market risk premium	4%				
Terminal growth rate of cash flow available to TransWorld	7%				

If the acquisition is made, it will occur on January 1, 1998. All cash flows shown in the income statements are assumed to occur at the end of the year. GCC currently has a capital structure of 40 percent debt, but TransWorld would increase that to 50 percent if the acquisition were made. GCC, if independent, would pay taxes at 20 percent, but its income would be taxed at 35 percent if it were consolidated. GCC's current market-determined beta is 1.40, and its investment bankers think that its beta would rise to 1.50 if the debt ratio were increased to 50 percent. The cost of goods sold is expected to be 65 percent of sales, but it could vary somewhat. Depreciation-generated funds would be used to replace worn-out equipment, so they would not be available to TransWorld's shareholders. The risk-free rate is 8 percent, and the market risk premium is 4 percent.
a. What is the appropriate discount rate for valuing the acquisition?
b. What is the terminal value? What is the value of GCC to TransWorld?

INTEGRATED CASE

SMITTY'S HOME REPAIR COMPANY

21-7 Merger Analysis Smitty's Home Repair Company, a regional hardware chain which specializes in "do-it-yourself" materials and equipment rentals, is cash rich because of several consecutive good years. One of the alternative uses for the excess funds is an acquisition. Linda Wade, Smitty's treasurer and your boss, has been asked to place a value on a potential target, Hill's Hardware, a small chain which operates in an adjacent state, and she has enlisted your help.

The table below indicates Wade's estimates of Hill's earnings potential if it came under Smitty's management (in millions of dollars). The interest expense listed here includes the interest (1) on Hill's existing debt, (2) on new debt that Smitty's would issue to help finance the acquisition, and (3) on new debt expected to be issued over time to help finance expansion within the new "H division," the code name given to the target firm. The retentions represent earnings that will be reinvested within the H division to help finance its growth.

Hill's Hardware currently uses 40 percent debt financing, and it pays federal-plus-state taxes at a 30 percent rate. Security analysts estimate Hill's beta to be 1.2. If the acquisition were to take place, Smitty's would increase Hill's debt ratio to 50 percent, which would increase its beta to 1.3. Further, because Smitty's is highly profitable, taxes on the consolidated firm would be 40 percent. Wade realizes that Hill's Hardware also generates depreciation cash flows, but she believes that these funds would have to be reinvested within the division to replace worn-out equipment.

Wade estimates the risk-free rate to be 9 percent and the market risk premium to be 4 percent. She also estimates that net cash flows after 2001 will grow at a constant rate of 6 percent. Smitty's management is new to the merger game, so

Wade has been asked to answer some basic questions about mergers as well as to perform the merger analysis. To structure the task, Wade has developed the following questions, which you must answer and then defend to Smitty's board.

a. Several reasons have been proposed to justify mergers. Among the more prominent are (1) tax considerations, (2) risk reduction, (3) control, (4) purchase of assets at below-replacement cost, (5) synergy, and (6) globalization. In general, which of the reasons are economically justifiable? Which are not? Which fit the situation at hand? Explain.

b. Briefly describe the differences between a hostile merger and a friendly merger.

c. Use the data developed in the table to construct the H division's cash flow statements for 1998 through 2001. Why is interest expense deducted in merger cash flow statements, whereas it is not normally deducted in a capital budgeting cash flow analysis? Why are earnings retentions deducted in the cash flow statement?

d. Conceptually, what is the appropriate discount rate to apply to the cash flows developed in Part c? What is your actual estimate of this discount rate?

e. What is the estimated terminal value of the acquisition; that is, what is the estimated value of the H division's cash flows beyond 2001? What is Hill's value to Smitty's? Suppose another firm were evaluating Hill's as an acquisition candidate. Would they obtain the same value? Explain.

f. Assume that Hill's has 10 million shares outstanding. These shares are traded relatively infrequently, but the last trade, made several weeks ago, was at a price of $9 per share. Should Smitty's make an offer for Hill's? If so, how much should it offer per share?

g. What merger-related activities are undertaken by investment bankers?

	1998	1999	2000	2001
Net sales	$60.0	$90.0	$112.5	$127.5
Cost of goods sold (60%)	36.0	54.0	67.5	76.5
Selling/administrative expense	4.5	6.0	7.5	9.0
Interest expense	3.0	4.5	4.5	6.0
Necessary retained earnings	0.0	7.5	6.0	4.5

COMPUTER-RELATED PROBLEM

Work the problem in this section only if you are using the computer problem diskette.

21-8
Merger analysis

Use the model in the File C21 to work this problem.

a. Refer back to Problem 21-6. Rework the problem assuming that sales in each year were $100,000 higher than the base-case amounts and that the cost of goods sold/sales ratio was 60 percent rather than 65 percent. What would be the value of GCC to TransWorld under these assumptions?

b. With sales and the cost of goods sold ratio at the levels specified in Part a, what would be GCC's value if its beta were 1.60, if k_{RF} rose to 9 percent, and if RP_M rose to 5 percent?

c. Leaving all values at their Part b levels, what would be the value of the acquisition if the terminal growth rate rose to 12 percent or dropped to 3 percent?

APPENDIX A

MATHEMATICAL TABLES

TABLE A-1   Present Value of $1 Due at the End of n Periods

Equation:

$$PVIF_{i,n} = \frac{1}{(1 + i)^n}$$

Financial Calculator Keys:

n — **N**   i — **I**   0 — **PV** (TABLE VALUE)   **PMT**   1.0 — **FV**

Period	1%	2%	3%	4%	5%	6%	7%	8%	9%	10%
1	.9901	.9804	.9709	.9615	.9524	.9434	.9346	.9259	.9174	.9091
2	.9803	.9612	.9426	.9246	.9070	.8900	.8734	.8573	.8417	.8264
3	.9706	.9423	.9151	.8890	.8638	.8396	.8163	.7938	.7722	.7513
4	.9610	.9238	.8885	.8548	.8227	.7921	.7629	.7350	.7084	.6830
5	.9515	.9057	.8626	.8219	.7835	.7473	.7130	.6806	.6499	.6209
6	.9420	.8880	.8375	.7903	.7462	.7050	.6663	.6302	.5963	.5645
7	.9327	.8706	.8131	.7599	.7107	.6651	.6227	.5835	.5470	.5132
8	.9235	.8535	.7894	.7307	.6768	.6274	.5820	.5403	.5019	.4665
9	.9143	.8368	.7664	.7026	.6446	.5919	.5439	.5002	.4604	.4241
10	.9053	.8203	.7441	.6756	.6139	.5584	.5083	.4632	.4224	.3855
11	.8963	.8043	.7224	.6496	.5847	.5268	.4751	.4289	.3875	.3505
12	.8874	.7885	.7014	.6246	.5568	.4970	.4440	.3971	.3555	.3186
13	.8787	.7730	.6810	.6006	.5303	.4688	.4150	.3677	.3262	.2897
14	.8700	.7579	.6611	.5775	.5051	.4423	.3878	.3405	.2992	.2633
15	.8613	.7430	.6419	.5553	.4810	.4173	.3624	.3152	.2745	.2394
16	.8528	.7284	.6232	.5339	.4581	.3936	.3387	.2919	.2519	.2176
17	.8444	.7142	.6050	.5134	.4363	.3714	.3166	.2703	.2311	.1978
18	.8360	.7002	.5874	.4936	.4155	.3503	.2959	.2502	.2120	.1799
19	.8277	.6864	.5703	.4746	.3957	.3305	.2765	.2317	.1945	.1635
20	.8195	.6730	.5537	.4564	.3769	.3118	.2584	.2145	.1784	.1486
21	.8114	.6598	.5375	.4388	.3589	.2942	.2415	.1987	.1637	.1351
22	.8034	.6468	.5219	.4220	.3418	.2775	.2257	.1839	.1502	.1228
23	.7954	.6342	.5067	.4057	.3256	.2618	.2109	.1703	.1378	.1117
24	.7876	.6217	.4919	.3901	.3101	.2470	.1971	.1577	.1264	.1015
25	.7798	.6095	.4776	.3751	.2953	.2330	.1842	.1460	.1160	.0923
26	.7720	.5976	.4637	.3607	.2812	.2198	.1722	.1352	.1064	.0839
27	.7644	.5859	.4502	.3468	.2678	.2074	.1609	.1252	.0976	.0763
28	.7568	.5744	.4371	.3335	.2551	.1956	.1504	.1159	.0895	.0693
29	.7493	.5631	.4243	.3207	.2429	.1846	.1406	.1073	.0822	.0630
30	.7419	.5521	.4120	.3083	.2314	.1741	.1314	.0994	.0754	.0573
35	.7059	.5000	.3554	.2534	.1813	.1301	.0937	.0676	.0490	.0356
40	.6717	.4529	.3066	.2083	.1420	.0972	.0668	.0460	.0318	.0221
45	.6391	.4102	.2644	.1712	.1113	.0727	.0476	.0313	.0207	.0137
50	.6080	.3715	.2281	.1407	.0872	.0543	.0339	.0213	.0134	.0085
55	.5785	.3365	.1968	.1157	.0683	.0406	.0242	.0145	.0087	.0053

TABLE A-1 continued

PERIOD	12%	14%	15%	16%	18%	20%	24%	28%	32%	36%
1	.8929	.8772	.8696	.8621	.8475	.8333	.8065	.7813	.7576	.7353
2	.7972	.7695	.7561	.7432	.7182	.6944	.6504	.6104	.5739	.5407
3	.7118	.6750	.6575	.6407	.6086	.5787	.5245	.4768	.4348	.3975
4	.6355	.5921	.5718	.5523	.5158	.4823	.4230	.3725	.3294	.2923
5	.5674	.5194	.4972	.4761	.4371	.4019	.3411	.2910	.2495	.2149
6	.5066	.4556	.4323	.4104	.3704	.3349	.2751	.2274	.1890	.1580
7	.4523	.3996	.3759	.3538	.3139	.2791	.2218	.1776	.1432	.1162
8	.4039	.3506	.3269	.3050	.2660	.2326	.1789	.1388	.1085	.0854
9	.3606	.3075	.2843	.2630	.2255	.1938	.1443	.1084	.0822	.0628
10	.3220	.2697	.2472	.2267	.1911	.1615	.1164	.0847	.0623	.0462
11	.2875	.2366	.2149	.1954	.1619	.1346	.0938	.0662	.0472	.0340
12	.2567	.2076	.1869	.1685	.1372	.1122	.0757	.0517	.0357	.0250
13	.2292	.1821	.1625	.1452	.1163	.0935	.0610	.0404	.0271	.0184
14	.2046	.1597	.1413	.1252	.0985	.0779	.0492	.0316	.0205	.0135
15	.1827	.1401	.1229	.1079	.0835	.0649	.0397	.0247	.0155	.0099
16	.1631	.1229	.1069	.0930	.0708	.0541	.0320	.0193	.0118	.0073
17	.1456	.1078	.0929	.0802	.0600	.0451	.0258	.0150	.0089	.0054
18	.1300	.0946	.0808	.0691	.0508	.0376	.0208	.0118	.0068	.0039
19	.1161	.0829	.0703	.0596	.0431	.0313	.0168	.0092	.0051	.0029
20	.1037	.0728	.0611	.0514	.0365	.0261	.0135	.0072	.0039	.0021
21	.0926	.0638	.0531	.0443	.0309	.0217	.0109	.0056	.0029	.0016
22	.0826	.0560	.0462	.0382	.0262	.0181	.0088	.0044	.0022	.0012
23	.0738	.0491	.0402	.0329	.0222	.0151	.0071	.0034	.0017	.0008
24	.0659	.0431	.0349	.0284	.0188	.0126	.0057	.0027	.0013	.0006
25	.0588	.0378	.0304	.0245	.0160	.0105	.0046	.0021	.0010	.0005
26	.0525	.0331	.0264	.0211	.0135	.0087	.0037	.0016	.0007	.0003
27	.0469	.0291	.0230	.0182	.0115	.0073	.0030	.0013	.0006	.0002
28	.0419	.0255	.0200	.0157	.0097	.0061	.0024	.0010	.0004	.0002
29	.0374	.0224	.0174	.0135	.0082	.0051	.0020	.0008	.0003	.0001
30	.0334	.0196	.0151	.0116	.0070	.0042	.0016	.0006	.0002	.0001
35	.0189	.0102	.0075	.0055	.0030	.0017	.0005	.0002	.0001	*
40	.0107	.0053	.0037	.0026	.0013	.0007	.0002	.0001	*	*
45	.0061	.0027	.0019	.0013	.0006	.0003	.0001	*	*	*
50	.0035	.0014	.0009	.0006	.0003	.0001	*	*	*	*
55	.0020	.0007	.0005	.0003	.0001	*	*	*	*	*

*The factor is zero to four decimal places.

TABLE   A - 2   Present Value of an Annuity of $1 per Period for n Periods

Equation:

$$PVIFA_{i,n} = \sum_{t=1}^{n} \frac{1}{(1+i)^t} = \frac{1 - \dfrac{1}{(1+i)^n}}{i} = \frac{1}{i} - \frac{1}{i(1+i)^n}$$

Financial Calculator Keys:

n	i		1.0	0
N	I	PV	PMT	FV
		TABLE VALUE		

NUMBER OF PERIODS	1%	2%	3%	4%	5%	6%	7%	8%	9%
1	0.9901	0.9804	0.9709	0.9615	0.9524	0.9434	0.9346	0.9259	0.9174
2	1.9704	1.9416	1.9135	1.8861	1.8594	1.8334	1.8080	1.7833	1.7591
3	2.9410	2.8839	2.8286	2.7751	2.7232	2.6730	2.6243	2.5771	2.5313
4	3.9020	3.8077	3.7171	3.6299	3.5460	3.4651	3.3872	3.3121	3.2397
5	4.8534	4.7135	4.5797	4.4518	4.3295	4.2124	4.1002	3.9927	3.8897
6	5.7955	5.6014	5.4172	5.2421	5.0757	4.9173	4.7665	4.6229	4.4859
7	6.7282	6.4720	6.2303	6.0021	5.7864	5.5824	5.3893	5.2064	5.0330
8	7.6517	7.3255	7.0197	6.7327	6.4632	6.2098	5.9713	5.7466	5.5348
9	8.5660	8.1622	7.7861	7.4353	7.1078	6.8017	6.5152	6.2469	5.9952
10	9.4713	8.9826	8.5302	8.1109	7.7217	7.3601	7.0236	6.7101	6.4177
11	10.3676	9.7868	9.2526	8.7605	8.3064	7.8869	7.4987	7.1390	6.8052
12	11.2551	10.5753	9.9540	9.3851	8.8633	8.3838	7.9427	7.5361	7.1607
13	12.1337	11.3484	10.6350	9.9856	9.3936	8.8527	8.3577	7.9038	7.4869
14	13.0037	12.1062	11.2961	10.5631	9.8986	9.2950	8.7455	8.2442	7.7862
15	13.8651	12.8493	11.9379	11.1184	10.3797	9.7122	9.1079	8.5595	8.0607
16	14.7179	13.5777	12.5611	11.6523	10.8378	10.1059	9.4466	8.8514	8.3126
17	15.5623	14.2919	13.1661	12.1657	11.2741	10.4773	9.7632	9.1216	8.5436
18	16.3983	14.9920	13.7535	12.6593	11.6896	10.8276	10.0591	9.3719	8.7556
19	17.2260	15.6785	14.3238	13.1339	12.0853	11.1581	10.3356	9.6036	8.9501
20	18.0456	16.3514	14.8775	13.5903	12.4622	11.4699	10.5940	9.8181	9.1285
21	18.8570	17.0112	15.4150	14.0292	12.8212	11.7641	10.8355	10.0168	9.2922
22	19.6604	17.6580	15.9369	14.4511	13.1630	12.0416	11.0612	10.2007	9.4424
23	20.4558	18.2922	16.4436	14.8568	13.4886	12.3034	11.2722	10.3711	9.5802
24	21.2434	18.9139	16.9355	15.2470	13.7986	12.5504	11.4693	10.5288	9.7066
25	22.0232	19.5235	17.4131	15.6221	14.0939	12.7834	11.6536	10.6748	9.8226
26	22.7952	20.1210	17.8768	15.9828	14.3752	13.0032	11.8258	10.8100	9.9290
27	23.5596	20.7069	18.3270	16.3296	14.6430	13.2105	11.9867	10.9352	10.0266
28	24.3164	21.2813	18.7641	16.6631	14.8981	13.4062	12.1371	11.0511	10.1161
29	25.0658	21.8444	19.1885	16.9837	15.1411	13.5907	12.2777	11.1584	10.1983
30	25.8077	22.3965	19.6004	17.2920	15.3725	13.7648	12.4090	11.2578	10.2737
35	29.4086	24.9986	21.4872	18.6646	16.3742	14.4982	12.9477	11.6546	10.5668
40	32.8347	27.3555	23.1148	19.7928	17.1591	15.0463	13.3317	11.9246	10.7574
45	36.0945	29.4902	24.5187	20.7200	17.7741	15.4558	13.6055	12.1084	10.8812
50	39.1961	31.4236	25.7298	21.4822	18.2559	15.7619	13.8007	12.2335	10.9617
55	42.1472	33.1748	26.7744	22.1086	18.6335	15.9905	13.9399	12.3186	11.0140

TABLE A - 2   continued

NUMBER OF PERIODS	10%	12%	14%	15%	16%	18%	20%	24%	28%	32%
1	0.9091	0.8929	0.8772	0.8696	0.8621	0.8475	0.8333	0.8065	0.7813	0.7576
2	1.7355	1.6901	1.6467	1.6257	1.6052	1.5656	1.5278	1.4568	1.3916	1.3315
3	2.4869	2.4018	2.3216	2.2832	2.2459	2.1743	2.1065	1.9813	1.8684	1.7663
4	3.1699	3.0373	2.9137	2.8550	2.7982	2.6901	2.5887	2.4043	2.2410	2.0957
5	3.7908	3.6048	3.4331	3.3522	3.2743	3.1272	2.9906	2.7454	2.5320	2.3452
6	4.3553	4.1114	3.8887	3.7845	3.6847	3.4976	3.3255	3.0205	2.7594	2.5342
7	4.8684	4.5638	4.2883	4.1604	4.0386	3.8115	3.6046	3.2423	2.9370	2.6775
8	5.3349	4.9676	4.6389	4.4873	4.3436	4.0776	3.8372	3.4212	3.0758	2.7860
9	5.7590	5.3282	4.9464	4.7716	4.6065	4.3030	4.0310	3.5655	3.1842	2.8681
10	6.1446	5.6502	5.2161	5.0188	4.8332	4.4941	4.1925	3.6819	3.2689	2.9304
11	6.4951	5.9377	5.4527	5.2337	5.0286	4.6560	4.3271	3.7757	3.3351	2.9776
12	6.8137	6.1944	5.6603	5.4206	5.1971	4.7932	4.4392	3.8514	3.3868	3.0133
13	7.1034	6.4235	5.8424	5.5831	5.3423	4.9095	4.5327	3.9124	3.4272	3.0404
14	7.3667	6.6282	6.0021	5.7245	5.4675	5.0081	4.6106	3.9616	3.4587	3.0609
15	7.6061	6.8109	6.1422	5.8474	5.5755	5.0916	4.6755	4.0013	3.4834	3.0764
16	7.8237	6.9740	6.2651	5.9542	5.6685	5.1624	4.7296	4.0333	3.5026	3.0882
17	8.0216	7.1196	6.3729	6.0472	5.7487	5.2223	4.7746	4.0591	3.5177	3.0971
18	8.2014	7.2497	6.4674	6.1280	5.8178	5.2732	4.8122	4.0799	3.5294	3.1039
19	8.3649	7.3658	6.5504	6.1982	5.8775	5.3162	4.8435	4.0967	3.5386	3.1090
20	8.5136	7.4694	6.6231	6.2593	5.9288	5.3527	4.8696	4.1103	3.5458	3.1129
21	8.6487	7.5620	6.6870	6.3125	5.9731	5.3837	4.8913	4.1212	3.5514	3.1158
22	8.7715	7.6446	6.7429	6.3587	6.0113	5.4099	4.9094	4.1300	3.5558	3.1180
23	8.8832	7.7184	6.7921	6.3988	6.0442	5.4321	4.9245	4.1371	3.5592	3.1197
24	8.9847	7.7843	6.8351	6.4338	6.0726	5.4509	4.9371	4.1428	3.5619	3.1210
25	9.0770	7.8431	6.8729	6.4641	6.0971	5.4669	4.9476	4.1474	3.5640	3.1220
26	9.1609	7.8957	6.9061	6.4906	6.1182	5.4804	4.9563	4.1511	3.5656	3.1227
27	9.2372	7.9426	6.9352	6.5135	6.1364	5.4919	4.9636	4.1542	3.5669	3.1233
28	9.3066	7.9844	6.9607	6.5335	6.1520	5.5016	4.9697	4.1566	3.5679	3.1237
29	9.3696	8.0218	6.9830	6.5509	6.1656	5.5098	4.9747	4.1585	3.5687	3.1240
30	9.4269	8.0552	7.0027	6.5660	6.1772	5.5168	4.9789	4.1601	3.5693	3.1242
35	9.6442	8.1755	7.0700	6.6166	6.2153	5.5386	4.9915	4.1644	3.5708	3.1248
40	9.7791	8.2438	7.1050	6.6418	6.2335	5.5482	4.9966	4.1659	3.5712	3.1250
45	9.8628	8.2825	7.1232	6.6543	6.2421	5.5523	4.9986	4.1664	3.5714	3.1250
50	9.9148	8.3045	7.1327	6.6605	6.2463	5.5541	4.9995	4.1666	3.5714	3.1250
55	9.9471	8.3170	7.1376	6.6636	6.2482	5.5549	4.9998	4.1666	3.5714	3.1250

TABLE   A - 3   Future Value of $1 at the End of n Periods

Equation:

$FVIF_{i,n} = (1 + i)^n$

Financial Calculator Keys:

n	i	1.0	0	
N	I	PV	PMT	FV

TABLE
VALUE

PERIOD	1%	2%	3%	4%	5%	6%	7%	8%	9%	10%
1	1.0100	1.0200	1.0300	1.0400	1.0500	1.0600	1.0700	1.0800	1.0900	1.1000
2	1.0201	1.0404	1.0609	1.0816	1.1025	1.1236	1.1449	1.1664	1.1881	1.2100
3	1.0303	1.0612	1.0927	1.1249	1.1576	1.1910	1.2250	1.2597	1.2950	1.3310
4	1.0406	1.0824	1.1255	1.1699	1.2155	1.2625	1.3108	1.3605	1.4116	1.4641
5	1.0510	1.1041	1.1593	1.2167	1.2763	1.3382	1.4026	1.4693	1.5386	1.6105
6	1.0615	1.1262	1.1941	1.2653	1.3401	1.4185	1.5007	1.5869	1.6771	1.7716
7	1.0721	1.1487	1.2299	1.3159	1.4071	1.5036	1.6058	1.7138	1.8280	1.9487
8	1.0829	1.1717	1.2668	1.3686	1.4775	1.5938	1.7182	1.8509	1.9926	2.1436
9	1.0937	1.1951	1.3048	1.4233	1.5513	1.6895	1.8385	1.9990	2.1719	2.3579
10	1.1046	1.2190	1.3439	1.4802	1.6289	1.7908	1.9672	2.1589	2.3674	2.5937
11	1.1157	1.2434	1.3842	1.5395	1.7103	1.8983	2.1049	2.3316	2.5804	2.8531
12	1.1268	1.2682	1.4258	1.6010	1.7959	2.0122	2.2522	2.5182	2.8127	3.1384
13	1.1381	1.2936	1.4685	1.6651	1.8856	2.1329	2.4098	2.7196	3.0658	3.4523
14	1.1495	1.3195	1.5126	1.7317	1.9799	2.2609	2.5785	2.9372	3.3417	3.7975
15	1.1610	1.3459	1.5580	1.8009	2.0789	2.3966	2.7590	3.1722	3.6425	4.1772
16	1.1726	1.3728	1.6047	1.8730	2.1829	2.5404	2.9522	3.4259	3.9703	4.5950
17	1.1843	1.4002	1.6528	1.9479	2.2920	2.6928	3.1588	3.7000	4.3276	5.0545
18	1.1961	1.4282	1.7024	2.0258	2.4066	2.8543	3.3799	3.9960	4.7171	5.5599
19	1.2081	1.4568	1.7535	2.1068	2.5270	3.0256	3.6165	4.3157	5.1417	6.1159
20	1.2202	1.4859	1.8061	2.1911	2.6533	3.2071	3.8697	4.6610	5.6044	6.7275
21	1.2324	1.5157	1.8603	2.2788	2.7860	3.3996	4.1406	5.0338	6.1088	7.4002
22	1.2447	1.5460	1.9161	2.3699	2.9253	3.6035	4.4304	5.4365	6.6586	8.1403
23	1.2572	1.5769	1.9736	2.4647	3.0715	3.8197	4.7405	5.8715	7.2579	8.9543
24	1.2697	1.6084	2.0328	2.5633	3.2251	4.0489	5.0724	6.3412	7.9111	9.8497
25	1.2824	1.6406	2.0938	2.6658	3.3864	4.2919	5.4274	6.8485	8.6231	10.835
26	1.2953	1.6734	2.1566	2.7725	3.5557	4.5494	5.8074	7.3964	9.3992	11.918
27	1.3082	1.7069	2.2213	2.8834	3.7335	4.8223	6.2139	7.9881	10.245	13.110
28	1.3213	1.7410	2.2879	2.9987	3.9201	5.1117	6.6488	8.6271	11.167	14.421
29	1.3345	1.7758	2.3566	3.1187	4.1161	5.4184	7.1143	9.3173	12.172	15.863
30	1.3478	1.8114	2.4273	3.2434	4.3219	5.7435	7.6123	10.063	13.268	17.449
40	1.4889	2.2080	3.2620	4.8010	7.0400	10.286	14.974	21.725	31.409	45.259
50	1.6446	2.6916	4.3839	7.1067	11.467	18.420	29.457	46.902	74.358	117.39
60	1.8167	3.2810	5.8916	10.520	18.679	32.988	57.946	101.26	176.03	304.48

TABLE   A - 3   continued

Period	12%	14%	15%	16%	18%	20%	24%	28%	32%	36%
1	1.1200	1.1400	1.1500	1.1600	1.1800	1.2000	1.2400	1.2800	1.3200	1.3600
2	1.2544	1.2996	1.3225	1.3456	1.3924	1.4400	1.5376	1.6384	1.7424	1.8496
3	1.4049	1.4815	1.5209	1.5609	1.6430	1.7280	1.9066	2.0972	2.3000	2.5155
4	1.5735	1.6890	1.7490	1.8106	1.9388	2.0736	2.3642	2.6844	3.0360	3.4210
5	1.7623	1.9254	2.0114	2.1003	2.2878	2.4883	2.9316	3.4360	4.0075	4.6526
6	1.9738	2.1950	2.3131	2.4364	2.6996	2.9860	3.6352	4.3980	5.2899	6.3275
7	2.2107	2.5023	2.6600	2.8262	3.1855	3.5832	4.5077	5.6295	6.9826	8.6054
8	2.4760	2.8526	3.0590	3.2784	3.7589	4.2998	5.5895	7.2058	9.2170	11.703
9	2.7731	3.2519	3.5179	3.8030	4.4355	5.1598	6.9310	9.2234	12.166	15.917
10	3.1058	3.7072	4.0456	4.4114	5.2338	6.1917	8.5944	11.806	16.060	21.647
11	3.4785	4.2262	4.6524	5.1173	6.1759	7.4301	10.657	15.112	21.199	29.439
12	3.8960	4.8179	5.3503	5.9360	7.2876	8.9161	13.215	19.343	27.983	40.037
13	4.3635	5.4924	6.1528	6.8858	8.5994	10.699	16.386	24.759	36.937	54.451
14	4.8871	6.2613	7.0757	7.9875	10.147	12.839	20.319	31.691	48.757	74.053
15	5.4736	7.1379	8.1371	9.2655	11.974	15.407	25.196	40.565	64.359	100.71
16	6.1304	8.1372	9.3576	10.748	14.129	18.488	31.243	51.923	84.954	136.97
17	6.8660	9.2765	10.761	12.468	16.672	22.186	38.741	66.461	112.14	186.28
18	7.6900	10.575	12.375	14.463	19.673	26.623	48.039	85.071	148.02	253.34
19	8.6128	12.056	14.232	16.777	23.214	31.948	59.568	108.89	195.39	344.54
20	9.6463	13.743	16.367	19.461	27.393	38.338	73.864	139.38	257.92	468.57
21	10.804	15.668	18.822	22.574	32.324	46.005	91.592	178.41	340.45	637.26
22	12.100	17.861	21.645	26.186	38.142	55.206	113.57	228.36	449.39	866.67
23	13.552	20.362	24.891	30.376	45.008	66.247	140.83	292.30	593.20	1178.7
24	15.179	23.212	28.625	35.236	53.109	79.497	174.63	374.14	783.02	1603.0
25	17.000	26.462	32.919	40.874	62.669	95.396	216.54	478.90	1033.6	2180.1
26	19.040	30.167	37.857	47.414	73.949	114.48	268.51	613.00	1364.3	2964.9
27	21.325	34.390	43.535	55.000	87.260	137.37	332.95	784.64	1800.9	4032.3
28	23.884	39.204	50.066	63.800	102.97	164.84	412.86	1004.3	2377.2	5483.9
29	26.750	44.693	57.575	74.009	121.50	197.81	511.95	1285.6	3137.9	7458.1
30	29.960	50.950	66.212	85.850	143.37	237.38	634.82	1645.5	4142.1	10143.
40	93.051	188.88	267.86	378.72	750.38	1469.8	5455.9	19427.	66521.	*
50	289.00	700.23	1083.7	1670.7	3927.4	9100.4	46890.	*	*	*
60	897.60	2595.9	4384.0	7370.2	20555.	56348.	*	*	*	*

*FVIF > 99,999.

TABLE   A - 4   Future Value of an Annuity of $1 per Period for n Periods

Equation:

$$FVIFA_{i,n} = \sum_{t=1}^{n} (1 + i)^{n-t} = \frac{(1 + i)^n - 1}{i}$$

Financial Calculator Keys:

n	i	0	1.0	
N	I	PV	PMT	FV

TABLE VALUE

NUMBER OF PERIODS	1%	2%	3%	4%	5%	6%	7%	8%	9%	10%
1	1.0000	1.0000	1.0000	1.0000	1.0000	1.0000	1.0000	1.0000	1.0000	1.0000
2	2.0100	2.0200	2.0300	2.0400	2.0500	2.0600	2.0700	2.0800	2.0900	2.1000
3	3.0301	3.0604	3.0909	3.1216	3.1525	3.1836	3.2149	3.2464	3.2781	3.3100
4	4.0604	4.1216	4.1836	4.2465	4.3101	4.3746	4.4399	4.5061	4.5731	4.6410
5	5.1010	5.2040	5.3091	5.4163	5.5256	5.6371	5.7507	5.8666	5.9847	6.1051
6	6.1520	6.3081	6.4684	6.6330	6.8019	6.9753	7.1533	7.3359	7.5233	7.7156
7	7.2135	7.4343	7.6625	7.8983	8.1420	8.3938	8.6540	8.9228	9.2004	9.4872
8	8.2857	8.5830	8.8923	9.2142	9.5491	9.8975	10.260	10.637	11.028	11.436
9	9.3685	9.7546	10.159	10.583	11.027	11.491	11.978	12.488	13.021	13.579
10	10.462	10.950	11.464	12.006	12.578	13.181	13.816	14.487	15.193	15.937
11	11.567	12.169	12.808	13.486	14.207	14.972	15.784	16.645	17.560	18.531
12	12.683	13.412	14.192	15.026	15.917	16.870	17.888	18.977	20.141	21.384
13	13.809	14.680	15.618	16.627	17.713	18.882	20.141	21.495	22.953	24.523
14	14.947	15.974	17.086	18.292	19.599	21.015	22.550	24.215	26.019	27.975
15	16.097	17.293	18.599	20.024	21.579	23.276	25.129	27.152	29.361	31.772
16	17.258	18.639	20.157	21.825	23.657	25.673	27.888	30.324	33.003	35.950
17	18.430	20.012	21.762	23.698	25.840	28.213	30.840	33.750	36.974	40.545
18	19.615	21.412	23.414	25.645	28.132	30.906	33.999	37.450	41.301	45.599
19	20.811	22.841	25.117	27.671	30.539	33.760	37.379	41.446	46.018	51.159
20	22.019	24.297	26.870	29.778	33.066	36.786	40.995	45.762	51.160	57.275
21	23.239	25.783	28.676	31.969	35.719	39.993	44.865	50.423	56.765	64.002
22	24.472	27.299	30.537	34.248	38.505	43.392	49.006	55.457	62.873	71.403
23	25.716	28.845	32.453	36.618	41.430	46.996	53.436	60.893	69.532	79.543
24	26.973	30.422	34.426	39.083	44.502	50.816	58.177	66.765	76.790	88.497
25	28.243	32.030	36.459	41.646	47.727	54.865	63.249	73.106	84.701	98.347
26	29.526	33.671	38.553	44.312	51.113	59.156	68.676	79.954	93.324	109.18
27	30.821	35.344	40.710	47.084	54.669	63.706	74.484	87.351	102.72	121.10
28	32.129	37.051	42.931	49.968	58.403	68.528	80.698	95.339	112.97	134.21
29	33.450	38.792	45.219	52.966	62.323	73.640	87.347	103.97	124.14	148.63
30	34.785	40.568	47.575	56.085	66.439	79.058	94.461	113.28	136.31	164.49
40	48.886	60.402	75.401	95.026	120.80	154.76	199.64	259.06	337.88	442.59
50	64.463	84.579	112.80	152.67	209.35	290.34	406.53	573.77	815.08	1163.9
60	81.670	114.05	163.05	237.99	353.58	533.13	813.52	1253.2	1944.8	3034.8

T A B L E   A - 4 continued

NUMBER OF PERIODS	12%	14%	15%	16%	18%	20%	24%	28%	32%	36%
1	1.0000	1.0000	1.0000	1.0000	1.0000	1.0000	1.0000	1.0000	1.0000	1.0000
2	2.1200	2.1400	2.1500	2.1600	2.1800	2.2000	2.2400	2.2800	2.3200	2.3600
3	3.3744	3.4396	3.4725	3.5056	3.5724	3.6400	3.7776	3.9184	4.0624	4.2096
4	4.7793	4.9211	4.9934	5.0665	5.2154	5.3680	5.6842	6.0156	6.3624	6.7251
5	6.3528	6.6101	6.7424	6.8771	7.1542	7.4416	8.0484	8.6999	9.3983	10.146
6	8.1152	8.5355	8.7537	8.9775	9.4420	9.9299	10.980	12.136	13.406	14.799
7	10.089	10.730	11.067	11.414	12.142	12.916	14.615	16.534	18.696	21.126
8	12.300	13.233	13.727	14.240	15.327	16.499	19.123	22.163	25.678	29.732
9	14.776	16.085	16.786	17.519	19.086	20.799	24.712	29.369	34.895	41.435
10	17.549	19.337	20.304	21.321	23.521	25.959	31.643	38.593	47.062	57.352
11	20.655	23.045	24.349	25.733	28.755	32.150	40.238	50.398	63.122	78.998
12	24.133	27.271	29.002	30.850	34.931	39.581	50.895	65.510	84.320	108.44
13	28.029	32.089	34.352	36.786	42.219	48.497	64.110	84.853	112.30	148.47
14	32.393	37.581	40.505	43.672	50.818	59.196	80.496	109.61	149.24	202.93
15	37.280	43.842	47.580	51.660	60.965	72.035	100.82	141.30	198.00	276.98
16	42.753	50.980	55.717	60.925	72.939	87.442	126.01	181.87	262.36	377.69
17	48.884	59.118	65.075	71.673	87.068	105.93	157.25	233.79	347.31	514.66
18	55.750	68.394	75.836	84.141	103.74	128.12	195.99	300.25	459.45	700.94
19	63.440	78.969	88.212	98.603	123.41	154.74	244.03	385.32	607.47	954.28
20	72.052	91.025	102.44	115.38	146.63	186.69	303.60	494.21	802.86	1298.8
21	81.699	104.77	118.81	134.84	174.02	225.03	377.46	633.59	1060.8	1767.4
22	92.503	120.44	137.63	157.41	206.34	271.03	469.06	812.00	1401.2	2404.7
23	104.60	138.30	159.28	183.60	244.49	326.24	582.63	1040.4	1850.6	3271.3
24	118.16	158.66	184.17	213.98	289.49	392.48	723.46	1332.7	2443.8	4450.0
25	133.33	181.87	212.79	249.21	342.60	471.98	898.09	1706.8	3226.8	6053.0
26	150.33	208.33	245.71	290.09	405.27	567.38	1114.6	2185.7	4260.4	8233.1
27	169.37	238.50	283.57	337.50	479.22	681.85	1383.1	2798.7	5624.8	11198.0
28	190.70	272.89	327.10	392.50	566.48	819.22	1716.1	3583.3	7425.7	15230.3
29	214.58	312.09	377.17	456.30	669.45	984.07	2129.0	4587.7	9802.9	20714.2
30	241.33	356.79	434.75	530.31	790.95	1181.9	2640.9	5873.2	12941.	28172.3
40	767.09	1342.0	1779.1	2360.8	4163.2	7343.9	22729.	69377.	*	*
50	2400.0	4994.5	7217.7	10436.	21813.	45497.	*	*	*	*
60	7471.6	18535.	29220.	46058.	*	*	*	*	*	*

*FVIFA > 99,999.

| | **TABLE   A - 5** | Values of the Areas under the Standard Normal Distribution Function | | | | | | | | |

z	0.00	0.01	0.02	0.03	0.04	0.05	0.06	0.07	0.08	0.09
0.0	.0000	.0040	.0080	.0120	.0160	.0199	.0239	.0279	.0319	.0359
0.1	.0398	.0438	.0478	.0517	.0557	.0596	.0636	.0675	.0714	.0753
0.2	.0793	.0832	.0871	.0910	.0948	.0987	.1026	.1064	.1103	.1141
0.3	.1179	.1217	.1255	.1293	.1331	.1368	.1406	.1443	.1480	.1517
0.4	.1554	.1591	.1628	.1664	.1700	.1736	.1772	.1808	.1844	.1879
0.5	.1915	.1950	.1985	.2019	.2054	.2088	.2123	.2157	.2190	.2224
0.6	.2257	.2291	.2324	.2357	.2389	.2422	.2454	.2486	.2517	.2549
0.7	.2580	.2611	.2642	.2673	.2704	.2734	.2764	.2794	.2823	.2852
0.8	.2881	.2910	.2939	.2967	.2995	.3023	.3051	.3078	.3106	.3133
0.9	.3159	.3186	.3212	.3238	.3264	.3289	.3315	.3340	.3365	.3389
1.0	.3413	.3438	.3461	.3485	.3508	.3531	.3554	.3577	.3599	.3621
1.1	.3643	.3665	.3686	.3708	.3729	.3749	.3770	.3790	.3810	.3830
1.2	.3849	.3869	.3888	.3907	.3925	.3944	.3962	.3980	.3997	.4015
1.3	.4032	.4049	.4066	.4082	.4099	.4115	.4131	.4147	.4162	.4177
1.4	.4192	.4207	.4222	.4236	.4251	.4265	.4279	.4292	.4306	.4319
1.5	.4332	.4345	.4357	.4370	.4382	.4394	.4406	.4418	.4429	.4441
1.6	.4452	.4463	.4474	.4484	.4495	.4505	.4515	.4525	.4535	.4545
1.7	.4554	.4564	.4573	.4582	.4591	.4599	.4608	.4616	.4625	.4633
1.8	.4641	.4649	.4656	.4664	.4671	.4678	.4686	.4693	.4699	.4706
1.9	.4713	.4719	.4726	.4732	.4738	.4744	.4750	.4756	.4761	.4767
2.0	.4773	.4778	.4783	.4788	.4793	.4798	.4803	.4808	.4812	.4817
2.1	.4821	.4826	.4830	.4834	.4838	.4842	.4846	.4850	.4854	.4857
2.2	.4861	.4864	.4868	.4871	.4875	.4878	.4881	.4884	.4887	.4890
2.3	.4893	.4896	.4898	.4901	.4904	.4906	.4909	.4911	.4913	.4916
2.4	.4918	.4920	.4922	.4925	.4927	.4929	.4931	.4932	.4934	.4936
2.5	.4938	.4940	.4941	.4943	.4945	.4946	.4948	.4949	.4951	.4952
2.6	.4953	.4955	.4956	.4957	.4959	.4960	.4961	.4962	.4963	.4964
2.7	.4965	.4966	.4967	.4968	.4969	.4970	.4971	.4972	.4973	.4974
2.8	.4974	.4975	.4976	.4977	.4977	.4978	.4979	.4979	.4980	.4981
2.9	.4981	.4982	.4982	.4982	.4984	.4984	.4985	.4985	.4986	.4986
3.0	.4987	.4987	.4987	.4988	.4988	.4989	.4989	.4989	.4990	.4990

SOLUTIONS TO SELF-TEST PROBLEMS

Note: Except for Chapter 1, we do not show an answer for ST-1 problems because they are verbal rather than quantitative in nature.

CHAPTER 1

ST-1   Refer to the marginal glossary definitions or relevant chapter sections to check your responses.

CHAPTER 2

ST-2   a.

EBIT	$5,000,000
Interest	1,000,000
EBT	$4,000,000
Taxes (40%)	1,600,000
Net income	$2,400,000

b.
$$\text{NCF} = \text{NI} + \text{DEP}$$
$$= \$2,400,000 + \$1,000,000 = \$3,400,000.$$

c.
$$\text{OCF} = \text{EBIT} (1 - T) + \text{DEP}$$
$$= \$5,000,000 (0.6) + \$1,000,000$$
$$= \$4,000,000.$$

d.
$$\text{EVA} = \text{EBIT} (1 - T) - (\text{Total capital}) (\text{After-tax cost of capital})$$
$$= \$5,000,000 (0.6) - (\$25,000,000) (0.10)$$
$$= \$3,000,000 - \$2,500,000 = \$500,000.$$

ST-3

Henderson's Taxes as a Corporation	1998	1999	2000
Income before salary and taxes	$52,700	$90,000	$150,000
Less: salary	(40,000)	(40,000)	(40,000)
Taxable income, corporate	$12,700	$50,000	$110,000
Total corporate tax	1,905[a]	7,500	26,150
Salary	$40,000	$40,000	$ 40,000
Less exemptions and deductions	(17,350)	(17,350)	(17,350)
Taxable personal income	$22,650	$22,650	$ 22,650
Total personal tax	3,398[b]	3,398	3,398
Combined corporate and personal tax:	$ 5,303	$10,898	$ 29,548
Henderson's Taxes as a Proprietorship			
Total income	$52,700	$90,000	$150,000
Less: exemptions and deductions	(17,350)	(17,350)	(17,350)
Taxable personal income	$35,350	$72,650	$132,650
Tax liability of proprietorship	$ 5,303[c]	$15,129	$ 33,002
Advantage to being a corporation:	$ 0	$ 4,232	$ 3,454

[a]Corporate tax in 1998 = (0.15)($12,700) = $1,905.
[b]Personal tax (if Henderson incorporates) in 1998 = (0.15)($22,650) = $3,398.
[c]Proprietorship tax in 1998 = (0.15)($35,350) = $5,303.

Notice that in 1998, both the corporate form of organization and the proprietorship form have the same tax liability; however, in 1999 and 2000, the corporate form has the lower tax liability. Thus, the corporate form of organization allows Henderson to pay the lowest taxes in each year. Therefore, on the basis of taxes over the 3-year period, Henderson should incorporate her business. However, note that to get additional money out of the corporation so she can spend it, Henderson will have to have the corporation pay dividends, which will be taxed to Henderson, and thus she will, sometime in the future, have to pay additional taxes.

CHAPTER 3

ST-2 Billingsworth paid $2 in dividends and retained $2 per share. Since total retained earnings rose by $12 million, there must be 6 million shares outstanding. With a book value of $40 per share, total common equity must be $40(6 million) = $240 million. Since Billingsworth has $120 million of debt, its debt ratio must be 33.3 percent:

$$\frac{\text{Debt}}{\text{Assets}} = \frac{\text{Debt}}{\text{Debt} + \text{Equity}} = \frac{\$120 \text{ million}}{\$120 \text{ million} + \$240 \text{ million}}$$

$$= 0.333 = 33.3\%.$$

ST-3 a. In answering questions such as this, always begin by writing down the relevant definitional equations, then start filling in numbers. Note that the extra zeros indicating millions have been deleted in the calculations below.

(1)
$$\text{DSO} = \frac{\text{Accounts receivable}}{\text{Sales}/360}$$

$$40 = \frac{\text{A/R}}{\$1,000/360}$$

$$\text{A/R} = 40(\$2.778) = \$111.1 \text{ million.}$$

(2)
$$\text{Quick ratio} = \frac{\text{Current assets} - \text{Inventories}}{\text{Current liabilities}} = 2.0$$

$$= \frac{\text{Cash and marketable securities} + \text{A/R}}{\text{Current liabilities}} = 2.0$$

$$2.0 = \frac{\$100 + \$111.1}{\text{Current liabilities}}$$

$$\text{Current liabilities} = (\$100 + \$111.1)/2 = \$105.5 \text{ million.}$$

(3)
$$\text{Current ratio} = \frac{\text{Current assets}}{\text{Current liabilities}} = 3.0$$

$$= \frac{\text{Current assets}}{\$105.5} = 3.0$$

$$\text{Current assets} = 3.0(\$105.5) = \$316.50 \text{ million.}$$

(4)
$$\text{Total assets} = \text{Current assets} + \text{Fixed assets}$$

$$= \$316.5 + \$283.5 = \$600 \text{ million.}$$

(5)
$$\text{ROA} = \text{Profit margin} \times \text{Total assets turnover}$$

$$= \frac{\text{Net income}}{\text{Sales}} \times \frac{\text{Sales}}{\text{Total assets}}$$

$$= \frac{\$50}{\$1,000} \times \frac{\$1,000}{\$600}$$

$$= 0.05 \times 1.667 = 0.0833 = 8.33\%.$$

(6)
$$\text{ROE} = \text{ROA} \times \frac{\text{Assets}}{\text{Equity}}$$

$$12.0\% = 8.33\% \times \frac{\$600}{\text{Equity}}$$

$$\text{Equity} = \frac{(8.33\%)(\$600)}{12.0\%}$$

$$= \$416.50 \text{ million.}$$

(7)
$$\text{Total assets} = \text{Total claims} = \$600 \text{ million}$$

$$\text{Current liabilities} + \text{Long-term debt} + \text{Equity} = \$600 \text{ million}$$

$$\$105.5 + \text{Long-term debt} + \$416.5 = \$600 \text{ million}$$

$$\text{Long-term debt} = \$600 - \$105.5 - \$416.5 = \$78 \text{ million.}$$

Note: We could have found equity as follows:

$$\text{ROE} = \frac{\text{Net income}}{\text{Equity}}$$

$$12.0\% = \frac{\$50}{\text{Equity}}$$

$$\text{Equity} = \$50/0.12$$

$$= \$416.67 \text{ million (rounding difference).}$$

Then we could have gone on to find current liabilities and long-term debt.

b. Kaiser's average sales per day were $1,000/360 = \$2.8$ million. Its DSO was 40, so A/R $= 40(\$2.8) = \$111.1$ million. Its new DSO of 30 would cause A/R $= 30(\$2.8) = \$83.3$ million. The reduction in receivables would be $\$111.1 - \$83.3 = \$27.8$ million, which would equal the amount of cash generated.

(1)
$$\text{New equity} = \text{Old equity} - \text{Stock bought back}$$

$$= \$416.5 - \$27.8$$

$$= \$388.7 \text{ million.}$$

Thus,

$$\text{New ROE} = \frac{\text{Net income}}{\text{New equity}}$$

$$= \frac{\$50}{\$388.7}$$

$$= 12.86\% \text{ (versus old ROE of 12.0\%).}$$

(2)
$$\text{New ROA} = \frac{\text{Net income}}{\text{Total assets} - \text{Reduction in A/R}}$$

$$= \frac{\$50}{\$600 - \$27.8}$$

$$= 8.74\% \text{ (versus old ROA of 8.33\%).}$$

(3) The old debt is the same as the new debt:

$$\text{Debt} = \text{Total claims} - \text{Equity}$$

$$= \$600 - \$416.5 = \$183.5 \text{ million.}$$

$$\text{Old total assets} = \$600 \text{ million.}$$

$$\text{New total assets} = \text{Old total assets} - \text{Reduction in A/R}$$

$$= \$600 - \$27.8$$

$$= \$572.2 \text{ million.}$$

Therefore,

$$\frac{\text{Debt}}{\text{Old total assets}} = \frac{\$183.5}{\$600} = 30.6\%,$$

while

$$\frac{\text{New debt}}{\text{New total assets}} = \frac{\$183.5}{\$572.2} = 32.1\%.$$

CHAPTER 4

ST-2 a. Average = (4% + 5% + 6% + 7%)/4 = 22%/4 = 5.5%.
 b. $k_{\text{T-bond}}$ = k* + IP = 2% + 5.5% = 7.5%.
 c. If the 5-year T-bond rate is 8 percent, the inflation rate is expected to average approximately 8% − 2% = 6% during the next 5 years. Thus, the implied Year 5 inflation rate is 8 percent:

$$6\% - (4\% + 5\% + 6\% + 7\% + I_5)/5$$
$$30\% = 22\% + I_5$$
$$I_5 = 8\%.$$

CHAPTER 5

ST-2 a. The average rate of return for each stock is calculated simply by averaging the returns over the 5-year period. The average return for each stock is 18.90 percent, calculated for Stock A as follows:

$$k_{\text{Avg}} = (-10.00\% + 18.50\% + 38.67\% + 14.33\% + 33.00\%)/5$$
$$= 18.90\%.$$

The realized rate of return on a portfolio made up of Stock A and Stock B would be calculated by finding the average return in each year as k_A(% of Stock A) + k_B(% of Stock B) and then averaging these yearly returns:

YEAR	PORTFOLIO AB's RETURN, k_{AB}
1993	(6.50%)
1994	19.90
1995	41.46
1996	9.00
1997	30.65
k_{Avg} =	18.90%

 b. The standard deviation of returns is estimated, using Equation 5-3a, as follows (see Footnote 5):

$$\text{Estimated } \sigma = S = \sqrt{\frac{\sum_{t=1}^{n} (\bar{k}_t - \bar{k}_{\text{Avg}})^2}{n - 1}}. \qquad (5\text{-}3a)$$

For Stock A, the estimated σ is 19.0 percent:

$$\sigma_A = \sqrt{\frac{(-10.00 - 18.9)^2 + (18.50 - 18.9)^2 + \cdots + (33.00 - 18.9)^2}{5 - 1}}$$
$$= \sqrt{\frac{1,445.92}{4}} = 19.0\%.$$

The standard deviation of returns for Stock B and for the portfolio are similarly determined, and they are as follows:

	STOCK A	STOCK B	PORTFOLIO AB
Standard deviation	19.0	19.0	18.6

c. Since the risk reduction from diversification is small (σ_{AB} falls only from 19.0 to 18.6 percent), the most likely value of the correlation coefficient is 0.9. If the correlation coefficient were -0.9, the risk reduction would be much larger. In fact, the correlation coefficient between Stocks A and B is 0.92.

d. If more randomly selected stocks were added to a portfolio, σ_p would decline to somewhere in the vicinity of 20 percent; see Figure 5-8. σ_p would remain constant only if the correlation coefficient were $+1.0$, which is most unlikely. σ_p would decline to zero only if the correlation coefficient, r, were equal to zero and a large number of stocks were added to the portfolio, or if the proper proportions were held in a two-stock portfolio with $r = -1.0$.

ST-3   a.

$$b = (0.6)(0.70) + (0.25)(0.90) + (0.1)(1.30) + (0.05)(1.50)$$

$$= 0.42 + 0.225 + 0.13 + 0.075 = 0.85.$$

b.

$$k_{RF} = 6\%;\ RP_M = 5\%;\ b = 0.85.$$

$$k = 6\% + (5\%)(0.85)$$

$$= 10.25\%.$$

c.

$$b_N = (0.5)(0.70) + (0.25)(0.90) + (0.1)(1.30) + (0.15)(1.50)$$

$$= 0.35 + 0.225 + 0.13 + 0.225$$

$$= 0.93.$$

$$k = 6\% + (5\%)(0.93)$$

$$= 10.65\%.$$

CHAPTER 6

ST-2   a.

$1,000 is being compounded for 3 years, so your balance on January 1, 2002, is $1,259.71:

$$FV_n = PV(1 + i)^n = \$1,000(1 + 0.08)^3 = \$1,259.71.$$

Alternatively, using a financial calculator, input N = 3, I = 8, PV = -1000, PMT = 0, and FV = ? FV = $1,259.71.

b.

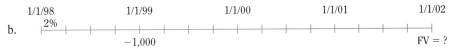

Use FVIF for 2%, 3 × 4 = 12 periods:

$$FV_{12} = \$1,000(FVIF_{2\%,12}) = \$1,000(1.2682) = \$1,268.20.$$

Alternatively, using a financial calculator, input N = 12, I = 2, PV = -1000, PMT = 0, and FV = ? FV = $1,268.24. (Note that since the interest factor is carried to only 4 decimal places, a rounding difference occurs.)

c.

1/1/98	8%	1/1/99	1/1/00	1/1/01	1/1/02
		250	250	250	250
					FV = ?

As you work this problem, keep in mind that the tables assume that payments are made at the end of each period. Therefore, you may solve this problem by finding the future value of an annuity of $250 for 4 years at 8 percent:

$$FVA_4 = PMT(FVIFA_{i,n}) = \$250(4.5061) = \$1,126.53.$$

Alternatively, using a financial calculator, input N = 4, I = 8, PV = 0, PMT = −250, and FV = ? FV = $1,126.53.

d.

1/1/98	8%	1/1/99	1/1/00	1/1/01	1/1/02
		?	?	?	?
					FV = 1,259.71

N = 4; I = 8; PV = 0; FV = 1259.71; PMT = ?; PMT = $279.56.

$$PMT(FVIFA_{8\%,4}) = FVA_4$$
$$PMT(4.5061) = \$1,259.71$$
$$PMT = \$1,259.71/4.5061 = \$279.56.$$

Therefore, you would have to make 4 payments of $279.56 each to have a balance of $1,259.71 on January 1, 2002.

ST-3   a. Set up a time line like the one in the preceding problem:

1/1/98	8%	1/1/99	1/1/00	1/1/01	1/1/02
		PV = ?			1,000

Note that your deposit will grow for 3 years at 8 percent. The fact that it is now January 1, 1998, is irrelevant. The deposit on January 1, 1999, is the PV, and the FV is $1,000. Here is the solution:

N = 3; I = 8; PMT = 0; FV = 1000; PV = ?; PV = $793.83.

$$FV_3(PVIF_{8\%,3}) = PV$$

PV = $1,000(0.7938) = $793.80 = Initial deposit to accumulate $1,000.

(Difference due to rounding.)

b.

1/1/98	8%	1/1/99	1/1/00	1/1/01	1/1/02
		?	?	?	?
					FV = 1,000

Here we are dealing with a 4-year annuity whose first payment occurs 1 year from today, on 1/1/99, and whose future value must equal $1,000. You should modify the time line to help visualize the situation. Here is the solution:

N = 4; I = 8; PV = 0; FV = 1000; PMT = ?; PMT = $221.92.

$$PMT(FVIFA_{8\%,4}) = FVA_4$$

$$PMT = \frac{FVA_4}{(FVIFA_{8\%,4})}$$

$$= \frac{\$1,000}{4.5061} = \$221.92 = \text{Payment necessary to accumulate } \$1,000.$$

c. This problem can be approached in several ways. Perhaps the simplest is to ask this question: "If I received $750 on 1/1/99 and deposited it to earn 8 percent, would I have the required $1,000 on 1/1/02?" The answer is no:

1/1/98	8%	1/1/99	1/1/00	1/1/01	1/1/02
		−750			FV = ?

$$FV_3 = \$750(1.08)(1.08)(1.08) = \$944.78.$$

This indicates that you should let your father make the payments rather than accept the lump sum of $750.

You could also compare the $750 with the PV of the payments:

$N = 4$; $I = 8$; $PMT = -221.92$; $FV = 0$; $PV = ?$; $PV = \$735.03$.

$$PMT(PVIFA_{8\%,4}) = PVA_4$$

$$\$221.92(3.3121) = \$735.02 = \text{Present value}$$
$$\text{of the required payments.}$$

(Difference due to rounding.)

This is less than the $750 lump sum offer, so your initial reaction might be to accept the lump sum of $750. However, this would be a mistake. The problem is that when you found the $735.02 PV of the annuity, you were finding the value of the annuity *today*, on January 1, 1998. You were comparing $735.02 today with the lump sum of $750 1 year from now. This is, of course, invalid. What you should have done was take the $735.02, recognize that this is the PV of an annuity as of January 1, 1998, multiply $735.02 by 1.08 to get $793.82, and compare $793.82 with the lump sum of $750. You would then take your father's offer to make the payments rather than take the lump sum on January 1, 1999.

d.

$N = 3$; $PV = -750$; $PMT = 0$; $FV = 1000$; $I = ?$; $I = 10.0642\%$.

$$PV(FVIF_{i,3}) = FV$$

$$FVIF_{i,3} = \frac{FV}{PV}$$

$$= \frac{\$1,000}{\$750} = 1.3333.$$

Use the Future Value of $1 table (Table A-3 in Appendix A) for 3 periods to find the interest rate corresponding to an FVIF of 1.3333. Look across the Period 3 row of the table until you come to 1.3333. The closest value is 1.3310, in the 10 percent column. Therefore, you would require an interest rate of approximately 10 percent to achieve your $1,000 goal. The exact rate required, found with a financial calculator, is 10.0642 percent.

e.

$N = 4$; $PV = 0$; $PMT = -186.29$; $FV = 1000$; $I = ?$; $I = 19.9997\%$.

$$PMT(FVIFA_{i,4}) = FVA_4$$

$$\$186.29(FVIFA_{i,4}) = \$1,000$$

$$FVIFA_{i,4} = \frac{\$1,000}{\$186.29} = 5.3680.$$

Using Table A-4 in Appendix A, we find that 5.3680 corresponds to a 20 percent interest rate. You might be able to find a borrower willing to offer you a 20 percent interest rate, but there would be some risk involved — he or she might not actually pay you your $1,000!

f.

1/1/98	4%	1/1/99		1/1/00		1/1/01		1/1/02
		400	?	?	?	?	?	?

FV = 1,000

Find the future value of the original $400 deposit:

$$FV_6 = PV(FVIF_{4\%,6}) = \$400(1.2653) = \$506.12.$$

This means that on January 1, 2002, you need an additional sum of $493.88:

$$\$1,000.00 - \$506.12 = \$493.88.$$

This will be accumulated by making 6 equal payments which earn 8 percent compounded semiannually, or 4 percent each 6 months:

$$N = 6; I = 4; PV = 0; FV = 493.88; PMT = ?; PMT = \$74.46.$$

$$PMT(FVIFA_{4\%,6}) = FVA_6$$

$$PMT = \frac{FVA_6}{(FVIFA_{4\%,6})}$$

$$= \frac{\$493.88}{6.6330} = \$74.46.$$

Alternatively, using a financial calculator, input $N = 6$, $I = 4$, $PV = -400$, $FV = 1000$, and $PMT = ?$ $PMT = \$74.46$.

g.

$$\text{Effective annual rate} = \left(1 + \frac{i_{Nom}}{m}\right)^m - 1.0$$

$$= \left(1 + \frac{0.08}{2}\right)^2 - 1 = (1.04)^2 - 1$$

$$= 1.0816 - 1 = 0.0816 = 8.16\%.$$

h. There is a reinvestment rate risk here because we assumed that funds will earn an 8 percent return in the bank. In fact, if interest rates in the economy fall, the bank will lower its deposit rate because it will be earning less when it lends out the funds you deposited with it. If you buy certificates of deposit (CDs) that mature on the date you need the money (1/1/02), you will avoid the reinvestment risk, but that would work only if you were making the deposit today. Other ways of reducing reinvestment rate risk will be discussed later in the text.

ST-4 Bank A's effective annual rate is 8.24 percent:

$$\text{Effective annual rate} = \left(1 + \frac{0.08}{4}\right)^4 - 1.0$$

$$= (1.02)^4 - 1 = 1.0824 - 1$$

$$= 0.0824 = 8.24\%.$$

Now Bank B must have the same effective annual rate:

$$\left(1 + \frac{i}{12}\right)^{12} - 1.0 = 0.0824$$

$$\left(1 + \frac{i}{12}\right)^{12} = 1.0824$$

$$1 + \frac{i}{12} = (1.0824)^{1/12}$$

$$1 + \frac{i}{12} = 1.00662$$

$$\frac{i}{12} = 0.00662$$

$$i = 0.07944 = 7.94\%.$$

Thus, the two banks have different quoted rates — Bank A's quoted rate is 8 percent, while Bank B's quoted rate is 7.94 percent; however, both banks have the same effective annual rate of 8.24 percent. The difference in their quoted rates is due to the difference in compounding frequency.

CHAPTER 7

ST-2   a. Pennington's bonds were sold at par; therefore, the original YTM equaled the coupon rate of 12%.

b.
$$V_B = \sum_{t=1}^{50} \frac{\$120/2}{\left(1 + \dfrac{0.10}{2}\right)^t} + \frac{\$1,000}{\left(1 + \dfrac{0.10}{2}\right)^{50}}$$

$$= \$60(PVIFA_{5\%,50}) + \$1,000(PVIF_{5\%,50})$$

$$= \$60(18.2559) + \$1,000(0.0872)$$

$$= \$1,095.35 + \$87.20 = \$1,182.55.$$

Alternatively, with a financial calculator, input the following: N = 50, I = 5, PMT = 60, FV = 1000, and PV = ? PV = $1,182.56.

c.
$$\text{Current yield} = \text{Annual coupon payment/Price}$$

$$= \$120/\$1,182.55$$

$$= 0.1015 = 10.15\%.$$

$$\text{Capital gains yield} = \text{Total yield} - \text{Current yield}$$

$$= 10\% - 10.15\% = -0.15\%.$$

d.
$$\$916.42 = \sum_{t=1}^{13} \frac{\$60}{(1 + k_d/2)^t} + \frac{\$1,000}{(1 + k_d/2)^{13}}.$$

Try $k_d = 14\%$:

$$V_B = INT(PVIFA_{7\%,13}) + M(PVIF_{7\%,13})$$

$$\$916.42 = \$60(8.3577) + \$1,000(0.4150)$$

$$= \$501.46 + \$415.00 = \$916.46.$$

Therefore, the YTM on July 1, 1997, was 14 percent. Alternatively, with a financial calculator, input the following: N = 13, PV = −916.42, PMT = 60, FV = 1000, and $k_d/2$ = I = ? Calculator solution = $k_d/2$ = 7.00%; therefore, k_d = 14.00%.

e.
$$\text{Current yield} = \$120/\$916.42 = 13.09\%.$$

$$\text{Capital gains yield} = 14\% - 13.09\% = 0.91\%.$$

f. The following time line illustrates the years to maturity of the bond:

| 1/1/97 | 7/1/97 | 1/1/98 | 7/1/98 | 1/1/99 | 12/31/03 |

3/1/97

Thus, on March 1, 1997, there were 13⅔ periods left before the bond matured. Bond traders actually use the following procedure to determine the price of the bond:

(1) Find the price of the bond on the next coupon date, July 1, 1997.

$$V_{B\ 7/1/97} = \$60(\text{PVIFA}_{7.75\%,13}) + \$1,000(\text{PVIF}_{7.75\%,13})$$
$$= \$60(8.0136) + \$1,000(0.3789)$$
$$= \$859.72.$$

Note that we could use a calculator to solve for $V_{B\ 7/1/97}$ or we could substitute $i = 7.75\%$ and $n = 13$ periods into the equations for PVIFA and PVIF:

$$\text{PVIFA} = \frac{1 - \dfrac{1}{(1 + i)^n}}{i} = \frac{1 - \dfrac{1}{(1 + 0.0775)^{13}}}{0.0775} = 8.0136.$$

$$\text{PVIF} = \frac{1}{(1 + k)^n} = \frac{1}{(1 + 0.0775)^{13}} = 0.3789.$$

(2) Add the coupon, $60, to the bond price to get the total value, TV, of the bond on the next interest payment date: TV = $859.72 + $60.00 = $919.72.

(3) Discount this total value back to the purchase date:

$$\text{Value at purchase date (March 1, 1997)} = \$919.72(\text{PVIF}_{7.75\%,4/6})$$
$$= \$919.72(0.9515)$$
$$= \$875.11.$$

Here

$$\text{PVIF}_{7.75\%,2/3} = \frac{1}{(1 + 0.0775)^{2/3}} = \frac{1}{1.0510} = 0.9515.$$

(4) Therefore, you would have written a check for $875.11 to complete the transaction. Of this amount, $20 = (⅓)($60) would represent accrued interest and $855.11 would represent the bond's basic value. This breakdown would affect both your taxes and those of the seller.

(5) This problem could be solved *very* easily using a financial calculator with a bond valuation function, such as the HP-12C or the HP-17B. This is explained in the calculator manual under the heading, "Bond Calculations."

ST-3 a. $100,000,000/10 = $10,000,000 per year, or $5 million each 6 months. Since the $5 million will be used to retire bonds immediately, no interest will be earned on it.

b. The debt service requirements will decline. As the amount of bonds outstanding declines, so will the interest requirements (amounts given in millions of dollars):

SEMIANNUAL PAYMENT PERIOD (1)	SINKING FUND PAYMENT (2)	OUTSTANDING BONDS ON WHICH INTEREST IS PAID (3)	INTEREST PAYMENT[a] (4)	TOTAL BOND SERVICE (2) + (4) = (5)
1	$5	$100	$6.0	$11.0
2	5	95	5.7	10.7
3	5	90	5.4	10.4
.	.	.	.	.
.	.	.	.	.
.	.	.	.	.
20	5	5	0.3	5.3

[a]Interest is calculated as (0.5)(0.12)(Column 3); for example: interest in Period 2 = (0.5)(0.12)($95) = $5.7.

The company's total cash bond service requirement will be \$21.7 million per year for the first year. The requirement will decline by $0.12(\$10,000,000) = \$1,200,000$ per year for the remaining years.

c. Here we have a 10-year, 9 percent annuity whose compound value is \$100 million, and we are seeking the annual payment, PMT. The solution can be obtained with a financial calculator. Input $N = 10$, $I = 9$, $PV = 0$, and $FV = 100000000$, and press the PMT key to obtain \$6,582,009.

We could also find the solution using this equation:

$$\$100,000,000 = \sum_{t=1}^{10} PMT(1 + k)^t$$

$$= PMT(FVIFA_{9\%,10})$$

$$= PMT(15.193)$$

$$PMT = \$6,581,979 = \text{sinking fund payment.}$$

The difference is due to rounding the FVIFA to 3 decimal places.

d. Annual debt service costs will be $\$100,000,000(0.12) + \$6,582,009 = \$18,582,009$.

e. If interest rates rose, causing the bond's price to fall, the company would use open market purchases. This would reduce its debt service requirements.

CHAPTER 8

ST-2 a. This is not necessarily true. Because G plows back two-thirds of its earnings, its growth rate should exceed that of D, but D pays higher dividends (\$6 versus \$2). We cannot say which stock should have the higher price.

b. Again, we just do not know which price would be higher.

c. This is false. The changes in k_d and k_s would have a greater effect on G; its price would decline more.

d. The total expected return for D is $\hat{k}_D = D_1/P_0 + g = 15\% + 0\% = 15\%$. The total expected return for G will have D_1/P_0 less than 15 percent and g greater than 0 percent, but $\hat{k}_G$ should be neither greater nor smaller than D's total expected return, 15 percent, because the two stocks are stated to be equally risky.

e. We have eliminated a, b, c, and d, so e should be correct. On the basis of the available information, D and G should sell at about the same price, \$40; thus, $\hat{k}_s = 15\%$ for both D and G. G's current dividend yield is $\$2/\$40 = 5\%$. Therefore, $g = 15\% - 5\% = 10\%$.

ST-3 The first step is to solve for g, the unknown variable, in the constant growth equation. Since D_1 is unknown but D_0 is known, substitute $D_0(1 + g)$ as follows:

$$\hat{P}_0 = P_0 = \frac{D_1}{k_s - g} = \frac{D_0(1 + g)}{k_s - g}$$

$$\$36 = \frac{\$2.40(1 + g)}{0.12 - g}.$$

Solving for g, we find the growth rate to be 5 percent:

$$\$4.32 - \$36g = \$2.40 + \$2.40g$$

$$\$38.4g = \$1.92$$

$$g = 0.05 = 5\%.$$

The next step is to use the growth rate to project the stock price 5 years hence:

$$\hat{P}_5 = \frac{D_0(1 + g)^6}{k_s - g}$$

$$= \frac{\$2.40(1.05)^6}{0.12 - 0.05}$$

$$= \$45.95.$$

[Alternatively, $\hat{P}_5 = \$36(1.05)^5 = \$45.95$.]

Therefore, Ewald Company's expected stock price 5 years from now, $\hat{P}_5$, is $45.95.

ST-4 a. (1) Calculate the PV of the dividends paid during the supernormal growth period:

$$D_1 = \$1.1500(1.15) = \$1.3225.$$

$$D_2 = \$1.3225(1.15) = \$1.5209.$$

$$D_3 = \$1.5209(1.13) = \$1.7186.$$

$$PV\ D = \$1.3225(0.8929) + \$1.5209(0.7972) + \$1.7186(0.7118)$$

$$= \$1.1809 + \$1.2125 + \$1.2233$$

$$= \$3.6167 \approx \$3.62.$$

(2) Find the PV of Snyder's stock price at the end of Year 3:

$$\hat{P}_3 = \frac{D_4}{k_s - g} = \frac{D_3(1 + g)}{k_s - g}$$

$$= \frac{\$1.7186(1.06)}{0.12 - 0.06}$$

$$= \$30.36.$$

$$PV\ \hat{P}_3 = \$30.36(0.7118) = \$21.61.$$

(3) Sum the two components to find the value of the stock today:

$$\hat{P}_0 = \$3.62 + \$21.61 = \$25.23.$$

Alternatively, the cash flows can be placed on a time line as follows:

Enter the cash flows into the cash flow register, I = 12, and press the NPV key to obtain $P_0 = \$25.23$.

b.
$$\hat{P}_1 = \$1.5209(0.8929) + \$1.7186(0.7972) + \$30.36(0.7972)$$

$$= \$1.3580 + \$1.3701 + \$24.2030$$

$$= \$26.9311 \approx \$26.93.$$

(Calculator solution: $26.93.)

$$\hat{P}_2 = \$1.7186(0.8929) + \$30.36(0.8929)$$

$$= \$1.5345 + \$27.1084$$

$$= \$28.6429 \approx \$28.64.$$

(Calculator solution: $28.64.)

c. YEAR	DIVIDEND YIELD	+	CAPITAL GAINS YIELD	=	TOTAL RETURN
1	$\dfrac{\$1.3225}{\$25.23} \approx 5.24\%$		$\dfrac{\$26.93 - \$25.23}{\$25.23} \approx 6.74\%$		$\approx 12\%$
2	$\dfrac{\$1.5209}{\$26.93} \approx 5.65\%$		$\dfrac{\$28.64 - \$26.93}{\$26.93} \approx 6.35\%$		$\approx 12\%$
3	$\dfrac{\$1.7186}{\$28.64} \approx 6.00\%$		$\dfrac{\$30.36 - \$28.64}{\$28.64} \approx 6.00\%$		$\approx 12\%$

CHAPTER 9

ST-2 a. A break point will occur when retained earnings are used up. Note that LEI has $24,000 of retained earnings:

$$\text{Retained earnings} = (\text{Total earnings})(1.0 - \text{Payout})$$
$$= \$34,285.72(0.7)$$
$$= \$24,000.$$

$$BP_{RE} = \frac{\text{Retained earnings}}{\text{Equity fraction}} = \frac{\$24,000}{0.6} = \$40,000.$$

b. Component costs are as follows:

$$k_s = \frac{D_1}{P_0} + g = \frac{D_0(1 + g)}{P_0} + g$$
$$= \frac{\$3.60(1.09)}{\$60} + 0.09$$
$$= 0.0654 + 0.09 \qquad\qquad = 15.54\%.$$

Common with F = 10%:

$$k_e = \frac{D_1}{P_0(1.0 - F)} + g = \frac{\$3.924}{\$60(0.9)} + 9\% \qquad\qquad = 16.27\%.$$

Preferred with F = 5%:

$$k_{ps} = \frac{\text{Preferred dividend}}{P_n} = \frac{\$11}{\$100(0.95)} \qquad\qquad = 11.58\%.$$

Debt at k_d = 12%:

$$k_d(1 - T) = 12\%(0.6) \qquad\qquad = 7.20\%.$$

c. WACC calculations within indicated total capital intervals:
   (1) $0 to $40,000 (debt = 7.2%, preferred = 11.58%, and retained earnings [RE] = 15.54%):

$$WACC_1 = w_d k_d(1 - T) + w_{ps}k_{ps} + w_{ce}k_s$$
$$= 0.25(7.2\%) + 0.15(11.58\%) + 0.60(15.54\%) = 12.86\%.$$

   (2) Over $40,000 (debt = 7.2%, preferred = 11.58%, and RE = 16.27%):

$$WACC_2 = 0.25(7.2\%) + 0.15(11.58\%) + 0.60(16.27\%) = 13.30\%.$$

d. See the graph of the MCC and IOS schedules for LEI on the next page.

e. LEI should accept Projects A, B, C, and D. It should reject Project E because its IRR does not exceed the marginal cost of funds needed to finance it.

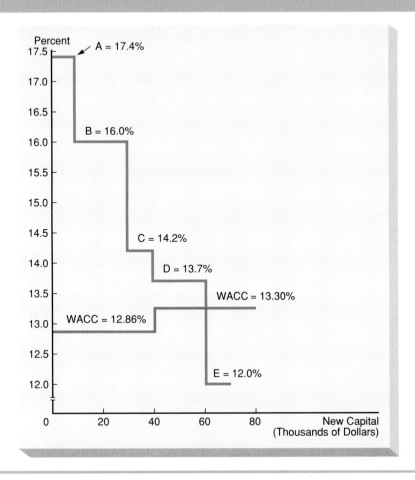

LEI: MCC and IOS Schedules

CHAPTER 10

ST-2   a. *Payback:*
To determine the payback, construct the cumulative cash flows for each project:

	CUMULATIVE CASH FLOWS	
YEAR	PROJECT X	PROJECT Y
0	($10,000)	($10,000)
1	(3,500)	(6,500)
2	(500)	(3,000)
3	2,500	500
4	3,500	4,000

$$\text{Payback}_X = 2 + \frac{\$500}{\$3,000} = 2.17 \text{ years.}$$

$$\text{Payback}_Y = 2 + \frac{\$3,000}{\$3,500} = 2.86 \text{ years.}$$

Net present value (NPV):

$$NPV_X = -\$10,000 + \frac{\$6,500}{(1.12)^1} + \frac{\$3,000}{(1.12)^2} + \frac{\$3,000}{(1.12)^3} + \frac{\$1,000}{(1.12)^4}$$

$$= \$966.01.$$

$$NPV_Y = -\$10,000 + \frac{\$3,500}{(1.12)^1} + \frac{\$3,500}{(1.12)^2} + \frac{\$3,500}{(1.12)^3} + \frac{\$3,500}{(1.12)^4}$$

$$= \$630.72.$$

Alternatively, using a financial calculator, input the cash flows into the cash flow register, enter I = 12, and then press the NPV key to obtain $NPV_X = \$966.01$ and $NPV_Y = \$630.72$.

Internal rate of return (IRR):
To solve for each project's IRR, find the discount rates which equate each NPV to zero:

$$IRR_X = 18.0\%.$$
$$IRR_Y = 15.0\%.$$

Modified internal rate of return (MIRR):
To obtain each project's MIRR, begin by finding each project's terminal value (TV) of cash inflows:

$$TV_X = \$6,500(1.12)^3 + \$3,000(1.12)^2$$
$$+ \$3,000(1.12)^1 + \$1,000 = \$17,255.23.$$
$$TV_Y = \$3,500(1.12)^3 + \$3,500(1.12)^2$$
$$+ \$3,500(1.12)^1 + \$3,500 = \$16,727.65.$$

Now, each project's MIRR is that discount rate which equates the PV of the TV to each project's cost, $10,000:

$$MIRR_X = 14.61\%.$$
$$MIRR_Y = 13.73\%.$$

b. The following table summarizes the project rankings by each method:

	PROJECT WHICH RANKS HIGHER
Payback	X
NPV	X
IRR	X
MIRR	X

Note that all methods rank Project X over Project Y. In addition, both projects are acceptable under the NPV, IRR, and MIRR criteria. Thus, both projects should be accepted if they are independent.

c. In this case, we would choose the project with the higher NPV at k = 12%, or Project X.

d. To determine the effects of changing the cost of capital, plot the NPV profiles of each project. The crossover rate occurs at about 6 to 7 percent (6.2%). See the graph on the next page.

If the firm's cost of capital is less than 6 percent, a conflict exists because $NPV_Y > NPV_X$, but $IRR_X > IRR_Y$. Therefore, if k were 5 percent, a conflict would exist. Note, however, that when k = 5.0%, $MIRR_X = 10.64\%$ and $MIRR_Y = 10.83\%$; hence, the modified IRR ranks the projects correctly, even if k is to the left of the crossover point.

e. The basic cause of the conflict is differing reinvestment rate assumptions between NPV and IRR. NPV assumes that cash flows can be reinvested at the cost of capital, while

NPV Profiles for Projects X and Y

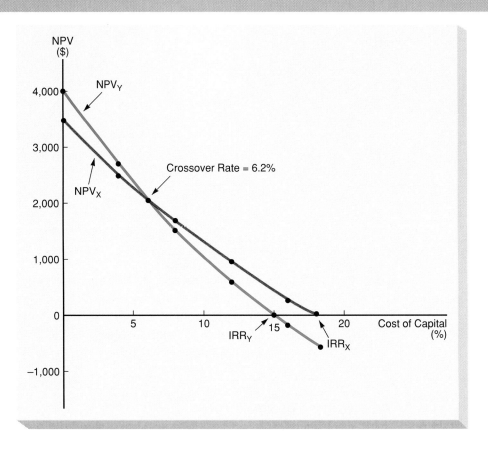

COST OF CAPITAL	NPV$_X$	NPV$_Y$
0%	$3,500	$4,000
4	2,545	2,705
8	1,707	1,592
12	966	631
16	307	(206)
18	5	(585)

IRR assumes reinvestment at the (generally) higher IRR. The high reinvestment rate assumption under IRR makes early cash flows especially valuable, and hence short-term projects look better under IRR.

CHAPTER 11

ST-2 a. *Estimated investment requirements:*

Price	($50,000)
Modification	(10,000)
Change in net working capital	(2,000)
Total investment	($62,000)

b. *Operating cash flows:*

	YEAR 1	YEAR 2	YEAR 3
1. After-tax cost savings[a]	$12,000	$12,000	$12,000
2. Depreciation[b]	19,800	27,000	9,000
3. Depreciation tax savings[c]	7,920	10,800	3,600
Operating cash flow (1 + 3)	$19,920	$22,800	$15,600

[a]$20,000 (1 − T).
[b]Depreciable basis = $60,000; the MACRS percentage allowances are 0.33, 0.45, and 0.15 in Years 1, 2, and 3, respectively; hence, depreciation in Year 1 = 0.33($60,000) = $19,800, and so on. There will remain $4,200, or 7 percent, undepreciated after Year 3; it would normally be taken in Year 4.
[c]Depreciation tax savings = T(Depreciation) = 0.4($19,800) = $7,920 in Year 1, and so on.

c. *Termination cash flow:*

Salvage value	$20,000
Tax on salvage value[a]	(6,320)
Net working capital recovery	2,000
Termination cash flow	$15,680

[a]Sales price	$20,000
Less book value	4,200
Taxable income	$15,800
Tax at 40%	$ 6,320

Book value = Depreciable basis − Accumulated depreciation
= $60,000 − $55,800 = $4,200.

d. *Project NPV:*

$$\text{NPV} = -\$62,000 + \frac{\$19,920}{(1.10)^1} + \frac{\$22,800}{(1.10)^2} + \frac{\$31,280}{(1.10)^3}$$

$$= -\$1,547.$$

Alternatively, using a financial calculator, input the cash flows into the cash flow register, enter I = 10, and then press the NPV key to obtain NPV = −$1,547. Because the earthmover has a negative NPV, it should not be purchased.

ST-3   *First determine the net cash flow at t = 0:*

Purchase price	($8,000)
Sale of old machine	3,000
Tax on sale of old machine	(160)[a]
Change in net working capital	(1,500)[b]
Total investment	($6,660)

[a]The market value is $3,000 − $2,600 = $400 above the book value. Thus, there is a $400 recapture of depreciation, and Dauten would have to pay 0.40($400) = $160 in taxes.
[b]The change in net working capital is a $2,000 increase in current assets minus a $500 increase in current liabilities, which totals to $1,500.

Now, examine the operating cash inflows:

Sales increase	$1,000
Cost decrease	1,500
Increase in pre-tax operating revenues	$2,500

After-tax operating revenue increase:

$$\$2,500(1 - T) = \$2,500(0.60) = \$1,500.$$

Depreciation:

YEAR	1	2	3	4	5	6
New[a]	$1,600	$2,560	$1,520	$ 960	$ 880	$ 480
Old	350	350	350	350	350	350
Change	$1,250	$2,210	$1,170	$ 610	$ 530	$ 130
Depreciation						
Tax savings[b]	$ 500	$ 884	$ 468	$ 244	$ 212	$ 52

[a]Depreciable basis = $8,000. Depreciation expense in each year equals depreciable basis times the MACRS percentage allowances of 0.20, 0.32, 0.19, 0.12, 0.11, and 0.06 in Years 1–6, respectively.
[b]Depreciation tax savings = T(Δ Depreciation) = 0.4(Δ Depreciation).

Now recognize that at the end of Year 6 Dauten would recover its net working capital investment of $1,500, and it would also receive $800 from the sale of the replacement machine. However, since the machine would be fully depreciated, the firm must pay 0.40($800) = $320 in taxes on the sale. Also, by undertaking the replacement now, the firm forgoes the right to sell the old machine for $500 in Year 6; thus, this $500 in Year 6 must be considered an opportunity cost in that year. No tax would be due because the $500 salvage value would equal the old machine's Year 6 book value.

Finally, place all the cash flows on a time line:

	0	1	2	3	4	5	6
Net investment	(6,660)						
After-tax revenue increase		1,500	1,500	1,500	1,500	1,500	1,500
Depreciation tax savings		500	884	468	244	212	52
Working capital recovery							1,500
Salvage value of new machine							800
Tax on salvage value of new machine							(320)
Opportunity cost of old machine							(500)
Net cash flows	(6,660)	2,000	2,384	1,968	1,744	1,712	3,032

The net present value of this incremental cash flow stream, when discounted at 15 percent, is $1,335. Thus, the replacement should be made.

CHAPTER 12

ST-2   a. First, find the expected cash flows:

YEAR	EXPECTED CASH FLOWS			
0	0.2(−$100,000)	+ 0.6(−$100,000)	+ 0.2(−$100,000)	= ($100,000)
1	0.2($20,000)	+ 0.6($30,000)	+ 0.2($40,000)	= $30,000
2				$30,000
3				$30,000
4				$30,000
5				$30,000
5*	0.2($0)	+ 0.6($20,000)	+ 0.2($30,000)	= $18,000

```
  0        1        2        3        4        5
 ├─10%─────┼────────┼────────┼────────┼────────┤
-100,000  30,000   30,000   30,000   30,000   48,000
```

Next, determine the NPV based on the expected cash flows:

$$NPV = -\$100,000 + \frac{\$30,000}{(1.10)^1} + \frac{\$30,000}{(1.10)^2} + \frac{\$30,000}{(1.10)^3}$$

$$+ \frac{\$30,000}{(1.10)^4} + \frac{\$48,000}{(1.10)^5} = \$24,900.$$

Alternatively, using a financial calculator, input the cash flows in the cash flow register, enter I = 10, and then press the NPV key to obtain NPV = $24,900.

b. For the worst case, the cash flow values from the cash flow column farthest on the left are used to calculate NPV:

```
  0        1        2        3        4        5
 ├─10%─────┼────────┼────────┼────────┼────────┤
-100,000  20,000   20,000   20,000   20,000   20,000
```

$$NPV = -\$100,000 + \frac{\$20,000}{(1.10)^1} + \frac{\$20,000}{(1.10)^2} + \frac{\$20,000}{(1.10)^3}$$

$$+ \frac{\$20,000}{(1.10)^4} + \frac{\$20,000}{(1.10)^5} = -\$24,184.$$

Similarly, for the best case, use the values from the column farthest on the right. Here the NPV is $70,259.

If the cash flows are perfectly dependent, then the low cash flow in the first year will mean a low cash flow in every year. Thus, the probability of the worst case occurring is the probability of getting the $20,000 net cash flow in Year 1, or 20 percent. If the cash flows are independent, the cash flow in each year can be low, high, or average, and the probability of getting all low cash flows will be

$$0.2(0.2)(0.2)(0.2)(0.2) = 0.2^5 = 0.00032 = 0.032\%.$$

c. The base-case NPV is found using the most likely cash flows and is equal to $26,142. This value differs from the expected NPV of $24,900 because the Year 5 cash flows are not symmetric. Under these conditions, the NPV distribution is as follows:

P	NPV
0.2	($24,184)
0.6	26,142
0.2	70,259

Thus, the expected NPV is 0.2(−$24,184) + 0.6($26,142) + 0.2($70,259) = $24,900. As is generally the case, the expected NPV is the same as the NPV of the expected cash flows found in Part a. The standard deviation is $29,904:

$$\sigma^2_{NPV} = 0.2(-\$24,184 - \$24,900)^2 + 0.6(\$26,142 - \$24,900)^2$$

$$+ 0.2(\$70,259 - \$24,900)^2$$

$$= \$894,261,126.$$

$$\sigma_{NPV} = \sqrt{\$894,261,126} = \$29,904.$$

The coefficient of variation, CV, is $29,904/$24,900 = 1.20.

d. Since the project's coefficient of variation is 1.20, the project is riskier than average, and hence the project's risk-adjusted cost of capital is 10% + 2% = 12%. The project now should be evaluated by finding the NPV of the expected cash flows, as in Part a, but using a 12 percent discount rate. The risk-adjusted NPV is $18,357, and, therefore, the project, should be accepted.

ST-3 a. *Cost using retained earnings:*

$$k_s = \hat{k}_s = \frac{D_1}{P_0} + g = \frac{(\$1.85)(1.08)}{\$50} + 0.08 = 12.0\%.$$

$$WACC_1 = 0.3(8\%)(0.6) + 0.7(12.0\%) = 9.84\%.$$

Cost using new common stock:

$$k_e = \hat{k}_e = \frac{D_1}{P_0(1 - F)} + g = \frac{(\$1.85)(1.08)}{(\$50)(0.85)} + 0.08 = 12.7\%.$$

$$WACC_2 = 0.3(8\%)(0.6) + 0.7(12.7\%) = 10.33\%.$$

Break point:

$$\text{Break point} = \frac{\$105,000(0.5)}{0.7} = \$75,000.$$

b. The MCC and IOS schedules are shown next:

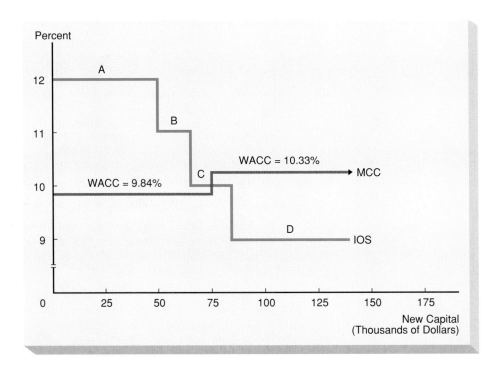

c. From this graph, we conclude that the firm should definitely undertake Projects A and B, assuming that these projects have about "average risk" in relation to the rest of the firm. Now, to evaluate Project C, recognize that one half of its capital would cost 9.84 percent, while the other half would cost 10.33 percent. Thus, the cost of the capital required for Project C is 10.09 percent:

$$0.5(9.84\%) + 0.5(10.33\%) = 10.09\%.$$

Since the cost is greater than Project C's return of 10 percent, the firm should not accept Project C.

d. The solution implicitly assumes (1) that all of the projects are equally risky and (2) that these projects are as risky as the firm's existing assets. If the accepted projects (A and B) were of above-average risk, this could raise the company's overall risk, and hence its cost of capital. Taking on these projects could result in a decline in the company's value.

e. If the payout ratio were lowered to zero, this would shift the break point to the right, from $75,000 to $150,000:

$$\text{Break point} = \frac{\$105,000(1.0)}{0.7} = \$150,000.$$

As the problem is set up, this would make Project C acceptable. If the payout were changed to 100 percent, the break point would shift to the left, from $75,000 to $0:

$$\text{Break point} = \frac{\$105,000(0.0)}{0.7} = \$0.$$

The optimal capital budget would still consist of Projects A and B. This assumes that the change in payout would not affect k_s or k_d; as we shall see in Chapter 14, this assumption may not be correct.

CHAPTER 13

ST-2 a.

EBIT	$4,000,000
Interest ($2,000,000 × 0.10)	200,000
Earnings before taxes (EBT)	$3,800,000
Taxes (35%)	1,330,000
Net income	$2,470,000

$$\text{EPS} = \$2,470,000/600,000 = \$4.12.$$
$$P_0 = \$4.12/0.15 = \$27.47.$$

b.
$$\text{Equity} = 600,000 \times (\$10) = \$6,000,000.$$
$$\text{Debt} = \$2,000,000.$$
$$\text{Total capital} = \$8,000,000.$$
$$\text{WACC} = w_d k_d (1 - T) + w_{ce} k_s$$
$$= (2/8)(10\%)(1 - 0.35) + (6/8)(15\%)$$
$$= 1.63\% + 11.25\%$$
$$= 12.88\%.$$

c.

EBIT	$4,000,000
Interest ($10,000,000 × 0.12)	1,200,000
Earnings before taxes (EBT)	$2,800,000
Taxes (35%)	980,000
Net income	$1,820,000

Shares bought and retired:

$$\Delta N = \Delta \text{Debt}/P_0 = \$8,000,000/\$27.47 = 291,227.$$

New outstanding shares:

$$N_1 = N_0 - \Delta N = 600,000 - 291,227 = 308,773.$$

New EPS:

$$\text{EPS} = \$1,820,000/308,773 = \$5.89.$$

New price per share:

$$P_0 = \$5.89/0.17 = \$34.65 \text{ versus } \$27.47.$$

Therefore, Gentry should change its capital structure.

d. In this case, the company's net income would be higher by $(0.12 - 0.10)$ ($2,000,000)(1 - 0.35) = \$26,000$ because its interest charges would be lower. The new price would be

$$P_0 = \frac{(\$1,820,000 + \$26,000)/308,773}{0.17} = \$35.18.$$

In the first case, in which debt had to be refunded, the bondholders were compensated for the increased risk of the higher debt position. In the second case, the old bondholders were not compensated; their 10 percent coupon perpetual bonds would now be worth

$$\$100/0.12 = \$833.33,$$

or $1,666,667 in total, down from the old $2 million, or a loss of $333,333. The stockholders would have a gain of

$$(\$35.18 - \$34.65)(308,773) = \$163,650.$$

This gain would, of course, be at the expense of the old bondholders. (There is no reason to think that bondholders' losses would exactly offset stockholders' gains.)

e.
$$\text{TIE} = \frac{\text{EBIT}}{\text{I}}.$$

$$\text{Original TIE} = \frac{\$4,000,000}{\$200,000} = 20 \text{ times.}$$

$$\text{New TIE} = \frac{\$4,000,000}{\$1,200,000} = 3.33 \text{ times.}$$

ST-3 a. (1) Determine the variable cost per unit at present, using the following definitions and equations:

$$Q = \text{units of output (sales)} = 5,000.$$
$$P = \text{average sales price per unit of output} = \$100.$$
$$F = \text{fixed operating costs} = \$200,000.$$
$$V = \text{variable costs per unit.}$$
$$\text{EBIT} = P(Q) - F - V(Q)$$
$$\$50,000 = \$100(5,000) - \$200,000 - V(5,000)$$
$$5,000V = \$250,000$$
$$V = \$50.$$

(2) Determine the new EBIT level if the change is made:

$$\text{New EBIT} = P_2(Q_2) - F_2 - V_2(Q_2)$$
$$= \$95(7,000) - \$250,000 - \$40(7,000)$$
$$= \$135,000.$$

(3) Determine the incremental EBIT:

$$\Delta\text{EBIT} = \$135,000 - \$50,000 = \$85,000.$$

(4) Estimate the approximate rate of return on the new investment:

$$\Delta\text{ROA} = \frac{\Delta\text{EBIT}}{\text{Investment}} = \frac{\$85,000}{\$400,000} = 21.25\%.$$

Since the ROA exceeds Olinde's average cost of capital, this analysis suggests that Olinde should go ahead and make the investment.

b. The change would increase the breakeven point. Still, with a lower sales price, it might be easier to achieve the higher new breakeven volume.

$$Old: Q_{BE} = \frac{F}{P - V} = \frac{\$200,000}{\$100 - \$50} = 4,000 \text{ units.}$$

$$New: Q_{BE} = \frac{F}{P_2 - V_2} = \frac{\$250,000}{\$95 - \$40} = 4,545 \text{ units.}$$

c. The incremental ROA is:

$$ROA = \frac{\Delta Profit}{\Delta Sales} \times \frac{\Delta Sales}{\Delta Assets}.$$

Using debt financing, the incremental profit associated with the investment is equal to the incremental profit found in Part a minus the interest expense incurred as a result of the investment:

$$\Delta Profit = New \text{ profit} - Old \text{ profit} - Interest$$
$$= \$135,000 - \$50,000 - 0.10(\$400,000)$$
$$= \$45,000.$$

The incremental sales is calculated as:

$$\Delta Sales = P_2 Q_2 - P_1 Q_1$$
$$= \$95(7,000) - \$100(5,000)$$
$$= \$665,000 - \$500,000$$
$$= \$165,000.$$

$$ROA = \frac{\$45,000}{\$165,000} \times \frac{\$165,000}{\$400,000} = 11.25\%.$$

The return on the new equity investment still exceeds the average cost of capital, so Olinde should make the investment.

CHAPTER 14

ST-2   a.

Projected net income	$2,000,000
Less projected capital investments	800,000
Available residual	$1,200,000
Shares outstanding	200,000

$$DPS = \$1,200,000/200,000 \text{ shares} = \$6 = D_1.$$

b. $EPS = \$2,000,000/200,000 \text{ shares} = \$10.$

Payout ratio $= DPS/EPS = \$6/\$10 = 60\%$, or

Total dividends/NI $= \$1,200,000/\$2,000,000 = 60\%$.

c. $$Currently, P_0 = \frac{D_1}{k_s - g} = \frac{\$6}{0.14 - 0.05} = \frac{\$6}{0.09} = \$66.67.$$

Under the former circumstances, D_1 would be based on a 20 percent payout on $10 EPS, or $2. With $k_s = 14\%$ and $g = 12\%$, we solve for P_0:

$$P_0 = \frac{D_1}{k_s - g} = \frac{\$2}{0.14 - 0.12} = \frac{\$2}{0.02} = \$100.$$

Although CMC has suffered a severe setback, its existing assets will continue to provide a good income stream. More of these earnings should now be passed on to the shareholders, as the slowed internal growth has reduced the need for funds. However, the net result is a 33 percent decrease in the value of the shares.

d. If the payout ratio were continued at 20 percent, even after internal investment opportunities had declined, the price of the stock would drop to $2/(0.14 − 0.06) = $25 rather than to $66.67. Thus, an increase in the dividend payout is consistent with maximizing shareholder wealth.

Because of the downward-sloping IOS curve (see Figure 14-4), the greater the firm's level of investment, the lower the average ROE. Thus, the more money CMC retains and invests, the lower its average ROE will be. We can determine the average ROE under different conditions as follows:

Old situation (with founder active and a 20 percent payout):

$$g = (1.0 − \text{Payout ratio})(\text{Average ROE})$$

$$12\% = (1.0 − 0.2)(\text{Average ROE})$$

$$\text{Average ROE} = 12\%/0.8 = 15\% > k_s = 14\%.$$

Note that the *average* ROE is 15 percent, whereas the *marginal* ROE is presumably equal to 14 percent. In terms of a graph like Figure 14-4, the intersection of the MCC and IOS curves would be 14 percent, and the average of the IOS curve above the intersection would be 15 percent.

New situation (with founder retired and a 60 percent payout):

$$g = 6\% = (1.0 − 0.6)(\text{ROE})$$

$$\text{ROE} = 6\%/0.4 = 15\% > k_s = 14\%.$$

This suggests that the new payout is appropriate and that the firm is taking on investments down to the point at which marginal returns are equal to the cost of capital. In terms of a graph like Figure 14-4, the IOS curve shifted to the left after the founder retired. Note that if the 20 percent payout was maintained, the *average* ROE would be only 7.5 percent, which would imply a marginal ROE far below the 14 percent cost of capital.

CHAPTER 15

ST-2   To solve this problem, we will define ΔS as the change in sales and g as the growth rate in sales, and then we use the three following equations:

$$\Delta S = S_0 g.$$

$$S_1 = S_0(1 + g).$$

$$\text{AFN} = (A^*/S_0)(\Delta S) − (L^*/S_0)(\Delta S) − MS_1(1 − d).$$

Set AFN = 0, substitute in known values for A^*/S_0, L^*/S_0, M, d, and S_0, and then solve for g:

$$0 = 1.6(\$100g) − 0.4(\$100g) − 0.10[\$100(1 + g)](0.55)$$

$$= \$160g − \$40g − 0.055(\$100 + \$100g)$$

$$= \$160g − \$40g − \$5.5 − \$5.5g$$

$$\$114.5g = \$5.5$$

$$g = \$5.5/\$114.5 = 0.048 = 4.8\%$$

$$= \text{Maximum growth rate without external financing.}$$

ST-3   Assets consist of cash, marketable securities, receivables, inventories, and fixed assets. Therefore, we can break the A^*/S_0 ratio into its components — cash/sales, inventories/sales, and so forth. Then,

$$\frac{A^*}{S_0} = \frac{A^* − \text{Inventories}}{S_0} + \frac{\text{Inventories}}{S_0} = 1.6.$$

We know that the inventory turnover ratio is sales/inventories = 3 times, so inventories/sales = 1/3 = 0.3333. Further, if the inventory turnover ratio can be increased to 4 times, then the inventory/sales ratio will fall to 1/4 = 0.25, a difference of 0.3333 − 0.2500 = 0.0833. This, in turn, causes the A^*/S_0 ratio to fall from $A^*/S_0 = 1.6$ to $A^*/S_0 = 1.6 − 0.0833 = 1.5167$.

This change has two effects: First, it changes the AFN equation, and second, it means that Weatherford currently has excessive inventories. Because it is costly to hold excess inventories, Weatherford will want to reduce its inventory holdings by not replacing inventories until the excess amounts have been used. We can account for this by setting up the revised AFN equation (using the new A^*/S_0 ratio), estimating the funds that will be needed next year if no excess inventories are currently on hand, and then subtracting out the excess inventories which are currently on hand:

Present conditions:

$$\frac{\text{Sales}}{\text{Inventories}} = \frac{\$100}{\text{Inventories}} = 3,$$

so

$$\text{Inventories} = \$100/3 = \$33.3 \text{ million at present.}$$

New conditions:

$$\frac{\text{Sales}}{\text{Inventories}} = \frac{\$100}{\text{Inventories}} = 4,$$

so

$$\text{New level of inventories} = \$100/4 = \$25 \text{ million.}$$

Therefore,

$$\text{Excess inventories} = \$33.3 − \$25 = \$8.3 \text{ million.}$$

Forecast of funds needed, first year:

$$\Delta S \text{ in first year} = 0.2(\$100 \text{ million}) = \$20 \text{ million.}$$
$$\text{AFN} = 1.5167(\$20) − 0.4(\$20) − 0.1(0.55)(\$120) − \$8.3$$
$$= \$30.3 − \$8 − \$6.6 − \$8.3$$
$$= \$7.4 \text{ million.}$$

Forecast of funds needed, second year:

$$\Delta S \text{ in second year} = gS_1 = 0.2(\$120 \text{ million}) = \$24 \text{ million.}$$
$$\text{AFN} = 1.5167(\$24) − 0.4(\$24) − 0.1(0.55)(\$144)$$
$$= \$36.4 − \$9.6 − \$7.9$$
$$= \$18.9 \text{ million.}$$

CHAPTER 16

ST-2   THE CALGARY COMPANY: ALTERNATIVE BALANCE SHEETS

	RESTRICTED (40%)	MODERATE (50%)	RELAXED (60%)
Current assets	$1,200,000	$1,500,000	$1,800,000
Fixed assets	600,000	600,000	600,000
Total assets	$1,800,000	$2,100,000	$2,400,000
Debt	$ 900,000	$1,050,000	$1,200,000
Equity	900,000	1,050,000	1,200,000
Total liabilities and equity	$1,800,000	$2,100,000	$2,400,000

THE CALGARY COMPANY: ALTERNATIVE INCOME STATEMENTS

	RESTRICTED	MODERATE	RELAXED
Sales	$3,000,000	$3,000,000	$3,000,000
EBIT	450,000	450,000	450,000
Interest (10%)	90,000	105,000	120,000
Earnings before taxes	$ 360,000	$ 345,000	$ 330,000
Taxes (40%)	144,000	138,000	132,000
Net income	$ 216,000	$ 207,000	$ 198,000
ROE	24.0%	19.7%	16.5%

ST-3 a. First, determine the balance on the firm's checkbook and the bank's records as follows:

	FIRM'S CHECKBOOK	BANK'S RECORDS
Day 1: Deposit $500,000; write check for $1,000,000	($500,000)	$500,000
Day 2: Write check for $1,000,000	($1,500,000)	$500,000
Day 3: Write check for $1,000,000	($2,500,000)	$500,000
Day 4: Write check for $1,000,000; deposit $1,000,000	($2,500,000)	$500,000

After Upton has reached a steady state, it must deposit $1,000,000 each day to cover the checks written 3 days earlier.

b. The firm has 3 days of float; not until Day 4 does the firm have to make any additional deposits.

c. As shown above, Upton should try to maintain a balance on the bank's records of $500,000. On its own books it will have a balance of *minus* $2,500,000.

CHAPTER 17

ST-2 a. and b.

INCOME STATEMENTS FOR YEAR ENDED DECEMBER 31, 1997 (THOUSANDS OF DOLLARS)

	VANDERHEIDEN PRESS		HERRENHOUSE PUBLISHING	
	a	b	a	b
EBIT	$ 30,000	$ 30,000	$ 30,000	$ 30,000
Interest	12,400	14,400	10,600	18,600
Taxable income	$ 17,600	$ 15,600	$ 19,400	$ 11,400
Taxes (40%)	7,040	6,240	7,760	4,560
Net income	$ 10,560	$ 9,360	$ 11,640	$ 6,840
Equity	$100,000	$100,000	$100,000	$100,000
Return on equity	10.56%	9.36%	11.64%	6.84%

The Vanderheiden Press has a higher ROE when short-term interest rates are high, whereas Herrenhouse Publishing does better when rates are lower.

c. Herrenhouse's position is riskier. First, its profits and return on equity are much more volatile than Vanderheiden's. Second, Herrenhouse must renew its large short-term loan every year, and if the renewal comes up at a time when money is very tight, when its business is depressed, or both, then Herrenhouse could be denied credit, which could put it out of business.

Chapter 20

ST-2   a. *Cost of leasing:*

	BEGINNING OF YEAR			
	0	**1**	**2**	**3**
Lease payment (AT)ᵃ	($ 6,000)	($6,000)	($6,000)	($6,000)
PVIFs (6%)ᵇ	1.000	0.9434	0.8900	0.8396
PV of leasing	($ 6,000)	($5,660)	($5,340)	($5,038)
Total PV cost of leasing =	($22,038)			

ᵃAfter-tax payment = $10,000(1 − T) = $10,000(0.60) = $6,000.
ᵇThis is the after-tax cost of debt: 10%(1 − T) = 10%(0.60) = 6.0%.

Alternatively, using a financial calculator, input the following data after switching your calculator to "BEG" mode: N = 4, I = 6, PMT = 6000, and FV = 0. Then press the PV key to arrive at the answer of ($22,038). Now, switch your calculator back to "END" mode.

b. *Cost of owning:*

$$\text{Depreciable basis} = \$40,000.$$

Here are the cash flows under the borrow-and-buy alternative:

	END OF YEAR				
	0	**1**	**2**	**3**	**4**
1. Depreciation schedule					
(a) Depreciable basis		$40,000	$40,000	$40,000	$40,000
(b) Allowance		0.33	0.45	0.15	0.07
(c) Depreciation		13,200	18,000	6,000	2,800
2. Cash flows					
(d) Net purchase price	($40,000)				
(e) Depreciation tax savings		5,280ᵃ	7,200	2,400	1,120
(f) Maintenance (AT)		(600)	(600)	(600)	(600)
(g) Salvage value (AT)					6,000
(h) Total cash flows	($40,000)	$ 4,680	$ 6,600	$ 1,800	$ 6,520
PVIFs	1.000	0.9434	0.8900	0.8396	0.7921
PV of owning	($40,000)	$ 4,415	$ 5,874	$ 1,511	$ 5,164
Total PV cost of owning =	($23,036)				

ᵃDepreciation (T) = $13,200(0.40) = $5,280.

Alternatively, input the cash flows for the individual years in the cash flow register and input I = 6, then press the NPV button to arrive at the answer of ($23,036). Because the present value of the cost of leasing is less than that of owning, the truck should be leased: $23,036 − $22,038 = $998, net advantage to leasing.

c. The discount rate is based on the cost of debt because most cash flows are fixed by contract and, consequently, are relatively certain. Thus, the lease cash flows have about the same risk as the firm's debt. Also, leasing is considered to be a substitute for debt. We use an after-tax cost rate because the cash flows are stated net of taxes.

d. Olsen could increase the discount rate on the salvage value cash flow. This would increase the PV cost of owning and make leasing even more advantageous.

APPENDIX C

ANSWERS TO END-OF-CHAPTER PROBLEMS

We present here some intermediate steps and final answers to selected end-of-chapter problems. Please note that your answer may differ slightly from ours due to rounding differences. Also, although we hope not, some of the problems may have more than one correct solution, depending upon what assumptions are made in working the problem. Finally, many of the problems involve some verbal discussion as well as numerical calculations; this verbal material is not presented here.

2-1 $1,000,000.

2-2 $3,600,000.

2-3 5.76%.

2-4 $21,950.

2-5 25%.

2-6 Tax = $107,855; NI = $222,145; Marginal tax rate = 39%; Average tax rate = 33.8%.

2-7 a. Tax = $3,575,000.
b. Tax = $350,000.
c. Tax = $105,000.

2-8 AT&T preferred stock = 5.37%.

2-9 Municipal bond; yield = 7%.

2-10 NI = $450,000; NCF = $650,000; OCF = $650,000.

2-11 a.

2-12 a. $584.
c. $1,520.

2-13 a. $2,400,000.

2-14 $2,500,000.

2-16 Tax_{1998} = $0; Tax_{2000} = $12,000,000; Tax_{2001} = $32,000,000; Tax_{2002} = $0 and receive refund of $44,000,000 for 2000 and 2001 taxes.

2-17 a. 1998 advantage as a corporation = $1,443; 1999 advantage = $4,693; 2000 advantage = $5,843.

2-18 a. Personal tax = $27,466.
c. Disney yield = 5.52%; choose FLA bonds.
d. 25%.

3-1 CL = $2,000,000; Inv = $1,000,000.

3-2 AR = $800,000.

3-3 D/A = 58.33%.

3-4 TATO = 5; EM = 1.5.

3-5 $\frac{NI}{S}$ = 2%; $\frac{D}{A}$ = 40%.

3-6 $262,500; 1.19×.

3-7 Sales = $2,592,000; DSO = 36 days.

3-8 TIE = 3.86×.

3-9 ROE = 23.1%.

3-10 7.2%.

3-11 a.

3-12 a. +5.54%.
b(2). +3.21%.
(3). +2.50%.

3-13 a. Current ratio = 1.98×; DSO = 75 days; Total assets turnover = 1.7×; Debt ratio = 61.9%.

3-14 A/P = $90,000; Inv = $90,000; FA = $138,000.

3-16 a. Quick ratio = 0.8×; DSO = 37 days; ROE = 13.1%; Debt ratio = 54.8%.

4-1 6%; 6.33%.

4-2 1.5%.

4-3 5.5%.

4-4 0.2%.

4-5 6.4%.

4-6 8.5%.

4-7 6.8%.

4-8 a. k_1 in Year 2 = 6%.

4-9 k_1 in Year 2 = 9%; Year 2 inflation = 7%.

4-10 1.5%.

4-11 6.0%.

4-12 a. k_1 = 9.20%; k_5 = 7.20%.

4-14 a. 8.20%.
b. 10.20%.
c. k_5 = 10.70%.

5-1 $\hat{k}$ = 11.40%; σ = 26.69%; CV = 2.34.

5-2 b = 1.12.

5-3 k_M = 11%; k = 12.2%.

5-4 k = 10.90%.

5-5 a. $\hat{k}_M = 13.5\%$; $\hat{k}_j = 11.6\%$.
 b. $\sigma_M = 3.85\%$; $\sigma_j = 6.22\%$.
 c. $CV_M = 0.29$; $CV_j = 0.54$.

5-6 a. $\hat{k}_Y = 14\%$.
 b. $\sigma_X = 12.20\%$.

5-7 a. $b_A = 1.40$.
 b. $k_A = 15\%$.

5-8 a. $k_i = 15.5\%$.
 b(1). $k_M = 15\%$; $k_i = 16.5\%$.
 c(1). $k_i = 18.1\%$.

5-9 $b_N = 1.16$.

5-10 $b_p = 0.7625$; $k_p = 12.1\%$.

5-11 $b_N = 1.1250$.

5-12 4.5%.

5-13 a. $0.5 million.

5-14 a. $k_i = 6\% + (5\%)b_i$.
 b. 15%.
 c. Indifference rate = 16%.

5-15 a. $\bar{k}_A = 11.30\%$.
 c. $\sigma_A = 20.8\%$; $\sigma_p = 20.1\%$.

5-16 a. $b_X = 1.3471$; $b_Y = 0.6508$.
 b. $k_X = 12.7355\%$; $k_Y = 9.254\%$.
 c. $k_p = 12.04\%$.

5A-1 a. $b = 0.62$.

5A-2 a. $b_A = 1.0$; $b_B = 0.5$.
 c. $k_A = 14\%$; $k_B = 11.5\%$.

6-1 $FV_5 = \$16,105.10$.

6-2 $PV = \$1,292.10$.

6-3 $n = 11.01$ years.

6-4 $i = 8.01\%$.

6-5 $FVA_5 = \$1,725.22$.

6-6 $FVA_{5\ Due} = \$1,845.99$.

6-7 $FVA_5 = \$1,725.22$.

6-8 $PV = \$923.98$; $FV = \$1,466.24$.

6-9 $i_{PER} = 2.25\%$; $i_{Nom} = 9\%$; EAR = 9.31%.

6-10 PMT = $444.89; EAR = 12.68%.

6-11 $1,000 today is worth more.

6-12 a. 15% (or 14.87%).

6-13 7.18%.

6-14 12%.

6-15 9%.

6-16 a. $33,872.
 b. $26,243.04 and $0.

6-17 $\approx$ 15 years.

6-18 6 years; $1,106.01.

6-19 $PV_{7\%} = \$1,428.57$; $PV_{14\%} = \$714.29$.

6-20 $893.16.

6-21 $984.88 $\approx$ $985.

6-22 57.18%.

6-23 a. FV = $1,432.02.
 b. PMT = $93.07.

6-24 $k_{Nom} = 15.19\%$.

6-25 PMT = $36,948.95 or $36,949.61.

6-26 a. $18.56 million.
 b. $86.49 million.
 c. PV = $17.18 million; FV = $80.08 million.

6-27 a. $666,669.35.
 b. $1,206,663.42.

6-28 $353,171.50.

6-29 $17,659.50.

6-30 $35.

6-31 $84.34.

6-32 a. $530.
 d. $445.

6-33 a. $895.40.
 b. $1,552.90.
 c. $279.20.
 d. $500.03; $867.14.

6-34 a. $\approx$ 10 years.
 c. $\approx$ 4 years.

6-35 a. $6,374.96.
 d(1). $7,012.46.

6-36 a. $2,457.84.
 c. $2,000.
 d(1). $2,703.62.

6-37 a. Stream A: $1,251.21.

6-38 b. 7%.
 c. 9%.
 d. 15%.

6-39 a. $881.15.
 b. $895.40.
 c. $903.05.
 d. $908.35.

6-40 a. $279.20.
 b. $276.85.
 c. $443.70.

6-41 a. $5,272.40.
b. $5,374.00.

6-42 a. 1st City = 7%; 2nd City = 6.14%.

6-43 a. PMT = $6,594.94.

6-44 a. Z = 9%; B= 8%.
b. Z = $558.39; $135.98; 32.2%; B = $1,147.20; $147.20; 14.72%.

6-45 a. $61,203.
b. $11,020.
c. $6,841.

7-1 $935.82.

7-2 12.48%.

7-3 YTM = 6.62%; YTC = 6.49%.

7-4 8.55%.

7-5 $1,028.60.

7-6 a. V_L at 5 percent = $1,518.97; V_L at 8 percent = $1,171.15; V_L at 12 percent = $863.79.

7-7 a. YTM at $829 $\approx$ 15%.

7-8 15.03%.

7-9 a. 10.37%.
b. 10.91%.
c. -0.54%.
d. 10.15%.

7-10 8.65%.

7-11 10.78%.

7-12 YTC = 6.47%.

7-13 a. $1,251.26.
b. $898.90.

7-15 a. YTM = 3.4%.
b. YTM $\approx$ 7%.
c. $934.91.

7-16 a. YTM = 8%; YTC = 6.1%.

7-17 10-year, 10% coupon = 6.75%;
10-year zero = 9.75%;
5-year zero = 4.76%;
30-year zero = 32.19%;
$100 perpetuity = 14.29%.

7-18 a. C_0 = $1,012.79; Z_0 = $693.04;
C_1 = $1,010.02; Z_1 = $759.57;
C_2 = $1,006.98; Z_2 = $832.49;
C_3 = $1,003.65; Z_3 = $912.41;
C_4 = $1,000.00; Z_4 = $1,000.00.

7A-1 5.4%.

7A-2 6.48%.

7A-3 12.37%.

7B-1 A/P = $816; First mortgage = $900; Subordinated debentures = $684; P/S = $0.

7B-2 a. Trustee = $281,250; N/P = $750,000; A/P = $375,000; Subordinated debentures = $750,000; Equity = $343,750.
b. Trustee = $281,250; N/P = $750,000; A/P = $318,750; Subordinated debentures = $525,000; Equity = $0.

8-1 D_1 = $1.5750; D_3 = $1.7364; D_5 = $2.1011.

8-2 P_0 = $6.25.

8-3 P_1 = $22.00; k_s = 15.50%.

8-4 k_{ps} = 8.33%.

8-5 $50.50.

8-6 g = 9%.

8-7 $\hat{P}_3$ = $27.32.

8-8 a. 13.3%.
b. 10%.
c. 8%.
d. 5.7%.

8-9 $23.75.

8-10 a. k_C = 10.6%; k_D = 7%.

8-11 $25.03.

8-12 P_0 = $19.89.

8-13 a. $125.
b. $83.33.

8-14 b. PV = $5.29.
d. $30.01.

8-15 a. 7%.
b. 5%.
c. 12%.

8-16 a(1). $9.50.
(2). $13.33.
b(1). Undefined.

8-18 a. Dividend 2000 = $2.66.
b. P_0 = $39.42.
c. Dividend yield 1998 = 5.10%; 2003 = 7.00%.

8-19 a. P_0 = $54.11.

8-20 a. P_0 = $21.43.
b. P_0 = $26.47.
d. P_0 = $40.54.

8-21 a. New price = $31.34.
b. beta = 0.49865.

9-1 $k_s = 13\%$.

9-2 $k_{ps} = 8\%$.

9-3 $k_s = 15\%$; $k_e = 16.11\%$.

9-4 $BP_{RE} = \$600,000$.

9-5 a. 13%.
b. 10.4%.
c. 8.45%.

9-6 7.80%.

9-7 11.94%.

9-8 a. $F = 10\%$.
b. $k_e = 15.8\%$.

9-9 $WACC = 12.72\%$.

9-10 $w_d = 20\%$.

9-11 a. $k_e = 14.40\%$.
b. $WACC = 10.62\%$.

9-12 7.2%.

9-13 $k_e = 16.51\%$.

9-14 a. 16.3%.
b. 15.4%.
c. 16%.

9-15 a. 8%.
b. \$2.81.
c. 15.81%.

9-16 a. \$18 million.
b. $BP_{RE} = \$45$ million.

9-17 a. $g = 3\%$.
b. $EPS_1 = \$5.562$.

9-18 a. \$67,500,000.
c. $k_s = 12\%$; $k_e = 12.4\%$.
d. \$27,000,000.
e. $WACC_1 = 9\%$; $WACC_2 = 9.2\%$.

9-19 a. $k_d(1 - T) = 5.4\%$; $k_s = 14.6\%$.
b. $WACC_1 = 10.92\%$.
d. $WACC_2 = 11.36\%$.

9-20 a. $BP_{RE} = \$2,000$.
b. $k_d = 7\%$; $k_{ps} = 10.20\%$; $k_s = 14.75\%$; $k_e = 15.72\%$.
c. $WACC_1 = 13.13\%$; $WACC_2 = 13.86\%$.
d. \$5,000.

10-1 4.34 years.

10-2 $NPV = \$7,486.20$.

10-3 $IRR = 16\%$.

10-4 $DPP = 6.51$ years.

10-5 $MIRR = 13.89\%$.

10-6 5%: $NPV_A = \$16,108,952$; $NPV_B = \$18,300,939$.
15%: $NPV_A = \$10,059,587$; $NPV_B = \$13,897,838$.

10-7 $NPV = \$174.90$.

10-8 $NPV_T = \$409$; $IRR_T = 15\%$; $MIRR_T = 14.54\%$; Accept;
$NPV_P = \$3,318$; $IRR_P = 20\%$; $MIRR_P = 17.19\%$;
Accept.

10-9 $NPV_E = \$3,861$; $IRR_E = 18\%$; $NPV_G = \$3,057$; $IRR_G = 18\%$; Purchase electric-powered forklift; it has a higher NPV.

10-10 $NPV_S = \$448.86$; $NPV_L = \$607.20$; $IRR_S = 15.24\%$;
$IRR_L = 14.67\%$; $MIRR_S = 14.67\%$; $MIRR_L = 14.37\%$.

10-11 b. $PV_C = -\$556,717$; $PV_F = -\$493,407$; Forklift should be chosen.

10-12 $MIRR_X = 13.59\%$.

10-13 $IRR_L = 11.74\%$.

10-14 $MIRR = 10.93\%$.

10-15 a. $NPV = \$136,578$; $IRR = 19.22\%$.

10-16 a. Payback = 0.33 year; $NPV = \$81,062.35$; $IRR = 261.90\%$.

10-17 a. No; $PV_{Old} = -\$89,910.08$; $PV_{New} = -\$94,611.45$.
b. \$2,470.80.
c. 22.94%.

10-18 b. $IRR_A = 18.1\%$; $IRR_B = 24.0\%$.
d(1). $MIRR_A = 15.10\%$; $MIRR_B = 17.03\%$.
(2). $MIRR_A = 18.05\%$; $MIRR_B = 20.49\%$.

10-19 a. $IRR_A = 20\%$; $IRR_B = 16.7\%$; Crossover rate $\approx$ 16%.

10-20 a. $NPV_A = \$14,486,808$; $NPV_B = \$11,156,893$;
$IRR_A = 15.03\%$; $IRR_B = 22.26\%$.

10-21 d. 9.54%; 22.87%.

10-22 a. A = 2.67 years; B = 1.5 years.
b. A = 3.07 years; B = 1.825 years.
d. $NPV_A = \$18,243,813$; choose A.
e. $NPV_B = \$8,643,390$; choose B.
f. 13.53%.
g. $MIRR_A = 21.93\%$; $MIRR_B = 20.96\%$.

11-1 \$12,000,000.

11-2 \$2,600,000.

11-3 \$4,600,000.

11-4 $NPV = \$15,301$; Buy the new machine.

11-5 $NPV = \$22,329$; Replace the old machine.

11-6 $NPV_{190-3} = \$20,070$; $NPV_{360-6} = \$22,256$.

11-7 $NPV_A = \$12.76$ million.

11-8 Machine A; Extended NPV_A = \$4.51 million; EAA_A = \$0.845 million.

11-9 a. −\$178,000.
b. \$52,440; \$60,600; \$40,200.
c. \$48,760.
d. NPV = −\$19,549; Do not purchase.

11-10 a. −\$126,000.
b. \$42,518; \$47,579; \$34,926.
c. \$50,702.
d. NPV = \$10,841; Purchase.

11-11 a. −\$88,500.
b. \$46,675; \$52,975; \$37,225; \$33,025; \$29,350.
c. −\$10,000.
d. NPV = \$42,407; Replace the old machine.

11-12 a. −\$792,750.
c. \$206,000; \$255,350; \$201,888; \$173,100; \$168,988.
d. \$118,925.
e. NPV = \$11,820; Purchase the new machine.

11A-1 PV = \$1,310,841.

11B-1 h. NPV = \$5,637,413.

11B-2 a. NPV = \$2,717,128.

12-1 E(NPV) = \$3 million; σ_{NPV} = \$23.622 million; CV_{NPV} = 7.874.

12-2 k_p = 8.5%; $b_{F, \text{New}}$ = 1.26; $k_{F, \text{new}}$ = 11.3%.

12-3 Accept Projects A, B, C, D, and E; Optimal capital budget = \$8 million.

12-4 Accept Projects A, B, D, and E; Optimal capital budget = \$6 million.

12-5 Accept Projects B, C, D, E, F, and G; Optimal capital budget = \$9 million.

12-6 a. 16%.
b. NPV = \$411; Accept.

12-7 a. 15%.
b. 1.48; 15.4%; 17%.

12-8 \$10 million.

12-9 \$42,000.

12-10 \$62,000.

12-11 a. Expected CF_A = \$6,750; Expected CF_B = \$7,650; CV_A = 0.0703.
b. NPV_A = \$10,037; NPV_B = \$11,624.

12-12 a. 14%.

12-13 NPV_5 = \$2,212; NPV_4 = −\$2,081; NPV_8 = \$13,329.

13-1 Q_{BE} = 500,000.

13-2 30% debt and 70% equity.

13-3 a(1). −\$75,000.
(2). \$175,000.
b. Q_{BE} = 140,000.

13-4 a(1). −\$60,000.
b. Q_{BE} = 14,000.

13-5 a(2). \$125,000.
b. Q_{BE} = 7,000.

13-6 a. P_0 = \$25.
b. P_0 = \$25.81.

13-7 a. ROE_{LL} = 14.6%; ROE_{HL} = 16.8%.
b. ROE_{LL} = 16.5%.

13-8 No leverage: ROE = 10.5%; σ = 5.4%; CV = 0.51; 60% leverage: ROE = 13.7%; σ = 13.5%; CV = 0.99.

13-9 a. 3,800 patients.

13-10 a. \$5.10.

13-11 a. EPS_{Old} = \$2.04; New: EPS_D = \$4.74; EPS_S = \$3.27.
b. 33,975 units.
c. $Q_{New, \text{Debt}}$ = 27,225 units.

13-12 Debt used: E(EPS) = \$5.78; σ_{EPS} = \$1.05; E(TIE) = 3.49×.
Stock used: E(EPS) = \$5.51; σ_{EPS} = \$0.85; E(TIE) = 6.00×.

13-13 a. FC_A = \$80,000; V_A = \$4.80/unit; P_A = \$8.00/unit.

13A-1 DOL = 2.67; ΔEBIT = 53.3%.

13A-2 DFL = 1.67; ΔNI = 167%.

13A-3 a. DOL = 1.2.
b. DFL = 1.11.
c. DTL = 1.33; Increase in NI = 13.33%.

13A-4 a. DOL_A = 2.80; DOL_B = 2.15; Method A.
b. DFL_A = 1.32; DFL_B = 1.35; Method B.
d. Debt = \$129,310; D/A = 5.75%.

14-1 Payout = 55%.

14-2 P_0 = \$60.

14-3 P_0 = \$40.

14-4 \$3,250,000.

14-5 Payout = 20%.

14-6 Payout = 52%.

14-7 D_0 = \$3.44.

14-8 Payout = 31.39%.

14-9 a(1). \$3,960,000.
(2). \$4,800,000
(3). \$9,360,000.
(4). Regular = \$3,960,000; Extra = \$5,400,000.
c. 15%.
d. 15%.

14-10 a. Payout = 63.16%; BP = \$9.55 million; $WACC_1$ = 10.67%; $WACC_2$ = 10.96%.
b. \$15 million.

15-1 AFN = \$410,000.

15-2 AFN = \$610,000.

15-3 AFN = \$200,000.

15-4 a. \$480,000.
b. \$18,750.

15-5 AFN = \$360.

15-6 ΔS = \$68,965.52.

15-7 a. \$13.44 million.
b. Notes payable = \$31.44 million.
c. Current ratio = 2.00×; ROE = 14.2%.
d(1). −\$14.28 million (surplus).
(2). Total assets = \$147 million; Notes payable = \$3.72 million.
(3). Current ratio = 4.25×; ROE = 10.84%.

15-8 Total assets = \$33,534; AFN = \$2,128.

15-9 a. 33%.
b. AFN = \$2,549.
c. ROE = 13.0%.

15-10 a. AFN = \$128,783.
b. 3.45%.

15-11 a. AFN = \$667.
b. Increase in notes payable = \$51; Increase in C/S = \$368.

16-1 \$10,000.

16-2 \$3,000,000.

16-3 A/R = \$59,500.

16-4 a. \$103,350.
b. \$97,500.

16-5 a. DSO = 28 days.
b. A/R = \$70,000.

16-6 a. ROE_T = 11.75%; ROE_M = 10.80%; ROE_R = 9.16%.

16-7 a. \$1,600,000.
c. Bank = \$1,200,000; Books = −\$5,200,000.

16-8 b. \$420,000.
c. \$35,000.

16-9 a. Feb. surplus = \$2,000.

16-10 a. Oct. loan = \$22,800.

16A-1 a. 32 days.
b. \$288,000.
c. \$45,000.

d(1). 30.
(2). \$378,000.

16A-2 a. 83 days.
b. \$356,250.
c. 4.8×.

16A-3 a. 56 days.
b(1). 1.875×.
(2). 11.25%.
c(1). 41 days.
(2). 2.03×.
(3). 12.2%.

17-1 k_{Nom} = 74.23%; EAR = 107.72%.

17-2 EAR = 8.37%.

17-3 \$7,500,000.

17-4 \$233.56.

17-5 EAR = 21.60%.

17-6 b. 14.69%.
d. 20.99%.

17-7 a. 44.54%.

17-8 a. k_d = 12%.
b. k_d = 11.25%.
c. k_d = 11.48%.
d. k_d = 14.47%. Alternative b has lowest interest rate.

17-9 Nominal cost = 14.69%; Effective cost = 15.66%.

17-10 Bank loan = 13.64%.

17-11 d. 8.3723%.

17-12 a. \$100,000.
c(1). \$300,000.
(2). Nominal cost = 36.73%; Effective cost = 43.86%.

17-14 a. \$300,000.

17-15 a. 11.73%.
b. 12.09%.
c. 18%.

17-16 b. \$384,615.
c. Cash = \$126.90; NP = \$434.60.

17-17 a(1). \$27,500.
(3). \$25,833.

17A-1 b. Total dollar cost = \$160,800; 15.12%.

17A-2 a. \$515,464.

17A-3 a. \$46,167.
b. \$40,667.

18-1 0.07425 yen per lira.

18-2 f_t = \$0.00907.

18-3 1 FF = $0.19724 or $1 = 5.07 FF.

18-4 0.6667 pound per dollar.

18-5 4.5455 FF.

18-6 8.85 francs per pound.

18-8 $480,000,000.

18-9 +$250,000.

18-10

	Dollars per 1,000 Units of:			
Marks	Lira	Yen	Pesos	Swiss Francs
$641.80	$0.65	$8.77	$127.26	$746.50

18-12 b. $17,192.80.

18-13 a. $2,709,339.
b. $2,689,121.
c. $3,200,000.

18-14 b. f_t = $0.5943.

18-15 $k_{Nom-U.S.}$ = 4.6%.

18-16 117 pesos.

18-17 e_0 = 20 yen per 1 FF, or 0.05 FF per 1 yen.

19-1 a. $5.00.
b. $2.00.

19-2 a, b, and c.

19-3 $1.82.

19-4 $27.00; $37.00.

19-5 k_d = 7.95%; $91,227.97.

19-6 b. Futures = +$1,969,105; Bond = −$1,101,851; Net = +$867,254.

20-1 55.6%; 50%.

20-2 $196.36.

20-3 CR = 25 shares.

20-4 a. PV cost of leasing = −$954,639; Lease equipment.

20-5 a. FV = −$3; FV = $0; FV = $4; FV = $49.
d. 9%; $90.

20-6 a. D/A_{J-H} = 50%; D/A_{M-E} = 67%.

20-7 a. PV cost of owning = −$185,112; PV cost of leasing = −$187,534; Purchase loom.

20-9 b. Percent ownership: Original = 80%; Plan 1 = 53%; Plans 2 and 3 = 57%.
c. EPS_0 = $0.48; EPS_1 = $0.60; EPS_2 = $0.64; EPS_3 = $0.86.
d. D/A_0 = 73%; D/A_1 = 13%; D/A_2 = 13%; D/A_3 = 48%.

21-1 P_0 = $37.04.

21-2 P_0 = $43.48.

21-3 $37.04 to $43.48.

21-4 a. 17%.
b. V = $14.65 million.

21-5 NPV = −$6,747.71; Do not purchase.

21-6 a. 14%.
b. T.V. = $1,143.4; V = $877.2.

SELECTED EQUATIONS AND DATA

CHAPTER 2

Net cash flow = Net income − Noncash revenues + Noncash charges.

Net cash flow = Net income + Depreciation.

Net cash flow = Operating cash flow − (Interest)(1 − T).

Operating cash flow = (Operating income)(1 − T) + Depreciation.

$$\text{Equivalent pre-tax yield on taxable bond} = \frac{\text{Muni yield}}{1 - T}.$$

MVA = Market value of equity − Equity capital supplied

= (Shares outstanding)(Stock price) − Total common equity.

EVA = EBIT(1 − T) − (Total capital)(After-tax cost of capital).

INDIVIDUAL TAX RATES FOR APRIL 1997

Single Individuals

IF YOUR TAXABLE INCOME IS	YOU PAY THIS AMOUNT ON THE BASE OF THE BRACKET	PLUS THIS PERCENTAGE ON THE EXCESS OVER THE BASE	AVERAGE TAX RATE AT TOP OF BRACKET
Up to $24,000	$ 0	15.0%	15.0%
$24,000–$58,150	3,600	28.0	22.6
$58,150–$121,300	13,162	31.0	27.0
$121,300–$263,750	32,738.50	36.0	31.9
Over $263,750	84,020.50	39.6	39.6

Married Couples Filing Joint Returns

IF YOUR TAXABLE INCOME IS	YOU PAY THIS AMOUNT ON THE BASE OF THE BRACKET	PLUS THIS PERCENTAGE ON THE EXCESS OVER THE BASE	AVERAGE TAX RATE AT TOP OF BRACKET
Up to $40,100	$ 0	15.0%	15.0%
$40,100–$96,900	6,015	28.0	22.6
$96,900–$147,700	21,919	31.0	25.5
$147,700–$263,750	37,667	36.0	30.1
Over $263,750	79,445	39.6	39.6

CORPORATE TAX RATES

IF A CORPORATION'S TAXABLE INCOME IS	IT PAYS THIS AMOUNT ON THE BASE OF THE BRACKET	PLUS THIS PERCENTAGE ON THE EXCESS OVER THE BASE	AVERAGE TAX RATE AT TOP OF BRACKET
Up to $50,000	$ 0	15%	15.0%
$50,000–$75,000	7,500	25	18.3
$75,000–$100,000	13,750	34	22.3
$100,000–$335,000	22,250	39	34.0
$335,000–$10,000,000	113,900	34	34.0
$10,000,000–$15,000,000	3,400,000	35	34.3
$15,000,000–$18,333,333	5,150,000	38	35.0
Over $18,333,333	6,416,667	35	35.0

CHAPTER 3

$$\text{Current ratio} = \frac{\text{Current assets}}{\text{Current liabilities}}.$$

$$\text{Quick, or acid test, ratio} = \frac{\text{Current assets} - \text{Inventories}}{\text{Current liabilities}}.$$

$$\text{Inventory turnover ratio} = \frac{\text{Sales}}{\text{Inventories}}.$$

$$\text{DSO} = \frac{\text{Days sales outstanding}}{} = \frac{\text{Receivables}}{\text{Average sales per day}} = \frac{\text{Receivables}}{\text{Annual sales}/360}.$$

$$\text{Fixed assets turnover ratio} = \frac{\text{Sales}}{\text{Net fixed assets}}.$$

$$\text{Total assets turnover ratio} = \frac{\text{Sales}}{\text{Total assets}}.$$

$$\text{Debt ratio} = \frac{\text{Total debt}}{\text{Total assets}}.$$

$$\text{D/E} = \frac{\text{D/A}}{1 - \text{D/A}}, \text{ and D/A} = \frac{\text{D/E}}{1 + \text{D/E}}.$$

$$\text{Debt ratio} = 1 - \frac{1}{\text{Equity multiplier}}.$$

$$\text{Times-interest-earned (TIE) ratio} = \frac{\text{EBIT}}{\text{Interest charges}}.$$

$$\frac{\text{Fixed charge}}{\text{coverage ratio}} = \frac{\text{EBIT} + \text{Lease payments}}{\text{Interest charges} + \text{Lease payments} + \dfrac{\text{Sinking fund payments}}{(1 - \text{Tax rate})}}.$$

$$\text{Profit margin on sales} = \frac{\text{Net income available to common stockholders}}{\text{Sales}}.$$

$$\text{Basic earning power ratio} = \frac{\text{EBIT}}{\text{Total assets}}.$$

$$\text{Return on total assets (ROA)} = \frac{\text{Net income available to common stockholders}}{\text{Total assets}}.$$

$$\text{ROA} = \left(\frac{\text{Profit}}{\text{margin}}\right)(\text{Total assets turnover}).$$

$$\text{Return on common equity (ROE)} = \frac{\text{Net income available to common stockholders}}{\text{Common equity}}.$$

$$\text{Price/earnings (P/E) ratio} = \frac{\text{Price per share}}{\text{Earnings per share}}.$$

$$\text{Book value per share} = \frac{\text{Common equity}}{\text{Shares outstanding}}.$$

$$\text{Market/book (M/B) ratio} = \frac{\text{Market price per share}}{\text{Book value per share}}.$$

$$\text{ROE} = \text{ROA} \times \text{Equity multiplier}$$

$$= \left(\frac{\text{Profit}}{\text{margin}}\right)\left(\frac{\text{Total assets}}{\text{turnover}}\right)\left(\frac{\text{Equity}}{\text{multiplier}}\right)$$

$$= \left(\frac{\text{Net income}}{\text{Sales}}\right)\left(\frac{\text{Sales}}{\text{Total assets}}\right)\left(\frac{\text{Total assets}}{\text{Common equity}}\right)$$

$$= \frac{\text{Net income}}{\text{Common equity}}.$$

CHAPTER 4

$$k = k^* + IP + DRP + LP + MRP.$$

$$k_{RF} = k^* + IP.$$

$$IP_n = \frac{I_1 + I_2 + \cdots + I_n}{n}.$$

CHAPTER 5

$$\text{Expected rate of return} = \hat{k} = \sum_{i=1}^{n} P_i k_i.$$

$$\text{Variance} = \sigma^2 = \sum_{i=1}^{n} (k_i - \hat{k})^2 P_i.$$

$$\text{Standard deviation} = \sigma = \sqrt{\sum_{i=1}^{n} (k_i - \hat{k})^2 P_i}.$$

$$CV = \frac{\sigma}{\hat{k}}.$$

$$\hat{k}_p = \sum_{i=1}^{n} w_i \hat{k}_i.$$

$$\sigma_p = \sqrt{\sum_{i=j}^{n} (k_{pj} - \hat{k}_p)^2 P_j}.$$

$$b_p = \sum_{i=1}^{n} w_i b_i.$$

$$SML = k_i = k_{RF} + (k_M - k_{RF})b_i.$$

$$RP_i = (RP_M)b_i.$$

$$b = \frac{Y_2 - Y_1}{X_2 - X_1} = \text{slope coefficient in } \bar{k}_{it} = a + b\,\bar{k}_{Mt} + e_t.$$

CHAPTER 6

$$FV_n = PV(1 + i)^n = PV(FVIF_{i,n}).$$

$$PV = FV_n \left(\frac{1}{1 + i}\right)^n = FV_n(1 + i)^{-n} = FV_n(PVIF_{i,n}).$$

$$\text{PVIF}_{i,n} = \frac{1}{\text{FVIF}_{i,n}}.$$

$$\text{FVIFA}_{i,n} = [(1 + i)^n - 1]/i.$$

$$\text{PVIFA}_{i,n} = [1 - (1/(1 + i)^n)]/i.$$

$$\text{FVA}_n = \text{PMT}(\text{FVIFA}_{i,n}).$$

$$\text{FVA}_n \text{ (Annuity due)} = \text{PMT}(\text{FVIFA}_{i,n})(1 + i).$$

$$\text{PVA}_n = \text{PMT}(\text{PVIFA}_{i,n}).$$

$$\text{PVA}_n \text{ (Annuity due)} = \text{PMT}(\text{PVIFA}_{i,n})(1 + i).$$

$$\text{PV (Perpetuity)} = \frac{\text{Payment}}{\text{Interest rate}} = \frac{\text{PMT}}{i}.$$

$$\text{PV}_{\text{Uneven stream}} = \sum_{t=1}^{n} \text{CF}_t \left(\frac{1}{1 + i} \right)^t = \sum_{t=1}^{n} \text{CF}_t(\text{PVIF}_{i,t}).$$

$$\text{FV}_{\text{Uneven stream}} = \sum_{t=1}^{n} \text{CF}_t (1 + i)^{n-t} = \sum_{t=1}^{n} \text{CF}_t(\text{FVIF}_{i,n-t}).$$

$$\text{FV}_n = \text{PV}\left(1 + \frac{i_{\text{Nom}}}{m} \right)^{mn}.$$

$$\text{Effective annual rate} = \left(1 + \frac{i_{\text{Nom}}}{m} \right)^m - 1.0.$$

$$\text{Periodic rate} = i_{\text{Nom}}/m.$$

$$i_{\text{Nom}} = \text{APR} = (\text{Periodic rate})(m).$$

$$\text{FV}_n = \text{PV}e^{in}.$$

$$\text{PV} = \text{FV}_n e^{-in}.$$

CHAPTER 7

$$V_B = \sum_{t=1}^{N} \frac{\text{INT}}{(1 + k_d)^t} + \frac{M}{(1 + k_d)^N}$$

$$= \text{INT}(\text{PVIFA}_{k_d,N}) + M(\text{PVIF}_{k_d,N}).$$

$$V_B = \sum_{t=1}^{2N} \frac{\text{INT}/2}{(1 + k_d/2)^t} + \frac{M}{(1 + k_d/2)^{2N}} = \frac{\text{INT}}{2}(\text{PVIFA}_{k_d/2,2N}) + M(\text{PVIF}_{k_d/2,2N}).$$

$$\text{Price of callable bond} = \sum_{t=1}^{N} \frac{\text{INT}}{(1 + k_d)^t} + \frac{\text{Call price}}{(1 + k_d)^N}.$$

$$\text{Accrued value at end of Year n} = \text{Issue price} \times (1 + k_d)^n.$$

$$\text{Interest in Year n} = \text{Accrued value}_n - \text{Accrued value}_{n-1}.$$

$$\text{Tax savings} = (\text{Interest deduction})(T).$$

CHAPTER 8

$$\hat{P}_0 = \text{PV of expected future dividends} = \sum_{t=1}^{\infty} \frac{D_t}{(1 + k_s)^t}.$$

$$\hat{P}_0 = \frac{D_0(1 + g)}{k_s - g} = \frac{D_1}{k_s - g}.$$

$$\hat{k}_s = \frac{D_1}{P_0} + g.$$

$$V_{ps} = \frac{D_{ps}}{k_{ps}}.$$

$$k_{ps} = \frac{D_{ps}}{V_{ps}}.$$

CHAPTER 9

After-tax component cost of debt = $k_d(1 - T)$.

$$\text{Component cost of preferred stock} = k_{ps} = \frac{D_{ps}}{P_n}.$$

$$k_s = \hat{k}_s = k_{RF} + RP = D_1/P_0 + g.$$

$$k_s = k_{RF} + (k_M - k_{RF})b_i.$$

$$k_s = \text{Bond yield} + \text{Risk premium}.$$

$$k_e = \frac{D_1}{P_0(1 - F)} + g.$$

$$g = (\text{Retention rate})(ROE) = (1.0 - \text{Payout rate})(ROE) = b(ROE).$$

$$WACC = w_d k_d(1 - T) + w_{ps}k_{ps} + w_{ce}(k_s \text{ or } k_e).$$

$$BP_{RE} = \frac{\text{Retained earnings}}{\text{Equity fraction}}.$$

CHAPTER 10

$$NPV = CF_0 + \frac{CF_1}{(1 + k)^1} + \frac{CF_2}{(1 + k)^2} + \cdots + \frac{CF_n}{(1 + k)^n}$$

$$= \sum_{t=0}^{n} \frac{CF_t}{(1 + k)^t}.$$

$$IRR: CF_0 + \frac{CF_1}{(1 + IRR)^1} + \frac{CF_2}{(1 + IRR)^2} + \cdots + \frac{CF_n}{(1 + IRR)^n} = 0$$

$$\sum_{t=0}^{n} \frac{CF_t}{(1 + IRR)^t} = 0.$$

$$MIRR: PV \text{ costs} = \sum_{t=0}^{n} \frac{COF_t}{(1 + k)^t} = \frac{\sum_{t=0}^{n} CIF_t(1 + k)^{n-t}}{(1 + MIRR)^n} = \frac{TV}{(1 + MIRR)^n}.$$

APPENDIX 11A

Recovery Allowance Percentage for Personal Property

OWNERSHIP YEAR	CLASS OF INVESTMENT			
	3-YEAR	5-YEAR	7-YEAR	10-YEAR
1	33%	20%	14%	10%
2	45	32	25	18
3	15	19	17	14
4	7	12	13	12
5		11	9	9
6		6	9	7
7			9	7
8			4	7
9				7
10				6
11				3
	100%	100%	100%	100%

CHAPTER 12

$$\sigma_{NPV} = \sqrt{\sum_{i=1}^{n} P_i[NPV_i - E(NPV)]^2}.$$

$$CV_{NPV} = \frac{\sigma_{NPV}}{E(NPV)}.$$

$$k_p = k_{RF} + (k_M - k_{RF})b_p.$$

CHAPTER 13

$$Q_{BE} = \frac{F}{P - V}.$$

$$EBIT = PQ - VQ - F.$$

$$EPS = \frac{(S - FC - VC - I)(1 - T)}{\text{Shares outstanding}} = \frac{(EBIT - I)(1 - T)}{\text{Shares outstanding}}.$$

APPENDIX 13A

$$DOL_Q = \frac{\dfrac{\Delta EBIT}{EBIT}}{\dfrac{\Delta Q}{Q}} = \frac{Q(P - V)}{Q(P - V) - F}.$$

$$DOL_S = \frac{S - VC}{S - VC - F}.$$

$$DFL = \frac{EBIT}{EBIT - I}.$$

$$DTL = \frac{Q(P - V)}{Q(P - V) - F - I} = \frac{S - VC}{S - VC - F - I} = (DOL)(DFL).$$

$$EPS_1 = EPS_0[1 + (DTL)(\%\Delta Sales)].$$

CHAPTER 15

$$AFN = (A^*/S_0)\Delta S - (L^*/S_0)\Delta S - MS_1(1 - d).$$

$$\text{Full capacity sales} = \frac{\text{Actual sales}}{\text{Percentage of capacity at which fixed assets were operated}}.$$

$$\text{Target FA/Sales ratio} = \frac{\text{Actual fixed assets}}{\text{Full capacity sales}}.$$

$$\text{Required level of FA} = (\text{Target FA/Sales ratio})(\text{Projected sales}).$$

CHAPTER 16

$$A/R = \frac{\text{Credit sales}}{\text{per day}} \times \frac{\text{Length of}}{\text{collection period}}.$$

$$ADS = \text{Annual sales}/360 = \frac{(\text{Units sold})(\text{Sales price})}{360}.$$

$$\text{Receivables} = (ADS)(DSO).$$

APPENDIX 16A

$$\frac{\text{Inventory conversion}}{\text{period}} = \frac{\text{Inventory}}{\text{Sales}/360}.$$

$$\frac{\text{Receivables collection}}{\text{period}} = DSO = \frac{\text{Receivables}}{\text{Sales}/360}.$$

$$\text{Payables deferral period} = \frac{\text{Payables}}{\text{Cost of goods sold}/360}.$$

$$\frac{\text{Inventory}}{\text{conversion}}_{\text{period}} + \frac{\text{Receivables}}{\text{collection}}_{\text{period}} - \frac{\text{Payables}}{\text{deferral}}_{\text{period}} = \frac{\text{Cash}}{\text{conversion.}}_{\text{cycle}}$$

CHAPTER 17

$$\text{Nominal cost of payables} = \frac{\text{Discount percent}}{100 - \text{Discount percent}} \times \frac{360}{\text{Days credit is outstanding} - \text{Discount period}}.$$

$$\text{Simple interest rate per day} = \frac{\text{Nominal rate}}{\text{Days in year}}.$$

$$\text{Simple interest charge for period} = (\text{Days in period})(\text{Rate per day})(\text{Amount of loan}).$$

$$\text{Face value}_{\text{Discount}} = \frac{\text{Funds received}}{1.0 - \text{Nominal rate (decimal)}}.$$

$$\text{Approximate annual rate}_{\text{Add-on}} = \frac{\text{Interest paid}}{(\text{Amount received})/2}.$$

$$\text{APR} = (\text{Periods per year})(\text{Rate per period}).$$

CHAPTER 18

$$\frac{f_t}{e_0} = \frac{(1 + k_h)}{(1 + k_f)}.$$

$$P_h = (P_f)(e_0).$$

$$e_0 = \frac{P_h}{P_f}.$$

CHAPTER 19

$$\text{Formula value} = \frac{\text{Current price}}{\text{of stock}} - \text{Strike price}.$$

$$V = P[N(d_1)] - Xe^{-k_{RF}t}[N(d_2)].$$

$$d_1 = \frac{\ln(P/X) + [k_{RF} + (\sigma^2/2)]t}{\sigma\sqrt{t}}.$$

$$d_2 = d_1 - \sigma\sqrt{t}.$$

CHAPTER 20

$$\frac{\text{Price paid for}}{\text{bond with warrants}} = \frac{\text{Straight-debt}}{\text{value of bond}} + \frac{\text{Value of}}{\text{warrants}}.$$

$$\text{Conversion price} = P_c = \frac{\text{Par value of bond given up}}{\text{Shares received}}.$$

$$\text{Conversion ratio} = CR = \frac{\text{Par value of bond given up}}{P_c}.$$

INDEX